*Contemporary Authors*®

# NEW REVISION SERIES

# Explore your options!

## Gale databases are offered in a variety of formats

™ **The information in this Gale publication is also available in** GALE **some or all of the formats described here. Your Gale Representative will be happy to fill you in. Call toll-free 1-800-877-GALE.**

### GaleNet
A number of Gale databases are now available on GaleNet, our new online information resource accessible through the Internet. GaleNet features an easy-to-use end-user interface, the powerful search capabilities of BRS/SEARCH retrieval software and ease of access through the World Wide Web.

### Diskette/Magnetic Tape

Many Gale databases are available on diskette or magnetic tape, allowing systemwide access to your most-used information sources through existing computer systems. Data can be delivered on a variety of mediums (DOS-formatted diskettes, 9-track tape, 8mm data tape) and in industry-standard formats (comma-delimited, tagged, fixed-field).

### CD-ROM

A variety of Gale titles are available on CD-ROM, offering maximum flexibility and powerful search software.

### Online

For your convenience, many Gale databases are available through popular online services, including DIALOG, NEXIS, DataStar, ORBIT, OCLC, Thomson Financial Network's I/Plus Direct, HRIN, Prodigy, Sandpoint's HOOVER, the Library Corporation's NLightN and Telebase Systems.

ISSN 0275-7176

# Contemporary Authors®

A Bio-Bibliographical Guide to
Current Writers in Fiction, General Nonfiction,
Poetry, Journalism, Drama, Motion Pictures,
Television, and Other Fields

**DANIEL JONES**
**JOHN D. JORGENSON**
Editors

## NEW REVISION SERIES
*volume* **68**

GALE

DETROIT • LONDON

# STAFF

Daniel Jones and John D. Jorgenson, *Editors, New Revision Series*

Thomas Wiloch, *Sketchwriting Coordinator and Online Research Specialist*

Tim Akers, Pamela S. Dear, Catherine V. Donaldson, Jeff Hunter, Jerry Moore, Deborah A. Schmitt, Polly A. Vedder, and Tim White, *Contributing Editors*

Mary Gillis, Joan Goldsworthy, Anne Janette Johnson, David Kroeger, Robert Miltner, Bryan Ryan, Susan Salter, Pamela L. Shelton, Arlene True, and Shanna Weagle, *Sketchwriters*

Shanna Weagle, *Copyeditor*

James P. Draper, *Managing Editor*

Victoria B. Cariappa, *Research Manager*

Jeffrey D. Daniels, Tamara C. Nott, Tracie A. Richardson Norma Sawaya, Cheryl L. Warnock, and Robert Whaley, *Research Associates*

Library of Congress Catalog Card Number 81-640179
ISBN 0-7876-2036-X
ISSN 0275-7176

Printed in the United States of America

10 9 8 7 6 5 4 3 2 1

# Contents

---

**Indexing note:** All *Contemporary Authors New Revision Series* entries are indexed in the *Contemporary Authors* cumulative index, which is published separately and distributed twice a year.

**As always, the most recent *Contemporary Authors* cumulative index continues to be the user's guide to the location of an individual author's listing.**

---

# Preface

The *Contemporary Authors New Revision Series* (*CANR*) provides updated information on authors listed in earlier volumes of *Contemporary Authors* (*CA*). Although entries for individual authors from any volume of *CA* may be included in a volume of the *New Revision Series, CANR* updates only those sketches requiring significant change. However, in response to requests from librarians and library patrons for the most current information possible on high-profile writers of greater public and critical interest, *CANR* revises entries for these authors whenever new and noteworthy information becomes available.

Authors are included on the basis of specific criteria that indicate the need for a revision. These criteria include a combination of bibliographical additions, changes in addresses or career, major awards, and personal information such as name changes or death dates. All listings in this volume have been revised or augmented in various ways and contain up-to-the-minute publication information in the Writings section, most often verified by the author and/or by consulting a variety of online resources. Many sketches have been extensively rewritten, often including informative new Sidelights. As always, a *CANR* listing entails no charge or obligation.

The key to locating an author's most recent entry is the *CA* cumulative index, which is published separately and distributed twice a year. It provides access to all entries in *CA* and *CANR*. Always consult the latest index to find an author's most recent entry.

For the convenience of users, the *CA* cumulative index also includes references to all entries in these Gale literary series: *Authors and Artists for Young Adults, Authors in the News, Bestsellers, Black Literature Criticism, Black Writers, Children's Literature Review, Concise Dictionary of American Literary Biography, Concise Dictionary of British Literary Biography, Contemporary Authors Autobiography Series, Contemporary Authors Bibliographical Series, Contemporary Literary Criticism, Dictionary of Literary Biography, Dictionary of Literary Biography Documentary Series, Dictionary of Literary Biography Yearbook, DISCovering Authors, DISCovering Authors: British, DISCovering Authors: Canadian, DISCovering Authors: Modules* (including modules for Dramatists, Most-Studied Authors, Multicultural Authors, Novelists, Poets, and Popular/Genre Authors), *Drama Criticism, Hispanic Literature Criticism, Hispanic Writers, Junior DISCovering Authors, Major Authors and Illustrators for Children and Young Adults, Major 20th-Century Writers, Native North American Literature, Poetry Criticism, Short Story Criticism, Something about the Author, Something about the Author Autobiography Series, Twentieth-Century Literary Criticism, World Literature Criticism, World Literature Criticism Supplement,* and *Yesterday's Authors of Books for Children.*

**A Sample Index Entry:**

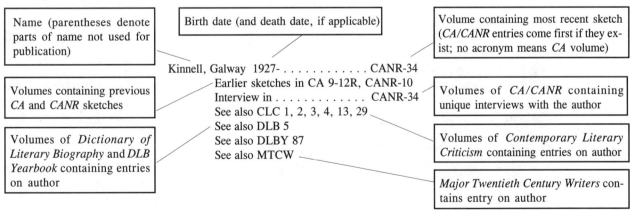

For the most recent *CA* information on Kinnell, users should refer to Volume 34 of the *New Revision Series,* as designated by "CANR-34"; if that volume is unavailable, refer to CANR-10. If CANR-10 is also unavailable, refer to CA 9-12R, published in 1974, for Kinnell's first revision entry.

# How Are Entries Compiled?

The editors make every effort to secure new information directly from the authors. Copies of all sketches in selected *CA* and *CANR* volumes previously published are routinely sent to listees at their last-known addresses, and returns from these authors are then assessed. For deceased writers, or those who fail to reply to requests for data, we consult other reliable biographical sources, such as those indexed in Gale's *Biography and Genealogy Master Index,* and biobibliographical sources, such as *Magazine Index, Newspaper Abstracts, LC MARC,* and a variety of online databases. Further details come from published interviews, feature stories, book reviews, online literary magazines and journals, author web sites, and often the authors' publishers supply material.

*\* Indicates that a listing has been compiled from secondary sources but has not been personally verified for this edition by the author under review.*


# What Kinds of Information Does an Entry Provide?

Sketches in *CANR* contain the following biographical and bibliographical information:

- **Entry heading:** the most complete form of author's name, plus any pseudonyms or name variations used for writing

- **Personal information:** author's date and place of birth, family data, ethnicity, educational background, political and religious affiliations, and hobbies and leisure interests

- **Addresses:** author's home, office, or agent's addresses, plus e-mail and fax numbers, as available

- **Career summary:** name of employer, position, and dates held for each career post; resume of other vocational achievements; military service

- **Membership information:** professional, civic, and other association memberships and any official posts held

- **Awards and honors:** military and civic citations, major prizes and nominations, fellowships, grants, and honorary degrees

- **Writings:** a comprehensive, chronological list of titles, publishers, dates of original publication and revised editions, and production information for plays, television scripts, and screenplays

- **Adaptations:** a list of films, plays, and other media which have been adapted from the author's work

- **Work in progress:** current or planned projects, with dates of completion and/or publication, and expected publisher, when known

- **Sidelights:** a biographical portrait of the author's development; information about the critical reception of the author's works; revealing comments, often by the author, on personal interests, aspirations, motivations, and thoughts on writing

- **Biographical and critical sources:** a list of books and periodicals in which additional information on an author's life and/or writings appears

# Related Titles in the *CA* Series

*Contemporary Authors Autobiography Series* complements *CA* original and revised volumes with specially commissioned autobiographical essays by important current authors, illustrated with personal photographs they provide. Common topics include their motivations for writing, the people and experiences that shaped their careers, the rewards they derive from their work, and their impressions of the current literary scene.

*Contemporary Authors Bibliographical Series* surveys writings by and about important American authors since World War II. Each volume concentrates on a specific genre and features approximately ten writers; entries list works written by and about the author and contain a bibliographical essay discussing the merits and deficiencies of major critical and scholarly studies in detail.

## Available in Electronic Formats

**CD-ROM.** Full-text bio-bibliographic entries from the entire *CA* series, covering approximately 101,000 writers, are available on CD-ROM through lease and purchase plans. The disc combines entries from the *CA, CANR,* and *Contemporary Authors Permanent Series* (*CAP*) print series to provide the most recent author listing. It can be searched by name, title, subject/genre, nationality/ethnicity, personal data, and as well as advanced searching using boolean logic. The disc is updated every six months. For more information, call 1-800-877-GALE. *CA* is also available on CD-ROM from SilverPlatter Information, Inc.

**Online.** The *Contemporary Authors* database is made available online to libraries and their patrons through online public access catalog (OPAC) vendors. Currently, *CA* is offered through Ameritech Library Services' Vista Online (formerly Dynix).

**GaleNet.** *CA* is available on a subscription basis through GaleNet, a new online information resource that features an easy-to-use end-user interface, the powerful search capabilities of the BRS/Search retrieval software, and ease of access through the World Wide Web. For more information, call 1-800-877-GALE.

**Magnetic Tape.** *CA* is available for licensing on magnetic tape in a fielded format. The database is available for internal data processing and nonpublishing purposes only. For more information, call 1-800-877-GALE.

## Suggestions Are Welcome

The editors welcome comments and suggestions from users on any aspects of the *CA* series. If readers would like to recommend authors for inclusion in future volumes of the series, they are cordially invited to write the editors; call toll-free at 1-800-347-GALE; fax at 1-313-961-6599; or email at john.jorgenson@gale.com or dan.jones@gale.com.

# *CA* Numbering System and Volume Update Chart

Occasionally questions arise about the *CA* numbering system and which volumes, if any, can be discarded. Despite numbers like "29-32R," "97-100" and "157," the entire *CA* print series consists of only 159 physical volumes with the publication of *CA* Volume 164. The following charts note changes in the numbering system and cover design, and indicate which volumes are essential for the most complete, up-to-date coverage.

**CA First Revision**
- 1-4R through 41-44R (11 books)
  *Cover:* Brown with black and gold trim.
  There will be no further First Revision volumes because revised entries are now being handled exclusively through the more efficient *New Revision Series* mentioned below.

**CA Original Volumes**
- 45-48 through 97-100 (14 books)
  *Cover:* Brown with black and gold trim.
- 101 through 164 (64 books)
  *Cover:* Blue and black with orange bands.
  The same as previous *CA* original volumes but with a new, simplified numbering system and new cover design.

**CA Permanent Series**
- *CAP*-1 and *CAP*-2 (2 books)
  *Cover:* Brown with red and gold trim.
  There will be no further *Permanent Series* volumes because revised entries are now being handled exclusively through the more efficient *New Revision Series* mentioned below.

**CA New Revision Series**
- *CANR*-1 through *CANR*-68 (68 books)
  *Cover:* Blue and black with green bands.
  Includes only sketches requiring significant changes; **sketches are taken from any previously published *CA*, *CAP*, or *CANR* volume**.

| If You Have: | You May Discard: |
|---|---|
| *CA* First Revision Volumes 1-4R through 41-44R **and** *CA Permanent Series* Volumes 1 and 2 | *CA* Original Volumes 1, 2, 3, 4 Volumes 5-6 through 41-44 |
| *CA* Original Volumes 45-48 through 97-100 **and** 101 through 164 | **NONE:** These volumes will not be superseded by corresponding revised volumes. Individual entries from these and all other volumes appearing in the left column of this chart may be revised and included in the various volumes of the *New Revision Series*. |
| *CA New Revision Series* Volumes *CANR*-1 through *CANR*-68 | **NONE:** The *New Revision Series* does not replace any single volume of *CA*. Instead, volumes of *CANR* include entries from many previous *CA* series volumes. All *New Revision Series* volumes must be retained for full coverage. |

# A Sampling of Authors and Media People
## Featured in This Volume

**Bill Barich**

A former staff writer for the *New Yorker,* Barich has enjoyed success among diverse audiences and has won acclaim for his interesting and entertaining prose style. One critic explains that Barich's "powerful reporting skills, evident throughout his work, show most clearly when he documents his most personal passions." Well-known for *Laughing in the Hills,* his semi-autobiographical debut documenting research on horse racing and the subculture surrounding the sport with reflections of his own life, Barich's other titles include *Traveling Light, Big Dreams: Into the Heart of California,* and *Carson Valley.*

**C. D. B. Bryan**

Though probably best-known as the author of the nonfiction work *Friendly Fire,* Bryan first attracted literary attention in 1965, when his book *P. S. Wilkinson* won the Harper Prize Novel award. Since his initial success, Bryan has written about a variety of topics, including an in-depth look at aviation history, the history of the National Geographic society, and an examination of alleged alien abduction stories. His titles include *The National Air and Space Museum* and *Beautiful Women; Ugly Scenes.*

**Barry Cole**

Praised for his "verbal precision, wit, exact ear for conversation, and his feeling for the elastic possibilities of language," Cole has been successful both as a novelist and as a poet. A self-described "frustrated lexicographer," Cole's works include *A Run across the Island, Blood Ties, The Search for Rita,* and *The Rehousing of Scaffardi.*

**Len Deighton**

With his early novels, especially *The Ipcress File* and *Funeral in Berlin,* Deighton established himself as one of the mainstays of modern espionage fiction. He is often ranked, along with Graham Greene, John le Carre, and Ian Fleming, among the foremost writers in the field. Known for his painstaking attention to accuracy in depicting espionage activities, his other titles include *Spy Hook, City of Gold,* and *Hope.*

**Elaine Feinstein**

Feinstein is an English poet, novelist, short story writer, playwright, biographer, and translator of several well-known Russian poets. Celebrated by one critic as "a writer of limitless simplicity and mistress of a musical prose that can apparently find rhythm anywhere," her works include *The Magic Apple Tree, The Ecstasy of Dr. Miriam Garner,* and *Daylight.*

**Carlos Fuentes**

Described by one critic as "without doubt one of Mexico's two or three greatest novelists" and by another as "the first active and conscious agent of the internationalization of the Spanish American novel," Fuentes gained widespread attention when his *The Old Gringo* became the first novel written by a Mexican to ever appear on the *New York Times* best-seller list. His other works include *A Change of Skin* and *Distant Relations.*

**John Kenneth Galbraith**

Galbraith is considered one of the twentieth century's foremost writers on economics and among its most influential economists. A prolific and diverse writer, whose more than thirty books range over a variety of topics, Galbraith is the author of such classic texts as *The Affluent Society* and *The New Industrial State.* In addition to his writings, he has held positions as a government economist, presidential advisor, foreign ambassador, and Harvard professor. His other titles include *The Triumph: A Novel of Modern Diplomacy* and *The Good Society: The Humane Dimension.*

**Marilyn Hacker**

In her National Book Award-winning collection, *Presentation Piece,* poet Hacker defined the dimensions of a poetic universe rooted in traditional poetic forms. Within these forms, Hacker couches the urgency of love, desire, and alienation in brash, up-to-the-minute language, writing from her perspective as a feminist, a lesbian, and a member of the extended family of women. Her other titles include *Love, Death, and the Changing of the Seasons* and *Winter Numbers.*

## Anita Lobel

Celebrated as both a talented artist and the creator of charming texts, Lobel is the author and illustrator of picture books, fantasies, retellings, and concept books that have as their hallmarks a theatrical approach and a keen sense of design. Her titles include *The Troll Music* and *Away from Home.*

## Barry Holstun Lopez

Lopez's early magazine articles and books established his reputation as an authoritative writer on the subject of natural history and he has been favorably compared to such distinguished naturalists/authors as Edward Hoagland, Peter Matthiessen, Edward Abbey, and Loren Eiseley. A recipient of the National Book Award for nonfiction in 1987 for his *Arctic Dreams: Imagination and Desire in a Northern Landscape,* Lopez's other works include *Of Wolves and Men, River Notes: The Dance of the Herons,* and *Field Notes: The Grace Note of the Canyon Wren.*

## James Michener

One of a handful of writers who enjoyed both critical and popular success, Michener penned short stories, nonfiction, bestselling novels, and received the Pulitzer Prize for fiction in 1948 for *Tales of the South Pacific.* Praised by one critic as "the literary world's Cecil B. DeMille" and by another as "a popular novelist with an awesome audience for his epic narratives, an unpretentious, solid craftsman," his titles included *Hawaii, Centennial, Alaska, The Novel,* and *This Noble Land: My Vision for America.* Michener died in 1997.

## N. Scott Momaday

Momaday's poetry and prose reflect his Kiowa Indian heritage in structure and theme, as well as in subject matter. His Pulitzer Prize-winning novel *House Made of Dawn* is described by one critic as "an attempt to transliterate Indian culture, myth, and sensibility into an alien art form without loss." Frequently concerned with the Native American perception of the human relationship to nature, Momaday's titles include *The Way to Rainy Mountain, In the Presence of the Sun: A Gathering of Shields,* and *Circle of Wonder: A Native American Christmas Story.*

## Iris Murdoch

Well-known and respected for her novels full of characters embroiled in philosophical turmoil, Murdoch was originally aligned with the existentialist movement. Her philosophy quickly broadened, however, and critics now primarily regard her works as "novels of ideas." In addition, her plays and nonfiction works encompass similar philosophical themes and add to her reputation as one of her generation's most prolific and important writers. Her titles include *Under the Net, The Sea, The Sea,* and *The Green Knight.*

## Andre Norton

Although she has published numerous books of historical fiction and mystery, Norton is best-known and admired for her science fiction and fantasy. Women writers were rare in the genre when she published *Star Man's Son, 2250 A.D.* in 1952, yet Norton quickly became a popular favorite, with some of her books selling over a million copies each. Her works include *The Time Traders, Victory on Janus, Tales of the Witch World,* and *The Monster's Legacy.*

## Linus Pauling

"Pauling is one of that select group of individuals whose lives have made a discernible impact on the contemporary world," proclaimed one critic. Similarly lauded as "the only American chemist whose name is a household word," Pauling received both a Nobel Prize for chemistry and a Nobel Peace Prize in addition to publishing many works prior to his death in 1994. His titles include *No More War!, Science and World Peace, Vitamin C, the Common Cold, and the Flu,* and *A Lifelong Quest for Peace: A Dialogue.*

## Nancy Willard

Loved by her readers, well-respected by critics, and admired by her students, Willard is an accomplished author of poetry, children's literature, and adult fiction. Although her first published works were books of poetry followed by two collections of short stories and a volume of literary criticism, most of her recent writings have been aimed at young readers. Her works include *Household Tales of Moon and Water, The Ballad of Biddy Early, The Tortilla Cat,* and *The Magic Cornfield.*

# A

*Indicates that a listing has been compiled from secondary sources believed to be reliable but has not been personally verified for this edition by the author sketched.*

**ADAMS, Daniel**
**See NICOLE, Christopher (Robin)**

\* \* \*

**ALLISON, Sam**
**See LOOMIS, Noel M(iller)**

\* \* \*

**ANASTASIO, Dina 1941-**

*PERSONAL:* First name is pronounced *Die*-nah; born October 9, 1941, in Des Moines, IA; daughter of William H. Brown (a sportscaster) and Jean (a writer; maiden name, Stout) Kinney; married Ernest J. Anastasio (a director of research), June 30, 1964 (divorced); children: Kristine, Trey. *Education:* Rutgers University, B.A., 1973.

*CAREER:* Author, 1971—; Sesame Street Publications, New York City, editor of *Sesame Street* Magazine, 1980-84.

*MEMBER:* Authors Guild.

*WRITINGS:*

FOR CHILDREN

*My Own Book,* Price, Stern (Los Angeles), 1975.
(Editor) *Who Puts the Care in Health Care?,* illustrated by John Freeman, Random House (New York City), 1976.

(Editor) *Who Puts the Plane in the Air?,* illustrated by John Freeman, Random House, 1976.
*My Secret Book,* Price, Stern, 1977.
*My Special Book,* Price, Stern, 1978.
*A Question of Time,* illustrated by Dale Payson, Dutton (New York City), 1978.
*Conversational Kickers,* Price, Stern, 1979.
*My Private Book,* Price, Stern, 1979.
*My Personal Book,* Price, Stern, 1980.
*My Own Book, Number Six,* Price, Stern, 1981.
*My School Book,* Price, Stern, 1981.
*My Wish Book,* Price, Stern, 1981.
*My Family Book,* Price, Stern, 1981.
*Count All the Way to Sesame Street,* illustrated by Richard Brown, Western Publishing (New York City), 1985, published as *Sesame Street Counting Book,* 1985.
*Big Bird Can Share,* illustrated by Tom Leigh, Western Publishing with Children's Television Workshop (New York City), 1985.
*The Romper Room Book of 1, 2, 3s,* illustrated by Nancy Stevenson, Doubleday (New York City), 1985.
*The Romper Room Book of ABCs,* illustrated by Nancy Stevenson, Doubleday, 1985.
*The Romper Room Book of Colors,* illustrated by A. O. Williams, Doubleday, 1985.
*The Romper Room Book of Shapes,* illustrated by A. O. Williams, Doubleday, 1985.
*Baby Piggy and Giant Bubble,* illustrated by Tom Cooke, Muppet Press (New York City), 1986.
*The Best Nickname,* illustrated by Tom Garcia, Golden Book (New York City), 1986.
*The Fisher-Price Picture Dictionary,* illustrated by Dick Codor and Carol Bouman, Marvel Books (New York City), 1987.
(Compiler and adapter) *Bedtime Stories,* illustrated by Lucinda McQueen, Grosset & Dunlap (New York City), 1987.

*Pass the Peas, Please: A Book of Manners,* illustrated by Katy Keck Arnsteen, Warner Books (New York City), 1988.

*Roger Goes to the Doctor,* illustrated by Cathy Beylon, Marvel Books, 1988.

(Adapter) *Walt Disney's Mickey and the Beanstalk,* illustrated by Sharon Ross, Western Publishing, 1988.

(With others) *Cars and Planes, Trucks and Trains: Featuring Jim Henson's Sesame Street Muppets,* illustrated by Richard Brown and others, Western Publishing with Children's Television Workshop, 1989.

*Twenty School Mini-Mysteries,* illustrated by George Parkin, Hippo, 1991.

*Ghostwriter: Courting Danger and Other Stories,* illustrated by Eric Velasquez, Bantam (New York City), 1992.

(Reteller) *Joy to the World: The Story of the First Christmas,* illustrated by Bettina Paterson, Platt & Munk (New York City), 1992.

*It's about Time,* illustrated by Mavis Smith, Grosset & Dunlap, 1993.

*The Teddy Bear Who Couldn't Do Anything,* illustrated by Karen Loccisano, Penguin Books (New York City), 1993.

*Dolly Dolphin and the Strange New Something: A Book about Cooperation,* illustrated by William Langley Studios, Third Story Books (Bridgeport, CT), 1994.

*Kissyfur and His Dad* (tie-in with television specials), illustrated by Phil Mendez, Scholastic, Inc. (New York City), 1994.

*Virtual Reality Magician* (based on teleplays for the *VR Troopers* series), Price, Stern, 1994.

*Virtual Reality Spy* (based on teleplays for the *VR Troopers* series), Price, Stern, 1994.

*The Case of the Glacier Park Swallow,* Roberts Rinehart, 1994.

*The Case of the Grand Canyon Eagle,* Roberts Rinehart, 1994.

(Adapter) *Apollo 13: The Junior Novelization* (based on the motion picture screenplay by William Broyles, Jr., Al Reinert, and John Sayles, and the book *Lost Moon* by Jim Lovell and Jeffrey Kluger), Grosset & Dunlap, 1995.

*Flipper: Junior Novelization* (based on the motion picture screenplay by Alan Shapiro), Price, Stern, 1996.

*Dark Side of the Sun,* HarperCollins (New York City), 1996.

*The Enemy,* HarperCollins, 1996.

*Pirates,* illustrated by Donald Cook, Grosset & Dunlap, 1997.

*Fly Trap,* illustrated by Jerry Smath, Grosset & Dunlap, 1997.

*"WRITE-IT-YOURSELF" SERIES; PUBLISHED BY PRICE, STERN*

*Dear Priscilla, I Am Sending You a Pet . . . for Your Birthday,* 1980.

*Everybody's Invited to Dudley's Party Except . . . ,* 1980.

*Georgina's Two . . . for Her Own Good, and Someday She's Going to Be Very Sorry,* 1980.

*Somebody Kidnapped the Mayor and Hid Her In . . . ,* 1980.

*Watch It Sarah (The . . . Is Right behind You),* 1980.

*Crazy Freddy's in Trouble Again and His Parents Are Going To . . . ,* 1981.

*Careful Melinda, That Footstep Belongs To . . . ,* in press.

*Something Weird Is Happening to Matthew, and He's a Little . . . ,* in press.

*OTHER*

Contributor to *Sesame Street Parents Newsletter, Parents,* and *Ladies' Home Journal.*

*SIDELIGHTS:* Dina Anastasio has written books for children of all ages, from simple board books for pre-readers to ecological mysteries for teens. In *A Question of Time,* a novel for children, she focuses on the adjustment problems of Sydell Stowe, who reluctantly moves with her family from her beloved New York City to the rural Minnesota town where her great-grandfather grew up. Unhappy and isolated in her new environment, she stumbles on an apparent mystery when she finds a set of antique dolls in a toy shop and subsequently meets Laura, who inexplicably resembles one of the dolls. Her investigation of this coincidence leads to a connection between the dolls, the dollmaker, a long-ago murder, and her own family ghosts. Barbara Elleman wrote in *Booklist* that "the mystery-ghost element snags attention, and Syd is a likable heroine." A reviewer in the *Bulletin of the Center for Children's Books* noted, "The fantastic and realistic elements are nicely meshed," and added, "the writing style is capable." A *School Library Journal* critic found the denouement "well handled" and describes the book as "briskly written and plotted."

Anastasio's *The Case of the Grand Canyon Eagle* and *The Case of the Glacier Park Swallow* introduce seventeen-year-old Juliet Stone, an amateur detective and aspiring veterinarian. Mary Harris Veeder commented in *Booklist,* "If Nancy Drew had wanted to be a veterinarian, she'd have been Juliet Stone." In these works, Anastasio tackles ecological mysteries in which "the settings play prominent roles," according to Sister Bernadette Marie Ondus in *Kliatt.* In *The Case of the Grand Canyon,* Juliet must identify the culprit who has stolen an eagle's eggs, while in *The Case of the Glacier Park Swallow,* Juliet attempts to determine the person responsible for disturbing the behavior of certain bird species. Cheryl Cufari observed in *School Library Journal* that each of the mysteries "has a degree of suspense and adventure that will keep readers intrigued." Ondus stated that Juliet's "excursions into nature and her encounters with the denizens of the wild, animal and human, are the heart of the stories."

## BIOGRAPHICAL/CRITICAL SOURCES:

### PERIODICALS

*Booklist,* July 1, 1977, p. 1649; October 1, 1978, p. 287; May 15, 1988, pp. 1601-602; December 1, 1994, p. 669.
*Books for Keeps,* November, 1991, p. 10.
*Bulletin of the Center for Children's Books,* March, 1979, p. 109.
*Horn Book Guide,* spring, 1993, p. 88; fall, 1993, p. 357.
*Kirkus Reviews,* November 15, 1978, p. 1246.
*Kliatt,* November, 1994, p. 4.
*Publishers Weekly,* July 3, 1978, p. 65; April 25, 1986, p. 79; September 7, 1992, p. 67; March 29, 1993, p. 57.
*School Library Journal,* December, 1978, p. 68; April, 1986, pp. 67-68; March, 1988, p. 180; October, 1994, p. 118.*

\*   \*   \*

## ANDENAES, Johannes 1912-

*PERSONAL:* Born September 7, 1912, in Innvik, Norway; son of Mads (a minister) and Signe (a housewife; maiden name, Mydland) Andenaes; married Ida Roeren, June 10, 1939; children: Mads, Bente, Ulf, Ellen. *Education:* University of Oslo, Cand. Jur., 1935, Dr. Jur., 1943; attended University of Munich, 1937-38.

*ADDRESSES: Home*—Generallunden 23, 0381 Oslo 3, Norway. *Office*—Karl Johansgate 47, Oslo 1, Norway.

*CAREER:* University of Oslo, Oslo, Norway, assistant professor, 1939-45, professor of law, 1945-82, dean of law faculty, 1959-60 and 1969, rector of the university, 1970-72. Visiting professor at University of Pennsylvania, 1963, University of Chicago, 1968, and University of Minnesota, 1974; Oxford University, visiting fellow of All Souls College, 1971. Chairperson of Commission of Criminal Procedure, 1957-67, and Penal Code Commission, 1981-87.

*MEMBER:* Norwegian Academy of Science and Letters (president, 1977-81), Finnish Academy of Sciences, Rotary International.

*AWARDS, HONORS:* Friddjof Nansen Award from Norwegian Academy of Science and Letters, 1964, for legal scholarship; Dr. Jur. from University of Copenhagen, 1970, University of Uppsala, 1977, and University of Bergen, 1996; Sellin-Glueck Award from American Society of Criminology, 1979; Knut og Alice Wallenbergs Stiftelsen Nordic Prize, 1981; Henrik-Steffens Prize from University of Kiel, 1983; Anders Sandoe Oersted Honorary Gold Medal from University of Copenhagen, 1984.

*WRITINGS:*

*Straffbar unnlatelse* (title means "Criminal Omissions"), Tanum, 1942.
*Statsforfatningen i Norge* (title means "The Constitution of Norway"), Tanum, 1945, 8th edition, Tano, 1998.
*Formuesforbrytelsene* (title means "Property Crimes"), Universitetsforlaget, 1953, 6th edition, 1996.
*Alminnelig strafferett,* Akademisk Forlag, 1956, 4th edition, Universitetsforlaget, 1997, translation published as *The General Part of the Criminal Law of Norway,* Fred Rothman, 1965.
(With Olav Riste and Magne Skodvin) *Norway and the Second World War,* Tanum, 1966, 3rd edition, 1983.
*Punishment and Deterrence,* introduction by Norval Morris, University of Michigan Press, 1974.
*Innfoering i rettsstudiet* (title means "Introduction to the Study of Law"), Groendahl, 1979, 4th edition, 1994.
*Det vanskelige oppgjoeret* (title means "The Difficult Reckoning"), Tanum-Norli, 1979.
(With Anders Bratholm) *Spesiell strafferett* (title means "The Special Part of Criminal Law"), Universitetsforlaget, 1983, 3rd edition, 1996.
*Norsk straffeprosess* (title means "Norwegian Criminal Procedure"), Universitetsforlaget, Volume 1, 1984, Volume 2, 1987, 2nd edition, 1994.

*Et liv blant paragrafer* (autobiography; title means "A Life in Law"), Gyldendal, 1987.
*Straffen som problem* (title means "The Problem of Punishment"), Exil forlag, 1994, 2nd edition, 1996.

Contributor to law and criminology journals.

*SIDELIGHTS:* Johannes Andenaes told *CA* that his international reputation is based largely upon his contributions to the theory of deterrence (or general prevention) in criminal law. The author wrote: "For more than three decades, I have been an active participant in the public discussion of current problems, especially in matters related to criminal law, criminal procedure, and criminology. The book *The Difficult Reckoning* describes the dealings with quislings and war criminals after the German occupation of Norway and the end of World War II, and my own role as a spokesman for moderation and fair trial. I have participated extensively in the preparation of legislation in criminal law and criminal procedure. The autobiography *Et liv blant paragrafer* gives an outline of controversial legal questions where I have been involved in public discussion. In recent years I have devoted a great deal of work to the question of punishment of drunk driving, criticizing the overly harsh treatment of this offense in Norwegian law. My efforts have had a limited success in the statutory amendments of 1988.

"In my latest book, *The Problem of Punishment*, I present my philosophy of criminal law and, more specifically, take issue with the drug policy of the Scandinavian countries, the United States, and most other countries of the western world."

*BIOGRAPHICAL/CRITICAL SOURCES:*

*PERIODICALS*

*Journal of Criminal Law and Criminology*, Volume 66, number 1, 1975.

\*      \*      \*

**ANGELO, Valenti 1897-**

*PERSONAL:* Born June 23, 1897, in Massarosa, Tuscany, Italy; came to the United States, 1905; son of Augustino and Viclinda (Checchi) Angelo; married Maxine Grimm, July 23, 1923; children: Valdine,

Peter. *Education:* Attended schools in Italy and California. *Religion:* Catholic.

*CAREER:* Author and illustrator. Worked in a paper mill at the age of fifteen; later worked as a laborer in rubber, steel, and glass works; employed for three years at a photoengraving firm; began illustrating books for Grabhorn Press, 1926; became a free-lance artist, 1933; turned to writing children's books, 1937.

*AWARDS, HONORS:* Since 1927, thirty-seven books illustrated by Angelo have been included in the American Institute of Graphic Arts' Fifty Books of the Year Exhibits.

*WRITINGS:*

*SELF-ILLUSTRATED*

*Nino,* Viking (New York City), 1938.
*Golden Gate,* Viking, 1939, reprinted, Arno, 1975.
*Paradise Valley,* Viking, 1940.
*A Battle in Washington Square,* Golden Cross Press, 1942.
*Hill of Little Miracles,* Viking, 1942.
*Look Out Yonder,* Viking, 1943.
*The Rooster Club,* Viking, 1944.
*The Bells of Bleecker Street,* Viking, 1949, reprinted, 1969.
*The Marble Fountain,* Viking, 1951.
*Big Little Island,* Viking, 1955.
*The Acorn Tree,* Viking, 1958.
*The Honey Boat,* Viking, 1959.
*The Candy Basket,* Viking, 1960.
*Angelino and the Barefoot Saint,* Viking, 1961.
*The Merry Marcos,* Viking, 1963.
*The Tale of a Donkey,* Viking, 1966.

*ILLUSTRATOR*

Walt Whitman, *Leaves of Grass,* Random House (New York City), 1930.
Alexandre Dumas, *Three Musketeers,* Illustrated Editions Co., 1935.
Nathaniel Hawthorne, *House of the Seven Gables,* Limited Editions Club, 1935.
Ruth Sawyer, *Roller Skates,* Viking, 1936.
Charles George Soulie, editor and translator, *Chinese Love Tales,* Illustrated Editions Co., 1936.
Richard Francis Burton, *F. Kasidah of Haji Abdu el-Yezdi: A Lay of the Higher Law,* Limited Editions Club, 1937.
Clement Clarke Moore, *Visit from St. Nicholas,* Hawthorne, 1937.

Charles K. Scott Moncrieff, translator, *Song of Roland,* Limited Editions Club, 1938.

Marguerite Vance, *Paula,* Dodd (New York City), 1939.

John Fante, *Dago Red,* Viking, 1940.

Sawyer, *Long Christmas,* Viking, 1941.

Bret Harte, *Luck of Roaring Camp and Other Stories,* Peter Pauper Press (New York City), 1943.

*Psalms of David in the King James Version,* Peter Pauper Press, 1943.

Annie Thaxter Eaton, *The Animals' Christmas,* Viking, 1944, reprinted, 1966.

Elizabeth Barrett Browning, *Sonnets from the Portuguese,* Heritage Press (Baltimore, MD), 1945.

Edwin Arnold, *Light of Asia,* Peter Pauper Press, 1946.

Burton, translator, *Book of the Thousand Nights and a Night,* Heritage Press, 1946.

Floy Perkinson Gates, *Hey, Mr. Grasshopper!,* privately printed, 1949.

Clyde Robert Bulla, *Song of St. Francis,* Crowell (New York City), 1952.

Sterling North, *Birthday of Little Jesus,* Grosset, 1952.

Delos Wheeler Lovelace, *Journey to Bethlehem,* Crowell, 1953.

Francis Thompson, *Hound of Heaven,* Peter Pauper Press, 1953.

Eaton, *Welcome Christmas,* Crowell, 1955.

William Shakespeare, *The Tragedy of Hamlet,* Peter Pauper Press, 1956.

*The Book of Proverbs,* Heritage Press, 1963.

Bulla, *St. Valentine's Day,* Crowell, 1965.

Hawthorne, *Twice-Told Tales,* edited by Wallace Stegner, Limited Editions Club, 1966.

Also illustrator of *Benito,* by Bulla, published by Crowell.

*SIDELIGHTS:* As a child growing up in Italy, Valenti Angelo was encouraged by the village wood-carver to become an artist. He followed that encouragement and went on to decorate and illustrate more than two hundred children's books. When he was forty years old, Angelo also began writing stories, based largely on his own childhood memories. Reviewers frequently characterized his work as charming and evocative. M. L. Becker, a writer for *Books,* referred to *Golden Gate,* one of Angelo's first books, as filled with "sensitiveness to beauty . . . a landscape with figures seen in a dream." A *Library Journal* contributor found the story "quiet but arresting," and A. T. Eaton, writing in the *New York Times,* stated that the book was designed "with beauty and distinction,"

combining "to a remarkable degree humor, action and interest."

*The Bells of Bleecker Street* is a portrait of Italian immigrant life in New York City. L. S. Bechtel, a reviewer for *New York Herald Tribune Book Review,* termed that story "a complete success," thanks to the author's great feeling for setting, for "his remarkable insight into the hearts of small boys," his understanding of Italians, and his love of craftsmen and their work. Bechtel further praised "his keen artist's eye for detail, and his ability to write fluid, lively good English." A *New York Times* critic was similarly enthusiastic, confiding: "Only grand opera, I have always felt, could do full justice to New York's Bleecker Street . . . but Mr. Angelo has come very close to it. . . . A book full of warmth, vitality and fun."

*BIOGRAPHICAL/CRITICAL SOURCES:*

*PERIODICALS*

*America,* November 16, 1963.
*Atlantic,* December, 1960.
*Best Sellers,* January 15, 1964.
*Booklist,* September, 1939; April 1, 1949; September 1, 1951; November 15, 1959; January 1, 1962.
*Bookmark,* October, 1969.
*Books,* July 2, 1939, p. 8.
*Canadian Forum,* December, 1960.
*Catholic World,* December, 1949.
*Chicago Sun,* May 7, 1949.
*Chicago Sunday Tribune,* September 30, 1951; December 3, 1961, p. 28.
*Christian Science Monitor,* September 8, 1960, p. 7.
*Cleveland Open Shelf,* August, 1939, p. 16; July, 1951, p. 13.
*Commonweal,* December 1, 1939; November 13, 1959; November 10, 1961; November 15, 1963.
*Horn Book,* July, 1939; May, 1949; February, 1960; December, 1961; December, 1963.
*Kirkus Reviews,* March 1, 1949; March 1, 1951; July 15, 1959; July 15, 1960; July 1, 1961.
*Library Journal,* September 1, 1939; November 1, 1939; May 1, 1949; October 15, 1951; January 15, 1960; November 15, 1960; January 15, 1962; September 15, 1963.
*New York Herald Tribune Book Review,* March 20, 1949, p. 6; July 15, 1951, p. 9; January 3, 1960, p. 11; September 25, 1960, p. 13; December 10, 1961, p. 13.
*New York Times,* July 23, 1939, p. 10; April 3, 1949, p. 29; November 11, 1951, p. 28.

*New York Times Book Review,* December 3, 1951, p. 68.

*New Yorker,* November 25, 1939; December 3, 1949; December 1, 1951.

*San Francisco Chronicle,* August 13, 1951, p. 16; November 11, 1951, p. 9; November 8, 1959, p. 14; November 13, 1960, p. 4; November 12, 1961, p. 2.

*Saturday Review,* August 15, 1964.

*Saturday Review of Literature,* November 18, 1939; July 9, 1949; June 2, 1951; November 10, 1951.

*Wilson Library Bulletin,* April, 1949; September, 1951; January, 1960; January, 1961.

\* \* \*

### ANGOFF, Charles 1902-1979
### (Richard W. Hinton)

*PERSONAL:* Born April 22, 1902, in Minsk, Russia; brought to the United States in 1908, naturalized in 1923; died May 3, 1979, in New York, NY; son of Jacob Joseph (a tailor) and Anna (Pollack) Angoff; married Sara F. Freedman, June 13, 1943; children: Nancy Carol (Mrs. Richard G. Gallin). *Education:* Harvard University, A.B., 1923.

*CAREER:* Newspaper reporter in Boston, MA, 1923; *American Mercury,* member of editorial staff, 1925-31, managing editor, 1931-34, 1943-50, editor, 1934-35; member of board of editors, *Nation,* 1935; editor, *American Spectator,* 1935-36; contributing editor, *North American Review,* 1938-40; also wrote in this period for *Living Age* and *Scribner's;* executive editor, Mercury Publications, 1950-51; Fairleigh Dickinson University, Rutherford, NJ, professor of English, 1954-76, editor of *Literary Review,* beginning 1957, chief editor of Fairleigh Dickinson University Press, beginning 1967. Lecturer in English at University of Kansas City, 1949-50, and University of New Hampshire, 1951-61; adjunct professor at Wagner College, 1955-56, and New York University, 1958-66; visiting professor of English, Yeshiva University, beginning 1975; University of Vermont, scholar-in-residence, 1976, visiting professor of English, 1977-79. Adviser, Jewish Book Guild, beginning 1949. Research director, radio-TV program *Meet the Press,* 1945-55.

*MEMBER:* Poetry Society of America (president, 1969-72), Jewish Academy of Arts and Sciences (fellow), Authors League, International PEN.

*AWARDS, HONORS:* Daroff Memorial Fiction Award for best Jewish novel, 1954, for *In the Morning Light;* Charles Angoff Collection established at Boston University Libraries, 1964; Litt. D., Fairleigh Dickinson University, 1966; humanitarian award, Fairleigh Dickinson University, 1973; Ellis Island Award for significant contributions to adopted country, 1977.

*WRITINGS:*

*A Literary History of the American People,* Knopf (New York City), 1931.

*Palestrina: Savior of Church Music,* Knopf, 1944.

*Adventures in Heaven,* Ackerman, 1945, reprinted, Books for Libraries Press, 1970.

*Handbook of Libel,* Duell, Sloan & Pearce, 1946, revised edition published as *The Book of Libel,* A. S. Barnes (San Diego, CA), 1966.

*Fathers of Classical Music,* Beechhurst, 1947, reprinted, Books for Libraries Press, 1969.

*When I Was a Boy in Boston,* Beechhurst, 1947, reprinted, Books for Libraries Press, 1970.

*Journey to the Dawn,* Beechhurst, 1951.

*In the Morning Light,* Beechhurst, 1952.

*The Sun at Noon,* Beechhurst, 1955.

*Something about My Father and Other People,* Yoseloff, 1956.

*H. L. Mencken: A Portrait from Memory,* Yoseloff, 1956.

*Between Day and Dark,* Yoseloff, 1959.

*The Bitter Spring,* Yoseloff, 1961.

*Summer Storm,* Yoseloff, 1963.

*The Tone of the Twenties and Other Essays,* Yoseloff, 1966.

*The Bell of Time* (poetry), Manyland Books, 1966.

*Memoranda for Tomorrow* (poetry), Yoseloff, 1968.

*Memory of Autumn,* Yoseloff, 1968.

*Winter Twilight,* Yoseloff, 1970.

*Season of Mists,* Yoseloff, 1971.

*Prayers at Midnight* (prose poetry), Manyland Books, 1971.

(Author of introduction) George J. Nathan, *The Theatre Book of the Year,* Fairleigh Dickinson University Press (East Brunswick, NJ), 1971.

*Mid-Century,* A. S. Barnes, 1973.

*Toward the Horizon,* A. S. Barnes, 1978.

*Emma Lazarus: Poet, Jewish Activist, Pioneer Zionist* (monograph), Jewish Historical Society of New York (New York City), 1979.

*EDITOR*

(Under pseudonym Richard W. Hinton) *Arsenal for Skeptics,* Knopf, 1934.

(And translator) Helen Tinyanova, *Stradivari: The Violin Maker,* Knopf, 1938.

(With Joseph H. Smyth) *World Over: 1938,* Harrison-Hilton, 1939.

(With Leon B. Bloch) *World Over: 1939,* Harrison-Hilton, 1940.

(With Lawrence E. Spivak) *The "American Mercury" Reader,* Blakiston, 1944, reprinted, AMS Press, 1979.

(And author of introduction) *The World of George Jean Nathan,* Knopf, 1952.

(With Clarence R. Decker) *Modern Stories from Many Lands,* Manyland Books, 1963, 2nd edition, 1972.

*The Humanities in the Age of Science,* Fairleigh Dickinson University Press, 1968.

*George Sterling: A Centenary Memoir-Anthology,* A. S. Barnes, 1969.

*Stories from the "Literary Review,"* Fairleigh Dickinson University Press, 1969.

(With John Povey) *African Writing Today: Ethiopia, Ghana, Kenya, Nigeria, Sierra Leone, Uganda, Zambia,* Manyland Books, 1969.

(With Meyer Levin) *The Rise of American Jewish Literature: An Anthology of Selections from the Major Novels,* Simon & Schuster (New York), 1970.

*The Diamond Anthology,* A. S. Barnes, 1971.

Conrad Cherry and others, *Jonathan Edwards: His Life and Influence,* Fairleigh Dickinson University Press, 1974.

Emily M. Wallace and Kenneth Burke, *William Carlos Williams,* Fairleigh Dickinson University Press, 1974.

Nathan Hershey, *Biology and the Future of Man,* Fairleigh Dickinson University Press, 1978.

(And author of foreword) *Twenty Years of the "Literary Review": Essays, Stories, Poems, Plays, Epigrams,* Fairleigh Dickinson University Press, 1979.

PLAYS

*Something to Sing About,* produced by Pasadena Playhouse, 1940.

*Moment Musical,* produced in New York, 1943.

OTHER

Contributor of poems, articles, and stories to over one hundred magazines and newspapers.

SIDELIGHTS: Charles Angoff was praised by H. L. Mencken as "the best managing editor in America," but Angoff was better known as the author of a series of autobiographical novels featuring a character named David Polonsky. Like Angoff, Polonsky was part of a large, close-knit Russian-Jewish family that came to America in the early 1900s.

The Polonsky books were foreshadowed by a book of semi-fictional memoirs entitled *When I Was a Boy in Boston.* Commenting on that volume, Mary McGrory wrote in the *New York Times* that the author's respect for his elders was obvious, and his recollection of his early years was "completely in focus." She opined that the book was probably too "low-pitched and solemn to be widely popular," but praised it as a moving portrait of a simple, rich way of life.

Angoff introduced the Polonsky family in *Journey to the Dawn.* In this book, his alter ego David is just a young boy who is enthusiastic about his new home in Boston. Reviews of the novel were mixed but generally favorable. Anna Yezierska, a contributor to the *New York Times,* judged that it was "over-written in places" and packed with too many characters, but she concluded that "these minor defects cannot mar its over-all impact" and named it "a pioneering work in American fiction." Eliezer Greenberg predicted in *Nation* that Angoff's series would become "one of the few significant portrayals in American literature of authentic Jewish life," while a *Springfield Republican* critic called it "a gentle novel, fondly told" and "a novel rich in the promise of books to come."

Angoff did fulfill that promise in the following volumes of his series, in the opinion of many reviewers. Discussing *Sun at Noon,* the third Polonsky book, Yezierska stated that the series "achieves a cumulative artistic effect that is extraordinary." *Between Day and Dark,* the next book, was "Angoff at his best," in her opinion. S. L. Simon, a *Library Journal* reviewer, also praised that volume as "a worthy effort," noting that Angoff's prose "is always warm in tone; his mood one of reflection and inquiry."

Not all comment on the series was positive, however; some reviewers disliked the dated style of the novels. For example, a *Times Literary Supplement* critic wrote of *Winter Twilight:* "The dialogue alone is enough to prevent the reader [from] getting past the first chapter; stickily emotional, it nonetheless manages to be as brittle as an official communique." Yet numerous reviewers found the books to be important chronicles of Jewish life in America. Harry

Roskolenko wrote in the *New York Times Book Review:* "In Angoff's continuous chronicles, the two salient moral events are the creation of Israel and the relationship of American Jews to Israel. . . . David Polonsky is somewhat romantic: but he is recording events that matter. . . . It is Polonsky against everybody—and his commentary as an adjunct to fiction. For every sort of man is here—from the opportunist to the hero as hero. . . . Angoff, the chronicler, sets a pace that staggers. . . . [The book] has the concerned scholar's desire for immediacy and continuity."

*BIOGRAPHICAL/CRITICAL SOURCES:*

BOOKS

Benton, J. T., *World of Charles Angoff: On the Occasion of His 75th Birthday,* Jewish Book Council of America, 1977.

PERIODICALS

*Booklist,* December 15, 1947; May 1, 1956.
*Bookmark,* March, 1951; May, 1959.
*Books Abroad,* summer, 1967; spring, 1968; winter, 1971.
*Book Week,* November 4, 1945, p. 9.
*Chicago Sunday Tribune,* July 1, 1956, p. 2.
*Christian Century,* April 8, 1959.
*Christian Science Monitor,* August 23, 1947, p. 11.
*Cleveland Open Shelf,* July, 1951, p. 16.
*Commonweal,* July 27, 1956.
*Library Journal,* June 15, 1956; April 1, 1959.
*Nation,* March 10, 1951; March 19, 1955; June 23, 1956.
*New York Herald Tribune Book Review,* December 7, 1947, p. 56; June 17, 1956, p. 4.
*New York Times,* August 3, 1947, p. 5; February 18, 1951, p. 16; January 16, 1955, p. 4; June 17, 1956, p. 5; March 8, 1959, p. 42.
*New York Times Book Review,* February 8, 1970.
*San Francisco Chronicle,* August 10, 1947, p. 12.
*Saturday Review,* January 15, 1955; May 12, 1956; July 7, 1956.
*Saturday Review of Literature,* March 10, 1951.
*Springfield Republican,* December 30, 1945, p. 4D; April 8, 1951, p. 6D.
*Time,* July 2, 1956.
*Times Literary Supplement,* August 21, 1970.
*Yale Review,* autumn, 1956.

OBITUARIES:

PERIODICALS

*AB Bookman's Weekly,* May 21, 1979.
*New York Times,* May 4, 1979.
*Time,* May 14, 1979.*

\*    \*    \*

## ANTHONY, Edward 1895-1971
### (Edar)

*PERSONAL:* Born August 4, 1895, in New York, NY; died August 16, 1971; son of Robert and Rose (Friedman) Anthony; married Esther H. Howard (an artist and editor), December 17, 1928; children: Richard W.

*CAREER:* Writer, newspaperman, and publisher. Member of the staff of the *Bridgeport Herald* and the *New York Herald;* became publisher of *Woman's Home Companion,* 1943, and *Collier's,* 1949. Publicity director of Herbert Hoover's presidential campaign, 1928.

*MEMBER:* National Press Club, PEN, Dutch Treat Club, Players Club.

*WRITINGS:*

*Merry-Go-Roundelays,* Century (New York City), 1921.
*The Pussycat Princess* (for children), Century, 1922.
(With Joseph Anthony) *The Fairies Up-to-Date* (illustrated by Jean de Bosschere), Little, Brown (Boston), 1923.
*"Razzberry!",* Holt (New York City), 1924.
(Editor) *How to Get Rid of a Woman: Being an Intimate Record of the Remarkable Love Affairs of Wilton Olmsted, Esq., Man of the World and Student of Life, Together with His Revealing Impressions of Women and His Amazing Discoveries Concerning the Sex* (illustrated by George de Zayas), Bobbs-Merrill (New York City), 1928.
(With Frank Buck) *Bring 'Em Back Alive,* Simon & Schuster (New York City), 1930.
(With Buck) *Wild Cargo,* Simon & Schuster, 1932.
(With Clyde Beatty) *The Big Cage,* Century, 1933.
(With Gordon B. Enders) *Nowhere Else in the World,* Farrar, Straus (New York City), 1935.

(With Abel A. Schechter) *I Live on Air,* F. A. Stokes, 1941.

*The Sex Refresher* (illustrated by George Price), Howell, Soskin, 1943.

*Every Dog Has His Say* (poems; illustrated by Morgan Dennis), Watson-Guptill (New York City) 1947.

(For children) *Oddity Land* (illustrated by Erik Blegvad), Doubleday (New York City), 1957.

*This Is Where I Came In: The Impromptu Confessions of Edward Anthony* (autobiography), Doubleday, 1960.

*O Rare Don Marquis: A Biography,* Doubleday, 1962.

(With C. Beatty) *Facing the Big Cats,* Doubleday, 1965.

(With Henry Trefflich) *Jungle for Sale,* Hawthorn Books, 1967.

(With Eric Sloane) *Mr. Daniels and The Grange,* Funk (New York City), 1968.

*Astrology and Sexual Compatibility,* Essandes, 1971.

*ADAPTATIONS:* Universal Pictures adapted Anthony's and Clyde Beatty's work, *The Big Cage,* as a motion picture in 1933.

*SIDELIGHTS:* Edward Anthony wrote many types of books: biographies, memoirs, fiction, verse, and nonfiction. His first book, *Merry-Go-Roundelays,* was a collection of verse he had previously published in newspapers and periodicals. This light verse was "a joy," in the estimation of a *Boston Transcript* reviewer; a *Springfield Republican* critic called it "mirth-provoking," "refreshing," and "a real smile-book."

In *How to Get Rid of a Woman: Being an Intimate Record of the Remarkable Love Affairs of Wilton Olmsted, Esq., Man of the World and Student of Life, Together with His Revealing Impressions of Women and His Amazing Discoveries Concerning the Sex,* Anthony told the humorous tale of an incredibly beautiful yet stupid man with an active love life. Numerous reviewers rated it as a very satisfactory piece of light entertainment.

Anthony's newspaper work was once again collected in *"Razzberry!",* a collection of prose columns about sports and sports crowds. "Sharp, witty, incisive," judged a *Boston Transcript* writer, while a *New York Tribune* contributor described the book as full of "admirable fooling and ingenious delight." A *New York Times* writer had even higher praise, claiming that the book established Anthony as "a sports writer of the first rank."

*Oddity Land,* a book of nonsense verse, was reviewed by a *New York Herald Tribune* critic who wrote: "This is nonsense that will be enjoyed beyond the nursery. The antic rhymes, smooth and clever or mischievously odd, the artfully crazy images that seem to be created because a rhyme is necessary, are strung together in groups with brief rhyming introductions. It is just plain fooling and good fooling."

*Saturday Review*'s analysis of *I Live on Air* included: "Mr. Schechter and his co-author have an agreeable talent for story-telling, and a racy style marked by a fondness for homespun American idiom. They write from the inside with all the data at their disposal. The result is a readable, in parts highly entertaining volume on a subject that so far has not been adequately covered. Anyone interested in news coverage in general or radio in particular might do well to have a copy of [this book] on his desk." The *New York Times* added, "It is a scattered and hectic account, racy and enthusiastic and laid out on the carefree principle that when one good story reminds the teller of another, it should be told at once, even if it properly belongs in another chapter."

Anthony turned to his own life for the subject matter of *This Is Where I Came In.* A *New York Herald Tribune* review of the autobiography said, "Though he packs his book with the names of the famous and illustrious people he knew and worked with, Anthony himself emerges as an unpretentious humor-loving individual who makes no personal claim to fame. He has no recognizable philosophy; he has no deep meaning message; he possesses no great literary style. But he is highly enjoyable because he writes out of the richness of a full and varied life in the world of words he loves." R. W. Henderson called the book "decidedly interesting" in his *Library Journal* assessment, and Quentin Reynolds, writing in *Saturday Review,* added, "There isn't a dull page in *This Is Where I Came In* because there hasn't been a dull page in the life of Ed Anthony."

*BIOGRAPHICAL/CRITICAL SOURCES:*

*BOOKS*

Anthony, Edward, *This Is Where I Came In: The Impromptu Confessions of Edward Anthony,* Doubleday, 1960.

*PERIODICALS*

*Atlantic,* March, 1962.
*Booklist,* March 15, 1960; March 15, 1962.

*Bookmark,* May, 1960; July, 1962.

*Boston Transcript,* October 15, 1921, p. 8; June 7, 1924, p. 1; August 22, 1928, p. 6.

*Horn Book,* December, 1957.

*Kirkus Reviews,* May 1, 1957; January 15, 1960; December 1, 1961.

*Library Journal,* November 15, 1957; February 1, 1960; January 15, 1962.

*Literature Review,* October 15, 1921, p. 92.

*New Yorker,* February 24, 1962.

*New York Herald Tribune,* November 17, 1957; May 22, 1960.

*New York Herald Tribune Book Review,* November 17, 1957, p. 2; May 22, 1960, p. 12; February 4, 1962, p. 6.

*New York Times,* June 29, 1924, p. 12; August 12, 1928, p. 7; March 2, 1941; November 17, 1957, p. 52.

*New York Tribune,* July 20, 1924, p. 24.

*San Francisco Chronicle,* August 25, 1957, p. 22; February 14, 1962, p. 31.

*Saturday Review,* April 26, 1941; April 30, 1960; February 17, 1962.

*Springfield Republican,* December 7, 1921, p. 8; October 14, 1928, p. 7E; March 18, 1962, p. 4D.

*Wilson Library Bulletin,* July, 1960.

*OBITUARIES:*

*PERIODICALS*

*New York Times,* August 18, 1971.

*Publishers Weekly,* September 13, 1971.

*Washington Post,* August 20, 1971.*

\*          \*          \*

**ARLEN, Leslie**
    See NICOLE, Christopher (Robin)

\*          \*          \*

**ARTHUR, Burt**
    See SHAPPIRO, Herbert (Arthur)

\*          \*          \*

**ARTHUR, Herbert**
    See SHAPPIRO, Herbert (Arthur)

\*          \*          \*

**ASHLEY, Ellen**
    See GASPAROTTI, Elizabeth Seifert

# B

## BAKER, Alan 1951-

*PERSONAL:* Born November 14, 1951, in London, England; son of Bernard Victor (a welder) and Barbara Joan (a tracer; maiden name, Weir) Baker. *Education:* Attended Croydon Technical College, 1969-71, Hull University, 1971-72, and Croydon Art College, 1972-73; Brighton Art College, B.A. (Honors), 1976. *Religion:* Agnostic.

*ADDRESSES: Home and office*—St. Michaels, Telscombe Village, near Lewes, East Sussex, England.

*CAREER:* Author and freelance illustrator of children's books. Part-time teacher of illustration at Brighton University.

*AWARDS, HONORS:* Silver Award, Campaign Press Awards, 1990; Gold Award, Creative Circle Awards, 1990; Children's Choice selection, International Reading Association/Children's Book Council (IRA/CBC), 1996, for *Gray Rabbit's Odd One Out;* several of Baker's works have been selected for annual "Best Books" commendations.

*WRITINGS:*

*FOR CHILDREN; SELF-ILLUSTRATED*

*Benjamin and the Box,* Deutsch (London), 1977.
*Benjamin Bounces Back,* Harper (New York City), 1978.
*Benjamin's Dreadful Dream,* Harper, 1980.
*Benjamin's Book,* Deutsch, 1982, Lothrop (New York City), 1983.
*A Fairyland Alphabet,* Deutsch, 1984.

*Benjamin's Portrait,* Deutsch, 1986.
*One Naughty Boy,* Deutsch, 1989.
*Goodnight William,* Deutsch, 1990.
*Benjamin's Balloon,* Lothrop, 1990.
*Two Tiny Mice,* Kingfisher, 1990.
*Jason's Dragon,* BBC Publications, 1992.
*Where's Mouse?,* Kingfisher, 1992.
*Black and White Rabbits ABC,* Kingfisher, 1994.
*Brown Rabbit's Shape Book,* Kingfisher, 1994.
*Gray Rabbit's 1, 2, 3,* Kingfisher, 1994.
*White Rabbit's Colour Book,* Kingfisher, 1994.
*Brown Rabbit's Day,* Kingfisher, 1995.
*Gray Rabbit's Odd One Out,* Kingfisher, 1995.
*Little Rabbit's First Word Book,* Kingfisher, 1996.
*I Thought I Heard . . . ,* Copper Beach Books (Brookfield, CT), 1996.
*Mouse's Christmas,* Copper Beach Books, 1996.
*Mouse's Halloween,* Copper Beach Books, 1997.
*Little Rabbit's Play and Learn Book,* Kingfisher, 1997.
*Little Rabbit's Snacktime,* Kingfisher, 1998.
*Little Rabbit's Bedtime,* Kingfisher, 1998.
*Little Rabbit's First Number Book,* Kingfisher, 1998.

*ILLUSTRATOR*

Ann Philippa Pearce, *The Battle of Bubble and Squeak,* Deutsch, 1978.
*Heritage of Flowers,* Hutchinson, 1980.
*Mythical Beasts,* Hutchinson, 1981.
Rudyard Kipling, *The Butterfly That Stamped,* Macmillan (New York City), 1982.
Kate Petty, *Snakes,* Aladdin (New York City), 1984.
Kate Petty, *Dinosaurs,* Aladdin, 1984.
Kate Petty, *Frogs and Toads,* Aladdin, 1985, Franklin Watts, 1990.
Kate Petty, *Spiders,* Aladdin, 1985.

Michael Rosen, *Hairy Tales and Nursery Crimes,* Deutsch, 1985.

Gene Kemp, *Mr. Magus Is Waiting for You,* Faber & Faber (Winchester, MA), 1986.

Robin Lister, *The Odyssey,* Kingfisher, 1987.

Robin Lister, *The Story of King Arthur,* Kingfisher, 1988.

Verna Wilkins, *Mike and Lottie,* Tamarind, 1988.

Judith Nicholls, *Wordspells,* Faber & Faber, 1988.

Judith Nicholls, *What on Earth?: Poems with a Conservation Theme,* Faber & Faber, 1989.

Michael Rosen, *Mini Beasties,* Firefly, 1991.

Kate Petty, *Stop, Look and Listen, Mr. Toad!,* Hodder & Stoughton (London), 1991.

Kate Petty, *Mr. Toad to the Rescue,* Aladdin, 1992.

Joni Mitchell, *Both Sides Now,* Scholastic (New York City), 1992.

Kate Petty, *Mr. Toad's Narrow Escape,* Barrons, 1992.

Gloria Patrick, *A Bug in a Jug,* Heath (Lexington, MA), 1992.

Judy Bennett, *Sorry for the Slug,* Reed, 1994.

Dan Abnett, *Treasure Hunt in the Creepy Mansion,* Salamander Books (London), 1995.

Dan Abnett, *Treasure Hunt in the Lost City,* Salamander Books, 1996.

Judy Allen, *Hedgehog in the Garden,* Leopard, 1996.

*Fit-a-Shape: Animals; Colors; Opposites; Shapes; Bugs; Patterns; Cloths; Numbers,* Running Press (Philadelphia), 1996.

Anita Ganeri, *Dragons and Monsters,* Macdonald, 1996.

*ADAPTATIONS: Benjamin and the Box* was featured on the Canadian Broadcasting Corporation (CBC-TV) series, *The Friendly Giant,* in March and April of 1980, and on British and Norwegian television.

*SIDELIGHTS:* The hero of Alan Baker's first book, *Benjamin and the Box,* "is a beautifully observed, beautifully furry hamster," asserted a reviewer for *Junior Bookshelf.* Critics aver that Baker's success lies in combining realistically depicted animal characters, which appeal to young children, with gently humorous stories that preschoolers can identify with. Indeed, some commentators contend that, in the Benjamin books and others, Baker's simple texts are merely a vehicle for his extravagant illustrations. But, though the visual element often takes precedence in Baker's work, "I like to think of the writing as adding a further dimension to the illustrations," Baker once commented. "The words hold the storyline when the idea cannot be illustrated."

In *Benjamin and the Box* Baker introduces preschoolers to a hapless, nearsighted, persistent little hamster named Benjamin, a character based on a pet from Baker's childhood. In this first book, Benjamin comes upon a box, which he persistently tries to open, using tools, magic spells, and even dynamite. "It was love at first meeting," a reviewer for *Publishers Weekly* declared of *Benjamin and the Box.* In *Benjamin Bounces Back,* the nearsighted Benjamin fails to read the "NO ENTRY" sign on a door, and reluctantly embarks on a series of wild adventures after he pushes through the forbidden entrance. *Benjamin's Dreadful Dream* similarly finds the accident-prone hamster inadvertently touching off a pile of fireworks that blasts him into outer space, when all he really wanted was a midnight snack. "The tenuous story is clearly an excuse for the sparkling illustrations," observed a reviewer for *Junior Bookshelf,* but a *Publishers Weekly* critic maintained that "charmed readers won't forget this larky escapade."

The same brightly colored, realistically detailed illustrations characterize the other stories about Benjamin, including *Benjamin's Book,* in which the hamster accidentally puts a paw print on a clean sheet of paper. In his increasingly frantic attempts to repair the damage, the page gets ever messier, until Benjamin replaces the sheet altogether, but accidentally marks it with another paw print as he leaves. "This is visually appealing, has a quiet humor, and tells a story that's just right in length, scope, and familiarity for the preschool child," noted Zena Sutherland of the *Bulletin of the Center for Children's Books. Benjamin's Portrait* finds the determined hamster attempting a self-portrait after going to a portrait gallery. "Preschoolers will identify with Benjamin's eagerness to try things for himself, as well as his encounters with unexpected troubles," remarked Susan Nemeth McCarthy in *School Library Journal.* Benjamin flies off under the power of a purple balloon in *Benjamin's Balloon,* which Margery Fisher of *Growing Point* called a "gentle and congenial comedy."

Baker's other recurring animal characters include a number of rabbits featured in some highly regarded concept books that teach very young children about shapes, colors, letters, and numbers. Invariably, critics found that Baker's concept books give a fresh twist to familiar themes. *Black and White Rabbit's ABC* starts with an apple, as many alphabet books do, but then is transformed as a black and white rabbit enters the picture and attempts to paint the apple, beginning the reader on "a wry and often very messy journey from A to Z," according to a *Publishers*

*Weekly* reviewer. *Brown Rabbit's Shape Book* features balloons of different shapes, and *White Rabbit's Color Book* is "perhaps the best book of the bunch," according to Ilene Cooper of *Booklist.* In *White Rabbit's Color Book,* a white rabbit falls into a series of paint cans, demonstrating how primary colors mix to become other colors. Throughout each of these concept books, a *Publishers Weekly* critic noted, "sweet-natured humor infuses the clear, precise artwork."

Baker's subsequent "Rabbit" titles are also distinguished by a gently humorous text and striking illustrations combined with a unique slant on a learning concept. In *Brown Rabbit's Day* a simple story offers the opportunity for color and object identification, counting and telling time. In *Gray Rabbit's Odd One Out* preschoolers help Gray Rabbit find his favorite book while learning to sort objects according to a variety of schemes.

Baker introduces his readers to animals common to the English forest through which his little heroes travel in *Two Tiny Mice,* another self-illustrated picture book. A *Kirkus Reviews* critic singled out Baker's "expansive, delicately detailed illustrations" for special mention in a review of this work. Introducing animals also forms the basis for Baker's story *Where's Mouse,* in which Mother Mouse questions one forest animal after another in her search for Baby Mouse. *Where's Mouse* has accordion-fold pages whose holes give the illusion of three-dimensionality to the illustrations, which *School Library Journal* contributor Christine A. Moesch praised as "delicate and cleverly laid out." Baker employs a similar format in *Mouse's Christmas,* in which Mouse's friends plan a surprise party for him on Christmas Eve.

Baker's illustrations are acclaimed for their fine detail and for the humor they add to the author's simple tales. Baker perfected this combination in his popular "Benjamin" series; "Even when one sees only [Benjamin's] feet encased in a snowball, the comic character of the furry creature is unmistakable," remarked Lori A. Janick in the *School Library Journal.* Although some critics have found Baker's plots meager, especially when compared to his arresting artwork, reviewers of such concept books as *Gray Rabbit's 1,2,3* and *White Rabbit's Color Book* felt that Baker's plots were suitable for holding the attention of his preschool audience. *School Library Journal* contributor Marsha McGrath avowed that Baker's books are "instructional titles that are lots of fun for prereaders."

*BIOGRAPHICAL/CRITICAL SOURCES:*

*PERIODICALS*

*Booklist,* March 15, 1983, p. 962; March 1, 1987, p. 1011; April 15, 1991, p. 1645; July, 1994, p. 1952.
*Books for Keeps,* May, 1990, p. 29; May, 1994, p. 33.
*Bulletin of the Center for Children's Books,* July, 1983, p. 202; January, 1991, p. 110.
*Catholic Library World,* February, 1979, p. 311.
*Christian Science Monitor,* September 16, 1994, p. 10.
*Emergency Librarian,* November, 1995, p. 45; January, 1996, p. 42.
*Growing Point,* January, 1978, p. 3251; November, 1982, p. 3990; May, 1990, p. 5349; March, 1991, p. 5486.
*Horn Book,* July, 1990, p. 35; fall, 1991, p. 220; fall, 1994, p. 254; spring, 1996, pp. 11, 118.
*Junior Bookshelf,* June, 1978, p. 133; April, 1979, p. 91; October, 1980, p. 232; December, 1982, p. 218; April, 1990, p. 70.
*Kirkus Reviews,* February 1, 1979, p. 119; June 15, 1980, p. 773; January 15, 1987, p. 130; July 15, 1990, p. 1010; May 1, 1991, p. 611; December 1, 1992, p. 1500.
*New York Times Book Review,* April 27, 1980, p. 49.
*Publishers Weekly,* February 27, 1978, p. 156; December 11, 1978, p. 70; January 25, 1980, p. 340; May 17, 1991, p. 62; November 23, 1992, p. 61; March 7, 1994, p. 68; September 30, 1996, p. 90.
*School Library Journal,* December, 1978, p. 64; October, 1980, p. 119; November, 1980, p. 57; May, 1983, p. 56; May, 1987, p. 81; December, 1990, p. 70; May, 1991, p. 74; February, 1993, p. 68; March, 1996, p. 166.
*Times Educational Supplement,* February 3, 1978, p. 45; June 20, 1980, p. 44; March 30, 1990, p. B11.
*Times Literary Supplement,* December 2, 1977, p. 1411; March 28, 1980, p. 359; June 26, 1987, p. 700.

\* \* \*

**BANKS, James A(lbert) 1941-**

*PERSONAL:* Born September 24, 1941, in Marianna, AR; son of Matthew (a farmer) and Lula (Holt)

Banks; married Cherry A. McGee (a professor and author), February 15, 1969; children: Angela Marie, Patricia Ann. *Ethnicity:* "African American." *Education:* Chicago City Junior College, A.A., 1963; Chicago State College (now Chicago State University), B.Ed., 1964; Michigan State University, M.A., 1967, Ph.D., 1969. *Religion:* Methodist.

*ADDRESSES: Home*—1333 Northwest 200th St., Shore Line, WA 98177-2140. *Office*—110 Miller Hall, Box 353600, University of Washington, Seattle, WA 98195-3600; fax: 206-542-4218.

*CAREER:* Teacher in Joliet, IL 1965, and in Chicago, IL 1965-66; University of Washington, Seattle, assistant professor, 1969-71, associate professor, 1971-73, professor of education, 1973—, chairperson of curriculum and instruction, 1982-87, director of Center for Multicultural Education, 1992—. Visiting professor at University of Michigan, 1975, and University of Guam, 1979; distinguished scholar lecturer at Kent State University, 1978, University of Arizona, 1979, Indiana University—Bloomington, 1983, Humboldt State University, 1989, and University of North Carolina at Chapel Hill, 1989; Virginia State University, eminent scholar lecturer, 1981; British Academy, visiting lecturer, 1983; California State University, Fullerton, distinguished visiting lecturer, 1989; Syracuse University, Harry F. and Alva K. Ganders Memorial Fund Distinguished Lecturer, 1989; University of Minnesota—Twin Cities, James J. Hill Visiting Professor, 1991; Howard University, Charles F. Thompson Lecturer, 1995; Columbia University, Teachers College, Sachs Lecturer, 1996; Florida State University, Mack and Effie Campbell Tyner Eminent Scholar, 1998. National Advisory Council on Ethnic Heritage Studies, member, 1975-79; Social Science Education Consortium, member of board of directors, 1976-79.

*MEMBER:* Association for Supervision and Curriculum Development (member of board of directors, 1976-79), National Council for the Social Studies (member of board of directors, 1973-74 and 1980-85; chairperson of task force on Ethnic Studies Curriculum Guidelines, 1975-76; vice-president, 1980; president, 1982), American Educational Research Association (president, 1997-98).

*AWARDS, HONORS:* Spencer fellowship, National Academy of Education, 1973; named "Outstanding Young Man", Washington State Jaycees, 1975; Rockefeller Foundation research fellowship, 1980;

Kellogg Foundation national fellowship, 1980-83; named distinguished lecturer for 1982, Association of Teacher Educators; American Educational Research Association, named distinguished scholar/researcher on minority education, 1986, research review award, 1994, senior career scholar/researcher award, 1996; L.H.D. from Bank Street College of Education, 1993; Distinguished Book Award, National Association for Multicultural Education, 1997, for *Handbook of Research on Multicultural Education.*

*WRITINGS:*

(With Cherry A. McGee Banks) *March toward Freedom: A History of Black Americans,* Fearon, 1970, revised edition, 1978.
*Teaching the Black Experience: Methods and Materials,* Fearon, 1970.
*Ethnic Studies in the Social Context* (monograph), National Urban League, 1972.
(With Ambrose A. Clegg, Jr.) *Teaching Strategies for the Social Studies,* Addison-Wesley (Reading, MA), 1973, 4th edition, Longman (New York City), 1990.
*Teaching Strategies for Ethnic Studies,* Allyn & Bacon (Newton, MA), 1975, 6th edition, 1997.
(With Carlos E. Cortes, Geneva Gay, Ricardo L. Garcia and Anna S. Ochoa) *Curriculum Guidelines for Multiethnic Education,* National Council for the Social Studies, 1976, revised edition published as *Curriculum Guidelines for Multicultural Education,* 1992.
*Multiethnic Education: Practices and Promises,* Phi Delta Kappa Educational Foundation, 1977.
*Multiethnic Education: Theory and Practice,* Allyn & Bacon, 1981, 3rd edition, 1994.
(With Sam L. Sebesta) *We Americans: Our History and People,* two volumes, Allyn & Bacon, 1982.
*An Introduction to Multicultural Education,* Allyn & Bacon, 1994, 2nd edition, 1998.
*Educating Citizens in a Multicultural Society,* Teachers College Press (New York City), 1997.

*EDITOR*

(With William W. Joyce) *Teaching the Language Arts to Culturally Different Children,* Addison-Wesley, 1971.
(With Joyce) *Teaching Social Studies to Culturally Different Children,* Addison-Wesley, 1971.
(With Jean D. Grambs) *Black Self-Concept: Implications for Education and Social Science,* McGraw (New York City), 1972.

*Teaching Ethnic Studies: Concepts and Strategies,* National Council for the Social Studies, 1973.

*Education in the Eighties: Multiethnic Education,* National Education Association, 1981.

(And contributor) *Multicultural Education in Western Societies,* Holt (New York City), 1986.

(And contributor) *Multicultural Education: Issues and Perspectives,* Allyn and Bacon, 1989, 3rd edition, 1997.

(And contributor) *Handbook of Research on Multicultural Education,* Macmillan (New York City), 1995.

(And contributor) *Multicultural Education, Transformative Knowledge, and Action,* Teachers College Press, 1995.

Guest editor, *Phi Delta Kappan,* 1972, 1983, 1993, and *Social Education,* 1982. Member of editorial boards, *Teachers College Record* and *Race, Ethnicity, and Education.* Principal consultant, *Preparation in the Social Studies,* 1986; general consultant, *A World of Difference,* 1986.

*CONTRIBUTOR*

Contributor to numerous books on education, including *The Humanities in Precollegiate Education,* 1984, *Social Issues and Education: Challenge and Responsibility,* 1987, *Cultural and Ethnic Factors in Learning and Motivation: Implications for Education,* 1988, *Black Adolescents,* 1989, *Review of Research in Education,* 1993, *Education for Cultural Diversity: The Challenge for a New Era,* 1993, *Handbook of Research on the Education of Young Children,* 1993, *Realizing Our Common Destiny,* 1995, *Making Schooling Multicultural: Campus and Classrooms,* 1996, *Encyclopedia of African-American Culture and History,* 1996, *Handbook of Tests and Measurements for Black Populations,* Volumes 1-2, 1996, *Inside Ethnic America: An Ethnic Studies Reader,* 1996, *Improving Schooling for Language-Minority Children: A Research Agenda,* 1997, *Handbook for Research on Teacher Education,* and *Handbook for Research on Social Studies Teaching and Learning.* Also contributor to *International Encyclopedia of Education,* Volumes 6 and 9, 1985. Contributor of more than ninety articles and reviews to professional journals, including *Educational Leadership, Social Studies, New Era, Educational Review,* and *Journal of Negro Education.*

*WORK IN PROGRESS: Teaching Strategies for the Social Studies,* 5th edition, with Clegg and C. A. M. Banks, for Addison-Wesley.

**BARICH, Bill 1943-**

*PERSONAL:* Born August 23, 1943, in Winona, MN; son of Russell (a magazine distribution executive) and Lois (a homemaker; maiden name, Petercon) Barich; married Diana Shugart, May 12, 1972. *Education:* Colgate University, B.A., 1965. *Politics:* Independent. *Avocational interests:* Hiking, fishing, music, travel.

*ADDRESSES: Agent*—c/o Amanda Urban, International Creative Management, 40 West 57th St., New York, NY 10019.

*CAREER:* U.S. Peace Corps volunteer in Nigeria and Biafra, 1966-67; Somerset Hills School, Somerset, NJ, teacher, 1967-69; L.S. Distributors, San Francisco, CA, stockperson and book salesperson, 1969-71; Alfred A. Knopf, San Francisco and New York City, publicity assistant and editorial assistant, 1972-75; *New Yorker,* New York City, staff writer, 1981-94. Instructor of creative writing at University of California, Berkeley and Santa Cruz campuses, Jack Kerouac School of Disembodied Poetics, and Naropa Institute (Boulder, CO). Faculty member of Squaw Valley Writers' Conference. President, Friends of Books and Comics, San Francisco Book Fair, 1971. Member of board of directors, Intersection for the Arts, San Francisco, 1987-91.

*MEMBER:* PEN.

*AWARDS, HONORS:* Guggenheim Fellow, 1985; Marin County Arts Council Fellow, 1995.

*WRITINGS:*

*Laughing in the Hills* (semi-autobiographical), Viking (New York City), 1980.

*Traveling Light* (travelogue essays), Viking, 1984.

*Hard to Be Good* (short stories), Farrar, Straus (New York City), 1987.

*Hat Creek and the McCloud,* Engdahl Typography, 1988.

*Big Dreams: Into the Heart of California* (nonfiction), Pantheon (New York City), 1994.

*Carson Valley* (novel), Pantheon, 1996.

*Crazy for Rivers,* Lyons Press (New York City), 1999.

Contributor of articles to various periodicals, including *New Yorker, Esquire, New York Times, Sports Illustrated* and *American Poetry Review.* Work represented in anthologies, including *Literary Journalists, Armchair Angler,* and *Best American Short Stories.*

*WORK IN PROGRESS: Divers in the Night: An African Memoir,* publication expected in 1998.

*SIDELIGHTS:* Bill Barich has enjoyed success among diverse audiences and has won acclaim for a prose style that has often been characterized as interesting as well as entertaining. Many of his articles and non-fiction books are based on his own observations and experiences, and as Edd Applegate noted in *Dictionary of Literary Biography,* the author's "powerful reporting skills, evident throughout his work, show most clearly when he documents his most personal passions. . . . His writing often presents in dramatic form his ceaseless search for some kind of meaning in what often appears to him a cruel and often absurd world." Barich once described his work to *CA:* "A great deal of my writing, some of it uncollected in book form, has appeared in the *New Yorker* over the past dozen years or so. It falls roughly into three categories: reportage (Northern Ireland, the Mexican border, board and care homes for chronic paranoid schizphrenics, etc.); essays (horse racing, boxing, fishing, travel pieces about England and Italy); and short fiction." He further told *CA:* "My mentor at the magazine was William Shawn, its legendary editor, whose fine and gentle guidance was an immense help to me."

Barich began writing his first book, *Laughing in the Hills,* when he was recovering from one of the lowest points of his life—his mother was dying of cancer, his wife had been misdiagnosed with a brain tumor and had undergone an unnecessary operation, and he had neither a job nor money. In the spring of 1978 Barich visited the racetrack, where he soon became fascinated with the subculture of horse racing and off-track betting. Barich subsequently left his rented mobile home in the country to live in a cheap motel near the Golden Gate Fields racetrack, close to San Francisco.

For a period of about ten weeks, Barich immersed himself in the world of horse racing and betting. He studied the trainers, jockeys, and grooms; he observed the regular wagerers, noticing that many enjoy a drink or two, eat when they can, and live in constant anticipation of the big win. Barich quickly managed to gain the trust of those behind the scenes of the sport, obtaining an in-depth education about thoroughbred racing and betting. Barich also discovered that the world of horse racing, with its neat, continuous

track and code of conduct, offered a much-needed sense of order to his then-tumultuous life.

*Laughing in the Hills* is semi-autobiographical, combining Barich's research on horse racing with reflections on his life. The work was serialized in the *New Yorker,* where Barich was on staff for fourteen years. Critics such as Gary L. Fisketjon, writing in *Esquire,* applauded the balance achieved between documentary and life story. "*Laughing in the Hills* wisely shies from weeping, gnashing of teeth, and impertinent autobiography," Fisketjon wrote, "much of it is devoted to the history, breeding, and training of horses, the routine and finances of the track, and all manner and variety of information that directly pertains only to itself." Noting that Barich's book "extends in many directions," Fisketjon applauded the author's handling of the material. Calling the book "moving, graceful, and spirited," the critic stated: "Instead of dogging the meaning of it all, [Barich] experienced a great deal with humor and sensitivity, every so often cashing in a ticket to boot."

*Laughing in the Hills* also garnered praise from Heywood Hale Broun in a review for *Book World.* He described Barich's work as "an odd and patchy book, sometimes seeming a simple instructional manual on the ins and outs of thoroughbred racing, sometimes a cry of pain quickly to be stilled by a salve of scholarship or an account of Wednesday's fifth race or Thursday's third." Joe Flaherty, writing for the *New York Times Book Review,* offered similar comments about *Laughing in the Hills.* Flaherty found that Barich's meshing of personal reflection with facts about the track gave the book a "wonderful dimension. Under the guise of 'a race track book' . . . Barich offers a touching portrait of a young man in trouble." The author, according to Flaherty, achieved success because "in a dismal period of his life he went out and fashioned art."

Barich's next book, *Traveling Light,* is a collection of essays, many of them first published in *New Yorker* magazine. The works chronicle Barich's journeys to various locales in the United States and Europe. Unlike conventional travelogues, however, Barich's journal describes what he considers simple pleasures of life, including fishing, searching for the best taverns in London, and perusing the race tracks. Also included are profiles of interesting and often eccentric people he met during his eighteen-month long tour.

With *Traveling Light,* Barich again received favorable reviews. *Washington Post* travel editor James T.

Yenckel stated: "What [Barich] set out to do in these pieces—and what he has accomplished beautifully—is to capture the ordinariness of the places he visited, rightfully aware that 'the character of any given place is best reflected in its daily routines.'" This, according to Yenckel, "is travel at its most interesting and most rewarding." The critic noted that "one learns quite a lot in Barich's deceptively simple stories, which is a quality of good travel writing."

Also assessing *Traveling Light* was Christopher Lehmann-Haupt of the *New York Times*. The reviewer compared *Traveling Light* to Barich's first book, *Laughing in the Hills:* "Both books share a lively curiosity and a keen eye for detail." *Time*'s John Skow also issued praise for *Traveling Light,* assessing that "Barich is especially good at the travel writer's peculiar con—getting the reader to enjoy his enjoyment." After expressing an appreciation for Barich's essay on pub shopping in London, Skow concluded: "The reader, by now quite thirsty but no longer a stranger, feels that *Traveling Light* has ended far too soon. He is moved to urge Barich onward. Take more trips, he wants to say, for those of us whose luggage has grown too heavy to lug." Also among fans of *Traveling Light* is Jonathan Elukin, who remarked in the *New York Times Book Review:* "This thin volume and the measured, informal style of Mr. Barich's prose belie[s] the amount of knowledge and humor packed into *Traveling Light.*"

Before publication of any of his previous works, Barich had to his credit half a dozen unreleased novels. He furthered his skill at creating fiction in his third published book, *Hard to Be Good,* a collection of short stories, many of which profile young men grappling with reality as they enter adulthood. All of Barich's characters share some similarities, among them disillusionment, the ability to dream, and the need for a second chance at success. Shane, the lead character in the title story, for example, is a sixteen-year-old who has a run-in with the law and, consequently, is sent to live with his mother and her new husband, a former marijuana farmer who has now reformed. Despite all efforts to stay out of trouble, Shane discovers that it is "hard to be good."

The volume fared well with critics, including William Murray, who reviewed the book for the *Los Angeles Times Book Review.* Murray described Barich's writing in general as "brilliantly entertaining," and wrote that Barich "cares deeply about his characters and the depth of this emotion is what gives his writing strength. He makes us see and hear each one of them

vividly, as if we had discovered them ourselves. It's a gift that cannot be taught in any creative-writing class and that distinguishes the work of only the very best authors." *Chicago Tribune* critic John Blades also enjoyed *Hard to Be Good,* especially the tales set in Italy. "Here and elsewhere," Blades suggested, "Barich catches the spirit of the country as whimsically as John Cheever did in his Italian tales." He added, "Judging by these three books [*Laughing in the Hills, Traveling Light,* and *Hard to Be Good*], it seems hard for Bill Barich not to be good."

Barich took to the road again in the writing of *Big Dreams: Into the Heart of California,* criss-crossing the state in a rented Ford Taurus and touring the land where many believe their dreams will come true. Chatting with farmers, migrant workers, fishermen, loggers, illegal immigrants, and others, Barich presents a seldom-seen look at the Golden State along with reflections about his own life and dreams. The result is another critically acclaimed book, with reviewers praising Barich's choice of subject and style of presentation. Applauding Barich's "scrupulous but passionate" voice, *New York Times* critic Margo Jefferson declared: "*Big Dreams* works because Mr. Barich keeps crossing the borders between history, reportage and reverie." Barich elicited further approval from David Traxel, who reviewed *Big Dreams* for the *New York Times Book Review:* "Barich . . . has a good eye and a delightful way with language. Using a style notable for its clarity, grace and energy, he gives us short biographies of historical figures . . . while weaving in interesting bits of information about native tribes, explorers and settlers." Still, Applegate found that despite Barich's laudable effort to "explain and capture California's appeal in his impressive prose style. . .the size and complexity of the state were sometimes overwhelming, and, despite the general praise for the book, some reviewers felt that Barich's depictions of some of the characters he met should have been more vivid."

In 1997, Barich published his first novel, *Carson Valley.* Set in California's wine country, it tells the story of Anna Torelli, a divorcee who returns to California to care for her aging, ailing parents. To Anna's surprise, she becomes romantically involved with the grandson of one of her father's best friends. "Barich, having lived in the area about which he writes, knows the characters and landscape well, and he provides readers with a realistic romantic novel," declared Applegate. Linda Gray Sexton also mentioned the realism of *Carson Valley* in her *New York Times* review of the book, and added that "there is also a sense of magic. Mr. Barich pulls in fate and luck with an elegant sleight of hand that guides his characters to their difficult destinies."

*BIOGRAPHICAL/CRITICAL SOURCES:*

*BOOKS*

Anderson, Chris, editor, *Literary Nonfiction: Theory, Criticism, Pedagogy,* Southern Illinois University Press (Carbondale), 1989.
*Dictionary of Literary Biography,* Volume 185: *American Literary Journalists, 1945-1995, First Series,* Gale (Detroit), 1997.
Sims, Norman, editor, *The Literary Journalists,* Ballantine (New York City), 1984, pp. 321-339.

*PERIODICALS*

*Book World,* July 27, 1980, p. 4.
*Chicago Tribune,* December 4, 1987.
*Esquire,* May, 1980, p. 92.
*Globe and Mail* (Toronto), April 27, 1985.
*Los Angeles Times Book Review,* December 6, 1987.
*New York Review of Books,* March 5, 1981, p. 39.
*New York Times,* February 17, 1984; May 18, 1994, p. C 21; March 3, 1997.
*New York Times Book Review,* June 15, 1980, pp. 7, 34; February 5, 1984, p. 19; March 3, 1985, p. 34; December 13, 1987; August 7, 1994, p. 6.
*People Weekly,* August 11, 1980.
*Time,* February 6, 1984, p. 72.
*Washington Post,* January 10, 1984.
*Washington Post Book World,* July 19, 1981, p. 12.*

\*    \*    \*

## BARLETT, Donald L(eon) 1936-

*PERSONAL:* Born July 17, 1936, in DuBois, PA; son of James L. and Mary V. (Wineberg) Barlett; married Shirley A. Jones (a nurse); children: Matthew J. *Education:* Attended Pennsylvania State University, 1954-55.

*ADDRESSES: Office*—Philadelphia Inquirer, P.O. Box 8263, Philadelphia, PA 19101.

*CAREER: Reading Times,* Reading, PA, general assignment and beat reporter, 1956-58, 1961-62; *Akron Beacon-Journal,* Akron, OH, general assignment and beat reporter, 1962-64; *Cleveland Plain Dealer,* Cleveland, OH, investigative reporter, 1965-66, 1969-70; *Chicago Daily News,* Chicago, investigative reporter, 1967-68; *Philadelphia Inquirer,* Philadelphia, investigative reporter, 1970—. *Military service:* U.S. Army, 1958-61; served as counterintelligence agent.

*AWARDS, HONORS:* George Polk Memorial Award for metropolitan reporting and Sigma Delta Chi Distinguished Service in Journalism award, 1971, for newspaper series on the Federal Housing Administration; George Polk Memorial Award for special reporting, Heywood Broun Award for public interest reporting, and Sidney Hillman Foundation Award, 1973, all for newspaper series "Crimes and Injustice"; Overseas Press Club award and Sigma Delta Chi Distinguished Service in Journalism award for foreign correspondence, 1974, for newspaper series "Foreign Aid: The Flawed Dream"; Pulitzer Prize for national reporting, 1975, for newspaper series "Auditing the IRS"; Honor Medal for distinguished service to journalism, University of Missouri, 1983.

*WRITINGS:*

(With James B. Steele) *Empire: The Life, Legend, and Madness of Howard Hughes* (biography), Norton (New York City), 1979.
(With Steele) *Forevermore: Nuclear Waste in America,* Norton, 1985.
(With Steele) *America: What Went Wrong?,* Andrews & McMeel (Kansas City), 1992.
(With Steele) *America: Who Really Pays the Taxes?,* Simon & Schuster (New York City), 1994.
(With Steele) *America: Who Stole the Dream?,* Andrews & McMeel, 1996.

Contributor to periodicals, including *Nation* and *New Republic.*

*SIDELIGHTS:* Since the early 1970s Donald L. Barlett and James B. Steele have collaborated as investigative reporters for the *Philadelphia Inquirer,* where their work together has garnered numerous awards, including a Pulitzer Prize. They also co-authored a highly acclaimed biography, *Empire: The Life, Legend, and Madness of Howard Hughes,* and have earned reputations for credible reporting by basing their stories on documentation rather than on scandal-hunting. According to reviewer Robert Sherrill in *Nation,* the pair constitutes "the finest team of investigative reporters west of *The Times of London.*"

Before teaming up with Steele at the *Inquirer,* Barlett was "a traditional scandal-hunting investigative reporter," according to Leonard Downie Jr. in *The New Muckrakers*. But while he had worked on a variety of newspapers and specialized in uncovering local corruption, Barlett had not been permitted to do the kind of aggressive investigative work he found most exciting. As a result, he eventually sought employment with the Knight newspaper chain, whose editors were said to support enterprising reporting. Barlett began work at the chain's Philadelphia paper, the *Inquirer,* in 1970—on the same day as future collaborator Steele—and was first assigned to write about narcotics traffic and phony business bankruptcies in the city. Before long, however, the two men were instructed to work together in the search for evidence of fraud in a Federal Housing Administration (FHA) subsidy program for rehabilitating and selling slum houses. The pair found they worked well together and after months of painstaking research—which included examining deeds and mortgages and interviewing families living in the substandard homes—Barlett and Steele published a thoroughly documented series of articles detailing abuse in the FHA program.

The award-winning FHA articles were the first of many successes for the two reporters. During subsequent investigations they disclosed inequities in Philadelphia's criminal courts and in tax law enforcement by the Internal Revenue Service; they revealed that the "oil crisis" of the early 1970s was largely the creation of policies designed by multinational firms and the U.S. government in order to control the supply of crude oil for their own ends; and they showed that funds of the U.S. Foreign Aid program more often ended up lining the pockets of the rich than helping the poor.

Especially fruitful for the two men was the time they spent systematically examining Howard Hughes' connections with the U.S. government. For eight months they searched through all kinds of records, including contracts, corporation documents, and financial statements, and finally assembled 10,000 pages of notes and documents—enough material not just for a series of articles, but for a book as well. The critics greeted *Empire: The Life, Legend, and Madness of Howard Hughes* with considerable fanfare. Critiquing for the *New York Times Book Review,* Ted Morgan declared: "Of all the books written about Howard Hughes, 'Empire' is easily the best . . . the authors have assembled the first fully documented, cradle-to-grave account of unique American life." And in *Newsweek,* reviewer Peter S. Prescot commented: "Donald L.

Barlett and James B. Steele . . . have made an impressive use of documents to fashion this longest, most responsible and authoritative biography of Hughes to date."

Their use of documentation has particularly distinguished Barlett and Steele. They are among the "new breed of muckraker," declared Downie. Their journalism goes beyond the old reliance on stories from informants and looks to the public record for evidence. "It reveals with expert analysis and thorough documentation what has systematically gone wrong with the powerful, complex institutions that affect so much of life today," explained Downie. "The best of this work reaches far enough beneath the skin of those institutions to enlighten even those who run them, thus improving the changes for change."

Documentation of sources would be especially important in Barlett and Steele's 1985 work, *Forevermore: Nuclear Waste in America.* Tackling an immense topic with dire implications—the problem of how to dispose of the growing amounts of high-level radioactive waste generated by nuclear power plants around the country—necessitated an authoritative factual basis, one which the authors gained through their eighteen-month investigation of nuclear waste disposal sites, interviews with key power-plant personnel, scientists, and other witnesses to the growing problem, and the search for documentation of the options currently being weighted U.S. policymakers with regard to the country's nuclear future. The author's central argument was, according to Mary Warnock in the *Times Literary Supplement:* because of the public's growing awareness, "it is the prime duty of policymakers to be open, to admit when decisions have been wrong, and . . . to establish categories of waste, from the most dangerous to the relatively safe" as a precursor to establishing regulated disposal methods. *Publishers Weekly* hailed it as "one of the most comprehensive studies to date of this important subject," and an *Economist* contributor, noting that the "out-of-sight, out-of-mind" philosophy characteristic of the industry has caused the book's authors to have "little hope that things will improve," added that Barlett and Steele "find it hard to absolve anybody involved in the fiasco. So too, will readers of this compelling testament to ignorance."

*America: What Went Wrong?,* which Barlett and Steele released in 1992 and which would serve as a jumping-off point for Bill Moyers' television series *Listening to America,* is gleaned from their essays published in the *Inquirer*'s editorial pages between

1978 and 1982, partially during the early years of President Ronald Reagan's administration. Targeting the tax cuts of the Reagan administration as the source of the economic ills of the 1980s, the authors contend that "the political system is corrupt, the Japanese have been eating our economic lunch, and the Mexicans will . . . do . . . the same" with NAFTA looming on the horizon, according to *Business Week* reviewer Howard Gleckman. However, arguing that increased spending rather than tax cuts were the root of the decade's recessionary problems, Gleckman contends that "Barlett and Steele, with their exclusive focus on fairness, are just barking up the wrong tree." The authors' central theme—that the economic standing of the middle class is ultimately being eroded by government policies put in place by Reagan and, later, Bush, to favor the rich and the corporate—held water with other critics, including *Los Angeles Times Book Review* writer Charles Solomon, who called *America: What Went Wrong?* an "important and profoundly disturbing book [that] should be required reading for voters."

Both Barlett and Steele credit their success to teamwork and the support they received from the *Inquirer.* Downie noted that Barlett believes it is important to have someone else to discuss ideas with; Barlett also thinks that he and Steele help prevent one another from becoming too personally involved in what they're reporting. Equally as important, the paper gives the two-man team the time and resources they need and has never yet killed a story because of pressure from its advertisers—even though that has occasionally meant losing advertisements. The journalists have also been given almost complete autonomy in their work. They might consult with an editor before embarking on a new project or when submitting their articles for final editing, but otherwise, they're pretty much on their own.

According to Barlett, this system suits him quite well. "When people ask me after each project we finish if I'm getting tired of this kind of work," he revealed to Downie, "I say, 'Are you kidding? How could I get tired of this?'" And from Barlett's point of view, it's just as well that he does like it. He believes that the kind of in-depth reporting he and Steele do on a single subject is "where newspaper circulation is going to be ten years from now."

See also: Steele, James B(ruce, Jr.). For a complete interview with Barlett, see *Contemporary Authors,* Volume 115.

*BIOGRAPHICAL/CRITICAL SOURCES:*

BOOKS

Downie, Leonard, Jr., *The New Muckrakers,* New Republic, 1976.
Dygert, James H., *The Investigative Journalist,* Prentice-Hall, 1976.

*PERIODICALS*

*Business Week,* May 4, 1992, pp. 14-16.
*Christian Science Monitor,* May 21, 1979.
*Economist,* October 19, 1985, pp. 103-04.
*Maclean's,* June 4, 1979.
*Library Journal,* March 1, 1986, p. 47.
*Los Angeles Times Book Review,* March 22, 1992, p. 10.
*Nation,* May 5, 1979.
*National Review,* April 27, 1979.
*Newsweek,* December 30, 1974; April 23, 1979.
*New West,* May 21, 1979.
*New York,* May 7, 1979.
*New York Review of Books,* May 31, 1979.
*New York Times Book Review,* May 6, 1979; November 25, 1979; March 22, 1981; March, 17, 1985, pp. 9-10; April 5, 1992, p. 9.
*Publishers Weekly,* April 26, 1976; January 18, 1985, p. 64; February 24, 1992, p. 50.
*Times Literary Supplement,* October 17, 1986, pp. 1155-56.
*Washington Monthly,* April, 1979.
*Washington Post Book World,* December 2, 1979.
*West Coast Review of Books,* July, 1979.*

\* \* \*

**BARNAO, Jack**
**See WOOD, Edward John**

\* \* \*

**BARNSTONE, Willis 1927-**

*PERSONAL:* Born November 13, 1927, in Lewiston, ME; son of Robert Carl (a businessman) and Dora (Lempert) Barnstone; married Helle Phaedra Tzapoulou (a painter), June 1, 1949; children: Aliki, Robert, Anthony. *Education:* Bowdoin College, B.A. (cum laude), 1948; graduate study at University of

Paris, 1948-49, and School of Oriental and African Studies, University of London, 1952-53; Columbia University, M.A. (with high honors), 1956; Yale University, Ph.D. (with distinction), 1960. *Politics:* Democrat.

*ADDRESSES: Home*—Heritage Woods, Bloomington, IN 47401. *Office*—Indiana University, Department of Comparative Literature, Bloomington, IN 47401.

*CAREER:* American Friends Service Committees, social worker in Mexico, 1945-46; Anavrita Academy, Anavrita, Greece, instructor in French and English, 1949; Les Editions Skira, Geneva, Switzerland, translator of French art texts, 1951; Wesleyan University, Middletown, CT, instructor, 1958-59; assistant professor of Romance languages, 1959-61; Indiana University, Bloomington, associate professor, 1962-66, professor, 1966-94, distinguished professor of Spanish, Portuguese, and comparative literature, 1994—. Visiting professor, University of California, Riverside, 1968-69; O'Connor professor of literature, Colgate University, 1973; Fulbright lecturer, Professorado de Avenida de Mayo, Buenos Aires, Argentina, 1975-76, and Foreign Studies University, Peking, 1984-85; visiting professor, Summer Institute of Literature, University of Texas, 1977. *Military service:* U.S. Army, 1954-56.

*MEMBER:* Modern Language Association of America, PEN.

*AWARDS, HONORS:* Danforth summer grant, 1960; Pulitzer Prize nomination in literature, 1960, for *From This White Island,* and 1977, for *China Poems;* Guggenheim fellowship, 1961-62; Cecil Hemley Memorial Award of the Poetry Society of America, 1968; American Council of Learned Societies, senior fellowship, 1969-70; Fulbright teaching fellowship, 1975; National Book Award nomination, 1977, for translation of *My Voice Because of You;* Lucille Medwick Memorial Award of the Poetry Society of America, 1978; National Endowment for the Arts, fellowship, 1979-80; Emily Dickinson Award, Poetry Society of America, 1985; W. H. Auden award, New York State Council on the Arts, 1986; D.Litt., Bowdoin College, 1981.

*WRITINGS:*

*POETRY*

*Poems for Exchange,* Institut Francais d'-Athenes, 1951.

*Notes for a Bible,* Hermanos Hernandez (Malaga), 1952.
*From This White Island,* Twayne, 1959.
*A Sky of Days,* Indiana University Fine Arts, 1967.
*Antijournal,* Sono Nis Press, 1971.
*A Day in the Country,* Harper, 1971.
*New Faces of China* (with photographs), Indiana University Press, 1973.
*China Poems,* University of Missouri Press, 1976.
*Wonders: A Sequence of 10 Fish Staring & Very Dumb,* privately printed, 1976.
*Stickball on 88th Street: A Child's NY Memorysongs,* illustrated by Karmen Effenberger, Colorado Quarterly, 1978.
*Overheard,* with drawings by wife, Helle Barnstone, Raintree Press, 1979.
*A Snow Salmon Reached the Andes Lake,* Curbstone Press, 1980.
*Ten Gospels & A Nightingale: A Sonnet Sequence Containing the Dedicatory Poem & Concluding Section of a Sequence of 202 Sonnets to Be Called the Book of Breath,* Triangular Press, 1981.
*The Alphabet of Night* (limited edition), F. Brewer, 1984.
*Five A.M. in Beijing,* Sheep Meadow Press, 1987.
*Funny Ways of Staying Alive,* University Press of New England, 1993.
*The Secret Reader: 501 Sonnets,* University Press of New England, 1996.
*Algebra of Night: New and Selected Poems, 1948-1998,* Sheep Meadow Press, 1998.

*CRITICISM*

(Contributor) Juan Marichal and Ivar Ivask, editors, *Luminous Reality: Critical Essays on the Poetry of Jorge Guillen,* University of Oklahoma Press, 1968.
*The Poetics of Ecstasy: Varieties of Ekstasis from Sappho to Borges,* Holmes & Meir, 1983.
*The Poetics of Translation: History, Theory, and Practice,* Yale University Press, 1993.
(And translator) *Six Masters of the Spanish Sonnet: Quevedo, Sor Juana Ines de la Cruz, Antonio Machado, Federico Garcia Lorca, Miguel Hernandez* (essays), Southern Illinois University Press, 1993.
(Co-editor with Tony Barnstone) *Literatures of Asia, Africa, and Latin America,* Prentice Hall, 1998.

*TRANSLATOR*

*Eighty Poems of Antonio Machado,* Las Americas, 1959.

(With wife, H. Barnstone) Margarita Liberaki, *The Other Alexander* (novel), Noonday, 1959.

(And editor) *Greek Lyric Poetry,* Bantam, 1962, enlarged edition, Indiana University Press, 1966.

(And author of introduction) Ignacio Bernal, *Mexico before Cortez: Art, History and Legend,* Dolphin Books, 1963.

Theobaldus Episcopus, *Physiologus Theobaldi Episcopi de Naturis Duodecim Animalium,* woodcuts and lithographs by Rudy Pozzatti, Indiana University Press, 1964.

*Sappho: Lyrics in the Original Greek with Translations,* Doubleday/New York University Press, 1965.

(And editor and author of introduction) *The Poems of Saint John of the Cross,* Indiana University Press, 1967.

Shir Hashirin, *The Song of Songs,* Kedros (Athens), 1970.

(With Ko Ching-po) *The Poems of Mao Tse-tung,* Harper, 1972.

(And author of introduction) Pedro Salinas, *My Voice Because of You,* preface by Jorge Guillen, State University of New York Press, 1975.

(And author of introduction) Fray Luis de Leon, *The Unknown Light: The Poems of Fray Luis de Leon,* State University of New York Press, 1979.

(With David Garrison) *A Bird of Paper: Poems of Vicente Aleixandre,* Ohio University Press, 1981.

Antonio Machado y Ruiz, *The Dream below the Sun: Selected Poems of Antonio Machado,* introduction by John Dos Passos, Crossing Press, 1981.

(And annotator) *Sappho and the Greek Lyrical Poets,* introduction by William E. McCulloh, drawings by H. Barnstone, Schocken Books, 1988.

(With son, Tony Barnstone, and Xu Haixen; critical introduction by W. Barnstone and T. Barnstone) *Laughing Lost in the Mountains: Poems of Wang Wei,* University Press of New England, 1992.

(With Bronislava Volkova) B. Volkova, *The Courage of the Rainbow: Selected Poems,* Sheep Meadow Press, 1993.

Sappho, *Sappho: A New Translation,* Sun & Moon Press, 1998.

*To Touch the Sky: Metaphysical and Spiritual Books in Translation,* New Directions, 1998.

*The New Testament* (with a study and literary translation), Penguin-Putnam, 1999.

Translator of plays in verse, including: Calderon de la Barca, *King Balshazzar's Feast,* produced in St. Leo, FL, 1969; Lope de Vega, *The Outrageous Saint,* produced in Nova Scotia, 1971; and Pablo Neruda, *Rage and Death of Joaquin Murieta,* 1972.

EDITOR

(With Hugh A. Harter) Miguel de Cervantes, *Riconete y Cortadillo,* Las Americas, 1960.

Luis de Gongora, *Soledades,* translated by Edward Wilson, Las Americas, 1965.

*Modern European Poetry: French, German, Greek, Italian, Russian, Spanish,* (anthology), Bantam, 1966, revised edition, 1978.

(And author of introduction) Edgar Lee Masters, *New Spoon River,* Macmillan, 1968.

(With Mary Ellen Solt) *Concrete Poetry: A World View,* Indiana University Press, 1969.

*Spanish Poetry from the Beginning through the Nineteenth Century* (anthology), Oxford University Press, 1970.

*Eighteen Texts: Writings by Contemporary Greek Authors,* Harvard University Press, 1972.

(With daughter, Aliki Barnstone) *A Book of Women Poets from Antiquity to Now,* Schocken Books, 1980, revised edition with A. Barnstone, Random House/Pantheon, 1992.

(And photographer) *Borges at Eighty: Conversations,* Indiana University Press, 1981.

*The Other Bible: Jewish Pseudepigrapha, Christian Noncanonical Apocrypha, and Gnostic Scriptures,* Harper, 1984.

OTHER

*With Borges on an Ordinary Evening in Buenos Aires: A Memoir,* University of Illinois Press, 1993.

*Sunday Morning in Fascist Spain: A European Memoir, 1948-1953,* Southern Illinois University Press, 1994.

Also author of play, *The Girl and the Poison Tree.* Contributor of numerous translations to anthologies and books, including: *The World's Love Poetry* (Greek, Latin, Portuguese sections), edited by Michael R. Martin, Bantam, 1960; *Anthology of Spanish Poetry,* edited by Angel Flores, Anchor, 1961; *Concise Encyclopaedia of Modern World Literature,* edited by Geoffrey Grigson, Hawthorn, 1963; Nikos Kazantzakis, *Spain* (poetry sections), translated by Amy Mims, Simon & Schuster, 1963; *Language of Love* (short stories), edited by Michael R. Martin, Bantam, 1964; *Genius of the Spanish Theater* (plays), edited by Robert O'Brien, Mentor Books, 1965; *Medieval Lyric Poetry,* edited by W. T. H. Jackson, Bantam, 1966; Helen Hill Miller, *Bridge to Asia,* Scribners, 1967; *Adventures in World Literature,* edited by Applegate, Browne, and others, Harcourt, 1970; *Poems of the Greek Anthology,* edited by Peter Jay, Penguin, 1973; Audrey Popping, *Dawn Wakes in the East,* Harper, 1974; and *For Neruda, for Chile,* edited by Walter Lowenfels, Beacon Press, 1974.

Original poems included in *New Campus Writing, Number 3,* Grove, 1959. Also contributor of original poems, verse translations, occasional prose translations, and articles to periodicals, including *Antioch Review, Arizona Quarterly, Columbia University Forum, Evergreen Review, Kenyon Review, Nation, New Republic, New York Book Review, New Yorker, New York Times Sunday Book Review, Nine* (London), *Points* (Paris), *Prairie Schooner, Sewanee Review, Triad, Tulane Drama Review,* and *Yale Review.* Editor-in-chief, *Artes Hispanicas Hispanic Arts,* published jointly by Indiana University and Macmillan.

*SIDELIGHTS:* Willis Barnstone is a writer of comparative literature, biblical studies, and poetry, as well as a translator. He has spent extended periods in Mexico, Spain, France, England, Greece, and China. He began writing poetry when he was twenty years old; his first published poem appeared in the Anglo-French periodical *Points.* His first book of poems published in the United States was *From This White Island,* reflecting on his time on an island in Greece. One of Barnstone's closest friends and mentors was author Jorge Luis Borges. In an essay written for *Contemporary Authors Autobiography Series,* Barnstone confides, "I see poetry, fiction, and scholarship as Borges did. They are the work of a writer and move into each other, separated by typography."

*BIOGRAPHICAL/CRITICAL SOURCES:*

BOOKS

*Contemporary Authors Autobiography Series,* Volume 15, Gale (Detroit), 1992.

\* \* \*

## BARRY, Jerome B(enedict) 1894-1975

*PERSONAL:* Born January 15, 1894, in Brooklyn, NY; died in 1975; son of Jerome Benedict and Mary Agnes (Reynolds) Barry; married Mary Eileen Williams, 1925. *Avocational interests:* Watercolor painting, chess, and playing the guitar.

*CAREER:* New York Telephone Co., Brooklyn, NY, draftsman, 1911-16; Bureau of Education, Philippine Islands, high school teacher, principal, superintendent of schools, 1916-20; W.J. Gallagher Advertising Agency, New York City, copy writer, office manager, 1954-75. Freelance fiction writer, 1920-75.

*MEMBER:* Mystery Writers of America, Salmagundi Club (New York).

*WRITINGS:*

*Murder with Your Malted,* Doubleday (Garden City, NY), 1941.
*Leopard Cat's Cradle,* Doubleday, 1942.
*Lady of Night,* Doubleday, 1944.
*Extreme License,* Doubleday, 1958.
*Malignant Stars,* Doubleday, 1960.
*Fall Guy,* Doubleday, 1960.
*Strange Relations,* Doubleday, 1962.

Contributor of short stories to *Saturday Evening Post, Collier's, New Yorker, Red Book, American Magazine,* and other magazines. Author of radio and television scripts.

*SIDELIGHTS:* Jerome Barry was an advertising executive who also wrote crime and mystery novels, all of which were set in his native New York City and its neighboring boroughs. Barry's settings were pulled from the places he knew best: busy lunch counters, large apartment dwellings, the streets and alleyways of Brooklyn, and even the quiet corridors of a metropolitan museum. Most of his works were published as part of the Doubleday Crime Club series, and they had to adhere to the standards set by the publisher. Nevertheless, *Weekly Book Review* critic Will Cuppy noted that Barry's books have "spells of what could be goofiness, but we think he does it on purpose—having, perhaps, a taste for the slightly grotesque in humble life."

Barry broke into book publishing with *Murder with Your Malted,* a mystery set in the improbable venue of a New York City lunch counter. The novel brims with the special argot of soda jerks and waitresses while also offering an unconventional means of murder—poisoned sandwiches. *New York Times* contributor Isaac Anderson called the book "a thoroughly enjoyable yarn, written in a breezy manner befitting the lunch-counter background."

Other mysteries set in New York followed, including *Lady of Night, Fall Guy,* and *Strange Relations.* The latter title, a story of an advertising executive struggling with a failing marriage, was described in the *San Francisco Chronicle* as having "all sorts of goings-on [and] a good thrilling climax. Mighty lively." One of Barry's better-known novels, *Malignant Stars,* plays on astrological signs for clues as a young woman attempts to prove her innocence of a murder committed in a museum. In *Malignant Stars,* wrote *New York Herald Tribune Book Review* correspondent James Sandoe, Barry "evokes [the suspects] with sharpness and in a texture to which he has not accustomed us in his earlier tales." The critic went on to suggest that the story is "handled with candor and without push." In the *New York Times Book Review,* Anthony Boucher likewise summed up *Malignant Stars* as being "agreeable as a damsel-in-distress tale . . . plausible as an 'inverted' study of a murderer."

*BIOGRAPHICAL/CRITICAL SOURCES:*

*PERIODICALS*

*Books,* December 21, 1941, p. 10.
*Book Week,* March 26, 1944, p. 10.
*Kirkus Reviews,* December 15, 1943, p. 561.
*New Yorker,* December 6, 1941, p. 17.
*New York Herald Tribune Book Review,* November 30, 1958, p. 32; February 14, 1960, p. 15; May 20, 1962, p. 15.
*New York Times Book Review,* December 21, 1941, p. 11; October 18, 1942, p. 18; November 23, 1958, p. 36; February 14, 1960, p. 18; November 27, 1960, p. 42; May 27, 1962, p. 22.
*San Francisco Chronicle,* January 4, 1959, p. 22; January 1, 1961, p. 22; June 17, 1962, p. 37.
*Springfield Republican,* January 11, 1941, p. E7.
*Time,* January 5, 1942, p. 72.
*Weekly Book Review,* February 20, 1944, p. 14.*

\*   \*   \*

**BARTLETT, Robert Merrill 1899-**

*PERSONAL:* Born December 23, 1899 (some sources say 1898), in Kingston, IN; son of Robert Alexander (a minister) and Minnie Lou (Dobson) Bartlett; married Theresa Sue Nuckols, August 9, 1923; children: Susan Jane (Mrs. Seward Weber), Mary Warren (Mrs. Fred J. Stare), Robert Hill. *Education:* Oberlin College, A.B., 1921; Yale University, B.D., 1924. *Politics:* Republican.

*ADDRESSES: Home*—Warwick Club, 280 Second Ave. S., Naples, FL 33940; and 1660 Bartlett House, R.F.D. 1, Brook Rd., Plymouth, MA (summer).

*CAREER:* Ordained minister of Congregational Church, 1924; Yenching University, Peiping, China, professor of comparative literature, 1924-27; First Congregational Church, Norwood, MA, minister, 1927-32; minister at First Church of Christ, Longmeadow, MA, and lecturer at Boston University and Springfield College, 1932-42; minister at Plymouth Congregational Church, Lansing, MI, and lecturer at Michigan State University, 1942-51; First Congregational Church, Shrewsbury, MA, minister, 1951-64. Organizer, Naples United Church of Christ, Naples, FL, 1972. Director, New Theological Library, Boston, MA. Lecturer on literature and world affairs at colleges in the United States; member of councils and seminars to Europe, Asia, and South America. Director of Massachusetts chapter, United Nations International Children's Fund; founder of Worcester chapter, National Council of Christians and Jews; chair, Massachusetts United Church Committee on Church Unity. *Military service:* U.S. Army, World War I, Field Artillery Officers Training.

*MEMBER:* English-Speaking Union, World Congress of Religions, Pilgrim Society (fellow), Society of Descendants of Robert Bartlett (president), Royal Society of Arts (fellow), Florida Society of Mayflower Descendents (elder), Massachusetts Society of Mayflower Descendents (member of board of assistants), Boston Authors, Phi Beta Kappa, Boston Fortnightly, Eel River Beach Club.

*AWARDS, HONORS:* D.D., Yankton College, 1940; Freedom Foundation Award, 1973.

*WRITINGS:*

*The Great Empire of Silence,* Pilgrim Press (Boston, MA), 1928.
*A Boy's Book of Prayers,* Pilgrim Press, 1930, reprinted, 1971.
*Builders of a New World,* Friendship (New York City), 1933.
*They Dared to Live,* Association Press, 1934, reprinted, Books for Libraries Press (Freeport, NY), 1969.
*Christian Conquests,* Abingdon (Nashville, TN), 1935.
*They Did Something about It,* Association Press, 1937, reprinted, Books for Libraries Press, 1969.

*Discovery—A Guidebook in Living,* Association Press, 1943.

*They Work for Tomorrow,* Association Press, 1944, reprinted, Books for Libraries Press, 1970.

*The Ascending Trail,* Association Press, 1945.

*Sky Pioneer—The Story of Igor I. Sikorsky,* Scribner (New York City), 1951.

*They Dare to Believe,* Association Press, 1952.

*They Stand Invincible—Men Who Are Reshaping Our World,* Crowell (New York City), 1959.

*With One Voice—Prayers from around the World,* Crowell, 1961.

*The Huguenots and Their Cross,* Whittemore, 1965.

*Thanksgiving Day,* Crowell, 1965.

*Pilgrim Robert Bartlett,* Leyden, 1966.

(Contributor) *They, Too, Belong,* Dell (New York City), 1970.

*The Pilgrim Way,* Pilgrim Press, 1971.

*Pilgrim House by the Sea,* Christopher House (North Quincy, MA), 1973.

*The Faith of the Pilgrims: An American Heritage,* United Church Press (New York City), 1978.

*My Corner of New England: Thoughts on Nature and Human Nature from a Pilgrim House on Cape Cod Bay,* P. E. Randall (Portsmouth, NH), 1984.

*Those Valiant Texans: A Breed Apart,* P. E. Randall, 1989.

*The Obstinate Illusion: A Historical Novel of China and America, 1920-1950,* P. E. Randall, 1991.

Contributor to religious and professional journals. Editor of *The Mayflower Quarterly,* 1964-67.

*SIDELIGHTS:* Few authors can boast a longer and more varied career than Robert Merrill Bartlett. Mayflower descendent, pastor and lecturer, world traveler, and writer, Bartlett published his first book at the age of thirty and his most recent at age ninety-two. In between he made a name for himself among young adult authors for his series of books profiling inspirational world leaders, as well as for his writings on the Pilgrims and their faith.

Bartlett may have been drawn to his career by his own background. The son of a pastor, he is also a descendent of Robert Bartlett, a Pilgrim who traveled to New England aboard the Mayflower. Inspired by his ancestor's adventures—and by the faith of his fathers—Bartlett undertook a long career as a Congregational minister, serving in Massachusetts, Michigan, and Florida. He also wrote numerous books, most aimed at young boys, on topics including Thanksgiving, Pilgrim philosophy and religion, and exploration of America.

Perhaps best known among Bartlett's books for young adults are the titles *They Dared to Live, They Did Something about It, They Work for Tomorrow, They Dare to Believe,* and *They Stand Invincible.* These books offer brief, inspirational profiles of outstanding international leaders in exploration, science, politics, and social welfare. In order to qualify as heroic in Bartlett's estimation, individuals had to work not for personal gain but for the common good—thus his inclusion of such notables as Jawaharlal Nehru, Mary McLeod Bethune, and Martin Luther King, Jr. In a review of *They Stand Invincible* for the *Christian Science Monitor,* Millicent Taylor wrote: "The concept of this inspiring book of miniature biographies of contemporary leaders is in itself a stroke of genius. . . . To learn how some unselfish dream can fill a person's life is a good thing for young people." *San Francisco Chronicle* reviewer Richard Cobden likewise noted: "Mr. Bartlett has presented his reshapers in a style aptly suited to the idealistic bent of the young mind." Cobden also deemed *They Stand Invincible* "indispensable" for youngsters searching for positive role models.

"Today's boys and girls want and need living heroes," declared a *Horn Book* contributor. Bartlett's books seek to fill that need and have been especially cited for that purpose. A *Springfield Republican* correspondent observed of the books: "These are not searching or critical portraits, but they make interesting and optimistic reading." And in *Survey,* H. W. Hintz concluded that Bartlett offers a service "in bringing within the compass of a comparatively few pages the essential concepts of [a] group of rather widely representative leaders."

*BIOGRAPHICAL/CRITICAL SOURCES:*

*PERIODICALS*

*Chicago Sunday Tribune,* October 26, 1952, p. 2.

*Christian Century,* May 13, 1959, p. 587.

*Churchman,* December 15, 1937, p. 16.

*Horn Book,* August, 1959, p. 293.

*Library Journal,* April 15, 1959, p. 1336.

*New York Times,* May 10, 1959, p. B14.

*San Francisco Chronicle,* May 17, 1959, p. 23.

*Springfield Republican,* December 6, 1937, p. 6; August 31, 1940, p. 6; February 6, 1944, p. E7; November 9, 1952, p. C8.

*Survey,* May, 1944, p. 262.*

## BARTLETT, (Charles) Vernon (Oldfeld) 1894-1983
## (Peter Oldfeld, joint pseudonym)

*PERSONAL:* Born April 30, 1894, in Westbury, Wiltshire, England; died January 18, 1983, in Yeovil, Tuscany; son of Thomas Oldfeld and Beatrice (Jacks) Bartlett; married Marguerite van den Bemden, September 25, 1917 (died 1966); married Eleanor Needham Ritchie, 1969; children: (first marriage) Dennis Oldfeld, Maurice Oldfeld. *Education:* Attended Blundell's School, Tiverton, Devon. *Avocational interests:* Viticulture and winemaking.

*CAREER:* Staff member with *London Daily Mail,* London, England, 1916, and Reuters Agency, 1917; *Times,* London, special correspondent in Switzerland, Germany, and Poland, 1919-20, correspondent in Rome, 1921-22; League of Nations, London director, 1922-32; British Broadcasting Corp., radio broadcaster on foreign affairs, 1928-34; *News Chronicle,* London, England, member of staff, 1934-54; *Straits Times,* Singapore, political commentator, 1954-61. Independent Progressive member of Parliament for Bridgewater, Somerset, 1938-50; founder, Vox Mundi Books, 1947; member of U.N. Advisory Committee of Experts, 1948. *Military service:* British Army during World War I; invalided home, 1916; served in Flanders and France; became first lieutenant.

*MEMBER:* Garrick Club, Beefsteak Club, Special Forces Club.

*AWARDS, HONORS:* Commander of the British Empire, 1956.

*WRITINGS:*

*Leaves in the Wind* (poetry), Morland, 1916.
*Mud and Khaki: Sketches from Flanders and France,* Simpkin, Marshall, 1917.
*Behind the Scenes at the Peace Conference,* Allen & Unwin (London), 1919.
*Songs of the Winds and Seas* (poetry), Elkin Mathews, 1920.
*The Brighter Side of European Chaos: A Journalist's Scrapbook,* Heath Cranton, 1925.
*Topsy-Turvy* (short stories), Constable (London), 1927, reprinted, Books for Libraries Press (Freeport, NY), 1970.
(With P. Jacobsson, under joint pseudonym Peter Oldfeld) *The Death of a Diplomat,* Washburn, 1928.
*Calf Love,* Lippincott (Philadelphia), 1929.

(With P. Jacobsson, under joint pseudonym Peter Oldfeld) *The Alchemy Murder,* Washburn, 1929.
*The Unknown Soldier,* Stokes, 1930.
(With Robert C. Sherriff) *Journey's End: A Novel,* Gollancz (London), 1930, reprinted, 1968.
*No Man's Land,* Allen & Unwin, 1930.
*The World—Our Neighbour,* Mathews & Marrot, 1931.
*Nazi Germany Explained,* Gollancz, 1933.
*If I Were Dictator,* Methuen (London), 1935.
*This Is My Life* (autobiography), Chatto & Windus (London), 1937.
*Intermission in Europe: The Life of a Journalist and Broadcaster,* Oxford University Press (Oxford, England), 1938.
*Tomorrow Always Comes,* Chatto & Windus, 1943, Knopf (New York City), 1944.
*Go East, Old Man,* Latimer House, 1948.
*East of the Iron Curtain,* Latimer House, 1949, M. McBride, 1950.
*Struggle for Africa,* Praeger (New York City), 1953.
*Report from Malaya,* Verschoyle, 1954, Criterion Books, 1955.
*And Now, Tomorrow,* Chatto & Windus, 1960.
*Tuscan Retreat,* Chatto & Windus, 1964, 3rd edition, 1966.
*A Book about Elba,* Chatto & Windus, 1965, 3rd edition, 1973.
(With John C. Caldwell) *Let's Visit Italy* (juvenile), Burke (London), 1966, John Day (New York City), 1968.
*Introduction to Italy,* Chatto & Windus, 1967.
*The Past of Pastimes,* Archon Books (Hamden, CT), 1969.
*The Colour of Their Skin,* Chatto & Windus, 1969.
*Tuscan Harvest,* Chatto & Windus, 1971.
*Central Italy,* Hastings House (New York City), 1972.
*Northern Italy,* Hastings House, 1973.
*I Know What I Liked,* Chatto & Windus, 1973.

Founder and editor, *World Review,* 1936-40.

*SIDELIGHTS:* Vernon Bartlett was a respected broadcast and print journalist, politician, and writer whose primary area of expertise was foreign affairs. A facility for foreign languages allowed Bartlett to travel widely in Europe, both prior to and after World War II, and he disseminated his opinions over radio and through the pages of such periodicals as the *Times* and *News Chronicle,* both in London. Having himself been wounded in the First World War, he carried throughout his life a conviction that war should be prevented by diplomatic means—and he served as

London director of the League of Nations from 1922 until 1932.

Bartlett began his writing career after receiving a medical discharge from active duty during World War I. By war's end he was covering the peace talks for the London *Daily Mail,* and in 1919 he joined the staff at the *Times* as a foreign correspondent. Three years later he moved to the League of Nations, and it was there that his broadcasting assignments began. From modest spots about the League, he moved onto radio with a more ambitious weekly program entitled *The Way of the World,* which was aired on the BBC (British Broadcasting Corporation). After some remarks he made in 1933 were interpreted as pro-Nazi, he was forced to resign from the BBC. He was not idle long. The London *News Chronicle* hired him as a foreign correspondent, and by the beginning of World War II he was back on the radio waves, this time as an international reporter.

Remarkably, Bartlett also spent the years surrounding World War II as an Independent Progressive member of Parliament for the district of Bridgewater, Somerset. He held the seat until 1950 and retired from the *News Chronicle* in 1954.

Despite his many other duties, Bartlett managed to publish numerous nonfiction and fiction titles during his lengthy career. As early as 1917 he found publishers for his poetry and field notes from the First World War, and by the mid-1920s he had garnered a reputation as an astute observer of international relations. He also used his own war experiences as grist for novels and short stories, among them the highly-regarded *Unknown Soldier.* "Vernon Bartlett has aimed squarely at that often elusive target, 'the intelligent general reader' and his aim is accurate," wrote R. A. Smith in the *New York Times.* "Since Mr. Bartlett is a veteran newspaper man as well as a former Member of Parliament, he could be expected to show both reportorial and political skills. He uses both to advantage."

Bartlett's best known works concern international relations in the World War II and Cold War period. He attended the peace talks that ended the war and traveled extensively in Eastern Europe during the early Cold War period. From these experiences came *Tomorrow Always Comes* and *East of the Iron Curtain,* both of which drew positive reviews on both sides of the Atlantic. A London *Times* reporter, for instance, deemed *Tomorrow Always Comes* a "shrewd and candid little volume," while *Nation* contributor Albert

Guerard called the same title "a generous, an entrancing book; and a wise one." A *New Yorker* correspondent likewise described *East of the Iron Curtain* as "one of the most levelheaded and responsible books yet published on the East European countries under the Soviet hegemony." In a *Springfield Republican* review of *East of the Iron Curtain,* a reporter concluded: "Mr. Bartlett's book will not please wishfulthinkers in every respect, but it appears to be an honest, careful piece of factual reporting and as such should be a valuable contribution toward understanding the factors that are shaping European history in our time."

After retiring from active journalistic work, Bartlett moved to Italy and wrote books while indulging in his hobby, wine-making. He died there in 1983. Later Bartlett titles include a popular history of games entitled *The Past of Pastimes.* This book in particular was cited for its style, which a *Choice* reviewer described as "freeflowing, informal and interesting," but critics also made note of the vast amount of information Bartlett infused into the text. "Without depreciating the earnest work of the academics, it is a rare relief occasionally to find a skilled writer treating a playful subject playfully," observed a *Times Literary Supplement* contributor. "A great mass of detailed information has passed before [Bartlett's] eyes; and one comes across many hints that he could have contributed, if he wished, to the critical study of the history of many games. But he has not chosen to join in the serious debates: he has set down the scraps of information that have amused him, and they will certainly amuse others."

## BIOGRAPHICAL/CRITICAL SOURCES:

### BOOKS

Bartlett, Vernon, *This Is My Life,* Chatto & Windus (London), 1937.
Bartlett, Vernon, *I Know What I Liked,* Chatto & Windus, 1974.

### PERIODICALS

*Book Week,* March 12, 1944, p. 6.
*Choice,* March 1970, p. 114.
*Christian Science Monitor,* May 17, 1930, p. 10.
*Kirkus Reviews,* April 15, 1950, p. 257.
*Library Journal,* April 15, 1950, p. 692; March 15, 1970, p. 1044.
*Nation,* March 25, 1944, p. 370; June 3, 1950, p. 553.

*New Republic,* March 6, 1944, p. 325; June 5, 1950, p. 20.

*New Yorker,* April 22, 1950, p. 124; April 9, 1955, p. 135.

*New York Times,* August 3, 1930, p. 7; June 11, 1950, p. 9; February 27, 1955, p. 10.

*Saturday Review,* February 8, 1930, p. 173.

*Saturday Review of Literature,* October 4, 1930, p. 177; September 16, 1950, p. 14.

*Spectator,* February 8, 1930, p. 206; March 3, 1944, p. 204; December 30, 1949, p. 926.

*Springfield Republican,* February 19, 1944, p. 6; May 7, 1950, p. C8.

*Times Literary Supplement,* January 30, 1930, p. 76; October 23, 1943, p. 508; September 24, 1954, p. 606; February 19, 1970, p. 199.

*OBITUARIES:*

*Times* (London), January 21, 1983.*

\*   \*   \*

**BEATON, Cecil (Walter Hardy) 1904-1980**

*PERSONAL:* Born January 14, 1904, in London, England; died January 18, 1980, in Broadchalke, Wiltshire, England; son of Ernest Walter Hardy (a timber merchant) and Esther (Sisson) Beaton. *Education:* Attended St. John's College, Cambridge, 1921-25. *Religion:* Church of England. *Avocational interests:* Scrapbooks, decoration, traveling, gardening, collecting modern paintings.

*CAREER:* Schmiegelow & Co., London, clerk, 1925-26; freelance portrait and fashion photographer, 1926-30; Conde Nast Publications, London and New York City, contract photographer, 1930-55; freelance photographer, 1955-80. Photographer to British Royal Family, 1939-80. Set and costume designer for plays, ballet, and films.

Selected exhibits include photography shows at Cooling Gallery (London, 1930) and National Portrait Gallery (London, 1968), costume show at Victoria and Albert Museum (London, 1971), and painting and stage design shows at the Redfern Gallery (London, 1936, 1958, 1965), the Sagittarius Gallery (New York, 1956), and the Lefevre Gallery (London, 1966). Work is in permanent collection at National Portrait Gallery, Imperial War Museum, and Sotheby's Belgravia (all London), Life Picture Collection in New York City, Boston Public Library, Yale University, Rhode Island School of Design, New Orleans Museum of Art, the University of Nebraska (Lincoln, NE), and the University of Texas at Austin. *Military service:* British Ministry of Information, 1939-45, official photographer in all theatres of war.

*AWARDS, HONORS:* Neiman Marcus Award, 1956; Antoinette Perry (Tony) Award for costume design, 1956, for *My Fair Lady,* and 1970, for *Coco;* Motion Picture Academy Award for costume design, 1958, for *Gigi,* for set and costume design, 1964, for *My Fair Lady;* Commander of the Order of the British Empire, 1957; Legion d'Honneur, 1960; Honor award from American Society of Magazine Photographers, 1963; created Knight of the Order of the British Empire, 1972.

*WRITINGS:*

*Cecil Beaton's Scrapbook,* Scribner (New York City), 1937.

*Cecil Beaton's New York,* Lippincott (Philadelphia, PA), 1938 (revised edition published in England as *Portrait of New York,* Batsford [London], 1948).

(With Baroness von Bulop) *My Royal Past,* Batsford, 1939, revised edition, John Day (New York City), 1960.

*Air of Glory* (wartime scrapbook), Her Majesty's Stationery Office (London), 1941.

*Time Exposure,* Batsford, 1941.

*Winged Squadrons,* Hutchinson (London), 1942.

*Near East,* Batsford, 1943.

*British Photographers,* Collins (London), 1944.

*Far East,* Batsford, 1945.

*Ashcombe,* Batsford, 1949.

*Ballet,* Doubleday (Garden City, NY), 1951.

*Photobiography* (autobiographical), Doubleday, 1951.

(With Kenneth Tynan) *Persona Grata,* Wingate, 1953, Putnam (New York City), 1954.

*The Glass of Fashion,* Doubleday, 1954.

*It Gives Me Great Pleasure,* Weidenfeld & Nicolson (London), 1955, published as *I Take Great Pleasure,* John Day, 1956.

*The Face of the World,* John Day, 1957.

*Japanese,* John Day, 1959.

*The Wandering Years* (diaries), Weidenfeld & Nicolson, 1961, Little, Brown (Boston, MA), 1962.

*Quail in Aspic,* Weidenfeld & Nicolson, 1962, Bobbs-Merrill (New York City), 1963.

*Cecil Beaton's Fair Lady,* Holt (New York City), 1964.

*The Years Between* (diaries), Holt, 1965.

*My Bolivian Aunt* (memoir), Weidenfeld & Nicolson, 1971.

*Cecil Beaton: Memoirs of the 40's* (diaries) McGraw-Hill (New York City), 1972 (published in England as *The Happy Years,* Weidenfeld & Nicolson, 1972).

*The Strenuous Years* (diaries), Weidenfeld & Nicolson, 1973.

(With Gail Buckland) *The Magic Image: The Genius of Photography from 1839 to the Present Day,* Little, Brown, 1975.

*The Restless Years* (diaries), Weidenfeld & Nicolson, 1976.

*The Parting Years* (diaries), Weidenfeld & Nicolson, 1978.

*Self Portrait with Friends: The Selected Diaries of Cecil Beaton, 1926-1974,* edited by Richard Buckle, Weidenfeld & NIcolson, 1979.

## BOOKS OF PHOTOGRAPHS

*The Book of Beauty,* Duckworth (London), 1930.

*History under Fire,* Batsford, 1941.

*Chinese Album,* Batsford, 1946, reprinted, Oxford University Press (New York City), 1991.

*Indian Album,* Batsford, 1946, reprinted as *Indian Diary and Album,* Oxford University Press, 1991.

*Royal Portraits,* Weidenfeld & Nicolson, 1963.

*Beaton Portraits,* Her Majesty's Stationery Office, 1968.

*The Best of Beaton,* Macmillan (New York City), 1968.

*The Photographs of Sir Cecil Beaton,* York, 1973.

(Contributor of drawings) C. Z. Guest, *First Garden,* Putnam, 1976.

(Contributor) Colin Ford, editor, *Happy and Glorious: 130 Years of Royal Photographs,* Macmillan, 1977 (published in England as *Happy and Glorious: Six Reigns of Royal Photography,* Angus & Robertson, 1977).

*Beaton,* edited by James Danziger, Viking (New York City), 1980.

(Contributor) Stanley Spencer, *Spencer in the Shipyard,* Arts Council of Great Britain (London), 1981.

*War Photographs, 1939-1945,* Imperial War Museum/Jane's (London), 1981.

*Cecil Beaton: A Retrospective,* edited by David Mellor, Little, Brown, 1986.

*Cecil Beaton: Photographs 1920-1970,* edited by Philippe Garner and David Mellor, Stewart, Tabori & Chang (New York City), 1995.

## PLAYS

*The Gainsborough Girls* (three-act), first produced in Brighton, England, at Theatre Royal, 1951.

*SIDELIGHTS:* The late Sir Cecil Beaton was one of the most renowned photographers and designers of his time. For more than thirty years the official photographer of the British royal family, Beaton also aimed his lens at several generations of the rich and famous, from T. S. Eliot, Winston Churchill, and Greta Garbo to Rudolph Nureyev, Mick Jagger, and Marlon Brando. Beaton was long associated with *Vogue* magazine, for which he shot fashion spreads and celebrity portraits. When his association with the magazine ended in the mid-1950s, he turned to his other passion—costume design—to produce the stunning Edwardian milieux in the films *Gigi* and *My Fair Lady.* "Beaton . . . was a leading arbiter in taste and fashion for much of the twentieth century," wrote Robert F. Jones in *Gay & Lesbian Biography.* "The epitome of the self-made man, with considerable talents founded on nothing further than instinct, and with even greater stamina and panache, Cecil Beaton stayed in the British limelight for nearly sixty years, through his innovative portraiture photography, bold set and costume designs, and by publishing over 30 works that chronicled twentieth-century fashion and design as well as his own impact on them."

Beaton grew up in an upper middle class background and was attracted to art and photography as a very young child. An indifferent student, he attended Cambridge University without earning a degree, but it was there that he began to cultivate the important friendships that would launch his career. By the age of twenty-five he had become sought after in London as an unconventional photographer of society hostesses and actresses, and the strength of these portraits—buttressed by his urbane personality—landed him a contract with *Vogue* magazine. According to Jones, Beaton's "ambition, easy wit, and natural self-assurance were assets that favored his climb."

Over the next twenty-five years, Beaton photographed celebrities and heroes, politicians and—during wartime—soldiers and victims. Among his most important clients were members of Britain's royal family, including Queen Elizabeth II and the Queen Mother. Beaton's professional association with the royals began in 1939 and continued into the 1970s, and, to quote Jones, "he may be credited with enhancing the royal family's image by giving them a more glamorous and popular look."

Busy as he was, Beaton kept diaries from his college days onward. In their pages he recorded his social life and observations of the famous, as well as details about his relationship with Greta Garbo and his infatuation with the wealthy Peter Watson. Needless to say, his name-dropping diaries found their way into print and were greeted with back-handed praise from reviewers. In a *San Francisco Chronicle* piece on *The Wandering Years,* for instance, William Hogan wrote: "No doubt the book will be a conversation piece in hightoned places. Beyond that it is a social document of rare implications, for I suspect Beaton represents the very best and the very worst of uppercrust Englishman in the period between the wars." A *Times Literary Supplement* reviewer likewise stated: "The social historian of the future could not find a more vivid description of cafe society." Naomi Bliven, commenting upon *The Years Between* in the *New Yorker,* noted that Beaton "is sensitive to people, and his book is dotted with word sketches that give magic pictures of their subjects' presences."

Among Beaton's greatest triumphs are the films *Gigi* and *My Fair Lady,* for which he designed sets and costumes. He won Academy Awards for both movies, as well as a Tony Award for the theatre version of *My Fair Lady.* His costumes for these and other stage performances were given a retrospective exhibition at the Victoria and Albert Museum in 1971. But it is for his photographs that he will be most remembered. "Beaton is important because what he did and what he does captures the imagination of the few, at first, and ultimately influences the many," declared *New York Times* correspondent Leo Lerman in 1951. "He was a cult: now he is a brand. Much of what he has done adds just a little bit of enchantment to the everyday world; makes us dream more richly, more variously."

The artist himself was much more circumspect about his work. In 1966 he wrote in his diary: "I don't really feel that I am going to come into my own, and justify myself and my existence by some last great gesture. I am likewise certain that nothing I have done is likely to live long after me." Beaton suffered a stroke in 1974, two years after being knighted by Elizabeth II. By 1979 he had recovered sufficiently to resume his work, but his return was short-lived: he died at his home in Broadchalke, England on January 18, 1980.

The ensuing decades have proven Beaton wrong about his work. Biographies have been written about his life, and his photographs have been collected and re-collected in well-received volumes. A *Times Literary Supplement* contributor concluded of his work: "In spite of the snobbery and the chi-chi effulgences, an unusual talent, which has its source in a rare zest for living, is displayed throughout."

*BIOGRAPHICAL/CRITICAL SOURCES:*

*BOOKS*

Beaton, Cecil, *The Parting Years,* Weidenfeld & Nicolson, 1978.
*Contemporary Photographers,* second edition, St. James Press (Detroit, MI), 1988.
Garner, Philippe, *Cecil Beaton,* Collins (London), 1982.
*Gay & Lesbian Biography,* St. James Press, 1997.
Ross, Josephine, *Beaton in Vogue,* Crown (New York City), 1986.
Souhami, Diana, *Greta and Cecil,* Harper (San Francisco, CA), 1994.
Spencer, Charles, *Cecil Beaton: Stage and Film Designs,* St. Martin's (New York City), 1975.
Strong, Roy C., *Cecil Beaton: The Royal Portraits,* Simon & Schuster (New York City), 1988.
Vickers, Hugo, *Cecil Beaton: A Biography,* Little, Brown (Boston, MA), 1985 (published in England as *Cecil Beaton: The Authorized Biography,* Weidenfeld & Nicolson, 1985).
Vickers, Hugo, *Loving Garbo: The Story of Greta Garbo, Cecil Beaton, and Mercedes de Acosta,* Random House (New York City), 1994.

*PERIODICALS*

*Atlantic,* April, 1973, p. 112.
*Best Sellers,* May 15, 1973, p. 75.
*Christian Science Monitor,* August 2, 1951, p. 7; May 30, 1973, p. 9.
*Guardian,* August 25, 1961, p. 5.
*Harper,* December, 1968, p. 130.
*Inter/View,* April, 1973.
*Life,* September 16, 1946.
*New Statesman,* July 28, 1961, p. 126; October 30, 1964, p. 657; July 23, 1965, p. 129.
*New Statesman & Nation,* June 23, 1951, p. 720.
*Newsweek,* May 12, 1969; April 16, 1973, p. 106.
*New Yorker,* January 22, 1966, p. 102.
*New York Herald Tribune Book Review,* July 29, 1951, p. 6.
*New York Herald Tribune Books,* January 14, 1962, p. 10.
*New York Times,* July 22, 1951, p. 7; November 25, 1951, p. 57; December 23, 1971.

*New York Times Book Review,* January 21, 1962, p. 6; November 7, 1965, p. 90; October 6, 1968, p. 6; May 6, 1973, p. 18.

*San Francisco Chronicle,* July 19, 1951, p. 12; January 3, 1962, p. 31.

*Saturday Review of Literature,* November 17, 1951, p. 67.

*Saturday Review of the Arts,* April, 1973, p. 88.

*Time,* July 30, 1951, p. 82.

*Times* (London), October 12, 1971.

*Times Literary Supplement,* May 18, 1951, p. 304; August 3, 1951, p. 480; July 21, 1961, p. 443; August 12, 1965, p. 692; November 28, 1968, p. 1331; May 26, 1972, p. 594.

*OBITUARIES:*

*PERIODICALS*

*Chicago Tribune,* January 19, 1980.

*Newsweek,* January 28, 1980.

*New York Times,* January 19, 1980.

*Times* (London), January 19, 1980.

*Washington Post,* January 19, 1980.*

\* \* \*

## BEAUMONT, Cyril William 1891-1976

*PERSONAL:* Born November 1, 1891, in London, England; died in 1976; son of Frederick John (a mechanical and electrical engineer) and Mary Adelaide (Balchin) Beaumont; married Alice Mari Beha, December 10, 1914. *Education:* Educated privately and at school in England. *Religion:* Church of England.

*CAREER:* Writer on the theater and dance. Antiquarian bookseller, London, England, 1910-65; Beaumont Press, London, founder and publisher, 1917-65; *Dance Journal,* London, editor, 1924-70. President, London Archives of the Dance (now part of Victoria and Albert Museum).

*MEMBER:* Royal Society of Literature (fellow), Royal Society of Arts (fellow), Imperial Society of Teachers of Dancing (honorary fellow; chair of Cecchetti Society branch, beginning 1924; chair of Imperial Society, 1958-70), Critics Circle (president, 1957).

*AWARDS, HONORS:* Gold Medal of Institute Historique et Heraldique de France, 1934; Officier d'Academie, 1934; Renaissance Francaise Gold Medal, 1938; Chevalier de la Legion d'Honneur, 1950; Imperial Award of Imperial Society of Teachers of Dancing, 1961; Queen Elizabeth II Coronation Award of Royal Academy of Dancing, 1962; Officer, Order of the British Empire, 1962; Knight Officer, Order of Merit (Italy), 1962.

*WRITINGS:*

*The Art of Lydia Lopokova,* Beaumont (London), 1920.

*The Art of Lubov Tchernicheva,* Beaumont, 1921.

(With Stanislas Idzikowski) *A Manual of the Theory and Practice of Classical Theatrical Dancing (Cecchetti Method),* Beaumont, 1922, Dover Publications (New York City), 1975.

*The Mysterious Toyshop, a Fairy Tale,* Beaumont, 1924, Holt (New York City), 1985.

*A Burmese pwe at Wembley; Some Impressions of Burmese Dancing,* Beaumont, 1924.

*The Art of Stanislas Idzikowski,* Beaumont, 1926.

*The Strange Adventures of a Toy Soldier* (juvenile), Beaumont, 1926.

*The History of Harlequin,* Beaumont, 1926, Benjamin Blom, 1967.

*The Wonderful Journey* (juvenile), Beaumont, 1927.

*The First Score: An Account of the Foundation and Development of the Beaumont Press,* Beaumont, 1927, N. T. Smith (Bronxville, NY), 1980.

*Sea Magic* (juvenile), John Lane (London), 1928.

(Compiler) *A Bibliography of Dancing,* Dancing Times (London), 1929, Benjamin Blom, 1963.

*Enrico Cecchetti; a Memoir,* Beaumont, 1929.

*Toys* (rhymes for children), Beaumont, 1930.

(With Margaret Craske) *The Theory and Practice of Allegro in Classical Ballet (Cecchetti Method),* Beaumont, 1930, Imperial Society of Teachers of Dancing (London), 1979.

*A History of Ballet in Russia (1613-1881),* Beaumont, 1930.

*Fanny Elssler (1810-1884),* Beaumont, 1931.

(Compiler) *A French-English Dictionary of Technical Terms Used in Classical Ballet,* Beaumont, 1931, 13th edition, 1959, reprinted, Imperial Society of Teachers of Dancing, 1977.

*Flash-back: Memories of My Youth,* Beaumont, 1931.

*A Primer of Classical Ballet for Children (Cecchetti Method),* Beaumont, 1933, revised edition, 1961.

*A Second Primer of Classical Ballet for Children,* Beaumont, 1935, revised edition, 1960.

*Michel Fokine and His Ballets,* Beaumont, 1935, 2nd edition, 1945.

*Design for the Ballet* (also see below), Studio Publications (New York City), 1937, revised edition, Studio (London), 1939.

*The Complete Book of Ballets; a Guide to the Principal Ballets of the Nineteenth and Twentieth Centuries,* Putnam (New York City), 1937, revised edition, 1949, *Supplement,* 1942.

(With Sacheverell Sitwell) *The Romantic Ballet in Lithographs of the Time,* Faber (London), 1938.

*Puppets and the Puppet Stage,* Studio Publications, 1938, Finch Press, 1973.

*Five Centuries of Ballet Design* (also see below), Studio Publications, 1939.

*The Diaghilev Ballet in London: A Personal Record,* Putnam, 1940, 3rd edition, A. & C. Black (London), 1951.

*A Third Primer of Classical Ballet for Children,* Beaumont, 1941, revised edition, 1967.

*The Ballet Called Giselle,* Beaumont, 1944, revised edition, 1945, reprinted, Dance Books (London), 1988.

(Author of introduction) *Leslie Hurry: Settings and Costumes for Sadler's Wells Ballets,* Faber, 1946.

*The Sleeping Beauty: The Sadler's Wells Ballet,* Beaumont, 1946.

*The Sadler's Wells Ballet, a Detailed Account of Works in the Permanent Repertory,* Beaumont, 1946, revised and enlarged edition, 1947.

*Ballet Design: Past and Present* (includes revisions of *Five Centuries of Ballet* and *Design for the Ballet*), Studio Publications (New York City), 1946.

*The Romantic Ballet as Seen by Theophile Gautier, Being His Notices of All the Principal Performances First Translated from the French,* Beaumont, 1947, reprinted, Dance Horizons (Brooklyn, NY), 1973.

*The Swan Lake,* Beaumont, 1948.

*Dancers Under My Lens,* Beaumont, 1949.

*Antonio: Impressions of the Spanish Dancer,* A. & C. Black, 1952.

*The Ballet Called Swan Lake,* Beaumont, 1952.

*Ballets of Today* (2nd supplement to *Complete Book of Ballets*), Putnam, 1954.

*Ballets, Past and Present* (3rd supplement to *Complete Book of Ballets*), Putnam, 1955, Dufour, 1964.

*Puppets and Puppetry,* Studio Publications, 1958.

*Bookseller at the Ballet: Memoirs 1891 to 1929,* Beaumont, 1975.

## EDITOR

(With M. T. H. Sadler) *New Paths,* 1918.

Valerian Svetlov, *Thamar Karsavina,* translated from the Russian by H. de Vere Beauclerk and Nadia Evrenov, 1922.

Vladimir Polunin, *The Continental Method of Scene Painting,* 1927.

(And author of preface) Gregorio Lambranzi, *New and Curious School of Theatrical Dancing,* translated from the German by Derra de Moroda, 1928.

Zelia Raye, *Rational Limbering,* 1929.

George D. Taylor, *Some Traditional Scottish Dances,* 1929.

Derra de Moroda, *The Csardas and Sor Tanc,* 1929.

Rikuhei Umemoto, *Some Classical Dances of Japan,* 1935.

Margaret Craske and Derra de Moroda, *The Theory and Practice of Advanced Allegro in Classical Ballet,* 1956, revised edition, 1971.

(And author of preface) Istvan Barlanghi, *Mime Training and Exercises,* 1959.

*A Bibliography of the Dance Collection of Doris Niles and Serge Leslie,* Part I, 1966, Part II, 1968, Part III, 1974.

D. I. Leshkov, *Marius Petipa,* 1971.

## TRANSLATOR FROM THE FRENCH

Francis de Miomandre, *Vaslav Nijinsky,* 1913.

Angelo Constantini, *The Birth, Life and Death of Scaramouch,* 1924.

Thoinot Arbeau, *Orchesography,* 1925, reprinted, Dance Horizons, 1965.

Andre Levinson, *Marie Taglioni,* Beaumont, 1930.

Jean G. Noverre, *Letters on Dancing and Ballets,* 1930.

Philippe Rameau, *Dancing-Master,* 1931.

Theophile Gautier, *Romantic Ballet,* 1932.

(And compiler) *A Miscellany for Dancers,* 1934.

Serge Lifar, *Ballet, Traditional to Modern,* Putnam, 1938.

## OTHER

Also author of "Impressions of the Russian Ballet," a series of twelve booklets, 1918-21, and of "Essays on Dancing and Dancers," a series of ten booklets, 1932-48. Ballet critic, *Dancing World,* 1921-24, and *Sunday Times,* 1950-59.

*SIDELIGHTS:* Cyril W. Beaumont was a distinguished authority on classical dance, especially the ballet. Beaumont combined his love of dance and puppetry with a career of writing and book-selling, operating his own publishing house as well as a popu-

*Chicago Sun Book Week,* May 18, 1947, p. 3.
*Chicago Sunday Tribune,* February 18, 1951, p. 2.
*Nation,* September 9, 1944, p. 304.
*New Yorker,* May 10, 1947, p. 104.
*New York Herald Tribune Book Review,* February 18, 1951, p. 8.
*New York Times,* June 8, 1941, p. 12; August 20, 1944, p. 4; February 18, 1951, p. 16.
*San Francisco Chronicle,* March 10, 1951, p. 10.
*Saturday Review of Literature,* September 30, 1944, p. 25; April 24, 1948, p. 36.
*Time,* February 19, 1951, p. 104.
*Times Literary Supplement,* September 20, 1947, p. 477.
*Weekly Book Review,* August 20, 1944, p. 6.

OBITUARIES:

PERIODICALS

*Milwaukee Journal,* July 1, 1986.*

*        *        *

BERGLAND, Martha 1945-

PERSONAL: Born September 16, 1945, in Oklahoma City, OK; daughter of Hugh Lennox Bond (a farmer) and Elizabeth Murphey (a painter; maiden name, Howard) Bergland; married Lawrence J. Barnett (a professor), December 30, 1984; stepchildren: Paul, John, Tom. *Education:* Benedictine College, B.A., 1967; University of Illinois at Urbana-Champaign, M.Ed., 1970; University of Wisconsin—Milwaukee, M.A., 1976.

ADDRESSES: *Home*—7460 Longview, Glendale, WI 53209. *Office*—Milwaukee Area Technical College—South, 6665 South Howell, Oak Creek, WI 53154; fax: 414-571-4668.

CAREER: St. Matthew Grade School, Champaign, IL, teacher, 1967-68; Institute for Advanced Study in Teaching Disadvantaged Youth, Urbana, IL, editor, 1968; University of Illinois Press, Champaign, assistant editor, 1968-70; Santiago College, Santiago, Chile, teacher, 1971-72; University of South Florida, Tampa, editor for U.S. Office of Education's Institute on Educational Reform, 1972; University of Wisconsin—Madison, research associate in Division of Urban Outreach, 1977-78; State University of New York at Albany, lecturer in freshman composition, 1979-80;

*Windsor Chronicle,* Windsor, VT, advertising and layout designer, 1980-81; University of Wisconsin—Milwaukee, lecturer in English, 1981; Marquette University, Milwaukee, lecturer in English and journalism, 1981-82; Milwaukee Area Technical College, Oak Creek, WI, part-time lecturer, 1982-84; Milwaukee Center for Photography, Milwaukee, lecturer in English, 1983-85; Milwaukee Area Technical College, instructor in English, 1984—, instructional chairperson, 1994—. Teacher at writers' workshops; gives poery and prose readings. Wisconsin Arts Board, member of literature panel, 1985 and 1989; Woodland Pattern Book Center, member of board of directors, 1985; Art Futures, member of board of directors, 1991.

MEMBER: National Council of Teachers of English, Authors Guild, American Federation of Teachers, Teachers and Writers Collaborative, Ozaukee Writers' Group.

AWARDS, HONORS: First prize for poetry, National LIT Creative Writing Contest, 1968, for "With Feathers of Other Poems"; Wisconsin Arts Board, fellow, 1976, 1981, and grants, 1986, 1988; Ragdale resident, 1982, 1983; Nancy Furstenberg Prize for fiction, *Plainswoman,* 1984, for "The Lessons"; *Primavera,* fiction award, 1985, for "Anna's Illinois," and poetry award, 1985, for "The Rabbit Killer"; first prize for short fiction, annual contest of Council for Wisconsin Writers, 1987, for "An Embarrassment of Ordinary Riches"; Milwaukee artists fellowship, 1989; award for best book-length fiction, Council for Wisconsin Writers, 1989, and Outstanding Achievement Award, Wisconsin Library Association, 1990, both for *A Farm under a Lake;* first prize, River Oak-Hemingway national Fiction Contest, 1996, for "The Feast of Basil the Great."

WRITINGS:

*Fish* (chapbook), Nemesis Press (Urbana, IL), 1975.
(Contributor) Larry Smith, editor, *From the Heartlands,* Bottom Dog Press (Huron, OH), 1988.
*A Farm under a Lake* (novel), Graywolf (St. Paul, MN), 1989.
(Contributor) Mark Vinz and Thom Tammaro, editors, *Imagining Home,* University of Minnesota Press (Moorhead, MN), 1995.
*Idle Curiosity* (novel), Graywolf, 1997.

Contributor of numerous poems and short stories to periodicals, including *First, Iris, New England Re-*

lar bookstore on Charing Cross Road in London. Decorated with the Order of the British Empire in 1962, he was recognized on two continents as one of ballet's most ardent enthusiasts. *Spectator* contributor Adrian Stokes wrote of Beaumont: "He is, for the most part, a monument of accuracy and of painstaking research, while the ease and stilted fluency of his style belongs to the common Victorian dignity of his thought."

Born in London in 1891, Beaumont became devoted to ballet after seeing Anna Pavlova dance in 1910. He published his first translation of a French dance book in 1913, and shortly thereafter his London bookstore became widely known for its collection of dance and theatre titles. Beaumont's other interests included puppetry and mime, but he was especially drawn to classical ballet. During his lifetime he published a voluminous amount of material on the subject. One of his best-known works, *The Complete Book of Ballet: A Guide to the Principal Ballets of the 19th and 20th Centuries,* was described in *New Statesman and Nation* as being "of biblical proportions, beautifully produced and illustrated."

In a *Books* review of *The Complete Book of Ballet,* Lloyd Morris observed: "Mr. Beaumont's redoubtable scholarship—from which every contemporary critic of the ballet has profited—is, in this book as in all his others, both unimpeachable and unobtrusive. But, over and above erudition, he possesses the ability to impart it stimulatingly. He is an ingratiating and persuasive writer, a critic whose wisdom about his chosen art is merely one facet of a love which—perhaps more than any other ballet-lover of today—he has succeeded in fully communicating."

Other Beaumont titles received equally laudatory reviews. A London *Times* contributor called *Design for the Ballet* "an entertaining picture book, and a valuable record of one of the most adventurous of the applied arts of today." And *Ballet Design, Past and Present,* was praised in the same periodical as "a valuable work of reference as well as a delight to the eye."

Beaumont began to ease back his work load as a bookseller and publisher in the 1960s so that he would have more time to write. He died in 1976, just a year after publishing a memoir about his early years in business. Many of his works, though first published in the 1930s, are still in print today.

BIOGRAPHICAL/CRITICAL SOURCES:

BOOKS

Beaumont, Cyril William, *Bookseller at the Ballet: Memoirs 1891-1929,* Beaumont (London), 1975.
Beaumont, Cyril William, *Flash-back: Memories of My Youth,* Beaumont, 1931.
Philpott, A. R., *Dictionary of Puppetry,* Plays (Boston, MA), 1969.

PERIODICALS

*Books,* May 15, 1938, p. 15.
*Boston Transcript,* October 30, 1937, p. 3; January 20, 1940, p. 1.
*Dance and Dancers,* December, 1961.
*Dance Magazine,* October, 1953.
*Dancing Times,* November, 1972.
*Manchester Guardian,* January 11, 1938, p. 5; December 9, 1938, p. 19.
*Nation,* May 28, 1938, p. 622.
*New Statesman and Nation,* February 19, 1938, p. 304; December 9, 1939, p. 836.
*New York Times,* April 24, 1938, p. 12.
*Saturday Review of Literature,* April 9, 1938, p. 21.
*Spectator,* February 11, 1938, p. 242.
*Theatre Arts,* December, 1937, p. 990; March, 1939, p. 231; November, 1947, p. 81.
*Times Literary Supplement,* November 6, 1937, p. 853; December 17, 1938, p. 798; December 2, 1939, p. 705; July 19, 1947, p. 362.*

*        *        *

BECK, Warren 1896-1986

PERSONAL: Born May 22, 1896 in Richmond, IN; died June 29, 1986 in Appleton, WI; son of Wilbur Henry and Lillian (Kemper) Beck; married Carmen Haberman, July 13, 1930 (divorced, 1956); children: James Peter. *Education:* Earlham College, B.A., 1921; Columbia University, M.A., 1926.

CAREER: Lawrence University, Appleton, WI, instructor, 1926-29, assistant professor, 1929-32, associate professor, 1932-37, professor of English, 1937-68, professor emeritus, 1968-86. Visiting professor at U.S. Army University, Shrivenham, England, 1945, University of Minnesota, 1956, and University of Colorado, 1957; member of faculty of Bread Loaf Graduate School of English, Middlebury College, summers, 1947-55; member of staff of writers' conferences at other colleges and universities.

*MEMBER:* Phi Beta Kappa.

*AWARDS, HONORS:* Friends of American Writers Award, 1945, for *Final Score;* Rockefeller Foundation grant to write fiction and criticism, 1948-59; Ford Foundation fellowship, 1952-53; Lit.D. from Earlham College, 1953; Ehrig Foundation Award for excellence in teaching, 1961; American Council of Learned Societies, fellowship, 1963, grant, 1969; *Joyce's "Dubliners": Substance, Vision, and Art* was chosen by Modern Language Association of America for inclusion in The Scholar's Library, 1970.

*WRITINGS:*

*The Blue Sash and Other Stories,* Antioch Press (Yellow Springs, OH), 1941.
*Final Score* (novel), Knopf (New York City), 1944.
*The First Fish and Other Stories,* Antioch Press, 1947.
*Pause under the Sky* (novel), Swallow & Morrow (New York City), 1947.
*The Far Whistle and Other Stories,* Antioch Press, 1951.
*Into Thin Air* (novel), Knopf, 1951.
*Huck Finn at Phelps Farm* (monograph), Archives des Lettres Modernes, 1958.
*Man in Motion: Faulkner's Trilogy,* University of Wisconsin Press (Madison, WI), 1961.
*The Rest Is Silence and Other Stories,* Swallow Press (Denver, CO), 1963.
*Joyce's "Dubliners": Substance, Vision, and Art,* Duke University Press (Durham, NC), 1969.
*Faulkner: Essays,* University of Wisconsin Press, 1976.

Work appears in *Best American Short Stories* and other anthologies. Contributor of stories, critical essays, and reviews to magazines and newspapers.

*SIDELIGHTS:* A scholarly author who preferred to call himself a "fictionist," Warren Beck published a number of short stories and novels during his long tenure as a professor of English at Wisconsin's Lawrence University. Beck used dramatic situations to explore social issues as varied as the isolation of old age and the trivialization of culture. Many of his works employed stream-of-consciousness or first person narrative, effectively telling stories within the story. To quote *Books* contributor Milton Rugoff,

"Warren Beck's is a personal and serious art in which every story is made to seek its own special form." The critic went on to state that Beck's work "reveals, in sum, a writer of considerable range, craft and sensitivity."

Beck established his literary reputation on his short stories, and he continued to write in that form throughout his career. Many of his stories appeared in literary magazines before they found their way between the covers of books, and they therefore varied greatly in theme and tone. His first collection, *The Blue Sash and Other Stories,* was declared "exciting and excellent" by *New York Times* reviewer E. H. Walton. Walton added that Beck "has extracted the best, for example, from the Hemingway tradition, yet has molded it to his own contemporary uses without any servile copying. His prose is clean, close-whittled, distinguished. Once one has read one of his stories, one looks forward with the sharpest anticipation to what he will make of the next." In a *Chicago Sun* piece on *First Fish and Other Stories,* the reviewer found Beck's short fiction to be "marked by broad human sympathy and brisk, economical artistry." *Saturday Review of Literature* correspondent Hollis Alpert cited the same book for "a clear and wise perceptiveness which pervades most of these stories," concluding: "Even when Mr. Beck fails— and it is unfair to expect perfection all of the time— his attempts are in themselves rewarding."

Beck's longer fictions include *Final Score,* the story of an ambitious reactionary; *Pause under the Sky,* about a pilot on leave from the Second World War; and *Into Thin Air,* a reminiscence by an old man as he watches the house next door being torn down. All three novels are essentially character studies with a moralist's eye for the hypocrisies and other failings of American society. In *Final Score,* for instance, the hero begins the novel as a suicide victim, and his story unfolds as two acquaintances chat over cocktails. *Book Week* contributor August Derleth deemed *Final Score* "eminently worth reading; it is not a great novel, it is not even an auspicious novel; but it is interesting with the fascination that all psychological explorations have, and it is more than competently done." In the *Saturday Review of Literature,* N. L. Rothman commented: "A more ambitious and timely subject could scarcely be undertaken. If Beck had succeeded in bringing it off he might have produced a first-class documentary novel; and even in his failure he has brought to the problem enough of honesty and vigor to make a provocative story of it."

*Pause under the Sky* explores how a pair of lovers are assaulted by the conformist culture in wartime Middle America. *New York Times* correspondent R. G. Davis found the characters "thoroughly sympathetic . . . sensitive and intelligent," but added nonetheless that Beck "has not been quite enough of a novelist, enough concerned with sensibility, imagination and dramatic projection." Conversely, a *New Yorker* essayist found *Pause under the Sky* to be "a vigorous, unsentimental book deeply imbued with sentiment."

Better reviews attended the publication of *Into Thin Air,* a fictitious memoir of adultery and disappointment from the point of view of a dying man. "One may not care for the method Warren Beck has chosen to tell [protagonist] Ralph Kempner's story," maintained Kelsey Guilfoil in the *Chicago Sunday Tribune.* "But it cannot be gainsaid that his story has a fullness and richness which a piling up of circumstances and incident might never have given it, and that what at last emerges from the gradual accretion of details of character is a triumph of narrative skill." According to James Hilton in the *New York Herald Tribune Book Review, Into Thin Air* "is a novel of quality; beautifully written, its rhythm beats a tune of sad purpose, and in the end the reader may find himself touched even if he is not moved."

"The finest virtue in Mr. Beck's [work] is the human accuracy," noted Paul Engle in the *Chicago Sunday Tribune.* "In a time when so much fiction asks the reader to accept the essential oddness, if not real eccentricity, of its characters, Mr. Beck's stories ask him to accept the varieties of the normal, the daily, the readily definable." In the *New York Times,* Donald Barr concluded that Beck's stories in particular "command respect by deep integrity, forthrightness of style, and compassion for the moderate soul in a nagging universe."

Beck once told *CA:* "For forty-two years at Lawrence, and elsewhere as visiting professor, I was an 'English teacher,' chiefly of 19th and 20th century literature, English and American, and at times a tutor in literary composition for selected students. Concurrently I have also been a writer of short stories and novels, and, more recently, literary criticism. I'm still trying to apply what I've taught, out of the examples of our betters, both precedent and contemporary. This holds not only in attempts to apply my extracted notions of the arts of fictional composition (my work in progress being a novel), but has held in my literary criticism on Joyce and Faulkner.

"My intention in this latter has been impressionistic rather than scholarly, in that it aims primarily at interpretive explication of the text in hand, and borrows from the learning of others very little except as that may expedite an understanding of the text's particulars at that point. (Conversely, on occasion a scholar quoted by an editor of an anthology or other text may have to be questioned and the student invited to consider whether a less strained, less remotely derived impression, and one nearer in line with the writer's manner and prevalent bent, doesn't give a clearer, more persuasive sense that best harmonizes with the whole passage. Indeed, in textually oriented study, use should be made of whatever exemplifies the words as a continuity of units that structure themselves into larger and larger conceptual entities which coalesce into the complete autonomous work of art.)

"At any rate, in teaching literary works to undergraduates and graduate students, through shared individual attention to the text, I've seen a number, from generations of students in a variety of American institutions, become spontaneously attentive to the particular subject and rapidly progressive in what they were learning to do for themselves as readers of literature. A welcome reassurance for the teacher that they had developed their own tasteful comparative judgments came at term's end when a poll of preferences among ten novels or several poets of a period showed choices scattered all over the list. The total experience didn't surprise me. Nor was I complacent in recalling the anecdote of Toscanini at a culminating rehearsal, when after going straight through the symphony as if in a concert the musicians broke into applause for their conductor, and he cried out, 'Gentlemen, it is not I, it is Beethoven!' But Toscanini, indubitably a genius, was also an eminently learned and severe scholar in music. More humbly, an impressionistic critic can make a similar gesture of deference to any text he feels inclined to promulgate, as teacher or writer, as best he can in its own terms and worth."

*BIOGRAPHICAL/CRITICAL SOURCES:*

*BOOKS*

*Indiana Authors and Their Books: 1917-1966,* Wabash College, 1974.

*PERIODICALS*

*Books,* October 5, 1941, p. 12.
*Book Week,* August 27, 1944, p. 3.
*Chicago Sun,* December 3, 1947, p. A16.

*view and Bread Loaf Quarterly, Primavera,* and *Plainswoman.* Editor of *Minnesota Review,* 1975-76; member of editorial committee, *Wisconsin Academy Review,* 1991-93.

*ADAPTATIONS:* The novel *A Farm under a Lake* was adapted for the stage by Mark Richard and Kelly Thompson, produced in Chicago, IL, at Live Bait Theater, 1992.

*SIDELIGHTS:* Martha Bergland told *CA:* "I keep coming back to a poem I wrote when I was twelve. I wrote it on my own; no one told me to write it. It must be the first thing I ever wrote that was not an assignment in school. I loved the poem, so I wrote several drafts of it and memorized it. When I told it to my little brothers, they were impressed—no easy thing to do with those two. I can see myself and my brothers. They are sitting on the bottom bunk in their bedroom, and I am standing in front of them declaiming the poem. (I am impressed too.) They listen raptly; I am having a wonderful time, and then they ask me to say it again. Later I told the poem to my parents. I think they asked me for a copy of it and asked me to say it aloud to some company.

"The poem was about talk. I still remember a part of it: 'How do grown-ups think up conversations? / Daddy says they should come in rations.'

"For more than twenty-five years since that first poem I have been writing poems, short stories, and essays. What is interesting to me is that there are things that were true of that poem that are still true of my writing today. First, I still write about talk. In many of my stories, especially, I am trying to answer questions concerning the importance of talk, how various people use talk, and what talk accomplishes. Second, I make up stuff. My father never said conversations should come in rations; as a matter of fact, he was and is a big talker and likes other people to be also. Now, in short stories and sometimes in poems and essays (I have to admit), I make things up. I try not to 'let truth stand in the way of a good story.' Third, I still use two voices, one of which is parenthetical and comments on the other, as the second line of that poem comments on the first. (In many of my stories and essays I think the most interesting things are said inside of the parentheses.) And fourth, I still love to mess with the sound of the words. In that poem I used rhyme, but now in stories I use alliteration and assonance, and I try to make sentences have interesting variations in pace and rhythm.

"Seeing these connections between what I was writing twenty-five years ago and what I write now has reinforced some of my beliefs about what is important in the process of learning to write. I can see from my own experience that it is important to have positive experiences with writing, and one of the most pleasurable and accessible experiences is to read aloud a piece you've written to an audience. It's wonderful to see the expressions on the faces of your listeners, and it's especially great when they want to hear it again. It is important also to play with words; revising is probably at first just messing around with the language: What would happen if I put this word here? What would happen if I repeated this sound? I think it is important, too, that we realize that we do not have to wait to 'get educated' before we have something to say. If a twelve-year-old can have something to say that people will want to listen to, it must be even truer of older people—people as old as eighteen or nineteen. But most of all, the continuity that I see in my writing over the years has made me realize that in learning to write we are not trying to say what we think but trying to clarify and strengthen and build on what may concern us for all of our lives."

*BIOGRAPHICAL/CRITICAL SOURCES:*

*PERIODICALS*

*Kirkus Reviews,* April 15, 1989.
*Los Angeles Times,* July 23, 1989.
*Milwaukee Journal,* May 21, 1989.
*New York Times Book Review,* July 9, 1989.
*Philadelphia Inquirer,* June 27, 1989.

\*     \*     \*

**BERGMAN, Tamar 1939-**

*PERSONAL:* Born January 29, 1939, in Tel Aviv, British Palestine (now Israel); daughter of Katriel Yaffe (a boat captain) and Fenia Sherman (a homemaker; maiden name, Oreloff); married Ze'ev Bergman (a psychologist), September 2, 1962; children: Opher, Sigal, Orit. *Education:* Hebrew University, Jerusalem, B.A., 1963, attended the Sorbonne, University of Paris, 1964-65. *Religion:* Jewish.

*ADDRESSES: Home and office*—6 Hanassi St., Jerusalem 92188, Israel.

*CAREER:* Israeli Broadcasting Authority, Jerusalem, Israel, radio play writer, 1970-82; writer.

*MEMBER:* Hebrew Writers Association.

*AWARDS, HONORS:* Berenstein Prize, Israeli Publishers' Association, and "Best Children's Book" citation, University of Haifa's Center for Literature for Children and Youth, both 1984, Notable Children's Trade Book in the Field of Social Studies, Children's Book Council, 1991, all for *The Boy from Over There;* Notable Children's Trade Book in the Field of Social Studies, Children's Book Council, and Ze'ev Prize, Israeli Ministry of Education, both 1988, both for *Along the Tracks;* Jerusalem Literary Award, 1994, for manuscript of "As a Polished Mirror"; ACUM Award, 1995, for manuscript of "Couch of Secrets."

*WRITINGS:*

*Hamassa Legan Hashoshanim* (title means "The Journey to the Rose Garden"), Massada, 1976.

*Danny Holeh Lemirpe'at Hashina'in* (title means "Danny Goes to the Dentist"), Israel Economist, 1976.

*Al Shumklum ye-'al Shumakom* (title means "About Nothing in Nowhere"), Hakibbutz Hameuchad, 1976.

*Mi Rotze Lehitarev?* (title means "Who Want's to Bet?"), Ministry of Health, 1977.

*Beshabat Baboker* (title means "On Saturday Morning"), Keter, 1979.

*Shinayim tsohakot* (title means "Laughing Teeth"), Keter, 1980.

(With Chemi Gutman) *Simlat Haksamim* (title means "The Magic Dress"), Keter, 1980.

*Kol Ehad Ha'ya Pa'am Yeled,* (title means "We Were All Children Once"), Sifriat Poalim, 1983.

*Ha Yeled mi-shamah,* Am Oved, 1983, published in English as *The Boy from Over There,* translated by Hillel Halkin, Houghton (Boston), 1988.

*Mehapsim Et Osnat,* (title means "Looking for Osnat"), Keter, 1985.

*Gozal Shel Aba Ve'ima* (title means "Mom and Dad's Chick"), Keter, 1987.

*Leoreh Hamessila,* Schocken, 1987, published in English as *Along the Tracks,* translated by Michael Swirsky, Houghton, 1991.

*Rav Hovel Shav Ela'ich* (title means "The Captain Has Returned"), Am Oved/Yad Ben-Zvi, 1990.

*Kemar'a Letusha* (title means "As a Polished Mirror"), Am Oved, 1996.

*Konchi'at Hassodot* (title means "Couch of Secrets"), Sifriat Poalim, 1996.

*The Boy from Over There* and *Along the Tracks* have been translated into other languages.

*SIDELIGHTS:* Israeli children's author Tamar Bergman has penned more than a dozen books in Hebrew, subtly interweaving incidents of her own childhood into the words she sets down for youngsters. In her novels, Bergman deals with difficult subject matter, such as coping with the death of a parent and the hurt of prejudice. Herself losing her father when she was two, Bergman creates protagonists who must deal with the loss or absence of a parent, as in *The Boy from Over There.* This book and *Along the Tracks* both draw upon the social and economic upheavals that occurred in Europe events stemming from the Nazis' rise to power in the late 1930s, the subsequent war, and slaughter of over six million Jews while Bergman was a child. Bergman's birthplace, Palestine (now Israel), became a refuge for the millions of Jewish refugees fleeing from the carnage in Europe.

Raised on a kibbutz, Bergman used this setting for *The Boy from Over There,* her first story translated into English. Avramik has finally reached Palestine after hiding from the war in Europe for most of his young life. Refusing to admit that his mother is dead, Avramik finds adjusting to life on a communal farm with his uncle very hard and the other children find his behavior-hoarding food, refusing to sleep, never speaking without shouting-odd, but understandable, because he is from "over there," a survivor of the war in Europe. However, the relative peace of the kibbutz is brief, as war breaks out in 1948 when Israel begins to fight for independence. Again under fire, Avramik must lead the children to safety and come to accept a new life in a different land.

Critics lauded Bergman for her touching portrayal of refugee life in Israel after the Second World War. Calling *The Boy from Over There* "potent," a reviewer in *Publishers Weekly* remarked that "Bergman develops strong characters and recreates Kibbutz life in rich detail." In *School Library Journal,* Louise L. Sherman also applauded the "realistic" characters and praised Bergman for her deft handling of life on a communal farm. Writing in the *New York Times Book Review,* Jenifer Levin proclaimed that the book "is a rewarding, consistently entertaining, multilayered book of emotions and ideas."

lar bookstore on Charing Cross Road in London. Decorated with the Order of the British Empire in 1962, he was recognized on two continents as one of ballet's most ardent enthusiasts. *Spectator* contributor Adrian Stokes wrote of Beaumont: "He is, for the most part, a monument of accuracy and of painstaking research, while the ease and stilted fluency of his style belongs to the common Victorian dignity of his thought."

Born in London in 1891, Beaumont became devoted to ballet after seeing Anna Pavlova dance in 1910. He published his first translation of a French dance book in 1913, and shortly thereafter his London bookstore became widely known for its collection of dance and theatre titles. Beaumont's other interests included puppetry and mime, but he was especially drawn to classical ballet. During his lifetime he published a voluminous amount of material on the subject. One of his best-known works, *The Complete Book of Ballet: A Guide to the Principal Ballets of the 19th and 20th Centuries,* was described in *New Statesman and Nation* as being "of biblical proportions, beautifully produced and illustrated."

In a *Books* review of *The Complete Book of Ballet,* Lloyd Morris observed: "Mr. Beaumont's redoubtable scholarship—from which every contemporary critic of the ballet has profited—is, in this book as in all his others, both unimpeachable and unobtrusive. But, over and above erudition, he possesses the ability to impart it stimulatingly. He is an ingratiating and persuasive writer, a critic whose wisdom about his chosen art is merely one facet of a love which—perhaps more than any other ballet-lover of today—he has succeeded in fully communicating."

Other Beaumont titles received equally laudatory reviews. A London *Times* contributor called *Design for the Ballet* "an entertaining picture book, and a valuable record of one of the most adventurous of the applied arts of today." And *Ballet Design, Past and Present,* was praised in the same periodical as "a valuable work of reference as well as a delight to the eye."

Beaumont began to ease back his work load as a book seller and publisher in the 1960s so that he would have more time to write. He died in 1976, just a year after publishing a memoir about his early years in business. Many of his works, though first published in the 1930s, are still in print today.

## BIOGRAPHICAL/CRITICAL SOURCES:

### BOOKS

Beaumont, Cyril William, *Bookseller at the Ballet: Memoirs 1891-1929,* Beaumont (London), 1975.
Beaumont, Cyril William, *Flash-back: Memories of My Youth,* Beaumont, 1931.
Philpott, A. R., *Dictionary of Puppetry,* Plays (Boston, MA), 1969.

### PERIODICALS

*Books,* May 15, 1938, p. 15.
*Boston Transcript,* October 30, 1937, p. 3; January 20, 1940, p. 1.
*Dance and Dancers,* December, 1961.
*Dance Magazine,* October, 1953.
*Dancing Times,* November, 1972.
*Manchester Guardian,* January 11, 1938, p. 5; December 9, 1938, p. 19.
*Nation,* May 28, 1938, p. 622.
*New Statesman and Nation,* February 19, 1938, p. 304; December 9, 1939, p. 836.
*New York Times,* April 24, 1938, p. 12.
*Saturday Review of Literature,* April 9, 1938, p. 21.
*Spectator,* February 11, 1938, p. 242.
*Theatre Arts,* December, 1937, p. 990; March, 1939, p. 231; November, 1947, p. 81.
*Times Literary Supplement,* November 6, 1937, p. 853; December 17, 1938, p. 798; December 2, 1939, p. 705; July 19, 1947, p. 362.*

\* \* \*

## BECK, Warren 1896-1986

*PERSONAL:* Born May 22, 1896 in Richmond, IN; died June 29, 1986 in Appleton, WI; son of Wilbur Henry and Lillian (Kemper) Beck; married Carmen Haberman, July 13, 1930 (divorced, 1956); children: James Peter. *Education:* Earlham College, B.A., 1921; Columbia University, M.A., 1926.

*CAREER:* Lawrence University, Appleton, WI, instructor, 1926-29, assistant professor, 1929-32, associate professor, 1932-37, professor of English, 1937-68, professor emeritus, 1968-86. Visiting professor at U.S. Army University, Shrivenham, England, 1945, University of Minnesota, 1956, and University of Colorado, 1957; member of faculty of Bread Loaf Graduate School of English, Middlebury College, summers, 1947-55; member of staff of writers' conferences at other colleges and universities.

*MEMBER:* Phi Beta Kappa.

*AWARDS, HONORS:* Friends of American Writers Award, 1945, for *Final Score;* Rockefeller Foundation grant to write fiction and criticism, 1948-59; Ford Foundation fellowship, 1952-53; Lit.D. from Earlham College, 1953; Ehrig Foundation Award for excellence in teaching, 1961; American Council of Learned Societies, fellowship, 1963, grant, 1969; *Joyce's "Dubliners": Substance, Vision, and Art* was chosen by Modern Language Association of America for inclusion in The Scholar's Library, 1970.

*WRITINGS:*

*The Blue Sash and Other Stories,* Antioch Press (Yellow Springs, OH), 1941.
*Final Score* (novel), Knopf (New York City), 1944.
*The First Fish and Other Stories,* Antioch Press, 1947.
*Pause under the Sky* (novel), Swallow & Morrow (New York City), 1947.
*The Far Whistle and Other Stories,* Antioch Press, 1951.
*Into Thin Air* (novel), Knopf, 1951.
*Huck Finn at Phelps Farm* (monograph), Archives des Lettres Modernes, 1958.
*Man in Motion: Faulkner's Trilogy,* University of Wisconsin Press (Madison, WI), 1961.
*The Rest Is Silence and Other Stories,* Swallow Press (Denver, CO), 1963.
*Joyce's "Dubliners": Substance, Vision, and Art,* Duke University Press (Durham, NC), 1969.
*Faulkner: Essays,* University of Wisconsin Press, 1976.

Work appears in *Best American Short Stories* and other anthologies. Contributor of stories, critical essays, and reviews to magazines and newspapers.

*SIDELIGHTS:* A scholarly author who preferred to call himself a "fictionist," Warren Beck published a number of short stories and novels during his long tenure as a professor of English at Wisconsin's Lawrence University. Beck used dramatic situations to explore social issues as varied as the isolation of old age and the trivialization of culture. Many of his works employed stream-of-consciousness or first person narrative, effectively telling stories within the story. To quote *Books* contributor Milton Rugoff,

"Warren Beck's is a personal and serious art in which every story is made to seek its own special form." The critic went on to state that Beck's work "reveals, in sum, a writer of considerable range, craft and sensitivity."

Beck established his literary reputation on his short stories, and he continued to write in that form throughout his career. Many of his stories appeared in literary magazines before they found their way between the covers of books, and they therefore varied greatly in theme and tone. His first collection, *The Blue Sash and Other Stories,* was declared "exciting and excellent" by *New York Times* reviewer E. H. Walton. Walton added that Beck "has extracted the best, for example, from the Hemingway tradition, yet has molded it to his own contemporary uses without any servile copying. His prose is clean, close-whittled, distinguished. Once one has read one of his stories, one looks forward with the sharpest anticipation to what he will make of the next." In a *Chicago Sun* piece on *First Fish and Other Stories,* the reviewer found Beck's short fiction to be "marked by broad human sympathy and brisk, economical artistry." *Saturday Review of Literature* correspondent Hollis Alpert cited the same book for "a clear and wise perceptiveness which pervades most of these stories," concluding: "Even when Mr. Beck fails—and it is unfair to expect perfection all of the time—his attempts are in themselves rewarding."

Beck's longer fictions include *Final Score,* the story of an ambitious reactionary; *Pause under the Sky,* about a pilot on leave from the Second World War; and *Into Thin Air,* a reminiscence by an old man as he watches the house next door being torn down. All three novels are essentially character studies with a moralist's eye for the hypocrisies and other failings of American society. In *Final Score,* for instance, the hero begins the novel as a suicide victim, and his story unfolds as two acquaintances chat over cocktails. *Book Week* contributor August Derleth deemed *Final Score* "eminently worth reading; it is not a great novel, it is not even an auspicious novel; but it is interesting with the fascination that all psychological explorations have, and it is more than competently done." In the *Saturday Review of Literature,* N. L. Rothman commented: "A more ambitious and timely subject could scarcely be undertaken. If Beck had succeeded in bringing it off he might have produced a first-class documentary novel; and even in his failure he has brought to the problem enough of honesty and vigor to make a provocative story of it."

*Pause under the Sky* explores how a pair of lovers are assaulted by the conformist culture in wartime Middle America. *New York Times* correspondent R. G. Davis found the characters "thoroughly sympathetic . . . sensitive and intelligent," but added nonetheless that Beck "has not been quite enough of a novelist, enough concerned with sensibility, imagination and dramatic projection." Conversely, a *New Yorker* essayist found *Pause under the Sky* to be "a vigorous, unsentimental book deeply imbued with sentiment."

Better reviews attended the publication of *Into Thin Air,* a fictitious memoir of adultery and disappointment from the point of view of a dying man. "One may not care for the method Warren Beck has chosen to tell [protagonist] Ralph Kempner's story," maintained Kelsey Guilfoil in the *Chicago Sunday Tribune.* "But it cannot be gainsaid that his story has a fullness and richness which a piling up of circumstances and incident might never have given it, and that what at last emerges from the gradual accretion of details of character is a triumph of narrative skill." According to James Hilton in the *New York Herald Tribune Book Review, Into Thin Air* "is a novel of quality; beautifully written, its rhythm beats a tune of sad purpose, and in the end the reader may find himself touched even if he is not moved."

"The finest virtue in Mr. Beck's [work] is the human accuracy," noted Paul Engle in the *Chicago Sunday Tribune.* "In a time when so much fiction asks the reader to accept the essential oddness, if not real eccentricity, of its characters, Mr. Beck's stories ask him to accept the varieties of the normal, the daily, the readily definable." In the *New York Times,* Donald Barr concluded that Beck's stories in particular "command respect by deep integrity, forthrightness of style, and compassion for the moderate soul in a nagging universe."

Beck once told *CA:* "For forty-two years at Lawrence, and elsewhere as visiting professor, I was an 'English teacher,' chiefly of 19th and 20th century literature, English and American, and at times a tutor in literary composition for selected students. Concurrently I have also been a writer of short stories and novels, and, more recently, literary criticism. I'm still trying to apply what I've taught, out of the examples of our betters, both precedent and contemporary. This holds not only in attempts to apply my extracted notions of the arts of fictional composition (my work in progress being a novel), but has held in my literary criticism on Joyce and Faulkner.

"My intention in this latter has been impressionistic rather than scholarly, in that it aims primarily at interpretive explication of the text in hand, and borrows from the learning of others very little except as that may expedite an understanding of the text's particulars at that point. (Conversely, on occasion a scholar quoted by an editor of an anthology or other text may have to be questioned and the student invited to consider whether a less strained, less remotely derived impression, and one nearer in line with the writer's manner and prevalent bent, doesn't give a clearer, more persuasive sense that best harmonizes with the whole passage. Indeed, in textually oriented study, use should be made of whatever exemplifies the words as a continuity of units that structure themselves into larger and larger conceptual entities which coalesce into the complete autonomous work of art.)

"At any rate, in teaching literary works to undergraduates and graduate students, through shared individual attention to the text, I've seen a number, from generations of students in a variety of American institutions, become spontaneously attentive to the particular subject and rapidly progressive in what they were learning to do for themselves as readers of literature. A welcome reassurance for the teacher that they had developed their own tasteful comparative judgments came at term's end when a poll of preferences among ten novels or several poets of a period showed choices scattered all over the list. The total experience didn't surprise me. Nor was I complacent in recalling the anecdote of Toscanini at a culminating rehearsal, when after going straight through the symphony as if in a concert the musicians broke into applause for their conductor, and he cried out, 'Gentlemen, it is not I, it is Beethoven!' But Toscanini, indubitably a genius, was also an eminently learned and severe scholar in music. More humbly, an impressionistic critic can make a similar gesture of deference to any text he feels inclined to promulgate, as teacher or writer, as best he can in its own terms and worth."

*BIOGRAPHICAL/CRITICAL SOURCES:*

*BOOKS*

*Indiana Authors and Their Books: 1917-1966,* Wabash College, 1974.

*PERIODICALS*

*Books,* October 5, 1941, p. 12.
*Book Week,* August 27, 1944, p. 3.
*Chicago Sun,* December 3, 1947, p. A16.

*Chicago Sun Book Week,* May 18, 1947, p. 3.
*Chicago Sunday Tribune,* February 18, 1951, p. 2.
*Nation,* September 9, 1944, p. 304.
*New Yorker,* May 10, 1947, p. 104.
*New York Herald Tribune Book Review,* February 18, 1951, p. 8.
*New York Times,* June 8, 1941, p. 12; August 20, 1944, p. 4; February 18, 1951, p. 16.
*San Francisco Chronicle,* March 10, 1951, p. 10.
*Saturday Review of Literature,* September 30, 1944, p. 25; April 24, 1948, p. 36.
*Time,* February 19, 1951, p. 104.
*Times Literary Supplement,* September 20, 1947, p. 477.
*Weekly Book Review,* August 20, 1944, p. 6.


*OBITUARIES:*

*PERIODICALS*

*Milwaukee Journal,* July 1, 1986.*


\*        \*        \*


**BERGLAND, Martha 1945-**

*PERSONAL:* Born September 16, 1945, in Oklahoma City, OK; daughter of Hugh Lennox Bond (a farmer) and Elizabeth Murphey (a painter; maiden name, Howard) Bergland; married Lawrence J. Barnett (a professor), December 30, 1984; stepchildren: Paul, John, Tom. *Education:* Benedictine College, B.A., 1967; University of Illinois at Urbana-Champaign, M.Ed., 1970; University of Wisconsin—Milwaukee, M.A., 1976.

*ADDRESSES: Home*—7460 Longview, Glendale, WI 53209. *Office*—Milwaukee Area Technical College—South, 6665 South Howell, Oak Creek, WI 53154; fax: 414-571-4668.

*CAREER:* St. Matthew Grade School, Champaign, IL, teacher, 1967-68; Institute for Advanced Study in Teaching Disadvantaged Youth, Urbana, IL, editor, 1968; University of Illinois Press, Champaign, assistant editor, 1968-70; Santiago College, Santiago, Chile, teacher, 1971-72; University of South Florida, Tampa, editor for U.S. Office of Education's Institute on Educational Reform, 1972; University of Wisconsin—Madison, research associate in Division of Urban Outreach, 1977-78; State University of New York at Albany, lecturer in freshman composition, 1979-80;

*Windsor Chronicle,* Windsor, VT, advertising and layout designer, 1980-81; University of Wisconsin—Milwaukee, lecturer in English, 1981; Marquette University, Milwaukee, lecturer in English and journalism, 1981-82; Milwaukee Area Technical College, Oak Creek, WI, part-time lecturer, 1982-84; Milwaukee Center for Photography, Milwaukee, lecturer in English, 1983-85; Milwaukee Area Technical College, instructor in English, 1984—, instructional chairperson, 1994—. Teacher at writers' workshops; gives poery and prose readings. Wisconsin Arts Board, member of literature panel, 1985 and 1989; Woodland Pattern Book Center, member of board of directors, 1985; Art Futures, member of board of directors, 1991.

*MEMBER:* National Council of Teachers of English, Authors Guild, American Federation of Teachers, Teachers and Writers Collaborative, Ozaukee Writers' Group.

*AWARDS, HONORS:* First prize for poetry, National LIT Creative Writing Contest, 1968, for "With Feathers of Other Poems"; Wisconsin Arts Board, fellow, 1976, 1981, and grants, 1986, 1988; Ragdale resident, 1982, 1983; Nancy Furstenberg Prize for fiction, *Plainswoman,* 1984, for "The Lessons"; *Primavera,* fiction award, 1985, for "Anna's Illinois," and poetry award, 1985, for "The Rabbit Killer"; first prize for short fiction, annual contest of Council for Wisconsin Writers, 1987, for "An Embarrassment of Ordinary Riches"; Milwaukee artists fellowship, 1989; award for best book-length fiction, Council for Wisconsin Writers, 1989, and Outstanding Achievement Award, Wisconsin Library Association, 1990, both for *A Farm under a Lake;* first prize, River Oak-Hemingway national Fiction Contest, 1996, for "The Feast of Basil the Great."

*WRITINGS:*

*Fish* (chapbook), Nemesis Press (Urbana, IL), 1975.
(Contributor) Larry Smith, editor, *From the Heartlands,* Bottom Dog Press (Huron, OH), 1988.
*A Farm under a Lake* (novel), Graywolf (St. Paul, MN), 1989.
(Contributor) Mark Vinz and Thom Tammaro, editors, *Imagining Home,* University of Minnesota Press (Moorhead, MN), 1995.
*Idle Curiosity* (novel), Graywolf, 1997.

Contributor of numerous poems and short stories to periodicals, including *First, Iris, New England Re-*

*view and Bread Loaf Quarterly, Primavera,* and *Plainswoman.* Editor of *Minnesota Review,* 1975-76; member of editorial committee, *Wisconsin Academy Review,* 1991-93.

*ADAPTATIONS:* The novel *A Farm under a Lake* was adapted for the stage by Mark Richard and Kelly Thompson, produced in Chicago, IL, at Live Bait Theater, 1992.

*SIDELIGHTS:* Martha Bergland told *CA:* "I keep coming back to a poem I wrote when I was twelve. I wrote it on my own; no one told me to write it. It must be the first thing I ever wrote that was not an assignment in school. I loved the poem, so I wrote several drafts of it and memorized it. When I told it to my little brothers, they were impressed—no easy thing to do with those two. I can see myself and my brothers. They are sitting on the bottom bunk in their bedroom, and I am standing in front of them declaiming the poem. (I am impressed too.) They listen raptly; I am having a wonderful time, and then they ask me to say it again. Later I told the poem to my parents. I think they asked me for a copy of it and asked me to say it aloud to some company.

"The poem was about talk. I still remember a part of it: 'How do grown-ups think up conversations? / Daddy says they should come in rations.'

"For more than twenty-five years since that first poem I have been writing poems, short stories, and essays. What is interesting to me is that there are things that were true of that poem that are still true of my writing today. First, I still write about talk. In many of my stories, especially, I am trying to answer questions concerning the importance of talk, how various people use talk, and what talk accomplishes. Second, I make up stuff. My father never said conversations should come in rations; as a matter of fact, he was and is a big talker and likes other people to be also. Now, in short stories and sometimes in poems and essays (I have to admit), I make things up. I try not to 'let truth stand in the way of a good story.' Third, I still use two voices, one of which is parenthetical and comments on the other, as the second line of that poem comments on the first. (In many of my stories and essays I think the most interesting things are said inside of the parentheses.) And fourth, I still love to mess with the sound of the words. In that poem I used rhyme, but now in stories I use alliteration and assonance, and I try to make sentences have interesting variations in pace and rhythm.

"Seeing these connections between what I was writing twenty-five years ago and what I write now has reinforced some of my beliefs about what is important in the process of learning to write. I can see from my own experience that it is important to have positive experiences with writing, and one of the most pleasurable and accessible experiences is to read aloud a piece you've written to an audience. It's wonderful to see the expressions on the faces of your listeners, and it's especially great when they want to hear it again. It is important also to play with words; revising is probably at first just messing around with the language: What would happen if I put this word here? What would happen if I repeated this sound? I think it is important, too, that we realize that we do not have to wait to 'get educated' before we have something to say. If a twelve-year-old can have something to say that people will want to listen to, it must be even truer of older people—people as old as eighteen or nineteen. But most of all, the continuity that I see in my writing over the years has made me realize that in learning to write we are not trying to say what we think but trying to clarify and strengthen and build on what may concern us for all of our lives."

*BIOGRAPHICAL/CRITICAL SOURCES:*

*PERIODICALS*

*Kirkus Reviews,* April 15, 1989.
*Los Angeles Times,* July 23, 1989.
*Milwaukee Journal,* May 21, 1989.
*New York Times Book Review,* July 9, 1989.
*Philadelphia Inquirer,* June 27, 1989.

\* \* \*

**BERGMAN, Tamar 1939-**

*PERSONAL:* Born January 29, 1939, in Tel Aviv, British Palestine (now Israel); daughter of Katriel Yaffe (a boat captain) and Fenia Sherman (a homemaker; maiden name, Oreloff); married Ze'ev Bergman (a psychologist), September 2, 1962; children: Opher, Sigal, Orit. *Education:* Hebrew University, Jerusalem, B.A., 1963, attended the Sorbonne, University of Paris, 1964-65. *Religion:* Jewish.

*ADDRESSES: Home and office*—6 Hanassi St., Jerusalem 92188, Israel.

*CAREER:* Israeli Broadcasting Authority, Jerusalem, Israel, radio play writer, 1970-82; writer.

*MEMBER:* Hebrew Writers Association.

*AWARDS, HONORS:* Berenstein Prize, Israeli Publishers' Association, and "Best Children's Book" citation, University of Haifa's Center for Literature for Children and Youth, both 1984, Notable Children's Trade Book in the Field of Social Studies, Children's Book Council, 1991, all for *The Boy from Over There;* Notable Children's Trade Book in the Field of Social Studies, Children's Book Council, and Ze'ev Prize, Israeli Ministry of Education, both 1988, both for *Along the Tracks;* Jerusalem Literary Award, 1994, for manuscript of "As a Polished Mirror"; ACUM Award, 1995, for manuscript of "Couch of Secrets."

*WRITINGS:*

*Hamassa Legan Hashoshanim* (title means "The Journey to the Rose Garden"), Massada, 1976.

*Danny Holeh Lemirpe'at Hashina'in* (title means "Danny Goes to the Dentist"), Israel Economist, 1976.

*Al Shumklum ye-'al Shumakom* (title means "About Nothing in Nowhere"), Hakibbutz Hameuchad, 1976.

*Mi Rotze Lehitarev?* (title means "Who Want's to Bet?"), Ministry of Health, 1977.

*Beshabat Baboker* (title means "On Saturday Morning"), Keter, 1979.

*Shinayim tsohakot* (title means "Laughing Teeth"), Keter, 1980.

(With Chemi Gutman) *Simlat Haksamim* (title means "The Magic Dress"), Keter, 1980.

*Kol Ehad Ha'ya Pa'am Yeled,* (title means "We Were All Children Once"), Sifriat Poalim, 1983.

*Ha Yeled mi-shamah,* Am Oved, 1983, published in English as *The Boy from Over There,* translated by Hillel Halkin, Houghton (Boston), 1988.

*Mehapsim Et Osnat,* (title means "Looking for Osnat"), Keter, 1985.

*Gozal Shel Aba Ve'ima* (title means "Mom and Dad's Chick"), Keter, 1987.

*Leoreh Hamessila,* Schocken, 1987, published in English as *Along the Tracks,* translated by Michael Swirsky, Houghton, 1991.

*Rav Hovel Shav Ela'ich* (title means "The Captain Has Returned"), Am Oved/Yad Ben-Zvi, 1990.

*Kemar'a Letusha* (title means "As a Polished Mirror"), Am Oved, 1996.

*Konchi'at Hassodot* (title means "Couch of Secrets"), Sifriat Poalim, 1996.

*The Boy from Over There* and *Along the Tracks* have been translated into other languages.

*SIDELIGHTS:* Israeli children's author Tamar Bergman has penned more than a dozen books in Hebrew, subtly interweaving incidents of her own childhood into the words she sets down for youngsters. In her novels, Bergman deals with difficult subject matter, such as coping with the death of a parent and the hurt of prejudice. Herself losing her father when she was two, Bergman creates protagonists who must deal with the loss or absence of a parent, as in *The Boy from Over There.* This book and *Along the Tracks* both draw upon the social and economic upheavals that occurred in Europe events stemming from the Nazis' rise to power in the late 1930s, the subsequent war, and slaughter of over six million Jews while Bergman was a child. Bergman's birthplace, Palestine (now Israel), became a refuge for the millions of Jewish refugees fleeing from the carnage in Europe.

Raised on a kibbutz, Bergman used this setting for *The Boy from Over There,* her first story translated into English. Avramik has finally reached Palestine after hiding from the war in Europe for most of his young life. Refusing to admit that his mother is dead, Avramik finds adjusting to life on a communal farm with his uncle very hard and the other children find his behavior-hoarding food, refusing to sleep, never speaking without shouting-odd, but understandable, because he is from "over there," a survivor of the war in Europe. However, the relative peace of the kibbutz is brief, as war breaks out in 1948 when Israel begins to fight for independence. Again under fire, Avramik must lead the children to safety and come to accept a new life in a different land.

Critics lauded Bergman for her touching portrayal of refugee life in Israel after the Second World War. Calling *The Boy from Over There* "potent," a reviewer in *Publishers Weekly* remarked that "Bergman develops strong characters and recreates Kibbutz life in rich detail." In *School Library Journal,* Louise L. Sherman also applauded the "realistic" characters and praised Bergman for her deft handling of life on a communal farm. Writing in the *New York Times Book Review,* Jenifer Levin proclaimed that the book "is a rewarding, consistently entertaining, multilayered book of emotions and ideas."

The saga of refugees is also discussed in Bergman's second novel translated into English, *Along the Tracks*. In this story, a young boy and his family flee Poland for the Soviet Union at the onset on World War II. After settling in a work camp there, the refugees find life becoming progressively harder, especially for young Yankele. When the Nazis invade the Soviet Union, Yankele is separated from his parents in the chaos and must learn to survive on his own. Forced to roam the countryside for the next few years, he bands together with other orphans and lives in railroad stations. Eventually Yankele finds his family and faces a new challenge of adjusting to a more settled life. In a *School Library Journal* review, Susan Knorr claimed that "Bergman poignantly shows the pain of separation and the remarkable determination of youth to survive." "The novel offers young readers plenty of action" according to *Horn Book* contributor Nancy Vasilakis, who went on to write that the book "excels particularly well in its evocation of setting."

"My writing once began with stories told to my children," Bergman once commented. "As they grew older, so did my readers. Now that my children are grown I find myself working on a novel for adults, but perhaps my future grandchildren will turn my imagination back to the enchanted realm of childhood.

"I have written more than a dozen books, most of them for ages five to eight, but the three of my books which are most meaningful for me are *The Boy from Over There, Along the Tracks,* and *The Captain Has Returned.* They were written for teenagers, but quite often I am accused by adults of keeping them up at night, while they finished a story they couldn't put down. . . .

"I have written . . . a biography of my father, Katriel Yaffe, who was born in British Palestine in 1909. It is the story of a man who dedicated his life to the sea, who from adolescence wanted to be a sea captain and could not because of poor eyesight, and who fulfilled his dream against all odds as a pioneer in creating the basis for the navy of the future state of Israel. Further, he achieved his goal in a remarkably short lifetime: In May, 1941, as captain of a commando boat, he disappeared with his crew of twenty-three while on a military mission. One of the highlights of the book occurs on September 1, 1939—the date World War II broke out. On that day he landed a ship on the Tel Aviv coast filled with illegal immigrants escaping the Nazi shadow that was spreading over Europe.

"*Along the Tracks* starts on this same day. It relates the odyssey of a young Jewish boy who found himself alone in Kazakhstan, U.S.S.R., during World War II. It is a fictional account of survival, full of incredible—yet real—adventures during which the boy changes from a frightened child of eight to a brave fourteen-year-old youth, resourceful, a great lover of the freedom of the endless horizon. For me it is a personal 'if' story: what might have happened to me if I had been born 'over there,' in Europe.

"*The Boy from Over There,* written first of the three books, starts at the end of World War II. It is also an 'if' story, based on my experience. I have a cousin who survived the holocaust and was then adopted by a Dutch couple in the Netherlands. My uncle eventually found the cousin, but she chose to stay with her adoptive parents. I wondered what would have happened if my cousin had instead gone to the kibbutz where we all lived. Like *Along the Tracks,* it is a novel based on historical fact."

"Although each of the three books stands alone, for me they form a kind of personal trilogy, created contrary to their chronological order."

*BIOGRAPHICAL/CRITICAL SOURCES:*

*PERIODICALS*

*Bulletin of the Center for Children's Books,* April, 1988, p. 150; October, 1991, pp. 30-31.
*Horn Book,* November/December, 1991, pp. 741-42.
*Kirkus Reviews,* April 1, 1988, p. 535; July 15, 1991, p. 928.
*New York Times Book Review,* May 8, 1988, p. 26.
*Publishers Weekly,* March 11, 1988, p. 104.
*Quill and Quire,* February, 1992, p. 36.
*School Library Journal,* June, 1988, p. 101; December, 1991, p. 135.
*Voice of Youth Advocates,* December, 1988, p. 234.

\*          \*          \*

**BIBESCO, Marthe Lucie 1887-1973**
**(Lucile Decaux)**

*PERSONAL:* Born January 28, 1887, in Bucharest, Romania; died November 29, 1973, in Paris, France; daughter of Jean (a diplomat) and Smaranda Mavrocordato Lahovary; married George Bibesco,

1903. *Education:* Educated in France. *Religion:* Catholic.

*CAREER:* Writer. *Military service:* Served as head nurse of hospital in Romania.

*AWARDS, HONORS:* Elected to Royal Belgian Academy; *Les Huits Paradis* was crowned by the French Academy.

*WRITINGS:*

*Les Huit Paradis: Perse, Asie Mineure, Constantinople,* 3rd edition, Hachette, 1911, translation published as *The Eight Paradises: Travel Pictures in Persia, Asia Minor, and Constantinople,* Dutton (New York City), 1923.

*Alexandre asiatique,* [France], 1912, translation by Enid Bagnold published as *Alexander of Asia,* Heinemann (London), 1935.

*Images d'Epinal,* Plon, 1915.

*Isvor: Le Pays des saules,* two volumes, Plon-Nourrit, 1923, translation by Hamish Miles published as *Isvor: The Country of Willows,* Heinemann, 1924.

*Le Perroquet vert* (novel), B. Grasset, 1924, translation by Malcolm Cowley published as *The Green Parrot,* Harcourt (New York City), 1929.

*Catherine—Paris* (novel), B. Grasset, 1927, translation by Cowley published as *Catherine—Paris* (Literary Guild selection), Harcourt, 1928.

*Une Victoire royale: Ferdinand de Roumanie,* [France], 1927, published as *Royal Portraits,* D. Appleton, 1928.

*Noblesse de robe,* B. Grasset, 1928.

*Au bal avec Marcel Proust,* 3rd edition, Gallimard, 1928, revised edition, 1956, translation by Anthony Rhodes published as *Marcel Proust at the Ball,* Citadel, 1956.

*Portraits d'hommes,* B. Grasset, 1929.

*Jour d'Egypte,* Flammarion, 1929, translation by Helen Everitt and Raymond Everitt published as *Egyptian Day,* Harcourt, 1930.

*Quatre Portraits,* [France], 1929, translation published as *Some Royalties and a Prime Minister: Portraits From Life,* D. Appleton, 1930.

*La Duchesse de Guermantes: Laure de Sade, comtesse de Chevigne,* Plon, 1930, translation by Edward Marsh published as *Proust's Oriane: A Diptych,* Falcon Press, 1952.

*Crusade for the Anemone: Letters From the Holy Land* (Catholic Book Club selection), translated by Thomas Kernan, Macmillan (New York City), 1932.

*Le Destin de Lord Thomson of Cardington,* Flammarion, 1932, published as *Lord Thomson of Cardington: A Memoir and Some Letters,* J. Cape (London), 1932.

*Une Fille inconnue de Napoleon,* Flammarion, 1935.

*Le Rire de la naide,* B. Grasset, 1935.

*Egalite* (novel), B. Grasset, 1935, translation by Pierce Butler, Jr. published as *Worlds Apart,* D. Appleton, 1935.

(Under pseudonym Lucile Decaux) *Charlotte et Maximilien: Les Amants chimeriques,* Gallimard, 1937, translation by John Ghika published as *Carlota: The Story of Charlotte and Maximilian of Mexico; A Historical Romance,* Heinemann, 1956.

(Under pseudonym Lucile Decaux) *Katia: Le Demon bleu de tsar Alexandre* (novel), Gallimard, 1938, translation by Priscilla Bibesco published as *Katia,* Doubleday (New York City), 1939.

(Under pseudonym Lucile Decaux) *Loulou: Prince Imperial,* Gallimard, 1938, translation by Roland Gant published as *Prince Imperial,* Grey Walls Press, 1949.

*Feuilles de calendrier,* Plon, 1939.

(Under pseudonym Lucile Decaux) *Pont-l'Abime; ou, La Grande Passion de la duchesse de Baume,* A. Fayard, 1947.

*Le Voyageur voile, Marcel Proust: Letters au duc de Guiche et documents inedits,* La Palatine, 1947, translation by Roland Gant published as *The Veiled Wanderer, Marcel Proust: Letters to the Duc de Guiche and Unpublished Papers,* Falcon Press, 1949.

*Tulips, Hyacinths, Narcissi,* Hyperion Press (New York City), 1948.

(Under pseudonym Lucile Decaux) *Caline: La Folle equipee de la duchesse de Berry,* Gallimard, 1948.

*La Vie d'une amitie: Ma correspondance avec l'abbe Mungnier, 1911-1944,* Plon, 1951.

*The Sphinx of Bagatelle,* translated by Marsh, Grey Walls Press, 1952.

*Theodore: La Cadeau de Dieu,* Editions francaises d'Amsterdam, 1953.

*Churchill; ou, Le Courage,* A. Michel, 1956, translation by Vladimir Kean published as *Sir Winston Churchill: Master of Courage,* J. Day, 1957.

*Elizabeth II,* A. Michel, 1957.

*La Nymphe Europe,* Plon, 1960.

*Le Confesseur et les poetes,* B. Grasset, 1970.

*Homage to Marcel Proust, 1871-1971,* Covent Garden Press, 1971.

*Echanges avec Paul Claudel,* Mercure de France, 1972.

Also author of *Balloons*, 1929.

*SIDELIGHTS:* Marthe Lucie Bibesco's many works of fiction and nonfiction were marked by a sophisticated prose style. A reviewer for the *New Statesman* once noted that Bibesco's writing possessed "smoothness and lightness and luxurious simplicity."

A member of the Romanian nobility, Bibesco often wrote of aristocratic characters. Her novel *Catherine-Paris,* for example, tells of the daughter of a Romanian noble who is educated in Paris, marries a Polish count, and goes to live on his family's vast estate. L. Galantiere in the *New York Herald Tribune Books* found the novel to be "the product of a fine analytical intelligence, an exquisite sensibility and a superior gift for the writing of delicately cadenced prose." F. L. Robbins of *Outlook* described the novel as "the work of an urbane wit, a sharp intelligence, a sensitive spirit, and an accomplished hand." Several critics noted how well Bibesco had done capturing the feeling of Paris. Rose Lee in *Bookman* claimed that "the atmosphere of Paris is distilled like an essence throughout the pages," while Robbins explained that "the book is permeated with the atmosphere of Paris."

In her novel *Green Parrot*, Bibesco tells the story of a Russian aristocratic family forever touched by the childhood death of their only son. The remaining daughter gives all her love to a pet parrot, only to lose him; following this loss, the girl finds herself unable to connect with other people. The reviewer for the *New York Times* labeled *Green Parrot* "a strange and beautiful story, with the faintly acrid charm of a miniature painted on the cover of a seventeenth century snuff box." The reviewer for *Outlook* believed that "Bibesco writes with poetic feeling, wit, delicacy, economy, and rare grace of expression."

In addition to fiction, Bibesco wrote several travel books, including *Egyptian Day* and *Crusade for the Anemone*. A three-month journey through Egypt inspired *Egyptian Day,* in which Bibesco recorded her impressions of the country, its people, and its customs. The many individual impressions, noted Lisle Bell in *Books,* combine to form "a rich mosaic." Konrad Bercovici in the *New York Evening Post* believed that "to have set down 200 pages of evocations of moods and people and places is a distinction very few modern writers attain. Marthe Bibesco stands out even among the brilliant company of these few blessed by the gods." *Crusade for the Anemone* consists of five letters written by Bibesco to her friends, recounting her visit to the Holy Land and the thoughts and emotions the journey inspired. The critic for the *Saturday Review* found the book to "embody the reactions of a quick and vivid soul, a mind well stored and reflective, and an imagination that invests the obvious with rich implications." Although noting that the book is ostensibly a travel memoir, the reviewer for the *Springfield Republican* judged that "it is the writer herself who is most interesting. Possessed of much erudition, deep sympathy and a gentle wit, Princess Bibesco reveals herself as a person whom it would be a privilege to know."

*BIOGRAPHICAL/CRITICAL SOURCES:*

*PERIODICALS*

*Booklist,* July, 1928, p. 24.
*Bookman,* August, 1928, p. 67; August, 1929, p. 69; July, 1930, p. 71; October, 1930, p. 72; May, 1932, p. 75.
*Books,* June 29, 1930, pp. 7, 14; May 15, 1932, p. 2; September 1, 1935, p. 5; May 14, 1939, p. 8.
*Boston Transcript,* November 17, 1923, p. 3; October 6, 1929, p. 1; August 16, 1930, p. 2; July 6, 1932, p. 2; August 28, 1935, p. 2.
*Catholic World,* July, 1932, p. 135.
*Christian Century,* September 24, 1930, p. 47.
*Cleveland Open Shelf,* March, 1929, p. 41.
*Commonweal,* July 13, 1932, p. 16.
*Current History,* July, 1930, p. 32.
*Independent,* June 30, 1928, p. 120.
*Literary Review,* December 27, 1924, p. 13.
*Manchester Guardian,* April 6, 1939, p. 5.
*Nation and Atheneum,* November 29, 1924, p. 36.
*New Republic,* December 24, 1924, p. 41; August 15, 1928, p. 55; August 14, 1929, p. 59.
*New Statesman,* November 22, 1924, p. 24.
*New York Evening Post,* June 23, 1928, p. 8; July 5, 1930, p. 5; May 14, 1932, p. 7.
*New York Herald Tribune Book Review,* May 31, 1959.
*New York Herald Tribune Books,* May 20, 1928, p. 3; January 27, 1929, p. 22; May 26, 1929, p. 5.
*New York Times,* January 13, 1924, p. 11; November 30, 1924, p. 16; May 13, 1928, p. 9; January 20, 1929, p. 10; May 19, 1929, p. 8; August 10, 1930, p. 11; August 31, 1930; July 31, 1932, p. 5; September 1, 1935, p. 6; May 7, 1939, p. 6.
*New York Tribune,* December 21, 1924, p. 5.
*New York World,* November 30, 1924, p. 8E; July 1, 1928, p. 7; June 2, 1929, p. 7.
*North America,* July, 1928, p. 226.
*Outlook,* June 20, 1928, p. 149; May 29, 1929, p. 152; May 21, 1930, p. 155.

*Saturday Review,* December 6, 1924, p. 138; May 26, 1928, p. 4; July 27, 1929, p. 6; May 7, 1932, p. 8; August 31, 1935, p. 12; May 6, 1939, p. 20.
*Spectator,* November 29, 1935, p. 155.
*Springfield Republican,* December 7, 1923, p. 14; August 11, 1929, p. 7E; June 12, 1932, p. 7E.
*Times Literary Supplement,* September 29, 1927, p. 664; November 7, 1929, p. 899; July 28, 1932, p. 539; December 21, 1935, p. 877; January 14, 1939, p. 29.
*Wisconsin Library Bulletin,* July, 1928, p. 24.

*OBITUARIES:*

*PERIODICALS*

*AB Bookman's Weekly* January 14, 1974.
*London Times,* November 30, 1973.*

\*    \*    \*

**BILL, Alfred Hoyt 1879-1964**

*PERSONAL:* Born May 5, 1879, in Rochester, NY; died August 10, 1964, in Princeton, NJ; son of Edward Clark (an Episcopal clergyman and a teacher) and Eliza Huline (Hoyt) Bill; married Florence Dorothy Reid, June 30, 1903; children: Alfred Reid (deceased), Florence Dorothy (Mrs. Gregory P. Tschebotarioff), Edward Clark. *Education:* Yale University, A.B., 1903. *Politics:* Republican. *Religion:* Episcopalian.

*CAREER:* Writer. Seabury Divinity School, Faribault, MN, instructor in English, 1910-1913; Bishop Seabury Mission and Shattuck School, Faribault, treasurer and teacher, 1916-21. *Military service:* National Guard, 1910-16; became captain and was regimental adjutant of 2nd Infantry. American Red Cross, 1918; captain and representative to 91st Division of American Expeditionary Forces.

*MEMBER:* American Historical Association, Society of American Historians, Minnesota Historical Society, Zeta Psi, Yale Club, Players Club (both New York City), Nassau Club (Princeton, NJ).

*WRITINGS:*

*Alas, Poor Yorick!: Being Three Hitherto Unrecorded Adventures in the Life of the Reverend Laurence*

*Sterne,* Little, Brown (Boston), 1927, reprinted, Books for Libraries, 1970.
*The Wolf in the Garden,* Longmans, Green (London), 1931.
*Astrophel; or, The Life and Death of the Renowned Sir Philip Sidney,* Farrar (New York City), 1937, reprinted, Arden Library, 1979.
*The Beleaguered City: Richmond, 1861-1865,* Knopf (New York City), 1946, reprinted, Greenwood Press, 1980.
*Rehearsal for Conflict: The War with Mexico, 1846-1848,* Knopf, 1947, reprinted, Cooper Square, 1970.
*The Campaign of Princeton, 1776-1777,* Princeton University Press (Princeton, NJ), 1948, reprinted, 1976.
*Valley Forge: The Making of an Army,* Harper (New York City), 1952.
(With Walter E. Edge) *A House Called Morven: Its Role in American History, 1701-1954,* Princeton University Press, 1954, new edition, 1978.
(With James Ralph Johnson) *Horsemen, Blue and Gray: A Pictorial History* (illustrated by Hirst D. Milhollen), Oxford University Press (New York City), 1960.
*New Jersey and the Revolutionary War,* Van Nostrand (New York City), 1964.

*CHILDREN'S BOOKS*

*The Clutch of the Corsican: A Tale of the Days of the Downfall of the Great Napoleon,* Atlantic Monthly Press (Boston), 1925.
*Highroads of Peril,* Little, Brown, 1926.
*The Red Prior's Legacy: The Story of the Adventures of an American Boy in the French Revolution* (illustrated by Henry Pitz), Longmans, Green, 1929.
*The Ring of Danger: A Tale of Elizabethan England* (illustrated by Frederick T. Chapman), Knopf, 1948.

*OTHER*

Contributor of articles to periodicals, including *American Heritage.*

*SIDELIGHTS:* Alfred Hoyt Bill wrote historical fiction and nonfiction, usually focusing on major military struggles in American history.

Bill's ability to combine a variety of historical details into a compelling nonfiction narrative was commented on by several critics of *Beleaguered City: Richmond,*

*1861-1865.* G. W. Wakefield in *Library Journal,* for example, noted that Bill displayed a "skillful weaving of innumerable facts into a memorable picture of Condederate life." Similarly, D. M. Potter in *Yale Review* called the book "a panorama . . . excellently executed. Based on careful research and written with considerable aptness of phrase, it recreates the sights, sounds, and smells of Confederate Richmond." Paul Kiniery of *Commonweal* judged the book "an unforgettable picture of war-time devastation, in all its horrible manifestations."

In *Rehearsal for Conflict: The War with Mexico, 1846-1848,* Bill presented a concise one-volume account of the war he argued brought the issue of slavery into national consciousness and thus was a precurser to the American Civil War. Bernard DeVoto in the *New York Herald Tribune Weekly Book Review* called *Rehearsal for Conflict* "sound, compact military history" and "zestful reading." J. H. Jackson of the *San Francisco Chronicle* concluded that "the book is carefully written, exceptionally readable . . . , an admirable example of what a book about a war should be." Holman Hamilton of the *American Historical Review* praised Bill for producing "an intensely readable book, capable of blasting some of the favorite myths, traditions, theories, and folklore embedded in the popular mind."

In his fiction, Bill's attention to historical accuracy was combined with a storytelling ability that brought the events of the past to life. *The Clutch of the Corsican* is set during the Napoleonic wars and concerns an American family captured by the French and forced to undergo a miserable captivity before managing a daring escape. While the reviewer for *Booklist* described the novel as "well told against a pictureful and historical background," the critic for the *Boston Transcript* labeled it "as convincing as an authoritative journal or autobiography." "The thrill and charm [of *The Clutch of the Corsican*]," wrote the critic for *Literary Review,* "lies in the author's ability to keep his action swiftly moving, tense and exciting."

## BIOGRAPHICAL/CRITICAL SOURCES:

### PERIODICALS

*American Historical Review,* April, 1948, p. 53; January, 1953, p. 58.
*Booklist,* July, 1925, p. 21; February 1, 1946, p. 42; November 15, 1947, p. 44; December 15, 1948, p. 45; June 1, 1952, p. 48; September 15, 1960, p. 57.
*Book Week,* January 27, 1946, p. 10.
*Boston Transcript,* April 18, 1925, p. 5.
*Chicago Sunday Tribune,* May 11, 1952, p. 3; October 30, 1960, p. 9.
*Christian Science Monitor,* January 31, 1946, p. 16; May 22, 1952, p. 11; July 22, 1954, p. 11.
*Commonweal,* February 8, 1946, p. 43; December 19, 1947, p. 47.
*Current History,* November, 1947, p. 13; March, 1948, p. 14; February, 1961, p. 40.
*Independent,* April 11, 1925, p. 114.
*International Book Review,* January, 1926, p. 134.
*Kirkus,* November 1, 1945, p. 13; August 15, 1947, p. 15; October 1, 1948, p. 16; March 1, 1952, p. 20; August 15, 1960, p. 28.
*Library Journal,* January 15, 1946, p. 71; September 1, 1947, p. 72; December 15, 1948, p. 73; May 1, 1952, p. 77.
*Literary Review,* April 18, 1925, p. 9.
*Nation,* November 15, 1947, p. 165.
*New Republic,* December 1, 1947, p. 117.
*New Yorker,* January 19, 1946, p. 21; January 17, 1953, p. 28.
*New York Herald Tribune Weekly Book Review,* October 26, 1947, p. 7; November 14, 1948, p. 8; May 25, 1952, p. 6; July 11, 1954, p. 12; April 9, 1961, p. 30.
*New York Times,* June 21, 1925, p. 12; January 20, 1946, p. 4; October 12, 1947, p. 7; November 14, 1948, p. 58; June 15, 1952, p. 3.
*New York Times Book Review,* December 25, 1960, p. 6.
*New York Tribune,* May 3, 1925, p. 6.
*Outlook,* April 22, 1925, p. 139.
*Political Science Quarterly,* September, 1948, p. 63.
*San Francisco Chronicle,* September 29, 1947, p. 14.
*Saturday Review of Literature,* February 9, 1946, p. 29; January 31, 1948, p. 31; June 5, 1948, p. 31; November 13, 1948, p. 31; May 24, 1952, p. 35.
*Social Education,* January, 1949, p. 13; February, 1953, p. 17.
*Springfield Republican,* August 23, 1925, p. 7A.
*Time,* February 18, 1946, p. 47.
*U.S. Quarterly Book Review,* September, 1952, p. 8.
*Weekly Book Review,* January 20, 1946, p. 1.
*Wisconsin Library Bulletin,* May, 1925, p. 21.
*Yale Review,* summer, 1946, p. 35.

## OBITUARIES:

### PERIODICALS

*New York Times,* August 12, 1964.*

## BLACK, Irma Simonton 1906-1972

*PERSONAL:* Born June 6, 1906, in Paterson, NJ; died June 18(?), 1972, of stab wounds, in New York, NY; daughter of John Vandervoort and Lida (Duke) Simonton; married James Hammond Black, 1934; children: Constance K. *Education:* Barnard College, A.B., 1927; Bank Street College of Education, graduate study, 1930-31; attended New York University, 1934-40. *Religion:* Protestant. *Avocational interests:* Travel, music, theater, books, swimming.

*CAREER:* Bank Street College of Education, New York, NY, nursery school teacher, 1931-36, testing and research, 1936-43, teacher of children's literature, 1945-72, chair of publications and communications, 1951-72.

*MEMBER:* National Association for Nursery Education, Phi Beta Kappa.

*AWARDS, HONORS:* Honorable mention, *Parents'* Magazine, for book for parents. The Irma S. and James H. Black Award for excellence in children's literature was established in 1973 by the Bank Street College of Education.

*WRITINGS:*

*JUVENILES*

*Hamlet: A Cocker Spaniel,* Holiday House (New York City), 1938.

*Kip, a Young Rooster* (illustrated by Kurt Wiese), Holiday House, 1939.

*Flipper, a Sea-Lion* (illustrated by Glen Rounds), Holiday House, 1940.

(Author of adaptation) *This Is the Bread That Betsy Ate,* W. R. Scott, 1945.

*Barbara's Birthday,* W. R. Scott, 1946.

*The Dog Doctor,* W. R. Scott, 1947.

*Toby, a Curious Cat* (illustrated by Zhenya Gay), Holiday House, 1948.

*Spoodles, the Puppy Who Learned* (illustrated by Johnny Whistle), W. R. Scott, 1948.

*Maggie, a Mischievous Magpie* (illustrated by Barbara Latham), Holiday House, 1949.

*Dusty and His Friends* (illustrated by Latham), Holiday House, 1950.

*Pudge, a Summertime Mixup,* Holiday House, 1953.

*Pete the Parakeet,* Holiday House, 1954.

*Night Cat* (illustrated by Paul Galdone), Holiday House, 1957.

*Busy Water* (illustrated by Jane Castle), Holiday House, 1958.

*The Troublemaker,* Knopf (New York City), 1959.

*Big Puppy and Little Puppy,* Holiday House, 1960.

*Castle, Abbey and Town: How People Lived in the Middle Ages* (illustrated by W. T. Mars), Holiday House, 1963.

*The Little Old Man Who Could Not Read* (illustrated by Seymour Fleishman), Albert Whitman (Chicago, IL), 1968.

*Busy Winds* (illustrated by Robert Quackenbush), Holiday House, 1968.

*Busy Seeds* (illustrated by Quackenbush), Holiday House, 1970.

*Little Old Man Who Cooked and Cleaned* (illustrated by Fleishman), Albert Whitman, 1970.

*Doctor Proctor and Mrs. Meriwether* (illustrated by Leonard Weisgard), Albert Whitman, 1971.

*Is This My Dinner?* (illustrated by Rosalind Fry), Albert Whitman, 1972.

(Editor with others) *Monsters and Wild Creatures: Prepared by the Bank Street College of Education,* Houghton (Boston, MA), 1979.

(With Lucy Sprague Mitchell and Jessie Stanton) *The Taxi That Hurried* (illustrated by Tibor Gergely), Western Publishing Co. (Racine, WI), 1992.

*ADULT BOOKS*

*Off to a Good Start: A Handbook for Modern Parents,* Harcourt (New York City), 1946, revised edition, 1953.

*Life and Ways of Seven- to Eight-Year-Olds,* Harcourt, 1952.

(Editor with Lucy Sprague Mitchell) *Believe and Make Believe,* Dutton (New York City), 1956.

*OTHER*

Columnist, *PM,* 1944-49, *Redbook,* 1950-59, and *Saturday Review,* 1959-61. Contributor of articles or reviews to *Ladies' Home Journal, Art in America, New York Times,* and other periodicals. Senior editor and contributor, "The Bank Street Readers," basic reading series for grades 1-3, Macmillan, 1966-72; senior editor and co-author, "Early Childhood Discovery" materials, Macmillan, 1968-72.

*SIDELIGHTS:* The late Irma Simonton Black was a successful children's writer and authority on early childhood development. Black combined teaching and writing duties throughout her career, and—from her classrooms at the Bank Street College of Education— tested her story ideas on student teachers as well as young readers. Black loved to write about animals. Her list of publications abounds with tales about dogs, cats, birds, and other creatures both wild and tame. She also was noted for her books on science for the youngest readers, books in which she introduced concepts such as the water cycle and the growth of plants from seeds.

Black's animal stories for beginning readers include *Spoodles, the Puppy Who Learned, Kip, a Young Rooster,* and *Night Cat.* These and other tales rely upon the true behavior of animals for story line, and they accent the responsibility inherent in owning a pet. In *Spoodles,* for instance, the mischievous pet is left at home unattended—and of course he gets into trouble. *New York Times* contributor S. C. Gross found *Spoodles* to be "an engaging story. . . . The funny name of this pup, Johnny Whistle's comical line drawings of Spoodles, guilty or triumphant; the humor and brevity of text per page all appeal to readers." In *Kip,* a young rooster yearns to crow like the barnyard ruler and works on his voice with determination. "This is a most successfully told story for the pre-school child as well as for the child who is beginning to read for himself," noted a *Wilson Library Bulletin* reviewer.

Nonfiction titles by Black include *Busy Water, Busy Winds,* and *Busy Seeds*—all easy-to-read science titles, and *Castle, Abbey, and Town: How People Lived in the Middle Ages.* A *Booklist* reviewer cited *Busy Water* for its "rhythmic text and pleasing pictures," adding: "A simple, general explanation . . . will satisfy the interest of young children." In the *New York Herald Tribune Book Review,* M. S. Libby wrote of *Busy Water:* "The very feel of an April day is in this fresh and charming . . . account of the water cycle. . . . Good simple science, attractively presented." *Castle, Abbey, and Town* shows how medieval life was lived through portraits of three different individuals. *New York Times Book Review* correspondent N. K. Burber deemed the book "one of the most attractive recent volumes dealing with this important, fascinating period."

Black's how-to books on parenting revealed her "refreshing premise that it is perfectly possible for a wonderful child to be the product of a quite ordinary American home," to quote Margaret Bevans in the *Weekly Book Review.* Black emphasized the need for children to engage in creative play and to broaden their social horizons as they grew; her books, such as *Off to a Good Start,* dealt with education at home and in school as well as effective, loving discipline. A

*Book Week* reviewer claimed: "Written with sincerity and a purposeful desire to help, [*Off to a Good Start*] makes accessible, especially to exhausted parents, easy-to-read suggestions." In *Library Journal,* A. I. Bryan concluded that *Off to a Good Start* provided "a worth-while contribution to the literature in this field."

*BIOGRAPHICAL/CRITICAL SOURCES:*

*PERIODICALS*

*Book Week,* November 10, 1946, p. 25; December 1, 1946, p. 47.
*Chicago Sun,* March 27, 1948.
*Chicago Sunday Tribune,* November 10, 1957, p. 12.
*Christian Science Monitor,* October 3, 1957, p. 11; October 3, 1963, p. 11.
*Kirkus Reviews,* August 15, 1946, p. 404; September 15, 1946, p. 455; July 15, 1957, p. 476.
*Library Journal,* February 15, 1940, p. 171; September 1, 1946, p. 1125; November 1, 1946, p. 1544; May 15, 1958, p. 1593; May 15, 1963, p. 2141.
*New Republic,* September 9, 1946, p. 301.
*New York Herald Tribune Book Review,* May 11, 1958, p. 25.
*New York Herald Tribune Books,* July 21, 1963, p. 9.
*New York Herald Tribune Weekly Book Review,* March 21, 1948, p. 6.
*New York Times,* November 10, 1946, p. 58; June 13, 1948, p. 21.
*New York Times Book Review,* May 12, 1963, p. 20.
*Saturday Review of Literature,* January 18, 1947, p. 30; April 27, 1963, p. 44.
*Weekly Book Review,* October 13, 1946, p. 21.
*Wilson Library Bulletin,* February 1940, p. 31.

*OBITUARIES:*

*PERIODICALS*

*New York Times,* June 19, 1972.*

\*　　\*　　\*

**BLAIR, Clay Drewry, Jr. 1925-**

*PERSONAL:* Born May 1, 1925, in Lexington, VA; married wife, Joan. *Education:* Attended Tulane University and Columbia University.

*ADDRESSES: Agent*—Scott Meredith Literary Agency, 845 Third Ave., New York, NY 10022.

*CAREER: Time* magazine, New York City, reporter, 1948-55; *Life* magazine, New York City, military correspondent, 1955-57; *Saturday Evening Post,* Indianapolis, IN, associate editor, 1957-61, assistant managing editor, 1961-62, managing editor, 1962-63, editor-in-chief, 1963-64; Curtis Publishing Co., senior vice-president, executive vice-president and director, editor-in-chief, 1962-64. Writer. *Military service:* Served in U.S. Navy during World War II; became quartermaster second class; received three battle stars.

*WRITINGS:*

*The Atomic Submarine and Admiral Rickover,* Henry Holt, 1954.
(With James R. Shepley) *The Hydrogen Bomb: The Men, the Menace, the Mechanism,* McKay (New York), 1954.
*Beyond Courage,* McKay, 1955.
(With William R. Anderson) *Nautilus 90, North,* World Publishing, 1959.
*Diving for Pleasure and Treasure,* World Publishing, 1960.
(With Albert Scott Crossfield) *Always Another Dawn: The Story of a Rocket Test Pilot,* World Publishing, 1960.
*The Board Room* (novel), Dutton (New York), 1969, published as *Magazine,* Cassell, 1970.
*The Strange Case of James Earl Ray, the Man Who Murdered Martin Luther King,* Bantam (New York), 1969.
*The Archbishop* (novel), World Publishing, 1970.
*Pentagon Country* (novel), McGraw (New York), 1971.
*Survive!,* Berkeley Publishing (New York), 1973.
*Silent Victory: The U.S. Submarine War against Japan,* Lippincott (Philadelphia), 1975.
(With wife, Joan Blair) *The Search for JFK,* Putnam (New York), 1976.
(With J. Blair) *Scuba!,* Bantam, 1977.
(With Omar N. Bradley) *A General's Life: An Autobiography,* Simon & Schuster (New York), 1983.
*Ridgway's Paratroopers: The American Airborne in World War II,* Dial Press (Garden City, NY), 1985.
*The Forgotten War: America in Korea, 1950-1953,* Times Books (New York), 1987.
*Hitler's U-Boat War: The Hunters, 1939-1942,* Random House (New York), 1996.

Also author of *Valley of the Shadow,* 1955.

*SIDELIGHTS:* Clay Blair has written numerous books about military subjects. He spearheaded a journalistic drive to keep Rear-Admiral Hyman G. Rickover—the staunchest supporter of the use of atomic energy in submarines—in the Navy after Rickover's career was threatened. Blair was rewarded for his successful crusade by being one of the first journalists allowed to go on a voyage of the *Nautilus,* the first atomic-powered submarine. His first book about the sub, *The Atomic Submarine and Admiral Rickover,* was described by R. E. Lapp, a writer for the *New York Times Book Review,* as "exciting reading for even the non-technically inclined. . . . A sound treatment meriting wide acceptance." H. W. Baehr, a contributor to the *New York Herald Tribune Book Review,* also praised the book as "a fascinating drama. It is well told and amply documented." Blair continued the story of the *Nautilus* in his book *Nautilus 90, North,* an account of the *Nautilus's* incredible, 1,830-mile journey beneath the polar ice cap. The book, which was published just five months after the completion of the voyage, was a bestseller and was published in twenty-six countries.

Blair has not confined himself to military subjects. In *Survive!,* he related the story of a harrowing plane crash in the Andes mountains. A *New York Times Book Review* critic wrote: "[It] cannot be called either intimate or definitive. Clearly this is an outsider's book. Blair writes as though he were himself in rarefied mountain air: short, breathless sentences, uninformed by any distinctive insight. Efficient enough, workmanlike: the excitement comes through. Blair corrects several widespread misunderstandings promulgated by early reportage. The Chilean plane crash was, in fact, an Argentinean plane crash. Much of the grisly details have been mitigated."

Blair and his wife Joan did extensive research for their joint effort *The Search for JFK.* Speaking of that book, a *New York Review of Books* critic stated: "Whatever the accuracy of the authors' interpretations of the evidence, they give a rich sense of the mixture of shyness, sensitivity, and callousness that characterized Kennedy; his deliberate use of what he called his 'BP'—Big Personality; and the disabilities of having a spectacularly amoral father. A book surprisingly free of malice or prurience."

Blair has also tried his hand at fiction. In his first novel, *The Board Room,* he drew on his own experience as editor-in-chief of the *Saturday Evening Post* to create the story of Lee Crawford, an editor-in-chief who accepts the challenge of breathing new life into a failing periodical. "The action is fast and the dialogue swift," approved J. Riccardi in *Library Journal,* yet that reviewer also believed that the book would appeal mainly to publishing insiders. Martin Levin, a contributor to *New York Times Book Review,* found *The Board Room* to be "a fascinating drama of publishing monkey business," and *Saturday Review* writer S. W. Little noted that "Blair is effective in dramatizing the editorial process."

In *The Archbishop,* another novel, Blair dramatized modern tensions in the Roman Catholic church. He wrote of a love affair between a priest and a nun, and of the liberated actions of a mother of nine after she begins taking birth control pills. John Deedy lambasted the book in *Critic,* stating that it "isn't an important book. It isn't even good fiction. . . . The character is pure caricature." He allowed that the basic ideas had the makings of "a first-rate novel," but charged that "Blair kicks it all away with his simple black-and-white imagery." *Library Journal* reviewer E. T. Smith did not agree with that view, praising *The Archbishop* as "a well-written, dramatic novel about today's Catholics and what happens when they confront their leaders who have forgotten Christ's teachings."

*BIOGRAPHICAL/CRITICAL SOURCES:*

*PERIODICALS*

*America,* November 15, 1975.
*Atlantic Monthly,* July, 1969.
*Best Sellers,* May 15, 1969; November 1, 1970.
*Booklist,* February 15, 1954; July 1, 1955; September 15, 1960.
*Bookmark,* February, 1954; June, 1955; October, 1960.
*Catholic World,* July, 1971.
*Chicago Sunday Tribune,* January 24, 1954, p. 3; August 21, 1955, p. 2.
*Choice,* July/August, 1975.
*Christian Century,* October 21, 1970.
*Christian Science Monitor,* January 9, 1954, p. 9.
*Critic,* January, 1971.
*Foreign Affairs,* July, 1954.
*Horn Book,* October, 1955.
*Kirkus Reviews,* November 15, 1953; April 1, 1955; June 15, 1960.
*Library Journal,* January 15, 1954; May 1, 1955; July, 1960; June 15, 1969; November 1, 1970.
*Nation,* February 6, 1954.

*New Republic,* January 25, 1954.
*Newsweek,* March 31, 1969.
*New York Herald Tribune Book Review,* February 7, 1954, p. 3; September 11, 1955, p. 7.
*New York Review of Books,* June 10, 1976.
*New York Times,* January 17, 1954, p. 3; June 26, 1955, p. 13.
*New York Times Book Review,* January 17, 1954; October 3, 1954; June 26, 1955; January 4, 1959; September 4, 1960; January 8, 1961; May 4, 1969; December 19, 1971; August 19, 1973; June 6, 1976.
*San Francisco Chronicle,* January 17, 1954, p. 24; December 11, 1960, p. 42.
*Saturday Review,* October 1, 1955; June 14, 1969.
*Springfield Republican,* February 14, 1954, p. 5C; May 22, 1955, p. 10C; September 11, 1960, p. 4D.
*Wilson Library Bulletin,* July, 1954.


\*      \*      \*


## BLASSINGAME, Wyatt Rainey 1909-1985
### (W. B. Rainey)

*PERSONAL:* Born February 6, 1909, in Demopolis, AL; died January 8, 1985, in Bradenton, FL; son of Wyatt Childs (a teacher) and Maud (Lurton) Blassingame; married Gertrude Olsen, 1936 (died, 1976); married Lenora Jeanne Toman; children: (first marriage) Peggy Diamant, April Lane. *Education:* Attended Howard College, 1926-28; University of Alabama, A.B., 1930, graduate study, 1931-33; New York University, graduate study, 1951-52. *Politics:* Independent. *Religion:* Protestant.

*CAREER:* Writer. *Montgomery Advertiser,* Montgomery, AL, reporter, 1930-31; University of Alabama, University, teaching fellow, 1931-33; Florida Southern College, Lakeland, FL, instructor, 1948-51. *Military service:* U.S. Navy, 1942-45; received Bronze Star and Presidential Unit Citation.

*AWARDS, HONORS:* Benjamin Franklin Magazine Award for best short story of 1956, for "Man's Courage," in *Harper's;* Outstanding Science Books for Children awards, National Science Teachers Association, for *Wonders of Alligators and Crocodiles, Science Catches the Criminal, Wonders of Raccoons,* and *Thor Heyerdahl.*

*WRITINGS:*

*NOVELS*

*For Better, for Worse,* Crowell (New York City), 1951.

*Live from the Devil,* Doubleday (New York City), 1959.

*The Golden Geyser,* Doubleday, 1961.

*Halo of Spears,* Doubleday, 1962.

*JUVENILE NONFICTION*

*Great Trains of the World,* Random House (New York City), 1953.

*The French Foreign Legion* (Junior Book-of-the-Month selection), Random House, 1955.

*His Kingdom for a Horse* (Junior Literary Guild selection), F. Watts (New York City), 1957.

*They Rode the Frontier,* F. Watts, 1959.

(With Richard Glendinning) *Frontier Doctors,* F. Watts, 1963.

*First Book of Florida,* F. Watts, 1963.

*The U.S. Frogmen of World War II* (Junior Book-of-the-Month selection), Random House, 1964, reprinted as *Underwater Warriors,* 1982.

*Naturalist-Explorers,* F. Watts, 1964.

*Stephen Decatur: Fighting Sailor,* Garrard (Champaign, IL), 1964.

*First Book of the Seashore,* F. Watts, 1964.

*First Book of American Expansion,* F. Watts, 1965.

*Ponce de Leon: A World Explorer,* Garrard, 1965.

*Sacagawea: Indian Guide,* Garrard, 1965.

(With Glendinning) *Men Who Opened the West,* Putnam (New York City), 1966.

*Franklin D. Roosevelt: Four Times President,* Garrard, 1966.

*Baden-Powell: Chief Scout of the World,* Garrard, 1966.

*Osceola: Seminole War Chief,* Garrard, 1967.

*Navy's Fliers in World War II,* Westminster (Philadelphia), 1967.

*Combat Nurses of World War II,* Random House, 1967.

*Bent's Fort: Crossroads of the Great West,* Garrard, 1967.

*Eleanor Roosevelt,* Putnam, 1967.

*The Look-It-Up Book of Presidents,* Random House, 1968.

*Story of the Boy Scouts,* Garrard, 1968.

*Story of the United States Flag,* Garrard, 1969.

*Medical Corps Heroes of World War II,* Random House, 1969.

*Jake Gaither: Winning Coach,* Garrard, 1969.

*William Tecumseh Sherman: Defender of the Union,* Prentice-Hall (Englewood Cliffs, NJ), 1970.

*Halsey: Five-Star Admiral,* Garrard, 1970.

*Joseph Stalin and Communist Russia,* Garrard, 1971.

*Ernest Thompson Seton, Scout and Naturalist,* Garrard, 1971.

*Diving for Treasure,* Macrae, 1971.

*Dan Beard: Scoutmaster of America,* Garrard, 1972.

*Wonders of Alligators and Crocodiles,* Dodd (New York City), 1973.

*Jim Beckwourth: Black Trapper and Indian Chief,* Garrard, 1973.

*The Everglades: From Yesterday to Tomorrow,* Putnam, 1974.

*Wonders of Frogs and Toads,* Dodd, 1975.

*Science Catches the Criminal,* Dodd, 1975.

*The Little Killers: Fleas, Lice, and Mosquitos,* Putnam, 1975.

*William Beebe: Underwater Explorer,* Garrard, 1976.

*Wonders of the Turtle World,* Dodd, 1976.

*Wonders of Raccoons,* Dodd, 1977.

*Wonders of Crows,* Dodd, 1979.

*Thor Heyerdahl: Viking Scientist,* Elsevier-Nelson (New York City), 1979.

*The Incas and the Spanish Conquest,* Messner (New York City), 1980.

*Skunks,* Dodd, 1981.

*Wonders of Egrets, Bitterns, and Herons,* Dodd, 1982.

*Porcupines,* Dodd, 1982.

*The Strange Armadillo,* Dodd, 1983.

*Wonders of Sharks,* Dodd, 1984.

*JUVENILE FICTION*

*John Henry and Paul Bunyan Play Baseball,* Garrard, 1971.

*How Davy Crockett Got a Bearskin Coat,* Garrard, 1972.

*Pecos Bill Rides a Tornado,* Garrard, 1973.

*Paul Bunyan Fights the Monster Plants,* Garrard, 1974.

*Bowleg Bill: Seagoing Cowboy,* Garrard, 1976.

*Pecos Bill Catches a Hidebehind,* Garrard, 1977.

*Pecos Bill and the Wonderful Clothesline Snake,* Garrard, 1978.

*OTHER*

(With Evans Cottman) *Out-Island Doctor* (nonfiction), Dutton (New York City), 1963.

Contributor, sometimes under pseudonym W. B. Rainey, of about six hundred stories and articles to national magazines; some stories reprinted in anthologies and textbooks in the United States and abroad.

*SIDELIGHTS:* Wyatt Rainey Blassingame wrote in several genres, including fiction and nonfiction for juvenile readers and adults. Many of his books were concerned with Florida, the state he called home for much of his life. An early adult novel, *Live from the Devil,* depicted the frontier days in Florida. Its central character was a lusty cattle baron, Matt Prescott. Reviewing *Live from the Devil* in the *Chicago Sunday Tribune,* H. T. Kane termed it a "lush narrative of men, cattle, and women." Kane noted that some readers might object to the author's "frank and vivid emphasis on sex," and warned that the book "may not be for the genteel," yet he also praised it as "a full blooded, sometimes gripping yarn." Henry Cavendish, a reviewer for the *New York Times,* admitted that some of the subject matter in the book was "crude," yet he found it to be "so simply handled as to cause little offense," and concluded that "the book will rouse the interest of those who like their literary fare rich and raw."

Blassingame was most productive in the field of children's nonfiction. His titles in that genre ranged from *Wonders of Raccoons* to *Ponce de Leon* to *Combat Nurses of World War II.* Reviewing *The French Foreign Legion,* a *Chicago Sunday Tribune* writer decided it was more gripping than any fiction, and L. S. Bechtel stated in the *New York Herald Tribune Book Review* that the author had done "a remarkable job" of explaining the origins, the goals, and the methods of the Legion.

Blassingame once commented to *CA:* "The one good thing about writing for a living is you can live wherever you wish." He noted that he had spent many years living on "Anna Maria, an island joined to the Florida mainland by a bridge. It is a fine place for fishing, swimming, and walking on the beach."

*BIOGRAPHICAL/CRITICAL SOURCES:*

PERIODICALS

*Booklist,* November 15, 1955; November 15, 1959.
*Chicago Sunday Tribune,* November 13, 1955, p. 38; June 21, 1959, p. 3; November 1, 1959, section 2, p. 36.
*Christian Science Monitor,* November 10, 1955, p. B6.
*Commonweal,* November 13, 1959; November 5, 1965; May 27, 1966; May 26, 1967.

*Kirkus Reviews,* July 15, 1955; March 1, 1959.
*Library Journal,* November 15, 1955; May 15, 1959; December 15, 1959; November 15, 1965; July, 1966; September 15, 1967.
*New York Herald Tribune Book Review,* October 30, 1955, p. 8.
*New York Times,* May 19, 1959, p. 28.
*New York Times Book Review,* July 9, 1967, p. 34.
*Saturday Review,* November 7, 1959.
*Wilson Library Bulletin,* March, 1960.

*OBITUARIES:*

PERIODICALS

*Sarasota Herald-Tribune,* January 10, 1985.*

\* \* \*

## BLOUGH, Glenn O(rlando) 1907(?)-

*PERSONAL:* Born September 5, 1907(?), in Edmore, MI; son of Levi and Catherine (Thomas) Blough. *Education:* Central Michigan University, student, 1925-26; University of Michigan, A.B., 1929, M.A., 1932; additional study at University of Chicago and Columbia University.

*ADDRESSES: Home*—2820 Ellicott St. N.W., Washington, DC 20008. *Office*—College of Education, University of Maryland, College Park, MD 20740.

*CAREER:* Teacher in secondary schools in Michigan, 1925-27, 1929-31; Eastern Michigan University, Ypsilanti, instructor in education, 1932-36; Colorado State College, Greeley, assistant professor of science education, 1937-38; University of Chicago, Chicago, IL, instructor in science education, 1939-42; U.S. Department of Health, Education, and Welfare, Washington, DC, specialist for elementary science, Office of Education, 1946-54; University of Maryland, College Park, 1956—, currently professor of education. Writer of books for young people and of textbooks. *Military service:* U.S. Navy, 1942-46; became lieutenant commander.

*MEMBER:* National Education Association, National Science Teachers Association (president, 1957-58), National Council for Elementary Science International (president, 1947), Phi Delta Kappa, Phi Sigma.

*AWARDS, HONORS:* LL.D. from Central Michigan University, 1950; Diamond Award, University of Maryland, 1950.

*WRITINGS:*

(With Wilbur L. Beauchamp and Mary Melrose) *Discovering Our World: A Course in Science for the Middle Grades,* Scott, Foresman (Glenview, IL), 1937-39, teachers edition, 1948.

(With Beauchamp and Melrose) *Teaching Manual* (to accompany Books 1-3 of *Discovering Our World*), Scott, Foresman, 1937-39.

*An Aquarium,* Row, 1943.

*Doing Work,* Row, 1943.

*The Insect Parade,* Row, 1943.

*Plants Round the Year,* Row, 1943.

*Water Appears and Disappears,* Row, 1943.

*Animals Round the Year,* Row, 1943.

*Teaching Manual* (to accompany the "Basic Science Education" series), Row, 1943.

*Animals and Their Young,* Row, 1945.

*Animals That Live Together,* Row, 1945.

*The Birds in the Big Woods,* Row, 1945.

(With Ida B. De Pencier) *How the Sun Helps Us,* Row, 1945.

*The Pet Show,* Row, 1945.

*Useful Plants and Animals,* Row, 1945.

*The Monkey with a Notion,* Holt (New York City), 1946.

*Beno, the Riverburg Mayor,* Holt, 1948.

(With Paul E. Blackwood) *Teaching Elementary Science: Suggestions for Classroom Teachers,* U.S. Office of Education, 1948.

(With Blackwood) *Science Teaching in Rural and Small Town Schools,* U.S. Office of Education, 1949.

(With Albert J. Huggett) *Elementary-School Science and How to Teach It,* Dryden Press (Hinsdale, IL), 1951, revised edition (with Huggett and Julius Schwartz), 1958, 4th edition (with Scwartz), Holt, 1969.

(With Huggett) *Methods and Activities in Elementary-School Science,* Dryden Press, 1951.

*The Tree on the Road to Turntown,* McGraw (New York City), 1953.

*Not Only for Ducks: The Story of Rain,* McGraw, 1954.

(With Marjorie H. Campbell) *Making and Using Classroom Science Materials in the Elementary School: Apparatus, Demonstrations, Equipment, Experiments,* Dryden Press, 1954.

(With Paul E. Garber) *Masters of the Air,* Smithsonian Institution (Washington, DC), 1954.

*Wait for the Sunshine: The Story of Seasons and Growing Things,* McGraw, 1954.

*Lookout for the Forest: A Conservation Story,* McGraw, 1955.

(With Campbell) *When You Go to the Zoo,* McGraw, 1955.

*After the Sun Goes Down: The Story of Animals at Night,* McGraw, 1956.

*Who Lives in This House?: A Story of Animal Families,* McGraw, 1957.

*It's Time for Better Elementary School Science* (report), National Science Teachers Association (Washington, DC), 1958.

(Editor) *Young People's Book of Science,* McGraw, 1958.

*Soon after September: The Story of Living Things in Winter,* McGraw, 1959.

*Discovering Dinosaurs,* McGraw, 1960.

*Christmas Trees and How They Grow,* McGraw, 1961.

*Who Lives at the Seashore?: Animal Life Along the Shore,* McGraw, 1961.

*Who Lives in This Meadow?: A Story of Animal Life,* McGraw, 1961.

*You, Your Child, and Science: A Handbook for Parents,* National Education Association (Washington, DC), 1963.

*Bird Watchers and Bird Feeders,* McGraw, 1963.

*Discovering Plants,* McGraw, 1966.

*Discovering Insects,* McGraw, 1967.

*Discovering Cycles,* McGraw, 1973.

Contributor of articles on science to national magazines. Chair of editorial board, *Science and Children* (magazine for elementary science teachers); member of editorial advisory board, *My Weekly Reader* (newspaper for children).

*SIDELIGHTS:* Glenn O. Blough has written many science books for children, as well as books on teaching science to elementary school students. In *Lookout for the Forest: A Conservation Story,* he presented information about fire prevention, firefighting, and conservation within a fictional context. E. T. Dobbins, a *Library Journal* reviewer, deemed the book "excellent," and a *New York Herald Tribune Book Review* contributor assured that it will "delight" younger readers. In *When You Go to the Zoo,* which was published at about the same time as *Lookout for the Forest,* Blough described how and where zoos acquire their animals and how they care for them. *Kirkus Reviews* rated this book "informative" and "succinctly presented," while a *Christian Science Monitor* writer noted with approval the wealth of "information of the sort you have often wondered where to find."

In *After the Sun Goes Down: The Story of Animals at Night,* Blough again combined scientific fact with a readable story that dispels many common myths and fears about the night and animals. "He gives us a sense of the hidden life teeming in the dark," stated a *New York Times* reviewer, and "makes it all sound . . . reasonable and natural." That critic believed that the book might be of value not only to budding naturalists, but also "to children who are timid about the night."

In the *Young People's Book of Science,* Blough presented excerpts from many science writers to cover a wide range of subjects, including weather, atomic energy, oceans, space travel, biology, and electronics. Numerous reviewers praised Blough's skill as editor, and a *Kirkus Reviews* writer called it "a book to convince even the most indifferent young reader of the excitement and drama of science."

For *Who Lives in This Meadow?: A Story of Animal Life,* Blough used a blend of storytelling and fact— much as he had in *After the Sun Goes Down*—to explore a meadow and a pond, and the habits and special adaptations of the animals who make their homes in such areas. "Everybody is in here," confided Millicent Taylor in *Christian Science Monitor,* ". . . rabbits, woodchucks, and moles . . . woodpeckers, grasshoppers, and spittlebugs." She approved of the storyline, told "with an air of breathless adventuring." A *New York Herald Tribune Lively Arts* writer also drew attention to Blough's "friendly simple style." A *Kirkus Reviews* writer summed up the appeal of Blough's books, referring to his "knack for combining pleasant conversation with sound scientific fact" to make "learning a pleasurable experience."

*BIOGRAPHICAL/CRITICAL SOURCES:*

*PERIODICALS*

*Atlantic,* December, 1946.
*Booklist,* November 15, 1946; April 15, 1955; September 15, 1955; September 15, 1956; July 15, 1958; September 1, 1960; July 15, 1961.
*Bookmark,* April, 1955.
*Book Week,* November 10, 1946, p. 8.
*Chicago Sunday Tribune,* November 13, 1955, p. 46; November 11, 1956, p. 11; November 2, 1958, part 2, p. 40; May 14, 1961, section 2, p. 2; December 10, 1961, p. 14.
*Christian Science Monitor,* May 12, 1955, p. 11; November 10, 1955, p. 3B; May 12, 1960, p. 5B; May 11, 1961, p. B6; November 16, 1961, p. B10.
*Kirkus Reviews,* October 1, 1946; August 15, 1955; June 15, 1956; May 1, 1958; September 15, 1961.
*Library Journal,* November 15, 1946; April 15, 1955; November 15, 1955; October 15, 1956; June 15, 1958; June 15, 1960; October 15, 1961.
*New York Herald Tribune Book Review,* May 15, 1955, p. 10; November 18, 1956, part 2, p. 30; May 8, 1960, section 12, p. 24.
*New York Herald Tribune Lively Arts,* May 14, 1961, section 12, p. 19.
*New York Times,* November 10, 1946, p. 48; November 4, 1956, p. 38; August 31, 1958, p. 16.
*New York Times Book Review,* May 14, 1961, part 2, p. 31; December 10, 1961, p. 46.
*San Francisco Chronicle,* May 22, 1955, p. 20; September 28, 1958, p. 24; November 12, 1961, p. 23.
*Saturday Review,* May 14, 1955; September 17, 1960; May 13, 1961.
*Saturday Review of Literature,* November 9, 1946.
*Weekly Book Review,* November 10, 1946, p. 14.
*Wilson Library Bulletin,* July, 1955.

\*    \*    \*

## BLUNT, Wilfrid (Jasper Walter) 1901-1987

*PERSONAL:* Born July 19, 1901, in Ham, Surrey, England; died January 8, 1987; son of Arthur Stanley Vaughan (a clergyman) and Hilda (Master) Blunt. *Education:* Attended Marlborough College, 1915-20, and Worcester College, Oxford, 1920-21; Royal College of Art, London, England, A.R.C.A., 1923. *Avocational interests:* Singing, travel.

*CAREER:* Haileybury College, Hertfordshire, England, art master, 1923-38; Eton College, Windsor, England, drawing master, 1938-59; Watts Gallery, Compton, Guildford, England, curator, 1959-85.

*MEMBER:* Linnean Society (fellow).

*AWARDS, HONORS:* Veitch Gold Medal, from the Royal Horticultural Society, for *The Art of Botanical Illustration.*

*WRITINGS:*

*The Haileybury Buildings,* privately printed, 1936.

*Desert Hawk,* Methuen (New York), 1947.

*The Art of Botanical Illustration,* Collins (London), 1950, Scribner (New York), 1951.

*Tulipomania,* Penguin (Harmondsworth, England), 1950.

*Black Sunrise: The Life and Times of Mulai Ismail, Emperor of Morocco,* Methuen, 1951.

*Sweet Roman Hand: Five Hundred Years of Italic Cursive Script,* J. Barrie, 1952.

*Japanese Colour Prints,* Faber, 1952.

*Georg Dionysius Ehret,* Traylen, 1953.

*Pietro's Pilgrimage,* J. Barrie, 1953.

*Sebastiano,* J. Barrie, 1956.

(With Sacheverell Sitwell and Patrick Synge) *Great Flower Books, 1700-1900,* Collins, 1956.

*A Persian Spring,* Dufour, 1957.

(With James Russell) *Old Garden Roses,* New York Graphic Society, 1957.

*Lady Muriel,* Methuen, 1962.

*Of Flowers and a Village,* Hamish Hamilton, 1963.

*Cockerell,* Hamish Hamilton, 1964, Knopf, 1965.

*Omar: A Fantasy for Animal Lovers,* Chapman & Hall (London), 1966, Doubleday (Garden City, NY), 1968.

*Isfahan: Pearl of Persia,* Stein & Day (New York), 1966.

*John Christie of Glyndebourne,* Theatre Arts (New York), 1968.

*The Dream King: Ludwig II of Bavaria,* Hamish Hamilton (London), 1970.

*The Compleat Naturalist: A Life of Linnaeus,* Viking (New York), 1971.

*The Golden Road to Samarkand,* Viking (New York), 1973.

*On Wings of Song: A Biography of Felix Mendelssohn,* Scribner, 1974.

*England's Michelangelo: A Biography of George Frederic Watts, O. M., R. A.,* Hamish Hamilton, 1975.

*The Ark in the Park: The Zoo in the Nineteenth Century,* Hamish Hamilton, 1976.

*Splendours of Islam,* Viking, 1976.

*In for a Penny: A Prospect of Kew Gardens, Their Flora, Fauna and Falballas,* Hamish Hamilton, 1978.

(Co-author) *The Illustrated Herbal,* Thames & Hudson (New York), 1979.

*Married to a Single Life: An Autobiography, 1901-1938,* Michael Russell (Wilton, England), 1983.

*Slow on the Feather: An Autobiography, 1938-1959,* Michael Russell, 1986.

(With Sacheverell Sitwell) *Great Flower Books, 1700-1900: A Bibliographical Record of Two Centuries of Finely-Illustrated Flower Books,* Atlantic Monthly Press (New York), 1990.

Contributor to *Captain Cook's Florilegium: A Selection of Engravings from the Drawings of Plants Collected by Joseph Banks and Daniel Solander on Captain Cook's First Voyage to the Islands of the Pacific,* Lion & Unicorn (London), 1973. Contributor of articles to journals.

*SIDELIGHTS:* Wilfrid Blunt wrote numerous biographies and books on botany. In one of his earliest works, *The Art of Botanical Illustration,* he presented a history of flower painting, beginning with the earliest known works in the genre (Egyptian bas-reliefs from the fifteenth century) and continuing through the twentieth century. A. S. Plaut called the book "a delight" in his *Library Journal* review. A *Manchester Guardian* contributor gave high marks to the author's style, declaring: "Mr. Blunt writes charmingly about a subject which requires great erudition and considerable taste." Geoffrey Taylor stated in *New Statesman & Nation:* "He has written a fascinating and a learned history."

In *Isfahan, Pearl of Persia,* Blunt turned his attention to the architecture of the former capital city of Persia. The book serves as an architectural commentary, a history, and a travel guide all in one, according to some critics. A *Times Literary Supplement* contributor asserted: "In his witty, graceful account of this unique city [Blunt] has done an inestimable service to all who will visit it in the future." Another book related to travel and history, *The Golden Road to Samarkand,* was similarly praised by many critics. *Best Sellers* contributor J. S. Phillipson called it a "beautiful book, engagingly written. . . . With a lucid and witty prose Mr. Blunt holds us charmed." A *Times Literary Supplement* writer declared that "as a guide to the region and as raconteur and historian combined, Mr. Blunt is always lively and informative."

In *The Compleat Naturalist: A Life of Linnaeus,* Blunt combined his skill for biography with his interest in botany. This book, about the famed Swedish botanist, examined both his personal life and his scientific achievements. E. C. Hall in *Library Journal* highly recommended the book, praising its "clear prose" and "wealth of fascinating detail." A *Times Literary Supplement* contributor also approved of *The*

*Compleat Naturalist* as a "very readable yet scholarly biography."

*BIOGRAPHICAL/CRITICAL SOURCES:*

*BOOKS*

Blunt, Wilfrid, *Married to a Single Life: An Autobiography, 1901-1938,* Michael Russell, 1983.
Blunt, Wilfrid, *Slow on the Feather: An Autobiography, 1938-1959,* Michael Russell, 1986.

*PERIODICALS*

*Best Sellers,* December 1, 1966; June 15, 1973; November 1, 1974.
*Booklist,* September 1, 1951; December, 1973.
*Choice,* December, 1967; April, 1971; October, 1974.
*Christian Science Monitor,* September 11, 1974, p. 11.
*Library Journal,* June 1, 1951; January 1, 1967; December 15, 1970; July 23, 1973; July, 1974.
*Manchester Guardian,* July 18, 1950, p. 4.
*Nation,* December 21, 1970.
*National Review,* December 29, 1970.
*New Statesman & Nation,* July 15, 1950.
*New Yorker,* July 23, 1973; August 19, 1974.
*New York Times,* October 13, 1968.
*Spectator,* June 30, 1950.
*Time,* December 20, 1971.
*Times Literary Supplement,* July 14, 1950, p. 435; August 17, 1967, p. 746; November 20, 1970, p. 1357; July 13, 1973, p. 810; June 21, 1974, p. 674; February 3, 1984; November 14, 1986.

*OBITUARIES:*

*PERIODICALS*

*Times* (London), January 12, 1987.*

\*          \*          \*

**BLYTHE, (William) LeGette 1900-**

*PERSONAL:* Born April 24, 1900, in Huntersville, NC; son of William Brevard and Hattye (Jackson) Blythe; married Esther Farmer, May 31, 1926; children: William Brevard, Samuel LeGette, Esther Lovelace Blythe Pugh. *Education:* University of North Carolina, B.A., 1921. *Politics:* Democrat. *Religion:* Presbyterian. *Avocational interests:* Sports, gardening.

*ADDRESSES: Home*—College St., Huntersville, NC 28078.

*CAREER:* Public school teacher in Greensboro, NC, 1921-22; *Charlotte News,* Charlotte, NC, reporter, 1922-25; *New York Evening Post* and other newspapers, New York, NY, reporter, 1925; *Mecklenburg Times,* Charlotte, editor, 1926-27; *Charlotte Observer,* Charlotte, reporter, columnist, editorial writer, feature writer, and literary editor, 1927-50; full-time writer, 1950—; University of North Carolina at Charlotte, writer-in-residence, 1967—. Member of Mayflower Award Jury, 1938, 1947, and 1952; member of governor's commission on library resources, 1964; chair of North Carolina Writers Conference, 1965. Chair of President Andrew Johnson Sesquicentennial Commission, 1958; member of Mecklenburg County Economic Development Commission, 1966—, and Huntersville Planning and Zoning Commission, 1967—; member of Charlotte Bicentennial Committee, 1968, and Charlotte-Mecklenburg Bicentennial Committee, 1975-76. Commissioner of general assembly, Presbyterian Church of the United States, 1952; Mecklenburg Presbytery, moderator, 1955-56, member of centennial commission, 1968; Presbyterian Synod of North Carolina, member of sesquicentennial observance committee, 1963, member of permanent commission on historical matters, 1967—. Member of board of directors, North Carolina Boys Home, 1971—.

*MEMBER:* North Carolina State Literary and Historical Association, North Carolina Society for the Preservation of Antiquities, North Carolina Folklore Society, Mecklenburg Historical Association (director), Phi Beta Kappa, Omega Delta, Sigma Upsilon, Delta Tau Delta, Huntersville Lions Club.

*AWARDS, HONORS:* Litt.D., Davidson College, 1950; Mayflower Society Awards, 1953 and 1961, for the best books by a North Carolinian; Huntersville Man of the Year Award, 1955; Cannon Cup for historical research, 1961; LL.D., University of North Carolina, 1969.

*WRITINGS:*

*The Chatham Rabbit* (play), first produced in Chapel Hill, NC, April 29, 1921.
*Marshall Ney: A Dual Life,* Stackpole (Harrisburg, PA), 1937.

*Alexandriana,* Stackpole, 1940.

*Bold Galilean,* University of North Carolina Press (Chapel Hill, NC), 1948, reprinted, Moody (Chicago, IL), 1993.

*William Henry Belk: Merchant of the South,* University of North Carolina Press, 1950.

*A Tear for Judas,* Bobbs-Merrill (New York City), 1951.

(With Mary Martin Sloop) *Miracle in the Hills,* McGraw (New York City), 1953.

*James W. Davis: North Carolina Surgeon,* Heritage House, 1956.

*The Crown Tree,* John Knox, 1957.

(With Mary Wilson Gee) *Yes, Ma'am, Miss Gee,* Heritage House, 1957.

(With Lucy Morgan) *Gift from the Hills,* Bobbs-Merrill, 1958.

*Call Down the Storm,* Holt (New York City), 1958.

(With Mabel Wolfe Wheaton) *Thomas Wolfe and His Family,* Doubleday (Garden City, NY), 1961.

*Hear Me, Pilate!,* Holt, 1961.

(With Charles Brockmann) *Hornets' Nest: The Story of Charlotte and Mecklenburg County,* McNally & Loftin (Charlotte, NC), 1961.

(With Septima Poinsette Clark) *Echo in My Soul,* Dutton (New York City), 1962.

*Mountain Doctor,* Morrow (New York City), 1964.

*Man on Fire,* Funk (New York City), 1964.

*Robert Lee Stowe: Pioneer in Textiles,* McNally & Loftin, 1965.

*38th Evac,* McNally & Loftin, 1966.

(With others) *Charlotte and Mecklenburg County, North Carolina Today,* Crabtree Press (Charlotte, NC), 1967.

*Brothers of Vengeance,* Morrow, 1969.

*Meet Julius Abernethy: Trader and Philanthropist,* Loftin (Charlotte, NC), 1970.

*When Was Jesus Born?,* Loftin, 1974.

*The Stableboy Who Stayed at Bethlehem: A Fantasy of the First Christmas* (illustrated by Barbara Allen Zepeda), Loftin, 1974.

*Looking to the One Beckoning Star,* Thomas Williams, 1979.

*SYMPHONIC DRAMAS*

*Shout Freedom!,* first produced in Charlotte, NC, May, 1948.

*Voice in the Wilderness* (first produced in Charlotte, 1955), Loftin, 1955.

*The Hornet's Nest* (first produced in Charlotte, June, 1968), McNally & Loftin, 1968.

*First in Freedom,* first produced in Charlotte, 1975.

*Thunder over Carolina,* first produced in Charlotte, 1976.

Contributor of articles, reviews, and short stories to magazines and newspapers.

*WORK IN PROGRESS:* Biblical novels; a series of children's books on biblical characters.

*SIDELIGHTS:* LeGette Blythe, a native of North Carolina, has published books about his home state as well as a number of novels based upon Biblical stories and situations. A longtime writer-in-residence at the University of North Carolina in Charlotte, Blythe has been writing fiction, history, and musical drama for more than fifty years. A reviewer in *Best Sellers* once noted of the author: "Mr. Blythe . . . is long overdue for national fame as a storyteller who can spin a fascinating tale." Indeed, national fame rarely eluded Blythe, as his Biblical novels in particular found a wide and loyal readership.

A very ambitious project marked Blythe's writing debut. In *Marshal Ney: A Dual Life,* he sought to prove that French nobleman Michel Ney eluded execution in 1815 and spent many years living in the Carolinas as Peter Stuart Ney. *Marshal Ney: A Dual Life* was given serious reviews, with most critics finding fault with Blythe's proposals. In *Books,* for instance, W. L. Langer wrote: "It is hard to imagine why the present book should ever have been written. It tells us nothing of consequence that has not been already known. . . . Where material is lacking, [Blythe's] luxuriant imagination serves to fill the gaps." Noted Geoffrey Bruun in *Nation:* "Satisfactory lives of Ney, the historic Ney, already exist in French and English. The main justification for Mr. Blythe's contribution depends, therefore, on the validity of its central thesis that Michel Ney and P. S. Ney were the same person. Yet Mr. Blythe offers little that is new and nothing that can be considered definitive to prove his thesis."

Far more favorable notices greeted Blythe's novels about Jesus Christ and the early days of Christianity in Roman-held Israel. Books such as *Crown Tree, Bold Galilean,* and *A Tear for Judas,* sought to recreate the atmosphere of Christ's times through the eyes of people who interacted with Jesus in various ways. "'The Crown Tree' tells a vivid, well-textured story of one Roman's experiences with his contemporaries and with his faith in Christianity's beginning years," noted Florence Girvin in the *New York Herald Tribune Book Review.* In another *Herald Tribune* review, F. H. Bullock found *A Tear for Judas* "a good historical novel [that] makes full use of the overtones and rich connotations inevitably present in the minds and memories of those for whom the New Testament scripture is a loved and significant part of our Christian culture." *Saturday Review of Literature* contributor Lon Tinkle called *Bold Galilean* "compelling drama extremely readable—both old and modern in its wisdom." In the *New York Herald Tribune,* P. J. Searles concluded of *Bold Galilean:* "Too often, unfortunately, a religious novel is overly-sentimental or overly-evangelical, but the author of 'Bold Galilean' avoids both pitfalls by admirable simplicity and sincerity, letting the message of Christ speak for itself without elaboration or paraphrase." A reviewer in *Best Sellers* deemed Blythe's *Brothers of Vengeance* "a story of early Christianity which is authentic, gripping and vibrant with life."

Most of Blythe's books about North Carolina were nonfiction—histories of certain counties, profiles of extraordinary people living and working among the mountain folk, or biographies of prominent citizens. In 1958, however, he released *Call Down the Storm,* a novel about the interaction of black and white residents on a plantation in the century after the Civil War. The plot revolves around the love affair between Dr. Claiborne Cardell, who owns the plantation, and his quadroon housekeeper, Sarah Gordon. How the children and grandchildren of this union fare in the twentieth century forms the crux of the story. A *Kirkus Reviews* correspondent cited *Call Down the Storm* for its "serious concern over Southern questions," adding that the book "handles its controversial questions sedately." In the *New York Times,* Henry Cavendish noted that the novel "treats the mixing of white and colored races from a reasoned attitude rather than through purpled verbalisms," and to quote Andrew Lytle in the *Saturday Review,* "the way [the characters] face the consequences of lust gives them dignity and the illusion of humanity." *Library Journal* contributor J. D. Marshall suggested that *Call Down the Storm* "is likely to prove somewhat controversial," but nevertheless concluded that the book provides "an absorbing story from first page to last."

*BIOGRAPHICAL/CRITICAL SOURCES:*

*BOOKS*

Henderson, Archibald, *North Carolina: The Old North State and the New,* Lewis, 1941.
Hoyle, Bernadette, *Tar Heel Writers I Know,* Blair (Winston-Salem, NC), 1956.

Kock, Frederick H., *Carolina Folk Plays,* Henry Holt (New York City), 1941.

*PERIODICALS*

*Best Sellers,* April 15, 1964, p. 34; August 1, 1969.
*Books,* March 28, 1937, p. 6.
*Chicago Sunday Tribune,* May 13, 1951, p. 3; July 13, 1958, p. 5.
*Christian Century,* February 2, 1949, p. 144; November 14, 1951, p. 1311.
*Christian Science Monitor,* November 18, 1948, p. 11.
*Commonweal,* May 14, 1937, p. 83.
*Kirkus Reviews,* October 1, 1948, p. 515; June 1, 1958, p. 388.
*Library Journal,* September 1, 1948, p. 1192; August 1958, p. 2177; March 1, 1964, p. 1104; June 15, 1964, p. 2673.
*Nation,* April 17, 1937, p. 443.
*New Republic,* July 14, 1937, p. 287.
*New Statesman & Nation,* December 4, 1937, p. 944.
*New York Herald Tribune Book Review,* May 6, 1951, p. 8; May 19, 1957, p. 5.
*New York Herald Tribune Weekly Book Review,* October 31, 1948, p. 12.
*New York Times,* April 4, 1937, p. 9; November 7, 1948, p. 30; June 24, 1951, p. 17; July 20, 1958, p. 22.
*San Francisco Chronicle,* July 29, 1951, p. 15.
*Saturday Review,* July 19, 1958, p. 30.
*Saturday Review of Literature,* June 12, 1937, p. 18; November 6, 1948, p. 29; July 22, 1950, p. 30; June 2, 1951, p. 30.
*Springfield Republican,* July 16, 1950, p. D6; July 13, 1958, p. C5.
*Times Literary Supplement,* October 16, 1937, p. 750.*

\* \* \*

**BOLITHO, (Henry) Hector 1897-1974
(Patrick Ney)**

*PERSONAL:* Born May 28, 1897, in New Zealand; died, 1974, in England; son of Henry and Ethelred Frances (Bregman) Bolitho. *Education:* Attended Seddon Memorial College, Auckland, New Zealand.

*ADDRESSES: Home*—No. 1, St. Nicholas Rd., Brighton, Sussex, England. *Agent*—A. M. Heath & Co. Ltd., 35 Dover St., London, England.

*CAREER:* Writer. Lecturer, especially in United States where he spoke more than a hundred times, beginning 1947. Chair, Committee for Writing and Reading Aids for the Paralyzed. *Military service:* Royal Air Force, Intelligence Corps, 1939-45; became squadron leader.

*MEMBER:* Royal Society of Arts (fellow), Royal Society of Literature (fellow), Athenaeum Club (London).

*WRITINGS:*

*The Island of Kawau: A Record, Descriptive and Historical,* Whitcombe & Tombs, 1919.

*With the Prince in New Zealand,* 1920.

*Fiji, Samoa, Tonga, the Islands of Wonder,* Whitcombe & Tombs, 1920.

(Editor with Albert V. Baillie) *Letters of Lady Augusta Stanley, a Young Lady at Court, 1849-1863,* George H. Doran, 1927.

*Solemn Boy* (novel), George H. Doran, 1927.

*The New Zealanders,* Dent (London), 1928.

*Thistledown and Thunder, a Higgledy-Piggledy Diary of New Zealand, the South Seas, Australia, Port Said, Italy, Paris, England, Madeira, Africa, Canada, and New York,* J. Cape (London), 1928.

*The Glorious Oyster: His History in Rome and in Britain, His Anatomy and Reproduction, How to Cook Him, and What Various Writers and Poets Have Written in His Praise,* Knopf (New York City), 1929.

*Judith Silver* (novel), Knopf, 1929.

(Editor with Baillie) *Later Letters of Lady Augusta Stanley, 1864-1876,* J. Cape, 1929.

(Editor) *The New Countries: A Collection of Stories and Poems by South African, Australian, Canadian, and New Zealand Writers,* J. Cape, 1929.

*The Flame on Ethirdova,* Cobden-Sanderson (London), 1930, Appleton (Norwalk, CT), 1931.

(Editor with Baillie) Arthur Penrhyn Stanley, *A Victorian Dean: A Memoir of Arthur Stanley, Dean of Westminister,* Chatto & Windus (London), 1930.

*Albert the Good and the Victorian Reign,* Appleton, 1932 (published in England as *Albert the Good,* Cobden-Sanderson, 1932).

*Alfred Mond, First Lord Melchett,* Appleton, 1933.

*Beside Galilee: A Diary in Palestine,* Appleton, 1933.

(Editor) *The Prince Consort and His Brother: Two Hundred New Letters,* Cobden-Sanderson, 1933, Appleton, 1934.

*Empty Clothes,* Centaur Press, 1934.

(Editor, contributor, and author of introduction) *Twelve Jews,* Rich & Cowan (London), 1934, Books for Libraries (Freeport, NY), 1967.

*The Romance of Windsor Castle,* Evans Brothers (London), 1934.

*Victoria, the Widow and Her Son,* Appleton, 1934.

*The Queen's Tact* (poetry), Centaur Press, 1934.

*Older People,* Appleton, 1935.

*The House in Half Moon Street and Other Stories,* Cobden-Sanderson, 1935, Appleton, 1936.

*James Lyle Mackay, First Earl of Inchcape,* J. Murray (London), 1936.

*Marie Tempest,* Eyre & Spottiswoode (London), 1936, Lippincott (Philadelphia, PA), 1937.

*King Edward VIII, an Intimate Biography,* Lippincott, 1937 (published in England as *King Edward VIII, His Life and Reign,* Eyre & Spottiswoode [London], 1937, 4th edition published as *Edward VIII—Duke of Windsor,* P. Owen [London], 1954).

*Royal Progress: One Hundred Years of British Monarchy* (includes material from *Albert the Good* and *Victoria, the Widow and Her Son*), Cobden-Sanderson, 1938.

*Victoria and Disraeli* (play for radio; first broadcast, 1938), Eyre & Spottiswoode, 1938.

(Editor) *Letters of Victoria, Queen of Great Britain, 1819-1901,* Yale University Press (New Haven, CT), 1938 (published in England as *Further Letters of Queen Victoria,* Butterworth & Co., 1938), reprinted, Kraus Reprint (Millwood, NY), 1976.

(With John Mulgan) *The Emigrants: Early Travellers to the Antipodes,* Selwyn & Blount, 1939, Books for Libraries, 1970.

*Roumania under King Carol,* Eyre & Spottiswoode, 1939, Longmans, Green (New York City), 1940.

*Haywire: An American Travel Diary,* Longmans, Green (New York City), 1939, new edition published as *America Expects: A Travel Diary,* Eyre & Spottiswoode, 1940.

*War in the Strand: A Notebook of the First Two and a Half Years in London,* Eyre & Spottiswoode, 1942.

(Editor) *A Batsford Century: The Record of a Hundred Years of Publishing and Bookselling, 1843-1943,* Batsford (London), 1943, 2nd edition, 1945.

*Combat Report: The Story of a Fighter Pilot,* Batsford, 1943.

*Command Performance: The Authentic Story of the Last Battle of Coastal Command, R.A.F.,* Howell, Soskin, 1946 (published in England as *Task for Coastal Command: The Story of the Battle of the*

*South-West Approaches,* Hutchinson [London], 1946).

*No Humour in My Love, and Two Other Stories,* Jenkins (London), 1946.

(Editor) *The British Empire,* Batsford, 1948.

*The Reign of Queen Victoria,* Macmillan (New York City), 1948.

*A Biographer's Notebook,* Longmans, Green (New York City), 1950.

*A Century of British Monarchy,* Longmans, Green (New York City), 1951, 2nd edition, 1953.

*Their Majesties,* Parrish, 1952, British Book Centre, 1953.

(With Derek Peel) *Without the City Wall: An Adventure in London Streetnames, North of the River,* J. Murray, 1952, Transatlantic (Albuquerque, NM), 1953.

*Jinnah, Creator of Pakistan,* J. Murray, 1954, Macmillan (New York City), 1955, reprinted, Greenwood Press (Westport, CT), 1981.

*A Penguin in the Eyrie: An R.A.F. Diary, 1939-1945,* Hutchinson, 1955.

*The Wine of the Douro* (booklet), Sidgwick & Jackson (London), 1956.

*No. 10 Downing Street, 1660-1900,* Hutchinson, 1957.

*The Glasshouse, Jamestown, Virginia,* (booklet), Jamestown Glasshouse Foundation (Jamestown, VA), 1957.

*The Angry Neighbours: A Diary of Palestine and Transjordan,* Arthur Barker (London), 1957.

*My Restless Years,* Parrish, 1962.

*A Summer in Germany: A Diary,* Wolff (London), 1963.

*The Galloping Third: The Story of the 3rd, the King's Own Hussars,* J. Murray, 1963, Transatlantic, 1964.

(Under pseudonym Patrick Ney) *An Animal Lover's Scrapbook,* Parrish, 1963.

*Albert, Prince Consort,* Parrish, 1964, Bobbs-Merrill (New York City), 1965, revised edition, David Bruce & Watson (London), 1970.

(With Peel) *The Drummonds of Charing Cross,* Allen & Unwin (London), 1967.

Contributor to magazines in England, United States, Germany, Pakistan, and other countries.

*SIDELIGHTS:* Hector Bolitho was a world traveler who traversed the globe at least three times and lived for periods in Portugal, Pakistan, the United States, Australia, England, Canada, South Africa, and Germany. Bolitho's output as a writer varied as much as his travel destinations: he authored biographies, edited collections of letters, wrote novels, stories, and poetry, and composed works based upon his sojourns. In the *New York Times,* Compton Pakenham wrote: "Hector Bolitho is of the fortunate of this earth, knows it and, with becoming modesty, says as much." The "becoming modesty" was particularly apparent in Bolitho's biographies of the British royal family, which were heralded as revealing but not salacious.

Though better known for his nonfiction, Bolitho published several novels and story collections during his lifetime. A *Boston Transcript* reviewer once noted that Bolitho's stories "reflect his care and interest in the meticulous placing of words, the smooth running of sentences, and the flavorsome definition of atmosphere." To quote *New York Evening Post* contributor Edwin Seaver, Bolitho's novel *Judith Silver* "is very fine . . . written with considerable grace and verve, an awareness of form and an irreproachable ear for the language." A *New York Times* correspondent likewise found *Judith Silver* "one of those rare books in which character and narrative and scene are fused into a beautiful and satisfying whole. Hector Bolitho reveals himself not only as a poet but as a man of deep understanding and originality of conception."

Bolitho also enjoyed doing research and, among other achievements, he unearthed a collection of letters written by Queen Victoria's consort prince, Albert, to his brother back in Germany. These letters helped Bolitho to construct his biographies of Prince Albert, including *Albert the Good, and the Victorian Reign, Albert, Prince Consort,* and *The Reign of Queen Victoria.* The author sought to clarify Albert's role in the creation of the Victorian Age, while also revealing the inner emotions that drove the outwardly stoic prince. In a review of *Albert the Good* for *New Statesman and Nation,* Hamish Miles declared: "This is a serious piece of biographical work—a little over-tender in its cadenced style, perhaps, but, nevertheless, careful in its detail and sympathetic in its feeling for the period and its problems." Wrote David Owen in the *Saturday Review of Literature:* "Mr. Bolitho's talents as a biographer are considerable. His style is effectively unassuming, and . . . he has made a genuine . . . addition to our knowledge of the century's most unselfish prince."

Other biographical works by Bolitho found similar respect. The vignettes in *Biographer's Notebook,* for instance, were considered "quite amusing" and "unusually diverting" by a *New Yorker* reviewer, and William MacDonald in *Books* declared *Alfred Mond, First Lord Melchett* "an admirable example of sympathetic biography." Concluded L. S. Bensusan in the *Saturday Review:* "Alfred Mond had splendid material successes in his life and has found fortune in his death—a gifted, eloquent, and enthusiastic biographer."

*BIOGRAPHICAL/CRITICAL SOURCES:*

*PERIODICALS*

*Booklist,* May, 1932, p. 386.
*Books,* May 14, 1933, p. 4; February 9, 1936, p. 12.
*Boston Transcript,* April 20, 1929, p. 1; April 20, 1932, p. 2; May 10, 1933, p. 3; March 7, 1936, p. 2.
*Christian Century,* August 3, 1932, p. 960; December 20, 1933, p. 1610.
*Christian Science Monitor,* December 16, 1933, p. 8; October 1, 1935, p. 16; September 19, 1951, p. 9.
*Commonweal,* June 15, 1932, p. 196.
*Nature,* October 7, 1933, p. 545.
*New Republic,* June 5, 1929, p. 80; July 27, 1932, p. 296.
*New Statesman and Nation,* May 7, 1932, p. 14; April 8, 1933, p. 454.
*New Yorker,* November 18, 1950, p. 190; September 22, 1951, p. 118.
*New York Evening Post,* March 16, 1929, p. 11.
*New York Herald Tribune Book Review,* October 29, 1950, p. 14.
*New York Times,* March 24, 1929, p. 8; April 10, 1932, p. 5; May 21, 1933, p. 9; November 26, 1933, p. 5; September 22, 1935, p. 5; February 9, 1936, p. 20; November 12, 1950, p. 44.
*Saturday Review,* March 19, 1932, p. 300; April 8, 1933, p. 344; July 13, 1935, p. 885.
*Saturday Review of Literature,* August 17, 1929, p. 62; July 29, 1933, p. 15; October 28, 1933, p. 220; October 12, 1935, p. 19.
*Spectator,* February 9, 1929, p. 210; March 19, 1932, p. 417; March 24, 1933, p. 431; July 7, 1933, p. 20.
*Time,* September 17, 1951, p. 114.
*Times Literary Supplement,* February 28, 1929, p. 165; March 17, 1932, p. 179; March 23, 1933, p. 193; June 29, 1933, p. 439; July 18, 1935, p. 463; November 23, 1935, p. 772; September 14, 1951, p. 575.*

## BONNER, Mary Graham 1890-1974

*PERSONAL:* Born September 5, 1890, in Cooperstown, NY; died February 12, 1974, in New York, NY; dual citizen of the United States and Canada; daughter of George William Graham (a bank manager) and Margaret Cary (Worthington) Bonner. *Education:* Attended Halifax Ladies' College and Halifax Conservatory of Music in Nova Scotia. *Avocational interests:* Playing basketball, hockey, and rounders (British baseball), swimming, high diving, skating, ice boating, and camping.

*CAREER:* Author of books, magazine articles, stories, and reviews.

*AWARDS, HONORS:* Constance Lindsay Skinner Award from the Women's National Book Association, 1943, for *Canada and Her Story*.

*WRITINGS:*

*Daddy's Bedtime Animal Stories* (illustrated by Florence Choate and Elizabeth Curtis), F. A. Stokes, 1916.
*Daddy's Bedtime Fairy Stories* (illustrated by Choate and Curtis), F. A. Stokes, 1916.
*Daddy's Bedtime Bird Stories* (illustrated by Choate and Curtis), F. A. Stokes, 1917.
*365 Bedtime Stories* (illustrated by Choate and Curtis), F. A. Stokes, 1923, reprinted, Derrydale Books (New York City), 1987.
*A Parent's Guide to Children's Reading,* Funk (New York City), 1926.
*The Magic Map* (illustrated by Luxor Price), Macaulay, 1927.
*Mrs. Cucumber Green* (illustrated by Janet L. Scott), Milton Bradley (East Longmeadow, MA), 1927.
*Magic Journeys* (illustrated by Price), Macaulay, 1928.
*Miss Angeline Adorable* (illustrated by Scott), Milton Bradley, 1928.
*Madam Red Apple* (illustrated by Scott), Milton Bradley, 1929.
*The Magic Music Shop* (illustrated by Price; with music by Harry Meyer), Macaulay, 1929.
*Etiquette for Boys and Girls: A Handbook for Use by Mothers, Governesses and Teachers,* McLoughlin, 1930.
*A Hundred Trips to Storyland* (illustrated by Hildegard Lupprian), Macaulay, 1930.
*The Magic Universe* (illustrated by Price), Macaulay, 1930.

*The Big Baseball Book for Boys* (edited by Alan Gould; introduction by Ty Cobb), McLoughlin, 1931.

*The Magic Clock* (illustrated by Price), Macaulay, 1931.

*The Animal Map of the World* (illustrated by Price), Macaulay, 1932.

*Adventures in Puddle Muddle* (illustrated by William A. Kolliker), Dutton (New York City), 1935.

*Rainbow at Night,* L. Furman, 1936.

*A World of Our Own* (illustrated by William A. Kolliker), Dutton, 1936.

(Editor) *Every Child's Story Book,* McLoughlin, 1938.

*A Story Teller's Holiday* (illustrated by Scott), McLoughlin, 1938.

(Editor) *A.B.C. Nursery Rhyme Book,* McLoughlin, 1939.

*Sir Noble, the Police Horse,* Knopf (New York City), 1940.

*Danger on the Coast: A Story of Nova Scotia,* Knopf, 1941.

*Canada and Her Story,* Knopf, 1942, 2nd edition, revised, 1950.

*Made in Canada,* Knopf, 1943.

*Couriers of the Sky: The Story of Pigeons,* Knopf, 1944, 2nd edition, revised, published as *Couriers of the Sky: Pigeons and Their Care,* 1952.

*The Surprise Place* (illustrated by Lois Lenski), Knopf, 1945.

*Something Always Happens* (illustrated by Avery Johnson), Knopf, 1946.

*Out to Win: A Baseball Story* (illustrated by Howard Butler), Knopf, 1947, reprinted, 1965.

*Hidden Village Mystery* (illustrated by Bob Meyers), Knopf, 1948.

*The Mysterious Caboose,* Knopf, 1949.

*The Haunted Hut: A Winter Mystery* (illustrated by Meyers), Knopf, 1950, published as *Mystery of the Haunted Hut* (illustrated by Norman Baer), Scholastic Books (New York City), 1969.

*Winning Dive: A Camp Story* (illustrated by Meyers), Knopf, 1950.

*The Base-Stealer* (illustrated by Meyers), Knopf, 1951.

*Wait and See* (illustrated by John N. Barron), Knopf, 1952.

*Dugout Mystery* (illustrated by Jonathan David), Knopf, 1953.

*Baseball Rookies Who Made Good,* Knopf, 1954.

*How to Play Baseball* (illustrated by Bernard Krigstein), Knopf, 1955.

(Editor) Rebecca McCann, *Complete Cheerful Cherub,* Crown (New York City), 1956.

*The Real Book about Crime Detection* (illustrated by Vincent Fodera), Garden City Books, 1957.

*Wonders around the Sun,* Lantern Press (Mt. Vernon, NY), 1957.

*The Real Book about Sports* (illustrated by Albert Orbaan), Garden City Books, 1958.

*Two-Way Pitcher* (illustrated by Victor Prezio), Lantern Press, 1958.

*Spray Hitter* (illustrated by Prezio), Lantern Press, 1959.

*The Real Book about Journalism* (illustrated by Albert Orbaan), Garden City Books, 1960.

*Wonders of Invention* (illustrated by Carol Cobbledick), Lantern Press, 1961.

*Mystery at Lake Ashburn,* Lantern Press, 1962.

*Wonders of Musical Instruments* (illustrated by Carol Cobbledick), Lantern Press, 1963.

Author of over 3,000 "Sundown Stories" syndicated daily by the Associated Press during a ten-year period.

*SIDELIGHTS:* Mary Graham Bonner undertook a busy and rather unconventional writing career. At a time when women rarely wrote about sports, Bonner turned out numerous titles, fiction and nonfiction, about baseball for boys. The work came natural for the author, as she herself played numerous competitive sports and enjoyed challenges as varied as ice skating and high diving.

Among Bonner's nine books about sports are *Baseball Rookies Who Made Good* and *Base Stealer. Baseball Rookies Who Made Good* profiles more than forty major league stars, documenting their early struggles and later successes. *Christian Science Monitor* contributor Harry Molter called the book "a solid hit for anyone who follows major league baseball," and *New York Times* reviewer David Dempsey deemed it "just the thing for young hero worshipers." *Base Stealer* is a novel about a youngster from a western state who finds himself in New York City for the summer. His depression turns to joy when he signs up to play baseball with the Police Athletic League. "All baseball fans should thrill to this story," noted Nelle McCalla in *Library Journal.* A *Saturday Review of Literature* correspondent described the novel as "more than a baseball story . . . well told in a natural style."

Storytelling was Bonner's chief occupation. Despite her affinity for sports, she was best known for her bedtime stories and other simple tales for the youngest listeners. Her *Adventures in Puddle-Muddle,* observed a *Boston Transcript* critic, "would appeal not only to the little ones but . . . [to] every older member of the family even unto the old maid auntie." The reviewer concluded that the story is "a much better treat than candy for good behavior." *Something Always Happens* revolves around nine-year-old Billy and his penchant for stirring up adventure. A *Kirkus Reviews* contributor found the book a "vivid, comfortable family story." Even more popular was Bonner's *Mysterious Caboose,* a mystery set against a railroading background. "Rarely does one find combined in one story so much adventure, action, and mystery," maintained Nelle McCalla in *Library Journal.* Another *Kirkus* reviewer called the book "thriller but credible . . . good yarn."

Bonner held dual citizenship in America and Canada, and a number of her titles concerned Canada, especially Nova Scotia. Her novel *Rainbow at Night,* one of the few she published for adults, concerns a young musical composer who visits Nova Scotia to write a symphony and the local girl who falls hopelessly in love with him. In *Books,* C. L. Skinner praised the novel for its "realistic detail and lack of reticence." In her *New York Times* review, Margaret Wallace concluded that Bonner "has drawn for us a number of picturesque characters and has rendered their idiomatic speech deftly and well. . . . [The novel] is a quiet and beautifully restrained love story which plumbs a depth of authentic and universal human emotion."

*BIOGRAPHICAL/CRITICAL SOURCES:*

*PERIODICALS*

*Booklist,* April, 1936, p. 232.
*Books,* October 6, 1935, p. 12; March 15, 1936, p. 22.
*Boston Transcript,* September 4, 1935, p. 2.
*Christian Science Monitor,* May 13, 1954, p. 12.
*Kirkus Reviews,* July 15, 1946, p. 325; August 15, 1949, p. 427; February 15, 1950, p. 97; March 1, 1951, p. 127.
*Library Journal,* September 1, 1946, p. 1130; September 15, 1949, p. 1333; May 15, 1950, p. 879.
*New York Herald Tribune Book Review,* June 25, 1950, p. 8; May 6, 1951, p. 10.
*New York Times,* October 27, 1929, p. 38; March 8, 1936, p. 6; August 28, 1949, p. 24; April 2, 1950, p. 28; August 5, 1951, p. 14; July 18, 1954, p. 16.
*San Francisco Chronicle,* November 10, 1946, p. 11.
*Saturday Review of Literature,* November 16, 1929, p. 428; September 28, 1935, p. 16; May 12, 1951, p. 54.

*OBITUARIES:*

*PERIODICALS*

*New York Times,* February 13, 1974.
*Publishers Weekly,* March 4, 1974.*

\*    \*    \*

**BOTHWELL, Jean (?)-1977**

*PERSONAL:* Born in Winside, NE; died March 2, 1977, in MO; buried in Lincoln, NE; daughter of James Millward (a minister) and Mary Emmeline (Batham) Bothwell. *Education:* Nebraska Wesleyan University, A.B., 1916. *Politics:* Republican. *Religion:* Methodist. *Avocational interests:* Collecting antique glass and stamps; historical movies and classical music; "interested in studying the effect of the environment on the progress of any given group of people."

*CAREER:* High school history teacher in Columbus, NE; served as business manager and missionary to India for the Methodist church; author in New York City.

*MEMBER:* Society of Women Geographers, Mystery Writers of America, Forum for Writers of Books for Young People, Nebraska Writers Guild, Nebraska State Historical Society, Metropolitan Women's Republican Club.

*AWARDS, HONORS:* Review Club Poetry Award, 1968; Children's Spring Book Festival Award and *New York Herald Tribune* award, both in 1946, both for *The Thirteenth Stone: A Story of Rajputana.*

*WRITINGS:*

*Little Boat Boy,* Harcourt (New York City), 1945.
*The Thirteenth Stone: A Story of Rajputana,* Harcourt, 1946.
*River Boy of Kashmir,* Morrow (New York City), 1946.
*Star of India,* Morrow, 1947.
*The Empty Tower,* Morrow, 1948.
*Little Flute Player,* Morrow, 1949.
*Onions without Tears* (adult cook book), Hastings House (New York City), 1950, published as *The Onion Cookbook,* Dover (New York City), 1976.
*Peter Holt, P.K.,* Harcourt, 1950.

*Sword of a Warrior,* Harcourt, 1951.

*Paddy and Sam,* Abelard (New York City), 1952.

*Story of India,* Harcourt, 1952.

*Lost Colony,* Winston, 1953.

*Golden Letter to Siam,* Abelard, 1953.

*The Wishing Apple Tree,* Harcourt, 1953.

*The Borrowed Monkey,* Abelard, 1953.

*Hidden Treasure,* Friendship (New York City), 1954.

*Flame in the Sky,* Vanguard, 1954.

*The Red Barn Club,* Harcourt, 1954.

*The First Book of Roads,* F. Watts (New York City), 1955.

*Cal's Birthday Present,* Abelard, 1955.

(With Phyllis Sowers) *Ranch of a Thousand Horns,* Abelard, 1955.

*Cobras, Cows, and Courage,* Coward, 1956 (published in England as *Men and Monsoons,* Chatto & Windus [London], 1962).

*Search for a Golden Bird,* Harcourt, 1956.

*Ring of Fate,* Harcourt, 1957.

*Tree House at Seven Oaks,* Abelard, 1957.

*Promise of the Rose,* Harcourt, 1958.

*The Missing Violin,* Harcourt, 1959.

*The Silver Mango Tree,* Harcourt, 1960.

*The Animal World of India,* F. Watts, 1961.

*The Mystery Key,* Dial (New York City), 1961.

*The Emerald Clue,* Harcourt, 1961.

*The Mystery Cargo,* Dial, 1962.

*The First Book of Pakistan,* F. Watts, 1962.

*The Red Scarf,* Harcourt, 1962.

*The Mystery Angel,* Dial, 1963.

*Omen for a Princess: The Story of Jahanara,* Abelard, 1963.

(With Irene Wells) *Fun and Festival from India,* revised edition, Friendship, 1963.

*The White Fawn of Phalera,* Harcourt, 1963.

*By Sail and Wind: The Story of the Bahamas,* Abelard, 1964.

*The Mystery Gatepost,* Dial, 1964.

*Romany Girl,* Harcourt, 1964.

*The Dancing Princess,* Harcourt, 1965.

*Lady of Roanoke,* Holt (New York City), 1965.

*The Mystery Egg,* Dial, 1965.

*The Mystery Clock,* Dial, 1966.

*The First Book of India,* F. Watts, 1966, 2nd revised edition, 1978.

*Ride, Zarina, Ride,* Harcourt, 1966.

*The Vanishing Wildlife of East Africa,* Abelard, 1967.

*The Mystery Box,* Dial, 1967.

*The Holy Man's Secret: A Story of India,* Abelard, 1967.

*Mystery at the House-of-the-Fish,* Harcourt, 1968.

*The Mystery Cup,* Dial, 1968.

*The Mystery Tunnel,* Dial, 1969.

*The Parsonage Parrot,* F. Watts, 1969.

*Defiant Bride,* Harcourt, 1969.

*African Herdboy: A Story of the Masai,* Harcourt, 1970.

*The Mystery Candlestick,* Dial, 1970.

*The Secret in the Wall,* Abelard, 1971.

A collection of Bothwell's books, papers, and memorabilia is housed at Boston University's Mugar Memorial Library.

*SIDELIGHTS:* Jean Bothwell was the author of numerous fiction and nonfiction books for young readers. Much of her writing focused on India, a country she knew firsthand from her work there as a Methodist missionary.

Bothwell's first book, *Little Boat Boy,* depicted everyday life in India through the story of a small boy named Hafiz. His tale, and Bothwell's portrait of India, was continued in *River Boy of Kashmir,* in which Hafiz enters the wider world when he begins attending a British-style school. "A quiet story with distinction and a real charm," approved Claire Nolte in *Library Journal.* A *New York Times* reviewer also enjoyed the book, noting that Hafiz lived in "a pleasant world . . . and a pleasant one for any child of 8 to 12 to share vicariously." That writer further noted: "Hafiz' adventures are small, everyday ones, but to him they are supremely dramatic. The author gets inside his earnest mind so successfully that we live . . . with him."

Bothwell was also praised by A. M. Jordan in *Horn Book* for "vividly" summoning up the sights and sounds of India in another book, *The Thirteenth Stone: A Story of Rajputana.* In this colorful tale, a boy named Jivan Singh shares a mud hut with his guardian. Jivan knows that he is part of an aristocratic warrior caste, but the rest of his past is a mystery to him—a mystery he is determined to unravel. "Although nothing can be more remote than this from the experience of American children," mused N. B. Baker in the *New York Times,* "it is Miss Bothwell's peculiar gift to make these Oriental youngsters as real as the boys in the next block." Baker went on to laud Bothwell for her "distinguished writing." Jivan's adventures were continued in *Search for a Golden Bird.* In that novel, the young protagonist—who has discovered that he is the grandson of the Prime Minister of Jaipur—searched with his cousin Dhuleep for a ruby-eyed, golden bird figure. The reviewer for *Horn Book* noted that the novel provided "clear and interesting" insights into political problems in India, and H. M.

Brogan, writing in *Library Journal,* deemed it a "well-written story with convincing characterization."

*BIOGRAPHICAL/CRITICAL SOURCES:*

*PERIODICALS*

*Booklist,* May 15, 1946; September, 1946; July 1, 1955; September 1, 1956; January 15, 1958; April 15, 1962.

*Bookmark,* April, 1955.

*Book Week,* July 21, 1946, p. 7; November 10, 1946, p. 3; March 15, 1955.

*Chicago Sunday Tribune,* November 14, 1954, p. 12; May 14, 1961, section 2, p. 12; May 13, 1962, section 2, p. 14.

*Christian Science Monitor,* November 15, 1956, part 2, p. 16; May 6, 1965, p. 5B.

*Churchman,* November 15, 1946.

*Cleveland Open Shelf,* May, 1946, p. 12.

*Horn Book,* May, 1946; September, 1946; June, 1955; December, 1956; February, 1958; June, 1961; June, 1962; February, 1965.

*Kirkus Reviews,* April 15, 1946; August 1, 1946; July 1, 1954; October 15, 1954; November 15, 1954; March 1, 1955; July 1, 1956; July 1, 1957; September 1, 1957.

*Library Journal,* June 1, 1946; November 1, 1946; November 15, 1954; December 15, 1954; April 15, 1955; May 15, 1955; September 15, 1956; January 15, 1958; February 15, 1958; May 15, 1961; May 15, 1962; February 15, 1965; June 15, 1966.

*New Yorker,* December 7, 1946.

*New York Herald Tribune Book Review,* November 18, 1956, part 2, p. 22; May 11, 1958, p. 8; August 5, 1962, p. 10.

*New York Times,* April 21, 1946, p. 14; November 10, 1946, p. 5; January 16, 1955, p. 28; September 23, 1956, p. 32; November 24, 1957, p. 36.

*New York Times Book Review,* May 14, 1961, part 2, p. 34; September 4, 1966, p. 16.

*San Francisco Chronicle,* May 22, 1955, pp. 20-21.

*Saturday Review,* November 17, 1956; February 15, 1958.

*Saturday Review of Literature,* July 13, 1946; November 9, 1946.

*Springfield Republican,* May 12, 1946, p. 4D; December 12, 1954, p. 9C.

*Weekly Book Review,* April 28, 1946, p. 7; October 27, 1946, p. 8.

*Wilson Library Bulletin,* July, 1946; October, 1946; November, 1954; May, 1955; January, 1958; July, 1962.*

## BOWEN, Catherine (Shober) Drinker 1897-1973

*PERSONAL:* Born January 1, 1897, in Haverford, PA; died of cancer November 1, 1973, in Haverford, PA; daughter of Henry Sturgis and Aimee Ernesta (Beaux) Drinker; married Ezra Bowen, 1919; married second husband, T. McKean Downs, July 1, 1939 (died, 1960); children: (first marriage) Ezra, Catherine Drinker Bowen Prince. *Education:* Attended Peabody Institute and Juilliard School of Music. *Avocational interests:* Skiing, skating, playing the violin.

*CAREER:* Writer; lecturer. Member, National Portrait Gallery Commission; trustee emeritus, Free Library System of Philadelphia.

*MEMBER:* National Institute of Arts and Letters (member of council, 1965-73), Royal Society of Literature (fellow), American Philosophical Society (fellow), Phi Beta Kappa.

*AWARDS, HONORS:* Philadelphia Award, 1957; Phillips Award, American Philosophical Society, 1957; National Achievement Award, 1958; National Book Award in nonfiction, 1958, for *The Lion and the Throne: The Life and Times of Sir Edward Coke;* Sarah Josepha Hale Award, 1961; Constance Lindsay Skinner Award from the Women's National Book Association, 1962; Litt.D. from Dickinson College, University of Rochester, University of North Carolina, Russell Sage College, Temple University, and Northeastern University.

*WRITINGS:*

*The Story of the Oak Tree,* Chemical Publishing (New York City), 1924.

*A History of Lehigh University,* Lehigh Alumni Bulletin (Lehigh, PA), 1924.

*Rufus Starbuck's Wife,* Putnam (New York City), 1932.

*Friends and Fiddlers,* Little, Brown (Boston, MA), 1935.

(With Barbara von Meck) *Beloved Friend: The Story of Tchaikowsky and Nadejda von Meck* (Book-of-the-Month Club selection), Random House (New York City), 1937, reprinted, Greenwood Press (Westport, CT), 1976.

*Free Artist: The Story of Anton and Nicholas Rubinstein,* Random House, 1939.

*Yankee from Olympus: Justice Holmes and His Family* (Book-of-the-Month Club selection), Atlantic-Little, Brown, 1944, reprinted with a new introduction by Louis Auchincloss, Book-of-the-Month Club (New York City), 1980.

*John Adams and the American Revolution* (Book-of-the-Month Club selection), Atlantic-Little, Brown, 1950, excerpts published as *The First Continental Congress: Carpenters' Hall, Philadelphia, 1774,* Girard Bank, 1973.

*The Lion and the Throne: The Life and Times of Sir Edward Coke* (Book-of-the-Month Club selection), Little, Brown, 1957, reprinted, 1990.

*Adventures of a Biographer,* Little, Brown, 1959.

(Contributor) *Four Portraits and One Subject: Bernard De Voto,* Houghton (Boston, MA), 1963.

*Francis Bacon: The Temper of a Man,* Little, Brown, 1963, reprinted, Fordham University Press (New York City), 1993.

*Miracle at Philadelphia: The Story of the Constitutional Convention, May to September, 1787* (Book-of-the-Month Club selection), Little, Brown, 1966, reprinted with new introduction by Henry Steele Commager and illustrations by Warren Chappel, Book-of-the-Month-Club, 1986.

(With Allan Nevins) *The Art of History,* Gertrude Clark Whittall Poetry and Literature Fund (Washington, DC), 1967.

*Biography: The Craft and the Calling,* Little, Brown, 1969, reprinted, Greenwood Press, 1978.

*Family Portrait,* Little, Brown, 1970.

*The Most Dangerous Man in America: Scenes from the Life of Benjamin Franklin,* Little, Brown, 1974.

Also author of booklets and published addresses, including *The Writing of Biography,* Writer, Inc., 1951, *The Biographer Looks for News,* 1958, and *The Nature of the Artist,* 1961, both published by Scripps College Press. Member of editorial board of *The Writer. Miracle at Philadelphia: The Story of the Constitutional Convention, May to September, 1787* has been translated into French. Bowen's family papers are collected at the Library of Congress, Washington, DC.

*ADAPTATIONS: Beloved Friend: The Story of Tchaikowsky and Nadejda von Meck* was adapted for the screen and produced as *The Music Lovers,* United Artists, 1971; Bowen was the subject of the film *Catherine Drinker Bowen: Other Peoples' Lives.*

*SIDELIGHTS:* Most of Catherine Drinker Bowen's writings are biographies of historical figures, many of them associated with the world of classical music. Her best known work, *Beloved Friend: The Story of*

*Tchaikowsky and Nadejda von Meck,* uses the voluminous letters between the composer and his patroness to construct their lives and the passion they held for one another. *Chicago Daily Tribune* reviewer Fanny Butcher called *Beloved Friend* "a strange and fascinating 'true story.' It is also a well documented record of a genius' life. And it is written with the true delicacy of feeling for music that only a fine musician can have." In the *Saturday Review of Literature,* W. J. Henderson wrote: "Mrs. Bowen has done her work well. The volume is a most valuable addition to the knowledge we possess of the celebrated Russian composer and to the large record of the peculiarities of men of genius."

Two years later, Bowen's biography of the Russian composers Anton and Nicholas Rubinstein drew similar praise for the author's combination of family history and music theory. "The most remarkable success of this book has been the manner by which Mrs. Bowen has conveyed to the reader Anton's genius as a pianist," declared Alexander Williams in *Atlantic. Boston Transcript* correspondent Charlotte Bassett maintained that Bowen, in *Free Artist: The Story of Anton and Nicholas Rubinstein,* "has managed . . . not only to convince a generation that knows him only as a mediocre composer of Anton Rubinstein's greatness as a pianist, but also to convey a distinct impression of how he played. The singing quality of Rubinstein's tones will be as audible to many readers as it was to his audiences." The critic concluded: "This book is not only superior to the usual run of musical chronicles: it is worthy to rank with the better biographies of any year."

Bowen also indulged her interest in politics by writing biographies of famous statesmen, from Sir Francis Bacon to Philadelphia's Benjamin Franklin. In a *New York Times Book Review* piece on *Francis Bacon: The Temper of a Man,* A. L. Rowse noted: "The portrait that the author presents of this Renaissance man is both more appealing and more perceptive than usual. With her admirable experience as a biographer, her conscientious care as a historian to document her study, and with her skill at precise delineation . . . she has seen farther into this difficult and rewarding man than anyone else has." Concluded *Library Journal* contributor J. L. Andrews: "All considered, this is a first-rate biography written in Mrs. Bowen's knowing style, which unquestionably accomplishes the foremost task of any biographer—to make his subject, no matter how remote in time, a living and breathing being."

In her 1969 book, *Biography: The Craft and the Calling,* Bowen talked about what is involved in writing about the lives of other people. Katherine Gauss Jackson said in a *Harper's* article that when "a distinguished biographer writes about the riddles, secrets, sorrows, and satisfactions of her metier it is good news indeed." Bowen, wrote Jackson, "is as delightful when talking about her trade as she is when professing it." According to Leon Edel's review of the volume in *Book World,* Bowen "has written several fine biographies, of subjects as disparate as Oliver Wendell Holmes, Francis Bacon and Tchaikovsky. Now she has written a fluent and candid little book that testifies to an interesting side of biography; that of the biographer himself, who is always playing second fiddle to his subject. . . . Bowen's book, rich in experience, offers a series of signposts to critics and students of biography and aspirants in that art."

In an excerpt from *Biography: The Craft and the Calling* published in *Writer,* Bowen noted which qualities she looked for in a good biography. "In the biographies I most admire, the story moves forward implacably, inevitably. The reader *believes* in [the subject]. . . . the reader cannot but believe. There are no awkward hurdles, no holes to fall through. Nothing is stretched too far or condensed to the point of collapse. The narrative—the plot—contains us, we know where we are going."

*BIOGRAPHICAL/CRITICAL SOURCES:*

*PERIODICALS*

*America,* September 28, 1963, p. 367; March 22, 1969, p. 341.
*Atlantic,* April, 1937; December, 1939.
*Atlantic Bookshelf,* July, 1935, p. 11.
*Atlantic Monthly,* March, 1970.
*Best Sellers,* July 1, 1963, p. 129; July 1, 1970.
*Books,* January 31, 1937, p. 3; November 26, 1939, p. 3.
*Book World,* February 9, 1969, p. 4.
*Boston Transcript,* December 1, 1939, p. 13.
*Chicago Daily Tribune,* February 6, 1937, p. 21.
*Christian Century,* September 7, 1960, p. 1023; June 10, 1970.
*Christian Science Monitor,* February 8, 1937, p. 18; January 20, 1940, p. 10; June 27, 1963, p. 11; February 6, 1969, p. 7; November 28, 1969.
*Critic,* August, 1963, p. 75.
*Harper's,* February, 1969, p. 104.
*Library Journal,* July, 1963, p. 2684.

*New Republic,* February 24, 1937, p. 86; May 29, 1944.
*New Statesman & Nation,* June 5, 1937, p. 928.
*Newsweek,* June 24, 1963, p. 118.
*New Yorker,* April 22, 1944; July 4, 1970; November 11, 1974.
*New York Herald Tribune,* June 16, 1935, p. 6.
*New York Herald Tribune Book Review,* July 9, 1950.
*New York Herald Tribune Books,* June 23, 1963, p. 3.
*New York Times,* March 31, 1935, p. 12; January 31, 1937, p. 3; November 26, 1939, p. 5; July 13, 1970.
*New York Times Book Review,* July 2, 1950; March 10, 1957; June 23, 1963, p. 1; December 6, 1970; April 6, 1975.
*Publishers Weekly,* March 5, 1962.
*Reporter,* August 15, 1963, p. 64.
*Saturday Review,* June 17, 1950; July 13, 1963, p. 30; March 15, 1969; March 29, 1969, p. 26.
*Saturday Review of Literature,* June 22, 1935, p. 22; January 30, 1937, p. 5; November 18, 1939, p. 6.
*Springfield Republican,* February 7, 1937, p. E7.
*Times Literary Supplement,* June 12, 1937, p. 443; November 28, 1963, p. 996.
*Virginia Quarterly Review,* autumn, 1970.
*Weekly Book Review,* April 23, 1944.
*Writer,* February, 1969.
*Yale Review,* October, 1963, p. 100.

*OBITUARIES:*

*PERIODICALS*

*Newsweek,* November 12, 1973.
*Publishers Weekly,* November 12, 1973.
*Time,* November 12, 1973.
*Washington Post,* November 6, 1973.*

\*        \*        \*

**BRADFORD, Ernle (Dusgate Selby) 1922-1986**

*PERSONAL:* Born January 11, 1922, in Cole Green, Norfolk, England; died in 1986; son of Jocelyn Ernle and Ada Louise (Dusgate) Bradford; married Janet Rushbury (a painter), 1948 (marriage ended, 1956); married Marie Blanche Thompson (a painter), 1957; children: (second marriage) Hugh Ernle. *Education:* Educated in England. *Politics:* Monarchist. *Religion:* Church of England.

*CAREER:* Writer. *Military service:* Royal Navy, 1940-46; became first lieutenant; mentioned in dispatches.

*MEMBER:* Royal Naval Sailing Association, Ocean Cruising Club.

*WRITINGS:*

### HISTORY

*The Mighty "Hood"*, Hodder & Stoughton (London), 1959, World Publishing (Cleveland), 1960.

(Translator) Francisco Balbi de Correggio, *The Great Siege: Malta, 1565*, Hodder & Stoughton, 1961, Harcourt (New York City), 1962.

*Wall of England: The Channel's Two Thousand Years of History*, Country Life (England), 1966, published as *Wall of Empire: The Channel's Two Thousand Years of History*, A. S. Barnes (San Diego, CA), 1967.

*The Great Betrayal: Constantinople, 1204*, Hodder & Stoughton, 1967.

*The Sundered Cross: The Story of the Fourth Crusade*, Prentice-Hall (Englewood Cliffs, NJ), 1967.

*Gibraltar: The History of a Fortress*, Hart-Davis (London), 1971, Harcourt (New York City), 1972.

*Mediterranean: Portrait of a Sea*, Harcourt, 1971.

*The Shield and the Sword: The Knights of St. John*, Hodder & Stoughton, 1972, Dutton (New York City), 1973, also published as *The Shield and the Sword: The Knights of Malta*, Collins (London), 1974.

*The Sword and the Scimitar: The Saga of the Crusades*, Putnam (New York City), 1974.

*The Year of Thermopylae*, Macmillan, 1980, published as *The Battle for the West: Thermopylae*, McGraw (New York City), 1980.

### BIOGRAPHIES

*A Wind From the North: The Life of Henry the Navigator*, Harcourt, 1960 (published in England as *Southward the Caravels: The Story of Henry the Navigator*, Hutchinson [London], 1961).

*The Wind Commands Me: A Life of Sir Francis Drake*, Harcourt, 1965 (published in England as *Drake*, Hodder & Stoughton, 1965).

*The Sultan's Admiral: The Life of Barbarossa*, Harcourt, 1968.

*Cleopatra*, Hodder & Stoughton, 1971, Harcourt, 1972.

*Christopher Columbus*, Viking (New York City), 1973.

*Paul the Traveller*, Allen Lane (London), 1974, Macmillan (New York City), 1976.

*Nelson: The Essential Hero*, Harcourt, 1977.

### OTHER

*Contemporary Jewellery and Silver Design*, John Heywood, 1950, Pitman, 1951.

*Four Centuries of European Jewellery*, Philosophical Library, 1953.

*The Journeying Moon* (personal account), Jarrolds (London), 1958.

*English Victorian Jewellery*, McBride, 1959.

*The Wind Off the Island* (travel), Hutchinson (London), 1960, Harcourt, 1961.

*The Touchstone*, Cassell (London), 1962.

*Antique Collecting*, English Universities Press, 1963.

*The Companion Guide to the Greek Islands* (travel), Harper (New York City), 1963, 3rd edition, Collins, 1975, also published as *The Greek Islands: A Travel Guide*, Harper, 1966.

*Dictionary of Antiques*, English Universities Press, 1963.

*Ulysses Found*, Hodder & Stoughton, 1963, Harcourt, 1964.

*The America's Cup*, Country Life, 1964.

*Three Centuries of Sailing*, Country Life, 1964.

*Antique Furniture*, English Universities Press, 1970.

Founder and editor of *Antique Dealer and Collectors' Guide*, and editor of *Watchmaker, Jeweller, and Silversmith*.

*ADAPTATIONS: Ulysses Found* was adapted as a television serial.

*SIDELIGHTS:* The late Ernle Bradford combined his passions for sailing and travel with a career writing books about his beloved Mediterranean and its various isles. Bradford's opus includes well-documented histories of seafaring communities as well as fanciful speculations about great literary voyages of the distant past. His own background in the British navy informed other works such as *The Mighty "Hood"* and *Wall of England: The Channel's Two Thousand Years of History*. According to *Guardian* contributor Jeremy Brooks, Bradford's writings "managed to distil the special poetry of the drifting, rootless sailor, whose boat is his home and whose journey has no purpose beyond the joy of voyaging."

Bradford's love of the Mediterranean began, oddly enough, while he was a commissioned Navy officer in World War II. Most of his three-and-a-half year tour of duty was spent in the Mediterranean theatre, and when he resigned from active duty he devoted himself to exploring the area in his own small boats. The adventure led to a series of books, most especially *Ulysses Found,* an attempt to reconstruct the legendary voyage of Ulysses as recorded in the Homeric poem. "Bradford's account is a fascinating one and his conclusions are well drawn and creditable," wrote a *Best Sellers* reviewer on *Ulysses Found.* "Anyone familiar with the Odyssey will find this a stimulating book." An *Economist* essayist wrote of the same title: "Mr. Bradford is a sailor, a lover of small ships; and every page of his book vibrates with the water-level slap and tang of the open sailing-boat such as Ulysses knew. . . . Here is a book to read, re-read and relish, either as a companion to the Odyssey, or better for its own salty sake."

The author's less speculative works include biographies of such notables as the pirate Barbarossa, Cleopatra, Prince Henry the Navigator, and Christopher Columbus. In these books Bradford also made use of his nautical expertise and his wide travels throughout maritime Europe. In a *Saturday Review* piece on *A Wind from the North: The Life of Henry the Navigator,* Gilbert Renault declared: "This book is the work of a sailor who renders homage to another sailor. A great salt breeze passes through his pages, and one senses that the heart of the author hides a secret regret: that of not having been born a little more than five centuries ago, when Henry of Portugal was sending courageous young captains to the far corners of the earth." *Best Sellers* reviewer V. J. Wathen wrote of Bradford's *Christopher Columbus:* "This story amazes us. . . . The book is beautifully printed and illustrated with contemporary maps, paintings and drawings. It would make a welcome gift, fascinating to read as well as to look at." A *Times Literary Supplement* correspondent concluded of the same work: "Bradford's accomplished biography . . . brings out well the curious tenacity with which Columbus pursued, in the face of constant rebuffs, his self-appointed destiny."

Bradford once told *CA:* "I have never wanted to do anything in my life but write. Although I had my first book accepted by Longman's when I was seventeen years old, unfortunately (or not), the Headmaster of my school persuaded both my father and the publisher that publication at so early an age would harm me. Hence I learned my trade on post-war Fleet Street

editing two specialist magazines. Journalism is great training, but if you want to be a writer, it's essential to know when to get out.

"Having spent so many years in Italy, Sicily, Spain, Greece, and the island of Malta, I think I have a more European than English mind. My books have been translated into most European languages from Swedish to Hungarian, and seem to sell best in Germany. This is explained by the fact that Germans are addicts of history and, particularly, Mediterranean subjects. It is curious to me that east European countries seem to like my writing since I am a Romantic, Imperialist, Royalist, and arch-Conservative.

"From my own experience with many people in many countries, a vast number would like to write. My advice is that unless you are driven by such a compulsion that you *have* to—forget it. As an old Greek saying has it: 'There are more bones around the altars of the Muses than around those of any other gods or goddesses.'"

## *BIOGRAPHICAL/CRITICAL SOURCES:*

### *PERIODICALS*

*Best Sellers,* February 1, 1964, p. 384; November 15, 1968, p. 341; December 15, 1973, p. 411.
*Book Week,* August 9, 1964, p. 12.
*Chicago Sunday Tribune,* May 1, 1960, p. 2.
*Christian Science Monitor,* May 16, 1960, p. 9; December 21, 1960, p. 9; March 5, 1964, p. 7; February 3, 1975.
*Economist,* July 27, 1963, p. 366; October 5, 1963, p. 53.
*Guardian,* July 1, 1960, p. 7.
*Horn Book,* December, 1972, p. 613.
*Library Journal,* December 1, 1963, p. 4637; February 1, 1964, p. 629; September 15, 1968, p. 3124; September 1, 1972, p. 2727.
*New York Herald Tribune Lively Arts,* November 27, 1960, p. 30.
*New York Times Book Review,* November 20, 1960, p. 56; March 12, 1961, p. 18; February 2, 1964, p. 7; October 28, 1968, p. 71; December 23, 1973, p. 10.
*Observer Review,* January 19, 1969.
*San Francisco Chronicle,* May 5, 1960, p. 33.
*Saturday Review,* December 17, 1960, p. 24; March 28, 1964, p. 33.
*Springfield Republican,* May 1, 1960, p. D4.
*Times Literary Supplement,* February 26, 1960, p. 131; June 24, 1960, p. 399; August 9, 1963, p.

607; December 5, 1963, p. 1010; September 10, 1971, p. 1092; April 5, 1974, p. 368; April 4, 1980.

*OBITUARIES:*

PERIODICALS

*Times* (London), May 14, 1986.*

\* \* \*

## BRANT, Irving (Newton) 1885-1976

*PERSONAL:* Born January 17, 1885, in Walker, IA; died, 1976; son of David (a newspaper editor) and Ruth (Hurd) Brant; married Hazeldean Toof, September 3, 1913; children: Ruth (Mrs. Jack Davis), Robin (Mrs. Kenneth Lodewick). *Education:* State University of Iowa, B.A., 1909. *Politics:* Democrat.

*CAREER: Iowa City Republican,* Iowa City, IA, reporter, later managing editor, 1909-14; *Clinton Herald,* Clinton, IA, editor, 1914-15; *Des Moines Register and Tribune,* Des Moines, Iowa, associate editor, 1915-18; *St. Louis Star,* St. Louis, MO, editorial writer, later editorial page editor, 1918-23; *St. Louis Star-Times,* St. Louis, MO, editorial page editor, 1930-38, contributing editor, 1938-41; *Chicago Sun,* Chicago, IL, editorial writer, 1941-43, foreign correspondent, 1945. Freelance writer and researcher, 1923-30, 1945-76. University of Virginia, Charlottesville, visiting scholar in history and political science, 1963-64; University of Oregon, Eugene, visiting professor, 1966. Director of National Public Housing Conference, New York, NY, 1935-44; U.S. Public Works Administration, consultant, 1938-40. Emergency Conservation Committee, New York City, treasurer, 1931-61.

*MEMBER:* Institute of Early American History and Culture (council, 1959-61), Society of American Historians, Overseas Writers (Washington, DC), American Civil Liberties Union, Delta Sigma Rho.

*AWARDS, HONORS:* E. B. MacNaughton Civil Liberties Award, American Civil Liberties Union, Oregon, 1971.

*WRITINGS:*

*Dollars and Sense,* John Day (New York City), 1933.

*Storm Over the Constitution,* Bobbs-Merrill (New York City), 1936, reprinted with a new introduction, 1963.

*James Madison,* six volumes, Bobbs-Merrill, Volume 1: *The Virginia Revolutionist,* 1941, Volume 2: *The Nationalist, 1780-1787,* 1948, Volume 3: *Father of the Constitution, 1787-1800,* 1950, Volume 4: *Secretary of State, 1800-1809,* 1953, Volume 5: *The President, 1809-1812,* 1956, Volume 6: *Commander in Chief, 1812-1836,* 1961, one-volume condensation of entire study published as *The Fourth President: A Life of James Madison,* Bobbs-Merrill, 1970.

*Road to Peace and Freedom,* Bobbs-Merrill, 1943.

*The New Poland,* International Universities Press (New York City), 1946 (published in England as *New Life in Poland,* Dobson, 1946).

*Friendly Cove* (historical novel), Bobbs-Merrill, 1963.

*The Free, Or Not So Free, Air of Pennsylvania,* Dickinson College (Carlisle, PA), 1964.

*The Books of James Madison, with Some Comments on the Reading of FDR and JFK* (address given at Tracy W. McGregor Library, 1964), University of Virginia (Charlottesville, VA), 1965.

*The Bill of Rights: Its Origin and Meaning,* Bobbs-Merrill, 1965.

*The Constitution and the Right to Know* (Harold L. Cross lecture given at University of Missouri, December 4, 1967), University of Missouri (Columbia, MO), 1967.

*James Madison and American Nationalism,* Van Nostrand (New York City), 1968.

*Impeachment: Trials and Errors,* Knopf (New York City), 1972.

*Adventures in Conservation with Franklin D. Roosevelt,* Northland (Flagstaff, AZ), 1989.

CONTRIBUTOR

Joseph F. Guffy, *How Liberal Is Justice Hughes?* (includes articles from *New Republic* by Brant), U.S. Government Printing Office (Washington, DC), 1937.

Harold L. Ickes, compiler, *Freedom of the Press Today,* Vanguard (New York City), 1941.

Bruce Bliven and A. G. Mazerik, editors, *What the Informed Citizen Needs to Know,* Duell, 1945.

W. Melville Jones, editor, *Chief Justice John Marshall: A Reappraisal,* Cornell University Press (Ithaca, NY), 1956.

Earl Schenck Miers, editor, *The American Story,* Channel Press, 1956.

John A. Garraty, editor, *The Unforgettable Americans,* Channel Press, 1960.

Edmond Cahn, editor, *The Great Rights,* Macmillan (New York City), 1963.

Robert B. Luce, editor, *The Faces of Five Decades,* Simon & Schuster (New York City), 1964.

(Author of introduction) Fowler V. Harper, *Justice Rutledge and the Bright Constellation,* Bobbs-Merrill, 1965.

John A. Garraty, editor, *Historical Viewpoints,* Volume 1 (to 1877), Harper (New York City), 1970.

Arthur Schlesinger, Jr., editor, *A History of American Presidential Elections,* Chelsea House (New York City), 1971.

*OTHER*

Contributor of articles to *New Republic,* and occasional contributor to law reviews, historical magazines, and encyclopedias. Writer of many pamphlets on conservation of wildlife and scenic areas published by Emergency Conservation Commission; author of a survey and report to Secretary of the Interior in 1938, on which basis President Roosevelt enlarged Olympic National Park in 1940.

*SIDELIGHTS:* Irving Brant was a journalist and constitutional historian who is best remembered for his six-volume biography of James Madison, the fourth president of the United States. Brant began his research for the Madison biography in 1937 and worked on it for the next twenty-three years, utilizing primary sources almost to the exclusion of all else. The resulting work was described by *Nation* contributor George Genzmer as "one of the most lastingly useful of American political biographies," and by *Library Journal* reviewer Herbert Cahoon as "a work of stature and permanent value."

Whole volumes in the Madison biography concern themselves with the statesman's role in framing the United States Constitution and determining the direction the American presidency would take. "With imagination and through diligence, Mr. Brant has presented a more complete and a more interesting Madison than has been done by any of his predecessors," declared *Christian Science Monitor* correspondent R. A. Brown. "The figure that does emerge is challenging." According to Nathan Schachner in the *American History Review,* Brant "has sometimes been too lavish with his material, going off into side paths which, however interesting, have only a tenuous connection with the onward march of his hero's story. . . . However, the sheer mass and research of Mr. Brant's

volumes make them the source to which all students of history must turn in the future for any extended study of Madison and his times. They will not easily be superseded." G. W. Johnson perhaps best summed up the critical response to the Madison biography, writing in the *New York Herald Tribune Book Review:* "For the ordinary reader what really matters is that here is a beautifully written book about a genuinely great man concerning whom few Americans know as much as they should."

In addition to his comprehensive Madison studies, Brant published several books on constitutional issues, including the well-received *The Bill of Rights: Its Origin and Meaning.* Examining no less than sixty-three separate rights and liberties denoted in various parts of the Constitution, Brant related these rights to Old English law and the special pressures of frontier life in America. To quote *New York Times Book Review* contributor M. R. Konvitz, the work is "a solid study of the origin (and only incidentally of the meaning) of our constitutional liberties. . . . Mr. Brant's book is history and at the same time a tract for the times. It is written argumentatively and will generate partisan debate. . . . This volume will remain indispensable." *Saturday Review* essayist Roger Baldwin offered a concurrent view. "This is not only a first-rate historical study written with anecdotal color," the critic wrote, "it is also an advocacy of the Bill of Rights as originally intended, to protect citizens from abuses of governmental power through intervention by the Supreme Court as the interpreter of the Constitution. . . . It is in the purest libertarian tradition."

*BIOGRAPHICAL/CRITICAL SOURCES:*

*PERIODICALS*

*American History Review,* October, 1948, p. 153; October, 1950, p. 124; October, 1954, p. 126.

*American Political Science Review,* October, 1948, p. 1026; September, 1950, p. 755.

*Atlantic,* December, 1941.

*Books,* September 28, 1941, p. 4.

*Book World,* May 7, 1972, p. 1.

*Chicago Sun,* March 18, 1948.

*Chicago Sunday Tribune,* April 23, 1950, p. 4.

*Choice,* September, 1970, p. 926.

*Christian Science Monitor,* April 2, 1948, p. 16; April 20, 1950, p. 18; November 18, 1953, p. 9.

*Commonweal,* May 7, 1948, p. 83.

*Economist,* August 15, 1970, p. 41.

*Ethics,* October, 1948, p. 49.

*Library Journal,* February 1, 1948, p. 195; March 15, 1970.

*Nation,* May 1, 1948, p. 482; August 19, 1950, p. 173; November 14, 1953, p. 405.

*New Republic,* January 19, 1942, p. 91; March 22, 1948, p. 27; September 4, 1950, p. 18; November 30, 1953, p. 17.

*New Yorker,* March 20, 1948, p. 119.

*New York Herald Tribune Book Review,* April 30, 1950, p. 5; November 1, 1953, p. 8.

*New York Herald Tribune Weekly Book Review,* February 29, 1948, p. 1.

*New Republic,* November 27, 1965, p. 38.

*New Yorker,* April 29, 1950, p. 107; November 7, 1953, p. 184.

*New York Times,* February 29, 1948, p. 3; April 9, 1950, p. 1; October 4, 1953, p. 3.

*New York Times Book Review,* December 12, 1965, p. 6.

*San Francisco Chronicle,* April 18, 1948, p. 15; June 18, 1950, p. 12.

*Saturday Review,* April 8, 1953; July 31, 1954, p. 37; January 1, 1966, p. 28; May 13, 1972, p. 83.

*Saturday Review of Literature,* May 15, 1948, p. 11; April 8, 1950, p. 9.

*Springfield Republican,* October 27, 1941, p. 6.

*Time,* March 15, 1948, p. 108.

*Times Literary Supplement,* October 30, 1970, p. 1278.

*U.S. Quarterly Book Review,* March, 1954, p. 2.*

\*　　\*　　\*

## BREUER, Lee 1937-

*PERSONAL:* Born February 6, 1937, in Philadelphia, PA; son of Joseph B. (an architect) and Sara (a designer; maiden name, Leopold) Breuer; married Ruth Maleczech (an actress and director), July 27, 1978; children: Clove Galilee, Lute Ramblin'. *Education:* University of California, Los Angeles, B.A., 1958; attended San Francisco State University; studied works of Berliner Ensemble and Growtowski, 1965-70.

*ADDRESSES: Home*—92 St. Marks Pl., No. 3, New York, NY 10009. *Office*—Mabou Mines, c/o Performing Arts Services, 325 Spring St., New York, NY 10013. *Agent*—Lynn Davis, Davis-Cohen Associates, 513A Avenue of the Americas, New York, NY 10011.

*CAREER:* San Francisco Actors' Workshop, San Francisco, CA, director, 1963-65, directing credits include *The House of Bernarda Alba,* 1963; director of plays in Europe, 1965-70, including *Mother Courage,* produced in Paris, 1967, *The Messingkauf Dialogues,* produced at Edinburgh Festival, 1968, and *Play,* produced in Paris and New York, 1969 and 1970; Mabou Mines, New York City, co-artistic director, 1970—, directing credits include *Red Horse Animation,* 1970 and 1972, *B. Beaver Animation,* 1974, *Mabou Mines Performs Samuel Beckett,* 1975, *Shaggy Dog Animation,* 1978, *A Prelude to Death in Venice,* 1980, and *Hajj,* 1982. Also director and choreographer of *The Saint and the Football Players,* produced at American Dance Festival, summer, 1976, director of *Lulu,* produced for American Repertory Theatre at Harvard University, 1980, and director of *The Tempest,* produced at New York Shakespeare Festival, 1981. Director with New York Shakespeare Festival, 1982—; co-artistic director of Re.Cher.Chez., a studio for the avant-grade performing arts. Member of faculties of Yale Drama School, 1978-80, Harvard Extension, 1981-82, and New York University, 1981-82. Lecturer at universities and colleges, including various campuses of University of California, and at art centers. Member of board of directors of Theatre Communications Group, 1979-81; panel member of National Endowment for the Arts and Inter-Art.

*MEMBER:* PEN, Dramatists Guild.

*AWARDS, HONORS:* Obie Award from *Village Voice* for best play, 1978, for *Shaggy Dog Animation,* and for writing and directing, 1980, for *A Prelude to Death in Venice;* fellowships from Creative Artists Public Service Program, 1980, Guggenheim Foundation, 1980, National Endowment for the Arts, 1980 and 1982, and Rockefeller Foundation, 1981; Los Angeles Drama Critics Circle Award, 1986; Tony Award, 1988; American Express/Kennedy Center's Fund for New American Plays grant, 1995.

*WRITINGS:*

*PLAYS*

(Adaptor) Samuel Beckett, *The Lost Ones,* first produced in New York City at Theatre for the New City, February 7, 1976, produced in Los Angeles, CA, at Mark Taper Theatre Forum, March 7, 1979.

*Animations* (animation scripts; contains *Red Horse Animation,* first produced in New York City at

Guggenheim Museum, November, 1970, revised version produced in New York City at La Mama Experimental Theatre Club, March, 1972; *B. Beaver Animation,* first produced in New York City at Whitney Museum of American Art, 1974, produced Off-Broadway at Public Theatre, March, 1977; *Shaggy Dog Animation,* first produced Off-Broadway at Public Theatre, February, 1978), P.A.J. Press, 1979.

*A Prelude to Death in Venice* (first produced Off-Broadway at Public Theatre, May 18, 1980), published in *New Plays U.S.A. No. 1,* edited by James Leverett, Theatre Communications Group, 1982.

*Sister Suzie Cinema,* first produced Off-Broadway at Public Theatre, June, 1980.

*Gospel at Colonnus* (adaptation of Sophocles' *Oedipus at Colonnus* as translated by Robert Fitzgerald), first produced at Brooklyn Academy of Music, November, 1983.

*Hajj* (a performance poem; first produced in 1982), P.A.J. Press, 1983.

*Sister Suzie Cinema: The Collected Poems and Performances, 1976-1986,* Theatre Communications Group (New York City), 1987.

*The Gospel at Colonus* (produced in New York City, 1983), Theatre Communications Group (New York City), 1989.

*The Warrior Ant,* produced in New York City, 1988.

*Lear* (based on Shakespeare's *King Lear*), produced in New York City, 1990.

*An Epidog,* produced in New York City, 1996.

Lyricist. Contributor of articles to periodicals, including *Village Voice* and *Soho Weekly News.*

SIDELIGHTS: As a writer and director interested in innovations in the performing arts, Lee Breuer works with a troupe which was originally part of the La Mama Experimental Theatre Company and is now an independent artistic collaborative. Mabou Mines, named after the Canadian mining community where the troupe rehearsed in 1970, presents productions that expand visual performances, adding another dimension to artistic experience. The group, "one of our most valuable experimental companies" in the eyes of *New York Times* critic Mel Gussow, "is explorative—extending the possibilities of theater into the visual arts." Juggling language and nonverbal imagery in a visual environment, Breuer concentrates on original writings and adaptations suitable for the "total theatre" of the Mabou Mines.

Writing in *Contemporary Dramatists,* Bill Coco described Breuer's approach to writing for the stage:

"The greater part of Breuer's dramatic writing is structured in the form of a labyrinthine monologue that he then 'animates' in a richly physicalized stage setting and performance. The monologues telescope many identities into a single voice that in turn splices together fragments of many linguistic worlds. . . . Through juxtaposition he develops a complex mode of irony, dominated by a sophisticated use of punning. This artistic strategy allows the poem and its speakers to subvert the efficacy of the expressive language of emotion without denying the reality of the emotion itself."

Breuer's first stage work, *Red Horse Animation,* sets out to construct an image. "This attempt at ritualistic theatre, bold and bald in its nameless imagery, had the sovereign merit of aspiration," noted Clive Barnes in a *New York Times* review. Following *Red Horse, B. Beaver Animation* is a stream of consciousness presentation of sea images and marine life. The stage of this production literally unfolds with the aquatic narrative. "The focus is the set," Gussow observed in another review, "an assemblage of boards, planks, poles and fabric" that transforms itself from a stage to the sea to a boat. "The work has a compulsive fascination," the critic wrote. "The words waft over us," he explained, "but the pictures are like optical illusions." Two actors, for instance, intertwine to create a giant crawling creature. Or, as one actor peers into a pail, the audience sees that it contains two amputated human feet submerged in water.

Like the set for *B. Beaver Animation,* the stage of *Shaggy Dog Animation* changes, too, from a cloud to a house to a cracked kitchen floor. A study of devotion, this work is a mechanized, acoustical "cascade of imagery" that parodies modern culture, including romance, through canine motifs. It "is a devious and difficult piece of theater," Gussow remarked, "which is as tantalizing as it is obfuscating." Commenting on Breuer, the critic noted that "he is a born punster, and not one double entendre about dogs escapes him. His cleverness with words is amply demonstrated in a long-winded comic monologue about the art world—an artist's hectic search for public and private support that ends with the discovery of a 'patron in a peartree.' "

Another Breuer production, *A Prelude to Death in Venice,* submitted Michael Feingold in the *Village Voice,* "is a violent shock—a triumph at the end of a long, dismal year in which the theatre has for the most part lacked not only glory but even mere competence and reason, a lush tropical plant rising unexpectedly out of a barren industrial waste." Loosely related to Thomas Mann's work of the same name, *Prelude* is the story of John, a large Bunraku puppet, plagued by the neuroses and obsessions of the modern spiritual crisis identified as contemporary life. Poised between two touch-tone pay telephones, John talks to his girlfriends, answering machines, his mother; at one point he punches out Bach's *G Major Prelude and Fugue* on the phones. The most critical props, "the phones," said Gerald Rabkin in the *New Statesman,* "become . . . [John's] hope, his succor, his escape, even his art."

In the work, Breuer attempts "to tickle and then to startle," Feingold maintained, "to resume tickling when the shock has worn off and then, suddenly jam an emotional knife in the very ribs that are being tickled." The author, on the other hand, contends that *Prelude,* wants "permission to subjectivise," thereby allowing ordinary theatrical productions to "wait for poetry." With *Prelude,* Breuer's ability with language becomes even more apparent. According to Feingold, "Breuer's brilliant gift for compressing it all into the life of one rattled, driven, assertive and terrified 'dummy' is poured into some of the richest language ever heard onstage in this country—not rich in the sense of conventional poetry, decorated in careful old images and trips to the dictionary for two-dollar words, but rich in its awareness of the living language that we speak, its flexibility, its multiple meanings and unconscious intents."

In the 1996 work *An Epidog* Breuer presented, according to Chris Haines in *American Theatre,* "the after-death account of a dog's life told through Japanese Bunraku puppetry." *An Epidog* was performed by Mabou Mines in conjunction with a revival of Breuer's *Red Horse Animation,* the two plays exploring new territory by combining such technologies as video-conferencing and a World Wide Web hook-up to create a live-action performance which was also viewed and interacted with by people from all over the world. Some videotaped actions by live actors were animated and broadcast during the live performance of the play, while a director was able to change and manipulate the virtual stage backgrounds broadcast over the Web. The result, Haines noted, approached the actor/audience configuration in startling ways."

Like his own productions, the works Breuer stages and directs are innovative and experimental. Though a recent directing endeavor, a classic by Shakespeare, met with critical trepidation because of its avant-garde rendition, "Breuer's work on *The Tempest,*"

commented Robert Brustein in the *New Republic,* "is an honest effort to create a Shakespeare for our time." Although Brustein mentions some reservations about Breuer's staging (that it "escapes classification," for one), he "came away from the production feeling rather exhilarated." And, despite the theatrical gadgetry and free interpretation, Breuer's *Tempest,* Jack Kroll commented in *Newsweek,* captures Shakespeare's idea of a reconciliation involving "the great globe itself," regardless of man-made imperialisms. Beneath all the hoopla, Kroll maintained, "there's a loving grasp of this play that's Shakespeare's final covenant with an intractable world."

Breuer told *CA:* "I write performance poetry. As a director, I am primarily concerned with my own work. At present, I am involved with the use of video and amplified sound in live performance. As a lyricist, I work with the composer Bob Telson and the doo-wop group Fourteen Karat Soul."

*BIOGRAPHICAL/CRITICAL SOURCES:*

BOOKS

*Contemporary Dramatists,* 5th edition, St. James Press (Detroit), 1993.
*Gale Theatre Annual, 1979-1980,* Gale (Detroit), 1981.

PERIODICALS

*American Film,* January-February, 1983.
*American Theatre,* January, 1996, p. 64.
*Nation,* August 8, 1981; May 19, 1997, p. 34.
*New Republic,* August 22-29, 1981.
*New Statesman,* August 1, 1980.
*Newsweek,* July 20, 1981.
*New York,* July 20, 1981.
*New York Times,* November 25, 1963, November 20, 1970, March 25, 1977, February 8, 1978, May 19, 1980, May 20, 1980.
*Time,* July 20, 1981.
*Variety,* July 15, 1981.
*Village Voice,* May 26, 1980.

\*     \*     \*

**BREWSTER, Elizabeth (Winifred) 1922-**

*PERSONAL:* Born August 26, 1922, in Chipman, New Brunswick, Canada; daughter of Frederick John and Ethel (Day) Brewster. *Education:* University of New Brunswick, Fredericton, B.A., 1946; Radcliff College, Cambridge, A.M., 1947; attended Kings College, London, 1949-50; University of Toronto, B.L.S., 1953; Indiana University, Ph.D., 1962.

*ADDRESSES: Home*—910 Ninth Street East, Apt. 206, Saskatoon, Saskatchewan S7H 0N1, Canada. *Office*—Department of English, University of Saskatchewan, Saskatoon, Saskatchewan S7N 0W0 Canada.

*CAREER:* Cataloger, Carleton University Library, Ottawa, Ontario, 1953-57, and Indiana University Library, Bloomington, 1957-58; University of Victoria, Victoria, British Columbia, member of English department, 1960-61; Mount Allison University, Sackville, New Brunswick, reference librarian, 1961-65; New Brunswick Legislative Library, Fredericton, cataloger, 1965-68; University of Alberta, Edmonton, cataloger of rare books in university library, 1968-70, visiting assistant professor of English, 1970-71; University of Saskatchewan, Saskatoon, assistant professor, 1972-75, associate professor, 1975-80, professor of English, 1980-90, professor emeritus, 1990—.

*AWARDS, HONORS:* Pratt Gold Medal and prize, Kings College, London, 1953; Senior Artists awards, Canada Council, 1971-72, 1976, 1978-79, and 1985-86; President's Medal, University of Western Ontario, 1979, for poetry; Litt.D., University of New Brunswick, 1982; Canadian Broadcasting Corporation (CBC) award for poetry, 1990, for poem sequence *Wheel of Change;* Lifetime Excellence in the Arts Award, Saskatchewan Arts Board, 1995; shortlisted for Governor General's award for poetry, 1996.

*WRITINGS:*

POETRY

*East Coast,* Ryerson (Toronto), 1951.
*Lillooet,* Ryerson, 1954.
*Roads and Other Poems,* Ryerson, 1957.
(With others) *Five New Brunswick Poets,* edited by Fred Cogswell, Fiddlehead (Fredericton, New Brunswick), 1962.
*Passage of Summer: Selected Poems,* Ryerson, 1969.
*Sunrise North,* Clarke, Irwin (Toronto), 1972.
*In Search of Eros,* Clarke, Irwin (Toronto), 1974.
*Sometimes I Think of Moving,* Oberon (Ottawa), 1977.
*The Way Home,* Oberon, 1982.
*Digging In,* Oberon, 1982.

*Selected Poems of Elizabeth Brewster, 1944-1984,* two volumes, Oberon, 1985.
*Entertaining Angels,* Oberon, 1988.
*Spring Again: Poems,* Oberon, 1990.
*Wheel of Change,* Oberon, 1993.
*Footnotes to the Book of Job,* Oberon, 1995.

PROSE

*The Sisters: A Novel,* Oberon, 1974.
*It's Easy to Fall on the Ice: Ten Stories,* Oberon, 1977.
*Junction* (novel), Black Moss (Windsor, Ontario), 1982.
*A House Full of Women* (short stories), Oberon, 1983.
*Visitations* (short stories), Oberon, 1987.
*The Invention of Truth* (memoir), Oberon, 1991.
*Away from Home,* Oberon, 1995.

OTHER

Contributor to periodicals, including *Canadian Forum, Canadian Literature, Dalhousie Review,* and *Fiddlehead.*

*SIDELIGHTS:* Canadian poet and novelist Elizabeth Brewster writes, as she herself has often noted, to better understand herself, her world, and those around her. Brewster's "genius for understatement" is, according to *Contemporary Women Poets* contributor John Robert Colombo, among the several qualities that make her verse "like a wine which improves with age; its taste mellows in memory." Colombo suggested that Brewster's two-volume *Selected Poems,* published in 1985, features some of her best work, and asserted that over the course of her career, the poet "has found a way to turn fancies and musings into meaningful subjects for poems, and she has mastered the casual aside."

In 1990's *Spring Again Poems,* Brewster's work "allows the reader to overhear the inner conversations that produce her poems," according to Anne Rayner writing in *Canadian Literature.* Much of the volume is a personal response to Ezra Pound's *Cantos,* and it has a distinctly journalistic, personal flavor. L. Maingon, writing in *Canadian Materials,* describes the tension in the poems as Brewster's "playing [of] her feminine reality against the chaos of Pound's . . . masculine world." In this volume, Rayner notes, Brewster explores the relationship between "sources of myth" and "twentieth-century Canadian prairie reality": "'I cannot make it new,'" Brewster exclaims, "'but I can make it Canadian.'"

*Wheel of Change,* published in 1993, in honor of Brewster's seventieth birthday, is a book of poems divided into sections in which each she meditates "on her life in [Canada] over the past fifty years," states Ian Dempsey in *Canadian Materials.* While Dempsey notes that Brewster seeks "intellectual insight . . . in [her] mild, elegiac meditations" he also adds that "she never achieves ecstasy, only wonder." The title sequence of poems, *Wheels of Change,* did win Brewster the CBC award for poetry in 1990.

In her 1991 memoir, *The Invention of Truth,* Brewster changes gears and offers her readers a text that is part fact, part imagination, part poetry, and part fiction. It is composed, according to Virginia Beaton's *Books in Canada* review, of "poems, some family photos, journal excerpts, and dreams," and it is largely "about memory, and the way truth changes over a lifetime." In Brewster's own words, reported by Barbara Pell in *Canadian Literature,* the book is a "'sidelong autobiography'" which explores family, friends, and Brewster's belief "that art elevates 'deliberate ordinariness . . . to the level of myth.'"

Both Pell and Beaton, however, lament the many gaps in *The Invention of Truth.* Pell finds the book ultimately "has too many unacknowledged gaps . . . and depths . . . to be satisfying," while Beaton more generously allows that "the overall tone of *The Invention of Truth* . . . tantalizes the reader because of what is left unsaid."

In spite of the faint praise which these critics have for Brewster's single attempt at non-fiction, she remains well known and well respected for her poetry and her prose. According to Maingon, Brewster is not merely another talented writer; in fact she is considered by the critic to be "one of Canada's major poets."

*BIOGRAPHICAL/CRITICAL SOURCES:*

*BOOKS*

*Contemporary Women Poets,* St. James Press (Detroit), 1997.
*Dictionary of Literary Biography,* Volume 60: *Canadian Writers since 1960, Second Series,* Gale (Detroit), 1987.

*PERIODICALS*

*Ariel,* July, 1973.
*Books in Canada,* May, 1992, p. 50; February, 1994, p. 45.

*Canadian Book Review Annual,* 1995, p. 44.
*Canadian Forum,* January, 1997, p. 46.
*Canadian Literature,* autumn, 1974; winter, 1992, pp. 137-39; spring, 1993, pp. 157-58.
*Canadian Materials,* November, 1990, pp. 291-92; March-April, 1994, pp. 42-43.
*Essays on Canadian Writing,* summer-fall, 1980.

\* \* \*

## BRYAN, C(ourtlandt) D(ixon) B(arnes) 1936-

*PERSONAL:* Born April 22, 1936, in New York, NY; son of Joseph III and Katharine (Barnes) Bryan; married Phoebe Miller, December 28, 1961 (divorced September, 1966); married Judith Snyder, December 21, 1967 (divorced July, 1978); children: (first marriage) J. St. George III, Lansing Becket; (second marriage) Amanda Barnes. *Education:* Yale University, B.A., 1958.

*ADDRESSES: Home*—19 Union St., Guilford, CT 06437. *Agent*—Lynn Nesbit, Janklow & Nesbit, 598 Madison Ave., New York, NY 10022. *Email*—cdbbryan@aol.com; fax: 203-453-6318.

*CAREER:* Writer. Editor, *Monocle* (magazine), beginning 1961. Colorado State University, writer-in-residence, winter, 1967; University of Iowa, visiting lecturer in writers workshop, 1967-69; Yale University, special editorial consultant, 1970; University of Wyoming, visiting professor, 1975; Columbia University, adjunct professor, 1976; Writers Community, New York City, fiction director, beginning 1977; University of Virginia, lecturer in English, spring, 1983; Bard College, Bard Center fellow, spring, 1984. *Military service:* U.S. Army, 1958-60, 1961-62.

*MEMBER:* Yale Club.

*AWARDS, HONORS:* Harper Prize Novel award, 1965, for *P. S. Wilkinson; Friendly Fire* named among top five nonfiction books of the year by *Time,* and rated best nonfiction book of the year by *New York Daily News,* both 1976; award from National Endowment for the Arts, 1979; Guggenheim fellow, 1986; George Foster Peabody Award (shared), for television production of *Friendly Fire.*

*WRITINGS:*

*P. S. Wilkinson* (novel; Literary Guild selection), Harper (New York City), 1965.

*The Great Dethriffe* (novel), Dutton (New York City), 1970.

*Friendly Fire* (nonfiction; Book-of-the-Month Club selected alternate), Putnam (New York City), 1976.

*The National Air and Space Museum* (nonfiction; Book-of-the-Month Club selected alternate), art by David Larkin, photographs by Michael Freeman, Robert Golden, and Dennis Rolfe, Abrams (New York City), 1979, second edition with photographs by Jonathan Wallen, 1988.

*Beautiful Women; Ugly Scenes* (novel; Literary Guild alternate), Doubleday (New York City), 1983.

*The National Geographic Society: 100 Years of Adventure and Discovery,* Abrams, 1987.

(Author of introduction) *In the Eye of Desert Storm: Photographers of the Gulf War,* Abrams, 1991.

*Close Encounters of the Fourth Kind: Alien Abduction, UFOs, and the Conference at M.I.T.,* Knopf (New York City), 1995.

Also author of narration for Swedish film, *The Face of War,* 1963. Contributor to *New York Times Magazine, New York Times Book Review, Harper's, Esquire, Saturday Review, New Yorker,* and other periodicals.

*ADAPTATIONS: Friendly Fire* was adapted as a television film by Fay Kanin for the American Broadcasting Co. (ABC), 1979.

*WORK IN PROGRESS: A History of the Mayo Clinic,* Abrams, 1999.

*SIDELIGHTS:* Though probably best known as the author of the nonfiction work *Friendly Fire,* C. D. B. Bryan first attracted literary attention in 1965, when his book *P. S. Wilkinson* won the Harper Prize Novel award. John Leonard describes the author's first work in the *New York Times* as "the story of a WASP-ish young man's groping toward a moral stance in the nineteen-fifties. Like the decade itself, it was cool and ambivalent, a series of skirmishes culminating in an overly tidy coming-to-awareness." *P. S. Wilkinson* is "entertainment of a high order," declares David Dempsey in the *Saturday Review,* adding that the virtues of the book are "numerous" and "accessible."

A number of reviewers were quick to identify the autobiographical elements in *P. S. Wilkinson.* A critic for the *Times Literary Supplement* writes: "Mr. Bryan organizes his abundant material with a true novelist's skill and expresses it in entirely adequate prose. [He] is a novelist who appears to rely largely on his pow-

ers of observation. Bryan seems to have an astonishing memory, rather than an ebulliently creative imagination. It is an exercise in total recall." Dempsey believes that Bryan "*is* P. S. Wilkinson, even to the insistence on those initials." Among the experiences the author and his character have in common: military service in Korea, graduation from Yale, and having been caught cheating in prep school.

Discussing his output with Joseph McLellan in the *Washington Post,* Bryan spoke about how the autobiographical elements in *P. S. Wilkinson* fit into the scope of his work: "You tend to put everything you know into the first novel, and then you rewrite it for the second. My first book was a novel, which encouraged me to write a second novel, which discouraged me from writing a third." That second novel was *The Great Dethriffe,* published in 1970.

Reflecting on the similarity in subject matter shared by *P. S. Wilkinson* and *The Great Dethriffe,* Leonard remarks: "On the evidence of [the latter], Mr. Bryan is prepared to be the historian of [the nineteen-fifties] generation. The book, a rewriting of 'The Great Gatsby' with a Gatsby who got what he wanted and couldn't abide it, is actually about a decade of illusions, unpreparedness and, ultimately, desperation." The story follows the disastrous marriage of George Dethriffe, "a gentlemanly young business sort," according to Jonathan Yardley in the *New York Times Book Review,* "whose detached exterior conceals a somewhat muted Gatsbyesque concern for the Daisy Buchanan of this novel. She is Alice Townsend, an incandescently beautiful Daisy-Zelda who turns out to be a classic bitch." A *New Republic* critic, after remarking upon the "laborious parallel between Scott Fitzgerald's characters and Bryan's," calls *The Great Dethriffe* "remarkable for its grace and depth of perception." Geoffrey Wolf of *Newsweek* notes the improvement of Bryan's second book over his first, calling *The Great Dethriffe* "droll" and "articulate." The reviewer for the *Times Literary Supplement* speaks of the "clever way Mr. Bryan has organized a prose which is a match for the specifically contemporary aspects of the narrative but which also harbours witty and relevant imitations of Fitzgerald."

*Friendly Fire,* perhaps Bryan's most acclaimed work to date, was published in 1976. A work of nonfiction, *Friendly Fire* relates the story of Michael Mullen, an American soldier accidentally killed in Vietnam by artillery fire from American troops—"misadventure" as a result of "friendly fire" in the parlance of the U.S. Army—and the profound effect his death had on his parents' perceptions of their government and the military. *New York Times* critic Christopher Lehmann-Haupt outlines the circumstances that eventually led Mrs. Mullen to reject her government's policies and become an anti-war activist: "Peg and Gene Mullen, two solid middle-American residents of Black Hawk County, Iowa . . . learned in February 1970 of the 'non-combat' death on an infantry mission of their oldest son, Michael, and were trying vainly to wrest from Washington a clear explanation of the [events] surrounding Michael's death. [The government seemed] obstinate and callous (the only word of sympathy from the White House had been a note from a minor Presidential aide attached to Xerox copies of President Nixon's 'Vietnamization' speeches), [and] determined to routinize and obscure Michael's sacrifice." Diane Johnson elaborates further in the *New York Review of Books,* explaining how "the army could not keep Michael's rank, the nature of his wounds, or even his personal effects straight. Sympathetic letters ostensibly from two different officers were really sent by some staff clerk using the same slightly awry date stamp. The army docked Michael's paycheck nine days, penalizing him for getting killed before he had served long enough to earn back his advance leave."

According to R. Z. Sheppard in *Time,* this state of affairs "radicalized [Michael's] parents—particularly his mother—because their basic conservative values had been shattered. As Peg Mullen became convinced that her son's life was wasted by an accident in a war that itself was a mistake, the line between her grief and fury vanished." And with nothing of substance forthcoming from the government to persuade them that they were not the victims of some sort of intrigue or coverup, the Mullens grew increasingly vehement as time passed. "They not only joined the national anti-war movement," writes Robert Sherrill in the *New York Times Book Review,* "but became a mini-movement of their own, buying newspaper ads to whip up public sentiment, churning out a storm of Xeroxed appeals and protests, adopting other soldiers' causes, keeping the phone lines hot to the Pentagon, marching on Washington. They were, in short, transformed." The Mullens took out a full-page advertisement in a Des Moines newspaper, one showing 714 crosses to stand for the 714 Iowans who had been killed in the war. They paid for the ad with their son's government life insurance.

Aside from the extensive interviews he conducted with the Mullens, Bryan set out to investigate the death of Michael on his own. His conclusions: that despite the overwhelming bureaucratic incompetence, insensitivity, and dishonesty to which the Mullens were subjected, there was not, as they had imagined, any concerted conspiracy to conceal or falsify the circumstances of Michael's death. He had died when gunners failed to take into account the height of the trees on the hill where he was sleeping. A round intended by artillerymen to clear the hill struck a tree, exploded, and killed him instantly in his sleep. Walter Clemons states in *Newsweek,* however: "It would be a gross misreading of what Bryan has accomplished if the reader, on finding that the Mullens were mistaken in their obsessive search for a conspiratorial coverup, were to conclude that they were unhinged troublemakers. Bryan's point is that Vietnam unhinged us all and inflicted unhealed wounds on this country." Peter Gardner agrees in the *Saturday Review* and sees the Mullens as representative of the "'silent majority,' who now had lost faith in their country. Explicitly and implicitly, it's a dramatic comment on what the war did to America."

Some critics have expressed doubts about Bryan's version of the actual events surrounding Michael Mullen's death, arguing that the author was too accepting of the explanations and attitudes of official authority, including a Lt. Colonel Norman Schwarzkopf—Mullen's battalion commander, who later went on to become the general in command of operations in the Persian Gulf war. Others have faulted him for his reconstructing conversations he himself did not hear, and for giving himself a role in the story. Commenting on this last point, R. Thomas Berner writes in *Dictionary of Literary Biography:* "One of the jolting aspects of *Friendly Fire* is the appearance of Bryan in the story. He changes from Bryan the author to Bryan the investigator or from Bryan the narrator to Bryan the character as he attempts to learn how Michael died. The story line changes from the third person and voice of Peg and Gene Mullen to the first person of Bryan and the mixed voice of Bryan and the Mullens." Yet, Berner decides, "once the jolt is over the reader begins to appreciate what Bryan has done. He does not let the story rest until he searches out his best notion of the truth. This is the method of a good journalist. Bryan uses the opening two-thirds of the book as a device to get the reader to the last third. . . . He admits that he structured the story as a mystery in order to hook the reader." The critic concludes that the "feeling that he had somehow violated his intention to be a journalist is false; he did behave as a journalist by seeking out the many sides of a dispute."

*Friendly Fire* has received praise from numerous reviewers. Berner reports that "some critics rated *Friendly Fire* one of the best works of nonfiction published in 1976, and Walter Clemons in *Newsweek* called it one of the three best books on the Vietnam War." Johnson believes that "From the interaction of the reporter, . . . the Mullens, and the military, there emerges a significant and subtle reflection on the moral conditions of the society which produced and variously tolerated or rejected, the war in Vietnam." "*Friendly Fire* is not another self-righteous lamentation about the U.S.'s tragic blunderings in Southeast Asia," writes Sheppard, "rather, it is as close to elemental tragedy as any nonfiction account to come out of the war."

Bryan's next work was to be of a decidedly different nature. According to McLellan, the author was chosen to write *The National Air and Space Museum* "because of his reputation as an all-purpose journeyman writer—one who could write to fit the prose between the pictures which are the book's major attraction." Published in 1979, *The National Air and Space Museum* is an illustrated record of a museum that is, as Bryan notes in his text, "more popular than the Lincoln Memorial, the Washington Monument, the United States Capitol, and the White House combined." With photographs by Dennis Rolfe, Michael Freeman, and Robert Golden, "the planes, black, yellow, silver, silhouetted against the white pages, seem to zoom out at you," says Henry S. F. Cooper, Jr. in the *New York Times Book Review.* "Many are works of art, the camera makes clear, as well as technology." Tom Zio of the *Washington Post* believes that the book, arranged as it is, "roughly organized to correspond with the museum's compartmentalization, [reads] as a sprightly history of flight. [It] brings a new sense of awe to America's most popular museum." Cooper calls *The National Air and Space Museum* "a lively and joyous celebration of one of the things Americans do best."

Though it has garnered mixed reviews, Bryan's third novel *Beautiful Women; Ugly Scenes* is seen by a number of critics to be the author's finest work of fiction. Assessing the work in the *Chicago Tribune Book World,* Mary Gray Hughes places *Beautiful Women; Ugly Scenes* in the context of Bryan's other novels: "In all three he has been concerned with links between emotional feelings and the quality of sexual experience with women. *Beautiful Women; Ugly Scenes* is very much Bryan's funniest, most pungent novel, and in it his concern for the complexity of relations between the sexes is most effectively pre-

sented." Though Michiko Kakutani finds that "the book is unwieldy, its prose at times opaque," in the *New York Times,* the reviewer feels that "its portrait of a man and his collapsing marriage is also powerful and disturbing, and it invests the familiar banalities of upper-middle class life with seriousness and art."

*Beautiful Women; Ugly Scenes* relates the story of a man close to Bryan's own age when he wrote the novel, a filmmaker who in his own words has come to the conclusion that "in a sense, I have been at war with women for most of my life." The novel, according to Alice Adams in the *New York Times Book Review,* is thus an attempt at "an honest account of one man's distress over what he reasonably sees as his failures in love: two finished marriages, innumerable unsatisfactory sexual encounters." The narrator's war with women has come to a halt in the person of his present companion, a Frenchwoman named Odette, and the substance of the book deals with his reflections on the slow, painful process he underwent on the way to finally establishing a meaningful relationship with a member of the opposite sex. The narration therefore, in the words of Charles Champlin in the *Los Angeles Times Book Review,* is "structurally a long flashback, with lesser flashbacks and flashforwards within to sustain a good deal of suspense. Will the unnamed protagonist have discovered enough about himself to hang on to the woman he demonstrably loves above all others?"

*Beautiful Women; Ugly Scenes* follows in the tradition of Bryan's earlier works of fiction in that critics have been swift to comment on his use of realistic detail in combination with a style of narration only one step removed from autobiography. In his comments Champlin focuses on the novelist's talent for translating life experience into art: "It is unsporting and essentially irrelevant to ponder how much personal experience (read anguish) has been required to populate and drive a work of fiction. But what makes *Beautiful Women; Ugly Scenes* especially readable is a suspicion that Bryan stood so close to the emotional heat, as witness or protagonist, that the story is surely memory, not dream."

Kakutani perceives a similar process at work. Bryan "seems to have a sad, knowing acquaintance with all the nasty inside jokes and sarcastic inflections that disaffected lovers employ," Kakutani asserts. "[He] often lets the marginal distance between himself and his hero collapse altogether; as a result there is little irony to the narrator's commentary, and much of the book sounds as though it had been blurted out instead of written." James Atlas of the *Atlantic* insists, however, that the author's techniques are far more sophisticated and conscious than such commentary would allow: "The very bluntness of Bryan's style . . . gives the novel a kind of sociological interest. It's as if he can't be bothered with literature; things are so bad he has to blurt out his story however he can. [His] way of confiding in the reader, thinking out loud, returning obsessively to crucial scenes like a patient on the couch, is a calculated literary tactic; I have rarely read a novel that so thoroughly suppressed all traces of its fictional design. The art is in the artlessness." Atlas finds the novel "utterly absorbing."

For a complete interview with Bryan, see *Contemporary Authors New Revisions,* Volume 13.

## BIOGRAPHICAL/CRITICAL SOURCES:

### BOOKS

Connery, Thomas B., editor, *Sourcebook of American Literary Journalism,* Greenwood Press (Westport, CT), 1992.

*Contemporary Literary Criticism,* Volume 29, Gale (Detroit), 1984.

*Dictionary of Literary Biography,* Volume 185: *American Literary Journalists, 1945-1995, First Series,* Gale, 1997.

Schroeder, Eric James, *Vietnam, We've All Been There: Interviews with American Writers,* Praeger (Westport, CT), 1992.

Sims, Norman, editor, *The Literary Journalists,* Ballantine (New York City), 1984, p. 3.

### PERIODICALS

*Atlantic,* July, 1976; August, 1983.

*Atlantic Monthly,* July, 1976, p. 93; August, 1983, pp. 96-98.

*Boston Herald,* June 13, 1995.

*Chicago Tribune Book World,* October 9, 1983.

*Christian Science Monitor,* June 11, 1976.

*Commonweal,* February 19, 1965, pp. 672-673.

*Los Angeles Times Book Review,* August 28, 1983.

*National Review,* April 20, 1971.

*New Republic,* November 7, 1970.

*Newsweek,* November 23, 1970; May 17, 1976.

*New Yorker,* July 31, 1995.

*New York Review of Books,* April 8, 1965; August 5, 1976, pp. 41-43.

*New York Times,* February 1, 1965; October 21, 1970; May 12, 1976; August 9, 1983.

*New York Times Book Review,* January 31, 1965, p. 4; November 1, 1970, pp. 46-47; May 9, 1976, pp. 1-2; October 14, 1979; August 28, 1983, pp. 10, 15; June 11, 1995.

*Publishers Weekly,* April 24, 1995.

*Saturday Review,* February 6, 1965; January 22, 1972; May 15, 1976.

*Time,* February 5, 1965, pp. 112, 114; April 19, 1976.

*Times Literary Supplement,* October 7, 1965; December 29, 1972, p. 1573.

*Washington Post,* October 24, 1979; June 5, 1995.

*Washington Post Book World,* December 27, 1970, p. 6; May 2, 1976, p. L5; August 21, 1983, p. 3.

# C

**CADE, Robin**
See NICOLE, Christopher (Robin)

*   *   *

**CANNAN, Denis 1919-**
(Denis Pullein-Thompson)

*PERSONAL:* Original name Denis Pullein-Thompson; name legally changed in 1964; born May 14, 1919, in Oxford, England; son of Harold James (an army officer; later secretary to Headmasters' Conference) and Joanna (an author; maiden name, Cannan) Pullein-Thompson; married Joan Ross, 1946 (marriage dissolved); married Rose Evansky, 1965; children: two sons, one daughter. *Education:* Attended Eton College.

*ADDRESSES: Home*—43 Osmond Rd., Hove, East Sussex BN3 1TF, England.

*CAREER:* Actor in repertory theater groups in England and Scotland, 1936-39 and 1946-51; performed in plays by George Bernard Shaw and others; appeared in television plays, 1948 and 1949; playwright, 1949—. *Military service:* British Army, Queen's Royal Regiment, 1939-45; mentioned in dispatches.

*WRITINGS:*

*PLAYS*

*Max* (three-act drama), produced at the Malvern Festival, Malvern, England, 1949.

*Captain Carvallo* (three-act comedy; produced in London at St. James Theatre, 1950), Hart-Davis (London), 1951, acting edition, Samuel French (New York City), 1951.

*Colombe* (adaptation of the play by Anouilh; produced in London at the New Theatre, 1951), Methuen (London), 1952.

*Misery Me!: A Comedy of Woe* (three-act comedy; produced on the West End at the Duchess Theatre, 1955), Samuel French, 1956.

*You and Your Wife* (three-act comedy; produced on the West End at the Old Vic Theatre, 1955), Samuel French, 1956.

(With Pierre Bost) *The Power and the Glory* (three-act drama; adaptation of the novel by Graham Greene; produced on the West End at the Phoenix Theatre, 1956; produced off-Broadway at the Phoenix Theatre, December 10, 1958), Samuel French, 1959.

*Who's Your Father?* (three-act comedy; produced on the West End at the Cambridge Theatre, 1958), Samuel French, 1959.

(With others) *US* (three-act drama; produced on the West End at the Aldwych Theatre, 1966), published as *Tell Me Lies: The Book of the Royal Shakespeare Production US/Vietnam/US/Experiment/Politics . . . ,* Bobbs-Merrill, 1968 (published in England as *US: The Book of the Royal Shakespeare Production US/Vietnam/US/Experiment/Politics . . . ,* Calder & Boyars, 1968).

*Ghosts* (adaptation of the play by Ibsen), produced on the West End at the Aldwych Theatre, 1967.

*One at Night* (three-act drama), produced in London at the Royal Court Theatre, April 13, 1971.

(With Colin Higgins) *Les Iks* (based on *The Mountain People,* by Colin Turnbull), produced in Paris, 1975, produced in London as *The Ik,* 1976.

*Dear Daddy* (produced on the West End at Ambassador's Theatre, 1976; produced in Philadelphia at the Annenberg Center, January 20, 1982), Samuel French, 1978.

SCREENPLAYS

(With Christopher Fry) *The Beggar's Opera,* 1953.
*Alive and Kicking,* 1959.
(With Frederic Raphael and Frederic Gotfurt) *Don't Bother to Knock,* 1961, also released as *Why Bother to Knock,* 1965.
*Tamahine,* 1963.
*Sammy Going South,* 1963, also released as *A Boy Ten Feet Tall,* 1965.
(With Roland Kibbee) *The Amorous Adventures of Moll Flanders,* 1965.
(With Stanley Mann and Ronald Harwood) *A High Wind in Jamaica,* 1965.
*Tell Me Lies,* 1968.
(With Terence Young) *Mayerling,* 1968.

RADIO PLAYS

*Headlong Hall,* 1950.
*The Moth and the Star,* 1950.
*The Greeting,* 1964.

TELEVISION SCRIPTS

(With Peter Brook) *Heaven and Earth,* 1956.
*One Day at a Time,* 1977.
*Home-Movies,* 1979.
*Fat Chance,* 1980.
*Picture of a Place,* 1980.
*The Best of Everything,* 1981.
*Way to Do It,* 1981.
*By George!,* 1982.
*The Absence of Emily,* 1982.
*The Memory Man,* 1983.
*The Last Bottle in the World,* 1986.

OTHER

Contributor to *Times Literary Supplement.*

SIDELIGHTS: Denis Cannan, according to Michael Billington in *Contemporary Dramatists,* is "the kind of dramatist who always has a tough time of it in the English theatre: one who attempts to mix the genres. His forte, particularly in the early 1950s, was intel-

ligent, satirical farce. . . . After a period of prolonged silence, he dropped the comic mask and launched a couple of direct, frontal assaults on the values of our society; but he still seems a dramatist of manifest talent who has been critically undervalued and unfairly neglected by the public."

Reviewing the Philadelphia production of Denis Cannan's play *Dear Daddy,* Mel Gussow of the *New York Times* calls the title character "an angry old man, a bitterly abusive critic of art, life, marriage and family. . . . If there is any real flaw in Mr. Cannan's malicious and mirthful play, it is that against all instinct and authorial guidance, we enjoy Bernard tremendously." Gussow continues: "*Dear Daddy* is an excoriating and literate look at a paterfamilias under siege."

Speaking of the play *One at Night,* in which a man has been confined to a mental asylum for having sex with an underage girl, Billington notes that the play "attacks certain aspects of our society with punitive vigour and sharp intelligence. . . . What gives the play its urgency is the feeling that Cannan isn't simply exploring a fashionable intellectual thesis (only the mad are sane) but that he is sharing with us a lived-through experience. And he makes, with some power, the point that in our society it is the scramble for wealth and material possessions that increases the incidence of insanity, but that it's the self-same scramble that produces the instant cure-alls and panaceas."

BIOGRAPHICAL/CRITICAL SOURCES:

BOOKS

*Contemporary Dramatists,* 5th edition, St. James Press (Detroit), 1993.

PERIODICALS

*New York Times,* January 24, 1982.

*       *       *

**CARTER, Elizabeth Eliot**
**See HOLLAND, Cecelia (Anastasia)**

## CARTLIDGE, Michelle 1950-

*PERSONAL:* Born October 13, 1950, in London, England; daughter of Haydn Derrick (director of transportation) and Barbara (a gallery director; maiden name, Feistmann) Cartlidge; married Richard Cook (an artist), June 25, 1982 (divorced, 1994); children: Theo. *Education:* Attended Hornsey College of Art, 1967-68, and Royal College of Art, 1968-70. *Avocational interests:* Travel abroad.

*ADDRESSES: Agent*—Laura Cecil, 17 Alwyne Villas, London N1 2HG, England.

*CAREER:* Artist, 1970—; writer and illustrator of books for children, 1978—.

*MEMBER:* Society of Authors.

*AWARDS, HONORS:* Mother Goose Award, Books for Your Children Booksellers, 1979, for *Pippin and Pod.*

*WRITINGS:*

MOUSE BOOKS; SELF-ILLUSTRATED

*Pippin and Pod,* Pantheon (New York City), 1978.
*A Mouse's Diary,* Lothrop (New York City), 1981, Dutton (New York City), 1994.
*Mousework,* Heinemann, 1982.
*Welcome to Mouseville,* Methuen (New York City), 1982.
*Baby Mouse,* Heinemann, 1984, Penguin (New York City), 1986.
*Mouse's Christmas Tree,* Penguin, 1985.
*Little Mouse Makes a Garden,* Walker, 1986.
*Little Mouse Makes a Mobile,* Walker, 1986.
*Little Mouse Makes Cards,* Walker, 1986.
*Little Mouse Makes Sweets,* Walker, 1986.
*A House for Lily Mouse,* Prentice-Hall (Englewood Cliffs, NJ), 1986, Methuen, 1987.
*Mouse House,* Dutton, 1990.
*Baby Mice,* Heinemann, 1991.
*Clock Mice,* Campbell, 1991.
*Mouse in the House,* Dutton, 1991.
*Mouse Time,* Dutton, 1991.
*Mouse's Christmas House: A Story/Activity Book,* Andrews and McMeel (Fairway, KS), 1991.
*Mouse Theater,* Dutton, 1992, published in England as *Theatre Mice,* Campbell, 1992.
*Baby Mice at Home,* Dutton, 1992.
*Mouse Letters,* Dutton, 1993.

*The Mouse Wedding: A Press-Out Model Book,* Andrew and McMeel, 1993.
*Mouse Birthday,* Dutton, 1994, published in England as *Birthday Mouse,* Campbell, 1994.
*Mouse's Scrapbook,* Dutton, 1995.
*Mouse Christmas,* Dutton, 1996.
*Mouse Magic,* Dutton, 1996, published in England as *Magic Mouse,* Campbell, 1996.
*The Mice of Mousehole: A Movable Picture Book,* Walker, Candlewick Press, 1997.
*School Mouse,* Campbell, 1997.

BEAR AND TEDDY BOOKS; SELF-ILLUSTRATED

*The Bears' Bazaar: A Story-craft Book,* Lothrop, 1979.
*Teddy Trucks,* Lothrop, 1981.
*Dressing Teddy* (cut-out book), Heinemann, 1983, Penguin, 1986.
*Teddy's Holiday,* Heinemann, 1984.
*Teddy's Birthday Party,* Penguin, 1985.
*Bear's Room: No Peeping,* Methuen, 1985.
*Teddy's Dinner,* Simon & Schuster (New York City), 1986.
*Teddy's Garden,* Simon & Schuster, 1986.
*Teddy's House,* Simon & Schuster, 1986.
*Teddy's Toys,* Simon & Schuster, 1986.
*Teddy's Christmas,* Simon & Schuster, 1986.
*Hello, Teddy,* Heinemann, 1991.
*Bear in the Forest,* Dutton, 1991.
*Bears on the Go,* Dutton, 1992.
*Good Night, Teddy,* Walker, Candlewick Press, 1992.
*Teddy's Friends,* Walker, Candlewick Press, 1992.
*Teddy's Cat,* Walker, Candlewick Press, 1996.

BUNNY BOOKS; SELF-ILLUSTRATED

*Playground Bunnies,* Walker Books (London), 1987.
*Seaside Bunnies,* Walker Books, 1987.
*Toy Shop Bunnies,* Walker Books, 1987.
*Birthday Bunnies,* Walker Books, 1987.
*Little Bunny's Picnic,* Dutton, 1990.
*Bunny's Birthday,* Dutton, 1992.

OTHER; SELF-ILLUSTRATED

*Little Boxes* (cut-out book), Heinemann, 1983.
*Munch and Mixer's Puppet Show: Presenting the Magic Lollipop,* Prentice-Hall, 1983.
*Little Shops,* Heinemann, 1985.
*Gerry's Seaside Journey,* Heinemann, 1988.
*Rabbit's Party,* Heinemann, 1991.
*Duck in the Pond,* Dutton, 1991.
*Elephant in the Jungle,* Dutton, 1991.

*Doggy Days,* Heinemann, 1991, Dutton, 1992.
*The Cats That Went to the Sea,* PictureLions, 1992.
*Fairy Letters,* Campbell, 1993.
*Michelle Cartlidge's Book of Words,* Dutton, 1994.

OTHER; ILLUSTRATED BY KIM RAYMOND AND RUTH BLAIR

*Bella's Birthday Party,* Heinemann, 1994.
*Boss Bear's Boat,* Heinemann, 1994.
*Gerry Kicks Off,* Heinemann, 1994.
*Gerry's Big Nose,* Heinemann, 1994.

Some of Cartlidge's works have been translated and published in Spanish, Japanese, French, German, Portuguese, and Welsh.

*SIDELIGHTS:* When her first book, *Pippin and Pod,* was published in 1978, Michelle Cartlidge was honored with the Mother Goose Award as the "most exciting newcomer to children's book illustration." Since that time, Cartlidge has created a number of children's picture books featuring anthropomorphized mice, bears, and bunnies. Cartlidge's books usually contain few words; they are known for her finely-detailed, delicate line drawings and warm pastel watercolors. While some critics have described her characters as static or have complained that it is difficult to tell them apart, many are charmed by the simple plots and cuddly animals Cartlidge portrays.

Cartlidge told *CA* that she began her career as an artist at an early age. She was just fourteen when she left school to work in a pottery studio. Later, Cartlidge studied pottery at the Hornsey School of Art and then the Royal College of Art. When she was twenty years old, she decided that her pottery "was becoming so fragile that I was the only person who could touch it with safety." Cartlidge began to devote her efforts to drawing. "To support myself, I did odd jobs, waitressing and washing up, but had the opportunity to show publisher and illustrator Jan Pienkowski a selection of cards I'd produced for my family and friends. This resulted in a commission to design a series of cards for Gallery Five."

Cartlidge told *CA* that she does her "best to create a world that a child will recognize, the kind of book he or she can step into to mingle with the characters portrayed." Throughout her career, Cartlidge has created picture books which provide activities, see-through windows, or movable parts, so that children "who have enjoyed reading about" her "characters can meet them again in active play." *Little Bunny's*

*Picnic,* for example, has windows on every other page that give children a peek at the next scene. Liza Bliss of *School Library Journal* described this as "a fun gimmick." *Mouse Birthday, Mouse Time, Mouse Theater, Mouse's Scrapbook,* and *Mouse Letters* are movable books; in the latter two books, attached envelopes contain letters and mementos relating to the story. For her younger fans, Cartlidge creates board books with watercolor teddy bears engaged in daily activities, from playing to eating lunch. While these books, which include *Teddy's Friends, Teddy's House, Teddy's Toys, Teddy's Garden,* and *Teddy's Dinner,* do not move, according to *School Library Journal* contributor Linda Wicher in a review of *Teddy's Friends,* they are "easy for young hands to hold."

Cartlidge's first book, *Pippin and Pod,* featuring "dainty line and watercolor" illustrations according to a *Kirkus Reviews* critic, was published in 1978. Set in Cartlidge's childhood neighborhood of Hampstead, London, the book follows the afternoon adventures of two mice. While their mother shops, the brothers wander through a colorfully rendered market, construction site, playground, and park. Then, as a critic for *Publishers Weekly* noted, the "wee mice suddenly realize they're lost and want to go home." The mice finally find their mother and all ends well. Barbara Elleman of *Booklist* complemented Cartlidge's illustrations in the book, stating that the pictures give "a warm feeling to this simply told tale."

*The Bears' Bazaar,* Cartlidge's next book, presents craft ideas and instructions within a tale about a bear sister and brother. A *Publishers Weekly* reviewer lauded the book as "a buoyant story with ideas for projects that can involve the whole family." Together with their parents, the bear siblings make a mobile, painted paperweights, paper dolls, gingerbread bears, and mustard men. Although a *Junior Bookshelf* critic voiced some concerns about the presentation of the projects, the reviewer described the overall work as "attractive, with seemingly inexhaustible detail." Writing in *Growing Point,* Margery Fisher called *The Bears' Bazaar* "the most attractive craft-book of last year."

After *The Bears' Bazaar,* Cartlidge continued to produce books about tiny mice or soft-looking bears, all with simple plots or scenes. *A Mouse's Diary* features a mouse girl who writes in her diary about such activities as going to the park, to ballet class, and on a nature walk. A critic for *Growing Point* appreciated how Cartlidge rendered fully detailed scenes with "bright paint and a strong sense of composition." According to a *Publishers Weekly* reviewer, the story "rolls along effortlessly." In *Bear's Room: No Peeping,* Bear is busy working in the house when the mice do their best to spy on him. In "crowded strip pictures," as a *Junior Bookshelf* critic described them, Cartlidge portrayed the large, dressed bear preparing treats, painting a mural in his room, and then taking a bath. At the end of the story, Bear invites the mice into his room for a party, and they take delight in the seesaw he has crafted for them.

*Michelle Cartlidge's Book of Words,* published in 1994, features a watercolor-rendered mouse family in a number of detailed everyday scenes on double-page spreads. As the mice get dressed, go to school, go grocery shopping, visit the playground and have fun at a birthday party, Cartlidge presents over 300 common words for young children and beginning readers. A *Kirkus Reviews* critic questioned the "conventional picture of mouse family life portrayed" in the book, and noted that the female mice were placed in some stereotypical female roles. Similarly, Patricia Pearl Dole of *School Library Journal* pointed out that the female characters were all in dresses, but observed that chores were "shared by both sexes."

Cartlidge once explained to *CA* how she goes about creating her books. "When planning a book, I like to decide on a location, do lots of sketches, and develop the story from them. The amount of detail I include appeals to children, and Theo, my small son, takes a lively and useful interest in my work. I find him a most useful critic."

*BIOGRAPHICAL/CRITICAL SOURCES:*

PERIODICALS

*Booklist,* October 1, 1978, pp. 290-91.
*Growing Point,* May, 1980, p. 3704; November, 1981, p. 3960; March, 1983, p. 4046.
*Horn Book Guide,* fall, 1994, p. 267.
*Junior Bookshelf,* June, 1980, p. 114; April, 1982; October, 1985, p. 211.
*Kirkus Reviews,* October 1, 1978, p. 1065; November 15, 1994, p. 1524.
*Publishers Weekly,* September 25, 1978, p. 141; March 28, 1980, p. 49; July 16, 1982, p. 78; October 28, 1983, p. 70.
*School Library Journal,* April, 1982, p. 56; August, 1990, p. 126; October, 1992, p. 85; January, 1995, pp. 82-83.

* * *

**CASTEL, Robert 1933-**

*PERSONAL:* Born March 27, 1933, in Brest, France. *Education:* University of Strassbourg, Licence de Philosophie; Sorbonne, University of Paris, Agregation de Philosophie and Doctorat d'Etat de Lettres et Sciences Humaines.

*ADDRESSES: Home*—8 rue Falguiere, 75015 Paris, France. *Office*—Centre d'Etudes des Mouvements Sociaux, Ecole des Hautes Etudes en Sciences Sociales, 54 bd. Raspail, 75006 Paris, France; fax: 0-14-954-2670.

*CAREER:* University of Lille, Lille, France, associate professor of philosophy, 1962-67; University of Paris, Sorbonne, Paris, France, associate professor of sociology, 1967-68; University of Paris VIII, Paris, associate professor, 1968-72, professor of sociology, 1973-90, director of studies at Ecole des Hautes Etudes en Sciences Sociales, 1990—, and director of Centre d'Etudes du Centre des Mouvements Sociaux. Mission interministerielle Recherche-experimentation, president of scientific council.

*MEMBER:* Societe internationale de sociologie de langue francaise, Societe international de sociologie, Societe francaise de sociologie.

*AWARDS, HONORS:* Officier des Palmes academiques, 1995; D.H.C., University of Lausanne, 1996.

*WRITINGS:*

*La Psychanalysme,* Editions Maspero, 1973.
(With Anne Lovell and Francoise Castel) *L'Ordre psychiatrique,* Editions de Minuit, 1976, translation by D. W. Halls published as *The Regulation of Madness,* Polity Press, 1988.
*La Societe psychiatrique avancee,* Grasset, 1979, translation by Arthur Goldhammer published as *The Psychiatric Society,* Columbia University Press (New York City), 1982.
*La Gestion des risques,* Editions de Minuit, 1981.
(With J. F. Lae) *Le revue minimum d'insertion: Une dette sociale,* L'Harmattan (Paris, France), 1991.
*Les Metamorphoses de la question sociale: Une chronique du salariat,* Fayard (Paris), 1995.

*BIOGRAPHICAL/CRITICAL SOURCES:*

PERIODICALS

*Times Literary Supplement,* June 18, 1982.

## CATALANOTTO, Peter 1959-

*PERSONAL:* Born March 21, 1959, in Atlanta, GA; son of Anthony (a printer) and Ella Virginia (a homemaker; maiden name, Lawrence) Catalanotto; married Jo-Ann Carrie Maynard (a photographer), August 8, 1989; children: Chelsea. *Education:* Pratt Institute, B.F.A., 1981. *Avocational interests:* Basketball, reading.

*ADDRESSES: Home*—4891 Edgewood Rd., Doylestown, PA 18901. *Office*—Orchard Books, 387 Park Ave. S., New York, NY 10016.

*CAREER:* Freelance illustrator, New York City, 1982-87; freelance writer and illustrator of children's books, New York City, 1987—. Catalanotto's work was displayed with the Mazza Collection in Findlay, OH, and has been with the permanent collection at Elizabeth Stone Gallery in Birmingham, MI, since 1991.

*AWARDS, HONORS:* Named "Most Promising New Artist," by *Publishers Weekly,* 1989; *Soda Jerk* was named an American Library Association "Best Book for Teens," 1990; *Cecil's Story* was honored as a "Keystone Book" for Pennsylvania, 1991; *All I See* and *Dylan's Day Out* both received Junior Literary Guild citations.

*WRITINGS:*

*SELF-ILLUSTRATED*

*Dylan's Day Out,* Orchard Books (New York City), 1989.
*Mr. Mumble,* Orchard Books, 1990.
*Christmas Always. . . ,* Orchard Books, 1991.
*The Painter,* Orchard Books, 1995.

*ILLUSTRATOR*

Judie Gulley, *Wasted Space,* Abingdon (Nashville, TN), 1988.
Cynthia Rylant, *All I See,* Orchard Books, 1988.
Rylant, *Soda Jerk* (poems), Orchard Books, 1990.
George Ella Lyon, *Cecil's Story,* Orchard Books, 1991.
Rylant, *An Angel for Solomon Singer,* Orchard Books, 1992.
Lyon, *Who Came Down That Road?,* Orchard Books, 1992.
Lyon, *Dreamplace,* Orchard Books, 1993.

SuAnn Kiser, *The Catspring Somersault Flying One-Handed Flip-Flop,* Orchard Books, 1993.
Susan Patron, *Dark Cloud Strong Breeze,* Orchard Books, 1994.
Lyon, *Mama Is a Miner,* Orchard Books, 1994.
Lyon, *A Day at Camp Damp,* Orchard Books, 1996.
Megan McDonald, *My House Has Stars,* Orchard Books, 1986.
Angela Johnson, *The Rolling Store,* Orchard Books, 1997.
Susan Marie Swanson, *Getting Used to the Dark,* D. K. Ink, 1997.

Illustrator of numerous young adult book jackets, including Judy Blume's *Just as Long as We're Together.* Contributor of illustrations to magazines and newspapers.

*SIDELIGHTS:* Peter Catalanotto commented: "I grew up in a household in East Northport, Long Island, where four of the five children went to art schools in New York City. I remember when I started school, I was amazed to learn everybody didn't draw like my family. I was a shy child. Although I had a lot of friends, I most enjoyed solitude, reading, doing jigsaw puzzles, or spending endless hours drawing. Comic book characters were my favorite things to draw, especially 'Spider-Man.'

"Throughout elementary school and high school, I found art classes frustrating, because they were taught at a level to accommodate all students. It wasn't until college that I found my abilities challenged. In fact, I failed tenth grade art strictly out of sheer boredom. At Pratt Institute I studied illustration, drawing, and painting. It was at Pratt that I developed the watercolor technique I still use today. I think it's important for an artist to find a medium that suits his or her personality. Watercolor allows me to stop and start without a lot of preparation. I can be loose or tight with my style with washes and rendering.

"After graduation from Pratt in 1981, I started freelance illustrating. My first clients were newspapers, and I did most of my painting in black and white. (This is what gave me the idea for *Dylan's Day Out,* the first picture book I wrote, where all black and white characters are painted on full-color backgrounds.) From the newspaper work, I started getting assignments from magazines like *Reader's Digest, Family Circle, Woman's Day,* and *Redbook.*

"In 1984 I started painting the covers of young adult book jackets and have done more than one hundred and fifty to date. In 1987 I did a couple of jackets for Orchard Books, including Judy Blumes's *Just as Long as We're Together.* The editor, Richard Jackson, offered me a picture-book manuscript, *All I See,* written by Cynthia Rylant. I became enamored with the process of creating paintings for an entire story. The research included spending time on a lake, since this was the setting for the story. I spent thirteen hours in a rowboat, sketching and photographing the lake at all angles and times of the day. Seasick and sunburned, I started my sketches. As the months on this project passed, Jackson and I became friends and had many discussions on writing and illustrating books for children.

"By 1988 these discussions had inspired me to begin writing. I was nervous at first—all of my formal training had been in drawing and painting. But using the thinking that I pass on in school visits today, I chose a topic that I was familiar with and one I loved. A dog became my main character. By following my dog around the house (this greatly confused him), I felt I understood his world and was fully prepared to write about it. There was nothing he loved more than going 'out.' So I created what I thought would be the ultimate adventure for him—a day every dog should have—in *Dylan's Day Out.*

"In 1989, I did the paintings for *Soda Jerk,* a collection of poems by Cynthia Rylant. Spending days in a soda shop/pharmacy (it took me weeks to find one), I sketched and photographed the people of Hudson, Ohio, as they entered looking for cold drinks and cold remedies. It was at this soda fountain that I first met Cynthia Rylant. This surprises many since we previously did *All I See* together. Usually the author and illustrator are kept apart (unless, of course, they collaborated initially before presenting the book to a publishing house). I agree with the tactic of keeping them separate. This way the illustrator's approach is different from the author's. I believe the illustrations for a text have to be more than just beautiful paintings. They should add new dimensions to the text, not merely repeat in pictures what the writer has said in words.

"In the fall of 1989 I started writing my second book, *Mr. Mumble.* My own shyness as a child inspired this off-beat tale of one being misunderstood—a feeling I think most people, especially children, can relate to. I tried to create a character I felt everybody knew, so when I'm approached and told 'Mr. Mumble is exactly like my grandfather,' I feel like I succeeded.

"I spent 1990 writing *Christmas Always. . . ,* a story of a girl who gets more visitors than she expects on Christmas Eve. When my parents would have parties on Christmas Eve, I was always sent to bed long before the party ended. This story is simply what I wished happened to me, instead of being in that bedroom all by myself.

"One of the things I stress to children in my school presentations is use of their imaginations—to write about what they wished would happen to them along with what really does. My 1992 book, *An Angel for Solomon Singer,* another volume with Cynthia Rylant, makes a strong statement about loneliness and how a friend can make life much nicer. The main character, Solomon, is painfully poor in New York City and is quite lonely. I was very poor for several years in New York City and understand the coldness Solomon experiences as well as his longing for familiar times and loved ones. I often found myself examining my life, wondering if I made the right choices. In hard times, I think this is quite common to do. This thinking gave me the idea of using a lot of reflections in my paintings—looking at our lives and examining our choices. Solomon stops into a cafe one night, and when a friendly waiter invites him to return, he does so night after night. Befriending the waiter, Angel, Solomon is able to see the city in a whole new light.

Catalanotto has illustrated several books by George Ella Lyon. The first was *Cecil's Story.* Catalanotto described it as an "incredibly powerful, yet simple poem about a boy whose father went off to fight in the Civil War. The poem speaks of his hopes and fears, leaving all the imagery up to me to create. The images her words evoked in my mind were endless, and I spent many nights editing and altering to create what I felt were the right ones." He told *Something about the Author Autobiography Series* (SAAS): "I love how much room she leaves between her words for me to fill in with pictures. Her writing is based on emotions and thoughts, not descriptions. How the characters look is left up to me." He added: "Some writers feel picture book manuscripts should be able to stand on their own. I'm not sure I agree. I think the most successful picture books are when the words and pictures are wed to create something bigger and better than when separate."

Another of Lyon's books is *Who Came Down That Road?,* in which a curious boy and his mother discover a pathway in the woods. The mother explains who uses the path nowadays, then goes on to describe the people who have walked there in days past. In

illustrating the story, Catalanotto told *SAAS:* "I love . . . movies where the story starts, then you see the title, then the story continues. . . . Before the title page [of *Who Came Down That Road?*] the story takes place in the 1990s. After the title page the story goes back in time to previous travelers of the road: great-grandparents, Civil War soldiers, buffalo, bear, mastodon, and others. . . . Since history is connected, as well as roads, I thought all the paintings should be connected too. On each double-page spread I showed the present, part of the past, and a hint of the future."

Catalanotto also illustrated Lyon's 1993 book *Dreamplace,* a poem about the Anasazi cliff dwellers of the southwestern United States. He wrote: "To illustrate *Dreamplace* . . . I visited Colorado and spent four days at Mesa Verde, sketching and photographing the Anasazi dwellings." A *Publishers Weekly* reviewer remarked, "Lyon and Catalanotto here offer an atmospheric, shimmering glance backwards. . . . Catalanotto's extraordinary watercolors clarify this journey through time." Another collaboration with Lyon resulted in *Mama Is a Miner,* for which the author and illustrator visited a modern-day coal mine in Kentucky. Catalanotto prefers site visits to library research. He commented: "I much prefer experiencing what I'm going to recreate for a book. The spirit of the Anasazi people and the plight of the miners haunted me as I painted their stories. I walked in the same place as my characters."

It was Catalanotto's own daughter Chelsea who inspired his self-illustrated book *The Painter.* Catalanotto's art studio was off-limits to the little girl, as he explained in *SAAS.* "I work with scissors, razor blades, sharp pencils, and spray cans, and I was terrified she would get hurt, so I never let her up there." When he finally allowed Chelsea, at the age of four, to enter the room under careful supervision, the child was almost too excited to move. This experience led to his story of a fictional girl who is also forbidden to visit her artist-father's studio. Not only that, when she wants to share his company outside the studio, the daddy is always too busy—working. In the story, the pair works out a solution that a *Publishers Weekly* reviewer called credible and "uplifting," adding that Catalanotto's "book subtly attests to the joy inherent in the creation of both life and art."

In recent years, Catalanotto has illustrated books by several other authors. One *Publishers Weekly* reviewer called the illustrations in SuAnn Kiser's book *The Catspring Somersault Flying One-handed Flip-Flop* "sun-drenched watercolors, as lush and complex

as ever," and *Horn Book* critic Nancy Vasilakis praised the "distinctive, impressionistic paintings" of a "tomboy whose facial expressions reveal her temperament." Vasilakis reported, again in the *Horn Book,* that Catalanotto's paintings for Susan Patron's *Dark Cloud Strong Breeze* "really capture attention," especially "the winsome informality of subjects caught off-guard" and the artist's use of "an unusual three-dimensional effect."

Catalanotto told *CA:* "I think writing and illustrating picture books suits my personality much more than simply illustrating book jackets and magazine articles. I can be quiet and subtle with my work while trying to catch someone's eye. A book jacket yells at you to take it off the shelf. An entire picture book slowly unfolds before you, almost inviting you to stay."

*BIOGRAPHICAL/CRITICAL SOURCES:*

*BOOKS*

*Something about the Author Autobiography Series,* Volume 25, Gale (Detroit), 1998.

*PERIODICALS*

*Booklist,* September 1, 1988, p. 83; October 1, 1989, p. 346.
*Horn Book,* September-October, 1993, p. 586; May-June, 1994, p. 318.
*New York Times Book Review,* June 3, 1990, p. 24.
*Publishers Weekly,* September 29, 1989, p. 65; July 13, 1990, p. 53; January 25, 1993, p. 86; July 26, 1993, p. 70; January 31, 1994, p. 88; July 11, 1994, p. 78; August 21, 1995, p. 64; August 26, 1996, p. 97; March 17, 1997, p. 82.
*School Library Journal,* September, 1990, p. 196.

\* \* \*

**CAYER, D. M.**
  **See DUFFY, Maureen**

\* \* \*

**CHARLES, Gerda 1914-**

*PERSONAL:* Born August 14, 1914, in Liverpool, England; daughter of Gertrude Lipson. *Education:*

Attended public schools in Liverpool, England. *Religion:* Jewish.

*ADDRESSES: Home*—22 Cunningham Ct., Maida Vale, London W9 1AE, England.

*CAREER:* Novelist, critic, and lecturer.

*AWARDS, HONORS:* James Tait Black Award, 1963, for *A Slanting Light;* Whitbread Literary Award, 1971, for *The Destiny Waltz;* Arts Council Award, 1972.

*WRITINGS:*

*The True Voice,* Eyre & Spottiswoode (London), 1959.
*The Crossing Point,* Eyre & Spottiswoode, 1960, Knopf (New York City), 1961.
*A Slanting Light,* Knopf, 1963.
(Editor and contributor) *Modern Jewish Stories,* Faber (London), 1963, Prentice-Hall (Engelwood Cliffs, NJ), 1965.
*A Logical Girl,* Eyre & Spottiswoode, 1966, Knopf, 1967.
*The Destiny Waltz,* Eyre & Spottiswoode, 1971, Scribner (New York City), 1972.

Also editor of *Great Short Stories of the World,* Hamlyn Publishing (London). Contributor of stories and reviews to numerous magazines and newspapers, including *New Statesman, Daily Telegraph, New York Times,* and *Jewish Chronicle.* Television columnist, *Jewish Observer and Middle East Review,* 1978.

*SIDELIGHTS:* Gerda Charles has described herself as a defender of the "ordinary" person. Her typical protagonist is what Frederick P. W. McDowell refers to in *Contemporary Novelists* as "the spiritual misfit in modern life"—isolated, alienated, ignored, and suffering in silence. Priscilla Martin explains in the *Dictionary of Literary Biography* that Charles's "fiction comprises a report, as indignant as it is compassionate, on the human jungle in which the weak—those deprived by virtue of sex, class, appearance, talent or its absence, personality, environment, or address—are savaged by the strong." Because Charles's novels reflect her own background—the characters and settings of her own experience—many critics have classified them as "Jewish novels," or reflections of Anglo-Jewish culture and society.

Charles's first novel, *The True Voice,* appeared in 1959 to critical acclaim. In the novel, McDowell

writes, "Charles develops a principal theme—the alienation felt by a person of talent when he is unable to articulate his aspirations and to communicate his inner intensities to others." The central character is Lindy Frome, a shy young woman attempting to improve her social standing by placing herself among people who, she believes, represent a better standard of life than her own. She fails, of course. Martin comments: "Her yearning to better her personal circumstances is matched by her inability to take advantage of any occasion for doing so. . . . She usually manages to muff any promising moment and . . . has to look on while less deserving opportunists reap the social rewards." Lindy learns, rather painfully, that her value as a person depends, not on her social standing or her proximity to people of value, but on her own internal qualities of endurance, patience, and strength.

Charles next wrote *The Crossing Point,* which she once nicknamed her Jewish novel and which McDowell considers, upon retrospection, to be her best book. The critic describes the novel as the author's testimony to Judaism as "the most viable of religions for human beings" in which "opposites such as asceticism and sensuousness, mysticism and secularism, idealism and practicality converge." The theme of patient suffering is central to this novel of Jewish family life in a London suburb; it is relentless in the sense that all of its characters are afflicted with it and driven by it into the very isolation and alienation that they wish to escape. "Sara's domestic martyrdom," writes Martin, " . . . is placed in larger and ancient contexts of oppression and endurance." The "novel paints a particularly bitter human experience. . . . The work also introduces an idea central to the later novels: the Jew as symbol of all the oppressed."

The symbol of oppression in the next novel, *A Slanting Light,* is Bernard Zold, "a psychically immolated American playwright" according to McDowell, "a sufferer rather than a doer." Though McDowell finds the characterization imprecise, he praises the work overall: "As a novel exploring entangled relationships it has distinction and force." Equally oppressed in this novel, according to Martin, is Bernard's housekeeper Ruth, who admires in her employer his "patience, his unfashionable nineteenth-century virtues, and . . . a mystical necessity to exemplify the suffering, the humane, the pacific . . . in the composite human nature of society." As a spectator of Bernard's suffering and isolation from the social milieu into which they both find themselves, Ruth must confront the dawning realization that what she had perceived as worthy goals—success and urbanity—might, in fact, be achievements worth resisting.

*A Logical Girl* tells the story of the 1943 Allied "invasion" of an English seaside town as seen through the eyes of Rose Morgan, an immature young woman who, along with her father and sister-in-law, runs a boarding house which serves American GIs. "Whatever else may be said for the underdog," writes Marilyn Gardner of the *Christian Science Monitor,* " . . . one fact remains too often sure: his still infrequent ability to come out on top. The 26-year-old underdog-narrator of [*A Logical Girl*] . . . is no exception to this, but [Miss Charles'] story makes exceptional reading just the same. . . . What gives the story vitality and sensitivity . . . is Miss Charles' deft appraisal of the internal changes Rosie undergoes. . . . Against the backdrop of a global conflict, her private war against falseness, dishonesty, and hypocrisy becomes a less futile cause."

R. G. G. Price of *Punch* writes: "*A Logical Girl* is so good that it's difficult to praise it without tearing bits off and holding them up for approval. It is a very ambitious novel and a very bold one. . . . Its many virtues include a swinging narrative vigour. . . . After I had finished, I kept seeing new points in what at the time of reading seemed to be just casual snatches of setting or amusing minor characters or even faults of tone. I admired, learned and enjoyed."

Not all the critics, however, were as equally impressed with the novel. Louise Armstrong of the *New York Times Book Review* calls Rose Morgan a "nonheroine" who is "one of the most tiresome women fiction has produced in a long time. . . . Rose's pattern of dream fancy and rude awakening treads monotonously on. Here is the most tenacious adolescence I have ever seen outside of real life." There is, however, a hint of faint praise for Charles' ability to create a vivid character. "Say this for Rosie—and for her author—she is so real, so specific, she details her relationships so minutely and makes her own limitations so clear, that in the end one is just annoyed and anxious to be rid of her, as though she had actually been around for months."

A reviewer in the *Nation* comments: "Miss Charles is an extremely gifted writer, a writer of unfashionable moral seriousness and exceptional narrative power, but *A Logical Girl* is the least impressive of her . . .

novels so far. One can take her female protagonist seriously, or regard her as an object for subtle satire: Miss Charles has not quite brought her themes and characters under the control of her hard, unsentimental intelligence, and there is an ambiguity at the core of *A Logical Girl* that is not willed."

A critic in *Newsweek* offers what is perhaps the best summation of the pros and cons of *A Logical Girl*: "Miss Charles charts Rose's futile puritanical reactions to the human frailties in her wartime world with an almost cruel satisfaction, which makes it rather difficult to sympathize with the poor girl. . . . Still, indelibly etched on our memory, we can never forget poor Rose—at least as a brilliant portrait of the arrested adolescent as compulsive old maid."

*A Logical Girl* may have marked the apex of Charles' popularity. It was followed by *The Destiny Waltz,* which McDowell calls her "longest and least satisfactory novel." It is the story of a television filmmaking venture, an attempt to document the achievements of an overlooked poet. McDowell reports that, while Charles's descriptions of the filmmaking process are confident, her characters fade in importance when compared to the moral lessons they intone: "Charles has overextended her materials for the value which accrues to them." Martin suggests as well that *The Destiny Waltz* reveals an increasingly ponderous emphasis on the author's moral theme, which had been noted in passing by critics of earlier works. Martin writes, "*The Destiny Waltz* seems . . . to state the other novels' premises pugnaciously and to combat the obvious criticisms of their indulgence in snobbishness, envy, and self-pity." The response of critics to this attitude was vexation, Martin adds. "Some . . . reviewers . . . reported that its opinionated tone was destructive of its great potential."

*The Destiny Waltz* is Charles's most recent novel to date. According to Martin, "Charles feels born into the wrong century. . . . Skeptical that human nature can be changed, she is contemptuous of the women's movement. . . . [H]er heroines sometimes expect an emotional welfare state, unearned benefits of personal fulfillment." Yet overall, McDowell concludes: "[Charles'] insight into human nature is penetrating. . . . [H]er prose is . . . perfectly modulated to convey a sense of Jamesian complexities . . . [and the] process whereby her protagonists determine 'how to be' is fraught with anguish, on occasion with muted triumph, always with the ring of truth."

*BIOGRAPHICAL/CRITICAL SOURCES:*

BOOKS

*Contemporary Novelists,* 6th edition, St. James Press (Detroit, MI), 1996.
*Dictionary of Literary Biography,* Volume 14: *British Novelists since 1960,* Gale (Detroit), 1983.

PERIODICALS

*Christian Science Monitor,* July 27, 1967.
*Critique,* winter, 1964-1965.
*Fincial Times,* April 15, 1971.
*Illustrated London News,* May 20, 1967.
*Jewish Quarterly,* spring, 1967; summer, 1971.
*Nation,* October 2, 1967.
*Newsweek,* July 14, 1967.
*New York Times Book Review,* June 6, 1967.
*Observer* (London), April 30, 1967.
*Punch,* May 24, 1967.
*Times Literary Supplement,* May 25, 1967; April 23, 1971.*

\* \* \*

## CHERRY, Kelly

*PERSONAL:* Born in Baton Rouge, LA; daughter of J. Milton (a violinist and professor of music theory) and Mary (a violinist and writer; maiden name, Spooner) Cherry; married Jonathan Silver, December 23, 1966 (divorced, 1969). *Education:* Mary Washington College, B.A., 1961; University of North Carolina at Greensboro, M.F.A., 1967; also attended New Mexico Institute of Mining and Technology, Virginia Polytechnic Institute (now Virginia Polytechnic Institute and State University), Richmond Professional Institute (now Virginia Commonwealth University), University of Richmond, and University of Tennessee.

*ADDRESSES: Home*—Madison, WI. *Office*—Department of English, University of Wisconsin—Madison, 600 N. Park St., Madison, WI 53706. *Agent*—Miriam Altshuler, Russell & Volkening, Inc, 50 West 29th St., Apt. 7E, New York, NY 10001.

*CAREER:* Behrman House, Inc. (publishers), New York City, editor and writer, 1970-71; Charles Scribner's (publishers), New York City, editor, 1971-72; John Knox Press, Richmond, VA, editor, 1973;

Southwest Minnesota State College (now Southwest State University), Marshall, writer-in-residence, 1974-75; University of Wisconsin—Madison, visiting lecturer, 1977-78, assistant professor, 1978-79, associate professor, 1979-82, professor of English and writer-in-residence, 1982—, Romnes Professor of English, 1983-88, Evjue-Bascom Professor in the Humanities, 1993—. Western Washington University, distinguished writer-in-residence, 1981; Rhodes College, distinguished visiting professor, 1985. Has taught at writers' conference workshops and presented numerous readings of her works at colleges and universities in both the U.S. and abroad, including Duke University, Bennington Writing Workshops, and Mount Holyoke Writers Conference.

*MEMBER:* PEN, Poetry Society of America, Poets and Writers, Associated Writing Programs (member, board of directors, 1990-93), Authors Guild, Authors League of America, National Book Critics Circle, American Academy of Poets, Phi Beta Kappa.

*AWARDS, HONORS:* University of Virginia Dupont Fellow in philosophy, 1962-63; Canaras Award for fiction, St. Lawrence University Writers Conference, 1974; Bread Loaf fellow, 1975; Pushcart Prize, 1977; Yaddo fellow, 1979 and 1989; National Endowment for the Arts fellowship, 1980; first prize for book-length fiction, Wisconsin Council of Writers, 1980, for *Augusta Played,* and 1991, for *My Life and Dr. Joyce Brothers;* PEN/Syndicated Fiction Award, 1983, for "Life at the Equator," 1987, for "Acts of Unfathomable Compassion," and 1990, for "About Grace"; Romnes fellowship, University of Wisconsin, 1983; fellowship, Wisconsin Arts Board, 1984 and 1989; Chancellor's Award, 1984; Ritz Paris Hemingway Award nomination, 1984, for *The Lost Traveller's Dream;* James G. Hanes Poetry Prize, Fellowship of Southern Writers, 1989, for distinguished body of work; Arts America Speaker Award (Republic of the Philippines), U.S. Information Agency, 1992.

*WRITINGS:*

FICTION

*Sick and Full of Burning,* Viking (New York City), 1974.
*Augusta Played,* Houghton (Boston), 1979.
*Conversion* (chapbook), Treacle Press (New Paltz, NY), 1979.
*In the Wink of an Eye,* Harcourt (San Diego), 1983.
*The Lost Traveller's Dream,* Harcourt, 1984.

*My Life and Dr. Joyce Brothers: A Novel in Stories,* Algonquin Books (Chapel Hill, NC), 1990.

POETRY

*Lovers and Agnostics,* Red Clay Books (Charlotte, NC), 1975, revised edition, Carnegie Mellon University Press, 1996.

*Relativity: A Point of View,* Louisiana State University Press (Baton Rouge), 1977.

*Songs for a Soviet Composer* (chapbook), Singing Wind Press (St. Louis), 1980.

*Natural Theology,* Louisiana State University Press, 1988.

*God's Loud Hand,* Louisiana State University Press, 1993.

*Benjamin John* (chapbook), March Street Press, 1993.

*Time out of Mind* (chapbook), March Street Press, 1994.

*Death and Transfiguration,* Louisiana State University Press, 1997.

NONFICTION

(Co-author and associate editor) *Lessons from Our Living Past* (textbook), Behrman House, 1972.

*Teacher's Guide for Lessons from Our Living Past* (textbook), Behrman House, 1972.

*The Exiled Heart: A Meditative Autobiography,* Louisiana State University Press, 1991.

*Writing the World* (essays), University of Missouri Press, 1995.

OTHER

*Where the Winged Horses Take Off into the Wild Blue Yonder* (recording), American Audio Prose Library (Columbia, MO), 1981.

(Contributorof translation) *Seneca: The Tragedies,* Volume 2, Johns Hopkins University Press (Baltimore), 1994.

Contributor to anthologies, including *The Girl in the Black Raincoat,* edited by George Garrett, Duell, Sloan & Pearce, 1966; *Pushcart Prize II,* edited by Bill Henderson, Avon, 1977; *Strong Measures: Recent American Poems in Traditional Forms,* edited by Philip Dacey and David Jauss, Harper, 1985; and *Prize Stories 1994: The O. Henry Awards,* Doubleday, 1994. Contributor of stories, poems, essays, and book reviews to periodicals, including *American Scholar, Anglican Theological Review, Atlantic Monthly, Commentary, Esquire, Fiction, Georgia Review, Gettysburg Review, Independent, Los Angeles Times Book Review, Ms., Mademoiselle, Midwest Quarterly, New Literary History, New York Times Book Review, North American Review, Parnassus, Red Clay Reader, Southern Poetry Review, Southern Review, Story Quarterly* and *Virginia Quarterly Review. Book Forum,* contributing editor, 1984-88; *Anglican Theological Review,* consultant to poetry editor, 1986—; *Shenandoah,* advising editor, 1988-92.

Cherry's works have been translated into numerous foreign languages, including Chinese, Czech, Dutch, Latvian, Lithuanian, Polish, Swedish, and Ukrainian.

*SIDELIGHTS:* Award-winning poet and novelist Kelly Cherry is concerned with philosophy; with, as she explains it, "the becoming-aware of abstraction in real life—since, in order to abstract, you must have something to abstract from." Within her novels, the abstract notions of morality become her focus: "My novels deal with moral dilemmas and the shapes they create as they reveal themselves in time," she once told *CA.* "My poems seek out the most suitable temporal or kinetic structure for a given emotion." Writing in the *Dictionary of Literary Biography Yearbook: 1983* of Cherry's fiction, Mark Harris concludes that "she manages to capture, in very readable stories, the indecisiveness and mute desperation of life in the twentieth century."

Cherry's collections of poetry, including *Lovers and Agnostics,* published in 1975, *Relativity: A Point of View,* published in 1977, and 1993's *God's Loud Hand,* have been widely praised by critics. "Her poetry is marked by a firm intellectual passion," begins the citation preceding her receipt of the James G. Hanes Poetry Prize in 1989, "a reverent desire to possess the genuine thought of our century, historical, philosophical, and scientific, and a species of powerful ironic wit which is allied to rare good humor." Reviewing *Relativity,* Patricia Goedicke notes in *Three Rivers Poetry Journal* that "her familiarity with the demands and pressures of traditional patterns has resulted . . . in an expansion and deepening of her poetic resources, a carefully textured over- and underlay of image, meaning and diction." Harris finds that Cherry's "ability to sustain a narrative by clustering and repeating images [lends] itself to longer forms, and 'A Bird's Eye View of Einstein,' the longest poem in [*Relativity*], is an example of Cherry at her poetic best."

Reviewers have praised Cherry's sense of humor and poetic language, as well as her keen observations on the human condition. In her novels, the author sometimes centers on female protagonists who cope with personal crises while searching for love, sexual fulfillment, and self-knowledge. Her first novel, *Sick and Full of Burning,* depicts the life and relationships of Mary "Tennessee" Settleworth, a newly-divorced medical student facing her thirtieth birthday. "Like many of Cherry's other heroines, Tennessee Settleworth is unable to enjoy more than a casual friendship with the men she meets," Harris writes. Tennessee's best male friend wants to live with her but refuses to make love to her; another male friend is eager to make love, but he has been impotent since his divorce. "The essential pessimism of the novel," writes Harris, "finds a certain anodyne in the protagonist's humorous attempts to relieve her sexual frustrations."

On the other hand, *Augusta Played,* published five years later in 1979, explores the dynamics of marriage and money through the tempestuous relationship between a young flutist and her musicologist husband, giving equal weight to both a male and a female point of view. Harris notes that *Augusts Played* "relies on improbable events and a series of misapprehensions much as the eighteenth-century comedy of manners did. . . . The mixture of realistic detail and improbable coincidence allows Cherry to explore a commonplace in our time—the breakdown of a marriage—in a refreshing and interesting manner." "Cherry's characters begin, as in high comedy, with stock types who gradually grow more and more complex," writes Robert Taylor in a review for the *Boston Globe.* "Behind them is the sad music of mortality . . . proclaiming that even our vanities possess absurd dignity and the absurd lies on the borderline of heartbreak."

The unique structure of Cherry's 1990 novel, *My Life and Dr. Joyce Brothers,* was also favorably received by critics. Subtitled "A Novel in Stories," the book relates, in the words of *Los Angeles Times Book Review* contributor Judith Freeman, "the plight of a middle-aged, unmarried woman named Nina who understands how the numbing jargon of self-help, so prevalent in our culture and epitomized by the philosophy of Dr. Joyce Brothers, can do nothing to alleviate a sense of deep-rooted alienation and loneliness." Freeman observes that the novel is "far too witty, too savvy, too lyrical and compassionate to resort to bitterness." She praises Cherry for performing "the admirable feat of taking hackneyed fates and infusing them with tremendous freshness."

The concerns Cherry addresses in her fiction are also reflected in her autobiography, *The Exiled Heart.* Having met and fallen in love with a Latvian musician named Imant Kalnin during the Cold War, Cherry was separated from him and the couple prevented from marrying by the Soviet government. She contemplated the nature and meaning of both love and justice while living in England and waiting for a visa to visit Kalnin. *The Exiled Heart* was the result: "One of the richest and most thoughtful books I have ever read," notes Fred Chappell in a review of the work in *Louisiana Literature.* "The integrity of thought and courage of vision it portrays are qualities that abide in the memory, steadfast as fixed stares. One day this book will come into its own and will be recognized, along with some other works by Kelly Cherry, for the masterwork that it is."

"I'm concerned with the shape of ideas in time," Cherry told *CA* in a discussion of her writing, "the dynamic configuration a moral dilemma makes, cutting through a novel like a river through rock; the way a philosophical statement bounces against the walls of a poem, like an echo in a canyon. A writer, poet or novelist, wants to create a contained, complete landscape in which time flows freely and naturally. The *poems* are where I live. It's in poetry that thought and time most musically counterpoint each other, and I like a world in which the elements sing."

"I think that the crucial unit of the poem is the line; in the story, it's sentence, or voice; and in the novel, it's scene," the novelist explained to *CA,* going on to add some thoughts on the inspiration for her works of fiction. "The hidden model for *Augusta Played* is *The Tempest;* the hidden model for *In the Wink of an Eye* is *A Midsummer Night's Dream.* Shakespeare and Beethoven, they're the main ones; the idea of an extended developmental passage—that's the root impetus for everything I write. I grew up on those two."

*BIOGRAPHICAL/CRITICAL SOURCES:*

*BOOKS*

*Authors in the News,* Volume 1, Gale (Detroit), 1976.
Cherry, Kelly, *The Exiled Heart: A Meditative Autobiography,* Louisiana State University Press, 1991.
*Dictionary of Literary Biography Yearbook: 1983,* Gale, 1984.
*Finding the Words: Conversations with Writers Who Teach,* Swallow Press, 1985.

*PERIODICALS*

*Book World,* April 7, 1991.
*Boston Globe,* March 17, 1979.
*Chicago Tribune,* April 1, 1979; May 20, 1984; April 17, 1990.
*Choice,* November, 1995, p. 461.
*Library Journal,* October 1, 1974.
*Los Angeles Times Book Review,* June 24, 1990; August 20, 1995, p. 3.
*Louisiana Literature,* April, 1991.
*New York Times Book Review,* April 22, 1984; May 27, 1990; October 6, 1991.
*Publishers Weekly,* February 15, 1993, p. 232; April 24, 1995, p. 57.
*Three Rivers Poetry Journal,* March, 1977.
*Writer's Digest,* July, 1996, p. 12.

\*　\*　\*

## CHOYCE, Lesley 1951-

*PERSONAL:* Born March 21, 1951, in Riverside, NJ; son of George (a mechanic) and Norma (a homemaker; maiden name, Willis) Choyce; married Terry Paul (a teacher); children: Sunyata, Pamela. *Education:* Rutgers University, B.A., 1972; Montclair State College, M.A. in American literature, 1974; City University of New York, M.A. in English literature, 1983.

*ADDRESSES: Home*—83 Leslie Rd., East Lawrencetown, Nova Scotia B2Z 1P8, Canada. *Office*—English Department, Dalhousie University, Halifax, Nova Scotia B3H 3J5, Canada.

*CAREER:* Writer, publisher, professor, television show host, music performer, surfer. Referrals Workshop, Denville, NJ, rehabilitation counselor, 1973-74; Bloomfield College, Bloomfield, NJ, coordinator of writing tutorial program, 1974; Montclair State College, Upper Montclair, NJ, instructor in English, 1974-78; Alternate Energy Consultants, Halifax, Nova Scotia, writer and consultant to Energy, Mines and Resources Canada, 1979-80; Dalhousie University, Halifax, 1981—, began as instructor, became professor of English. Founder of Pottersfield Press. Creative writing instructor, City of Halifax continuing education program, 1978-83; instructor at St. Mary's University, 1978-82, Nova Scotia College of Art and Design, 1981, and Mount St. Vincent University, 1982. Participant in creative writing workshops; public reader and lecturer; freelance broadcaster, 1972—; host of television talk show *Choyce Words,* beginning 1985.

*MEMBER:* International PEN, Atlantic Publishers Association, Canadian Periodical Publishers Association, Association of Canadian Publishers, Literary Press Group, Canadian Poetry Association, Writers' Union of Canada, Writers Federation of Nova Scotia.

*AWARDS, HONORS:* Canadian Science Fiction and Fantasy Award finalist, 1981; recipient, Order of St. John Award of Merit, 1986; Dartmouth Book Award, 1990, 1995, shortlist, 1991-93; *Event* magazine Creative Nonfiction winner, 1990; Ann Connor Brimer Award for Children's Literature, 1994; Manitoba Young Reader's Choice Award finalist, 1994; Authors Award, Foundation for the Advancement of Canadian Letters, co-winner, 1995.

*WRITINGS:*

*Eastern Sure,* Nimbus Publishing, 1981.
*Billy Botzweiler's Last Dance* (stories), Blewointment Press, 1984.
*Downwind,* Creative Publishers, 1984.
*Conventional Emotions* (stories), Creative Publishers, 1985.
*The Dream Auditor* (science fiction), Ragweed Press, 1986.
*Coming up for Air,* Creative Publishers, 1988.
*The Second Season of Jonas MacPherson,* Thistledown, 1989.
*Magnificent Obsessions* (photo-novel), Quarry Press, 1991.
*The Ecstasy Conspiracy,* Nuage Editions, 1992.
*Margin of Error* (stories), Borealis Press, 1992.
*The Republic of Nothing,* Goose Lane Editions, 1994.
*The Trap Door to Heaven* (science fiction), Quarry Press, 1996.
*Dance the Rocks Ashore,* Goose Lane Editions, 1997.
*Go for It, Carrie* (for children), Formac, 1997.

*FOR YOUNG ADULTS*

*Skateboard Shakedown,* Formac Publishing, 1989.
*Hungry Lizards,* Collier-Macmillan (Toronto), 1990.
*Wave Watch,* Formac Publishing, 1990.
*Some Kind of Hero,* Maxwell-Macmillan, 1991.
*Wrong Time, Wrong Place,* Formac Publishing, 1991.
*Clearcut Danger,* Formac Publishing, 1992.
*Full Tilt,* Maxwell-Macmillan, 1993.
*Good Idea Gone Bad,* Formac Publishing, 1993.
*Dark End of Dream Street,* Formac Publishing, 1994.

*Big Burn,* Thistledown, 1995.
*Falling through the Cracks,* Formac Publishing, 1996.

POETRY

*Reinventing the Wheel,* Fiddle Head Poetry Books, 1980.
*Fast Living,* Fiddle Head Poetry Books, 1982.
*The End of Ice,* Fiddle Head Poetry Books, 1982.
*The Top of the Heart,* Thistledown Press, 1986.
*The Man Who Borrowed the Bay of Fundy,* Brandon University, 1988.
*The Coastline of Forgetting,* Pottersfield Press (Lawrencetown Beach, Nova Scotia), 1995.

NONFICTION

*Edible Wild Plants of the Maritimes,* Wooden Anchor Press, 1977.
*An Avalanche of Ocean* (autobiography), Goose Lane Editions, 1987.
*December Six/The Halifax Solution,* Pottersfield Press, 1988.
*Transcendental Anarchy* (autobiography), Quarry Press, 1993.
*Nova Scotia: Shaped by the Sea,* Penguin (Toronto), 1996.

EDITOR

*The Pottersfield Portfolio,* Volumes 1-7, Pottersfield Press, 1971-1985.
*Alternating Current: Renewable Energy for Atlantic Canada,* Wooden Anchor Press, 1977.
*Chezzetocook* (fiction and poetry), Wooden Anchor Press, 1977.
(With Phil Thompson) *ACCESS,* Pottersfield Press, 1979.
(With John Bell) *Visions from the Edge,* Pottersfield Press, 1981.
*The Cape Breton Collection,* Pottersfield Press, 1984, 1989.
(With Andy Wainwright) Charles Bruce, *The Mulgrave Road,* Pottersfield Press, 1985.
*Ark of Ice: Canadian Futurefiction,* Pottersfield Press, 1985.
(With Rita Joe) *The Mi'kmaq Anthology,* Pottersfield Press, 1997.

OTHER

Contributor to more than one hundred magazines and anthologies.

*WORK IN PROGRESS: Cold Clear Morning,* a novel.

*SIDELIGHTS:* American-born Canadian author and editor Lesley Choyce, who has written numerous works of fiction (for both adults and young adults), nonfiction, science fiction, and poetry, shows no signs of slowing down. Choyce has worked some of his many passions—including nature and the environment, surfing, windsurfing, skateboarding, and music—into several novels for young adults. In his first effort, *Skateboard Shakedown* (1989), a skateboarder, his girlfriend, and a group of friends take on a corrupt mayor who wants to turn their favorite skateboard site into a shopping mall. Writing in *Quill & Quire,* reviewer Norene Smiley said that "this fast-paced novel marks the entrance of a new and refreshing voice for young readers."

In *Hungry Lizards* (1990), a sixteen-year-old rock band leader finds that the advantages of winning a performing contract at a local club can be outweighed by the realities of the entertainment business, the conflicting time demands of school and work, and the temptations of a questionable lifestyle. The book is designed for reluctant teen readers, and reviewer Kenneth Oppel concluded in *Quill & Quire* that the book's "tempered view of teenage street life and the rock 'n' roll underworld should appeal to young readers."

*Wrong Time, Wrong Place* (1991) explores racial tensions and social injustice through the story of Corey, a young man with one parent who is black and one who is white. Corey first becomes aware of his different status as a biracial youth when he is branded as a troublemaker and rebel and begins to notice how both students and faculty treat lighter-skinned students differently. Through his Uncle Larry's good example and Larry's stories of a black community in Halifax called Africville, Corey comes to identify with his black forebears. As described by *Canadian Children's Literature* reviewer Heidi Petersen, Corey "realizes that he must face injustices himself, and embraces a form of social activism which begins by keeping the past, the truth, alive."

In *Clearcut Danger* (1992), as in *Skateboard Shakedown,* two teenage protagonists take on adult greed, this time in the form of a joint government-business project to build a pollution-prone pulp and paper mill in a job-starved town. Praising Choyce's "strong and interesting" characterization and "good, strong story," reviewer Patty Lawlor concluded in *Quill &*

*Quire* that "booksellers, teachers, and librarians should talk this one up."

In *Dark End of Dream Street* (1994), Choyce takes up the problem of homeless youth in the person of Tara, who always thought her friend Janet was the one with problems until Tara's own life starts to spin out of control. *Quill & Quire* reviewer Fred Boer found the author's subplots—about Tara's friendship with an elderly woman, and both Tara's and Janet's problems with their boyfriends—somewhat distracting, and the absence of swearing oddly cautious. Boer nevertheless praised the book for being "entertaining and readable."

While most of Choyce's young adult novels are in the high interest/low vocabulary category, *Big Burn* appeals to a more sophisticated audience. Nevertheless, the main plot—two teens against a new incinerator that threatens to poison the atmosphere—is familiar Choyce terrain. In *Quill & Quire,* reviewer Maureen Garvie especially praised the "infectious" quality of the "outrage the author and his characters feel." Other strengths include the portrayal of John's "adolescent darknesses" and the death of a parent.

Discussing *An Avalanche of Ocean* and *Transcendental Anarchy,* his two autobiographies, Choyce once told *CA:* "[Although writing mostly fiction], as time went on I found that some of the facts of my own life were more revealing than the fictional truths I create. This came as a surprise and a shock to me. . . . When I grew into my skin as a writer, I pretended for awhile that *what I had to say* really was of importance. After a time, I started believing in the myth, and this convinced me to abandon fiction for awhile and get autobiographical.

"Since my life story would be exceedingly boring, I was forced to edit my personal history ruthlessly until there was something left worth sharing. My first fragmented history of the self came out as *An Avalanche of Ocean,* and I almost thought that I was done with autobiography. What more could I possibly say once I'd written about winter surfing, transcendental woodsplitting, and getting strip-searched for cod tongues in a Labrador airport? But then something happened to me that I can't quite explain. *Avalanche* had set off something in me—a kind of manic, magical couple of years where I felt like I was living on the edge of some important breakthrough. It was a time of greater compressed euphoria and despair than I'd ever felt before. Stuff was happening to me, images of the past were flooding through the doors, and I needed to get

it all down. Some of it was funny, some of it was not. Dead writers were hovering over my shoulder, saying, 'Dig deep; follow it through. Don't let any of it go.' And I didn't.

"So again I have the audacity to say that these things that happened to me are worth your attention. . . . In *Transcendental Anarchy* I celebrated the uncompromising passages of a midthirties male, admitting that I would never be an astronaut or a president, and instead finding satisfaction in building with wood, arguing a good cause, or even undergoing a successful vasectomy. . . . Write about what makes you feel the most uncomfortable, a voice in my head told me. So I tackled fear and my own male anger and my biggest failures. And, even more dangerous, I tried writing about the most ordinary of things: a morning in Woolco, an unexceptional day, the thread of things that keeps a life together."

About his writing, Choyce further told *CA:* "Throughout it all, there is, I hope, a record of a search for love and meaning fraught with failure and recovery. Maybe I've developed a basic mistrust of the rational, logical conclusions. I've only had the briefest glimpses beyond the surface, but I've seen enough to know that sometimes facts are not enough. There are times to make the leap, to get metaphysical, and suppose that we all live larger lives than appearances would suggest."

*BIOGRAPHICAL/CRITICAL SOURCES:*

*PERIODICALS*

*Books in Canada,* October, 1995, pp. 49-50.
*Canadian Children's Literature,* number 62, 1991, pp. 86-88; number 76, 1994, pp. 72-6.
*Canadian Materials,* January, 1991, p. 34; May, 1992, p. 165.
*Maclean's,* August 15, 1994, p. 44.
*Quill & Quire,* March, 1990, p. 22; August, 1990, p. 15; April, 1991, p. 18; May, 1993, pp. 33-34; March, 1995, p. 79; May, 1995, pp. 46-47.

\* \* \*

**CLARKE, Austin C(hesterfield) 1934-**

*PERSONAL:* Born July 26, 1934, in St. James, Barbados; son of Kenneth Trothan (an artist) and Gladys (a hotel maid) Clarke; married Trinity Collego (marriage ended); married Betty Joyce Reynolds, 1957; children: Janice, Loretta, Jordan (also known as Mphahlele). *Education:* Attended secondary school at Harrison College in Barbados; studied economics and politics at Trinity College, University of Toronto, beginning in 1955.

*ADDRESSES: Home*—62 McGill St., Toronto, Ontario M5B 1H2, Canada. *Agent*—Phyllis Westberg, Harold Ober Associates, 425 Madison Ave., New York, NY 10017.

*CAREER:* Coleridge-Parry Primary School, St. Peter, Barbados, teacher, three years prior to 1955; newspaper reporter in Timmins and Kirkland Lake, Ontario, 1959-60; Canadian Broadcasting Corp., Toronto, Ontario, producer and freelance broadcaster, beginning 1963; Barbados Embassy, Washington, DC, cultural and press attache, 1974-76; Caribbean Broadcasting Corp., St. Michael, Barbados, general manager, 1975-76. Also has worked as freelance journalist for *Toronto Globe and Mail* and Canadian Broadcasting Corp.

Yale University, New Haven, CT, Hoyt fellow, 1968, visiting professor of Afro-American literature and creative writing, 1968-71; Brandeis University, Waltham, MA, Jacob Ziskind Professor of Literature, 1968-69; Williams College, Williamstown, MA, Margaret Bundy Scott Visiting Professor of Literature, 1971; Duke University, Durham, NC, lecturer, 1971-72; University of Texas, Austin, visiting professor, 1973-74; Concordia University, Montreal, Quebec, writer in residence, 1977; University of Western Ontario, writer in residence, 1978. Rhode Island School of Design, Providence, member of board of trustees, 1970-75; Ontario Board of Censors, vice-chairperson, 1983-85; Immigration and Refugee Board of Canada, member, 1988.

*MEMBER:* Writers Guild, Writers' Union of Canada (founding member), Yale Club (New Haven).

*AWARDS, HONORS:* President's Medal for best story, University of Western Ontario, 1966; Belmont Short Story Award, 1965, for "Four Stations in His Circle"; Canada Council, senior arts fellowships, 1968, 1970, 1974, grant, 1977; Indiana University School of Letters, Bloomington, fellow, 1969; Cuba's Casa de las Americas Literary Prize, 1980; Toronto Arts Award, 1993; Toronto Pride Achievement Award, 1995.

*WRITINGS:*

*NOVELS*

*The Survivors of the Crossing,* McClelland & Stewart (Toronto, Ontario), 1964.
*Amongst Thistles and Thorns,* McClelland & Stewart, 1965.
*The Prime Minister,* General Publishing (Don Mills, Ontario), 1977.
*Proud Empires,* Gollancz (London), 1986, Viking-Penguin (Markham, Ontario), 1988.
*The Origin of Waves,* McClelland and Stewart, 1997.

*NOVELS; "THE TORONTO TRILOGY"*

*The Meeting Point,* Macmillan (Toronto), 1967, Little, Brown (Boston), 1972.
*Storm of Fortune,* Little, Brown, 1973.
*The Bigger Light,* Little, Brown, 1975.

*SHORT STORIES*

*When He Was Free and Young and He Used to Wear Silks,* Anansi (Toronto), 1971, revised edition, Little, Brown, 1973.
*When Women Rule,* McClelland and Stewart, 1985.
*Nine Men Who Laughed,* Penguin (New York City), 1986.
*In This City,* Exile Editions (Toronto), 1992.
*There Are No Elders,* Exile Editions, 1993.

Author of *Short Stories of Austin Clark,* 1984.

*OTHER*

*The Confused Bewilderment of Martin Luther King & the Idea of Non-Violence as a Political Tactic,* Watkins (Burlington, Ontario), 1986.
(Contributor) Lloyd W. Brown, editor, *The Black Writer in Africa and the Americas,* Hennessey & Ingalls (Los Angeles), 1973.
*Growing up Stupid under the Union Jack: A Memoir,* McClelland & Stewart, 1980.
Charlotte Stewart, compiler, *The Austin Clark Collection,* Mills Memorial Library, McMaster University (Hamilton, Ontario), 1982.
*A Passage Back Home: A Personal Reminiscence of Samuel Selvon,* Exile Editions, 1994.

Also author of *Myths and Memories, African Literature,* and other filmscripts for Educational Television (ETV), Toronto, beginning in 1968. Contributor to periodicals, including *Studies in Black Literature* and

*Canadian Literature.* Manuscript collection held at McMaster University, Hamilton, Ontario.

*SIDELIGHTS:* Austin C. Clarke's childhood in colonial Barbados and his experiences as a black immigrant to Canada have provided him with the background for most of his fiction. His writing is almost exclusively concerned with the cultural contradictions that arise when blacks struggle for success in a predominantly white society. Clarke's "one very great gift," in the words of a *New Yorker* critic, is the ability to see "unerringly into his characters' hearts," and this ability is what makes his stories memorable. Martin Levin writes in the *New York Times Book Review*: "Mr. Clarke is plugged into the fixations, hopes, loves and dreams of his characters. He converts them into stories that are charged with life."

Clarke's memoir, *Growing up Stupid under the Union Jack,* is an example of the author's typical theme and style. The narrator, Tom, is a young man from a poor village in Barbados. Everyone in the village is proud that Tom is able to attend the Combermere School, for it is run by a "real, true-true Englishman"—an ex-British army officer who calls his students "boy" and "darky" and who flogs them publicly. The students eagerly imitate this headmaster's morals and manners, for to them he represents "Mother England"; they are unaware that in England he would be looked down upon as a mere working-class soldier. The book is "a personal, captivating, provoking, and often humorous record of ignorance, inhumanity and lowly existence under colonial imperialism in World War II Barbados. . . . With its major emphasis on education and childhood, *Growing up Stupid under the Union Jack* continues to draw attention to one of the chief preoccupations of the anti-colonial Anglo-Caribbean novel," writes Robert P. Smith in *World Literature Today*. "The colonial situation is the essence of the absurd because it both causes and symbolizes the condition of being isolated from one's self, one's cultural and personal roots," explains *Contemporary Novelists* contributor Lloyd W. Brown, who declares "the most central, and universal, of all [Clarke's] themes [is] alienation." The theme is well rendered in what Darryl Pinckney calls in the *New York Review of Books* Clarke's "tender, funny, unpolemical style." This style emphasizes what Victor J. Ramraj describes in the *Dictionary of Literary Biography* as "his immense talent for capturing the feel and flow of Barbadian speech and his adeptness at creating hilariously comic scenes."

Clarke's early novels are also "set in Barbados and they explore the twin evils of colonial self-hatred and Caribbean poverty," Brown comments. *The Survivors of the Crossing* describes the attempts of Rufus, a worker at a white-owned sugar plantation, to lead a labor strike. He fails because the powerful white owners and the middle-class black islanders ally themselves against him, and even the poor, working-class laborers eventually thrust him from their midst. Rufus's inspiration to incite rebellion came from his perception of the American dream, in this case, the power of the working class in Canada. *Amongst Thistles and Thorns* is the story of a nine-year-old runaway who finds his birth father, spends a weekend with him, then returns home still alienated from his current lot in life, but filled with stories about the American land of opportunity, in particularly New York City's Harlem. However, as Ramraj summarizes: "What North America, in particular Canada, actually holds for the black migrant is not so pleasant, however, which is the concern of Clark's next three novels, the Toronto trilogy."

The trilogy, which is perhaps Clarke's best known work, details the lives of the Barbadian blacks who immigrate to Toronto hoping to better their lot. In these novels, *The Meeting Point, Storm of Fortune,* and *The Bigger Light,* "it is as if the flat characters of a Dickensian world have come into their own at last, playing their tragicomic roles in a manner which owes much to Clarke's extraordinary facility with the Barbadian dialect," writes Diane Bessai in *Canadian Literature.* Bessai also expresses eagerness for Clarke to "continue to create his Brueghel-like canvases with their rich and contrasting detail and mood." "The sense of defeat among the poor islanders is enlivened by the humour of the characters and their glowing fantasies about the presumed wealth of relatives and friends who make it big in the fatlands of the United States or Canada," writes John Ayre in *Saturday Night*. The reality for such immigrants, according to Brown, is that "West Indians must choose between being integrated into a strange culture—at the cost of their cultural uniqueness and racial integrity—or being so dedicated to maintaining their black, West Indian identity that they risk being cultural and economic outsiders in their adopted homeland."

The first two novels dwell mostly on Bernice Leach, a live-in maid at a wealthy Toronto home, and her small circle of fellow immigrants. Martin Levin writes in the *New York Times Book Review:* "Mr. Clarke is masterful at delineating the oppressive insecurities of Bernice and her friends, and the claustrophobic atmosphere that envelops such a mini-minority" as the Caribbean blacks in Toronto. In *The Meeting Point,* Ramraj writes, "these characters have to contend with inner as well as outer conflicts as they try to retain their black pride and identity and come to grips with self-hatred and beckoning materialism." In *Storm of Fortune,* he continues, some of the group have increased their "measure of economic success and feel they deserve acceptance into the system [but] now have to cope with more sharply felt social alienation."

The third novel, *The Bigger Light,* explores the life of Boysie, the most successful of this immigrant group, and his wife, Dots. Boysie has at last realized the dream that compelled him to leave Barbados; he owns a prosperous business and his own home. However, in the process of realizing his goals, he has become alienated from his wife and his community. "His economic successes have not protected him from emotional failure," explains Brown. Now he searches for a greater meaning to his life—a "bigger light." "*The Bigger Light* is a painful book to read," writes David Rosenthal in the *Nation.* It is "a story of two people with many things to say and no one to say them to, who hate themselves and bitterly resent the society around them. . . . Certain African novelists have also dealt with the isolation of self-made blacks, but none with Clarke's bleak intensity." A *New Yorker* writer praises the book further, citing Clarke's strong writing skill as the element that lifts the book beyond social comment: "The universal longings of ordinary human beings are depicted with a simplicity and power that make us grateful for all three volumes of this long and honest record."

In Clarke's later writing, according to Brown, "themes of isolation and self-conflict have increasingly been integrated with the issue of Canadian society and Canadian identity." The stories in the collection *When Women Rule* are about immigrants, both white and black, from a variety of cultural origins, who share similar anxieties and fears for the future. Brown remarks: "It is the central irony of this collection that the very idea of a Canadian mosaic, with its implicit promise of social harmony and individual success, binds Clarke's diverse Canadians together by virtue of its failure, rather than its fulfillment." In his introduction to the collection *Nine Men Who Laughed,* according to Ramraj, the author "rails against the Canadian system that perpetually perceives the West Indian immigrant as an outsider," and he also criticizes the immigrant who finally succeeds, then "becomes tolerant of abuses." These later stories,

Ramraj concludes, "show Clarke honing his skills as a short-story writer. Most of the stories achieve an ironic control, discipline, and aesthetic distance not evident in the earlier work."

Clarke has also written works that attack political corruption in his native Barbados. These include the novel *The Prime Minister* which, according to some critics, bears striking comparisons to Clarke's own experiences and observations in Barbados in 1975, when he served briefly as the general manager of the Caribbean Broadcasting Corporation. The novel *Proud Empire,* set in the 1950s, examines political corruption and middle-class values from the perspective of a teen-aged boy not yet tainted by the reality of island politics. It follows Boy through graduation, a period of study in Canada, and a return to Barbados, after which he enters politics himself, though now reluctant and with open eyes. "The novel confirms," Ramraj writes, "that Clarke's strength as a novelist lies not so much in his probing the psyche and inner development of his protagonists as in capturing the subtleties of the social and political behavior of his Barbadian characters, whether at home or abroad."

In 1997 Clarke published the novel *The Origin of Waves* which, according to John Bemrose in *Maclean's,* "contains some of Clarke's best writing ever." It follows a chance reunion of two old friends, of an age similar to that of the author, who have not seen each other since childhood. The two reminisce for hours in a local bar, enabling Clarke, through their stories, to express what Bemrose calls "a gentle melancholy and, finally, a spark of hopefulness" about the lot of the immigrant in Canadian society.

*BIOGRAPHICAL/CRITICAL SOURCES:*

*BOOKS*

Algoo-Baksh, Stella, *Austin C. Clarke: A Biography,* Press of the University of West Indies (Barbados), 1994.

Brown, Lloyd, *El Dorado and Paradise: A Critical Study of the Works of Austin Clarke,* Center for Social and Humanistic Studies, University of Western Ontario (London), 1989.

*Contemporary Authors Autobiography Series,* Volume 16, Gale (Detroit), 1992.

*Contemporary Literary Criticism,* Volume 8, Gale, 1978; Volume 53, 1989.

*Contemporary Novelists,* 6th edition, St. James Press (Detroit), 1996.

*Dictionary of Literary Biography,* Gale, Volume 53: *Canadian Writers since 1960, First Series,* 1986; Volume 125: *Twentieth-Century Caribbean and Black African Writers, Second Series,* 1993.

Gibson, Graeme, *Eleven Canadian Novelists,* Anansi, 1973, pp. 33-54.

*PERIODICALS*

*Books in Canada,* October, 1986, pp. 20-21.
*Canadian Literature,* summer, 1974; autumn, 1981, pp. 136-38; winter, 1982, pp. 181-85.
*College Language Association Journal,* September, 1985, pp. 9-32; December, 1992, pp. 123-33.
*Journal of Caribbean Studies,* fall 1985-spring 1986, pp. 71-78.
*Journal of Commonwealth Literature* (Leeds), July, 1970.
*Listener,* June 15, 1978.
*Maclean's,* April 21, 1997, p. 62.
*Nation,* November 1, 1975.
*New Yorker,* February 24, 1975.
*New York Review of Books,* May 27, 1982.
*New York Times Book Review,* April 9, 1972; December 9, 1973; February 16, 1975; August 23, 1987.
*Saturday Night,* October, 1971; June, 1975.
*Times Literary Supplement,* May 11, 1967, p. 404.
*World Literature Today,* winter, 1982.
*World Literature Written in English,* spring, 1986, pp. 115-127.*

* * *

## CLEMENTS, Bruce 1931-

*PERSONAL:* Born November 25, 1931, in New York, NY; son of Paul Eugene (a salesman) and Ruth (an editor; maiden name, Hall) Clements; married Hanna Charlotte Margarete Kiep (a community worker), January 30, 1954; children: Mark, Ruth, Martha, Hanna. *Education:* Columbia University, A.B., 1954; Union Theological Seminary, B.D., 1956; State University of New York at Albany, M.A., 1962. *Politics:* Democrat. *Religion:* Protestant.

*ADDRESSES: Office*—Department of English, Eastern Connecticut State College, Willimantic, CT 06226.

*CAREER:* Ordained minister of United Church of Christ; pastor in Schenectady, NY, 1957-64; Union College, Schenectady, NY, instructor, 1964-67; Eastern Connecticut State College, Willimantic, CT, professor of English and department chair, 1967—.

*AWARDS, HONORS:* National Book Award finalist, American Academy and Institute of Arts and Letters, 1975, and "Best of the Best, 1966-1978," *School Library Journal,* 1979, both for *I Tell a Lie Every So Often.*

*WRITINGS:*

*FICTION; FOR YOUNG PEOPLE; PUBLISHED BY FARRAR, STRAUS (NEW YORK CITY)*

*Two against the Tide,* 1967.
*The Face of Abraham Candle,* 1969.
*I Tell a Lie Every So Often,* 1974.
*Prison Window, Jerusalem Blue,* 1977.
*Anywhere Else but Here,* 1980.
*Coming About,* 1984.
*The Treasure of Plunderell Manor,* 1987.
*Tom Loves Anna Loves Tom,* 1990.

*NONFICTION; FOR YOUNG PEOPLE*

*From Ice Set Free: The Story of Otto Kiep,* Farrar, Strauss, 1972.
(With wife, Hanna Clements) *Coming Home to a Place You've Never Been Before,* Farrar, Strauss, 1975.

*OTHER*

Author of plays for radio and theatre.

*SIDELIGHTS:* The author of several well-received books for young people, Bruce Clements began writing in the late 1960s. His novels, which include *I Tell a Lie Every So Often, Anywhere Else but Here,* and *The Treasure of Plunderell Manor,* focus on the importance of caring for one's fellow man and, by extension, our society's need to be tolerant and supportive of other cultures. Mary Lystad remarked of Clements in *Twentieth-Century Young Adult Writers:* "His writing style is crisp and clear; in a few words and phrases Clements conjures up vivid images of people, places, and times in conflict." Lystad further noted that Clements's books are products of his extensive research, with carefully detailed historical and geographical settings. "Clements is not easy reading, but he is worth the effort," Lystad continued. "His stories are powerful, with strong characters facing basic human choices."

Clements was born in New York City in 1931, and was writing plays with a boyhood friend, before he had entered high school. While Clements dreamed of becoming a writer—as a way to become rich and famous, he admits—he later realized that "that *heaven of successful artists* doesn't exist"; as an adult, he studied theology and became a pastor instead. However, the writing bug never quite let go, and "after many years of writing plays, in 1965 I wrote a novel," he explained. "It was so awful that I still blush when I think about it. Writing it, however, taught me a lot about how to do something that long, and in 1966, I tried a second novel [*Two against the Tide*]."

*Two against the Tide* (1967) is set on an island off the rocky coast of Maine. The story concerns a community of nearly fifty residents who have been able to stop the aging process through the use of a drug discovered by a local doctor and nurse more than a century earlier. When a young brother and sister are gently "kidnapped" by their aunt in order to rejuvenate this island utopia, they are faced with the choice of arresting their development and remaining children forever or returning to society and confronting the attendant joys and sorrows of growing up and growing older. A *Booklist* reviewer called Clements's debut novel "a thought-provoking, sometimes frightening and suspenseful story," while *Horn Book* reviewer Mary Silva Cosgrave praised *Two against the Tide* as a "highly original first book for children."

One of Clements's most highly praised novels for young adults is *I Tell a Lie Every So Often* (1974). A finalist for the National Book Award, the story is based on the 1850 diary of one Thaddeus Culbertson, who Clements fictionalizes as a fourteen-year-old cooper's apprentice named Henry Desant. Almost a decade after his young cousin has mysteriously disappeared, Henry claims to have heard of a young woman resembling her living with a tribe of Native Americans in the Dakota Territory. This fib fuels older-brother Clayton's desire to find his cousin, and the two boys set out on a thousand-mile trek into the North American wilderness, traveling by steamboat, wagon, and horseback. Noting that Clayton's pomposity provides most of the book's humor, Zena Sutherland of the *Bulletin of the Center for Children's Books* asserted that "there's considerable humor and wit in other characters and they are all involved in dashing action."

*The Treasure of Plunderell Manor* (1987) is the adventure story that Clements always wanted to write.

Taking place in Victorian England, it features a fourteen-year-old serving girl named Laurel Bybank. Orphaned, she finds work with Lord and Lady Stayne, who, motivated by greed, have confined their wealthy teenage niece, Alice Plunderell, to the tower room of their large home. Ordered by the couple to convince Alice to reveal the whereabouts of the treasure hidden by her deceased parents, Laurel befriends the young woman instead, thwarting the couple's evil plans. Ilene Cooper praised the novel in *Booklist,* calling it a "Dickensian romp [that] is loads of fun, though Clements walks a thin line as he slyly parodies a familiar genre." *School Library Journal* contributor Michael Cart called Clements "a talented and convincing storyteller with a rich gift for characterization."

*Tom Loves Anna Loves Tom* (1990) is "an honest and direct, modern-day love affair," according to Lystad. Narrated by Tom, Clements's novel relates the two emotionally intense weeks that teens Tom and Anna share while Anna comes from out of town to visit her dying Aunt Barbara. "The question is not whether Tom and Anna will fall in love," noted Betsy Hearne of the *Bulletin of the Center for Children's Books.* "The question is how they will sustain each other through self-disclosures and mutual experiences." Commenting on the author's skillful pacing, Ilene Cooper noted in *Booklist* that "so much is embraced in that [two weeks] time—love, fear, regret, longing, death—that in many ways it does seem as if a lifetime has passed."

In addition to fiction, Clements has also written several works of nonfiction for younger readers. *From Ice Set Free: The Story of Otto Kiep* (1972) is the biographical account of Clements's father-in-law, a German-born Scot who returned to the country of his birth to serve in the German Army during World War I. A successful lawyer and diplomat by the dawn of the Second World War, Kiep courageously spoke out against Adolf Hitler until his execution at the hands of the Nazis in 1944. *Coming Home to a Place You've Never Been Before,* co-authored by his wife, Hanna, is a documentary account of a twenty-four-hour period in Perception House, a local half-way house for troubled young people where the authors have worked. "Essentially, it is a book about change," Clements noted, "and the slow attempts of change through interaction with others who have been in trouble."

"I write because I want to say to young people that life can be put together," Clements once explained, "that you can make sense out of yourself and the world around you, that you don't have to be a victim. The characters I write about are sometimes frightened and uncertain, but they don't give up. They make decisions and stick to them and survive."

*BIOGRAPHICAL/CRITICAL SOURCES:*

BOOKS

Holtze, Sally Holmes, editor, *Fifth Book of Junior Authors and Illustrators,* H. W. Wilson (Bronx, NY), 1983, pp. 71-72.
*Twentieth-Century Young Adult Writers,* St. James Press (Detroit), 1994, p. 136.

PERIODICALS

*Booklist,* January 1, 1968, p. 542; June 15, 1972, p. 902; October 15, 1977, p. 373; June 1, 1980, p. 1422; January 15, 1988, p. 861; October 1, 1990, p. 330.
*Bulletin of the Center for Children's Books,* February, 1970, pp. 93-94; November, 1974, p. 39; November, 1980, p. 49; December, 1990, p. 81.
*Horn Book,* October, 1967, pp. 587-88; April, 1974, pp. 151-52; April, 1978, p. 169.
*Kirkus Reviews,* August 15, 1967, p. 966; April 1, 1972, p. 412.
*Publishers Weekly,* November 24, 1969, p. 42; March 25, 1974, p. 57; July 13, 1990, p. 56.
*School Library Journal,* September, 1984, p. 126; March, 1988, p. 212.
*Voice of Youth Advocates,* February, 1985, p. 323; April, 1988, pp. 21-22; April, 1991, p. 28.

\*   \*   \*

**COALSON, Glo  1946-**

*PERSONAL:* Born March 19, 1946, in Abilene, TX; daughter of Bill L. (a teacher) and LaVerne (an elementary school teacher; maiden name, Bowles) Coalson. *Education:* Abilene Christian University, B.A. (art), 1968; also attended University of Colorado, University of Texas, and Columbia Teachers College. *Avocational interests:* Camping, sailing, snorkeling, "all watery things done on top of the water."

*ADDRESSES: Home*—Route 5, Box 860, Abilene, TX 79605.

*CAREER:* Writer and illustrator. Ed Triggs/Al Boyd—Graphic Designers, Austin, TX, graphic designer, 1969; artist in Kotzebue, AK, 1969-70; freelance illustrator in New York City, 1971-78, and Dallas, TX, 1978-80.

*AWARDS, HONORS:* Friends of American Writers award for illustration, 1974, for *The Long Hungry Night.*

*WRITINGS:*

ILLUSTRATOR

(And author) *Three Stone Woman* (for children), Atheneum (New York City), 1971.
Ann Herbert Scott, *On Mother's Lap,* McGraw (New York City), 1972, revised edition, Clarion (Boston), 1992.
E. C. Foster and Slim Williams, *The Long Hungry Night,* Atheneum, 1973.
Arnold Griese, *At the Mouth of the Luckiest River,* Crowell (New York City), 1973.
Clyde Robert Bulla, *Dexter,* Crowell, 1973.
Jonathan Gathorne-Hardy, *Operation Peeg,* Lippincott (Philadelphia), 1974.
Phyllis LaFarge, *Abby Takes Over,* Lippincott, 1974.
Helen S. Rodgers, *Morris and His Brave Lion,* McGraw, 1975.
Tom Robinson, *An Eskimo Birthday,* Dodd (New York City), 1975.
Hila Coleman, *That's the Way It Is, Amigo,* Crowell, 1975.
Gloria Skurzynski, *In a Bottle with a Cork on Top,* Dodd, 1976.
Gathorne-Hardy, *The Airship Lady Ship Adventure,* Lippincott, 1977.
Valentina P. Wasson, *The Chosen Baby,* Lippincott, 1977.
Griese, *The Wind Is Not a River,* Crowell, 1978.
Patricia C. Hass, *Windsong Summer,* Dodd, 1978.
Jay Leech and Zane Spencer, *Bright Fawn and Me,* Crowell, 1979.
Lee Bennett Hopkins, *By Myself,* Crowell, 1980.
Arnold Adoff, *Today We Are Brother and Sister,* Crowell, 1981.
Scott, *Hi!,* Philomel/Putnam (New York City), 1994.
Gina Willner-Pardo, *Daphne Eloise Slater, Who's Tall for Her Age,* Houghton (Boston), 1996.
Scott, *Brave as a Mountain Lion,* Clarion, 1996.
Jan Slepian, *Emily Just in Time,* Philomel (New York City), 1997.

*SIDELIGHTS:* Illustrator and author Glo Coalson grew up with a love of art and of the out-of-doors. It wasn't until she was almost ready to graduate from college that she decided to begin a career as a children's book illustrator and author. Since writing and illustrating *Three Stone Woman* in 1971, Coalson has used her talent with ink, watercolor, and oil pastels to illustrate numerous picture books and poetry collections for children. "In my book art, I try always to do things that people can identify with, the typical human experience," Coalson once explained. "I like to pack energy into my drawings, as much as is appropriate for each manuscript. In my personal art I keep exploring, playing off ever-accumulating life experiences, hoping for the satisfaction that comes with learning how to express more about myself in a visual way."

Coalson demonstrated creativity throughout her childhood—"All my life I've been making things—sculpture and pottery—and drawing things"—but never considered channeling her talents into illustration until 1968, when just before graduating college a classmate enthusiastically commented, "You should illustrate books!" Two years later, while Coalson was visiting Alaska, she collected some Eskimo folktales and designed several book proposals around them. In 1971, her first book, *Three Stone Woman,* was released. The book presents a folktale about a widowed woman, Ana, whose difficult circumstances force her to beg for food for her children from her brother and her sister-in-law, Tula. But instead of filling Ana's sack with food, the miserly Tula fills it with three stones. Fortunately, Ana eventually is helped by two strangers, who give her a magic sealskin pouch, which provides her and her family with more than enough food, and the entire village is well fed during the long winter months. *Library Journal* reviewer Marilyn McCulloch called *Three Stone Woman,* which Coalson illustrated with graphic black ink-and-brush, "an excellent choice for story hours and for units on Eskimo life."

Coalson has also garnered recognition for her work with author Ann Herbert Scott, publishing such books as *On Mother's Lap, Hi!,* and *Brave as a Mountain Lion.* First published in 1972, *On Mother's Lap* was reprinted twenty years later with new pastel illustrations replacing the original black ink drawings. The story follows a young Inuit boy as he discovers that his mother's lap, as well as his mother's heart, has room enough for both him and his new baby sister. Calling the book a "classic, re-illustrated with finesse," *Booklist* reviewer Carolyn Phelan remarks

that children reading the book for the first time will enjoy the story as much as a "rocking chair ride on a mother's lap." Writing in *School Library Journal,* Mollie Bynum claims that Coalson's new artwork "improves upon a fine original work," going on to say that they give the book "revitalized energy to reach a new generation of youngsters."

Coalson and Scott also produced *Hi!* and *Brave as a Mountain Lion. Hi!* is a story about young Margarita as she attempts to make contact with people waiting in line at the post office. Initially shouting a cheerful "hi" to everyone she sees, Margarita becomes less confident as no one returns her greetings. Finally, after whispering one last "hi," Margarita finds a happy recipient when the postal clerk responds with a smile and "hi" of her own. In *School Library Journal,* Anna Biagioni Hart wrote that Coalson's drawings capture "exactly what it is like to feel small and unnoticed." Describing Coalson's watercolors as "true-to-life," a reviewer in *Publishers Weekly* praised her illustrations which "affectionately portray a diverse, multiracial cast." In a *Booklist* review of *Brave as a Mountain Lion,* a story presenting a family's show of support to an anxious Shoshone boy prior to his spelling bee, Shelley Townsend-Hudson noted that Coalson's "subtle watercolor illustrations effectively evoke . . . the warmth of [a] family's love." Praising Coalson's subdued watercolor and pastel illustrations, Susan Hepler, writing in *School Library Journal,* suggested that the book would be useful for teachers looking to depict modern Native American families in their classrooms.

*BIOGRAPHICAL/CRITICAL SOURCES:*

*PERIODICALS*

*Booklist,* April 1, 1992, p. 1458; May 15, 1994, p. 1684; March 15, 1996, p. 1269.
*Horn Book,* July/August, 1994, p. 445.
*Kirkus Reviews,* August 1, 1971, p. 801.
*Library Journal,* October 15, 1971, p. 3457.
*Publishers Weekly,* May 30, 1994, p. 56; January 22, 1996, p. 73.
*School Library Journal,* May, 1992, p. 93; July, 1994, p. 89; April 1996, p. 118.*

\*    \*    \*

**COHEN, Anthea**
  **See SIMPSON, Doris**

## COLE, Barry 1936-

*PERSONAL:* Born November 13, 1936, in Woking, Surrey, England; son of Leslie Herbert and Jennifer (Ryder) Cole; married Rita Linihan, June, 1958; children: Celia, Rebecca, Jessica. *Education:* Attended secondary school in England until age fifteen. *Politics:* "Anarchic (but not anarchist)." *Religion:* None.

*ADDRESSES: Home*—68 Myddelton Square, London EC1R 1XP, England.

*CAREER:* Reuters (news agency), began as clerk, became writer, beginning in 1958; Central Office of Information, London, England, assistant information officer, beginning in 1964; Northern Arts fellow in literature at Universities of Durham and Newcastle-upon-Tyne, 1970-72; freelance writer, 1972-74; Central Office of Information, staff member, including work as senior editor, 1974-94. *Military service:* Royal Air Force, 1955-57.

*AWARDS, HONORS:* Poetry Book Society Recommendation, 1969, for *Moonsearch;* Arts Council of Great Britain award, 1969-70.

*WRITINGS:*

NOVELS

*A Run across the Island,* Methuen (London), 1968.
*Joseph Winter's Patronage,* Methuen, 1969.
*The Search for Rita,* Methuen, 1970.
*The Giver,* Methuen, 1971.
*Doctor Fielder's Common Sense,* Methuen, 1972.

POETRY

*Blood Ties,* Turret Books (London), 1968.
*Moonsearch,* Methuen, 1968.
*Ulysses in the Town of Coloured Glass,* Turret Books, 1968.
*The Visitors,* Methuen, 1970.
*Vanessa in the City,* Trigram Press (London), 1970.
*Pathetic Fallacies,* Methuen, 1973.
*Dedications,* Byron Press (Nottingham, England), 1975.
*The Rehousing of Scaffardi,* Keepsake Press (Richmond, Surrey, England), 1976.

Also author of *Inside Outside: New and Selected Poems,* 1998.

OTHER

(Contributor) M. Horovitz, editor, *Children of Albion,* Penguin (New York City), 1969.
(Contributor) E. Lucie-Smith, editor, *Post-War British Poetry,* Penguin, 1971.
(Contributor) B. S. Johnson and M. Drabble, editors, *London Consequences,* Greater London Arts Association, 1972.
(Contributor) P. Larkin, editor, *Oxford Book of Twentieth Century Verse,* Oxford University Press (Oxford, England), 1974.

Also contributor to other anthologies. Contributor of poems and reviews to numerous periodicals, including the *New Statesman, Spectator,* and *Times Educational Supplement.*

*SIDELIGHTS:* Barry Cole "considers himself more a poet than a novelist," Theresa M. Peter writes in the *Dictionary of Literary Biography,* but he "writes exceptionally precise and enjoyable prose. His novels involve colorful but very realistic people in familiar situations and surroundings, usually centered in London. Cole catches the essence of British life in the late 1960s and early 1970s in a style that is witty and fresh." According to Peter, the main character in his first novel *A Run across the Island* reveals a "deadpan wit and a nonchalance that allows for keen, objective descriptions. These two qualities are, of course, attributable to the author, and they are the hallmarks of all Barry Cole's fiction." John Lucas writes in *Contemporary Novelists,* "The majority of novelists lack Cole's gifts of verbal precision, wit, exact ear for conversation, and his feeling for the elastic possibilities of language."

Like *A Run across the Island,* Lucas reports, *Joseph Winter's Patronage* explores a theme "of loneliness, of the difficulties of establishing relationships, of the slippery impermanence of friendship and love." Unlike the earlier novel, however, it approaches the theme from the perspective of the elderly. "Joseph Winter is a very old man," Peter explains, and though he lives in a senior citizens' home, "he is also very spirited and unwilling to relinquish his authority." Joseph's reminiscences and those of other residents shift backward and forward in time, building upon each other until they reveal complete characters, who came to the home with full and varied lives behind them. Lucas praises Cole for his sensitivity to the ambience of the home and its residents: "*Joseph Winter's Patronage* is the most touching and warmly sympathetic novel that Cole has so far written." "The book ends on a note of indignation at the patronizing attitude of society toward the elderly," Peter reports, "and critics have praised the novel for isolating this signigicant concern."

Cole's novel *The Search for Rita,* "his favorite one so far, is his liveliest, wittiest, and cleverest," Peter says. "It deftly captures the spirit of London in the 1960s and while amusing, it also reveals sinister undertones. The plot is vague and subordinate to the characters, who are highly developed and vividly described." The mysterious narrator is "the central figure who emerges," Peter comments. "He treats the others objectively, includes passages about his own life, and makes sudden appearances in their lives. It is never certain whether he is an eccentric and lazy private eye, an unemployed man half-heartedly searching for his own vanished lover (the elusive Rita), or an amiable author who is attempting to please his characters." A *Times Literary Supplement* reviewer says that "the characters and their actions are connected carefully in the unity of their creator's mind and temperament in such a manner as to suggest that his purpose is to show how any brain seeks instinctively to put order and coherence into chaotic, unrelated experience." According to Lucas, the novel manages to be "glittering" and "elegant" without seeming "aloof from life." He adds: "It is rather that the mess of life is met by a keen-eyed wit that can be ironic, self-deprecatory, satiric, and bawdy by turns. Style means everything in a novel of this kind, and the novelist's style does not let him down."

"Cole's cleverness overruns his fourth novel, *The Giver,*" says Peter. "He admits that in writing it he was playing with words to an extreme, almost showing off. Many of the passages are turned around, transmuted, reexecuted." Moral principals and the nature of human relationships are explored in *The Giver,* "but quite obscurely," according to Peter. "There is no plot as such; the novel is more a prolonged exercise in syntax and phraseology." This novel was not as well received as his earlier efforts were, but as Peter points out, "though *The Giver* ultimately remains enigmatic" one should remember that "the same creative imagination, precise description, subtle absurdities, irony, and wit that characterize Barry Cole's other fiction are all present [here]."

As Cole says, "the only vital subjects in my writings are words and the meaning of words; man (meaning woman) and the meaning of man; life and the meaning of life; society and its reconstruction; pretentiousness and its eradication; pomposity and its deflation;

onions and their private peelings." And Peter points out that "although his work lacks the social significance usually prerequisite for literary immortality, this is deliberate. Cole's novels provide insight into human nature and relationships—love, friendships, rejection, isolation—but draw no lofty conclusions. Words are everything to him; he calls himself a 'frustrated lexicographer' and challenges anyone to find a solecism in his work."

*BIOGRAPHICAL/CRITICAL SOURCES:*

*BOOKS*

*Contemporary Novelists,* sixth edition, St. James Press (Detroit), 1996.
*Dictionary of Literary Biography,* Volume 14: *British Novelists since 1960,* Gale (Detroit), 1983.
Johnson, B. S., editor, *The Evacuees,* Gollancz, 1969.

*PERIODICALS*

*Listener,* May 23, 1968; February 5, 1970.
*New Statesman,* December 13, 1968; September 25, 1970.
*Observer Review,* May 26, 1968.
*Times Literary Supplement,* January 9, 1969; February 5, 1970; October 30, 1970.

\*    \*    \*

## COLE, Sheila R(otenberg) 1939-

*PERSONAL:* Born January 5, 1939, in Toronto, Ontario, Canada; daughter of Benjamin (a grocer) and Helen (Weiss) Rotenberg; married Michael Cole (a research psychologist and university professor), December 18, 1957; children: Jennifer, Alexander. *Education:* Attended University of California, Los Angeles, 1957-59; Indiana University, B.A., 1961; Columbia University, M.S., 1965. *Avocational interests:* Cooking, reading, gardening, sailing, hiking.

*ADDRESSES: Home*—522 Glencrest Dr., Solana Beach, CA 92075. *Agent*—Jennifer Flannery, 1140 Wickfield Court, Naperville, IL 60563.

*CAREER:* Writer. *Sunnyvale Daily Standard,* Sunnyvale, CA, reporter, 1963-64; Community Progress,

Inc., New Haven, CT, public information officer, 1965-66; *Newport Beach Daily Pilot,* Newport Beach, CA, reporter, 1966-67; University of California, Irvine, research assistant, 1968-69; freelance writer, 1969—; Deutsch, Shea & Evans, Inc., New York City, director of communications, 1977; University of California, San Diego, consultant on interview techniques, 1979-80. Has also worked as a staff writer for an advertising agency and as an editor for the U.S. Government Office of Education.

*MEMBER:* Society of Children's Book Writers and Illustrators, Southern California Council on Literature for Children and Young People.

*AWARDS, HONORS:* Golden Kite Honor Book, Society of Children's Book Writers and Illustrators, 1974, for *Meaning Well;* Notable Children's Trade Book in the Field of Social Studies, National Council for the Social Studies and Children's Book Council (NCSS-CBC), and Junior Literary Guild Selection, both for *Working Kids on Working;* "Pick of the Lists," American Booksellers Association, and "Science for the Young Child List," *Booklist,* both for *When the Tide Is Low;* Notable Children's Trade Book in the Field of Social Studies, NCSS-CBC, Outstanding Science Trade Book for Children, and Perrot Library Young Critics' Choice, all for *The Dragon in the Cliff; What Kind of Love? The Diary of a Pregnant Teenager* was selected for the "Quick Picks for Reluctant Young Adult Readers" list by the Young Adult Library Services division of the American Library Association, 1996.

*WRITINGS:*

*FOR YOUNG PEOPLE*

*Meaning Well,* illustrated by Paul Raynor, F. Watts (New York City), 1974.

*Working Kids on Working* (nonfiction), photographs by Victoria Beller-Smith, Lothrop (New York City), 1980.

*When the Tide Is Low,* illustrated by Virginia Wright-Frierson, Lothrop, 1985.

*The Dragon in the Cliff: A Novel Based on the Life of Mary Anning,* illustrated by T. C. Farrow, Lothrop, 1991.

*When the Rain Stops,* illustrated by Henri Sorensen, Lothrop, 1991.

*The Hen That Crowed,* illustrated by Barbara Rogoff, Lothrop, 1993.

*What Kind of Love? The Diary of a Pregnant Teenager,* Lothrop, 1995.

*OTHER*

(Editor with husband, Michael Cole) A. R. Luria, *The Making of Mind: A Personal Account of Soviet Psychology* (autobiography), Harvard University Press (Cambridge, MA), 1979.

(With Michael Cole) *The Development of Children* (college textbook), W. H. Freeman (New York City)/Scientific American Books, 1989, revised editions, 1992, 1996.

Contributor to *The International Cook's Catalogue,* Random House (New York City), 1977. Also a contributor of articles and book reviews to *Psychology Today, Ms., New York Times Sunday Magazine, New York Times Book Review, Ladies' Home Journal, Human Nature, Nation, Chicago Tribune,* and *Banking.*

*WORK IN PROGRESS: The Canyon,* a novel for children.

*SIDELIGHTS:* Sheila R. Cole has written everything from picture books to young adult novels to nonfiction works for both children and adults. While Cole takes on a complex issue for a teenage audience in *What Kind of Love? The Diary of a Pregnant Teenager,* she also uses simple stories to convey information to very young readers. *When the Tide Is Low,* for example, is a picture book about a little girl and her mother at the beach that helps teach children about sea life. *When the Rain Stops* uses a similar approach to introduce youngsters to the sights and sounds of nature. Cole has also written a nonfiction book for young adults: *Working Kids on Working,* which is a collection of interviews with working teens discussing their first job experiences. More recently, the author has decided to do another nonfiction project. "I am currently working on a nonfiction book about the history of childhood," she once told *CA.* "I am fascinated by how different it is to be a child today from what it was like 300, 150, even sixty years ago. One of the great pleasures of this project is that it allows me to indulge in one of my favorite pastimes: reading history books and historical novels."

In a number of Cole's books a common pattern appears. From her Golden Kite Honor Book, *Meaning Well,* to one of her more recent novels for teens, *What Kind of Love?,* Cole demonstrates an empathy for the outsider, the person estranged from those who are considered normal. That her sympathies lie with such outsiders, both real and fictional, is no accident, for as a child Cole herself was keenly aware of her differences from other children in her Toronto neighborhood. The daughter of Jewish immigrants from Eastern Europe, Cole was self-conscious that her family was not like those of her friends. Her parents did not speak English very well, and her mother, unlike other mothers at the time, had a job. Cole, however, learned to blend in very well in American culture, but her fascination with what makes people different from one another remained. She and her husband lived for a time in what was then the Soviet Union, and they later spent time in Liberia, the Yucatan in Mexico, and London. "With each of these moves," she wrote in a publicity release for her publisher, Lothrop, "has come a new experience of feeling 'different' and the need to find out everything about the place so I can make sense of it."

Being different is the subject of Cole's first book for children ages eight and older, *Meaning Well* (1974). This story is about a girl named Lisa and quiet Peggy, who is a loner. Though Lisa wants to befriend Peggy, her desire to have the popular, pretty Susan for a friend gets in the way. When Susan begins to taunt Peggy for being "weird," Lisa feels pressured to take Susan's side. The conclusion, noted a *Publishers Weekly* reviewer, "to the author's credit, is decidedly not a happy one," for Peggy moves away before Lisa takes the important step of extending a friendship to a deserving girl and defying her selfish classmates.

Cole touched on the theme of the outsider again in a more recent book for young children, *The Hen That Crowed* (1993). "A refreshing, inventive plot . . . make[s] this story something to crow about," asserted Ellen Fader in *Horn Book*. The author sets the tale in the town of Bean Blossom, where no roosters are allowed because everyone likes to sleep late. But when kind-hearted farmer Goodhart accidentally buys a chick that grows up to be a cockle-doodle-doo-ing rooster, he unsuccessfully tries to fool the bird by blindfolding it rather than making it into chicken soup. One morning, however, the rooster mistakes the light that comes through a hole in the shed as the sun. It is actually a fire, and Charlene's crowing alerts the townspeople into avoiding disaster. Naturally, Charlene becomes a hero.

In an interesting mix of fact and fiction, Cole brings the story of another outsider to life in her biographical novel, *The Dragon in the Cliff: A Novel Based on the Life of Mary Anning*. A poor British girl from the nineteenth century, Anning discovered some of the first dinosaur fossils ever uncovered. Her findings,

however, only brought her ridicule. As Cole explained to *CA*, "I was moved to write *The Dragon in the Cliff* by the condescending tone of something I read about Anning in a natural history magazine. It made me wonder what it was like for a poor girl with little education to make the momentous paleontological discoveries she did. How did she feel about her discoveries, the questions they raised, and the people they brought her into contact with? Since the only written record from that time comes from the gentlemen who used her discoveries to make their names in science, I had to make up her side of the story." Using what researched facts she could find, Cole pieced together Anning's story.

Most critics agreed that *The Dragon in the Cliff* is an engaging and well-researched historical novel that faithfully describes the world in which Mary lived. "Cole does a wonderful job of describing Anning's struggles to overcome the biases of the times, the English town in which she lived, and its prejudices," asserted *School Library Journal* contributor Cathryn Camper, who added that "by including the societal instigators of [Anning's] many problems—classism and sexism—Cole refuses to write down to her audience, or to simplify history." Anna K. Behrensmeyer, writing in *Science* magazine, maintained that "Cole gives her readers a lasting image of how intelligence, necessity, and determination combined to shape Mary Anning's life and give her a significant place in the history of paleontology." *Booklist* reviewer Candace Smith praised *The Dragon in the Cliff* as a "readable and enjoyable historical novel," noting that "Mary shines through as a spunky and believable heroine."

Cole takes on an even tougher story of rejection in her 1995 novel, *What Kind of Love? The Diary of a Pregnant Teenager*. The author wrote this story in an attempt to better understand what it is like for young people to go through an unwanted pregnancy. "When I began my young adult novel," Cole once told *CA*, "I couldn't understand how a girl could bring herself to give up her baby for adoption. The novel was my attempt to work out a plausible explanation of what might bring someone to do such a thing." Cole uses the device of a diary to get inside Valerie's, the story's fifteen-year-old protagonist, thoughts over a six month period as she goes through the adoption process. Valerie has the opportunity to pursue a possible career in music as a violinist, and she comes to realize that giving up the baby will not only help her achieve her own potential, but it will also be more fair to her child.

*What Kind of Love?* is full of factual information, ranging from frank discussions about sex and the discomforts of pregnancy to what is involved in putting a baby up for adoption and tips about how to childproof a home. "Quite often, these facts come adroitly camouflaged," remarked a *Publishers Weekly* reviewer. Cole, as Stephanie Zvirin observed in her *Booklist* review, manages to convey this information within an interesting story line: "[It is] Val's determination to hang on to her romantic vision that drives the story." Zvirin praised Cole's characterization and her ability to avoid "shrill preachiness." *School Library Journal* contributor Dona Weisman applauded the book's unresolved conclusion, maintaining that by not revealing whether Valerie will actually go through with the adoption, Cole compels readers "to relate to [Valerie's] dilemma and to ponder the consequences of her decision."

*BIOGRAPHICAL/CRITICAL SOURCES:*

*PERIODICALS*

*Booklist,* January 15, 1981, pp. 697-98; March 1, 1991, p. 1383; September 1, 1991, p. 60; March 15, 1995, p. 1322.
*Bulletin of the Center for Children's Books,* April, 1995, p. 268.
*Horn Book,* April, 1981, pp. 202-203; June, 1993, p. 313.
*Kirkus Reviews,* February 1, 1974, p. 109; May 15, 1985, p. J25; May 1, 1991, p. 603.
*Publishers Weekly,* May 27, 1974, p. 65; March 15, 1993, p. 86; April 17, 1995, p. 61.
*School Library Journal,* May, 1985, p. 71; September, 1991, p. 250; January, 1992, p. 89; August, 1993, p. 140; May, 1995, p. 118.
*Science,* April 16, 1993, pp. 376-77.

\*    \*    \*

## COMMAGER, Henry Steele 1902-

*PERSONAL:* Born October 25, 1902, in Pittsburgh, PA; son of James Williams and Anna Elizabeth (Dan) Commager; married Evan Carroll, July 3, 1928; married Mary E. Powlesland, July 14, 1979; children: (first marriage) Henry Steele (deceased), Nellie Thomas McColl, Elisabeth Carroll. *Education:* University of Chicago, Ph.B., 1923, M.A., 1924, Ph.D., 1928; attended University of Copenhagen; Cambridge University, M.A.; Oxford University, M.A. *Politics:* Independent Democrat.

*ADDRESSES: Home*—405 South Pleasant St., Amherst, MA 01002. *Office*—Department of History, Amherst College, Amherst, MA 01002.

*CAREER:* New York University, New York City, instructor in history, 1926-29, assistant professor, 1929-30, associate professor, 1930-31, professor, 1931-38; Columbia University, New York City, professor of American history, 1939-56, adjunct professor, 1956-59, Speranza Lecturer, 1960; Amherst College, Amherst, MA, Smith Professor of History, 1956-72, Simpson Lecturer, beginning 1972, then professor emeritus. Pitt Professor of American History, Cambridge University, 1941, 1947-48; Bacon Lecturer, Boston University, 1943; Richards Lecturer, University of Virginia, 1944; Harmsworth Professor of American History, Oxford University, 1952-53; Gottesman Lecturer, Uppsala University, 1953; Ziskind Professor, Brandeis University, 1955; Commonwealth Lecturer, University of London, 1963; Harris Lecturer, Northwestern University, 1964; Patton Lecturer, Indiana University, 1977. Visiting professor or lecturer at several universities in the United States and abroad. Member of War Department Commission on History of the War; travelled to Britain for War Department, Office of War Information, summer, 1943, and to France and Belgium, 1945. *Military service:* Served with U.S. Army Information and Education Division, 1945.

*MEMBER:* American Academy of Arts and Letters, American Scandinavian Society (fellow), American Antiquarian Society, Massachusetts Historical Society, Phi Beta Kappa, Century Association, St. Botolph's (Boston), Athenaeum Club (London).

*AWARDS, HONORS:* Herbert B. Adams Award of the American Historical Association, 1929; special award from Hillman Foundation, 1954, for *Freedom, Loyalty, Dissent*; Guggenheim fellowship, 1960-61; Gold Medal Award for history from American Academy and Institute of Arts and Letters, 1972; Sarah Josepha Hale Award, 1973; decorated Knight, Order of Dannebrog. Honorary degrees from numerous colleges and universities.

*WRITINGS:*

*The Literature of the Pioneer West,* [Saint Paul], 1927.

(With Samuel Eliot Morison) *The Growth of the American Republic,* Oxford University Press, 1931, 7th edition, 1980, abbreviated and newly revised edition published as *A Concise History of the American Republic,* 1977.

*Our Nation's Development,* Harper, 1934.

*Theodore Parker,* Little, Brown, 1936, reissued with a new introduction, Beacon Press, 1960.

(With Allan Nevins) *America: The Story of a Free People,* Little, Brown, 1942, Oxford University Press, 1976, reissued in paperback as *The Pocket History of the United States,* Pocket Books, 1943, revised edition, 1982.

*Majority Rule and Minority Rights,* Oxford University Press, 1943.

(With Nevins) *A Short History of the United States,* Modern Library, 1945, 6th edition, Knopf, 1976.

*The American Mind: An Interpretation of American Thought and Character since the 1880s,* Yale University Press, 1950.

(With others) *Civil Liberties under Attack,* University of Pennsylvania Press, 1951.

(Contributor) Courtlandt Canby, editor, *The World of History,* New American Library, 1954.

(With Geoffrey Brunn) *Europe and America since 1492,* Houghton, 1954.

*Freedom, Loyalty, Dissent,* Oxford University Press, 1954.

*Federal Centralization and the Press,* University of Minnesota, 1956.

(Contributor) *Conference on the American High School,* University of Chicago Press, 1958.

(With Robert W. McEwen and Brand Blanshard) *Education in a Free Society,* University of Pittsburgh Press, 1961.

*The Nature and the Study of History,* C. E. Merrill, 1965.

*The Role of Scholarship in an Age of Science,* Laramie, 1965.

*Freedom and Order: A Commentary on the American Political Scene,* Braziller, 1966.

*The Study of History,* C. E. Merrill, 1966.

(With Elmo Giordonetti) *Was America a Mistake?: An Eighteenth-Century Controversy,* Harper, 1967.

*The Search for a Usable Past, and Other Essays in Historiography,* Knopf, 1967.

(With Richard B. Morris) *Colonies in Transition,* Harper, 1968.

*The Commonwealth of Learning,* Harper, 1968.

*The Defeat of America: Presidential Power and the National Character,* Simon & Schuster, 1974.

*Britain through American Eyes,* McGraw, 1974.

*Jefferson, Nationalism, and the Enlightenment,* Braziller, 1974.

*The Empire of Reason: How Europe Imagined and America Realized the Enlightenment,* Doubleday, 1977.

(Author of text) *Mort Kuenstler's Fifty Epic Paintings of America,* Abbeville Press, 1979.

(With Raymond H. Muessig) *The Study and Teaching of History,* Merrill, 1980.

(Author of introduction) *The Civil War Almanac,* Facts on File, 1983.

(Author of introduction) *Of America East and West: From the Writings of Paul Horgan,* Farrar, Straus, 1984.

(Contributor) John Grafton, editor, *America: A History of the First 500 Years,* Crescent Books (New York City), 1992.

*Commager on Tocqueville,* University of Missouri Press (Columbia), 1993.

*The Odes of Horace: A Critical Study,* University of Oklahoma Press (Norman), 1995.

*EDITOR*

*Documents of American History* (Volume 1, to 1898; Volume 2, from 1865), F. S. Crofts, 1934, 10th edition, Prentice-Hall, 1988.

(With Nevins) *The Heritage of America,* Little, Brown, 1939, revised and enlarged edition, 1949.

(And author of historical narrative) *The Story of the Second World War,* Little, Brown, 1945, Brassey's (Washington), 1991.

(And author of introduction and notes) *America in Perspective: The United States through Foreign Eyes,* Random House 1947, abridged edition, New American Library, 1959.

Alexis de Tocqueville, *Democracy in America,* translated by Henry Reeve, Oxford University Press, 1947.

*Selections from "The Federalist,"* Appleton, 1949.

(With others) *Years of the Modern: An American Appraisal,* Longmans, Green, 1949.

*The Blue and the Gray: The Story of the Civil War as Told by Participants,* two volumes, Bobbs-Merrill, 1950, revised and abridged, Meridian (New York City), 1994.

William Dean Howells, *Selected Writings,* Random House 1950.

(And author of commentary) *Living Ideas in America,* Harper, 1951, enlarged edition, 1967.

(With Morris) *The Spirit of '76: The Story of the American Revolution as Told by the Participants,* two volumes, Bobbs-Merrill, 1958, bicentennial edition, Harper, 1975.

*Official Atlas of the Civil War,* Yoseloff, 1958.

*Living Documents of American History,* [Washington], 1960.

*The Era of Reform, 1830-1860,* Van Nostrand, 1960.

*Theodore Parker: An Anthology,* Beacon Press, 1960.

James Bryce, *Reflections on American Institutions: Selections from "The American Commonwealth,"* Fawcett, 1961.

*Immigration and American History: Essays in Honor of Theodore C. Blegen,* University of Minnesota Press, 1961.

Chester Bowles, *The Conscience of a Liberal,* Harper, 1962.

Winston Churchill, *History of the English-Speaking Peoples* (one volume of a four volume series), Bantam, 1963.

*Noah Webster's American Spelling Book,* Teachers College Press, 1963.

*The Defeat of the Confederacy: A Documentary Survey,* Van Nostrand, 1964.

*Fifty Basic Civil War Documents,* Van Nostrand, 1965.

(Consulting editor) *Encyclopedia of American History,* Harper, 1965.

*Lester Ward and the Welfare State,* Bobbs-Merrill, 1966.

*The Struggle for Racial Equality: A Documentary Record,* Harper, 1967.

Churchill, *Marlborough: His Life and Times,* Scribner, 1968.

(With others) *The West: An Illustrated History,* Promotory Press, 1976.

Edward M. Kennedy, *Our Day and Generation: The Words of Edward M. Kennedy,* Simon & Schuster, 1979.

(With others) *Illustrated History of the American Civil War,* Orbis, 1979.

Also editor with Morris of the "New American Nation" series, published by Harper; editor-in-chief of *The American Destiny: An Illustrated Bicentennial History of the United States,* twenty volumes, published by Danbury Press.

*FOR CHILDREN*

(With Eugene Campbell Barker) *Our Nation,* Row, Peterson, 1941.

(Editor) *St. Nicholas Anthology,* Random House, 1948.

(Editor) *Second St. Nicholas Anthology,* Random House, 1950.

*America's Robert E. Lee,* Houghton, 1951, Marshall Cavendish Corporation (North Bellmore, NY), 1991.

*Chestnut Squirrel,* Houghton, 1952.

*The First Book of American History,* illustrated by Leonard Everett Fisher, F. Watts, 1957.

*The Great Declaration,* Bobbs-Merrill, 1958.

*A Picture History of the United States of America,* F. Watts, 1958.

*The Great Proclamation,* Bobbs-Merrill, 1960.

*The Great Constitution,* Bobbs-Merrill, 1961.

*Crusaders for Freedom,* Doubleday, 1962.

*OTHER*

Contributor of essays to scholarly and popular journals, including *Book Week, New York Times Book Review, New Republic, Saturday Review, New York Review of Books,* and *American Scholar.*

*WORK IN PROGRESS:* Editing "The Rise of the American Nation," a projected fifty-volume series.

*SIDELIGHTS:* Henry Steele Commager is revered by many as among America's most preeminent historians of the twentieth century. His writings include textbooks for children and college students, edited compilations of historical source material, original studies of the nature of U.S. democracy, and biographies of prominent U.S. citizens. As Lawrence Wells Cobb explains in the *Dictionary of Literary Biography,* Commager "has devoted his energies to making it easier for scholars and lay readers both to 'get at' the sources of the American historical record and to understand their heritage more fully. He has undertaken these tasks so that his readers might become more informed and responsible participants in the great experiment launched in the eighteenth century to make a free, democratic, and bountiful society a reality on the North American continent." *New Republic* contributor Alexander R. Butler calls Commager "one of America's most distinguished historians," an educator and scholar whose "excellent reputation" stems from his "simple, straightforward, and assertive" style. Behind that style lies serious conviction, however. Butler notes that Commager is "convinced that the reader can learn from history" and profit from the lessons of the usable past. Cobb likewise observes that in his writings the historian demands "that Americans live responsibly and prove worthy of their heritage." Commager's sprightly style, his eye for the illuminating vignette, his catholic knowledge, and his optimistic perspective have served him well in bringing his insights to generations of readers.

Commager's best known book is *The Growth of the American Republic,* a title he co-authored with

Samuel Eliot Morison. First published in 1931, the work continues to be read by students of U.S. history. According to *New York Times Book Review* correspondent Esmond Wright, the "limpidly clear style and the easy marshaling of arguments . . . have made 'The Growth of the American Republic' one of the most unusual and certainly one of the most readable of textbooks." Commager's other books for lay readers include 1941's *Our Nation* for high school students, and the popular study *America: The Story of a Free People,* co-authored by Allan Nevins in 1942. Commager's aim, in Cobb's words, has been "always to provide the facts within the matrix of an unobtrusive liberal interpretation and to provoke thought on the part of the reader." As early as 1934 Commager also began the editing duties for which he has become well known; his *Documents of American History* collects in two volumes the important primary sources on the creation and development of the United States. Cobb calls the work "the best single-volume source book in its field." Throughout the following forty years Commager has continued to publish anthologies of historical source material; his efforts have produced, among others, *The Blue and the Gray: The Story of the Civil War as Told by Participants, The Era of Reform, 1830-1860,* and *The Struggle for Racial Equality: A Documentary History.* Cobb claims that such collections are "intended to put the words and ideas that shaped America within easy reach of both the generalist and interested layman." In the *New York Herald Tribune Book Review,* Bernard DeVoto contends that these books provide "a way of experiencing the nation's most tremendous experience. No one can read [them] without being impelled to think searchingly about the American people, the American nation, the American past and future."

As a scholar Commager has sought to define the strengths of democracy. Cobb suggests that the historian's theses "always revolved around Jeffersonian liberalism: give the public the maximum amount of information and the people can be trusted to make the right decisions in the long run." Such a view stresses the importance of education as well as the necessity for free speech and dissent; not surprisingly, Commager would become one of the strongest opponents of the intellectual purges of the communist-fearing McCarthy Era conformity of the 1950s. His comment in the 1951 volume *Civil Liberties under Attack* has since become famous: "The great danger that threatens us is neither heterodox thought nor orthodox thought, but the absence of thought." Throughout the following decade, as the Vietnam War and social unrest escalated, Commager continued to argue for

the preservation of free speech and inquiry. According to Cobb, the historian "reminded visitors, distressed to see all the unrest in America, . . . that the idealism of the 1960s was a reassertion, not a repudiation, of our Revolutionary ideals of liberty and equality." Since then, in such essentially optimistic books as *Jefferson, Nationalism, and the Enlightenment* and *The Empire of Reason: How Europe Imagined and America Realized the Enlightenment,* Commager has maintained that America is an ongoing experiment in the practical implementation of philosophy; the nation's continued strength depends on its forging a link with the ideals of the founding generation. As Cobb puts it, history is "definitely a usable past for citizens of the United States, and this history [is] also a living proof to all the people of the world that such 'good things' as continental self-government and socio-economic mobility [are] possible."

Commager's 1993 work, *Commager on Tocqueville,* provides another link with the past that has much to teach modern America. Based on the classic *Democracy in America,* a political study of the young American republic written by French historian Alexis de Tocqueville in 1835 and translated by Commager in 1947, *Commager on Tocqueville* focuses on several areas of concern in the historic nineteenth-century critique of early democracy. While the French historian evinced concern by what he perceived as the potential for a tyranny of the majority, the difficulty of finding an equilibrium between individuality and equality, the role of a military arm of government within a democratic state, and the advocacy of personal liberty by a central ruling body, Commager contends that many of these concerns have been proven to be unfounded. However, he warns, such things as the overly large federal and state governmental bureaucracies and the extreme economic inequity that have manifested themselves in the United States over the past century may be symptomatic of some of de Tocqueville's concerns. While D. J. Maletz dubs *Commager on Tocqueville* "an ardent defense of all the institutions of the contemporary liberal welfare state," Commager maintains throughout the work that the problems facing the United States at the close of the millennia—including environmental depredations, overpopulation over much of the earth's inhabitable surface, and chronic political upheavals—call for a revisioning of democratic government along global rather than nationalistic boundaries.

In his continued commitment to educating the public, Commager attempts to offer readers a spectrum of facts, thereby enabling them to judge history objectively. Critics such as *New York Times* columnist Herbert Mitgang note, however, that the educator's enthusiasm for history, coupled with his "crystalline clarity of [his] writing," causes "explosions in the reader's mind," resulting in "history to be pondered and cherished." Cobb sees Commager as a popularizer of the love of history, an author who has "kindled a love for the spectacle of history and personality in thousands of young minds" through his juvenile literature and his many source books. *Atlantic* contributor C. J. Rolo also contends that Commager's value as a writer "is that he combines an exhilarating enthusiasm for his subject with a keenly critical viewpoint and an absence of cant that is becoming increasingly rare."

A prolific writer, Commager has continued to edit and compile historical texts that reveal both the benefits and the challenges of democratic government since retiring from his professorial duties at Amherst College. In the *New York Times Book Review*, Arthur Schlesinger Jr. concludes that in Henry Steele Commager, "learning and reason are at the service of a mind whose understanding of democracy gains brilliance and power from a passion for democratic freedom."

*BIOGRAPHICAL/CRITICAL SOURCES:*

*BOOKS*

Commager, Henry Steele, with others, *Civil Liberties under Attack,* University of Pennsylvania Press, 1951.
*Dictionary of Literary Biography,* Volume 17: *Twentieth Century American Historians,* Gale (Detroit), 1983.
Garraty, John, *Interpreting American History: Conversations with Historians,* Macmillan, 1970.
Hyman, Harold M. and Leonard W. Levy, editors, *Freedom and Reform: Essays in Honor of Henry Steele Commager,* Harper, 1967.

*PERIODICALS*

*Atlantic,* May, 1950.
*Choice,* November, 1993, p. 535.
*Christian Century,* July 5, 1950; October 24, 1962.
*Christian Science Monitor,* April 6, 1936; March 18, 1950.
*Commonweal,* May 5, 1950.
*Library Journal,* May 15, 1993, p. 81; October 15, 1995, p. 96.

*Nation,* April 22, 1950; December 23, 1950.
*New Republic,* April 24, 1950; May 24, 1954; May 20, 1967; December 21, 1974.
*New Statesman,* June 2, 1967.
*Newsweek,* November 15, 1948.
*New York Herald Tribune Book Review,* March 12, 1950; November 19, 1950; May 30, 1954.
*New York Times,* March 12, 1950; November 12, 1950; June 7, 1977.
*New York Times Book Review,* March 12, 1950; October 23, 1966; June 25, 1967; November 26, 1967; August 14, 1977; November 4, 1979; April 8, 1984.
*San Francisco Chronicle,* March 24, 1950; November 26, 1950.
*Saturday Review,* March 11, 1950; December 2, 1950; May 1, 1954; January 28, 1967; May 14, 1977.
*Survey,* April, 1950.
*Time,* December 11, 1950.
*Times Literary Supplement,* November 17, 1950; July 23, 1954; September 27, 1974; August 4, 1978.
*Yale Review,* summer, 1950.*

\*    \*    \*

## COOK, Michael 1933-

*PERSONAL:* Born February 14, 1933, in London, England; came to Canada, 1966; naturalized Canadian citizen, 1971; son of George William Cook (a civil servant); married Joyce Horner, 1951 (divorced, 1966); married Janis Jones, 1967 (divorced, 1973); married Madonna Decker (a researcher), December 28, 1973; children: Michael, Diane, Graham, Elaine, Adrian, Etain, Rowena, Christopher, Sarah, Sebastian, Fergus, Perdita. *Education:* University of Nottingham, T.T.C. (with honors), 1966.

*ADDRESSES: Home*—Box 327, R.R. 1, Petley, Random Island, Trinity Bay, Newfoundland AOE IJO, Canada. *Office*—Department of English, Memorial University, P. O. Box 4200, St. John's, Newfoundland A1C 5S7, Canada. *Agent*—Playwrights Union of Canada, 8 York St., 6th Floor, Toronto, Ontario M5J 1R2, Canada.

*CAREER:* Steelworker and farmer in Nottinghamshire, England, 1961-63; Memorial University, St. John's, Newfoundland, drama adviser, 1967-69, lecturer, 1969-74, assistant professor, 1974-79, associate professor of English, 1979—. Playwright in residence, Banff Festival, 1978, and Stratford Festival, 1987. Host and scriptwriter of *Our Man Friday* (weekly television review), Canadian Broadcasting Corp. (CBC-TV), 1971-72; *St. John's Evening Telegram,* St. John's, Newfoundland, drama critic and television columnist, 1967-77. Artistic director of St. John's Summer Festival of the Arts, 1968-75; director of Newfoundland Arts and Culture Centre productions, 1971-74; occasional actor. Member of executive board of *Canadian Theatre Review;* governor of Canadian Conference of the Arts, 1975-79; member of grants and awards committee of Department of Cultural Affairs, 1979—. *Military service:* British Army, Royal Electrical and Mechanical Engineers and Intelligence Corps, 1949-61; served in Korea, Japan, Malaya, and Europe; became staff sergeant.

*MEMBER:* Guild of Canadian Playwrights (vice-president, 1978-80), Playwright's Canada, Association of Canadian Radio and Television Artists, Newfoundland Arts Council.

*AWARDS, HONORS:* Canada Council senior arts grant, 1973 and 1979, for significant contribution to the arts; Labatt Award for the best Canadian play, 1974, for *Head, Guts, and Soundbone Dance,* 1975, for *Jacob's Wake,* 1978, for *On the Rim of the Curve,* and 1979, for *The Gayden Chronicles;* Queen's Silver Jubilee Medal, 1979, for service to the arts; Newfoundland and Labrador Government Award, 1985.

*WRITINGS:*

PLAYS

*The J. Arthur Prufrock Hour,* produced in St. John's, Newfoundland, 1968.
*Colour the Flesh the Colour of Dust* (two-act; produced in Ottawa, Ontario, at National Arts Centre, 1972), Simon & Pierre (Toronto), 1972.
*Tiln* (one-act), produced in Toronto, 1972.
*The Head, Guts, and Soundbone Dance* (two-act; produced in Montreal, Quebec, at Saidye Bronfman Centre, 1974), Breakwater (St. John's), 1974.
*Jacob's Wake* (three-act; produced in St. John's, Newfoundland, 1974), Talonbooks (Vancouver), 1975.
*The Fisherman's Revenge* (one-act; produced in Trinity Bay, Newfoundland, 1976), Playwrights (Toronto), 1985.
*Not as a Dream* (two-act; produced in Halifax, Nova Scotia, at Dalhousie University, 1976), Playwrights, 1976, Doubleday (New York City), 1979.

*Tiln and Other Plays,* Talonbooks, 1976.
*On the Rim of the Curve,* produced in Gander, Newfoundland, 1977.
*Quiller* [and] *Therese's Creed* (both one-act; produced in Montreal, Quebec, at Centaur Theatre, 1977), Talonbooks, 1977.
*Three Plays* (contains *On the Rim of the Curve, The Head, Guts and Soundbone Dance* and *Therese's Creed*), Breakwater (Portugal Cove, Newfoundland), 1977.
*The Gayden Chronicles* (three-act; produced in Lennoxville, ON, 1977; produced in Waterford, CT, at O'Neill Centre, 1978), Playwrights, 1979.
*The Apocalypse Sonata: Sex and St. John* (two-act), produced in Regina, Saskatchewan, 1980.
*The Deserts of Bohemia,* produced in San Francisco, 1980.
*The Great Harvest Festival,* produced in Stratford, Ontario, 1986.

RADIO PLAYS

*He Should Have Been a Pirate,* Canadian Broadcasting Corp. (CBC), 1967.
*No Man Can Serve Two Masters,* CBC, 1967.
*Or the Wheel Broken,* CBC, 1968.
*A Walk in the Rain,* CBC, 1968.
*The Concubine,* CBC, 1969.
*The Illiad* (adapted from the work by Homer), CBC, 1967.
*Midsummer Night's Dream* (adapted from the play by William Shakespeare), CBC, 1969.
*A Time for Doors,* CBC, 1970.
*The Truck,* CBC, 1970.
*To Inhabit the Earth Is Not Enough,* CBC, 1971.
*Love Is a Walnut,* CBC, 1971.
*Enemy of the People* (adapted from the play by Ibsen), CBC, 1971.
*A Walk Into the Unknown,* CBC, 1972.
*The Ballad of Patrick Docker,* CBC, 1972.
*Tiln,* CBC, 1972.
*There's a Seal at the Bottom of the Garden,* CBC, 1973.
*Colour the Flesh the Colour of Dust,* CBC, 1973.
*Apostles for the Burning,* CBC, 1974.
*Travels with Aunt Jane,* CBC, 1974.
*Knight of Sorrow, Lady of Darkness,* CBC, 1975.
*The Head, Guts, and Soundbone Dance,* CBC, 1975.
*Ireland's Eye,* CBC, 1976.
*The Producer, the Director,* CBC, 1976.
*On the Rim of the Curve,* CBC, 1977.
*Quiller,* CBC, 1978.
*The Gentleman Amateur,* CBC, 1978.
*All a Pack o' Lies,* CBC, 1979.

*The Hunter,* CBC, 1980.

*The Preacher,* CBC, 1981.

*The Terrible Journey of Frederick Douglas,* CBC, 1982.

*The Sweet Second Summer of Kitty Malone,* CBC, 1983.

*This Damned Inheritance,* CBC, 1984.

*The Bailiff and the Women,* CBC, 1984.

*The Ocean Ranger,* CBC, 1985.

*The Saddest Barn Dance Ever Held,* CBC, 1985.

*The Hanging Judge,* CBC, 1985.

*The Moribundian Memorandum,* CBC, 1986.

OTHER

*In Search of Confederation* (television script), CBC-TV, 1971.

*Daniel, My Brother,* CBC-TV, 1979.

*The C.F.A.,* CBC-TV, 1980.

*The Course of True Love,* CBC-TV, 1980.

*The Island of Fire* (novel), Doubleday (Toronto), 1980.

Also author of an autobiographical novel, *The Elusive Conversationalist,* held in Canadian Archives at University of Calgary, 1966, and a juvenile, *The Fogo Island Caper,* 1972, both unpublished.

Work represented in anthologies, including *The Blasty Bough,* Breakwater, 1967; *Tiln and Other Plays,* Tallonbooks, 1976; *Cues and Entrances,* Gage, 1977; *Transitions I: Short Plays,* Commcept, 1978; *31 Newfoundland Poets,* Breakwater, 1979; and *And What Are You Going to Do for Us?,* Simon & Pierre, 1980. Contributor of reviews, articles, and short stories to periodicals, including *Macleans, Performing Arts in Canada, Canadian Theatre Review, Vie Des Arts,* and Canadian Broadcasting Corp. (CBC)-Radio.

*ADAPTATIONS:* Many of Cook's radio plays have been translated for broadcast on Radio Berlin and Radio Switzerland.

*SIDELIGHTS:* Michael Cook is best known for his "so-called Newfoundland Trilogy," according to Reid Gilbert in *Contemporary Dramatists.* These three plays—*Colour the Flesh the Colour of Dust, The Head, Guts and Soundbone Dance* and *Jacob's Wake*—are based in Newfoundland history. Cook, writes Chris Johnson in the *Dictionary of Literary Biography,* is "the Newfoundland playwright best known outside his own province and a major contributor to the rise of regional theater in Canada during the 1970s." Writing in *Canadian Literature,* Brian Parker claims that "at the poetic heart of [Cook's] work, lies an intensely imagined experience of Newfoundland life, presented with such integrity that at its best it rises to comment on the human condition."

In *Colour the Flesh the Colour of Dust,* Cook sets his story in 18th century Newfoundland when the English and the French vied for control of the area. The town of St. John's changed hands on several occasions. "In his play," writes Johnson, "Cook uses one of these cycles, English to French to English again, to demonstrate the insignificance of political definition where the real authority is vested in sea, rock, and fog and where the inhabitants adopt values in reaction to those constants, recognizing no other authority." Martin Fishman, writing in *Canadian Drama/L'Art dramatique canadien,* notes how Cook has in this play, "in a theatrical and well structured manner, juxtaposed the ideas and themes of honour and survival and recorded poetically the resulting human actions and reactions."

*The Head, Guts and Soundbone Dance* is set in a declining Newfoundland village where an elderly fisherman named Skipper Pete gathers each day with his son-in-law John and his retarded son Absalom to recall his past glory as a sea captain. The Skipper, notes Gilbert, "rails against modern society, the decline of traditional industry and values, and the loss of a patriarchal society." The past remembered by the Skipper, explains Patrick Treacher in *Canadian Drama/L'Art dramatique canadien,* "consists entirely of shoals of fish, and his ability to appear an iron master of lesser men. That they were men in their own right is not relevant—he was Master. . . . The Skipper makes the supreme mistake—he believes his own fantasy, and goes mad."

In *Jacob's Wake* Cook tells of Skipper Blackburn, an elderly fishing captain who is dying while his family gathers for a wake. "A storm grows in intensity throughout the play," Johnson writes, "mirroring both the Skipper's visionary frenzy and the turmoil of his family. At the play's conclusion, the Skipper dies, and, in a surreal sequence, his ghost steers the house into darkness and chaos as he once drove his sealing ship into the ice floes." Gilbert calls the play "the story of a modern New Foundland of unemployment, alcoholism, welfare, empty religious values, and destructive gender roles."

Cook told *CA:* "If you are committed to the living theatre, why the hell live so far away from anywhere that theatre is happening? I get letters from friends in

New York asking 'When are you coming?'—as if it is the only place to be. I *know* professionally it is a hell of a place to be. But I also know my own nature and given that amount of stimulus, I'd probably blow up or scatter myself in all directions or become a faded story teller in bars.

"Looking back over this hodge podge of literary and dramatic activity, though, I'm astonished to discover that virtually none of it took place before I emigrated to Canada, more specifically, Newfoundland, in 1966. Twelve years in the army, any army I suppose, although providing a not always pleasant treatment book on the magnificent corruption of life, isn't exactly conducive to reflection, prompting instead alternate moods of anger and despair, which bouts of absurdity and alcohol do not always dissipate.

"This is the place I love. It informs my sensibility and I suppose I cling, desperately, to the old belief that if I write anything good enough, it will get done somewhere out there. Certainly Canada has been good to me, and the stuff has been done out there—if not as often as I've liked simply because I am not readily available. It is a conscious choice, and one that I agonize over every year. But I'm still here.

"Perhaps most important to me is the fact that Newfoundland is itself a stage, afloat in the Atlantic, a rocky plug in the fundament of the St. Lawrence River, beautiful and savage at once, whose people, isolated for centuries, kept their own seventeenth- and eighteenth-century idioms of speech and a brand of humor that was, in the face of a merciless environment, exploitive colonialism, black and cruel and ribald. Artaud would have loved it. Although I doubt if he could have lived there.

"Myself, half Irish, half English, the island, itself half and half, acted as a catalyst. It was like coming home, both physically and emotionally, and the people and the environment seemed to open an artistic floodgate. I had always known I was a playwright. And now I was surrounded by the artifacts to make that boast either come to fruition or die.

"Initially, my emotional and theatrical response was to the brutal effects of the inevitable patterns of change that took place when, to quote one of our premiers, 'Newfoundland was dragged kicking and screaming into the twentieth century.' Since then my base has broadened, as it must, but still at some point, no matter what I'm writing, this often bleak and stormbound island, littered with the droppings of millions of sea birds, stirs the true and ancient Celtic responses which at the core of the subconscious inform all of my work. Which is also to say, myself."

*BIOGRAPHICAL/CRITICAL SOURCES:*

*BOOKS*

Anthony, Geraldine, *Stage Voices: Twelve Canadian Playwrights Talk about Their Lives and Work,* Doubleday (Toronto), 1978, pp. 207-232.

*Contemporary Dramatists,* 5th edition, St. James Press (Detroit), 1993.

*Contemporary Literary Criticism,* Volume 58, Gale (Detroit), 1990.

*Dictionary of Literary Biography,* Volume 53: *Canadian Writers since 1960, First Series,* Gale, 1986.

Peck, Edward, editor, *Transitions I: Short Plays,* Commcept (Toronto), 1978, pp. 245-247.

Perkyns, Richard, editor, *Major Plays of the Canadian Theatre, 1934-1984,* Irwin (Toronto), 1984.

Rubin, Don, editor, *Canada on Stage: Canadian Theatre Review Yearbook 1977,* Canadian Theatre Review Publications (Toronto), 1978, pp. 282-284.

Rubin, *Canada on Stage: Canadian Theatre Review Yearbook 1978,* Canadian Theatre Review Publications, 1979, pp. 18-19.

Rubin, *Canada on Stage: Canadian Theatre Review Yearbook 1979,* Canadian Theatre Review Publications, 1980, pp. 23-25.

Rubin, *Canada on Stage: Canadian Theatre Review Yearbook 1980-1981,* Canadian Theatre Review Publications, 1981, pp. 29-30.

Wallace, Robert and Cynthia Zimmerman, *The Work: Conversations with English-Canadian Playwrights,* Coach House Press (Toronto), 1982, pp. 156-171.

Whittaker, Herbert, *Whittaker's Theatre: A Critic Looks at Stages in Canada and Thereabouts, 1944-1975,* Whittaker Project (Greenbank, Ontario), 1985, pp. 149-151.

*PERIODICALS*

*Canadian Drama/L'Art Dramatique Canadien,* fall, 1976, pp. 176-187; spring, 1985, pp. 2-229.

*Canadian Literature,* summer, 1980, pp. 22-41, 126-128; summer, 1984, pp. 72-78.

*Canadian Theatre Review,* summer, 1974, pp. 125-127; spring, 1975, pp. 117-120; summer, 1975, pp. 136-138; spring, 1976, pp. 87-91; fall, 1977, pp. 26-31; summer, 1982, pp. 132-134; fall, 1982, pp. 85-101.

*Performing Arts in Canada,* winter, 1976, pp. 26-29.

### COOKSON, Catherine (McMullen) 1906-
### (Catherine Marchant)

*PERSONAL:* Born June 20, 1906, in Tyne Dock, South Shields, England; mother's name, Catherine Fawcett; married Thomas H. Cookson (a schoolmaster), June 1, 1940.

*ADDRESSES: Home*—Bristol Lodge, Langley on Tyne, Northumberland, England. *Agent*—Anthony Sheil Associates Ltd., 43 Doughty St., London WC1N 2LF, England.

*CAREER:* Writer. Lecturer for women's groups and other organizations.

*MEMBER:* Society of Authors, PEN (England), Authors Guild (USA), Authors League of America, Women's Press Club (London).

*AWARDS, HONORS:* Winifred Holtby Award for best regional novel from Royal Society of Literature, 1968, for *The Round Tower;* Order of the British Empire, 1985; recipient of Freedom of the County Borough of South Shields in recognition of her services to the city; honorary Master's and Doctorate degrees from the University of Newcastle, England, 1983.

*WRITINGS:*

*Kate Hannigan,* Macdonald & Co., 1950, reprinted, Macdonald & Jane's, 1979.
*Fifteen Streets* (also see below), Macdonald & Co., 1952, reprinted, Corgi Books, 1979.
*Colour Blind,* Macdonald & Co., 1953, reprinted, Macdonald & Jane's, 1975, published as *Color Blind,* New American Library, 1977.
*Maggie Rowan,* Macdonald & Co., 1954, New American Library, 1975.
*Rooney,* Macdonald & Co., 1957, reprinted, Macdonald & Jane's, 1974.
*The Menagerie,* Macdonald & Co., 1958, reprinted, Macdonald & Jane's, 1974.
*Slinky Jane,* Macdonald & Co., 1959, reprinted, Macdonald & Jane's, 1979.
*Fenwick Houses,* Macdonald & Co., 1960, reprinted, Macdonald & Jane's, 1979.
*The Garment,* Macdonald & Co., 1962, New American Library, 1974.
*The Blind Miller* (also see below), Macdonald & Co., 1963, reprinted, Heinemann, 1979.
*Hannah Massey,* Macdonald & Co., 1964, New American Library, 1973.

*The Long Corridor,* Macdonald & Co., 1965, New American Library, 1976.
*The Unbaited Trap,* Macdonald & Co., 1966, New American Library, 1974.
*Katie Mulholland,* Macdonald & Co., 1967, reprinted, Macdonald & Jane's, 1980.
*The Round Tower* (also see below), Macdonald & Co., 1968, New American Library, 1975.
*The Nice Bloke,* Macdonald & Co., 1969, published as *The Husband,* New American Library, 1976.
*Our Kate: An Autobiography,* Macdonald & Co., 1969, Bobbs-Merrill, 1971, published as *Our Kate: Catherine Cookson—Her Personal Story,* Macdonald & Jane's, 1974.
*The Glass Virgin,* Macdonald & Co., 1970, Bantam, 1981.
*The Invitation,* Macdonald & Co., 1970, New American Library, 1974.
*The Dwelling Place,* Macdonald & Jane's, 1971.
*Fanny McBride,* Corgi Books, 1971, reprinted, Macdonald & Jane's, 1980.
*Feathers in the Fire* (also see below), Macdonald & Co., 1971, Bobbs-Merrill, 1972.
*Pure as the Lily,* Macdonald & Co., 1972, Bobbs-Merrill, 1973.
*The Invisible Cord* (also see below), Dutton, 1975.
*The Gambling Man* (also see below), Morrow, 1975.
*The Tide of Life,* Morrow, 1976.
*The Girl* (also see below), Morrow, 1977.
*The Cinder Path* (also see below), Morrow, 1978.
*Tilly Trotter,* Heinemann, 1978, published as *Tilly,* Morrow, 1980.
*Selected Works,* Heinemann/Octopus, Volume 1 (contains *Fifteen Streets, The Blind Miller, The Round Tower, Feathers in the Fire,* and *A Grand Man* [also see below]), 1978, Volume 2 (contains *The Mallen Streak* [also see below], *The Invisible Cord, The Gambling Man, The Girl,* and *The Cinder Path*), 1980.
*The Man Who Cried,* Morrow, 1979.
*Tilly Wed,* Morrow, 1981 (published in England as *Tilly Trotter Wed,* Heinemann, 1981).
*Tilly Alone,* Morrow, 1982 (published in England as *Tilly Widowed,* Heinemann, 1982).
*The Whip,* Summit Books, 1982.
*Hamilton* (comic), Heinemann, 1983.
*The Black Velvet Gown,* Summit Books, 1984.
*Goodbye Hamilton,* Heinemann, 1984.
*The Bannaman Legacy,* Summit Books, 1985 (published in England as *A Dinner of Herbs,* Heinemann, 1985).
*Harold,* Heinemann, 1985.

*The Moth,* Summit Books, 1986, also published as *The Thorman Inheritance: A Novel,* Summit Books (New York City), 1986.

*Bill Bailey,* Heinemann, 1986.

*Catherine Cookson Country,* Heinemann, 1986.

*The Parson's Daughter,* Summit Books, 1987.

*The Baily Chronicles,* Summit Books, 1988.

*The Harrogate Secret,* Summit Books, 1988.

*Let Me Make Myself Plain,* Bantam, 1988.

*The Black Candle: A Novel,* Summit Books (New York City), 1989.

*The Spaniard's Gift: A Novel,* Summit Books (New York City), 1989.

*The Gillyvors,* Bantam (New York City), 1990.

*The Wingless Bird,* Summit (New York City), 1990.

*Bill Bailey's Lot,* G. K. Hall (Boston), 1990.

*Bill Bailey's Daughter,* G. K. Hall (Boston), 1990.

*The Love Child: A Novel,* Summit Books (New York City), 1990.

*My Beloved Son,* Bantam (New York City), 1991.

*The Iron Facade,* Bantam, 1991.

*The Rag Nymph,* Bantam (New York City), 1991.

*The House of Women,* Bantam, 1992.

*The Maltese Angel: A Novel,* Simon & Schuster (New York City), 1992.

*The Forester Girl: A Novel,* Simon & Schuster (New York City), 1993.

*The Golden Straw: A Novel,* Simon & Schuster (New York City), 1993.

*The Year of the Virgins: A Novel,* Simon & Schuster (New York City), 1993.

*Justice Is a Woman,* Bantam, 1995.

*The Obsession,* Bantam Press, 1995.

*Plainer Still,* Bantam, 1995.

*A Ruthless Need* Bantam, 1995.

*Three Complete Novels* (includes *The Love Child, The Maltese Angel,* and *The Year of the Virgins*), Wings (New York City), 1996.

*Tinker's Girl,* Bantam Press, 1996.

### "MARY ANN" SERIES

*A Grand Man,* Macdonald & Co., 1954, Macmillan, 1955, reprinted, Morrow, 1975.

*The Lord and Mary Ann,* Macdonald & Co., 1956, reprinted, Macdonald & Jane's, 1974, Morrow, 1975.

*The Devil and Mary Ann,* Macdonald & Co., 1958, Morrow, 1976.

*Love and Mary Ann,* Macdonald & Co., 1961, Morrow, 1976.

*Life and Mary Ann,* Macdonald & Co., 1962, Morrow, 1977.

*Marriage and Mary Ann,* Macdonald & Co., 1964, Morrow, 1978.

*Mary Ann's Angels,* Macdonald & Co., 1965, Morrow, 1978.

*Mary Ann and Bill,* Macdonald & Co., 1966, Morrow, 1979.

*Mary Ann Omnibus* (contains all novels in "Mary Ann" series), Macdonald & Jane's, 1981.

### "MALLEN NOVELS" TRILOGY

*The Mallen Streak* (also see below), Heinemann, 1973.

*The Mallen Girl* (also see below), Heinemann, 1974.

*The Mallen Lot,* Dutton, 1974 (published in England as *The Mallen Litter* [also see below], Heinemann, 1974).

*The Mallen Novels* (contains *The Mallen Streak, The Mallen Girl,* and *The Mallen Litter*), Heinemann, 1979.

### JUVENILE NOVELS

*Matty Doolin,* Macdonald & Co., 1965, New American Library, 1976.

*Joe and the Gladiator,* Macdonald & Co., 1968.

*The Nipper,* Bobbs-Merrill, 1970.

*Blue Baccy,* Macdonald & Jane's, 1972, Bobbs-Merrill, 1973.

*Our John Willie,* Morrow, 1974.

*Mrs. Flanagan's Trumpet,* Macdonald & Jane's, 1977, Lothrop, 1980.

*Go Tell It to Mrs. Golightly,* Macdonald & Jane's, 1977, Lothrop, 1980.

*Lanky Jones,* Lothrop, 1981.

### UNDER PSEUDONYM CATHERINE MARCHANT

*Heritage of Folly,* Macdonald & Co., 1963, reprinted, Macdonald & Jane's, 1980.

*The Fen Tiger,* Macdonald & Co., 1963, Morrow, 1979.

*House of Men,* Macdonald & Co., 1964, Macdonald & Jane's, 1980.

*Evil at Roger's Cross,* Lancer Books, 1965, revised edition published as *The Iron Facade,* Heinemann, 1976, Morrow, 1980.

*Miss Martha Mary Crawford,* Heinemann, 1975, Morrow, 1976.

*The Slow Awakening,* Heinemann, 1976, Morrow, 1977.

Other titles include: *The Cultured Handmaiden,* 1988, and the children's books *Rory's Fortune, Nancy*

*Nutall and the Mongrel,* and *Bill and the Mary Ann Shaughnessy.*

*SIDELIGHTS:* Catherine Cookson is a prolific British author with a large following. Her family sagas, for which she is most noted, are read in some thirty countries. A frequent name on the best-seller list, in the early 1980s Cookson was commemorated by Corgi Books for exceeding the 27 million mark in paperback sales alone. According to Anne Duchene in the *Times Literary Supplement,* "these days there are never fewer than fifty Cookson titles in print in English at any time; they are translated into fifteen languages; and new books are still readily produced." In a London *Times* interview with Caroline Moorehead, Cookson emphasizes that she never has trouble coming up with ideas for her historical novels: "I've always been a jabberer. I just talked. I see everything in images. The plot sort of unfolds. Even the dialogue. In the morning, it's all there to put down." As Duchene observes: "[Cookson] writes stories in which her readers can gratefully recognize experiences and emotions of their own—heightened, to be sure, by greater comedy or greater violence than their own lives normally vouchsafe, but based on all their own affections, furies, aspirations and reactions."

Born the illegitimate daughter of an alcoholic mother, Cookson lived with her mother in her grandparents' strict, Catholic household during most of her childhood. By the age of eighteen, Cookson had been working as a laundry checker, although she longed for an education. Cookson's success in overcoming her disadvantaged childhood, critics note, is one source of her broad appeal. Anita Brookner of *Observer* comments: "[Cookson] brings comfort to millions and one can see the reason why: she represents the strong woman of various mythologies, a Mother Courage with no children but [more than 57] titles. She is an entirely remarkable person." Published in 1969, Cookson's autobiography *Our Kate* documented the difficulties she experienced during her childhood, and became a popular and critical success. A later autobiographical work, *Let Me Make Myself Plain,* presents essays, poetry, and paintings, each of which draw upon the author's personal reflections and experiences.

Cookson's experience of life in the working-class, industrial environment of Tyneside has also provided material for her numerous novels. Autobiographical elements strongly inform the narrative of *The Love Child,* for example, which portrays a nineteenth-century girl who is tormented by the hostility of villagers and the disapproval of the church pastor due to her illegitimate status. An example of Cookson's use of the "family saga" form, *The House of Women,* focuses on four generations of women living in the same house in Tyneside and chronicles their experience of hypochondria, an unhappy marriage, and teenaged pregnancy, among other trials. Along with their treatment of northern English settings and British class structures, Cookson's novels are noted for their portrayal of appealing female characters. *The Wingless Bird,* for instance, depicts Agnes Conway, the daughter of an English shop-keeper, who must choose between an unhappy marriage or spinsterhood. Her life changes unexpectedly, however, when she falls in love with an upper-class man and subsequently finds the courage and the means to escape her family's oppressive treatment.

The character Mary Ann Shaughnessy has reappeared in eight of Cookson's novels, which have been published together in a single volume titled *The Mary Ann Omnibus.* Mary Ann is eight years old in *A Grand Man,* the first novel of the series, and the twenty-seven-year-old mother of twins in *Mary Ann and Bill,* the final story. "In the earlier books Mary Ann bounces through her own and other people's lives like a cross between a deus (or dea) ex machina and a gremlin, interfering in situations and people with blithe impartiality, generally for the benefit of her beloved, drunken father Mike Shaughnessy," notes Judith Rhodes in *Romance and Historical Writers.* "Few of Cookson's other novels demonstrate her capacity for comedy as this series does; not only does Mary Ann herself create a number of amusing situations, but her grannie McMullen . . . is a wonderful comic character."

Cookson is also well-established as an author of children's books, several of which draw upon historical and autobiographical themes. Set in England during the 1850s, her juvenile novel *Our John Willie,* for example, portrays two brothers who manage to survive poverty and exploitation at the hands of mine-owners. While some objected to the extreme sentimentality of the story, others commented favorably on Cookson's treatment of her historical subject. Like many of her novels for adults, Cookson's children's stories often draw upon her experience of the English community of Tyneside. *Joe and the Gladiator,* for example, is set in the Tyneside shipyards and depicts a hard-working young man who is plagued with financial and family problems that grow worse when an elderly man dies, leaving an old horse in Joe's care. Although recently bedridden due to health problems and disabled by seriously declining eyesight, Cookson has continued to create fiction, dictating her stories to a tape-recorder, and working in collaboration with her husband during the editing process. The author is also well-known as a philanthropist.

*BIOGRAPHICAL/CRITICAL SOURCES:*

*BOOKS*

Cookson, Catherine, *Our Kate: An Autobiography,* Macdonald & Co., 1969, Bobbs-Merrill, 1971, published as *Our Kate: Catherine Cookson—Her Personal Story,* Macdonald & Jane's, 1974.

*PERIODICALS*

*Booklist,* February 1, 1984, p. 769; January 15, 1991, p. 979; September 1, 1991, p. 28; November 1, 1992, p. 466.
*Books,* November, 1990; July 1991, p. 10.
*Catholic World,* June, 1955.
*Chicago Tribune,* November 27, 1994, p. 9.
*Kirkus Reviews,* August 1, 1969, p. 793; May 15, 1978, p. 562; February 1, 1981, p. 140; October 1, 1992, p. 1203; October 1, 1993, p. 1219; September 1, 1994, p. 1148; February 1, 1995, p. 86.
*Kliatt,* September, 1990, p. 6.
*Library Journal,* June 1, 1975, p. 1152; May 15, 1985, p. 78; March 15, 1987, p. 400; April 15, 1987, p. 96; April 15, 1990, p. 141; September 1, 1991; October 1, 1994, p. 112, 228.
*London Review of Books,* June 27, 1991, p. 22.
*New York Times,* January 7, 1955.
*New York Times Book Review,* October 20, 1974, p. 41; April 2, 1984, p. 25; June 30, 1985, p. 20.
*Observer* (London), April 1, 1984; November 27, 1988.
*Publishers Weekly,* July 21, 1969, p. 53; November 17, 1975, p. 95; August 16, 1976, p. 118; March 22, 1985, p. 51; March 28, 1986, p. 52; March 27, 1987, p. 37; February 10, 1989, p. 53; March 16, 1990, p. 60; January 25, 1991, p. 48; August 9, 1991, p. 44; October 12, 1992, p. 64; October 11, 1993, p. 70; October 3, 1994, p. 52; February 20, 1995, p. 195.
*School Library Journal,* August, 1990, p. 174.
*Spectator,* July 6, 1991, p. 26; October 12, 1991, p. 39.
*Times* (London), August 15, 1983.

*Times Literary Supplement,* January 7, 1955; June 6, 1968; June 19, 1969; March 29, 1974; July 24, 1981, p. 830.
*Washington Post Book World,* April 1, 1990.*

\*     \*     \*

## COOPER, Lettice (Ulpha) 1897-1994

*PERSONAL:* Born September 3, 1897, in Eccles, Lancashier, England; died July 24, 1994, Coltishall, England; daughter of Leonard (an engineer) and Agnes Helena (Fraser) Cooper. *Education:* Lady Margaret Hall, Oxford, B. A. *Politics:* Socialist.

*CAREER:* Writer. *Time and Tide,* London, editorial assistant and drama critic, 1939-40; Ministry of Food, London, public relations officer, 1940-45.

*MEMBER:* International PEN (president, 1977-79), English PEN (vice-chair, 1975-78, and president, 1979-81), Authors' Society, Writers' Guild; Robert Louis Stevenson Club (president, 1958-74).

*AWARDS, HONORS:* Arts Council bursary, 1968 and 1979; Eric Gregory traveling scholarship, 1977; Order of British Empire (O.B.E.) officer, 1980.

*WRITINGS:*

*NOVELS*

*The Lighted Room,* Hodder & Stoughton (London), 1925.
*The Old Fox,* Hodder & Stoughton, 1927.
*Good Venture,* Hodder & Stoughton, 1928.
*Likewise the Lyon,* Hodder & Stoughton, 1929.
*The Ship of Truth,* Little, Brown (Boston), 1930.
*Private Enterprise,* Hodder & Stoughton, 1931.
*Hark to Rover!,* Hodder & Stoughton, 1933.
*We Have Come to a Country,* Gollancz (London), 1935.
*The New House,* Gollancz, 1936, Macmillan (New York City), 1937, with a new introduction by Maureen Duffy, Penguin Books—Virago Press (New York City), 1988.
*National Provincial,* Macmillan, 1938.
*Black Bethlehem,* Macmillan, 1947.
*Fenny* (Book Society selection), Gollancz, 1953, with an introduction by Francis King, Penguin (New York City), 1988.
*Three Lives,* Gollancz, 1957.

*A Certain Compass,* Gollancz, 1960.
*The Double Heart,* Gollancz, 1962.
*Late in the Afternoon,* Gollancz, 1971.
*Tea on Sunday,* Gollancz, 1973.
*Snow and Roses,* Gollancz, 1976.
*Desirable Residence,* Gollancz, 1980.
*Unusual Behavior,* Gollancz, 1986.

FOR CHILDREN

*Great Men of Yorkshire (West Riding),* Lane (London), 1955.
*The Young Florence Nightingale,* Lane, 1960, Roy (New York City), 1961.
*The Young Victoria,* Parrish (London) 1961, Roy, 1962.
*Blackberry's Kitten* (fiction), Brockhampton Press (Leicester), 1961, Roy, 1963.
*The Bear Who Was Too Big* (fiction), Parrish, 1963, Follett (Chicago), 1966.
*Bob-a-Job* (fiction), Brockhampton Press, 1963.
*James Watt,* A. & C. Black (London), 1963.
*Contadino* (fiction), J. Cape (London), 1964.
*Garibaldi,* Methuen (London), 1964, Roy, 1966.
*The Young Edgar Allan Poe,* Parrish, 1964, Roy, 1965.
*The Twig of Cypress* (fiction), Deutsch (London), 1965, Ives Washburn (New York City), 1966.
*The Fugitive King,* Parrish, 1965.
*We Shall Have Snow* (fiction), Brockhampton Press, 1966.
*A Hand Upon the Time: A Life of Charles Dickens,* Pantheon (New York City), 1968.
*Gunpowder, Treason and Plot,* Abelard-Schuman (London & New York City), 1970.
*Robert the Spy Hunter* (fiction), Kaye & Ward (London), 1973.
*Parkin* (fiction), Harrap (London), 1977.

OTHER

"Frowning Caryatid" (short story), published in *London Calling,* by Storm Jameson, Harper (New York City), 1942.
*Robert Louis Stevenson,* Home & Van Thal (London), 1947, A. Swallow (Denver), 1948, second edition, Arthur Barker (London).
*Yorkshire West Riding,* R. Hale (London), 1950, Macmillan, 1951.
*George Eliot,* Longmans, Green (London), 1951, revised edition, 1960, 1964, 1969.
(Author of introduction) Edward George Lytton, *The Last Days of Pompeii,* Norton (London), 1959.

Contributor to *Times Literary Supplement, Observer, Spectator, Critical Quarterly,* and other journals and newspapers in England. Associate editor, *Time and Tide,* 1939-40. Manuscript collection held at Eccles Public Library, Lancashire.

*SIDELIGHTS:* Lettice Cooper first gained popularity as a novelist in 1925 with the publication of *The Lighted Room,* and her subsequent works of the 1920s and 1930s were well-received by critics and the public, praised for their stylistic simplicity and perceptive characterizations. Later, during the 1960s, she wrote a series of successful children's books, and in the 1980s some of her early works became the focus of renewed interest when they were reissued by her publisher. Cooper was also active in a variety of professional and social causes and many of her works reflect her liberal political ideals. Her writings include the novels *National Provincial, Fenny, Snow and Roses,* and *Unusual Behavior,* as well as children's biographies of Queen Victoria, Florence Nightingale, and Edgar Allan Poe.

Describing Cooper's novels, Isabel Quigly wrote in *Contemporary Novelists:* "Their settings are domestic, though their domesticity varies. . . . Two places are of primary importance in her novels-her native Yorkshire . . . [and] Italy, and more specifically Tuscany. . . . the action, as a rule, is unadventurous, in the sense of undramatic—except in terms of feelings and personalities. But this might be said, of course, of the majority of English fiction written by women. . . . She deals . . . with the basic issues and problems: love and indifference, parental selfishness, the young's longing for escape, moral dilemmas, varying standards of behavior, of loyalty and truth."

Cooper's fifth novel, *The Ship of Truth,* follows Clement Dyson, a clergyman who loses his faith and latter rediscovers it. "The cause of Clement Dyson's actual reconversion is somewhat vague," noted an *Outlook* critic who believed the novel is "competently written but not particularly impressive." K. G. David also remarked on the lack of "insight . . . [into] Dyson's belief or disbelief," however, in *Saturday Review of Literature* he praised *The Ship of Truth* for being "well written, without religious bias, and certainly it stimulates both conjecture and discussion." A *New York Times* critic positively noted the "human elements" of the novel. In *New Republican,* a critic remarked on the story's "warmth and candor" and stated: "[Cooper] tells her tale competently and pleasantly, but she never really comes to grips with the shattering experience which she describes."

Cooper's ninth novel, *The New House,* is "inescapably appealing" according to *New York Times* critic Dorothea Kingsland, who commented: "There is in it tender appreciation for the common utensils of living and their influence upon human minds. There is also a warm understanding of the inconsistencies and doublecrossings within those minds." "To take one day in the lives of a group of people and to make from it a dramatic story is very difficult, but Miss Cooper has done it with great success," stated a *Times Literary Supplement* review. Although "inexperience" shows in the writing, remarked a critic for *Saturday Review of Literature, The New House* is "perceptive and sensible, showing excellent observation and talent for characterization . . . a good book by a good writer."

"Characterization, unerring and exact in its revealing of human complexity, is Miss Cooper's strongest point," proclaimed Ruth Bower in a *Books* review of *National Provincial,* Cooper's tenth novel. This political novel "fits in everything from Ethiopia to the march of the Clack Shirts," recognized a *New Yorker* contributor who continued: "[Cooper] does it cleverly and her characters seem really moved and affected by what is happening. Serious but not heavy reading." Critics commonly remarked on it's long length, but general recognized, as Evelyn Waugh did in a *Spectator* review, "the book is well worth persevering with because the authoress's talent again and again transcends the self-imposed limits." Waugh also stated Cooper "exploit[s]" the interesting subject matter, usually unsuitable for novels, "to its fullest." An unfavorable review appeared in *Times Literary Supplement,* reporting: "The illumination or vision that one looks for in the novel to-day, the poetry or the tragic sense—of this there is no trace. It is a hard thing to say of so truthful and scrupulous a study, but *National Provincial* is wanting in what is commonly called art." J. S. Southron perceived the novel differently, in the *New York Times* he commented: "Emotional strength has, no doubt, been sacrificed to breadth of treatment; but it would be difficult to overpraise *National Provincial* as a floodlight illuminating contemporary English social and political history."

"Cooper [wrote] novels for many years, and social historians of the future may well study them for their careful reflection of middle-class English life at various stages of this century. The worlds she described in her younger days may have gone, but this does not mean that the novels themselves have dated: technically and psychologically they still stand up well," remarked Quigly. Quigly further summarized: "Noth-

ing in Cooper's novels is put in without a point or a place in the action, without being properly inserted and made familiar. Cooper is always professional, a writer whose care, and whose respect for her readers, deserve respect. . . . In what seems a straightforward way she concentrates much into seemingly simple scenes and passages; her strength lying in an intelligent understanding of human nature; in warmth tempered with briskness and humor, and in an intuitive interpretation of events, psychological and spiritual."

*BIOGRAPHICAL/CRITICAL SOURCES:*

BOOKS

*Contemporary Novelists,* sixth edition, St. James Press (Detroit), 1996.

PERIODICALS

*Books,* June 8, 1930; October 25, 1936; October 23, 1938.
*New Republican,* May 21, 1930.
*New Yorker,* October 22, 1938.
*New York Times,* April 27, 1930; October 18, 1936; October 23, 1938.
*Observer Review,* July 20, 1971; May 2, 1976.
*Outlook,* April 9, 1930.
*Saturday Review of Literature,* May 24, 1930; October 17, 1936; November 5, 1938.
*Spectator,* June 24, 1938.
*Times Literary Supplement,* May 23, 1936; June 18, 1938; October 30, 1970; July 2, 1971; July 23, 1971; April 6, 1973; July 9, 1976.

*OBITUARIES:*

PERIODICALS

*Times* (London), July 26, 1994, p. 17.*

\*          \*          \*

**CORTEZ, Jayne 1936-**

*PERSONAL:* Born May 10, 1936, in Fort Huachuca, Arizona; married Ornette Coleman (a jazz musician), 1954 (divorced, 1964); married Melvin Edwards (a sculptor and illustrator), 1975; children: (first marriage) Denardo Coleman.

*ADDRESSES: Home*—c/o Bola Press, Box 96, Village Station, New York, NY 10014.

*CAREER:* Poet and performance artist. Watts Repertory Theatre Company, Los Angeles, co-founder, 1964; Bola Press, New York City, founder, 1972; has lectured and read her poetry alone and with musical accompaniment at universities, including Dartmouth College, Howard University, Queens College, Wesleyan University, and throughout Europe, Africa, Latin America, and the Caribbean.

*AWARDS, HONORS:* Creative Artists Program Service poetry awards, New York State Council on the Arts, 1973 and 1981; National Endowment for the Arts fellowship in creative writing, 1979-86; American Book Award, 1980; New York Foundation for the Arts Award, 1987; Before Columbus Foundation Award, 1987; Fannie Lou Hammer Award, 1994; Afrikan Poetry Theatre tribute and award, 1994.

*MEMBER:* Organization of Women Writers of Africa (co-founder).

*WRITINGS:*

POETRY

*Pissstained Stairs and the Monkey Man's Wares,* Phrase Text (New York City), 1969.
*Festivals and Funerals,* illustrated by husband, Mel Edwards, Bola Press (New York City), 1971.
*Scarifications,* illustrated by Edwards, Bola Press, 1973.
*Mouth on Paper,* Bola Press, 1977.
*Firespitter,* illustrated by Mel Edwards, Bola Press, 1982.
*Coagulations: New and Selected Poems,* Thunder's Mouth Press (New York City), 1982.
*Poetic Magnetic,* illustrated by Edwards, Bola Press, 1991.
*Somewhere in Advance of Nowhere,* Serpent's Tail (London), 1997.

OTHER

*Celebrations and Solitudes: The Poetry of Jayne Cortez* (sound recording), Strata-East Records, 1975.
*Unsubmissive Blues* (sound recording), Bola Press, 1980.
*There It Is* (sound recording), Bola Press, 1982.
*War against War* (performance piece), UNESCO (Paris), 1982.

*Poetry in Motion* (screenplay), Sphinx Productions (Toronto, Ontario, Canada), 1983.
*Maintain Control* (sound recording), Bola Press, 1986.
*Everywhere Drums* (sound recording), Bola Press, 1991.
*Mandela Is Coming* (music video), Globalvision, 1991.
*Taking the Blues Back Home* (sound recording), with band the Firespitters, Harmolodic/Verve, 1997.

Contributor to anthologies, including *We Speak as Liberators,* edited by Orde Coombs, Dodd, 1970; *The Poetry of Black America,* edited by Arnold Adoff, Harper, 1972; *Homage a Leon Gontran Damas,* Presence Africaine, 1979; *Black Sister,* edited by Erlene Stedson, Indiana University Press, 1981; *Women on War,* edited by Daniela Gioseffi, Simon & Schuster, 1988; and *Daughters of Africa,* Pantheon, 1992. Contributor to numerous periodicals, including *Free Spirits, Mother Jones, UNESCO Courier, Black Scholar, Heresies,* and *Mundus Artium.* Guest editor, *Black Scholar,* 1988, and *Drumvoices Revue,* 1994.

*SIDELIGHTS:* Poet and performance artist Jayne Cortez began her creative explorations as an actress, publishing her first volume of poetry, *Pissstained Stairs and the Monkey Man's Wares,* in 1969. Her work, which reflects the politics and culture of African Americans, is characterized by a dramatic intensity, causing D. H. Melhem to note in an introduction to an interview with Cortez published in *Heroism in the New Black Poetry,* that "Her fine ear for music, her dynamic imagery, and her disposition to orchestrate in a broad cultural span, both African and American, have led her social and political concerns into unique and risk-taking forms." Recording and performing around the world, often with backing by blues musicians, Cortez "has forged connections . . . that help us see how our histories . . . whether we life in Chile, Harlem or Nigeria, are related," in the opinion of Barbara T. Christian, writing in *Callaloo.* "The result is a poetry as wide in its scope as it is compelling in its craft."

In a review of Cortez's debut work, *Pissstained Stairs and the Monkey Man's Wares* for *Negro Digest* Nikki Giovanni remarks: "We haven't had many jazz poets who got inside the music and the people who created it. We poet about them, but not of them. And this is Cortez's strength. She can wail from Theodore Navarro and Leadbelly to Ornette [Coleman, Cortez' first husband] and never lose a beat and never make a mistake. She's a genius and all lovers of jazz will need this book—lovers of poetry will want it." The jazz elements threaded throughout Cortez' body of work have caused *Dictionary of Literary Biography* essayist Jon Woodson to remark that she remains "a creative artist uniquely able to reach audiences for whom books of poetry have little appeal."

Although the influence of music is readily evident throughout Cortez's body of work, the poet also pointedly seeks to convey a message. Reviewing the 1984 collection *Coagulations,* Barbara T. Christian states in *Callaloo* that "it is eminently clear . . . that Jayne Cortez is a blatantly political poet—that her work intends to help us identify those who control our lives and the devastating effects such control has on our lives, and she rouses us to do something about it. . . . Like the poets and warriors whose words and actions it celebrates, Jayne Cortez's *Coagulations* is a work of resistance."

Citing influences such as Amiri Bakara, Langston Hughes, Aime Cesaire, Margaret Walker, and Pablo Neruda, John F. Roche notes in an essay in *Contemporary Women Poets* that Cortez' free verse is characterized by its "impassioned crescendo," as well as the use of anaphora, repetition, alliteration, and modulated spoken tones. "She often combines African iconology, American colloquialisms, and leftist political themes with surrealist body imagery," explains Roche, adding that her more recent verse has begun to explore the patterned typesetting characteristic of the concrete poetry of the 1960s. Commenting on Cortez' 1996 collection, *Somewhere in Advance of Nowhere,* a *Publishers Weekly* critic comments on Cortez' ability to write in a manner that remains rhythmic while providing "an unflinching glimpse at life's ugliness" that nonetheless ends with the ability to survive. "This resilience animates Cortez's work and supports the unwavering, and compelling directness with which she confronts the world," the critic adds.

In an interview with Melhem, Cortez outlined what she believes to be the responsibilities inherent in her craft: "I think that poets have the responsibility to be aware of the meaning of human rights, to be familiar with history, to point out distortions, and to bring their thinking and their writing to higher levels of illumination." An acknowledgement of Cortez' success at meeting these standards was made in 1994, when she received the Fannie Lou Hammer award for her "outstanding contribution through her poetry to the struggle for justice, equality, and the freedom of the human spirit."

In addition to her work as a published author, Cortez has distinguished herself as an internationally acclaimed performance artist, and has several recorded performances to her credit, including *Everywhere Drums* (1990), *Cheerful and Optimistic* (1994), and 1996's *Taking the Blues Back Home.* Commenting on *Unsubmissive Blues,* a 1980 recording of the poet reading her works accompanied jazz musicians Bill Cole, Joe Daley, Bern Nix, and Cortez's son Denardo Coleman, Warren Woessner asserts in *Small Press Review* that the record "is the most accomplished collaboration between a poet and jazz group that I've listened to in recent years." He continues: "*Unsubmissive Blues* is an unqualified success. The sum of this collaboration is always greater than its individual pieces."

*BIOGRAPHICAL/CRITICAL SOURCES:*

*BOOKS*

*American Women Writers: From Colonial Times to the Present,* Volume 5, Continuum, 1994.
*Contemporary Women Poets,* St. James Press (Detroit), 1997.
*Dictionary of Literary Biography,* Volume 41: *Afro-American Poets since 1955,* Gale (Detroit), 1985.
Melhem, D. H., *Heroism in the New Black Poetry,* University Press of Kentucky, 1990.

*PERIODICALS*

*Black World,* March, 1975.
*Callaloo,* winter, 1986, pp. 235-39.
*Greenfield Review,* summer/fall, 1983.
*MELUS,* spring, 1996, pp. 71-79.
*Negro Digest,* December, 1969.
*Publishers Weekly,* June 3, 1996, p. 74.
*Small Press Review,* March, 1981.

*OTHER*

*Jane Cortez Biography,* www.harmolodic.com/bios/cortezbio.html (May 31, 1997).

\*      \*      \*

## CRAIG, Helen 1934-

*PERSONAL:* Born August 30, 1934, in London, England; daughter of Edward (a writer and designer for theater and films) and Helen (maiden name, Godfrey)

Craig; children: Ben Norland. *Education:* Attended King Alfred's School, London, England. *Avocational interests:* Collecting children's books, etching, working with ceramic sculpture and in her garden.

*ADDRESSES: Home*—Vine Cottage, Harroell, Long Crendon, Aylesbury, Buckinghamshire HP18 9AQ, England.

*CAREER:* Gee & Watson (commercial photographers), London, England, apprentice, 1950-56; owner and operator of photographic studio in Hampstead, London, 1956-63; sculptor and artist in southern Spain, 1964-66; freelance potter and photographer in London, 1967-69; began illustrating children's books, 1969—; Garland Compton (advertising agency), London, photographer, 1969-72; freelance photographer, potter, and Chinese wallpaper restorer, 1972-74; OXFAM, England, photographer, 1975-77.

*AWARDS, HONORS:* Award from Society of Illustrators (United States), 1977, for *The Mouse House ABC* foldout concertina; Kentucky Blue Grass Award, 1985, for *Angelina Ballerina;* Smarties Book Prize shortlist, 1992, for *The Town Mouse and the Country Mouse.* Three of Craig's books have been chosen for the British Book Design and Production exhibitions, of which *Angelina's Birthday* won a category award in 1990.

*WRITINGS:*

*SELF-ILLUSTRATED CHILDREN'S BOOKS*

*A Number of Mice,* Aurum Press, 1978.
*The Little Mouse Learning House: ABC,* Simon & Schuster (New York City), 1983.
*The Little Mouse Learning House: 123,* Simon & Schuster, 1983.
*Susie and Alfred in the Knight, the Princess, and the Dragon,* Knopf (New York City), 1985.
*Susie and Alfred in the Night of the Paper Bag Monsters,* Knopf, 1985.
*Susie and Alfred in a Welcome for Annie,* Walker, 1986.
*Susie and Alfred in a Busy Day at Town,* Walker, 1986.
*The Town Mouse and the Country Mouse,* Walker, 1992, Candlewick, 1992.
*I See the Moon and the Moon Sees Me: Helen Craig's Book of Nursery Rhymes,* Harper, 1992.
*Charlie and Tyler at the Seashore,* Candlewick, 1995, published in England as *Charlie and Tyler at the Seaside,* Walker, 1995.

*"THE MOUSE HOUSE" SERIES; SELF-ILLUSTRATED; FOLD-OUT CONCERTINA BOOKS; PUBLISHED BY RANDOM HOUSE (NEW YORK CITY)*

*The Mouse House ABC,* 1978.
*The Mouse House 123,* 1980.
*The Mouse House Months of the Year,* 1981.
*The Mouse House The Days of the Week,* 1982.

*ILLUSTRATOR*

Robert Nye, *Wishing Gold,* Macmillan (New York City), 1970.
Tanith Lee, *Animal Castle,* Farrar, Straus (London), 1972.
Lee, *Princess Hynchatti and Some Other Surprises,* Macmillan, 1972.
Katharine Holabird, *Angelina Ballerina,* C. N. Potter (New York City), 1983.
Holabird, *Angelina and the Princess,* C. N. Potter, 1984.
Holabird, *Angelina Goes to the Fair,* C. N. Potter, 1985.
Holabird, *Angelina's Christmas,* C. N. Potter, 1985.
Margaret Mahy, *JAM: A True Story,* Atlantic Monthly Press, 1985.
Sarah Hayes, *This Is the Bear,* Candlewick, 1986.
Judy Corbalis, *The Wrestling Princess,* Deutsch (London), 1986.
Holabird, *Angelina on Stage,* C. N. Potter, 1986.
Nigel Gray, *The One and Only Robin Hood,* Little, Brown (Boston), 1987.
Blake Morrison, *The Yellow House,* Harcourt (San Diego), 1987.
Holabird, *Angelina and Alice,* C. N. Potter, 1987.
Hayes, *This Is the Bear & the Picnic Lunch,* Candlewick, 1988.
Corbalis, *Porcellus the Flying Pig,* Dial (New York City), 1988.
Holabird, *Alexander and the Dragon,* C. N. Potter, 1988.
Holabird, *Angelina's Birthday,* Aurum Press, 1989, published as *Angelina's Birthday Surprise,* C. N. Potter, 1989.
Hayes, *Crumbling Castle,* Candlewick, 1989.
Hayes, *Mary Mary,* McElderry, 1989.
Mahy, *The Pumpkin Man and the Crafty Creeper,* Lothrop (New York City), 1990.
Holabird, *Alexander and the Magic Boat,* C. N. Potter, 1990.
Hayes, *This Is the Bear and the Scary Night,* Candlewick, 1991.
Holabird, *Angelina's Baby Sister,* C. N. Potter, 1991.
Jenny Nimmo, *The Stone Mouse,* C. N. Potter, 1993.

Holabird, *Angelina Ice Skates,* C. N. Potter, 1993.

Hayes, *This Is the Bear and the Bad Little Girl,* Candlewick, 1995.

Martin Waddell, *My Aunty Sal and the Mega-Sized Moose,* Candlewick, 1996.

Phyllis Root, *One Windy Wednesday,* Candlewick, 1996.

Mara Bergman, *Bears Bears, Everywhere,* Orchard, 1997.

Charlotte Zolotow, *The Bunny Who Found Easter,* Houghton (Boston), 1998.

Hayes, *This Is the Bear and the Scary Night,* Candlewick, 1998.

Root, *Turnover Tuesday,* Candlewick, 1998.

Joyce Dunbar, *Gander's Pond,* Candlewick, 1998.

Dunbar, *The Secret Friend,* Candlewick, 1998.

Dunbar, *Panda's New Toy,* Candlewick, 1999.

Dunbar, *Pomegranate Seeds,* Candlewick, 1999.

Also contributed illustrations to *Stories for a Prince,* Hamish Hamilton (London), 1983, to *The Children's Book,* in aid of Save the Children, Walker, 1985, and to *The Tail Feathers of Mother Goose,* Walker, 1988.

*SIDELIGHTS:* Helen Craig is the writer-illustrator or illustrator of over fifty books for children, and "can be compared favorably to all of the other great artists of anthropomorphic mice," according to Jean Hammond Zimmerman in *School Library Journal.* Craig, an English illustrator, is perhaps best known for her "Angelina Mouse" character, written by Katharine Holabird. She teamed up with Sarah Hayes for "This Is the Bear" series, in which she created a lovable, cuddly stuffed bear. In addition, Craig is writer-illustrator for her popular "Susie and Alfred" series of picture books featuring a pair of porcine pals, and her "Charlie and Tyler" series about a country mouse and a town mouse.

Craig once told *CA,* "It had always been my ambition that one day I would be a creative artist of some sort." Craig began illustrating children's books while raising her son as a single mother. "I bought Maurice Sendak's book, *Where the Wild Things Are,* for my small son, and that really gave me direction," she told *CA.* "As a child I had been strongly impressed by the books I looked at and read, and I can still recall those feelings and try to remember them when working." Craig first illustrated for books by Tanith Lee, but by the late 1970s she had developed her own series of foldout concertina books called "The Mouse House." These first picture books taught alphabet and number skills, as well as months of the year and days of the week.

In 1983, Craig teamed up with Katharine Holabird for *Angelina Ballerina,* the first of a series of Angelina books. The "Angelina" series has proven popular enough to support eight further titles and spin-offs such as the Angelina Doll (which Craig designed) and miniature Angelina books. In these books, such childhood themes as jealousy, shyness, birthday happiness, dedication, wonderment, and even despair are explored in a light format centering around the adventures of the balletic mouse, Angelina. *Angelina and the Princess,* for example, is the story of Angelina's ballet class which has been chosen to dance for Her Royal Highness. Angelina works so hard she becomes ill and does poorly in tryouts, but comes through on the final night with a marvelous dance. Even though the story was "predictable," *Horn Book* contributor Anita Silvey felt Craig's illustrations were "extraordinary." Silvey noted Craig's "ever so slight a line" "magnificently delineates character" in pictures "alive with movement, vitality, and humor." *School Library Journal*'s Zimmerman commented that "Craig's pastel colored ink drawings . . . steal the show." *Publishers Weekly* concluded that "Craig's gently humorous pastel pictures will appeal to little ones."

Another title in the ongoing "Angelina" series is *Angelina's Christmas,* in which she enlists a lonely postman to become the school Santa. *Kirkus Reviews* commented that Craig's "cheerful pastel scenes are delicate but not sentimental." Peggy Forehand, reviewing the book in *School Library Journal,* noted that the character of Angelina "has charmed readers with her sensitivity and tenderness without melodrama," and that Craig's art reveals "unusual attention to tone and detail." She concluded both author and illustrator have again provided "simple lessons that create a real celebration."

According to *Horn Book*'s Silvey, "Craig steals the show" in *Angelina and Alice,* a story in which the little mouse applies her talents to gymnastics. Silvey noted also the "marvelous things [Craig] accomplishes with the arc of a mouse tail." Angelina is happily surprised by a new red bicycle in *Angelina's Birthday Surprise,* another team effort in which "text and illustrations work together beautifully," according to Jane Gardner Connor in *School Library Journal.* Craig has also partnered with Holabird on two non-mouse books, *Alexander and the Dragon* and *Alexander and the Magic Boat.*

Craig has also collaborated extensively with the writer Sarah Hayes, notably with *This Is the Bear* and its sequels. Intended as read-alouds, the books are written with chanting rhyme and follow the adventures of a little boy, his stuffed bear, and the dog who, although jealous of the bear, quite often comes to his rescue. The first title in the series sets the tone for the rest: Bear is mistakenly put into a garbage bin and ends up at the dump where the boy and his dog eventually save him. Judith Glover noted in *School Library Journal* that "Bear's face is wonderfully expressive." Barbara Elleman, writing in *Booklist,* commented that "The softly colored economical drawings are framed in thin, coordinated borders. . . . Sure to be a winner with the toddler crowd." More adventures follow in *This Is the Bear and the Picnic Lunch,* in which Craig's delicate and expressive artwork "nicely counterpoint the rollicking text," according to *Kirkus Reviews.* Bear is carelessly left out in the park overnight in *This Is the Bear and the Scary Night,* a "spare story" with just the correct "sequencing," according to Trev Jones in *School Library Journal.* Jones went on to comment that all "the action takes place in Craig's pictures." Martha V. Parravano, reviewing the fourth title in the series, *This Is the Bear and the Bad Little Girl,* concluded that Hayes's "chantable, mock-cumulative text" is well-matched by Craig's "humorous, airy" illustrations and "droll" speech balloons. Craig and Hayes also produced *Crumbling Castles,* three stories about a wizard named Zeb, and *Mary Mary,* a contrary girl who befriends a lonely giant.

Craig's solo efforts as both author and illustrator are highlighted by the "Susie and Alfred" books. The mischievous piglet neighbors who "dress, live and behave like middle-class human children of fifty years ago," described a reviewer for *The Junior Bookshelf,* experience a variety of adventures in the series, from a fancy dress party to welcoming a new neighbor. *Susie and Alfred in the Night of the Paper Bag Monsters,* for example, has the duo preparing for a party. When Alfred spills green paint all over Susie's fancy dress clothes, they must come up with alternative dress. Margery Fisher, writing in *Growing Point,* noted that this small glimpse into neighborhood life is borne out by appropriate "humanization in the dress, posture and facial expressions" of the two featured piglets. With *The Town Mouse and the Country Mouse,* however, Craig went back to her beloved mice and to an interesting format for the retelling of the familiar fable by Aesop. "I have always liked comic books where the action is shown in a sequence of pictures," Craig told *CA.* "I looked to the work of Windsor McKay, whom I really admire, for inspiration when designing the sequence of image and type." The resulting book was well received, shortlisted for

England's prestigious Smarties Prize in 1992. Kathryn Jennings in *Bulletin of the Center for Children's Books* dubbed it a "cozy version" of the traditional tale. "The pen-and-wash illustrations have a comic-book-format appeal and a bucolic air."

"I enjoyed the two mice characters so much," Craig told *CA,* "that I followed it up with another adventure using the same 'comic book' style layout." *Charlie and Tyler at the Seaside* tells the tale of Tyler, the town mouse, and Charlie from the country, who spend a day together at the seashore. They are flown there by Mrs. Pigeon, and immediately find themselves in adventures galore. They are nearly washed out to sea in a tiny boat, become members of a toy theater company, and narrowly avoid becoming dinner for a predator. Cynthia Anthony, writing in *Magpies,* concluded that "Craig's cozy illustrations and her depiction of two very different mice, jaunty Tyler and the more cautious Charlie, are sure to please."

"I was exploring many relationships and contrasts in these books," Craig explained to *CA.* "Not only the 'child-giant' theme—here represented by the 'mouse-human,' but also the small secret 'unknown' fantastical world of the mice existing within the giant 'known' world of humans with which every child is familiar. Also the relationship of the swaggering Tyler Townmouse contrasting with the retiring quality of the timid Charlie Country Mouse. At the same time, one double-page spread has, in a sense, two contrasting time scales. The dining table where Tyler invites Charlie to eat shows the whole table as one picture but is also divided into little moments in time in which Charlie is being offered a new tasty treat."

"Recently," Craig continued, "I have been experimenting with a new technique which I used for *One Windy Night* written by Phyllis Root. The original pictures were drawn in fine line on a very small scale and then enlarged a number of times on a photocopier. This gave them a very bold quality—they were then coloured. I hope to use this more often." It is this spirit of innovation and creative endeavor that comes through in Craig's illustrations and that has made her a favorite with young readers.

*BIOGRAPHICAL/CRITICAL SOURCES:*

*PERIODICALS*

*Booklist,* April 1, 1986, p. 1141.
*Bulletin of the Center for Children's Books,* January, 1985, p. 87; September, 1985, p. 5; January,

1986, pp. 86-7; June, 1986. p. 183; February, 1987, p. 108.

*Bulletin of the Center for Children's Books,* January, 1993, pp. 138-9.

*Growing Point,* September, 1988, p. 5041.

*Horn Book,* January/February, 1985, p. 46; March, 1987, p. 202; March/April, 1988, pp. 192-3; January/February, 1989, p. 54; November/December, 1989, p. 760; September/October, 1992, pp. 575-6; January, 1993, p. 103; November/December, 1995, p. 760

*Junior Bookshelf,* August, 1986, pp. 146-7; February, 1987, p. 20; April, 1993, p. 63.

*Kirkus Reviews,* October, 1985, p. 211; January, 1986, pp. 86-7; April 15, 1989, p. 624.

*Library Journal,* October, 1985, p. 190; December, 1989, p. 82.

*Los Angeles Times Book Review,* February 17, 1985, p. 7; April 19, 1987, p. 4.

*Magpies,* September, 1995, pp. 27-8.

*New York Times Book Review,* November 11, 1984, p. 55.

*Publishers Weekly,* November 30, 1984, p. 89.

*School Library Journal,* January, 1985, p. 65; September, 1986, p. 122; April, 1992, p. 92.

*Times Educational Supplement,* June 21, 1985, p. 25; February 14, 1992, p. 27; July 7, 1995, p. R2.

—*Sketch by J. Sydney Jones*

\*　　\*　　\*

## CRAMER, Richard Ben 1950-

*PERSONAL:* Born June 12, 1950, in Rochester, NY; son of A. Robert and Blossom (Lackritz) Cramer. *Education:* Johns Hopkins University, B.A., 1971; Columbia University, M.S., 1972.

*CAREER: Sun,* Baltimore, MD, reporter, 1973-76; *Philadelphia Inquirer,* Philadelphia, PA, reporter, 1976-78, foreign correspondent in Europe, Africa, and the Middle East, beginning in 1978; freelance journalist and writer. Has worked as a contributing editor for *Esquire.*

*MEMBER:* Pen and Pencil, Stampa Estere d'Italia.

*AWARDS, HONORS:* Pulitzer Prize for international reporting, 1979, for reports from the Middle East; Sigma Delta Chi award for foreign correspondence, 1980; Ernie Pyle Award, Scripps Howard News Service, 1980; Hal Boyle Award, Overseas Press Club of America, 1981, for coverage of Afghan guerrillas fighting the Russians; American Society of Newspaper Editors award for excellence in writing.

*WRITINGS:*

*Ted Williams: The Season of the Kid,* photo essays by John Thorn, Prentice-Hall (Englewood Cliffs, NJ), 1991.

*What It Takes: The Way to the White House,* Random House (New York City), 1992.

*Bob Dole,* Vintage (New York City), 1995.

Contributor to anthologies, including *Best Newspaper Writing,* edited by Roy Peter Clark, Modern Media Institute (St. Petersburg, FL), 1980; *The Pulitzer Prize Archive,* Volume 1, edtied by Heinz-Dietrich Fischer, K. G. Saur (Munich), 1987; and *The Best American Essays 1987,* edited by Gay Talese, Ticknor & Fields (New York City), 1987. Also contributor to newspapers and periodicals, including the *New York Times, New York Times Book Review, Esquire,* and *Rolling Stone.*

*SIDELIGHTS:* During his award-winning career as a newspaper journalist, Richard Ben Cramer spent most of his time covering affairs outside the United States. As the *Philadelphia Inquirer*'s correspondent for Europe, Africa, and the Middle East, he spent many years overseas, reporting on both the civil war in Lebanon and the fighting between Soviet troops and Afghan guerrillas. In the years since he left the *Inquirer,* however, Cramer has been concerned with uniquely American subjects. His 1992 book, *What It Takes: The Way To the White House,* presents a study of six of the 1988 presidential candidates. He has also focused on the sports world of his native country, producing *Ted Williams: The Season of the Kid* in 1991. Both books have been praised by critics for delivering an unusual glimpse of their prominent and powerful subjects.

In profiling baseball legend Williams, Cramer was faced with a man who was renowned for his exploits on the field but who was uncomfortable with his role as a superstar. As the last professional player to hold a season batting average of .400, Williams has been touted by many experts as the best hitter to ever play the game. His career was also marred by incidents in which he spit at fans and threw his bat into the crowd to silence hecklers. *Ted Williams: The Season of the Kid* opens with an account of Cramer's visit to the aging star in his Florida retirement home, then chronicles Williams's career and personal life. *Newsweek* reviewer Charles Leerhsen proclaimed the book "a timeless piece of journalism" that results in "a brilliantly crafted profile" of Williams, a man, Cramer writes, who "wanted fame . . . but could not stand celebrity."

The celebrities in *What It Takes,* Cramer's second book, are also involved in a competitive American pastime: politics. The author studies six of the candidates in the 1988 presidential campaign: Gary Hart, Joseph Biden, Richard Gephardt, Michael Dukakis, Bob Dole, and George Bush. Cramer was not content in writing a conventional political analysis of the race, however. "I wanted to know not about the campaign, but about the campaigners," the author notes in his introduction to the book. "Who are these guys. . . . What happened to their idea of themselves? What did *we do to them,* on the way to the White House?" In order to answer these questions Cramer worked on the book for a total of six years, before, during, and after 1988. He conducted over 1,000 interviews with people involved in the campaign, including extensive discussions with each of the six candidates. The resulting book is over 1,000 pages in length, providing an extensive study of the men who aspired to be president.

"Cramer renders his representative men with specificity and sensitivity," judged *Dictionary of Literary Biography* contributor Robert Schmuhl. "He captures their strengths, limitations, habits, and idiosyncrasies, and even seems to empathize with them for what they are forced to endure. The politicians, in fact, have a stature just short of heroic." Devoting seven chapters to the alleged extramarital affair of Gary Hart and its effect on Hart's career, Cramer exposes "more monkey business by journalists than sexual shenanigans by the former Colorado senator," advised Schmuhl. "But the intense coverage is enough to make Hart withdraw. Hart's experience allows Cramer to focus on the importance of character and the involvement of the media in presidential politics."

Douglas Bell, reviewing the book in the Toronto *Globe & Mail,* noted that "Cramer zeroes in and with surgical precision dissects layer upon layer of his subject's persona." These insights stem, in part, from the details the author relates about the candidates. The book pictures Biden as he shops for real estate between political rallies, discusses Hart's choice of cocktails at a campaign stopover, and describes the mysterious tune that Bob Dole continually whistles and hums throughout the primaries. "Cramer has a particularly sensitive ear for dialogue," Bell continued, "capturing not just what the candidate said but the way he said it." In addition to documenting the behavior of the candidates, *What It Takes* also provides the author's assessment of the campaign's headline stories. Cramer defends the two candidates who withdrew from the race after allegations of impropriety—Biden, who plagiarized a campaign speech, and Hart, who was accused of having an extramarital affair. In both cases Cramer feels the candidates were the victims of an overzealous news media who were hungry for sensational stories.

The media are only one of many forces that impact the candidates in Cramer's account. The author also considers the so-called "handlers"—the group of analysts, pollsters, and image consultants that help manage each candidate's campaign. Jack Shafer, reviewing the book in the *Washington Post Book World,* noted that "the subtext of *What It Takes* is that a candidate must maintain his vigilance lest the handlers (Cramer calls them 'the white men') take over." The author also describes the closed world that the candidates exist in, a claustrophobic environment created by their non-stop travel and carefully orchestrated appearances. This quality is made clear, according to *Time* reviewer Walter Shapiro, in the book's depiction of George Bush on the campaign trail. "Where Cramer excels," wrote Shapiro, "is in portraying Bush's sterile life inside the bubble—the Secret-Service-secure world of motorcades, advancemen, rope lines, and step-by-step schedules." Cramer argues that such elements created a campaign environment where Bush would "never see one person who was not a friend, or someone whose sole purpose it was to serve or protect him."

The epic length of *What It Takes* became an issue for critics reviewing the book. Some, such as *New Statesman & Society* reviewer Boyd Tonkin, found the book excessively detailed. "No one ever stopped to think that this project might have worked better at 300 pages than at *1046,*" Tonkin complained. "Few will finish it, and no skimmer can use its information, as it lacks an index." Shapiro conceded that "only the dust jacket is terse" in *What It Takes,* but he found that the length of the book was justified. "Despite its heft," Shapiro wrote, "the prose is a joyous journey" that results in an "artful reworking" of the campaign.

Cramer's writing style in the book—his use of numerous exclamation points and capitalized words, for instance—was singled out by many reviewers and compared to the writing of other experimental journalists such as Tom Wolfe and Hunter S. Thompson. *Newsweek*'s Joe Klein addressed another aspect of Cramer's technique, noting that the author doesn't cite his sources as is the normal journalistic practice. Because of this, Klein speculated that *What It Takes* "is bound to cause a fair amount of controversy among the political and media priesthoods, as it blithely skirts the boundaries of responsibility and good taste." Despite this danger, the critic felt that the book succeeded in its quest to explain the political candidates. "Even if only semi-journalistic," Klein wrote, "this is still great fun and . . . far more insightful about pols and political tradecraft than the common run of campaign effluvia."

In the end, the book suggests that "what it takes" to be president is a willingness to give all. Shapiro, summing up Cramer's views, wrote that the president must be "so driven in his pursuit of the White House that he jettisons family, friends, any semblance of privacy or normal human existence." And a similar question was addressed by the critics who reviewed Cramer's study: did the book have "what it takes" to be worthwhile reading? The *Globe & Mail*'s Bell was one of many who felt it did, citing the author's "deft mix of insight and breathtaking reportage." The critic went on to proclaim the book an important document of the campaign, declaring that "Cramer's delightfully unexpected insights capture the tenor and the timbre of his political times."

In 1995, the minibiography of Senator Dole that made up part of *What It Takes* was published separately as *Bob Dole.* A fifteen-page introduction also provides new information gathered during a speaking trip and an interview with Dole. According to Schmuhl, *What It Takes* and *Bob Dole* "enhanced Cramer's reputation as a detail-oriented reporter who writes with imagination and originality. The people he selects to write about are at the heart of his work, and they frequently come to life as characters in a well-wrought piece of fiction do. His willingness to test established journalistic forms yields creative approaches that a reader sees from his earliest newspaper days to his magazine articles and books. Journalism often simplifies complexity. With Cramer's in-depth probing of subjects, clear and precise explanation illumines what is complex, and the presentation is engagingly distinctive."

*BIOGRAPHICAL/CRITICAL SOURCES:*

*BOOKS*

Connery, Thomas B., editor, *A Sourcebook of American Literary Journalism: Representative Writers in an Emerging Genre,* Greenwood Press (Westport, CT), 1992, pp. 331-41.
Cramer, Richard Ben, *Ted Williams: The Season of the Kid,* Prentice Hall, 1991.
Cramer, *What It Takes: The Way to the White House,* Random House, 1992.
*Dictionary of Literary Biography,* Volume 185: *American Literary Journalists, 1945-1995, First Series,* Gale (Detroit), 1997.

*PERIODICALS*

*Chicago Tribune,* July 14, 1992, section 2, pp. 1-2.
*Esquire,* October, 1984, p. 7.
*Globe & Mail* (Toronto), July 11, 1992, p. C5.
*New Statesman & Society,* July 31, 1992, p. 37.
*Newsweek,* October 28, 1991, p. 62; July 6, 1992, p. 55.
*Philadelphia Inquirer,* September 2, 1992, pp. E1, 5.
*Style,* fall, 1982, pp. 427-447.
*Time,* July 13, 1992, pp. 78-80.
*Washington Post,* July 6, 1992, pp. D1, 4.
*Washington Post Book World,* June 28, 1992, pp. 1, 10.*

*        *        *

## CROSBY, Alfred W., Jr. 1931-

*PERSONAL:* Born January 15, 1931, in Boston, MA; son of Alfred W. (a commercial artist) and Ruth (Coleman) Crosby; married second wife, Barbara Stevens, June 27, 1964; children: (first marriage) Kevin R.; (second marriage) Carolyn J. *Education:* Harvard University, A.B., 1952, A.M.T., 1956; Boston University, Ph.D., 1961.

*ADDRESSES: Office*—Department of American Studies, University of Texas, Austin, TX 78712.

*CAREER:* Albion College, Albion, MI, instructor in history, 1960-61; Ohio State University, Columbus, instructor in history, 1961-65; San Fernando Valley State College (now California State University, Northridge), assistant professor of history, 1965-66; Washington State University, Pullman, associate professor of history, 1966-77; University of Texas at Austin, professor of American studies, 1977—. Fellow, National Institutes of Health, 1971-73; fellow, Humanities Institute, 1975-76. *Military service:* U.S. Army, 1952-55; became sergeant.

*MEMBER:* American Historical Association.

*WRITINGS:*

*America, Russia, Hemp and Napoleon,* Ohio State University Press (Columbus), 1965.

*The Columbian Exchange: Biological and Cultural Consequences of 1492,* Greenwood Press (Westport, CT), 1972.

*Epidemic and Peace, 1918,* Greenwood Press, 1976, reprinted with a new preface as *America's Forgotten Pandemic: The Influenza of 1918,* Cambridge University Press (New York City), 1989.

(Contributor) June E. Osborn, editor, *Influenza in America, 1918-1976: History, Science, and Politics,* Prodist (New York City), 1977.

*Ecological Imperialism: The Biological Expansion of Europe, 900-1900,* Cambridge University Press, 1986.

*The Columbian Voyages, the Columbian Exchange, and their Historians,* American Historical Association (Washington, DC), 1987.

*Germs, Seeds, and Animals: Studies in Ecological History,* M.E. Sharpe (Armonk, NY), 1994.

*The Measure of Reality: Quantifications and Western Society, 1250-1600,* Cambridge University Press, 1997.

Contributor to *American Neptune, Pennsylvania Magazine of History and Biography, Hispanic American Review, Sexual Behavior,* and *American Anthropologist.*

*SIDELIGHTS:* In his works of nonfiction, historian Alfred W. Crosby, Jr., looks beyond the people and events, the leaders and wars, that provide the framework for most histories, to the natural forces that shape human history. What he uncovers are the profound effects that plants, animals, and diseases have had upon the course of history. In his 1976 book, *Epidemic and Peace, 1918* (revised and published in 1989 as *America's Forgotten Pandemic: The Influenza of 1918*), Crosby examines the outbreak of Spanish influenza that occurred as World War I was coming to a close. The pandemic engulfed the world, killing over 20 million people (more than 500,000 in the United States), making it more deadly than the war and the worst disease since the Black Plague of the Middle Ages. In the United States, the influenza first spread among sailors and soldiers back from the fighting in Europe. Its symptoms began like those of the common cold with a fever but quickly progressed in many cases to pneumonia and then death. "Crosby has written a lively and informative account of three waves of devastation wrought in 1918 by the Spanish influenza," observes William K. Beatty in *Library Journal.* "He draws on individual and institutional records to paint a picture that conveys the magnitude, terror, and speed of the flu and its companion pneumonia." The quality of his research, "rich in detail," is all the more noteworthy, remarks Allan M. Brandt in the *Times Literary Supplement,* "given incomplete and inconsistent record-keeping."

Brandt recognizes the fundamental difference between Crosby's work and that of most historians. "While most historians are eager to chart human conflicts," Brandt writes, "Crosby seeks to detail those of human beings against nature. Influenza is for him the preeminent force causing historical change after the war." For Brandt, however, by giving the pandemic such a major role, Crosby goes too far. He finds that "Crosby tends to trivialize historical change." Yet, a number of reviewers note that Crosby makes a strong case for the impact of influenza because the 1918 pandemic has been overlooked and runs the risk of being forgotten. And, for *Publishers Weekly* contributor Albert H. Johnston, the world needs a reminder. The reviewer suggests in a 1976 piece that Crosby's book is "especially relevant now when we may be threatened by a recurrence" [the swine flu scare of the mid-1970s]. More recent reviewers have compared the 1918 pandemic to the AIDS epidemic of the eighties and nineties.

In *Ecological Imperialism: The Biological Expansion of Europe, 900-1900,* Crosby again attempts to look beyond the traditional focus of history, this time to reveal in greater breadth the consequences of European exploration and immigration. As Crosby argues, European explorers, conquistadors, and traders were not the only agents of devastation upon the new lands they encountered. Animals, plants, and diseases that came along with the Europeans "rapidly established biological empires of their own," observes David Arnold in the *Times Literary Supplement,* "at times outstripping the Europeans in the speed of their advancing colonization." Much of the work of subduing these new lands was done for humans by these biological agents. In addition, Crosby maintains that the impact of these environmental elements also explains "why Europeans were successful in becoming the dominant majority in certain places—the Americas, Australia, New Zealand, and South Africa—but not in most of Africa and Asia, although they also tried to gain control in those places," F. N. Egerton points out in *Choice.* In temperate climates where the plants, animals, and relatively sparse population of indigenous people had had little exposure to such potent ecological invaders, the Europeans replaced the native ecology with their own. Tropical climates, teeming with their own biological agents, withstood the European onslaught more effectively.

*Ecological Imperialism,* "based on information from various disciplines, is a wide-ranging and well-documented synthesis," offers Joseph Hannibal in *Library Journal.* And, the effect of placing biological factors and their consequences on European expansion at the center of Crosby's history, according to Sean French in the *Observer,* is one of "telling an old story from a startling new vantage point, in which humans are blown about by forces, outside and inside, of whose existence they can scarcely comprehend." The reviewer concludes, "This is a revolutionary work of history, eloquently written with a dry irony befitting its appalling subject, a thousand years of genocide occurring over and over again wherever the Old World met the new."

*BIOGRAPHICAL/CRITICAL SOURCES:*

PERIODICALS

*Booklist,* January 1, 1997, p. 811.
*Choice,* September, 1976, p. 848; April, 1987, p. 1266; April, 1993, p. 1277; September, 1994, p. 49.
*Journal of the American Medical Association,* January 16, 1991, p. 403.
*Library Journal,* March 1, 1976, p. 712; October 1, 1986, p. 103; March 15, 1990, p. 119; January, 1997, p. 118.
*Natural History,* December, 1986, p. 74.
*Nature,* October 16, 1986, p. 103.
*New York Review of Books,* January 28, 1993, p. 38.
*New York Times Book Review,* October 19, 1986, p. 20; January 26, 1997, p. 7.
*Observer* (London), November 14, 1993, p. 22.
*Publishers Weekly,* May 17, 1976, p. 49; November 25, 1996, p. 62.
*Times Literary Supplement,* February 27, 1987, p. 208; October 26, 1990, p. 1158.
*Whole Earth Review,* spring, 1988, p. 48.

## CROZIER, Lorna 1948-
### (Lorna Uher, a pseudonym)

*PERSONAL:* Born May 24, 1948, in Swift Current, Saskatchewan, Canada; daughter of Emerson and Peggy Crozier; companion of Patrick Lane (a poet). *Education:* University of Saskatchewan, B.A., 1969; University of Alberta, M.A., 1980.

*ADDRESSES: Office*—c/o McClelland & Steward, 481 University Avenue, Suite 900, Toronto, Ontario M5G 2E9, Canada.

*CAREER:* High school English teacher in Swift Current, Saskatchewan, 1970-77; Cypress Hills Community College, Swift Current, writer-in-residence, 1980-81; Saskatchewan Department of Culture and Recreation, Regina, director of communications, 1981-83; Regina Public Library, Regina, writer-in-residence, 1983-84; University of Saskatchewan, Saskatoon, special lecturer, 1986-91; University of Toronto, Toronto, Ontario, writer-in-residence, 1988-90; University of Victoria, Victoria, British Columbia, associate professor of English, 1991—. Canadian Broadcasting Corporation (CBC) Radio, broadcaster and writer, 1986.

*MEMBER:* League of Canadian Poets, Saskatchewan Writers' Guild (vice president, 1977-79), Saskatchewan Artists' Colony (committee president, 1982-84).

*AWARDS, HONORS:* Poetry prize, Saskatchewan Department of Culture and Youth, 1978, for *Crow's Black Joy;* poetry manuscript prize, Saskatchewan Writers' Guild, 1983, for *The Weather,* and 1985, for *The Garden Going on without Us;* nomination for Governor General's Award for Poetry, 1985, for *The Garden Going on without Us,* and 1988, for *Angels of Flesh, Angels of Silence;* first prize for poetry, Canadian Broadcasting Corp. (CBC), and second prize, *Prism International* poetry competition, both 1987, both for "Fear of Snakes"; Nellie Award for best public radio program, 1988, for "Chile"; Governor General's award for poetry, and Canadian Authors award, both 1992, both for *Inventing the Hawk;* League of Canadian Poets Pat Lowther Award, 1992, for *Inventing the Hawk,* and 1996, for *A Saving Grace;* National Magazine Gold Medal Award for Poetry, 1996; Mothertongue Chapbook winner, 1996, for *The Transparency of Grief.*

*WRITINGS:*

*POETRY*

(As Lorna Uher) *Inside Is the Sky,* Thistledown Press (Saskatoon), 1975.

(As Lorna Uher) *Crow's Black Joy,* NeWest Press (Edmonton, Alberta), 1978.

(As Lorna Uher, with Patrick Lane) *No Longer Two People,* Turnstone Press (Winnipeg, Manitoba), 1979.

(As Lorna Uher) *Animals of Fall,* Very Stone House (Vancouver), 1979.

(As Lorna Uher) *Humans and Other Beasts* (poetry), Turnstone Press, 1980.

*The Weather,* Coteau (Moose Jaw, Saskatchewan), 1983.

*The Garden Going on without Us,* McClelland & Stewart (Toronto), 1985.

*Angels of Flesh, Angels of Silence,* McClelland & Stewart, 1988.

*Inventing the Hawk,* McClelland & Stewart, 1992.

*Everything Arrives at the Light,* McClelland & Stewart, 1995.

*A Saving Grace: The Collected Poems of Mrs. Bentley,* McClelland & Stewart, 1996.

*The Transparency of Grief,* Mothertongue Press (Ganges), 1996.

*OTHER*

(With others) *If We Call This the Girlie Show, Will You Find It Offensive?* (three-act play), produced in Regina, Saskatchewan, 1984.

(Editor, with Lane) *Breathing Fire: The New Generation of Canadian Poets,* Harbour (Madeira Park, BC), 1995.

(Editor, with Lane) *The Selected Poems of Alden Nowlan,* Anansi (Toronto), 1995.

Also author of "Chile" (radio program), broadcast on CBC-Radio. Contributor to anthologies, including *Full Moon,* Quadrant, 1984; *Anything Is Possible,* Mosaic, 1984; *Canadian Poetry Now,* House of Anansi, 1984; *Ride off Any Horizon,* NeWest, 1984; and *The New Canadian Poets,* edited by Dennis Lee, McClelland & Stewart, 1985. Contributor of poems and reviews to periodicals, including *Quarry* and *Saturday Night.* Poetry editor, *NeWest Review.*

*SIDELIGHTS:* Associated with Canada's so-called Moose Jaw Movement that took place during the mid-1970s in the central plains area that bears its name,

poet Lorna Crozier has become well known for work that combines a sharp, penetrating wit with deft portraits of human feeling and intuition. As Bruce Meyer wrote in an essay in *Contemporary Women Poets,* Crozier "is not the typical prairie poet. Her terrain . . . is the realm of metaphysics and the metaphysical complexities of time, place, history, thought, and emotions." Beginning her writing career publishing under the name Lorna Uher, Crozier has authored several collections of verse, including *Animals of Fall, The Garden Going on without Us,* and the 1992 volume *Inventing the Hawk,* winner of Canada's prestigious Governor General's award.

As influences on her work Crozier cites Sinclair Ross's *As for Me and My House,* as well as works by Rainer Maria Rilke and Pablo Neruda, who inspired her to expand "the limits of my imagination and beyond, to get in touch with the interior landscape of the soul." Of Ross's work, she once explained to *CA* that "It was the first book I read that was set in the landscape where I grew up, the southwest corner of Saskatchewan. It made me realize that someone from my area could actually be a writer and, in some ways, it gave me the courage to try."

A self-authored work that would be cited by several reviewers as pivotal in Crozier's career is 1979's *No Longer Two People,* which the poet co-authored with long-time companion Patrick Lane. In contrast to her early, politically based works, the poems published in the wake of *No Longer Two People* would exhibit a greater tendency toward "playfulness," according to Meyer. Noting that the volume was given little consideration by critics when it was first published, Meyer maintained that *No Longer* is pivotal in Crozier's career because "it shifted the focus of her work onto the details of the male/female relationship and allowed her to redefine her own femininity and her partner's masculinity within that context; and it brought to her work an idea of 'metamorphosis' that has become a key element" in the poet's more recent work.

In *Angels of Flesh, Angels of Silence,* the influence of myth becomes evident, as images of Icarus and other classical elements intertwine in her verses. As Meyer noted, Crozier's ability to intermix mythology and dream elements with aspects of everyday life "humanizes" her subjects. "It is that sense, . . . of making the real more real by making it magical and believable, that gives Crozier's work its life," maintained the critic.

"The landscape of southwestern Saskatchewan has definitely influenced my writing," Crozier once explained to *CA*. "I've tried to thread the wind and sky into my poems, to make them breathe the way the prairie does. But the influence of place goes beyond the recurrence of images particular to a certain landscape. The mutability and the extremes of the natural world in Saskatchewan have given rise to my sense of the fragility of happiness, love, and life itself. Our hold on things and on each other is so tenuous. My poems, I think, express the fearful hope I feel for the human—for our capability to return to love through pain and for our journey towards that sense of unity with all things, with the mule deer I startled from feeding in the coulee yesterday, and with the mute explosions of lichens on the stones in my grandfather's pasture. If the magic that is poetry can't lead us to that oneness, then I hope it at least can make us feel less alone."

*BIOGRAPHICAL/CRITICAL SOURCES:*

BOOKS

*Contemporary Women Poets,* St. James Press (Detroit), 1997.

*PERIODICALS*

*Books in Canada,* May, 1996, p. 8; March, 1997, p. 12.
*Canadian Book Review Annual,* 1996, p. 228.
*Canadian Literature,* summer, 1996, p. 201.
*Quill & Quire,* September, 1996, p. 66.*

\*          \*          \*

**CURTIS, Sharon 1951-**
    **(Robin James, Laura London, joint pseudonyms)**

*PERSONAL:* Born March 6, 1951, in Dahran, Saudi Arabia; father was a geologist, mother a magazine editor and historian; immigrated to the United States, naturalized citizen; married Thomas Dale Curtis (a writer and trucker), 1970; children: two. *Education:* Attended University of Wisconsin—Madison.

*ADDRESSES: Home*—Wisconsin.

*CAREER:* Writer and bookstore manager.

*WRITINGS:*

ROMANCE NOVELS; WITH HUSBAND, THOMAS DALE CURTIS, UNDER JOINT PSEUDONYM LAURA LONDON; EXCEPT AS INDICATED

*A Heart Too Proud,* Dell (New York City), 1978.
*The Bad Baron's Daughter,* Dell, 1978.
*Moonlight Mist,* Dell, 1979.
*Love's a Stage,* Dell, 1980.
*The Gypsy Heiress,* Dell, 1981.
(As Sharon Curtis and Tom Curtis) *Sunshine and Shadow,* Bantam (New York City), 1986.
*Keepsake,* Jove (New York City), 1987.

Also author of *Lightning That Lingers,* 1991 and *The Windflower,* 1994; also author of *The Golden Touch,* 1992, and *The Testimony,* 1993, both as Robin James. Contributor to anthology *When You Wish,* edited by Jane Feather, Bantam, 1997.

*WORK IN PROGRESS:* A novel set during the Spanish Civil War.

*SIDELIGHTS:* Sharon Curtis and her husband Tom Curtis have written numerous popular romance novels, most under the joint pseudonym Laura London and a few as Robin James. They began to work together when both were in their early twenties. Both were fond of Jane Austen and Regency romance writer Georgette Heyer, so they first tried writing a Regency. In about six months, the husband-and-wife team had completed the manuscript for *A Heart Too Proud.* Curtis then went to a bookstore, found that the Dell publishing house produced numerous Regencies, and looked up Dell's phone number. After chatting with someone at the company, she sent the manuscript to the Regency editor, and *A Heart Too Proud* was bought almost immediately.

Many romance aficionados consider *The Windflower* to be the best book written under the London pseudonym—even one of the best historical romances ever written. The book has been described by its authors as a coming-of-age story. It follows the character development of a young woman who is kidnaped by pirates when she is eighteen years old. Inspiration for the story came after Curtis read an eighteenth-century document that listed names, ages, and descriptions of pirates executed at a public hanging. Her imagination and sympathy were aroused by the youth of many on the list, and the fact that so many were poor, orphaned, or both.

Curtis thought back to her childhood for the background of *Sunshine and Shadow,* which is set in an Amish community. Curtis's grandfather lived in an Amish area in southwestern Wisconsin. After completing that novel, the Curtises took an extended sabbatical from writing, working at other jobs and focusing on family issues. They returned to romance writing in the late-1990s with a novella published in the Bantam romance anthology *When You Wish.* Each story in the collection features a magical bottle that is found by various characters. Other contributors to the book include Patricia Potter, Suzanne Robinson, Elizabeth Elliot, and Patricia Coughlin.*

# D

## D'ALPUGET, Blanche 1944-

*PERSONAL:* Surname is pronounced Dal-pu-*jay;* born January 3, 1944, in Sydney, Australia; daughter of Louis Albert (a journalist) and Josephine (Curgenuen) d'Alpuget; married Anthony Ian Camden Pratt (a civil servant), November 22, 1965; children: Louis Pratt. *Education:* Sydney Church of England Girls' Grammar School. *Politics:* Labor.

*ADDRESSES: Home*—18 Urambi Village, Kambah, Australian Capital Territory 2902, Australia. *Agent*—Robert Gottlieb, William Morris Agency, 1350 Avenue of the Americas, New York, NY 10019.

*CAREER:* Journalist in Sydney, London, Paris, Djakarta (Indonesia), Kuala Lumpur (Malaysia), and Canberra (Australia), 1962-74; writer. Member of Women's Electoral Lobby.

*MEMBER:* Women's International League for Peace and Freedom, International PEN (Sydney Centre), Australian Labor Party, Oral History Association of Australia (president of Australian Capital Territory branch, 1980-81), Australian Society of Authors, Women's Electoral Body.

*AWARDS, HONORS:* Novel of the Year Award from *The Age* (Australian newspaper), 1981, Golden Jubilee Award from PEN, Sydney Centre, 1981, Biennial Award for Literature from South Australian Government, 1982, and Braille Book of the Year award, 1982, all for *Turtle Beach;* New South Wales Premier's Award and Braille Book of the Year Award, both 1983, both for *Robert J. Hawke: A Biography.*

*WRITINGS:*

*NOVELS*

*Monkeys in the Dark,* J. Cape (London), 1980.
*Turtle Beach,* Penguin, 1981, Simon & Schuster (New York City), 1983.
*Winter in Jerusalem,* Simon & Schuster, 1986.
*White Eye,* Simon & Schuster, 1994.

*OTHER*

*Mediator: A Biography of Sir Richard Kirby,* Melbourne University Press (Melbourne), 1977.
*Robert J. Hawke: A Biography,* Schwartz with Landsdowne Press (East Melbourne), 1982.

*SIDELIGHTS:* In the novel *Turtle Beach* Blanche d'Alpuget introduces Judith Wilkes, an Australian journalist assigned to cover the arrival of boatloads of Vietnamese refugees into Malaysia in 1979. The world the presswoman encounters in postcolonial Kuala Lumpur is a strange mingling of East and West, full of disturbing juxtapositions and ironies: the people she meets in this chaotic environment are a curious mix as well. As Wilkes reports on the tragic plight of the boat people in a country that does not want them and incarcerates them in cruel camps, she also observes the intricate lives of those she has met and engages in her own journey of self-discovery. Gene Lyons, writing in *Newsweek,* described *Turtle Beach* as "the sort of novel one encounters at very rare intervals: broad in scope, ambitious almost to a fault, yet written with a crisp, breezy intelligence that enlivens the story without concealing for a moment its grave implications. . . . 'Turtle Beach' makes us witness to history in the raw—the human tidal wave of Southeast Asia," he added, "without peddling phony guilt or easy answers."

Other critics concurred with Lyons, praising the gripping plot of *Turtle Beach,* its well-drawn characters, and the skillfulness of d'Alpuget's writing. Toronto *Globe and Mail* reviewer Anne Montagnes remarked that "Blanche d'Alpuget writes in a simple, gripping style. Pages flip over as the reader plunges into the concerns of her characters." Suzanne Freeman repeated the observation in a *Washington Post* critique, noting that d'Alpuget "is a strong writer with a particularly sharp sense of character. In a few deft behind-the-scene scenes, we get a good look right into the souls of the people in this book." The critic added that "the sheer force of her story is enough to sweep us along to the end. And it's well worth the trip. The final scenes on Turtle Beach are powerful and haunting." And Joe Klein, writing in the *New York Times Book Review,* reflected: "Mrs. d'Alpuget seems able to enter effortlessly the heads of her characters, both Western and Eastern. . . . Her observations are made all the more powerful by a graceful style of writing that is, at once, lucid and coy. . . . This is an auspicious American debut for Blanche d'Alpuget, and it raises two immediate questions: What else has she written, and when do we get to see it?"

D'Alpuget's fourth novel, *White Eyes,* received less enthusiastic reviews. Although written as a thriller, according to *New York Times Book Review* critic Nina Sonenberg, the story is "disappointing" and "packs little suspense." Laurie Clancy described the novel in *Contemporary Novelists:* " Although written in a deliberately plain and simple style the novel has an extraordinarily intricate plot, involving illegal trafficking in chimpanzees between Thailand and Australia, genetic engineering, and an attempt to destroy the world. . . . The protagonist, Diana Pembridge, is a quintessential d'Alpuget heroine, thirty-two years old, beautiful and patrician in appearance, but vulnerable and unfulfilled in reality. She is a passionate lover of nature without being a fanatic. . . . Against her is pitted John Parker, a deeply misogynistic man whose disgust with a proliferating human race drives him to invent a vaccine that will prevent it breeding." Both Sonenberg and Clancy agreed that, in the words of Clancy, "some of the finest writing in the novel is devoted to accounts of [Diana] falconing and her struggle to heal and release a wounded wedgetail eagle."

A *Publishers Weekly* review of *White Eyes* faulted d'Alpuget for "striv[ing] so hard to press her fine

style and character insights into the thriller genre" and further noted: "More problematic is the way characters drop in and out of the plot without developing cogent relationships." Clancy's summary of the novel also recognized weaknesses in character relations: "Like all of d'Alpuget's work, *White Eye* is a carefully and thoroughly researched novel that at times indeed wears its learning a little ostentatiously. It alternates scenes of lyrical evocation of landscape and the beauty of the colony of birds that Diana looks after with descriptions of violence and cruelty. Like *Winter in Jerusalem* it suffers from a rushed ending in which Diana and a charismatic photographer cum environmentalist meet and fall in love in what seems seconds. D'Alpuget has admitted that she has difficulty in writing scenes of sexual love and this is evident here. . . . However, d'Alpuget does save a couple of ingenious twists in the plot till right near the end."

d'Alpuget told *CA:* "The Muses were the daughters of Jupiter and Memory. Memory, I think, exists within imagination as the grain in timber. Uncovering it— and memory for me remains utterly mysterious—is a delight."

*BIOGRAPHICAL/CRITICAL SOURCES:*

*BOOKS*

*Contemporary Novelists,* sixth edition, St. James Press (Detroit), 1996.

*PERIODICALS*

*Globe and Mail,* (Toronto), December 3, 1983.
*Los Angeles Times,* February 3, 1984.
*Newsweek,* November 14, 1983.
*New York Times Book Review,* October 23, 1983; August 14, 1994.
*Publishers Weekly,* June 6, 1994.
*Washington Post,* September 20, 1983.*

\* \* \*

## DAVIDSON, Sara 1943-

*PERSONAL:* Born February 5, 1943, in Los Angeles, CA; daughter of Marvin H. (a realtor) and Alice S. (Wass) Davidson; married Jonathan Schwartz (a disc jockey and author), January 26, 1968 (divorced, 1975); married second husband; divorced; children (second marriage): Andrew, Rachel. *Education:* University of California, B.A., 1964; Columbia University, M.S., 1965.

*ADDRESSES: Home*—Venice, CA. *Agent*—Lynn Nesbit, International Creative Management, 40 West 57th St., New York, NY 10019.

*CAREER: Boston Globe,* Boston, MA, reporter, 1965-67, correspondent in New York City, 1967-69; freelance writer, 1969—. Notable assignments include coverage of youth and the counterculture, rock groups, radical activists, the Robert Kennedy assassination, and the 1968 political conventions. Writer and producer for television. Co-executive producer of *Dr. Quinn, Medicine Woman* (CBS), 1994—.

*WRITINGS:*

*Loose Change: Three Women of the Sixties* (nonfiction), Doubleday (New York City), 1977.
*Real Property* (nonfiction), Doubleday, 1980.
*Friends of the Opposite Sex* (novel), Doubleday, 1984.
(With Rock Hudson) *Rock Hudson: His Story* (biography), Morrow (New York City), 1986.

Contributor to periodicals, including *Harper's, Atlantic, Life, Rolling Stone, New Woman, Esquire, Ms., New York Times* magazine, and *New York Times Book Review.*

*ADAPTATIONS: Loose Change* has been adapted as a miniseries on NBC-TV, 1978.

*SIDELIGHTS:* Sara Davidson "has been taking the pulse of her generation" since she began writing for the University of California newspaper in the 1960s, according to *Dictionary of Literary Biography* contributor Ginger Rudeseal Carter. "Davidson's work spans not only four decades but also diverse media. She has moved from newspapers to magazines, from nonfiction to fiction, and from print to television. Her creative work seems to fit whatever medium is most popular at the time, and her subjects seem to be reminiscent of the mood of the decade in which they appear." Carter went on to declare that at least every ten years, Davidson published an article that served as a benchmark for the decade: "From *Loose Change: Three Women of the Sixties* . . . to her article 'Love with a Proper Cowboy' (1995), her work as a literary journalist has provided a vivid illumination of the times she describes."

"In the Sixties, I often felt that I was caught between two worlds: the Establishment and the counterculture," Davidson herself wrote. "In the first, I was viewed as a youth spokesman and in the second, I was seen as a representative of the bourgeois capitalist press. I could move in both worlds, but I did not fit in either.

"In 1972, I had a chance meeting in an elevator with a young woman I had known at Berkeley. It was this meeting which led me to seek out others from my past, to see if, by tracing our stories, I might piece together a social history of the Sixties and gain an understanding of what happened to us—and our country—in this time."

After the surprise reunion with her former apartment-mate, Davidson sought out the other woman who had lived with them at Berkeley, and convinced the two to tell their stories. Davidson spent six months interviewing Natasha in New York and six months interviewing Susie in Berkeley (their names are fictional).

"We would meet once a week and spend all day," Davidson wrote. "Often I would ask them to go very deep. For instance I'd ask Susie to reconstruct the time she and Jeff broke up. All she could say was: 'I remember. We had a terrible fight and then he left.'

"I would ask her: 'What was the fight about? Who said what? What were you wearing?' She kept saying: 'I don't remember.' So I had to invent it, invent all that texture, from what I knew of Susie at the time, and what I knew of Berkeley.

"Which gets to the question of: is it still nonfiction? I decided it was, if you were using the facts and details that were real and if you were taking the plot from history. But I was certainly filling it out, filling in the skeleton, with my memory."

Malcolm Cowley called *Loose Change* "the liveliest account of the era" yet written and found that "the mood of the times is vividly suggested." However, some critics complained that the book did little to elucidate the meaning of the Sixties. While many reviewers were impressed by Davidson's journalistic skills, they were bothered by her lack of insight into the social and political upheavals of the decade. "It is as if the author expected the mere invocation of the events to carry their own emotional weight," Erica Jong noted. Jong admired Davidson's attempt to be "descriptive rather than judgmental," and praised Davidson for her "engaging sense of adventure, a willingness to try anything once, a real lust for life. She is a risk-taker, willing to be a fool if in the process she may find enlightenment."

*Time* judged Davidson "an acute observer and ironist," but decried the book's confusion of sex and politics, which it termed "countercultural soap opera." Other reviewers, however, found that she handled the subject of sex with honesty and delicacy.

"Sara Davidson's book is like a loaf that has been taken out of the oven too soon—crisp and brown on the outside, rather runny and shapeless within," commented Lucinda Franks. "There is no doubt that Davidson is a fine reporter: she paints a colorful era in broad, bright strokes; she has an eye for the bizarre, the ironic, the tiny detail," Franks continued. "Her fundamental problem lies in her failure, after four years of researching and writing the book, to discover the inner logic to analyze the meaning of an event."

In anticipation of the criticism *Loose Change* would receive, Davidson wrote in the epilogue: "I'm afraid I will be criticized for copping out. . . . But the truth is, I have not found answers and I'm not sure I remember the questions."

"If you follow the book, people in it learn no answers," she told Barry Siegel. "There are just different interpretations. If you asked me why my marriage broke up when it was happening, I'd have said one thing; a year later, something else."

"The point is, we all used to believe in certain interpretations that explained everything. When one interpretation wouldn't work, we'd change and get another. I've grown wary of explanations. No explanation ever closes all accounts."

Davidson's second book, *Real Property,* illuminates her life after her divorce. "The tone of *Real Property* is distinctly different from that of *Loose Change,* much as the music of the 1960s is different from that of the 1970s, more hip and knowledgeable, less bare and vulnerable," observed Carter. "The change is also materialistic, as the quote from Ron Koslow at the beginning of the article suggests: 'What marijuana was to the sixties, real estate is to the seventies.'" In the book, Davidson confessed that despite a comfortable, even luxurious, lifestyle, she felt unsatisfied.

After *Real Property* was published, Davidson continued to write nonfiction for periodicals, but she also tried her hand at writing a novel. *Friends of the Opposite Sex* was published in 1984. According to Carter, it is "a story of friendship, romance, and travel abroad to countries that include war-torn Israel. The themes are reminiscent of both *Real Property* and *Loose Change* jumbled together."

Davidson's next book project was co-authoring the biography of actor Rock Hudson. For years the film star had kept his private life well-guarded. But as he neared death from AIDS, he decided to publicly reveal his homosexuality and his battle with AIDS in the hope that doing so might help others. "The book is not graphic about Hudson's homosexuality, but it is frank," advised Carter. "Davidson does not avoid talking about the men who filtered through the actor's life, but she keeps details discreet and minimal. Hudson is pictured as a Hollywood playboy, hard drinking, and sexually voracious, all of whose love interests are men."

In the late 1980s, Davidson began to focus on television work, while continuing to write nonfiction for major periodicals. "Davidson, like her writing and her subjects, has grown and matured over her years as a journalist," concluded Carter. "After several decades of work she continues to write with the same depth of research and immersion-style reporting that first marked her work as literary journalism in the late-1960s."

*BIOGRAPHICAL/CRITICAL SOURCES:*

*BOOKS*

*Contemporary Literary Criticism,* Volume 9, Gale (Detroit), 1978.
*Dictionary of Literary Biography,* Volume 185: *American Literary Journalists, 1945-1995, First Series,* Gale, 1997.
*The Literary Journalists,* Ballantine (New York City), 1992.

*PERIODICALS*

*Atlantic,* June, 1977.
*Chicago Tribune Book World,* May 22, 1977.
*Commentary,* August, 1977.
*Los Angeles Times,* March 24, 1977.
*Mademoiselle,* October, 1977.
*New Republic,* August 20, 1977.
*Newsweek,* May 30, 1977.
*New Times,* May 13, 1977.
*New Yorker,* July 11, 1977.

*New York Post,* May 21, 1977.
*New York Times,* May 15, 1977; June 1, 1977.
*New York Times Book Review,* May 21, 1977.
*Rolling Stone,* July 28, 1977.
*Saturday Review,* May 28, 1977.
*Time,* July 11, 1977.*

\* \* \*

## DAVIS, Donald (D.) 1944-

*PERSONAL:* Born June 1, 1944, in Waynesville, NC; son of Joseph (a banker) and Lucille (a teacher; maiden name, Walker) Davis; married Merle Smith (a teacher), April 16, 1992; children: Douglas, Patrick, Kelly, Jonathan. *Education:* Davidson College, B.A., 1966; Duke University, M.Div., 1969.

*ADDRESSES: Home and office*—Storyteller, Inc., P.O. Box 397, Ocracoke Island, NC 27960.

*CAREER:* Christ United Methodist Church, High Point, NC, minister, 1967-89; storyteller, lecturer, and writer, 1967—. Appeared at numerous storytelling festivals, conferences, and teachers' workshops in the United States and abroad, including National Storytelling Festival, Sierra Storytelling Festival, and Three Apples Storytelling Festival.

*MEMBER:* National Association for the Preservation and Perpetuation of Storytelling (member of board of directors, 1982-89; chairperson of board of directors, 1983-89).

*AWARDS, HONORS:* Anne Izard Storyteller's Choice Award, 1992, and South Carolina Middle-School Young Reader's Award, both for *Listening for the Crack of Dawn;* Anne Izard Storyteller's Choice Award, 1994, for *Jack Always Seeks His Fortune;* D.H.L., La Grange College, 1994; selected for "Circle of Excellence" by National Storytelling Association, 1996.

*WRITINGS:*

### RECORDED STORIES

*Storytelling Festival,* two volumes, NAPPS, 1983.
(With Pat Floyd) *Old Testament Stories to Hear and Tell,* Graded Press, 1983.
*Live and Learn,* Weston Woods, 1984.

*Jack Tales: More Than a Beanstalk,* Weston Woods, 1985.
*Listening for the Crack of Dawn,* August House (Little Rock, AR), 1991.
*Rainy Weather,* August House, 1992.
*Jack's First Job,* August House, 1992.
*Uncle Frank Invents the Electron Microphone,* August House, 1992.
*Party People,* August House, 1993.
*Miss Daisy,* August House, 1993.
*Christmas at Grandma's,* August House, 1994.
*The Southern Bells,* August House, 1994.
*Walking Through Sulphur Springs,* August House, 1995.
*Jack and the Animals: An Appalachian Folktale,* August House, 1995.
*Grandma's Lap Stories,* August House, 1995.
*Mrs. Rosemary's Kindergarten,* August House, 1995.
*See Rock City,* August House, 1996.
*Stanley Easter,* August House, 1997.
*Granny Ugly,* August House, 1997.
*Dr. York, Miss Winnie, and the Typhoid Shot,* August House, 1997.

### OTHER

*My Lucky Day: Stories of a Southern Appalachian Storyteller,* Johnson Publishing (Chicago, IL), 1984.
*Listening for the Crack of Dawn,* August House, 1990.
*Barking at a Fox-Fur Coat,* August House, 1991.
*Jack Always Seeks His Fortune: Authentic Appalachian Jack Tales,* August House, 1992; reprinted as *Southern Jack Tales,* 1997.
*Telling Your Own Stories: A Guide to Family, Classroom, and Personal Storytelling,* August House, 1993.
*Thirteen Miles From Suncrest,* August House, 1994.
*Jack and the Animals: An Appalachian Folktale,* illustrated by Kitty Harvill, August House, 1995.
*See Rock City: A Story Journey Through Appalachia,* August House, 1996.

Also author of *My Uncle Frank Used to Say.* Contributor to books, including *Jack in Two Worlds,* edited by William Bernard McCarthy, University of North Carolina Press, 1994. Contributor to periodicals, including *Utne Reader, Teacher, Parenting, Time,* and *Mother Earth News.*

*SIDELIGHTS:* Although he has published a variety of books for adults and children, Donald Davis considers himself foremost a storyteller. Born in the mountainous region of western North Carolina in 1944, Davis told Robert Jordan of the *Winston-Salem Journal* that storytelling was an element of his daily life growing up, particularly as part of his relationship with his Grandma Walker. "My grandmother did lots of telling," Davis recalls. "I remember hearing those stories, and I remember by the time I was in the second grade telling other kids in school stories I'd heard my grandmother tell."

Davis's storytelling has led to several successful publishing outlets, including the use of audio recordings. His stories have been recorded on more than thirty albums and videotapes. Some of his recorded works feature the ubiquitous fairy tale figure of Jack. Well-known from such stories and nursery rhymes as "Jack and the Beanstalk" and "Jack and Jill," this hero stars in Davis's audio cassette *Jack's First Job*. Retold as part of the Appalachian oral tradition, Davis's rich versions of various classic tales demonstrate the importance of humor in children's stories and the endearing, universal qualities of Jack.

Jack also appears in Davis's written stories, including *Jack and the Animals*. Davis sets this Scottish parallel to the Grimm Brothers' tale "The Bremen Town Musicians" in the Appalachian Mountains. Using simple, direct language, he recounts the story of Jack's adoption of five animals, all of whom seem to have outgrown any usefulness. He happens upon an aging cow, for example, and learns that she can no longer produce milk. She and the other animals join Jack on his adventures in search of fortune. When they happen upon a band of robbers, Jack and these formerly valueless creatures foil their lawless plot and save the day.

Many of Davis's other writings are rendered from more personal sources. In his novel *Thirteen Miles from Suncrest* (1994), he presents a slice-of-life story set in the mountains of North Carolina early in the nineteenth century. Its narrator, Medford Henry McGee, was born at the turn of the century. On his tenth birthday his father gives him a journal, and Medford chronicles his experiences between the years 1910 and 1913 in the pages of his diary. His stories record the gradual encroachment of the "modern world" into the western regions of North Carolina. Judy Sokoll, writing in *School Library Journal*, observed that "Medford is a captivating narrator—sensitive, trusting, loving, natural, and filled with wide-eyed curiosity about the world. All of the characters are wonderfully created and the sense of a simpler time is masterfully crafted." A *Publishers Weekly*

critic likewise praised the work, noting that "the novel's themes—hardship and tragedy set against the strength and beauty of family love—prove affecting and timeless."

*See Rock City* (1996) represents another of Davis's forays into the history of his native North Carolina. Transporting the reader to 1948, the year Davis entered kindergarten, *See Rock City* follows his life and the tales of his family through his second year of college. "After a slow start, the narrative moves gently, smoothly, and charmingly with the cadence of a master storyteller," asserted *School Library Journal* contributor Judy Sokoll.

As Davis mines the tales of his life, retells the classic stories of the past, and creates his own legends, his activities as a writer and traveling storyteller show no sign of slowing. In fact, he believes that both of these occupations are common aspects of life for everyone. As he told Robert Jordan of the *Winston-Salem Journal,* "Any time you tell somebody about a place you've been that you wish they could go, you're telling a story. A lot of it is just realizing that it is a very natural process."

*BIOGRAPHICAL/CRITICAL SOURCES:*

*PERIODICALS*

*Booklist,* September 15, 1994, p. 111; October 1, 1995, p. 322.
*Kirkus Reviews,* July 1, 1994, p. 864.
*Publishers Weekly,* August 8, 1994, p. 380.
*School Library Journal,* January, 1995, p. 183; January, 1996, p. 100; September, 1996, p. 240.
*Winston-Salem Journal,* November 24, 1995, pp. C9-10.

\*    \*    \*

## DAWSON, Jennifer

*PERSONAL:* Married Michael Hinton, 1964. *Education:* St. Anne's College, Oxford, B.A. (history), 1952; attended University of London. *Politics:* Labour Party.

*ADDRESSES: Home*—Hinton, Fisher's Ln., Charlbury, Oxfordshire, England. *Agent*—c/o Virago Press, 20-23 Mandela Street, London NW1 0HQ, England.

*CAREER:* Social worker in a mental hospital; Clarendon Press, Oxford, England, proofreader and indexer; teacher; domestic; novelist and short-story writer.

*MEMBER:* Campaign for Nuclear Disarmament.

*AWARDS, HONORS:* Dawes-Hicks Scholarship, 1959; James Tait Black Memorial Prize for Fiction, 1962, for *The Ha-Ha;* Cheltenham Festival Award for Fiction, 1963; Fawcett prize, 1990, for *Judasland.*

*WRITINGS:*

*NOVELS*

*The Ha-Ha,* Little, Brown (Boston), 1961, reprinted, Virago (London), 1985.
*Fowler's Snare,* Anthony Blond (London), 1962.
*The Cold Country,* Anthony Blond, 1965.
*Strawberry Boy,* Quartet Books (London), 1976.
*A Field of Scarlet Poppies,* Quartet Books, 1979.
*The Upstairs People,* Virago, 1988.
*Judasland,* Virago, 1989.

*SHORT STORIES*

(Contributor) E. J. Burnley, editor, *Penguin Modern Stories 10,* Penguin (London), 1972.
*Hospital Wedding: Stories,* Quartet Books, 1978.

Also author, with E. Mitchell, of *The Queen of Trent,* 1961.

*ADAPTATIONS: The Ha-Ha* was adapted for radio in 1964, adapted for the stage and produced in London in 1968 and in Jerusalem in 1996-97, and adapted for television in 1969.

*SIDELIGHTS:* Jennifer Dawson's critically acclaimed, award-winning first novel, *The Ha-Ha,* is set in a mental hospital and is narrated by Josephine, a schizophrenic "slowly recovering from a breakdown," wrote Judy Cooke in *Contemporary Novelists.* After progressing and gaining some independence, Josephine digresses. "The inevitable relapse is brought about by her first real relationship, a love relationship," described Cooke, "a love affair with another patient. Alastair is critical of doctors and routines; he alarms [Josephine] by telling her the true nature of her illness and she panics when he leaves the hospital. She runs away."

*The Ha-Ha,* according to Miriam Ylvisaker in *Library Journal* is "a first novel by a young English writer whose restraint and economical, vivid scenes and gentle characters make this an admirable small book-not just another macabre story of madness." "The scenes of almost mystic exhilaration on [Josephine's] return are macabre but brilliantly convincing, and Josephine's comments on insiders provide some very funny satire," stated a *Times Literary Supplement* reviewer, noting "only the seducer does not quite come off, the outcome of his interest too obviously foreseen." Martin Levin, in the *New York Times Book Review,* similarly recognized the story's satire in his praise: "[Josephine's] varying levels of consciousness as they oscillate from and to reality as crystallized in a hospital love affair are beautifully delineated by Miss Dawson in a kind of cool 'Wind-in-the-Willows' style tinged with a delicate wit. A wit, by the way that is at the expense of the sane."

Dawson's sensitive portrayal of mental illness was positively noted by critics. Many reviews echoed Norman Shrapnel's *Guardian* statement: "Miss Dawson handles [the dangerous subject of schizophrenia] in a serious and unsensational way and indeed does a service to the mentally afflicted." A *New Yorker* contributor agreed that "Miss Dawson's writing is clear and gentle and sensitive, and she shows admirable sympathy for and understanding of the mental patient, Josephine," however he faulted Dawson, continuing, "but sympathy and understanding in a novel should provoke more than admiration for themselves, and all we feel for the unfortunate Josephine is a helpless pity that leaves us no nearer to her on the last page than we were on the first." Cooke commented: "The schizophrenic is sometimes hailed [by modern writers] as a prophet, whose view of life is not only as valid as that of his doctors but also morally superior to the standards they uphold. Dawson shares this fashionable, essentially romantic, attitude but her writing is without the stridency of propaganda. The parallels with Sylvia Plath's *The Bell Jar* are many and the prose is equally fine. Dawson has written further explorations of her subject but has not yet matched the sustained brilliance of this first novel."

*BIOGRAPHICAL/CRITICAL SOURCES:*

*BOOKS*

*Contemporary Novelists,* sixth edition, St. James Press (Detroit), 1996.

*PERIODICALS*

*Booklist,* November 15, 1961.
*Guardian,* February 3, 1961.
*Library Journal,* October 1, 1961.
*New Statesman,* February 3, 1961.
*New Yorker,* December 16, 1961.
*New York Herald Tribune Books,* November 19, 1961.
*New York Times Book Review,* October 22, 1961.
*Spectator,* February 3, 1961.
*Times Literary Supplement,* February 10, 1961.

\* \* \*

**DECAUX, Lucile**
  **See BIBESCO, Marthe Lucie**

\* \* \*

**DEIGHTON, Len**
  **See DEIGHTON, Leonard Cyril**

\* \* \*

**DEIGHTON, Leonard Cyril 1929-**
  **(Len Deighton)**

*PERSONAL:* Born February 18, 1929, in Marylebone, London, England; married Shirley Thompson (an illustrator), 1960. *Education:* Attended St. Martin's School of Art, London, three years; Royal College of Art, graduate.

*ADDRESSES: Office*—25 Newman St., London W.1, England.

*CAREER:* Author. Worked as a railway lengthman, an assistant pastry cook at the Royal Festival Hall, 1951, a manager of a gown factory in Aldgate, England, a waiter in Piccadilly, an advertising man in London and New York City, a teacher in Brittany, a co-proprietor of a glossy magazine, and as a magazine artist and news photographer; steward, British Overseas Airways Corporation (BOAC), 1956-57; producer of films, including *Only When I Larf,* based on his novel of the same title, 1969.

*WRITINGS:*

UNDER NAME LEN DEIGHTON

*Only When I Larf* (novel), M. Joseph, 1968, published as *Only When I Laugh,* Mysterious Press, 1987.
*Oh, What a Lovely War!* (screenplay), Paramount, 1969.
*Bomber: Events Relating to the Last Flight of an R.A.F. Bomber Over Germany on the Night of June 31, 1943* (novel), Harper, 1970.
*Declarations of War* (story collection), J. Cape, 1971, published as *Eleven Declarations of War,* Harcourt, 1975.
*Close-Up* (novel), Atheneum, 1972.
*SS-GB: Nazi-Occupied Britain, 1941* (novel), J. Cape, 1978, Knopf, 1979.
*Goodbye, Mickey Mouse* (novel; Book-of-the-Month Club selection), Knopf, 1982.
*Winter: A Novel of a Berlin Family* (Book-of-the-Month Club alternate selection), Knopf, 1988.

Also author of television scripts *Long Past Glory,* 1963, and *It Must Have Been Two Other Fellows,* 1977. Also author of weekly comic strip on cooking, *Observer,* 1962—.

ESPIONAGE NOVELS; UNDER NAME LEN DEIGHTON

*The Ipcress File,* Fawcett, 1962, reprinted, Ballantine, 1982.
*Horse Under Water* (Literary Guild selection), J. Cape, 1963, Putnam, 1967.
*Funeral in Berlin,* J. Cape, 1964, Putnam, 1965.
*The Billion Dollar Brain,* Putnam, 1966.
*An Expensive Place to Die,* Putnam, 1967.
*Spy Story,* Harcourt, 1974.
*Yesterday's Spy,* Harcourt, 1975.
*Twinkle, Twinkle, Little Spy,* J. Cape, 1976, published as *Catch a Falling Spy,* Harcourt, 1976.
*XPD,* Knopf, 1981.
*Berlin Game,* Knopf, 1983.
*Mexico Set* (Literary Guild selection), Knopf, 1985.
*London Match,* Knopf, 1985.
*Spy Hook* (Book-of-the-Month Club selection), Knopf, 1988.
*Spy Line,* Knopf, 1989.
*Spy Sinker,* HarperCollins, 1990.
*MAMista,* HarperCollins, 1991.
*City of Gold,* HarperCollins, 1992.
*Violent Ward,* HarperCollins, 1993.
*Faith,* HarperCollins, 1995.
*Hope,* HarperCollins (New York City), 1995.

*NONFICTION; UNDER NAME LEN DEIGHTON*

(Editor) *Drinks-man-ship: Town's Album of Fine Wines and High Spirits,* Haymarket Press, 1964.

*Ou est le garlic; or, Len Deighton's French Cookbook,* Penguin, 1965, revised edition published as *Basic French Cooking,* J. Cape, 1979.

*Action Cookbook: Len Deighton's Guide to Eating,* J. Cape, 1965.

*Len Deighton's Cookstrip Cook Book,* Bernard Geis Associates, 1966.

(Editor with Michael Rand and Howard Loxton) *The Assassination of President Kennedy,* J. Cape, 1967.

(Editor and contributor) *Len Deighton's London Dossier,* J. Cape, 1967.

*Len Deighton's Continental Dossier: A Collection of Cultural, Culinary, Historical, Spooky, Grim and Preposterous Fact,* compiled by Victor and Margaret Pettitt, M. Joseph, 1968.

*Fighter: The True Story of the Battle of Britain,* J. Cape, 1977, Knopf, 1978.

(With Peter Mayle) *How to Be a Pregnant Father,* Lyle Stuart, 1977.

(With Arnold Schwartzman) *Airshipwreck,* J. Cape, 1978, Holt, 1979.

(With Simon Goodenough) *Tactical Genius in Battle,* Phaidon Press, 1979.

*Blitzkrieg: From the Rise of Hitler to the Fall of Dunkirk,* Coward, 1980.

*Battle of Britain,* Coward, 1980.

*ABC of French Food,* Bantam (New York City), 1990.

*Blood, Tears, and Folly: An Objective Look at World War II,* HarperCollins, 1993.

*ADAPTATIONS: The Ipcress File* was filmed by Universal in 1965, *Funeral in Berlin* by Paramount in 1966, *The Billion Dollar Brain* by United Artists in 1967, and *Only When I Larf* by Paramount in 1969; *Spy Story* was filmed in 1976; film rights to *An Expensive Place to Die* have been sold. Deighton's nameless British spy hero was given the name Harry Palmer in the film adaptations of his adventures.

*SIDELIGHTS:* With his early novels, especially *The Ipcress File* and *Funeral in Berlin,* Len Deighton established himself as one of the mainstays of modern espionage fiction. He is often ranked—along with Graham Greene, John le Carre, and Ian Fleming—among the foremost writers in the field. Deighton shows a painstaking attention to accuracy in depicting espionage activities, and in his early novels this realism was combined with a light ironic touch that set

his work apart. Deighton, David Quammen remarks in the *New York Times Book Review,* is "a talented, droll and original spy novelist."

Deighton's early novels are written in an elliptical style that emphasizes the mysterious nature of the espionage activities portrayed. They feature a nameless British intelligence officer who is quite different from the usual fictional spy. This officer is a reluctant spy, cynical, and full of wisecracks. Unlike many other British agents, he is also, Julian Symons states in *Mortal Consequences: A History—From the Detective Story to the Crime Novel,* "a working-class boy from Brunley, opposed to all authority, who dislikes or distrusts anybody outside his own class. He is set down in a world of terrifying complexity, in which nobody is ever what he seems." "The creation of this slightly anarchic, wise-cracking, working-class hero," T. J. Binyon writes in the *Times Literary Supplement,* "was Deighton's most original contribution to the spy thriller. And this, taken together with his characteristic highly elliptical expositional manner, with his fascination with the technical nuts and bolts of espionage, and with a gift for vivid, startling description, make the first seven [of Deighton's spy] stories classics of the genre." Peter S. Prescott of *Newsweek,* speaking of the early novels featuring Deighton's nameless hero, finds that the style, marked by "oblique narration, nervous laughter and ironic detachment, . . . effectively transformed [Deighton's] spy stories into comedies of manners."

Deighton's elliptical style in these early books is clipped and episodic, deliberately omitting vital explanations of what his characters are discussing or thinking. This style, Robin W. Winks writes in the *New Republic,* makes Deighton's "plots seem more complex than they are. . . . Because very little is stated explicitly, sequences appear to begin in mid-passage, and only through observation of the action does one come to understand either the motives of the villains, or the thought processes of the heroes." In these novels, Winks concludes, "Deighton had patented a style in which every third paragraph appeared to have been left out." Although this style confuses some readers—Prescott claims that Deighton's "specialty has always been a nearly incoherent plot"—Pearl K. Bell finds it well suited to the subject matter of Deighton's novels. Writing in *New Leader,* Bell states that Deighton's "obsessive reliance on the blurred and intangible, on loaded pauses and mysteriously disjointed dialogue, did convey the shadowy meanness of the spy's world, with its elusive loyalties, camouflaged identities and weary brutality."

Deighton was an immediate success with his first novel, *The Ipcress File,* a book that the late Anthony Boucher of the *New York Times Book Review* admits "caused quite a stir among both critics and customers in England." Introducing Deighton's nameless protagonist in an adventure that takes him to a nuclear testing site on a Pacific atoll, to the Middle East, and behind the Iron Curtain, the book continues to be popular for its combination of a serious espionage plot with a parody of the genre. As Richard Locke observes in the *New York Times Book Review, The Ipcress File* possesses "a Kennedy-cool amorality. . . , a cross of Hammett and cold war lingo."

Critics praise the book's gritty evocation of intelligence work, ironic narrative, and comic touches. Boucher calls it "a sharply written, ironic and realistic tale of modern spy activities." Deighton's humor attracts the most attention from John B. Cullen of *Best Sellers,* who claims that in *The Ipcress File* "Deighton writes with a tongue-in-cheek attitude. . . . No one is spared the needle of subtle ridicule, but the author still tells a plausible story which holds your attention throughout." However, for Robert Donald Spectar of the *New York Herald Tribune Book Review* Deighton's humor ruins the espionage story. "Deighton," Spectar writes, "has combined picaresque satire, parody, and suspense and produced a hybrid more humorous than thrilling." But this opinion is disputed by G. W. Stonier in the *New Statesman.* Comparing Deighton with James Bond creator Ian Fleming, Stonier finds Deighton to be "a good deal more expert and twice the writer" and believes "there has been no brighter arrival on the shady scene since Graham Greene." Even in 1979, some seventeen years after the book's initial publication, Julian Symons of the *New York Times Book Review* was moved to call *The Ipcress File* "a dazzling performance. The verve and energy, the rattle of wit in the dialogue, the side-of-the-mouth comments, the evident pleasure taken in cocking a snook at the British spy story's upper-middle-class tradition—all these, together with the teasing convolutions of the plot, made it clear that a writer of remarkable talent in this field had appeared."

Deighton's reputation as an espionage writer was enhanced by *Funeral in Berlin,* a story revolving around an attempt to smuggle a defecting East German biologist out of Berlin. With the assistance of a high-ranking Russian agent, former Nazi intelligence officers, and a free-lance operator of doubtful allegiance, Deighton's unnamed hero arranges the details of the defection. The many plot twists, and

Deighton's enigmatic presentation of his story, prompt Stephen Hugh-Jones of *New Statesman* to admit, "I spent most of the book wondering what the devil was going on." Boucher finds the mysterious goings-on to be handled well. "The double and triple crosses involved," Boucher writes, "are beautifully worked out." Published at the same time as John le Carre's classic espionage tale *The Spy Who Came in From the Cold,* a novel also set in Germany's divided city, *Funeral in Berlin* compares favorably with its competitor. Boucher calls its plot "very nearly as complex and nicely calculated," while Charles Poore of the *New York Times* maintains it is "even better" than le Carre's book. It is, Poore concludes, "a ferociously cool fable of the current struggle between East and West." Andy East of *Armchair Detective* claims that *Funeral in Berlin* "has endured as Deighton's most celebrated novel."

Since these early novels, Deighton's style has evolved, becoming more expansive and less oblique. His "approach has grown more sophisticated," Mark Schorr relates in the *Los Angeles Times Book Review.* "His more recent writings offer a deft balance of fact, scene-setting and the who-can-we-trust paranoia that makes spy novels engrossing." Peter Elstob of *Books and Bookmen* elaborates on the change. Deighton "develops with each new book," Elstob believes. "He could have gone on repeating the formula of *The Ipcress File* with undoubted success, but instead he tried for more subtlety, for more convincing, more substantial characters."

Of his later espionage novels, perhaps his most important work has been the trilogy comprised of *Berlin Game, Mexico Set,* and *London Match.* Here, Deighton spins a long story of moles (agents working within an enemy intelligence organization), defection, and betrayal that also comments on his own writing career, the espionage genre, and the cold war between East and West that has inspired such fiction. Derrick Murdoch of the Toronto *Globe and Mail* calls the trilogy "Deighton's most ambitious project; the conventional spy-story turned inside-out."

The first novel of the trilogy, *Berlin Game,* opens with two agents waiting near the Berlin Wall for a defector to cross over from East Berlin. "How long have we been sitting here?" asks Bernie Samson, British agent and the protagonist of the trilogy. "Nearly a quarter of a century," his companion replies. With that exchange Deighton underlines the familiarity of this scene in espionage fiction, in his own early work and in the work of others, while commenting on the continuing relevance of the Berlin Wall as a symbol of East-West conflict, notes Anthony Olcott in the *Washington Post Book World.* Deighton, Olcott argues, "is not only aware of this familiarity, it is his subject. . . . Berlin and the Wall remain as much the embodiment of East-West rivalry as ever. . . . To read *Berlin Game* is to shrug off 25 years of acclimatization to the Cold War, and to recall what espionage fiction is about in the first place."

In *Berlin Game,* Samson works to uncover a Soviet agent secretly working at the highest levels of British intelligence. This, too, is a standard plot in spy fiction, inspired by the real-life case of Soviet spy Kim Philby. But, as the *New Yorker* critic points out, "Deighton, as always, makes the familiar twists and turns of spy errantry new again, partly by his grip of narrative, partly by his grasp of character, and partly by his easy, sardonic tone." Prescott claims that the novel does not display the wit of Deighton's earlier works, but the book overcomes its faults because of Deighton's overall skill as a storyteller. "Each scene in this story," Prescott writes, "is so adroitly realized that it creates its own suspense. Samson, the people who work for him, his wife, even the twits who have some reason to be working for Moscow, are interesting characters; what they say to each other is convincing. Besides, the book is full of Berlin lore: we can easily believe that Samson did grow up there and thinks of it as home." In like terms, Christopher Lehmann-Haupt of the *New York Times* holds that in *Berlin Game* "the immediate scene is always brilliantly clear, thanks mostly to Mr. Deighton's intimate familiarity with the Berlin landscape. Every building and street seems to have resonance for him, which he imparts to the reader." Olcott judges *Berlin Game* to be "among Deighton's best books" because "his Berlin, his characters, the smallest details of his narrative are so sharp." Olcott concludes that it is "a book to strip away the age-withered, custom-staled betrayals of all that quarter century of novels, perhaps even of history, and once again make painful, real, alive, the meaning of treason."

*Mexico Set* continues the story begun in *Berlin Game.* In the first book, Samson uncovers the spy in British intelligence—his own wife—and she defects to East Germany. To redeem himself in the eyes of his superiors, who now harbor understandable doubts about his own loyalty, Samson works in *Mexico Set* to convince a Russian KGB agent to defect. But the agent may only be a plant meant to further discredit Samson and destroy his credibility. If Samson cannot convince him to defect, his superiors may assume that he is secretly working for the Russians himself. But the Russian may defect only to provide British intelligence with "proof" of Samson's treason. As in *Berlin Game,* Deighton relates this novel back to the origins of the cold war and, "just when you've forgotten what the Cold War was all about, Len Deighton takes you right back to the [Berlin] Wall and rubs your nose on it," as Chuck Moss writes in the *Detroit News.*

Samson's efforts to persuade the Russian agent to defect take him from London to Mexico, Paris, and Berlin. "Every mile along the way," Noel Behn writes in the *Chicago Tribune,* "objectives seem to alter, friends and enemies become indistinguishable, perils increase, people disappear, people die." Behn finds it is Deighton's characters that make the story believable: "They strut forward one after the other—amusing, beguiling, arousing, deceiving, threatening—making us look in the wrong direction when it most behooves the prestidigitator's purpose." Ross Thomas also sees Deighton's characters as an essential ingredient in the novel's success. Writing in the *Washington Post Book World,* Thomas reports that Deighton "serves up fascinating glimpses of such types as the nearly senile head of British intelligence; a KGB major with a passion for Sherlock Holmes; and Samson's boyhood friend and Jewish orphan, Werner Volkmann," all of whom Thomas finds to be "convincing characters." Thomas concludes that *Mexico Set* is "one of [Deighton's] better efforts," while Behn calls the novel "a pure tale, told by an author at the height of his power."

In the final novel of the trilogy, *London Match,* the Russian agent has defected to the British. But Samson must now decide whether the defector is telling the truth when he insists that a high-ranking member of British intelligence is a Russian mole. The situation grows more complicated when the suspected mole, one of Samson's superiors, comes to Samson for help in clearing his name. *London Match* "is the most complex novel of the trilogy," Julius Lester writes in the *New York Times Book Review.*

But Lester finds *London Match*'s complexity to be a liability. He thinks "the feeling it conveys of being trapped in a maze of distorting mirrors is almost a cliche in spy novels now." Similarly, Gene Lyons of *Newsweek* calls *London Match* "not the most original spy story ever told." In his review of the book for the *Washington Post Book World,* J. I. M. Stewart criticizes Deighton's characterization. He states that "the characters, although liable to bore a little during their frequently over-extended verbal fencings, are tenaciously true to themselves even if not quite to human nature."

But even critics with reservations about some of the novel's qualities find aspects of the book to praise. Stewart lauds Deighton's ability to recreate the settings of his story. "The places, whether urban or rural, can be described only as triumphs alike of painstaking observation and striking descriptive power," Stewart writes. Lester finds this strength, too, calling "the best character" in the book "the city of Berlin. It is a living presence, and in some of the descriptions one can almost hear the stones breathing."

More favorable critics point to Deighton's handling of characters as one of the book's best features. Schorr, for example, believes that "Deighton gives a skilled and believable portrait of Samson. . . . Samson maintains his professional cool, but there is a sense that emotions are repressed, and not nonexistent, as with too many other spy heroes." Margaret Cannon of the Toronto *Globe and Mail* has nothing but praise for *London Match.* She calls the trilogy "some of [Deighton's] best work," and *London Match* "a brilliant climax to the story."

Deighton continues Samson's adventures in the 1988 *Spy Hook,* the first story in a second trilogy about the British intelligence agent. In this thriller, Samson is charged with accounting for the disappearance of millions in Secret Service funds. At first, he suspects his ex-wife—who defected in the earlier *Berlin Game*—as the thief, but later Samson learns that his superiors have begun to suspect him for the crime. *Spy Hook* was chosen as a Book-of-the-Month Club selection and became a best-seller. Critical reception of the work was generally favorable, with reviewers praising the book's carefully developed and intricate plot, detailed settings, and suspenseful atmosphere. A number of reviewers, however, reacted negatively to the book's ending, which they feel is too ambiguous. "Deighton's craftsmanship—his taut action and his insightful study of complex characters under pressure—is very much in place here, but many. . . unanswered questions raised in *Spy Hook* remain just that at the novel's conclusion," states Don G. Campbell, for example, in the *Los Angeles Times Book Review.* Several critics, though, share Margaret Cannon's Toronto *Globe and Mail* assessment of *Spy Hook* as matching Deighton's previous achievements in the espionage genre. The novel, she writes, "promises to be even better than its terrific predecessors and

proves that Deighton, the old spymaster, is still in top form."

Deighton followed *Spy Hook* with the trilogy's second installment, *Spy Line,* in 1989 and the concluding book, *Spy Sinker,* in 1990. *Spy Sinker* focuses on the clandestine efforts of Samson's wife to effect the fall of the Berlin Wall from inside East Germany. As it turns out, Samson's wife was working as a double-agent all along. Her earlier defection and callous abandonment of her husband was ordered by British Intelligence as part of a long-term strategic plan to subvert East German internal order. "Here *Spy Sinker* shows Deighton at the top of his form, in his concentration upon the one player in this series whose story is not yet told," writes Anthony Olcott in *Washington Post Book World.* Olcott adds, "Deighton is able now to close in *Spy Sinker* by exploring what betrayal costs the betrayer, a woman who for higher loyalties leaves husband, home, and country, to incur even more betrayals in a cycle which may, in the end, destroy her."

According to Albert Hunt in *New Statesmen & Society,* "Everything slots together beautifully—Len Deighton has done as professional a job as Bernard Samson ever did." A *Time* reviewer similarly praises *Spy Sinker,* noting that Deighton accomplishes the near impossible—"winding up a closely plotted six-volume thriller . . . and still writing a credible novel. He makes a good job of it with a clever change of focus." However, *New York Times Book Review* contributor Morton Kondracke strongly disagrees: "As a stand-alone spy novel, this book is implausible, often incomprehensible and, altogether, downright dull." Though acknowledging the rather convenient resolution achieved by Deighton as the omnipotent narrator, Hunt remarks, "Manipulation, rather than the Berlin Wall, is what these books are about—that, and the way what Bernard calls 'marital, professional and political' betrayals are enmeshed."

Deighton initiated another Samson trilogy with *Faith* and *Hope* in 1995. Set in Berlin in 1987, *Faith* involves Samson's participation in the defection of a Communist spy and relates complicated domestic circumstances surrounding the return of his wife after their long separation. "What raises Deighton's genre to art," according to Andy Solomon in *Washington Post Book World,* "is not only his absorbing characters but his metaphoric grace. . . droll wit. . . command of technical detail. . . and sure sense of place." Despite such praise, *New York Times Book Review* contributor Newgate Callendar describes *Faith* as "dull and turgid." Likewise *Kirkus Reviews* criticizes Deighton's "vapid characters, murky plot, and infelicitous descriptions." While noting slow passages concerning Samson's marital difficulties and Intelligence agency politics, *Times Literary Supplement* reviewer John-Paul Flintoff writes, "Deighton throws in plenty of plausible details—tricks of the trade, gun specifications, a picture of Berlin as a local would see it."

Deighton followed with *Hope,* in which Samson pursues his Polish brother-in-law despite official evidence of his death at the hands of Russian army deserters. Commenting on the strained relationship depicted between Samson and his wife, a *Times Literary Supplement* reviewer describes *Hope* as "an unexpectedly ambiguous novel, complicated by repressed emotions and jealousies as well as by double crosses and false identities." Scott Veale complains in the *New York Times Book Review,* "there's more secrecy than action in this novel, and too often it's easy to get lost in the plot's numerous byways." However, Chris Petrakos praises *Hope* in Chicago *Tribune Books,* noting that "as usual" Deighton puts forth "a taut, enigmatic effort." *Publishers Weekly* also commends *Hope* and hails Deighton as "the only author other than le Carre who deserves to be known as 'spymaster.'"

Although Deighton is best known for his espionage fiction, he has also written best-selling novels outside the espionage field, as well as books of military history. These other novels and books of history are usually concerned with the events and figures of the World War II. Among the most successful of his novels have been *SS-GB: Nazi-Occupied Britain, 1941* and *Goodbye, Mickey Mouse: The True Story of the Battle of Britain* has earned Deighton praise as a writer of military history. Deighton's writing in other fields has shown him, Symons writes, to be "determined not to stay within the conventional pattern of the spy story or thriller."

*SS-GB* takes place in an alternative history of World War II, a history in which England lost the crucial Battle of Britain and Nazi Germany conquered the country. The story takes place after the conquest when Scotland Yard superintendent Douglas Archer investigates a murder and finds that the trail leads to the upper echelons of the Nazi party. An underground plot to rescue the king of England, who is being held prisoner in the Tower of London, and the ongoing efforts of the Nazis to develop the atom bomb also complicate Archer's problems. "As is usual with Mr.

Deighton," John Leonard writes in *Books of the Times,* "there are as many twists as there are betrayals."

Deighton's ability to fully render what a Nazi-occupied Britain would be like is the most widely-noted strength of the book. "The atmosphere of occupied England," Michael Demarest writes in his review of *SS-GB* for *Newsweek,* "is limned in eerie detail. . . . In fact, Deighton's ungreened isle frequently seems even more realistic than the authentic backgrounds of his previous novels." "What especially distinguishes 'SS-GB,'" Leonard believes, "is its gritty atmosphere, the shadows of defeat on every page. Yes, we think, this is what martial law would feel like; this is the way the Germans would have behaved; this is how rationing and the black market and curfews and detention camps would work; this is the contempt for ourselves that we would experience."

Although Michael Howard of the *Times Literary Supplement* agrees that "there can be little doubt that this is much the way things would have turned out if the Germans had won the war in 1940," he nonetheless concludes that "on this level of imaginative creation Mr. Deighton is so good that the second level, the plot itself, seems by comparison unnecessarily silly and confused." This criticism of the novel's plot is shared by Paul Ableman of the *Spectator,* who complains: "From about Page 100, the subversive thought kept surfacing: what is the point of this kind of historical 'might have been'?. . . I fear [the novel] ultimately lost its hold on me. We could have been given the same yarn set in occupied France."

But Symons and many other reviewers judge *SS-GB* a successful and imaginative novel. It is, Symons writes, "a triumphant success. It is Mr. Deighton's best book, one that blends his expertise in the spy field with his interest in military and political history to produce an absorbingly exciting spy story that is also a fascinating exercise in might-have-been speculation." And Demarest concludes his review by predicting that *SS-GB* "is on its way to becoming a worldwide classic of the 'What If?' genre."

*Goodbye, Mickey Mouse,* another Deighton novel about World War II, concerns a group of American pilots in England who run fighter protection for the bombers making daylight runs over Germany. It is described by Thomas Gifford of the *Washington Post Book World* as "satisfying on every imaginable level, but truly astonishing in its recreation of a time and place through minute detail." Equally high praise comes from Peter Andrews, who writes in his review for the *New York Times Book Review:* "Deighton's latest World War II adventure novel is such a plain, old-fashioned, good book about combat pilots who make war and fall in love that it defies a complicated examination. . . . 'Goodbye, Mickey Mouse' is high adventure of the best sort but always solidly true to life."

Not all reviewers were so enthusiastic, but even those with reservations about the novel's ultimate quality were impressed with the way Deighton presented the scenes of aerial combat. "As long as he keeps his propellers turning," Prescott allows in his *Newsweek* review, "Deighton's book lives. He understands the camaraderie of pilots and to a lesser degree the politics of combat. . . . It's a pity that his people, like his prose, are built from plywood." Similarly, the reviewer for *Harper's* reports that "the book is oddly anemic—except on the subject of fighter planes. Deighton's obsession with planes makes the combat sequences lurid and exciting. If only the rest of the book were too."

While sharing the belief that Deighton writes extremely well about aerial combat, Lehmann-Haupt sees a more serious side to the novel which, for him, raises it "above the merely entertaining." Deighton, Lehmann-Haupt writes, "has an almost uncanny ability to make war action in the air come visually alive. . . . But what is most intriguing about 'Goodbye, Mickey Mouse' is that it explores a profound but little noticed aspect of war—namely, the necessity it creates for parents to send their children off to death." The book's title, the last words of a dying pilot to his friend, Lieutenant Morse, nicknamed Mickey Mouse, are "also an expression of farewell to childhood and its trivialities, as well as what a father or mother might say to a departing son," Lehmann-Haupt concludes. Gifford, too, interprets the novel on a more serious level. Speaking of the generation who fought in the Second World War, many of whom are "approaching the time when they will one by one pass into our history," Gifford finds Deighton's novel a tribute to that generation and its monumental fight. "Some of them," Gifford writes, "are fittingly memorialized in Deighton's hugely assured novel."

The crucial Battle of Britain, which figures prominently in *SS-GB,* and the air battles of that period, which appear in *Goodbye, Mickey Mouse,* are further explored in the nonfiction *Fighter,* a history of the Royal Air Force defense of England during the Battle of Britain. A highly acclaimed popular account of what Noble Frankland of the *Times Literary Supplement* calls "among the handful of decisive battles in British history," *Fighter* "is the best, most dispassionate story of the battle I have read," Drew Middleton states in the *New York Times Book Review,* "and I say that even though the book destroyed many of my illusions and, indeed, attacks the validity of some of what I wrote as an eyewitness of the air battle 38 years ago."

The Battle of Britain took place over several months of 1940. After overrunning France, the Nazi leadership focused their attention on softening up England for a land invasion. They launched extensive bombing raids against the British Isles, attacking the city of London, air bases, factories, and seaports. The Royal Air Force, vastly outnumbered by their opponents, bravely fought the Germans to a standstill which resulted in the proposed invasion being delayed and ultimately canceled. Or so most historians relate the story.

Deighton dispels some of the myths about the Battle of Britain still widely believed by most historians. He shows, for example, that a major reason for the failure of the German offensive was the decision to shift the main attack from British airfields to the city of London. The Nazis hoped that bombing the civilian population would cause Britain to sue for peace. But leaving the airfields alone only allowed the Royal Air Force to launch their fighter planes against the German bombers. And when bomber losses rose too high, the Nazi invasion plans were called off.

Other insights into the Battle of Britain include the facts "that British anti-aircraft fire was ineffective, that some R.A.F. ground personnel fled under fire, that the Admiralty provoked costly skirmishes. . . . The book resounds with exploded myths," Leonard Bushkoff writes in the *Washington Post Book World.* Deighton also shows that British estimates of German losses were far higher than they actually were, while British losses were reported to be less serious than was actually the case. But Bushkoff sees the importance of these revelations to be inconsequential. "Is debunking sufficient to carry a book that essentially is a rehash of earlier works?" he asks. Frankland admits that Deighton is sometimes "prone to get his technicalities wrong," but finds that "the Battle of Britain after all is a very difficult subject. No two people seem quite to agree about when it began, when it ended, what were its turning points or why they occurred. . . . Len Deighton cuts through this fog incisively and utterly correctly." In his article for the *Saturday Review,* George H. Reeves reports that "there is a profusion of detail in *Fighter . . .* that will delight the military history specialist, and Deighton's well-paced narrative and techniques of deft characterization will also hold the attention of the general reader." He believes that Deighton "has turned his hand with commendable results to the writing of military history."

In all of his writing, whether fiction or nonfiction, Deighton shows a concern for an accurate and detailed presentation of the facts. He has included appendices in several novels to explain to his readers such espionage esoterica as the structure of foreign intelligence organizations and the effects of various poisons. Howard claims that Deighton "takes enormous, almost obsessional care to get the background to his books exactly right."

Part of Deighton's research involves extensive travel throughout the world; he is reported to have contacts in cities as far-flung as Anchorage and Casablanca. These research trips have sometimes proven dangerous. Hugh Moffett notes that Deighton was once "hauled into police barracks in Czechoslovakia when he neglected to renew his visa." And Russian soldiers once took him into custody in East Berlin. For *Bomber: Events Relating to the Last Flight of an R.A.F. Bomber Over Germany on the Night of June 31, 1943,* Deighton made three trips to Germany and spent several years in research, gathering some half million words in notes. Research for the books *Fighter* and *Blitzkreig: From the Rise of Hitler to the Fall of Dunkirk* took nearly nine years. But these efforts have paid off. MacLeish believes that in a Deighton novel, "the atmospherics ring forever true. Deighton seems to know the places he writes about." Speaking of *XPD,* Les Whitten of the *Washington Post Book World* finds that "the research on exotic guns, cars, poisons, trains, wall safes, foliage is shining and satisfying evidence of the hard work Deighton has done to make his background genuine and informative."

Deighton turns to historical fiction in his 1987 book *Winter: A Novel of a Berlin Family.* The story of a well-to-do German family led by a banker and war financier, *Winter* depicts how cultural and historical factors influence the attitudes of his two sons, one of whom joins the murderous Nazi party, while the other moves to the United States and marries a Jewish woman. The mixed criticism for *Winter* revolves around Deighton's sympathetic portrayals of his Nazi

characters and around the novel's wide historical scope, which some reviewers feel is inadequately represented, mainly through dialogue rather than plot.

"Unlike much of Deighton's work," writes Gary Dretzka in Chicago *Tribune Books,* "'Winter' isn't much concerned with military strategy, suspense and spies as with people and relationships." According to Elizabeth Ward in *Washington Post Book World,* "*Winter* is neither fiction nor history but docudrama, running like a film script in a series of dutifully dated vignettes from New Year's Eve 1899. . . to 1945." Favorably describing *Winter* as a fictional counterpart to William L. Shirer's acclaimed historical work *The Rise and Fall of the Third Reich,* Ward maintains that "*Winter* is an altogether silkier, less demanding and more entertaining read," adding, "Len Deighton certainly knows how to move a narrative along, build suspense and weave mysteries, even if history did write the larger plot for him." While praising Deighton's "scholarship and attention to detail," Dretzka notes, "In the end, it's almost as if the enormity of World War II devours the context of the novel, leaving little for the reader to feel except pity—which is fine for TV, but not enough for a serious, well-written piece of fiction about such a shocking period in history."

Deighton also produced *City of Gold* in 1992, another volume of historical fiction based on events during the Second World War. This novel is set in Cairo at the height of Nazi domination of North Africa under the command of General Erwin Rommel. The protagonist is Corporal Jim Ross, a British soldier who escapes court-martial by assuming the identity of Major Bert Cutler, a British Intelligence agent who dies of a heart attack on a train. With his new identity and security clearance, Ross (as Cutler) is assigned to uncover the source of Rommel's detailed information about Allied forces and their movements. Though critical of Deighton's unusually large cast of stereotyped characters, Michael Kernan writes in *Washington Post Book World,* "The action scenes in the desert are as good as anything he has written." *Kirkus Reviews* praises Deighton's "terrific return" to the Second World War and the "rich drama of heroes and villains" in *City of Gold.* "In the finest Deighton form," writes Dick Roraback in the *Los Angeles Times Book Review,* "the master sets up his row of people then surrounds them with the authentic sights, sounds, smells, the moods and mores of their locale."

Deighton's position as one of the most prominent of contemporary espionage writers is secure. Cannon describes him as "one of the finest living writers of espionage novels." Schorr relates that it was Rudyard Kipling who "first called espionage the 'Great Game,' and no one is more adept at providing a fictional play-by-play than Len Deighton." Writing in *Whodunit?: A Guide to Crime, Suspense and Spy Fiction* about his life as a writer, Deighton reveals: "I have no formal training and have evolved a muddled sort of system by trial and error. . . . My own writing is characterized by an agonizing reappraisal of everything I write so that I have to work seven days a week. . . . The most difficult lesson to learn is that thousands and thousands of words must go into the waste paper basket." Summing up his feelings about being a best-selling author, Deighton concludes, "It's not such a bad job after all; except for sitting here at this damned typewriter."

*BIOGRAPHICAL/CRITICAL SOURCES:*

*BOOKS*

*Bestsellers 89,* Issue 2, Gale (Detroit), 1989.
*Concise Dictionary of British Literary Biography: Contemporary Writers, 1960 to Present,* Gale, 1992.
*Contemporary Literary Criticism,* Gale, Volume 4, 1975; Volume 7, 1977; Volume 22, 1982; Volume 46, 1988.
*Dictionary of Literary Biography,* Volume 87: *British Mystery and Thriller Writers since 1940,* First Series, Gale, 1989.
Keating, H. R. F., editor, *Whodunit?: A Guide to Crime, Suspense and Spy Fiction,* Van Nostrand, 1982.
Symons, Julian, *Mortal Consequences: A History—From the Detective Story to the Crime Novel,* Harper, 1972.

*PERIODICALS*

*Armchair Detective,* winter, 1986.
*Best Sellers,* November 15, 1963; January 1, 1968.
*Booklist,* June 1-15, 1993.
*Books and Bookmen,* September, 1967; December, 1971.
*Books of the Times,* February, 1979; August, 1981.
*British Book News,* December, 1980.
*Chicago Tribune Book World,* March 18, 1979; January 19, 1986.
*Detroit News,* February 3, 1985; February 9, 1986.
*Globe and Mail* (Toronto), December 1, 1984; December 14, 1985.
*Harper's,* November, 1982.

*Kirkus Reviews,* May 1, 1992, p. 555; October 15, 1994, p. 1364.
*Life,* March 25, 1966.
*London Review of Books,* March 19-April 1, 1981.
*Los Angeles Times,* November 26, 1982; March 23, 1987.
*Los Angeles Times Book Review,* March 17, 1985; February 16, 1986; November 22, 1987; August 19, 1990, p. 8; July 26, 1992, p. 9.
*New Leader,* January 19, 1976.
*New Republic,* December 13, 1975.
*New Statesman,* December 7, 1962; September 8, 1964; May 12, 1967; June 18, 1976; August 25, 1978.
*New Statesman and Society,* September 14, 1990; September 6, 1991.
*Newsweek,* January 18, 1965; January 31, 1966; June 26, 1972; October 14, 1974; February 19, 1979; December 27, 1982; December 19, 1983; February 11, 1985; January 13, 1986.
*New Yorker,* February 3, 1968; May 7, 1979; February 6, 1984.
*New York Herald Tribune Book Review,* November 17, 1963.
*New York Times,* January 12, 1965; October 17, 1970; October 16, 1976; September 20, 1977; May 13, 1981; June 21, 1981; December 7, 1982; December 12, 1983; December 21, 1987.
*New York Times Book Review,* November 10, 1963; January 17, 1965; May 21, 1967; January 14, 1968; October 4, 1970; April 13, 1975; July 9, 1978; February 25, 1979; May 3, 1981; November 14, 1982; January 8, 1984; March 10, 1985; December 1, 1985; January 10, 1988; December 25, 1988; September 2, 1990, p. 6; June 28, 1992; August 15, 1993; January 29, 1995, p. 21; February 25, 1996, p. 21.
*Playboy,* May, 1966.
*Publishers Weekly,* November 27, 1995, p. 53.
*Saturday Review,* January 30, 1965; June 10, 1978.
*Spectator,* September 24, 1977; September 2, 1978; April 18, 1981.
*Time,* March 12, 1979; April 27, 1981; January 13, 1986; December 28, 1987; December 5, 1988; September 17, 1990, p. 79.
*Times Literary Supplement,* February 8, 1963; June 1, 1967; June 22, 1967; September 25, 1970; June 16, 1972; May 3, 1974; October 28, 1977; September 15, 1978; March 13, 1981; October 21, 1983; October 21, 1994; October 6, 1995.
*Tribune Books* (Chicago), February 24, 1985; December 27, 1987; January 1, 1989; January 8, 1989; January 21, 1996, p. 6.
*Village Voice,* February 19, 1979.

*Wall Street Journal,* May 21, 1980.

*Washington Post,* October 9, 1970; December 20, 1987; December 13, 1988; December 12, 1989; July 12, 1992.

*Washington Post Book World,* September 29, 1974; June 4, 1978; March 20, 1979; April 14, 1981; November 7, 1982; January 8, 1984; January 27, 1985; December 15, 1985; December 20, 1987; September 23, 1990; February 12, 1995.*

\*    \*    \*

## DEWHURST, Keith 1931-

*PERSONAL:* Born December 24, 1931, in Oldham, England; son of J. F. and Lily (Carter) Dewhurst; married Eve Pearce, July 14, 1958 (divorced, 1980); married Alexandra Cann, November 4, 1980; children: (first marriage) Alan, Emma, Faith. *Education:* Peterhouse, Cambridge, B.A. (with honors), 1953.

*ADDRESSES: Home*—2 King Edwards Mansions, Fulham Rd., London SW6, England. *Agent*—Alexandra Cann Representation, 68E Redcliffe Gardens, London SW10 9HE, England.

*CAREER:* Lancashire Cotton Corp., Romiley, England, yarn tester, 1953-55; *Manchester Evening Chronicle,* Manchester, England, sportswriter, 1955-59; Granada Television Ltd., London, England, presenter of television programs, 1968-69; *The Guardian,* London, arts columnist, 1969-72. Presenter of British Broadcasting Corp. (BBC-TV) television arts program, *Review,* 1972. Writer-in-residence, West Australian Academy of Performing Arts, 1984.

*AWARDS, HONORS:* Japan Prize, 1968, for *The Last Bus.*

*WRITINGS:*

*PLAYS*

*Rafferty's Chant,* produced in London at Mermaid Theatre, June 28, 1967.

*Pirates,* produced in London at Royal Court Theatre, December 13, 1970.

*Brecht in '26,* produced in London at Theatre Upstairs, 1971.

*Corunna!,* produced in London at Theatre Upstairs, 1971.

*Kidnapped* (adaptation of novel by Robert Louis Stevenson), produced in Edinburgh at Royal Lyceum Theatre, 1972.

*The Miser* (adaptation from Moliere), produced in Edinburgh at Royal Lyceum Theatre, May 25, 1973.

*The Magic Island,* produced at Birmingham Repertory Theatre, December 19, 1974.

*The Bomb in Brewery Street,* produced in Sheffield at Crucible Theatre, May 8, 1975.

*One Short,* produced in Sheffield at Crucible Theatre, January 22, 1976.

*Luggage,* produced in London at Natural Theatre Platform, 1977.

*The World Turned Upside Down* (adaptation of novel by Christopher Mill), produced in London at Coltesloe Theatre, November, 1978.

*Lark Rise* (adaptation of novel by Flora Thompson; produced in London at Coltesloe Theatre, March, 1978), Hutchinson (London), 1980.

*Candleford* (adaptation of novel by Thompson; produced in London at Coltesloe Theatre, March, 1978), Hutchinson, 1980.

*San Salvador,* produced in Louisville, KY, 1980.

*Don Quixote* (adaptation of novel by Miguel de Cervantes), produced in London at Olivier Theatre, June, 1982.

*Batavia,* produced in Perth, Western Australia, 1984.

*Black Snow* (adaptation of a novel by Mikhail Bulgakov; produced in London, 1991), Absolute Press (Bath, England), 1991.

*Lark Rise to Candleford: Two Plays,* Samuel French (New York City), 1995.

*TELEVISION PLAYS*

*Think of the Day,* 1960.

*A Local Incident,* 1961.

*Albert Hope,* 1962.

*The Chimney Boy,* 1964.

*The Life and Death of Lovely Karen Gilhooley,* 1964.

*The Siege of Manchester,* 1965.

*The Towers of Manhattan,* 1966.

*The Last Bus,* 1968.

*Men of Iron,* 1969.

*Why Danny Misses School,* 1969.

*It Calls for a Great Deal of Love,* 1969.

*Helen,* 1970.

*The Sit-In,* 1972.

*Lloyd George,* 1973.

*End Game,* 1974.

*The Great Alfred,* 1975.

*Our Terry,* 1975.

*Two Girls and a Millionaire,* 1978.

*The Battle of Waterloo,* 1983.
*What We Did in the Past,* 1986.

Also author of scripts for television series, including *Z Cars, Just William, Joe Wilson, Knight Errant, Skyport, Love Story, Front Page Story, The Villains, The Emigrants, Dominic, Juliet Bravo, Van der Valk, Casualty,* and *Making News.*

*RADIO PLAYS*

*Drummer Delaney's Sixpence,* 1971.
*That's Charlie George over There,* 1972.
*Dick Turpin,* 1976.
*Mother's Hot Milk,* 1979.

*OTHER*

*Captain of the Sands* (novel), Viking (New York City), 1982.
*McSullivan's Beach* (novel), Angus & Robertson (London), 1985.
*The Empty Beach* (screenplay), 1985.

Work appears in anthologies, including *Plays of the Year 33,* Elek, 1967; *Z Cars: Four Scripts from the Television Series,* Longman, 1968; and *Scene Scripts,* Longman, 1972.

*SIDELIGHTS:* Keith Dewhurst, writes Christopher Smith in *Contemporary Dramatists,* "is a highly skilled and conscientious dramatic craftsman." His work has ranged from experimental theatre to television detective series. Dewhurst, according to Smith, "insists that drama can and ought to be an artistic medium which appeals to a wide range of people in a number of different ways. In this, . . . Dewhurst proclaims a wide sympathy with the great mass of humanity."

Smith points out that Dewhurst "has done some of his most original work in adaptations." In *Carunna!,* Dewhurst presents an operatic story of the Napoleonic wars featuring only five characters and a rock band. His adaptations of works by Cervantes, Flora Thompson and Robert Louis Stevenson exhibit, according to Smith, Dewhurst's aim "to find a dramatic representation of these works which functions in performance with all the different means of communication that are available in the theatre when, without the trammels and clutter of old-fashioned realism, the imagination is engaged and provoked into providing whatever may be sensed as needed to colour the pictures that are sketched before our eyes. The success of the produc-

tions of *Lark Rise* and *Candleford* is ample justification for the enterprise that Dewhurst has embarked upon."

*BIOGRAPHICAL/CRITICAL SOURCES:*

*BOOKS*

*Contemporary Dramatists,* 5th edition, St. James Press (Detroit), 1993.

\*     \*     \*

**DOBSON, James (Clayton, Jr.) 1936-**

*PERSONAL:* Born April 21, 1936, in Shreveport, LA; son of James C. and Myrtle (G.) Dobson; married Shirley Deere, August 27, 1960; children: Danae, Ryan. *Education:* Pasadena College, B.A., 1958; University of Southern California, M.S., 1962, Ph.D., 1967; graduate study, University of California, Berkeley, 1963, University of California, Los Angeles, 1964.

*ADDRESSES: Home*—348 Harvard Dr., Arcadia, CA 91006. *Office*—Focus on the Family, Pomona, CA 91799.

*CAREER:* Teacher and counselor in public schools in Hacienda, CA, and Covina, CA, 1960-64; Charter Oak Unified School District, Covina, CA, psychologist and coordinator of Pupil Personnel Services, 1964-66; University of Southern California, School of Medicine, Los Angeles, 1966-83, began as assistant professor, became associate clinical professor of pediatrics; Focus on the Family, Pomona, CA, founder, 1977, president, 1977—. Co-director of Research, Division of Medical Genetics, Children's Hospital of Los Angeles. Appointed by President Carter to task force for White House conferences on the family, and by President Reagan to National Advisory Council, Office of Juvenile Justice and Delinquency Prevention, 1983.

*WRITINGS:*

*Dare to Discipline,* Tyndale (Wheaton), 1970, revised edition published as *The New Dare to Discipline,* 1992.
(Editor and contributor with Richard Koch) *The Mentally Retarded Child and His Family: A Multidisciplinary Handbook,* Brunner, 1971.

*Symposium on Phenylketonuria: Present Status and Future Developments,* Verlag Thieme Publications (Heidelberg), 1971.

*Discipline with Love,* Tyndale, 1972.

*Hide or Seek,* Revell, 1974, 3rd edition, 1979.

*What Wives Wish Their Husbands Knew about Women,* Tyndale, 1975.

*Prescription for a Tired Homemaker,* Tyndale, 1978.

*The Strong-Willed Child: Birth through Adolescence,* Tyndale, 1978.

*Preparing for Adolescence,* Vision House, 1978, updated, Tyndale (Wheaton), 1992.

(With daughter, Danae Dobson) *Woof!: A Bedtime Story about a Dog,* illustrations by Dennis Bellile, Word, 1979.

*Emotions: Can You Trust Them?,* Regal, 1980.

*Straight Talk to Men and Their Wives,* illustrations by Bellile, Word, 1980, revised, 1991.

*Dr. Dobson Answers Your Questions,* Tyndale, 1982.

*Love Must Be Tough: New Hope for Families in Crisis,* Word, 1983.

*Dr. Dobson Answers Your Questions about Confident, Healthy Families,* Tyndale, 1986.

*Dr. Dobson Answers Your Questions about Marriage and Sexuality,* Tyndale, 1986.

*Dr. Dobson Answers Your Questions about Raising Children,* Tyndale, 1986.

*Temper Your Child's Tantrums,* Tyndale, 1986.

*Love for a Lifetime: Building a Marriage That Will Go the Distance,* Multnomah, 1987.

*Parenting Isn't for Cowards,* Word, 1987.

*Christ in Christmas: A Family Advent Celebration,* NavPress (Colorado Springs), 1989.

*Romantic Love,* Regal (Ventura), 1989.

(With Gary L. Bauer) *Children at Risk: The Battle for the Hearts and Minds of Our Kids,* Word (Dallas), 1990.

*Help for Home and Family,* Tyndale (Wheaton), 1990.

*Dr. Dobson Answers Your Questions* (includes *Dr. Dobson Answers Your Questions about Marriage and Sexuality, Dr. Dobson Answers Your Questions about Confident, Healthy Families,* and *Dr. Dobson Answers Your Questions about Raising Children*), Living Books (Wheaton), 1992.

*Emotions, Can You Trust Them?,* Tyndale (Wheaton), 1992.

*When God Doesn't Make Sense,* Tyndale (Wheaton), 1993.

*Life on the Edge: A Proven Plan for a Life of Meaning and Fulfillment,* Word (Dallas), 1995.

Contributor to *Educational and Psychological Measurement, Journal of Developmental Reading, New England Journal of Medicine, Hospital Topics, Lancet,* and *Journal of Pediatrics.* Consulting editor, *Journal of International Neurosciences Abstracts.*

*SIDELIGHTS:* Child psychologist and author James Dobson is also founder and president of Focus on the Family, an organization that produces nationally broadcast radio programs on domestic issues. Dobson's books cover such topics as helping adolescents understand their sexuality and building stronger marital relationships. Dobson once told *CA:* "My mission in writing is to help preserve the health and vitality of the American family, which is undergoing a serious threat to its survival. It is my view that our society can be no more stable than the foundation of individual family units upon which it rests. Our government, our institutions, our schools . . . indeed, our way of life is dependent on healthy marriages and loyalty to the vulnerable little children around our feet. Thus, my professional life is devoted to the integrity of the family and the God who designed it."

Dobson displays this devotion in his titles *Children at Risk: The Battle for the Hearts and Minds of Our Kids,* co-authored with lawyer Gary L. Bauer, and *Preparing for Adolescence* originally published by Vision House in 1978, then updated and published by Tyndale in 1992. In *Children at Risk,* Dobson and Bauer rally readers to "battle [secularism] . . . for the hearts and minds of our children." Specifically, Dobson calls for the reestablishment of a nuclear family which includes both father and mother and that is guided by Christian values in order to provide children with the backbone to combat the cultural absence of a Biblical-based morality. A contributor to the *West Coast Review of Books* found the book to be "on target, although a bit preachy and heavy-handed." *Preparing for Adolescence* continues Dobson's emphasis on Christian values in its coverage of the psychological and physiological changes of adolescence. Dobson steers clear of issues such as birth control and notes homosexuality as "abnormal." However, he does include biological facts on sexuality and admits normal adolescent issues such as masturbation while "acknowledging the controversy within the Christian community," commented a contributor to the *School Library Journal.* The result, the critic continued, is that "those faithful to their religious beliefs can resolve most difficulties."

*Life on the Edge: A Proven Plan for a Life of Meaning and Fulfillment,* published in 1995, picks up where *Preparing for Adolescence* left off, bringing Dobson's "family focus" to bear on issues facing teenagers and young adults, such as choosing a marital partner, school and career decisions, and sexuality. Dobson continues to emphasize "fundamentalist Christianity," commented Ray Olson in *Booklist,* "but also [displays] a genuine counselor's understanding of human weakness and extension of sympathy." A *Publishers Weekly* contributor found "His conservative approach may make some readers uneasy. . .but he offers credible and useful insight into major life choices for young seekers." A *Library Journal* reviewer was somewhat more critical, commenting that "Dobson's tone is often arrogant, his demeanor sexist, and his attitude narrow-minded" but conceding, "he has a large and dedicated following." Olson viewed the title differently, stating, "despite the bad rap the Religious Right. . .gets, there is not a hateful word in the book."

*BIOGRAPHICAL/CRITICAL SOURCES:*

*BOOKS*

Zettersten, Rolf, *Dr. Dobson: Turning Hearts Toward Home: The Life and Principles of America's Family Advocate,* Word (Dallas), 1989.

*PERIODICALS*

*Booklist,* March 15, 1995, p. 1282.
*Library Journal,* May 1, 1995, p.102.
*Publishers Weekly,* March 13, 1995, p. 34.
*School Library Journal,* August, 1981, p. 31.
*West Coast Review of Books,* Volume 16, number 2, 1991, p. 45.*

\* \* \*

**DOLAN, Edward F(rancis), Jr. 1924-**

*PERSONAL:* Born February 10, 1924, in Oakland, CA; son of an engineer. *Education:* Attended University of Southern California, San Francisco State College, and University of San Francisco. *Avocational interests:* Travel, the theater.

*CAREER:* Has worked as a freelance radio and television writer, teacher of communications, reporter, and director of publications.

*AWARDS, HONORS:* Children's Books of the Year, Child Study Association of America (CSAA), 1965, for *The Camera,* 1979, for *Kyle Rote, Jr.: American-*

Born Soccer Star, 1980, for *The Bermuda Triangle and Other Mysteries of Nature,* 1984, for *Great Mysteries of the Air,* 1986, for *Anti-Semitism,* 1992, for *Our Poisoned Sky,* and 1996, for both *The American Revolution: How We Fought the War of Independence,* and *Your Privacy: Protecting It in a Nosy World*; Best Books for Young Adults, American Library Association (ALA), 1977, for *How to Leave Home—And Make Everybody Like It,* and 1981, for *Adolph Hitler: A Portrait of Tyranny.*

*WRITINGS:*

*Pasteur and the Invisible Giants,* Dodd (New York City), 1958.
*Green Universe: The Story of Alexander von Humboldt,* Dodd, 1959.
*Jenner and the Miracle of Vaccine,* Dodd, 1960.
*White Background: The Conquest of the Arctic,* Dodd, 1961.
*Vanquishing Yellow Fever: Dr. Walter Reed,* Britannica Press, 1962.
*Adventure with a Microscope: A Story of Robert Koch,* Dodd, 1964.
*The Camera,* Messner (New York City), 1965.
*Disaster 1906: The San Francisco Earthquake and Fire,* Messner, 1967.
(With H.T. Silver) *William Crawford Gorgas: Warrior in White,* Dodd, 1968.
*Explorers of the Arctic and Antarctic,* Crowell-Collier (New York City), 1968.
*The Explorers: Adventures in Courage,* Reilly & Lee, 1970.
*Inventors for Medicine,* Crown (New York City), 1971.
*Engines Work Like This,* McGraw (New York City), 1971.
*Legal Action: A Layman's Guide,* Regnery, 1972.
(With Frederick J. Hass) *What You Can Do About Your Headaches,* Regnery, 1973.
(With Hass) *The Foot Book,* Regnery, 1973.
*A Lion in the Sun: A Background Book for Young People on the Rise and Fall of the British Empire,* Parents Magazine Press (New York City), 1973.
*The Complete Beginner's Guide to Bowling,* Doubleday (New York City), 1974.
*The Complete Beginner's Guide to Ice Skating,* Doubleday, 1974.
*Starting Soccer: A Handbook for Boys and Girls,* illustrated with photographs by Jameson C. Goldner, Harper (New York City), 1976.
*Basic Football Strategy: An Introduction for Young Players,* foreword by Duffy Daugherty, Doubleday, 1976.

*Amnesty: The American Puzzle,* F. Watts (New York City), 1976, revised edition, 1977.

*The Complete Beginner's Guide to Making and Flying Kites,* Doubleday, 1977.

*The Complete Beginner's Guide to Magic,* Doubleday, 1977.

*How to Leave Home—And Make Everybody Like It,* Dodd, 1977.

(With Richard B. Lyttle) *Archie Griffin,* Doubleday, 1977.

(With Lyttle) *Bobby Clarke,* Doubleday, 1977.

(With Lyttle) *Martina Navratilova,* Doubleday, 1977.

(With Lyttle) *Scott May: Basketball Champion,* Doubleday, 1978.

(With Lyttle) *Fred Lynn: The Hero from Boston,* Doubleday, 1978.

(With Lyttle) *Janet Guthrie: First Woman Driver at Indianapolis,* Doubleday, 1978.

*Gun Control: A Decision for Americans,* F. Watts, 1978, revised edition, 1982.

(With Lyttle) *Dorothy Hamill: Olympic Skating Champion,* Doubleday, 1979.

(With Lyttle) *Jimmy Young: Heavyweight Challenger,* Doubleday, 1979.

(With Lyttle) *Kyle Rote, Jr.: American-Born Soccer Star,* Doubleday, 1979.

*Matthew Henson, Black Explorer,* Dodd, 1979.

*Child Abuse,* F. Watts, 1980, revised edition, 1992.

*The Complete Beginner's Guide to Gymnastics,* illustrated with photographs by James Stewart, Doubleday, 1980.

*The Bermuda Triangle, and Other Mysteries of Nature,* F. Watts, 1980.

*Let's Make Magic,* Doubleday, 1980.

*Adolf Hitler: A Portrait in Tyranny,* Dodd, 1981.

*Calling the Play: A Beginner's Guide to Amateur Sports Officiating,* Atheneum (New York City), 1981.

*It Sounds Like Fun: How to Use and Enjoy Your Tape Recorder and Stereo,* Simon & Schuster (New York City), 1981.

*Great Moments in the World Series,* F. Watts, 1982.

*Great Moments in the Indy 500,* F. Watts, 1982.

*Great Moments in the Super Bowl,* F. Watts, 1982.

*Great Moments in the NBA Championships,* F. Watts, 1982.

*Bicycle Touring and Camping,* Simon & Schuster, 1982.

*Matters of Life and Death,* F. Watts, 1982.

*Protect Your Legal Rights: A Handbook for Teenagers,* Simon & Schuster, 1983.

*Great Mysteries of the Air,* Dodd, 1983.

*History of the Movies,* Bison, 1983.

(With Shan Finney) *The New Japan,* F. Watts, 1983.

(With Finney) *Youth Gangs,* Simon & Schuster, 1984.

*Great Mysteries of the Sea,* Dodd, 1984.

*The Insanity Plea,* F. Watts, 1984.

*The Simon & Schuster Sports Question and Answer Book,* Simon & Schuster, 1984.

*Be Your Own Man,* Prentice-Hall (Englewood Cliffs, NJ), 1984.

*International Drug Traffic,* F. Watts, 1985.

*Anti-Semitism,* F. Watts, 1985.

*Great Mysteries of the Ice and Snow,* Dodd, 1985.

*Hollywood Goes to War,* Bison, 1985.

*Money Talk,* Messner, 1986.

*Animal Rights,* F. Watts, 1986.

*Drugs in Sports,* F. Watts, 1986, revised edition, 1992.

*Famous Builders of California,* Dodd, 1987.

(With Margaret M. Scariano) *Cuba and the United States: Troubled Neighbors,* F. Watts, 1987.

(With Scariano) *The Police in American Society,* F. Watts, 1988.

*The Old Farmer's Almanac Book of Weather Lore: The Fact and Fancy behind Weather Predictions, Superstitions, Old-Time Sayings, and Traditions* (foreword by Willard Scott), Yankee Books (Dublin, NH), 1988.

*Victory in Europe: The Fall of Hitler's Germany,* F. Watts, 1988.

*Missing in Action: A Vietnam Drama,* F. Watts, 1989.

*Famous Firsts in Space,* Dutton (New York City), 1989.

*America After Vietnam: Legacies of a Hated War,* F. Watts, 1989.

(With Scariano) *Nuclear Waste: The 10,000-Year Challenge,* F. Watts, 1990.

*Our Poisoned Sky,* Cobblehill Books, 1990.

*Panama and the United States: Their Canal, Their Stormy Years,* F. Watts, 1990.

*Drought: The Past, Present, and Future Enemy,* F. Watts, 1990.

*America in World War II: 1941,* Millbrook (Brookfield, CT), 1991.

*Animal Folklore: From Black Cats to White Horses,* Ivy Books, 1992.

*America in World War II: 1943,* Millbrook, 1992.

*The American Wilderness and its Future: Conservation versus Use,* F. Watts, 1992.

*Folk Medicine Cures and Curiosities,* Ivy Books, 1993.

*Teenagers and Compulsive Gambling,* F. Watts, 1994.

*America in World War II: 1945,* Millbrook, 1994.

(With Scariano) *Guns in the United States,* F. Watts, 1994.

(With Scariano) *Illiteracy in America,* F. Watts, 1995.

*The American Revolution: How We Fought the War of Independence,* Millbrook Press, 1995.

*Your Privacy: Protecting It in a Nosy World,* Cobblehill, 1995.

*In Sports, Money Talks,* Twenty-First Century Books, 1996.

*America in World War I,* Millbrook Press, 1996.

(With Scariano) *Shaping U.S. Foreign Policy: Profiles of Twelve Secretaries of State,* F. Watts, 1996.

*The American Civil War: A House Divided,* Millbrook, 1997.

*Our Poisoned Waters,* Cobblehill, 1997.

*America in the Korean War,* Millbrook, 1998.

*SIDELIGHTS:* Edward F. Dolan is among the most prolific authors of nonfiction for children. Dolan started writing at the age of twelve, and by age sixteen he published his first story. Since the publication of his first book in 1958, Dolan has written over seventy nonfiction books and co-authored nearly twenty more. While many of his titles deal with sports or science, he has also widely written on topics in history, social studies, the environment, health, law, and on contemporary problems like drugs, gun control, and compulsive gambling.

Dolan's first published book was *Pasteur and the Invisible Giants,* but his first title to receive special note was *The Camera* in 1965, which was praised by the Child Study Association as an "exciting history." Dolan's next book, *Disaster 1906: The San Francisco Earthquake and Fire* was a selection of the Junior Library Guild. Marion Marx, writing in *Horn Book,* concluded that the book will "appeal to the science-oriented child as well as to the child with an interest in the human drama and tragedy resulting from natural disasters."

*The Complete Beginner's Guide to Bowling* was the first of many books Dolan has written or co-authored in the field of sports. Praised in *Booklist* as perhaps "the next best thing to private lessons," the book was also singled out by *Kirkus Reviews* for its "attention to fundamentals" and "detailed instruction." Dolan has written similar how-to books on ice-skating, soccer, football, kitemaking, gymnastics, and officiating. *The Complete Beginner's Guide to Gymnastics* was recommended in *Booklist* as a "valuable primary resource" for beginning gymnasts. Dolan has won equal attention for his series (co-authored with R. B. Lyttle) on sports heroes in sports ranging from tennis to

baseball, racing car driving, soccer, ice skating, and boxing. The Child Study Association singled out *Kyle Rote, Jr.: American-Born Soccer Star* as a "lively biography" with "action-packed photographs." Dolan has also written several titles in the general category of sports-related information books. *The Simon & Schuster Sports Question and Answer Book* was cited by a *Bulletin of the Center for Children's Books* reviewer for its "good job" in answering questions about twelve different sports.

Dolan began tackling contemporary problems in his books in 1977, when he published *Amnesty: The American Puzzle.* The book, described *Booklist,* is a "straightforward examination" of Vietnam-era war evaders or deserters. After summarizing the history of amnesty in the United States, Dolan examines the arguments for and against amnesty. *Booklist* found the book "useful for students of American history and government." That same year, Dolan received his first major recognition when the American Library Association (ALA) named *How to Leave Home—And Make Everybody Like It* a Notable Book selection for young adults. The book is a guide to leaving home and living independently, including how to tell one's family, find a job, and handle finances. The author also discusses the pros and cons of running away. In *Gun Control: A Decision For Americans,* Dolan explores the background and conflicting viewpoints on this controversial subject, analyzing present gun control laws and surveying public opinion. The book was described as "thorough and objective" by Zena Sutherland of the *Bulletin of the Center for Children's Books.*

In *Child Abuse,* Dolan discusses the various manifestations of this problem, its psychological causes, and the sources of help that are available for victims and abusers. *School Library Journal* contributor Linda Rombough commended the book for the "firm, straightforward" manner and "honesty and sensitivity" with which it handles a difficult topic. Zena Sutherland of the *Bulletin of the Center for Children's Books* also noted the book's "serious but not heavy" writing and "objective tone." The revised edition was praised in *Booklist* by Carolyn Phelan as a "good resource." *School Library Journal* contributor Libby K. White commented: "The author writes clearly, putting the problem of abuse in proper perspective. . . . He aims to inform, not to frighten."

Nolan's interest in history, especially that of the World War II era, blossomed with *Adolph Hitler: A Portrait in Tyranny,* which garnered the author's second ALA Notable Book honor. The book was praised by Ethel R. Twichell in *Horn Book* as a "solid and well-researched biography" written in "sober and workmanlike style." While finding fault with the author's occasionally "tortured" writing style and inferior organization, Lorraine Douglas, writing in *School Library Journal,* nevertheless found the book an "absorbing and graphic description of Hitler."

A decade later, Dolan followed up his interest in World War II with the first in a series of books, each devoted to one year in the conflict. The first, *America in World War II: 1941,* was commended by Eldon Younce in *School Library Journal* as a "readable introduction" with "well-written" text, "well-chosen" photographs and an "attractive overview" of the period. The same reviewer also praised the "clear and concise writing" of the third book in the series, covering the year 1943. In a similar vein, *Booklist* contributor Ilene Cooper noted Dolan's "straightforward" approach and "accessible text." Extending this same historical treatment to World War I, Dolan's *America in World War I* was recognized by David A. Lindsey in *School Library Journal* as a "concise introductory survey" marked by the author's "taut and seemingly effortless" prose. The work was also praised by *Booklist*'s Susan Dove Lempke as "fine work" proceeding in an "understandable, orderly fashion."

Dolan applied a more thematic approach to a broad subject in *Anti-Semitism,* dividing the topic into three forms: personal prejudice, discrimination, and persecution. *School Library Journal* contributor Ruth Horowitz found this approach too "abstract," while a *Bulletin of the Center for Children's Books* commentator complained that the book "lacks personality." Nevertheless, the latter reviewer also noted the advantage of its "objective tone" in dealing with sensitive issues like Black anti-Semitism in the United States. The Child Study Committee gave the work one of its Children's Books of the Year citations in 1986.

In general, Dolan has been praised for the balanced point of view he takes toward controversial topics, ranging from the police (*The Police in American Society*) to guns in the United States (*Gun Control: A Decision for Americans*) to issues of privacy (*Your Privacy: Protecting It in a Nosy World*). In other works like *Animal Rights,* however, the author has taken a strong advocacy position—in this case, in favor of more humane treatment. On the whole, Dolan's large body of work has won an impressive number of favorable assessments for its breadth and conciseness.

BIOGRAPHICAL/CRITICAL SOURCES:

*PERIODICALS*

*Booklist,* September 1, 1974, p. 39; May 15, 1976, pp. 1329-30; March 1, 1980, p. 935; October 15, 1986, p. 342; October 10, 1991, p. 319; January 1, 1993, p. 888; June 1, 1996, p. 1708.
*Bulletin of the Center for Children's Books,* March, 1979, p. 113; November, 1980, pp. 50-51; April, 1985, p. 145; March, 1986, p. 125; April, 1997, p. 280.
*Horn Book,* April, 1968, pp. 191-92; February, 1982, p. 63.
*Kirkus Reviews,* September 1, 1967, p. 1061; March 1, 1974, p. 255; April 1, 1997, p. 553.
*School Library Journal,* September, 1980, p. 82; February, 1981, p. 64; October, 1981, p. 119; February, 1986, p. 94; January, 1987, p. 82; September, 1991, p. 268; May, 1992, p. 121; January, 1993, p. 136; May 5, 1996, p. 137.
*Voice of Youth Advocates,* February, 1983, pp. 48-49; April, 1986, p. 45; June, 1989, p. 122; October, 1995, p. 245.
*Wilson Library Bulletin,* June, 1987, p. 65.*

\*   \*   \*

## DONDERS, Jozef G(erardus) 1929-

*PERSONAL:* Born March 11, 1929, in Tilburg, Netherlands; immigrated to United States, 1984; son of Jan Piet Jan (an architect) and Riet (a teacher; maiden name, Panhuysen) Donders. *Ethnicity:* "European." *Education:* Attended College of Philosophical and Theological Studies, 1950-56, and International Scholasticate, Jedburgh, Scotland, 1956-57; Pontifical Gregorian University, Rome, Italy, M.A., 1958, Ph.D., 1961.

*ADDRESSES: Home*—1624 21st St. N.W., Washington, DC 20009. *Office*—Washington Theological Union, 6896 Laurel St. N.W., Washington, DC 20012. *E-mail*—sjef@aul.com.

*CAREER:* Entered Society of Missionaries of Africa, 1956, ordained Roman Catholic priest, 1957; Philosophicum St. Charles, Esch, Netherlands, teacher of systematic philosophy and history of philosophy, 1960-66; College of Philosophical and Theological Studies, Haaren, Netherlands, visiting lecturer, 1964-66; University of Tilburg, Gemeenschappelijk

Instituut voor Theologie, Tilburg, Netherlands, professor of philosophy, 1966-68; conducted lecture tours through Tanzania and Uganda, including visiting lectures at Pastoral Institute of Eastern Africa, 1968-70; Nairobi University, Nairobi, Kenya, lecturer, 1970-73, professor of philosophy, 1973-81, part-time professor, 1981-84, chaplain to Catholic students, 1973-84; Africa Faith and Justice Network, Washington, DC, executive director, 1984-88; Washington Theological Union, Washington, DC, chairperson of mission and cross-cultural studies, 1988—. Catholic Youth Council of Kenya, national youth chaplain, 1983-84. Producer of Dutch and British television programs on human evolution and history, catechism, the pentecostal movement in East Africa, and cross-cultural philosophy.

*MEMBER:* Thomistische Vereniging, American Association of Catholic Theologians, Teilhard de Chardin Association, Philosophical Association of Kenya.

*AWARDS, HONORS:* National Religious Book Award from Religious Book Review and OMNI Communications, 1979, for *Jesus, the Stranger;* Religious Book Award from Catholic Press Association, 1997, for *Pope John Paul II: The Encyclicals in Everyday Language.*

*WRITINGS:*

IN ENGLISH

*How to Study,* Uzina Press (Nairobi, Kenya), 1974.
*The Expatriate Jesus,* Gazelle Books (Nairobi), 1975.
*Don't Fence Us In: The Liberating Role of Philosophy,* University of Nairobi, 1977.
*Jesus, the Stranger,* Orbis Books (Maryknoll, NY), 1979.
*Jesus, the Way,* Orbis Books, 1979.
*Jesus: Heaven on Earth,* Orbis Books, 1980.
*The Jesus Community,* Orbis Books, 1981.
*The Jesus Option,* Orbis Books, 1982.
*The Peace of Jesus,* Orbis Books, 1983.
*Beyond Jesus,* Orbis Books, 1984.
*Non-Bourgeois Theology,* Orbis Books, 1985.
*Empowering Hope,* Twenty-Third (Mystic, CT), 1985.
*Creation and Human Dynamism,* Twenty-Third, 1985.
*Bread Broken,* Gaba (Eldoret, Kenya), 1985.
(With S. Smith) *Refugees Are People,* Gaba, 1986.
*Wars and Rumors of War,* Gaba, 1986.
*Christ, the Divine Network,* Orbis Books, 1986.
*The Global Believer,* Twenty-Third, 1986.

*Liberation, the Jesus Mode,* Orbis Books, 1987.
*Praying and Preaching the Sunday Gospel* (Catholic Book Club selection), Orbis Books, 1988.
*Gathering All Nations,* Gaba, 1988.
(With Elizabeth Byrne) *Original Joy,* Twenty-Third, 1989.
*Risen Life,* Orbis Books, 1990.
*Scriptural Reflections Day by Day,* Twenty-Third, 1992.
*Charged with the Spirit: Mission Is for Everyone,* Orbis Books, 1993.
*Pope John Paul II: The Encyclicals in Everyday Language,* Orbis Books, 1996.
*The Fullness of Time,* CAFOD (London, England), 1997.

OTHER

*Schepping en Evolutie* (title means "Creation and Evolution"), Vereniging voor Thomistische Wijsbegeerte, 1964.
(With A. G. Weiler and Marga Kerklaan) *Wie zijn toch die Mensen* (title means "Who Are We Humans?"), Het Wereldvenster, 1970.
*In God's Naam nu inspelen op de Toekomst* (title means "To Begin the Future in the Name of God"), Altiora (Aberbode, Belgium), 1970.
*Het Lichaam waar het om gaat* (title means "The Body That Counts"), Altiora, 1971.
*De voorlopigheid van de Stad* (title means "The Provisional Nature of Urbanism"), Nelissen (Bilthoven, Netherlands), 1971.
*Het Westen is de Navel niet* (title means "The West Is Not the Center"), Nelissen, 1973.
*Wie na Jezus* (title means "Who After Jesus"), Altiora, 1974.
*Mbinu za kujifunza* (title means "How to Study"), TMP (Tabora, Tanzania), 1975.
*Meewerken aan het Leven op grond van de schepping* (title means "Cooperate in Life As It Is God-Given"), Altiora, 1977.
*Gered uit de Tempel* (title means "Saved from the Temple"), Bijeen (Deurne, Netherlands), 1977.
*Jinsi ya kuhubiri* (title means "How to Preach"), Peramiho (Tanzania), 1983.
*So Einfach is das Evangelium: Ungewoehnliche Texte fuer das Kirchenjahr* (title means "The Gospel Is Simple As This"), Herder, 1986.
*Bijbels Bezien,* Katholieke Bijbelstichting ('s Hertogenbosch, Netherlands), Volume I: *Lucas,* 1991, Volume II: *Marcus,* 1992, Volume III: *Matteus,* 1993.
*Il Vangelo della Domenica,* three volumes, Edizioni Messagero Padova (Padova, Italy), 1994-96.

Contributor of more than a hundred-fifty articles to philosophy and theology journals.

*SIDELIGHTS:* Jozef G. Donders told *CA:* "An issue that intrigues me is that while more and more people are witnesses to religious experiences, the influence of institutionalized religion is diminishing. A similar phenomenon is observable in politics. People are 'coming into their own' religiously and civically. This means that new stories are told, and a new language is spoken.

"It was in Africa that I was first confronted by totally unalienated people. It seems to me that the western way of working out humanity's reality should be revised. According to statistics, ninety-five percent of Americans do not realize that all that is given to us is given to each one of us. All my writings center around these issues."

*BIOGRAPHICAL/CRITICAL SOURCES:*

PERIODICALS

*Critic,* summer, 1978.

\* \* \*

**DONKIN, Nance (Clare) 1915-**

*PERSONAL:* Born in 1915, in West Maitland, New South Wales, Australia; daughter of Archie T. Pender and Clara Russell; married Victor Donkin, 1939; children: Nicola Williams, Richard Donkin.

*ADDRESSES: Home*—8/8 Mooltan Avenue, Balaclava, Victoria 3183, Australia.

*CAREER: Maitland Daily Mercury,* Maitland, New South Wales, Australia, journalist, 1932-1935; *Newcastle Morning Herald,* Newcastle, New South Wales, journalist, 1935-1939; writer, 1946—. Broadcaster for Australian Broadcasting Commission program, *Women's Session; Melbourne Herald,* children's book reviewer, 1970—; Council of Adult Education, Melbourne, tutor, 1975—. Children's Book Council, Victoria, president, 1968-1975, vice-president, 1975-1979.

*MEMBER:* Australian Society of Authors, Fellowship of Australian Writers, Women Writers Society, National Trust of Australia, Gallery Society of Victoria.

*AWARDS, HONORS:* Australian Arts Council travel grant, 1972, and senior fellowship, 1980; A.M. (General Division of Order of Australia), 1986, for services to children's literature and adult education.

*WRITINGS:*

FICTION; FOR CHILDREN

*Araluen Adventures,* illustrated by Edith B. Bowden, Cheshire (Palo Alto, CA), 1946.
*No Medals for Meg,* illustrated Bowden, Cheshire, 1947.
*Julie Stands By,* illustrated by Joan Turner, Cheshire, 1948.
*Blue Ribbon Beth,* Oxford University Press (Melbourne), 1951.
*House by the Water,* illustrated by Astra Lacis Dick, Angus & Robertson (London), 1969.
*Johnny Neptune,* Angus & Robertson (Sydney), 1971.
*A Friend for Petros,* illustrated by Gavin Rowe, Hamish Hamilton (London), 1974.
*Patchwork Grandmother,* illustrated by Mary Dinsdale, Hamish Hamilton, 1975, published as *Patchwork Mystery,* Beaver, 1978.
*Green Christmas,* illustrated by Rowe, Hamish Hamilton, 1976.
*Yellowgum Girl,* illustrated by Margaret Loxton, Hamish Hamilton, 1976.
*The Best of the Bunch,* illustrated by Edwina Bell, Collins (Sydney), 1978.
*The Maidens of Petka,* illustrated by Bruce Treloar, Methuen (Sydney), 1979.
*Nini,* Rigby (Adelaide), 1979.
(Reteller) Aeneas Gunn, *We of the Never Never,* Hutchinson (Victoria), 1983.
*Two at Sullivan Bay,* illustrated by Margaret Senior, Kangaroo Press, 1985.
*A Family Affair,* illustrated by Lyn Sikiotis, Martin, 1988.

Contributor to anthologies, including *The Cool Man,* Angus & Robertson (London), 1973; and *A Handful of Ghosts,* Hodder & Stoughton (London), 1976.

NONFICTION; FOR CHILDREN

*Sheep,* illustrated by Jocelyn Jones, Oxford University Press, 1967.
*Sugar,* illustrated by Jones, Oxford University Press, 1967.
*An Emancipist,* illustrated by Jane Robertson, Oxford University Press, 1968.

*A Currency Lass,* illustrated by Jane Walker, Oxford University Press, 1969.

*An Orphan,* illustrated by Anne Culvenor, Oxford University Press, 1970.

*Margaret Catchpole,* illustrated by Bell, Collins, 1974.

*Blackout* (reader), illustrated by Dandra Laroche, Macmillan (Melbourne), 1987.

OTHER

(Editor) *The Australian Children's Annual* Lothian (Melbourne), 1963.

*A Writer at Work* (lecture), Children's Book Council of Australia, 1975.

*Stranger and Friend: The Greek-American Experience,* Dove (Victoria, Australia), 1983.

*The Women Were There: Nineteen Women Who Enlivened Australia's History,* Collins Dove, 1988.

*Always a Lady: Courageous Women of Colonial Australia,* Collins Dove, 1990.

*SIDELIGHTS:* A journalist and writer for sixty-five years, Nance Donkin has written or edited over two dozen books of fiction and nonfiction for children and four works of nonfiction for adults. Her special interest in Australian history and in the problems of immigrants has supplied themes for many of her books. Commenting about her main interest in Australia's past, Donkin has written: "I hope to help [children] see, even vaguely, that 'history is people like you.'. . . I expect to keep on with this kind of historical 'digging' for the rest of my writing life. There is buried treasure there in fabulous nuggets."

As a child, the author was perhaps influenced by what Donkin herself calls the "web of words spun by my father, a natural story-teller of the yarn and the tall story ender," according to *Twentieth-Century Children's Writers* critic Nancy Shepherdson. Her early works from the 1940s have been criticized by Shepherdson as having "uninspired plots and much digressive conversation," but the same critic notes that her later books, beginning with *House by the Water,* are more interesting because of her special passion for Australia's history and geography. *House by the Water* is set in Sydney in 1811 and is based on a real family who lived in the early convict settlement there. Writing in the *Times Literary Supplement,* one critic praised the book for its realism, saying it was "well researched but unpretentious and fast-moving."

*Johnny Neptune,* praised in *Times Literary Supplement* for the "ring of truth" of many of its incidents,

is set in Sydney in 1790. The novel describes the tough life of an orphan, born to a dying convict, who must fight against the odds to survive in the new colony. Johnny is adopted by a young woman who is herself a convict—not surprising since Australia in its early colonial days was a dumping ground for criminals of all kinds. Johnny succeeds in growing up honest, even in pulling the rest of the family up to his standard. The family leaves Sydney and starts a farm, only to have an unexpected flood destroy their efforts, yet they do not lose hope and resolve to begin again.

Donkin's interest in the Australian Bush is evident in *Green Christmas.* The story is about a contemporary English girl whose family has moved to Australia at Christmas and who misses snow and holly. Lorna soon forgets her homesickness, however, when she meets Patsy Holden and her brother James, who show her a secret cave with wall paintings that are thousands of years old. *Junior Bookshelf* critic J. Russell praised the story for being "well written, exciting, amusing and about 'real' people." The Australian Bush is also the setting of *Yellowgum Girl,* which is about a city boy's vacation near a nature reserve where "desert mice that move quicker than a flash nibble silky tea tree blossoms." Nancy Shepherdson praised the book for its "appreciation and knowledge" of this fascinating part of Australia.

In *The Best of the Bunch,* Donkin returns to the historical genre that had served her well in *Johnny Neptune* and *Margaret Catchpole,* Donkin's 1974 biography about a young English girl jailed for horse-stealing and deported to New South Wales. *The Best of the Bunch* is set in Sydney around 1820, the year England's King George III died. Girlie, an orphan with a notable ability to cry, has been rescued from abject poverty by Old Sal, a reformed female thief. Girlie hopes her redcoat father will come for her one day, but his arrival does not turn out the way she expected. The novel was praised by M. Hobbs in *Junior Bookshelf* for its "effortlessly conveyed" setting and historical background and its "convincingly drawn" characters.

Donkin's interest in Greece, growing from her acquaintance with Greek immigrants in Australia as well as several long visits to Greece, presents itself in four books. *A Friend for Petros* and *Nini* are both about Greek children in contemporary Australia. *The Maidens of Petka* concerns an Australian family on a Greek island. Finally, *Stranger and Friend* is an adult nonfiction book about what Donkin once called "the Greek-Australian experience."

*BIOGRAPHICAL/CRITICAL SOURCES:*

*BOOKS*

Donkin, Nance, *Yellowgum Girl,* Hamish Hamilton (London), 1976.
*Twentieth-Century Children's Writers,* 4th edition, St. James Press (Detroit), 1995, pp. 300-01.

*PERIODICALS*

*Growing Point,* November, 1976, p. 3005.
*Junior Bookshelf,* February, 1975, p. 60; April, 1977, p. 91; October 1979, p. 270.
*Times Literary Supplement,* April 16, 1970, p. 426; April 28, 1972, p. 480.

\*   \*   \*

**DOVE, Rita (Frances) 1952-**

*PERSONAL:* Born August 28, 1952, in Akron, OH; daughter of Ray A. (a chemist) and Elvira E. (Hord) Dove; married Fred Viebahn (a writer) March 23, 1979; children: Aviva Chantal Tamu Dove-Viebahn. *Education:* Miami University, B.A. (summa cum laude), 1973; attended Universitaet Tuebingen, West Germany, 1974-75; University of Iowa, M.F.A., 1977.

*ADDRESSES: Office*—Department of English, University of Virginia, Charlottesville, VA, 22903.

*CAREER:* Arizona State University, Tempe, assistant professor, 1981-84, associate professor, 1984-87, professor of English, 1987-89; University of Virginia, Charlottesville, professor of English 1989-93, Commonwealth Professor of English, 1993—; United States Poet Laureate, 1994-95. Writer-in-residence at Tuskegee Institute, 1982. National Endowment for the Arts, member of literature panel, 1984-86, chair of poetry grants panel, 1985. Commissioner, Schomburg Center for the Preservation of Black Culture, New York Public Library, 1987—; judge, Walt Whitman Award, Academy of American Poets, 1990, Pulitzer Prize in poetry, 1991, Ruth Lilly Prize, 1991, National Book Award (poetry), 1991, Anisfield-Wolf Book Awards, 1992—.

*MEMBER:* PEN, Associated Writing Programs (member of board of directors, 1985-88; president, 1986-87), Academy of American Poets, Poetry Society of America, Poets and Writers, Phi Beta Kappa, Phi Kappa Phi.

*AWARDS, HONORS:* Fulbright fellow, 1974-75; grants from National Endowment for the Arts, 1978, and Ohio Arts Council, 1979; International Working Period for Authors fellow for West Germany, 1980; Portia Pittman fellow at Tuskegee Institute from National Endowment for the Humanities, 1982; John Simon Guggenheim fellow, 1983; Peter I. B. Lavan Younger Poets Award, Academy of American Poets, 1986; Pulitzer Prize in poetry, 1987, for *Thomas and Beulah;* General Electric Foundation Award for Younger Writers, 1987; Bellagio (Italy) residency, Rockefeller Foundation, 1988; Ohio Governor's Award, 1988; Mellon fellow, National Humanities Center, North Carolina, 1988-89; Ohioana Award, 1991, for *Grace Notes;* Literary Lion citation, New York Public Libraries, 1991; inducted Ohio Hall of Fame, 1991; Women of the Year Award, Glamour Magazine, 1993; NAACP Great American Artist Award, 1993; Harvard University Phi Beta Kappa poetry award, 1993; U.S. Poet Laureate, 1994-1995; Distinguished Achievement medal, Miami University Alumni Association, 1994; Renaissance Forum Award for leadership in the literary arts, Folger Shakespeare Library, 1994; Carl Sandburg Award, International Platform Association, 1994; honorary literary doctorates: Miami Univeristy, 1988, Knox College, 1989, Tuskegee University, 1994, University of Miami, 1994, Washington University, St. Louis, 1994, Case Western Reserve Univeristy, 1994, University of Akron, 1994, Arizona Atate University, 1995, Boston College, 1995, Dartmouth College, 1995.

*WRITINGS:*

*Ten Poems* (chapbook), Penumbra Press, 1977.
*The Only Dark Spot in the Sky* (poetry chapbook), Porch Publications, 1980.
*The Yellow House on the Corner* (poems), Carnegie-Mellon University Press, 1980.
*Mandolin* (poetry chapbook), Ohio Review, 1982.
*Museum* (poems), Carnegie-Mellon University Press, 1983.
*Fifth Sunday* (short stories), Callaloo Fiction Series, 1985.
*Thomas and Beulah* (poems), Carnegie-Mellon University Press, 1986.
*The Other Side of the House* (poems), photographs by Tamarra Kaida, Pyracantha Press, 1988.
*Grace Notes* (poems), Norton (New York City), 1989.

*Through the Ivory Gate* (novel), Pantheon Books (New York City), 1992.

*Selected Poems,* Pantheon, 1993.

*Lady Freedom among Us,* (poem; read on the occasion of the return of the statue "Freedom" to the Capitol, October 23, 1993; limited edition), Janus Press (West Burke, VT), 1993.

*The Darker Face of the Earth: A Verse Play in Fourteen Scenes,* Story Line Press, 1994.

*Stepping Out: The Poet in the World* (recorded lecture; also see below), Library of Congress (Washington, DC), 1994.

*A Handful of Inwardness: The World in the Poet* (recorded lecture; also see below), Library of Congress, 1994.

*Mother Love: Poems,* Norton, 1995.

(Author of foreword) *Multicultural Voices: Literature from the United States,* ScottForesman (Glenview), 1995.

*The Poet's World* (lectures; contains *Stepping Out: The Poet in the World* and *A Handful of Inwardness: The World in the Poet*) Library of Congress (Washington, DC), 1995.

Also author of *The 1979 Aquatic Plant Quarantine Project.* Work represented in anthologies. Contributor of poems, stories, and essays to magazines, including *Agni Review, Antaeus, Georgia Review, Nation,* and *Poetry.* Member of editorial board, *National Forum,* 1984—; poetry editor, *Callaloo,* 1986—; advisory editor, *Gettysburg Review,* 1987—, and *TriQuarterly,* 1988—.

SIDELIGHTS: Award-winning writer Rita Dove, former U.S. Poet Laureate, has been described as a quiet leader, a poet who does not avoid race issues, but does not make them her central focus. As Dove herself explains in the *Washington Post:* "Obviously, as a black woman, I am concerned with race. . . . But certainly not every poem of mine mentions the fact of being black. They are poems about humanity, and sometimes humanity happens to be black. I cannot run from, I won't run from any kind of truth." As the first black poet laureate, Dove notes that, though it has less personal significance for her, "it is significant in terms of the message it sends about the diversity of our culture and our literature."

Born in Akron, Ohio, in 1952, Dove was a National Merit Scholar at Miami University in Ohio, after which she received a Fulbright Fellowship to attend the University of Tubingen and then completed an M.F.A. at the Iowa Writers' Workshop. Although Dove published two chapbooks of poetry in 1977 and

1980, she made her formal literary debut in 1980 with the poetry collection *The Yellow House on the Corner,* which received praise for its sense of history combined with individual detail. Dove's next volume, *Museum,* also received praise for its lyricism, its finely crafted use of language, and its detailed depiction of images drawn from Dove's travels in Europe. Alvin Aubert of *American Book Review,* however, faults the volume for an avoidance of personal issues and experiences, such as that of ethnicity. "I would like to know more about Rita Dove as a woman, including her ethnicity, and on her home ground," he asserts. Calvin Hernton of *Parnassus,* in contrast, praises the "universal" sensibility of the poems in *Museum,* which, he notes, "lack anything suggesting that they were written by a person of African, or African-American, artistic or cultural heritage."

Dove turned to prose fiction with the publication of *Fifth Sunday,* a short story collection. Reviewers emphasized Dove's minimalist style and her interest in what a critic for *Southern Humanities Review* called "the fable-like aspects of middle class life." While considered promising, the volume generally received mixed reviews, with many critics finding the quality and detail of the writing uneven.

Dove is best known for her book of poems *Thomas and Beulah,* which garnered her the 1987 Pulitzer Prize in poetry. The poems in *Thomas and Beulah* are loosely based on the lives of Dove's maternal grandparents, and are arranged in two sequences: one devoted to Thomas, born in 1900 in Wartrace, Tennessee, and the other to Beulah, born in 1904 in Rockmart, Georgia. *Thomas and Beulah* is viewed as a departure from Dove's earlier works in both its accessibility and its chronological sequence that has, to use Dove's words, "the kind of sweep of a novel." On the book's cover is a snapshot of the author's grandparents, and *New York Review of Books* contributor Helen Vendler observes that "though the photograph, and the chronology of the lives of Thomas and Beulah appended to the sequence, might lead one to suspect that Dove is a poet of simple realism, this is far from the case. Dove has learned . . . how to make a biographical fact the buried base of an imagined edifice."

In the *Washington Post,* Dove describes the poems this way: "The poems are about industrialization, discrimination sometimes—and sometimes not—love and babies—everything. It's not a dramatic story— nothing absolutely tragic happened in my grandparents' life. . . . But I think these are the people who often are ignored and lost." Peter Stitt expresses a similar view in the *Georgia Review:* "The very absence of high drama may be what makes the poems so touching—these are ordinary people with ordinary struggles, successes, and failures." He concludes: "There is a powerful sense of community, residing both in a family and in a place, lying at the heart of this book, and it is this that provides a locus to the poems. Rita Dove has taken a significant step forward in each of her three books of poems; she must be recognized as among the best young poets in the country today."

The poems in *Grace Notes,* Dove's fourth book, are largely autobiographical. Alfred Corn remarks in *Poetry* that "glimpses offered in this collection of middle-class Black life have spark and freshness to them inasmuch as this social category hasn't had poetic coverage up to now." In *Parnassus,* Helen Vendler describes Dove's poems as "rarely without drama," adding, "I admire Dove's persistent probes into ordinary language of the black proletariat." Jan Clausen notes in *The Women's Review of Books* that Dove's "images are elegant mechanisms for capturing moods and moments which defy analysis or translation." In the *Washington Post Book World,* A. L. Nielsen finds that the poems "abound in the unforgettable details of family character" and adds that Dove "is one of those rare poets who approach common experience with the same sincerity with which the objectivist poets of an earlier generation approached the things of our world."

A later work, the novel *Through the Ivory Gate,* tells the story of Virginia King, a gifted young black woman who takes a position as artist in residence at an elementary school in her hometown of Akron, Ohio. The story alternates between past and present as Virginia's return stirs up strong, sometimes painful memories of her childhood. Barbara Hoffert observes in the *Library Journal* that the "images are indelible, the emotions always heartfelt and fresh," and in the *New York Times Book Review,* Geoff Ryman notes: "*Through the Ivory Gate* is mature in its telling of little stories—Virginia's recollections of life with a troupe of puppeteers, of visiting the rubber factory where her father worked, of neighborhood boys daubing a house so that it looked as if it had measles." He concludes: "The book aims to present the richness of a life and its connections to family and friends, culture, place, seasons, and self. In this it succeeds."

In 1993 Dove published *Selected Poems,* which contains three of Dove's previously published volumes:

*The Yellow House on the Corner, Museum,* and *Thomas and Beulah.* Reviewing the collection for *The Women's Review of Books,* Akasha (Gloria) Hull remarks, "In the guise of poet, [Dove] becomes many types of women and men, and takes us readers into their consciousness, helping us to feel whatever it is we all share that makes those journeys possible." In recognition of her achievements as a poet, Dove was appointed to the prestigious post of United States Poet Laureate, a position she held from 1994 to 1995.

Dove explores yet another genre with her first full-length play, *The Darker Face of the Earth..* "[T]here's no reason to subscribe authors to particular genres," comments Dove in *Black American Literature*; "I'm a writer, and I write in the form that most suits what I want to say." Depicting the events that ensue when a wealthy white woman named Amalia gives birth to slave's child, *The Darker Face of the Earth* imbues the theme of slavery with the high drama as well as the murderous elements reminiscent of classical Greek drama. Hull, again writing for *The Women's Review of Books,* comments: "[*The Darker Face of the Earth*] transfers the oedipal myth of patricide and maternal incest to antebellum South Carolina, and though we can guess the end from the very beginning, we read with continuing interest, sustained by Dove's poetic dialogue."

While Dove's forays into fiction and drama have been well-received, some critics, such as Helen Vendler in *The New Yorker,* comment that Dove is "primarily a poet" because her greatest concern is language itself. Dove returned to writing poetry with her most recent volume, *Mother Love.* Dedicated to Dove's daughter Aviva, the volume takes its unifying structure from the Greek mother-daughter myth of Demeter and Persephone. Vendler praises Dove's unsentimental portrayal of motherhood, emphasizing her often wry and sometimes startling tone. "Dove brings into close focus the pained relation between mothers and daughters," notes Vendler. "Dove's handling of the variety of voices and styles woven through the book shows a wonderful control of register and music," affirms Sarah Maguire in *Times Literary Supplement.*

*BIOGRAPHICAL/CRITICAL SOURCES:*

*BOOKS*

*Contemporary Authors Autobiography Series,* Volume 19, Gale (Detroit), 1994.
*Contemporary Literary Criticism,* Gale, Volume 50, 1988, Volume 81, 1994.

*Dictionary of Literary Biography,* Volume 120: *American Poets since World War II,* Third Series, Gale, 1992.

*Poetry Criticism,* Volume 6, Gale, 1993.

Vendler, Helen Hennessy, *The Given and the Made: Strategies of Poetic Redefinition,* Harvard Univeristy Press (Cambridge), 1995.

*PERIODICALS*

*American Book Review,* July, 1985.

*American Poetry Review,* January, 1982, 36.

*American Visions,* April-May, 1994, p. 33.

*Belles Lettres,* winter 1993-94, pp. 38-41.

*Black American Literature Forum,* fall, 1986, pp. 227-40.

*Booklist,* February 1, 1981, p. 743; August, 1983; March 15, 1986, p. 1057.

*Callaloo,* winter, 1986; spring, 1991.

*Detroit Free Press,* July 24, 1993, pp. 5A, 7A.

*Georgia Review,* summer, 1984; winter, 1986.

*Kliatt,* March, 1994, p. 25.

*Library Journal,* August, 1992; November 15, 1993, p. 81; March 1, 1994, p. 88.

*Michigan Quarterly Review,* spring, 1987, pp. 428-38.

*New Yorker,* May 15, 1995.

*New York Review of Books,* October 23, 1986.

*New York Times Book Review,* October 11, 1992.

*North American Review,* March, 1986.

*Parnassus: Poetry in Review,* spring, 1985; summer, 1985; fall, 1985; winter, 1985; Volume 16, number 2, 1991.

*Poetry,* October, 1984; October, 1990, pp. 37-9.

*Publishers Weekly,* August 3, 1992; January 31, 1994, p. 83.

*Southern Humanities Review,* winter, 1988, p. 87.

*Times Literary Supplement,* February 18, 1994; November 17, 1995, p. 29.

*USA Weekend,* March 25-27, 1994, p. 22.

*Virginia Quarterly Review,* spring, 1988, pp. 262-76.

*Washington Post,* April 17, 1987; May 19, 1993.

*Washington Post Book World,* April 8, 1990, p. 4; July 30, 1995, p. 8.

*Women's Review of Books,* July, 1990, pp. 12-13; May, 1994, p. 6.*

\*    \*    \*

## DREWNOWSKI, Jan  1908-

*PERSONAL:* Surname is pronounced "Drev-*nov*-ski"; born January 30, 1908, in Wilno, Poland; son of Jozef (a farmer and manager) and Helena (Plawska) Drewnowski; married Jadwiga Brzozowski, December 27, 1947; children: Adam, Zofia. *Ethnicity:* "Polish." *Education:* Attended London School of Economics and Political Science, London, 1933-35; Szkola Glowna Handlowa (also known as Warsaw School of Economics), Warsaw, Poland, Dr.Econ.Sc., 1936. *Religion:* Roman Catholic.

*ADDRESSES: Home*—81 Harvest Bank Rd., West Wickham, Kent BR4 9DP, England.

*CAREER:* Warsaw School of Economics, Warsaw, Poland, professor of economics, 1946-61; University of Ghana, Legon, professor of economics, 1961-64; United Nations Research Institute for Social Development, Geneva, Switzerland, program director, 1964-69; Institute of Social Studies, The Hague, Netherlands, professor of economics, 1969-79. Central Planning Office of Poland, divisional director, 1946-48; member of State Economic Planning Commission and Economic Council of Poland, 1957-61; consultant to World Health Organization and United Nations Development Program. Helped to organize and direct Congress of Polish Culture in London, England, 1985. *Military service:* Polish Army, 1939 and 1945; became second lieutenant.

*MEMBER:* Polskie Towarzystwo Ekonomiczne, British National Association for Soviet and East European Studies, Royal Economic Society, Royal Institute of International Affairs, American Economic Association.

*AWARDS, HONORS:* D.H.C., Warsaw School of Economics, 1994.

*WRITINGS:*

*Proba ogolnej teorii gospodarki planowej* (title means "An Attempt at a General Theory of a Planned Economy"), [Warsaw, Poland], 1938.

(Translator into Polish) David Ricardo, *The Principles of Political Economy and Taxation,* PWN (Warsaw), 1957.

(Contributor) W. A. Leeman, editor, *Market Socialism and Central Planning,* Houghton (Boston, MA), 1963.

*On Measuring and Planning the Quality of Life,* Mouton, 1974.

*O mysl polityczna* (title means "Toward Political Thinking"), Odnova (London, England), 1976.

*Wladza i opozycja* (title means "Authority and Opposition"), Veritas (London), 1979.

(Editor and contributor) *Crisis in the East European Economy,* St. Martin's (New York City), 1982.

(Editor and contributor) *Polska 1983* (title means "Poland 1983"), Polska Fundacja Kulturalna (London), 1984.

(Editor and contributor) *Samorzutne procesy rozkladu systemow typu sowieckiego* (title means "Self-Generating Deterioration Processes in Soviet-Type Systems"), PUNO (London), 1989.

*Rozklad i upadek sowietyzmu w Polsce* (title means "Decline and Fall of the Soviet System in Poland"), Norbertinum (Lublin, Poland), 1991.

Contributor to periodicals, including *Journal of Political Economy.*

*WORK IN PROGRESS:* A volume of essays on social indicators and the quality of life, in English.

*SIDELIGHTS:* Jan Drewnowski told *CA:* "My work and writings refer to two fields which may seem far apart, yet in fact are meaningfully linked by a common element—namely the concern for human welfare. The first covers the theory of centrally planned economies, their shortcomings and attempts at reforms, comparing the merits of various economic systems and explaining the decline of Soviet-type systems with special attention to economic and political problems of Poland. The second one is the elaboration of social indicators and their application to the measurement of levels of living, of the quality of life, and of the quality of society itself."

*BIOGRAPHICAL/CRITICAL SOURCES:*

PERIODICALS

*Times Literary Supplement,* September 16, 1983.

\*      \*      \*

**DREXLER, Rosalyn 1926-**
    **(Julia Sorel)**

*PERSONAL:* Born November 25, 1926, in New York; married Sherman Drexler, 1946; children: one daughter, one son.

*ADDRESSES: Home*—131 Greene St., New York, NY 10012. *Agent*—Georges Borchardt, 136 East 57th St., New York, NY 10022 (literary); Helen Harvey Asso-

ciates, 410 West 24th St., New York, NY 10011 (drama).

*CAREER:* Playwright, novelist, and painter. Taught at Writer's Workshop, University of Iowa, 1976-77; taught art at University of Colorado. Has held one woman art shows at galleries in New York City, Boston, and Provincetown, RI; her work has been included in group shows at Martha-Jackson, Pace Gallery, Washington Gallery of Modern Art, Guggenheim Museum, and Whitney Museum.

*MEMBER:* New Dramatists, New York Theatre Strategy, Dramatists Guild, PEN, Actors Studio.

*AWARDS, HONORS:* Obie Award from *Village Voice,* 1964, for *Home Movies,* 1979, and 1985; MacDowell fellowship, 1965; Rockefeller grant, 1965, 1968, and 1974; humor prize from *Paris Review,* 1966, for short story, "Dear"; Guggenheim fellowship, 1970-71; Emmy Award for writing excellence from Academy of Television Arts & Sciences, 1974, for *The Lily Show.*

*WRITINGS:*

NOVELS

*I Am the Beautiful Stranger,* Grossman (New York City), 1965.

*One or Another,* Dutton (New York City), 1970.

*To Smithereens,* New American Library (New York City), 1972, published as *Submissions of a Lady Wrestler,* Mayflower (London), 1976.

*The Cosmopolitan Girl,* M. Evans (New York City), 1974.

*Starborn: The Story of Jenni Love,* Simon & Schuster (New York City), 1979.

*Tomorrow Is Sometimes Temporary When Tomorrow Rolls Around,* Simon & Schuster, 1979.

*Bad Guy,* Dutton, 1982.

*Art Does (Not) Exist,* Northwestern University Press (Evanston), 1996.

*Dear,* Applause (New York City), 1997.

UNDER PSEUDONYM JULIA SOREL

*Dawn: Portrait of a Teenage Runaway,* Ballantine (New York City), 1976.

*Alex: Portrait of a Teenage Prostitute,* Ballantine, 1977.

*Rocky,* Ballantine, 1977.

*See How She Runs,* Ballantine, 1978.

*PLAYS*

*The Line of Least Existence and Other Plays,* introduction by Richard Gilman, (includes *Home Movies* [produced in New York City at Judson Poet's Theatre, 1964], *Hot Buttered Roll* [produced in New York City at New Dramatists Committee, 1966], *The Investigation* [produced in Boston at Theatre Co. of Boston; first produced in New York City at New Dramatists Committee, 1966], *The Bed Was Full* [produced at New Dramatists Committee, 1967], *The Line of Least Existence* [produced at Judson Poets' Theatre, March 15, 1968], and *Softly, and Consider the Nearness* [produced in New York City at St. Luke's Church, 1969]), Random House (New York City), 1967.

(With others) *Collision Course* (twelve plays; includes *Skywriting* by Drexler; produced together in New York City at Cafe au Go Go, May 8, 1968), Random House, 1968.

*The Investigation* [and] *Hot Buttered Roll,* Methuen (London), 1969.

*Was I Good?,* produced by New Dramatists Committee, 1972.

*The Ice Queen,* produced in Boston at The Proposition, 1973.

*She Who Was He,* produced in Richmond, Va., at Virginia Commonwealth University, 1974.

*Travesty Parade,* produced in Los Angeles at Center Theatre Group, 1974.

*Vulgar Lives,* produced in New York City at Theatre Strategy, 1979.

*The Writer's Opera,* produced in New York City at TNC, 1979.

*Graven Image,* produced in New York City, 1980.

*Starburn,* produced in New York City, 1983.

*Room 17-C,* produced in Omaha, 1983.

*Delicate Feelings,* produced in New York City, 1984.

*Transients Welcome,* Broadway Play Publishing (New York City), 1986.

*A Matter of Life and Death,* produced in New York City, 1986.

*What Do You Call It?,* produced in New York City, 1986.

*The Heart That Eats Itself,* produced in New York City, 1987.

*OTHER*

*Rosalyn Drexler: Intimate Emotions,* Grey Art Gallery, New York University (New York City), 1986.

Work represented in anthologies, including *The Bold New Women,* Fawcett, 1966; *New American Review,* New American Library, 1969; and *The Off-Off Broadway Book,* 1972. Author of screenplay *Naked Came the Stranger* and of television script *The Lily Show.* Contributor of articles and reviews to periodicals, including *Esquire, Village Voice,* and *Mademoiselle.* Film reviewer for *Vogue.*

*SIDELIGHTS:* Rosalyn Drexler's dramatic work is based in "a reaction against the intellectualism and pretentiousness which surrounded the theatre of the absurd," as Howard McNaughton writes in *Contemporary Dramatists.* Her own dramatic works display a verbal dexterity and a delight in lampooning the avant garde art world. "Few contemporary playwrights can equal her verbal playfulness, fearless spontaneity, and boundless irreverence," Michael Smith writes. "Few in fact, share her devotion to pure writing, preferring their language functional, meaningful, or psychologically 'real.'" Jack Kroll comments: "Drexler presents the spectacle of a playwright with a brilliant gift, not only for language, but for making language work on many levels with the ease and excitement of a Cossack riding his horse everywhere but in the saddle." Drexler's novels are humorous slapstick romps which critics have compared to both Kafka and the Marx Brothers.

The play *The Line of Least Existence,* which Kroll finds to be "about the total dissonance that occurs whenever living creatures find themselves in any sort of relationship," was deemed by him to be evidence of Drexler's "sweet shrewdness that seems to be talking straight to the most hidden part of you. She has the great and necessary gift of fashioning a new, total innocence out of the total corruption that she clearly sees. With lots of laughs." McNaughton notes in *The Line of Least Existence* "an utterly unpretentious playfulness, in which words are discovered and traded just for their phatic values."

Drexler's play *Hot Buttered Roll* features an aging billionaire, a callgirl hired to entertain him, and a female bodyguard. "The play's central image," McNaughton admits, "is never clearly stated, but seems to be that of (gendered) man as a sort of transplant patient, his facilities being monitored externally, his needs being canvassed through a huge mail-order system." Benedict Nightingale praises how Drexler uses a preoccupation with "sterile hedonism and dead feelings" to create "arresting dramatic terms."

Speaking of Drexler's novel *One or Another,* Christopher Lehmann-Haupt in the *New York Times* writes: "Rosalyn Drexler may very well be the first Marx Sister." Lehmann-Haupt describes the novel as being filled with "so many sight, sound and word gags, so many sillinesses and surrealistic—not to mention little grinning obscenities—that the reader soon begins to flinch in anticipation of the next verbal skit and to bark with relieved laughter when it works." Kroll contends that Drexler belongs with Donald Barthelme and Thomas Pynchon as representatives of the "new literary voice." He explains: "The new literary voice comes from some odd and perilous psychic area still being charted, some basic metabolic flashpoint where the self struggles to convert its recurrent breakdowns into new holds on life and reality. . . . Drexler is . . . funny, scary, preternaturally aware she is at the exact center where the new sensibility is being put together cell by cell."

Drexler's exuberant style does not always earn critical acclaim. The novel *To Smithereens* fared less well with critics. Michael Wood praises the humor and intelligence of the novel and notes that the language "has confidence in its capacity to render precisely the perceptions it is supposed to render." But Anatole Broyard writes that Drexler "seems almost to strain for irrelevancy, to struggle through a strenuous willed-free association in search of a fashionable zaniness." A critic for the *Times Literary Supplement* finds that "the strength of Miss Drexler's writing is in the energy of her prose: every joke is cleancut. And yet she refuses to go inside, to go deeper into her characters' psyches. She has a natural eye and ear but her mistake is in assuming that the number of empty gaps, the things *not* said, will indicate, or evoke, the emptiness of the lives she has created."

Sara Blackburn assesses Drexler's work as a novelist: "She's an absolute original who can take all of the ingredients that usually characterize 'serious' fiction . . . and use them with inventiveness, playfulness, and even hilarity. Wonderfully, it works, and the result is admirable not only for its style and wit, but for its lack of pretense, for the respect it grants its reader in not straining beyond its materials, and for what it achieves; art which is also high entertainment."

*BIOGRAPHICAL/CRITICAL SOURCES:*

*BOOKS*

*Contemporary Dramatists,* 5th edition, St. James Press (Detroit), 1993.

*Contemporary Literary Criticism,* Gale (Detroit), Volume 2, 1974, Volume 6, 1976.
Drexler, Rosalyn, *Rosalyn Drexler: Intimate Emotions,* Grey Art Gallery, New York University, 1986.

*PERIODICALS*

*American Theatre,* December, 1993, p. 58.
*Books and Bookmen,* June, 1967.
*Book World,* March 19, 1972.
*Ms.,* July, 1975.
*Nation,* August 31, 1970.
*Newsweek,* April 1, 1968; February 9, 1970; June 1, 1970; March 10, 1975.
*New Statesman,* February 27, 1969.
*New York Review of Books,* August 10, 1972.
*New York Times,* June 5, 1970; February 21, 1972.
*New York Times Book Review,* June 28, 1970; March 30, 1975.
*Publishers Weekly,* February 12, 1996, p. 59.
*Times Literary Supplement,* September 14, 1973.
*Village Voice,* March 28, 1968.

\*     \*     \*

**DRIVING HAWK, Virginia**
**See SNEVE, Virginia Driving Hawk**

\*     \*     \*

**DUFFY, Maureen 1933-**
**(D. M. Cayer)**

*PERSONAL:* Born October 21, 1933, in Worthing, Sussex, England; daughter of Cahia Patrick Duffy and Grace Rose Wright. *Education:* King's College, London, B.A. (with honors), 1956. *Politics:* Socialist. *Religion:* None.

*ADDRESSES: Home*—18 Fabian Road, London SW6 7TZ, England. *Agent*—Jonathan Clowes, 22 Prince Albert Rd., London NW1, England.

*CAREER:* Novelist. Teacher of creative writing in England, 1951-53, 1956-60; has also taught adult classes in Amherst and London. Co-founder, Writers Action Group, 1972.

*MEMBER:* Writers Guild of Great Britain (deputy chair; joint chair, 1978-79), British Copyright Council (vice chair, 1980-86, chair, 1989—), Authors Lending and Copyright Society (chair, 1982-94), Copyright Licensing Agency (chair, 1986—), Beauty without Cruelty (vice president).

*AWARDS, HONORS:* City of London Festival Playwright's Award, 1962, for *The Lay-Off;* Arts Council of Great Britain bursary, 1963, 1966, 1975; Society of Authors travelling scholarship, 1976; fellow, Royal Society of Literature, 1985.

*WRITINGS:*

NOVELS

*That's How It Was,* Hutchinson (London), 1962, Dial (New York City), 1984.
*The Single Eye,* Hutchinson, 1964.
*The Microcosm,* Simon & Schuster (New York City), 1966.
*The Paradox Players,* Hutchinson, 1967, Simon & Schuster, 1968.
*Wounds,* Knopf (New York City), 1969.
*Love Child,* Knopf, 1971.
*All Heaven in a Rage,* Knopf, 1973, published as *I Want to Go to Moscow,* Hodder & Stoughton (London), 1973.
*Capital,* Cape (London), 1975, Braziller (New York City), 1976.
*Housespy,* Hamish Hamilton (London), 1978.
*Gor Saga,* Methuen (London), 1981, Viking (New York City), 1982.
(As D. M. Cayer) *Scarborough Fear,* Macdonald (London), 1982.
*Londoners: An Elegy,* Methuen, 1983.
*Change,* Methuen, 1987.
*Illuminations,* Flamingo (London), 1991.
*Occam's Razor,* Flamingo, 1993.

PLAYS

*The Lay-Off,* produced at the City of London Festival, 1961.
*The Silk Room,* produced in England at Watford Civic Theatre, 1966.
*Rites* (produced by the National Theatre Repertory Co. in London, 1969), Methuen, 1969.
*Solo, Olde Thyme,* produced in Cambridge, England, 1970.
*A Nightingale in Bloomsbury Square,* produced at Hampstead Theatre, 1974.

POETRY

*Lyrics for the Dog Hour,* Hutchinson, 1968.
*The Venus Touch,* Weidenfeld & Nicolson (London), 1971.
*Actaeon,* Sceptre Press (Rushden, Northamptonshire) 1973.
*Evesong,* Sapppho (London), 1975.
*Memorials of the Quick and the Dead,* Hamish Hamilton, 1979.
*Collected Poems,* Hamish Hamilton, 1985.

OTHER

(Translator) Domenico Rea, *A Blush of Shame,* Barrie & Rockliff (London), 1963.
*The Erotic World of Faery,* Hodder & Stoughton, 1972.
*The Passionate Shepherdess: Aphra Behn* (biography), J. Cape (London), 1977.
(Editor with Alan Brownjohn) *New Poetry* (anthology), Arts Council of Great Britain, 1977.
*Inherit the Earth* (social history), Hamish Hamilton, 1979.
*Men and Beasts: An Animal Rights Handbook,* Paladin, 1984.
(Editor and author of introduction) Aphra Behn, *Oroonoko and Other Stories,* Methuen, 1986.
*A Thousand Capricious Chances: A History of the Methuen List 1889-1989,* Methuen, 1989.
(Editor) Aphra Behn, *Five Plays,* Methuen, 1990.
*Henry Purcell,* Fourth Estate (London), 1994.

Fiction editor, *Critical Quarterly,* 1987.

*SIDELIGHTS:* A poet, playwright, novelist, and historian, writer Maureen Duffy reflects within her work the loneliness experienced by those living on the fringes of a judgmental and sometimes hostile "society"; her characters—lesbians, the homeless, political radicals, displaced intellectuals—are frustrated by aspirations unfulfilled and emotional, sexual, or other needs unmet. Novels such as *The Microcosm, All Heaven in a Rage,* and *Illuminations* exhibit inventive plots and deft characterization, while nonfiction works such as the 1972 Freudian literary study *The Erotic World of Faery* also speak to the author's creative talents. Duffy has been praised by critics for her ability to create vivid characters and evoke a sense of place. Commenting on the comparison by several British reviewers of her work with that of author Virginia Woolf, a critic for *Time* noted that "both have the knack of tuning the physical world precisely to the pitch of the characters' emotions. Miss Duffy has a special talent for describing landscape, seascape and weather."

Duffy's ability to handle description and develop characters is perhaps most apparent in her fourth novel, *The Paradox Players.* Taking place on a houseboat floating on the Thames during a winter in the 1960s, *The Paradox Players* details the voluntary isolation of the writer Sym. Thinking to abandon his "square" lifestyle, which includes a wife and child, Sym buys an old, forty-foot boat called "Mimosa" and attempts to keep it afloat while also endeavoring to "find a point to work from" in his writing. A critic for the *New Yorker* writes that "no one character in . . . [*The Paradox Players*] is outstanding, although each human being and each animal is impeccably drawn and treated with thorough understanding. As a study in gray, animated and given sad meaning by the slow movement of gray figures, gray weather, and fateful gray light, her book is a work of art."

Although praising the author's eye for detail, some reviewers were disturbed by what they perceived to be a lack of focus in Duffy's early work. Reviewing her 1969 novel, *Wounds,* for example, a critic for the *Times Literary Supplement* regretted the uncertainty he found in the "larger implications" of Duffy's fiction because she "handles detail so beautifully and can suggest what her characters see, imagine and remember with such precision and life." And a reading of the complex, fantasy-based *Love Child* caused another reviewer for the same periodical to remark of the 1971 work: "Duffy has created a novel of sparkling details and surfaces, yet its hollowness goes deeper than its theme. . . . Fairy tales are usually harsh, but this one has lost its edge through glossiness and a too obvious cunning." However, a *Washington Post Book World* critic disagreed, noting that the young but brilliant narrator's "epicenism"—her "snotty remarks"—becomes in fact "a most effective metaphor . . . [for] a cult of 'understanding' and ultra-permissiveness, a world whose emotional values have been eradicated by the intellect."

Duffy's 1973 novel *All Heaven in a Rage,* published in England as *I Want to Go to Moscow,* reflects one of the author's personal concerns: the proper treatment of animals. The novel's main character, an incarcerated felon named Jarvis Chuff, is sprung from prison by a group of anti-vivisectionist vegetarians who promise to give Chuff his freedom if he will help them free a number of animals from captivity. Calling the novel a "romp" on the order of writer P. G. Wodehouse, *New York Times Book Review* critic Paul

Theroux added that *All Heaven in a Rage* features a plot that "is at best only amusing and at worst quite preposterous." Maintaining that the work shows a lack of focus, Anatole Broyard added in the *New York Times* that Duffy's seventh novel contains "a topical message delivered without urgency, a romance that is well above average in its arbitrariness, a teetering between suspense fiction and morality tale, . . . an intermittent flaring up of fine writing. The book," Broyard concluded, "consistently refuses to settle on one level and stay there."

A scruffy, self-taught historian of the Dark Ages named Meepers is the protagonist of 1976's *Capital.* Odd in character, Meepers has determined to single-mindedly pursue proof that the Dark Ages were not a break in civilization in Britain after the departure of the occupying Roman legions; rather, he believes, London society survived and has progressed along a steady path since the end of the island's Roman occupation. When an article he writes fails to get publication, Meepers shadows the rejecting editor, a professor at Queen's College who serves in the novel as a representative of modern, "schooled" historical methodology. The knowledgeable but unschooled Meepers attends the professor's classes, and the two eventually meet; this meeting represents what Jan Miller deemed in the *Times Literary Supplement* as conflicting interpretations of "the nature of the historical imagination and its relation to the historian's needs and expectations." "Duffy is as much interested in language as in story," Valentine Cunningham commented in the *New Statesman.* "And *Capital*'s celebration of London doesn't just recollect the past but tries to recreate it in the styles of the past,. . . . The room Maureen Duffy's proceedings allows her for irony is immense, and opportunities for sly humour rarely go unexploited." Anatole Broyard agreed in the *New York Times.* "In brilliant bits of contrapuntal virtuosity, we see and hear Saxons, Romans, Elizabethans, Victorian pickpockets and whores, people in the blitz," Broyard wrote, adding that *Capital* "is a wonderful idea . . . . [that] is gratifyingly realized in its most appealing ramifications. Miss Duffy's prose style rises to each occasion."

*Londoners,* published in 1983, deals with the possibility that society is an amalgam of individuals living in close-quartered solitude rather than groupings based on familial relationships or sexual bonds. Duffy's protagonist, the writer Al, inhabits what *New Statesman* reviewer Angela McRobbie called "a gay underworld characterized less by fantasy and bravado than by anonymity, fleeting pleasure, timidity, fear and the search for comfort." *Londoners,* noted McRobbie, views non- mainstream sexual preference as "a burden, a sleight of hand of nature, a force which seeks solace in an environment where pain can be transformed into neither pleasure or anger." Noting that the book features dense prose and a narrative structure containing a number of "loose ends—glimpses of brown or ivory skin, fragments of 'colorful' conversation," Lorna Sage concluded in the London *Observer* that *Londoners* "suggests that it's not by pastoral myth-making about communities, but by acceptance of our crowded solitudes, that we make a possible society."

Duffy's 1991 novel, *Illuminations,* follows retired history lecturer Hetty Deardon's travels to newly reunified Germany, where she gains a lesbian lover, the political agitator Helge Eggesen. While in Germany, Hetty attempts to reconstruct the life and work of Tetta, an eighth-century British nun whom the historian sees as an alter ego of sorts. Drawing a parallel between Europe as it existed during the reign of Emperor Charlemagne during the Middle Ages and as it appears in the twentieth century—in a state of post-Cold War flux—Duffy "inclines to historical pastiche in the Anglo-Saxon chronicle style," noted Janet Barron in *New Statesman.* While maintaining that the subplot detailing the life of Tetta distracts from the novel overall, Barron added that *Illuminations* "has some wonderful passages of eroticism and warm affection, and it is a kindly and ultimately optimistic book." In her review for the *Times Literary Supplement,* Lorna Sage dubbed the novel "an elaborate piece of *bricolage";* writing that the mysticism underlying the plot is not reflected in the matter-of-fact prose style, Sage concluded that "*Illuminations* is both ingenious and frustrating, a rich and complicated frame for a blurred and hesitant picture."

Like *Illuminations* and *Capital,* 1993's *Occam's Razor* also moves back and forth along a historical timeline. Through the characters Pearse and Orazio, Duffy juxtaposes both the early- and late-twentieth-century histories of I.R.A. terrorism and the activities of the Italian mafia. Both Pearse, an Irishman, and the Italian Orazio, old men who now spend their days playing chess, inhabit their separate pasts more than they do their collective present. "Slowly the turbulent histories of the two old men unfold,. . . . Past and present violently collide," explained Mary Scott in *New Statesman & Society.* Comparing the novel's plot to a "gripping chess game," Shena Mackay wrote in the *Times Literary Supplement* that Duffy's "portraits of eccentric and ordinary people are masterly, and

*Occam's Razor*'s two old heroes, Orazio and Pearse, are plausible and touching men . . . impressive in their solidity and solidarity." Ruth Pavey likewise praised the novel in the London *Observer,* noting that the novel's "careful plotting . . . is not only ingenious and entertaining, it is also touching."

In addition to fictional work, Duffy has also written plays as well as works of poetry and nonfiction, including biographies of several creative individuals of the seventeenth century. *Henry Purcell,* a biography of the seventeenth-century British composer published in 1994, was praised for showing "tact and understanding in [Duffy's] consideration of the few events in his life we know about, or are almost certain we know about," by *Times Literary Supplement* critic Paul Griffiths. Praising her thoroughness, Griffiths deemed Duffy "a digger in the archives" who "characteristically ploughs her own furrow, and comes up with a good deal of new information."

Duffy's poetry and plays comprise a large portion of her early career as a writer. Her first work for the stage, 1962's *The Lay-Off,* coincided with her first novel, *That's How It Was,* and would be followed by two more plays before the end of the decade. As she told Leah Fritz in *Women's Review of Books,* her plays were "intended to make up for the dearth of strong theatrical roles available to women." Her nonfiction work *Henry Purcell* inspired a stage play, titled *The Masque of Henry Purcell,* which was performed in London in 1995. Duffy's work has also appeared on radio and television in Great Britain.

Beginning with 1968's *Lyrics for the Dog Hour,* Duffy has also gained recognition for her work as a poet. With such volumes as *Evesong* and *Memorials of the Quick and the Dead,* she composes verse that revolves around themes of love in its many facets. "Its passion imbues the bulk of her poetry," maintained *Contemporary Women Poets* essayist Geoff Sadler; "collections like *Lyrics for the Dog Hour, The Venus Touch,* and *Evesong* [are] almost totally given over to an expression of its strength, its violence, and its ultimate fulfillment." Within the career-spanning *Collected Poems* are revealed Duffy's roots in Great Britain's working class, wherein she was raised in relative poverty by a single mother battling tuberculosis. Citing the lines of the poem "Going like a Man" that read "I walk as working men walk, / a little stiff, weight thrown back on the heels, / . . . coat tails aswing, heavy with dust and age," Fritz opined that "The image of hopelessness Duffy evokes . . . is relieved by the hearty sense of humor which also marks her work and has undoubtedly been a saving grace in her life as well. . . . [She] seems to have wrested freedom for herself out of the most difficult of circumstances, to find challenge and reason for optimism even in the fact that she was forced at a very early age and in dire poverty to be, as she puts it, the "man of the family."

Citing Duffy's "passionate interest in history and in language," Shena Mackay commended the versatile author's oeuvre in the *Times Literary Supplement*. With numerous books to her credit that span the genres of history, literary criticism, poetry, and fiction, Duffy's later works, according to Mackay, "should consolidate her reputation as a writer, an imaginative poet of the city and someone who is committed to the cause of both human and animal rights." Sadler echoed such praise, noting of Duffy's poetry that "the variety of subjects covered, and the pure, intense clarity of her vision lift her work above the ordinary, giving to it the quality of a personal testament."

## BIOGRAPHICAL/CRITICAL SOURCES:

### BOOKS

*Contemporary Literary Criticism,* Volume 37, Gale (Detroit), 1986.
*Contemporary Women Poets,* St. James Press (Detroit), 1997.
*Dictionary of Literary Biography,* Volume 14: *British Novelists since 1960,* Gale, 1983.
*Feminist Writers,* St. James Press, 1996.

### PERIODICALS

*Books and Bookmen,* October, 1967; November, 1967.
*Bookseller,* March 27, 1971.
*London Review of Books,* December 22, 1983; January 18, 1984, p. 15.
*Nation,* October 7, 1968, p. 346.
*New Statesman & Society,* July 4, 1969, pp. 21-22; April 30, 1971, p. 604; September 9, 1975, p. 342; November 20, 1981, p. 22; October 21, 1983, p. 24; May 17, 1991, pp. 36-37; July 16, 1993, p. 40.
*New Yorker,* October 5, 1968, pp. 181-82.
*New York Times,* August 17, 1969; April 19, 1973; March 19, 1976.
*New York Times Book Review,* March 6, 1966; August 11, 1968, pp. 20-21; September 23, 1968;

August 17, 1969, p. 32; May 27, 1973, pp. 16-17.
*Observer,* September 17, 1967; October 16, 1983, p. 33; June 27, 1993, p. 62; April 30, 1995, p. 20.
*Publishers Weekly,* May 13, 1996, p. 70.
*Spectator,* October 13, 1967; May 1, 1971; October 29, 1983, p. 28.
*Time,* September 13, 1968.
*Times Literary Supplement,* May 26, 1966; September 28, 1967; July 3, 1969; July 5, 1971, p. 521; November 10, 1972; June 8, 1973; September 19, 1975; April 7, 1978; November 6, 1981; October 7, 1983; May 15, 1987, p. 515; August 11, 1989; May 17, 1991, p. 18; June 25, 1993, p. 22; September 15, 1995, pp. 3-4.
*Washington Post Book World,* August 31, 1969, p. 8; April 11, 1971, p. 2; May 23, 1976.
*Women's Review of Books,* November, 1987, pp. 24-25.*

\*    \*    \*

## DUTTON, Geoffrey (Piers Henry) 1922-

*PERSONAL:* Born August 2, 1922, in Anlaby, Kapunda, South Australia; son of Henry Hampden (one of South Australia's pioneer colonizers and pastoralists) and Emily (Martin) Dutton; married Ninette Trott (an enameler), July 31, 1944 (divorced, 1985); married Robin Lucas (a writer), April 4, 1985; children: (first marriage) Francis, Teresa, Sam. *Education:* Attended University of Adelaide, 1940-41; Magdalen College, Oxford, B.A., 1949.

*ADDRESSES: Agent*—Curtis Brown Ltd., P.O. Box 19, Paddington, New South Wales 2021, Australia.

*CAREER:* Writer in Europe and Australia, 1949-54; University of Adelaide, Adelaide, South Australia, Australia, lecturer, 1954-58, senior lecturer in English, 1958-62; Penguin Books Ltd., Melbourne, Victoria, Australia, editor, 1961-65; writer and farmer, 1962—; Sun Books Pty. Ltd. (paperback publishers), Melbourne, co-founder with Brian Stonier, 1965, editorial director, 1965-80. Co-founder, *Australian Letters,* Adelaide, 1957, *Literary Quarterly,* 1957, and *Australian Book Review* (fortnightly), Kensington Park, 1962; University of Leeds, Commonwealth Fellow, lecturer in Australian Literature, 1960; Kansas State University, Manhattan, visiting professor, 1962. Member, Australian Council for the Arts, 1968-70, Commonwealth Literary Fund Advisory Board, 1972-73, Australian Literature Board, 1973-78, and Australian National University. Has appeared on television. *Military service:* Royal Australian Air Force, pilot, 1941-45; became flight lieutenant.

*AWARDS, HONORS:* Grace Leven prize, 1959; officer, Order of Australia, 1976; L. C. Weickhardt Award, 1978, F. A. W. Christopher Brennan award for poetry, 1994.

*WRITINGS:*

*POEMS*

*Nightflight and Sunrise,* Reed & Harris (Melbourne), 1944.
*Antipodes in Shoes,* Edwards & Shaw (Sydney), 1958.
*Flowers and Fury,* F. W. Cheshire (Melbourne), 1962.
*On My Island: Poems for Children,* F. W. Cheshire, 1967.
*Poems Soft and Loud,* F. W. Cheshire, 1967.
*Findings and Keepings: Selected Poems, 1940-70,* Australian Letters (Adelaide), 1970.
*New Poems to 1972,* Australian Letters, 1972.
*A Body of Words,* Edwards & Shaw, 1977.
*Selective Affinities,* Angus & Robertson (Sydney), 1985.
*New and Selected Poems,* Angus & Robertson, 1993.

Also author of *Night Fishing,* Australian Letters.

*NOVELS*

*The Mortal and the Marble,* Chapman & Hall (London), 1950.
*Andy,* Collins (Sydney), 1968.
*Tamara,* Collins, 1970.
*Queen Emma of the South Seas,* St. Martin's (New York City), 1976.
*The Eye-Opener,* University of Queensland Press (St. Lucia, Australia), 1982.
*Flying Low,* University of Queensland Press, 1992.

*EDITOR*

*The Literature of Australia,* Penguin (Melbourne), 1964, revised edition, 1976.
*Modern Australian Writing,* Fontana (London), 1966.
*Australia and the Monarchy: A Symposium,* Sun Books (Melbourne), 1966.

(With Max Harris) *The Vital Decade: Ten Years of Australian Art and Letters,* Sun Books, 1968.
(With Harris) *Australia's Censorship Crisis,* Sun Books, 1970.
(With Harris) *Sir Henry Bjelke: Don Baby, and Friends,* Sun Books, 1971.
*The Australian Uppercrust Book,* Sun Books, 1971.
*Australian Verse from 1805: A Continuum,* Rigby (Adelaide), 1975.
*Republican Australia?,* Sun Books, 1977.
*The Illustrated Treasury of Australian Stories,* Nelson (Melbourne), 1986.
*The Australian Bedside Book: A Selection of Writings from the Australian Literary Supplement,* Macmillan (Melbourne), 1987.
*The Poetic Language: An Anthology of Great Poems of the English Speaking World,* Macmillan, 1987.
(With Dennis Haskell) Kenneth Slessor, *Collected Poems,* Angus & Robertson, 1994.

Also, editor, *Australian Letters,* 1957, *Verse in Australia* (annual anthology of poetry), 1958-61, Australian Writers and Their Work Series, 1962-66, Australian Poetry 1962, 1962, *Bulletin Literary Supplement,* Sydney, 1980-85, *The Australian Literary Quarterly,* Sydney, 1984-88, and *Australian* (literary magazine).

*TRANSLATOR*

(With Igor Mezhakoff-Koriakin) Yevgeny Evtushenko, *The Bratsk Station and Other Poems,* Sun Books, 1966, Doubleday (New York City), 1967.
(With Mezhakoff-Koriakin) Bella Akhmadulina, *Fever and Other Poems,* Sun Books, 1968, Morrow (New York City), 1969.
Robert Ivanovich Rozhdestvenskii, *A Poem on Various Points of View and Other Poems,* Sun Books, 1968.
Evtushenko, *Bratsk Station, The City of Yes and the City of No, and Other Poems,* Sun Books, 1970.
(With Mezhakoff-Koriakin) Andre Andreevich Voznesenskii, *Little Woods: Recent Poems,* Sun Books, 1972.
(With Eleanor Jacka) Evtuschenko, *Kazan University and Other New Poems,* Sun Books, 1973.

*JUVENILE*

*Tisi and the Yabby,* Collins (Sydney & London), 1965.
*Seal Bay,* Collins, 1966.
*Tisi and the Pageant,* Rigby, 1968.
*The Prowler,* Collins (Sydney), 1982.

*OTHER*

*A Long Way South* (travel), Chapman & Hall, 1953.

*Africa in Black and White* (travel), Chapman & Hall, 1956.

*States of the Union* (travel), Chapman & Hall, 1958.

*Founder of a City: The Life of William Light* (historical biography), F. W. Cheshire, 1960.

*Patrick White* (critical study), Landsdowne Press (Melbourne), 1961, 4th edition, Oxford University Press (London & New York City), 1971.

*Walt Whitman* (critical study), Grove (New York City), 1961.

(Author of introduction and commentaries) Samuel Thomas Gill, *Paintings of S. T. Gill* (art criticism), Rigby (Adelaide), 1962.

*Russell Drysdale* (art criticism), Thames & Hudson (London), 1964, revised edition, 1969, revised edition published as *Russell Drysdale: A Biographical and Critical Study,* Angus & Robertson (Sydney and London), 1981.

*The Hero as Murderer: The Life of Edward John Eyre, Australian Explorer and Governor of Jamaica, 1815-1901* (historical biography), F. W. Cheshire, 1967, published as *Edward John Eyre: The Hero as Murderer,* Penguin (London), 1977.

*Australia's Last Explorer: Ernest Giles* (historical biography), Barnes & Noble (New York City), 1970.

*Australia since the Camera: From Federation to War 1901-1914,* F. W. Cheshire, 1971, published as *From Federation to War,* Longman Cheshire (Melbourne), 1972.

*Swimming Free: On and below the Surfaces of Lake, River, and Sea,* St. Martin's, 1972.

*White on Black: The Australian Aborigine Portrayed in Art* (art criticism), Macmillan (Melbourne), 1974.

*A Taste of History: Geoffrey Dutton's South Australia,* Rigby, 1978.

*Patterns of Australia* (photographs by Harri Peccinotti), Macmillan, 1980.

*The Wedge-Tailed Eagle,* Macmillan, 1980. *The Australian Heroes,* Angus & Robertson (Sydney), 1981.

*Impressions of Singapore* (photographs by Peccinotti), Macmillan (London & Melbourne), 1981.

*S.T. Gill's Australia,* Macmillan (Melbourne), 1981.

*Country Life in Old Australia,* O'Neill (South Yarra, Victoria), 1982.

*In Search of Edward John Eyre,* Macmillan, 1982.

*Snow on the Saltbush: The Australian Literary Experience* (art and literary history), Viking (Ringwood, Victoria), 1984.

*The Australian Collection: Australia's Greatest Books,* Angus & Robertson, 1985.

*The Squatters: An Illustrated History of Australia's Pastoral Pioneers,* O'Neill, 1985.

*Sun, Sea, Surf, and Sand: The Myth of the Beach,* Oxford University Press (Melbourne), 1985.

*The Beach,* Oxford University Press, 1985.

*The Innovators: The Sydney Alternatives in the Rise of Modern Art, Literature, and Ideas* (art and literary history), Macmillan, 1986.

*The Book of Australian Islands,* Macmillan, 1986.

*Arthur Streeton, 1867-1943: A Biographical Sketch,* Oz (Brisbane), 1987. *Famous Australian Art: Fredrick McCubbin,* Oz, 1987.

*Kenneth Slessor* (biography), Ashton Scholastic (Gosford, New South Wales), 1987, Viking (Ringwood, Victoria & New York City), 1991.

*Tom Roberts, 1856-1931: A Biographical Sketch,* Oz, 1987, Mallard Press (Moorebank, NSW), 1989.

*Henry Lawson,* Ashton Scholastic, 1988.

*Waterways of Sydney: A Sketchbook,* Dent (Melbourne), 1988.

(Compiler and author of introduction and notes) Havelock Ellis, *Kanga Creek: Havelock Ellis in Australia,* Picador (Sydney), 1989.

*Images of Melbourne: A Sketchbook* (illustrated by Kay Stewart), Houghton Mifflin (Ferntree Gully, Victoria), 1989.

*Russel Drysdale, 1912-1981: A Biographical Sketch,* Mallard Press, 1989.

(Selector and author of introduction) *Artists' Portraits,* National Library of Australia (Canberra), 1992.

*Country Childhoods* (autobiographical), University of Queensland Press, 1992.

*Out in the Open: An Autobiography,* University of Queensland Press, 1994.

*A Rare Bird: Penguin Books in Australia, 1946-96,* Penguin (Ringwood, Victoria & New York City), 1996.

Manuscript collection held at Australian National Library, Canberra.

*SIDELIGHTS:* "Geoffrey Dutton is one of Australia's most versatile writers: poet, biographer, novelist, short story writer, editor, travel writer, literary and art critic and essayist. . . . Dutton's six novels to date reflect this versatility and a cosmopolitanism that stems from his upbringing . . . his education . . . his wide travels, about which he has written extensively; and, especially, his several sojourns in Russia. . . . Perhaps Dutton's main achievement as a novelist is that with his erudite, polished, and uninhibited writing (exemplified also in his many short stories) he has brought new dimensions of sophistication to modern Australian fiction," Clement Semmler described in *Contemporary Novelists.*

Discussing Dutton's novels, Semmler wrote: "Dutton's first and the least considerable of his novels [is] *The Mortal and the Marble.*. . . But he was on sure ground with his next novel, *Andy,* a lively, picaresque tale. . . . that explores the sheer beauty and exhilaration of flying. . . . If the novel occasionally borders on farce it is nevertheless a shrewdly observed and often disturbing account of the excesses and follies of warfare. . . . For his third novel, *Tamara,* Dutton turned to his Russian travels and experiences, and his appreciation of Russian poetry. . . . This is a novel about poets by a poet: in its simplicity, its lyricism, its rich yet economical evocations of Georgia and the Georgians, it is, in the truest sense, a deeply romantic story. Dutton's sensitive evocations of Russian mores and idiosyncrasies emerge in many fine passages. . . . *Queen Emma of the South Seas.* . . . fashion[s] a colorful slice of history into an exotic and remarkable novel, [and] deftly handl[es] the technique of recording Emma's story through narratives by herself [and others]. . . . Finally, Dutton has extended his versatility to that of satirist in *The Eye-Opener.* . . . it is at once a clever comic creation and a shrewd examination of life in Australia."

Dutton's poetry, according to Bruce Beaver in *Contemporary Poets,* is "remarkable for its intrinsic light-heartedness . . . [and] has tended to be underrated by most critics, while a growing audience of appreciative readers testifies to its inherent qualities." Beaver specified: "Despite his lightheartedness, the poet is capable of extended lyrical meditations of a uniquely beautiful nature. . . . His comments in verse on the Vietnamese War show him to be capable of clear-headed and compellingly written poems of protest, but it is in the longer autobiographical poem ["Abandoned Airstrip, Northern Territory"] imbued with lyrical insights and quiet humor that this fine poet's best work is found."

*BIOGRAPHICAL/CRITICAL SOURCES:*

*BOOKS*

*Contemporary Novelists,* sixth edition, St. James Press (Detroit), 1996.
*Contemporary Poets,* sixth edition, St. James Press, 1996.

*PERIODICALS*

*Best Sellers,* September, 1978.
*Books & Bookmen,* June, 1966; March, 1970.
*New Statesman,* January 12, 1968.
*Observer,* February 1, 1970; December 19, 1976.
*Spectator,* June 3, 1966; January 17, 1970.
*Times Literary Supplement,* January 4, 1968; October 2, 1970; August 16, 1974; November 12, 1976.*

# E

**EAGLETON, Terence (Francis) 1943-**
**(Terry Eagleton)**

*PERSONAL:* Born February 22, 1943, in Salford, England. *Education:* Trinity College, Cambridge, B.A., 1964; Jesus College, Cambridge, Ph.D., 1968. *Avocational interests:* Poetry, theatre, Irish music.

*ADDRESSES: Home and office*—St. Catherine's College, Oxford University, Oxford, 0X1 3UJ England.

*CAREER:* Cambridge University, Jesus College, Cambridge, England, fellow, 1964-69; Oxford University, Wadham College, Oxford, England, fellow and tutor in poetry, 1969-89, lecturer in critical theory, 1989-92; Oxford University, St. Catherine's College, Thomas Warton professor of English and Literature, 1992—. Selector for Poetry Book Society, 1969-71; judge, Sinclair Fiction Prize, 1985.

*MEMBER:* Society for the Study of Narrative Literature (president).

*AWARDS, HONORS:* D. Litt., Salford, 1993.

*WRITINGS:*

UNDER NAME TERRY EAGLETON

(Editor) *Directions: Pointers for the Post-Conciliar Church* (essays), Sheed, 1968.
(Editor with Brian Wicker) *From Culture to Revolution: The Slant Symposium, 1967* (essays), Sheed, 1968.
*The Body as Language: Outline of a "New Left" Theology,* Sheed, 1970.

*Exiles and Emigres: Studies in Modern Literature,* Schocken, 1970.
*Myths of Power: A Marxist Study of the Brontes,* Barnes & Noble, 1975.
*Marxism and Literary Criticism,* University of California Press, 1976.
*Criticism and Ideology: A Study in Marxist Literary Theory,* Verso, 1976, Schocken, 1978.
*Walter Benjamin; or, Towards a Revolutionary Criticism,* Schocken, 1981.
*The Rape of Clarissa: Writing, Sexuality and Class Struggle in Samuel Richardson,* University of Minnesota Press, 1982.
*Literary Theory: An Introduction,* University of Minnesota Press, 1983, second edition, Blackwell (Cambridge, MA), 1996.
*The Function of Criticism: From the Spectator to Post-Structuralism,* Verso, 1984.
(Editor) Laura Brown, *Alexander Pope,* Basil Blackwell, 1985.
(Editor) James Kavanaugh, *Emily Bronte,* Basil Blackwell, 1985.
(Editor) Stan Smith, *W. H. Auden,* Basil Blackwell, 1985.
*William Shakespeare,* Basil Blackwell, 1986.
*Against the Grain: Selected Essays, 1975-1985,* Verso, 1986.
*Saints and Scholars* (novel), Verso, 1987.
*Myths of Power: A Marxist Study of the Brontes,* second edition, Macmillan, 1988.
(Editor) *Raymond Williams: A Critical Reader,* Northeastern University Press, 1989.
*The Ideology of the Aesthetics,* Blackwell (Oxford, UK), 1990.
(With Fredric Jameson and Edward W. Said) *Nationalism, Colonialism, and Literature,* University of Minnesota Press (Minneapolis), 1990.

*Saint Oscar* (play), first produced in London, 1990.

*Ideology: An Introduction,* Verso (London), 1991.

*Wittgenstein: The Terry Eagleton Script, the Derek Jarman Film,* BFI (London), 1993.

*Heathcliff and the Great Hunger: Studies in Irish Culture,* Verso (London), 1995.

*The Illusions of Postmodernism,* Blackwell (Cambridge, MA), 1996.

(Editor) *Marxist Literary Theory: A Reader,* Blackwell (Cambridge, MA), 1996.

OTHER

*The New Left Church* (essays), Helicon, 1966.

*Shakespeare and Society: Critical Studies in Shakespearean Drama,* Schocken, 1967.

Contributor to *Slant, Times Literary Supplement, Stand, Commonweal,* and other periodicals. Poetry reviewer, *Stand,* 1968—. Delivered lecture "The Crisis of Contemporary Culture" before the University of Oxford, 1992, published by Clarendon Press (Oxford), 1993.

*SIDELIGHTS:* Terry Eagleton is "widely regarded as the foremost young Marxist literary thinker in England," writes a *Washington Post Book World* contributor. Concerned with the ideologies found in literature, Eagleton examines the role of Marxism in discerning these ideologies. "Always alert to the underside or reversible lining of any intellectual model, Eagleton tracks the cross-currents and strategies of literary criticism with a uniquely agile understanding," states Chris Baldick in the *Times Literary Supplement.* Eagleton's books have not only clarified arcane critical theories of literature for the novice but have also posed provocative questions to the specialists. His polemical expositions in literary theory have generated a spirited critical response, and even those opposed to his stance speak readily about his "accessible" and persuasive prose. "Unlike too many other theorists, Marxist or otherwise," says Steven G. Kellman in *Modern Fiction Studies,* "Eagleton writes with grace, clarity, and force." In *Thought,* Walter Kendrick points also to Eagleton's "sprightly style and. . . lively sense of humor, rare commodities in his field."

Eagleton's brief but concise *Marxism and Literary Criticism* discusses the author of a work as producer, as well as the relationships between literature and history, form and content, and the writer and commitment. As George Woodcock observes in the *Sewanee Review,* Eagleton perceives Marxist criticism to be "part of a larger body of theoretical analysis that aims to understand *ideologies*—the ideas, values and feelings by which men experience their societies at various times. And certain of those ideas, values and feelings are available to us only in literature." Woodcock praises Eagleton's clear and vigorous writing, adding that he is "brisk and specific, and tells us a great deal. . . about the more important continental European Marxist critics, their books, and their theories." Peter Conrad, however, sees a need for more textual examples in *Marxism and Literary Criticism,* and he refers to it in the *Spectator* as "a case of theory talking about itself." Michael Wilding similarly finds the book "academic and self-referential," suggesting in *Modern Language Review* that Eagleton approaches Marxist literary criticism "as a subject, rather than as an instrument for revealing other subjects." Nevertheless, noting that the book avoids "pseudo-philosophical jargon," R. Berg-Pan maintains in *World Literature Today* that Eagleton "introduces the neophyte to a very complex set of problems with ease and great skill." Moreover, Woodcock says that Eagleton is "one of the few Marxist theoreticians willing to see Marxism itself not as a self-sufficient doctrine but as part of a spectrum of related doctrines."

According to Jonathan Culler in *Poetics Today,* Eagleton's academic best-seller, *Literary Theory: An Introduction,* is a "vigorous articulation of what has become a common theme today in the realm of critical theory: the call for criticism and for literary theory to assume a relationship to history, both by confronting the question of their insertion in social and political history and by taking account of their own history." As John Lucas notes in a *Times Literary Supplement* review of *Against the Grain: Selected Essays, 1975-1985,* Eagleton is "one of a number of critics and theorists on the left who have necessarily drawn attention to improper or at least ideologically-based privileging of certain authors and texts." In *Literary Theory,* Eagleton begins with the observation that "literary criticism is by nature a political act, even (or especially) when it eschews direct political engagement," writes Kendrick, and in this volume, Eagleton connects each school of literary study with the ideology of its particular time and place.

*Literary Theory* is a "remarkable and important book," writes Charles Sugnet in *American Book Review,* adding that it "does what a good introduction should do—it synthesizes tendencies already in the air and makes them widely accessible in clear prose." Culler believes it to be Eagleton's "best work: provocative, efficient, and for the most part well-informed." Praising the stylistic grace and precision with which Eagleton distills complex theories of literature, critics especially address the book's provocative premise. "A Marxist with wit, Terry Eagleton is magisterial in his deployment of a wide range of ideas, but rarely dispassionate. . . ," says Kellman. "After patient scrutiny of the writings of numerous contemporary critics, Eagleton confesses that he has not come to praise theory but to bury it."

"Under cover of writing a primer on current literary criticism," writes Sugnet, ". . .Eagleton dissolves his own field of inquiry by arguing that there is no such thing as 'literature,' and therefore no 'literary theory.'" As Lennard J. Davis explains in *Nation,* "Literature and the cult of the literary are ideologies that exalt high cultural artifacts like novels, poems and plays over other forms of writing and representation." Eagleton would prefer to replace literature, as it is presently being studied, with the more encompassing discipline of rhetoric as it was practiced from Greek and Roman times until the eighteenth century. "Literature would be, of course, only a branch of this study," summarizes Kendrick. "It would share the field with polemics, journalism, and even the labels on beer cans. . . . A rhetorical approach to literary texts would at least acknowledge one important fact about them that all current critical methodologies tend to ignore: that they are modes of persuasion, designed to elicit some response, even if only complacency, in their readers. That response, like the text which provokes it, must be political in the widest sense."

David Forgacs questions Eagleton's proposal of subsuming literature into a wider study and wonders in *Poetics Today,* "Who is going to supply the methodologies and the courses, and with what claims to expertise in the field." Among other criticisms, Denis Donoghue in the *New York Review of Books* faults Eagleton for failing to adequately define "history" or how it "proves invulnerable to the irony he so relentlessly directs against other ultimate categories." But in *South Atlantic Quarterly,* Wallace Jackson thinks that Eagleton "de-mythologizes the high-cultural pretensions of literary study in the university, recognizes that in fact such study underwrites the practices of state capitalism, and effectively nullifies whatever radical power literature may have as an instrument of social criticism and social change." Kendrick notes in the *New York Times Book Review* that while *Literary Theory* is intended for a nonacademic audience, "academics will be unable to ignore it. . . . Eagleton's expositions render even the most jargon-ridden of

contemporary theories accessible to the ordinary educated person, and the questions posed by *Literary Theory* will have to be answered, either by the theoreticians themselves or by those who validate them by accepting their authority." Kellman, who believes that Eagleton successfully assimilates "a motley crowd of structuralists, feminists, hermeneuticians, psychoanalysts, and deconstructionists to his argument that there are no innocent readings, that every literary experience is shaped by ideology," recommends that it "ought to be read with the same blend of enthusiasm and wariness with which it was written, but it ought to be read by anyone concerned with contemporary theory."

Eagleton's *The Function of Criticism: From the Spectator to Post-Structuralism* augments *Literary Theory* in that it traces the history of English literary criticism "from its earliest recognizable appearance around the turn of the eighteenth century to its present institutionalized form," writes Kendrick in the *Voice Literary Supplement.* It is a "polemical history, not of criticism as such," observes Patrick Parrinder in the *London Review of Books,* "but of the 'critical institution' within which it acquired what Eagleton recognises as social significance." And David Montrose points out in the *New Statesman* that Eagleton "seeks to 'recall criticism to its traditional role'—engagement in cultural politics—from what he considers a position of crisis, where it is narrowly preoccupied with literary texts and estranged from social life through confinement to Academe and 'the literary industry.'" "But the heart of this book," says Christopher Norris in *British Book News,* "is clearly to be found in Eagleton's use of the 'public sphere' as a concept to articulate and clarify the relation between criticism and ideology."

Eagleton further articulates his theoretical positions in *Saints and Scholars,* a novel of ideas whose characters are philosopher Ludwig Wittgenstein, Irish revolutionary James Connolly, Leopold Bloom from James Joyce's *Ulysses,* and Nikolai Bakhtin, brother of famed Marxist literary critic Mikhail. Their fictitious conversations while gathered together in an Irish cottage during 1916 serve as a forum for Eagleton to debate the practical and theoretical limitations of thought and social action. Though noting that "facts blended with fiction make a difficult genre, and the connections between realism and surrealism are not always easily made," Roy Foster praises the novel in the *Times Literary Supplement* as "ingenious, erudite and entertaining." *Observer* contributor Maureen Freely commends Eagleton's courage to write such a book, described by Freely as "an experimental, non-bourgeois anti-novel" whose "*raison d'etre* is discourse, and the subject of the discourse is revolution."

Eagleton followed with *The Ideology of Aesthetics,* which, according to *Times Literary Supplement* reviewer Sebastian Gardner, "is Terry Eagleton's most substantial work to date, . . . a comprehensive engagement with the history of modern philosophical aesthetics." Eagleton's analysis considers the work of Immanuel Kant, G. W. F. Hegel, Friedrich Nietzsche, Walter Benjamin, Martin Heidegger, and Theodor Adorno, among other major philosophers and social theorists, in an attempt to further penetrate and reveal the interplay of social and political forces in the formation of aesthetic thought. While challenging conventional Marxist principles and the "libertarian pessimism" of post-structuralism, as Frank Kermode writes in the *London Review of Books,* "Eagleton states his own faith in a community purged of the imperialism of the bourgeois aesthetic—a community in which all will recognise that 'our shared material conditions bind us ineluctably together, and in doing so open up the possibilities of friendship and love.'" As Paul Tyndall concludes in *Canadian Literature,* "it seems safe to say that subsequent histories of modern aesthetic theory will have to begin with *The Ideology of Aesthetics.*"

With *Heathcliff and the Great Hunger: Studies in Irish Culture* Eagleton launched an assault on the perceived revisionism of Irish history that, in his view, denies the impact of the great potato famine and nineteenth century colonial politics on Victorian English literature and subsequent writers such as Oscar Wilde and W. B. Yeats. The book consists of a series of eight essays on Irish culture and society from the period of the famine, referred to by Eagleton as "the Irish Auschwitz," through the early decades of the twentieth century. Commenting on Eagleton's interpretation of Heathcliff, a character from Emily Bronte's *Wuthering Heights,* as an Irish famine victim, Andrew Hadfield writes in the *Times Literary Supplement,* "This is Eagleton at his best: lucid, original and witty, goading the reader to challenge his unmasking of the complacent assumptions we all, probably, share." Hadfield continues, "Elsewhere in the work, he explores a fundamental paradox: why was Ireland, the most backward nation in nineteenth-century Europe, able to produce some of the most avant-garde writing? Answer: mainland Britain was too wedded to an ideology of organic progress which allowed realism to flourish as a genre, whereas in

Ireland, traumatized by the famine, nature and culture were out of sympathy and no one dominant tradition emerged, rather, a whole range of genres flourished."

Citing Eagleton's greatest strength as "his tenacity in pursuing a contradiction through its every shifting guise and permutation," Baldick adds: "Of all living Marxist critics, he is most emphatically the dialectician. . . and it is the resulting stress upon contradiction which ensures that his historical placings of writers highlight rather than erase their particular features." Norris suggests, however, that at times the polemics are too forceful and reduce his opponents to "so many shadowy figures in a dance-like routine of ingenious argumentation." But understanding the book to concern "all that is wrong with professionalism," Gary Wihl indicates in *South Atlantic Quarterly* that it "enables us to keep in mind its overriding revolutionary point; it attempts to draw us out of our narrowly sanctifying view of literary history and reminds us of our predicament as critics." Baldick believes that in the "urgency and integrity of this view, Terry Eagleton has marked out a position which further discussions of the state of criticism will have to address if they are to take their historical bearings."

Norris concludes in *Southern Humanities Review* that "Eagleton is a stylist of great resource whose arguments derive much of their power from the presently embattled situation of literary theory." And Parrinder suggests that while "one does not go to Eagleton's works for true judgment, by and large, and it is hard to know what contribution he has made to the emancipation of the masses," he nonetheless maintains that "Eagleton remains one of the most spectacular orators in the park, and English criticism would be a good deal less entertaining without his pamphlets."

*BIOGRAPHICAL/CRITICAL SOURCES:*

*BOOKS*

*Contemporary Literary Criticism,* Volume 63, Gale (Detroit), 1991.

*PERIODICALS*

*American Book Review,* May-June, 1985.
*British Book News,* February, 1985.
*Canadian Literature,* autumn, 1992, p. 108.
*Commentary,* March, 1984.
*London Review of Books,* February 7, 1985; September 3, 1987, p. 19; April 5, 1990, p. 14.
*Modern Fiction Studies,* summer, 1984.

*Modern Language Review,* January, 1979; April, 1985.

*Nation,* December 24, 1983; January 21, 1984.

*New Republic,* November 10, 1986; June 20, 1994, p. 34; August 21, 1995, p. 42.

*New Statesman,* June 3, 1983; October 5, 1984; October 6, 1989, p. 42; June 21, 1991, p. 44; June 16, 1995, p. 37.

*New York Review of Books,* July 21, 1983; December 8, 1983; November 6, 1986.

*New York Times,* April 18, 1986.

*New York Times Book Review,* September 4, 1983; October 18, 1987; August 18, 1991, p. 14.

*Observer* (London), September 13, 1987; March 4, 1990, p. 64.

*Poetics Today,* Volume 5, number 1, 1984; Volume 5, number 2, 1985; Volume 7, number 1, 1986.

*Sewanee Review,* fall, 1978.

*South Atlantic Quarterly,* summer, 1985; spring, 1986.

*Southern Humanities Review,* summer, 1985.

*Spectator,* August 21, 1976.

*Thought,* December, 1984.

*Times Literary Supplement,* July 13, 1967; January 23, 1969; August 14, 1970; October 23, 1970; May 20, 1977; November 12, 1982; February 4, 1983; June 10, 1983; November 23, 1984; July 4, 1986; September 4, 1987, p. 947; March 30-April 5, 1990, p. 337; July 7, 1995, p. 24.

*Voice Literary Supplement,* June, 1983; March, 1985.

*Washington Post Book World,* October 2, 1983.

*World Literature Today,* winter, 1977.*

\* \* \*

**EAGLETON, Terry**
  **See EAGLETON, Terence (Francis)**

\* \* \*

**EDAR**
  **See ANTHONY, Edward**

\* \* \*

**EPERNAY, Mark**
  **See GALBRAITH, John Kenneth**

**ERICKSON, Steve 1950-**

*PERSONAL:* Born Stephen Michael Erickson, April 20, 1950, in Santa Monica, CA; son of Milton Ivan (a printer and photographer) and Joanna (a theater director; maiden name, DeGraff) Erickson. *Education:* University of California, Los Angeles, B.A., 1972, M.A., 1973.

*CAREER:* Freelance editor and writer in London, Paris, Rome, Venice, Amsterdam, and Los Angeles, 1973-86; arts editor, *Los Angeles Weekly,* 1989-91.

*AWARDS, HONORS:* Samuel Goldwyn Award for fiction from University of California, Los Angeles, 1972; fellowship from National Endowment for the Arts, 1987.

*WRITINGS:*

*Days between Stations,* Poseidon (New York City), 1985.

*Rubicon Beach,* Poseidon, 1986.

*Tours of the Black Clock,* Poseidon, 1989.

*Leap Year* (nonfiction), Poseidon, 1989.

*Arc d'X,* Poseidon, 1993.

*American Nomad* (nonfiction), Holt (New York City), 1997.

Author of column "Guerrilla Pop" and contributing editor for *Los Angeles Reader,* 1982-85; film columnist for *California Magazine,* 1989—. Contributor to *Esquire, Los Angeles Times, Los Angeles Herald Examiner, Chicago Reader, Free Paper* (Washington, DC), *East Bay Express* (Berkeley, CA), *L.A. Weekly, PSA Magazine,* and *Rolling Stone.*

*SIDELIGHTS:* Readers of Steve Erickson's novels frequently find themselves lost in time. Like a disjointed dream sequence, historical characters appear in the present as prisoners of an enduring fate while those born in the here and now can find themselves just as suddenly displaced to a past they never knew they had. Erickson's work stretches the limit of the novel form in its attempt to incorporate the qualities of other media, such as film and art.

In his first novel, *Days between Stations,* futuristic lovers Lauren and Michel travel the post-apocalyptic world in search of the latter's pre-amnesic identity. A reel of silent film recorded by his Parisian grandfather is the only clue Michel possesses of his past; his bleak European journey, in which he finds Paris plunged into primeval darkness, reveals little about his past or his current situation. Writing in the *New York Times Book Review,* Frederika Randall observed, "There is a healthy dose of cinematic surrealism in . . . Erickson's moody first novel," its narrative unfolding "with the magical ease of a movie that floats back and forth in space and time." *Los Angles Times* critic Carolyn See also noted that *Days between Stations* "demands concentration and a very close reading [as] characters change names at the drop of a hat . . . incidents repeat themselves, [and] . . . diction shifts."

See further stated that Erickson's interest in "the essential duality of things, image versus reality, past versus present, dreams versus wakening," is plotted logically, but that the book defies a "symbolic exegesis or a plot summary." Deeming the book a serious, risk-taking endeavor, See predicted a distinguished future for the author.

Discussing Erickson's second novel, *Rubicon Beach,* in the *New York Times Book Review,* Paul Auster observed that the author has again "shunned the strictures of realistic fiction." Describing the work as "part science fiction, part surrealist love story, [and] part political fable," Auster noted that its three distinct parts often intersect and ultimately converge. "Characters vanish from one world and reappear in another . . . names and identities slide" and "imagery is far more important . . . than plot." Noting the "Jungian tonality" of the book's events, Auster suggested that *Rubicon Beach* "is in some sense intended as a warning to those who lack the courage to cross the Rubicon of their imaginations." While the reviewer acknowledged "moments when [Erickson's] energies outstrip his ideas," Auster nonetheless judged the work a success. "One does not think twice about following him down the labyrinthine paths of his bizarre and striking tale." The critic praised the author's prose as well, concluding that Erickson "is a young writer to be watched."

*Tours of the Black Clock,* Erickson's third novel, blends future with past and history with fantasy. The plot concerns Banning Jainlight, who becomes Adolf Hitler's pornographer. Erickson "effectively creates a brooding, self- enclosed world of driven sensuality," remarked Tom Clark in *Los Angeles Times Book Review,* adding that the novelist's "effort to engage history on a cosmic scale . . . is affected negatively by a serious case of overreaching." Kathy Acker, however, praised Erickson in her *New York Times Book Review* article, saying that the novel "is more than a story: it becomes a meditation on evil, on 'the

most evil man in the world.' Since the narrator of this meditation is himself a murderer, hardly free of the taint of evil, the *absolute* quality of evil is being questioned." Acker pronounced the novel "a gorgeous argument against a culture of absolutes and for a way of life based on questioning."

In *Arc d'X,* Erickson expounds on a favorite theme: the lost ideals and dreams of America. The book takes place during Thomas Jefferson's diplomatic sojourn in Paris, though it is Jefferson's slave and reputed lover, Sally Hemings, who is the focus of attention. In Paris, Sally is a free woman, but love proves more important to her than freedom, and she accompanies Jefferson back to America and remains his slave.

The plot shifts from eighteenth-century France to an apocalyptic city ravaged by religious extremists, then again to Berlin in 1999 where Jefferson reappears to kill the novelist, who is a character in his own work of fiction. "Characters, objects, and events jump across time and space," commented Walt Bode of the *Voice Literary Supplement.* While Bode found some of Erickson's writing confusing, he added that "there is luminous and sensual prose about bodies, the weather and revolution; there are breathtaking leaps of the imagination, but too often obliqueness seems to be the goal." For Michiko Kakutani of the *New York Times, Arc d'X* has "moments of genuine brilliance," including "haunting descriptions of pre-Revolutionary Paris and post-unification Berlin and imaginative depictions of a futuristic city-state perched precariously between ruin and redemption."

In his interview with Erickson for *HotWired,* John Alderman called the author's sixth novel, *Amnesiascope,* "bleakly funny," particularly in its "nightmarish" depiction of a futuristic Los Angeles. "*Amnesiascope* seems to describe not just an architecture of the imagination but an urban sprawl of the imagination," Alderman commented. While the book is clearly a work of science fiction, it is also a semi-autobiographical account that contains scenes that Alderman noted "are embarrassing to read" because they are so intensely personal.

The protagonist of *Amnesiascope* is, as Erickson once was, a film critic for an alternative local newspaper, a position that leaves the former novelist artistically and financially dissatisfied. S, as the character is called, roams a divided Los Angeles, encircled by rings of fire to separate it from the rest of the country, to visit the city's underside of prostitution, drugs and strip joints. Alvin Lu of the *San Francisco Bay*

*Guardian* found the book "dazzling" and "mind-blowing," but mentioned what he considers a recurrent fault of the author's work: "at times his articulation is impatient, unwilling to work out the details; ultimately the brilliance becomes blinding."

Kakutani of the *New York Times* complained that *Amnesiascope*'s series of "peculiar events" never become a coherent story. These events are S and his girlfriend's plans to kidnap a stripper, a review of an imagined movie that somehow everyone in Los Angeles thinks is real, and S's efforts to track down the woman of his dreams after spotting her on a billboard. Kakutani wrote that these events "feel like the sort of drug-induced riffs college students like to spin out for one another late at night." Despite this criticism, Kakutani observed that *Amnesiascope* reveals "passages far more emotionally intimate—and in some cases, far more engaging—than anything he has written before."

In the category of nonfiction, Erickson produced two books recounting his experiences covering two presidential elections. But, as G. Michael O'Toole warned in his *West Coast Review of Books* article, no one should expect from Erickson "your standard 'Making-of-the-President'-type fare." The first of these works, *Leap Year,* finds the author on the road with the 1988 campaign. "He was in Atlanta for the Democratic convention, but mainly bagged the event by television in his hotel room," noted *Los Angeles Times Book Review* writer Charles Bowden. "He was in New Orleans for the Republican Convention, but split before it began in order to take in the music and bars of Austin, Tex. . . .He was periodically hounded by Sen. Albert Gore and his wife Tipper—they kept showing up either wasted or demented as Erickson hallucinated his way across the landscape of the United States."

The author, Bowden continued, uses the election and the candidates "as props in his discussion of what's gone wrong with this country. And his novelist's feel for the language is a relief from either the dead newspaper prose or poli-sci jargon that lurks in election books." In devoting an entire article to Erickson's works, *Village Voice* writer Greg Tate singled out *Leap Year* as the author's "most melancholic work, a *Mr. Smith Goes to Washington* for the '90s."

An unexpected character in *Leap Year* materializes in the ghost of Sally Hemings—the same historical figure who also appeared in the novel *Arc d'X*. Hemings' voice, according to Tate, "is symbolic of all those

locked out of Jefferson's vision of democracy by his ofay will to power." Hemings is portrayed searching for Jefferson and locating him during the election year 1988, living in a Hopi Reservation.

Journalist and critic David Yepsen, for one, found elements of *Leap Year* rough going; as he told *Washington Post Book World,* what with the ghost of Hemings and the author's side trips "the book gets so confused. . .[that] the political junkie looking for some counterculture insights will find [*Leap Year*] to be too much work." Still, Yepsen acknowledged, Erickson "makes some worthwhile points about all the rot of the 1988 campaign that aren't often made by those of us who covered it."

With *American Nomad,* Erickson covered the 1996 Oval Office race; this time he was on assignment for *Rolling Stone* magazine. "For a while [Erickson carried] off the pretense of being a more or less normal campaign correspondent," remarked Barbara Ehrenbach. But he was subsequently fired by publisher Jann Wenner for what was perceived as increasingly bizarre dispatches.

No matter, as Ehrenbach continued in her *New York Times Book Review* piece. In *American Nomad* the author retains "his eagle eye for the ambient madness, rage and yearning of the Presidential election season. He understands the cheap redemption white America sought in Colin Powell and how, when another high-profile African-American was acquitted of murder, white America decided to blow off redemption and stick with resentment and guilt."

At his best, the critic added, Erickson "functions like some high-tech psycho-medical sensing devise inserted into the ravaged soul of American politics." Less impressed was *Washington Post Book World*'s Jonathan Yardley, who deemed *American Nomad* a book "overloaded with sweeping, cosmic generalizations almost none of which is capable of holding more than a couple ounces of water." While he cited the author for areas of "clear, straight thinking," Yardley also pointed to passages like "America had [become] a country of nomads, who wandered the hallways of the American soul not sure if they were in a funhouse or a cancer ward" as evidence that Erickson "simply cannot resist the formulation of glib oversimplifications that quickly reach the level of *reductio ad absurdum.*"

To a *Kirkus Review* critic, on the other hand, *American Nomad* "operates brilliantly as both a political chronicle and a zany memoir." And in Ehrenbach's view, Erickson "establishes one thing in this beautiful, crazed and weirdly patriotic book: [in firing Erickson] Jann Wenner made a big mistake."

*BIOGRAPHICAL/CRITICAL SOURCES:*

BOOKS

*Contemporary Literary Criticism,* Volume 64, Gale (Detroit), 1991.

PERIODICALS

*Atlanta Journal and Constitution,* March 5, 1989.
*Boston Globe,* December 30, 1988.
*HotWired,* April 18-20, 1997.
*Kirkus Reviews,* March 15, 1997, p. 434.
*L.A. Weekly,* May 17, 1985; August 29, 1986; January 13, 1989.
*Los Angeles Herald Examiner,* August 20, 1985.
*Los Angeles Times,* May 20, 1985; September 8, 1986.
*Los Angeles Times Book Review,* January 29, 1989; October 15, 1989, pp. 3-7.
*New Statesman & Society,* April 8, 1994, p. 40.
*New York Times,* January 7, 1989; April 6, 1993, p. C17; June 11, 1996, p. B2.
*New York Times Book Review,* May 12, 1985; September 21, 1986; March 5, 1989; May 2, 1993, p. 9; June 6, 1993, p. 37; June 8, 1997, p. 6.
*Philadelphia Inquirer,* August 8, 1985; October 26, 1986.
*Publishers Weekly,* March 22, 1993, p. 59; March 25, 1996, p. 60.
*San Francisco Bay Guardian,* May 29, 1996.
*San Francisco Chronicle,* March 19, 1989.
*Village Voice,* October 7, 1986; April 3, 1990, p. 75.
*Voice Literary Supplement,* May, 1993, p. 5.
*Wall Street Journal,* March 13, 1989.
*Washington Post Book World,* October 8, 1989; May 9, 1993, p. 4; May 4, 1997.
*West Coast Review of Books,* November-December, 1989, p. 41.

\*    \*    \*

**ESQUIVEL, Laura 1951(?)-**

*PERSONAL:* Born c. 1951, in Mexico; daughter of Julio Caesar Esquivel (a telegraph operator) and Josephina Esquivel; married Alfonso Arau (a film director); children: Sandra. *Education:* Attended Escuela Normal de Maestros, Mexico. *Avocational interests:* Cooking.

*ADDRESSES: Home*—Mexico City, Mexico. *Agent*—c/o Crown Publishing Group, 201 E. 50th St., New York, NY 10022.

*CAREER:* Novelist and screenwriter; writer and director for children's theater. Worked as a teacher for eight years.

*AWARDS, HONORS:* Ariel Award nomination for best screenplay, Mexican Academy of Motion Pictures, Arts and Sciences, for *Chido One.*

*WRITINGS:*

NOVELS

*Como agua para chocolate: novela de entregas mensuales con recetas, amores, y remedios caseros,* Editorial Planeta Mexicana, 1989, translation by Carol Christensen and Thomas Christensen published as *Like Water for Chocolate: A Novel in Monthly Installments, with Recipes, Romances, and Home Remedies* (also see below), Doubleday (New York City), 1991.
*La ley del amor,* Plaza and Janes (Barcelona), 1995, translation by Margaret Sayers Peden published as *The Law of Love,* Crown Publishers (New York City), 1996.

Esquivel's work has been translated into numerous languages.

SCREENPLAYS

*Como agua para chocolate* (based on Esquivel's novel of the same title), Instituto Mexicano de Cinematografia, 1992, released in the United States as *Like Water for Chocolate,* Miramax, 1992.

Also author of *Chido One,* released in 1985, and *Little Ocean Star,* a children's feature, released in 1994.

*WORK IN PROGRESS: Regina,* a screenplay of a film about a female Christ, based on Antonio Belasco Pina's novel of the same name.

*SIDELIGHTS:* Mexican author Laura Esquivel, who gained international recognition with her first novel, *Como agua para chocolate (Like Water for Choco-*

*late*), began her literary career as a screenwriter. Working in partnership with her husband, the Mexican director Alfonso Arau, Esquivel wrote the screenplay for a 1985 Mexican release *Chido One,* which Arau directed. The film's success prompted the couple to continue their collaboration, and Arau became the director when Esquivel adapted *Like Water for Chocolate* for the screen. Both the novel and movie have been enormously popular. A number one best-seller in Mexico in 1990, the book has been translated into numerous languages, including an English version, which enjoyed a longstanding run on the *New York Times Book Review* best-seller list in 1993. The movie, according to *Publishers Weekly,* has reported record-breaking attendance, to become one of the highest-grossing foreign films of the decade. Employing in this work the brand of magic realism that Gabriel Garcia Marquez popularized, Esquivel blends culinary knowledge, sensuality, and alchemy with fables and cultural lore to capture what *Washington Post* reviewer Mary Batts Estrada calls "the secrets of love and life as revealed by the kitchen."

*Like Water for Chocolate* is the story of Tita, the youngest of three daughters born to Mama Elena, the tyrannical owner of the De La Garza ranch. Tita is a victim of tradition: as the youngest daughter in a Mexican family she is obliged to remain unmarried and to care for her mother. Experiencing pain and frustration as she watches Pedro, the man she loves, marry her older sister Rosaura, Tita faces the added burden of having to bake the wedding cake. But because she was born in the kitchen and knows a great deal about food and its powers, Tita is able to bake her profound sense of sorrow into the cake and make the wedding guests ill. "From this point," as James Polk remarks in the *Tribune Books,* "food, sex and magic are wondrously interwoven." For the remainder of the novel, Tita uses her special culinary talents to provoke strange reactions in Mama Elena, Rosaura, Tita's other sister, Gertrudis, and many others.

Food has played a significant role in Esquivel's life since she was a child. Remembering her early cooking experiences and the aromas of foods cooked in her grandmother's house, she told Molly O'Neill of the *New York Times* that "I watch cooking change the cook, just as it transforms the food. . . . Food can change anything." For Esquivel, cooking is a reminder of the alchemy between concrete and abstract forces. Esquivel's novel of cooking and magic has

been well-received by critics. Writing in the *Los Angeles Times Book Review,* Karen Stabiner remarks that Esquivel's novel "is a wondrous, romantic tale, fueled by mystery and superstition, as well as by the recipes that introduce each chapter." James Polk, in the *Chicago Tribune,* writes that "*Like Water for Chocolate* (a Mexican colloquialism meaning, roughly, agitated or excited) is an inventive and mischievous romp—part cookbook, part novel."

Esquivel followed with *The Law of Love,* a highly imaginative novel that features reincarnation, cosmic retribution, and attests to the primacy of love. The story opens with the sixteenth century Spanish conquest of Tenochtitlan, the future site of Mexico City, and the rape of an Aztec princess atop a temple. Many centuries later the principal actors of this earlier drama reappear as astro-analyst Azucena, her missing soul mate Rodrigo, and planetary presidential candidate Isabel in a confrontation that finally breaks the cycle of vengeance and hatred with love and forgiveness. The text is accompanied by a compact disc with music and cartoon illustrations. This "multimedia event," as described by Lilian Pizzichini in the *Times Literary Supplement,* incorporates elements of magic realism, science fiction, and New Age philosophy. "The result," writes *Library Journal* reviewer Barbara Hoffert, "is at once wildly inventive and slightly silly, energetic and cliched." Pizzichini concludes, "Esquivel dresses her ancient story in a collision of literary styles that confirm her wit and ingenuity. She sets herself a mission to explore the redemptive powers of love and art and displays boundless enthusiasm for parody."

*BIOGRAPHICAL/CRITICAL SOURCES:*

*PERIODICALS*

*Kirkus Reviews,* July 1, 1996, p. 917.
*Library Journal,* January, 1996, p. 81; July, 1996, p. 156.
*Los Angeles Times Book Review,* November 1, 1992, p. 6.
*Nation,* June 14, 1993, p. 846.
*New Republic,* March 1, 1993, pp. 24-25.
*New Yorker,* June 27, 1994, p. 80.
*New York Times,* March 31, 1993, pp. C1, C8.
*Time,* April 5, 1993, pp. 62-63.
*Times Literary Supplement,* October 18, 1996, p. 23.
*Tribune Books* (Chicago), October 18, 1992, p. 8.
*Washington Post,* September 25, 1992, p. B2.
*World Press Review,* February, 1996, p. 43.*

**ESZTERHAS, Joe**
  **See ESZTERHAS, Joseph A.**


*       *       *


**ESZTERHAS, Joseph A.**
  (Joe Eszterhas)

*PERSONAL:* Born in November 23, 1944, in Csak-anydoroszlo, Hungary; immigrated to United States, naturalized citizen; married first wife Geri (a police reporter; divorced); married Naomi Baka; children (first marriage): Steven, Susie.

*ADDRESSES: Agent*—Rosalie Swedlin, Creative Artists Agency, 1888 Century Park E., Suite 1400, Los Angeles, CA 90067.

*CAREER:* Reporter for *Cleveland Plain Dealer,* Cleveland, OH, in early 1970s; *Rolling Stone,* San Francisco, CA, 1971-74, began as staff writer, became senior editor; screenwriter, novelist, and freelance journalist, 1974—.

*WRITINGS:*

NONFICTION UNDER NAME JOE ESZTERHAS

(With Michael D. Roberts) *Thirteen Seconds: Confrontation at Kent State,* Dodd (New York City), 1970.
*Charlie Simpson's Apocalypse,* Random House (New York City), 1974.
*Nark!: A Tale of Terror,* Straight Arrow (San Francisco), 1974.

SCREENPLAYS UNDER NAME JOE ESZTERHAS

(With Sylvester Stallone) *F.I.S.T.* (also see below), United Artists, 1978.
*Flashdance,* Paramount, 1983.
*Jagged Edge,* Columbia Pictures, 1985.
*Hearts of Fire,* Lorimar, 1986.
*Big Shots,* Twentieth Century-Fox, 1987.
*Betrayed,* Metro-Goldwyn-Mayer/United Artists, 1988.
*Checking Out,* Handmade Films, 1989.
*Music Box,* Tri-Star Pictures, 1990.
*Basic Instinct,* Tri-Star, 1992.
*Sliver,* Paramount, 1993.
(With Leslie Bohem and Randy Feldman) *Nowhere to Run,* Columbia, 1993.

*Showgirls,* MGM, 1995.
*Jade,* Paramount, 1995.

OTHER

*F.I.S.T.,* (novel; based on screenplay of the same title), Dell (New York), 1978.

Contributor of articles to newspapers and magazines.

*SIDELIGHTS:* Joe Eszterhas has achieved widespread fame as a top Hollywood screenwriter, whose successes include such films as *Flashdance* and *Basic Instinct.* Yet before he conquered the movie world, Eszterhas had already established himself as a cutting-edge, radical journalist. He wrote his first book, *Thirteen Seconds: Confrontation at Kent State,* with Michael D. Roberts in 1970. *Thirteen Seconds* is a widely praised investigation of the massacre of student anti-war demonstrators by the Ohio National Guard at Kent State University in May of 1970. The authors interviewed numerous witnesses and participants in the tragic confrontation to tell the story with "relentless honesty," remarked *Newsweek* reviewer Peter S. Prescott.

Eszterhas wrote two additional books on controversial social themes while working as a reporter for *Rolling Stone* magazine in the early 1970s. *Charlie Simpson's Apocalypse* examines the social context of a seemingly senseless act of violence by an alienated youth in a small Missouri town in early 1972. Charlie Simpson, a volatile, long-haired farm boy with what Eszterhas terms "revolutionary" pretensions, killed several townspeople and himself with an M-1 carbine following months of petty conflict between Simpson's band of youthful hippies and their conservative elders. According to Toby Thompson in the *Washington Post,* Eszterhas insightfully explores the prejudices, thoughtlessness, and penchant for violence on both sides of this small-town generation gap in a "beautifully researched, finely wrought, narratively blessed piece of American journalism." In *Nark!: A Tale of Terror,* his 1974 probe of the Federal Bureau of Narcotics/Drug Enforcement Administration, Eszterhas "gives solid evidence of the corruption and inhumanity" among narcotics agents, noted *New York Times Book Review* critic Robert Sherrill. The author argues that the antidrug force devotes excessive attention to small-time marijuana raids while generally leaving major hard drug dealers alone.

Eszterhas turned to screenwriting in the mid-1970s, co-authoring the story and original screenplay for

United Artists' *F.I.S.T.*, a drama starring Sylvester Stallone. The author later reworked his story into a novel that Dell published under the same title in 1978. The narrative traces the rise and fall of labor leader Johnny Kovak, a son of Hungarian immigrants who organizes truckers in Cleveland in the 1930s, rises to become a powerful national figure, and is ultimately undone by his connections with organized crime. *Washington Post Book World* critic Joseph McLellan deemed *F.I.S.T.* "a very good novel" with "fine atmosphere and a fair degree of complexity."

Subsequent films written by Eszterhas have garnered mixed reviews while doing well at the box office. *Flashdance,* about the coming-of-age of a young woman steelworker in Pittsburgh who dreams of becoming a dancer, was generally judged superficial in plot but rich in visual appeal. Some reviewers of *Jagged Edge,* a 1985 murder mystery starring Glenn Close and Jeff Bridges, credited Eszterhas with providing enough narrative twists to keep the audience guessing but considered the film short on characterization.

Like several other movie reviewers, *Los Angeles Times* critic Michael Wilmington found *Big Shots,* an adventure-comedy about two twelve-year-olds in the inner city, "entertaining" if somewhat "overblown." Eszterhas's story centers on a white suburban boy named Obie who joins forces with Scam, a street-smart black youth, in an attempt to recover Obie's stolen watch, a keepsake from his recently deceased father. What begins as an alliance of convenience blossoms into friendship as the boys discover shared interests and concerns despite their very different backgrounds. Eszterhas took a darker look at American race relations in the 1988 release *Betrayed,* which was directed by Constantin Costa-Gavras. The film concerns a Midwestern white supremacist organization recruiting members from among the region's destitute farmers. The undercover FBI agent assigned to infiltrate the group inadvertently falls in love with its handsome, virile, seemingly forthright leader while seeking to betray him. *Washington Post* critic Rita Kempley judged the story somewhat implausible but still found the movie well paced and suspenseful. Most critics, however, were disappointed with Eszterhas's farcical screenplay for the 1989 film *Checking Out,* about a young man's obsessive fear of death. In the 1990s, scripts for the highly successful sexual dramas *Basic Instinct* and *Sliver* placed Eszterhas high in the Hollywood elite, while *Showgirls,* a flimsy but visually riveting story about exotic dancers, echoed the success of *Flashdance* a decade before. These scripts made Eszterhas as much as $3 million per picture.

"How to reconcile the millionaire screenwriter and the rebellious, experimental journalist?" queried Jack Lule in the *Dictionary of Literary Biography.* "Rather than a radical departure from his early work, his film career drives home the point that literary journalism, for Eszterhas, was an expressive vehicle, a channel for his narrative and dramatic talents." Lule concluded that it was natural for Eszterhas to move from journalism to screenwriting, because "his work simply could not be confined to the conventional news story. The traditional journalistic report is derived from language determinedly dispassionate and apolitical. . . . Language orders experience, Eszterhas knew, and he resisted having his experience ordered in traditional ways. His work can be understood as a challenge to the benefit and possibility of objective, unbiased, apolitical reporting. Instead, he celebrated passion, commitment, and engagement."

"The writing of Joe Eszterhas makes the confrontation between traditional and literary journalism difficult to ignore," asserted Lule. "His precise rendering of scenes, his experimentation with point of view, and his dramatization of differences with other reporters—all these challenged conventions of journalism and showed once again the power of a story well told by its teller."

## BIOGRAPHICAL/CRITICAL SOURCES:

### BOOKS

*Dictionary of Literary Biography,* Volume 185: *American Literary Journalists, 1945-1995, First Series,* Gale (Detroit), 1997.
Love, Robert, *The Best of Rolling Stone: 25 Years of Journalism on the Edge,* Doubleday (New York City), 1993.
Wolfe, Tom, and E. W. Johnson, editors, *The New Journalism,* Harper (New York City), 1973.

### PERIODICALS

*Chicago Tribune,* April 18, 1983; August 28, 1988; January 19, 1990.
*Esquire,* May 9, 1978, pp. 78-82.
*Los Angeles Times,* April 15, 1983; October 4, 1985; October 2, 1987; August 26, 1988; October 30, 1989.
*Newsweek,* November 28, 1970; January 14, 1974.

*New York Times,* April 15, 1983; October 4, 1985; October 2, 1987; May 30, 1993, section 2, p. 9.

*New York Times Book Review,* January 27, 1974; July 7, 1974.

*San Francisco Chronicle,* June 5, 1994, pp. 6, 21.

*Time,* May 31, 1993, pp. 64-65.

*Washington Post,* January 26, 1974; October 10, 1985; August 26, 1988; January 19, 1990.*

# F

**FEINSTEIN, Elaine 1930-**

*PERSONAL:* Born October 24, 1930, in Bootle, England; daughter of Isidore and Fay (Compton) Cooklin; married Arnold Feinstein (an immunologist), July 22, 1957; children: Adam, Martin, Joel. *Education:* Cambridge University, B.A., 1952, M.A., 1955.

*ADDRESSES: Agent*—Gill Coleridge, Rogers, Coleridge & White, 20 Powis Mews, London W11, England; (plays and film) Lemon Unna & Durbridge, 24-32 Pottery Lane, London W11 4LZ, England.

*CAREER:* Cambridge University Press, London, England, editorial staff member, 1960-62; Bishop's Stortford Training College, Hertfordshire, England, lecturer in English, 1963-66; University of Essex, Wivenhoe, England, assistant lecturer in literature, 1967-70; writer, 1971—. Writer-in-residence, British Council in Singapore, 1993, and for the British Council in Tromsoe. Has also worked as a journalist.

*MEMBER:* Poetry Society, Eastern Arts Association, Royal Society of Literature (fellow).

*AWARDS, HONORS:* Arts Council grants, 1970, 1979, 1981; Daisy Miller Prize, 1971, for fiction; Kelus poetry prize, 1978; fellow, Royal Society of Literature, 1980; Cholmodeley Poets Award, 1990; D.Litt., Leicester University, England, 1990.

*WRITINGS:*

*POETRY*

*In a Green Eye,* Goliard Press (London), 1966.
*The Magic Apple Tree,* Hutchinson (London), 1971.

*At the Edge,* Sceptre Press (Northamptonshire, England), 1972.
*The Celebrants and Other Poems,* Hutchinson, 1973.
*Some Unease and Angels,* Green River Press (University Center, MI), 1977, 2nd edition, Hutchinson, 1982.
*The Feast of Euridice,* Faber (London), 1981.
*Badlands,* Hutchinson, 1986.
*City Music,* Hutchinson, 1990.
*Selected Poems,* Carcanet (Manchester), 1994.
*Daylight,* Carcanet, 1997.

*NOVELS*

*The Circle,* Hutchinson, 1970.
*The Amberstone Exit,* Hutchinson, 1972.
*The Glass Alembic,* Hutchinson, 1973, published as *The Crystal Garden,* Dutton, 1974.
*The Children of the Rose,* Hutchinson, 1974.
*The Ecstasy of Dr. Miriam Garner,* Hutchinson, 1976.
*The Shadow Master,* Hutchinson, 1977, Simon & Schuster, 1978.
*The Survivors,* Hutchinson, 1982.
*The Border,* Hutchinson, 1984.
*Mother's Girl,* Dutton, 1988.
*All You Need,* Hutchinson, 1989.
*Loving Brecht,* Hutchinson, 1992.
*Dreamers,* Macmillan (London), 1994.
*Lady Chatterley's Confession,* Macmillan, 1995.

*SHORT STORIES*

*Matters of Chance,* Covent Garden Press, 1972.
*The Silent Areas,* Hutchinson, 1980.

*PLAYS*

*Breath* (teleplay), British Broadcasting Corporation (BBC), 1975.

*Lear's Daughters,* produced in London, 1987.

*The Diary of a Country Gentlewoman* (twelve-part television series, based on the novel by Edith Holden), ITV, 1984.

Also author of radio plays, including *Echoes.* 1980; *A Late Spring,* 1982; *A Captive Lion,* 1984; *Maria Tsvetayeva: A Life,* 1985; *A Day Off* (based on the novel by Storm Jameson), 1986; *If I Ever Get on My Feet Again,* 1987; *The Man in Her Life,* 1990; *Foreign Girls,* 1993; *Winter Meeting,* 1994; *Women in Love* (based on the novel by D. H. Lawrence); and a radio adaptation of her own novel *Lady Chatterly's Confession.* Author of teleplays, including *Lunch,* 1982; *A Brave Face,* 1985; *The Chase,* 1988; and *A Passionate Woman* (series), 1989.

*OTHER*

(Editor) *Selected Poems of John Clare,* University Tutorial Press, 1968.

(Editor) *The Selected Poems of Marina Tsvetayeva,* Oxford University Press, 1971.

(Translator) *Three Russian Poets: Margarita Aliger, Yunna Moritz, and Bella Akhmadulina,* Carcanet Press, 1979.

(Editor with Fay Weldon) *New Stories Four,* Arts Council of Great Britain, 1979.

*Bessie Smith* (biography), Viking, 1986.

*A Captive Lion: The Life of Marina Tsvetayeva,* Dutton, 1987.

(Translator with Antonina W. Bouis) Nika Turbina, *First Draft: Poems,* M. Boyars (London), 1988.

(Editor) *PEN New Poetry,* Quartet (London), 1988.

*Lawrence's Women: The Intimate Life of D. H. Lawrence,* HarperCollins (New York City), 1993.

Contributor to periodicals, including *Times Literary Supplement.*

*SIDELIGHTS:* Elaine Feinstein is an English poet, novelist, short story writer, playwright, biographer, and translator of several well-known Russian poets. Such diversity of interest and talent is relatively rare, but, according to Michael Schmidt in the *Times Literary Supplement,* all of Feinstein's disparate writings speak with "very much one voice." The granddaughter of Jews who fled persecution in Tsarist Russia, Feinstein retains a strong preoccupation with her background and upbringing; this fascination with her Eastern European origins informs both her poetry and the majority of her novels. As Jennifer Birkett notes in *Contemporary Women Poets,* "Landscapes of exile, suffering, and loss" characterize Feinstein's verse.

*Dictionary of Literary Biography* contributor Peter Conradi calls Feinstein "a writer who has made fragmentation and deracination her special topics" and adds that she "has developed a language of formidable efficiency for evoking each, and for searching for authentication in the teeth of each. If her earliest books defamiliarized the ordinary world and the domestic self, her later books appropriately domesticated the exotic." *New Yorker* essayist George Steiner likewise notes that a "pulse of narrative and of dramatic voice is vivid in [Feinstein's] verse"; and in the *New Statesman,* Peter Buckman calls the author "a discovery, a writer of limitless simplicity and mistress of a musical prose that can apparently find rhythm anywhere."

Feinstein was born in Bootle, Lancashire, and brought up in the industrial town of Leicester in the English Midlands. Her father owned a factory, and his success with it fluctuated dramatically. Although her family was never destitute, Feinstein experienced some genteel poverty in her childhood. An only child, she was raised to respect religion, but it was only after World War II that she came to realize what being Jewish meant for her. Feinstein noted in an essay in *Contemporary Authors Autobiography Series* (*CAAS*) that her childhood sense of security "was exploded, once and for all, at the war's end, when I read what exactly had been done to so many children, as young as I was, in the hell of Hitler's camps. You could say that in that year I became Jewish for the first time. That is not something I regret. But no doubt the knowledge of human cruelty damaged me. For a very long time afterwards, I could feel no ordinary human emotion without testing it against that imagined experience, and either suspecting it or dismissing it." Conradi puts it another way. After the war, he writes, Feinstein came "to an understanding of the degree to which being Jewish could mean to suffer and live in danger."

Feinstein was educated with a grant provided by the Butler Education Act of 1944, receiving both her bachelor's and master's degrees from Cambridge University. In 1957, two years after leaving Cambridge, she married Arnold Feinstein, an immunologist. For several years thereafter she devoted herself to rearing the couple's three sons, but she was also able to work as an editor for Cambridge University

Press and as a part-time English lecturer at several colleges. Her first volume of poetry, *In a Green Eye,* was published in 1966. According to Deborah Mitchell in the *Dictionary of Literary Biography,* the book "already shows an unassuming sureness of diction and imagery. . . . The poems are simple and generously affectionate—she is always anxious to do justice to whomever she is 'portraying' as well as to express her own relationship with the individual. There is also an unsentimental recognition that, in human relationships, people are tied to one another, pushing and pulling toward and away from one another in mutual dependency."

For a time in the late 1960s Feinstein joined a poetry group in an effort to clarify her approach and better understand her own poetic voice. The group helped her to do this in an oblique way: she came to disagree with its insistence on "Englishness" as a motivating characteristic. Conradi suggests that members of the group "wished to de-Europeanize themselves, to make a cult of and to explore the history of their particular Englishness. This helped [Feinstein] define herself against any such cult, as a person who had never definitely 'settled' in England, and whose roots, if she had them and was not nomadic, were certainly not to be discovered in a nationalist version of 'Little England.'" Thereafter Feinstein's work began to explore her ancestry and heritage as well as the horrors inflicted on modern Jews. Her poetry was especially influenced by the verse of Marina Tsvetayeva, a Russian author of the early twentieth century.

Feinstein told *CA:* "I began to write poetry in the '60's very *consciously* influenced by American poets; at a time when the use of line, and spacing, to indicate the movement of poetry, was much less fashionable than it is now among young British poets. It was my translations from the Russian of Marina Tsvetayeva, however, that gave me my true voice, or at least made me attend to a strength and forward push, *against* and *within* a formal structure, that I could have only learnt from Tsvetayeva herself. In the wholeness of her self exposure, she opened a whole world of experience. Without her, I should never have written novels, still less plays."

Feinstein's early novels "came out of domestic and personal experience whose woes and wonders they to some degree make lyrical," to quote Conradi. A favorite early theme of Feinstein's is a woman's search for identity within and outside of familial relationships. In the *Times Literary Supplement,* D. M. Thomas observes that Feinstein wants to show "that women's dreams are common and commonplace, because of their depressed lives." Both *The Circle* and *The Amberstone Exit* feature young women so mired in domestic or family responsibilities that they cannot fully explore themselves. Mitchell contends that Feinstein's early work, with its feminist slant, "concerned [as it is] with the world of personal emotion and relationships and with the domestic environment, is remarkable for its economy, its stringent emotional honesty, and tough ironic humor, as well as [for] an intensity and richness of metaphor unusual with this sort of subject matter."

Most critics agree that the death of Feinstein's parents in 1973 marks the beginning of Feinstein's movement into new thematic territory. Conradi states: "It was about this time that she began to enquire into Jewish history more systematically and enlarge her reading. A wish to make her characters more securely substantial also entered into this investigation; the result was not merely more substantial characterization, but also more satisfying mythmaking." To quote *Times Literary Supplement* correspondent Susannah Clapp, Feinstein's characters began to be "not just incidentally irritated or pleased by their dreams and memories, but changed and controlled by them. . . . Some of [her] most persuasive writing . . . describes people in the grip of flashback or nightmare."

Mitchell writes: "In a complex process Feinstein has combined traditional myths with myths she has created out of themes that arose originally from direct reactions to her personal experience and that have been gradually clarified and set into a broader historical perspective." In works such as *The Shadow Master, The Ecstasy of Dr. Miriam Garner,* and *The Border,* Feinstein leaves not only the boundaries of England but the constraints of realism; characters confront the drama of Jewish history, and one way or another it begins to control their lives. Lorna Sage describes Feinstein's intentions in the *Times Literary Supplement:* "Elaine Feinstein has long been obsessed with the persistence of the past in her characters' lives. . . . The last war, the holocaust, the webs of violence, fanaticism, exile and betrayal that make up recent history (especially Jewish history) reach out to reclaim her cosmopolitan, clever, 'free' people again and again." Conradi observes that in many of Feinstein's novels "someone falls dangerously ill, sick beyond the reach even of modern pharmacy, and it is often the past which can be said figuratively to have sickened them, and which has returned to get them." In *New Statesman,* Clapp contends that this obsession with the past is represented by ghostly visitations. "Now the spectres have been unleashed," Clapp concludes, "and, though it's not easy to give whole-hearted assent to their original necessity, the open acknowledgment of their presence brings remarkable release."

One of Feinstein's best known novels is *The Survivors,* a multi-generational story of two Jewish families who flee Odessa for turn-of-the-century Liverpool. In the *Times Literary Supplement,* Peter Lewis describes the families: "The Gordons are extremely well-to-do and middle-class, and have been assimilated to a considerable extent into English social life. The Katz family is working class, belongs to the Liverpool equivalent of a ghetto (within a slum area), and is orthodox in religion." The tale revolves around a marriage between the Gordon and Katz families, and the subsequent offspring of that union. Lewis notes a good probability that Feinstein "has transmuted her family and personal history into fiction in *The Survivors,* which is full of insights into the changing patterns of Jewish life during this century." *Listener* contributor John Mellors finds more to praise than just the novel's story, however. "It is the poet's precision and verbal fastidiousness which make *The Survivors* far more than just another family chronicle," Mellors writes. Neil Philip offers a similar opinion in *British Book News. The Survivors,* concludes Philip, "is an exceptional novel: intimate, engrossing, economical, yet covering sixty years, two world wars and immense social change. It is Elaine Feinstein's remarkably sure grip on her material which enables her to treat such large themes, to encompass three generations, to manage such a large cast, without losing sight of the personal, the individual, the sense of the minute as well as the year. . . . Fiction as rich and rewarding as this is rare."

In her 1989 novel *All You Need,* Feinstein chose a very contemporary setting—London in the late 1980s—and a highly cosmopolitan cast of characters-successful businessmen, television producers, literary stars—and produced a work in which the focus is less on the past than it is on the present and near future. The main character is a suburban housewife named Nell who moves to London with her teenage daughter after her husband is arrested and sent to jail for somewhat mysterious reasons. Like her previous novels, *All You Need* focuses on the self-discovery and reawakening of the female protagonist. Unlike Feinstein's previous work, however, this one employs the reawakened protagonist as an observer of the contemporary British cultural scene, rather than as a psychological and spiritual conduit to the past. For this reason, most critics were somewhat disappointed by *All You Need.* Jan Dalley in the *Observer* calls the book "good-natured but rather bland," and Nicci Gerrard in the *New Statesman and Society*—while generally liking the novel—misses "the elegiac notes that make Elaine Feinstein's earlier works so haunting."

From the contemporaneity of *All You Need* Feinstein then examined—in *Dreamers*—Vienna in the Habsburg period of the mid-nineteenth century. This novel presents an intellectual and thematic portrait of the time and place, focusing on how Jews lived and contributed to the society and culture of central Europe at a time when anti-Semitism was becoming institutionalized. As Ruth Padel summarizes the novel's themes in the *New Statesman and Society,* Feinstein examines questions such as: "How should Jews live in a liberalising Christian empire, with anti-Semitism rising as Jews contribute to everything the city values? Disguise themselves, or keep marks of difference? Converting, as Heine did, is useless. Assimilation is never enough. Hitler's dream backlights everything." The novel depicts various responses to these questions, following a wide range of characters during a fifteen-year period. Padel notes that in *Dreamers* "you get Vienna through its ideas, soldiers, prostitutes, poets, bankers, singers, cooks, social injustices and changes—until the closing paragraph. There, the two themes—political change in nineteenth-century Europe and the *impasse* of its Jews—merge in a last shot." She concludes that the "novel is beautifully plotted, but moments of relationship, and of meditation on them, are where [Feinstein's] lyric perception always soars."

In 1993 Feinstein wrote a biography of D. H. Lawrence titled *Lawrence and the Women: The Intimate Life of D. H. Lawrence.* This study focuses on the women in his life and his troubled relationships with them. Two years later she wrote a sequel to one of Lawrence's most famous novels, *Lady Chatterley's Lover,* called *Lady Chatterley's Confession.* Writing in the *Times Literary Supplement,* Miranda Seymour concludes that "Feinstein, with sturdy pragmatism, recognizes that sex would never have kept this relationship [between the eponymous heroine and Mellors, her upper-class paramour] alive for long and that, without it, Lady Chatterley is a lost woman. It is not a romantic conclusion to the story but it is a perfectly convincing one." Craig Brown in *The Spectator* argues that Feinstein appears not to have grasped some of the comedy of Lawrence's original. He concludes: "Lawrence, who always had more of an eye for Mellors' manhood than Lady C's womanhood, would not, I think, approve of Feinstein's novel. On the other hand, it is far more plausible as a sequel than anything he would have written."

Her novels and short stories have eclipsed the attention given to hear early verse, but, but Feinstein has drawn praise and respect in British literary circles for her poetry. In *Spectator,* Emma Tennant calls the author "a powerful poet, whose power lies in the disarming combination of openness and sibylline cunning, a fearless and honest eye on the modern world, the smallest domestic detail, the nerve-bare feelings of people lashed together in marriage, parental and filial relationships—and then, suddenly, like a buried sketch emerging from under an accepted picture and proving to be of a totally different subject, terrifying, uneasy, evoking the old spells that push us this way and that in our lives of resisted superstitions." Tennant adds that the works "have lives of their own, they are very delicately observed. And, in poems which can seem at first spare and slight, there is a powerful undertow of sane love." Mitchell expresses a similar opinion. "The poems come from a familiar world but there is nothing cozy or reassuringly safe about Feinstein's domesticity," Mitchell writes, adding that Feinstein's "poems are faithful to the actual experience described . . . but she is less interested, finally, in realism for its own sake than in the 'making strange' of familiar experience to enable the reader to recognize its importance once more." Schmidt discusses Feinstein's style, noting that her language "evokes a memory, thought or perception in just the way it came to consciousness—brokenly, or in a pondered fashion, or suddenly in a flash. This is not language miming experience, but miming rather the process by which experience is registered and understood. Thus the freshness of her writing, the occasional obscurities, and the sense that despite the apparent self-consciousness of style, she is paradoxically the least artificial, the least *literary* of writers. The poems are composed . . . not to *be* poems but to witness accurately to how she experiences."

Feinstein's interest in the poet Maria Tsvetayeva, who she calls "my teacher of courage," has continued for more than twenty years. Feinstein has not only translated Tsvetayeva's poetry, she has also written a biography titled *A Captive Lion: The Life of Marina Tsvetayeva.* In a *Spectator* review, Peter Levi contends that the work "as it now stands is like the ultimate Tsvetayeva poem, a painful extension of the painful life, with its final focus on a nail used for tethering horses from which she hung herself. It is not the kind of truth one enjoys hearing." Most critics have praised Feinstein's English translations from the Russian—a difficult undertaking given the disparities between the two languages. Levi observes that some of the resultant works "are magnificent poems that do not look like translations at all, they are so good." *Spectator* correspondent Emma Fisher writes: "The thought, the feeling, even the wit, [Feinstein] transfers into plain but intense English, sometimes using rhyme, assonance and regular metres, but often preferring to let the words make their own awkward, blatant shapes on the page." According to Ellendea Proffer in the *New York Times Book Review,* readers "can only be grateful for her work in bringing this difficult poet [Tsvetayeva] into English, and certainly it can be said that these are the best translations available."

Conradi feels that Feinstein's "impressive progress as a novelist can be seen . . . as an emancipation of prose from a provincial sense of its limits," a discovery the author gleaned from her work on Tsvetayeva. Feinstein "wants to write novels which *move* her readers, as the great novels of the past have done," adds the critic, "and to involve them in the fate of her characters so that they will care about what happens to them." Addressing herself to Feinstein's poetic contributions, Mitchell writes: "The mature achievement of her verse has been recognized by a small number of diverse critics, [although] . . . the very individuality which is so refreshing in her work, as well as its diversity, has puzzled a sometimes parochial English reading public." Nevertheless, concludes Mitchell, Feinstein is "something of a rarity among writers—equally at home in verse and fiction, being too well aware of the distinct qualities of each form to make one an adjunct of the other. The cross-fertilization between narrative and lyric means that she is continually developing new and enriching approaches to writing poetry." Schmidt declares that in her more mature work, Feinstein has become the creator of "a richly *moral* art" that "eschews facile effect, focuses on its subject, not its audience." In Peter Lewis's opinion, Feinstein "is well on the way to being a writer of infinite variety."

*BIOGRAPHICAL/CRITICAL SOURCES:*

*BOOKS*

*Contemporary Authors Autobiography Series,* Volume 1, Gale (Detroit), 1984.
*Contemporary Literary Criticism,* Volume 36, Gale, 1986.

*Contemporary Women Poets,* St. James Press (Detroit), 1997.

*Dictionary of Literary Biography,* Gale, Volume 14: *British Novelists since 1960,* 1983, Volume 40: *Poets of Great Britain and Ireland since 1960,* 1985.

Schmidt, Michael, and Grevel Lindop, editors, *British Poetry since 1960,* Carcanet Press, 1972.

Schmidt, Michael and Peter Jones, editors, *British Poetry since 1970,* Carcanet Press, 1980.

*PERIODICALS*

*Books,* October, 1970.

*British Book News,* July, 1982.

*Contemporary Review,* January, 1979.

*Economist,* March 29, 1997, pp. 92-93.

*Encounter,* September-October, 1984.

*Globe and Mail* (Toronto), March 15, 1986.

*Harper's,* June, 1974.

*Listener,* August 20, 1970; November 28, 1974; September 28, 1978; March 11, 1982.

*Literary Review,* April, 1982.

*London Review of Books,* July 5-19, 1984; November 9, 1989; March 25, 1993.

*Los Angeles Times,* June 6, 1985.

*Los Angeles Times Book Review,* December 11, 1988.

*Nation,* June 25, 1988.

*New Statesman,* August 21, 1970; May 7, 1971; August 4, 1972; April 11, 1975; June 4, 1976; September 15, 1989, p. 34; January 22, 1993, p. 37; August 12, 1994, p. 39.

*New Yorker,* June 3, 1974; April 29, 1985; May 3, 1993, p. 115.

*New York Review of Books,* October 8, 1987.

*New York Times,* February 25, 1974; August 21, 1987.

*New York Times Book Review,* May 19, 1974; November 4, 1979; August 21, 1997, p. 23; September 27, 1987; March 28, 1993, p. 25; December 27, 1987, p. 22.

*Observer* (London), August 16, 1970; August 20, 1972; May 27, 1973; April 20, 1975; March 1, 1992; July 17, 1994.

*Publishers Weekly,* February 1, 1991, p. 64; February 1, 1993, p. 84.

*Poetry Nation Review,* number 101, 1994.

*Spectator,* June 5, 1976; September 24, 1977; September 23, 1978; June 16, 1979; February 9, 1980; March 7, 1987; December 16, 1995.

*Times* (London), November 9, 1985; April 2, 1987; January 21, 1988.

*Times Literary Supplement,* August 28, 1970; August 11, 1972; June 29, 1973; December 7, 1973; April 25, 1975; June 4, 1976; February 3, 1978; October 6, 1978; January 18, 1980; February 22, 1980; February 26, 1982; June 8, 1984; July 17, 1987; July 31, 1987; January 22, 1988; November 16, 1990; January 15, 1993; July 15, 1994; October 13, 1995.

*Tribune Books* (Chicago), December 29, 1985.

*Village Voice,* May 27, 1986.*

\* \* \*

**FERBER, Edna 1885-1968**

*PERSONAL:* Born August 15, 1885, in Kalamazoo, MI; died of cancer, April 16, 1968, in New York, NY; daughter of Jacob Charles (Hungarian-born small businessman) and Julia (Newmann) Ferber. *Education:* Graduated from Ryan High School, Appleton, WI.

*CAREER:* Writer. *Appleton Daily Crescent,* Appleton, WI, reporter, 1902-04; *Milwaukee Journal,* Milwaukee, WI, writer and reporter, 1905-08; also writer and reporter for *Chicago Tribune. Military service:* During World War II, served in civilian capacity as war correspondent for U.S. Army Air Forces.

*MEMBER:* National Institute of Arts and Letters, American Academy, Authors League of America, Authors Guild, Dramatists Guild.

*AWARDS, HONORS:* Pulitzer Prize for Fiction, 1924, for *So Big;* Litt.D., Columbia University and Adelphi College.

*WRITINGS:*

*NOVELS*

*Dawn O'Hara, the Girl Who Laughed,* Stokes (New York City), 1911.

*Fanny Herself,* Stokes, 1917.

*The Girls,* Doubleday (New York City), 1921.

*So Big,* Doubleday, 1924, with introduction by Maria K. Mootry, University of Illinois Press (Urbana), 1995.

*Show Boat,* Doubleday, 1926.

*Cimarron,* Doubleday, 1930, revised edition, Grosset (New York City), 1942, new edition by Frederick H. Law, Globe, 1954.

*American Beauty,* Doubleday, 1931.

*Come and Get It,* Doubleday, 1935.
*Nobody's In Town* (two novellas, including *Trees Die at the Top*), Doubleday, 1938.
*Saratoga Trunk,* Doubleday, 1941.
*Great Son,* Doubleday, 1945.
*Giant,* Doubleday, 1952.
*Ice Palace,* Doubleday, 1958.

*STORY COLLECTIONS*

*Buttered Side Down,* Stokes, 1912.
*Roast Beef, Medium: The Business Adventures of Emma McChesney,* Stokes, 1913.
*Personality Plus: Some Experiences of Emma McChesney and Her Son, Jock,* Stokes, 1914.
*Emma McChesney & Co.,* Stokes, 1915.
*Cheerful, by Request,* Doubleday, 1918.
*Half Portions,* Doubleday, 1920.
*Gigolo* (includes "Old Man Minick"), Doubleday, 1922; published in England as *Among Those Pressent,* Nash and Grayson (London), 1923.
*Mother Knows Best: A Fiction Book,* Doubleday, 1927.
*They Brought Their Women: A Book of Short Stories,* Doubleday, 1933.
*No Room at the Inn,* Doubleday, 1941.
*One Basket: Thirty-One Short Stories,* Simon & Shuster (New York City), 1947.

*PLAYS*

(With George V. Hobart) *Our Mrs. McChesney,* first produced in New York at Lyceum Theater, October 19, 1915.
(With Newman Levy) *$1200 a Year,* Doubleday, 1920.
(With George S. Kaufman) *Minick* (dramatization of her short story, "Old Man Minick"), first produced in New York at Booth Theater, September 24, 1924.
*The Eldest: A Drama of American Life,* Appleton (New York City), 1925.
(With Kaufman) *The Royal Family* (first produced in New York at Selwyn Theater, December 28, 1927; produced as television play, 1954), Doubleday, 1928; produced in England as *Theatre Royal,* London, 1935, Samuel French (London), 1936.
(With Kaufman) *Dinner at Eight* (first produced on Broadway at Music Box Theater, October 22, 1932), Doubleday, 1932.
(With Kaufman) *Stage Door* (first produced on Broadway at Music Box Theater, October 22, 1936), Doubleday, 1936.

(With Kaufman) *The Land Is Bright* (first produced on Broadway at Music Box Theater, October 28, 1941), Doubleday, 1941.
(With Kaufman) *Bravo!* (first produced in New York at Lyceum Theater, November 11, 1948), Dramatists Play Service (New York City), 1949.

*OTHER*

*A Gay Old Dog* (filmscript), Pathe Exchange, 1919.
(Contributor) *My Story That I Like Best,* International Magazine Co., 1924.
*Old Man Minick* [and] *Minick* (the story and the play; the latter with Kaufman), Doubleday, 1924.
(With Kaufman) *Welcome Home* (filmscript), Paramount, 1925.
*A Peculiar Treasure* (autobiography), Doubleday, 1939.
*Your Town,* World, 1948.
*Show Boat, So Big,* [and] *Cimarron: Three Living Novels of American Life,* Doubleday, 1962.
*A Kind of Magic* (autobiography; sequel to *A Peculiar Treasure* ), Doubleday, 1963.

A collection of Ferber's papers is housed at the State Historical Society of Wisconsin.

*WORK IN PROGRESS:* At the time of her death, Ferber was collecting material for a book on American Indians but, according to *Variety,* "it is not believed that anything was actually written."

*ADAPTATIONS:* The following films were based on Ferber's work: *Our Mrs. McChesney,* Metro, 1918; *No Woman Knows* (based on *Fanny Herself*), Universal, 1921; *Classified* (based on her short story of the same title), Corinne Griffith Productions, 1925; *Gigolo,* Cinema Corporation of America, 1926; *Mother Knows Best,* Fox, 1928; *The Home Girl* (based on a short story), Paramount, 1928; *Show Boat,* Universal, 1929, remade by Universal, 1936, and MGM, 1951; *The Royal Family of Broadway* (based on the play *The Royal Family,* by Ferber and Kaufman), Paramount, 1930; *Cimarron,* RKO, 1931, remade by MGM, 1960; *The Expert* (based on her short story, *Old Man Minick*), Warner Bros., 1932; *So Big,* Warner Bros., 1932, remade by Warner Bros., 1953; *Dinner at Eight* (based on play written with Kaufman), MGM, 1933; *Come and Get It,* United Artists, 1936; *Stage Door,* RKO, 1937; *No Place to Go* (based on the play, *Minick,* by Ferber and Kaufman), Warner Bros., 1939; *Saratoga Trunk,* Warner Bros., 1945; *Giant,* Warner Bros., 1956; *Ice Palace,* Warner Bros., 1960. *Show Boat* was adapted for the stage with music by Jerome Kern, and was first produced in New York at Ziegfeld Theater, December 27, 1927. *Saratoga Trunk* was adapted for a musical, *Saratoga,* with a libretto by Harold Arlen; it was first produced on Broadway at Winter Garden Theater, December 7, 1959.

*SIDELIGHTS:* Edna Ferber was a novelist, short-story writer, and playwright whose works clearly reflected her love for middle-class America. Her best-known works are her novels, including *So Big, Giant,* and *Cimarron.* These books depict the western movement of American civilization, and she is, according to *Dictionary of Literary Biography* contributor Paula Reed, "remembered chiefly as a chronicler and critic of American cultural history." The optimistic, senti-mental tone that pervades her work typifies the na-tional mood of the early decades of this century. In her novels and stories, Ferber frequently featured strong female characters who, when thrown into diffi-cult situations, rise heroically to the occasion. One of her most popular creations is Emma McChesney, a spirited divorcee who makes her living selling women's undergarments. McChesney, featured in numerous short stories by Ferber, is often cited as one of the first truly liberated women in American fiction. The author's male characters tend to be dreamier and more ineffectual than her heroines.

Critical assessment of Ferber's work has varied greatly from one decade to the next, and from one reviewer to another. During the 1920s and 1930s, she was frequently hailed as one of the greatest of Ameri-can woman writers; she was awarded the Pulitzer Prize for her novel *So Big.* Her books were once standards of high school and college reading lists, a fact Ferber often noted with pride. Yet as the years went on her work was taken less seriously, and was more frequently characterized as mere entertainment. Reed mused: "A clumsy didacticism prevalent in her writing is partially responsible for this change in sta-tus. Still, from a sociological perspective her care-fully researched novels are of importance in affording a panoramic view of American growth and develop-ment during the nineteenth and twentieth centuries; in her best work, her portrayals of familial relationships, and the problematic demands produced within them, especially the condition we now refer to as the "gen-eration gap,' are particularly insightful."

Ferber was born in Kalamazoo, Michigan, to Jewish parents who moved frequently, due to her father's repeated failures in business. They finally settled in Appleton, Wisconsin, where she graduated from high school at the age of 17. The family could not afford to send Edna to college although she deeply wished to attend; instead, she took a job as a reporter for her local newspaper, eventually moving on to the *Milwau-kee Journal.* Her journalism background is evident in her keen observations and her sharp ear for dialogue. She sold her first short story in 1910 and her first novel, *Dawn O'Hara,* in 1911. Contemporary review-ers were kind in their comments, but Ferber would later disparage the book, which is dismissed by Reed as "sentimental and sloppily written." Her short-story output was prolific in the early years of her career; between 1911 and 1915 she published four volumes of stories, all of them previously published. Most of these featured the popular Emma McChesney charac-ter.

In 1912 Ferber moved to New York, which served as her home base for most of the rest of her life. Work-ing with George V. Hobart, she created a stage ver-sion of her McChesney stories, which was produced with the famed actress Ethel Barrymore in the lead role. Some years later, she collaborated successfully with George S. Kaufman on several other plays, in-cluding *The Royal Family, Dinner at Eight, Stage Door,* and *Bravo!* In 1921 she published *The Girls,* her first truly mature novel. It describes three genera-tions of unmarried women—a great-aunt, aunt, and niece—and the ways they handled the restrictions of society in their respective eras. The subject was one close to Ferber. Though she was rumored to be ro-mantically linked with several men, she never mar-ried.

*So Big* was published in 1924. It is the story of Selina DeJong, a gambler's daughter who marries a farmer and, after his death, turns his debt-ridden farm into a success. *So Big* was a resounding critical and popular success. Like most of Ferber's work, it speaks out for the value of hard work. Typically, it also portrayed a woman surviving despite being surrounded by men who are less capable than herself. Selina's father is a wastrel; her husband is plodding and inept; and her son, Dirk, disappoints her with his choice of the easy road in life. Steven P. Horowitz and Miriam J. Landsman explained in *Dictionary of Literary Biogra-phy:* "Dirk . . . represents the type of person who sacrifices principles for materialistic success." Ferber followed *So Big* with *Show Boat,* a lively story of life on a floating theater on the Mississippi River. In 1927, *Show Boat* was adapted into a musical that remains popular today.

*Cimarron,* published in 1930, is frequently cited as being Ferber's best novel. "Certainly it contains her most subtly rendered depiction of differences between the sexes and between generations," offered Reed. The backdrop is the settlement of Oklahoma, beginning with the great Land Rush of 1889 and continuing through the discovery of oil. "Ferber has distilled from the heady, strong mash of those days a draught that gives the reader such an intoxication as those days were themselves," enthused Fanny Butcher in *Chicago Daily Tribune.* "It certainly is the most thrilling thing that ever has come from the pen of Miss Ferber." "Read it . . . for its splendidly kaleidoscopic view of a young American city coming into existence, with its shifting social patterns and its broad diversity of types, with its background of disinherited Indians coming at last, by an ironic turn of fate, into that bewildering wealth which oil brought to them," urged a *New York Times* reviewer.

Ferber continued to be a prolific writer of short stories, and she also wrote many more historical adventure novels, including *Saratoga Trunk,* which featured a Creole lady and a Texas cowboy in a scheme to bilk the wealthy people of Saratoga Springs; and *Great Son,* which was set in Seattle and the Klondike region. *Giant* appeared in 1952, and became one of her most famous works after being made into a film—the last one actor James Dean appeared in before his death. *Giant* was "far superior to anything Ferber had published since *Cimarron,*" declared Reed. It illustrated life in Texas, in a fashion that enraged many of the inhabitants of that state. "'Giant' will be joyfully received in forty-seven states and avidly though angrily read in Texas," remarked William Kittrell in *Saturday Review.*

During the last years of her life, Ferber developed an extremely painful condition known as *tic douloureux.* Her writing output dropped sharply, but she did produce one more significant book. *Ice Palace* is set in Alaska and revolves around Christine Storm, whose two grandfathers—once friends—are now bitter enemies, because one wishes to preserve the pristine quality of Alaska while the other believes in exploiting its natural resources. *Ice Palace* is credited as being one of the deciding factors in the approval of Alaskan statehood in 1959.

Though a *Dial* reviewer expressed a typical criticism of Ferber—her "talents go to polishing the bright pebbles of life, rather than to touching the bedrock of reality"—this comment could just as well be taken as a compliment to her talent. Ferber gave us a fragment of life important to her. Her "sentimentality" was typical of an era we may never see again. William Allen White believed that "the historian will find no better picture of America in the first three decades of this century than Edna Ferber has drawn." Her own philosophy continues to help the talented young writers in whom she was so interested: "Life," she said, "can't ever really defeat a writer who is in love with writing, for life itself is a writer's lover until death— fascinating, cruel, lavish, warm, cold, treacherous, constant; the more varied the moods the richer the experience."

*BIOGRAPHICAL/CRITICAL SOURCES:*

*BOOKS*

*Authors in the News,* Volume 1, Gale (Detroit), 1976.

*Contemporary Literary Criticism,* Volume 18, Gale, 1981, Volume 93, 1996.

Cournos, John, and Sybil Norton (pseudonym of H. S. N. K. Cournos), *Famous American Modern Novelists,* Dodd (New York City), 1952.

Fain, John Tyree, *The Spyglass: Views and Reviews, 1924-1930,* Vanderbilt University Press (Nashville, TN), 1963, pp. 70-74.

Dickinson, R., *Edna Ferber,* Doubleday, 1925.

*Dictionary of Literary Biography,* Gale, Volume 9: *American Novelists, 1910-1945,* 1981, Volume 28: *Twentieth-Century American-Jewish Fiction Writers,* 1984, Volume 86: *American Short-Story Writers, 1910-1945, First Series,* 1989.

Dodd, Loring Holmes, *Celebrities at Our Hearthside,* Dresser, 1959.

Ferber, Edna, *A Peculiar Treasure,* Doubleday, 1939.

Ferber, *A Kind of Magic,* Doubleday, 1963.

Gilbert, Julie Goldsmith, *Edna Ferber: A Biography,* Doubleday, 1978.

Gray, James, *On Second Thought,* University of Minnesota Press (Minneapolis), 1946, pp. 154-64.

Lawrence, Margaret, *The School of Femininity,* Kennikat (Port Washington, NY), 1966, pp. 183-209.

*Literary Spotlight,* Doran, 1924, pp. 135-45, pp. 135-45.

Nathan, George Jean, *The Theatre Book of the Year: 1948-1949,* Knopf (New York City), 1949, pp. 153-62.

Shaughnessy, Mary Rose, *Women and Success in American Society in the Works of Edna Ferber,* Gordon Press (New York City), 1977.

*Twentieth-Century Western Writers,* St. James Press (Chicago), 1991.

Van Gelder, Robert, *Writers and Writing,* Scribner (New York City), 1946.

Williams, Blanche Colton, *Our Short-Story Writers,* Dodd (New York City), 1941, pp. 146-59.

Witham, W. Tasker, *Panorama of American Literature,* Doubleday, 1947.

*PERIODICALS*

*Atlantic,* November, 1912; December, 1941; October, 1952; May, 1958, pp. 78, 80.

*Atlantic Bookshelf,* May, 1930, p. 22; December, 1931; October, 1952, pp. 100-101.

*Booklist,* November, 1926; May, 1930; January, 1937; October 1, 1952.

*Bookman,* July, 1911, p. 534; September, 1926, pp. 91-92; July, 1930, p. 440.

*Books,* March 23, 1930, p. 7.

*Boston Transcript,* August 21, 1926, p. 2; March 29, 1930, p. 3.

*Catholic World,* January, 1937; January, 1953.

*Chicago Daily Tribune,* March 22, 1930, p. 11.

*Chicago Sunday Tribune,* September 28, 1952, p. 3.

*Chicago Sunday Tribune Book Review,* March 30, 1958.

*Christian Science Monitor,* March 29, 1930, p. 10; October 2, 1952, p. 6; March 27, 1958.

*Commonweal,* November 6, 1936, p. 51; October 17, 1952.

*Dial,* November 20, 1950.

*Kirkus Reviews,* July 15, 1952.

*Library Journal,* October 1, 1952.

*Literary Journal,* November 1, 1941.

*Literary Review,* October 28, 1922; August 21, 1926.

*Midwestern Miscellany,* Volume 7, 1980, pp. 82-93.

*Nation,* April 23, 1930; October 28, 1931, pp. 462-63; November 7, 1936, pp. 557-58.

*New Republic,* January 4, 1922, pp. 158-59; September 15, 1926; April 30, 1930; November 11, 1936.

*New Statesman,* November 6, 1926; May 24, 1930.

*New Statesman and Nation,* June 24, 1939, pp. 998, 1000.

*New Yorker,* August 22, 1926, p. 5; December 5, 1926, p. 5; September 28, 1952, p. 4; October 4, 1952; February 4, 1939.

*New York Herald Tribune Book Review,* August 22, 1926, p. 3; October 18, 1931, p. 3; May 7, 1933, p. 6; February 24, 1935, p. 3; February 13, 1938, p. 5; November 2, 1941, p. 5; September 28, 1952, p. 1; March 30, 1958, p. 1; September 8, 1963, p. 6.

*New York Times,* October 30, 1921, p. 16; March 23, 1930, p. 13; January 17, 1937, p. 14.

*New York Times Book Review,* April 20, 1913, p. 232; September 20, 1914, p. 386; October 17, 1915, pp. 390, 396; October 7, 1917, p. 380; September 22, 1918, pp. 399, 408; May 9, 1920, p. 236; November 5, 1922, p. 10; August 22, 1926; April 17, 1927, p. 2; March 23, 1930, p. 841; October 18, 1931, p. 7; May 14, 1933; February 24, 1935, p. 6; February 5, 1939, pp. 1, 30; November 2, 1941, p. 4; January 28, 1945, p. 5; February 16, 1947, p. 3; September 28, 1952, pp. 4-5; March 30, 1958, p. 4; April 17, 1968.

*New York World,* March 20, 1930.

*Outlook,* September 15, 1926; April 9, 1930.

*San Francisco Chronicle,* October 12, 1952, p. 20.

*Saturday Review,* August 21, 1926, pp. 49, 54; October 17, 1931; September 27, 1952; March 29, 1958.

*Saturday Review of Literature,* August 21, 1926; March 22, 1930; October 17, 1931, p. 201; November 22, 1941, p. 18; January 27, 1945, p. 24.

*Spectator,* November 6, 1926, p. 824; May 31, 1930; November 21, 1952.

*Springfield Republican,* March 2, 1924; September 5, 1926, p. F7; June 1, 1930, p. E7; October 26, 1952, p. D11.

*Time,* September 29, 1952.

*Times* (London), April 17, 1968.

*Times Literary Supplement,* November 11, 1926, p. 792; May 1, 1930, p. 368; December 5, 1952, p. 789.

*United States Quarterly Booklist,* September, 1947.

*Variety,* April 24, 1968.

*Wilson Library Bulletin,* October, 1926.

*OBITUARIES:*

*PERIODICALS*

*Newsweek,* April 29, 1968.

*New York Times,* April 17, 1968.

*Publishers Weekly,* April 29, 1968.

*Time,* April 26, 1968.

*Times* (London), April 17, 1968.

*Washington Post,* April 17, 1968.*

\* \* \*

**FERNANDEZ, Roberto G. 1951-**

*PERSONAL:* Born September 24, 1951, in Sagua la Grande, Cuba; immigrated to United States, 1961;

naturalized citizen, 1972; son of Jose Antonio (a certified public accountant) and Nelia G. (a homemaker; maiden name, Lopez) Fernandez; married Elena Reyes (a psychologist), July 7, 1978 (divorced, April 26, 1983; remarried Elena Reyes, 1990); children: Tatiana. *Education:* Florida Atlantic University, B.A., 1970, M.A., 1973; Florida State University, Ph.D., 1977. *Religion:* Roman Catholic.

*ADDRESSES: Home*—Tallahassee, FL. *Office*—Department of Modern Languages, Florida State University, Tallahassee, FL 32306.

*CAREER:* Florida State University, Tallahassee, instructor of Spanish literature, 1975-78; University of South Alabama, Mobile, assistant professor of Spanish, 1978-80; Florida State University, associate professor of Spanish and Spanish literature, 1980—.

*MEMBER:* American Association of Teachers of Spanish and Portuguese, Modern Language Association of America, Associated Writing Programs, Florida Arts Council.

*AWARDS, HONORS:* Florida Artist fellowship and Cintas fellowship, both 1986-87, for fiction writing; writer in residence at University of Texas at El Paso, 1989; King-Chavez-Parks Visiting Professorship at Western Michigan University, 1990.

*WRITINGS:*

*Cuentos sin rumbos* (short stories), Ediciones Universal (Miami), 1975.
*El jardin de la luna* (short stories), Ediciones Universal, 1976.
*La vida es un special .75* (novel), Ediciones Universal, 1981.
(With Jose B. Fernandez) *Indice bibliografico de autores cubanos (Diaspora, 1959-1979): literatura* (nonfiction; title means "Bibliographical Index of Cuban Authors (Diaspora, 1959-1979): Literature"), Ediciones Universal, 1983.
*La montana rusa* (novel), Arte Publico (Houston), 1985.
*Raining Backwards* (novel), Arte Publico, 1988.
*Holy Radishes!,* Arte Publico, 1995.

Contributor to periodicals, including *Apalachee Quarterly, Florida Review, Linden Lane,* and *West Branch.*

*SIDELIGHTS:* Roberto Fernandez has published several novels and short story collections in his native Spanish since the mid-1970s, but it is his first English language novel, *Raining Backwards* (1988), that has earned him attention from critics. Praised for its humor and affectionate tone, *Raining Backwards* challenges notions of cultural assimilation and identity among Cuban exiles in Miami. Fernandez's ability to satirize both the immigrant community and the reluctance of the American majority to accept minority cultures gives his narrative a foundation of realism and strong social commentary under the hyperbolic, humorous behavior of his characters. The novel was praised as an important contribution to the development of the North American Latino voice, which has lagged behind the development of South American literature.

Roberto Fernandez was born on September 24, 1951 in Sagua la Grande, Cuba, the son of an accountant and a homemaker. In 1961, Fernandez immigrated to the United States, becoming a naturalized citizen in 1972. He attended Florida Atlantic University for undergraduate and graduate work, and earned a Ph.D. at Florida State University in 1977. Fernandez published two collections of short stories, *Cuentos sin rumbos* (1975) and *El jardin de la luna* (1976), while earning his doctorate and teaching Spanish Literature. In 1978, he married Elena Reyes, a psychologist; they divorced five years later, only to remarry in 1990. Fernandez published two Spanish language novels in the early eighties, *La vida es un special .75* (1981) and *La montana rusa* (1985). In 1988, *Raining Backwards* brought Fernandez an expanded audience and favorable critical reception. He has received the Florida Artists fellowship and Cintas fellowship for fiction writing (1986-1987), and has been the writer in residence at the University of Texas at El Paso and a visiting professor at Western Michigan University. Today, Fernandez continues to teach Spanish and Spanish Literature at Florida State University while contributing to publications and writing novels.

Fernandez's early stories and novels chronicled the Cuban community in Miami with humor, satire, and a lively use of colloquial language and colorful characters. In the struggle to assimilate into the American mainstream while retaining an unique cultural identity, Fernandez's characters often yearn for an idealized Cuba. Mary Vasquez writes of his early work, "Beneath the carnivalesque vibrance and color, the entrepreneurial successes and the outrageous humor, the effort to preserve a heritage and the sometimes equally fervent attempt to embrace another, is heard a long and deep lament for an uprooted people." These themes are echoed and developed in Fernandez's most successful novel, *Raining Back-*

*wards,* in which every aspect of the exile experience is parodied, sometimes to outrageous proportions. The novel is populated with characters on the fringe of sanity and normalcy: a drug dealer who forms a guerilla unit in the Everglades, a woman who makes her fortune selling guava pastries, an old maid who seduces a young boy and pines for the diamond dusted beaches of her native Cuba. Fernandez's narration relies on shifting points of view, letters, and telephone calls. The prevailing tone of the novel is one of restless transition, of desiring acceptance and success while clinging to a homeland elevated to mythical status.

Critics consider Fernandez's early works to be blueprints for themes more thoroughly and successfully developed in *Raining Backwards.* Some commentators criticized the narrative style of *Raining Backwards,* contending that it renders the plot confusing at times, and some found the colloquial language less vibrant than in earlier works. However, most critics lauded Fernandez's lively characters and vivid portrayal of the struggle for identity among Cuban exiles in their attempts to transcend their community while retaining their heritage.

Fernandez followed *Raining Backwards* with *Holy Radishes!* As with the author's previous efforts, the novel is set in South Florida-this time in the Everglades community of Belle Glade. The satiric plot concerns the lives of former aristocrats now working at a radish-processing plant. Fernandez again uses shifting narrative and exuberant dialogue. While some critics felt that the author's attempt at satire failed, others praised the novel for its intriguing mix of characters and colorful plot.

*BIOGRAPHICAL/CRITICAL SOURCES:*

*BOOKS*

*Hispanic Writers,* Gale (Detroit), 1991.

*PERIODICALS*

*Americas Review,* spring-summer, 1994, p. 106.
*Booklist,* October 1, 1995, p. 252.
*Confluencia,* fall, 1990.
*Hispanic,* March, 1989.
*Kirkus Reviews,* August 1, 1995, p. 1043.
*New York Times Book Review,* August 14, 1988.
*Philadelphia Inquirer,* December 6, 1988
*San Francisco Chronicle,* April 14, 1988.

*USA Today,* January 3, 1989.
*Vista,* September 3, 1988.*

\* \* \*

## FISHER, Vardis (Alvero) 1895-1968

*PERSONAL:* Born March 31, 1895, in Annis, ID; died July 9, 1968; son of Joseph Oliver and Temperance (Thornton) Fisher; married Leona McMurtrey, September 10, 1918 (died September 8, 1924); married Margaret Trusler, 1928 (divorced, 1929); married Opal Laurel Holmes, April 16, 1940; children: (first marriage) Grant, Wayne; (second marriage) Thornton Roberts. *Education:* University of Utah, A.B., 1920; University of Chicago, A.M., 1922, Ph.D. (magna cum laude), 1925. *Avocational interests:* Horticulture, photography, and wildlife.

*CAREER:* University teacher for eleven years, including University of Utah, Salt Lake, assistant professor of English, 1925-28, and New York University, New York City, assistant professor of English, 1928-31; Federal Writers Project, Idaho State director, 1935-39, general editor for Rocky Mountain states, 1938-39. Columnist for group of western newspapers, 1941-68. *Military service:* U.S. Army, World War I.

*AWARDS, HONORS:* Harper Prize Novel Award, 1939, for *Children of God;* Wrangler Award for best Western historical novel, National Cowboy Hall of Fame, 1965, for *Mountain Man: A Novel of Male and Female in the Early American West;* Western Writers of American Spur award for novel, 1966, and for nonfiction, 1969.

*WRITINGS:*

*"VRIDAR HUNTER" TETRALOGY*

*In Tragic Life,* Caxton (Caldwell, ID), 1932 (published in England as *I See No Sin,* Boriswood [London], 1934).
*Passions Spin the Plot,* Doubleday (New York City), 1934.
*We Are Betrayed,* Doubleday, 1935.
*No Villain Need Be,* Doubleday, 1936.

*"THE TESTAMENT OF MAN" SERIES*

*Darkness and Deep,* Vanguard (New York City), 1943.

*The Golden Rooms,* Vanguard, 1944.

*Intimations of Eve,* Vanguard, 1946.

*Adam and the Serpent,* Vanguard, 1947.

*The Divine Passion,* Vanguard, 1948.

*The Valley of Vision,* Abelard (New York City), 1951.

*The Island of the Innocent,* Abelard, 1952.

*A Goat for Azazel,* A. Swallow (Denver, CO), 1956.

*Jesus Came Again: A Parable,* A. Swallow, 1956.

*Peace Like a River: A Novel of Christian Asceticism,* A. Swallow, 1957, reprinted as *The Passion Within,* Pyramid (New York City), 1960.

*My Holy Satan: A Novel of Christian Twilight,* A Swallow, 1958.

*Orphans in Gethsemane,* A. Swallow, 1960, reprinted in two volumes as *For Passion, For Heaven* and *The Great Confession,* Pyramid, 1962.

### AMERICAN HISTORICAL NOVELS

*Children of God,* Harper (New York City), 1939.

*City of Illusion,* Harper, 1941.

*The Mothers: An American Saga of Courage,* Vanguard, 1943.

*Pemmican: A Novel of the Hudson's Bay Company,* Doubleday, 1956.

*Tale of Valor: A Novel of the Lewis and Clark Expedition,* Doubleday, 1958.

*Mountain Man: A Novel of Male and Female in the Early American West,* Morrow (New York City), 1965.

### OTHER

*Sonnets to an Imaginary Madonna,* Vinal (New York City), 1927.

*Toilers of the Hills,* Houghton (Boston), 1928, reprinted as *The Wild One,* Pyramid (New York City), 1952.

*Dark Bridwell,* Houghton, 1931.

*The Neurotic Nightingale* (essays), Casanova Press (Milwaukee, WI), 1935.

*Odyssey of a Hero,* Ritten House (Philadelphia), 1937.

*April: A Fable of Love,* Caxton, 1937, Doubleday, 1937.

*Forgive Us Our Virtues: A Comedy of Evasions,* Caxton, 1938.

*The Caxton Printers in Idaho: A Short History,* Society of Bibliosophers (Cincinnati, OH), 1944.

*God or Caesar?: The Writing of Fiction for Beginners,* Caxton, 1953.

*Love and Death: The Complete Short Stories of Vardis Fisher,* Doubleday, 1959.

*Suicide or Murder?: The Strange Death of Governor Meriwether Lewis,* A. Swallow, 1962.

*Thomas Wolfe as I Knew Him, and Other Essays,* A. Swallow, 1963.

(With Opal Laurel Holmes) *Gold Rushes and Mining Camps of the Early American West,* Caxton, 1968.

General editor and contributor to *Idaho: A Guide in Word and Picture,* Caxton, 1937, *Idaho Encyclopedia,* Caxton, 1938, and *Idaho Lore,* Caxton, 1939. Contributor of articles and short stories to magazines and journals.

*ADAPTATIONS: Mountain Man* was filmed as *Jeremiah Johnson,* starring Robert Redford and directed by Sydney Pollack, Warner, 1972.

*SIDELIGHTS:* Vardis Fisher was a prolific, ambitious writer who was determined to question every facet of the human psyche. Although numerous critics have conceded that his reach exceeded his grasp, his body of work nevertheless has a significant place in American literature. His best known works describe the rugged conditions of life in the American West during the frontier days. Frequently, these books are based on real-life events. *The Mothers: An American Saga of Courage* relates the story of the Donner party, trapped by snow in the high Sierras while trying to reach California; *Tale of Valor: A Novel of the Lewis and Clark Expedition* is the epic of the explorers' journey west; and *Mountain Man: A Novel of Male and Female in the Early American West* is a fictionalized autobiography of "Liver Eating" Johnson, a legendary frontiersman. Fisher's "Vridar Hunter" books are based on his own life and search for meaning and truth, while the "Testament of Man" series undertakes no less than a complete retelling of the physical, intellectual, and spiritual evolution of man from prehistoric times to the present day. His other work included poetry, essays, and volumes of historical nonfiction.

Fisher has been constantly compared to Thomas Wolfe, and the comparison is in many ways apt. The two writers, both one-time instructors at New York University, were good friends, and both produced sprawling, autobiographical works. Fisher once said of Wolfe: "I had more in common with him that I have ever had with any other friend." Elizabeth Nowell, Wolfe's literary agent, wrote to Fisher: "I think [Wolfe] felt that you had never got the recognition you deserved, and that was one reason he was always FOR you, suggesting you to me . . . 'talking you up'. . . . Think he identified you with himself, sort of: two guys trying to write books from really inside, and long series of them, and so up against it to get recognized for what they were." Fisher, however, always remained in Wolfe's shadow.

Writing in *Dictionary of Literary Biography,* Joseph M. Flora named Fisher "the first American Writer from the Rocky Mountains to create significant literature about that region. But Fisher's place in American literature does not rest solely on his being a regional writer. Alfred Kazin has called him America's last authentic novelist of the frontier. Unquestionably Fisher demands attention for his regional writings: his frontier isolation made him unique among twentieth-century writers." The author was born in a Mormon pioneer settlement in Idaho, but when he was six years old, his family moved to a remote property in the foothills of the Big Hole Mountains, near the Snake River. They lived in almost total isolation, with their nearest neighbors some ten miles away on the other bank of the river. Fisher's schooling came from his mother until he was sixteen years old; at that time, he and his sister moved into a hut outside the nearest small town so that they could attend high school there. Fearful and shy, Fisher was nevertheless highly competitive. After entering the University of Utah, he even made the football team, but his main focus was intellectual life. He decided to become a teacher, and eventually moved with his wife and two young sons to Chicago to do graduate work there.

In 1924 Fisher's wife committed suicide, an event that filled him with guilt and intensified his desire to find meaning in the human condition. His first published book, *Sonnets to an Imaginary Madonna,* was his response to the tragic ending of his first marriage. A year later, in 1928, he published his first novel, *Toilers of the Hills.* It was basically the story of his youth—"a realistic account of frontier farming struggles, with leavening humor," in Flora's words. The follow-up novel, *Dark Bridwell,* published in 1931, was based on the life of Charley Wheaton, the neighbor who had lived across the river during Fisher's youth. "In presenting Charley's history, Fisher created one of his most powerful works," asserted Flora. John Milton, a contributor to *Midwest Quarterly,* asserted that "*Dark Bridwell* is . . . not only Fisher's best novel . . . but one of the masterpieces of the American novel. It is a true tragedy of the end of the American frontier; it achieves the status of myth, although firmly anchored in the Idaho soil; and Charley Bridwell, through his peculiar strengths and weaknesses, becomes an American

Lear." Fisher's alter ego Vridar Hunter is introduced in this story, as a sensitive, fearful little boy. About the time *Dark Bridwell* was published, Fisher—who had remarried—returned to live in Idaho once more.

His third novel, *In Tragic Life,* was similar in theme to the first two, yet it also marked the beginning of a larger venture, the four-volume series based on his own life—which was completed by *Passions Spin the Plot, We Are Betrayed,* and *No Villain Need Be.* The titles of the tetralogy come from one of George Meredith's sonnets, a Fisher influence, and appropriately suggest the theme, since Fisher is analyzing a tragic love experience." 'Tis morning: but no morning can restore / What we have forfeited. I see no sin: / The wrong is mixed. In tragic life, God wot, / No villain need be! Passion spins the plot: We are betrayed by what is false within." The sensitive honesty of the books struck a responsive chord, and Fisher's "prose and hard-hitting themes seemed right to meet the demands of the 1930s, an era impatient with frills and pretense," noted Flora.

Despite the public's enthusiasm for his books, Fisher experienced a sense of failure after writing the tetralogy. He felt that exploring a man's childhood was not sufficient for explaining the man that came to be. "After I had read in the records many years and had come to a fair notion of my ignorance I wrote my publisher that Schulberg had not been able to tell us what made Sammy run, Wolfe had not known what made Gant-Webber run, and I had not known what made Vridar run. The matter, I had come to suspect, was not the simple one of the adult's childhood; it was the complex matter of his entire history, which is the history not only of mankind but of the whole plant and animal world. Writers may never be able to tell their readers what makes Sammy run, but after thirty years of reading about the past I knew more about Vridar . . . than I had known when I wrote his story." He eventually revised and edited this work and it became *Orphans in Gethsemane,* the last volume of "The Testament of Man."

With "The Testament of Man," Fisher aimed to present the evolution of man's soul from the beginning of time to the present day. He began the series, which would eventually grow to twelve volumes, in 1943. Less than a decade had passed since the Fisher had been in the literary limelight, but his fortunes had changed considerably. Critical response to "The Testament of Man" was scant, and on the whole it was judged overly didactic and repetitious. Flora elaborated: "When the first few books of ["The Testament of Man"] appeared, a few critics noticed them with interest. However, they received nothing like the attention Fisher got in the depression decade. Even his first two novels received more notice. But midway through the series, Fisher was receiving almost no attention. He had become a historical curiosity; he was dismissed as a writer whose interest belonged essentially to the troubled decade of the 1930's." Eventually Fisher's original publisher abandoned the project, but it was revived by Alan Swallow, who was firmly convinced of the importance of the author's work. Milton called the "Testament" "one of the most monumental fictional projects ever undertaken in America" and further described it as "frighteningly ambitious."

Commenting on the "Testament," Fisher said: "Now that the task is completed I feel, in looking back, that it was too big for me. I think that if a writer were to attempt what I attempted his preparation should begin early and his education should be directed toward his goal. I started late, very late, and so abused my eyes and health and drove myself at a pace that only my wife was ever allowed to see, realizing more clearly as the years passed that I'd never had enough time to assimilate and reflect on the countless wonderful facts and implications in the learned articles and more than two thousand books that I read. I developed a case of chronic mental indigestion. . . . I knew from the first that I'd want to write a novel about the ape-man. I think I was not half so successful as I had wished to be in projecting myself into the small dim world of those stooped short-legged hairy ancestors, who were learning to walk in an upright position. . . . The second novel, with its theme . . . of the ghost and the grave, satisfied me no more; or the third . . . nor the fourth." Critic Edmund Fuller was much more impressed than the author himself, declaring: "I am in utter disagreement with all of Fisher's philosophy, yet I respect him. . . . He is hard-working, he is courageous; he is expanding his talents unstintingly to try to answer the great questions that haunt him."

Fisher's most famous novel is *Children of God,* the story of the Mormons. "This was an enormous task, an opportunity to make an enormous achievement," commented Mark Schorer. Yet he deemed Fisher ultimately unsuccessful, claiming that "here and there . . . the novel comes up to the nearly excellent; but usually, in every important respect, Mr. Fisher fails to bring his novel up to the level of his ambitions." Clifton Fadiman, however, reflected the more enthusiastic attitude of many critics: "*Children of God* is one of the most extraordinarily interesting stories I have ever read and . . . I have rarely encountered a book whose faults one is more eager and easily able to condone." Financially successful, the book is still the most widely read of Fisher's works. The author capitalized on its popularity by following it with a string of other novels set in the old West. *City of Illusion* tells of the Comstock lode and the early days of Nevada; *The Mothers* recounted the Donner party disaster, in which the survivors were reduced to cannibalism; and *Pemmican: A Novel of the Hudson's Bay Company* recreates the Pemmican War of the early nineteenth century, in which the Hudson's Bay Company and the North West Company battled for supremacy in the fur trade. Most of these books were well-reviewed. For example, *Library Journal* contributor M. P. McKay classified *The Mothers* as "fictionized biography at its best," featuring "excellent writing and characterization"; and a writer for the *Boston Transcript* wrote of *City of Illusion:* "One doubts if a better book could be written on the subject. . . . It is an intensely alive book."

Flora summarized Fisher's stature as a writer thus: "In a prolific career, Fisher has not been a static writer, and he cannot, therefore, be easily labeled. His work has more complexity than summary treatments of him have usually indicated. If he is a hard-boiled Naturalist, he is also a humanitarian—and though many critics missed it—a humorist. If he sometimes is overly didactic, he has written novels in which he has been quite detached. . . . He has not only written novels on many subjects but he has experimented with form; he has unfortunately, however, never developed the technical excellence of most of our major figures. . . . As a poet, essayist, and novelist, Fisher is a writer of range, imagination, and mind. . . . Clearly Fisher is not every man's writer, and it is quite conceivable that readers will approve him in one kind of novel—or genre—and not in another, in itself a tribute to his range."

*BIOGRAPHICAL/CRITICAL SOURCES:*

*BOOKS*

Chatterton, Wayne, *Vardis Fisher: The Frontier and Regional Works,* Idaho State University Press (Boise), 1972.
*Contemporary Literary Criticism,* Volume 7, Gale (Detroit), 1977.
*Dictionary of Literary Biography,* Volume 9: *American Novelists, 1910-1945,* Gale, 1981.
Flora, Joseph M., *Vardis Fisher,* Twayne (New York City), 1965.

Grover, Dorys C., *A Solitary Voice: Vardis Fisher,* Revisionist Press (New York City), 1973.

Grover, *Vardis Fisher: The Novelist as Poet,* Revisionist Press (New York City), 1973.

Milton, John, editor, *Three West,* Dakota Press (Vermillion, SD), 1970.

Rein, David, *Vardis Fisher: Challenge to Evasion,* Black Cat (New York City), 1938.

Snell, Dixon, *Shapers of American Fiction, 1798-1947,* Dutton (New York City), 1947, pp. 276-88.

*Twentieth-Century Western Writers,* 2nd edition, St. James Press (Detroit), 1991.

Strong, Lester, *The Past in the Present: Two Essays on History and Myth in Fisher's Testament of Man,* Revisionist Press (New York City), 1979.

Thomas, Alfred K., *The Epic of Evolution: Its Ideology and Art: A Study of Vardis Fisher's "Testament of Man",* Revisionist Press, 1973.

*PERIODICALS*

*American Book Collector,* September, 1963, pp. 9-12.

*Arts and Science,* spring, 1962.

*Booklist,* November 1, 1943; May 1, 1941.

*Books,* March 30, 1941, p. 5.

*Book Week,* March 21, 1943, p. 4; October 10, 1943, p. 2; December 10, 1944, p. 4; April 21, 1946, p. 6.

*Boston Transcript,* September 9, 1939; March 29, 1941, p. 2.

*Chicago Sunday Tribune,* June 24, 1951, p. 2.

*Dialogue: A Journal of Mormon Thought,* autumn, 1969, pp. 48-55.

*Kirkus Reviews,* September 15, 1944; January, 1946; August 15, 1948.

*Library Journal,* February 1, 1941; September 1, 1943; November 1, 1944; September 15, 1948; May 1, 1951.

*Manchester Guardian,* September 26, 1941, p. 3.

*Midwest Quarterly,* July, 1976, pp. 369-84.

*MD,* November, 1961.

*Nation,* March 27, 1943; October 30, 1943.

*New Republic,* May 19, 1941.

*New Yorker,* September 2, 1939; March 29, 1941; March 13, 1943; October 9, 1943; April 13, 1946; October 2, 1948; June 9, 1951.

*New York Herald Tribune Book Review,* August 26, 1939, p. 3; June 3, 1951, p. 7; June 22, 1952, p. 10.

*New York Herald Tribune Weekly Book Review,* October 31, 1948, p. 11.

*New York Times,* April 6, 1941, p. 6; March 21, 1943, p. 5; October 3, 1943, p. 6; December 3, 1944, p. 6; March 31, 1946, p. 12; September 19, 1948, p. 21; June 3, 1951, p. 16; April 13, 1952, p. 17.

*Prairie Schooner,* winter, 1938, pp. 294-309.

*San Francisco Chronicle,* December 12, 1948, p. 22; April 20, 1952, p. 25.

*Saturday Review,* November 6, 1965, pp. 33-34.

*Saturday Review of Literature,* August 26, 1939, p. 41; April 19, 1941; March 27, 1943; November 6, 1943; April 20, 1946; October 2, 1948; August 18, 1951.

*Southern Review,* autumn, 1937, pp. 56-65.

*Spectator,* October 10, 1941.

*Springfield Republican,* June 1, 1952, p. 19A.

*Time,* August 12, 1946; April 14, 1941; April 8, 1946; July 2, 1951.

*Times Literary Supplement,* September 27, 1941, p. 481.

*Weekly Book Review,* March 21, 1943, p. 6; October 3, 1943, p. 3; April 28, 1946, p. 6.

*Western American Literature,* winter, 1967, pp. 285-96; spring, 1970; summer, 1970, pp. 121-128.*

\*          \*          \*

**FO, Dario 1926-**

*PERSONAL:* Born March 24, 1926, in San Giano, Lombardy, Italy; son of Felice (a railroad stationmaster) and Pina (Rota) Fo; married Franca Rame (a playwright and actress), June, 1954; children: three. *Education:* Attended Accademia di Belle Arti, Milan.

*ADDRESSES: Home*—Milan, Italy. *Agent*—Maria Nadotti, 349 East 51st St., New York, NY 10022.

*CAREER:* Playwright, director, actor, and theatrical company leader. Has written more than forty plays, many of which have been translated and performed in more than thirty countries, beginning in 1953; performs plays in Italy, Europe, and the United States, and runs classes and workshops for actors, 1970s—. Worked as a member of small theatrical group, headed by Franco Parenti, performing semi-improvised sketches for radio before local audiences, 1950; wrote and performed comic monologues for his own radio program, *Poer nana* ("Poor Dwarf"), broadcast by the Italian national radio network RAI, 1951; formed revue company, *I Dritti* ("The Stand-Ups"), with Giustino Durano and Parenti, 1953; screenwriter in Rome, 1956-58; formed improvisational troupe *Compagnia Fo-Rame,* with wife, Franca Rame, 1958;

named artistic director of Italian state television network's weekly musical revue, *Chi l'ha visto?* ("Who's Seen It?"), and writer and performer of sketches for variety show *Canzonissima* ("Really Big Song"), 1959; formed theater cooperative *Nuova Scena,* with Rame, 1968, and *La Comune,* 1970.

*AWARDS, HONORS:* Recipient of Sonning Award, Denmark, 1981; Obie Award, 1987; Nobel Prize in Literature, 1997.

*WRITINGS:*

PLAYS

*Teatro comico,* Garzanti, 1962.

*Le commedie,* Einaudi, 1966, enlarged edition published as *Le commedie di Dario Fo,* 6 volumes, Einaudi, 1974, reprinted, 1984.

*Vorrei morire anche stasera se dovessi pensare che no e servito a niente,* E.D.B., 1970.

*Morte e resurrezione di un pupazzo,* Sapere Edizioni, 1971.

*Ordine! Per Dio,* Bertani, 1972.

*Pum, pum! Chi e? La polizia!* (title means "Knock, Knock! Who's There? Police!"), Bertani, 1972.

*Tutti uniti! Tutti insieme! Ma scusa quello non e il padrone?* (title means "United United We Stand! All Together Now! Oops, Isn't That the Boss?"), Bertani, 1972.

*Guerra di popolo in Cile* (title means "The People's War in Chile"), Bertani, 19), Bertani, 1973.

*Mistero buffo* (title means "The Comic Mystery"; first produced in Milan, 1969; produced on Broadway at the Joyce Theater, May 27, 1986), Bertani, 1973, revised, 1974.

*Ballate e canzoni* (title means "Ballads and Songs"), introduction by Lanfranco Binni, Bertani, 1974, reprinted, Newton Compton, 1976.

*Morte accidentale di un anarchico* (first produced in Milan, December, 1970; produced on Broadway at Belasco Theater, November 15, 1984), Einaudi, 1974, translation by Gavin Richards published as *Accidental Death of an Anarchist,* Pluto Press, 1980.

*Non si paga, non si paga* (first produced in Milan, 1974), La comune, 1974, translation by Lino Pertite published as *We Can't Pay? We Won't Pay!,* adapted by Bill Colvill and Robert Walker, Pluto Press, 1978, translation by Pertite reprinted as *Can't Pay? Won't Pay!,* Pluto Press, 1982, North American version by R. G. Davis published as *We Won't Pay! We Won't Pay!,* Samuel French, 1984.

*La guillarata,* Bertani, 1975.

*Il Fanfani rapito,* Bertani, 1975.

*La marjuana della mamma e la piu bella,* Bertani, 1976.

*La signora e da buttare* (title means "The Old Girl's for the Scrapheap"), Einaudi, 1976.

*Il teatro politico,* G. Mazzotta, 1977.

(With wife, Franca Rame) *Tutta casa, letto e chiesa* (title means "All House, Bed, and Church"), Bertani, 1978, translation published as *Orgasmo Adulto Escapes from the Zoo,* Bertani, 1978, translation by Estelle Parsons, Broadway Play Publishing, 1985.

*La storia di un soldato,* photographs by Silvia Lelli Masotti, commentary by Ugo Volli, Electa, 1979.

*Storia vera di Piero d'Angera: Che alla crociata non c'era,* La comune, 1981.

OTHER PLAYS; IN ENGLISH TRANSLATION

(With Rame) *Female Parts: One Woman Plays,* translated by Margaret Kunzle and Stuart Hood, adapted by Olwen Wymark, Pluto Press, 1981.

*Car Horns, Trumpets and Raspberries* (first produced in Milan, January, 1981; produced in the United States at the Yale Repertory Theater as *About Face,* 1981), translated by R. C. McAvoy and A. H. Giugni, Pluto Press, 1981, reprinted, 1984.

(With Rame) *The Open Couple—Wide Open Even,* Theatretexts, 1984.

*The Tale of a Tiger,* Theatretexts, 1984.

*One Was Nude and One Wore Tails,* Theatretexts, 1985.

*The Open Couple and an Ordinary Day,* Heinemann, 1990.

*The Pope and the Witch,* Heinemann, 1993.

(With Rame) *Plays, Two* (contains *Can't Pay? Won't Pay!, The Open Couple,* and *An Ordinary Day*), Methuen (London), 1994.

Also author of *The Devil with Boobs.*

OTHER PLAYS; PRODUCED ONLY

*Il dito nell'occhio* (title means "A Finger in the Eye"), first produced in Milan at Piccolo Teatro, June, 1953.

*I sani da legare* (title means "A Madhouse for the Sane"), first produced in Milan at Piccolo Teatro, 1954.

*Ladri, manachini e donne nude* (title means "Thieves, Dummies, and Naked Women"), first produced in Milan at Piccolo Teatro, 1958.

*Gli arcangeli non giocano a flipper* (title means "Archangels Don't Play Pinball", first produced in Milan at Teatro Odeon, September, 1959.

*Isabella, tre caravelle, e un cacciaballe* (title means "Isabella, Three Ships, and a Con Man"), first produced in Milan at Teatro Odeon, 1963.

Also author of numerous other plays produced in Italy, including *Aveva due pistole con gli occhi bianchi e neri* (title means "He Had Two Pistols with White and Black Eyes"), 1960; *Grande pantomima con bandiere e pupazzi piccoli e medi* (title means "Grand Pantomime with Flags and Small and Medium-Sized Puppets"), October, 1968; *Fedayn,* 1971; *Il fabulazzo osceno* (title means "The Obscene Fable"), 1982; *Quasi per caso una donna: Elisabetta* (title means "A Woman Almost by Chance: Elizabeth"), 1984; and *Hellequin, Arlekin, Arlechino,* 1986. Other stage credits include an adaptation of Bertolt Brecht's *Threepenny Opera,* for Teatro Stabile di Torino and Teatro Il Fabbricone of Prato, and *Patapumfete,* for the clown duo I Colombaioni.

*OTHER*

*Manuale minimo dell'attore* (title means "Basic Handbook for the Actor"), Einuadi, 1987.

*The Tricks of the Trade,* translation by Joe Farrell, Routledge, 1991.

*SIDELIGHTS:* Noted Italian playwright and Nobel laureate Dario Fo began refining his animated method of storytelling as a child, listening to the tales told by the locals in San Giano, the small fishing village in northern Italy where he was born. After leaving Milan's Academy of Fine Arts without earning a degree, Fo wrote and performed with several improvisational theatrical groups. He first earned acclaim as a playwright in 1953 with *Il dito nell'occhio* (*A Finger in the Eye*), a socially satiric production that presented Marxist ideas against a circus-like background. His 1954 attack on the Italian government in *I sani de legare* (*A Madhouse for the Sane*), in which Fo labeled several government officials fascist sympathizers, resulted in the cutting of some material from the original script and the mandated presence of state inspectors at each performance of the play to insure that the country's strict libel laws were not violated.

Following a brief stint as a screenwriter in Rome, Fo, together with his wife, actress Franca Rame, returned to the theater and produced a more generalized, less explicitly political brand of social satire. Widely regarded as his best work during this phase of his ca-

reer, *Gli arcangeli non giocano a flipper* (*Archangels Don't Play Pinball*) was the first of Fo's plays to be staged outside of Italy. As quoted by Irving Wardle in the London *Times,* the heroic clown in *Archangels* voices the playwright's basic contention, stating, "My quarrel is with those who organize our dreams."

In 1968 Fo and Rame rejected the legitimate theater as an arm of the bourgeoisie and, backed by the Italian Communist party, they formed Nuova Scena, a noncommercial theater group designed to entertain and inform the working class. The plays produced by this company centered on political issues and grew increasingly radical in tone. The communist government withdrew its support from Nuova Scena after the staging of *Grande pantomima con bandiere e pupazzi piccoli e medi* (*Grand Pantomime with Flags and Small and Medium-Sized Puppets*), a satire of Italy's political history in the wake of World War II. The highly symbolic play depicts the birth of capitalism (portrayed by a beautiful woman) from fascism (a huge monster puppet) and the subsequent seduction of communism by capitalism. Through the play Fo demonstrated his disenchantment with the authoritative, antirevolutionary policies of the Italian Communist party, allowing communism to succumb to capitalism's enticement.

Steeped in an atmosphere of political and social unrest, the 1960s proved to be a decade of increased popularity for Fo, providing him with new material and a receptive audience. He first performed *Mistero buffo,* generally considered his greatest and most controversial play, in 1969. An improvised production based on a constantly changing script, the play is a decidedly irreverent retelling of the gospels that indicts landowners, government, and, in particular, the Catholic church as public oppressors. Fo based the show's format on that of the medieval mystery plays originally parodied by *giullari,* strolling minstrel street performers of the Middle Ages. *Mistero buffo* was written in Italian as a series of sketches for a single actor—Fo—to perform on an empty stage. The playwright introduces each segment of the work with an informal prologue to establish a rapport with his audience. He links together the satiric religious narratives, portraying up to a dozen characters at a time by himself. The sketches include a reenactment of Lazarus's resurrection, complete with opportunists who pick the pockets of the awestruck witnesses; the tale of a contented cripple's efforts to avoid being cured by Jesus; an account of the wedding feast at Cana as told by a drunkard; and an especially dark portrait of the corrupt Pope Boniface VIII.

Jenkins considered Fo's black humor and "sense of moral indignation" most effectively illuminated in a fable from *Mistero buffo* titled "The Birth of the Giullare," which explains how the minstrel received his narrative gift. A former peasant, the *giullare* had been humiliated and victimized by corrupt politicians, priests, and landowners. In his despair, he decides to kill himself but is interrupted by a man asking for water. The man is Jesus Christ, who, in kissing the peasant's lips gives him the facility to mesmerize an audience—and deflate the very authorities that had oppressed him—with his words. Jenkins remarked, "Fo performs the moment of the miracle with an exhilarating sense of musicality. . . . The triumph of freedom over tyranny is palpable in [his] every sound and movement."

According to Charles C. Mann in *Atlantic Monthly,* Fo took pleasure in the Vatican's description of the play, which was taped and broadcast on television in 1977, as "the most blasphemous" program ever televised. *Mistero buffo* was nevertheless a critical and popular success throughout Europe. The staging of the play in London in 1983 singlehandedly saved from bankruptcy the financially ailing theater in which it was performed. Despite the reception of his masterpiece abroad, Fo was unable to perform the play in the United States until 1986 when he and Rame were finally granted permission to enter the country. The couple had been denied visas in 1980 and 1984 because of their alleged involvement in fund-raising activities for an Italian terrorist organization. Fo and his wife dismissed the accusation and maintained their innocence. Through the efforts of civil libertarian and cultural groups in Europe and the United States, Fo and Rame ultimately received visas, and *Mistero buffo* opened in New York in the spring of 1986. Jenkins termed the play "a brilliant one-man version of biblical legends and church history" whose comedy "echo[es] the rhythms of revolt."

Fo's penchant for justice prompted him to compose the absurdist play *Morte accidentale di un anarchico* (*Accidental Death of an Anarchist*) in response to the untimely death of anarchist railway man Giuseppi Pinelli in late 1969. Pinelli's death was apparently connected to efforts by right-wing extremists in Italy's military and secret service agencies to discredit the Italian Communist party by staging a series of seemingly leftist-engineered bombings. The railway worker was implicated in the worst of these bombings, the 1969 massacre at Milan's Agricultural Bank. While being held for interrogation, Pinelli

fell—it was later shown that he was pushed—from the fourth-floor window of Milan's police headquarters.

In *Accidental Death* Fo introduces a stock medieval character, the maniac, into the investigation of the bombing to illuminate the truth. Fo commented in *American Theatre,* "When I injected absurdity into the situation, the lies became apparent. The maniac plays the role of the judge, taking the logic of the authorities to their absurd extremes," thus demonstrating that Pinelli's death could not have occurred in the way the police had described. John Lahr reported in the *Los Angeles Times* that because of their part in the exposure of the police cover-up, Fo was assaulted and jailed and Rame kidnapped and beaten in the first few years that the play was staged.

*Accidental Death of an Anarchist* was a smash hit in Italy, playing to huge crowds for more than four years. When officials pressured a theater in Bologna to halt plans for production, the play was alternatively staged in a sports stadium for an audience of more than six thousand people. After receiving rave reviews throughout Europe—Lahr, writing in *New Society,* called the show "loud, vulgar, kinetic, scurrilous, smart, [and] sensational. . . . Everything theatre should be"—and enjoying a thirty-month run in London, *Accidental Death* opened in the United States in 1984, only to close a short time later.

Because Fo's plays are often either loosely translated or performed in Italian and center on historical, political, and social events that bear more significance for audiences in Italy than in the States, American versions of the playwright's works are frequently considered less dazzling than their Italian counterparts. In an article for the *New York Times* Mel Gussow pointed out that "dealing with topical Italian materials in colloquial Italian language . . . presents problems for adapters and directors." For instance, a few critics found the presence of a translator on stage during *Mistero buffo* mildly distracting. And many reviewers agreed that the English translation of *Accidental Death* lacked the power of the Italian production. Frank Rich insisted in the *New York Times* that adapter Richard Nelson's introduction of timely American puns into the *Accidental Death* script "wreck[ed] the play's farcical structure and jolt[ed] both audience and cast out of its intended grip."

Fo's 1978 collaboration with Rame, *Tutta casa, letto e chiesa,* produced in the United States as *Orgasmo Adulto Escapes from the Zoo,* also "may have lost some of its punch crossing the Atlantic," asserted David Richards in the *Washington Post*. A cycle of short sketches written for a single female player, *Orgasmo* focuses on women's status in a patriarchal society. Richards felt that, to an American audience in the mid-1980s (when the play was produced in the United States), "the women in *Orgasmo* seem to be fighting battles that have long been conceded on these shores." Still, if not timely, the performances were judged favorably for their zest and honesty in portraying Italian sexism.

*The Tricks of the Trade,* published in 1991, is a collection of notes, talks, and workshop transcripts by Fo that deal with numerous aspects of the theater and their historical origins and modern roles: mimes and clowns, masks, and puppets and marionettes. Fo also discusses his own plays and his distinctive approach to playwriting and performing. "*The Tricks of the Trade* offers inspiration for theatre practitioners of all sorts, while celebrating a revival of the power and predominance of the politically inspired clown," remarked James Fisher in *Drama Review*. Writing in *World Literature Today,* Giovanni d'Angelo commented that the book "is technically robust and exhaustive" and termed Fo's style "fluent and graceful."

Gussow noted, "For Mr. Fo, there are no sacred cows, least of all himself or his native country," and concluded that Fo's social commentary is more "relevant" than "subversive." Commenting on the underlying philosophy that shapes and informs his works, Fo asserted in *American Theatre,* "My plays are provocations, like catalysts in a chemical solution. . . . I just put some drops of absurdity in this calm and tranquil liquid, which is society, and the reactions reveal things that were hidden before the absurdity brought them out into the open."

## BIOGRAPHICAL/CRITICAL SOURCES:

### BOOKS

Artese, Erminia, *Dario Fo parla di Dario Fo,* Lerici, 1977.
*Contemporary Literary Criticism,* Gale (Detroit), Volume 32, 1985, Volume 109, 1998.
McAvoy, R. C., editor, *Fo Dario and Franca Rame: The Theatre Workshops at Riverside Studios,* Red Notes, 1983.
Mitchell, Tony, *Dario Fo: People's Court Jester,* Methuen, 1984.

### PERIODICALS

*American Theatre,* June, 1986.
*Atlantic Monthly,* September, 1985.
*Choice,* March, 1992, p. 1090.
*Drama,* summer, 1979.
*Drama Review,* winter, 1992, p. 171.
*Los Angeles Times,* January 16, 1983; January 21, 1983.
*National Catholic Reporter,* November 13, 1992.
*New Republic,* December 17, 1984.
*New Society,* March 13, 1980.
*New Statesman,* August 7, 1981.
*New Yorker,* February 23, 1981.
*New York Times,* December 18, 1980; April 17, 1983; August 5, 1983; August 14, 1983; August 27, 1983; February 15, 1984; October 31, 1984; November 16, 1984; May 29, 1986; May 30, 1986; May 9, 1987; November 27, 1987.
*New York Times Book Review,* February 2, 1998, p. 31.
*Opera News,* October, 1993.
*Times* (London), November 17, 1984; September 22, 1986; September 25, 1986.
*Times Literary Supplement,* December 18, 1987.
*Variety,* August 4, 1982; May 11, 1992.
*Washington Post,* August 27, 1983; November 17, 1984; January 17, 1985; June 12, 1986.
*World Literature Today,* autumn, 1992, p. 707.*

\* \* \*

## FOREMAN, Michael 1938-

*PERSONAL:* Born March 21, 1938, in Lowestoft, England; son of Walter Thomas (a crane operator) and Gladys (Goddard) Foreman; married Janet Charters, September 26, 1959 (divorced, 1966); married Louise Phillips, 1980; children: (first marriage) Mark; (second marriage) Ben Shahn, Jack. *Education:* Lowestoft School of Art, National Diploma in Design (painting), 1958; Royal College of Art, A.R.C.A. (with first honors), 1963.

*ADDRESSES: Home*—5 Church Gate, London SW6, England. *Agent*—John Locke, 15 East 76th St., New York, NY 10021.

*CAREER:* Graphic artist, children's author. Lecturer in graphics at St. Martin's School of Art, London, England, 1963-66, London College of Printing, 1966-68, Royal College of Art, London, 1968-70, and

Central School of Art, London, 1971-72. Art director of *Ambit,* 1960—, *Playboy,* 1965, and *King,* 1966-67. Work exhibited at individual show, Royal Festival Hall, London, 1985, and in Europe, America, and Japan.

*AWARDS, HONORS:* Schweppes traveling scholarship to United States, 1961-63; Gimpel Fils Prize for young painters, 1962; Festival International du Livre Silver Eagle Award, France, 1972; Francis Williams Memorial Award, Victoria and Albert Museum, 1972, and 1977, for *Monkey and the Three Wizards;* Kate Greenaway Commended Book, British Library Association, 1978, for *The Brothers Grimm: Popular Folk Tales;* Carnegie Medal, British Library Association, 1980, Kate Greenaway Highly Commended Book, 1980, and Graphics Prize, International Children's Book Fair, Bologna, Italy, 1982, for *City of Gold and Other Stories from the Old Testament;* Kate Greenaway Medal and Kurt Maschler/Emil Award, Book Trust of England, both 1982, for *Sleeping Beauty and Other Favourite Fairy Tales;* Kate Greenaway Medal, 1982, for *Longneck and Thunderfoot;* Federation of Children's Book Groups award, England, 1983, for *The Saga of Erik the Viking;* Kate Greenaway Commended Book and *New York Times* Notable Book, both 1985, for *Seasons of Splendour: Tales, Myths and Legends of India;* runner-up, Maschler Award, 1985, for *Shakespeare Stories;* runner-up, Maschler Award, 1986, and *Signal* Poetry award, 1987, for *Early in the Morning: A Collection of New Poems;* Kate Greenaway Medal and W. H. Smith/Books in Canada Award, both 1990, for *War Boy: A Country Childhood;* Smarties Prize, 1993.

*WRITINGS:*

*Winter's Tales,* illustrated by Freire White, Doubleday (New York City), 1979.

*SELF-ILLUSTRATED*

*The Perfect Present,* Coward (New York City), 1967.
*The Two Giants,* Pantheon (New York City), 1967.
*The Great Sleigh Robbery,* Hamish Hamilton (London), 1968, Pantheon, 1969.
*Horatio,* Hamish Hamilton, 1970, published as *The Travels of Horatio,* Pantheon, 1970.
*Moose,* Hamish Hamilton, 1971, Pantheon, 1972.
*Dinosaurs and All That Rubbish,* Hamish Hamilton, 1972, Crowell (New York City), 1973.
*War and Peas,* Crowell, 1974.
*All the King's Horses,* Hamish Hamilton, 1976, Bradbury (Scarsdale, NY), 1977.

*Panda's Puzzle, and His Voyage of Discovery,* Hamish Hamilton, 1977, Bradbury, 1978.
*Panda and the Odd Lion,* Hamish Hamilton, 1979.
*Trick a Tracker,* Philomel (New York City), 1981.
*Land of Dreams,* Holt (New York City), 1982.
*Panda and the Bunyips,* Hamish Hamilton, 1984, Schocken (New York City), 1988.
*Cat and Canary,* Andersen (London), 1984, Dial (New York City), 1985.
*Panda and the Bushfire,* Prentice-Hall (Englewood Cliffs, NJ), 1986.
*Ben's Box,* Hodder and Stoughton (London), 1986.
*Ben's Baby* (picture book), Andersen, 1987, Harper (New York City), 1988.
*The Angel and the Wild Animal,* Andersen, 1988, Atheneum (New York City), 1989.
*One World,* Andersen, 1990, Arcade (New York City), 1991.
*War Boy: A Country Childhood,* Arcade, 1990.
*Michael Foreman,* Beetles, 1990.
(Editor) *Michael Foreman's World of Fairy Tales,* Pavilion (London), 1990, Arcade, 1991.
(Editor) *Michael Foreman's Mother Goose,* Harcourt (San Diego, CA), 1991.
(With Richard Seaver) *The Boy Who Sailed with Columbus,* Pavilion, 1991, Arcade, 1992.
*Jack's Fantasic Voyage,* Harcourt, 1992.
*War Game,* Pavilion, 1993.
*Grandfather's Pencil and the Room of Stories,* Harcourt, 1994.
*Dad! I Can't Sleep,* Harcourt, 1995.
*Surprise Surprise,* Harcourt, 1995.
*After the War Was Over,* Arcade, 1996.

*ILLUSTRATOR*

Janet Charters, *The General,* Dutton (New York City), 1961.
Cledwyn Hughes, *The King Who Lived on Jelly,* Routledge & Kegan Paul (London), 1963.
Eric Partridge, *Comic Alphabets,* Routledge & Kegan Paul, 1964.
Derek Cooper, *The Bad Food Guide,* Routledge & Kegan Paul, 1966.
Leonore Klein, *Huit Enfants et un Bebe,* Abelard, 1966.
Mabel Watts, *I'm for You, You're for Me,* Abelard, 1967.
Sergei Vladimirovich Mikalkov, *Let's Fight!, and Other Russian Fables,* Pantheon (New York City), 1968.
Donald Davie, *Essex Poems,* 1969.
William Ivan Martin, *Adam's Balm,* Bowmar (Los Angeles, CA), 1970.

C. O. Alexander, *Fisher v. Spassky,* Penguin (New York City), 1972.

William Fagg, editor, *The Living Arts of Nigeria,* Studio Vista, 1972.

Barbara Adachi, *The Living Treasures of Japan,* Wildwood House, 1973.

Janice Elliott, *Alexander in the Land of Mog,* Brockhampton Press, 1973.

Elliott, *The Birthday Unicorn,* Penguin, 1973.

Sheila Burnford, *Noah and the Second Flood,* Gollancz (London), 1973.

Jane H. Yolen, *Rainbow Rider,* Crowell (New York City), 1974.

Georgess McHargue, *Private Zoo,* Viking (New York City), 1975.

Barbara K. Walker, *Teeny-Tiny and the Witch-Woman,* Pantheon, 1975.

Cheng-en Wu, *Monkey and the Three Wizards,* translated by Peter Harris, Collins & World (London), 1976.

Alan Garner, *The Stone Book,* Collins & World, 1976.

Garner, *Tom Fobble's Day,* Collins & World, 1976.

Garner, *Granny Reardun,* Collins & World, 1977.

Hans Christian Andersen, *Hans Christian Andersen: His Classic Fairy Tales,* translated by Erik Haugaard, Gollancz, 1977.

K. Bauman, *Kitchen Stories,* Nord Sud, 1977, published as *Mickey's Kitchen Contest,* Andersen (London), 1978.

Garner, *The Aimer Gate,* Collins & World, 1978.

Bryna Stevens, reteller, *Borrowed Feathers and Other Fables,* Random House (New York City), 1978.

Brian Alderson, translator, *The Brothers Grimm: Popular Folk Tales,* Gollancz, 1978.

Oscar Wilde, *The Selfish Giant,* Kaye & Ward, 1978.

*Seven in One Blow,* Random House, 1978.

Garner, *Fairy Tales of Gold,* Collins & World, 1979, Volume 1: *The Golden Brothers,* Volume 2: *The Girl of the Golden Gate,* Volume 3: *The Three Golden Heads of the Well,* Volume 4: *The Princess and the Golden Mane.*

Bill Martin, *How to Catch a Ghost,* Holt (New York City), 1979.

Anthony Paul, *The Tiger Who Lost His Stripes,* Andersen Press, 1980, Harcourt, 1995.

Ernest Hemingway, *The Faithful Bull,* Emme Italia, 1980.

Aldous Huxley, *After Many a Summer,* Folio Society, 1980.

Allen Andrews, *The Pig Plantagenet,* Hutchinson (London), 1980.

Peter Dickenson, *City of Gold and Other Tales from the Old Testament,* Gollancz, 1980.

Terry Jones, *Terry Jones' Fairy Tales* (also see below) Pavilion, 1981, Puffin (New York City), 1986.

John Loveday, editor, *Over the Bridge,* Penguin, 1981.

Robert McCrum, *The Magic Mouse and the Millionaire,* Hamish Hamilton, 1981.

Rudyard Kipling, *The Crab That Played with the Sea: A Just So Story,* Macmillan (New York City), 1982.

Angela Carter, selector and translator, *Sleeping Beauty and Other Favourite Fairy Tales,* Gollancz, 1982, Schocken, 1984.

Helen Piers, *Longneck and Thunderfoot,* Kestrel, 1982.

McCrum, *The Brontosaurus Birthday Cake,* Hamish Hamilton, 1982.

Jones, *The Saga of Erik the Viking,* Pavilion, 1983, Puffin, 1986.

Charles Dickens, *A Christmas Carol,* Dial, 1983.

Nanette Newman, *A Cat and Mouse Love Story,* Heinemann (London), 1983.

Robert Louis Stevenson, *Treasure Island,* Penguin, 1983.

Kit Wright, editor, *Poems for 9-Year-Olds and Under,* Puffin, 1984.

Helen Nicoll, editor, *Poems for 7-Year-Olds and Under,* Puffin, 1984.

Wright, editor, *Poems for 10-Year-Olds and Over,* Puffin, 1985.

Roald Dahl, *Charlie and the Chocolate Factory,* Puffin, 1985.

Madhur Jaffrey, *Seasons of Splendour: Tales, Myths and Legends of India,* Pavilion, 1985.

McCrum, *Brontosaurus Superstar,* Hamish Hamilton, 1985.

Leon Garfield, *Shakespeare Stories,* Gollancz, 1985, Houghton (Boston, MA), 1991.

William McGonagall, *Poetic Gems,* Folio Society, 1985.

Stevenson, *A Child's Garden of Verses,* Delacorte (New York City), 1985.

Nigel Gray, *I'll Take You to Mrs. Cole!* (picture book), Bergh, 1986, Kane/Miller (Brooklyn, NY), 1992.

Edna O'Brien, *Tales for the Telling: Irish Folk and Fairy Tales,* Pavilion, 1986, Puffin, 1988.

Eric Quayle, *The Magic Ointment and Other Cornish Legends,* Andersen, 1986.

Jones, *Nicobobinus,* Pavilion, 1986.

Michael Moorcock, *Letters from Hollywood,* Harrap (London), 1986.

Charles Causley, *Early in the Morning,* Kestrel, 1986, Viking (New York City), 1987.

Kipling, *Just So Stories,* Kestrel, 1987.

Kipling, *The Jungle Book,* Kestrel, 1987.

Jan Mark, *Fun,* Gollancz, 1987, Viking, 1988.

Daphne du Maurier, *Classics of the Macabre,* Gollancz, 1987.

Clement C. Moore, *The Night before Christmas,* Viking, 1988.

Jones, *The Curse of the Vampire's Socks,* Pavilion, 1988.

J. M. Barrie, *Peter Pan and Wendy,* Pavilion, 1988.

Martin Bax, *Edmond Went Far Away,* Harcourt, 1989.

David Pelham, *Worms Wiggle,* Simon & Schuster (New York City), 1989.

Eric Quayle, editor, *The Shining Princess and Other Japanese Legends,* Arcade, 1989.

Ann Turnbull, *The Sand Horse* (picture book), Macmillan, 1989.

Kiri Te Kanawa, *Land of the Long White Cloud,* Arcade, 1990.

*The Puffin Book of Twentieth-Century Children's Stories,* Viking, 1991.

Jonathan Shipton, *Busy Busy Busy,* Delacorte, 1991.

Alderson, translator, *The Arabian Nights, or, Tales Told by Sheherezade during a Thousand Nights and One Night,* Gollancz, 1992.

Jones, *Fantastic Stories,* Viking, 1993.

Newman, *Spider the Horrible Cat,* Harcourt, 1993.

Newman, *There's a Bear in the Bath,* Harcourt, 1994.

Harrison Troon, *The Long Weekend,* Andersen, 1993, Harcourt, 1994.

Jones, *The Beast with a Thousand Teeth* (first appeared in *Terry Jones' Fairy Tales),* P. Bedrick (New York City), 1994.

Jones, *A Fish of the World* (first appeared in *Terry Jones' Fairy Tales),* P. Bedrick, 1994.

Jones, *The Fly-by-Night* (first appeared in *Terry Jones' Fairy Tales),* P. Bedrick, 1994.

Jones, *The Sea Tiger* (first appeared in *Terry Jones' Fairy Tales),* P. Bedrick, 1994.

Garfield, *Shakespeare Stories II,* Houghton, 1995.

Michael Morpurgo, *Arthur, High King of Britain,* Harcourt, 1995.

Morpurgo, *Robin of Sherwood,* Harcourt, 1996.

Sally Grindley, *Peter's Place,* Harcourt, 1996.

Louise Borden, *The Little Ships,* Margaret K. McElderry (New York City), 1997.

Also illustrator of *Making Music* by Gwen Clemens, 1966; *The Birthday Unicorn* by Janet Elliott, 1970; *The Pushcart War* by Jean Merrill, 1976; *The Nightingale and the Rose* by Oscar Wilde, 1981; and *The Young Man of Cury* by Charles Causley, Macmillan. Also creator of animated films for television in England and Scandinavia.

*SIDELIGHTS:* Michael Foreman has enjoyed a long and far-ranging career as an author and illustrator of books for children. A world traveler who has visited every continent in search of material for his books, Foreman has illustrated for Indian, Chinese, and Arabian folktale collections—but he is equally well known for his closely-observed books about his own childhood and youth in England. As Elaine Moss put it in the *Times Literary Supplement,* Foreman "goes from strength to strength, always exploring, through his picture books, fresh ways of expanding the readers' visual and philosophical perception." *Twentieth-Century Children's Writers* contributor Jennifer Taylor deemed Foreman "one of the outstanding creators of children's picture books working today. . . . He combines a distinctive style of flowing watercolor with a genius for conveying atmosphere, and the visual richness of his work is always a feast for the eye."

Foreman has tackled some deep issues in his stories, from Cold War politics to the need to conserve natural resources. For many years he was regarded as a polemical writer who managed to get his point across with whimsical characters and engaging illustrations. Works such as *Moose, The Two Giants, All the King's Horses,* and *One World* reveal an author concerned with teaching his readers lessons while simultaneously entertaining them. "I decided to do [books] which would raise issues children could in turn raise with adults, at home and in the classroom," Foreman recalled in *Something about the Author Autobiography Series.* "To some extent I feel I am not doing books for children, but for the next generation of adults."

Foreman also draws upon his real-life experiences when writing and illustrating books. He once told *CA,* "I was born in a fishing village on the east coast [of England] and grew up there during the war. My first book, *The General,* was set there and the local people recognise the church, the ice cream hut, and other scenes in the pictures. By the time *The General* was published, I was living in London and my second book, *The Perfect Present,* contained many London scenes. Since then I have been to many parts of the world and the sketches I bring back become the backgrounds for new books. *Rainbow Rider* is set in New Mexico and Arizona, for example, *Panda and the Odd Lion* in Africa and Venice.

"Sometimes the story is about travelling to many places, as with *Horatio* or *Trick a Tracker*. Occasionally, I get the idea for a story while travelling, but usually it takes a long time to get the right place, the right story, and the right character to meet. Much of my time I am illustrating the work of other writers, and the subject matter varies from the Bible to Shakespeare to stories set in contemporary Britain or the future. My own books are never really about a place or country, but about an idea which is hopefully common to the dreams of everyone, one which works best, however, against a particular background."

Foreman began his formal art studies at the age of fifteen and continued them at London's Royal College of Art. While still a student he published his first children's book, *The General,* one of many stories inspired by his pacifist perspective. A span of six years elapsed before his next book appeared, but in that time he worked as a magazine illustrator and freelance illustrator for other people's books. He began to be inspired by his world travels, his exposure to other cultures, and his continuing concern for creating in future generations a greater commitment to disarmament and ecology.

"The thing that gives me most pleasure in being an illustrator now is that almost everything I do in the normal course of life has a bearing on the work in progress," Foreman noted in *SAAS.* "It's all totally enmeshed, and anything that affects you in the newspapers or on television or in your own personal experience can be a jumping-off point. Whereas, had I remained an abstract painter—and I'm certain, in any case, that I wouldn't be abstract any longer by now—there would still be a division between pursuing a very narrow aesthetic path on the one hand and living a normal life on the other."

Those "normal life" experiences—be they traveling, reminiscing, or merely engaging in fatherhood duties—have enlivened Foreman's work both in his own books and as illustrator for others' work. A *Junior Bookshelf* contributor called Foreman "one of the most intelligent of modern book-artists," adding: "There is no doubt at all about his vision, or his feeling for atmosphere." In a *School Librarian* review, Gabrielle Maunder observed that the author "has the courage and ability to present children with illusory and elusive pictures which command the eye and challenge the intelligence."

Foreman's books often use creatures—mythical or real—to illustrate deep philosophical points. In *Moose,* for instance, a kindly moose who is caught in the crossfire between a warring bear and eagle draws other animals to a shelter he's erected to avoid the conflict. *War and Peas* follows the efforts of King Lion to get food for his starving countrymen. In *Dinosaurs and All That Rubbish,* a throng of angry dinosaurs clean up the mess left on earth by a rocket-building industrialist. According to Donnarae MacCann and Olga Richard in the *Wilson Library Bulletin,* Foreman "is good at mixing a dab of logic with volumes of imagination and then finding a thoroughly satisfying finale."

Addressing the content of some of his children's stories in his *SAAS* essay, Foreman declared: "I assume our early years stamp us all. But why did topical or political issues feed *my* work and not that of my illustrator contemporaries who also grew up during the [Second World War]? I think it is because in my family we had no books, but we did sell newspapers in our shop. . . . As a small boy, I wallowed in the picture papers and magazines of the day. . . . My imagination lived off real life. Not fairy stories."

Nevertheless, Foreman has edited and illustrated numerous editions of fairy tales both ancient and modern, from the traditional Mother Goose to an international collection that he compiled himself from his travels. He has also done extensive work for author Terry Jones, whose modern fairy tales are quite popular in England especially. More recently, a collaboration with Michael Morpurgo has produced new children's books about King Arthur and Robin Hood. "Working with other writers' stories is both a privilege and a challenge," Foreman observed in *SAAS.* "They are often writing about subjects of which I have little knowledge or experience. I have to research the background and substance of the subject. This is another kind of journey and can be just as rewarding."

Foreman's three autobiographical books have helped to personalize the author-illustrator for his readers. *War Boy: A Country Childhood,* which received the Kate Greenaway Medal in 1990, is a memoir of his boyhood growing up in England during World War II. Said reviewer Christopher Lehmann-Haupt in the *New York Times:* "Though his memories are haunted by enemy bombers and V1 and V2 rockets, the author recalls in delicate watercolors the many joys of being a shopkeeper's child under siege: the licorice comforts that left your teeth stained black, or the millions of flower seeds that were exploded out of gardens and showered around the district so that 'the following spring and summer, piles of rubble burst into bloom.'" To quote Phyllis G. Sidorsky in *School Library Journal*, "Foreman's recollections are sharp and graphic as he poignantly recalls the servicemen who crowded into his mother's shop, grateful for her welcoming cup of tea and a place to chat." *War Boy* proved so popular that Foreman wrote a prequel, *War Game*, dedicated to the four uncles he lost in World War I, and *After the War Was Over*, which describes his life as a young teen. In a *Chicago Tribune Books* review of the latter title, Mary Harris Veeder wrote: "The pull of this book is as hard to describe as it is strong. You'll pick it up unsure why you would be interested in it, and you'll finish every page."

Another topic announced itself to Foreman as the 1990s progressed—fatherhood. His two growing sons have inspired a number of titles, including *Dad! I Can't Sleep* and *Ben's Baby*, both of which aim at easing a younger child's anxieties about life issues. In his *SAAS* essay, the author concluded: "You don't need to cross the ocean to find ideas—just look across the kitchen table at your family, or in the attic and the memories of your childhood. . . . You don't need to travel here, there, and everywhere. But I'm awfully glad I did!"

"My books are not intended for any particular age group," Foreman once commented, "but the type is large and inviting for young readers who like to explore the pages after the story has been read to them. In addition I want the story to have some relevance for the adult reader. Less a question of age—more a state of mind."

*BIOGRAPHICAL/CRITICAL SOURCES:*

*BOOKS*

*Children's Literature Review*, Volume 32, Gale (Detroit), 1994, pp. 76-107.
Kingman, Lee, *Illustrators of Children's Books, 1967-1976*, Horn Book (Boston, MA), 1977.
Martin, Douglas, *The Telling Line: Essays on Fifteen Contemporary Book Illustrators*, Julia MacRae (New York City), 1989, pp. 291-311.
*Something about the Author Autobiography Series*, Volume 21, Gale, 1996, pp. 121-35.
*Twentieth-Century Children's Writers*, St. James Press (Detroit), 1995, pp. 361-63.

*PERIODICALS*

*Booklist*, March 1, 1995, p. 1247; May 15, 1996, p. 1582.

*Books and Bookmen*, December, 1983, p. 29.
*Books for Keeps*, May, 1990, pp. 4-5; November, 1990, p. 26; November, 1992, p. 7.
*Books for Your Children*, May, 1975, p. 2.
*Chicago Tribune Books*, April 14, 1996, p. 7.
*Growing Point*, January, 1981, pp. 3802-03.
*Junior Bookshelf*, February, 1981, p. 27; February, 1982, p. 14; February, 1990, pp. 10-11.
*Isis*, November, 1966.
*New Statesman*, November 27, 1987, p. 34.
*New York Times*, December 3, 1990.
*New York Times Book Review*, April 28, 1985, p. 26; January 15, 1995, p. 25.
*Publishers Weekly*, April 25, 1994, p. 78.
*School Library Journal*, June, 1983, p. 128-29; May, 1990, p. 116; November, 1992, p. 69.
*Times* (London), August 29, 1991, p. 14.
*Times Educational Supplement*, November 14, 1986, p. 41; March 11, 1988, p. 24; June 3, 1988, p. 46; October 13, 1989, p. 28; September 21, 1990, p. R22.
*Times Literary Supplement*, December 2, 1977, p. 1411; November 26, 1982; November 30, 1984, p. 1379; June 6, 1986, p. 630; November 25, 1988, p. 1321; August 3, 1990, p. 833.
*Washington Post Book World*, September 11, 1988, p. 9; July 9, 1989, p. 10; July 7, 1996, p. 15.
*Wilson Library Bulletin*, March, 1991, pp. 107-09.

\*    \*    \*

## FRANCIS, Dick 1920-

*PERSONAL:* Full name, Richard Stanley Francis; born October 31, 1920, in Tenby, Pembrokeshire, Wales; son of George Vincent (a professional steeplechase rider and stable manager) and Molly (Thomas) Francis; married Mary Brenchley (a teacher and assistant stage manager), June 21, 1947; children: Merrick, Felix. *Education:* Attended Maidenhead County School. *Religion:* Church of England. *Avocational interests:* Boating, fox hunting, tennis.

*ADDRESSES: Home*—P.O. Box 30866 SMB, George Town, Grand Cayman, West Indies.

*CAREER:* Novelist. Amateur steeplechase rider, 1946-48; professional steeplechase jockey, 1948-57; *Sunday Express*, London, England, racing correspondent, 1957-73. Exercises racehorses in winter; judges hunters at horse shows in summer. *Military service:*

Royal Air Force, 1940-46; became flying officer (pilot).

*MEMBER:* Crime Writers Association (chair, 1973-74), Mystery Writers of America, Writers of Canada, Detection Club, Racecourse Association.

*AWARDS, HONORS:* Steeplechase jockey championship, 1954; Silver Dagger Award, Crime Writers Association, 1965, for *For Kicks;* Edgar Allan Poe Award, Mystery Writers of America, 1969, for *Forfeit,* and 1980, for *Whip Hand;* Gold Dagger Award, Crime Writers Association, 1980, for *Whip Hand;* Order of the British Empire, 1984; L.H.D., Tufts University, 1991; Grand Master Award and Best Novel award for *Come to Grief,* both from the Mystery Writers of America, both 1996.

*WRITINGS:*

*MYSTERY NOVELS*

*Dead Cert,* Holt (New York City), 1962.
*Nerve,* Harper (New York City), 1964.
*For Kicks,* Harper, 1965.
*Odds Against,* M. Joseph (London), 1965, Harper, 1966.
*Flying Finish,* M. Joseph, 1966, Harper, 1967.
*Blood Sport,* Harper, 1967.
*Forfeit,* Harper, 1968.
*Enquiry,* Harper, 1969.
*Rat Race,* Harper, 1970.
*Bonecrack,* Harper, 1971.
*Smokescreen,* Harper, 1972.
*Slay-ride,* Harper, 1973.
*Knockdown,* Harper, 1974.
*High Stakes,* Harper, 1975.
*In the Frame,* Harper, 1976.
*Risk,* Harper, 1977.
*Trial Run,* Harper, 1978.
*Whip Hand,* Harper, 1979.
*Reflex,* M. Joseph, 1980, Putnam (New York City), 1981.
*Twice Shy,* M. Joseph, 1981, Putnam, 1982.
*Banker,* M. Joseph, 1982, Putnam, 1983.
*The Danger,* M. Joseph, 1983, Putnam, 1984.
*Proof,* M. Joseph, 1984, Putnam, 1985.
*Break In,* M. Joseph, 1985, Putnam, 1986.
*Bolt,* M. Joseph, 1986, Putnam, 1987.
*Hot Money,* M. Joseph, 1987, Putnam, 1988.
*The Edge,* M. Joseph, 1988, Putnam, 1989.
*Straight,* Putnam, 1989.
*Longshot,* Putnam, 1990.
*Comeback,* Putnam, 1991.

*Driving Force,* Putnam, 1992.
*Wild Horses,* Putnam, 1994.
*Coming to Grief,* Putnam, 1995.
*Colour Scheme,* Putnam, 1996.
*To the Hilt,* Putnam, 1996.

*OTHER*

*The Sport of Queens* (racing autobiography), M. Joseph, 1957.
(Editor with John Welcome) *Best Racing and Chasing Stories,* Faber, 1966.
(Editor with Welcome) *Best Racing and Chasing Stories II,* Faber, 1969.
*The Racing Man's Bedside Book,* Faber, 1969.
*A Jockey's Life: The Biography of Lester Piggott,* Putnam, 1986, published in England as *Lester, the Official Biography,* M. Joseph, 1986.
(Editor with Welcome) *The New Treasury of Great Racing Stories,* Norton, 1991.
(Editor with Welcome) *The Dick Francis Treasury of Great Racing Stories,* G. K. Hall (Boston), 1991.

Contributor to anthologies, including *Winter's Crimes 5,* edited by Virginia Whitaker, Macmillan, 1973; *Stories of Crime and Detection,* edited by Joan D. Berbrich, McGraw, 1974; *Ellery Queen's Crime Wave,* Putnam, 1976; and *Ellery Queen's Searches and Seizures,* Davis, 1977. Contributor to periodicals, including *Horseman's Year, Sports Illustrated, In Praise of Hunting,* and *Stud and Stable.*

Francis's works have been translated into Japanese, Norwegian, and Czechoslovakian.

*ADAPTATIONS: Dead Cert* was filmed by United Artists in 1973; *Odds Against* was adapted for Yorkshire Television as *The Racing Game,* 1979, and also broadcast by the PBS-TV series *Mystery!,* 1980-81; Francis's works adapted for television series *Dick Francis Mysteries* by Dick Francis Films Ltd., 1989; *Blood Sport* was adapted for television as *Dick Francis: Blood Sport* by Comedia Entertainment, 1989. Many of Francis's books have been recorded on audiocassette.

*SIDELIGHTS:* When steeple jockey Dick Francis retired from horseracing at age thirty-six, he speculated in his autobiography that he would be remembered as "the man who didn't win the National," England's prestigious Grand National steeplechase. If he hadn't turned to fiction, his prediction might have been correct, but with the publication of his first novel, *Dead*

*Cert,* in 1962, Francis launched a second career that was even more successful than his first: he became a mystery writer.

Since that time, Francis has averaged a thriller a year, astounding critics with the fecundity of his imagination and garnering awards such as Britain's Silver Dagger (in 1965 for *For Kicks*) and two Edgars (for *Forfeit* in 1969 and *Whip Hand* in 1980). However, talking about his books and their success Francis says in *Sport of Queens,* his autobiography, that, "I still find the writing . . . grindingly hard, and I approach Chapter 1 each year with deeper foreboding." Gina MacDonald, writing in the *Dictionary of Literary Biography,* says that Francis's method of writing his books is very precise. He usually thinks of a plot by midsummer, and spends the rest of the year researching the book. He finally starts writing the following year and finishes the book by spring. Since most of his books concern horses, racing still figures in his life. His affinity for the racetrack actually enhances his prose, according to Julian Symons, who writes in the *New York Times Book Review* that "what comes most naturally to [Francis] is also what he does best—writing about the thrills, spills and chills of horse racing."

Before he began writing, Francis experienced one of racing's most publicized "spills" firsthand. In 1956, when he was already a veteran jockey, Francis had the privilege of riding Devon Loch—the Queen Mother's horse—in the annual Grand National. Fifty yards from the finish line, with the race virtually won, the horse inexplicably faltered. Later examination revealed no physical injury and no clue was ever found. "I still don't have the answer," Francis told Peter Axthelm of *Newsweek.* "Maybe he was shocked by the noise of 250,000 people screaming because the royal family's horse was winning. But the fact is that with nothing wrong with him, ten strides from the winning post he fell. The other fact is," he added, "if that mystery hadn't happened, I might never have written all these other ones."

Though each of his novels deals with what many consider a specialized subject, Francis's books have broad appeal. One explanation, offered by Judith Rascoe in the *Christian Science Monitor,* is that "you needn't know or care anything about racing to be his devoted reader." And, writing in the *New York Times,* book reviewer John Leonard agrees: "Not to read Dick Francis because you don't like horses is like not reading Dostoyevsky because you don't like

God. . . . Race tracks and God are subcultures. A writer has to have a subculture to stand upon." Francis's ability to make this subculture come alive for his reader—to create what Rascoe calls "a background of almost Dickensian realism for his stories"—is what sets him apart from other mystery writers. "In particular," observes Charles Champlin in the *Los Angeles Times,* "his rider's view of the strains and spills, disappointments and exaltations of the steeplechase is breathtaking, a far cry from the languid armchair detecting of other crime solvers." Writing in the *London Magazine,* John Welcome expresses similar admiration, praising especially Francis's ability to infuse his races with a significance that extends beyond the Jockey Club milieu: "One can hear the smash of birch, the creak of leather and the rattle of whips. The sweat, the strain, the tears, tragedies and occasional triumphs of the racing game are all there, as well as its seductive beauty. In this—as in much else—no other racing novelist can touch him. He has made racing into a microcosm of the contemporary world."

While critics initially speculated that Francis's specialized knowledge would provide only limited fictional opportunities, most have since changed their minds. "It is fascinating to see how many completely fresh and unexpected plots he can concoct about horses," marvels Anthony Boucher in the *New York Times Book Review.* Philip Pelham takes this approbation one step further, writing in *London Magazine* that "Francis improves with every book as both a writer of brisk, lucid prose and as a concocter of ingenious and intricately worked-out plots." His racetrack thrillers deal with such varied story lines as crooks transporting horses by air (*Flying Finish*), stolen stallions (*Blood Sport*), and a jockey who has vanished in Norway (*Slay-ride*). To further preserve the freshness of his fiction, Francis creates a new protagonist for each novel and often develops subplots around fields unrelated to racing. "His books," notes Axthelm, "take him and his readers on global explorations as well as into crash courses in ventures like aviation, gold mining and, in *Reflex,* amateur photography."

Notwithstanding such variations in plot and theme, Francis is known as a formula writer whose novels, while well-written, are ultimately predictable. In all the Francis novels, writes Welcome, "the hard-done-by chap [is] blindly at grips with an unknown evil, the threads of which he gradually unravels. Frequently—perhaps too frequently—he is subjected to physical torture described in some detail. His heroes are hard men used to injury and pain and they learn to dish it out as once they had to learn to take it. Racing has made them stoics."

Barry Bauska, writing in the *Armchair Detective,* offers a more detailed version of the "typical" Francis thriller: "At the outset something has happened that looks wrong (a jockey is set down by a board of inquiry that seemed predetermined to find him guilty; a horse falls going over a final hurdle it had seemed to clear; horses perfectly ready to win consistently fail to do so). The narrator protagonist (usually not a detective, but always inherently curious) begins to poke around to try to discover what has occurred. In so doing he inevitably pokes too hard and strikes a hornets' nest. The rest of the novel then centers on a critical struggle between the searcher-after-truth and the mysterious agent of evil, whose villainy had upset things in the first place."

Despite the formulaic nature of his work, Francis deals with problems prevalent in modern society, says Marty Knepper in *Twelve Englishmen of Mystery.* He feels that Francis's works deal with social and moral issues "seriously and in some depth . . . including some topics generally considered unpleasant." For example, in *Blood Sport* the hero is struggling with his own suicidal urges. In Knepper's words, "To read *Blood Sport* . . . is to learn what it feels like to be lonely, paranoid and suicidal."

Character development also plays an important part in Francis's novels. Knepper says that biographical similarities between Francis's heroes may blind the reader to the important differences between them. For example, Francis's heroes have a wide variety of professions. This gives him a chance to examine professionalism, and the responsibilities that accompany it, in fields other than racing and detection. Each of Francis's heroes, according to Knepper, is "a unique person, but each hero . . . changes as a result of his adventures." In the end, characters learn from their experiences and have evolved.

While a number of Francis's books include a love story, a much more pressing theme, according to Axthelm, is that of pain. "Again and again," he writes in *Newsweek,* the author's "villains probe the most terrifying physical or psychic weakness in his heroes. A lifetime's most treasured mementos are destroyed by mindless hired thugs; an already crippled hand is brutally smashed until it must be ampu-

tated. The deaths in Francis novels usually occur 'off-camera.' The tortures are more intimate affairs, with the reader forced to watch at shudderingly close range."

The prevalence of such violence, coupled with Francis's tendency to paint the relationship between hero and villain as a confrontation between good and evil, makes some reviewers uneasy. In his *Times Literary Supplement* review of *Risk,* for example, Alex de Jong comments that "characterization is sometimes thin and stylized, especially the villains, out to inflict pain upon the accountant who has uncovered their villainy, crooked businessmen and trainers, all a little too well dressed, florid and unexpectedly brutal bullies, created with a faint hint of paranoia." Francis, however, justifies the punishment he metes out to his characters as something his fans have come to expect. "Somehow the readers like to read about it," he told Judy Klemesrud in the *New York Times Book Review.* "But I don't subject them to anything I wouldn't put up with myself. This old body has been knocked around quite a bit."

While the violence of his early novels is largely external, his later novels emphasize more internal stress, according to critics who believe that this shift has added a new dimension to Francis's work. Welcome, for instance, comments that in *Reflex* Francis's lessened emphasis on brutality has enabled him to "flesh out his characters. The portrait of Philip More, the mediocre jockey nearing the end of his career, is created with real insight; as is the interpretation of his relations with the horses he rides." MacDonald comments that Francis's later books "concentrate more specifically on psychological stress." In her opinion, his writing has gone beyond the "dramatic presentation of heroic action" to a deeper level, where the hero "is less a man who can endure torture than one who has the strength to face self-doubt, fear, and human inadequacy and still endure and thrive." And Bauska expresses a similar view when he says that Francis's later works, although not that different in the plot, focus on the protagonist. According to Bauska, Francis is increasingly "considering what goes into the making not so much of a 'hero' as of a good man." The focus of Francis's work is no longer the war outside, though the books are still action-packed, but on the struggle within the protagonist's mind and his attempts to conquer his own doubts and fears. Bauska attributes this shift in focus to Francis's own growing distance from his racing days. The result, he says, "is that Dick Francis is becoming less a writer of thrillers and more a creator of literature."

While not all reviewers find Francis's work to be the stuff of literature, his ability to relate a fresh racing murder-mystery each year that retains a creative spark in its focus and technique are continually remarked upon. Patricia Craig comments in the *Times Literary Supplement,* "Unreality aside, the Dick Francis story line works through a combination of energy and amiability, the doggedness and right-thinking of the central character, and a certain expertise in the evocation of atmosphere." Citing Francis's *Driving Force* as an example, Craig continues, "Francis shows that he has such a hold on his readers that he can dwell on the properties of horseboxes without fear of being judged uncompelling." Even when Francis returns to the same protagonist, Sid Halley (*Odds Against, Whip Hand,* and *Come to Grief,*), he manages to shed new light on the character. Dick Adler, contributing to the *Chicago Tribune,* finds, "In spite of a certain predictability in the plot . . . *Come to Grief* is in fact one of [Francis's] most engrossing recent efforts."

Francis's consistent ability to continually engage both new readers and old fans alike in his stories is perhaps his greatest strength. Christopher Wordsworth, reviewing *Wild Horses* for the London *Observer,* calls Francis "an institution." Indeed, as Elizabeth Tallent notes in the *New York Times Book Review,* while Francis's former position as jockey for the Queen Mother is often mentioned in reviews of the writer, "At this point in his illustrious writing career, the Queen Mother might wish to note in her *vita* that the writer Dick Francis once rode for her."

*BIOGRAPHICAL/CRITICAL SOURCES:*

BOOKS

Bargainnier, Earl F., editor, *Twelve Englishmen of Mystery,* Bowling Green University Popular Press, 1984, pp. 222-48.

Barnes, Melvyn, *Dick Francis,* Ungar, 1986.

*Bestsellers 89,* Issue 3, Gale (Detroit), 1989.

*Contemporary Literary Criticism,* Gale, Volume 2, 1974; Volume 22, 1982; Volume 42, 1987; Volume 102, 1998.

Davis, J. Madison, *Dick Francis,* Twayne, 1989.

*Dictionary of Literary Biography,* Gale, Volume 87: *British Mystery and Thriller Writers since 1940, First Series,* Gale, 1989.

Francis, Dick, *The Sport of Queens,* M. Joseph, 1957.

PERIODICALS

*Architectural Digest,* Volume 42, June, 1985.

*Armchair Detective,* July, 1978; spring, 1982; winter, 1986; summer, 1993; winter, 1996, p. 102.

*Atlantic Monthly,* March, 1969.

*Booklist,* January 15, 1986.

*British Book News,* October, 1984.

*Chicago Tribune,* October 2, 1994, p. 9; September 3, 1995, p. 4.

*Christian Science Monitor,* July 17, 1969; July 17, 1969.

*Family Circle,* July, 1970.

*Forbes,* November 21, 1994, p. 26.

*Globe and Mail* (Toronto), November 16, 1985; August 12, 1989.

*Kirkus Reviews,* July 15, 1995, p. 986.

*Life,* June 6, 1969.

*London Magazine,* February-March, 1975; March, 1980; February-March, 1981.

*Los Angeles Times,* March 27, 1981; April 9, 1982; September 12, 1984.

*National Review,* January 20, 1992.

*Newsweek,* April 6, 1981.

*New Yorker,* March 15, 1969; April 16, 1984; April 22, 1985.

*New York Times,* March 6, 1969; April 7, 1971; March 20, 1981; December 18, 1989.

*New York Times Book Review,* March 21, 1965; March 10, 1968; March 16, 1969; June 8, 1969; July 26, 1970; May 21, 1972; July 27, 1975; September 28, 1975; June 13, 1976; July 10, 1977; May 20, 1979; June 1, 1980; March 29, 1981; April 25, 1982; February 12, 1989; March 27, 1983; March 18, 1984; March 24, 1985; March 16, 1986; October 18, 1992, p. 32; October 2, 1994, p. 26.

*New York Times Magazine,* March 25, 1984.

*Observer* (London), October 2, 1994, p. 18.

*People Weekly,* June 7, 1976; November 23, 1982; January 24, 1994, p. 32.

*Publishers Weekly,* January 24, 1986.

*School Library Journal,* January, 1995, p. 145.

*Sports Illustrated,* November 15, 1993.

*Time,* March 11, 1974; July 14, 1975; May 31, 1976; July 7, 1978; May 11, 1981.

*Times* (London), December 18, 1986.

*Times Literary Supplement,* October 28, 1977; October 10, 1980; December 10, 1982; October 30, 1992, p. 21; October 7, 1994, p. 30; November 17, 1995, p. 28.

*U.S. News and World Report,* March 28, 1988.

*Washington Post,* October 3, 1986.

*Washington Post Book World,* April 30, 1972; February 18, 1973; April 19, 1980; April 18, 1982;

March 27, 1983; March 17, 1985; February 21, 1988; February 5, 1989.*

\*   \*   \*

## FRANK, Anne(lies Marie) 1929-1945

*PERSONAL:* Born June 12, 1929, in Frankfurt on the Main, Germany; died of typhoid fever and malnutrition in March, 1945, in the Bergen-Belsen concentration camp near Belgen, Germany; daughter of Otto (banker and business owner) and Edith Frank.

*WRITINGS:*

*Het achterhuis* (diary; foreword by Annie Romein-Verschoor), Contact (Amsterdam), 1947, translation from the Dutch by B. M. Mooyaart-Doubleday published as *Diary of a Young Girl,* introduction by Eleanor Roosevelt, Doubleday, 1952; with new preface by George Stevens, Pocket Books, 1958; published as *Anne Frank: The Diary of a Young Girl,* Washington Square Press, 1963; published as *The Diary of Anne Frank,* foreword by Storm Jameson, illustrations by Elisabeth Trimby, Heron Books, 1973; published as *The Diary of Anne Frank: The Critical Edition,* edited by David Barnouw and Gerrold van der Stroom, translated by Arnold J. Pomerans and B. M. Mooyaart-Doubleday, introduction by Harry Paape, Gerrold van der Stroom, and David Barnouw, Doubleday, 1989; published as *The Diary of Anne Frank: The Definitive Edition,* edited by Otto Frank and Mirjam Pressler, Doubleday, 1995.
*The Works of Anne Frank* (also see below), introduction by Ann Birstein and Alfred Kazin, Doubleday, 1959.
*Tales from the House Behind: Fables, Personal Reminiscences, and Short Stories* (also see below), translation from the original Dutch manuscript, *Verhalen rondom het achterhuis,* by H. H. B. Mosberg and Michel Mok, World's Work, 1962; with drawings by Peter Spier, Pan Books, 1965.
*Anne Frank's Tales from the Secret Annex* (portions previously published in *The Works of Anne Frank* and *Tales from the House Behind*), with translations from the original manuscript, *Verhaaltjes en gebeurtenissen uit het Achterhuis,* by Ralph Manheim and Michel Mok, Doubleday, 1983.

Anne Frank's diary has been translated into many languages, including German, French, Italian, Spanish, Russian, and Polish.

*ADAPTATIONS:* Frances Goodrich and Albert Hackett adapted *Anne Frank: Diary of a Young Girl* as a two-act stage play titled *Diary of Anne Frank,* first produced in New York, 1955, published with a foreword by Brooks Atkinson, Random House, 1956; the diary was also adapted as the film *The Diary of Anne Frank,* released by Twentieth Century-Fox, 1959, and as a television movie of the same name, starring Melissa Gilbert, 1980; selections of the diary were read by Julie Harris for a recording by Spoken Arts, 1974, and by Claire Bloom for a recording by Caedmon, 1977.

*SIDELIGHTS:* Anne Frank, a victim of the Holocaust during World War II, became known throughout the world through her eloquent diary, describing the two years she and seven others hid from Nazis in an attic above her father's business office in Amsterdam. In the diary Anne relates the fear of being discovered and the aggravations of life in hiding as well as the feelings and experiences of adolescence that are recognized by people everywhere. Anne received the first notebook as a present from her parents on her thirteenth birthday in 1942, about a month before the family went into hiding. She wrote in the diary until the discovery of the hiding place in August, 1944. Anne's father, Otto Frank, the only one of them to survive the concentration camps to which they were sent, agreed to publish the diary in 1946.

Since then, Anne has been for many people a source of inspiration, a model of courage, and a symbol of the persecution, tragic suffering, and loss of life inflicted by the Nazis. Meyer Levin declared in the *New York Times Book Review,* "Because the diary was not written in retrospect, it contains the trembling life of every moment—Anne Frank's voice becomes the voice of six million vanished Jewish souls." This is not because there were no other journals found from that time. Upon reading a copy of Anne's diary in 1946, Jan Romein declared in the Dutch newspaper *Het Parool:* "The Government Institute for War Documentation is in possession of about two hundred similar diaries, but it would amaze me if there was *one* among them as pure, as intelligent, and yet as human as [Anne's]."

The Franks moved from Frankfort, Germany—where Anne was born—to Amsterdam in 1933 after Germany ruled that Jewish and German children had to attend segregated schools. In July, 1942, after Anne's sister Margot received notice to report to the Dutch Nazi organization, the Franks immediately went into hiding in the "Secret Annex," as Anne dubbed the attic of the Amsterdam warehouse. Soon after, Mr. and Mrs. Frank and their two girls welcomed Mr. and Mrs. Van Daan (pseudonymous names used by Anne) and their son Peter into their rooms, and lastly Mr. Dussel, an elderly dentist. In an entry about her family's flight into hiding, Anne wrote that the diary was the first thing she packed. It meant a great deal to her; she viewed the diary as a personal friend and confidant, as she remarked June 20, 1942, in a reflection about the diary itself: "I haven't written for a few days, because I wanted first of all to think about my diary. It's an odd idea for someone like me to keep a diary; not only because I have never done so before, but because it seems to me that neither I—nor for that matter anyone else—will be interested in the unbosomings of a thirteen-year-old schoolgirl. Still, what does that matter? I want to write, but more than that, I want to bring out all kinds of things that lie buried deep in my heart. . . . [T]here is no doubt that paper is patient and as I don't intend to show this . . . 'diary' to anyone, unless I find a real friend, boy or girl, probably nobody cares. And now I come to the root of the matter, the reason for my starting a diary; it is that I have no such real friend. . . . [I]t's the same with all my friends, just fun and joking, nothing more. I can never bring myself to talk of anything outside the common round. . . . Hence, this diary. . . . I don't want to set down a series of bald facts in a diary as most people do, but I want this diary itself to be my friend, and I shall call my friend Kitty."

"What child of 13 hasn't had these feelings, and resolved to confide in a diary?" wrote Levin. Apart from interest in the diary for its historical value and for the extreme circumstances under which it was written, some have admired the diary for its accurate, revealing portrait of adolescence. "She described life in the 'Annex' with all its inevitable tensions and quarrels," wrote L. De Jong in *A Tribute to Anne Frank*. "But she created first and foremost a wonderfully delicate record of adolescence, sketching with complete honesty a young girl's feelings, her longings and loneliness."

At the age of thirteen, when Anne began the diary, she was struggling with the problems of growing up. Lively and vivacious, she was chastised at school—

and later in the annex—for her incessant chattering. In the annex she was forced to whisper throughout the day. It was a great trial for Anne, who wrote on October 1, 1942, "We are as quiet as mice. Who, three months ago, would ever have guessed that quicksilver Anne would have to sit still for hours—and, what's more—could?" After a year of this silence, combined with confinement indoors, she expressed her feelings of depression, writing on October 29, 1943, "The atmosphere is so oppressive, and sleepy and as heavy as lead. You don't hear a single bird singing outside, and a deadly close silence hangs everywhere, catching hold of me as if it will drag me down deep into an underworld. . . . I wander from one room to another, downstairs and up again, feeling like a songbird whose wings have been clipped and who is hurling himself in utter darkness against the bars of his cage."

The eight people lived in constant fear of being discovered. Their concerns were heightened by seeing and hearing about other Jews who were rounded up in Amsterdam, and by burglars at the warehouse who threatened to find them accidentally. These fears, in addition to the stress of close confinement, resulted in great tension and many quarrels. Anne could be headstrong, opinionated, and critical—especially of her mother. Generally cheerful and optimistic, she adored her father and attempted to get along with the others, but she was sensitive to criticism, explaining in her diary that no one criticized her more than she herself. The diary thus traces her development from an outgoing, popular child to an introspective, idealistic young woman. Her entry on July 11, 1943, illustrates her developing tact: "I do really see that I get on better by shamming a bit, instead of my old habit of telling everyone exactly what I think." Anne herself described the two sides of her personality in her final entry: "I have, as it were, a dual personality. One half embodies my exuberant cheerfulness, making fun of everything, my high-spiritedness, and above all, the way I take everything lightly. . . . This side is usually lying in wait and pushes away the other, which is much better, deeper and purer."

It is this introspection and ability to express her various moods that distinguishes her diary, Pommer noted: "Any diary of a young girl who hid in Amsterdam during the Nazi occupation, who described her first protracted love affair, and who was a person of breeding, humor, religious sensitivity, and courage might well interest us. But Anne had one further trait of the utmost importance for her own maturity and for what she wrote: an unusual ability for self-analysis. She knew she had moods, and she could write eloquently about them—about loneliness for example. But she could also step outside her moods in order to evaluate them."

Her friend Lies Goslar later attributed Anne's rapid maturity to the many hours of quiet reflection encouraged by hiding, the severity of her situation, and her tender relationship with Peter Van Daan. A former teacher expressed surprise at the transformation in her character and writing because Anne had not been an exceptional student. Even Anne's father admitted "I never knew my little Anna was so deep." She meditated on religion, developed a strong sense of morality, and deliberately set about improving her own character. On July 15, 1944, she wrote: "It's really a wonder that I haven't dropped all my ideals, because they seem so absurd and impossible to carry out. . . . I simply can't build up my hopes on a foundation consisting of confusion, misery and death. I see the world gradually being turned into a wilderness, I hear the ever approaching thunder, which will destroy us too, I can feel the sufferings of millions and yet, if I look up into the heavens, I think that it will all come right, that this cruelty too will end, and that peace and tranquility will return again. . . . In the meantime, I must uphold my ideals, for perhaps the time will come when I shall be able to carry them out." She vowed to make a difference, writing on April 6, 1944: "I know what I want, I have a goal, an opinion, I have a religion and love. . . . I know that I'm a woman, a woman with inward strength and plenty of courage. If God lets me live . . . I shall not remain insignificant, I shall work in the world and for mankind!"

During the course of writing the diary, Anne became certain she wanted to be a writer. She envisioned a novel based on her diary. Additionally she wrote stories, later collected in *The Works of Anne Frank* and *Tales From the House Behind.* According to *New York Times Book Review* critic Frederick Morton, the stories "show that Anne followed instinctively the best of all platitudes: Write whereof you know. Not even her little fairy tales are easy escapes into make-believe, but rather pointed allegories of reality—the two elves who are imprisoned together to learn tolerance; or Blurry the Baby who runs away from home to find the great, free, open world, and never does. . . . Still none of these . . . , not even a charming little morality tale like "The Wise Old Dwarf," has the power of any single entry in the diary."

The diary ends August 1, 1944, three days before the group was arrested and sent to the concentration camp at Auschwitz, Poland. They were separated, and Margot and Anne were later transferred to Bergen-Belsen. According to a survivor who knew her at the concentration camp, Anne never lost her courage, deep sensitivity, or ability to feel. An excerpt of Ernst Schnabel's *Anne Frank: A Portrait in Courage,* reprinted in *A Tribute to Anne Frank,* states that "Anne was the youngest in her group, but nevertheless she was the leader of it. She also distributed the bread in the barracks, and she did it so well and fairly that there was none of the usual grumbling. . . . Here is another example. We were always thirsty. . . . And once, when I was so far gone that I almost died because there was nothing to drink, Anne suddenly came to me with a cup of coffee. To this day I don't know where she got it." The woman continued: "She, too, was the one who saw to the last what was going on all around us. . . . we were beyond feelings. . . . Something protected us, kept us from seeing. But Anne had no such protection, to the last. I can still see her standing at the door and looking down the camp street as a herd of naked gypsy girls was driven by, to the crematory, and Anne watched them going and cried. And she cried also when we marched past the Hungarian children who had already been waiting half a day in the rain in front of the gas chambers, because it was not yet their turn. And Anne nudged me and said: 'Look, look. Their eyes. . . .'"

Both Anne and Margot died of typhoid fever at Bergen-Belsen in March, 1945. Their mother had died earlier at Auschwitz. Otto Frank, liberated from Auschwitz by Russian troops in 1945, returned to Amsterdam. He already knew of his wife's death, but he had hope that Margot and Anne were alive. He soon received a letter informing him of their deaths. It was then that Miep Gies, who had worked for Mr. Frank as a secretary and helped hide the family, gave Anne's writings to him. Gies had discovered the diaries strewn on the floor after the Franks' arrest, and she kept the writings at her home but did not read them. It took Anne's father several weeks to read the diary as he could only bear to read a little at a time. Urged by friends, he published an edited version of the diary, deleting a number of passages he thought too personal.

Fifty years after the diary was first published, a new edition was published that included the passages Otto had originally deleted. Titled *The Diary of Anne Frank: The Definitive Edition* and edited by German author Mirjam Pressler, the new version includes thirty percent more material than the original publication. Writing in the *New York Times Book Review,* Patricia Hampl remarked, "There are more searching passages about her erotic feelings and her urgent curiosity about sexuality, more emphatic distancing from her dignified but apparently critical mother."

Mr. Frank, who received numerous letters in response to the diary, cautioned in the preface to *A Tribute to Anne Frank,* "However touching and sincere the expressions of sympathy I receive may be, I always reply that it is not enough to think of Anne with pity or admiration. Her diary should be a source of inspiration toward the realization of the ideals and hopes she expressed in it."

The Anne Frank Foundation has preserved the Franks' hiding place in Amsterdam, and schools in several countries, as well as a village at Wuppertal, West Germany, have been named for Anne.

*BIOGRAPHICAL/CRITICAL SOURCES:*

*BOOKS*

*Authors and Artists for Young Adults,* Volume 12, Gale (Detroit), 1994.
Bettelheim, Bruno, *Surviving and Other Essays,* Knopf, 1979.
Berryman, John, *The Freedom of the Poet,* Farrar, Straus, 1976.
Ehrenberg, Ilya, *Chekhov, Stendhal, and Other Essays,* translated by Tatiana Shebunia and Yvonne Kapp, Knopf, 1963.
Dunaway, Philip, and Evans, Melvin, editors, *Treasury of the World's Great Diaries,* Doubleday, 1957.
*Encyclopedia of the Third Reich,* McGraw, 1976.
Fradin, Dennis B., *Remarkable Children: Twenty Who Made History,* Little, Brown, 1987.
Frank, Anne, *The Diary of a Young Girl,* Doubleday, 1967.
Gies, Miep, and Alison Leslie Gold, *Anne Frank Remembered: The Story of the Woman Who Helped to Hide the Franks,* Simon & Schuster, 1987.
Goodrich, Frances, and Albert Hackett, *Diary of Anne Frank,* Random House, 1956.
Graver, Lawrence, *An Obsession with Anne Frank: Meyer Levin and The Diary,* University of California Press (Berkeley, CA), 1995.
*Her Way: Biographies of Women for Young People,* American Library Association, 1976.

Katz, Sandor, *Anne Frank,* Chelsea House (New York City), 1996.
*The Reader's Encyclopedia,* 2nd edition, Crowell, 1965.
*Something about the Author,* Gale, Volume 42, 1986, Volume 87, 1996.
Schnabel, Ernst, *Anne Frank: A Portrait in Courage,* translated from German by Richard and Clara Winston, Harcourt, 1958, published in England as *Footsteps of Anne Frank,* Longmans, 1959.
Steenmeijer, Anna G., editor, in collaboration with Otto Frank and Henri van Praag, *A Tribute to Anne Frank,* Doubleday, 1970.
*Twentieth-Century Literary Criticism,* Volume 17, Gale, 1985.
*Twentieth-Century Writing: A Reader's Guide to Contemporary Literature,* Transatlantic, 1969.
Tridenti, Lina, *Anne Frank,* translated by Stephen Thorne, Silver Burdett, 1985.

*PERIODICALS*

*Christian Century,* May 6, 1959.
*Commonweal,* October 31, 1958.
*Horn Book,* November-December, 1994, p. 706.
*Ladies' Home Journal,* September, 1967.
*Life,* August 18, 1958.
*Los Angeles Times,* April 13, 1984.
*McCall's,* July, 1958.
*New Statesman and Nation,* May 17, 1952.
*Newsweek,* June 25, 1979.
*New York Times Book Review,* June 15, 1952; September 20, 1959; May 10, 1987; July 2, 1989; March 5, 1995.
*New York Times Magazine,* April 21, 1957.
*People Weekly,* September 16, 1984.
*Saturday Review,* July 19, 1952.
*Time,* June 16, 1952; February 17, 1958; January 30, 1984.
*Women's Review of Books,* January, 1996, p. 12.*

\* \* \*

**FRANZKE, Andreas 1938-**

*PERSONAL:* Born September 27, 1938, in Breslau, Germany (now Wroclaw Poland); son of Walter and Erna (Gloede) Franzke; children: Hendrikje, Titus. *Education:* Attended University of Heidelberg, 1962-63, and University of Wurzburg, 1963-64; University of Marburg, Ph.D., 1969. *Religion:* Protestant.

*ADDRESSES: Home*—A.M. Rueppurrer Schloss 3A, Karlsruhe D-76199, Germany. *Office*—Reinhold-Frank-Strasse 81, Karlsruhe D-76133, Germany; fax: 72-184-8150.

*CAREER:* Staatliche Akademie der Bildenen Kuenste, Karlsruhe, Germany, professor of art history, 1969—, dean, 1988—. University of Michigan, guest professor, 1985.

*WRITINGS:*

*Jean Dubuffet,* Beyeler, 1975.
*Antoni Tapies Werk und Zeit* (title means "The Work and Life of Antoni Tapies"), Hatje, 1979.
*Dubuffet Zeichnungen* (title means "Drawings by Dubuffet"), Rogner & Bernard, 1980.
*Dubuffet,* Abrams (New York City), 1981.
*Skulpturen und Objekte von Malern des 20. Jahrhunderts* (title means "Sculptures and Objects by Painters of the Twentieth Century"), Dumont, 1982.
*Max Beckmann Skulpturen,* Piper, 1987.
*Jean Dubuffet: Petites Statues de la vie precaire* (includes English translation; title means "Jean Dubuffet: Small Statues of Precarious Life"), Gachnang & Springer, 1988.
*George Baselitz,* Prestel, 1988, English translation, Prestel, 1989.
*Jean Dubuffet,* Dumont, 1990.
*Antoni Tapies,* Prestel, 1992, English translation, Prestel, 1992.
*Stephan Balkenhol,* Cantz Edition, 1996.
*Lucian Freud, Radierungen* (etchings; includes English translation), Kerber Verlag, 1997.

*SIDELIGHTS:* Andreas Franzke told *CA:* "As a student I became familiar with the art and the ideas of Jean Dubuffet. Later on I became a friend of the artist, and I worked with him for many years. He considerably influenced my ideas about art. In my opinion Dubuffet is one of the leading painters of post-World War II Europe, and his impact and influence on American artists is substantial. He was discovered by collectors and museums in America far earlier than in his native France."

*BIOGRAPHICAL/CRITICAL SOURCES:*

*PERIODICALS*

*New York Times Book Review,* March 28, 1982.

**FUENTES, Carlos 1928-**

*PERSONAL:* Born November 11, 1928, in Panama City, Panama; Mexican citizen; son of Rafael Fuentes Boettiger (a career diplomat) and Berta Macias Rivas; married Rita Macedo (a movie actress), 1959 (divorced, 1969); married Sylvia Lemus (a television journalist), 1973; children: (first marriage) Cecilia; (second marriage) Carlos Rafael, Natasha. *Education:* National University of Mexico, LL.B., 1948; graduate study, Institute des Hautes Etudes, Geneva, Switzerland. *Politics:* Independent leftist. *Avocational interests:* Reading, travel, swimming, visiting art galleries, listening to classical and rock music, motion pictures, the theater.

*ADDRESSES: Home*—716 Watchung Rd., Bound Brook, NJ 08805. *Office*—401 Boylston Hall, Harvard University, Cambridge, MA 02138.

*CAREER:* Writer. International Labor Organization, Geneva, Switzerland, began as member, became secretary of the Mexican delegation, 1950-52; Ministry of Foreign Affairs, Mexico City, Mexico, assistant chief of press section, 1954; National University of Mexico, Mexico City, secretary and assistant director of cultural dissemination, 1955-56, head of department of cultural relations, 1957-59; Mexico's ambassador to France, 1975-77; Cambridge University, Norman Maccoll Lecturer, 1977, Simon Bolivar professor, 1986-87; Barnard College, New York City, Virginia Gildersleeve Professor, 1977; Columbia University, New York City, Henry L. Tinker Lecturer, 1978; Harvard University, Cambridge, MA, Robert F. Kennedy Professor of Latin American studies, 1987—. Fellow at Woodrow Wilson International Center for Scholars, 1974; lecturer or visiting professor at University of Mexico, University of California at San Diego, University of Oklahoma, University of Concepcion in Chile, University of Paris, University of Pennsylvania, and George Mason University; Modern Humanities Research Association, president, 1989—; member of Mexican National Commission on Human Rights.

*MEMBER:* American Academy and Institute of Arts and Letters (honorary).

*AWARDS, HONORS:* Centro Mexicano de Escritores fellowship, 1956-57; Biblioteca Breve Prize from Seix Barral (publishing house; Barcelona), 1967, for *Cambio de piel*; Xavier Villaurrutia Prize (Mexico), 1975; Romulo Gallegos Prize (Venezuela), 1977, for *Terra Nostra*; Alfonso Reyes Prize (Mexico), 1979, for body of work; National Award for Literature (Mexico), 1984, for *Orchids in the Moonlight;* nominated for *Los Angeles Times* Book Award in fiction, 1986, for *The Old Gringo*; Miguel de Cervantes Prize from Spanish Ministry of Culture, 1987; Ruben Dario Order of Cultural Independence (Nicaragua) and literary prize of Italo-Latino Americano Institute, both 1988, for *The Old Gringo*; Medal of Honor for Literature, National Arts Club, New York City, 1988; Rector's Medal, University of Chile, 1991; Casita Maria Medal, 1991; Order of Merit (Chile), 1992; French Legion of Honor, 1992; Menedez Pelayo International Award, University of Santander, 1992; named honorary citizen of Santiago de Chile, Buenos Aires, and Veracruz, 1993; Principe de Asturias Prize, 1994; Premiio Grinzane-Cavour, 1994; candidate for Neustadt International Prize for Literature, 1996; honorary degrees from Bard College, Cambridge University, Columbia College, Chicago State University, Dartmouth College, Essex University, Georgetown University, Harvard University, and Washington University.

*WRITINGS:*

NOVELS

*La region mas transparente,* Fondo de Cultura Economica, 1958, translation by Sam Hileman published as *Where the Air Is Clear,* Ivan Obolensky, 1960, Hileman's translation published as *Where the Air Is Clear: A Novel,* Farrar, Straus, 1982.

*Las buenas consciencias,* Fondo de Cultura Economica, 1959, translation published as *The Good Conscience,* Ivan Oblensky, 1961, reprinted, Farrar, Straus, 1981.

*La muerte de Artemio Cruz,* Fondo de Cultura Economica, 1962, reprinted, 1983, translation by Hileman published as *The Death of Artemio Cruz,* Farrar, Straus, 1964.

*Aura* (also see below), Era, 1962, reprinted, 1982, translation by Lysander Kemp, Farrar, Straus, 1965.

*Zona sagrada,* Siglo XXI, 1967, translation by Suzanne Jill Levine published as *Holy Place* (also see below), Dutton, 1972.

*Cambio de piel,* Mortiz, 1967, translation by Hileman published as *A Change of Skin,* Farrar, Straus, 1968.

*Cumpleanos,* Mortiz, 1969, translation published as *Birthday* (also see below).

*Terra Nostra* (also see below), Seix Barral, 1975, translation by Levine, afterword by Milan Kundera, Farrar, Straus, 1976.

*La cabeza de hidra,* Mortiz, 1978, translation by Margaret Sayers Peden published as *Hydra Head,* Farrar, Straus, 1978.

*Una familia lejana,* Era, 1980, translation by Peden published as *Distant Relations,* Farrar, Straus, 1982.

*El gringo viejo,* Fondo de Cultura Economica, 1985, translation by Peden and Fuentes published as *The Old Gringo,* Farrar, Straus, 1985.

*Christopher Unborn* (translation of *Cristobal Nonato*), Farrar, Straus, 1989.

Also author of *Holy Place & Birthday: Two Novellas,* Farrar, Straus.

SHORT STORIES

*Los dias enmascarados* (also see below), Los Presentes, 1954, reprinted, Era, 1982.

*Cantar de ciegos* (also see below), Mortiz, 1964.

*Dos cuentos mexicanos* (title means "Two Mexican Stories"; two short stories previously published in *Cantar de ciegos*), Instituto de Cultura Hispanica de Sao Paulo, Universidade de Sao Paulo, 1969.

*Poemas de amor: Cuentos del alma,* Imp. E. Cruces (Madrid), 1971.

*Chac Mool y otros cuentos,* Salvat, 1973.

*Agua quemada* (anthology), Fondo de Cultura Economica, 1981, translation by Peden published as *Burnt Water,* Farrar, Straus, 1980.

*Constancia and Other Stories for Virgins,* Farrar, Straus, 1989.

*Diana, the Goddess Who Hunts Alone,* introduction by Alfred J. Mac Adam, Farrar, Straus, & Giroux (New York City), 1995.

PLAYS

*Todos los gatos son pardos* (also see below), Siglo XXI, 1970.

*El tuerto es rey* (also see below; first produced [in French], 1970), Mortiz, 1970.

*Los reinos originarios* (contains *Todos los gatos son pardos* and *El tuerto es rey*), Seix Barral, 1971.

*Orquideas a la luz de la luna* (first produced in English as *Orchids in the Moonlight* at American Repertory Theater in Cambridge, MA, June 9, 1982), Seix Barral, 1982.

NONFICTION

*The Argument of Latin America: Words for North Americans,* Radical Education Project, 1963.

(Contributor) *Whither Latin America?* (political articles), Monthly Review Press, 1963.

*Paris: La revolucion de mayo,* Era, 1968.

*La nueva novela hispanoamericana,* Mortiz, 1969.

(Contributor) *El mundo de Jose Luis Cuevas,* Tudor (Mexico City), 1969.

*Casa con dos puertas* (title means "House with Two Doors"), Mortiz, 1970.

*Tiempo mexicano* (title means "Mexican Time"), Mortiz, 1971.

*Cervantes; o, La critica de la lectura,* Mortiz, 1976, translation published as *Don Quixote; or, The Critique of Reading,* Institute of Latin American Studies, University of Texas at Austin, 1976.

*On Human Rights: A Speech,* Somesuch Press (Dallas), 1984.

*Latin America: At War with the Past,* CBC Enterprises, 1985.

*Myself with Others: Selected Essays,* Farrar, Straus, 1988.

*A New Time for Mexico,* Farrar, Straus, & Giroux, 1996.

*OTHER*

(Editor and author of prologue) Octavio Paz, *Los signos en rotacion, y otros ensayos,* Alianza, 1971.

*Cuerpos y ofrendas* (anthology; includes selections from *Los dias enmascarados, Cantar de ciegos, Aura,* and *Terra Nostra,*) introduction by Octavio Paz, Alianza, 1972.

(Author of introduction) Milan Kundera, *La vida esta en otra parte* (Spanish translation of *Life Is Elsewhere*), Seix Barral, 1977.

(Author of introduction) Omar Cabezas, *Fire from the Mountain,* Crown, 1988.

*Valiente Mundo Nuevo,* Fondo de Cultura Economica (Mexico City), 1990.

*The Campaign,* Farrar, Straus, 1991.

*Buried Mirror: Reflections on Spain in the New World,* Houghton, 1992.

*Geografia de la novela,* Fondo de Cultura Economica (Mexico City), 1993.

*El naranjo, o los circulos del tiempo,* Alfaguara, Mexico, 1993.

*The Orange Tree,* introduction by Mac Adam, Farrar, Straus, & Giroux, 1994.

*La frontera de cristal,* Alfaguara, Mexico, 1995.

*The Writings of Carlos Fuentes,* edited by Raymond L. Williams, University of Texas Press (Austin), 1996.

Collaborator on several film scripts, including *Pedro Paramo,* 1966, *Tiempo de morir,* 1966, and *Los caifanes,* 1967. Work represented in numerous anthologies, including *Antologia de cuentos hispanoamericanos,* Nueva Decada (Costa Rica), 1985. Contributor to periodicals in the United States, Mexico, and France, including *New York Times, Washington Post,* and *Los Angeles Times.* Founding editor, *Revista Mexicana de Literatura,* 1954-58; coeditor, *El Espectador,* 1959-61, *Siempre,* 1960, and *Politica,* 1960.

*ADAPTATIONS:* Two short stories from *Cantar de ciegos* were made into films in the mid-1960s; *The Old Gringo* was adapted into a film of the same title by Fonda Films, 1989.

*WORK IN PROGRESS:* A novel about the assassination of Emiliano Zapata.

*SIDELIGHTS:* "Carlos Fuentes," states Robert Maurer in *Saturday Review,* is "without doubt one of Mexico's two or three greatest novelists." He is part of a group of Latin American writers whose writings, according to Alistair Reid's *New Yorker* essay, "formed the background of the Boom," a literary phenomenon Reid describes as a period in the 1960s when "a sudden surge of hitherto unheard-of writers from Latin America began to be felt among [U.S.] readers." Fuentes, however, is singled out from among the other writers of the Boom in Jose Donoso's autobiographical account, *The Boom in Spanish American Literature: A Personal History,* in which the Chilean novelist calls Fuentes "the first active and conscious agent of the internationalization of the Spanish American novel." And since the 1960s, Fuentes has continued his international influence in the literary world: his 1985 novel, *The Old Gringo,* for example, was the first written by a Mexican to ever appear on the *New York Times* best-seller list.

Although, as Donoso observes, early worldwide acceptance of Fuentes's novels contributed to the internationalization of Latin American literature, his work is an exploration of the culture and history of one nation, his native Mexico. Critics note the thematic presence of Mexico in nearly all Fuentes's writing. Robert Coover comments in the *New York Times Book Review* that in *The Death of Artemio Cruz,* for instance, Fuentes delineates "in the retrospective details of one man's life the essence of the post-Revolutionary history of all Mexico." Mexico is also present in Fuentes's novel *Terra Nostra,* in which, according to *Washington Post Book World* contributor Larry Rohter, "Fuentes probes more deeply into the origins of Mexico—and what it means to be a Mexican—than ever before." Fuentes's *Old Gringo*—published more than twenty years after *The Death of Artemio Cruz*—returns to the same theme as it explores Mexico's relationship with its northern neighbor, the United States.

Fuentes explains his preoccupation with Mexico, and particularly with Mexican history, in a *Paris Review* interview. "Pablo Neruda used to say," he told Alfred MacAdam and Charles Ruas, "that every Latin American writer goes around dragging a heavy body, the body of his people, of his past, of his national history. We have to assimilate the enormous weight of our past so that we will not forget what gives us life. If you forget your past, you die." Fuentes also notes that the development of the same theme in his novels unifies them so that they may be considered part of the same work. The author observes in the same interview, "In a sense my novels are one book with many chapters: *Where the Air Is Clear* is the biography of Mexico City; *The Death of Artemio Cruz* deals with an individual in that city; [and] *A Change of Skin* is that city, that society, facing the world, coming to grips with the fact that it is part of civilization and that there is a world outside that intrudes into Mexico."

Along with thematic unity, another characteristic of Fuentes's work is his innovative narrative style. In a *New Yorker* review, Anthony West compares the novelist's technique to "a rapid cinematic movement that cuts nervously from one character to another." Evan Connell states in the *New York Times Book Review* that Fuentes's "narrative style—with few exceptions—relies on the interruption and juxtaposition of different kinds of awareness." Reviewers Donald Yates and Karen Hardy also comment on Fuentes's experimental style. In the *Washington Post Book World* Yates calls Fuentes "a tireless experimenter with narrative techniques and points of view," while in *Hispania* Hardy notes that in Fuentes's work "the complexities of a human or national personality are evoked through . . . elaborate narrative devices."

Fuentes's novels *The Death of Artemio Cruz* and *Terra Nostra* are especially good examples of his experimental techniques. The first narrative deals with a corrupt Mexican millionaire who on his deathbed relives his life in a series of flashbacks. In the novel Fuentes uses three separate narrations to tell the story, and for each of these narrations he uses a different narrative person. *New York Review of Books* contributor A. Alvarez explains the three-part narration of the novel: "Cruz's story is told in three per-

sons. 'I' is the old man dying on his bed; 'you' is a slightly vatic, 'experimental' projection of his potentialities into an unspecified future . . . ; 'he' is the real hero, the man whose history emerges bit by bit from incidents shuffled around from his seventy-one years." In John S. Brushwood's *Mexico in Its Novel: A Nation's Search for Identity,* the critic praises Fuentes's technique, commenting: "The changing narrative viewpoint is extremely effective, providing a clarity that could not have been accomplished any other way. I doubt that there is anywhere in fiction a character whose wholeness is more apparent than in the case of Artemio Cruz."

Coover observes that in *Terra Nostra* Fuentes once again uses a variety of narrators to tell his story. Commenting favorably on Fuentes's use of the "you" narrative voice in the novel, Coover writes: "Fuentes's second person [narration] is not one overheard on a stage: the book itself, rather than the author or a character, becomes the speaker, the reader or listener a character, or several characters in succession." Spanish novelist Juan Goytisolo similarly states in *Review:* "One of the most striking and most successful devices [in *Terra Nostra*] is the abrupt shift in narrative point of view (at times without the unwary reader's even noticing), passing from first-person narration to second, . . . and simultaneously rendering objective and subjective reality in one and the same passage with patent scorn for the rules of discourse that ordinarily govern expository prose." In the *Paris Review* Fuentes comments on his use of the second person narrative, calling it "the voice poets have always used and that novelists also have a right to use."

Fuentes's use of the second person narrative and other experimental techniques makes his novels extremely complex. The author's remarks in a *New York Times Book Review* interview with Frank MacShane concerning the structure of *Terra Nostra* describe the intricacy of the work: "My chief stylistic device in 'Terra Nostra' is to follow every statement by a counter statement and every image by its opposite." This deliberate duplicity by the author, along with the extensive scope of the novel, causes some reviewers to criticize *Terra Nostra* for being unaccessible to the average reader. Maurer, for instance, calls the novel "a huge, sprawling, exuberant, mysterious, almost unimaginably dense work of 800 pages, covering events on three continents from the creation of man in Genesis to the dawn of the twenty-first century," and adds that "*Terra Nostra* presents a common reader with enormous problems simply of understanding what is going on." *Newsweek*'s Peter S. Prescott notes: "To talk about [*Terra Nostra*] at all we must return constantly to five words: excess, surreal, baroque, masterpiece, [and] unreadable."

Other critics, however, have written more positive reviews, seeing *Terra Nostra* and other Fuentes works as necessarily complex. *Village Voice* contributor Jonah Raskin finds Fuentes is at his best when the novelist can "plunge readers into the hidden recesses of his characters' minds and at the same time allow language to pile up around their heads in thick drifts, until they feel lost in a blizzard of words that enables them to see, to feel, in a revolutionary way." Fuentes also defends the difficulty of his works in a *Washington Post* interview with Charles Truehart. Recalling the conversation with the Mexican author, Truehart quotes Fuentes as saying: "I believe in books that do not go to a ready-made public. . . . I'm looking for readers I would like to *make*. . . . To *win* them, . . . to *create* readers rather than to give something that readers are expecting. That would bore me to death."

In 1992 Fuentes produced, *The Buried Mirror: Reflections on Spain in the New World,* a historical work that discusses the formation and development of the Latin American world. The title refers to polished rocks found in the tombs of ancient Mediterranean and Amerindian peoples, presaging, in Fuentes's view, the convergence of these distant cultures. Fuentes writes that his book is "dedicated to a search for the cultural continuity that can inform and transcend the economic and political destiny and fragmentation of the Hispanic world." Attempting to disentangle the complex legacy of Spanish settlement in the New World, Fuentes first addresses the mixed ethnicity of the Spanish conquerors, whose progeny include Celts, Phoenicians, Greeks, Romans, Arabs, and Jews, and the consequent diversity produced in Latin America through war, colonization, and miscegenation.

Praising Fuentes's intriguing though broad subject, Nicolas Shumway writes in the *New York Times Book Review,* "The range of the book is both its principal defect and its chief virtue. Beginning with the prehistoric cave paintings at Altamira in Spain and ending with contemporary street art in East Los Angeles, Mr. Fuentes seeks to cover all of Spanish and Spanish-American history, with frequent digressions on a particular artist, political figure, novel or painting." *The Buried Mirror,* according to David Ewing Duncan in a *Washington Post Book World* review, is "invigorated by the novelist's sense of irony, paradox and

sensuality. Here is a civilization, he says, that defies whatever stereotypes we may hold, a society at once erotic and puritanical, cruel and humane, legalistic and corrupt, energetic and sad." Guy Garcia notes in *Time* that the book "represents an intellectual homecoming for Fuentes, who conceived of the project as 'a fantastic opportunity to write my own cultural biography.'"

Four years later Fuentes followed with *A New Time for Mexico,* a collection of essays on the internal injustice and international indignity suffered by Mexico. Viewed as a sequel to his 1971 publication *Tiempo mexicano* ("Mexican Time"), Fuentes addresses current events in his native country, including political reform, the Chiapas rebellion, social inequities, and the significance of the North American Free Trade Agreement (NAFTA) for Mexico and its perception in the United States. Though noting the bias of Fuentes's strong nationalism, Roderic A. Camp maintains in *Library Journal* that his "brief cultural vignettes" are "appealing and insightful." A *Publishers Weekly* reviewer commends Fuentes's "lapidary, lyrical meditations on Mexico as a land of continual metamorphosis."

In *The Orange Tree* Fuentes offers five novellas whose subjects span several centuries, each connected by the image of the orange and its perennial source. For Fuentes the orange tree signifies the possibilities of beauty, sustenance, transplantation, and rejuvenation, as its seeds were introduced to Spain through Roman and Moorish invaders, reached the New World with the conquistadors, and have flourished since. Fuentes illustrates various manifestations of violence, deception, and suffering by recounting episodes from the conquest of Roman Iberia and Mexico, a contemporary corporate takeover, and the death wish of an American actor.

"In all this intercourse between Old World and New, Rome and Africa and Spain, past and present," Alan Cheuse writes in Chicago *Tribune Books,* "Fuentes makes the older material resonate with all of the exotic and yet familiar attraction of compelling human behavior." Michael Kerrigan praises the work in a *Times Supplement Review,* noting that "The challenge and opportunity *The Orange Tree* presents its reader are those of escaping from 'a more or less protected individuality' into a wider existence of multiple possibility and a cyclical history which holds past and present in simultaneity and in ceaseless renewal." Kerrigan concludes, "What strikes the reader first in Fuentes' work may be his erudition and intellectual rigour, but what remains in the mind is his sympathy, his concern to commemorate the countless lives sacrificed in pain and obscurity so that we might live."

In 1995 Fuentes published *Diana, the Goddess Who Hunts Alone,* a semi-autobiographical novel that follows a love affair between an unnamed, married Mexican novelist and an American film actress, Diana Soren. The fictional romance, however, contains obvious parallels to the author's real-life affair with film actress Jean Seberg. Mirroring actual events surrounding the liaison between Fuentes and Seberg, the writer meets Soren at a New Year's Eve party in 1969 and follows her to a Santiago film location where they enjoy a passionate, albeit brief, relationship. After several months of literary conversation and tenuous intimacy, the self-absorbed writer is abandoned by the unstable actress who maintains a second relationship via telephone with a Black Panther and keeps a photograph of her last lover, Clint Eastwood, by her bed.

Though the book received mixed reviews, Rosanne Daryl Thomas observes in Chicago *Tribune Books* that the novel reveals "the tensions between imagination, language and reality, between generosity born of love and the profound selfishness often found in artists." Thomas concludes, "Carlos Fuentes takes off the mask of literary creation and reveals a man nakedly possessed by a desperate passion. Then he raises the mask to his face and tells a fascinating, frightening tale of heartbreak."

While Fuentes's innovative use of theme and structure has gained the author an international reputation as a novelist, he believes that only since *Terra Nostra* has he perfected his craft. "I feel I'm beginning to write the novels I've always wanted to write and didn't know how to write before," he explains to Philip Bennett in a *Boston Globe Magazine* interview. "There were the novels of youth based on energy, and conceptions derived from energy. Now I have the conceptions I had as a young man, but I can develop them and give them their full value."

*BIOGRAPHICAL/CRITICAL SOURCES:*

*BOOKS*

*Authors and Artists for Young Adults,* Volume 4, Gale (Detroit), 1990.
*Authors in the News,* Volume 2, Gale, 1976.
Brushwood, John S., *Mexico in Its Novel: A Nation's Search for Identity,* University of Texas Press, 1966.

*Contemporary Literary Criticism,* Gale, Volume 3, 1975, Volume 8, 1978, Volume 10, 1979, Volume 13, 1980, Volume 22, 1982, Volume 41, 1987, Volume 60, 1991.
*Dictionary of Literary Biography,* Volume 113: *Modern Latin American Fiction Writers, First Series,* Gale, 1992.
Donoso, Jose, *The Boom in Spanish American Literature: A Personal History,* Columbia University Press, 1977.
*Hispanic Literature Criticism,* Gale, 1994.
Plimpton, George, editor, *Writers at Work: The Paris Review Interviews, Sixth Series,* Penguin Books, 1984.
*Short Story Criticism,* Gale, Volume 24, 1997.
*World Literature Criticism,* Gale, 1992.

*PERIODICALS*

*Boston Globe Magazine,* September 9, 1984.
*Hispania,* May, 1978.
*Kirkus Reviews,* April 15, 1996, p. 575.
*Library Journal,* January, 1994, p. 96; January, 1995, p. 77; January, 1996, p. 81; May 1, 1996, p. 112.
*London Review of Books,* May 10, 1990, p. 26.
*Los Angeles Times Book Review,* April 10, 1994, p. 6.
*Nation,* February 17, 1992, p. 205.
*New Perspectives,* spring, 1994, p. 54.
*New Statesman and Society,* August 26, 1994, p. 37; September 29, 1995, p. 57.
*Newsweek,* November 1, 1976.
*New Yorker,* March 4, 1961; January 26, 1981; February 24, 1986.
*New York Review of Books,* June 11, 1964.
*New York Times Book Review,* November 7, 1976; October 19, 1980; October 6, 1991, p. 3; April 26, 1992, p. 9; October 22, 1995, p. 12.
*Observer* (London), April 1, 1990, p. 67.
*Paris Review,* winter, 1981.
*Publishers Weekly,* April 15, 1996, p. 55.
*Review,* winter, 1976.
*Saturday Review,* October 30, 1976.
*Time,* June 29, 1992, p. 78.
*Times Literary Supplement,* June 10, 1994, p. 23; September 29, 1995, p. 27.
*Tribune Books* (Chicago), April 19, 1992; April 11, 1994, p. 6; December 17, 1995, p. 3.
*Village Voice,* January 28, 1981; April 1, 1986.
*Washington Post,* May 5, 1988.
*Washington Post Book World,* October 26, 1976; January 14, 1979; March 29, 1992.
*World Literature Today,* autumn, 1994, p. 794.*

# G

## GALBRAITH, John Kenneth 1908-
### (Mark Epernay, Herschel McLandress)

*PERSONAL:* Born October 15, 1908, in Iona Station, Ontario, Canada; naturalized United States citizen, 1937; son of William Archibald (a politician and farmer) and Catherine (Kendall) Galbraith; married Catherine Atwater, September 17, 1937; children: John Alan, Peter, James, Douglas (deceased). *Education:* University of Toronto, B.S. (agriculture), 1931; University of California, Berkeley, M.S., 1933, Ph.D. (economics), 1934; attended Cambridge University, 1937-38. *Politics:* Democrat.

*ADDRESSES: Home*—30 Francis Ave., Cambridge, MA 02138; Newfane, VT (summer); Gstaad, Switzerland (winter). *Office*—207 Littauer Center, Harvard University, Cambridge, MA 02138.

*CAREER:* Harvard University, Cambridge, MA, instructor and tutor, 1934-39; Princeton University, Princeton, NJ, assistant professor of economics, 1939-42; U.S. Office of Price Administration, Washington, D.C., administrator in charge of price division, 1941-42, department administrator, 1942-43; *Fortune* magazine, member of board of editors, 1943-48; Harvard University, lecturer, 1948-49, professor, 1949-59, Paul M. Warburg Professor of Economics, 1959-75, Paul M. Warburg Professor emeritus, 1975—. Reith Lecturer, 1966; Trinity College, Cambridge, visiting fellow, 1970-71. Director of U.S. Strategic Bombing Survey, 1945, and Office of Economic Security Policy, U.S. Department of State, 1946; presidential adviser to John F. Kennedy and Lyndon B. Johnson; U.S. Ambassador to India, 1961-63. Affiliated with television series *The Age of Uncer-*

*tainty,* on the British Broadcasting Corporation (BBC), 1977.

*MEMBER:* American Academy and Institute of Arts and Letters (president, 1984-87), American Academy of Arts and Sciences (fellow), American Economic Association (president, 1972), Americans for Democratic Action (chairman, 1967-69), American Agricultural Economics Association, Twentieth Century Fund (trustee), Century Club (New York City), Federal City Club (Washington, DC), Harvard Club (New York City), Saturday Club (Boston).

*AWARDS, HONORS:* Research fellowship, University of California, 1931-34; Social Science Research Council fellowship, 1937-38; Medal of Freedom, 1946; Sarah Josepha Hale Award, Friends of the Richards Free Library, 1967; President's Certificate of Merit; honorary degrees include LL.D., Bard College, 1958, Miami University (Ohio), 1959, University of Toronto, 1961, Brandeis University, 1963, University of Massachusetts, 1963, University of Guelph, 1965, University of Saskatchewan, 1965, Rhode Island College, 1966, Boston College, 1967, Hobart and William Smith Colleges, 1967, University of Paris, 1975, Harvard University, 1988, Moscow State University, 1988, Smith College, 1989, and Oxford University, 1990.

*WRITINGS:*

(With Henry Sturgis Dennison) *Modern Competition and Business Policy,* Oxford University Press, 1938.

*A Theory of Price Control,* Harvard University Press, 1952, reprinted with new introduction by Galbraith, 1980.

*American Capitalism: The Concept of Countervailing Power,* Houghton, 1952, reprinted with new introduction by Galbraith, M. E. Sharpe, 1980, revised edition, Transaction Publishers, 1993.

*Economics and the Art of Controversy,* Rutgers University Press, 1955.

*The Great Crash, 1929,* Houghton, 1955, reprinted with new introduction by Galbraith, 1988.

(With Richard H. Holton and others) *Marketing Efficiency in Puerto Rico,* Harvard University Press, 1955.

*Journey to Poland and Yugoslavia,* Harvard University Press, 1958.

*The Affluent Society,* Houghton, 1958, 4th edition, 1984.

*The Liberal Hour,* Houghton, 1960.

*Economic Development in Perspective,* Harvard University Press, 1962, revised edition published as *Economic Development,* 1964.

(Under pseudonym Mark Epernay) *The McLandress Dimension* (satire), Houghton, 1963, revised edition, New American Library, 1968.

*The Scotch* (memoir), Houghton, 1964, 2nd edition, 1985 (published in England as *Made to Last,* Hamish Hamilton, 1964, and as *The Non-potable Scotch: A Memoir on the Clansmen in Canada,* Penguin, 1964).

*The Underdeveloped Country* (text of five radio broadcasts), Canadian Broadcasting Corp., 1965.

*The New Industrial State,* Houghton, 1967, 4th edition, 1985.

*How to Get Out of Vietnam: A Workable Solution to the Worst Problem of Our Time,* New American Library, 1967.

*The Triumph: A Novel of Modern Diplomacy,* Houghton, 1968.

(With Mohinder Singh Randhawa) *Indian Painting: The Scene, Themes and Legends,* Houghton, 1968.

*How to Control the Military,* Doubleday, 1969.

*Ambassador's Journal: A Personal Account of the Kennedy Years,* Houghton, 1969.

(Author of introduction) David Levine, *No Known Survivors: David Levine's Political Prank,* Gambit, 1970.

*Who Needs the Democrats, and What It Takes to Be Needed,* Doubleday, 1970.

*A Contemporary Guide to Economics, Peace, and Laughter* (essays), edited by Andrea D. Williams, Houghton, 1971.

*Economics and the Public Purpose,* Houghton, 1973.

*A China Passage,* Houghton, 1973.

(Author of introduction) Frank Moraes and Edward Howe, editors, *India,* McGraw-Hill, 1974.

*Money: Whence It Came, Where It Went,* Houghton, 1975, revised edition, 1995.

*The Age of Uncertainty* (based on the 1977 BBC television series), Houghton, 1977.

*The Galbraith Reader: From the Works of John Kenneth Galbraith,* selected and with commentary by the editors of *Gambit,* Gambit, 1977.

(With Nicole Salinger) *Almost Everyone's Guide to Economics,* Houghton, 1978.

*Annals of an Abiding Liberal,* edited by Williams, Houghton, 1979.

*The Nature of Mass Poverty,* Harvard University Press, 1979.

*A Life in Our Times: Memoirs,* Houghton, 1981.

*The Anatomy of Power,* Houghton, 1983.

*The Voice of the Poor: Essays in Economic and Political Persuasion,* Harvard University Press, 1983.

*A View from the Stands: Of People, Politics, Military Power, and the Arts,* edited by Williams, Houghton, 1986.

*Economics in Perspective: A Critical History,* Houghton, 1987, published as *A History of Economics,* 1987.

(With Stanislav Menshikov) *Capitalism, Communism and Coexistence: From the Bitter Past to a Better Present,* Houghton, 1988.

*A Tenured Professor* (novel), Houghton, 1990.

*The Culture of Contentment,* Houghton, 1992.

(Editor and author of introduction) Thomas H. Eliot, *Recollections of the New Deal: When the People Mattered,* Northeastern University Press, 1992.

*A Short History of Financial Euphoria: A Hymn of Caution,* Whittle Books/Viking, 1993.

*The Triumph: A Novel of Modern Diplomacy,* Houghton, 1993.

*A Journey through Economic Time: A Firsthand View,* Houghton, 1994.

*The World Economy since the Wars: An Eyewitness Account,* Houghton, 1994.

*The Good Society: The Humane Dimension,* Houghton, 1996.

Contributor to books, including *Can Europe Unite?,* Foreign Policy Association (New York City), 1950, and *The Past Speaks to the Present,* by Yigael Yadin, Granada TV Network Limited, 1962. Author of drafts of speeches for political leaders, including Franklin D. Roosevelt, Adlai Stevenson, John F. Kennedy, Lyndon B. Johnson, and Robert Kennedy. Editor of "Harvard Economic Studies" series, Harvard University Press. Contributor to scholarly journals. Reviewer, under pseudonym Herschel McLandress, of *Report from Iron Mountain.*

Galbraith's works have been translated into numerous languages.

*SIDELIGHTS:* John Kenneth Galbraith is considered one of the twentieth century's foremost writers on economics and among its most influential economists. A prolific and diverse writer, whose more than forty books range over a variety of topics, Galbraith is the author of such classic texts as *The Affluent Society* and *The New Industrial State.* In addition to his writings, he has also held positions as a government economist, presidential adviser, and foreign ambassador, and for more than fifteen years he was the Paul M. Warburg Professor of Economics at Harvard University. Galbraith's blend of skills make him a rarity among economists. "As a raconteur and a literary stylist, he stands with the best," stated James Fallows in the *New York Times Book Review,* while "as a thinker," noted Lowell Ponte in the *Los Angeles Times Book Review,* "Galbraith has made major contributions to the economic arguments of our time." In addition to originating several terms that are part of the vernacular of economists and laymen alike—such as "affluent society," "conventional wisdom," and "countervailing power"—Galbraith is famous as a witty guide to twentieth-century economics. A *New Yorker* reviewer called him "a wizard at packing immense amounts of information into a style so entertaining that the reader does not realize he is being taught." Eugene D. Genovese wrote in the *New York Times Book Review* that Galbraith "has admirably demonstrated that respect for the English language provides everything necessary to demystify economics and render its complexities intelligible."

Galbraith's writing abilities, including his accessibility to non-economist audiences, have at times overshadowed his achievements as an economist. "Galbraith's irreverent wit and lucid style lead many to underestimate his importance in the history of economic thought," Walter Russell Mead notes in the *Los Angeles Times Book Review.* "Like Adam Smith . . . Galbraith has spent a career attacking the entrenched errors of conventional wisdom." Galbraith is well known as a formidable critic of modern economic policies and economists. Richard Eder in the *Los Angeles Times* depicted him as "liberal, witty, polemical and a man who tends to charm his antagonists because the dunce caps he fits on them are so finely made that they almost flatter." As a critic, Galbraith has made significant contributions to economics by highlighting its shortcomings. According to Genovese, Galbraith's "services" include: "his early warnings that Keynesians were paying inadequate at-

tention to the danger of inflation; his thoughtful if not always convincing discussions of the political and economic relationship of the free market sector to the managed sector; his bold exploration of the possibilities and actualities of socialism; and his humane concern for the problems of women, the poor, the blacks and others conveniently forgotten by most academic economists." Godfrey Hodgson, in the *Washington Post Book World,* compared Galbraith to eighteenth-century French satirist Voltaire, "a man whose sardonic wit and careful urbanity are worn like masks to hide both the anger he feels for sham and complacent greed, and the pity he feels for their victims."

The son of a Canadian politician and farmer, Galbraith became interested in the study of economics during the Depression. In the 1930s and early 1940s, he taught at both Harvard University and Princeton University and became influenced by economist John Maynard Keynes. In 1941, at the age of 33, he was appointed administrator of the price operations of the U.S. Office of Price Administration and was responsible for setting prices in the United States. His 1952 book *A Theory of Price Control* outlines many of Galbraith's fundamental economic principles, as does another early book, *American Capitalism: The Concept of Countervailing Power,* which explores postwar American economy and the role of labor as a countervailing force in a market economy. Samuel Lubell in the *New York Herald Tribune Book World* called *American Capitalism* "one of the most provocative economic essays since the writings of the late John Maynard Keynes," adding that "even where one disagrees, [Galbraith's] ideas stimulate a spring cleaning of old beliefs and outworn, if cherished, notions—which is perhaps all that can be asked of any new theory." Galbraith commented to Victor Navasky in the *New York Times Book Review* on his decision to write about economics: "I made up my mind I would never again place myself at the mercy of the technical economists who had the enormous power to ignore what I had written. I set out to involve a large community. I would involve economists by having the larger public say to them 'Where do you stand on Galbraith's idea of price control?' They would *have* to confront what I said."

Galbraith broadened his readership with his 1955 book *The Great Crash, 1929,* which recounts the harried days leading up to the stock market crash and Great Depression. Written at the suggestion of historian Arthur Schlesinger, Jr., who queried Galbraith as to why no one had ever written an economic account of the depression, *The Great Crash, 1929* was praised for being both illuminating and readable. "Economic writings are seldom notable for their entertainment value, but this book is," C. J. Rolo commented in *Atlantic Monthly,* adding, "Galbraith's prose has grace and wit, and he distills a good deal of sardonic fun from the whopping errors of the nation's oracles and the wondrous antics of the financial community." R. L. Heilbroner wrote in the *New York Herald Tribune Book Review:* "Galbraith has told the tale of the great bust with all the verve, pace, and suspense, of a detective story. . . . For any one who is interested in understanding the recent past or attempting to achieve a perspective on the future of American economic history, . . . this book will be of great interest."

Following these books, Galbraith wrote the bestseller *The Affluent Society.* A major assessment of the U.S. economy, *The Affluent Society* questions priorities of production and how wealth is to be divided. As Galbraith stated in the book: "The final problem of the productive society is what it produces. This manifests itself in an implacable tendency to provide an opulent supply of some things and a niggardly yield of others. This disparity carries to the point where it is a cause of social discomfort and social unhealth." According to Heilbroner, Galbraith raised three important issues: "One of these is the moral problem of how an Affluent Society may be prevented from becoming merely a Rich one. A second is the efficacy of Mr. Galbraith's reforms to offset the inertia and the vested interests of a powerful social structure. A third is what form of social cohesion can replace our troublesome but useful absorption in Production." Heilbroner called *The Affluent Society* "as disturbing as it is brilliant. . . . with which it is easy to cavil or to disagree, but which it is impossible to dismiss."

Galbraith's 1967 bestseller *The New Industrial State,* a sequel to *The Affluent Society,* examines the diminishing role of individual choice in the market enterprise. "I reached the conclusion that in 'The Affluent Society' I had only written half the book I should have," Galbraith commented to the *New York Times Book Review.* "'The Affluent Society' says the more you have the more you want. And for obvious reasons, as people become richer it is easier to persuade them as to their wants. But I hadn't really examined the role of the great corporations, the industrial system, in the persuasion process." Arthur Selwyn Miller commented in the *New Republic:* "If Galbraith is correct—and I am inclined to agree in large part with him—then we . . . are ruled by nameless and faceless managers in the technostructures of the private governments of the supercorporations and their counterparts in the public bureaucracy. That's an event of considerable significance." Raymond J. Saulnier in the *New York Times Book Review* called *The New Industrial State* "a tightly organized, closely reasoned book, notable for what it says about the dynamics of institutional change and for certain qualities of its author: a sardonic wit, exercised liberally at the expense of conservatives, and unusual perception."

In his 1973 book *Economics and the Public Purpose* Galbraith, according to Leonard Silk in the *New York Times,* goes "beyond his earlier books to describe the whole modern capitalist economy, which he sees as split roughly in twain between 'the planning system' and what he calls 'the market system'—a collection of imperfect competitors and partial monopolists that includes such producers as farmers, television repairmen, retailers, small manufacturers, medical practitioners, photographers and pornographers." The *New Yorker's* Naomi Bliven commented that Galbraith "offers his account of the American economic system and his ideas of how to correct—a word he uses frequently—its irrationality." She added that although "his intensity sometimes makes his wit painfully abrasive. . . . because his work is intelligent, stimulating, and comprehensive—Galbraith knows (in fact, insists) that an economic theory implies an ethical system, a political purpose, and a psychological hypothesis—one forgives this unrelenting critic."

In addition to more than twenty-five other books on economics, the prolific Galbraith is also the author of novels and acclaimed volumes of memoirs. As in his other books, critics found that these writings display Galbraith's characteristic wit and insight. His 1968 novel *The Triumph,* set amidst a revolution in a fictional Latin American nation, depicts the bungled efforts of U.S. foreign policy officials to put an acceptable leader in power. Robert Brown in the *New Republic,* while expressing reservations about the novel's tone, which he described as "loftily condescending and relentlessly witty," called the book "quite devastating" and acknowledged Galbraith's "detailed knowledge of the scene." Galbraith's 1990 novel, *A Tenured Professor,* is the tale of a professor who, with his wife, develops a successful stock forecasting mechanism that makes them very wealthy. With their new money, the couple begins supporting various liberal causes, such as identifying companies that do not employ women in top executive positions. "Lurking in the background of his story is enough economics to satisfy Wall Street game players and enough of a cheerful fairy tale for grown-ups to please the most liberal dreamers," notes Herbert Mitgang in the *New York Times.* "A whimsical fellow is John Kenneth Galbraith, who knows that money makes people and institutions jump through hoops and over their own cherished principles." He added: "Readers who know and admire the author as an acerbic political voice are not shortchanged in his biting new novel. . . . Satirical one-liners and paragraphs fall lightly from the pen of the author and from the lips of his characters all through the story."

Galbraith's memoirs give insights into his diverse career as economist, writer, and participant in the political scene. Regarding *A Life in Our Times,* Ward Just commented in the *Chicago Tribune Book World:* "[Galbraith] has rarely been at the center of events, though he has been on the fringes of most everything, so this is not a memoir of the and-then-I-told-the-President variety. . . . The charm and consequence of this book is not the career as such, but the manner in which the author has chosen to describe it, with singular range, style, and wit, and a sure grasp of absurdity and pomposity, particularly as they apply to government and politics." Regarding the essays in *A View from the Stands: Of People, Politics, Military Power, and the Arts,* Richard Eder wrote in the *Los Angeles Times* that Galbraith "has a priceless sense of the absurd. . . . [Yet,] for someone who makes an art out of polite irreverence, Galbraith manages to be equally artistic in his strong admirations. . . . His portraits of, among others, Ambassador Chester Bowles, President Lyndon B. Johnson and First Lady Eleanor Roosevelt are both warm and strikingly perceptive." *A View from the Stands* reveals a man, according to John Freeman in the *Times Literary Supplement,* who is "substantial, interesting, frequently perverse, occasionally silly, almost always stimulating—at least hardly ever a bore—opinionated, funny, fastidious, loyal, on the whole generous and magnificently infallible even when he is wrong."

In *The Culture of Contentment,* Galbraith "scathingly denounces a society in which the affluent have come to dominate the political arena, guaranteeing their continued comfort while refusing to address the needs of the less fortunate," claimed Victor Dwyer in *Maclean's.* Galbraith asserted that satisfied citizens—those whose earning are in the top twenty percent and who live a moneyed lifestyle—tend, by their very prosperity, to guarantee their eventual downfall by ignoring the fundamental requirements of the

underclasses. Their blindness to social reform has historically led to inflation and the need for greater government intervention, the author maintained, thereby causing a resulting eventual decline in economic security even for the elite. Galbraith warned that the upper class ignores economic, political, and social necessities of the lower classes at its own peril. Galbraith told Dwyer that *The Culture of Contentment* exceeds the scope of his other books: "'What I am attempting is to formulate the political consequences of self-satisfied well-being,' said Galbraith. 'In the wake of Mr. Reagan and Mr. Bush,' he added, 'it seemed that the time was right.'" Robert N. Bellah observed in the *New York Times Book Review,* "'The Culture of Contentment' is certainly no savage jeremiad. It is a very amusing volume, but by the end one's laughter has turned hollow and one wants to weep. For all its gentle appearances, it is a bombshell of a book, and the story it tells is one of devastation." Aidan Rankin commented in the *Times Literary Supplement:* "The reassuring, old-fashioned elegance of John Kenneth Galbraith's prose is at once the most striking and the most disturbing feature of *The Culture of Contentment.* Striking, because it contrasts so markedly with the jargon and euphemism of modern economics, disturbing in the force and clarity of its critique of contemporary democracy."

About *A Short History of Financial Euphoria: A Hymn of Caution,* Robert Krulwich explained in the *New York Times Book Review* that it "is John Kenneth Galbraith's quick tour through four centuries of financial bubbles, panics and crashes, with an eye toward instructing today's investors on how to see cautionary signs before it is too late." The book describes, through myriad examples, a historic pattern of financial ebb and flow creating highs and lows in the economic climate. Galbraith denounces the oblivious attitude engendered by successful investments, blinding individuals to warning signs and potential disasters. As Krulwich put it, "How people become blockheads is the real subject of his treatise." He concluded that Galbraith reminds readers that "rich people aren't smart. They're just lucky."

*A Journey through Economic Time: A Firsthand View* traces economic development from the time of World War I (or the "Great War") through the highlights of the twentieth century, including other wars and military conflicts, the philosophies of influential pundits, and the practices and ideologies of various presidential administrations. "Somehow, with an astonishing and no doubt deceptive ease, Mr. Galbraith is able to compress eras, reducing their unwieldy bulk to grasp-able essence and extracting coherence from their the-matic tangle," remarked Alan Abelson in the *New York Times Book Review*. Abelson admired the read-ability of the book, asserting, "He's opinionated, in-corrigibly sardonic and murder on fools. . . . In a profession in which statistical surfeit, abused syntax and impenetrable prose are prerequisites to standing, Mr. Galbraith's lucidity and grace of articulation are excommunicable offenses." Donald McCloskey hailed Galbraith's tome in the Chicago *Tribune Books,* sum-marizing, "What makes it good is the Old Economist showing you page after page how to think like one," ultimately urging readers to "buy it or borrow it. You'll be a better citizen and will not believe so easily the latest economic idiocy from Washington or the Sierra Club or the other fonts of conventional wisdom."

William Keegan noted in *New Statesman and Society* that *The World Economy since the Wars: An Eyewit-ness Account* "can be thoroughly recommended to those interested in the economic debate, but [who are] not quite sure where to start." Galbraith's efforts involve "sifting and reducing a lifetime's observations to an essential core," described Keegan. While the reviewer suggested that much of this volume had al-ready appeared in other forms in earlier books, he nevertheless maintained, "This is a highly engaging memoir, which holds the attention even of people, such as myself, who are thoroughly familiar with most of Galbraith's work."

Two years after the Republican party won control of Congress in the 1994 elections, Galbraith produced *The Good Society: The Humane Dimension,* reiterat-ing his economic and political vision for the creation of a just and equitable society. While suggesting that big government and the welfare state are the products of historical forces rather than liberal policies, Galbraith advocated reform on behalf of the poor and disenfranchised, including health care, unemployment compensation, government regulation of working con-ditions, education, environmental protection, and pro-gressive taxation. As Paul Craig Roberts summarized in the *National Review,* Galbraith "defines 'the good society' as one that is politically organized to coerce 'the favored' for the poor. The instrument for this coercion 'must be the Democratic Party.'" According to Todd Gitlin in *The Nation,* "Galbraith has written perhaps the most chastened manifesto in American history. Deliberately so. His goal in this brief hand-book is to sketch 'the achievable, not the perfect.'" *The Good Society,* as Matthew Miller observed in the

*New York Times Book Review,* contains "Mr. Galbraith's vintage cultural complaints. He denounces the equation of wealth with intelligence, the role of advertising in ginning up consumer desire, the injus-tice of private affluence alongside public squalor . . . and, of course, the perils of bureaucracy."

For more than half a century, Galbraith has proven himself a brilliant writer, critical thinker, perspica-cious social analyst, and astute economic observer/commentator. Rankin opined in the *Times Literary Supplement* that "Galbraith has contributed substan-tially to the liberal tradition in the United States and the social democratic tradition in Western Europe." About the author's multiple interests and abilities, McCloskey commented in the *Chicago Tribune Books,* "As much as he would rather be a writer, converting people to his government-loving faith, he [is] an economist down to his shoes." Dwyer described Galbraith in *Maclean's* as "America's foremost lib-eral thinker," adding that he "is most passionate about the state of American society." McCloskey concluded, "We need more of him because he's an economist who can speak to non-economists. . . . Galbraith is one of a handful of professors who can make the Dismal Science sing."

An interview with Galbraith appears in *Contemporary Authors New Revision Series,* Volume 34.

*BIOGRAPHICAL/CRITICAL SOURCES:*

*BOOKS*

*Contemporary Issues Criticism,* Volume 1, Gale (De-troit), 1982.

Galbraith, John Kenneth, *The Affluent Society,* Houghton, 1958.

Galbraith *The Scotch,* Houghton, 1964.

Galbraith, *A Life in Our Times: Memoirs,* Houghton, 1981.

Galbraith, *A View from the Stands: Of People, Poli-tics, Military Power, and the Arts,* Houghton, 1986.

Galbraith, *A Journey through Economic Time: A Firsthand View,* Houghton, 1994.

Galbraith, *The World Economy since the Wars: An Eyewitness Account,* Houghton, 1994.

Reisman, D. A., *Galbraith and Market Capitalism,* New York University Press, 1980.

Reisman, *Tawney, Galbraith, and Adam Smith,* St. Martin's, 1982.

Stanfield, J. Ron, *John Kenneth Galbraith,* St. Mar-tin's, 1996.

*PERIODICALS*

*American Economic Review,* December, 1952.
*Atlantic Monthly,* June, 1955; January, 1987.
*Chicago Tribune,* June 1, 1958.
*Chicago Tribune Book World,* April 19, 1981.
*Fortune,* June 13, 1994, p. 149.
*Kirkus Reviews,* February 15, 1996, p. 273.
*Library Journal,* May 15, 1993, pp. 78-79.
*Look,* March 27, 1970.
*Los Angeles Times,* December 3, 1986.
*Los Angeles Times Book Review,* May 24, 1981;
    November 11, 1987; March 4, 1990; June 19,
    1994, pp. 4, 11.
*Maclean's,* May 25, 1992, pp. 61-62.
*Nation,* July 30, 1955; May 6, 1996, p. 28.
*National Review,* October 10, 1994, p. 75; June 17,
    1996, p. 52.
*New Republic,* June 9, 1958; July 8, 1967; May 4, 1968.
*New Statesman and Society,* January 28, 1994, p. 14;
    February 18, 1994, p. 24; July 22, 1994, p. 47.
*Newsweek,* June 26, 1967; July 3, 1967.
*New Yorker,* January 6, 1968; December 31, 1973;
    May 2, 1977.
*New York Herald Tribune Book Review,* June 29,
    1952; April 24, 1955; June 9, 1958.
*New York Review of Books,* May 26, 1994, p. 40.
*New York Times,* June 1, 1958; September 18, 1973;
    February 24, 1990.
*New York Times Book Review,* June 25, 1967; Sep-
    tember 7, 1975; May 3, 1981; February 11,
    1990; April 5, 1992, p. 10; July 18, 1993, p. 8;
    June 19, 1994, p. 9.
*Playboy* (interview), June, 1968.
*Publishers Weekly,* May 17, 1993, p. 58.
*Spectator,* November 10, 1967.
*Time,* February 16, 1968.
*Times Literary Supplement,* March 13, 1987; May 29,
    1992, p. 26.
*Tribune Books* (Chicago), February 18, 1990; Sep-
    tember 25, 1994, p. 4.
*Washington Monthly,* July-August, 1994, p. 20.
*Washington Post Book World,* October 21, 1979;
    February 11, 1990.*

*    *    *

## GASPAROTTI, Elizabeth Seifert 1897-1983
### (Elizabeth Seifert; Ellen Ashley, a pseudonym)

*PERSONAL:* Born June 19, 1897, in Washington,
MO; died June 18, 1983, in Moberly, MO; daughter
of Richard Chester and Anna (Sanford) Seifert; married John J. Gasparotti, February 3, 1920 (deceased);
children: John Joseph, Richard Seifert, Paul Anthony,
Anna Gasparotti Felter. *Education:* Washington University, St. Louis, MO, B.A., 1918. *Religion:* Episcopalian.

*CAREER:* Writer, 1938-83. St. Barnabas Episcopal
Church, Moberly, MO, clerk and member of vestry.

*MEMBER:* Authors League of America, Women's
Book Association, American Association of University Women, Missouri Welfare Association (life member), Missouri Historical Society, State Historical
Society of Missouri, Beta Sigma Phi, Sorosis Club.

*AWARDS, HONORS:* First Novel Award from *Redbook* and Dodd, Mead, 1938, for *Young Doctor
Galahad.*

*WRITINGS:*

UNDER NAME ELIZABETH SEIFERT; PUBLISHED BY DODD
(NEW YORK CITY) EXCEPT AS INDICATED

*Young Doctor Galahad,* 1938, published in England
    as *Young Doctor,* Collins (London), 1939.
*A Great Day,* 1939.
*Thus Doctor Mallory,* 1940, published in England as
    *Doctor Mallory,* Collins, 1941.
*Hillbilly Doctor,* 1940, published in England as *Doc-
    tor Bill,* Collins, 1941.
*Bright Scalpel,* 1941, published in England as *Healing
    Hands,* Collins, 1942, published as *The Doctor's
    Healing Hands,* Severn House (London), 1982.
*Army Doctor,* 1942.
*Surgeon in Charge,* 1942.
*A Certain Doctor French,* 1943.
*Bright Banners,* 1943.
*Girl Intern,* 1944, published in England as *Doctor
    Chris,* Collins, 1946.
*Dr. Ellison's Decision,* 1944.
*Dr. Woodward's Ambition,* 1945.
*Orchard Hill,* 1945.
*Old Doc,* 1946.
*Dusty Spring,* 1946.
*Take Three Doctors,* 1947.
*So Young, So Fair,* 1947.
*The Glass and the Trumpet,* 1948.
*Hospital Zone,* 1948.
*The Bright Coin,* 1949, published in England as *The
    Doctor Dares,* Collins, 1950.
*Homecoming,* 1950.
*The Story of Andrea Fields,* 1950.

*Pride of the South,* Collins, 1950.

*Miss Doctor,* 1951, published in England as *Woman Doctor,* Collins, 1951.

*Doctor of Mercy,* 1951.

*The Strange Loyalty of Dr. Carlisle,* 1952, published in England as *The Case of Dr. Carlisle,* Collins, 1953.

*The Doctor Takes a Wife,* 1952.

*Doctor Mollie,* Collins, 1952.

*The Doctor Disagrees,* 1953.

*Lucinda Marries the Doctor,* 1953.

*Doctor at the Crossroads,* 1954.

*Marriage for Three,* 1954.

*A Doctor in the Family,* 1955.

*Challenge for Doctor Mays,* 1955, published in England as *Doctor Mays,* Collins, 1957.

*A Doctor for Blue Jay Cove,* 1956, published in England as *Doctor's Orders,* Collins, 1958.

*A Call for Dr. Barton,* 1956.

*Substitute Doctor,* 1957.

*The Doctor's Husband,* 1957.

*The New Doctor,* 1958, published in England as *Doctor Jamie,* Collins, 1959.

*Love Calls the Doctor,* 1958.

*Hometown Doctor,* 1959.

*Doctor on Trial,* 1959.

*When Doctors Marry,* 1960.

*Doctors on Parade* (omnibus), 1960.

*The Doctor's Bride,* 1960.

*The Doctor Makes a Choice,* 1961.

*Doctor Jeremy's Wife,* 1961.

*The Honor of Doctor Shelton,* 1962.

*The Doctor's Strange Secret,* 1962.

*Katie's Young Doctor,* 1963, Thorndike, 1989.

*Doctor Scott: Surgeon on Call,* 1963, published in England as *Surgeon on Call,* Collins, 1965.

*Legacy for a Doctor,* 1963.

*Doctor Samaritan,* 1964.

*A Doctor Comes to Bayard,* 1964.

*Ordeal of Three Doctors,* 1965.

*Pay the Doctor,* 1966.

*Hegerty, M.D.,* 1966.

*The Rival Doctors,* 1967.

*Doctor with a Mission,* 1967.

*To Wed a Doctor,* 1968.

*The Doctor's Confession,* 1968.

*For Love of a Doctor,* 1969.

*Bachelor Doctor,* 1969.

*The Doctor's Two Lives,* 1970.

*Doctor's Kingdom,* 1970.

*Doctor in Judgment,* 1971.

*The Doctor's Second Love,* 1971.

*Doctor's Destiny,* 1972.

*The Doctor's Reputation,* 1972.

*The Two Faces of Doctor Collier,* 1973.

*The Doctor's Private Life,* 1973.

*Doctor in Love,* 1974.

*The Doctor's Daughter,* 1974.

*The Doctor and Mathilda,* 1974.

*Four Doctors, Four Wives,* 1975.

*The Doctor's Affair,* 1975.

*The Doctor's Desperate Hour,* 1976.

*Two Doctors and a Girl,* 1976.

*Doctor Tuck,* 1977.

*The Doctor on Eden Place,* 1977.

*The Doctors Were Brothers,* 1978.

*Rebel Doctor,* 1978.

*The Doctor's Promise,* 1979.

*The Problems of Doctor A,* 1979.

*Two Doctors, Two Loves,* 1982.

OTHER

(Under pseudonym Ellen Ashley) *Girl in Overalls: A Novel of Women in Defense Today,* Dodd, 1943.

*SIDELIGHTS:* Elizabeth Seifert Gasparotti began writing under her maiden name, Elizabeth Seifert, at the age of forty. Over the next forty years, she produced more than eighty novels. Seifert's books revolved almost exclusively around doctors and the medical profession, although her own medical training was confined to a brief period at Washington University, followed by work at St. Louis hospitals. Her first novel, *Young Doctor Galahad,* earned the author a ten-thousand-dollar prize and set the stage for a long and successful writing career.

*Young Doctor Galahad* is set, like many of Seifert's novels, in the American midwest. The young doctor of the novel's title plies his trade as a surgeon at the local hospital, participating in typical small-town life and courting not one, but two local women. It is not the romance that captured reviewers' attention, however; in fact, a *Time* critic wrote: "Her hero's two love affairs are not very convincing."

Marion Hanscom, writing in *Twentieth-Century Romance and Historical Writers,* attributed Seifert's overall success to her earnest and realistic characterizations of doctors and their families as ordinary people, not unlike her avid readers themselves: "Her books are easy to read and consist almost entirely of brief descriptions and dialogue. . . . We learn about the characters by how they look, what they wear, what they say . . . [a]nd we know these people." The books are not so much about the medical profession as they are about "people who happen to be doctors,"

Hanscom wrote, adding, "Seifert's male characters are apt to be heroic and larger than life, but she is right on target with women, their strengths and weaknesses, their hopes and fears." Mary Ross commented in a similar vein in *Books,* "In her portraits of the doctors—old and young, good and bad—Mrs. Seifert pictures men who are individual and convincing."

*Young Doctor Galahad* "shows fine promise," Peter M'Nab wrote in the *Boston Transcript.* "Mrs. Seifert is sincere, her study is honestly written." Set as it is in the post-depression midwest, the novel explores a theme that was controversial at the time: socialized medicine in a clinic environment. "As a sincere and apparently well-founded argument for medical reform," Beatrice Sherman contributed in the *New York Times,* "it deserves attention." Ross predicted that many doctors, "perusing it privately, will find it fair and honest, if disturbing."

The elements that contributed to Seifert's original success appeared in varying proportions throughout most of her subsequent writings as well. *A Great Day* is the story of a pharmacy clerk who builds his fortune on the large-scale manufacture of patent medicines, sacrificing ethics and consumer safety along the way. In *Books,* critic Lisle Bell praised the novel as "a bitter indictment of the inner workings of a drug factory that cunningly sidesteps the intent of the law and reaps gigantic profits." *Thus Doctor Mallory* provides a contrast to controversy, relating a shy young man's struggle, against multiple adversities, to become a doctor. *Books* reviewer D. B. Shapiro called it a "charming story with a happy ending and a strain of sincere nobility . . . nicely told with a lot of little interwoven plots."

*Hillbilly Doctor* revives the idealistic spirit in the character of a young doctor committed to injecting modern sanitation and public health standards deep into the heart of the Ozarks. Published in 1942, *Army Doctor* offers, according to the *New York Times,* "a realistic picture of the problems of new citizen soldiers." *Surgeon in Charge,* published later that year, marks a return to the soap opera flavor of romance among doctors and hospital administrators. Mysterious plots resurface in *A Certain Doctor French,* which Charlotte Dean of the *New York Times* called Seifert's "best book to date," an example of "good straight story telling." Hanscom summarized Seifert's work by commenting that the "stories do not reflect the changing influences and current events of half a century, nor do they keep up with the many technological advances. But human nature does not change

with the times." Seifert's books were nearly as popular in England as they were in the United States. They have been published in more than a dozen other countries, and numerous reprints as recently as the 1980s have brought even her earliest works to a new generation of readers.

*BIOGRAPHICAL/CRITICAL SOURCES:*

*BOOKS*

*Twentieth-Century Romance and Historical Writers,* 3rd edition, St. James Press (Detroit, MI), 1994.

*PERIODICALS*

*Books,* October 30, 1938, p. 2; October 15, 1939, p. 12; March 10, 1940, p. 11.
*Boston Transcript,* November 5, 1938, p. 2.
*New York Times,* November 13, 1938, p. 7; September 24, 1939, p. 7; March 8, 1942, p. 24; April 11, 1943, p. 14.
*Time,* November 14, 1938.

*OBITUARIES:*

*PERIODICALS*

*Chicago Tribune,* June 19, 1983.
*New York Times,* June 21, 1983.
*Publishers Weekly,* July 8, 1983.
*Washington Post,* June 22, 1983.*

\*    \*    \*

**GAVIN, Jamila 1941-**

*PERSONAL:* Born August 9, 1941, in Mussoorie, India; daughter of Terence (a retired Indian civil servant) and Florence Jessica (a teacher; maiden name, Dean) Khushal-Singh; married Barrie Gavin (a television producer) in 1971 (divorced, 1990); children: Rohan Robert, Indra Helen. *Education:* Trinity College of Music, L.T.C.L. in piano performance and drama instruction; studied piano in Paris; attended Hochschul fuer Musik, Berlin, Germany. *Politics:* Labour Party. *Avocational interests:* Theater.

*ADDRESSES: Home*—"The Laurels," All Saints Rd., Uplands Stroud, Gloucestershire GL5 1TT, England.

*Agent*—Jacqueline Korn, David Higham Associates, 5-8 Lower John St., Golden Square, London W1R 4HA, England.

*CAREER:* Freelance writer and lecturer. British Broadcasting Corporation (BBC), London, radio studio manager, then television production assistant, 1964-71. Member, Stroud Town Council; member of advisory committee, Cheltenham Literary Festival. Writer and co-director, Taynton House Children's Opera Group; affiliated with Children's Drama Group, Niccol Center, Cirencester.

*MEMBER:* PEN, West of England Writers, Writers Guild.

*AWARDS, HONORS: Guardian* award runner-up, 1993, for *The Wheel of Surya; Guardian* award special runner-up and Carnegie Medal nomination, both 1995, both for *The Eye of the Horse.*

*WRITINGS:*

*"SURYA" SERIES*

*The Wheel of Surya,* Methuen, 1992.
*The Eye of the Horse,* Methuen, 1994.
*The Track of the Wind,* Methuen, 1997.

*"GRANDPA CHATTERJI" SERIES*

*Grandpa Chatterji,* illustrated by Mei-Yim Low, Methuen, 1993.
*Grandpa's Indian Summer,* illustrated by Yow, Methuen, 1995.

*OTHER*

*The Magic Orange Tree and Other Stories,* illustrated by Ossie Murray, Methuen (New York City), 1979.
*Double Dare and Other Stories,* illustrated by Simon Willby, Methuen, 1982.
*Kamla and Kate* (short stories), illustrated by Thelma Lambert, Methuen, 1983.
*Digital Dan,* illustrated by Patrice Aitken, Methuen, 1984.
*Ali and the Robots,* illustrated by Sally Williams, Methuen, 1986.
*Stories from the Hindu World,* illustrated by Joanna Troughton, Macdonald, 1986, Silver Burdett (Morristown, NJ), 1987.
*The Hideaway,* illustrated by Jane Bottomley, Methuen, 1987.

(Reteller) *Three Indian Princesses: The Stories of Savitri, Damayanti, and Sita,* illustrated by Govinder Ram, Methuen, 1987.
*The Singing Bowls,* Methuen, 1989.
*I Want to Be an Angel,* Methuen, 1990.
*Kamla and Kate Again* (short stories), illustrated by Rhian Nest-James, Methuen, 1991.
*Deadly Friend,* Heinemann, 1994.
*A Fine Feathered Friend,* illustrated by Carol Walters, Heinemann, 1996.
*The Mango Tree,* illustrated by Nest-James, Heinemann, 1996.
*Presents,* illustrated by Nest-James, Heinemann, 1996.
*Who Did It?,* illustrated by Nest-James, Heinemann, 1996.
*The Wormholers,* Methuen, 1996.
(Contributor with James Riordan and Margaret Nash) *The Wolf and the Kids; The Straw House; Lake of the Stars; The Ugly Duckling,* 4 volumes, Heinemann Educational (Exeter, NH), 1996.
*Grandma's Surprise,* illustrated by Nest-James, Heinemann, 1996.
*Our Favourite Stories: Children Just Like Me Storybook,* Dorling Kindersley (London), 1997.
*Out of India: An Anglo-Indian Childhood* (memoir), Pavilion (London), 1997.

Also author of the books *The Temple by the Sea,* Ginn; *The Demon Drummer,* Pavillion; *Pitchou; The Girl Who Rode on a Lion,* Ginn; *Forbidden Dreams,* Mammoth; *All Aboard,* Heinemann; *A Singer from the Desert,* Pavillion; *Forbidden Clothes,* Methuen; and *Just Friends,* Mammoth. Also author of the musical *The Green Factor,* music by Nigel Stephenson.

*ADAPTATIONS: The Demon Drummer* was adapted as a play, Cheltenham Literary Festival, 1994; *Grandpa Chatterji* was adapted for television, 1996; six-part adaptation of *The Wheel of Surya,* BBC-TV, 1996.

*WORK IN PROGRESS: Starchild on Clark Street* for Oxford University Press.

*SIDELIGHTS:* Jamila Gavin brings her understanding of the special concerns of children with a multicultural heritage to her stories and novels for young readers. Born in India of an Indian father and a British mother, Gavin has focused on her Indian heritage in such books as *Three Indian Princesses: The Stories of Savitri, Damayanti, and Sita* as well as in her highly praised epic trilogy that begins with the 1992 novel *The Wheel of Surya.* In addition to her novels and short fiction for middle-school readers,

Gavin, who has worked in television and in theater for many years, has also authored plays for younger viewers. Several of her works have been adapted for broadcast on British television. "I began writing to be published, rather than for fun in 1979, when I realized how few books for children reflected the multicultural society in which they lived," Gavin once explained to *CA*. "As someone of mixed Indian and British origins, I wanted to see my mirror image, and felt that every child, no matter what their race or colour, was entitled to see their mirror image."

Among Gavin's first books was *Kamla and Kate,* a collection of short stories featuring a young girl named Kate who gains a best friend when six-year-old Kamla and her family move from India to Kate's boy-dominated street. While engaging together in tasks and activities common to young British children, Kate joins her new friend in celebrating the Indian Festival of Light, or Diwali. The book reflects the author's belief that "people with different customs and beliefs [need] to find common ground," while also celebrating their differences, according to Margery Fisher of *Growing Point.* The two best friends return in *Kamla and Kate Again,* a second collection of stories that *School Librarian* contributor Julie Blaisdale cited as showing "with sensitivity and understanding" the many ways in which young people can "share in and celebrate a diversity of cultural influences."

Other books by Gavin are steeped in Indian culture and tradition. In *The Singing Bowls,* a mixed Anglo-Indian teen named Ronnie delves into the mystery surrounding three wooden bowls that have mystical properties rooted in Tibetan history. The sixteen-year-old hopes that the bowls can help him find his Indian father, who disappeared ten years ago. While noting that the writing is "slightly uneven," a *Junior Bookshelf* reviewer praised *The Singing Bowls* for evoking "the dust, heat and beauty of India" and presenting a "revealing and thought-provoking" portrait of the multi-layered generations of Indian society. Indian culture also plays a significant role in *Grandpa Chatterji,* a collection of stories about Sanjay and Neeta, sisters who get to know their Indian grandfather when he makes a long-awaited visit from his home in Calcutta. A man of traditional, old-fashioned values, "Grandpa Chatterji is a wonderful character . . . with his warmth and enthusiasm for life," according to *School Librarian* contributor Teresa Scragg. A *Junior Bookshelf* reviewer agreed, noting that Gavin's "charming" book paints the portrait of a family with strong ties to two diverse cultures "and

offers the hope that its members will draw the best from both."

First published in England in 1992, Gavin's *Wheel of Surya* is the first book of her "Surya" trilogy. Taking place in a small Indian village in the Punjab on the eve of India's war for independence, the novel follows the adventures of Marvinder and Jaspal Singh, siblings whose mother decides to bring the family to England to join her husband, who has been absent for many years in an effort to further his education. During the trip the children's mother and grandmother both die, but the brother and sister remain determined to find the father whom they hardly remember. With little money, the pair find their way to Bombay and stow away aboard an ocean liner bound for England. When at last they find their father, Govind, he is not at all the person they expected to find—he has married an Irishwoman and has a son—and the two children must adjust to both a new family and a new culture. In a review of *The Wheel of Surya* for *School Librarian,* Linda Saunders praised Gavin for "the power of her descriptions and her portrayal of two different societies." A *Junior Bookshelf* critic called the novel "a tribute to the stubbornness of children the world over whose instinct is for survival first and prosperity second."

In the sequels to *The Wheel of Surya*—*The Eye of the Horse* and *The Track of the Wind*—readers continue to follow the adventures of Mavinder and her brother Jaspal. *The Eye of the Horse* finds the children's father released from jail after a conviction for dealing in stolen goods; on the heels of his release, now abandoned by his Irish wife, Govind gathers his children together and returns to his native India, which is now free of British domination. The story threads in and out of many historic events of the 1940s, including the death of Mohandas Gandhi and the religious and political turmoil that racked India during the decade. In a review for *Books for Your Children,* Val Bierman dubbed the novel a "powerful book of betrayal, sadness and anger" that also reveals the "power of healing and forgiveness." In a *School Librarian* review, Peter Hollindale praised it as "an immensely readable, exciting story."

Of her more recent works, Gavin told *CA:* "Perhaps, of all my books, *The Wormholers* represents my exploration of the inner world, but inspired by the glorious theories and astro-physical world of the physicist Stephen Hawking. That is the joy of writing; that there are so many doors waiting to be opened and be a source of inspiration."

*BIOGRAPHICAL/CRITICAL SOURCES:*

*PERIODICALS*

*Books for Keeps,* May, 1986, p. 20; March, 1989; May, 1991; January, 1996.

*Books for Your Children,* summer, 1986, p. 8; summer, 1989, p. 12; summer, 1993, p. 10; spring, 1995, p. 12.

*Growing Point,* September, 1979, p. 3578; September, 1982, p. 3943; May, 1983, p. 4089.

*Junior Bookshelf,* October, 1979, p. 271; April, 1988, p. 93; October, 1989, p. 237; April, 1992, p. 62; August, 1992, p. 153; June, 1993, pp. 96-97; August, 1994, p. 134; February, 1995, pp. 35-36.

*School Librarian,* February, 1988, p. 20; November, 1989, p. 160; November, 1991, p. 144; November, 1992, pp. 157-58; August, 1993, p. 108; November, 1994, p. 165.

*Times Educational Supplement,* August 26, 1983, p. 20.

* * *

## GERINGER, Laura 1948-

*PERSONAL:* Born February 23, 1948, in New York, NY; daughter of Benjamin and Ann Geringer. *Education:* Barnard College, B.A., 1968; Yale University, M.F.A., 1975.

*CAREER:* Author of books for children and young adults. Also worked as an editor of children's books, Harper and Row Publishers, Inc., New York City, beginning in 1980.

*MEMBER:* Women's National Book Association, New York Critics Circle.

*WRITINGS:*

*PICTURE BOOKS*

*Seven True Bear Stories,* illustrated by Carol Maisto, Hastings, 1978.

*A Three Hat Day,* illustrated by Arnold Lobel, Harper (New York City), 1985.

*Molly's New Washing Machine,* illustrated by Petra Mathers, Harper, 1986.

*The Cow Is Mooing Anyhow: A Scrambled Alphabet Book to Be Read at Breakfast,* illustrated by Dirk Zimmer, HarperCollins (New York City), 1991.

*Look Out, Look Out, It's Coming,* illustrated by Sue Truesdell, HarperCollins, 1992.

*Yours 'til the Ice Cracks: A Book of Valentines,* illustrated by Andrea Baruffi, HarperCollins, 1992.

*The Pumpkin,* illustrated by Holly Berry, Scholastic (New York City), 1999.

*"MYTH MEN" SERIES; PUBLISHED BY SCHOLASTIC*

*Andromeda: The Flying Warrior Princess,* illustrated by Peter Bollinger, 1996.

*Hercules: The Strong Man,* illustrated by Bollinger, 1996.

*Perseus: The Boy with Super Powers,* illustrated by Bollinger, 1996.

*Ulysses: The Soldier King,* illustrated by Bollinger, 1996.

*Theseus: Hero of the Maze,* illustrated by Bollinger, 1997.

*Atalanta: The Wild Girl,* illustrated by Bollinger, 1997

*Iole: The Girl with Super Powers,* illustrated by Bollinger, 1997.

*Castor and Pollux: The Fighting Twins,* illustrated by Bollinger, 1997.

*OTHER*

*Silverpoint* (young adult novel), HarperCollins, 1991.

(Reteller) Jacob and Wilhelm Grimm, *The Seven Ravens,* illustrated by Edward S. Gazsi, HarperCollins, 1994.

(Reteller) *The Pomegranate Seeds: A Classic Greek Myth,* illustrated by Leonid Gore, Houghton (Boston), 1995.

(With Bruce Brooks) *Shark* (for children), Harpercrest, 1998.

(With Brooks) *Billy* (for children), Harpercrest, 1998.

Contributor of book reviews to periodicals, including *Saturday Review* and *Newsweek.*

*SIDELIGHTS:* Laura Geringer is the author of several original picture books for children, a novel for young adults, and a number of retellings of classic myths and folktales. In reviews of her works, critics have commented favorably on her rich use of language and her ability to entertain readers with zany details.

Like many of Geringer's picture books, *Molly's New Washing Machine* features an unusual premise and lively action. According to *Booklist* contributor Denise M. Wilms, the story is "an odd tale with an originality that is beguiling." One day, two burly brown rabbits unexpectedly deliver a washing machine to a human named Molly. Soon three of her animal friends—a dog named Bongo, a fox named Click, and a mole named Pocket—show up to do their laundry. When they turn the machine on, it begins to make funny, rhythmic noises that compel the friends to dance around the suds-filled kitchen with abandon until they finally collapse from exhaustion. Later, the two rabbits show up to reclaim the washing machine, explaining that they delivered it to Molly by mistake. A *Publishers Weekly* reviewer stated that the book "is sure to have both adults and children laughing with delight."

*A Three Hat Day,* another offbeat Geringer picture book, features the somewhat quirky Pottle clan, in particular R. R. Pottle the Third and his wife Isabel, who indulge their love of hats in comic fashion. "Although the characters are adult right up to the last page, they share the compelling urge to collect, which seems instinctive to most children," noted a reviewer for the *Bulletin of the Center for Children's Books.* *School Library Journal* contributor Judith Gloyer offered a favorable assessment of the "fun-filled story," praising the "richness and rhythm of the language." Other uniquely Geringer picture-book offerings include *The Cow Is Mooing Anyhow: A Scrambled Alphabet Book to Be Read at Breakfast,* featuring letters that are *not* in alphabetical order, and *Yours 'til the Ice Cracks: A Book of Valentines,* with whimsical professions of love that the accompanying illustrations reveal to be not quite as enduring as they sound.

*Silverpoint,* Geringer's novel for middle graders, was dubbed "an unusually fine first novel" by a *Kirkus Reviews* critic. *Silverpoint* focuses on twelve-year-old Cora, abandoned at an early age by her father. Cora and her best friend, Charley, similarly distressed by his own father's death, search for information about Cora's father while masking their loneliness in a world of games, rituals, and fantasy. "The events are sparse in this carefully constructed, beautifully written story, but Cora's inner life is fascinating, rich with interconnected leitmotifs," stated the *Kirkus Reviews* commentator. In another favorable assessment, Maeve Visser Knoth of *Horn Book* praised Geringer's "intricately drawn, sympathetic characters," adding: "Geringer's prose is filled with imagery, and Cora's dream and fantasy lives are as strong and rich as her everyday life. . . . Her impressive first novel is remarkable for its restrained storytelling and deft characterization."

For her 1995 book, *The Pomegranate Seeds,* Geringer retold and updated the classic Greek myth that ex-

plains the origin of the four seasons of the year. In Geringer's version, Persephone becomes an outspoken, modern young woman who is kidnapped by her uncle, Hades, not to become his bride, but merely to provide him with company in his lonely underworld kingdom. Persephone's overprotective mother, Demeter, is so distressed by her daughter's disappearance that she uses her powers to make the earth barren. Zeus finally intervenes to offer a compromise to the gods of the earth and the underworld. Persephone will be returned to her mother on the earth's surface, but since she has been tricked into eating three pomegranate seeds by Hades, she will be required to spend three months of each year with her uncle in the underworld. Thus the earth is barren for three months in winter, then blooms in joyous spring when Persephone returns to the surface, and eventually begins to wither as the time nears for her to rejoin Hades in fall. A *Publishers Weekly* reviewer commented that "despite the updating, [Geringer] captures the timeless, bittersweet atmosphere of the ancient tale." Jennifer Fleming, writing in *School Library Journal,* called *The Pomegranate Seeds* "a moving, evocative retelling . . . that is at once contemporarily relevant and solidly classic."

### BIOGRAPHICAL/CRITICAL SOURCES:

*PERIODICALS*

*Booklist,* September 15, 1986, p. 128; September 1, 1994, p. 45.
*Bulletin of the Center for Children's Books,* January, 1986, pp. 85-86; October, 1991, p. 37; October, 1994, p. 48.
*Horn Book,* January-February, 1992, pp. 69-70.
*Kirkus Reviews,* February 1, 1991, p. 182; September 1, 1991, p. 1160; December 15, 1991, p. 1590.
*Publishers Weekly,* April 30, 1979, p. 114; July 25, 1986, p. 186; March 8, 1991, p. 74; July 25, 1994, p. 55; November 13, 1995, p. 61.
*School Library Journal,* November, 1985, p. 70; December, 1986, p. 86; January, 1992, p. 102; March, 1996, p. 208.

\*       \*       \*

### GLENN, Mel 1943-

*PERSONAL:* Born May 10, 1943, in Zurich, Switzerland (U.S. citizen born abroad, moved to U.S. in 1945, raised in Brooklyn, NY); son of Jacob B. (a physician) and Elizabeth (Hampel) Glenn; married Elyse Friedman (a teacher), September 20, 1970; children: Jonathan, Andrew. *Education:* New York University, A.B., 1964; Yeshiva University, M.S., 1967. *Religion:* Jewish.

*ADDRESSES: Home*—4288 Bedford Ave., New York, NY 11229. *Office*—Abraham Lincoln High School, Brooklyn, NY 11235.

*CAREER:* U.S. Peace Corps, Washington, DC, volunteer English teacher in Sierra Leone, 1964-66; English teacher at a public junior high school, New York City, 1967-70; Abraham Lincoln High School, New York City, English teacher, 1970—.

*MEMBER:* Society of Children's Book Writers and Illustrators, Authors Guild.

*AWARDS, HONORS:* Best Books for Young Adults, American Library Association (ALA), 1982, and Golden Kite Honor Book plaque, Society of Children's Book Writers, both for *Class Dismissed! High School Poems;* Best Books, *School Library Journal,* 1986, and Christopher Award, 1987, both for *Class Dismissed II: More High School Poems;* Best Books for Young Adults, ALA, 1992, for *My Friend's Got This Problem, Mr. Candler: High School Poems;* Top Ten Best Books for Young Adults, ALA, 1997, for *Who Killed Mr. Chippendale? A Mystery in Poems.*

*WRITINGS:*

*POETRY*

*Class Dismissed! High School Poems,* illustrated with photographs by Michael J. Bernstein, Clarion (Boston), 1982.
*Class Dismissed II: More High School Poems,* illustrated with photographs by Bernstein, Clarion, 1986.
*Back to Class,* illustrated with photographs by Bernstein, Clarion, 1989.
*My Friend's Got This Problem, Mr. Candler: High School Poems,* illustrated with photographs by Bernstein, Clarion, 1991.
*Who Killed Mr. Chippendale? A Mystery in Poems,* Lodestar (New York City), 1996.
*The Taking of Room 114: A Hostage Drama in Poems,* Lodestar, 1997.

*Jump Ball: A Basketball Season in Poems,* Lodestar/Dutton (New York City), 1997.

*FICTION*

*One Order to Go,* Clarion, 1984.
*Play-by-Play,* Clarion, 1986.
*Squeeze Play: A Baseball Story,* Clarion, 1989.

*SIDELIGHTS:* Teacher and writer Mel Glenn is noted especially for books that address the day-to-day concerns of teenagers in a unique manner—through poetry. Written in free verse, using uncomplicated language that makes them accessible to many students who would otherwise steer clear of the genre, Glenn's poems "echo the voices of young adults who are struggling in two separate worlds: the world of adults and the world of children," notes Teri S. Lesesne in *Twentieth-Century Young Adult Writers.* Glenn's verse, Lesesne adds, "capture[s] the essence of the adolescent: the emotions which sometimes seem to run out of control, the changing relationships with parents and other adults as the adolescent struggles for independence."

Writing books for young adults was a natural extension of Glenn's interest in teaching. The inspiration for his first book, the poetry collection *Class Dismissed! High School Poems,* was *Spoon River Anthology,* a collection of original verse by poet Edgar Lee Masters. The motivation behind sitting down and actually writing the book was a challenge Glenn gave himself one New Year's eve. "Another teacher had shown me his unpublished manuscript, and I said to myself that if he could write a book, so could I." Glenn set up a schedule for himself and completed the manuscript in only six months. "The source for the book came easily: I have always prided myself on the fact that I am a good listener, and surrounding me were hundreds of stories—some sad, some happy, some tragic—but all terribly real and poignant. Though styles and fashions may change, there are certain common denominators in being a teenager that connect all generations—the feelings of being alone, different, in love, in conflict with parents. No matter how old we grow there will always be a part of us that will be sixteen years old."

Each of the poems in *Class Dismissed!,* as well as such sequels as 1986's *Class Dismissed II* and 1989's *Back to Class,* are written in the first person using free verse. Each is titled using the name of the fictional author, a teen from Glenn's fictional "class."

Each poem is a brief look into the mind of a teen as he or she tries to grapple with a problem that is of momentary uppermost concern. In "Hildy Ross," for example, a young girl writes about her need to cover up the true cause of a bruise on her cheek: she is being beaten by an abusive father. Other adolescent concerns revolve around finding a summer job, the hard work of being an unwed teen parent, frustrations with preoccupied, out-of-touch parents, deciding which colleges to apply to, and even how to finagle the keys to the family car for a date. While *Voice of Youth Advocates* reviewer Tony Manna questions whether or not Glenn's verse contains "the kind of universals that we expect good poetry to illuminate" and ponders "whether many of the revelations are in fact poetry rather than the rendering of personal feelings," Candy Bertelson notes in *School Library Journal* that Glenn's works "deal with engaging, very 'real' kids, who are easy to identify with," and should "reach many young people who don't ordinarily read poetry."

Glenn has always taken his subject matter from his direct experiences with young people growing up in Brooklyn. His second book, the young adult novel *One Order to Go,* takes place in a candy store that the author recalled from his own youth: "the old kind where you can get a real malted and an egg cream." The story concerns seventeen-year-old Richie Linder, who hates school and wants to drop out and lead the exciting life of a news correspondent. His strict father will hear nothing of Richie's plans; instead, he fills his son's free time by making him man the counter at his luncheonette. A friendship with Lana finally gives Richie the courage to confront his domineering father with his own aspirations and make plans for an independent future. "I am sure that a large part of [*One Order to Go*] is autobiographical," Glenn once confided to *CA,* "but, in the larger sense, what writing isn't? You bring to your characters a sense of your own personal values and memories."

In *Play-by-Play,* Glenn wrote a story for younger readers. In this work, fourth grader Jeremy is constantly bested by his own best friend, Lloyd, a natural athlete who uses his talent to assume an air of superiority over those around him, Jeremy included. Through Jeremy's narration the reader watches as a new sport—soccer—and some new teammates—the fourth-grade girls—make both boys more tolerant of others. The two friends are reunited as sixth graders in *Squeeze Play: A Baseball Story,* in which a new coach seems more like a drill sergeant in his manage-

ment of a school-wide baseball team. "Again, the material was all around me," Glenn told *CA* of his inspiration. "My son, Jonathan, was actively involved in a local soccer league, and between practices and games on cold Saturday mornings I learned about this 'foreign' sport. As a writer, I tried to pay a close attention to the language, characteristics, and social mores of nine-year-olds."

In his 1991 poetry collection, *My Friend's Got This Problem, Mr. Candler,* Glenn presents the day-to-day triumphs and tragedies that make up the life of a high school guidance counselor. *Who Killed Mr. Chippendale? A Mystery in Poems* is a unique whodunit, as students, teachers, and others involved express through free-verse poetry their reaction to the tragic death of a high school English teacher in a random shooting. Several suspects emerge—a fellow teacher who was a former girlfriend, a high schooler who claims she was the murdered man's lover, and an emotionally unstable student whose negative attitude towards Mr. Chippendale and other circumstantial evidence call his alibi strongly into question. "Not only do the poems clue readers into the characters' personalities and sensibilities," noted Sharon Korbeck in a *School Library Journal* review, "but they also provide a telling commentary on the attitudes toward violence reflected in our society at large."

*BIOGRAPHICAL/CRITICAL SOURCES:*

*BOOKS*

*Twentieth-Century Young Adult Writers,* St. James Press (Detroit), 1994, pp. 248-49.

*PERIODICALS*

*ALAN Review,* winter, 1997.
*Booklist,* October 1, 1984, p. 211; December 1, 1986, p. 567; September 15, 1991, p. 134; June 1, 1996, p. 1688.
*Bulletin of the Center for Children's Books,* September, 1982, p. 9; April, 1986, p. 148; February, 1987, p. 107; July/August, 1989, p. 275; March, 1997, p. 247.
*Kirkus Reviews,* October 15, 1988, p. 1527; February 15, 1989, p. 292; May 1, 1996.
*Publishers Weekly,* July 8, 1996, p. 85.
*School Library Journal,* October, 1982, p. 160; December, 1984, p. 89; August, 1986, p. 92; July, 1996, p. 98.
*Voice of Youth Advocates,* February, 1989, pp. 300-01.

## GLUCK, Robert 1947-

*PERSONAL:* Surname rhymes with "look;" born February 2, 1947, in Cleveland, OH; son of Morris and Dorothy (Philips) Gluck. *Ethnicity:* "White/Jewish/gay." *Education:* Attended University of California, Los Angeles, 1964-66, and University of Edinburgh, 1966-67; University of California, Berkeley, B.A., 1969; California State University, San Francisco (now San Francisco State University), M.A., 1973. *Politics:* "Left."

*ADDRESSES: Home and office*—4303 20th St., San Francisco, CA 94114. *E-mail*—chrisko@sirius.com.

*CAREER:* Small Press Traffic (book store and literary center), San Francisco, CA, writer in residence, 1977-85; San Francisco State University, assistant director of Poetry Center, 1985-88, director, 1988-91. Teacher at San Francisco State University and San Francisco Art Institute.

*AWARDS, HONORS:* Award from Academy of American Poets, 1973, for *Andy;* Monoclonal Antibodies, Inc., fellowship in literature, Djerassi Foundation, 1989; fellow of Fund for Poetry, 1991.

*WRITINGS:*

*Andy* (poetry), Panjandrum (Los Angeles, CA), 1973.
*Metaphysics* (poetry and prose), Hoddypoll, 1977.
*Family Poems,* Black Star Publishing (New York City), 1979.
(Translator with Bruce Boone) *La Fontaine,* Black Star Publishing, 1981.
*Elements of a Coffee Service* (stories), Four Seasons Foundation (San Francisco, CA), 1982.
(Editor) *Saturday Afternoon,* Black Star Series, 1985.
*Jack the Modernist* (novel), Sea Horse (New York City), 1985.
*Reader* (poetry and prose), Lapis Press, 1989.
*Margery Kempe* (novel), Serpent's Tail, 1996.

Contributor to anthologies, including *Writing/Talks, Men on Men, High Risk, New Directions Anthology,* and *The Faber Book of Gay Short Fiction,* Faber. Contributor of stories, poems, articles, and reviews to periodicals, including *Social Text, Poetics Journal, Zyzzyva, Sulfur, San Diego Reader, Metropolitan Home, Nest,* and *City Lights Review.*

*WORK IN PROGRESS: Denny Smith,* a book of stories; a short novel.

*SIDELIGHTS:* Robert Gluck told *CA:* "My work can be seen as an elaboration of the old feminist maxim, 'The Personal is Political,' with a great deal of pressure applied to both terms, so that the equal sign between them breaks down. That is, on the one hand my work explores how we exist in language, in our bodies, and in our societies, and on the other hand it explores moral life and the ways we assign meanings to experience, from gossip to the largest political structures.

"I am an autobiographer, and I think that any life, intensely examined, can reveal a whole society, in the same way that a dinosaur femur, properly studied, can suggest the whole animal. I am a gay man, and I record an intense life inside my community and identity, with the understanding that both are still rather new and experimental. I hope that looking at the particulars will give me access to a larger picture. One of my models is Isaac Bashevis Singer. His work relates to a small Jewish community, and it appeared first in Jewish publications. Yet, through intensity of engagement with his world and with the materials of writing itself—language and literary form—he created stories and novels that speak to almost any reader.

"I often write about sex and the extremes of romantic obsession, because they interest me. Why? I guess because at these limits the self is not stable, and it yields its secrets. What secrets? That we are not very well assembled in the first place, that beyond us nothingness exists—a silence, say, or nameless something beyond language and beyond life—which is vital for us to experience through writing."

\*    \*    \*

## GODFREY, Martyn N. 1949-

*PERSONAL:* Born April 17, 1949, in Birmingham, England; immigrated to Canada, 1957, naturalized citizen; son of Sidney (an engineer) and Helen (a secretary; maiden name, Brown) Godfrey; married Carolyn Boswell, 1973 (divorced, 1985); children: Marcus, Selby. *Education:* University of Toronto, B.A. (with honors), 1973, B.Ed., 1974.

*ADDRESSES: Agent*—Joanne Kellock, 11017—80th Ave., Edmonton, Alberta, Canada T6G 0R2.

*CAREER:* Teacher at elementary schools in Kitchener and Waterloo, Ontario, 1974-77, Mississauga, Ontario, 1977-80, and Assumption, Alberta, 1980-82; junior high school teacher in Edson, Alberta, 1983-85; writer, 1985—.

*MEMBER:* Writers Union of Canada, Writers Guild of Alberta (vice-president, 1986; president, 1987).

*AWARDS, HONORS:* Metcalf Award for best children's short story from Canadian Authors Association, 1985, and award for best children's book from University of Lethbridge, 1987, both for *Here She Is, Ms. Teeny-Wonderful;* runner-up, Geoffrey Bilson Award, 1989, for *Mystery in the Frozen Lands;* Manitoba Young Reader's Choice Award, 1993, for *Can You Teach Me to Pick My Nose?*

*WRITINGS:*

*JUVENILE*

*The Vandarian Incident* (science fiction), Scholastic-TAB, 1981.
*Alien Wargames* (science fiction), Scholastic-TAB, 1984.
*The Beast,* EMC Publishing, 1984.
*Spin Out,* EMC Publishing, 1984.
*Here She Is, Ms. Teeny-Wonderful,* Scholastic-TAB, 1985.
*Ice Hawk,* EMC Publishing, 1985.
*Fire! Fire!,* EMC Publishing, 1985.
*The Things,* OZ New Media, 1985.
*Mall Rats,* OZ New Media, 1985.
*Plan B Is Total Panic,* Lorimer, 1986.
*The Last War,* illustrated by Greg Ruhl, Macmillan, 1986.
*It Isn't Easy Being Ms. Teeny-Wonderful,* Scholastic-TAB, 1987.
*Wild Night,* EMC Publishing, 1987.
*More Than Weird,* Macmillan (New York City), 1987.
*Rebel Yell,* EMC Publishing, 1987.
*It Seemed Like a Good Idea at the Time,* Tree Frog Press, 1987.
*Baseball Crazy,* Lorimer, 1987.
*Send in Ms. Teeny-Wonderful,* Scholastic-TAB, 1988.
*In the Time of the Monsters,* Macmillan, 1988.
*Mystery in the Frozen Lands* (historical fiction), Lorimer, 1988.
*Break Out,* Collier-Macmillan (New York City), 1988.
*Why Just Me?,* McClelland & Stewart (London), 1989.

*Can You Teach Me to Pick My Nose?,* Avon (New York City), 1990.
*I Spent My Summer Vacation Kidnapped into Space,* Scholastic (New York City), 1990.
*Monsters in the School,* Scholastic, 1991.
(With Frank O'Keefe) *There's a Cow in My Swimming Pool,* Scholastic, 1991.
*Wally Stutzgummer, Super Bad Dude,* Scholastic, 1992.
*Is It Okay If This Monster Stays for Lunch?,* Oxford, 1992.
*Don't Worry about Me, I'm Just Crazy,* General, 1992.
*The Great Science Fair Disaster,* Scholastic, 1992.
*Please Remove Your Elbow from My Ear,* Avon, 1993.
*Monsters in the School II,* Scholastic, 1997.

*"JAWS MOB" SERIES; JUVENILE*

*Meet You in the Sewer,* Scholastic, 1993.
*Just Call Me Boom Boom,* Scholastic, 1994.

*"ADVENTURES IN PIRATE COVE" SERIES; JUVENILE*

*The Mystery of Hole's Castle,* Avon, 1996.
*The Hunt for Buried Treasure,* Avon, 1996.
*The Desperate Escape,* Avon, 1997.

*SIDELIGHTS:* Martyn N. Godfrey is a prolific Canadian writer of juvenile and young adult novels who blends humor with often serious subjects ranging from peer pressure and single-parenting to teenage suicide and atomic disasters. A former teacher, Godfrey writes dialogue that critics have said rings true and leavens his message with comic overtones and action-adventure sequences in books such as *Plan B Is Total Panic, Send in Ms. Teeny-Wonderful, Can You Teach Me to Pick My Nose?,* and *There's a Cow in My Swimming Pool.* Godfrey has also written historical fiction for the young adult audience, with his *Mystery in the Frozen Lands.* According to Lyle Weis, writing in *Canadian Children's Literature,* "Godfrey's strength as a writer for juveniles lies in his ability to blend serious issues with an action-oriented plot, something he accomplishes by placing ordinary kids in demanding or unusual circumstances." Godfrey employs a simple rule of thumb for his fiction: "Writers have to grab their readers in the first few sentences," he once concluded. "You know, the last thing I ever write in a novel is the first paragraph. Hook the reader as fast as possible, and then don't let go."

While an elementary school teacher, Godfrey was challenged to become a writer by one of his difficult students. "I can truthfully say that I wouldn't have become an author of books for young adults, if it wasn't for a twelve-year-old student of mine named Tom. A science fiction fan who hated school, Tom challenged: 'I think that if I'm writing a story for you, then you should write a story for me, Mr. G. Why don't you write a space story for me?'" Godfrey took up the challenge, initially simply to get Tom to work harder on his work. However, the story soon took on more importance and resulted in Godfrey's first publication, *The Vandarian Incident.* The novel is an action-packed sci-fi tale about the attempts of the Vandarian Confederation to stop the signing of a treaty between the Galaxy Union and the Andromuse Empire. These efforts result in an attack upon an academy on a desert planet which leaves only three survivors—two cadets and their instructor. While noting flaws in the characters and plot, Adele Ashby, writing in *Quill and Quire,* nonetheless commented that young sci-fi fans would be unlikely to notice such deficits, as the book offered "lots of action, strange beings and spectacular intergalactic battles."

"I knew very little about science fiction," Godfrey once reported. "What I did know was school and kids." And those are the subjects he has been writing about ever since his third novel. The change in subject matter better suited Godfrey. "Now I only write about what I know," he once commented. "In my books you'll find incidents about a fluoride rinse disaster, a student with a raisin caught in his nose, a bear attack, spiders in a cheeseburger, and so on. They're all true. I just twist reality a little on my computer screen to make them more interesting." For example, *Plan B Is Total Panic* is the story of Nicholas Clark, a boy who considers himself a wimp and an outsider, but who secretly longs to dance with Sandra Travis. Nicholas finally proves himself on a hunting expedition on an Indian reserve in this "simple, effective, rattling good yarn," according to *School Librarian*'s Mike Hanoye. Peter Carver, reviewing the novel in *Quill and Quire,* commented that Godfrey "is swiftly becoming the most prolific children's writer in the country . . . he reveals considerable skill with witty dialogue and fast-moving, realistic plots."

Inspired by a young female bike-jumping enthusiast in his neighborhood, Godfrey came up with the idea for *Here She Is, Ms. Teeny-Wonderful,* a what-if about a beauty contest similar to Miss America, but for young girls. He placed his feisty tomboy heroine, Carol Weatherspoon, as an unwilling contestant in such a pageant. Joan Yolleck, commenting in *Quill and Quire,* noted that Godfrey "successfully turns his talents to humor" in this book, while Marjorie Gann, writing in *Canadian Children's Literature,* commented that Godfrey further illuminated the contemporary theme of "traditional vs. liberated female roles, but he does this with a light touch." Gann also pointed out Godfrey's "natural" dialogue and his use of "fresh, precise language" in his descriptions. Wally, Carol's friend in *Here She Is, Ms. Teeny-Wonderful* and its sequels, is one example of how Godfrey sometimes plays with the traditional conceptions of boy/girl relations. Brent and Cheryl in *Baseball Crazy* are another example. According to Brenda M. Schmidt, writing in *Canadian Children's Literature, Baseball Crazy* deals with "growing up and the mixed emotions of adolescence," and the relations between the boy and girl are realistic: "[They] tease each other, turn to each other for help with their problems and face danger together, but they are not sentimental nor are there any overt romantic overtones."

The 1991 book *There's a Cow in My Swimming Pool* bears a whimsical title but actually treats a serious theme—the aftermath of death and the adjustments a family makes, including remarriage. Joanne Findon in *Quill and Quire* found it to be a "light, fun book, that nevertheless attempts to address some of the anxieties teens face when a parent remarries." Another story given a whimsical title, *Please Remove Your Elbow from My Ear,* tells the tale of the Dregs, a floor hockey team that is not exactly of top athletic quality, yet which must make a good showing in the annual school trophy game. In the course of their efforts, the members of the team come to discover their own unique worth. The book is "wholeheartedly recommended for any preteen who ever thought he or she was 'different' while desperately wishing to be 'normal'," concluded Faye H. Gotschall in her *Voice of Youth Advocates* review.

Something of a departure for Godfrey was his *Mystery in the Frozen Lands,* about the search for an expedition attempting to find a passage to the Pacific via the Arctic Circle. In this "compelling page-turner," as described by *Canadian Children's Literature* contributor Mary Ellen Binder, Godfrey blended factual historical elements to create a fictional account of the rescue mission, narrated by an adolescent aboard the rescue ship. The historical background for the novel is the expedition of Sir John Franklin, who in 1847 set out to discover the Northwest Passage. Franklin was never heard from again, and twelve years later another voyage was set up in search of Franklin and his crew. Godfrey's novel tells the story of a ship's boy, Peter Griffin, and his Inuit friend, Anton, and the rest of the crew sent to discover what had become of Franklin. The hardships of Arctic life are shown in Peter's diary, as well as the budding romance with his cousin, Elisabeth. According to Binder, "Godfrey's novel offers enough mystery and suspense to keep the reader interested," providing a history lesson in the process.

*Meet You in the Sewer* and *Just Call Me Boom Boom*, novels in the "JAWS Mob" series, are about a writing club which meets in a Toronto school. The club takes its name from the acronym for their school, the John Allen Watson School, and the first novel introduces JB Lunn, a student writer who tells of adventures on a scavenger hunt, a sewer exploration, and a fire. Related in the language of an eighth-grader, the book provides some of the "fastest and funniest dialogue in recent Canadian children's fiction," according to Ken Setterington in *Quill and Quire*. A reviewer for *Canadian Materials* commented that "Godfrey excels at this type of atmosphere/character melange and proceeds to racket along with a plot full of action and challenge." Of the second book in the series, *Just Call Me Boom Boom*, Setterington wrote in *Quill and Quire* that "Godfrey deserves credit for more than just a fun story. . . . The JAWS Mob series is sure to be successful, and the books deserve the attention they will receive."

Godfrey has also penned several short novels in various high-low reading series, titles which include *Mall Rats, More Than Weird, Fire! Fire!,* and *Ice Hawk.* These books have been favorably reviewed as providing a quick read for reluctant readers. *Ice Hawk* is about a hockey player trying to go professional who is faced with a moral dilemma when his coach wants him to deliberately hurt an opposing player. *Fire! Fire!* is set in British Columbia and looks at the lives of a Native fire-fighting team. Both books offer a "good blend of action, excitement, and information without being stiff, dry, or pedantic," according to Nancy Black in *Quill and Quire. Mall Rats* is the story of teens who congregate at the local mall and run into trouble with gangs. Setterington in *Quill and Quire* felt that young readers would care about the characters because "Godfrey has identified realistic teenage lives and tells their stories in interesting, unintimidating ways."

*BIOGRAPHICAL/CRITICAL SOURCES:*

*BOOKS*

Clute, John, and Peter Nichols, editors, *Encyclopedia of Science Fiction,* St. Martin's (New York City), 1993.
Godfrey, Martyn N., *Plan B Is Total Panic,* Lorimer, 1986.

*PERIODICALS*

*Booklist,* February 1, 1987, p. 839; May 1, 1990, p. 1696; March 15, 1994, p. 1360.
*Bulletin of the Center for Children's Books,* May, 1989, p. 213.
*Canadian Children's Literature,* number 43, 1986, pp. 98-99; number 45, 1987, pp. 72-74; number 56, 1989, pp. 78-80, 91-93.
*Canadian Materials,* May, 1994, p. 75.
*Kliatt,* September, 1990, p. 10.
*Quill and Quire,* June, 1981, pp. 33-34; June, 1985, p. 22; February, 1986, p. 21; December, 1986, p. 17; November, 1991, p. 28; October, 1993, p. 41; March, 1994, p. 82; July, 1994, p. 58.
*School Librarian,* February, 1991, p. 30.
*School Library Journal,* June, 1989, p. 122; July, 1992, p. 46; July, 1996, p. 84.
*Voice of Youth Advocates,* October, 1990, p. 217; December, 1993, p. 290.

\*    \*    \*

## GOLDSTEIN, Richard 1944-

*PERSONAL:* Born June 19, 1944, in New York, NY; son of Jack (a postal worker) and Molley (Maurer) Goldstein; married Judith Mipaas (an editor), May 31, 1967. *Education:* Hunter College of the City University of New York, B.A., 1965; Columbia University, M.S., 1966. *Religion:* Unitarian.

*CAREER:* Bantam Books, New York City, editor of *US* (magazine), 1968—; *Village Voice,* New York City, writer. Guest lecturer in journalism, Columbia University, spring, 1969.

*WRITINGS:*

*One in Seven: Drugs on Campus,* Walker & Co. (New York City), 1966.

*The Poetry of Rock,* Bantam (New York City), 1969.

*Goldstein's Greatest Hits: A Book Mostly about Rock 'n' Roll* (articles that appeared in the *New York Times, Village Voice,* and other publications, 1966-68), Prentice-Hall (Englewood Cliffs, NJ), 1970.

*Reporting the Counterculture,* Unwin Hyman (Boston), 1989.

Author of columns in *Vogue, New York,* and *Village Voice.*

SIDELIGHTS: "Richard Goldstein's precocious career in literary journalism in the 1960s filled the underground niche of counterculture reportage and rock and roll criticism," asserted A. J. Kaul in the *Dictionary of Literary Biography.* The critic went on to enumerate what he considered some of Goldstein's most significant contributions to American culture: "His 'Pop Eye' column in the *Village Voice* was credited with helping launch serious and incisive popular criticism of rock music and the conterculture of the 1960s. The 'counter reportage' he invented probed the images of what he called 'pseudo events,' creating 'a field of his own in which to exercise his critical faculties.'" Writing in *Saturday Review,* Ellen Sander maintained that by the end of the 1960s, Goldstein was generally recognized "not only as the most astute rock critic of his times and one of the decade's most promising young writers but as one of the most creative, colorful, and scholarly journalists alive."

"'The sacred squeal of now' is how Richard Goldstein refers to rock in the introduction to his definitive collection of rock lyrics [*The Poetry of Rock*]. Goldstein is not only the reigning Namer of rock but also so good a writer that the book is a pleasure even for those to whom Twentieth Century Fox is just a studio or Mabellene, a misspelled mascara," said a *New York* writer. Goldstein commented on the 50's in the book: "When matters of taste were at hand, you simply arched your back against the lamppost, fixed the buckle of your garrison belt across your hip, and drawled with a hint of spittle across your teeth: 'I like it. It's got a good beat. Y'can dance to it.'"

*Goldstein's Greatest Hits: A Book Mostly about Rock 'n' Roll* collected thirty-seven critical essays written between 1966 and 1968. "The essays reflect his virginal innocence and his captivation with popular culture," asserted Kaul, and trace "his viewpoint and tone from, as Goldstein writes in the introduction, "wonder in my early columns to the reserve which came later, when being a 'critic' had already become

a profession and a task." Kaul praised the "compression, insight, and style" with which Goldstein interpreted many of rock music's figureheads, including Janis Joplin, Bob Dylan, Jim Morrison, and Mick Jagger.

Goldstein generated a great deal of controversy—and lost some of his standing as a rock critic—with his assessment of the Beatles' album *Sergeant Pepper's Lonely Hearts Club Band.* Many commentators judged this elaborately produced album to be the band's greatest achievement, but Goldstein dismissed it as unoriginal music, overlaid with dazzling special effects. Goldstein also offered unflattering assessments of celebrity gurus such as Marshall McLuhan, Timothy Leary, and the Maharishi Mahesh Yogi.

The 1989 publication *Reporting the Counterculture* reprinted many of the pieces collected in *Goldstein's Greatest Hits* but began with what Kaul described as "an insightful retrospective introduction, 'First Person, Past Tense,' that deftly situates Goldstein's writing in historical and literary perspective." Kaul summarized: "From Goldstein's vantage point the 1960s counterculture spawned a hybrid form of journalism, a 'counter-reportage' infused with hip jargon and hyperbole, a mix of essay, narrative, criticism, and memoir. . . . His own writing about the counterculture evolved into an extended case study of hip culture's commercial co-optation in an expansionist economy. . . . Goldstein's counter-reportage was, like his brief career in literary journalism, a magic moment in the experimental journalistic style of the 1960s."

Goldstein once confessed to *CA* that he digs "sloths and groundhogs. Also late night horror movies and melted popsicles." He said he became a writer because "my mother used to hit me over the knuckles with a ruler to improve my penmanship."

BIOGRAPHICAL/CRITICAL SOURCES:

BOOKS

*Dictionary of Literary Biography,* Volume 185: *American Literary Journalists, 1945-1995, First Series,* Gale (Detroit), 1997.

McAuliffe, Kevin Michael, *The Great American Newspaper: The Rise and Fall of the Village Voice,* Scribners (New York City), 1978.

Wolf, Daniel, and Edwin Fancher, editors, *The Village Voice Reader,* Grove (New York City), 1963.

*PERIODICALS*

*Book World,* October 26, 1969.
*Harper's,* September, 1969.
*Newsweek,* March 3, 1969.
*New York,* February 10, 1969; March 24, 1969.
*New York Times,* May 23, 1969.
*Saturday Review,* July 31, 1971.
*Village Voice,* March 6, 1969.
*Washington Post,* March 20, 1970.*

\*   \*   \*

## GOODMAN, George J(erome) W(aldo) 1930-
### (Adam Smith)

*PERSONAL:* Born August 10, 1930, in St. Louis, MO; son of Alexander Mark and Viona (Cremer) Goodman; married Sallie Cullen Brophy, October 6, 1961; children: Alexander Mark, Susannah Blake. *Education:* Harvard University, B.A. (magna cum laude), 1952; attended Oxford University (Rhodes scholar), 1952-54.

*CAREER:* Reporter for *Collier's,* 1956, and *Barron's,* 1957; *Time* and *Fortune,* New York City, associate editor, 1958-60; Lincoln Fund, New York City, portfolio manager and vice president, 1960-62; screenwriter in Los Angeles, CA, 1962-65; *New York* magazine, New York City, cofounder, 1967, contributing editor and vice president, 1967—; *Institutional Investor* (magazine), New York City, charter editor, 1967-72; editorial chair, *NJ Monthly,* 1976-79; *New York Times,* New York City, member of editorial board, 1977; *Esquire,* New York City, executive editor, 1978-81; chair, Continental Fidelity Group, 1980—. Executive vice president and director, Institutional Investor Systems, 1969-72; director, Hyatt Hotels, 1977-81, USAIR, Inc., and Cambrex, Inc.; member of advisory committee (publications), U.S. Tennis Association, 1978-83; host and editor-in-chief of *Adam Smith's Money World,* broadcast on public television nationwide, 1984-97. Glassboro State College, Glassboro, NJ, trustee, 1967-71, co-chair of presidential selection committee, 1968; Princeton University, member of advisory council, economics department, 1970-89; Harvard University, member of representative committee on shareholder responsibility, 1971-74, member of visiting committee, psychology and social relations department, 1974-80, occasional lecturer; trustee, C. J. Jung Foundation and Urban Insti-

tute, Washington, DC, 1986—; member of visiting committee, Middle East Institute. *Military service:* U.S. Army, 1954-56.

*MEMBER:* Writer's Guild of America (West), Authors Guild, Authors League of America (director), Association of Harvard Alumni (director, 1972-75), Harvard Club (New York City), Century Association (New York City).

*AWARDS, HONORS:* G. M. Loeb Award for Distinguished Achievement in Writing about Business and Finance, University of Connecticut, 1969; media award for economic understanding, Amos Tuck School, Dartmouth College, 1978, for television documentary, *The Forty-Five Billion Dollar Connection;* Emmy Award nomination for outstanding interviewer, 1985, and five Emmy awards for news and public affairs broadcasting, including 1986, 1987, and 1988, all for *Adam Smith's Money World.*

*WRITINGS:*

*NOVELS*

*The Bubble Makers,* Viking (New York City), 1955.
*A Time for Paris,* Doubleday (New York City), 1957.
(With Winthrop Knowlton) *A Killing in the Market,* Doubleday, 1958.
*The Wheeler Dealers* (also see below), Doubleday, 1959.

*SCREENPLAYS*

*The Wheeler Dealers* (based on Goodman's novel of the same title), Metro-Goldwyn-Mayer (MGM), 1963.
*The Americanization of Emily,* MGM, 1964.

*NONFICTION; UNDER PSEUDONYM ADAM SMITH*

*The Money Game* (Literary Guild alternate selection), Random House (New York City), 1968.
*Supermoney* (Literary Guild selection), Random House, 1972.
*Powers of Mind* (Book-of-the-Month Club selection), Random House, 1975.
*Paper Money* (Book-of-the-Month Club selection), Summit Books (New York City), 1981.
*The Roaring Eighties* (Literary Guild alternate selection), Summit Books, 1988.
(With Piet Schreuders and Mark Lewisohn) *The Beatles London,* St. Martin's (New York City), 1994.

*OTHER*

*Bascombe, the Fastest Hound Alive* (juvenile), with pictures by Paul Galdone, Morrow (New York City), 1958.

Author of introduction to *The Money Managers,* edited by Gilbert Edmund Kaplan and Chris Welles, Random House, 1969. Occasional columnist, *Newsweek,* 1973; author of column, "Unconventional Wisdom," *Esquire,* 1979-88. Contributor to *Readings in Economics,* edited by Paul Samuelson, and many other anthologies. Contributor of articles to periodicals.

Goodman's papers are housed in Special Collections, Mugar Library, at Boston University.

*SIDELIGHTS:* In addition to his career as a journalist, writer and editor, George J. W. Goodman, formerly affiliated with magazines such as *Time, Fortune* and *Esquire,* has enjoyed a two-stage career as an author. During the first stage he wrote fiction and a children's book published under his own name; in the second stage, he wrote a string of bestselling nonfiction books on money, published under the name "Adam Smith." Goodman the journalist is "a thorough and conscientious reporter"; Goodman the novelist "is clever, urbane, good-humored, [and] eloquent," comments Jeff Riggenbach of the *Los Angeles Times.* And his "Adam Smith" books on the inner workings of contemporary American economics are well known around the world.

Goodman has done his best-known work as "Adam Smith," but he has proven himself in "nearly every venue available to feature writers," declares John J. Pauly in the *Dictionary of Literary Biography.* "As the older mass magazines died, he found a niche in the expanding market for business journalism. During the 1960s he achieved fame as a practitioner of the 'New Journalism' at the first and most influential of the new city magazines. With much less fanfare he directed a bold and irreverent trade magazine for investors and fund managers. During the 1980s his stylish columns helped redefine a struggling men's magazine. Through all this work has run an appealing and recognizable persona—that of a witty, urbane dinner guest, a droll observer of human affairs as comfortable discussing group psychology and cultural myths as he is business."

In the 1950s and early 1960s, Goodman was a reporter for *Collier's* and *Barron's.* During this time he

also published several well-received satires on upper-class life. *The Bubble Makers,* which follows the conflict between a Harvard student and his wealthy grandfather, is an "original and entertaining first novel," says Dan Wickenden in the *New York Herald Tribune Book Review.* Wickenden also appreciates the author's "uncommonly sound style" and "a notable ability to create character." *A Time for Paris* looks in on two American graduates who fall in love on a cruise ship headed for Europe. *New York Times* contributor Judith Quehl commends Goodman for his skillfully combined "lunatic escapades, a handful of warm and witty characters and an undeniable gift for a clever turn of phrase."

*A Killing in the Market,* written with Winthrop Knowlton, combines information on the stock market with international intrigue. A broker's assistant sets out to rescue the boss's daughter after she has been kidnapped by a mysterious European investor in an aerospace firm. *San Francisco Chronicle* critic L. G. Offord describes this battle between rich Americans and Russian agents as "both exciting and funny." James Sandoe of the *New York Herald Tribune Book Review* comments, "The authors, working with such highly topical stuff as guided missiles, seem to have had as much fun with this as they provide for us."

Goodman's fourth generally well-received novel also displays his bent for comedy and his ear for dialogue. *The Wheeler Dealers,* a story about the pyrotechnics that develop when a Texas oil baron meets a lady broker, is "a skillful blend of sophisticated repartee, belly laughs, and satirical observation, topped with an invaluable lesson on how to push up the price of a stock," Jerry Cowle notes in the *Chicago Sunday Tribune.* A children's book Goodman wrote in 1958, however, has been read perhaps more often than his novels. *Bascombe, the Fastest Hound Alive* has been extremely popular among young readers for nearly twenty years. "I wish my other books had so long a life," he tells *New York Times* writer Edwin McDowell.

During the sixties, Goodman left his position as associate editor for *Time* and *Fortune* magazines to become vice president of the Lincoln Fund. Then he spent a few years in Los Angeles, writing a screenplay for a film based on *The Wheeler Dealers.* Though the comedy was a success, he returned to New York to be the editor of *Institutional Investor* magazine. Goodman identifies himself as a person who follows a variety of interests. He tells Frances

Lear in a *Lear's* interview, "I think I'm a person who likes to learn things. I do the things I do because I like learning about them. The only reason I know anything about Wall Street is that I was curious to know why some people make money and others don't."

Goodman's writing about money management in the early 1960s brought him a new identity and fame. He was contributing articles on Wall Street to *New York* magazine, a *New York Herald Tribune* supplement, when he inadvertently became the namesake of an eighteenth-century American economist. Back at Oxford, where Goodman was a Rhodes scholar, he had noticed that Governors of the Bank of England signed their articles with names from Roman history; he followed suit, and signed the name "Procrustes" to an article about securities analysts, so that he could write freely without losing his welcome among his sources. The article appeared, however, with the byline "Adam Smith." Incensed, Goodman demanded to know which editor had given him that name, but no one confessed until some time after he became a best-selling writer.

*The Money Game,* Goodman's first venture into book-length nonfiction, was a bestseller a week after its release in 1968 and remained so for a year. Its overnight success established the reputation of "Adam Smith." Eric Berne of the *New York Times Book Review* relates that *The Money Game* benefits from the author's wide range of expertise. Smith "has tried everything, knows everything and everybody, and has read everything, that a man in the marketplace should," writes Berne. "He knows about games, and intuition, and anxiety, and identity, and he knows that a personality profile can be inferred from a stock portfolio. . . . And he knows that the stock market behaves like a woman, although it is run by men." However, Berne attributes the book's phenomenal success, for the most part, to its author's sense of humor. Previously, the topic of money had been handled with intimidating language spoken in serious tones. "But now comes Smith . . . laughing not only all the way to the bank, but also inside the bank, which takes as much courage as laughing at a funeral or in church, since for most people solemnity is the essence of money, and it is believed that if you laugh, Mammon will get sulky and bounce your check," Berne states. Because it demystifies the hallowed halls of high finance, *The Money Game,* he feels, is "the best book there is about the stock market and all that goes with it."

"It could be argued that [the author's] particular perspective gives excessive emphasis to [Wall] Street's jazzier phenomena," notes C. J. Rolo in *Book World.* For this reason, *The Money Game* may be more appealing to adventuring neophytes than to conventional investors, states Rolo. But he deems it required reading for anyone who seeks insight into the human elements of Wall Street activity. The human factors of investing seldom turn out according to expectations, Goodman relates. "Of course, people who make a lot of money frequently don't think about money. They only think about the game they're playing," he told Lear. "Even people on Wall Street are playing a game: They're concerned about what they make, what the other guy makes, but the money *as* money doesn't mean anything." Furthermore, he says in his book, some players will consistently set themselves up to lose, or spend small gains instead of using them to build wealth.

The gap between people who have wealth and those who do not is widening, and the possession of "supercurrency" makes the difference, Goodman says in the first section of *Supermoney,* his next bestseller. Business owners who can sell, merge, or go public with their companies at a rate based on a multiple of their earnings have "supercurrency," he explains. "Compounding net worth, not just increasing income or finding new tax-shelters, is the name of this particular game, and it is what has made the recently really rich really rich," Eliot Fremont-Smith writes in *Saturday Review.* "The same zesty style" makes *Supermoney* as readable as prior books, says the reviewer, yet "nervousness licks at the edges of its charm. The message of *Supermoney* is not simply that nobody really knows how to play the game, but that the game may be ending." Later sections of *Supermoney* explain that sudden major losses such as were sustained in 1970 threaten the whole economy; that some "sure thing" investments can and do go wrong; and that several attitudes fundamental to business are changing. Goodman shows that many people feel that if they defer gratification they may lose it altogether; business itself supports this attitude through advertising. The expectation that work leads to certain rewards is also no longer to be taken for granted.

Reviewers note that much of what Goodman relates in *Paper Money* is bad news as well. In it, Goodman explains "the international monetary system and . . . the largest transfer of wealth in history, which is taking place between the oil-importing and exporting nations," McDowell writes. Goodman takes his readers through a series of disasters to explain how each has contributed to the perilous condition of the American dollar. A reviewer for the *Economist* maintains that *Paper Money* "is just as racy, just as good a mixture of anecdote and research [as *The Money Game*], but it is much harder to laugh this time. . . . The money game has got crazier in a disturbing way; the rulebook has been discarded and nobody knows how to rewrite it." The realities which economics must describe and predict fluctuate, consensus regarding America's actual position in the world economy and how to make the most of it difficult to achieve. In the midst of this, comments Leonard Silk in the *New York Times Book Review,* Goodman "strives for sanity," balancing the bad news with the possibility of a better future. "Along the way, we've seen money lose its value, banking catastrophes, mass unemployment, the poisoning of once healthy societies, the collapse of the international economic system and the breeding of monstrous wars in the swamps of rotting economies. History tells us that there is plenty to be scared about, but also that we might get through, if we are not too selfish or stupid," Silk summarizes. Writing in the *Washington Post Book World,* Robert Lekachman offers the consolation that "Goodman's bad news is delivered in prose that is a pleasure to read."

In *The Roaring Eighties* Goodman tackles the aftershocks of the spending and debt that characterized the decade. After speaking to people at all levels of economic power, he relates their experiences, responding with questions about the future. Fortunes are being made—and lost—in new and surprising ways, and the changed economic climate is not an improvement on the past, Goodman maintains. *Newsweek* reviewer Bill Powell and others comment that *The Roaring Eighties* is not the "analysis of these remarkable times" they had expected. Suggests Powell, many of the issues described may be familiar due to greater coverage of business news in the media, so that the book does not have the flavor of inside information that enhances the other books. Susan Lee of the *New York Times Book Review,* however, defends the author's treatment of the times: "We could not ask for a more genial, knowledgeable companion for a tour of the national financial landscape. . . . He is able to describe events in a common-sense way that makes them accessible and that puts him way ahead of most financial commentators."

Goodman's style also animates *Powers of Mind,* a book that relates his personal quest for relaxation techniques to share with his colleagues in the marketplace, says Elsa First in the *New York Times Book Review.* Goodman "writes with enough pizzazz, jump-cutting, and Woody Allen one-liners to keep even the weariest commodities trader alert," she notes. His tour through the realm of psychic experience, transcendental meditation, Esalen, and Zen highlights its humorous aspects. Martin Gardner, a *New York Review of Books* contributor, cites the author's interview with EST (Erhard Seminars Training) proponent Jack Rosenberg, now known as Erhard. Erhard told Goodman that what participants get from a seminar is the assurance that whatever already exists is perfect as it is, and beyond that, there is no greater idea to "get." "You lose, of course, your 250 initiation fee, that's what EST gets," Gardner quips, rephrasing Goodman's punchline. Though some critics feel the author's quick tour leaves some relevant ground uncovered, in the end Goodman expresses some valuable connections between the mysteries of subatomic particle physics, poetry, and religion, *Time* reviewer R. Z. Sheppard notes. Sheppard comments, "Given his subject matter, the author could have settled for far less. Instead he provides a bestseller with a considerable educational function as well as high entertainment"— a comment which sums up the appeal of nearly all of Goodman's books.

"*Powers of Mind* is further evidence that [Goodman's] publishing instincts are like those of a surfer who knows just when to catch the curl of the wave," Sheppard notes. Even Goodman's lesser acclaimed works of "participatory journalism," as Sheppard calls them, have reached millions of appreciative readers. And *The Money Game,* now published in seventeen languages, is read around the world.

Pauly muses that in many ways, "Goodman's influence has greatly exceeded that of other literary journalists. He opened the eyes of publishers, writers, and readers to a feature approach now widely used by business journalists. He left a distinctive mark on every publication with which he was closely associated, from *New York* to *Institutional Investor* to *Esquire.* And, most improbably, he is the only noted literary journalist in U.S. history to have made an equally successful career in television. For historians, at least, there will be no telling the story of literary journalism in the late twentieth century without speaking about Jerry Goodman."

*BIOGRAPHICAL/CRITICAL SOURCES:*

BOOKS

*Dictionary of Literary Biography,* Volume 185: *American Literary Journalists, 1945-1995, First Series,* Gale (Detroit), 1997.

Quirt, John, *The Press and the World of Money,* Anton/California Courier (Byron, CA), 1993, pp. 110-25.

PERIODICALS

*Avenue,* October, 1987, pp. 110-25.
*Book World,* June 2, 1968.
*Chicago Sunday Tribune,* September 6, 1959.
*Commonweal,* November 29, 1968; March 17, 1973.
*Economist,* March 28, 1981.
*Esquire,* February, 1989.
*Lear's,* September, 1989.
*Life,* December 20, 1968.
*Los Angeles Times,* April 10, 1981; March 24, 1985.
*National Observer,* June 10, 1968.
*New Statesman,* March 16, 1973.
*Newsweek,* June 17, 1968; December 5, 1988.
*New York,* April 7, 1969; August 18, 1969.
*New York Herald Tribune Book Review,* August 28, 1955; November 17, 1957; May 11, 1958.
*New York Review of Books,* December 11, 1975.
*New York Times,* August 28, 1955; December 8, 1957; May 4, 1958; March 9, 1981.
*New York Times Book Review,* September 27, 1959; May 26, 1968; July 14, 1968; October 15, 1972; November 2, 1975; March 22, 1981; March 29, 1981; November 27, 1988.
*Publishers Weekly,* January 15, 1979.
*San Francisco Chronicle,* June 22, 1958; January 11, 1969.
*Saturday Review,* June 21, 1968; September 9, 1972; October 21, 1972; February, 1981.
*Time,* November 27, 1972; October 27, 1975.
*Times Literary Supplement,* October 24, 1968; August 3, 1973.
*Virginia Quarterly Review,* winter, 1969.
*Washington Post Book World,* February 22, 1981.*

\* \* \*

**GRANGE, Peter**
　**See NICOLE, Christopher (Robin)**

**GRANT, Nicholas**
　**See NICOLE, Christopher (Robin)**

\* \* \*

**GRAVES, John (Alexander III) 1920-**

*PERSONAL:* Born August 6, 1920, in Fort Worth, TX; son of John Alexander and Nancy (Kay) Graves; married Jane Marshall Cole, 1958; children: Helen, Sally. *Education:* Rice University, B.A., 1942; Columbia University, M.A., 1948. *Avocational interests:* Natural history, the outdoors.

*ADDRESSES: Home*—P.O. Box 667, Glen Rose, TX 76043.

*CAREER:* Freelance writer. University of Texas at Austin, instructor in English, 1948-50; Texas Christian University, Fort Worth, adjunct professor of English, 1958-65; employed with U.S. Department of Interior, 1965-68. *Military service:* U.S. Marine Corps, 1941-45; became captain; received Purple Heart.

*MEMBER:* PEN, Nature Conservancy, Audubon Society, Texas Institute of Letters (president, 1984), Phi Beta Kappa.

*AWARDS, HONORS:* Collins Award of Texas Institute of Letters, 1961, for *Goodbye to a River: A Narrative;* Guggenheim fellow, 1963; Rockefeller fellow, 1972; Parkman Prize of Texas Institute of Letters, 1974, for *Hard Scrabble: Observations on a Patch of Land;* Distinguished Alumni Award from Rice University, 1983; Barbara McCombs/Lon Tinkle Memorial award, Texas Institute of Letters, 1983; D.Litt., Texas Christian University, 1983.

*WRITINGS:*

"BRAZOS TRILOGY"

*Goodbye to a River: A Narrative,* Knopf (New York), 1960.
*Hard Scrabble: Observations on a Patch of Land,* Knopf, 1974.
*From a Limestone Ledge: Some Essays and Other Ruminations about Country Life in Texas,* Knopf, 1980.

*OTHER*

*Home Place: A Background Sketch in Support of a Proposed Restoration of Pioneer Building in Fort Worth, Texas,* Pioneer Texas Heritage Committee (Fort Worth, TX), 1958.

*The Creek and the City: Urban Pressures on a Natural Stream, Rock Creek Park and Metropolitan Washington,* Department of the Interior (Washington, DC), 1967.

*The Nation's River,* U.S. Government Printing Office (Washington, DC), 1968.

(With Robert Boyle and T. H. Watkins) *The Water Hustlers,* Sierra Club (San Francisco), 1971, revised edition, 1973.

(With others) *Growing Up in Texas,* Encino Press (Austin, TX), 1972.

*The Last Running,* Encino Press, 1974.

(With Jim Bones, Jr.) *Texas Heartland: A Hill Country Year,* Texas A&M University Press (College Station), 1975.

(Editor with John Walsh) *The River Styx, Salt Spring Cave System,* Texas Cave Report Series (San Antonio), 1976.

(Author of introduction) *Landscapes of Texas,* Texas A&M University Press, 1980.

(Editor) Gail W. Starr, *Mall,* Envision Commission, 1980.

(With others) *The American Southwest, Cradle of Literary Art,* Southwest Texas State University (San Marcos), 1981.

*Blue and Some Other Dogs,* Encino Press, 1981.

*Of Birds and Texas,* Gentling Editions (Fort Worth), 1986.

*A John Graves Reader,* University of Texas Press (Austin), 1996.

Contributor to *The Best American Short Stories 1960,* Houghton (Boston), 1960, and to *Prize Stories: The O. Henry Awards,* 1955 and 1962. Contributor to numerous magazines. Collections of Graves's manuscript are housed at the Humanities Research Center, University of Texas, Austin, and Southwest Texas State University.

*SIDELIGHTS:* A native Texan naturalist, John Graves writes primarily of his home state and of his experiences as the owner of Hard Scrabble Ranch, four hundred acres of arid land near Fort Worth. He is best known for a trio of books called the "Brazos Trilogy": *Goodbye to a River: A Narrative, Hard Scrabble: Observations on a Patch of Land,* and *From a Limestone Ledge: Some Essays and Other Ruminations about Country Life in Texas.*

*Goodbye to a River* began as a magazine article for *Holiday* magazine, about a canoe trip the author took down the Brazos River. It is the third largest river in Texas and the largest between the Red River and the Rio Grande. Graves was inspired to take the trip in 1957, after learning that the Brazos was scheduled to be dammed by the federal government. After completing his magazine piece, Graves had so much material left over that he put together a book. It is, according to *Dictionary of Literary Biography Yearbook* contributor Timothy Dow Adams, "part autobiography, part history, part philosophy, and part woodlore, loosely tied to the erratic but steady flow of John Graves's canoe down twists of the river through both yellow-blue and rain-ruined November days and on into December snow and freezing northers." Adams deems Graves's writing style "highly polished and literate, reflecting the wide variety of influence alluded to in chapter headings and in the body of the book itself, writers such as [Henry David] Thoreau, [William Butler] Yeats, [William] Shakespeare, Thorstein Veblen, George Herbert, and the author of *Sir Gawain and the Green Knight.*" Adams adds, however, that "for all his literary ancestors, Graves's style is peculiarly his own, his syntax characterized by rhythmic stops and starts, like a boat caught momentarily on an obstruction in the current, now catching and spinning backward, now speeding downstream."

Despite the highly favorable critical response to *Goodbye to a River,* more than a decade passed before Graves's next major book. According to a reviewer in the *Atlantic Monthly, Hard Scrabble: Observations on a Patch of Land,* a book of essays, is "a rumination tinctured with [Graves's] love of history, his inquisitiveness about his neighbors, and his shrewd knowledge of the natural world." A *New Yorker* critic finds that Graves's subjects, which include everything from "hired help [to] armadillos, . . . come to us reshaped and reenlivened by his agreeably individual . . . notions." Edward Hoagland calls the book "galloping [and] spontaneous" in the *New York Times Book Review* and points out that "what the best [naturalists], like Graves, do have . . . and what can give their books exceptional staying power, is a tone that suits the book . . . a life, a grace, an impetus [that] is lent to their efforts" by their unique perspective.

In the third part of the "Brazos Trilogy," *From a Limestone Ledge: Some Essays and Other Ruminations about Country Life in Texas,* Graves presented essays previously printed in *Texas Monthly* magazine.

Many of these functioned as sequels to subjects introduced in *Hard Scrabble*. Referring to *From a Limestone Ledge,* Susan Wood of the *Washington Post* says that Graves "writes about Texas and Texans with full attention to the complex peculiarities that distinguish the region; but because he so lovingly particularizes, rather than generalizes, his thoughts come to us in larger terms, made universal by the art of language and feeling. Although permeated with a sense of place, Graves's writing translates Texas as though it were Anywhere." Bill Marvel, reviewing the book in the *Detroit News,* claims that the "ruminative essay on country life is a tradition in American letters, . . . and it is [here] that John Graves's *From a Limestone Ledge* takes its place."

Adams declared: "John Graves has outgrown his strong regional identification and emerged as an important American writer in the naturalist mode. To the list of recent writers such as Edward Hoagland, Annie Dillard, Noel Perrin, John McPhee, and Wendell Berry, who have inherited that particularly American combination of autobiography-natural history-philosophy handed down from Thoreau and William Bartram through Louis Bromfield, Joseph Wood Krutch, and John Muir, the name of John Graves should be added."

*BIOGRAPHICAL/CRITICAL SOURCES:*

*BOOKS*

Bennett, Patrick, *Talking with Texas Writers: Twelve Interviews,* Texas A&M University Press, 1981, pp. 63-88.
*Dictionary of Literary Biography Yearbook: 1983,* Gale (Detroit), 1984.
Grover, Dorys Crow, *John Graves,* Boise State University (Boise, ID), 1989.
*Twentieth-Century Western Writers,* 2nd edition, St. James Press (Chicago), 1991.

*PERIODICALS*

*Atlantic Monthly,* August, 1974.
*Detroit News,* January 25, 1981.
*New Yorker,* August 19, 1974; December 29, 1980.
*New York Times Book Review,* May 19, 1974.
*Washington Post,* December 27, 1980.

\*    \*    \*

**GRAY, Caroline**
   **See NICOLE, Christopher (Robin)**

# H-J

## HACKER, Marilyn 1942-

*PERSONAL:* Born November 27, 1942, in New York, NY; daughter of Albert Abraham (a management consultant) and Hilda (a teacher; maiden name, Rosengarten) Hacker; married Samuel R. Delany (a writer), August 22, 1961 (separated, 1974; divorced, 1980); partner of Karyn London, 1986—; children: Iva Alyxander Hacker-Delany. *Education:* New York University, B.A., 1964. *Politics:* "Progressive, feminist, socialist."

*ADDRESSES: Office*—230 West 105 St., Apt. 10-A, New York, NY 10025. *Agent*—Frances Collin, P.O. Box 33, Wayne, PA 19087-0033.

*CAREER:* Poet, editor. Worked variously as a teacher, mail sorter, and editor. Antiquarian bookseller in London, England, 1971-76. Jenny McKean Moore Chair in Writing, George Washington University, Washington, DC, 1974; Columbia University, New York City, American Studies Institute, writer-in-residence, 1988; University of Cincinnati, Cincinnati, OH, George Elliston poet-in-residence, 1988; American University, Washington, DC, distinguished writer-in-residence, 1989; Barnard College, New York City, visiting professor, 1995; Brandeis University, Waltham, MA, Fannie Hurst Visiting Professor of Poetry, 1996, Washington University, St. Louis, MO, Fannie Hurst Writer-in-Residence, 1997; Hofstra University, Professor of English, 1997—.

*MEMBER:* PEN, Poetry Society of America, Authors Guild, Feminist Writers Guild.

*AWARDS, HONORS:* Lamont Poetry Selection, Academy of American Poets, for *Presentation Piece,* and New York YWHA Poetry Center Discovery award, for "new" poets, both 1973; National Endowment for the Arts grant, 1974, 1985, 1995; National Book Award in Poetry, 1975, for *Presentation Piece;* New York State Foundation for the Arts Creative Artists Public Service grant, 1979-80; Guggenheim Foundation award, 1980-81; Coordinating Council of Little Magazines' editor's fellowship, 1984; Ingram Merrill Foundation Award, 1985; Robert F. Winner Memorial Award, 1987, for "Letter from Goose Creek: April," and 1989, for "Two Cities"; Lambda Literary Award in Poetry, 1991, for *Going Back to the River;* John Masefield Memorial Award and B. F. Conners Award, both 1994, both for "Cancer Winter"; Reader's Choice Award, 1995; Lambda Literary Award in Poetry and Lenore Marshall Poetry Prize, Academy of American Poets, both 1995, both for *Winter Numbers;* Poet's Prize, 1996, for *Selected Poems.*

*WRITINGS:*

POETRY

*The Terrible Children,* privately printed, 1967.
(With Thomas M. Disch and Charles Platt) *Highway Sandwiches,* privately printed, 1970.
*Presentation Piece,* Viking (New York City), 1974.
*Separations,* Knopf (New York City), 1976.
*Taking Notice,* Knopf, 1980.
(Editor) *Woman Poet: The East,* Women in Literature (Reno, NV), 1982.
*Assumptions,* Knopf, 1985.
*Love, Death, and the Changing of the Seasons,* Arbor House (New York City), 1986.
*Going Back to the River,* Random House (New York City), 1990.

*The Hang-Glider's Daughter: New and Selected Poems,* Onlywomen Press (London), 1990.

*Selected Poems, 1965-1990,* Norton (New York City), 1994.

*Winter Numbers,* Norton, 1994.

(Translator) *Edge* (poems), by Claire Malroux, Wake Forest University Press (Wake Forest, NC), 1996.

*OTHER*

(Editor, with husband, Samuel R. Delany) *Quark I-IV,* four volumes, Paperback Library (New York City), 1970-71.

*The Poetry and Voice of Marilyn Hacker* (sound recording) Caedmon, 1976.

*Treasury of American Jewish Poets Reading Their Poems* (sound recording), edited by Paul Kresh, Spoken Arts Recordings, 1979.

*Marilyn Hacker* (sound recording), University of Missouri, New Letters, 1979.

Contributor to periodicals, including *Nation, Paris Review,* and *Women's Review of Books.* Editor, *City,* 1967-70, *Quark* (speculative fiction quarterly), 1970-71, *Little Magazine,* 1977-80, *Thirteenth Moon,* 1982-86, and *Kenyon Review,* 1990-94. Editor of special issue of *Ploughshares,* winter 1989-90 and spring 1996.

*SIDELIGHTS:* In her award-winning first book, *Presentation Piece,* poet Marilyn Hacker defined the dimensions of a poetic universe that she would continue to explore in her later work. Verse forms included in the book are sonnets, sestinas, villanelles, blank verse, and heroic couplets. Hacker largely stays within these formal boundaries in her subsequent books. Within these traditional poetic forms, Hacker couches the urgency of love, desire and alienation in brash, up-to-the minute language, writing from her perspective as a feminist, a lesbian, and a member of the extended family of women. Judith Barrington, in the *Women's Review of Books,* identified Hacker as a "radical formalist" to describe that juxtaposition of the traditional and the vernacular.

Carol S. Oles has interpreted Hacker's formalism as a political device. She observed in the *Nation:* "When she writes in forms associated with the primarily male poets canonized by literary history, it is as if she were slipping, in broad daylight, into a well-guarded preserve. She uses the decorous sonnet, sestina and villanelle to contain a vernacular, often racy speech." Hacker herself might not agree with that analysis, as

she commented in an interview with Karla Hammond in *Frontiers,* "The language that we use was as much created and invented by women as by men." According to Felicia Mitchell, in the *Dictionary of Literary Biography,* Hacker "has insisted and shown that the traditional poetic forms are as much women's as they are men's—even if men were acclaimed and published more frequently in the past."

A native of New York City, Hacker attended New York University in the early 1960s, earning her B.A. in 1964. In 1961 she married writer Samuel R. Delany; despite Delany's homosexuality, the couple remained married for thirteen years, during which time they had a daughter. In the 1970s, Hacker spent much of her time living in London and working as a book dealer. She returned to the United States in 1976 but has divided her time since then between the United States and France, editing literary periodicals such as *Ploughshares* and *Kenyon Review,* and teaching at a number of colleges and universities. Openly lesbian since the late 1970s, Hacker has created a poetry that is "feminist in its themes as it reveals how the personal is political," noted Mitchell.

Mitchell suggested that Hacker's first three books, *Presentation Piece, Separations,* and *Taking Notice,* can be viewed as a trilogy. While all three are concerned with "a modern woman's psyche, played against the context of city streets and personal memories," the third collection, published in 1980, showed signs of increasing "self-awareness." The poems "grew richer and less arcane. Her tone softened, even hinted at joy." According to Mitchell, reviews of *Taking Notice* suggested that "the breadth of Hacker's vision was increasing as her experiences gave her more depth of emotion, and that her blend of formal structure and informal speech seemed less contrived and more natural." The poems in *Taking Notice* "betray their imprisonment in the material present," Mary Kinzie stated in *American Poetry Review.* "There is here no beauty that makes the heart yearn, no broad consciousness guiding the verses, and no spiritual truth. There are only things." She concluded that the collection "is work that practically dares us to find a fault with its skill, and I find little to mitigate my judgment that the gauge is thrown by poems in which failed irony, dull lists, turgid diction, and a superficial formalism are artlessly exaggerated." While criticizing those poems in the collection that stray from the sonnet form, a *Washington Post Book World* reviewer remarked that "at her best no one handles the colloquial sublime . . . better than Marilyn Hacker. She is a master of progressive pentameter, of measuring, interrupting and holding the line, and of letting it go on, of letting it pile into sentences and juxtapositions."

Several critics characterized Hacker's 1985 collection, *Assumptions,* as a personally revealing and compassionate work. Here the poet's concerns revolve around relationships among women: as mother and daughter, as friends, as lovers, and as mythic figures which inform women's consciousness. In the book's first section, Hacker's relationship with her own mother is explored, precipitated by the poet's efforts to explain herself to her own daughter, Iva. Hacker had written about her mother and her daughter in earlier collections, but as Oles notes in *Assumptions,* acceptance, and finally forgiveness have occurred. It is that autobiographical note of Hacker's verse which J. D. McClatchy praised in the *New York Times Book Review:* "how relationships evolve, how love changes from passion to friendship, how we watch ourselves come clear or obscured in the eyes of others—these problems are traced in a remarkable series of epistolary poems to her ex-lovers and portraits of her family." In *Women's Review of Books,* contributor Kathleen Aguero wrote, "Hacker's voice manages to be intimate and intellectual at the same time. The forms she uses so expertly lend her just enough distance to be personal and self-conscious about craft, about language as a repository of meaning, without being self-indulgent."

Oles pointed out that the title *Assumptions* can be read as a reference to Catholicism, and that the collected verses contain similar references to "communicants," "sin," and "salvation." Oles concluded that Hacker is advocating "the creation of a new faith for unbelievers in the old." Along these lines, the book's final section, "The Snow Queen," uses the characters of Hans Christian Andersen to create a new feminist mythology. Hacker gives new life to Andersen's characters as portraits of women's possibilities, whose ultimate quest is to define themselves. The Snow Queen, a powerfully evil figure in Andersen's tale, is here redefined as one of the admirable "bad old ladies" who takes charge of her own life and is rewarded when her "daughters slog across the icecap to get drunk" with them. These literary figures are in the end part of the extended family of women—mothers and daughters—to whom Hacker feels a debt and a connection.

Hacker's next book, *Love, Death and the Changing of the Seasons,* is an extended narrative comprised mainly of sonnets that describes the arc of a love affair between a poet living in New York and France and a younger woman. Kathleen West described it in *Prairie Schooner* as "the unfolding of a grand passion that is in no way lessened by its entanglement with twentieth-century angst and American self-deprecatory humor." The characters meet in a poetry class taught by the older woman, Hack. Their relationship develops against a backdrop of what West called "New York freneticism, trans-Atlantic travel, and the energy of love." Hacker mainly uses Petrarchan sonnets to tell the story, peppering it with English and French slang, strong erotic language, the details of everyday life, a wide-ranging set of friends, and literary allusions—especially to Shakespeare, whose sonnets to a younger lover are an obvious reference point. As West points out, Hacker can combine Penelope, Persephone, French phrases, and the Shirelles in a single poem. Marilyn French, in a review in the *Nation,* summed up the book as "deeply satisfying. It allows the reader, in the concentrated and vivid way only poetry provides, to be immersed in the texture of one woman's actuality. . . . Unlike any other love poems I know, Hacker's sequence provides a context that offers a tacit explanation of how one can go on when the heart is shattered."

In 1990's *Going Back to the River,* Hacker again published a collection of formally constructed poems grouped into sections and based on personal themes. Elizabeth Alexander wrote in the *Voice Literary Supplement* that the collection addresses "themes that have long absorbed Marilyn Hacker: geographies, languages, the marking of her own places across various landscapes, and the creation of rituals." Alexander opined that the book falls short of Hacker's earlier work, that the autobiographical focus that had previously provided such a rich source of material, fails in this collection. "Hacker fans . . . will want to read this volume to see what she's thinking about and eating. . . . But only a few of the poems show what she's capable of." One poem that Alexander did praise, however, is the final poem, "Against Silence," addressed to Hacker's former mother-in-law, Margaret Delany. Delany had been an early hero of Hacker's, as a woman who earned her own living, "unduped and civilized." As a victim of stroke, the elderly Delany is less and less able to speak, leaving the poet "mourning your lost words . . . at a loss/ for words to name what my loss of you is."

Judith Barrington, reviewing *Going Back* for the *Women's Review of Books,* found Hacker's "brilliant" form to be an integral aspect of the poetry's meaning. She quotes, as an example, the poem "Cultural Exchange," in which an Hispanic woman muses on the contradictions she sees in the behavior of her employers: North Americans who think that women are "all one class" yet who still employ a domestic. The sestina form, noted Barrington, is "perfect for conveying the nature of cross-cultural exchanges, with their moments of connection and their odd near-misses."

Some reviewers have commented that Hacker's adherence to formal structure has resulted in poems that are nothing more than technical exercises. Ben Howard found in *Poetry* that the more formal poems of *Presentation Piece* "fall victim to artifice," while finding the poems in freer forms to be "more convincing."

However, as Hacker has continued to develop her distinctive combination of traditional forms and radical themes, many reviewers have appreciated her accomplishments. By the time *Going Back to the River* was published, Hacker was so well known for her adherence to traditional forms that Alexander could refer to her "familiar technical dexterity." Alexander went on to note that while the poet uses "tightly rhymed and metered structures such as sestinas and villanelles, she nonetheless brings a colloquial ease and grace to the forms. She builds her rhythm on the rhyme itself, which forges connections between unlike quantities, and she uses her language to make those unlikely companions jibe."

Hacker has also been praised for her use of language. Howard noted of *Presentation Piece*, "Over and again one encounters images of the body, especially the tongue; of salt upon the tongue; of the sea, cliffs, a beach; of lovers awakening. And it becomes apparent that the poet is attempting to formulate, in these and related images, a language of instinct and feeling—of a woman's bodily awareness—and to express the body's longings, including its 'inadmissible longings' as they are shaped and repressed in personal relationships." In *Contemporary Women Poets,* contributor Jane Augustine described the poet's language as "hard-edged," "darkly jewel-encrusted, redolent of a devastated inner world of difficult loving, tangled sexuality, and convoluted relationships. Semiprecious gems—onyx, amethyst, alexandrite—express the hardness, mystery, and richness of experience," Augustine noted of Hacker's early work in particular.

*Selected Poems, 1965-1990* is a collection of poems from five previous books (all except *Love, Death, and the Changing of the Seasons*). In addition to highlight-

ing Hacker's formal skill, "this retrospective collection documents the extent to which she has consistently articulated the complexities of contemporary culture, as a feminist, as a lesbian, and simply as a politically aware human being," noted *Lambda Book Report* contributor Sue Russell. Observing that Hacker's signature style is traceable from her earliest works, a *Publishers Weekly* reviewer praised the collection "for its great heart and its embrace of the female condition." *Library Journal* reviewer Steve R. Ellis commented on Hacker's unique ability in "negotiating the boundary of the feminist and lesbian canon while generating a buzz around [her] early work." And Lawrence Joseph declared in the *Voice Literary Supplement,* "Part of Hacker's genius is her use of traditional forms, or variations on them, as an integral level of expression." Writing in the *New York Times Book Review,* David Kirby stated: "There are no ticktock rhymes in her work; her use of enjambment, slant rhyme and metrical variation produces a line so lissome and fluid that, once engaged, the reader glides on as swiftly as a child in a water slide."

Published at the same time as *Selected Poems,* 1994's *Winter Numbers* "represents a darker vision than one is accustomed to from Hacker," according to Russell. Russell found "the same clear image of women's bodies, together or alone, this time augmented by a starkly vivid physical consciousness of aging and disease in the self or others." *Women's Review of Books* contributor Adrian Oktenberg noted that Hacker's typical scenes and characters in this collection are now "almost always tinged with a deeper sense of brevity, mutability and loss; and the sense of a future, both individual and collective, is now very much in doubt." Joseph remarked, "Hacker's voices are more mellifluously startling and alive than ever" as "the central motifs of her poetry . . . revolve around, simultaneously, the destruction of one's own body and that of the body politic." "As a Jew who lives part-time in Paris, her 'chosen diaspora,' Hacker writes hauntingly of the Holocaust. As a lesbian who lives part-time in America, Hacker writes with tremendous force about bigotry, AIDS, and breast cancer," explained Matthew Rothschild in the *Progressive.* The critic summarized: "It is the specter of death that lends this work its unforgettable power." "Although I am hesitant to equate 'darker' with 'deeper,' or even 'better,' as if the experience of human suffering in itself entitled one to added respect," remarked Russell, "I can say without hesitation that *Winter Numbers* is a stunning achievement bound to be quoted widely, and, one hopes, read by a broadening audience." Kirby declared, "Once again Ms. Hacker's supple formalism gives backbone to ideas and images that might overwhelm a lesser poet, and once again one sees how good this poet is, so good that anyone else trying to do what she does would only look foolish." "Dark as her subject is, Hacker's poems illuminate," commented a reviewer from *Publishers Weekly*. Oktenberg summarized: "The news in *Winter Numbers* is that one remains oneself in illness, and perhaps becomes more so."

*Winter Numbers* garnered Hacker the prestigious Lenore Marshall Poetry Prize in 1995; as Maxine Kumin noted of her award in *Nation*, "Love and grief come together in Hacker's poems, infused with passion and wit and rendered in intricately woven formal patterns that stun the ear with their vernacular grace." Summarizing Hacker's work in *Feminist Writers*, contributor Renee Curry noted that "Much of Hacker's life work has been to frame the nameless inside the names, to work on providing forms for the formless." Hacker's significance to modern poetry, Curry added, "is synonymous with her persistent contribution of her own life experiences and her own life's wisdom to the feminist lesbian canon."

*BIOGRAPHICAL/CRITICAL SOURCES:*

BOOKS

*Contemporary Literary Criticism,* Gale (Detroit), Volume 5, 1976, Volume 9, 1978, Volume 23, 1983, Volume 72, 1992, Volume 91, 1996.
*Contemporary Women Poets,* St. James Press (Detroit), 1997.
*Dictionary of Literary Biography,* Volume 120: *American Poets since World War II, Third Series,* Gale, 1992.
*Feminist Writers,* St. James Press, 1996.

PERIODICALS

*American Poetry Review,* July, 1981, pp. 13-14; May/June, 1996, pp. 23-27.
*AWP Chronicle,* March/April, 1996.
*Belles Lettres,* spring, 1991, p. 52; winter, 1996, pp. 34-35.
*Bloomsbury Review,* March, 1996, p. 23.
*Choice,* September, 1976, p. 822.
*Frontiers,* fall, 1981, pp. 22-27.
*Hudson Review,* summer, 1995, p. 339.
*Kliatt,* fall, 1985, p. 29.
*Ms.,* April, 1975; March, 1981, p. 78.
*Lambda Book Report,* November, 1994, p. 27.

*Library Journal,* September 15, 1994, p. 73; April 1, 1997, p. 95.
*Los Angeles Times Book Review,* December 28, 1980, p. 7; June 30, 1985, p. 4; October 19, 1986, p. 8; September 2, 1990, p. 9.
*Nation,* September 18, 1976, p. 250; April 27, 1985; November 1, 1986; November 7, 1994, p. 548; December 26, 1994, p. 813; December 18, 1995, p. 800.
*New Republic,* September 7, 1974, p. 24.
*New Yorker,* November 21, 1994, p. 133.
*New York Times,* November 22, 1995, p. B4.
*New York Times Book Review,* January 12, 1975, p. 2; August 8, 1976, pp. 12, 16; October 12, 1980, p. 14; May 26, 1985; June 21, 1987, p. 13; March 12, 1995; December 3, 1995, p. 80.
*Poetry,* April, 1975, p. 44; February, 1977, p. 285; July, 1981, p. 231.
*Prairie Schooner,* winter, 1987; fall, 1992, pp. 129-31.
*Progressive,* January, 1995, pp. 43-44.
*Publishers Weekly,* August 29, 1994, p. 67; September 26, 1994, p. 58.
*Times Literary Supplement,* October 29, 1976, p. 1348; July 10, 1987, p. 748; December 1, 1995, p. 10.
*Tribune Books,* May 26, 1974; January 11, 1981, p. 3.
*Voice Literary Supplement,* April, 1990, pp. 6-7; February, 1995, p. 25.
*Washington Post Book World,* November 2, 1980, p. 11; February 1, 1987, p. 6.
*Women's Review of Books,* September, 1985, p. 13; July, 1990, p. 28; April, 1995, pp. 10-11.\*

\*   \*   \*

**HANNAH, Barry 1942-**

*PERSONAL:* Born April 23, 1942, in Meridian, MS; son of William (an insurance agent) and Elizabeth (King) Hannah; divorced; children: Barry, Jr., Ted, Lee. *Education:* Mississippi College, Clinton, B.A. in pre-med, 1964; University of Arkansas, M.A., 1966, M.F.A. in creative writing, 1967. *Politics:* Democrat. *Religion:* Baptist. *Avocational interests:* Playing the trumpet, fishing.

*ADDRESSES: Home*—1413 Van Buren Ave., Oxford, MS 38655. *Office*—University of Mississippi, English Department, University, MS 38677.

*CAREER:* Writer. Clemson University, Clemson, SC, teacher of literature and fiction, 1967-73; Middlebury College, Middlebury, VT, writer in residence, 1974-75; University of Alabama, Tuscaloosa, AL, teacher of literature and fiction, 1975-80; worked as writer with filmmaker Robert Altman in Hollywood, CA, 1980; University of Iowa, Iowa City, writer in residence, 1981; University of Mississippi, Oxford, writer in residence, 1982, 1984-85; University of Montana, Missoula, writer in residence, 1982-83.

*AWARDS, HONORS:* Bellaman Foundation award in fiction, 1970; Atherton fellowship from Bread Loaf Writers Conference, 1971; nomination for National Book Award, 1972, for *Geronimo Rex*; Arnold Gingrich Award for short fiction from *Esquire*, 1978, for *Airships*; special award from American Academy of Arts and Letters, 1978; Guggenheim Award, 1983; Mississippi Governor's Award in the Arts, 1986; Award in Fiction, Mississippi Institute of Arts and Letters, 1994.

*WRITINGS:*

NOVELS

*Geronimo Rex,* Knopf (New York City), 1972.
*Nightwatchmen,* Viking (New York City), 1973.
*Ray,* Knopf, 1981.
*The Tennis Handsome,* Knopf, 1983.
*Hey Jack!,* Dutton (New York City), 1987.
*Boomerang,* Houghton/Seymour Lawrence (Boston), 1989.
*Never Die,* Houghton/Seymour Lawrence, 1991.
*High Lonesome,* Atlantic Monthly Press (New York City), 1996.

OTHER

*Airships* (short stories), Knopf, 1978.
*Two Stories* (short stories), Nouveau Press, 1982.
*Black Butterfly* (short stories), Palaemon Press, 1982.
*Power and Light* (novella), Palaemon Press, 1983.
*Captain Maximus* (short stories), Knopf, 1985.
*Bats Out of Hell* (short stories), Houghton/Seymour Lawrence, 1993.

Contributor to periodicals, including *Esquire*.

*SIDELIGHTS:* Barry Hannah is among the most prominent writers to emerge from the American South since World War II. His novels and short stories reveal a preoccupation with violence and sex that marks him as a disturbing and often demanding author. His first novel, *Geronimo Rex,* details the struggles and adventures of Harry Monroe, a romantic youth with literary aspirations in Louisiana. Amid the turbulent racial struggle of the early 1960s, Monroe abandons his plans to write and begins a period of disappointment and depravity with a succession of local prostitutes. At his spiritual nadir, he desperately adopts the legendary Indian warrior Geronimo as his inspiration. "What I especially liked about Geronimo," Monroe declares, "was that he had cheated, lied, stolen, usurped, killed, burned, raped. . . . I thought I would like to get into that line of work." At college, Monroe befriends Bobby Dove Fleece, a pallid youth cowed by domineering parents. The two students eventually oppose an avid racist, Whitfield Peter, in a wild shootout culminating in the bigot's defeat. Monroe then marries and enrolls in graduate school.

*Geronimo Rex* was greeted with great enthusiasm by most critics and was nominated for a National Book Award. Jim Harrison, writing in the *New York Times Book Review,* called it "almost a totally successful book" and declared, "the writing is intricate enough to make it hard to believe that it's really a first novel." Although John Skow, in the *Washington Post,* protested that the book's momentum was disrupted by its subplots, he agreed that the language was "raucously good" and anticipated Hannah's next work.

Hannah returned to Harry Monroe in the following novel, *Nightwatchmen.* While studying for his doctorate, Monroe meets Thorpe Trove, a rich but strange figure whose estate functions as a meeting place for several of Monroe's fellow students. Thorpe is obsessed with the Knocker, a mysterious killer plaguing the academic community of Southern Mississippi University. *Nightwatchmen* focuses on Thorpe's efforts to expose the Knocker, for which purpose he recruits an equally eccentric detective, the elderly Howard Hunter. *Nightwatchmen* abounds in scenes or speeches of mutilation and death. In taped accounts, provided by acquaintances of the Knocker's victims, gruesome acts are related in a manner that both reinforces the notion of society as violent and underscores its callous acceptance of mayhem. In addition, hurricane Camille wreaks havoc on the area, accounting for more grisly death and chaos. Perhaps because of these sensational aspects, *Nightwatchmen* failed to entice critics and was ultimately ignored.

In 1978 Hannah produced his first collection of short stories, *Airships.* Equally comprising new work and stories previously featured in *Esquire,* the volume served to confirm Hannah's standing as a unique

Southern writer. Several stories in *Airships* were culled from Hannah's abandoned novel on the adventures of Confederate General Jeb Stuart. Centering on the recollections of maimed survivors of Stuart's campaigns, these stories range in subject from the brutality of war to the obsessive love for Stuart harbored by a homosexual Confederate. In the particularly unsettling "Eating Wives and Friends," Hannah portrays an impending world in which the 1930s are referred to as the "Mild Depression." It is a nightmare of ghoulish depravity, however humorously represented, in which trespassers on private property are shot and eaten, and in which impoverished wanderers are compelled to eat grass and even poison ivy to survive. Writing in the *New York Times Book Review,* Michael Wood hailed the collection's longer works for their "careful, sympathetic wit [in depicting] the string of unlikely shocks and half-hearted enthusiasms that often make up a life." *Time*'s Paul Gray noted that most of the tales "are artfully rounded-off vignettes humping with humor and menace."

Hannah's third novel, *Ray,* recounts the experiences of an apparently immortal, and slightly unhinged, protagonist who served in both the Civil War and the Vietnam War and who also worked in Alabama as a doctor. Like the preceding novels and *Airships, Ray* emphasizes violence and death as its title character recalls a gruesome event in Vietnam, contemplates suicide, and reflects on a defeat suffered in Virginia during the Civil War. *Newsweek*'s Walter Clemons described Ray as "a griper, but also an accepter," adding that "he wakes up every morning voracious for more sex, more fights, more disappointments." Clemons characterized the novel as a work "of brilliant particulars, dizzying juxtapositions and no reassuring narrative transitions." Benjamin DeMott was exuberant in praising *Ray* as "the funniest, weirdest, soul-happiest work by a genuinely young American writer that I've read in a long while."

In *The Tennis Handsome,* Hannah further pursued his interest in graphic, and often absurd, violence. Ostensibly concerned with the exploits of an incredibly attractive tennis player, French Edward, and his twisted mentor, Baby Levaster, *The Tennis Handsome* abounds in scenes of perverse mayhem—including a woman raped by a walrus—and absurdist humor. Reviewer Jack Beatty, in the *New Republic,* complained that the overwhelmingly violent nature of the novel resulted in "a lurid gumbo of inconsequence," lacking in plot, character growth, or logic of development. Ivan Gold, writing in the *New York Times Book Review,* was less critical, conceding that *The Tennis*

*Handsome* might not be Hannah's best book, but that "it's as good a place to start as any." Gold was impressed with the bizarre tone of the novel, and noting that it was partially derived from works first featured in *Airships,* said that "the stories are worth repeating." But Christopher Lehmann-Haupt in the *New York Times* was exhausted by the novel's frantic pace. Observing that Hannah's flamboyant language "palls eventually" and that the book lacked credible characters, Lehmann-Haupt added, "Finally, the only living thing in 'The Tennis Handsome' is the author's fierce determination to stun us with his zaniness."

Hannah's 1985 story collection, *Captain Maximus,* represented for some reviewers a powerful step forward from the failings of *The Tennis Handsome.* One widely noticed story in the collection, "Idaho," is a semiautobiographical work about Hannah's meeting with the late Montana poet Richard Hugo, and features such other well-known writers as Thomas McGuane. Another story, "Power and Light," is an assemblage of "quick camera cuts," in the words of the *Washington Post Book World* critic Doris Betts, among a cast of Seattle characters. George Stade, in the *New York Times Book Review,* claimed that "Power and Light" "is evidence that Mr. Hannah has more than one way of writing like no one else. The prose now is cool, distant, mostly without personal inflection. . . . Anything written by Mr. Hannah is well worth having." While reprising some of the violence of earlier books and once again showcasing Hannah's "vital" prose, *Captain Maximus* also features "more narrative movement" than *Ray* and *The Tennis Handsome,* according to Lehmann-Haupt. Placing Hannah "at the forefront of America's latest crop of experimental writers" alongside Raymond Carver and Frederick Barthelme, Peter Ross in the *Detroit News* felt that Hannah "serves up an unimpeachably original imagination, a mature sense of self-mockery and an abundance of technical and pyrotechnic skill."

In 1987, Hannah emerged with a new novel, *Hey Jack!* Featuring an antiheroic character named Homer, who goes nameless until the last page, the novel showed "in graphic detail," according to Michiko Kakutani in the *New York Times,* "just how short, brutish and nasty life in a small Southern town can be." In this fictional town—which strongly resembles the university community of Oxford, Mississippi—"there are exactly five topics of conversation," Kakutani observed, "money, Negroes, women, religion, and Elvis Presley." Kakutani opined that the novel was made up of rehashed versions of previous

Hannah characters, adding up to a set of misfits without meaning. Jonathan Yardley, in the *Washington Post,* felt that Hannah had "dug himself into a rut" with the book. Thomas R. Edwards, in the *New York Times Book Review,* suggested that "geography, culture, and a sense of his precursors—especially Faulkner—seem to be interfering with [Hannah's] performance." However, Richard Eder in the *Los Angeles Times Book Review* called *Hey Jack!* a "compelling novella," finding that "Homer's wandering cogitations, his tales, his pleasures and his anguish all ramble to a purpose. They test and reveal the tensile strength of a cord that is never really loosed . . . that binds his Southern community and perhaps all communities to their own."

The 1989 *Boomerang* was termed a "brief, minor but brilliant autobiographical novel" by *New York Times Book Review* critic Joanne Kennedy. In this book, the narrator ruminates about his life in a series of episodes which are "held together by three boomerang-throwing sessions." Southern boyhood, failed marriages, drinking, and dogs feature prominently, as do celebrities such as film director Robert Altman, actor Jack Nicholson, and singer-writer Jimmy Buffett. Stating that the book broke no new ground, Kennedy observed, "what we get from Mr. Hannah is instinct and impact over plot, as always. And in clean, spare prose and a distinctive raconteur's voice that could only be Southern, there is originality, power, pain and deadpan humor." Alex Raskin, in the *Los Angeles Times Book Review,* singled out Hannah's satirical characterizations for praise, calling *Boomerang* "a fortuitous blend of novel and autobiography."

Hannah's next novel, *Never Die,* is set in Nitburg, Texas, in 1910, and presents "a surreal version" of the old West, in the words of *Washington Post Book World* reviewer Richard Gehr. Calling the book "entertaining," Gehr raised serious reservations about its "static" characters and its many narrative quirks. Janet Kaye, in the *New York Times Book Review,* was unsettled by the book's combination of violence and parody, as well as its "undeveloped" characters and its plot's lack of conviction.

"There are a thousand discoveries at hand in any book by Barry Hannah, not the least of which are the noble and amazing tricks he can perform with language," Marianne Wiggins wrote in a review of Hannah's short-story collection *Bats Out of Hell* in *The Nation.* She observed, "several [of the stories are] wildly surrealist apocalyptic and postapocalyptic" and "everything, *everything,* Hannah seems to suggest has its double, its doubt, its own mirror image." Most of the protagonists in the stories are angry men who are disillusioned and often violent. A *Los Angeles Times Book Review* critic noted that while the stories often begin humorously, Hannah inevitably clouds "the landscape with pitch-black turns of plot." Richard Burgin asserted in *Washington Post Book World* that although Hannah "is a virtuoso writer with a singular perspective" and that "most of the stories, considered individually, succeed, . . . one wishes that . . . more of them didn't end in such predictable, all-encompassing despair."

Describing his own work for *CA,* Hannah admitted its autobiographical bent, saying, "the main part of my stories always comes out of life. I'm terribly affected by something, obsessed with it, or find a situation I can't forget, and then the rest is imagination. . . . I have to do quite a bit of life or I just don't feel I've anything to say. . . . I don't come in at eight o'clock and hit the typewriter till two every day like some writers. I have to feel something." He has expressed admiration for other writers, such as Ernest Hemingway and Walker Percy, and gratitude to his teachers and literary friends at the University of Arkansas, Bill Harrison, Ben Kimpel, and Jim Whitehead. Hannah credits his graduate school experience with helping make him a writer: "I found my 'soul' in the writing classes I took . . . it turned my whole life around. Even if you just get self-educated around a university, it's good to have a few props and know some good books."

*BIOGRAPHICAL/CRITICAL SOURCES:*

*BOOKS*

*Contemporary Literary Criticism,* Gale, Volume 23, 1983, Volume 38, 1986, Volume 90, 1996.
*Dictionary of Literary Biography,* Volume 6: *American Novelists since World War II,* Second Series, Gale, 1980.

*PERIODICALS*

*Chicago Tribune Book World,* November 23, 1980; July 3, 1983.
*Detroit News,* August 4, 1985.
*Los Angeles Times Book Review,* September 6, 1987, p. 3; September 13, 1987; May 7, 1989, p. 6; February 28, 1993, p. 3.
*Nation,* November 29, 1980; June 1, 1985, pp. 677-79; June 7, 1993, p. 804.
*New Republic,* December 13, 1980; April 18, 1983, p. 39.

*Newsweek,* May 8, 1978; December 1, 1980.

*New York,* May 16, 1983, p. 66.

*New Yorker,* September 9, 1972.

*New York Review of Books,* April 23, 1978; June 27, 1985, pp. 33-34.

*New York Times,* April 15, 1978; April 18, 1983, p. C15; April 29, 1985, p. C18; November 18, 1987.

*New York Times Book Review,* May 14, 1972, April 23, 1978; May 21, 1978; November 16, 1980; December 21, 1981; May 1, 1983, pp. 11, 19; June 9, 1985, p. 14; November 1, 1987; May 14, 1989, p. 19, July 7, 1991, p. 18.

*Saturday Review,* June 10, 1978; November, 1980; March 7, 1993, p. 8.

*Studies in Short Fiction,* summer, 1994, p. 504.

*Time,* May 15, 1978; January 12, 1981; July 22, 1985, p. 70.

*Washington Post,* April 19, 1972; August 26, 1987.

*Washington Post Book World,* June 23, 1985, p. 11; March 16, 1986; August 17, 1986, June 2, 1991, p. 3; March 14, 1993, p. 8.*

*    *    *

## HARRISON, Kathryn 1961-

*PERSONAL:* Born March 20, 1961, in Los Angeles, CA; daughter of Edward M. and Carole Cecile (Jacobs) Lang; married Colin Harrison (an editor and novelist); children: two. *Education:* Attended Stanford University and University of Iowa Writers' Workshop.

*ADDRESSES: Home*—Brooklyn, NY. *Office*—c/o Kate Medina, Random House, 201 East 50th St., New York, NY 10022. *Agent*—Amanda Urban, International Creative Management, 40 West 57th St., New York, NY 10019.

*CAREER:* Writer. Former editor at Viking Publishers, New York City.

*AWARDS, HONORS:* James Michener Fellowship, 1989; artists' fellowship, New York Foundation for the Arts, 1994.

*WRITINGS:*

*Thicker than Water* (novel), Random House (New York City), 1991.

*Exposure* (novel), Random House, 1993.

*Poison* (historical novel), Random House, 1995, published in England as *A Thousand Orange Trees,* Fourth Estate (London), 1995.

*The Kiss* (memoir), Random House, 1997.

*SIDELIGHTS:* With the publication of her 1997 memoir, *The Kiss,* Kathryn Harrison placed herself at the center of a firestorm of controversy. In this personal tale, the novelist tells the story of how with a passionate kiss her father started an incestuous relationship with her that lasted four years, until the death of her mother. What makes Harrison's story different from other exposes of incest, and what raised the controversy, is that Harrison was twenty years old when the kiss occurred. Over the next four years, the once estranged father and daughter carried on an affair, secret meetings in places far from Harrison's college and her father's community, where he had a new wife and family, and a position as a preacher.

Harrison's frank talk about this incestuous affair drew immediate and pointed criticism. One line of criticism accuses the author of using this serious breach of social mores to titillate the masses in order to sell more books, increasing her financial and literary capital. Jonathan Yardley's blunt assessment of Harrison's book represents this view. He writes in the *Washington Post,* "*The Kiss* is trash from the first word to the last, self-promotion masquerading as literature." Other critics fault Harrison for turning a cathartic confrontation of past demons into an exercise in raising the kiss-and-tell bar to absurd heights. "The point is," maintains James Wolcott in the *New Republic,* "just because she wrote it doesn't mean she had to publish it. It is assumed today that all secrets are bad, that withholding them is unhealthy; secrets denied the light of day will only fester." But, according to Wolcott, "There is a big difference between getting something out of your system and putting it on the market." Similarly, for other reviewers, *The Kiss* represents an act of narcissism and evasion of responsibility on Harrison's part.

Harrison and *The Kiss* have not been without their defenders, however. "What's really going on in this memoir," suggests Diane Roberts in the *Atlanta Journal and Constitution,* "has to do with the shifty issues of power, possession, how families live and lie, how the role of parent is not God-given or inviolate, how a child can be both victim and collaborator." And, according to Christopher Lehmann-Haupt in the *New York Times,* Harrison does not sidestep the issues of narcissism and responsibility. He writes: "Ms. Harrison, while not analytical, spins a complex web of clues involving narcissism, repressed desire, her mother's emotional inaccessibility, her father's hunger to recapture the past and her own need for substantiation."

*Harper's Bazaar* contributor Mary Gordon rejects the notion that Harrison's novel is just another kiss-and-tell expose contrived to appeal to the basest of human instincts. She maintains: "*The Kiss* stands out from a welter of recent sensational memoirs because of the complexity of Harrison's moral views; her refusal to allow her carefully crafted 'I' the simple role of victim; and her near absolute avoidance of the prurient—the description of the kiss and another scene . . . are the extent of the sexual specifics." It is not "trash" in Roberts's view. Rather, she declares *The Kiss* "an extraordinary book," "exquisite" and written "the way a poet writes." Notes Lehmann-Haupt: "Her narrative is spare and stark, written in a present tense that perfectly conveys how her experience happened." Harrison stands by her effort to write about that experience and to publish it. As she told Gordon, "There is only one real incest taboo: talking about it. . . . The people who judge me about this book don't judge me for what I did, just for talking about it."

In addition to stirring a controversy among critics, *The Kiss* also confirmed in the minds of some reviewers that, despite the author's prior comments to the contrary, Harrison was mining her own family experience for the material for her first two novels. Carolyn See of the *Los Angeles Times* describes the plot of Kathryn Harrison's first novel, *Thicker than Water,* as "the story of a particular California nightmare: The child who is born in easy, even luxurious circumstances, and soon, way too soon, notices that her fate on Earth is to be discarded and loathed." Isabel, the protagonist of *Thicker than Water,* is abandoned first by a father she's never met and then by her mother, who is not interested in taking care of a child. She is raised quietly by her grandparents in a wealthy suburb of Los Angeles and subjected to regular and frequent visits from her mother, who abuses her. When her father appears, late in her adolescence, he completes a pattern of sexual assault by raping her repeatedly over the two-year period during which her mother struggles with cancer.

Scott Spencer of the *New York Times Book Review* characterizes *Thicker than Water* as "odd but beautifully written." The novel has similarly struck other reviewers, who point to Harrison's lyrical prose, which encompasses such horrifying acts as incest and physical degradation. Sally Emerson explains in the

*Washington Post Book World,* "It is . . . not so much the plot which is compelling, but the mesmeric writing and the control with which the author moves back and forth through different time frames." Michiko Kakutani of the *New York Times* calls the effect of Harrison's writing "devastating." Kakutani adds, "[*Thicker than Water*] is a story written in hallucinatory, poetic prose, yet a story that possesses the harrowing immediacy—and visceral impact—of a memoir." Similarly, Spencer comments, "[Harrison] has produced a beautifully written, unsparingly honest novel."

Spencer then wonders in his 1991 review of *Thicker than Water* (six years before Harrison's public admission in *The Kiss*) if this first novel is more honest than the author is willing to admit. "The first two words of *Thicker than Water* are 'In truth,'" Spencer writes, "and as the novel plunges into a woman's painfully frank and unsparing revelations about her miserable childhood, and her struggle to awaken from its dank, hypnotic spell, this reader felt, at times, that he was reading a harrowing, fully imagined work of nonfiction. There is very little traditional narrative flow, yet the reader remains spellbound not only by the artistry of the writing but by its persistent and often horrifying matter-of-factness." Kakutani echoes this observation, writing, "There is almost no authorial distance between Isabel and her creator, almost no indication that this is a novel we're reading." Even so, as Kakutani finds remarkable, the story successfully presents more than just the tragedy experience by a child, "it also manages to wring from its heroine's story the hope and possibility of transcendence." Harrison's second novel, *Exposure,* also centers on an abnormal relationship between a parent and child; in this case, a photographer-father takes eerily suggestive and morbid pictures of his daughter throughout her childhood and adolescence. Harrison told Patricia A. O'Connell of *Publishers Weekly:* "I wrote about a photographer because I wanted a relationship between a parent and a child in which the former stole something from the latter, and the thing taken was somewhat slippery." The main action of the story takes place during the weeks before a retrospective of Edgar Rogers's work is scheduled at the Museum of Modern Art. Through a variety of perspectives, including first-person monologues, court and private detective reports, and newspaper articles, Harrison constructs the demise of the daughter as she becomes addicted to crystal methedrine and begins to shoplift. The author explained this choice of narrative exposition to interviewer O'Connell: "I had a character who was going through crisis and change; although intelligent, she was not self-aware. I needed a number of mechanisms by which we could see into her . . . because she's not good at telling us about herself."

Critical response to *Exposure* has been warm, both for the issue of artistic freedom versus artistic integrity the novel raises and for Harrison's unconventional method of exposition. Mindi Dickstein of the *Chicago Tribune Book World* remarks: "At their best, stories expose the secrets we live with but cannot utter, and the best writers preserve the unsayable nature of those secrets while capturing them long enough for us to gaze upon their mystery. Kathryn Harrison is such a writer." While noting that "at times Ms. Harrison is heavy-handed and comes close to making a didactic look-what-you've-done-to-this-girl argument," Howard Coale of the *New York Times Book Review* concludes: "Ms. Harrison does not allocate blame without a full analysis of all the ironies and all the nooks and crannies of responsibility." Wendy Smith of the *Washington Post Book World* describes Harrison's "accomplishment" in *Exposure* as "the delineation, in superbly modulated prose, of a woman's painful, tentative journey toward self-knowledge." Of her own work, Harrison commented to O'Connell: "I'm not a doctor, so clinical diagnosis is not my realm. But both physical and mental illnesses are factors in my work. I hope that my imagination in some way illuminates the human condition."

In her third work of fiction, *Poison,* Harrison achieves some artistic distance between herself and her work by setting the story in seventeenth century Spain. Her blending of historical fact and fiction has impressed a number of reviewers. "The historical novel is a vigorously evolving form," observes Laura Argiri in the *Village Voice.* "And Kathryn Harrison's *Poison* is a lively example of that evolution." For *New York Times Book Review* contributor Janet Burroway, "Ms. Harrison's voluminous research is everywhere evident, but so seamlessly matched by invention that the reader neither knows nor cares which is which." Ron Hansen offers a similar evaluation in the *Los Angeles Times Book Review.* He writes, "It's gratifying to find that in this book she's handled the forbidding obligations of historical fiction so well."

Harrison's story follows two women, Maria Luisa and Francisca, who lead very different lives; even so, both women are consumed by a Spain in a period of decline. Maria Luisa (born Marie Louise de Bourbon, the niece of France's king Louis XIV) is an historical figure. She is sent from her homeland to become the queen to Spain's Carlos II and to bear him an heir. Carlos is a boy, retarded and crippled, who lives off of breast milk supplied to him by a team of wet nurses. The daughter of one of these wet nurses and a failed silkworm farmer is Francisca de Luarca. Maria Luisa fails to produce an heir for her incompetent or impotent husband and is poisoned. Francisca pursues forbidden love with a priest and is imprisoned. From her prison cell, Francisca becomes Maria Luisa's biographer, reconstructing the story of the queen, abandoned and destroyed in a strange land. "In a novel of less authority this might be clumsy," comments Burroway, "but in Ms. Harrison's hands it raises, instead, serious questions about the power of imagination and the nature of history."

*Poison* captures the events of Spanish history swirling around these two women as well as the public lives that they live in the Spanish capital; but, it also offers insight into the intimate lives of women in the seventeenth century. For Francisca, there is love. And, in the opinion of Judith Dunford in *Tribune Books,* Harrison's portrayal of this love is "remarkable—crystalline prose perfumed (but not too much; she knows just when to stop) with musky eroticism, bigger enough than life to carry you away." For Maria Luisa, there is no love; there is only duty. "If Harrison writes meltingly about sexual love," adds Dunford, "she does even better at sexual loathing . . . the mixture of disgust, longing, pity and duty in the couplings of Charles [Carlos] and Maria Luisa."

The result of Harrison's blending of fact and fiction to create the lives and loves of these two women "is a fascinating, feminist princess-and-pauper story, gorgeously written and hauntingly told," concludes Hansen. "It is a tale of passion, hopelessness and thwarted ambitions in a harsh and hate-filled century that was, as in all fine historical fiction, quite different than and disturbingly like our own."

## BIOGRAPHICAL/CRITICAL SOURCES:

### BOOKS

*Contemporary Literary Criticism,* Volume 70, Gale (Detroit), 1992.

### PERIODICALS

*Atlanta Journal and Constitution,* March 30, 1997, p. K12.
*Booklist,* May 1, 1995, p. 1551; March 1, 1997, p. 1094.

*Chicago Tribune,* June 4, 1995, p.3.

*Chicago Tribune Book World,* February 21, 1993, p. 5.

*Cosmopolitan,* May, 1995, p. 44.

*Entertainment Weekly,* May 26, 1995, p. 79; March 21, 1997, pp. 30-31.

*Glamour,* May, 1995, p. 172.

*Guardian Weekly,* July 31, 1994, p.28.

*Harper's Bazaar,* April, 1997, p. 136.

*Insight in the News,* June 26, 1995, pp. 24-25.

*Los Angeles Times,* March 18, 1991, p. E3.

*Los Angeles Times Book Review,* June 18, 1995, p. 8.

*New Republic,* March 31, 1997, p. 32.

*New Statesman & Society,* July 28, 1995, p. 40.

*Newsweek,* February 17, 1997, p. 62.

*New York Times,* April 26, 1991, p. C30; February 27, 1997, p. C18.

*New York Times Book Review,* April 21, 1991, pp. 13-14; March 14, 1993, p. 10; December 5, 1993, p. 60; May 29, 1994, p. 20; May 14, 1995, p. 12; September 8, 1996, p. 36; March 30, 1997, p. 11.

*People Weekly,* May 29, 1995, p. 27; March 17, 1997, p. 33.

*Publishers Weekly,* March 1, 1993, pp. 33-34; March 6, 1995, p. 53; February 10, 1997, p. 71.

*Time,* May 29, 1995, p. 71; March 10, 1997, p. 90.

*Tribune Books* (Chicago), July 17, 1994, p. 8; June 4, 1995, p. 3; December 10, 1995, p. 1.

*USA Today,* May 25, 1995, p. D4; March 13, 1997, p. D4.

*Vanity Fair,* February, 1997, pp. 54-58.

*Village Voice,* May 16, 1995, p. 82.

*Wall Street Journal,* March 4, 1997, p. A16.

*Washington Post,* June 9, 1991, p. 11; June 16, 1993, pp. B1, B4; March 5, 1997, p. D2.

*Washington Post Book World,* March 7, 1993, p. 7; April 30, 1995, p. 9.*

*       *       *

## HEARNE, Betsy Gould 1942-

*PERSONAL:* Born October 6, 1942, in Wilsonville, AL; daughter of Kenneth (a doctor) and Elizabeth (Barrett) Gould; married Michael Claffey; children: Joanna Hearne, Elizabeth Claffey. *Education:* Wooster College, B.A., 1964; University of Chicago, M.A., 1968, Ph.D., 1985.

*ADDRESSES: Home*—Urbana, IL. *Agent*—Philippa Brophy, The Sterling Lord Agency, Inc., 660 Madison Ave., New York, NY 10021. *Office*—Graduate School of Library and Information Science, 501 East Daniel, Champaign, IL 61820. *E-mail*—hearne@alexia.lis.uiuc.edu.

*CAREER:* Wayne County Public Library, Wooster, OH, children's librarian, 1964-65; University of Chicago Laboratory Schools, Chicago, IL, children's librarian, 1967-68; *Booklist,* Chicago, children's books editor, 1973-85; *Bulletin of the Center for Children's Books,* children's books editor, 1985-92. University of Illinois at Urbana-Champaign, professor, 1992—. Judge, National Book Awards, 1975, and American Book Awards, 1981.

*MEMBER:* American Library Association (member, Mildred Batchelder Committee, 1973-77, Newbery-Caldecott Award Committee; consultant, Notable Books Committee), Children's Reading Round Table.

*AWARDS, HONORS:* Agnes Sayer Klein Award for Graduate Study, American Library Association, 1979; Children's Reading Round Table Award, 1982.

*WRITINGS:*

*NONFICTION*

(Editor with Marilyn Kaye) *Celebrating Children's Books: Essays on Children's Literature in Honor of Zena Sutherland* (reference), Lothrop (New York City), 1981.

*Choosing Books for Children: A Commonsense Guide* (reference), Delacorte (New York City), 1981, revised edition, 1990.

*Beauty and the Beast: A Study of Aesthetic Survival* (thesis), University of Chicago, 1985.

*Love Lines: Poetry in Person* (poetry for young adults and adults), Simon & Schuster (New York City), 1987.

*Beauty and the Beast: Visions and Revisions of an Old Tale,* University of Chicago Press, 1989.

(Editor with Zena Sutherland and Roger Sutton) *The Best in Children's Books: The University of Chicago Guide to Children's Literature, 1985-1990,* University of Chicago Press, 1991.

*Polaroid and Other Poems of View* (poetry for young adults and adults), photographs by Peter Kiar, Simon & Schuster Children's Books, 1991.

(Editor with Roger Sutton) *Evaluating Children's Books: A Critical Look,* University of Illinois, 1993.

(Editor) *The Zena Sutherland Lectures, 1983-1992,* Houghton (Boston), 1993.

*CHILDREN'S BOOKS*

*South Star,* illustrated by Trina Schart Hyman, Atheneum (New York City), 1977.

*Home,* illustrated by Hyman, Atheneum, 1979.

*Eli's Ghost,* illustrated by Ronald Himler, Simon & Schuster Children's Books, 1987.

(Editor) *Beauties and Beasts,* illustrated by Joanne Caroselli, Oryx (Phoenix), 1993.

*Eliza's Dog,* illustrated by Erica Thurston, Simon & Schuster Children's Books, 1996.

*Seven Brave Women,* illustrated by Bethanne Andersen, Greenwillow (New York City), 1997.

*Listening for Leroy,* Margaret K. McElderry), 1998.

*Beauty and the Beast* (picture book translated from the French), illustrated by Hyman, Holiday House (New York City), in press.

*Mr. Trouble* (picture book), illustrated by Hyman, Holiday House, in press.

*South of the Sun and Moon,* Macmillan/Margaret K. McElderry (New York City), in press.

*OTHER*

Also contributor of articles, reviews, and editorials to periodicals such as *Library Quarterly* and *Signal.* Recordings include "Evaluating Children's Books," Children's Book Council, 1979, and videorecording, *Sharing Books with Young Children,* American Library Association, 1986.

*SIDELIGHTS:* Since Betsy Gould Hearne began work as a children's librarian in the 1960s, she has made a variety of contributions to children's literature. During her career, Hearne worked as a critic, editor, scholar, and children's book writer, and she has also earned advanced degrees and developed her talents as a poet. Hearne's commentaries on children's books can be found in *Booklist* and *The Bulletin of the Center for Children's Books* (where she has worked as a children's book editor). Her books for educators, librarians, and parents include *Choosing Books for Children: A Commonsense Guide* and *Evaluating Children's Books: A Critical Look* (which she edited with Roger Sutton) among others; given this work, Humphrey Carpenter of the *New York Times Book Review* described Hearne as "a distinguished cataloger of children's books." Many of Hearne's children's books, such as *South Star, Eli's Ghost,* and *Beauties and Beasts,* have been well received. This latter book developed from Hearne's historical and interpretive work on the many permutations of the "Beauty and the Beast" tale. Finally, Hearne's two

volumes of poetry have been recommended for mature young adults.

A *Publishers Weekly* critic described Hearne's first book, *South Star,* as "an exciting fantasy." It tells the story of Megan, a young giant girl who has escaped her family's castle, and the Screamer which has frozen the castle and her parents in ice. As Megan flees across a plain from the terrible Screamer, she is befriended and aided by a boy, Randall, who is also on his own. A bear helps the pair find the southern star to follow, and they begin a difficult journey. They finally find a valley populated by Megan's relatives and led by her sister. According to Ethel L. Heins of *Horn Book,* Hearne "successfully creates suspense and casts an atmosphere of primeval magic" in *South Star.*

*Home,* the sequel to *South Star,* returns to Megan's story to find her living with her sister. When Megan dreams that her sister's missing husband is calling for help, she leaves the peaceful valley to find him. While she waits at the seaside for the storms to go away, and to train for a trip across the sea, she once again encounters her friend Randall. They journey across the sea to a desert land ruled by lion people, where Megan's brother-in-law is alive in prison. After battling the king of the land, the three return to the valley. "Both Brendan and Megan return home with a new appreciation for the people and places they left" and "better knowledge of themselves," explained Karen M. Klockner of *Horn Book.* Writing in *School Library Journal,* Margaret A. Dorsey commented that this book is "greatly superior to" *South Star* and "good stuff for growing girls."

Despite its title, *Eli's Ghost* "is definitely not scary," according to Elizabeth S. Watson of *Horn Book.* The action, set in the southern United States, begins when Eli runs away to a swamp to find his long-lost mother. When Eli falls into the water, his mother arrives just in time to save him. Still, Eli's ghost escapes his body and has some fun with the rescue party that arrives. Furthermore, Eli's ghost is nothing like him. "For Eli Wilson," observed a critic in *Bulletin of the Center for Children's Books,* "life will never be the same." Watson concluded in *Horn Book,* "the humor and suspense" of *Eli's Ghost* "will appeal to intermediate readers."

As a reviewer noted in *Publishers Weekly,* "Hearne shapes a convincing portrait of a feisty, resourceful girl" in *Eliza's Dog.* Eliza, who has always wanted a dog, finds a border collie while on vacation with her parents in Ireland. Although Eliza manages to convince her parents to let her keep the dog, she worries that it will grow too large to fit in its carry-cage for the trip back home from Ireland. In addition, Eliza must learn to deal with her new pet and his many needs. "This book has appeal," wrote a *Kirkus Reviews* critic, "mainly for other dog-obsessed children." "The story clearly sends the message that owning a dog entails hard work," pointed out Carol Schene in *School Library Journal.*

In 1979, Hearne went back to graduate school; by 1985, she had completed a dissertation. She published this work, in revised form, in 1989 as *Beauty and the Beast: Visions and Revisions of an Old Tale.* This work traces the beauty and the beast motif from its origins, and takes a look at how it has been revised by various authors, storytellers, and illustrators throughout time for children. "Hearne's conclusions are provocative, illuminating, and stimulating," commented Mary M. Bush of *Horn Book.* "This book is a fine example of critical analysis of a traditional tale" and "offers a wealth of material for adults to use in fostering critical thinking in children," explained Jane Anne Hannigan in *School Library Journal.* Hearne's related book for children, *Beauties and Beasts,* features twenty-seven beauty and the beast folktales from different cultures and time periods. According to Judy Constantinides of *School Library Journal,* this book "will attract the attention of older primary grade children" and it will be useful to those adults "teaching multiculturalism."

More than a critic, editor, scholar and children's book writer, Hearne is also the author of two volumes of poetry. *Love Lines: Poetry in Person* includes fifty-nine poems about love, family, and friends that Hearne wrote over the course of twenty-five years. According to Becki George in *Voice of Youth Advocates,* the work provides "quickly readable free verse" and "includes many sexual references." "None of the book's three sections . . . seems to speak directly to young adult readers," observed Kathleen Whalin of *School Library Journal.* A critic for *Kirkus Reviews* asserted that the volume, "rich in ideas and imagery," "should appeal to anyone mature enough to yearn after love." *Polaroid and Other Poems of View* contains forty-three poems. Many critics enjoyed the black-and-white photos by Peter Kiar, which help introduce each section of poetry. This volume, in the words of Brooke Selby Dillon of *Voice of Youth Advocates,* "will enthrall and delight the mature poetry reader." The "rhythms . . . are capricious and compelling," and the poems are "clearly the work of an

artist in control of her medium," related Nancy Vasilakis of *Horn Book.*

*BIOGRAPHICAL/CRITICAL SOURCES:*

*PERIODICALS*

*Booklist,* October 1, 1993, p. 358; April 1, 1996, p. 1364.
*Bulletin of the Center for Children's Books,* March, 1987, p. 126.
*Horn Book,* December, 1977, pp. 662-63; June, 1979, p. 301; August, 1981, p. 447; September/October, 1987, p. 612; May/June, 1990, pp. 353-54; July/August, 1991, p. 471; September/October, 1997, pp. 558-59.
*Kirkus Reviews,* April 1, 1979, p. 388; January 1, 1987, p. 56; August 1, 1987, p. 1157; May 1, 1991, p. 604; March 15, 1996, p. 448.
*Library Quarterly,* July, 1990, p. 264.
*New York Times Book Review,* March 22, 1987, p. 33; March 25, 1990, p. 25.
*Publishers Weekly,* September 19, 1977, p. 146; September 25, 1987, p. 113; March 18, 1996, p. 70.
*School Library Journal,* October, 1977, pp. 112-13; May, 1979, p. 62; November, 1981, p. 41; February, 1988, p. 88; February, 1990, p. 38; September, 1991, p. 288; June, 1994, p. 55; May, 1996, p. 113.
*Voice of Youth Advocates,* February, 1988, p. 296; August, 1991, p. 189.

\*   \*   \*

## HEBBLETHWAITE, Margaret 1951-

*PERSONAL:* Born June 16, 1951, in London, England; daughter of George (a puppeteer and writer) and Mary (a museum education officer) Speaight; married Peter Hebblethwaite (a writer), July 21, 1974 (deceased); children: Dominic, Anna Cordelia, Benedict. *Ethnicity:* "White." *Education:* Lady Margaret Hall, Oxford, B.A., 1975, M.A., 1977. *Religion:* Roman Catholic.

*ADDRESSES: Home*—45 Marston St., Oxford OX4 1JU, England.

*CAREER:* Writer and broadcaster, 1975—. Oxford University, catechist of Exeter College, 1994—.

*MEMBER:* Society of Authors, European Society of Women for Theological Research, Catholic Theological Association of Great Britain (member of committee, 1984-86).

*WRITINGS:*

(With Kevin Donovan) *The Theology of Penance,* Mercier Press, 1979.

*Motherhood and God,* Geoffrey Chapman, 1984.

*Through Lent with Luke,* Bible Reading Fellowship, 1986.

*Finding God in All Things: Praying with St. Ignatius,* Collins Fount, 1987.

*Basic Is Beautiful: Basic Ecclesial Communities from Third World to First World,* HarperCollins Fount, 1993.

*Base Communities: An Introduction,* Geoffrey Chapman, 1993.

*Six New Gospels: New Testament Women Tell Their Stories,* Geoffrey Chapman, 1994.

Contributor to magazines and newspapers, including *Theology, Way, She, New Blackfriars, Doctrine and Life, Independent, Guardian,* and *Priests and People.* Assistant editor, *Tablet,* 1991—.

*WORK IN PROGRESS: Conversations on Christian Feminism,* with Elaine Storkey, publication by HarperCollins expected in 1999.

*SIDELIGHTS:* Margaret Hebblethwaite told *CA:* "I am committed to the development of the lay ministry in the church, particularly through the means of Ignatian retreats in daily life and the development of base communities throughout the church. I am also a firm supporter of women's ordination and of the ongoing task of developing women's contribution to theology, particularly through discovering female images for God."

\*     \*     \*

**HERBERT, Arthur**
  **See SHAPPIRO, Herbert (Arthur)**

\*     \*     \*

**HERR, Michael 1940(?)-**

*PERSONAL:* Born c. 1940.

*ADDRESSES: Home*—New York, NY.   *Office*—c/o Alfred A. Knopf, Inc., 201 East 50th St., New York, NY 10022.

*CAREER:* Writer.

*WRITINGS:*

*Dispatches* (nonfiction; also see below), Knopf (New York City), 1977.

(Author of narration) Francis Coppola and John Milius, *Apocalypse Now* (screenplay), United Artists, 1979.

(With Guy Peellaert) *The Big Room,* Summit Books (New York City), 1986.

(With Gustav Hasford and Stanley Kubrick) *Full Metal Jacket* (screenplay), Warner Bros., 1987.

*Walter Winchell: A Novel,* Knopf, 1990.

Contributor of articles to *Rolling Stone, Esquire,* and *New American Review.*

*ADAPTATIONS: Dispatches* was adapted into a musical by Elizabeth Swados and produced in New York City at the Martinson Hall/Public Theater, April 18, 1979.

*WORK IN PROGRESS:* A novel about a friendship that spans 25 years.

*SIDELIGHTS: Dispatches,* Michael Herr's book about the Vietnam War, has been hailed not only as perhaps the finest book about Vietnam, but as one of the best books ever written about war. When Herr left the United States in 1967 to serve as war correspondent for *Esquire* magazine, his writing experience was not too impressive: he had worked on the literary magazine at Syracuse University (where he eventually dropped out), had written some travel pieces for *Holiday* magazine, and had held a nonpaying film-criticism job at *New Leader*—which he eventually lost because of his unconventional taste in films. Yet *Dispatches*—published ten years after Herr's return from the fields of war—was hailed as a masterpiece as soon as it appeared in 1977, and critical opinion of it has not waned since that time.

"Major literary scholars of that war are unanimous in their judgments that this "rock 'n' roll work of literary journalism is perhaps the single most powerful book to come out of that war, and the book is almost universally considered a landmark," asserted Donald J. Ringnalda in *Dictionary of Literary Biography.* "Dust jacket blurbs rarely reflect a scholarly consensus, but they do in the case of *Dispatches*. Gloria Emerson claimed that Herr surpassed Stephen Crane in writing about war. Tom Wolfe still maintains that *Dispatches* rivals Erich Maria Remarque's 1929 masterpiece, *All Quiet on the Western Front.*. . . . John Le Carre calls it "the best book I have ever read on men and war in our time."

Reporting the war was a difficult task. "I went to cover the war," Herr noted, "and the war covered me." Herr discovered that he actually enjoyed being there. As Paul Gray wrote, "Herr came to realize that Viet Nam was the most intense experience life was ever likely to offer him." Reveling in the danger of war, Herr wrote: "There were choices everywhere, but they were never choices that you could hope to make. There was even some small chance for personal style in your recognition of the one thing you feared more than any other. You could die in a sudden bloodburning crunch as your chopper hit the ground like dead weight, you could fly apart so that your pieces would never be gathered, you could take one neat round in the lung and go out hearing only the bubble of the last few breaths, you could die in the last stage of malaria with that faint tapping in your ears, and that could happen to you after months of firefights and rockets and machine guns. . . . You could be shot, mined, grenaded, rocketed, mortared, sniped at, blown up and away so that your leavings had to be dropped into a sagging poncho and carried to Graves Registration, that's all she wrote. It was almost marvelous."

As a correspondent, Herr was an oddity in Vietnam for he was there by choice. "A GI would walk clear across a firebase for a look at you if he'd never seen a correspondent before," wrote Herr, "because it was like going to see the Geek, and worth the walk." Another passage reflects the disbelief Herr encountered among soldiers: "'Oh man, you *got* to be kidding me. You guys *asked* to come here?' 'Sure.' 'How long do you have to stay?' he asked. 'As long as we want.' 'Wish *I* could stay as long as *I* want,' the Marine called Love Child said. '*I'd* been home las' March.' 'When did you get here?' I asked. 'Las' March.'"

Although he romanticized many of his own experiences in Vietnam, Herr was still able to see the war as a "story that was as simple as it had always been, men hunting men, a hideous war and all kinds of victims." He wrote of one soldier who escaped death by hiding under the corpses of his fellow soldiers

while the enemy went about bayoneting the dead. In another episode, American troops escaping by helicopter were forced to shoot their Vietnamese allies who'd jeopardized the take-off by also trying to jump aboard.

Herr's writing throughout is oddly detached yet subjective. "He preaches no sermons, draws no morals, enters no ideological disputes," declared Gray. "He simply suggests that some stories must be told—not because they will delight and instruct but because they happened." However, John Leonard called *Dispatches* "a certain kind of reporting come of age—that is, achieving literature. It is the reporting of the 1960's at last addressing itself to great human issues, subjective, painfully honest, scaled of abstractions down to the viscera, the violence and the sexuality understood and transcended." He concluded with one word: "Stunning."

Critics also praise Herr's ear for dialogue. Alfred Kazin wrote, "Herr caught better than anyone else the kooky, funny, inventively desperate code in which the men in the field showed that they were well and truly in shit." Another critic, Geoffrey Wolff, reported that Herr "had ears like no one else's ears over there, and he brought an entire language back alive." Typical of the dialogue in *Dispatches* is one GI's comment when he learns that another soldier will only be in Vietnam for four months. "'Four Months?'" comes the reply. "'Baby, four *seconds* in this whorehouse'll get you greased.'" Another soldier exclaims, "'A dead buddy is some tough shit, but bringing your own ass out alive can sure help you to get over it.'"

Kazin reserved his highest praise for the political aspects of *Dispatches*. Despite his enthusiasm for the language, Kazin claimed that Herr's "big effort is not literary but political. To his generation, Vietnam did come down to so much self-enclosed, almost self-deafened, despair. No one gets above that specific cruel environment." He cites one soldier's rationale for being in Vietnam, "I mean, if we can't shoot these people, what . . . are we doing here?" Explaining why he can't die in Vietnam, another soldier contends, "'Cause it don't exist." Herr contrasts his own position with that of a "young soldier speaking in all bloody innocence, saying, 'All that's just a *load,* man. We're here to kill gooks. Period.'" Herr amends the soldier's comment by insisting that that "wasn't at all true of me. I was there to watch."

Upon returning to America, Herr had to deal with his memories of the war. "Was it possible that they were there and not haunted?," he wondered of his friends from the war. "No, not possible, not a chance. I know I wasn't the only one. Where are they now? (Where am I now?) I stood as close to them as I could without actually being one of them, and then I stood as far back as I could without leaving the planet." While sharing departure with other correspondents, Herr observed: "A few extreme cases felt that the experience there had been a glorious one, while most of us felt that it had been merely wonderful. I think that Viet Nam was what we had instead of happy childhoods."

Gray concluded his review of *Dispatches* by noting, "Herr dared to travel to that irrational place and to come back with the worst imaginable news: war thrives because men still love it." But Bryan defended Herr's position: "To Michael Herr's credit he never ceased to feel deeply for the men with whom he served; he never became callous, always worried for them, agonized over them, on occasion even took up arms to defend them. His greatest service, I'm convinced, is this book."

After completing *Dispatches,* Herr contributed to the screenplay for the movie *Apocalypse Now,* Francis Ford Coppola's celebrated work about the Vietnam War. Herr later contributed to the screenplay for another Vietnam-themed movie, Stanley Kubrick's 1987 film *Full Metal Jacket.* Also in 1987, Herr published *The Big Room,* a collection of biographical sketches of celebrities who had some connection to Las Vegas. Each of the sketches is accompanied by a painting by Guy Peellaert.

Among the people profiled in *The Big Room* is Walter Winchell, the famed newspaper columnist and television broadcaster who was known for his acerbic wit. Herr used his short sketch of Winchell as the basis for a screenplay about the man; after unsuccessful attempts to get a movie made from his screenplay, Herr altered the text into a novel. The result, *Walter Winchell: A Novel,* was published in 1990. It is not a standard novel but rather a combination of novel and screenplay, complete with camera directions, flashbacks, and other cinematic devices. The book follows Winchell from his early vaudevillian days to his first column-a Broadway gossip column-in the 1920s and his growing fame and influence in the 1930s and 1940s. Herr also traces Winchell's decline in the 1950s; despite his earlier courageous opposition to

Hitler and various mobsters, Winchell cooperated with Senator Joseph McCarthy during his notorious anti-Communist witch hunts in the 1950s. Reviewers had mixed opinions of the novel. *Times Literary Supplement* reviewer Philip French remarked that "Herr's book is enjoyable enough, but one would rather have seen the movie." But Chicago *Tribune Books* critic Joseph Coates declared, "Even slightly modified to novel form, this is a brilliant screenplay, full of punchy dialogue, colorful people and places, and period movie devices like spinning headlines that convey both the highly charged era it portrays and the vitality of the times as Winchell himself incarnated it." Similarly, *New York Times Book Review* contributor Judith Rascoe exclaimed that "Herr's screenplay-novel in the style of the 40's not only captures what we've come to think of as the flavor of that era; it also evokes the same ghostly feelings we get while watching a 40's movie today—of actors vigorously alive in an immortal present tense, yet more inaccessible than creatures in a fairy tale."

Herr has not proved to be a prolific author, but as Ringnalda asserted, "That should not in the least minimize the singular and astounding achievement of *Dispatches.* Stephen Crane also wrote only one great book [*The Red Badge of Courage*], about a different divisive war, and one hundred years later his fame remains secure. Many believe that *Dispatches* will have similar staying power."

## BIOGRAPHICAL/CRITICAL SOURCES:

### BOOKS

*American Myth and the Legacy of Vietnam,* Columbia University Press (New York City), 1986, pp. 150-60.

Beidler, Philip D., *American Literature and the Experience of Vietnam,* University of Georgia Press (Athens), 1982, pp. 64, 141-48.

Connery, Thomas B., editor, *A Sourcebook of American Literary Journalism: Representative Writers in an Emerging Genre,* Greenwood Press (Westport, CT), 1992, pp. 281-95.

*Dictionary of Literary Biography,* Volume 185: *American Literary Journalists, 1945-1995, First Series,* Gale (Detroit), 1997.

Gilman, Owen W., Jr., and Lorrie Smith, editors, *America Rediscovered: Critical Essays on Literature and Film of the Vietnam War,* Garland (New York City), 1990, pp. 189-204.

Hayles, N. Katherine, editor, *Chaos and Order,* University of Chicago Press (Chicago), 1991.

Herr, Michael, *Dispatches,* Knopf, 1977.

Limon, John, *Writing after War,* Oxford University Press (Oxford, England), 1994.

Myers, Thomas, *Walking Point: American Narratives of Vietnam,* Oxford University Press, 1988, pp. 146-71.

Ringnalda, Donald J., *Fighting and Writing the Vietnam War,* University Press of Mississippi (Jackson), 1994, pp. 71-89.

Schroeder, Eric James, *Vietnam, We've All Been There,* Praeger (New York City), 1992, pp. 33-49.

*PERIODICALS*

*Atlantic,* January, 1978.

*Book World,* November 6, 1977.

*Critic,* July, 1978, pp. 4-5.

*Esquire,* March 1, 1978.

*Los Angeles Times,* June 21, 1987; June 26, 1987; April 15, 1990, p. 22.

*Los Angeles Times Book Review,* September 20, 1987, p. 18.

*Nation,* June 18, 1990, p. 862.

*New Republic,* November 5, 1990, p. 27.

*New Statesman,* September 14, 1990. p. 37.

*Newsweek,* November 14, 1977; June 29, 1987.

*New Times,* November 11, 1977.

*New York Review of Books,* December 8, 1977, pp. 34-35; November 22, 1990, p. 16.

*New York Times,* October 28, 1977; April 19, 1979; June 26, 1987; May 14, 1990.

*New York Times Book Review,* November 20, 1977; May 20, 1990, p. 12.

*Observer,* September 16, 1990, p. 55.

*Publishers Weekly,* March 30, 1990, p. 33; February 20, 1995, p. 118.

*Saturday Review,* January 7, 1978.

*South Atlantic Quarterly,* 79, 1980, pp. 141-151.

*Time,* November 7, 1977; June 29, 1987.

*Times Literary Supplement,* September 14, 1990, p. 970.

*Tribune Books* (Chicago), January 3, 1988, p. 6; May 13, 1990, p. 3.

*Washington Post,* November 4, 1977, p. D1; June 26, 1987; June 28, 1987; June 12, 1990, p. E1.

*Washington Times,* May 31, 1990, p. E1.

*OTHER*

*Back in the World: Writing after Vietnam* (videotape), American Arts Project (New York City), 1984.*

## HILL, Lee Sullivan 1958-

*PERSONAL:* Born September 2, 1958, in Hartford, CT; daughter of Philip Richard Sullivan (a physician) and Nancy Doyle Lee (a systems manager; maiden name, Doyle); married Gary William Hill (a construction purchasing manager), May 8, 1982; children: Adam Doherty, Colin James. *Education:* Lafayette College, A.B., Engineering, 1980. *Politics:* Registered Democrat. *Religion:* Episcopalian.

*CAREER:* Office of Robert Cameron, Dedham, MA, member of land surveying crew, 1978; Ford Motor Co., Steel Division, Dearborn, MI, summer intern, 1979; Turner Construction Co., Washington, DC, 1980-87, began as field engineer for the construction of a wastewater treatment plan, became senior estimator; Turner Construction Co., Shelton, CT, part-time estimator, 1995-96; writer, 1996—. Riding teacher, Woodland Horse Center, Silver Spring, MD; trainer and exerciser, Something Extra Arabian Farm, Salisbury, CT. Volunteer at local schools and libraries.

*MEMBER:* Society of Children's Book Writers and Illustrators, Foundation for Children's Books, Children's Reading Round Table, National Trust for Historic Preservation, Nature Conservancy.

*WRITINGS:*

*"BUILDING BLOCK BOOKS"; PUBLISHED BY CAROLRHODA (MINNEAPOLIS, MN)*

*Bridges Connect,* 1997.

*Roads Take Us Home,* 1997.

*Towers Reach High,* 1997.

*Dams Give Us Power,* 1997.

*Canals Are Water Roads,* 1997.

*Farms Feed the World,* 1997.

*Parks Are to Share,* 1997.

*Libraries Take Us Far,* 1998.

*Schools Help Us Learn,* 1998.

*WORK IN PROGRESS:* Six volumes in the series "Get Around Books," including *Get Around in the City, Get Around in the Country, Get Around in Air and Space, Get Around on Water, Get Around for Fun,* and *Get Around with Cargo,* publication by Carolrhoda expected in fall, 1998; several nonfiction books; a folk tale; a historical novel.

*SIDELIGHTS:* Lee Sullivan Hill told *CA:* "I write because I love putting thoughts on paper, creating beautiful books. I love to share my dreams and ideas and knowledge with people everywhere—especially children. The more I write, the more I want [and love] to write.

"As a child I never said, 'I want to be a writer when I grow up.' I always planned to be an architect or a veterinarian, but I did adore reading. My list of favorite authors included Robert Louis Stevenson, P. D. Eastman, Laura Ingalls Wilder, J. R. R. Tolkien, C. S. Lewis . . . the list could go on and on. . . . It's not that I couldn't write; the thought of writing as a profession just didn't occur to me. In fact, a teacher at Wellesley High School once wrote a note on a fairy tale I had written, 'Lee, have you ever considered a career writing books for children?' At the time, I laughed, pleased with the grade of 'A plus.' But write? You know the old saying, to write what you know. I couldn't imagine that anyone would want to read about my boring life. How could I write?

"I began to write because I loved to read—and to save my sanity. I had taken a leave of absence from my construction estimating job when my first child was born, and I continued to stay at home with my second. I enjoyed my babies, but felt my brain power slipping away. So I began to write. Once I started, I found I couldn't stop!

"When I became serious about my writing, I took a class and joined the Society of Children's Book Writers and Illustrators, whose conferences gave me the specialized knowledge to compete in the field of children's literature. By the way—there was never any question for whom I would write. Stories for children just came naturally to me. I could even see the books in my hands.

"I didn't have to wait long to see a real book. The first piece I submitted to editors was accepted on the third try. *Bridges Connect* expresses my love of structures, my love of engineering. Carolrhoda Books recognized this. In fact, the publisher decided to launch a whole series that became the 'Building Block Books.'"

*       *       *

**HIMMELMAN, John C. 1959-**

*PERSONAL:* Born October 3, 1959, in Kittery, ME; son of John A. (manager, New York Stock Exchange)

and Pauline (a receptionist; maiden name, Nault) Himmelman; married Elizabeth Shanahan (an art teacher), September 6, 1982; children: Jeffrey Carl, Elizabeth Ann. *Education:* School of Visual Arts, B.F.A., 1981. *Politics:* Independent. *Religion:* Christian. *Avocational interests:* Nature photography, backpacking, travel.

*ADDRESSES: Home and office*—67 Schnoor Road, Killingworth, CT 06419. *E-mail*—jhimmel@connix.com.

*CAREER:* Writer and illustrator, 1981—. Teacher of children's book writing and illustration, lecturer on nature topics. Worked variously as a cook and carpenter.

*MEMBER:* Society of Children's Book Writers and Illustrators, The Lepidopterists Society, Connecticut Butterfly Association (co-founder and director), Connecticut Botanical Society, Connecticut Entomological Society, Connecticut Ornithological Society, New Haven Bird Club (director and past president), Killingworth Land Trust (director).

*AWARDS, HONORS:* A Book Can Develop Empathy Award, New York State Humane Association, 1991, for *Ibis, A True Whale Story.*

*WRITINGS:*

*SELF-ILLUSTRATED; FOR YOUNG PEOPLE*

*Talester the Lizard,* Dial (New York City), 1982.
*Amanda and the Witch Switch,* Viking (New York City), 1985.
*Amanda and the Magic Garden,* Viking, 1986.
*The Talking Tree, or, Don't Believe Everything You Hear,* Viking, 1986.
*Montigue on the High Seas,* Viking, 1988.
*The Ups and Downs of Simpson Snail,* Dutton (New York City), 1989.
*The Day-Off Machine,* Silver Burdett (Morristown, NJ), 1990.
*Ellen and the Goldfish,* Harper (New York City), 1990.
*The Great Leaf Blast-Off,* Silver Burdett, 1990.
*Ibis, A True Whale Story,* Scholastic (New York City), 1990.
*The Clover County Carrot Contest,* Silver Burdett, 1991.
*A Guest Is a Guest,* Dutton, 1991.
*The Super Camper Caper,* Silver Burdett, 1991.
*Simpson Snail Sings,* Dutton, 1992.
*Wanted: Perfect Parents,* Troll (Mahwah, NJ), 1993.

*I'm Not Scared! A Book of Scary Poems,* Scholastic, 1994.

*Lights Out!,* Troll, 1995.

*J.J. Versus the Babysitter,* Troll, 1996.

*Honest Tulio,* Troll, 1997.

*The Animal Rescue Club,* HarperCollins (New York City), 1998.

*A Salamander's Life,* Children's Press (New York City), 1998.

*A Ladybug's Life,* Children's Press, 1998.

*A Luna Moth's Life,* Children's Press, 1998.

*A Slug's Life,* Children's Press, 1998.

*A Dandelion's Life,* Children's Press, 1998.

*A Wood Frog's Life,* Children's Press, 1998.

*ILLUSTRATOR; FOR YOUNG PEOPLE*

Barbara Ware Holmes, *Charlotte Cheetham, Master of Disaster,* Harper, 1985.

Marjorie Sharmat, *Go to Sleep, Nicholas Joe,* Harper, 1986.

Michele Stepto, *Snuggle Piggy and the Magic Blanket,* Dutton, 1986.

Holmes, *Charlotte the Starlet,* HarperCollins, 1988.

Holmes, *Charlotte Shakespeare and Annie the Great,* HarperCollins, 1989.

Marcia Leonard, *Rainboots for Breakfast,* Silver Burdett, 1989.

Leonard, *Shopping for Snowflakes,* Silver Burdett, 1989.

Julia Hoban, *Buzby,* HarperCollins, 1990.

Leonard, *What Next?,* Silver Burdett, 1990.

Eric Carpenter, *Young Christopher Columbus: Discoverer of New Worlds,* Troll, 1992.

Andrew Woods, *Young George Washington: America's First President,* Troll, 1992.

Leslie Kimmelman, *Hanukkah Lights, Hanukkah Nights,* HarperCollins, 1992.

Hoban, *Buzby to the Rescue,* HarperCollins, 1993.

Wendy Lewison, *Let's Count,* Joshua Morris, 1995.

Carolyn Graham, *The Story of Myrtle Marie,* Harcourt, 1995.

Graham, *The Story of the Fisherman and the Turtle Princess,* Harcourt, 1995.

Claire Nemes, *Young Thomas Edison: Great Inventor,* Troll, 1995.

Kimmelman, *Hooray, It's Passover!,* HarperCollins, 1996.

Kimmelman, *Uncle Jake Blows the Shofar,* HarperCollins, 1998.

Kimmelman, *Sound the Shofar!: A Story for Rosh Hashanah and Yom Kippur,* HarperCollins, 1998.

*OTHER*

Also author of *Ben's Birthday Wish* and *Sarah and the Terns,* published by Harcourt; illustrator of *Animal Countdown* and *The Christmas Star,* published by Joshua Morris, and *The Myrtle Marie Chant Book,* published by Harcourt; illustrator of *Ugrashimataro* (a children's animated video), ALC Press. Contributor of articles to *Birdwatcher's Digest* and illustrations to *Wildlife Conservation Magazine.*

*WORK IN PROGRESS:* Eight books for the "Nature Up-Close" series for Grolier, each of which will feature an insect, plant, or animal as it goes through the cycle of life; *Animal Rescue Club,* for Harper, about a group of children who rescue and rehabilitate injured and orphaned wildlife.

*SIDELIGHTS:* John C. Himmelman has written or illustrated more than forty books for young people. After considering a career as an artist or veterinarian, Himmelman choose art and enrolled at the School of Visual Arts in 1977. He took courses in cartooning, advertising, and creative writing, but found that "the prospect of making a living in these fields was frightening!" as he recalled to *CA.* "By the last half of my fourth and last year of college, I still had no idea of how I was going to make a living as an artist. Then, for the fun of it, I took a course in writing and illustrating children's books. It was taught by Dale Payson. One of the assignments was to write and illustrate your own book. (This was close to the end of the course.) I did a story about a lizard named Talester. My teacher liked it and showed it to her editor at Dial Publishers, and *Talester the Lizard* became my first published book! I now knew what I wanted to do."

A reviewer for *Publishers Weekly* noted that Himmelman's first self-illustrated work, *Talester the Lizard,* was "sure to please tots and beginning readers." *Talester* tells the story of a pop-eyed green lizard who lives inside a curled-up leaf that hangs over a pond. Every day, he peeks out of his house to see his reflection in the water below, which he thinks is another lizard. But one day, the pond dries up and his friend disappears. Talester then sets out on a comic adventure in search of his missing friend, but is unable to find him. He returns home in a rainstorm, and is amazed to find that his friend has reappeared. "Pastel pictures, spare in composition, make it clear that Talester sees his reflection," stated Zena Sutherland of the *Bulletin of the Center for Children's Books,* "and children can enjoy the superiority of knowing that."

Another of Himmelman's early successes came with his "Amanda" books, *Amanda and the Witch Switch* and *Amanda and the Magic Garden.* Both stories center around a well-meaning witch who encounters trouble despite her best efforts. In the first book, Amanda walks through the woods using her magic for good things. She meets a toad and grants his wish to become a witch. The toad, however, uses his powers badly, turning Amanda into a toad, and making a bee become the size of a bear. After the bee attacks him, the toad asks Amanda to restore him to his old self. A reviewer for *Publishers Weekly* called the story "entrancing, graced by witty, almost speaking pictures in brilliant hues." In the second book, Amanda plants magic seeds that grow giant vegetables, only to find that any animals eating the vegetables become huge as well. She finally finds another spell that undoes the damage: she grows tiny vegetables that restore the animals to their original size. Although Barbara Peklo of *School Library Journal* called the story "strained," Denise M. Wilms of *Booklist* commented that "the changing proportions add a comical element that will appeal to children."

Himmelman's self-illustrated book, *Wanted: Perfect Parents,* tells the story of a young boy named Gregory who posts a "help wanted" sign on his bedroom door. When his parents ask him about it, he provides them with a detailed description of the qualities that he felt would make up ideal parents. Perfect parents would never make their children clean their rooms, for example, but would allow them to purchase 117 pets. Gregory's descriptions become more and more outrageous until finally he comes up with the most important requirement: perfect parents would tuck their children into bed, wish them sweet dreams, and check under the bed for monsters. Writing in *Booklist,* Deborah Abbott stated that "the read-aloud crowd will love the fantasies of this 'perfect' world, made thoroughly enticing by Himmelman's whimsical color drawings."

In addition to writing and illustrating his own books, Himmelman has helped other people to become published authors. Along with an author-illustrator friend, Kay Kudlinski, he established a "traveling school" known as Storycraft Studios for this purpose. "Over the years, several of our students have gotten published, which is as exciting to me as getting one of my own books published," he related to *CA.* Himmelman also visits schools and libraries to teach children the basics of creating stories and to present slide shows about birds, butterflies, moths, and amphibians. He also enjoys watching and photographing animals, particularly the annual migration of birds along the coast of Connecticut. "So many natural events," Himmelman concluded, "so many stories to be inspired by them."

*BIOGRAPHICAL/CRITICAL SOURCES:*

*PERIODICALS*

*Booklist,* March 1, 1987, p. 1013; March 15, 1988, p. 1258; December 1, 1989, p. 751; June 1, 1991, p. 1883; October 15, 1993.
*Bulletin of the Center for Children's Books,* June, 1982, p. 188; January, 1986, p. 87; February, 1988, p. 118.
*Kirkus Reviews,* January 1, 1988, p. 54; August 1, 1989, p. 1158; November 1, 1989, p. 1602; August 15, 1990, p. 1176; June 1, 1991, p. 736; January 1, 1997, p. 59.
*Publishers Weekly,* February 5, 1982, p. 387; June 28, 1985, p. 75; December 11, 1987, p. 64; January 15, 1988, p. 97; June 29, 1990, p. 101; March 8, 1991, p. 74; September 7, 1992, p. 62; May 1, 1995, p. 58.
*School Library Journal,* October, 1985, p. 155; August, 1987, p. 69; December, 1988, p. 87; January, 1991, p. 86; March, 1991, p. 173; October, 1992, p. 42; May, 1996, p. 92.

\*   \*   \*

**HINTON, Richard W.**
**See ANGOFF, Charles**

\*   \*   \*

**HIRSCHI, Ron 1948-**

*PERSONAL:* Name pronounced "Hershey"; born May 18, 1948, in Bremerton, WA; son of Glenn W. (a lumber mill mechanic) and Doris (Hoffman) Hirschi; married Brenda Dahl (a grocery clerk), July 19, 1969; children: Nichol. *Education:* University of Washington, B.S., 1974, graduate research in wildlife ecology, 1974-76. *Politics:* Independent. *Religion:* Independent.

*ADDRESSES: Office*—Point No Point Treaty Council, 7850 Northeast Little Boston Rd., Kingston, WA 98346.

*CAREER:* Washington Game Department, Seattle, biologist, 1976-81; North Kitsap Schools, Poulsbo, WA, counselor in Indian education program, 1984-85; author, 1985—; Point No Point Treaty Council, Kingston, WA, biologist, 1988—.

*MEMBER:* National Audubon Society.

*AWARDS, HONORS: Headgear* and *One Day on Pika's Peak* were each chosen one of Child Study Association's Children's Books of the Year, 1986; Outstanding Science Trade Book for Children, National Science Teachers Association, 1986, for *Headgear,* and 1987, for *City Geese, Who Lives in . . . the Forest?,* and *What Is a Bird?*

*WRITINGS:*

*FOR CHILDREN*

*Headgear,* photographs by Galen Burrell, Dodd (New York City), 1986.
*One Day on Pika's Peak,* photographs by Burrell, Dodd, 1986.
*City Geese,* photographs by Burrell, Dodd, 1987.
*What Is a Bird?,* photographs by Burrell, Walker (New York City), 1987.
*Where Do Birds Live?,* photographs by Burrell, Walker, 1987.
*The Mountain Bluebird,* Dodd, 1988.
*What Is a Horse?,* photographs by Linda Quartman Younker, Walker, 1989.
*Where Do Horses Live?,* photographs by Younker, Walker, 1989.
*What Is a Cat?,* photographs by Younker, Walker, 1991.
*Where Do Cats Live?,* photographs by Younker, Walker, 1991.
*Harvest Song,* illustrated by Deborah Haeffele, Cobblehill (New York City), 1991.
*Loon Lake,* photographs by Daniel J. Cox, Cobblehill, 1991.
*Seya's Song,* illustrated by Constance R. Bergum, Sasquatch Books (Seattle), 1992.
*Hungry Little Frog,* photographs by Dwight Kuhn, Cobblehill, 1992.
*Turtle's Day,* photographs by Kuhn, Cobblehill, 1994.
*Dance with Me,* photographs by Thomas D. Mangelsen, Cobblehill, 1995.

*When the Wolves Return,* photographs by Mangelsen, Cobblehill, 1995.
*People of Salmon and Cedar,* illustrated by Deborah Cooper, Cobblehill, 1995.

Contributor to periodicals, including *Owl.*

*"WHERE ANIMALS LIVE" SERIES; FOR CHILDREN; PHOTOGRAPHS BY BURRELL*

*Who Lives in . . . the Forest?,* Dodd, 1987.
*Who Lives in . . . Alligator Swamp?,* Dodd, 1987.
*Who Lives in . . . the Mountains?,* Putnam (New York City), 1988.
*Who Lives on . . . the Prairie?,* Putnam, 1988.

*"HOW ANIMALS LIVE" SERIES; FOR YOUNG PEOPLE; PHOTOGRAPHS BY MANGELSEN; PUBLISHED BY COBBLEHILL*

*A Time for Babies,* 1993.
*A Time for Sleeping,* 1993.
*A Time for Playing,* 1994.
*A Time for Singing,* 1994.

*"WILDLIFE SEASONS" SERIES; FOR YOUNG PEOPLE; PHOTOGRAPHS BY MANGELSEN; PUBLISHED BY COBBLEHILL*

*Winter,* 1990.
*Spring,* 1991.
*Summer,* 1991.
*Fall,* 1991.

*"DISCOVER MY WORLD" SERIES; FOR YOUNG PEOPLE; ILLUSTRATED BY BARBARA BASH; PUBLISHED BY BANTAM (NEW YORK CITY)*

*Forest,* 1991.
*Ocean,* 1991.
*Desert,* 1992.
*Mountain,* 1992.

*"ONE EARTH" SERIES; FOR YOUNG PEOPLE; PHOTOGRAPHS BY ERWIN AND PEGGY BAUER, EXCEPT AS NOTED*

*Where Are My Bears?,* Bantam, 1992.
*Where Are My Prairie Dogs and Black-Footed Ferrets?,* Bantam, 1992.
*Where Are My Puffins, Whales, and Seals?,* Bantam, 1992.
*Where Are My Swans, Whooping Cranes, and Singing Loons?,* Bantam, 1992.

*Save Our Forests,* National Audubon Society (New York City), 1993.

*Save Our Oceans and Coasts,* photographs by E. and P. Bauer and others, Delacorte (New York City), 1993.

*Save Our Prairies and Grasslands,* Delacorte, 1994.

*Save Our Wetlands,* Delacorte, 1994.

*"WILDLIFE WATCHER'S FIRST GUIDE" SERIES; FOR YOUNG PEOPLE; PHOTOGRAPHS BY MANGELSEN; PUBLISHED BY COBBLEHILL*

*Faces in the Forest,* 1997.

*Faces in the Mountains,* 1997.

SIDELIGHTS: Wildlife biologist and writer Ron Hirschi once recalled to *CA*: "When I was growing up, I spent *all* my free time in the woods, at the beach, or out on the water in boats my father made for me. It was a wonderful childhood and a great way to learn about animals and their needs." As it would prompt his later choice of a career, so these early experiences of nature would also direct him toward becoming a children's author by inspiring such books as *One Day on Pika's Peak, When the Wolves Return,* and several series of nature guides for young people. With numerous books on plants, animals, and their habitats to his credit, Hirschi has opened a wide window to the world of nature for young readers. As *School Library Journal* reviewer Eva Elisabeth Von Ancken commented of his contributions to the National Audubon Society-sponsored "One Earth" series for children, "books such as these may be vital steps in saving what remains of the Earth's once abundant species."

An idea for an article he submitted to *Owl* magazine, a publication of the Canadian Young Naturalist Foundation, would eventually become Hirschi's first published book for children. "The idea I submitted to *Owl* was about horns and antlers. My editor thought it wasn't quite right for the magazine, but she liked the concept and wrote a few thoughts that triggered my imagination enough to rewrite the idea as a nonfiction book." That rejected idea became *Headgear,* which was published in 1986.

Hirschi's "Where Animals Live" series was based on a set of books he wrote for adults while he was employed by the Washington State Game Department. Including the titles *Who Lives in . . . the Mountains?* and *Who Lives on . . . the Prairie?,* the series is designed to appeal to a preschool audience, with its color photographs of animals in their habitats and a

prose style that Nancy Vasilakis praised in a *Horn Book* review as "brief and expressive, never talking down to its young audience." Each volume includes a supplement for adults and older children that provides further information on the many animals that Hirschi features in each book—from such common creatures as a chipmunk to exotic birds like egrets and the gallinule. While noting the basic approach of the "Where Animals Live" books, Jacqueline Elsner commented in a *School Library Journal* review that Hirschi's work "is sure to inspire an appreciation for wildlife and conservation in the very young."

In addition to his "Where Animals Live" books, Hirschi has authored several other nature book series, including "Discover My World," each illustrated by artist Barbara Bash. Featuring titles like *Ocean, Forest,* and *Mountain,* each book is designed in a question-and-answer format. Detailed watercolor drawings of a particular animal's features—eyes, legs, teeth—encourage up-close observation by budding scientists so they can hypothesize what animal each picture represents, in answer to the question "Who am I?" that is posed on every double-page spread. Other series by Hirschi include "The One Earth," which encourages young readers to actively engage in protecting and preserving the Earth's endangered areas, and "Wildlife Seasons," each book of which documents the myriad of seasonal changes that occur in the natural world through beautiful color photographs by Thomas D. Mangelsen.

Picture books featuring animal characters in realistic natural settings are another way Hirschi has promoted a love of the natural world, especially to really young audiences. His *Hungry Little Frog* uses a tiny spring peeper's quest for dinner as the basis for a counting book: one ladybug, four strawberries, five robin's eggs, and so on. In *Harvest Song,* published in 1991, he shows the passages of the seasons as viewed through the eyes of a young girl visiting her grandmother's farm. Hirschi's *Turtle's Day,* illustrated with color photographs by nature photographer Dwight Kuhn, follows an eastern box turtle as he makes his daily rounds, scouting around for food, keeping out of the way of hungry bobcats, and righting himself after being turned over onto his back. "Hirschi conveys basic facts in a direct, lively manner that provides immediacy" to young readers, noted Diane Nunn in her review of *Turtle's Day* for *School Library Journal.*

One of many well-illustrated books on birds that Hirschi has written, 1989's *The Mountain Bluebird* presents readers with a complete portrait of a bird whose numbers have been steadily decreasing due to the influence of mankind on its Rocky Mountain habitat. Praising the work as having "tremendous application as a reference tool," an *Appraisal* reviewer added that *The Mountain Bluebird* "is perfect for pleasure reading. Both young and old will enjoy the beauty of the bluebirds and their surroundings as portrayed in this wonderful book."

In 1988 Hirschi accepted a job with Washington State's S'Klallam Indian Tribe, acting to protect and help enforce the S'Klallam tribe's treaty rights to fish and wildlife in reservation areas, especially against deforestation. Story is one way that the S'Klallam preserve their cultural traditions, and Hirschi reflects those rich traditions in 1993's *Seya's Song*. Using words of native S'Klallam speakers, a young girl describes the life cycle of the region's salmon against the changes wrought by the seasons and the activities of her tribe. With his characteristic fluid prose, which Janice Del Negro characterized in a *Booklist* review as "simple, poetic, and concrete," Hirschi paints a portrait of a rare Native American culture and language that reflects its origins in nature.

"When I think about the inspiration for my books, the connection with my childhood experiences always comes through," Hirschi explained to *CA*. "But, my experiences as a biologist are also important in shaping the book themes. Now, I write nonfiction almost exclusively. I still pursue some fiction, but I remain a biologist and have a strong need to communicate through children's books all the ideas I have about our relationship with animals and the land."

*BIOGRAPHICAL/CRITICAL SOURCES:*

*PERIODICALS*

*Appraisal,* spring 1987, pp. 31-32; fall, 1987, pp. 32-3; fall 1988, pp. 31-33; summer, 1990, pp. 25-26; winter 1991, pp. 29-30; winter 1992, p. 70; winter 1993, pp. 60-61; fall 1994, pp. 76-77.
*Booklist,* October 15, 1990, p. 444; August 1991, p. 2149; September 15, 1991, pp. 160-62; December 15, 1992, p. 739; January 1, 1993, p. 806; April 1, 1994, pp. 1453, 1457; April 15, 1994, p. 1530.
*Bulletin of the Center for Children's Books,* May 1987, pp. 168-69; February 1988, pp. 117-18.
*Horn Book,* May-June, 1987, pp. 356-57; January-February, 1988, p. 85; March-April, 1988, pp. 223-24.

*Kirkus Reviews,* December 1, 1987, p. 1675; July 1, 1989, p. 990; July 15, 1991, p. 938.
*Publishers Weekly,* October 4, 1991, p. 89; November 9, 1992.
*School Library Journal,* January, 1988, pp. 72-73; November, 1990, p. 103; January, 1993, p. 92; February, 1994, p. 110; July, 1994, pp. 94-95; February, 1995, p. 107; October, 1995, p. 148.*

\*          \*          \*

**HOFFMAN, Lee 1932-**
   **(Georgia York)**

*PERSONAL:* Born August 14, 1932, in Chicago, IL; daughter of William E. and Vera (Ray) Hoffman; married Larry Shaw (a science fiction editor; divorced)*. Education:* Armstrong Junior College, A.A., 1951. *Politics:* "Confused."

*ADDRESSES: Home*—401 Sunrise Trail N.W., Port Charlotte, FL 33952. *Agent*—Henry Morrison, Inc., 58 West Tenth St., New York, NY 10011.

*CAREER:* Freelance writer, 1965—. Employed in various jobs, principally in the printing industry. Active in amateur publishing, 1950—. Instructor for Writers Workshop.

*MEMBER:* International Fortean Organization.

*AWARDS, HONORS:* Spur Award, Western Writers of America, for best western novel of 1967, for *The Valdez Horses;* guest of honor at World Science Fiction Convention, 1982.

*WRITINGS:*

*In and Out of Quandry* (bound with *Up to the Sky in Ships* by A. Bertram Chandler), edited by Charles J. Hitchcock, New England Science Fiction Association (Cambridge, MA), 1982.

*WESTERN NOVELS*

*Gunfight at Laramie,* Ace Books (New York City), 1966.
*The Legend of Blackjack Sam,* Ace Books, 1966.
*Bred to Kill,* Ballantine (New York City), 1967.
*The Valdez Horses,* Doubleday (New York City), 1967.

*Dead Man's Gold,* Ace Books, 1968.
*The Yarborough Brand,* Avon (New York City), 1968.
*West of Cheyenne,* Doubleday, 1969.
*Wild Riders,* Signet Books (New York City), 1969.
*Return to Broken Crossing,* Ace Books, 1969.
*Loco,* Doubleday, 1969.
*Wiley's Move,* Dell (New York City), 1973.
*The Truth about the Cannonball Kid,* Dell, 1975.
*Fox,* Doubleday, 1976.
*Trouble Valley,* Ballantine, 1976.
*Nothing but a Drifter,* Doubleday, 1976.
*Sheriff of Jack Hollow,* Dell, 1977.
*The Land Killer,* Doubleday, 1978.

SCIENCE FICTION NOVELS

*Telepower,* Belmont Publishing (New York City), 1967.
*The Caves of Karst,* Ballantine, 1969.
*Always the Black Knight,* Avon, 1970.
*Change Song,* Doubleday, 1970.

HISTORICAL ROMANCE NOVELS; UNDER PSEUDONYM GEORGIA YORK

*Savage Key,* Fawcett (New York City), 1979.
*Savannah Grey,* Fawcett, 1981.
*Savage Conquest,* Fawcett, 1983.

OTHER

Contributor to science fiction anthologies, including *Orbit 9,* edited by Damon Knight, Putnam (New York City), 1971, *Again Dangerous Visions,* edited by Harlan Ellison, Doubleday, 1972, and *Earth in Transit,* edited by Sheila Schwartz, Dell, 1976. Contributor to magazines, including *Cars* and *Miniatures and Dollhouse World.* Editor and publisher, *Quandry,* 1950-53; *Science Fiction Five Yearly,* editor and publisher, 1951-71, co-editor and co-publisher, 1971-76; assistant editor, *Infinity Science Fiction* and *Science Fiction Adventures,* both 1956-58.

ADAPTATIONS: *The Valdez Horses* was adapted as the movie *Chino* (released in England under the title *Valdez, the Halfbreed*), which was produced by Intercontinental Films in 1973 and starred Charles Bronson and Jill Ireland.

SIDELIGHTS: Lee Hoffman has written in a variety of genres, including science fiction, historical romance, and westerns. She is best known for her work in the latter category, and is one of the most successful female authors of westerns. In a *Contemporary Authors Autobiography Series* essay, she recalls that while growing up in the 1930s, her favorite radio programs were *Tom Mix* and *The Lone Ranger,* and her "favorite activities were pony riding and playing *cowboy.* Going to the fairgrounds so I could ride a pony was a Sunday-afternoon ritual." Hoffman also remembered that at a very young age, she insisted on telling bedtime stories to her mother, and that she did her first writing in the sixth grade. It was a Nancy Drew-style mystery, which she worked on during school hours. "I turned out dozens of [adventure stories] which I passed around among classmates," she wrote. "I wasn't thinking about writing as a possible career. I was too naive for that. I did them for my own entertainment and to entertain my companions. At the time, my ambition was to own a horse ranch."

Hoffman's first experience in the world of publishing was as an editor of science-fiction magazines. Despite her years of work in the science fiction field, however, when her first book was published in the mid-1960s, it was a western, *Gunfight at Laramie.* "Although it has a rather unremarkable storyline, it demonstrates Hoffman's ability to create interesting, credible, and sympathetic characters," averred Vicki Piekarski in *Twentieth-Century Western Writers.* Because of the ambiguous gender of her name, Hoffman found easy acceptance from male readers who made up most of the audience for westerns, and many more books in that genre followed. Piekarski remarked that the author's heroes are "particularly engaging because of their very human qualities—guilt, fear, and upon occasion, stupidity. . . . Hoffman is not reticent to write about fist fights, gun battles, lynchings, and elaborate chase scenes; in fact, her books never want for fast-paced, suspenseful action sequences." Piekarski described Hoffman's award-winning novel about a Mexican horse breeder, *The Valdez Horses,* as "a carefully structured, evocative story" and further noted: "The reader becomes attached to the vividly drawn horses. . . . It is a perfect blending of plot, characterization, and mood."

BIOGRAPHICAL/CRITICAL SOURCES:

BOOKS

*Contemporary Authors Autobiography Series,* Volume 10, Gale (Detroit), 1989.
*Twentieth-Century Western Writers,* second edition, St. James Press (Chicago), 1991.

PERIODICALS

*Analog,* August, 1983.
*Library Journal,* January 15, 1972.
*Publishers Weekly,* December 6, 1971; October 30, 1981.

\*    \*    \*

## HOFFMAN, Mary (Margaret) 1945-
### (Mary Lassiter)

*PERSONAL:* Born April 20, 1945, in Eastleigh, Hampshire, England; daughter of Origen Herman (in telecommunications) and Ivegh (a homemaker; maiden name, Lassiter) Hoffman; married Stephen James Barber (a social worker), December 22, 1972; children: Rhiannon, Rebecca, Jessica. *Education:* Newnham College, Cambridge, B.A. (with honors), 1967; University of London, diploma in linguistics, 1970. *Politics:* Green. *Religion:* Anglo-Catholic.

*ADDRESSES: Home*—28 Crouch Hall Rd., London N8 8HJ, England. *Agent*—Deborah Rogers Ltd., 49 Blenheim Cres., London W11 2EF, England.

*CAREER:* Open University, Milton Keynes, England, lecturer in education, 1975-80; writer, 1980—. Member of The Other Award Panel, 1980-87; reading consultant to BBC-TV.

*MEMBER:* International Board on Books for Young People, National Union of Journalists, Society of Authors.

*WRITINGS:*

FOR ADULTS

*Reading, Writing, and Relevance,* Hodder & Stoughton, 1976.
(Under pseudonym Mary Lassiter) *Our Names, Our Selves,* Heinemann, 1983.

Also author of course materials for Open University. Former columnist for *Mother.* Contributor to periodicals.

FOR CHILDREN

*White Magic,* Rex Collings, 1975.
(With Chris Callery) *Buttercup Busker's Rainy Day,* Heinemann, 1982.
(With Willis Hall) *The Return of the Antelope,* Heinemann, 1985.
*Beware, Princess!,* Heinemann, 1986.
*The Second-Hand Ghost,* Deutsch, 1986.
*A Fine Picnic,* Macdonald, 1986.
*King of the Castle,* Hamish Hamilton, 1986.
*Animal Hide and Seek,* Macdonald, 1986.
(With Trevor Weston) *Dangerous Animals,* Brimax Books, 1986.
*Whales and Sharks,* Brimax Books, 1986.
*The Perfect Pet,* Macdonald, 1986.
*Clothes for Sale,* Silver Burdett, 1986.
*Nancy No-Size,* Methuen, 1987.
*Specially Sarah,* Methuen, 1987.
*My Grandma Has Black Hair,* Dial, 1988.
*Dracula's Daughter,* Heinemann, 1988.
*All About Lucy,* Methuen, 1989.
*Min's First Jump,* Hamish Hamilton, 1989.
*Mermaid and Chips,* Heinemann, 1989.
*Dog Powder,* Heinemann, 1989.
*Catwalk,* Methuen, 1989.
*Just Jack,* Methuen, 1990.
(Editor) *Ip, Dip, Sky Blue,* Collins, 1990.
*Leon's Lucky Lunchbreak,* Dent, 1991.
*The Babies' Hotel,* Dent, 1991.
*Amazing Grace,* illustrated by Caroline Binch, Dial (New York City), 1991.
*Max in the Jungle,* Hamish Hamilton, 1991.
*The Ghost Menagerie,* Orchard Books (New York City), 1992.
*The Four-Legged Ghosts,* illustrated by Laura L. Seeley, Orchard Books, 1993.
*Amazing Mammals Kit,* Dorling Kindersley, 1993.
*Henry's Baby,* Dorling Kindersley, 1993.
*Cyril MC,* Viking, 1993.
*Bump in the Night,* Collins, 1993.
*Boundless Grace,* illustrated by Binch, Dial, 1995 (published in England as *Grace and Family,* Frances Lincoln, 1995).
*Earth, Fire, Water, Air,* illustrated by Jane Ray, Dutton (New York City), 1995 (published in England as *Song of the Earth,* Orion, 1995).
*Trace in Space,* Hodder & Stoughton, 1995.
*A Vanishing Tail,* Orchard Books, 1996.
*Quantum Squeak,* Orchard Books, 1996.
*Special Powers,* Hodder & Stoughton, 1997.
*A First Bible Storybook,* Dorling Kindersley, 1997.
*An Angel Just like Me,* Frances Lincoln, 1997, Dial, 1998.

*Comet,* Orchard Books, 1997.
*Sun, Moon, and Stars,* Orion, 1998.
*A Twist in the Tail,* Frances Lincoln, 1998.

### "ANIMALS IN THE WILD" SERIES

*Animals in the Wild: Tiger,* Belitha/Windward, 1983.
*Animals in the Wild: Monkey,* Belitha/Windward, 1983.
*Animals in the Wild: Elephant,* Belitha/Windward, 1983.
*Animals in the Wild: Panda,* Belitha/Windward, 1983.
*Animals in the Wild: Lion,* Belitha/Methuen, 1985.
*Animals in the Wild: Zebra,* Belitha/Methuen, 1985.
*Animals in the Wild: Hippo,* Belitha/Methuen, 1985.
*Animals in the Wild: Gorilla,* Belitha/Methuen, 1985.
*Animals in the Wild: Wild Cat,* Belitha/Methuen, 1986.
*Animals in the Wild: Snake,* Belitha/Methuen, 1986.
*Animals in the Wild: Giraffe,* Belitha/Methuen, 1986.
*Animals in the Wild: Bear,* Belitha/Methuen, 1986.
*Animals in the Wild: Wild Dog,* Belitha/Methuen, 1987.
*Animals in the Wild: Seal,* Belitha/Methuen, 1987.
*Animals in the Wild: Antelope,* Belitha/Methuen, 1987.
*Animals in the Wild: Bird of Prey,* Belitha/Methuen, 1987.

*SIDELIGHTS:* "Whenever I write, I am in touch with the five-year-old or seven-year-old or nine-year-old who is still inside me," Mary Hoffman wrote for *Something about the Author Autobiography Series.* In her long essay, she described many of the memorable childhood events and friendships that molded the writer she is today. A recurring motif in the essay is Hoffman's ongoing fascination with play-acting and the invention of playlets and pantomimes. In the traditional British pantomime, she explained, there is always (at least) a leading male character (played by a woman) and an unappealing female character (played by a man). Hoffman's problem, she commented, was that she always wanted to play the lead, or all of the "good" parts combined, leaving her companions with the leftovers. She also noticed that many of the best parts were intended for boys.

The book that has won Hoffman the greatest recognition, on both sides of the Atlantic, is *Amazing Grace.* "Grace is really me," she declared in *SATA,* "a little girl who loved stories and who loved acting them out." Grace also wanted to play the leading parts, even when people told her she could not appear in a male role. Hoffman once told *CA,* "I am a feminist

and first got involved in children's books by assessing them in terms of their attitudes toward sex roles." In her recent essay, she commented, "Because things have moved on a bit in equality between the sexes since I was Grace's age, I added another level of challenge by making her Black." This gave people even more opportunities to try to dissuade Grace from pursuing her goal of playing Peter Pan. *Amazing Grace* was particularly well received in the United States, where it was adapted for the stage and produced by the Children's Theatre Company in Minneapolis, Minnesota. *Horn Book* reviewer Mary M. Burns called the story "a dynamic introduction to one of the most engaging protagonists in contemporary picture books."

Hoffman wrote a sequel, *Boundless Grace,* because, as she stated in her *SATA* essay, "Grace had become a role model for hundreds of thousands of children around the world, and if she could come to terms with a situation experienced by . . . many children today, it could really be helpful." Grace, now twelve years old, must face the separation and divorce of her parents. Hoffman and her illustrator, Caroline Binch, had to travel to the West African nation of Gambia to meet with the girl who had served as a photographic model for the first "Grace" book. Because of the photographic technique involved in creating the illustrations, no other model would do. It was natural, then, for the older Grace to move to Africa, too, to visit her father and his new wife and two step-siblings. She flies there with her grandmother, filled with anxiety about her reception into this new family. The lesson of the story, writes a *Publishers Weekly* reviewer, is "that 'families are what you make of them,'" concluding that *Boundless Grace* "is as assured and uplifting as its predecessor." Burns reported that "this story, like Grace, transcends social, cultural, and geographic boundaries."

Grace introduced many American readers to Hoffman, but she had written nearly forty books by 1991, when Grace first appeared. More than a dozen of these are titles in the "Animals in the Wild" series. "I have been a vegetarian since 1969," Hoffman told *CA,* "and I like animals, particularly cats and reptiles." According to her *SATA* essay, Hoffman's first book was *White Magic,* a story "about two cousins, a boy and a girl . . . who find a unicorn and have to look after it." Recent titles include *The Four-Legged Ghosts,* the tale of a pet mouse who somehow revives the ghosts of all past animal residents of the house where he lives, to the consternation of his "keepers" Carrie and Alex. A *Publishers Weekly* reviewer recommended the fantasy: ". . .[R]eaders will enjoy the mounting tension . . . and they will eagerly anticipate the resolution." Hoffman also wrote *Earth, Fire, Water, Air,* a wide-ranging miscellany of facts, poems, and stories about the elements that reflect what a *Publishers Weekly* critic called "a general reverence for the natural world." She followed this with *Sun, Moon, and Stars,* a similar collection of material on the luminaries of the sky.

Hoffman told *CA:* "I have three daughters, and I have a good marriage. I worked through the whole period of having and raising babies, and have never had a nanny or au pair. I'm proud of my achievements and could never imagine not working."

*BIOGRAPHICAL/CRITICAL SOURCES:*

BOOKS

*Something about the Author Autobiography Series,* Volume 24, Gale (Detroit, MI), 1997.

PERIODICALS

*Horn Book,* July-August, 1995, p. 450.
*Publishers Weekly,* July 12, 1993, p. 80; May 8, 1995, p. 294; December 18, 1995, p. 54.

\* \* \*

**HOLDEN, Anthony (Ivan) 1947-**

*PERSONAL:* Born May 22, 1947, in Southport, England; son of John (a company director) and Margaret Lois (Sharpe) Holden; married Amanda Juliet Warren (a musician), May 1, 1971 (marriage dissolved, 1988); married Cynthia Blake, 1990; children: (first marriage) Sam, Joe, Ben. *Education:* Merton College, Oxford, M.A. (with honors), 1970. *Avocational interests:* Poker.

*ADDRESSES: Office*—c/o Rogers Coleridge White, 20 Powis Mews, London W11 1JN, England. *Agent*—Curtis Brown Ltd., 575 Madison Ave., New York, NY 10022.

*CAREER:* Thomson Regional Newspapers, Hemel Hempstead, England, reporter, 1970-73; *London Sunday Times,* London, England, staff writer and author of column, *Atticus,* 1973-79; *Observer,* London, chief U.S. correspondent, 1979-81; *Times,* London, fea-

tures editor and assistant editor, 1981-82; freelance author, 1982-85; *Today,* New York City, executive editor, 1985-86; writer, 1986—. Columnist, *Punch* magazine, 1979-81.

*MEMBER:* National Union of Journalists.

*AWARDS, HONORS:* Named young journalist of the year by National Council for Training of Journalists, 1973, for local newspaper work; named news reporter of the year by British Press, 1977, for work in Ulster, and columnist of the year, 1978, for *Atticus.*

*WRITINGS:*

(Translator) *Aeschylus' Agamemnon,* Cambridge University Press (Cambridge, England), 1969.
(Editor and translator) *Greek Pastoral Poetry,* Penguin (London), 1974.
*The St. Albans Poisoner: The Life and Crimes of Graham Young,* Hodder & Stoughton (London), 1974.
*Prince Charles: A Biography,* Atheneum (New York City), 1979 (published in England as *Charles, Prince of Wales,* Weidenfeld & Nicolson [London], 1979).
*Their Royal Highnesses: The Prince and Princess of Wales,* Weidenfeld & Nicolson, 1981.
(Author of introduction) *Great Royal Front Pages,* Collins (London), 1983.
*Of Presidents, Prime Ministers, and Princes: A Decade in Fleet Street,* Atheneum, 1984.
*Olivier,* Weidenfeld & Nicolson, 1988, published in the U.S. as *Laurence Olivier,* Atheneum, 1988.
*King Charles III: A Biography,* Weidenfeld & Nicolson (New York City), 1988.
*Big Deal: A Year as a Professional Poker Player,* Viking (New York City), 1990.
*A Princely Marriage: Charles and Diana, the First Ten Years,* Bantam (New York City), 1991.
*Behind the Oscar: The Secret History of the Academy Awards,* Simon & Schuster (New York City), 1993.
*The Tarnished Crown: Princess Diana and the House of Windsor,* Random House (New York City), 1993.
*Tchaikovsky: A Biography,* Random House, 1995.

Contributor to magazines in the United States and England, including *Punch, New Statesman, Spectator,* and *National Geographic.*

*WORK IN PROGRESS:* Nonfiction work on the United States; a novel.

*SIDELIGHTS:* Anthony Holden ranks among the foremost authorities on the English royal family, having followed the fortunes of Prince Charles especially closely since the late 1970s. Unlike many royal-watchers, however, Holden has not restricted himself merely to biographies on the House of Windsor—his varied output includes a book about poker playing, an encyclopedic history of the Academy Awards, and highly-regarded biographies of actor Laurence Olivier and composer Pyotr Ilyich Tchaikovsky. An accomplished journalist who has worked for press outlets on both sides of the Atlantic, Holden has been commended for both his reportage and his writing style in his book-length works.

Holden went to work as a newspaper reporter right out of college, and within three years had won a position—and a column—at the *London Sunday Times*. In 1979 he published his first royal biography, *Prince Charles*. Released to coincide with the Prince of Wales's thirtieth birthday, the book was soon overshadowed by a momentous event: the marriage of Charles to Lady Diana Spencer. Holden was one of many who wrote intimate biographies of Charles and Diana at the time of their engagement, but Holden's prior relationship with the prince allowed him a closer view of the couple than most other writers were afforded. Thus it was that Holden, with his wealth of background material on the couple, stood in a good position to assess the marriage as it began to disintegrate. Called upon to discuss the royals on television and radio, he also penned another biography of Charles on the prince's fortieth birthday and two more books on the royal marriage and its impact on the House of Windsor.

Ironically, Holden's reputation rests less on his works about the royals than upon his other books. In 1988 he published a 504-page biography of noted actor Sir Laurence Olivier that garnered favorable reviews even though the actor had been the subject of almost a half dozen previous biographies. "Mr. Holden, to his everlasting credit, resists the spurious and gives us a scrupulously fair portrait of a great artist at war with himself," wrote Bryan Forbes in the *New York Times Book Review*. "Inevitably, he cannot avoid tracts of familiar ground in tracing Laurence Olivier's progress from childhood to glory, but marshals and presents his material in a way that compels the reader forward. . . . Here we have not just the fascinating details of an extraordinary career, but a compassionate stripping away of the public mask to reveal the face of insecurity." In a *London Review of Books*

essay on *Laurence Olivier,* contributor Ronald Bryden commented: "Holden comes well-equipped. He has assembled all the facts available from previous biographies, as well as scores of entertaining new ones from his own researches and interviews with Olivier's friends and co-workers. It is the largest compilation between covers of what is known about the actor, and that is its value, a real one."

Reviewers found equal favor with Holden's biography of Tchaikovsky, the popular Russian composer whose works include *The Nutcracker Suite*. In the biography Holden reveals the musician's deep-seated self-loathing and fear of scandal, brought on by his homosexuality. As Ted Libbey put it in the *Washington Post Book World,* the work "is the chronicle of an artist who might have said, as Pushkin does in *Eugene Onegin,* 'Love passed, the muse appeared, the weather of mind got clarity newfound; now free, I once more weave together emotion, thought, and magic sound.' Only Tchaikovsky was never free. And while this book is about his life, its importance is in the story it tells of his death, by far the best treatment of that sad event yet to emerge." *Spectator* correspondent Fiona Maddocks declared: "Anthony Holden's biography, acknowledging a debt to [other] scholars, is a noble attempt at a psychologically informed portrait of a neurotic, troubled genius. The author makes no pretence at unearthing new facts, which in itself will attract scorn from some circles. Rather, he draws together the latest findings into a readable . . . narrative which anyone with an interest in the composer, or in the Russian 19th-century landscape he inhabited, would do well to read."

*BIOGRAPHICAL/CRITICAL SOURCES:*

*PERIODICALS*

*Chicago Tribune Books,* October 16, 1988; January 14, 1990.
*London Review of Books,* September 1, 1988, pp. 4-6; August 19, 1993, pp. 8-9.
*New Republic,* April 12, 1993, pp. 39-42.
*New Statesman,* July 24, 1981, pp. 16-17.
*New York Times,* March 18, 1993, p. C21; July 9, 1993, p. C27.
*New York Times Book Review,* October 23, 1988, p. 14; January 7, 1990, p. 28.
*Observer,* June 6, 1993, p. 62; September 24, 1995.
*Punch,* July 16, 1991, p. 44.
*Spectator,* July 25, 1981, pp. 20-21; December 30, 1995, p. 30.
*Time,* November 19, 1990, p. 110.

*Times Literary Supplement,* June 10-16, 1988, p. 652; November 11, 1988, p. 1254; November 16-22, 1990, p. 1239; June 14, 1991, p. 6.
*Washington Post Book World,* March 21, 1993, p. 3; March 31, 1996, p. 4.

\*   \*   \*

## HOLLAND, Cecelia (Anastasia) 1943-
### (Elizabeth Eliot Carter)

*PERSONAL:* Born December 31, 1943, in Henderson, NV; daughter of William Dean (an executive) and Katharine (Schenck) Holland. *Education:* Pennsylvania State University, student, 1961-62; Connecticut College, B.A., 1965. *Politics:* Anarchist. *Religion:* Atheist.

*ADDRESSES: Home*—Fortuna, CA.

*CAREER:* Writer. Visiting professor of English at Connecticut College, 1979.

*AWARDS, HONORS:* Guggenheim fellowship, 1981-82.

*WRITINGS:*

NOVELS

*The Firedrake,* Atheneum (New York City), 1966.
*Rakossy,* Atheneum, 1967.
*The Kings in Winter,* Atheneum, 1968.
*Until the Sun Falls,* Atheneum, 1969.
*Antichrist: A Novel of the Emperor Frederick II,* Atheneum, 1970, published in England as *The Wonder of the World,* Hodder & Stoughton (London), 1970.
*The Earl,* Knopf (New York City), 1971, published in England as *Hammer for Princes,* Hodder & Stoughton, 1972.
*The Death of Attila,* Knopf, 1973.
*Great Maria,* Knopf, 1974.
*Floating Worlds,* Knopf, 1976.
(Under pseudonym Elizabeth Eliot Carter) *Valley of the Kings,* Dutton (New York City), 1977, published in England under her own name by Gollancz (London), 1978.
*Two Ravens,* Knopf, 1978.
*City of God: A Novel of the Borgias,* Knopf, 1979.
*Home Ground,* Knopf, 1981.
*The Sea Beggars,* Knopf, 1982.

*The Belt of Gold,* Knopf, 1984.
*Pillar of the Sky,* Knopf, 1985.
*The Lords of Vaumartin,* Houghton (Boston), 1988.
*The Bear Flag,* Houghton, 1990.
*Pacific Street,* Houghton, 1992.
*Jerusalem,* Forge (New York City), 1996.

JUVENILE

*Ghost on the Steppe,* Atheneum, 1970.
*The King's Road,* Atheneum, 1971.

*SIDELIGHTS:* From ancient Byzantium to Stonehenge, from the Crusades to early California, Cecelia Holland's historical novels have skillfully depicted many eras, through stories that blend real events with fictional plots. "Read history books to learn the facts about a given age, but read Holland to soak up the atmosphere," advised Marion Hanscom in *Twentieth-Century Romance and Historical Writers.* Holland's first novel, *The Firedrake*—which was set in England just prior to the Norman conquest—was published a year after the author graduated from college, and she has kept up a steady output of well-reviewed fiction ever since.

*Firedrake* "was criticized for the use of very short, plain, often abrupt language and simple sentence structure," recounted Hanscom, "but praised for the sound research about England." As the years have passed, Holland's "style has not changed and in fact her disdain for the ornate language often found in historical novels has become a hallmark of her work, which is now frequently praised for the immediacy her prose brings to her stories." Holland has also been lauded for her willingness to explore many new territories rather than sticking to one familiar setting.

In her novel *City of God,* Holland "proves that there can be more to historical thrillers than swordplay and seduction," according to a *Time* critic. *City of God* is set in the Rome of the Borgias, between 1500 and 1503, and is told from the point of view of Nicholas, a secretary to the Florentine ambassador to Rome. Holland "convincingly pictures Renaissance Rome, the sumptuousness of the costumes and furnishings, the squalor and menace of the streets," noted Audrey Foote in the *Washington Post Book World.* Furthermore, she "adroitly leads the reader through the tangle of dynastic ambitions and shifting alliances. Best of all, she creates a fascinating focal character in Nicholas."

In *The Belt of Gold,* Holland delved into ninth-century Byzantium and a power struggle between Empress Irene and her enemies. A *Times Literary Supplement* reviewer called it Holland's best at the time of publication, noting that it besides a good plot and skillful writing, "its main triumph lies in the way it manages to bring to life a civilization even more alien and incomprehensible to Westerners than to the Turks who destroyed it." *Pillar of the Sky,* Holland's tale of the creation of Stonehenge, is applauded for its "scholarship, insight and invention" by *Washington Post Book World* contributor Valerie FitzGerald, who further noted: "For those unwilling to acknowledge that superior technology is not synonymous with heightened intelligence, this book will prove a surprise; to those who find some comfort in believing that their remote forebears were not all that much different from themselves, it will give reassurance. . . . [It] is informative, entertaining and uncommonly easy to read."

Holland broached the subject of the plague in *The Lords of Vaumartin,* set in fourteenth-century Brittany. The plot concerns a man and his nephew, who are separated during a battle. The manner in which Holland chronicles their fates is "strong," judged Edna Stumpf in the *New York Times Book Review,* "proclaiming that in this death-haunted century the ideals of chivalry are being abandoned and the verities of the church are failing. . . .The contrast between these two men's inner lives carries a somber esthetic richness. Such rewards are always present in Ms. Holland's books. . . . [She] eloquently demonstrates for us the precariousness and preciousness of life."

The author jumped to early California for her next two novels. *The Bear Flag* illuminated the war between the Mexicans and Americans that eventually resulted in California statehood. The main character is Catherine Reilly, a proper Bostonian woman who must learn the basics of survival when she loses everything, even her husband, in an attempt to cross the Sierra Nevadas. "Written in a vigorous, spirited style, Holland organises her complex material with admirable skill," affirmed Kathy O'Shaughnessy of *Observer Review.* A writer for *West Coast Review of Books* declared that the book mixed "fact and fiction in such a wonderful way, neither the historian nor the romantic will be disappointed." In *Pacific Street,* Holland moved on to the Gold Rush years in San Francisco. The story is "thick with plot and suspense," according to the *Rapport* reviewer, and Sybil Steinberg noted in *Publishers Weekly* that "Holland's

grasp of history is neatly matched by her skills as a storyteller." Reviewing the author's body of work, Hanscom summarized: "Holland is above all a storyteller who has a wonderful way of transporting herself back in time and taking us along with her."

*BIOGRAPHICAL/CRITICAL SOURCES:*

*BOOKS*

*Twentieth-Century Romance and Historical Writers,* 3rd edition, St. James Press (Detroit), 1994.

*PERIODICALS*

*Atlantic,* June, 1977; July, 1990, p. 104.
*Booklist,* February 15, 1992, p. 1088; January 1, 1996, p. 786.
*Chicago Tribune,* June 30, 1985, section 14, p. 35.
*Chicago Tribune Book World,* February 25, 1979.
*Kirkus Reviews,* November 15, 1991, pp. 1432-33.
*Library Journal,* June 15, 1990, p. 134; January, 1992, p. 174; April 1, 1993, p. 136; November 20, 1995, p. 67; January, 1996, p. 142.
*New Yorker,* August 20, 1984.
*New York Review of Books,* September 27, 1979.
*New York Times Book Review,* July 8, 1984, p. 20; July 21, 1985, p. 22;. December 25, 1988, p. 16; January 28, 1996, p. 20.
*Observer Review,* September 5, 1990.
*Publishers Weekly,* December 20, 1991, p. 64.
*Rapport,* Volume 17, number 1, 1992.
*School Library Journal,* August, 1990, p. 174; November, 1992.
*Spectator,* October 22, 1977.
*Time,* April 9, 1979.
*Times Literary Supplement,* August 3, 1984, p. 875; November 2, 1990, p. 1182.
*Washington Post Book World,* March 12, 1979; June 16, 1985, pp. 1-2; April 26, 1986, p. 12; November 6, 1988, p. 8; April 30, 1989, p. 10; March 10, 1996, p. 7.
*West Coast Review of Books,* Volume 15, number 4, 1990, p. 26.

\*    \*    \*

## HOROWITZ, David (Joel) 1939-

*PERSONAL:* Born January 10, 1939, in New York, NY; son of Philip (an activist) and Blanche (Brown)

Horowitz; married Elissa Krauthamer, June 14, 1959 (divorced); children: Jonathan, Sarah, Benjamin, Anne. *Education:* Columbia University, A.B., 1959; University of California, Berkeley, M.A., 1961, graduate study, 1962; London School of Economics and Political Science, University of London, graduate study, 1964.

*CAREER:* Writer. Bertrand Russell Peace Foundation, London, England, former director of research and publications; *Ramparts* (magazine), Berkeley, CA, editor, 1969-74; founder and co-director of Second Thoughts Project, Washington, DC, 1986—; co-director, Center for the Study of Popular Culture; editor, *Heterodoxy*. Alternate delegate, Republican Party National Convention, 1996.

*WRITINGS:*

*Student,* Ballantine (New York City), 1962.

*Shakespeare: An Existential View,* Hill & Wang (New York City), 1965.

*The Free World Colossus,* Hill & Wang, 1965, revised edition, 1971 (published in England as *From Yalta to Vietnam: American Foreign Policy in the Cold War,* Penguin, 1967).

*Hemispheres North and South: Economic Disparity among Nations,* Johns Hopkins University Press (Baltimore, MD), 1966.

(Editor) *Containment and Revolution,* Beacon Press (Boston, MA), 1967 (published in England as *Containment and Revolution: Western Policy towards Social Revolution, 1917 to Vietnam,* Blond, 1967).

(Compiler) *Marx and Modern Economics,* Monthly Review Press (New York City), 1968.

*Empire and Revolution: A Radical Interpretation of Contemporary History,* Random House (New York City), 1969 (published in England as *Imperialism and Revolution,* Allen Lane [London], 1969).

(Editor) *Corporations and the Cold War,* Monthly Review Press, 1970.

(Editor) *Issac Deutscher: The Man and His Work,* Macdonald & Co., 1971.

(Compiler) *Radical Sociology: An Introduction,* Canfield Press, 1971.

(Compiler with Michael Lerner and Craig Pyes; and contributor) *Counterculture and Revolution,* Random House, 1972.

*The Enigma of Economic Growth: A Case Study of Israel,* Praeger (New York City), 1972.

*The Fate of Midas and Other Essays,* Ramparts Press (Palo Alto, CA), 1973.

*The First Frontier: The Indian Wars and America's Origins, 1607-1776,* Simon & Schuster (New York City), 1978.

(With Peter Collier) *The Kennedys: An American Drama,* Summit Books (New York City), 1984.

(With Collier) *The Fords: An American Epic,* Summit Books, 1987.

*The Rockefellers: An American Dynasty,* Summit Books, 1989.

(With Collier) *Destructive Generation: Second Thoughts about the Sixties,* Summit Books, 1989.

(Editor with Collier) *Second Thoughts: Former Radicals Look Back at the Sixties,* Madison Books (Lanham, MD), 1989.

(Editor with Collier) *Second Thoughts about Race in America,* Madison Books, 1991.

(With Collier) *Deconstructing the Left: From Vietnam to the Persian Gulf,* Second Thoughts Books (Lanham, MD), 1991.

(With Collier) *The Roosevelts: An American Saga,* Simon & Schuster, 1994.

(Editor with Collier) *The Heterodoxy Handbook: How to Survive the PC Campus,* Regnery (Lanham, MD), 1994.

*Radical Son: A Generational Odyssey,* Free Press, 1997.

(Editor with Collier) *The Race Card: White Guilt, Black Resentment, and the Assault on Truth and Justice,* Prima Publications (Rocklin, CA), 1997.

Contributor to *Nation* and *Studies on the Left.*

*SIDELIGHTS:* David Horowitz and his collaborator Peter Collier are best known in political circles as the founders of the Second Thoughts Project, an association of former Sixties radicals who have since denounced the agenda of the New Left. Perhaps no other conservative writers are more ideally suited for this task: Horowitz and Collier began their association while on the editorial board of the radical *Ramparts* magazine in the late 1960s, and they were avowed left wingers who wrote numerous books and magazine articles in the service of radical causes. Today they are equally enthusiastic about conservatism and a free market economy, and they have presented their ideas in such works as *Destructive Generation: Second Thoughts about the Sixties* and *Deconstructing the Left: From Vietnam to the Persian Gulf. National Review* correspondent Joseph Sobran observed that Horowitz and Collier are producing "must reading" about the lasting national effects of Sixties radicalism, "and they write about it with intelligence, gossipy intimacy, and a sort of savage introspection." Sobran concluded: "There's not a trace of sentimentality about the Left's 'idealism,' which they correctly interpret as malicious fantasizing."

Horowitz's unconventional childhood prepared him for left wing politics and socialist idealism. He was born and raised in Queens by parents who belonged to the Communist Party, and his childhood memories include comic book-burnings at a communist-run summer camp for children. Later, both of Horowitz's parents lost their teaching jobs in the McCarthy era. Their travails were not lost on young David, who began writing political commentary in the early 1960s. "As members of a new radical generation, our political identity was virginal," the author recalled in his autobiography, *Radical Son: A Generational Odyssey.* "We had the benefit of everybody's doubt. We could position ourselves as radical critics of American society without having to defend the crimes committed by the Soviet bloc. . . . And we could express our moral outrage at Communist excesses."

"Moral outrage" defined the tenor of much of Horowitz's writing. In *Free World Colossus,* his first widely-read book, he denounced the United States as the architect of the Cold War in its pursuit of a monopoly on international power. "The heaviest price exacted by the cold war has been the moral contamination of people," wrote Arnold S. Kaufman in the *Nation.* "Perhaps one should accept the toll with reflective calm. David Horowitz has refused to do so. The result is a book that describes and interprets the history of the cold war in a way that challenges, excites, provokes, angers and inspires. Horowitz has written a sincere and important book, which says much that desperately needs saying in these times of madness."

In 1968 Horowitz established himself in Berkeley, California, and began working as an editor of *Ramparts,* a radical magazine that served as a forum for the political views of the New Left. Among the other causes championed by *Ramparts* was the Black Panther Party, and Horowitz became personally acquainted with many of the most important Panther leaders. His eventual disillusionment with the Left began with his realization that Black Panther violence was being overlooked by left wing journalists in the same way that Josef Stalin's crimes had been overlooked by an earlier generation of committed revolutionaries. Horowitz "became convinced," explained George Cantor in the *Detroit News,* "that [Black

Panther leader] Huey Newton had ordered a hit on a bookkeeper Horowitz had placed in a job with the party. Although Newton's complicity was widely suspected, no one wanted to look any further. Especially the mainstream media. The Panthers had been made heroes by these publications and networks. . . . The possibility that [the Panthers] may have been a street gang using Marxism as their hustle was something the media did not care to deal with." "Like all radicals, I lived in some fundamental way in a castle in the air," Horowitz recalled in his autobiography. "Now I had hit the ground hard, and had no idea how to get up."

In fact, Horowitz did not founder for long. He formed a partnership with Collier, and the two wrote three well-received family biographies: one about the Kennedys, one about the Rockefellers, and one about the Henry Ford dynasty. "Chronicles of great 20th-century American families tend to fall into two divided camps: on the one side, foot-stomping denunciations of the depredations and corruptions of the powerful; on the other, . . . saccharine, flowery treatments that are often the work of kept biographers," declared Carter Cooper in *Books in Review.* "Peter Collier and David Horowitz, in lively chronicles of the Rockefellers, the Kennedys, and now the Fords, have avoided both pitfalls." Cooper contended that in the Collier-Horowitz biographies, the authors demonstrate "a novelistic flair for pacing and the effective use of anecdote, [producing] exciting [portraits] that will not fail to satisfy even the heartiest appetite for the perversities and extravagances of the powerful."

Far more provocative are the political writings Horowitz has produced since becoming a conservative in the early 1980s. With Collier, or on his own, Horowitz has challenged both the left wing politics of the 1960s and what he sees as the lasting ill effects of those politics in American society today. *Destructive Generation: Second Thoughts about the Sixties* was widely reviewed in the nation's political magazines, with opinions on the work varying according to the reviewer's own ideology. Not surprisingly, Saul Landau in the leftist *Progressive* labeled Horowitz and Collier "defective defectors" and characterized their book as "disconnected and bilious." Paul Berman perhaps presented a more reasonable approach in the *New Republic* when he noted that the authors "have produced pieces of lasting value. These chapters go to the heart of the matter, to the explosive quality of the New Left, to the notion, so crucial to the New Left's appeal, that you can batter down your own limitations, that conventions are oppressions, that an existential choice can turn you into something better, more heroic, more powerful."

In *Leaders from the 1960s,* Thomas R. West stated that Collier and Horowitz may have broken from left wing politics, but their new right wing views have proven equally strident. *Destructive Generation,* the critic declared, "is the report of a conversion. Collier and Horowitz discovered human imperfection, but this did not make them humble. Instead, they insisted, with an aggressive self-righteousness, that everyone should be judged by their new standards. . . . Even if the reader is not convinced, however, the book does illustrate something about the uses of critical introspection in the forming of a politics that is at once personal and responsible."

Horowitz gives more personal details about his political conversion in his biography, *Radical Son.* "Many intellectuals have made the voyage from Left to Right in recent decades," observed Christopher Caldwell in *Commentary.* "But few have come from as deep inside the hard Left as Horowitz, and none has retained more of the 60's style. . . . *Radical Son,* his memoir, charts a trek from one political commitment to something approaching its opposite, and the events that propelled him on his way." *Reason* magazine correspondent Steven Hayward noted: "Taken as a whole, *Radical Son* is a compelling story, because it goes farther than many of the previous narratives in conveying how deeply radicalism cuts into one's character and psychology. The supposedly redemptive power of radical ideology, Horowitz makes clear, reaches into every corner of the soul, thus making a break from radicalism a desperate and personally devastating matter." In *Commonweal,* Julia Vitullo-Martin stated: "This is an American journey of sorts—traveling the short road from authoritarian left to demagogic right. But does the journey, excruciatingly detailed in *Radical Son,* have anything to tell the rest of us? The answer is yes, in part because the story of a red-diaper American childhood has seldom been told, and perhaps never so well."

Horowitz and Collier are currently running the California-based Center for the Study of Popular Culture and are publishing their views in a monthly broadsheet called *Heterodoxy.* Steven Hayward concluded of the former radical: "Horowitz has not changed that much since the 1960s; he is still at war with the dominant culture. So in the end he is in harmony with his essential political being."

*BIOGRAPHICAL/CRITICAL SOURCES:*

*BOOKS*

Horowitz, David, *Radical Son: A Generational Odyssey,* Free Press, 1997.
*Leaders from the 1960s,* Greenwood Press (Westport, CT), 1994, pp. 349-53.

*PERIODICALS*

*American History,* April, 1995, p. 27.
*Booklist,* January 1, 1997, pp. 9-10.
*Commentary,* October, 1984, p. 66; March, 1988, pp. 78-82; June, 1997, pp. 64-67.
*Commonweal,* May 23, 1997, pp. 26-27.
*Cosmopolitan,* June, 1994, p. 18.
*Detroit News,* June 4, 1997; October 4, 1997.
*Entertainment Weekly,* July 8, 1994, p. 50.
*Journal of American History,* June, 1995, p. 284.
*Library Journal,* December, 1996, p. 104.
*Los Angeles Times,* June 2, 1992, p. E1; April 14, 1993, p. B1; February 28, 1997, p. E1.
*Los Angeles Times Book Review,* March 19, 1989, p. 2.
*Maclean's,* July 16, 1984, p. 50.
*Mother Jones,* August-September, 1984, p. 56; January, 1988, p. 10.
*Nation,* February 21, 1966, pp. 214-16; April 6, 1985, p. 388; October 31, 1987, p. 475; November 27, 1989, pp. 630-32; February 17, 1997, pp. 30-33.
*National Review,* March 24, 1989, pp. 43-44; June 13, 1994, pp. 65-68; March 24, 1997, pp. 50-51.
*New Leader,* December 16, 1996, pp. 5-8.
*New Republic,* August 27, 1984, pp. 31-34; April 24, 1989, pp. 26-34; June 26, 1989, pp. 38-42.
*Newsweek,* July 2, 1984, p. 25.
*New York Times,* April 23, 1989, p. 18; June 1, 1989, p. C19; July 16, 1989.
*New York Times Book Review,* March 4, 1979, p. 11; June 19, 1994, p. 13; February 16, 1997, p. 34.
*People,* August 29, 1994, p. 29.
*Progressive,* May, 1985, p. 4; August, 1989, pp. 37-38.
*Publishers Weekly,* December 30, 1996, p. 49; May 5, 1997, p. 188.
*Reason,* March, 1997, pp. 62-63.
*Time,* July 25, 1994, p. 67.
*Times Literary Supplement,* September 9, 1965, p. 773.
*Wall Street Journal,* August 13, 1996, p. A14; February 3, 1997, p. A12.
*Washington Monthly,* May, 1989, p. 44.

*Washington Post Book World,* June 5, 1994, p. 3; February 9, 1997, p. 3.
*Whole Earth Review,* fall, 1989, p. 102.

\* \* \*

**HUGHES, Sara**
**See SAUNDERS, Susan**

\* \* \*

**HUMPHREY, William 1924-**

*PERSONAL:* Born June 18, 1924, in Clarksville, TX; father's name Clarence; married; wife's name Dorothy; children: one daughter. *Education:* Attended Southern Methodist University and University of Texas.

*ADDRESSES: Home*—Lexington, VA.

*CAREER:* Writer. Former lecturer and teacher at Washington and Lee University, University of Texas at El Paso, and Smith College.

*AWARDS, HONORS:* Texas Institute of Letters award, 1958, for *Home from the Hill,* and 1965, for *The Ordways;* National Institute of Arts and Letters grant, 1962.

*WRITINGS:*

*STORY COLLECTIONS*

*The Last Husband and Other Stories,* Morrow (New York City), 1953.
*A Time and a Place: Stories,* Knopf (New York City), 1968, published in England as *A Time and a Place: Stories of the Red River Country,* Chatto & Windus (London), 1969.
*The Collected Stories of William Humphrey,* Delacorte (New York City), 1985.

*NOVELS*

*Home from the Hill,* Knopf, 1958.
*The Ordways,* Knopf, 1965.
*Proud Flesh,* Knopf, 1973.
*Hostages to Fortune,* Delacorte, 1984.

*No Resting Place,* Delacorte, 1989.
*September Song,* Houghton (Boston), 1992.

*OTHER*

*The Spawning Run: A Fable,* Knopf, 1970.
*Ah, Wilderness: The Frontier in American Literature,* Texas Western Press (El Paso), 1977.
*Farther off from Heaven* (memoir), Knopf, 1977.
*My Moby Dick,* Doubleday (New York City), 1978.
*Open Season: Sporting Adventures,* Delacorte, 1986.

Contributor of short stories to *Esquire, New Yorker, Harper's Bazaar, Accent, Sewanne Review, Quarterly Review of Literature* and *Saturday Evening Post.*

*ADAPTATIONS: The Spawning Run* and *My Moby Dick* have been produced as sound recordings by Christopher Enterprises (Mt. Pleasant, SC), 1986.

*SIDELIGHTS:* In his short stories, novels, and other writings, William Humphrey looks at how an individual's identity is shaped by family, society, and the environment. Many of his books, including some of those that have drawn the most favorable comment from reviewers, are set in and around Clarksville, Texas, where the author grew up. His powerful evocation of this place is often pointed to as one of his greatest strengths as a writer. "It is a region of small farmers and their workworn wives, small businessmen and their families, and large landowners and their retainers, all of whom are pictured in acute detail," informed James W. Lee in *Twentieth-Century Western Writers.* "And nobody writing about the southwest has ever been better than Humphrey at rendering the speech patterns and the landscape of the region."

*The Last Husband and Other Stories,* the author's first published book, was an impressive debut. "Mr. Humphrey successfully brings off the usually awkward match of satire with sympathy," wrote D. M. Culhane about a few of the stories. And Pearl Kazin of the *New York Times* noted that Humphrey "has the kind of skilled and persuasive originality which only the most respected practitioners of the short-story art can claim." *Home from the Hill,* his first novel, brought Humphrey widespread critical attention. The plot concerns a young man, Theron, who is torn between loyalty to his powerful, masculine father and his equally powerful—yet very prim—mother. Theron loathes his father's infidelities, but is in awe of his prowess as a woodsman. Eventually, Theron's father is gunned down by the father of a girl who is pregnant by Theron. The young man then takes revenge on his father's killer. Lee judged the plot to be somewhat "ordinary" and "too melodramatic," but added: "What saves the work, and makes it a Texas classic, is Humphrey's ability to make the folklore, the customs, and the speech of the people of Red River County, Texas seem totally real to the reader." Reviewing the novel for the *Chicago Tribune,* Fanny Butcher deemed Humphrey "a major American novelist in the making." Butcher also noted that "he has in his writing qualities which every novelist strives for."

*The Ordways,* Humphrey's next book, is also set in Red River County. It follows a family's story through four generations, from the Civil War to the 1920s. This book also garnered considerable critical praise. A *Time* review summed it up lavishly: "Good writing is rare enough. Storytelling is an even rarer skill. A genuinely comic vision is beyond price. *The Ordways* has all three." In a *Dictionary of Literary Biography* essay, James W. Lee commented: "In *The Ordways* the family is symbolic of the South. And much of the novel is an attempt to explain the loyal and proud family and the equally proud land." Lee found some fault with the book, however, because "some of the point of the theme gets lost when Humphrey allows the adventures of Sam Ordway to take over the book."

The stories in Humphrey's second short fiction collection, *A Time and a Place,* are again set in the area where Humphrey spent his childhood. Commenting on the characters that populate Humphrey's this book, Janice Elliott wrote that Humphrey "writes beautifully . . . of oil prospectors, farmers, Indians, children, in a deceptive, lolloping style that is in fact precise, and, for all its good humour, carries a sombre message." And Granville Hicks referred to Humphrey's characters as "rough people in a rough age, but there was drama in their lives, and Humphrey knows how to reveal it to us."

Many of Humphrey's writings are compared to those of William Faulkner. In reviewing *Home from the Hill,* William Hogan wrote: "*Home from the Hill* is a kind of lucid Faulkner in this serious novel which observes the mental and physical crack-up of an East Texas small-town. It is a kind of healthy *As I Lay Dying* . . . in which a young author's cosmos is less awry than Faulkner's, and his syntax is far more agreeable." Walter Allen commented on the similarity to Faulkner in *New Statesman.* "What Mr. Humphrey gives us," Allen wrote, "is a piece of Faulkner in which the obscurities have been clarified and the crooked made straight." And in a review of *A Time and A Place,* Granville Hicks commented, "Humphrey is a storyteller in the tradition of Mark Twain and William Faulkner." But Hicks also distinguished between Faulkner and Humphrey. "He [Humphrey] forgives more, grieves less torturedly, converts more to folklore. . . ." Perhaps Elizabeth Janeway established the relation between Faulkner and Humphrey when she wrote of Humphrey: "He's too good a writer to copy Faulkner, any more than he's copying Chekhov or Mark Twain, both of whom are recalled by various pages in *The Ordways.* What Humphrey does is accept the vision that Faulkner and others have bequeathed to their heirs, and build on it."

Humphrey abandoned the "Faulknerian" style in *The Spawning Run.* The story of the salmon's journey to its spawning place was also a critical success for Humphrey. Christopher Lehmann-Haupt wrote, "What Humphrey has done in his chronicle of a fishing trip to Wales is to artfully compare the life cycle of the salmon with that of elderly British fishermen."

In *Farther off from Heaven,* Humphrey returned to Texas for the locale. An autobiographical story of his years in Texas before the death of his father, *Farther off from Heaven* earned more praise for Humphrey. Thomas Lask called attention to Humphrey's "prose that is precise and exact in detail, yet one that imparts to the events a feeling of distance, of happenings far away." And *Saturday Review*'s Peter Shaw praised Humphrey's "incomparable portrait of small-farm and small-town America, both as they looked on the outside and felt on the inside." Lee judged *Farther off from Heaven* to be "perhaps the best" of the author's books.

The critic was less enthusiastic about *Hostages to Fortune,* a novel set not in Texas, but in upstate New York, where Humphrey lived for several decades. The story concerns a young man's suicide and its effect on his family. "The subject is, needless to say, sad, but Humphrey's treatment of the family's suffering is not well sustained throughout the novel," complained Lee. "Also missing are the effects of place that made Humphrey's early novels critical successes." Jonathan Yardley was more generous in his assessment of the novel, calling it in *Washington Post Book World* "powerful if rather lugubrious." He deemed Humphrey's use of flashbacks "artful" and concluded: "William Humphrey is a marvellously accomplished writer, one of the best we have. . . . Any book of his commands the most serious attention.

That is no less true of *Hostages to Fortune* than it is of his finest work, *Farther off from Heaven*. The voice in these books is intelligent, compassionate, civilized; we could hardly ask for more."

*BIOGRAPHICAL/CRITICAL SOURCES:*

*BOOKS*

Anderson, John Q., Edwin W. Gaston and James W. Lee, editors, *Southwestern American Literature: A Bibliography*, Swallow Press (Chicago), 1980, p. 322.

*Contemporary Literary Criticism*, Volume 45, Gale (Detroit), 1987.

*Dictionary of Literary Biography*, Volume 6: *American Novelists since World War II, Second Series*, Gale, 1980.

Hoffman, Frederick J., *The Art of Southern Fiction*, Southern Illinois University Press (Carbondale), 1967, pp. 103-106.

Lee, James W., *William Humphrey*, Steck Vaughn (Austin, TX), 1967.

Rubin, Louis D., Jr., *The Curious Death of the Novel: Essays in American Literature*, Louisiana State University Press (Baton Rouge), 1967, pp. 262-281.

Rubin, editor, *A Bibliographical Guide to the Study of Southern literature*, Louisiana State University Press, 1969, pp. 224-225.

*Twentieth-Century Western Writers*, second edition, St. James Press (Chicago), 1991.

Winchell, Mark Royden, *William Humphrey*, Boise State University (Boise, ID), 1992.

*PERIODICALS*

*Book World*, November 3, 1968.
*Chicago Tribune*, January 12, 1958.
*Commonweal*, May 8, 1953, p. 127; February 28, 1958, p. 571.
*Kirkus Reviews*, September 1, 1986, pp. 1347-48.
*National Observer*, January 20, 1969, p. 21.
*New Leader*, December 30, 1968.
*New Statesman*, April 12, 1958; February 28, 1969.
*Newsweek*, October 30, 1978, p. 96.
*New York Times*, April 12, 1953, p. 27; November 5, 1970; June 15, 1977.
*New York Times Book Review*, January 12, 1958, p. 4; January 31, 1965, pp. 1, 40; November 3, 1968, pp. 5, 47; April 4, 1973, p. 41; April 29, 1973, pp. 26-27; May 22, 1977, pp. 7, 31; October 17, 1984, p. 38; June 22, 1985, p. 16; August 18, 1985, p. 3.

*Observer*, March 2, 1969, p. 30.
*Observer Review*, November 20, 1970.
*San Francisco Chronicle*, January 30, 1958.
*Saturday Review*, July 25, 1953, pp. 33-34; January 11, 1958, p. 15; February 6, 1965, pp. 25-26; November 9, 1968; May 28, 1977.
*Southwest Review*, winter, 1978, pp. 84-86.
*Sunday Herald Tribune Book Week*, January 31, 1965, pp. 5, 19.
*Time*, February 5, 1965; December 8, 1986, p. 94.
*Times Literary Supplement*, December 11, 1970, p. 1470; August 3, 1973, p. 893; March 15, 1985, p. 284.
*Washington Post Book World*, December 17, 1978, p. E7; September 16, 1984, p. 3; July 14, 1985, pp. 3, 7.
*Wilson Library Bulletin*, November, 1985, p. 71.

\*   \*   \*

## HURD, (John) Thacher 1949-

*PERSONAL:* Born March 6, 1949, in Burlington, VT; son of Clement G. (an illustrator of children's books) and Edith (an author of children's books; maiden name, Thacher) Hurd; married Olivia Scott (co-owner with husband of Peaceable Kingdom Press), June 12, 1976; children: Manton, Nicholas. *Education:* Attended University of California, Berkeley, 1967-68; California College of Arts and Crafts, B.F.A., 1972.

*ADDRESSES: Home*—188 Tamalpais Rd., Berkeley, CA 94708. *Agent*—Marilyn Marlow, Curtis Brown Ltd., 10 Astor Pl., New York, NY 10003.

*CAREER:* Writer and illustrator of children's books. Grabhorn-Hoyem Press (now Arion Press), apprentice printer, 1967, 1969; self-employed builder, designer, and cabinetmaker, 1972-78; teacher of writing and illustrating children's books at California College of Arts and Crafts and Dominican College, 1981-86; co-owner with wife, Olivia Hurd, of Peaceable Kingdom Press (a children's greeting card publishing company), 1983—. Artist with group show at California College of Arts and Crafts, 1972; one-man show in Monkton, VT, 1973. Lecturer and guest speaker at seminars, conferences, and schools.

*MEMBER:* Society of Children's Book Writers and Illustrators.

*AWARDS, HONORS: Boston Globe-Horn Book* award for illustration, 1985, for *Mama Don't Allow.*

*WRITINGS:*

(With mother, Edith Hurd) *Little Dog Dreaming* (juvenile), illustrated by father, Clement G. Hurd, Harper (New York City), 1965.

(With John Cassidy) *Watercolor for the Artistically Undiscovered,* Klutz (Stanford, CA), 1992.

*SELF-ILLUSTRATED JUVENILE BOOKS*

*The Old Chair,* Greenwillow (New York City), 1978.

*The Quiet Evening,* Greenwillow, 1978, reissued, 1992.

*Hobo Dog,* Scholastic Book Services (New York City), 1980.

*Axle the Freeway Cat,* Harper, 1981.

*Mystery on the Docks,* Harper, 1983.

*Hobo Dog's Christmas Tree,* Scholastic Inc., 1983.

*Mama Don't Allow,* Harper, 1984.

*Hobo Dog in the Ghost Town,* Scholastic Inc. (New York City), 1985.

*Pea Patch Jig,* Crown, 1986, published with cassette, Random House/McGraw Hill (New York City), 1988, HarperCollins (New York City), 1995.

*A Night in the Swamp* (pop-up book), Harper, 1987.

*Blackberry Ramble,* Crown, 1989, HarperCollins, 1995.

*Little Mouse's Big Valentine,* Harper, 1990.

*Tomato Soup,* Crown (New York City), 1991.

*Little Mouse's Birthday Cake,* HarperCollins, 1992.

*Art Dog,* HarperCollins, 1996.

*Zoom City* (board book), HarperCollins, 1998.

*Santa Mouse and the Ratdeer,* HarperCollins, 1998.

*ILLUSTRATOR*

Ida Luttrell, *Mattie and the Chicken Thief,* Dodd (New York City), 1988.

Dayle Ann Dodds, *Wheel Away!,* Harper, 1989.

Carolyn Otto, *Dinosaur Chase,* HarperCollins, 1991.

Komaiko, Leah, *Fritzi Fox Flew in from Florida,* HarperCollins, 1995.

*ADAPTATIONS: Mystery on the Docks* was adapted for television and broadcast on *Reading Rainbow,* Public Broadcasting Service (PBS-TV), 1984. *Mama Don't Allow* was adapted for television and broadcast on *Reading Rainbow,* PBS-TV, 1984, and on *CBS Storybreak,* Columbia Broadcasting System, Inc. (CBS-TV), 1986; was adapted for videocassette, Random House, 1988; and was adapted for a children's

opera, *Muskrat Lullaby,* performed by the Los Angeles City Opera, October 6, 1989.

*SIDELIGHTS:* Author-illustrator Thacher Hurd combines a love of music, indefatigable tongue-in-cheek humor, and vibrantly bright colors to create children's books that provide lessons and chuckles. In titles such as *Hobo Dog* and its sequels, in *Mama Don't Allow, Peach Patch Jig, Blackberry Ramble,* and the "Little Mouse" books, Hurd serves up simple stories with cartoon-like artwork that make for excellent read-aloud books. Hurd's ambitions for his children's books are straightforward, as Hurd himself explained to *CA:* "To make a book exciting, to make the pages turn, to make a child laugh, to bring out a child's sense of wonder: these are what I am aiming at in my books. I believe that children's books should be for children, and not for the coffee tables of educators and librarians. I remember I loved to read as a child, and I think I try to write . . . something that could draw me into another world: an alive, vibrant world of energy and wild, bursting color."

Hurd is the son of the children's book illustrator, Clement Hurd, and the children's book author, Edith Thacher Hurd. Hurd once explained to *CA* about his informal apprenticeship with his parents: "My father never sat me down and said 'Learn this' or 'This is how you must draw.' I took everything at my own pace, and when the time was right I started to do my own books." At age sixteen, Hurd collaborated with his mother on *Little Dog Dreaming,* which was illustrated by his father. Other artists and writers also figured in his development: Maurice Sendak and his *Where the Wild Things Are;* Don Freeman and his *Pet of the Met;* Margaret Wise Brown and her *Sailor Dog;* Taro Yashima and his *Crow Boy;* and William Steig.

One of Hurd's first solo efforts, *The Quiet Evening,* was a bedtime book describing the sounds and sights of a day drawing to a close. A child lies in bed "thinking quiet thoughts," not only of home but of distant places made safe by the security felt at home. "The simple text" has accompanying illustrations rendered in "clear, dark colors. . ." noted a reviewer for *Horn Book.* Martha Davis Beck, writing in *Hungry Mind Review,* commented that Hurd "splendidly makes the link between the worlds inside and outside a house at night. His illustrations are gorgeous, but also friendly."

"I love picture books that are real adventures, full of daring and danger," Hurd once said. Though raised a country boy, Hurd possesses an urban sensibility.

Herd once told *CA:* "I try to create characters in my books who are part of the tough, fast world of the city but who are still able to make their own cozy lives within that world. . . . I find myself drawn to characters on the fringes of life: drifters, hoboes, short-order cooks, gangsters, litter collectors. . . . Music also seems to play an important part in my books. The rhythms of music spark the rhythms of a picture book and music always seems to creep into my books." And music does find its way into many of his books: the protagonist of *Axle the Freeway Cat* plays a harmonica; Ralph in *Mystery on the Docks* sings opera; and Miles plays the saxophone in *Mama Don't Allow.*

Hurd's award-winning *Mama Don't Allow* was inspired by the theme music for a show on a local radio station. The old jazz song of that name "sounded like the most raucous, wonderful thing I had ever heard and I couldn't stop thinking about it," Hurd noted in *Harper Highlights.* The lyrics to the song sounded like a natural for a children's book, and inspired Hurd to write the story of Miles, the saxophone-playing possum. In this "engaging and nonsensical romp," according to *Bulletin of the Center for Children's Books,* Miles drives his parents and neighbors crazy with his loud practicing, and soon forms a combo with three other animals called the Swamp Band. The alligators invite the band to perform at their party, to be their entertainment and main course. The band manages to escape, however, by playing a lullaby that sends the alligators off to dreamland with empty stomachs. The reviewer for *Bulletin of the Center for Children's Books* concluded that the story was "ebullient, fast-paced, and funny."

Swamps also figure in Hurd's pop-up book, *A Night in the Swamp,* which represents the activities of swamp animals between sundown and sunrise. Yvonne A. Frey in *School Library Journal* noted that the book was "exceptionally well engineered and nicely illustrated," with flaps that reveal animals underneath a wheel on one page which, when turned, makes a catfish family swim and fireflies flicker on the following page. "This is a delightful book for children of any age," Frey concluded. Writing in *Publishers Weekly,* a reviewer concluded that Hurd's "delightful" pop-up creation supplied plenty of tabs to lift or pull, which provided "a fun lesson" on animals of the night, at the same time "fancifully capturing night's many moods."

"Children often identify so completely with the characters they read about in books that they live through these characters and see themselves as the charac-

ters," Hurd once noted, "So I feel that the main character in a picture book should be strong and full of energy with a spirit of adventure and a sense of his own power to solve whatever comes his way." A family of such characters are presented in *Pea Patch Jig* and its sequels, *Blackberry Ramble* and *Tomato Soup.* Father Mouse, Mother Mouse, and Baby Mouse, who is a born troublemaker, live near Farmer Clem's garden. In the first of the books, the family is involved in a trio of adventures involving lettuce, tomatoes, and a pea shooter employed by the precocious Baby Mouse in scaring off a fox. The colors are brilliant primaries and the text simple. Music is again in attendance, with a rendition of "The Pea Patch Jig" concluding the capers. "Energy pulsates throughout the whole book," noted Ann A. Flowers in *Horn Book,* going on to describe the story as "a festive salad of a book, filled with snap, crackle, and crunch." Roger Sutton, in *Bulletin of the Center for Children's Books,* commented that "bright, jazzy shapes and colors complement this sprightly ode to vegetables." A *Publishers Weekly* critic concluded that Hurd's "kaleidoscopic colors and mischievous sense of humor make this book ripe for picking."

In *Blackberry Ramble,* Baby Mouse is once again troublesome, celebrating the arrival of spring by bothering Farmer Clem's animals, in particular, Becky the Cow. Mary Lou Budd, writing in *School Library Journal,* concluded that the "vibrant watercolor illustrations . . . are the attraction here." Sutton in *Bulletin of the Center for Children's Books* felt that though Baby Mouse's antics were "amusing," the book lacked "the vibrancy of the first." Baby Mouse makes a return visit in *Tomato Soup,* in which the little rodent is sick in bed upstairs while its parents are out planting. The doctor is called, but Baby Mouse is no friend of doctors and escapes, only to be pursued by George the cat. *Booklist*'s Ilene Cooper commented that "a bright, witty text meets its match in good-size colorful pencil illustrations."

Hurd's penchant for mice carried him through two further books: *Little Mouse's Big Valentine* and *Little Mouse's Birthday Cake.* Little Mouse makes a big valentine in the first of these, but has trouble finding the right recipient until Gloria the Mouse comes along. However, the two finally figure out an even better solution: They cut up the giant valentine into many smaller ones and distribute them to everybody. Cooper dubbed this easy-to-read book "simple yet sweet," and a critic in *Kirkus Reviews* commented that "this beguiling fable is both told and illustrated with disarming simplicity." In the second Little

Mouse adventure, it seems that his friends have forgotten his birthday and so he goes off skiing by himself. Lost for a time, he is found by his three friends who have a surprise party waiting for him. *School Library Journal*'s Budd noted that young readers would feel "the warmth and kindness of friendship through the sweeping watercolor illustrations and anticipatory text." Karen Hutt of *Booklist* concluded that "With a minimum of detail, Hurd conveys the beauty of solitude and the warmth of friendship."

With his 1996 *Art Dog,* Hurd created a superhero dog who solves problems and finds happiness through art. When the famous Mona Woofa painting is stolen from the Dogopolis Museum of Art, Art Dog goes in search of the thieves. Famous artists in the museum include Vincent Van Dog and Henri Muttisse, all joining forces with Art Dog to create an adventure that "has a camp, cartoonish Batman zaniness to it that kids will sink their canines into," according to Deborah Stevenson, writing in *Bulletin of the Center for Children's Books.* Virginia Golodetz in *School Library Journal* noted that "Hurd infuses every page of this book with dramatic watercolors," and a contributor to *Kirkus Reviews* concluded that "Art Dog is a superhero for all times." Hurd has also illustrated books for other authors, most recently Leah Komaiko's *Fritzi Fox Flew in from Florida.* Patricia Pearl Dole in *School Library Journal* commented that the text of the book was "enhanced by Hurd's bold, watercolor cartoons."

## BIOGRAPHICAL/CRITICAL SOURCES:

### BOOKS

Hurd, Thacher, *The Quiet Evening,* Greenwillow (New York City), 1978.

### PERIODICALS

*Booklist,* January 1, 1990, p. 916; November 15, 1991, p. 630; May 1, 1992, p. 1608; January 1 & 15, 1996, p. 845.

*Bulletin of the Center for Children's Books,* October, 1984, p. 28; October, 1986, p. 28; January, 1990, pp. 110-11; February, 1996, p. 191.

*Horn Book,* January, 1985, p. 72; November-December, 1986, p. 735; January/February, 1990, p. 89; March, 1992, p. 219; November-December, 1992, p. 741.

*Hungry Mind Review,* summer, 1993, p. C-16.

*Kirkus Review,* January 15, 1987, p. 131; July 1, 1989, p. 991; January 1, 1990, p. 46; December 1, 1991, p. 1541; May 15, 1992, p. 671; November 15, 1995.

*Los Angeles Times Book Review,* May 29, 1994, p. 13.

*New York Times Book Review,* February 15, 1987, p. 41.

*Publishers Weekly,* June 27, 1986, p. 86; January 16, 1987, p. 72; August 11, 1989, p. 457; December 8, 1989, p. 53; November 29, 1991, p. 51; December 20, 1991, p. 83; May 11, 1992, p. 71; January 9, 1995, p. 63; December 18, 1995, p. 53.

*School Library Journal,* April, 1987, p. 84; November, 1989, p. 84; February, 1992, p. 74; March, 1995, p. 182; February, 1996, pp. 85-6.

\*     \*     \*

## JACQUES, Brian 1939-

*PERSONAL:* Surname is pronounced "Jakes"; born June 15, 1939, in Liverpool, England; son of James (a truck driver) and Ellen Jacques; married; wife's name, Liz (a former school teacher); children: David, Marc. *Education:* Attended St. John's School, Liverpool, England. *Politics:* "Humanitarian/socialist." *Religion:* Roman Catholic. *Avocational interests:* Opera, walking his dog, crossword puzzles.

*ADDRESSES: Home*—Liverpool, England. *Office*—BBC-Radio Merseyside, 55 Paradise St., Liverpool L1 3BP, England.

*CAREER:* Worked in numerous occupations, including seaman, 1954-57, railway fireman, 1957-60, longshoreman, 1960-65, long-distance truck driver, 1965-75, docks representative, 1975-80, as well as logger, bus driver, boxer, policeman, postmaster, stand-up comic, and member of folk singer group, The Liverpool Fisherman; freelance radio broadcaster, 1980—. Radio broadcasts for BBC-Radio Merseyside include the music programs "Jakestown" and "Saturday with Brian Jacques"; six half-hour programs for junior schools, "Schools Quiz"; ten half-hour programs on cinematic knowledge, "Flixquiz"; and documentaries "We All Went Down the Docks," "Gangland Anthology," "The Eternal Christmas," "Centenary of Liverpool," "An Eyefool of Easter," "A Lifetime Habit," and "The Hollywood Musicals," a six-part series; contributor to the "Alan Jackson" show;

broadcaster for BBC-Radio and BBC-Radio 2; member of BBC Northwest Television Advisory Council. Presents humorous lectures at schools and universities. Patron of Royal Wavertree School for the Blind.

*AWARDS, HONORS:* National Light Entertainment Award for Radio from Sony Company, 1982, for BBC-Radio Merseyside's "Jakestown"; Rediffusion Award for Best Light Entertainment Program on Local Radio, 1982, and Commendation, 1983; Parents' Choice Honor Book for Literature, 1987, for *Redwall; Booklist* Editor's Choice, 1987, for *Redwall;* Children's Book of the Year Award from Lancashire County (England) Library, 1988, for *Redwall,* and also for *Mossflower* and *Salamandastron;* Western Australian Young Readers' Award, for *Redwall, Mossflower,* and *Mattimeo;* Carnegie Medal nominations, for *Redwall, Mossflower, Mattimeo,* and *Salamandastron; Redwall* was also selected as an American Library Association Best Book for Young Adults, and a *School Library Journal* Best Book.

*WRITINGS:*

*"REDWALL" SERIES*

*Redwall,* illustrated by Gary Chalk, Hutchinson (London), 1986, Philomel (New York City), 1987, anniversary edition illustrated by Troy Howell, Philomel, 1997.

*Mossflower,* illustrated by Chalk, Hutchinson, 1988, Philomel, 1988.

*Mattimeo,* illustrated by Chalk, Hutchinson, 1989, Avon, 1989.

*The Redwall Trilogy* (contains *Redwall, Mossflower,* and *Mattimeo*), three volumes, Red Fox, 1991.

*Mariel of Redwall,* illustrated by Chalk, Hutchinson, 1991, Philomel, 1991.

*Salamandastron,* illustrated by Chalk, Hutchinson, 1992, Philomel, 1992.

*Martin the Warrior,* illustrated by Chalk, Hutchinson, 1993, Philomel, 1993.

*The Bellmaker,* illustrated by Allan Curless, Hutchinson, 1994, Philomel, 1995.

*The Outcast of Redwall,* illustrated by Curless, Hutchinson, 1995, Philomel, 1995.

*The Great Redwall Feast* (rhymes excerpted from previously published material), illustrated by Christopher Denise, Philomel, 1995.

*Pearls of Lutra,* illustrated by Curless, Hutchinson, 1996, Philomel, 1997.

*The Long Patrol,* illustrated by Curless, Philomel, 1997.

*OTHER*

*Seven Strange and Ghostly Tales,* Philomel, 1991.

Also author of numerous documentaries and plays for television, radio, and the stage; stage plays include *Brown Bitter, Wet Nellies,* and *Scouse,* all performed in Liverpool, England, at the Everyman Theatre. Columnist for *Catholic Pictorial.*

*ADAPTATIONS:* Jacques narrated the cassette recording of *Seven Strange and Ghostly Tales,* Listening Library, 1996; *Redwall* and *Mossflower* have been released on audio cassette, Recorded Books, 1996.

*SIDELIGHTS:* Once planned by their author to be only a trilogy—and, before that, not intended for publication at all—the "Redwall" books by English radio personality Brian Jacques have blossomed into a nine-novel phenomenon with a growing fandom on both sides of the Atlantic. Jacques began a career as a radio personality, playwright, poet, and storyteller. By the time he was in his early forties, Jacques had found his niche as an entertainer and he now has a successful weekly radio show, "Jakestown," that airs Sundays on BBC Radio Merseyside and features selections from Jacques' favorite operas. Jacques enjoys performing and giving humorous lectures before children and adults, and he explains that this was how the story of Redwall first came into being. "I did not write my first novel, *Redwall,* with publication in mind," he once commented. "It was mainly written as a story for [the Royal Wavertree School for the Blind in Liverpool,] where I am a patron. Luckily it was picked up by a reputable author [Alan Durband, my former English teacher] and sent to Hutchinson." And so the Redwall series was born—and there is currently no end in sight to the saga of Redwall Abbey and the series' resident gentlebeasts.

The Redwall fantasy novels feature a broad cast of anthropomorphized animals who follow the author's successful good-versus-evil formula that appeals to both young and older readers. Jacques heroes and heroines can be counted on to be brave, true, and kind, while the villains are always appropriately wicked, violent, and depraved and, much to the reader's satisfaction, are dutifully defeated by the end of each novel. Some critics have argued that Jacques' characters are more animal than human, despite the fact that they wear clothes, construct buildings, and sail ships. Jane Inglis, writing in *Books for Your*

*Children,* felt that the author's "creatures are true first and foremost to their animal natures." Looking deeper into the nature of the first book in the series, *School Library Journal* contributor Susan M. Harding observed that *Redwall* is more than merely a classic story of good versus evil; it is also a study of the *nature* of the two sides of this coin. Jacques, Harding explained, does not create characters who are merely "personifications of attributes," for the heroes do have flaws, and even the reprehensible Cluny has his admirable points. The "rich cast of characters, the detailed accounts of medieval warfare, and Jacques' ability to tell a good story *and* make readers think" all make the author's first novel a worthwhile book, Harding concluded.

With *Redwall* Jacques created a flavorful recipe with admirable heroes and contemptible villains in classic battles between good and evil. This distinction between good and evil, right and wrong, is carried out deliberately by Jacques, who once remarked: "In writing children's books, I feel that a 'good yarn' is essential, keeping in mind a strong moral sense of values for children." *Voice of Youth Advocates* contributor Katharine L. Kan summarized the basic plotline as: "goodbeast sanctuary threatened by nogood vermin and/or natural disaster, young untested heroes to the rescue." The world of Redwall, according to Selma Lanes in the *New York Times Book Review,* is "a credible and ingratiating place, one to which many young readers will doubtless cheerfully return." "Jacques," Sawyer concluded, "is writing for an audience who want—even need—clearly identifiable labels for their moral signposts." While such a device can be reassuring to readers, who always know what to expect when they pick up a Redwall book, it also has a downside, as Ruth S. Vose pointed out in her *School Library Journal* review of *Mossflower:* "Suspense does not arise from the situation itself," she remarked, "for the end is never really in doubt." Marcus Crouch, also writing about *Mossflower* in *Junior Bookshelf,* felt that, although Jacques demonstrates narrative skill in the way he weaves different subplots together, the author goes into too much unnecessary detail, his style is filled with "narrative cliches," and the characters "are mostly stereotypes."

One of the more common complaints about Jacques' stories concerns the author's delight in describing sumptuous Redwall feasts in great detail and at great length. Not a story is told without at least one of these festive soirees of fish, vegetables, fruit, fresh breads, and luscious desserts. The Redwallers' "love of food . . . makes for a persistent and slightly repetitious theme in all the books," commented Katherine Bouton in the *New York Times Book Review.* More emphatically, Kan lamented, "*Why* do English authors spend so much time describing meals in such excruciating detail?" But "the repasts are not the only part of the story that go on too long," wrote one *Publishers Weekly* contributor in a review of *Outcast of Redwall,* who complained that the qualities of each character is fixed by his or her species: the hares are all upper class, foppish but brave warriors; the moles are all rural types who speak in a difficult-to-interpret dialect; the children (or "dibbuns") are all rascally mischief-makers; the hawks all speak with Scottish accents; the sparrows are all primitive barbarians who speak a sort of pidgin English, and so on.

Nevertheless, there are also many positives to the Redwall series. While admitting that the stories are "formulaic," Bouton asserted that they are also "wonderfully imaginative in their variety of plot and character." Jacques approaches his subject, not with a heavy hand in an attempt to suggest some epic struggle, but rather finds plenty of opportunity for levity. As Andy Sawyer remarked in his *School Librarian* review of *Outcast of Redwall,* not only is there much jollity in the regular feasts in which the gentlebeasts partake, but there is also plenty of "hearty japes, slapstick humour and swashbuckling action [that is] pitched perfectly at the intended readership." Much of the humor comes from the antics of the mischievous dibbuns, but also from Jacques' satirical jibes at English upper crust military types who take the form of hares in his books. A satiric air is lent even to the villains, as *School Librarian* critic Peter Andrews observed: "Evil as they may be, none of the villains can be taken seriously because most are of the pantomime variety."

Another feature of Jacques' books that critics have admired is his complete lack of chauvinism: there are just as many brave and daring heroines in the series as there are heroes; likewise, the villains are often vixens or female wildcats who are just as treacherous as their male counterparts. "The author must be commended for creating a world of equal-opportunity adventuring," commented one *Publishers Weekly* reviewer. "For once," Carolyn Cushman wrote in her *Locus* assessment of *Mariel of Redwall,* "it's not just the boys who get to hear the spirit of Martin the Warrior—the ladies really get their chance this outing. Having a valiant female protagonist is a nice touch."

Inevitably, comparisons have been drawn between *Redwall* and other English books with anthropomorphized animal characters like Richard Adams' *Watership Down* and Kenneth Grahame's *The Wind in the Willows,* though about the only common feature of these books is that they include animal protagonists exhibiting human-like behavior to greater or lesser degrees. Citing the comparison with *Watership Down,* Margery Fisher perceptively noted in her *Growing Point* assessment of *Redwall* that for "all the similarities of idiom, alert sophisticated narrative and neat humanization, *Redwall* has an intriguing and unusual flavour of its own."

*BIOGRAPHICAL/CRITICAL SOURCES:*

BOOKS

*Seventh Book of Junior Authors and Illustrators,* H. W. Wilson (Bronx, NY), 1996, pp. 150-51.

PERIODICALS

*Booklist,* March 1, 1996, p. 1182; October 15, 1996, p. 424.
*Books for Your Children,* spring, 1988, p. 31.
*Bulletin of the Center for Children's Books,* January, 1994, p. 157; March, 1996, pp. 30-31.
*Growing Point,* March, 1987, pp. 4756-57.
*Horn Book,* May-June, 1992, p. 340.
*Junior Bookshelf,* December, 1988, pp. 304-05.
*Kirkus Reviews,* February 1, 1994, p. 144.
*Locus,* March, 1992, p. 64.
*New York Times Book Review,* August 23, 1987, p. 27; February 27, 1994, p. 24.
*Publishers Weekly,* February 20, 1995, p. 206; January 15, 1996, pp. 462-63; April 15, 1996, p. 34; August 19, 1996; December 30, 1996, p. 67.
*School Librarian,* November, 1994, p. 151; February, 1996.
*School Library Journal,* August, 1987, p. 96; November, 1988, pp. 125-26; March, 1993, p. 198; May, 1996, p. 113.
*Voice of Youth Advocates,* June, 1993, p. 102.*

\*      \*      \*

**JAMES, Robin**
    **See CURTIS, Sharon**

**JENNINGS, Sharon (Elizabeth) 1954-**

*PERSONAL:* Born January 21, 1954, in Toronto, Ontario, Canada; daughter of Alfred Joseph (a mechanic) and Eileen Estella (a homemaker; maiden name, Coull) Jennings; married Anthony DiLena (a lawyer), October 20, 1979; children: Adrian, Guy, Mia. *Education:* University of York, M.A., 1978; University of Toronto, diplomas in speech arts, 1978 and 1979.

*ADDRESSES: Home*—34 Evans Ave., Toronto, Ontario, Canada M6S 3V6.

*CAREER:* Harcourt Brace Jovanovich, Toronto, Ontario, senior editor, 1982-1986; Nelson Canada, Toronto, senior editor, 1986-87; writer.

*MEMBER:* International Board of Books for Young People (IBBY-Canada), Canadian Society of Composers, Authors, Illustrators and Publishers (CANS-CAIP), Writers' Union of Canada, Canadian Children's Book Centre.

*AWARDS, HONORS:* Best Kids' Books of the Year citation, *Parents* magazine, 1990, for *Jeremiah and Mrs. Ming.*

*WRITINGS:*

FOR CHILDREN; ILLUSTRATED BY MIREILLE LEVERT; PUBLISHED BY ANNICK PRESS

*Jeremiah and Mrs. Ming,* 1990.
*When Jeremiah Found Mrs. Ming,* 1992.
*Sleep Tight, Mrs. Ming,* 1993.

*SIDELIGHTS:* "As a young adult I studied drama and belonged to theater groups," Sharon Jennings once recalled. "This led to many part-time jobs teaching drama to children. After receiving a master's degree in English literature, I was able to combine my interests and edit language and dramatic arts textbooks. Now, with three children of my own, I am very much drawn to writing for children."

Jennings came up with the idea for her first book, *Jeremiah and Mrs. Ming,* when her first child wouldn't go to sleep one night. In the story, Jeremiah tells Mrs. Ming he can't sleep, each time for a different reason: his shoes "are tap dancing," his books "are reading their stories," and so on. Meanwhile, Mrs. Ming herself pursues a variety of activities: baking cookies, practicing her ballet, reading the newspaper. Yet each time she is interrupted by Jeremiah, she patiently accompanies him to his room, where she announces loudly, "When I open the door . . . ," and asks each noisemaker in turn to quiet down. Finally, Jeremiah is soothed enough to go to sleep. This "simple, cumulative, and repetitive" story has a "mysterious" effect, commented *Horn Book* reviewer Sarah Ellis. "The world is crazy but safe, say the pictures. . . . This is the world of bedtime that Jennings and Levert celebrate in this delicate and resonant picture book." Also praising the book was art professor Jetske Sybesma, who noted in *Canadian Children's Literature* that "Mrs. Ming is not at all a stereotyped immigrant functioning in a subordinate role. . . . The text and pictures succeed in presenting a positive attitude" toward Canada's ethnic diversity. The book was cited by *Parents* magazine as one of the year's best.

*When Jeremiah Found Mrs. Ming* grew out of the time the author's children, standing in middle of a pile of many toys, announced that they had nothing to do. When Jeremiah presents the marvelous Mrs. Ming with the same problem, he is rewarded with a series of wacky adventures. "Jennings has clearly captured a small child's idea of a good time," said Ellis in *Quill & Quire*. Writing in *Canadian Materials,* reviewer Ila D. Scott noted that the book "reinforces the strong message that whenever there is nothing to do, reading is a way to bring many exciting things to pass."

According to her publisher, *Sleep Tight, Mrs. Ming* "was inspired by Sharon's own many sleepless nights." Once again the reluctant sleeper Jeremiah calls on Mrs. Ming to deal with the usual variety of nighttime problems and fears. Then comes a surprise ending in which Mrs. Ming, finally asleep herself, is awakened by a thunderstorm and turns to Jeremiah for comfort. Mireille Levert's artwork earned the book a Governor General's Award for illustration, and in the *Canadian Book Review Annual* Steve Pitt remarked that "This is the third terrific book about the enigmatic relationship between Mrs. Ming and Jeremiah." In recommending the book, the critic concluded that the pair "seem destined for a long relationship."

*BIOGRAPHICAL/CRITICAL SOURCES:*

*PERIODICALS*

*Books in Canada,* November, 1992, p. 36.
*Canadian Book Review Annual,* 1990, p. 6046.
*Canadian Children's Literature,* Number 62, 1991, pp. 99-100.
*Canadian Materials,* October, 1992, p. 263; November, 1993, p. 218.
*Horn Book,* January/February, 1991, p. 110.
*Quill & Quire,* June, 1990; September, 1992, p. 71.

# K

## KNUDTSON, Peter M(ichael) 1947-

*PERSONAL:* Born February 28, 1947, in Bethesda, MD; son of Kenneth P. (a physician) and Ruth (Higdon) Knudtson. *Education:* University of California, Riverside, B.A., 1969; graduate study at University of North Carolina at Chapel Hill, 1969-70; California State University, Arcata, M.A., 1974; further graduate study at University of California, Berkeley, 1982-83.

*ADDRESSES: Home*—605-1508 Mariner's Walk, Vancouver, British Columbia, Canada V6J 4X9.

*CAREER:* U.S. Forest Service, naturalist in California and Alaska, 1972-74; U.S. Fish and Wildlife Service, Anchorage, AK, wildlife biologist, 1975-76; technical writer for solar energy education group, 1977-78; science teacher at an alternative high school in Ketchikan, AK, 1979-81; free-lance writer, 1974—. Technical writer for computer software industry, 1983-85.

*MEMBER:* National Association of Science Writers, Writers Union of Canada.

*AWARDS, HONORS:* Writing grants, Ontario Arts Council, 1987, and Canada Council, 1987, 1993, 1997; second prize, Canadian Authors Awards, Foundation for the Advancement of Canadian Letters, 1988, for *David Suzuki Talks about AIDS.*

*WRITINGS:*

*The Wintun Indians of California,* Naturegraph (Healdsburg, CA), 1977.

(With David Suzuki and Eileen Thalenberg) *David Suzuki Talks about AIDS,* General Publications (Toronto, Ontario), 1987.

(With Suzuki) *Genethics: The Ethics of Engineering Life,* Stoddart (Don Mills, Ontario), 1988, published as *Genethics: The Clash between the New Genetics and Human Values,* Harvard University Press (Cambridge, MA), 1989.

*A Mirror to Nature: Reflections on Science, Scientists, and Society* (collected essays), Stoddart, 1991.

(With Suzuki) *Wisdom of the Elders: Honoring Sacred Native Visions of Nature,* Bantam (New York City), 1992.

*Orca: Visions of the Killer Whale,* Sierra Books (San Francisco, CA), 1997.

*The World of the Walrus,* Sierra Books, 1998.

Contributor to periodicals, including *Natural History, Alaska, Science 85, Equinox, California Living,* and *Oceans.* Books have been bestsellers in Canada and Australia.

*BIOGRAPHICAL/CRITICAL SOURCES:*

*PERIODICALS*

*Globe and Mail* (Toronto), July 16, 1988.
*Journal of the American Medical Association,* January 5, 1990.
*Los Angeles Times,* February 7, 1989.
*San Francisco Chronicle,* February 29, 1989.
*Times Literary Supplement,* December 15, 1989.
*Washington Post Book World,* March 26, 1989.

**KONSTAN, David 1940-**

*PERSONAL:* Born November 1, 1940, in New York, NY; son of Harry (a store manager) and Edythe (a school board president; maiden name, Wahrman) Konstan; children: Eve Anna, Geoffrey. *Education:* Columbia University, B.A. (cum laude), 1961, M.A., 1963, Ph.D., 1967.

*ADDRESSES: Home*—92 Ivy St., Providence, RI 02906. *Office*—Department of Classics, Brown University, Providence, RI 02912; fax 401-863-7484. *E-mail*—dkonstan@brownvm.brown.edu.

*CAREER:* Hunter College of the City University of New York, New York City, lecturer in classics, 1964-65; Brooklyn College of the City University of New York, Brooklyn, NY, instructor in classics, 1965-67; Wesleyan University, Middletown, CT, assistant professor, 1967-72, associate professor, 1972-77, Jane A. Seney Professor of Greek, 1977-87, chairperson of department of classics, 1975-77, 1978-80, director of humanities program, 1972-74; Brown University, Providence, RI, professor, 1987—, John Rowe Workman Distinguished Professor of the Classics and the Humanistic Tradition, 1992—, chairperson of department of classics, 1989-92. American University in Cairo, visiting professor, 1981-83; University of Texas at Austin, visiting scholar, 1986-90; University of California, Los Angeles, visiting professor, 1987; Monash University, Fulbright senior lecturer, 1988; University of Sydney, visiting professor, 1990-91; University of Natal, visiting professor, 1993; University of La Plata, visiting professor, 1997. Programme MENTOR, member of international scientific committee, 1988—.

*MEMBER:* American Philological Association, Classical Association of New England (state president, 1979), Phi Beta Kappa.

*AWARDS, HONORS:* Fellow, National Endowment for the Humanities, 1978 and 1990, and American Council of Learned Societies, 1991; award for outstanding academic book, *Choice,* 1989-90, for the translation *On Aristotle's Physics Six;* Guggenheim fellow, 1994; fellow at National Humanities Center, 1995.

*WRITINGS:*

*Some Aspects of Epicurean Psychology,* E. J. Brill (Leiden, Netherlands), 1973.

*Catullus' Indictment of Rome: The Meaning of Catullus 64,* Hakkert (Amsterdam, Netherlands), 1977.
*Roman Comedy,* Cornell University Press (Ithaca, NY), 1983.
(Editor) Menander, *Dyskolos,* Bryn Mawr Commentaries (Bryn Mawr, PA), 1983.
(Contributor) John P. Anton and Anthony Preus, editors, *Essays in Ancient Greek Philosophy,* Volume 2, State University of New York Press (Albany, NY), 1983.
(Contributor) Hugh Curtler, editor, *What Is Art?,* Haven Publishing, 1983.
(Contributor) Berel Lang, editor, *The Death of Art: Critical Essays in Philosophy,* Haven Publishing, 1984.
(Contributor) Bertell Ollman and Edward Vernoff, editors, *The Left Academy,* Volume 2, Praeger (New York City), 1984.
(Editor with Michael Roberts) *Apollonius of Tyre,* Bryn Mawr Commentaries, 1985.
(Translator) Simplicius, *On Aristotle's Physics Six,* Cornell University Press, 1989.
*Sexual Symmetry: Love in the Ancient Novel and Related Genres,* Princeton University Press (Princeton, NJ), 1994.
*Greek Comedy and Ideology,* Oxford University Press (New York City), 1995.
*Friendship in the Classical World,* Cambridge University Press (Cambridge, England), 1997.
(Translator with Diskin Clay, Clarence Glad, and others, and author of commentary) *Philodemus Peri Parrhesias,* Society of Biblical Literature Texts and Translations (Atlanta, GA), 1997.

Contributor of more than one-hundred articles and reviews to scholarly journals. *Arethusa,* guest editor, 1980, associate editor, 1990—; member of editorial board, *Diaspora: Journal of Transnational Studies,* 1989—; member of editorial advisory board, *Scholia: Natal Studies in Classical Antiquity,* 1991-93.

*WORK IN PROGRESS: Greek Literature,* in the series "The Classical Idiom," for Routledge (New York City).

*SIDELIGHTS:* David Konstan told *CA:* "Among my original motives for pursuing the classics were these: that one could study a few texts lovingly, and that all disciplines, it seemed, lay open to one who commanded the languages. I have been fortunate: I have had the chance to spend months with a few dozen verses of Catullus, to meditate on why atoms fall and how slavery transformed the Roman world. I approach the ancient world as an anthropologist. True,

I cannot ask direct questions of the Greeks and Romans, but they have left us a marvelous set of documents.

"The classical world was not all glory and grandeur. It marginalized women, foreigners, slaves, the dependant poor. Part of our task is [to] demystify the past, and understand it in a critical way.

"I have had the pleasure, in recent years, of studying laughter, sexuality, and friendship in the ancient world. I am contemplating devoting the next few years to investigating the history of pity. I don't know if there is a deeper significance to this intellectual trajectory, but it is certainly not boring."

\*    \*    \*

**KRAMER, Jane 1938-**

PERSONAL: Born August 7, 1938, in Providence, RI; daughter of Louis (a physician) and Jessica (Shore) Kramer; married Vincent Crapanzano (professor and writer), April 30, 1967; children: Aleksandra. *Education:* Vassar College, B.A., 1959; Columbia University, M.A., 1961.

ADDRESSES: *Home*—New York, NY. *Office*—*New Yorker,* 25 West 43rd St., New York, NY 10036. *Agent*—Lynn Nesbit, International Creative Management, 40 West 57th St., New York, NY 10019.

CAREER: *Morningsider,* New York City, founder and writer, 1961-62; *Village Voice,* New York City, writer, 1962-63; *New Yorker,* New York City, writer, 1963—. Member of Council on Foreign Relations; member of Journalists Human Rights Committee; associate of Environmental Defense Fund. Consultant to German Marshall Fund, 1981.

MEMBER: Writers Guild of America (East; board member, 1963-65), Authors League of America, Authors Guild, PEN, Book Critics Circle, Phi Beta Kappa.

AWARDS, HONORS: Emmy award from National Academy of Television Arts and Sciences, 1966, for documentary, "This Is Edward Steichen"; named woman of the year by *Mademoiselle,* 1968; Front Page award from *New Yorker,* 1977, for best magazine feature, "The Invandrare"; National Book Award for best paperback nonfiction book, 1981, for *The*

Last Cowboy; National Magazine Award for feature writing, 1993, for *Whose Art Is It?.*

*WRITINGS:*

*NONFICTION*

*Off Washington Square: A Reporter Looks at Greenwich Village,* Duell, Sloan & Pearce (New York City), 1963.

*Allen Ginsberg in America,* Random House (New York City), 1969 (published in England as *Paterfamilias,* Gollancz, 1970).

*Honor to the Bride Like the Pigeon That Guards Its Grain Under the Clove Tree,* Farrar, Straus (New York City), 1970.

*The Last Cowboy,* Harper (New York City), 1978.

*Unsettling Europe,* Random House, 1980.

*Europeans,* Farrar, Straus, 1988.

*Whose Art Is It?,* Duke University Press (Durham, NC), 1994.

*The Politics of Memory: Looking for Germany in the New Germany,* Random House, 1996.

Contributor to periodicals, including the *New Yorker, New York Times Book Review* and *New York Review of Books.*

SIDELIGHTS: "In her thirty years at the *New Yorker* Jane Kramer has written shrewd profiles of Italian peasants, Moroccan teenagers, Texas cowboys, German skinheads, New York City artists, and European heads of state," said John J. Pauly in *Dictionary of Literary Biography.* "Reviews of her books in popular magazines and newspapers have praised the grace and clarity of her writing. Yet this cosmopolitan body of work, with an intellectual depth unmatched in contemporary journalism, has received almost no scholarly attention. Such recognition is long overdue, for Kramer has written eloquently about the politics of cultural identity . . . that have characterized the late twentieth century."

Kramer's first widely reviewed book, *Allen Ginsberg in America,* met with a mixed reception. Many critics complained that Kramer's biographical portrait was too sketchy and admiring. Malcolm Muggeridge in the *Observer* called the author "sentimental, whimsical, sprawling" and explained that what the book "is lacking is any serious critical estimate of Ginsberg and his work." Similarly, Steve Lerner of the *Village Voice* observed "that while the book is an up, easy-flowing, often informative narrative about a colorful man, it lacks the tension and deep, often uncomfortable probing that a good biography requires in order to adequately depict a public figure." Lerner added, however, that even though Kramer in *Allen Ginsberg in America* "is repetitious of the flower-bedecked caricature we all know and love, she also manages to present enough new information, describe enough scenes that the television cameras missed, and hear enough good words that were inaudible to the masses to piece together a living Ginsberg. This, in itself, is enough of a recommendation to make the book worth reading for an audience of post beat-early hip generation who have missed the real article in person."

*Honor to the Bride,* Kramer's next book, is about the kidnapping and violation of a thirteen-year-old girl from her Arab family living in Meknes, Morocco. She is the family's most valuable asset, for her virginal state will bring in a substantial bride price. Therefore, when she is returned to her relatives, her family comically endeavors to legally reestablish her virginity. *Times*'s Martha Duffy highly praised *Honor to the Bride*. It "is an excellent example of the 'nonfiction novel,'" she commented. "Beyond its entertainment value, the book offers a remarkable glimpse into . . . Arab attitudes toward justice, money and women. . . . Thanks to the author's effortless narrative, the reader hurtles through an exotic world, not realizing until the end that he has been taken on a fascinating trip through the Arab mind."

*The Last Cowboy* is the story of Henry Blanton, a cowboy who lives and works on a ranch in the Texas panhandle. With motion picture star Glen Ford as his model, Blanton has embodied the image of the proud cowboy to such a degree that he has become a caricature. Henry McDonald of the *Washington Post* explained that Blanton is seen "as an anomaly, not so much because he seems bigoted, chauvinistic and unpredictably violent. Rather, his oddity stems from his determination to live out a fantasy of himself as a rugged and heroic cowboy in a land which devalues such qualities." The *New York Times*'s John Leonard complimented the author on her portrait of Blanton and remarked: "It is a measure of Jane Kramer's immense skill that we come to like Henry almost in spite of himself. . . . We aren't poked in the tearducts; we merely watch and eavesdrop. . . . She [Kramer] is incapable of contempt, although the sadness has spurs." McDonald concurred and described *The Last Cowboy* as an "insightful, unsentimental and handsomely crafted work."

Similarly, *Unsettling Europe* also received favorable reviews from critics. Irving Howe of the *New York*

*Times Book Review* explained that "this accomplished book consists of four social-historical sketches— suavely but sturdily composed—about people in Europe who have been uprooted from their natural communities and thrust into alien, sometimes hostile settings." Featured are a Yugoslav family living in Sweden, French Algerians living in Provence, Ugandan Muslims dwelling in a London ghetto, and Italian Communists who feel their Party has forsaken them and the revolution. *Nation*'s Thomas Flanagan assessed that "Kramer's intention is to break down the exhausted, conventional categories in which sociology and journalism solicit us to consider contemporary Europe, by creating for us the bitter, absurd, fractured lives of 'people who fell into the cracks of history.'" James N. Baker of *Newsweek* agreed that Kramer's "is no-nonsense journalism at its best: direct, finely detailed portraits of four troubled families . . . by a writer who combines the skills of a social historian with those of a novelist."

Kramer deepened her portrait of Europe and its people in her 1988 book *Europeans,* which is made up of *New Yorker* pieces written between 1978 and 1988. It includes sketches of cities, descriptions of ordinary people, long stories about controversial news events, obituaries and sketches of famous citizens, and comic and serious reflections. "Reviewers agreed that *Europeans* was a superb piece of writing," reported Pauly. "They called it 'masterful,' 'exquisite,' 'polished,' 'distinguished,' and 'brilliant.'" Pauly declared that "*Europeans* interprets politics of cultural identity as it is played out in national policy, cultural mythology, news coverage, local prejudice, and family history. Kramer understands European politics as a symbolic drama and treats political events as cultural texts. Particularly new and notable are the book's ambitious profiles of five major cities—Hamburg, Paris, Zurich, London, and West Berlin. These city essays are among the most accomplished and opinionated pieces Kramer has ever written."

For her next book, *Whose Art Is It?,* Kramer turned her attention back to the United States. The book, originally published as a long article in the *New Yorker,* details a conflict that arose over publicly funded sculpture in the Bronx. Internationally known sculptor John Ahearn was awarded a commission from New York City's Percent for Art Program to install three statues in front of a police station. He chose to depict a man with a pit bull, a man with a basketball and a boom box, and a girl on roller skates. Protests arose on the grounds that the figures were stereotypes, demeaning to Bronx residents, and Ahearn voluntarily removed the statues less than a week after they were installed. Pauly called it "a stylistic tour de force . . . [that] displays the dense, graceful, complex narrative that Kramer has spent years perfecting." He further commented that "ultimately, *Whose Art Is It?* examines the social conflicts often referenced by shorthand terms such as *multiculturalism* and *political correctness.*"

Applauding Kramer's body of work, Pauly declared: "Over three decades she has developed one of the most elegant and distinctive voices in American literary journalism. She has written with depth and sophistication about an extraordinary range of topics. She has earned the admiration of careful readers and other professional writers. She has refused to traffic in celebrity, speculation, or shallow controversy. She writes eloquently of her subjects virtues and vices, regardless of their social standing. Yet for all the praise of her beautiful writing style, Kramer remains underappreciated as a reporter and analyst." Pauly conjectured that if Kramer were a man, if she wrote "in a more ponderously theoretical style . . . if she promoted herself as shamelessly as others do, she would find herself being heralded by the newsweeklies as a 'public intellectual.'"

Pauly concluded: "The profession of journalism is mythically devoted, in equal measure, to objectivity and publicity, to detachment and fame, and journalists, like women, struggle to make themselves visible. The worst journalists settle for notoriety, serving as television pundits, currying favor with the powerful, surfing the tides of public opinion. The best, like Kramer, cherish their independence but want something more. They seek to make their presence felt, to serve as witnesses rather than remain just observers."

*BIOGRAPHICAL/CRITICAL SOURCES:*

*BOOKS*

Connery, Thomas B., editor, *A Sourcebook of American Literary Journalism: Representative Writers in an Emerging Genre,* Greenwood Press (New York City), 1992, pp. 323-329.
*Dictionary of Literary Biography,* Volume 185: *American Literary Journalists, 1945-1995, First Series,* Gale (Detroit), 1997.
McAuliffe, Kevin M., *The Great American Newspaper: The Rise and Fall of the* Village Voice, Scribners (New York City), 1978, pp. 71-73.

*PERIODICALS*

*Christian Science Monitor,* July 17, 1969.
*Nation,* May 31, 1980.
*New Statesman,* August 13, 1971.
*Newsweek,* June 9, 1980.
*New York Review of Books,* August 14, 1980.
*New York Times,* May 17, 1969; January 24, 1978.
*New York Times Book Review,* May 11, 1969; May 18, 1980.
*Observer,* February 8, 1970.
*Time,* August 8, 1969; January 4, 1971.
*Village Voice,* September 4, 1969.
*Washington Post,* April 1, 1978.*

\*      \*      \*

## KRAMER, Mark (William) 1944-

*PERSONAL:* Born April 14, 1944, in New York, NY; son of Sidney B. (an attorney and publisher) and Esther (a book store operator; maiden name, Schlansky) Kramer. *Education:* Brandeis University, B.A., 1966; Columbia University, M.A., 1967; graduate study at Indiana University, 1967-68.

*ADDRESSES: Agent*—Georges Borchardt, Inc., 136 East 57th St., New York, NY 10022.

*CAREER:* Farmer in western Massachusetts, 1969-81; Smith College, Northampton, MA, writer-in-residence, 1980-90; Boston University, Boston, MA, professor and writer-in-residence, 1990—. Visiting lecturer at University of Massachusetts, 1976-79.

*AWARDS, HONORS:* Rockefeller Foundation humanities fellowship, 1976-78; blue ribbon from American Film Festival, 1979, for writing and co-directing *Crisis in Yankee Agriculture;* Ford Foundation fellowship for nonfiction, 1980-81.

*WRITINGS:*

*Mother Walker and the Pig Tragedy,* Knopf (New York City), 1972.
*Three Farms: Making Milk, Meat, and Money from the American Soil,* Atlantic Monthly Press (Boston), 1980, revised edition, Harvard University Press (Cambridge, MA), 1987.

*Invasive Procedures: A Year in the World of Two Surgeons,* Harper (New York City), 1983.

(Editor with Norman Sims, and contributor) *The Literary Journalists,* Ballantine (New York City), 1985.

*Travels with a Hungry Bear: A Journey to the Russian Heartland,* Houghton (Boston), 1996.

Author of introduction, *The Growth of Industrial Art* (picture book), edited by Benjamin Butterworth, Knopf, 1973. Contributor of articles and reviews to *Atlantic Monthly, New York Times,* and *National Geographic.* Also author of documentary film *Crisis in Yankee Agriculture,* released by Cambridge Media Resources.

*SIDELIGHTS:* Mark Kramer once told *CA:* "I am writing about people whose lives are tangled up with changing technology and new businesses. I am as interested in style and structure as I am in my topics." Kramer's *Three Farms: Making Milk, Meat, and Money from the American Soil* examines the economic pressures that are besieging the American farm industry. In order to research the book, Kramer spent several years visiting the farms he chose to profile—a small dairy farm in Massachusetts, a larger hog farm in Iowa, and an extensive corporate farm in California. In all three cases, he found a concern for updating technology in order to expand production and profitability. Noel Perrin, reviewing *Three Farms* in the *New York Times Book Review,* feels that Kramer's background as a small farmer helped to formulate "an enthralling book." "Mr. Kramer does two remarkable things in this book," Perrin writes. "One is to capture the true feel of country life in a high-technology era. . . . Kramer's other triumph is to see what scarcely anyone else has seen so clearly: that the villain in the destruction of rural life is not . . . cold-hearted agri-businessmen or greedy distributors, but simply the capital-intensive nature of technology itself."

In *Invasive Procedures: A Year in the World of Two Surgeons,* Kramer continues his technique of writing based upon longterm observations. Having followed two doctors on their rounds, into the operating rooms, and even into their homes, Kramer reports on the quality of life his subjects achieve within their demanding professions. William A. Nolen, himself a surgeon, says in the *Washington Post Book World:* "Kramer's book gives, I think, a realistic view of how surgeons in private practice live and work. His descriptions of operating-room scenes, including the interplay between the nurses, anesthetists and doctors, [are] vivid and dramatic, but the drama isn't grossly exaggerated as is so often the case when the medical world is portrayed." In the *New York Times Book Review,* Joe McGinniss calls Kramer's work "frequently engrossing, though naggingly uneven," and goes on to comment that Kramer's "reportorial skill, combined with a prose style that . . . is as clean and sharp as one of his subjects' scalpel blades, has produced a book that gives an intriguing and often insightful look behind the scenes of a world that both fascinates and repels."

Kramer's agricultural background served him well for the writing of *Travels with a Hungry Bear: A Journey to the Russian Heartland.* In it, he takes "an evocative look at the sad state of agriculture in the former Soviet Union," advises Jim Collins in *Dictionary of Literary Biography.* "He attempts to answer the question 'How can a country of eleven time zones of wheat fields not feed itself?'" As in *Three Farms* and *Invasive Procedures,* Kramer takes the reader into a foreign world and looks at the dramatic changes taking place in it. "The result," says Collins, "is a compelling tale that is part travelogue, part social and political commentary, part agricultural criticism, part historical document, and part psychological portraiture."

Kramer made six trips to the Soviet Union to research the book, visiting numerous state farms. Unfortunately for the author, the Soviet Union collapsed just as he completed his first draft, making much of what he had written out-of-date. "It was," Collins quotes him as saying, "as if I'd made a huge mosaic out of tiny pieces, and someone had come along and tipped the whole thing over, leaving the pieces in a jumble on the floor. I could use bits of the information I'd gathered, but now I had to start over and put them back together in a new order." He did just that, and the result, says Collins, "is a condemnation of state-run agriculture on a large scale but a sympathetic portrait of everyday people who struggle to live within a system of entrenched bureaucracy, underground markets, and chronic shortages of everything from food staples to fertilizer and basic tractor parts."

*BIOGRAPHICAL/CRITICAL SOURCES:*

*BOOKS*

*Dictionary of Literary Biography,* Volume 185: *American Literary Journalists, 1945-1995, First Series,* Gale (Detroit), 1997.

PERIODICALS

*New York Times Book Review,* March 30, 1980; September 18, 1983.
*Washington Post Book World,* August 28, 1983.*

\*   \*   \*

## KRIPPNER, Stanley (Curtis) 1932-

*PERSONAL:* Born October 4, 1932, in Edgerton, WI; son of Carroll Porter (a farmer) and Ruth (Volenberg) Krippner; married Lelie Harris, June 25, 1966; children: (stepchildren) Caron Harris, Robert Harris. *Ethnicitiy:* "EuroAmerican." *Education:* University of Wisconsin—Madison, B.S., 1954; Northwestern University, M.A., 1958, Ph.D., 1961. *Politics:* Independent. *Religion:* "Presbyterian, Taoist." *Avocational interests:* Cinema, theater, jogging.

*ADDRESSES: Home*—79 Woodland Rd., Fairfax, CA 94930. *Office*—Saybrook Institute, 450 Pacific Ave., No. 300, San Francisco, CA 94123; fax 415-433-9271. *E-mail*—skrippner@ige.ape.org.

*CAREER:* Speech therapist for city of Warren, IL, 1954-55, and for public schools of Richmond, VA, 1955-56; Kent State University, Kent, OH, director of Child Study Center, 1961-64; Maimonides Medical Center, Brooklyn, NY, director of dream laboratory, 1964-73; Saybrook Institute, San Francisco, CA, professor of psychology, 1973—. State University of West Georgia, adjunct professor, 1976; visiting professor or lecturer at universities and academies in the United States and abroad, including University of California, Los Angeles, 1968, and U.S.S.R. Academy of Pedagogical Sciences, 1971. Academy of Religion and Psychical Research, member of board of trustees; member of advisory boards of foundations, schools, and health centers, including Foundation for Mind Research and Center for Attitudinal Healing; Menninger Foundation, member.

*MEMBER:* International Association for Psychotronic Research (vice-president, 1973-77), International Society for General Semantics, Inter-American Psychological Association, National Society for the Study of Education, National Association for Gifted Children (vice-president, 1968-74), American Society for Clinical Hypnosis (fellow), American Psychological Association (fellow; division president, 1980-81, 1997-98), American Psychological Society (fellow), American Society for Psychical Research, American Association for the Advancement of Science, American Educational Research Association, American Counseling Association, Association for Humanistic Psychology (president, 1974-75), Association for the Psychophysiological Study of Sleep, Association for Biofeedback and Applied Psychophysiology, Association for the Study of Dreams (president, 1995-96), Council for Exceptional Children, Parapsychological Association (president, 1983), Psychologists for Social Action, Society for Clinical and Experimental Hypnosis (fellow), Society for the Scientific Study of Sexuality (fellow), Society for the Scientific Study of Religion (fellow).

*AWARDS, HONORS:* Service to Youth Award, Young Men's Christian Association, 1959; citations of merit, National Association for Gifted Children, 1972, and National Association for Creative Children and Adults, 1975; certificate of recognition, U.S. Office of the Gifted and Talented, 1976; Maurice Volker Award, 1980, for contributions to parapsychology; honorary doctorate, University for Humanistic Studies, 1982.

*WRITINGS:*

(With Montague Ullman) *Dream Studies and Telepathy* (monograph), Parapsychological Foundation, 1970.
*Shamlet,* Exposition (Smithtown, NY), 1971.
(Editor with Daniel Rubin) *Galaxies of Life: The Human Aura in Acupuncture and Kirlian Photography,* Gordon & Breach (New York City), 1973.
(With Ullman and Alan Vaughan) *Dream Telepathy: Experiments in Nocturnal E.S.P.,* Macmillan (New York City), 1973, 2nd edition, McFarland & Co. (Jefferson, NC), 1989.
(Editor with Rubin) *The Kirlian Aura,* Doubleday (New York City), 1974.
(Editor with Rubin) *The Energies of Consciousness: Explorations in Acupuncture, Auras, and Kirlian Photography,* Gordon & Breach, 1975.
*Song of the Siren: A Parapsychological Odyssey,* Harper (New York City), 1975.
(With Alberto Villoldo) *The Realms of Healing,* Celestial Arts (Berkeley, CA), 1976.
(With Roy Dreistadt) *The Psychology of Societies* (monograph), Kishkam Press, 1976.
(With Eleanor Criswell) *Physiology of Consciousness* (monograph), Kishkam Press, 1976.
(Editor) *Advances in Parapsychological Research,* Volume 1: *Psychokinesis,* Plenum (New York City), 1977, Volume 2: *Extrasensory Perception,*

Plenum, 1978, Volume 3, Plenum, 1982, Volume 4, McFarland & Co., 1984, Volume 5, McFarland & Co., 1987, Volume 6, McFarland & Co., 1990, Volume 7, McFarland and Co., 1994.

(Editor with John White) *Future Science: Life Energies and the Physics of Paranormal Phenomena,* Anchor Press (New York City), 1977.

(With Dreistadt and Judith Malamud) *The Measurement of Behavior* (monograph), Kishkam Press, 1977.

(With Dreistadt) *Cognitive Functions of Human Intentionality* (monograph), Kishkam Press, 1977.

(With Brian Leibovitz) *Drug-Related Altered States of Consciousness* (monograph), Kishkam Press, 1978.

(Editor) *Psychoenergetic Systems: The Interaction of Consciousness, Energy and Matter,* Gordon & Breach, 1979.

*Human Possibilities,* Anchor Press, 1980.

(With David Feinstein) *Personal Mythology: The Psychology of Your Evolving Self,* J. P. Tarcher (Los Angeles, CA), 1988.

(With Joseph Dillard) *Dreamworking: How to Use Your Dreams for Creative Problem Solving,* Bearly (Buffalo, NY), 1988.

(Editor) *Dreamtime and Dreamwork,* J. P. Tarcher, 1990.

(With Patrick Welch) *Spiritual Dimensions of Healing,* Irvington (New York City), 1992.

(With Denny Thong and Bruce Carpenter) *Psychiatrist in Paradise,* White Lotus Press, 1994.

(With Feinstein) *The Mythic Path,* J. P. Tarcher/Putnam, 1997.

(Editor with Susan Powers) *Broken Images, Broken Selves,* Brunner (New York City), 1997.

Contributor to psychology texts and other books, including *Issues in Urban Education and Mental Health,* 1971, and *The Emotional Stress of War, Violence, and Peace,* 1972. Contributor of more than six-hundred articles to journals in psychology, education, psychiatry, and parapsychology. Editor in chief, *Advances in Parapsychological Research: A Biennial Review;* member of editorial or advisory boards, *Journal of Indian Psychology, Journal of Humanistic Psychology,* and *Journal of Transpersonal Psychology.*

*SIDELIGHTS:* In 1971 Stanley Krippner gave the first lecture on parapsychology ever presented at the U.S.S.R. Academy of Pedagogical Sciences in Moscow, and in 1972 in Tokyo he read the first paper on parapsychology ever accepted by the International Congress of Psychology. In 1981 he gave an invited lecture on parapsychology before the Chinese Academy of Sciences in Peking, the first such presentation. His main research interest has been the understanding of exceptional human experiences and their function in altered states of consciousness. He has also studied gifted and exceptional children, with an interest in the relationship between creativity and human consciousness.

\* \* \*

## KUBINYI, Laszlo 1937-

*PERSONAL:* Born December 20, 1937, in Cleveland, OH; son of professional artists; married to Suzanne Kubinyi (a special education teacher). *Education:* Attended School of the Museum of Fine Arts in Boston, and School of Visual Arts and the Art Students League in New York City.

*ADDRESSES: Home and office*—115 Evergreen Pl., Teaneck, NJ 07666-4920.

*CAREER:* Author and illustrator of children's books; illustrator for editorial, advertising, and medical fields. Has traveled throughout the world, and played a *dumbek* (a Middle-Eastern drum) in Armenian, Turkish, and Arabic musical groups.

*AWARDS, HONORS:* Grammy Award nomination, National Academy of Recording Arts and Sciences, 1967, for "best album cover"; Canadian Library Association award, 1969, for *And Tomorrow the Stars: The Story of John Cabot* by Kay Hill; American Library Association Notable Book and New York Times Notable Book, both 1972, both for *The Haunted Mountain* by Maureen Mollie Hunter McIlwraith; Children's Book Showcase award, 1974, for *Peter the Revolutionary Tsar,* by Peter Brock Putnam; Fifty Books of the Year, AIGA, 1974, for *Our Fathers Had Powerful Songs,* edited by Natalia Maree Belting; "Certificate of Excellence," AIGA, 1977, for *The Town Cats and Other Tales,* written by Lloyd Alexander; Andy Award of Merit, 1979.

*WRITINGS:*

*SELF-ILLUSTRATED*

*The Cat and the Flying Machine,* Simon & Schuster (New York City), 1970.

*Zeki and the Talking Cat Shukru,* Simon & Schuster, 1970.

*ILLUSTRATOR*

Paul Anderson, *The Fox, the Dog, and the Griffin,* Doubleday (New York City), 1966.

Cristoforo Columbo, *Across the Ocean Sea: A Journal of Columbus's Voyage,* edited by George Sanderlin, Harper (New York City), 1966.

William C. Harrison, *Dr. William Harvey and the Discovery of Circulation,* Macmillan (New York City), 1967.

Kay Hill, *And Tomorrow the Stars: The Story of John Cabot,* Dodd (New York City), 1968.

Coralie Howard, *What Do You Want to Know?,* Simon & Schuster, 1968.

Martin Gardner, *Perplexing Puzzles and Tantalizing Teasers,* Simon & Schuster, 1969.

Robert Froman, *Science, Art, and Visual Illusions,* Simon & Schuster, 1969.

Jeanne B. Hardendorff, *Witches, Wit, and a Werewolf,* Lippincott (Philadelphia), 1971.

Betty Jean Lifton, *The Silver Crane,* Seabury (New York City), 1971.

Adrien Stoutenburg, *Haran's Journey,* Dial (New York City), 1971.

Tony Hillerman, *The Boy Who Made Dragonfly: A Zuni Myth,* Harper, 1972.

Maureen Mollie Hunter McIlwraith, *The Haunted Mountain,* Harper, 1972.

F. N. Monjo, *Slater's Mill,* Simon & Schuster, 1972.

Morton Friend, *The Vanishing Tungus: The Story of a Remarkable Reindeer People,* Dial, 1972.

David C. Knight, *Poltergeists: Hauntings and the Haunted,* Lippincott, 1972.

Arthur S. Gregor, *Witchcraft and Magic: The Supernatural World,* Scribner, 1972.

Peter Brock Putnam, *Peter the Revolutionary Tsar,* Harper, 1973.

Felice Holman, *I Hear You Smiling, and Other Poems,* Scribner (New York City), 1973.

Maia Wojciechowska, *Winter Tales from Poland,* Doubleday, 1973.

Natalia Maree Belting, editor, *Our Fathers Had Powerful Songs,* Dutton (New York City), 1974.

Lloyd Alexander, *The Wizard in the Tree,* Dutton, 1975.

Margaret Greaves, *The Dagger and the Bird: A Story of Suspense,* Harper, 1975.

Ellen Pugh, *The Adventures of Yoo-Lah-Teen: A Legend of the Salish Coastal Indians,* Dial, 1975.

Miriam Anne Bourne, *Patsy Jefferson's Diary,* Coward, 1975.

Gardner, *More Perplexing Puzzles and Tantalizing Teasers,* Archway (New York City), 1977.

Alexander, *The Town Cats and Other Tales,* Dutton, 1977.

Brigid Clark and Christopher Noel, *The Gingham Dog and the Calico Cat: Season of Harmony,* Rabbit Ears Books, 1990.

Tom Roberts, adaptor, *Goldilocks,* Rabbit Ears Books, 1990.

Roberts, adaptor, *Red Riding Hood,* Rabbit Ears Books, 1991.

Nomi Joval, *Room of Mirrors,* Wonder Well, 1991.

Mary Blount Christian, *Who'd Believe John Colter?,* Macmillan, 1993.

Joval, *Color of Light,* Wonder Well, 1993.

Joval, *Power of Glass,* Wonder Well, 1993.

Mihai Spariosu and Dezso Benedek, retellers, *Ghosts, Vampires, and Werewolves: Eerie Tales from Transylvania,* Orchard, 1994.

Roy Edwin Thomas, compiler, *Come Go with Me: Old-Timer Stories from the Southern Mountains,* Farrar, Straus (New York City), 1994.

Roger B. Swain, *Earthly Pleasures: Tales from a Biologist's Garden,* Lyons & Burford, 1994.

*Sea of Cortes, Copper Canyon* (travel guide), Secretaria de Turismo, Mexico, 1994.

Kelly Trumble, *Cat Mummies,* Clarion Books (Boston), 1996.

*ADAPTATIONS: Goldilocks* and *Red Riding Hood,* narrated by Meg Ryan and containing over two hundred illustrations by Kubinyi, and *The Gingham Dog and the Calico Cat: Season of Harmony,* narrated by Amy Grant with illustrations also by Kubinyi, were originally produced as videotapes.

*SIDELIGHTS:* Laszlo Kubinyi believes children are influenced by the literature they read and that he, as a children's book illustrator, must be careful not to convey racism, sexism, or unnecessary violence in his work. Kubinyi's self-illustrated storybooks for children include *The Cat and the Flying Machine* and *Zeki and the Talking Cat Shukru.* Although the latter title was not widely reviewed, *The Cat and the Flying Machine* was noted for its far-fetched, whimsical story. This picture book centers on the adventures of Shukru, a talking cat who gets involved in a revolution while trying to rescue an alchemist from the dungeon of an evil Count. Kubinyi's illustrations are "soft-toned and pleasant," according to a reviewer in *New York Times Book Review.*

Primarily an illustrator, Kubinyi has contributed to numerous picture books, some of which, like his own stories, feature cats as main characters. Notable among these is *Cat Mummies,* by Kelly Trumble, a nonfiction exploration of the role of cats in the lives of the ancient Egyptians. In a laudatory review in *Booklist*, Ilene Cooper singled out Kubinyi's illustrations as an "enormous help" to the author who has to introduce unfamiliar terms and an ancient, foreign culture without losing her audience. "The delightful watercolors not only visually expand the text," Cooper contended, "but also have an easy, inviting quality to them that draws readers right in."

While the reviewer of *Cat Mummies* for *Kirkus Reviews* failed to echo Cooper's high estimation of the author's abilities, it was stated that "Kubinyi's highly detailed, softly colored drawings bring immediacy to ancient events and objects." Likewise, other critics view Kubinyi's illustrations as enhancements to the text. Thus, though a critic in *Kirkus Reviews* complained that Mary Blount Christian's text in *Who'd Believe John Colter?* contains the author's conjectures about the inner thoughts and feelings of historical figures, the critic stated that Kubinyi's drawings, "recalling 19th-century engravings, contribute nicely to an inviting format." Well-regarded works, such as *Come Go with Me: Old-Timer Stories from the Southern Mountains,* Roy Edwin Thomas's collection of tales about life among mountain people in the late part of the nineteenth century, are similarly considered to be augmented by what *Bulletin of the Center for Children's Books* reviewer Betsy Hearne referred to as Kubinyi's "incisive pen-and-ink crosshatch drawings."

## BIOGRAPHICAL/CRITICAL SOURCES:

### PERIODICALS

*Booklist,* September 15, 1996, p. 236.

*Bulletin of the Center for Children's Books,* November, 1969, p. 46; November, 1973, p. 50; March, 1994, pp. 235-36.

*Kirkus Reviews,* July 1, 1968, p. 701; October 15, 1970, p. 1148; June 1, 1993, p. 717; May 1, 1994, pp. 637-38; July 15, 1996, p. 1057.

*New York Times Book Review,* February 21, 1971, p. 22.

*Publishers Weekly,* May 31, 1993, p. 55; February 21, 1994, p. 256.

*School Library Journal,* August, 1993, p. 170; October, 1994, p. 140.

# L

LASSITER, Mary
   See HOFFMAN, Mary (Margaret)


                    *    *    *


LEIGH, Mike  1943-

*PERSONAL:* Born February 20, 1943, in Salford, Lancashire, England; son of Alfred Abraham and Phyllis Pauline (Cousin) Leigh; married Alison Steadman (an actress), September 15, 1973; children: Toby, Leo. *Education:* Attended Royal Academy of Dramatic Art, 1960-62, Camberwell School of Arts and Crafts, 1963-64, Central School of Art and Design, 1964-68, and London Film School, 1965.

*ADDRESSES: Agent*—Peters, Fraser, & Dunlop, The Chambers, Chelsea Harbor Lots Rd., London SW1O 0XF, England.

*CAREER:* Filmmaker. Dramagraph (a production company), London, England, co-founder, 1965; Midlands Art Centre for Young People, Birmingham, England, associate director, 1965-66; Victoria Theatre, Stoke-on-Trent, England, actor, 1966; assistant director of Royal Shakespeare Co., 1967-68; creator of movies, plays, television movies, and radio dramas, 1968—. Director of plays, including *Little Malcolm and His Struggle against the Eunuchs,* 1965, and *The Knack,* 1967. Lecturer, Sedgely Park College, 1968-69, De La Salle College, 1968-69, and London Film School, 1970-73.

*AWARDS, HONORS:* Golden Hugo Award, Chicago Film Festival, and Golden Leopard Award, Locarno Film Festival, both 1972, both for *Bleak Moments;* George Divine Award, 1973; Best Comedy Award, *Evening Standard,* and Best Comedy Award, *Drama,* both 1981, both for *Goose-Pimples; Evening Standard* Award, 1982, and 1989; People's Award, Berlin Film Festival, 1984, for *Meantime;* International Critics' Prize from Venice Film Festival, 1988, "Best Film Coup de Coeur" from Geneva Film Festival, 1989, and Peter Sellers Best Comedy Film Award from *London Evening Standard,* 1990, all for *High Hopes;* National Society of Film Critics Best Film Award, 1991; best director award from Cannes Film Festival, 1993, for *Naked;* named to Order of British Empire, 1993; Palm d'Or from Cannes Film Festival, 1996, for *Secrets and Lies.*

*WRITINGS:*

PLAYS

*The Box Play,* first produced in Birmingham, England, at Midlands Art Centre Theatre, 1965.
*My Parents Have Gone to Carlisle,* first produced in Birmingham, 1966.
*The Last Crusade of the Five Little Nuns,* first produced at Midland Arts Centre Theatre, 1966.
*Waste Paper Guards,* first produced in Birmingham, 1966.
*NENAA,* first produced in Stratford-upon-Avon, England, 1967.
*Individual Fruit Pies,* first produced in Loughton, England, at East-15 Acting School Theatre, 1968.
*Down Here and Up There,* first produced in London at Theatre Upstairs, 1968.
*Big Basil,* first produced in Manchester, England, at Manchester Youth Theatre, 1968.

*Epilogue,* first produced in Manchester, 1969.

*Glum Victoria and the Lad with Specs,* first produced at Manchester Youth Theatre, 1969.

*Bleak Moments* (also see below), first produced in London at Open Space Theatre, 1970.

*A Rancid Pong,* first produced in London at Basement Theatre, 1971.

*Wholesome Glory,* first produced at Theatre Upstairs, 1973.

*The Jaws of Death,* first produced in Edinburgh, Scotland, at Traverse Theatre, 1973.

*Dick Whittington and His Cat,* first produced in London, 1973.

*Babies Grow Old,* first produced in Stratford-upon-Avon at the Other Place, 1974.

*The Silent Majority,* first produced in London at Bush Theatre, 1974.

*Abigail's Party* (also see below; first produced in London at Hampstead Theatre, 1977), Samuel French, 1979.

*Ecstasy* (also see below), first produced at Hampstead Theatre, 1979.

*Goose-Pimples* (also see below; first produced at Hampstead Theatre, 1981), Samuel French, 1982.

*Abigail's Party and Goose-Pimples,* Penguin, 1983.

*Smelling a Rat and Ecstasy,* Nick Hern Books (London), 1989.

*Greek Tragedy,* first produced in Sydney, Australia, 1989; produced in London, 1990.

*Too Much of a Good Thing* (radio play), first aired on British Broadcasting Corporation (BBC) radio, 1992.

*It's a Great Big Shame!,* first produced at Theatre Royal, Stratford East, London, 1993.

*TELEVISION SCREENPLAYS*

*A Mug's Game,* British Broadcasting Corp. (BBC-TV), 1973.

*Hard Labour,* BBC-TV, 1973.

*The Permissive Society,* BBC-TV, 1975.

*Knock for Knock,* BBC-TV, 1976.

*Nuts in May,* BBC-TV, 1976.

*The Kiss of Death,* BBC-TV, 1977.

*Abigail's Party* (adapted from own play), BBC-TV, 1977.

*Who's Who,* BBC-TV, 1978.

*Grown-Ups,* BBC-TV, 1980.

*Home Sweet Home,* BBC-TV, 1982.

*Meantime,* BBC-TV, 1983.

*Four Days in July,* BBC-TV, 1984.

*The Short and Curlies,* BBC-TV, 1987.

*A Sense of History,* BBC-TV, 1992.

*FILMS; ALSO DIRECTOR*

*Bleak Moments,* Contemporary (London), 1971.

*High Hopes,* Film Four (London), 1988.

*Life Is Sweet,* Thin Man Films (London), 1991.

*Naked,* Thin Man Films, 1993.

*Secrets and Lies,* Thin Man Films, 1996.

*Career Girls,* Thin Man Films, 1997.

Also author of "Five Minute Plays" for television, including "The Birth of the 2001 FA Cup Finale Goalie," "Old Chums," "Probation," "A Light Snack," and "Afternoon," all 1982.

*SIDELIGHTS:* Mike Leigh once told *CA:* "All my plays and films have evolved from scratch entirely by rehearsal through improvisation; thus it is inherent in my work that I always combine the jobs of author and director, and I never work with any other writers or directors. I have been pioneering this style of work in England, beginning with the 'Box Play' in 1965." John O'Leary writes in *Contemporary Dramatists:* "Leigh produces his work through a process that is, broadly speaking, collaborative. A group of actors is selected and each is presented with a germ of a character. They are often asked to go away and develop these characters, using their own experience and imagination. At the end of several weeks, or months, they are reassembled and, under Leigh's direction, a play is put together."

From pioneering playwright-director to highly regarded filmmaker, Leigh has taken his improvisatory style into movies with quite successful results. *Chicago Tribune* critic Michael Wilmington called Leigh "one of the world's most original filmmakers . . . also one of the best," an artist whose works "all portray recognizable British working and middle-class people with terrific humor, depth and sympathy." *Los Angeles Times Magazine* contributor Kenneth Turan, himself a film critic, noted that Leigh is "considered by many critics the preeminent filmmaker in the English-speaking world," adding of the writer-director: "He's a man who works in a way completely and totally his own, going well below the surface to create an unmatched level of emotional intensity and, in the process, stretching the boundaries of psychological truth on film as far as they will go."

Leigh was not well known outside of Great Britain until the 1990s, when his feature films such as *Life Is Sweet, Naked,* and *Secrets and Lies* received international distribution and prestigious awards from the European film festivals, including the coveted Palm d'Or from Cannes in 1996. Critics and moviegoers alike have applauded Leigh's grimly realistic tales of extraordinary moments in ordinary lives, and much comment has been generated over the filmmaker's unique working style. As for Leigh himself, he told the *Washington Post:* "My ongoing preoccupation is with families, relationships, parents, children, sex, work, surviving, being born and dying. I'm totally intuitive, emotional, subjective, empirical, instinctive. I'm not an intellectual filmmaker. Primarily my films are a response to the way people are, the way things are as I experience them. In a way, they are acts of taking the temperature."

Conventional filmmaking begins with a developed screenplay through which actors and actresses can chart the fortunes of their characters. Producers receive funding from film companies after the executives have studied the screenplay and approved of it. Leigh works completely outside this system. "My job," he commented in the *New Yorker,* "is to gather the resources, then go out there and find the film by making it." With only a basic vision of a situation or circumstance in his mind, Leigh hires character actors and exhorts them to give their own flesh-and-blood interpretation to the role they're assigned. The actors immerse themselves in their characters, down to the most minute details of everyday life. Months of improvisational rehearsals follow, in which the actors—in character—react to one another as they would in "real life" situations. From the many hours of extemporaneous interplay, Leigh finally concocts a finished script based upon the improvisational dialogue.

"I'm always walking around with certain feelings and ideas kicking around, and I put myself in the position any artist can understand: Here is the space, here is the canvas," Leigh declared in the *Los Angeles Times Magazine.* "Every decision I make, starting with choosing actors, gives you different combinations, stimulates you. What I'm doing is looking for the film, testing what is going on against what I think I'm doing. It's an elusive combination of what I know and what I don't know, and no one should underestimate the importance of the fact that I'm only answerable to myself, even if I don't know what I'm doing."

This idiosyncratic style has been nurtured by Leigh's middle-class upbringing, his training as an actor, painter, and improvisational playwright, and his dedication to revealing aspects of British culture and society often overlooked by more conventional, more commercial filmmakers. According to many critics,

Leigh has made a huge success for himself without compromising on his artistic vision. To quote Stuart Klawans in *The Nation,* "Because of his practice of developing the characters and dialogue in collaboration with the actors, over a long period of rehearsal . . . each performer carries onto the soundstage an accumulation of lived experience. So, unless you're high-handed enough to judge someone else's life as superfluous, you can't very well dismiss any of the actors. Each seems to have an absolute right to exist on the screen; and each turns out to be playing a consequential role, no matter how small or unshowy."

Leigh created his first feature film, *Bleak Moments,* in 1971. The film was not widely seen or reviewed, but those critics who did watch it commended it highly. Nevertheless, it would be seventeen years before Leigh made his second feature film. The years in between were spent working on projects for BBC-TV. These reached large audiences in the United Kingdom while they also helped Leigh to perfect his method. "We complained about this and that, but the BBC was brilliant," he contended in the *Los Angeles Times Magazine.* "It was good news. When I got the films, boy, it was carte blanche. Nobody ever interfered with casting or editing. I never made a cut that wasn't mine."

In 1988 Leigh returned to cinematic films with *High Hopes,* a drama that explores the conflict between working class and upper crust citizens in Margaret Thatcher's Britain. He followed that film with *Life Is Sweet,* a family drama revolving around a bulimic teenager and her parents' eccentric friends. In *The Nation,* Klawans cited *Life Is Sweet* for its "uncommon richness of character" and "all-too-rare spontaneity." That same spontaneity features prominently in *Naked,* the sexually-charged story of a young drifter who finds his personal apocalypse in lower-class London. Leigh received the best director award from the Cannes Film Festival in 1993 for *Naked.* In his *New Statesman & Society* review, Jonathan Romney concluded: "Watching *Naked* is like being trapped for two hours in a railway carriage with a charismatic preacher who might possibly have an axe under his coat. It's utterly compelling, but you never get so much as a glance out of the window."

Leigh is best known in America for his 1996 film *Secrets and Lies,* the story of a successful black woman who, in the wake of her adoptive mother's death, seeks out her birth mother and becomes acquainted with a new—and troubled—family. *Christian*

*Science Monitor* reviewer David Sterritt cited *Secrets and Lies* for its "sensitive story, superb performances, and compassionate approach to a potentially troubling subject." The film won the Palm d'Or at the 1996 Cannes Film Festival as best picture of the year, which assured it a wider distribution in the United States. "Transcendent and moving, not to mention blisteringly funny, *Secrets and Lies* is something very special indeed," remarked Peter Travers in *Rolling Stone*. ". . . The writer and director handles the . . . explosion of laughs, tears, rage and reconciliation with rare skill and immediacy. Leigh [is] a world-class filmmaker at the top of his form."

According to John Lahr in the *New Yorker,* Leigh's gift "is for the drama of behavior in an unkempt, ordinary world, and it has made him something of a cult figure: he is the maestro of the mundane." Lahr continued: ". . . His England is a place of claustrophobia and collapse, where people measure out their lives in cups of tea and trips to the pub. The characters and the rooms they inhabit seem jerry-built: they have rough edges, bright, make-do surfaces, cracks that can't be filled in. Leigh riffles through this banal world with the avidity of a pensioner at a jumble sale. His films have a particular density of detail, and an almost ruthless focus on that drab intersection of working-class and middle-class life: a zone of impoverishment, resignation, and aggression where a large part of the English population lives." In the *Los Angeles Times,* Turan concluded: "It is Leigh's greatest strength . . . that rarely if ever has a filmmaker understood his subjects as intimately as he does his. . . . When it comes to hearing and understanding the voices of the nominally inarticulate, to knowing how much people are saying when they don't seem to be saying very much at all, Leigh is very much one of a kind. He has such an exact ear for the nuances of (invariably lower-class) speech, such a restless eye for the vagaries of interpersonal connection, the way people talk at each other without really communicating, that words like empathy barely describe what he is able to pull off."

*BIOGRAPHICAL/CRITICAL SOURCES:*

*BOOKS*

Clements, Paul, *The Improvised Play: The Work of Mike Leigh,* Methuen (New York City), 1983.
*Contemporary Dramatists,* 5th edition, St. James Press (Detroit), 1993.
Coveney, Michael, *The World According to Mike Leigh,* HarperCollins (New York City), 1996.

*PERIODICALS*

*Chicago Tribune,* October 27, 1996, p. 12.
*Christian Science Monitor,* September 27, 1996.
*Detroit News,* May 21, 1996.
*Entertainment Weekly,* January 28, 1994, pp. 34-36.
*Los Angeles Times,* March 9, 1989; June 21, 1992, p. 23; December 23, 1993, p. 4.
*Los Angeles Times Magazine,* September 22, 1996, p. 14.
*Nation,* December 2, 1991, pp. 717-20; October 7, 1996, pp. 34-36.
*New Republic,* September 30, 1996, pp. 30-32.
*New Statesman & Society,* November 5, 1993, pp. 34-35.
*Newsweek,* January 6, 1992, p. 52; December 27, 1993, pp. 47-48.
*New Yorker,* November 4, 1991, pp. 101-04; September 23, 1996, pp. 50-54.
*New York Review of Books,* January 13, 1994, pp. 7-11.
*New York Times,* February 19, 1989; September 22, 1996, section 2, pp. 1, 22-23.
*Rolling Stone,* November 14, 1991; October 1996, pp. 142-43.
*Time,* December 20, 1993, p. 62.
*Washington Post,* April 7, 1989; January 30, 1994, p. G1; October 13, 1996, p. G4.*

*      *      *

## Le TORD, Bijou 1945-

*PERSONAL:* Born January 15, 1945, in St. Raphael, France; immigrated to the United States, 1966; daughter of Jacques (an artist) and Paule (Pigoury) Le Tord. *Education:* Attended Ecole des Beaux Arts, Lyon, France. *Religion:* Protestant. *Avocational interests:* Poetry, fine arts, music, people, travel in Europe.

*ADDRESSES: Home*—P.O. Box 2226, Sag Harbor, NY 11963.

*CAREER:* Author and illustrator of children's books. Fashion Institute of Technology, New York City, instructor, 1978-1982.

*MEMBER:* Beatrix Potter Society, Society of Children's Book Writers and Illustrators.

*AWARDS, HONORS:* American Institute of Graphic Arts Bookshow award, 1977, for *The Generous Cow;* Notable Children's Trade Book in the Field of Social Studies, National Council for the Social Studies and Children's Book Council (NCSS-CBC), 1986, for *Joseph and Nellie;* "Pick of the Lists," American Booksellers Association, 1987, for *My Grandma Leonie;* "Books Can Develop Empathy" citation, 1990, for *A Brown Cow.*

*WRITINGS:*

FOR CHILDREN; SELF-ILLUSTRATED

*A Perfect Place to Be,* Parents Magazine Press (New York City), 1976.

*The Generous Cow,* Parents Magazine Press, 1977.

*Rabbit Seeds,* Four Winds (Bristol, FL), 1978.

*Merry Christmas, Hooper Dooper,* Random House (New York City), 1979.

*Nice and Cozy,* Four Winds, 1980.

*Picking and Weaving,* Four Winds, 1980.

*Arf, Boo, Click: An Alphabet of Sounds,* Four Winds, 1981.

*Good Wood Bear,* Bradbury (Scarsdale, NY), 1985.

*Joseph and Nellie,* Bradbury, 1986.

*My Grandma Leonie,* Bradbury, 1987.

*The Little Hills of Nazareth,* Bradbury, 1988.

*A Brown Cow,* Little, Brown (Boston), 1989.

*The Deep Blue Sea,* Orchard, 1990.

*The Little Shepherd: The Twenty-Third Psalm,* Delacorte (New York City), 1991.

(Compiler) *Peace on Earth: A Book of Prayers from Around the World,* Delacorte, 1992.

*Elephant Moon,* Doubleday (New York City), 1993.

*The River and the Rain: The Lord's Prayer,* Doubleday, 1994.

*A Blue Butterfly: A Story about Claude Monet,* Doubleday, 1995.

*Sing a New Song: A Book of Psalms,* Eerdmans (Grand Rapids, MI), 1997.

*God's Little Seeds: A Book of Parables,* Eerdmans, 1998.

*SIDELIGHTS:* Bijou Le Tord is an author/illustrator whose books for young readers have been called minimalist in design and content. As described by Anita Silvey in *Horn Book,* Le Tord's work involves "simple lines and shapes which she uses to tell an engaging story." Le Tord takes simplicity as her maxim. As she once told *CA:* "In my books I try to show or explain it all in a simple way. Simplicity means honesty to me. And that is what I try to be at all times, honest. I hope that my books carry this

message more than anything else. You could call me a champion of truth!" The creator of picture books and books for children in early elementary grades, Le Tord writes and illustrates works that characteristically have their roots in childhood experiences or attempt to introduce young audiences to some aspect of nature or animal life; she is also well known for her spiritual writings. Praised for the charm, interest, and succinctness of her works, Le Tord is also recognized for the quality of her art, which she renders most often as watercolors or black and white line drawings.

Born in St. Raphael, France, Le Tord grew up on the French Riviera. She arrived in New York at age eighteen and set to work, initially designing silk textiles for such couture designers as Oscar de la Renta and Bill Blass. She was a designer for several years and also taught at the Fashion Institute of Technology. However, her childhood dream of becoming a writer had not left her. "One day, it came time for me to sit down and write a story," Le Tord explained to *CA.* "I did write a story, illustrated it, published it and I have never stopped since." That first story, *A Perfect Place to Be,* is a quiet story of the small pleasures that Jeremiah M. Coolin remembers from growing up in the valley town of Hillsley, his boyhood home: the peaceful countryside, the weekly trip to town, meeting with his friend Charlotte, and getting to choose a wooden toy for helping out around the house. *Booklist* noted that "the comfortable ambiance of this picture book suggests its suitability for quiet one-to-one sharing. . . . Le Tord's pictures extend the text's serenity."

From the outset, Le Tord had hit on a signature simplicity in both text and pictures. Other early books by Le Tord include *The Generous Cow* and *Nice and Cozy.* The former title tells the story of a milk cow in sparse language and illustrations; *Nice and Cozy* is the tale of a pig who wishes to fly before he settles down to married life. While *Kirkus Reviews* called the story "silly" and "inane," a point perhaps reflecting the risks taken by the writer in stripping her story down to bare essentials, *Booklist,* in favor of Le Tord's "breezy, free-floating" approach, thought that "younger pre-schoolers will find much to enjoy in this brief nonsense tale."

With her later titles, more reviewers appear to have caught on to what Le Tord was attempting with her minimalist picture books. *Good Wood Bear* tells the story of how Goose and Bear build a house, from drawing up plans to choosing wood and constructing the building. *Horn Book* reviewer Silvey noted that there was a "great deal of humor" in Le Tord's line drawings, and that *Good Wood Bear* and Le Tord's earlier title, *Rabbit Seeds,* demonstrated that "wonderful books for children can be created out of the simplest of components." *Joseph and Nellie* is a picture book that recounts a day in the life of two companions who make their livelihood from fishing. *School Library Journal* reviewer Kathy Piehl noted that Le Tord's watercolors, "with muted shadings and her simple portrayals of activity suit the subject matter admirably." Comparing Le Tord's work to the "quiet charm" of M. B. Goffstein and the "ingenious naivet" of Lois Lenski "while remaining a unique creation in its own right," Mary M. Burns called the book "elegantly simple" and a "small but perfect gem" in her *Horn Book* review, and concluded that "this gentle tribute to a particular way of life warms the heart with a glow derived from the artist's appreciation for the subject."

Le Tord's texts are generally as simplified as her illustrations, but that does not imply that her meanings are small. In *My Grandma Leonie,* for example, Le Tord examines the generational links between a young child and her grandmother. Based on Le Tord's experience of coping with the death of her own grandmother, the book is a "moving tribute to the special love which connects grandchildren and grandparents," according to Burns in *Horn Book.* "Sometimes less is more," Burns concluded, "and this small book, with its simplicity and charm, touches the heart more poignantly than many an erudite elegy." Another of Le Tord's books, *A Brown Cow,* frames a cow in a window and is accompanied by the text of a little girl describing the attributes of the cow that lives in her backyard. "Affecting but not sentimental," says *Horn Book*'s Burns, and "as calming as it is delightful." Ilene Cooper commented in *Booklist* that the book "will appeal most to those who appreciate Le Tord's minimalist design, and that includes young children—the natural audience for this quiet story." Le Tord's love of nature and animals comes to the fore with her *Elephant Moon,* "a quiet paean to an endangered creature," according to Cynthia K. Richey in *School Library Journal.*

Several of Le Tord's books have dealt with the presentation of religious topics: retellings of the creation story in *The Deep Blue Sea* and collections of prayers and psalms in *Peace on Earth, The River and the Rain,* and *The Little Shepherd. Peace on Earth* is a collection of prayers and devotional poetry from

around the world organized in various categories such as children, animals, and the sea. Writing in *School Library Journal,* Susan Scheps noted that Le Tord's "childlike paintings in pale, blue-dominated watercolors on creamy paper, give the book a soft peaceful quality," while *Kirkus Reviews* concluded that the book is a "thoughtful, beautifully produced collection." *The River and the Rain,* a simplified rendition of the Lord's Prayer with an ecological message, includes illustrations that depict humanity's destruction of the rain forest. "This understated but definite reminder that our stewardship of the Earth is at risk is properly and effectively combined with the all-embracing prayer," noted Patricia Pearl Dole in *School Library Journal.*

Le Tord's palette is generally subdued, and she does not necessarily try to reproduce colors exactly from nature. "The color itself is not what matters to me," she explained to *CA.* "What is important is the mood of the book, what it implies. And if I have to change nature's colors to express it, to suit the book, I just do it. I let paint show me where the source of the light is. And I go for it!" With *A Blue Butterfly,* Le Tord challenged herself to tell a story about the impressionist painter Claude Monet by using Monet's colors to reflect his work. A *Publishers Weekly* reviewer commented on Le Tord's "haiku-like text" and concluded that "Le Tord does herself, and Monet, proud."

Le Tord once summed up her approach to books and their creation to *CA:* "I think a book should be like a relationship where you take in as much as you need at the time. Just like a friend with whom you exchange ideas, feelings, experiences. I like to leave plenty of room in my books for a child to find himself or herself, get a sense of his or her own space. Room for him or her to grow in, express his or her taste. Not mine! I hope that my books are and have done just that."

*BIOGRAPHICAL/CRITICAL SOURCES:*

*BOOKS*

*Sixth Book of Junior Authors and Illustrators,* H. W. Wilson (Bronx, NY), 1989, pp. 168-69.

*PERIODICALS*

*Booklist,* May 1, 1976, p. 1266; December 1, 1980, p. 514; May 15, 1989, p. 1651; December 1, 1992, p. 98; September 15, 1993, p. 158; November 1, 1994, p. 502; October 15, 1996, p. 406; December 15, 1996, p. 730.

*Horn Book,* January-February, 1986, p. 51; September-October, 1986, p. 583; November-December, 1987, pp. 726-27; May-June, 1989, p. 360; March, 1995, p. 215.

*Kirkus Reviews,* October 1, 1980, p. 1294; October 15, 1992, p. 1311.

*New York Times Book Review,* May 2, 1976, p. 47; November 9, 1980, p. 71; April 1, 1984, p. 29; August 24, 1986, p. 21.

*Publishers Weekly,* September 18, 1995, p. 130.

*School Library Journal,* September, 1986, p. 124; May, 1990, p. 98; December, 1992, p. 98; August, 1993, pp. 146-47; January, 1995, p. 101; November, 1995, p. 91.

*—Sketch by J. Sydney Jones*

\* \* \*

## LOBEL, Anita (Kempler) 1934-

*PERSONAL:* Surname is pronounced "*Lo*-bel"; born June 3, 1934, in Cracow, Poland; immigrated to the United States, 1952; naturalized citizen, 1956; daughter of Leon and Sofia (Grunberg) Kempler; married Arnold Stark Lobel (an author and illustrator) April, 1955 (died December 4, 1987); children: Adrianne, Adam. *Education:* Pratt Institute, B.F.A., 1955; attended Brooklyn Museum Art School, 1975-76.

*ADDRESSES: Home*—New York, NY.

*CAREER:* Freelance textile designer, 1957-64; writer and illustrator of children's books, 1964—. *Exhibitions:* Lobel's art and papers are included in the Kerlan Collection at the University of Minnesota.

*AWARDS, HONORS:* Best Illustrated Book selection, *New York Times,* 1965, for *Sven's Bridge,* and 1981, for *Market Street;* Spring Book Festival Award (picture book), 1972, for *Little John;* Children's Book Showcase Award, 1974, for *A Birthday for the Princess,* and 1977, for *Peter Penny's Dance;* Outstanding Book selection, *New York Times,* 1976, for *Peter Penny's Dance,* 1977, for *How the Rooster Saved the Day,* and 1981, for *On Market Street;* Boston Globe/Horn Book Award (illustration), 1981, for *On Market Street,* and 1984, for *The Rose in My Garden;* Caldecott Honor Book Award, and American Book Award finalist, both 1982, both for *On Market Street.*

*WRITINGS:*

*SELF-ILLUSTRATED*

*Sven's Bridge,* Harper (New York City), 1965, Greenwillow (New York City), 1992.

*The Troll Music,* Harper, 1966.

*Potatoes, Potatoes,* Harper, 1967.

*The Seamstress of Salzburg,* Harper, 1970.

*Under a Mushroom,* Harper, 1970.

*A Birthday for the Princess,* Harper, 1973.

(Reteller) *King Rooster, Queen Hen,* Greenwillow, 1975.

(Reteller) *The Pancake,* Greenwillow, 1978.

(Adapter) *The Straw Maid,* Greenwillow, 1983.

*Alison's Zinnia,* Greenwillow, 1990.

*The Dwarf Giant,* Holiday, 1991.

*Pierrot's ABC Garden,* Western, 1992.

*Away from Home,* Greenwillow, 1994.

*ILLUSTRATOR; BY HUSBAND, ARNOLD LOBEL; PUBLISHED BY GREENWILLOW*

*How the Rooster Saved the Day,* 1977.

*A Treeful of Pigs,* 1979.

*On Market Street,* 1981.

*The Rose in My Garden,* 1984.

*ILLUSTRATOR*

Paul Kapp, *Cock-a-Doodle Doo! Cock-a-Doodle Doo!,* Harper (New York City), 1966.

Meindert De Jong, *Puppy Summer,* Harper, 1966.

*The Wishing Penny and Other Stories* (anthology), Parents Magazine Press (New York City), 1967.

F. N. Monjo, *Indian Summer,* Harper, 1968.

Alice Dalgliesh, *The Little Wooden Farmer,* Macmillan (New York City), 1968.

Benjamin Elkin, *The Wisest Man in the World,* Parents Magazine Press, 1968.

Barbara Borack, *Someone Small,* Harper, 1969.

Doris Orgel, *The Uproar,* McGraw (New York City), 1970.

Mirra Ginsburg, editor, *Three Rolls and One Doughnut: Fables from Russia,* Dial (New York City), 1970.

Elkin, *How the Tsar Drinks Tea,* Parents Magazine Press, 1971.

Theodore Storm, *Little John,* retold by D. Orgel, Farrar, 1972.

John Langstaff, editor, *Soldier, Soldier, Won't You Marry Me?,* Doubleday (New York City), 1972.

Cynthia Jameson, *One for the Price of Two,* Parents Magazine Press, 1972.

Elizabeth Shub, adapter, *Clever Kate,* Macmillan, 1973.

Carolyn Meyer, *Christmas Crafts: Things to Make the Days Before Christmas,* Harper, 1974.

Janet Quin-Harkin, *Peter Penny's Dance,* Dial, 1976.

Penelope Lively, *Fanny's Sister,* Dutton (New York City), 1980.

Jane Hart, compiler, *Singing Bee! A Collection of Favorite Children's Songs,* Lothrop, 1982, published in England as *Sing a Song of Sixpence! The Best Song Book Ever,* Gollancz (London), 1983.

Clement Clarke Moore, *The Night Before Christmas,* Knopf (New York City), 1984.

Harriet Ziefert, *A New Coat for Anna,* Knopf, 1986.

B. P. Nichol, *Once: A Lullaby,* Greenwillow, 1986.

Steven Kroll, *Looking for Daniela: A Romantic Adventure,* Holiday House (New York City), 1988.

Charlotte S. Huck, reteller, *Princess Furball,* Greenwillow, 1989.

Charlotte Zolotow, *This Quiet Lady,* Greenwillow, 1992.

Ethel L. Heins, reteller, *The Cat and the Cook and Other Fables of Krylov,* Greenwillow, 1995.

Huck, reteller, *Toads and Diamonds,* Greenwillow, 1995.

Charlotte Pomerantz, *Mangaboom,* Greenwillow, 1997.

Carl Sandburg, *Not Everyday an Aurora Borealis for Your Birthday: A Love Poem,* Knopf, 1998.

Miela Ford, *My Day in the Garden,* Greenwillow, 1998.

*OTHER*

*No Pretty Pictures: A Child of War,* Greenwillow, 1998.

*ADAPTATIONS: The Little Wooden Farmer* was adapted as a filmstrip with cassette by Threshold Filmstrips, 1974; *Peter Penny's Dance* was adapted as a filmstrip with cassette by Weston Woods, 1978; *A New Coat for Anna* was adapted as a filmstrip with cassette by Random House, 1987; A *Treeful of Pigs* and *On Market Street* have been adapted as filmstrips with audiocassettes by Random House; *King Rooster, Queen Hen* and *The Rose in My Garden* have been adapted as audiocassettes by Random House; *On Market Street* has been adapted as a videocassette by Random House.

*SIDELIGHTS:* Celebrated as both a talented artist and the creator of charming texts, Lobel is the author and illustrator of picture books, fantasies, retellings, and concept books that have as their hallmarks a theatrical approach and a keen sense of design. She has also provided the pictures for more than twenty-five texts by writers such as Meindert De Jong, Doris Orgel, Clement Clarke Moore, Penelope Lively, John Langstaff, and Charlotte Zolotow. Several of Lobel's works, both as author/illustrator and illustrator, are considered tour de forces. As an artist, Lobel is well known for creating evocative, detailed paintings in line-and-wash or watercolor and gouache that reflect her signature style of richly patterned landscapes, opulent costumes and tapestries, and colorful flowers. As a writer, Lobel characteristically uses the traditions of the folk and fairy tale, such as "once-upon-a-time" settings and happy endings, to structure her stories, which are usually filled with humor; however, she underscores several of her works with serious themes, such as the nature of war and the results of parental neglect. As a creator of concept books, Lobel is credited for her originality and inventiveness, especially in her contributions to the alphabet book genre. Four of Lobel's works were created with her late husband Arnold; their third collaboration, *On Market Street* (1981), received several prizes, including the *Boston Globe/Horn Book Award* for illustration and designation as a Caldecott Medal honor book. Writing of Anita Lobel's career in *Twentieth Century Children's Writers,* Jacqueline L. Gmuca concludes, "Lobel ably illustrates the meaning of a statement she made to *Publishers Weekly* in 1971: 'It's nice to tell a tale that is pleasant for a child to read, be diverting, and at the same time have some kind of substance to it.' Her books are clearly informed by the pleasant, substantial spirit of which she speaks."

"For several years after graduation [from Pratt Institute]," Lobel related in *Junior Library Guild,* "I worked as a textile designer. Then Susan Hirschman, who had 'discovered' [my husband] Arnold, asked me to do a book. I thought I couldn't, but Susan and Arnold encouraged me and I came through with *Sven's Bridge.*" Published in 1965, Lobel's first book as an author/illustrator grew from an idea that came to her about a goodhearted man; the story also includes examples of Swedish folk designs that the illustrator remembered from her childhood. *Sven's Bridge,* Lobel stated in the *Third Book of Junior Authors,* "started with pictures and the words followed." In contrast, the illustrations followed the text in her fourth book, *The Seamstress of Salzburg* (1970). "At first, I thought only of illustrating stories by other authors but found, with a little effort, I, too, could supply a story to go with the pictures," she told *Books Are by People,* adding, "When I begin a book,

I have a specific style in mind, for instance a historical period." Lobel also incorporates a love of embroidery and tapestry and drawing flowers and large figures into her work. *The Troll Music* (1966), she says, "was mainly inspired by the bottom parts of medieval tapestries with all the vegetation and little animals running around."

Lobel's third book, *Potatoes, Potatoes* (1967), is considered one of her most affecting works. The story, which was inspired, Lobel says, "partly from childhood memories in Poland," describes how two brothers who become enemies in war are brought together by their mother, who refuses to give the boys something to eat until they and their comrades stop fighting. As Jacqueline L. Gmuca describes her in *Twentieth Century Children's Writers,* the mother "not only serves to protect her sons from joining in the fighting for a number of years but also functions as a peacemaker when she reminds them, and the opposing armies they lead, of their former lives of contentment." A reviewer in the *Times Literary Supplement* calls the book "beautifully executed," while *New York Times Book Review* critic Barbara Wersba remarks, "Lobel's illustrations . . . [are] excellent picture-book fare, finely drawn and colored." Lobel told *Books Are By People,* "I like *Potatoes, Potatoes* because of its theme. But I do not take it as seriously as some of the reviewers have."

Lobel and her husband Arnold first combined their talents on *How the Rooster Saved the Day* (1977), a book written by Arnold. Their second collaboration, *A Treeful of Pigs* (1979), was, Anita told *Junior Library Guild,* "written specifically for me to illustrate, the way an author might write a star part for an actress. There were a few noises of objection coming in my direction during the execution of the pictures. The nice thing about having the illustrator and the author together in the same studio is that we can decide to change or rethink little details while the work is in progress. For many years we tried to keep our work separate but, when we discovered this extra bonus, we nodded and bowed graciously to each other and giggled with a sense of a new discovery. That discovery, I felt, is especially a gift to me." Before Arnold's death in 1987, the Lobels collaborated on a total of four books.

Lobel's first book as an author and illustrator since the death of her husband is *Alison's Zinnias* (1990), which Caroline Ward of *School Library Journal* describes as a "luscious-looking alphabet book." The

text links a girl's name with a verb and a flower, all starting with a letter of the alphabet, before coming back to the beginning; each page features a painting and a line of type, below which is a large letter and a smaller storyboard that shows the flower chosen by each child. Zena Sutherland of *Bulletin of the Center for Children's Books* calls *Alison's Zinnias* "an unusual alphabet book" and a "dazzling display of floral painting"; *Horn Book Magazine* reviewer Mary M. Burns calls it, "a book to brighten the dreariest of days. . . . What could have been just another clever idea becomes . . . a tour de force."

A companion piece to *Alison's Zinnias,* Lobel's *Away from Home* (1994) is an alphabet book which focuses on little boys rather than little girls and, in the words of a *Publishers Weekly* reviewer, "takes the reader on a globe-trotting adventure as Lobel sets the stage—literally—to introduce letters and various world cities as well." On each page, a small boy stands under the spotlight before a child audience, who responds to alliterative sentences like "Adam arrived in Amsterdam" and "Henry hoped in Hollywood." A *Publishers Weekly* contributor commends the accuracy, romanticism, and informativeness of the illustrations, while *Booklist* reviewer Hazel Rochman notes that "an all-male cast pulls you into imagining each character's story and making the journey to each exciting place."

Lobel's *The Dwarf Giant* (1991) is a story set in ancient Japan in which an evil dwarf, intending to take over a peaceful kingdom, is defeated by the resourcefulness of the country's princess after her husband is bewitched; although the dwarf is stopped, the story ends in a minor key with other visitors waiting outside the palace. *Kirkus Reviews* calls *The Dwarf Giant* "a deeply felt variant on a classic theme that more often ends in tragedy," and adds that Lobel's illustrations, graceful paintings that reflect Japanese art and architecture, reveal a new direction "for this fine illustrator, their allusive power reinforcing the Faustian subtext. . . ."

With *The Quiet Lady* (1992), Lobel provides the illustrations for a tender picture book by Charlotte Zolotow in which a little girl looks at photographs of her mother in the various stages of her life; the book ends with the birth and baby picture of the young narrator. Each of Lobel's double-page spreads includes a small, darkly hued painting of the little girl and richly colored paintings of her mother. Writing in *Publishers Weekly,* a critic calls *The Quiet Lady* an "excellent choice for quiet mother-child sharing [that is] sure to invite genealogy lessons filled with fond memories." *Booklist* reviewer Carolyn Phelan notes: "The exceptional talents of Zolotow and Lobel combine in this celebration of life. . . . Lobel's sense of design and her signature use of costume and flowers find apt expression in this series of portraits."

As both author and illustrator, Lobel created *Pierrot's ABC Garden* (1993), an alphabet book in which Pierrot the clown packs a huge basket with alphabetically gathered produce—both familiar and exotic—and musical instruments for a picnic with his friend Pierrette. Described by *Kirkus Reviews* as "another enchanting alphabet from the illustrator," *Pierrot's ABC Garden*—a new edition of a Little Golden Book—is called "simple and pleasing" by Carolyn Phelan in *Booklist,* who concludes that preschoolers will love it, "whether or not they care about the ABCs or vegetables."

With *The Cat and the Cook and Other Fables of Krylov* (1995), Lobel illustrates twelve Russian fables retold by Ethel L. Heins, several of which are prose versions of poems by popular fabulist Ivan Andreevich Krylov. The artist paints vigorous folk-art paintings that are noted both for their theatrical quality and evocation of the works of Marc Chagall. In her *Booklist* review, Julie Corsaro claims that Lobel "outdoes herself" with "paintings that are brilliantly colored and wonderfully composed." *School Library Journal* reviewer Cheri Estes adds, "the artist adeptly captures the essence of each tale. . . . [The] paintings will entice youngsters to read this collection independently." *Toads and Diamonds* (1996) is a retelling of a classic French folktale by Charlotte S. Huck, whose popular *Princess Furball* (1989) is also illustrated by Lobel. In *Toads and Diamonds,* lovely Renee lives with her nasty stepmother and stepsisters, who treat her as a lowly servant. When Renee goes to the well, she brings water to an old woman, who rewards her with flowers and jewels every time she speaks; she wins the heart of a handsome prince, who appreciates her for herself and not for her jewels. "Full of life, color, and grace, Lobel's paintings create a sense of magic within everyday reality," writes Carolyn Phelan in *Booklist,* while Maria B. Salvadore of the *Horn Book Magazine* concludes, "This is some of Anita Lobel's best work, each picture in close harmony with the text to move quickly to a satisfying conclusion. . . ."

In 1968, Lobel wrote in *Illustrators of Children's Books: 1957-1966*: "I feel very strongly that an artist working in the field of children's book illustration should by no means compromise on the graphic design quality of his work. Our senses are bombarded by so much ugliness from our earliest days that it is to be hoped that picture books do open a child's eyes and start at least a germ for a future aesthetic sense. I have always loved to draw flowers and I love needlework and tapestries as well as embroidery. During my years as an art student, I spent most of my time drawing and painting monumental figures. When I had to make a living, I became a textile designer. Picture books have opened to me an opportunity to bring back some of my old fat friends and put them in landscapes filled with floral design! I usually plan a book as a play. The pictures become 'scenes' with 'principals' and 'chorus' grouped and regrouped according to what is then happening in the story."

As she alludes above, the theme perhaps most prevalent in Lobel's character as an artist and creator of children's books is her great affection for the theater. She told *Books Are by People,* "I wanted to be in the theatre at one time. When I am illustrating a manuscript, I do it as if it might be a stage play." She told John F. Berry in *Book World,* "Picture books are like screenplays. How do you translate very terse text into some kind of visual context? Really and truly, if you don't know anything about the theatre, it is very difficult to illustrate children's books." She comments in *Twentieth Century Children's Writers,* "Writing and illustrating books for children is a form of drama for me. I approach the construction of a picture book as if it were a theatre piece to be performed, assigning dialogue, dressing the characters, and putting them into an appropriate setting. Some books take the form of zany farces (*King Rooster, Queen Hen,* and *The Pancake*). Others, like *Peter Penny's Dance,* are a bit like *Around the World in Eighty Days,* a sort of movie or musical. *The Seamstress of Salzburg* and *A Birthday for the Princess* are more like operettas. *On Market Street* was constructed like a series of solos in a ballet, held together by a prologue and epilogue, with an implied divertimento for the score."

Lobel has been able to modify her schedule so that she can finish studio work by 2:00 p.m., then put her energy into other interests, such as the theater. As a result, she has landed roles in several Off-Broadway shows. "My ideal day now," she told John F. Berry in *Book World,* "is to work from nine until two in the afternoon at my drawing desk, then go to rehearsal—if I'm lucky enough to have a part."

*BIOGRAPHICAL/CRITICAL SOURCES:*

*BOOKS*

Cummins, Julie, editor, *Children's Book Illustration and Design,* PBC International, 1992.
de Montreville, Doris and Donna Hill, editors, *Third Book of Junior Authors,* Wilson, 1972, pp. 180-81.
Hopkins, Lee Bennett, editor, *Books Are by People,* Citation Press (New York City), 1969.
Kingman, Lee and others, editors, *Illustrators of Children's Books: 1957-1966,* Horn Book (Boston), 1968, *1967-1976,* 1978.
Lanes, Selma G., *Down the Rabbit Hole,* Atheneum (New York City), 1971.
*Major Authors and Illustrators for Children and Young Adults,* Gale (Detroit), 1993.
Silvey, Anita, editor, *Children's Books and Their Creators,* Houghton (Boston), 1995.
*Twentieth Century Children's Writers,* 2nd edition, St. James Press (Detroit), 1983, 3rd edition, 1989, 4th edition, 1995.

*PERIODICALS*

*Booklist,* April 1, 1991; May 1, 1992, p. 1599; November 15, 1993, p. 632; August, 1994, p. 2054; March 15, 1995, p. 1330; November 1, 1996, p. 496.
*Bulletin of the Center for Children's Books,* October, 1990, p. 36.
*Horn Book Magazine,* February, 1971; August, 1981; November-December, 1990, p. 730; July-August, 1995; November-December, 1996, p. 751.
*Junior Library Guild,* March, 1979.
*Kirkus Reviews,* April 15, 1991, p. 537; October 1, 1993, p. 1276.
*New York Times Book Review,* October 1, 1967; April 26, 1981; April 1, 1984.
*Publishers Weekly,* May 17, 1971, pp. 11-13; June 1, 1992, p. 61; July 4, 1994, pp. 60-61; March 20, 1995; July 24, 1996.
*School Library Journal,* October, 1990, p. 96; May, 1991; June, 1992; April, 1995, pp. 142-43; September, 1996.
*Times Literary Supplement,* June 26, 1969.
*Washington Post Book World,* June 13, 1982.

**LOGAN, Mark**
**See NICOLE, Christopher (Robin)**

\*      \*      \*

**LONDON, Laura**
**See CURTIS, Sharon**

\*      \*      \*

**LOOMIS, Noel M(iller) 1905-1969**
   **(Sam Allison, Benj. Miller, Frank Miller, Silas Water)**

*PERSONAL:* Born April 3, 1905, in Wakita, OK; died September 7, 1969; son of LeRoy Parker and Florida Bess (Miller) Loomis; married Dorothy Moore Green, 1945; children: James LeRoy, Mary Nell Liljenberg. *Education:* Attended Clarendon College, 1921, University of Oklahoma, 1930.

*CAREER:* Freelance writer, 1929-79; San Diego State College, San Diego, CA, instructor in English, 1958-69, director of Writers' Workshop, 1963-69. Did national survey of writers' incomes, 1953, and of terms in writers' contracts, 1955-56. President, Hulburd Grove Improvement Association. Early in life worked as printer, editor, and worked as newspaperman all over the American West.

*MEMBER:* Western Writers of America (president and secretary), American Academy of Political and Social Science, American Association of University Professors, American Historical Association, PEN, California Writers' Guild, Westerners Club (New York, Washington, DC, Chicago), Longhorn Cowboy Club (Duesseldorf, Germany).

*AWARDS, HONORS:* Western Writers of American, Silver Spur awards for best Western novel, 1958, for *Short Cut to Red River,* for best Western short story, 1959, for "Grandfather Out of the past" (in *Frontiers West*).

*WRITINGS:*

*WESTERN NOVELS*

*Rim of the Caprock,* Macmillan (New York City), 1952, published as *Battle for the Caprock,* Collins (London), 1959.

(As Frank Miller) *Tejas Country,* Bouregy and Curl, 1953.

(As Sam Allison) *Trouble on Crazyman,* Lion Books (New York City), 1953, published as *Wyoming War,* Lion Books, 1957.

*The Buscadero,* Macmillan, 1953, published as *Trouble Shooter,* Collins, 1953.

*North to Texas,* Ballantine (New York City), 1955, published as *Texas Rebel,* Corgi (London), 1956.

*West to the Sun,* Gold Medal (New York City), 1955, published as *Rifles on the River,* Collins, 1957.

*Johnny Concho,* Gold Medal, 1956.

*The Twilighters,* Macmillan, 1956.

*Wild Country,* Pyramid (New York City), 1956.

(With Paul Leslie Peil) *Hang the Men High,* Gold Medal, 1957.

*The Maricopa Trail,* Gold Medal, 1957.

*Short Cut to Red River,* Macmillan, 1958, published as *Connelly's Expedition,* Collins, 1959.

*The Leaden Cache,* Collins, 1958, published as *Cheyenne War Cry,* Avon (New York City), 1959.

*Above the Palo Duro,* Gold Medal, 1959.

*A Time for Violence,* Macmillan, 1960.

*Have Gun, Will Travel* (based on the television series by same name, CBS, 1957-63), Dell (New York City), 1960.

*Bonanza* (based on the television series by same name, NBC, 1959-73), Popular Library (New York City), 1960.

*Ferguson's Ferry,* Avon, 1962.

### OTHER

*Murder Goes to Press* (novel), Phoenix Press (New York City), 1937.

*Murder Beats the Drums,* published by *Star Weekly* (Toronto), 1938.

*A Dead Man Signs a Will,* published by *Star Weekly,* 1939.

*City of Glass* (novel), Thrilling Publications, 1942.

*Iron Men,* Thrilling Publications, 1943.

(As Silas Water) *The Man with Absolute Motion* (novel), Rich and Cowan (London), 1953.

(Editor) *Holsters and Heroes,* Macmillan (New York City), 1954.

*Wells Fargo, Danger Station* (for children, based on the television series *Tales of Wells Fargo,* NBC, 1957-62), Whitman (Racine, WI), 1958.

*The Linecasting Operator-Machinist* (technical book), Stockton (Pittsburgh), 1958.

*The Texan-Santa Fe Pioneers,* University of Oklahoma Press (Norman), 1958.

(With Abraham P. Nasatir) *Pedro Vial and the Roads to Santa Fe,* University of Oklahoma Press, 1967.

*Wells Fargo* (company history), Clarkson N. Potter (New York City), 1968.

Also, editor of *The Overland Dispatch* and *Narrative of the Captivity and Adventures of John Tanner During Thirty Years Residence Among the Chippewa, Ottawa, and Objibwa Tribes* by Edwin James, published by Ross & Haines (Wayzata, MN); historical editor, *Western Country.* Contributor to *Western Review, The Texans,* and *Western American Literature.* Short stories published in numerous periodicals, including *Exciting Western, Zane Grey's Western 32, Gunsmoke,* and *Texas Rangers.* His novels and short stories have been translated into several languages.

*ADAPTATIONS: Johnny Concho* (directed by Don McGuire), United Artists, 1956.

*SIDELIGHTS:* Noel Loomis' books are classified variously within the western, science fiction, mystery, and historical genres. According to Jeff Sadler in *Twentieth-Century Western Writers:* "[Loomis'] reputation rests--justly--on the handful of novels produced under his own name between 1952 and 1959, when his creative powers were at their peak. Five outstanding works, whose merits indicate their author as the foremost in his field, are *Rim of the Caprock, The Twilighters, Rifles on the River, The Leaden Cache,* and *Connelly's Expedition.* In each of these novels, Loomis selects a precise time and place, and brings them stunningly alive. The 'feel' of the period is magnificently caught—in description, in attitudes revealed by the laconic dialogue, most of all in full-blooded action which at times takes the breath away." *A Time for Violence,* published in 1960 after Loomis' award-winning novel and "five outstanding works," is "brightly grounded in drama," according to a *New York Times Book Review* reviewer, and represented at the time "the author's best performance to date."

*The Twilighters,* a novel based on an earlier short story, is "brutal and forceful" noted a *Kirkus* reviewer. *New York Times'* Hoffman Birney "found the original short story as morbidly gruesome as anything he had ever read" and stated in his review that "*The Twilighters,* while well written, is equally unpleasant." According to Sadler: "Violence shapes the work of Noel M. Loomis. There is a savage force at work in his novels, evoking the atmosphere of a harsh untamed land. His writing captures the taste and scent of another time, when danger stalked a man with every stride and life hung by a thread. Yet the violence is not all. Against the cruelty of man and nature Loomis sets his heroes, tough, honest men embodying the frontier virtues, strong enough to face the challenge of the land and tame it." Sadler noted that "though brutality is part of the world he describes, Loomis does not rely on it for his effects. His plots are authentic and imaginative, often with a strong historical basis."

Sadler summarized Loomis' western writing, stating: "The work of Loomis is far ahead of its time. No other western writer of the 1950s depicts so honestly the nature of the land and its people, or renders them so alive. Avoiding comment, he concentrates on the atmosphere of time and place. One experiences with him the smell of Indian camps and frontier trading posts, the breathtaking vision of the Caprock, the sudden terror of a surprise attack. Loomis, in his swift character sketches, his striking descriptions, his lithe effective style, brings that world to life before our eyes. In the field he chose, he has yet to be surpassed."

*Wells Fargo,* a history of the Wells Fargo company, and *Pedro Vial and the Roads to Santa Fe,* a description of Pedro Vial's exploratory expeditions, are both historical non-fiction books. *Wells Fargo,* stated O. O. Winther in the *Journal of American History,* "is not in any sense a scholarly, monographic study . . . [but] it is so rich in interesting miscellaneous and fairly well-documented tidbits of historical information that it is not without some conceivable value to professional historians. . . . It is regrettably a hodge-podge of historical information. Moreover, the author has overextended the scope of his book." In some contrast, Marco Thorne commented in *Library Journal* that *Wells Fargo* is written in a "scholarly but easy-to-read style. . . . This latest work is more complete than previous books . . . about the firm." In another issue of *Library Journal,* Donald Powell reviewed *Pedro Vial and the Roads to Santa Fe* as "an essential work for all academic libraries and any others interested in the story of the American West." Powell noted, however, that the book "is not always easy reading." Brian Garfield echoed that thought in *Saturday Review,* stating: "The book's weight of detail, while of value to historians, may tend to blur events in the mind of the casual reader. . . . If the reader is patient with documentation, he will be well rewarded."

*BIOGRAPHICAL/CRITICAL SOURCES:*

BOOKS

*Twentieth-Century Western Writers,* second edition, St. James (Chicago), 1991.

PERIODICALS

*Booklist,* December 1, 1960.
*Journal of American History,* September, 1969.
*Kirkus,* February 1, 1955; June 15, 1960.
*Library Journal,* May 15, 1967; December 15, 1968.
*New York Times,* April 3, 1955.
*New York Times Book Review,* October 2, 1960.
*Saturday Review,* June 10, 1967.

*OBITUARIES:*

PERIODICALS

*New York Times,* September 9, 1969.
*Publishers Weekly,* October 20, 1969.*

\* \* \*

## LOPEZ, Barry Holstun 1945-

*PERSONAL:* Born January 6, 1945, in Port Chester, NY; son of Adrian Bernard and Mary (Holstun) Lopez; married Sandra Landers (a bookwright), June 10, 1967. *Education:* University of Notre Dame, A.B. (cum laude), 1966, M.A.T., 1968; University of Oregon, graduate study, 1969-70.

*CAREER:* Full-time writer, 1970—. Columbia University, New York City, associate at Gannett Foundation Media Center, 1985—; Eastern Washington University, Cheney, WA, Distinguished Visiting Writer, 1985; University of Iowa, Iowa City, Ida Beam Visiting Professor, 1985; Carleton College, Northfield, MN, Distinguished Visiting Naturalist, 1986; University of Notre Dame, Notre Dame, IN, W. Harold and Martha Welch Visiting Professor of American Studies, 1989. Sino-American Writers Conference in China, delegate, 1988. Correspondent, *Outside,* 1982—.

*MEMBER:* PEN American Center, Authors Guild, Poets and Writers.

*AWARDS, HONORS:* John Burroughs Medal for distinguished natural history writing, Christopher Medal for humanitarian writing, and Pacific Northwest Booksellers award for excellence in nonfiction, all 1979, and American Book Award nomination, 1980, all for *Of Wolves and Men;* Distinguished Recognition Award, Friends of American Writers, 1981, for *Winter Count;* National Book Award in nonfiction (formerly American Book Award), Christopher Book Award, Pacific Northwest Booksellers award, National Book Critics Circle award nomination, *Los Angeles Times* book award nomination, American Library Association notable book citation, *New York Times Book Review* "Best Books" listing, and American Library Association "Best Books for Young Adults" citation, all 1986, and Francis Fuller Victor Award in nonfiction from Oregon Institute of Literary Arts, 1987, all for *Arctic Dreams: Imagination and Desire in a Northern Landscape*; Award in Literature from American Academy and Institute of Arts and Letters, 1986, for body of work; Guggenheim fellow, 1987; L.H.D., Whittier College, 1988; Parents' *Choice* Award, 1990, for *Crow and Weasel*; Lannan Foundation Award in nonfiction, 1990, for body of work; Governor's Award for Arts, 1990; Best Geographic Educational Article, National Council for Geographic Education, 1990, for "The American Geographies; L.H.D., University of Portland, 1994; Award in Fiction from Pacific Northwest Booksellers, 1995."

*WRITINGS:*

*Desert Notes: Reflections in the Eye of a Raven* (fictional narratives), Andrews & McMeel, 1976.
*Giving Birth to Thunder, Sleeping with His Daughter: Coyote Builds North America* (Native American trickster stories), Andrews & McMeel, 1978.
*Of Wolves and Men* (nonfiction), Scribner, 1978.
*River Notes: The Dance of Herons* (fictional narratives), Andrews & McMeel, 1979.
*Desert Reservation* (chapbook), Copper Canyon Press, 1980.
*Winter Count* (fiction), Scribner, 1981.
*Arctic Dreams: Imagination and Desire in a Northern Landscape* (nonfiction), Scribner, 1986.
*Crossing Open Ground* (essays), Scribner, 1988.
*Crow and Weasel* (fable), illustrated by Tom Pohrt, North Point Press, 1990.
*The Rediscovery of North America* (essay), University Press of Kentucky, 1991.
*Field Notes: The Grace Note of the Canyon Wren,* A. A. Knopf, 1994.

*OTHER*

Contributor to numerous books, including *Wonders: Writings and Drawings for the Child in Us All,* edited by Jonathan Cott and Mary Gimbel, Rolling Stone Press, 1980; *Resist Much, Obey Little: Some Notes on Edward Abbey,* edited by James Hepworth and Gregory McNamee, Dream Garden, 1985; *Before and After: The Shape and Shaping of Prose,* edited by D. L. Emblen and Arnold Solkov, Random House, 1986; *Best American Essays,* edited by Gay Talese and Robert Atwan, Ticknor and Fields, 1988; *Bighorse the Warrior,* by Tiana Bighorse, University of Arizona Press, 1990; *Helping Nature Heal: A Whole Earth Catalogue,* edited by Richard Nilson, Ten Speed Press, 1991; *Contemporary Voices,* edited by Rick Bass, Texas A & M University Press, 1992.

Contributor to numerous periodicals, including *Harper's, North American Review, New York Times, Orion Nature Quarterly, Antaeus, National Geographic,* and *Outside.* Contributing editor, *North American Review,* 1977—, and *Harper's,* 1981-82, 1984—; guest editor of special section, "The American Indian Mind," for *Quest,* September/October, 1978; advisory editor, *Antaeus,* autumn, 1986.

Lopez's books have been translated into Chinese, Dutch, Finnish, French, German, Italian, Japanese, Norwegian, Portuguese, Russian, Spanish, and Swedish.

*ADAPTATIONS:* Composer John Luther Adams consulted with Lopez and others to create a stage adaptation of *Giving Birth to Thunder,* which was performed in Juneau, Alaska, in 1987; three stories from *River Notes* have been recorded with accompanying music by cellist David Darling; portions of *Desert Notes* and *Arctic Dreams* have been adapted for the stage by modern dance companies.

*WORK IN PROGRESS:* A work of fiction, set on the northern plains in the eighteenth century; a work of nonfiction about landscapes remote from North America; essays, articles, and short fiction for magazines.

*SIDELIGHTS:* Barry Holstun Lopez's early magazine articles and books established his reputation as an authoritative writer on the subjects of natural history and the environment. He has been favorably compared to such distinguished naturalist/authors as Edward Hoagland, Peter Matthiessen, Edward Abbey, Sally Carrighar, and Loren Eiseley. Lopez's later works are praised for their philosophical content as well, for in such works as *Of Wolves and Men* and *Arctic Dreams: Imagination and Desire in a Northern Landscape* the author uses natural history as a metaphor for discussing some larger moral issues. "A writer has a certain handful of questions," Lopez explained to Nick O'Connell in a *Seattle Review* interview. "Mine seem to be the issues of tolerance and dignity. You can't sit down and write directly about those things, but if they are on your mind and if you're a writer, they're going to come out in one form or another. The form I feel most comfortable with, where I do a lot of reading and aimless thinking, is in natural history."

Lopez spent most of his first ten years in Southern California—"before it became a caricature of itself," he told *Western American Literature* interviewer Jim Aton. By the time the family moved back to Lopez's birthplace in New York, he had formed a strong emotional attachment to the West Coast, and so he returned to live there when he was twenty-three years old. Lopez's graduate studies in folklore led him to write his first book, a retelling of Native American stories featuring the coyote as a trickster figure. It was published some time later as *Giving Birth to Thunder, Sleeping with His Daughter: Coyote Builds North America.* Deciding that life as a writer was preferable to life as a scholar, Lopez left the university in 1970, settled with his wife on the McKenzie River in western Oregon, and devoted himself to writing full-time.

A 1974 assignment for *Smithsonian* magazine led to Lopez's first major book, *Of Wolves and Men.* His research for that article "catalyzed a lot of thinking about human and animal relationships which had been going on in a vague way in my mind for several years," he said in a *CA* interview. "I realized that if I focused on this one animal, I might be able to say something sharp and clear." In his book, Lopez attempts to present a complete portrait of the wolf. He includes not only scientific information but also wolf lore from aboriginal societies and an overview of the animal's role in literature, folklore, and superstition.

The result, say many critics, is a book that succeeds on several levels. First, Lopez has gathered "an extraordinary amount of material," writes a contributor to the *New York Review of Books,* making *Of Wolves and Men* one of the most comprehensive sources of information on these animals ever published. Second, in showing readers the many diverse images of the wolf, the author reveals how man "creates" animals by projecting aspects of his own personality onto them. Third, Lopez illustrates how undeserved is Western civilization's depiction of the wolf as a ruthless killer. His observations showed him that the Eskimos' conception of the wolf is much closer to the truth; among them, wolves are respected and emulated for their intelligence and strong sense of loyalty. What society thinks about the wolf may reveal some-

thing about itself, concludes Lopez, for while Western man has reviled the wolf as a wanton killer, he himself has brutally and pointlessly driven many animals to extinction. Whitley Streiber, writing for the *Washington Post,* believes that *Of Wolves and Men* is "a very important book by a man who has thought much on his subject. Above all he has listened to many people who claim to know about wolves. In coming to terms with the difference between what we know and what we imagine about the wolf, Lopez has shed light on some painful truths about the human experience. By laying no blame while facing the tragedy for what it is, he has made what we have done to the wolf a source of new knowledge about man."

Lopez found that he was strongly drawn to the Arctic even after *Of Wolves and Men* was completed. Over the next four years he made several more trips there, and in 1986 he published an account of his travels entitled *Arctic Dreams: Imagination and Desire in a Northern Landscape.* While the book provides a wealth of factual information about the Arctic region, it is, says the *New York Times*'s Michiko Kakutani, "a book about the Arctic North in the way that 'Moby-Dick' is a novel about whales." In *Arctic Dreams* Lopez restates the deeper themes found in *Of Wolves and Men,* but while *Of Wolves and Men* focused tightly on man's relationship with a specific animal, *Arctic Dreams*'s scope is wider, exploring man's relationship with what Lopez refers to as "the landscape." He explained to Jim Aton, "By landscape I mean the complete lay of the land—the animals that are there, the trees, the vegetation, the quality of soils, the drainage pattern of water, the annual cycles of temperature, the kinds of precipitation, the sounds common to the region."

*Arctic Dreams* drew many favorable reviews, both for its vivid descriptions of the North and for the questions it raises about man's place in nature. "The writing, at times, is luminous, powerful and musical. Lopez infuses each sentence with grace," asserts George Tombs in the Toronto *Globe & Mail.* "It is a lyrical geography and natural history, an account of Eskimo life, and a history of northern explorations," finds *Los Angeles Times Book Review* contributor Richard Eder. "But mainly, it is a . . . reflection about the meaning of mankind's encounter with the planet. . . . Its question, starting as ecology and working into metaphysics, is whether civilization can find a way of adapting itself to the natural world, before its predilection for adapting the natural world to itself destroys self and world, both." Lopez elaborated on the feelings that prompted him to write *Arc-*

*tic Dreams* in his interview with Aton: "I think if you can really see the land, if you can lose your sense of wishing it to be what you want it to be, if you can strip yourself of the desire to order and to name and see the land entirely for itself, you see in the relationship of all its elements the face of God. And that's why I say the landscape has an authority."

Man's interactions with "the landscape" are often highlighted in Lopez's fiction as well as in his nonfiction. His short story collections are praised by many reviewers. For example, in a *Detroit News* review of *River Notes: The Dance of Herons,* David Graber writes: "Lopez delicately surveys the terrain of shared experience between a man and place, in this case a river in the Pacific Northwest. . . . [The author] has an unsentimental naturalist's knowledge combined with profound love-of-land. . . . [His] writing has a dreamlike quality; the sensuality of his words, his . . . playful choice of simile serve as counterpoint to his precisely accurate portrayals of salmon spawning and herons fishing, of Douglas fir falling to the chainsaw and willow crowding the riverbank." Edith Hamilton of the *Miami Herald* says that in *River Notes* "Lopez transmogrifies the physical characteristics of the river—the bend, the falls, the shallows, the rapids—into human experience: the bend as a man seriously ill for a long time who suddenly, for no reason as the river bends for no reason, decides he will recover. The falls is a strangely gothic convolution of the original fall from grace, brought up to date by a vagabond with mythic yearnings who ends his search at the high brink of the river's falls. . . . Lopez's nice shallows become deep reflecting mirrors, their images multiplying beyond ease. . . . Not since Ken Kesey's drastically different novel, *Sometimes a Great Notion,* has a writer so caught and pinned the mossy melancholy of Oregon." In his *Progressive* review, David Miller makes the point that, despite the book's deceptively simple title, it is no mere study of herons. He writes that *River Notes* "is about a small world of relationships among people, herons, salmon, cottonwoods—and all creatures drawn to this rushing, tumbling, powerful, and endangered emblem of natural life, the river. . . . [The book ] is a thing of beauty in itself, as tantalizingly real and yet as otherworldly as your own reflection on a river's surface. . . . It is a rare achievement; perhaps—I've never said this before and know that only time will tell—it is a work of genius."

*Saturday Review* writer Alan Cheuse believes that *Winter Count,* another collection of short fiction, is the book that will win for Lopez "recognition as a writer who like, say, Peter Matthiessen or Edward Hoagland, goes to the wilderness in order to clarify a great deal about civilization." Cheuse commends Lopez for weaving "a style reminiscent of some important contemporary Latin American magical realists" and for turning "the sentiments of a decade's worth of ecology lovers into a deeply felt and unnervingly powerful picture of reality." *Los Angeles Times* reviewer Elaine Kendall writes: "There's a boundary, no wider than a pinstripe, where fact and fiction barely touch. With so much room on either side and assorted areas where overlap is expected, few writers choose to confine themselves to that fine line where the two simply meet. Lopez is one of those few. He makes that delicate border his entire territory. *Winter Count* is a small and perfectly crafted collection of just such encounters between imagination and reality. . . . Lopez's observations are so acute the stories expand of their own accord, lingering in the mind the way intense light lingers on the retina." Finally, David Quammen, in a *New York Times Book Review* article, says that *Winter Count* is "full of solid, quiet, telling short works. Each of the stories . . . is as economical in design, as painstakingly crafted and as resonant as a good classical guitar." Quammen concludes that Lopez's fiction "is as spare, as pared down and elemental as the lives it describes, the values it celebrates. One of his characters says, 'I've thrown away everything that is no good,' and this perilously righteous algorithm seems a key part of the author's own epic."

In *Field Notes* Lopez presents a collection of twelve stories, completing a trilogy that also includes *Desert Notes* and *River Notes*. Critics emphasized the collection's portrayal of civilized man at odds with the natural world, noting Lopez's imaginative combination of elements of folklore, myth, and natural science. Ruth Coughlin in *New York Times Book Reivew* praises the "purity and power of Mr. Lopez's imagery."

Discussing his fiction with Aton, Lopez commented: "My interest in a story is to illuminate a set of circumstances that bring some understanding of human life, enough at least so that a reader can identify with it and draw some vague sense of hope or sustenance or deep feeling and in some way be revived. . . . It's important to me . . . to go into a story with a capacity for wonder, where I know I can derive something 'wonder-full' and then bring this into the story so that a reader can feel it and say, 'I am an adult. I have a family, I pay bills, I live in a world of chicanery and subterfuge and atomic weaponry and inhumanity and round-heeled politicians and garrulous, insipid television personalities, but still I have wonder. I have been brought to a state of wonder by contact with something in a story.'" Lopez again emphasized the centrality of writing and story-telling in his life in a *Publishers Weekly* interview with Douglas Marx: "My themes will always be dignity of life, structures of prejudice, passion, generosity, kindness and the possibility of the good life in dark circumstances."

*BIOGRAPHICAL/CRITICAL SOURCES:*

BOOKS

Lopez, Barry Holstun, *Arctic Dreams: Imagination and Desire in a Northern Landscape* (nonfiction), Scribner, 1986.

Lueders, Edward, editor, *Writing Natural History: Dialogues with Authors,* University of Utah Press, 1989.

O'Connell, Nicholas, *At the Field's End: Interviews with Twenty Pacific Northwest Writers* (excerpted in *Seattle Review*), Madrona, 1987.

Paul, Sherman, *Hewing to Experience: Essays and Reviews on Recent American Poetry and Poetics, Nature and Culture,* University of Iowa Press, 1989.

PERIODICALS

*Bloomsbury Review,* January/February, 1990.
*Chicago Tribune,* November 5, 1978; March 30, 1986.
*Chicago Tribune Book World,* November 23, 1979.
*Christian Science Monitor,* February 12, 1979.
*Detroit News,* November 4, 1979.
*English Journal,* April, 1989.
*Environmental Journal,* January/February, 1991.
*Esquire,* November, 1994, p. 136.
*Globe & Mail* (Toronto), May 31, 1986.
*Harper's,* December, 1984.
*Los Angeles Times,* November 12, 1978; May 9, 1981.
*Los Angeles Times Book Review,* March 2, 1986; February 14, 1988; April 2, 1995, p. 6; September 17, 1995, p. 8.
*Miami Herald,* September 30, 1979; March 29, 1986.
*Missouri Review,* Volume 11, number 3, 1988.
*Nation,* November 11, 1978.
*New Republic,* June 30, 1979.
*Newsweek,* October 16, 1978.
*New Yorker,* February 26, 1979; March 17, 1986; November 26, 1990.
*New York Review of Books,* October 12, 1978.

*New York Times,* January 4, 1979; February 12, 1986; March 29, 1986.
*New York Times Book Review,* November 19, 1978; June 14, 1981; February 16, 1986; April 24, 1988; November 25, 1990; November 20, 1994, p. 22.
*North Dakota Quarterly,* winter, 1988.
*Observer,* June 24, 1979.
*Orion Nature Quarterly,* summer, 1990.
*Pacific Northwest,* March/April, 1980.
*Progressive,* May, 1980.
*Publishers Weekly,* October 11, 1985; June 23, 1989; July 27, 1990; September 26, 1994, p. 41.
*Saturday Review,* April, 1981.
*Seattle Review,* fall, 1985.
*Time,* March 10, 1986; October 10, 1994, p. 90.
*Times Literary Supplement,* December 7, 1979; August 8, 1986.
*Washington Post,* November 27, 1978; November 18, 1986; November 24, 1986.
*Washington Post Book World,* March 9, 1986.
*Western American Literature,* spring, 1986.*

\*    \*    \*

## LUDLUM, Robert 1927-
### (Jonathan Ryder, Michael Shepherd)

*PERSONAL:* Born May 25, 1927, in New York, NY; son of George Hartford (a businessman) and Margaret (Wadsworth) Ludlum; married Mary Ryducha (an actress), March 31, 1951; children: Michael, Jonathan, Glynis. *Education:* Wesleyan University, B.A., 1951. *Politics:* Independent.

*ADDRESSES: Home*—Naples, FL. *Agent*—Henry Morrison, Box 235, Bedford Hills, NY 10507.

*CAREER:* Writer, 1971—. Actor on Broadway and on television, 1952-60; North Jersey Playhouse, Fort Lee, NJ, producer, 1957-60; producer in New York City, 1960-69; Playhouse-on-the-Mall, Paramus, NJ, producer, 1960-70. *Military service:* U.S. Marine Corps, 1944-46.

*MEMBER:* Authors Guild, Authors League of America, American Federation of Television and Radio Artists, Screen Actors Guild.

*AWARDS, HONORS:* New England Professor of Drama Award, 1951; awards and grants from American National Theatre and Academy, 1959, and from

Actors' Equity Association and William C. Whitney Foundation, 1960; Scroll of Achievement, American National Theatre and Academy, 1960.

*WRITINGS:*

*The Scarlatti Inheritance,* World Publishing, 1971.
*The Osterman Weekend,* World Publishing, 1972.
*The Matlock Paper,* Dial, 1973.
(Under pseudonym Jonathan Ryder) *Trevayne,* Delacorte, 1973.
(Under pseudonym Jonathan Ryder) *The Cry of the Halidon,* Delacorte, 1974.
*The Rhinemann Exchange,* Dial, 1974.
(Under pseudonym Michael Shepherd) *The Road to Gandolfo,* Dial, 1975, reprinted under name Robert Ludlum, Bantam, 1982.
*The Gemini Contenders,* Dial, 1976.
*The Chancellor Manuscript,* Dial, 1977.
*The Holcroft Covenant,* Richard Marek, 1978.
*The Matarese Circle,* Richard Marek, 1979.
*The Bourne Identity,* Richard Marek, 1980.
*The Parsifal Mosaic,* Random House, 1982.
*The Aquitaine Progression,* Random House, 1984.
*The Bourne Supremacy,* Random House, 1986.
*The Icarus Agenda,* Random House, 1988.
*The Bourne Ultimatum,* Random House, 1990.
*The Road to Omaha,* Random House, 1992.
*The Scorpio Illusion,* Bantam, 1993.
*Three Complete Novels: The Ludlum Triad,* Wings Books, 1994.
*The Apocalypse Watch,* Bantam, 1995.
*The Matarese Countdown,* Bantam, 1997.

*ADAPTATIONS: The Rhinemann Exchange* was adapted as a television miniseries by NBC, 1977; *The Osterman Weekend* was filmed by EMI, 1980; *The Bourne Supremacy,* read by Michael Prichard, was released on cassette tape by Books on Tape, 1986; an abridged version of *The Bourne Identity,* read by Darren McGavin, was released on cassette tape by Bantam, 1987, and was adapted for television, c. 1989; *The Icarus Agenda,* read by Prichard, was released on cassette by Books on Tape, 1988; *The Bourne Ultimatum,* read by Prichard, was released on cassette by Books on Tape, 1990; *The Road to Omaha,* read by Joseph Campanella, was released by Random House, 1992; *The Scarlatti Inheritance* was filmed by Universal Pictures.

*SIDELIGHTS:* Suspense novelist Robert Ludlum "has his share of unkind critics who complain of implausible plots, leaden prose, and, as a caustic reviewer once sneered, an absence of 'redeeming literary val-

ues to balance the vulgar sensationalism,'" Susan Baxter and Mark Nichols noted in *Maclean's.* "But harsh critical words have not prevented Robert Ludlum . . . from becoming one of the most widely read and wealthiest authors in the world." In fact, with sales of his books averaging 5.5 million copies each, Ludlum is "one of the most popular living authors [writing] in the English language," Baxter and Nichols concluded.

Authorship came as a second career for Ludlum, who worked in the theater and found success as a producer before writing his first novel at age forty-two. His most notable production, Bill Manhoff's *The Owl and the Pussycat,* featured then unknown actor Alan Alda, who later gained fame for his role in the television series, *M*A*S*H.* The play was performed at Playhouse-on-the-Mall in Paramus, New Jersey, the country's first theater in a shopping center, which Ludlum opened in 1960. After serving as producer at the Playhouse for ten years, Ludlum found himself bored and frustrated with the pressures of theater work. Finally, he gave in to his wife's admonition to try his hand at writing.

*The Scarlatti Inheritance,* Ludlum's first novel, was written around an old story idea and outline, drafted years earlier and finally fleshed out when he left the theater. Based on Ludlum's curiosity at the wealth of one group of Germans during that country's economic collapse and skyrocketing inflation following World War I, *The Scarlatti Inheritance* follows several financiers, including some Americans, who fund Hitler's Third Reich. The book set the pattern for Ludlum's career: the story of espionage and corruption became a best-seller. Criticism of *The Scarlatti Inheritance* also foreshadowed that of future works. The book was described by Patricia L. Skarda in *Dictionary of Literary Biography Yearbook: 1982* as having a "somewhat erratic pace and occasionally melodramatic characterizations" but was nonetheless "a thrilling, compelling tale"—pronouncements typical of each of Ludlum's novels.

In his next work, *The Osterman Weekend,* a television reporter is convinced by the CIA that his friends are involved in a conspiracy to control the world economy and agrees to gather evidence against them, but finds himself in over his head when his wife and children are threatened. Though the book's ending is considered disappointing by several reviewers, William B. Hill, writing in *Best Sellers,* noted, "If the ending is a bit weak, it is chiefly because it lets the rider down off a very high horse." Skarda pointed out that the story "exposes the inadequacies of American intelligence operations and our deepest fears that our friends cannot be trusted." Government agents again use a civilian as an investigator in a situation beyond his expertise in *The Matlock Paper.* Professor Matlock is pushed "into an untenable and dangerous situation" while snooping around campus for information on a group of crime bosses, Kelly J. Fitzpatrick related in *Best Sellers.* "The climax is effective and leaves the reader wondering, 'Can it be so?'" Yet Newgate Callendar countered in the *New York Times Book Review,* "The basic situation is unreal—indeed, it's unbelievable—but a good writer can make the reader suspend his disbelief, and Ludlum is a good writer."

*Trevayne* and *The Cry of the Halidon,* both written under the pseudonym Jonathan Ryder, feature protagonists who discover they were hired not for their skills, but in hopes that they would be unable to uncover the truth about their employers. Andrew Trevayne, appointed to investigate spending by the U.S. Defense Department, uncovers a company so powerful that even the president of the United States is controlled by it. "There is no doubt that big business exerts an inordinate amount of pressure," Callendar contended in a *New York Times Book Review.* "But how much pressure? Who is really running the country?" Reviewing *The Cry of the Halidon,* in which a young geologist is sent to Jamaica to conduct an industrial survey and winds up in the crossfire of British Intelligence, the corporation that hired him, and various underground factions, Callendar disparaged Ludlum's "rather crude and obvious writing style," and commented, "[Ludlum] is not very good at suggesting real characters, and his hero is a cutout composite of a number of sources." A reviewer for *Publishers Weekly* found that, early on in *The Cry of the Halidon,* "cleverness ceases to look like a virtue and becomes an irritant. If the writing were as rich or subtle as the plot is involved the reader might more happily stay the course . . . , but the writing is in fact rather bare." Ludlum's final pseudonymous offering (this time writing as Michael Shepherd), *The Road to Gandolfo* is "a strange, lurching amalgam of thriller and fantasy," Henri C. Veit contended in *Library Journal.* Involving the Pope, the Mafia, and the U.S. Army, the book is intended to be funny, but falls short, Veit continued. A *Publishers Weekly* reviewer similarly noted that the book "comes crammed with zaniness and playful characters, but, unhappily, neither asset produces comedy or the black humor indictment of the military mind the author intended."

*The Rhinemann Exchange* contains "one extremely ingenious plot gimmick," according to Callendar in *New York Times Book Review,* in which the United States and Germany arrange a trade—industrial diamonds for Germany, a weapons guidance system for the United States. Despite the author's "commonplace and vulgar style apparently much relished by his vast audience," Veit predicted in a *Library Journal* review that the book would be a success. In a review of the audio version of *The Rhinemann Exchange,* a *Publishers Weekly* contributor believed Ludlum fans "will find exactly what they're looking for—in a format already quite familiar." A secret with devastating consequences, described by Irma Pascal Heldman in *New York Times Book Review* as "absolutely within the realms of authenticity and fascinating to contemplate," is the key to *The Gemini Contenders.* Twin brothers, compelled by their father's deathbed wish to find a hidden vault containing a volatile document, unleash the secret on the world. Despite criticizing the plot, characters, and period detail of *The Gemini Contenders,* reviewer T. J. Binyon commented in the *Times Literary Supplement* that Ludlum "has the ability to tell a story in such a way as to keep even the fastidious reader unwillingly absorbed."

In *The Chancellor Manuscript* Ludlum returned to remaking history as he had in *The Scarlatti Inheritance.* J. Edgar Hoover's death is found to be an assassination, not the result of natural causes as was previously believed. The murder was carried out to prevent Hoover from releasing his secret files, which, *Christian Science Monitor*'s Barbara Phillips noted, "contain enough damaging information to ruin the lives of every man, woman and child in the nation." A group of prominent citizens join forces to retrieve the files but find half have already been stolen. An unsuspecting decoy is deployed, as in many other Ludlum stories, to lead the group to the thieves. The message of *The Chancellor Manuscript* is familiar to Ludlum fans, as the book "seems to justify our worst nightmares of what really goes on in the so-called Intelligence Community in Washington," Richard Freedman maintained in the *New York Times Book Review.*

*The Bourne Identity,* which introduced a trilogy of books, follows Bourne, a spy who awakens in a doctor's office with amnesia; the story is played out as a remarkable number of killers and organizations attempt to finish Bourne off before he realizes his true identity. "Some of Mr. Ludlum's previous novels were so convoluted they should have been packaged with bags of bread crumbs to help readers keep track of the plot lines," Peter Andrews mused in the *New York Times Book Review*. "But *The Bourne Identity* is a Ludlum story at its most severely plotted, and for me its most effective." The second volume, *The Bourne Supremacy,* forces Bourne to face his past when his wife is kidnapped. The final story in the "Bourne" trilogy, *The Bourne Ultimatum,* finds Bourne drawn into one last battle with his arch-enemy, the Jackal. The *Los Angeles Times Book Review*'s Don G. Campbell praised the third "Bourne" book as an example of "how it *should* be done," concluding that "in the pulse-tingling style that began so many years ago with *The Scarlatti Inheritance,* we are caught up irretrievably."

A woman comes back from the dead and a spy in the White House threatens humanity's continued existence in *The Parsifal Mosaic.* "Certainly, millions of entranced readers tap their feet in time to his fiction, and I'm positive this new adventure will send his legions of fans dancing out into the streets," Evan Hunter remarked in the *New York Times Book Review.* "Me? I must be tone-deaf." A world takeover is again imminent in *The Aquitaine Progression,* this time at the hands of five military figures. "Ludlum's hero, Joel Converse, learns of a plot by generals in the United States, Germany, France, Israel and South Africa to spawn violent demonstrations. Once the violence bursts out of hand, the generals plan to step in and take over," Charles P. Wallace wrote in the *Los Angeles Times Book Review. The Icarus Agenda* features a similar plot. This time, five wealthy, powerful figures arrange the election of the next United States president. "There is a sufficient amount of energy and suspense present in *The Icarus Agenda* to remind the reader why Mr. Ludlum's novels are best sellers," Julie Johnson commented in the *New York Times Book Review.* "Ludlum is light-years beyond his literary competition in piling plot twist upon plot twist," Peter L. Robertson commented in the Chicago *Tribune Books,* "until the mesmerized reader is held captive, willing to accept any wayward, if occasionally implausible, plotting device." In a more recent offering, *The Road to Omaha,* Ludlum departs from the seriousness of his espionage thrillers with a follow-up to *The Road to Gandolfo* that continues that novel's farcical tone. The Hawk and Sam, Ludlum's heroes in *Gandolfo,* return to fight the government for a plot of land legally belonging to an Indian tribe. In a review of the audio version of *The Road to Omaha,* a *Publishers Weekly* reviewer noted, "Hardcore Ludlum fans may be taken aback at first, but they stand to be won over in the listening."

*The Scorpio Illusion* returns to more familiar Ludlum territory: terrorism, international intrigue, mayhem, and death. In this novel, Amaya Bajaratt, a beautiful Basque terrorist, ignites a plot to assassinate the leaders of Israel, England, France, and the United States. Supported in her plot by a secret society of assassins known as the Scorpios, Bajaratt ventures to the United States to carry out the prize murder--the assassination of the U.S. president. The killer runs into resistance in the form of Tye Hawthorne, a former Naval intelligence officer, who is the only person capable of stopping the scheme. *The Apocalypse Watch,* Ludlum's next novel, covers similar serious territory, as a well-funded group of neo-Nazis attempts to create a Fourth Reich and achieve world domination. This intricately plotted novel features Harry Latham, who infiltrates the evil group only to be implanted with a memory chip of false information about prominent supporters of the group. When Harry is killed by the neo-Nazis, his brother Drew must pick up the fight against the group. Aided by the beautiful and mysterious Karin de Vries, Drew dodges assassination attempts and thwarts the neo-Nazis' ploy for world-domination.

The key elements of Ludlum's books—corruption in high places, elaborate secret plans, and unsuspecting civilians drawn into the fray—are what keep Ludlum fans waiting for his next offering. His writing, characterized by the liberal use of exclamation points, italics, sentence fragments, and rhetorical questions, has been described by some critics as crude, but others acknowledge that the style is popular with millions of readers and has proven difficult to duplicate, leaving Ludlum with little copycat competition. Still, reviewers often point to Ludlum's use of mixed metaphors and illogical statements as serious flaws in his books. Horror novelist Stephen King, in a somewhat tongue-in-cheek review of *The Parsifal Mosaic* for the *Washington Post Book World,* highlighted some of Ludlum's "strange, wonderful, and almost Zen-like thoughts: 'We've got . . . a confluence of beneficial prerogatives.' 'What I know is still very operative.' 'I'll get you your cover. But not two men. I think a couple would be better.'"

Journalist Bob Woodward, writing in the *Washington Post Book World,* summarized the media's view of Ludlum in a review of *The Icarus Agenda:* "Ludlum justifiably has a loyal following. Reviews of most of his previous books are critical but conclude, grudgingly, that he has another inevitable bestseller." In a review of *The Bourne Identity* for *Washington Post Book World,* Richard Harwood opined, "Whether reviewers are universally savage or effusive seems irrelevant: the book is bound to be a best seller. *The Bourne Identity* . . . is already on both the national and *Washington Post* best-seller lists and the damned thing won't officially be published [for three more days]. So much for the power of the press." Despite reviewers' advice, readers have voiced their approval of Ludlum in sales figures. As Baxter and Nichols noted in *Maclean's,* "For all his imperfections, Ludlum manages—by pumping suspense into every twist and turn in his tangled plots and by demanding sympathy for well-meaning protagonists afflicted by outrageous adversity—to keep millions of readers frantically turning his pages."

*BIOGRAPHICAL/CRITICAL SOURCES:*

BOOKS

*Bestsellers 89,* Issue 1, Gale, 1989.
*Bestsellers 90,* Issue 3, Gale, 1990.
*Contemporary Literary Criticism,* Gale, Volume 22, 1982, Volume 43, 1988.

PERIODICALS

*Best Sellers,* April 15, 1973, p. 41; April, 1972, p. 5.

*Christian Science Monitor,* March 31, 1977, p. 31.
*Library Journal,* October 1, 1974, p. 2504; April 1, 1975, pp. 694-695.
*Los Angeles Times Book Review,* March 11, 1984, p. 3; March 23, 1986, p. 3; March 18, 1990, p. 8.
*Maclean's,* April 9, 1984, pp. 50-52.
*New Republic,* November 25, 1981, p. 38; September 20, 1982, p. 43.
*New York,* May 9, 1988, pp. 74-75.
*New Yorker,* June 20, 1988, pp. 90-92.
*New York Review of Books,* May 8, 1986, pp. 12-13.
*New York Times,* March 13, 1978, p. C19.
*New York Times Book Review,* January 28, 1973, p. 20; May 6, 1973, p. 41; August 4, 1974, p. 26; October 27, 1974, p. 56; March 28, 1976, p. 18; March 27, 1977, p. 8; April 8, 1979, p. 14; March 30, 1980, p. 7; March 21, 1982, p. 11; April 22, 1984, p. 14; March 9, 1986, p. 12; March 27, 1988, p. 16; June 20, 1993, p. 16.
*Publishers Weekly,* April 8, 1974, p. 76; February 10, 1975, p. 52; March 1, 1991, pp. 49-50; March 2, 1992; April 19, 1993, p. 48; April 17, 1995, p. 37; May 29, 1995, p. 37.
*Times Literary Supplement,* October 1, 1976, p. 1260.
*Tribune Books* (Chicago), February 28, 1988, Section 14, p. 7.
*Washington Post Book World,* March 23, 1980, p. 3; March 7, 1982, p. 1; February 21, 1988, p. 1.*

# M-P

MARCHANT, Catherine
See COOKSON, Catherine (McMullen)

*    *    *

MARLOW, Max
See NICOLE, Christopher (Robin)

*    *    *

MATHIEU, Joe
See MATHIEU, Joseph P.

*    *    *

MATHIEU, Joseph P. 1949-
(Joe Mathieu)

PERSONAL: Born January 23, 1949, in Springfield, VT; son of Joseph A. (a car dealer) and Patricia (Biner) Mathieu; married Melanie Gerardi, September 7, 1970; children: Kristen, Joey. *Education:* Rhode Island School of Design, B.F.A., 1971. *Avocational interests:* Bicycling (especially touring the New England states), jazz and ragtime.

ADDRESSES: Home—64 Pheasant Lane, Brooklyn, CT 06234.

CAREER: Author and illustrator of books for children. Designer of album covers for Stomp Off records.

AWARDS, HONORS: Best Books selection, American Institute of Graphic Arts, 1973, for *The Magic Word Book, Starring Marko the Magician!;* Children's Choice selection, International Reading Association, 1982, for *Ernie's Big Mess.*

WRITINGS:

SELF-ILLUSTRATED; AS JOE MATHIEU

*The Amazing Adventures of Silent "E" Man,* Random House (New York City), 1973.
*The Magic Word Book, Starring Marko the Magician!* Random House, 1973.
*Big Joe's Trailer Truck,* Random House, 1974.
*I Am a Monster* (a "Sesame Street" book), Golden Press (New York City), 1976.
*The Grover Sticker Book,* Western Publishing (New York City), 1976.
*The Count's Coloring Book,* Western Publishing, 1976.
*The Sesame Street Mix or Match Storybook: Over Two Hundred Thousand Funny Combinations,* Random House, 1977.
*Who's Who on Sesame Street,* Western Publishing, 1977.
*Busy City* (nonfiction), Random House, 1978.
*The Olden Days* (nonfiction), Random House, 1981.
*Bathtime on Sesame Street,* edited by Jane Schulman, Random House, 1983.
*Big Bird Visits the Dodos,* Random House, 1985.
*Fire Trucks,* Random House, 1988.
*Trucks in Your Neighborhood,* Random House, 1988.
*Sesame Street 123: A Counting Book from 1 to 100,* Random House, 1991.
*Colors,* photographed by George Siede, Donna Preis, and Brian Warling Photography, Publications International (Lincolnwood, IL), 1997.

*Counting,* photographed by Siede, Preis, and Brian Warling Photography, Publications International, 1997.

*On the Go,* photographed by Siede, Preis, and Brian Warling Photography, Publications International, 1997.

*Sounds,* photographed by Siede, Preis, and Brian Warling Photography, Publications International, 1997.

ILLUSTRATOR; "SESAME STREET" SERIES; AS JOE MATHIEU; PUBLISHED BY RANDOM HOUSE, EXCEPT AS NOTED

Robinson, *Matt Robinson's Gordon of Sesame Street Storybook,* 1972.

Emily Perl Kingsley and others, *The Sesame Street 1,2,3 Storybook,* 1973.

Norman Stiles and Daniel Wilcox, *Grover and the Everything in the Whole Wide World Museum: Featuring Lovable, Furry Old Grover,* 1974.

Jeffrey Moss, Stiles, and Wilcox, *The Sesame Street ABC Storybook,* 1974.

Anna Jane Hays, *See No Evil, Hear No Evil, Smell No Evil,* Western Publishing, 1975.

Kingsley, David Korr, and Moss, *The Sesame Street Book of Fairy Tales,* 1975.

Stiles, *Grover's Little Red Riding Hood,* Western Publishing, 1976.

Stiles, *The Ernie and Bert Book,* Western Publishing, 1977.

Patricia Thackray, *What Ernie and Bert Did on Their Summer Vacation,* Western Publishing, 1977.

Kingsley, *The Exciting Adventures of Super-Grover,* Golden Press, 1978.

Sharon Lerner, *Big Bird's Look and Listen Book,* 1978.

Thackray, *Grover Visits His Granny,* 1978.

Daniel Korr, *Cookie Monster and the Cookie Tree,* Western Publishing, 1979.

Valjean McLenigham, *Ernie's Work of Art,* Western Publishing, 1979.

Linda Hayward, *The Sesame Street Dictionary,* 1980.

Sarah Roberts, *Ernie's Big Mess,* 1981.

Jon Stone and Joe Bailey, *Christmas Eve on Sesame Street* (based on the television special "Christmas Eve on Sesame Street"), 1981.

Roberts, *Nobody Cares about Me!,* 1982.

Dan Elliott, *Ernie's Little Lie,* 1983.

Elliott, *A Visit to the Sesame Street Firehouse,* 1983.

Roberts, *Bert and the Missing Mop Mix-Up,* 1983.

Stiles, *I'll Miss You, Mr. Hooper,* 1984.

Elliott, *Two Wheels for Grover,* 1984.

Lerner, *Big Bird's Copycat Day,* 1984.

Elliott, *My Doll Is Lost,* 1984.

Roberts, *The Adventures of Big Bird in Dinosaur Days,* 1984.

Roberts, *I Want to Go Home,* 1985.

Deborah Hautzig, *A Visit to the Sesame Street Hospital,* 1985.

Lerner, *Big Bird Says,* 1985.

Hautzig, *A Visit to the Sesame Street Library,* 1986.

Judy Freudberg and Tony Geiss, *Susan and Gordon Adopt a Baby,* 1986.

Liza Alexander, *A Visit to the Sesame Street Museum,* 1987.

Molly Cross, *Wait for Me,* 1987.

Hautzig, *It's Easy,* 1988.

Virginia Holt, *A My Name Is Alice,* 1989.

Hautzig, *Get Well, Granny Bird,* 1989.

Hautzig, *Grover's Bad Dream,* 1990.

Alexander, *How to Get to Sesame Street,* Western Publishing, 1990.

Hautzig, *Ernie and Bert's New Kitten,* 1990.

Hautzig, *Big Bird Plays the Violin,* 1991.

Alexander, *Bird Watching with Bert,* Western Publishing, 1991.

Bobbi Jane Kates, *We're Different, We're the Same,* 1992.

Elizabeth Rivlin, *Elmo's Little Glowworm,* 1994.

Anna Ross, *Elmo's Big Lift-and-Look Book,* 1994.

Stiles, *Around the Corner on Sesame Street,* 1994.

Lou Berger, *Sesame Street Stays up Late,* 1995.

Annie Cobb, *B Is for Books,* 1996.

Ross, *Elmo's Lift-and-Peek around the Corner Book,* 1996.

Eleanor Hudson, *Can You Tell Me How to Get to Seasame Street,* 1997.

ILLUSTRATOR; AS JOE MATHIEU

Ossie Davis, *Purlie Victorious,* Houghton (Boston), 1973.

Scott Corbett, *Dr. Merlin's Magic Shop,* Little, Brown (Boston), 1973.

Genevieve Gray, *Casey's Camper,* McGraw (New York City), 1973.

Byron Preiss, *The Electric Company: The Silent "E's" from Outer Space,* Western Publishing, 1973.

Corbett, *The Great Custard Pie Panic,* Little, Brown, 1974.

Suzanne W. Bladow, *The Midnight Flight of Moose, Mops, and Marvin,* McGraw, 1975.

Howard Liss, *The Giant Book of Strange But True Sports Stories,* Random House, 1976.

Hedda Nussbaum, *Plants Do Amazing Things* (nonfiction), Random House, 1977.

Katy Hall and Lisa Eisenberg, *A Gallery of Monsters,* Random House, 1981.

Cindy West, *The Superkids and the Singing Dog,* Random House, 1982.

Harold Woods and Geraldine Woods, *The Book of the Unknown* (nonfiction), Random House, 1982.

Liss, *The Giant Book of More Strange But True Sports Stories,* Random House, 1983.

Deborah Kovacs, *Brewster's Courage,* Simon & Schuster (New York City), 1992.

Leslie McGuire, *Big Dan's Moving Van,* Random House, 1993.

Laura Joffe Numeroff, *Dogs Don't Wear Sneakers,* Simon & Schuster, 1993.

Numeroff, *Chimps Don't Wear Glasses,* Simon & Schuster, 1995.

McGuire, *Big Frank's Fire Truck,* Random House, 1995.

Tish Rabe, *The King's Beard* (adapted from a script by Will Ryan, based on the television series "The Wubbulous World of Dr. Seuss"), Random House, 1997.

Lori Haskins, *Too many dogs!,* Random House, 1998

Also contributor, as illustrator under the names of Joe Mathieu and Joseph Mathieu, to series of Sesame Street publications, such as: *The Sesame Street Treasury* and *The Sesame Street Library.*

*SIDELIGHTS:* Joe Mathieu has made a career illustrating many of the numerous books for children that feature Jim Henson's Muppets from the award-winning children's program, *Sesame Street.* Although he began his career illustrating books he had also written, such as *The Magic Word Book, Starring Marko the Magician!* and *The Amazing Adventures of Silent "E" Man,* the majority of his work has appeared in books written by others. Among these are *Elmo's Lift-and-Peek around the Corner Book,* in which numbers, opposites, and matching concepts are taught with the aid of Mathieu's "loudly colored, chaotic-looking pages," in the estimation of a *Publishers Weekly* reviewer.

Joe Mathieu once told *CA:* "As a youngster, I became enamored of Jim Henson and the Muppets long before they were really famous. I would beg permission to miss the bus if they were going to appear on the 'Dave Garroway Show' or I'd get special permission to stay up late if they were scheduled for Jack Parr. When Random House and CTW (Children's Television Workshop) started looking for illustrators to interpret the Muppet characters from 'Sesame Street,' I just fell into it and I love drawing them. The 'Sesame Street' characters are my favorites of all the many Muppet characters."

*Sesame Street* tie-in books illustrated by Mathieu include *We're Different, We're the Same,* in which Mathieu's drawings of the Muppets "cavort cheerfully with people of all sizes, shapes and ethnicities," according to a *Publishers Weekly* critic. In *A Visit to the Sesame Street Hospital,* Grover is given a tour of the hospital where he will stay during a tonsillectomy operation. In *Get Well, Granny Bird,* Big Bird visits his grandmother when she gets a cold, and though his attempts to help out generally fail he learns that just his being there is a treat to Granny Bird. Mathieu's illustrations "are typical" of the *Sesame Street* books, that is, "realistically drawn and in full color," Sharron McElmeel observed in *School Library Journal.*

Mathieu has also illustrated a number of books outside the *Sesame Street* tie-in industry. A *Publishers Weekly* critic praised the "exuberant art" in Laura Numeroff's *Dogs Don't Wear Sneakers,* in which pictures of animals in implausible situations accompany the author's nonsensical rhymes. Indeed, according to Lori A. Janick of *School Library Journal,* "It's Mathieu's wacky and inventive illustrations that really carry the show." The book's sequel, *Chimps Don't Wear Glasses,* was deemed less successful by a *Kirkus Reviews* critic, who nonetheless noted Mathieu's "busy, literal cartoons." Deborah Kovacs's picture book, *Brewster's Courage,* features a ferret who travels to Louisiana to enjoy the zydeco music and learns how to make friends in a new situation. It also bears Mathieu's "amusing drawings," which accompany "a story with appeal for anyone who has ever felt like an outsider," according to a *Kirkus Reviews* commentator.

Joe Mathieu once told *CA:* "I became addicted to drawing pictures at about three years old. I was never interested in drawing completely straight. It's almost impossible for me to avoid humor, caricature and lots of action.

"I don't feel that an artist has to be particularly encouraged to draw. I think he'll draw no matter what. The same with a writer or a musician for that matter."

*BIOGRAPHICAL/CRITICAL SOURCES:*

*PERIODICALS*

*Booklist,* September 1, 1995, p. 89.

*Kirkus Reviews,* June 15, 1992, p. 780; August 1, 1995, p. 1115.

*Publishers Weekly,* November 23, 1992, p. 61; January 29, 1996, p. 99; August 19, 1996, p. 69.

*School Library Journal,* August, 1989, p. 122; September, 1992. p. 254; January, 1994, p. 96.

\*    \*    \*

## MAYO, Margaret (Mary) 1935-

*PERSONAL:* Born May 10, 1935, in London, England; daughter of William John and Anna (maiden name, Macleod) Cumming; married Peter Robin Mayo (a university lecturer), July 28, 1958; children: Roderick, Katrina, Andrew. *Education:* University of Southampton, B.Sc. (with honors), 1956, certificate in education, 1957.

*ADDRESSES: Home*—85 Peacock Lane, Brighton, Sussex BN1 6WA, England.

*CAREER:* Writer, 1974—. Teacher at numerous schools in England, 1957-61, 1969-71, 1973-75, and 1975-80.

*AWARDS, HONORS:* Aesop Accolade, Children's Folklore Society of the American Folklore Society, for *When the World Was Young: Creation and Pourquois Tales,* 1996.

*WRITINGS:*

*FOLKTALE COLLECTIONS*

(Compiler) *If You Should Meet a Crocodile and Other Verse,* illustrated by Carol Barker, Kaye & Ward (London), 1974.

(Reteller) *The Book of Magical Horses,* illustrated by Victor Ambrus, Kaye & Ward, 1976, Hastings House (New York City), 1977.

(Reteller) *The Book of Magical Birds,* illustrated by Fiona French, Kaye & Ward, 1977.

(Reteller) *The Book of Magical Cats,* illustrated by Ambrus, Kaye & Ward, 1978.

*Saints, Birds, and Beasts,* illustrated by Cara Lockhart Smith, Kaye & Ward, 1980.

*The Italian Fairy Book,* illustrated by Smith, Kaye & Ward, 1981.

*Fairy Tales from France,* illustrated by Smith, Kaye & Ward, 1983.

(Reteller) *The Orchard Book of Magical Tales,* illustrated by Jane Ray, Orchard, 1993, published in the United States as *Magical Tales from Many Lands,* Dutton (New York City), 1993.

(Reteller) *How to Count Crocodiles,* illustrated by Emily Bolam, Orion, 1994, published in the United States as *Tortoise's Flying Lesson: Animal Stories,* Harcourt (San Diego), 1995.

(Reteller) *First Fairy Tales,* illustrated by Selina Young, Orchard, 1994, Barnes & Noble Books (New York City), 1996.

(Reteller) *The Orchard Book of Creation Stories,* illustrated by Louise Brierley, Orchard, 1995, published in the United States as *When the World Was Young: Creation and Pourquois Tales,* Simon & Schuster (New York City), 1996.

(Reteller) *The Orchard Book of Mythical Birds and Beasts,* illustrated by Jane Ray, Orchard, 1996, published in the United States as *Mythical Birds and Beasts from Many Lands,* Dutton (New York City), 1997.

*OTHER; FOR CHILDREN*

*Little Mouse Twitchy Whiskers,* illustrated by Penny Dann, Orchard, 1992.

(Reteller) *First Bible Stories,* illustrated by Nicole Smee, Barron's (Hauppauge, NY), 1998.

*WORK IN PROGRESS: First Bible Stories.*

*SIDELIGHTS:* Margaret Mayo's contribution to children's literature comes in a familiar form: the folktale collection. Yet Mayo's work is distinguished by her careful selection of little-known but delightful tales from around the world, by her talent for engaging narration, and by her passion for her work. As she once told *CA,* Mayo is intent on preserving the oral tradition of storytelling and unique stories that merit attention from contemporary children. She selects "stories that have passed the most difficult of tests—the test of time," she explained, tales that "can still entertain and satisfy emotionally like no others. They are a precious part of our common heritage, and if our children are also to share it, then the tales must be told afresh to them."

Mayo began her career as a writer for children in the mid-1970s with *If You Should Meet a Crocodile and Other Verse.* This book is a compilation of short rhymes, poems, and limericks written by both famous and anonymous poets. According to a critic writing in *Growing Point,* this book was "designed for the very young." Mayo's first book for older readers contains thirteen fairytales about horses. *The Book of Magical Horses* tells of an enchanted mule, a winged horse, and even a water horse. A reviewer for *Junior Bookshelf* described the stories as "typically vigorous and full of action," and a *Booklist* contributor wrote that they are "told in an assured, conventional style." Mayo spent the last years of the seventies working on similar collections featuring magical birds and cats.

Mayo's *Saints, Birds, and Beasts* was published in 1980. This book tells the stories of sixteen saints with an emphasis on their relationships with animals. St. Jerome deals with a lion, St. Ailbe is raised by a wolf, and St. George fights his fabled dragon. In addition to the tales, Mayo provides brief biographies of the saints. According to a *Junior Bookshelf* contributor, the work displays "Mayo's considerable gifts as a storyteller."

*Magical Tales from Many Lands,* which includes fourteen folktales and comes complete with endnotes citing origins and sources, appeared in 1993. The emphasis in this work is the magic that works wonders for people around the world, from Arabians and Australians to Zulus. There is a story about a king from the Caribbean, a Baba Yaga tale from Russia, a Native American tale about the morning star, a story from Peru and another from China. "The stories read aloud well," observed Carolyn Phelan in a *Booklist* review. A critic writing in *Kirkus Reviews* described the book as a "remarkably felicitous collection" and lauded Mayo's story selection: "Mayo has chosen splendidly." A *Publishers Weekly* contributor appreciated Mayo's "lively vocabulary" and "fine sense of theater." According to this critic, the collection is "a winner" whether read piece by piece or all at once. "Mayo's book will work its magic on all who open it," asserted Barbara Chatton in *School Library Journal. How to Count Crocodiles,* like Mayo's earlier work, *If You Should Meet a Crocodile and Other Verses,* is a collection for young children. According to *Magpies* contributor Nola Allen, these stories are told with "exuberance." Eight stories, from Africa, Indonesia, Japan, and other countries, feature a monkey, an eagle, a tortoise, crocodiles, rabbits, elephants, a hippopotamus, bears, a lion, and other animals. The tales, reported a *Junior Bookshelf* critic, "include many amusing incidents, animal noises, tricks and games." The collection, published in the United States as *Tortoise's Flying Lesson: Animal Stories,* "brims with both vigor and cheer," wrote a contributor to *Publishers Weekly.* "What an engaging collection!" exclaimed Harriett Fargnoli in a *School Library Journal* review.

Mayo's *When the World Was Young: Creation and Pourquois Tales* received similar attention. This book, published in 1996, provides ten retold tales which explain some familiar aspect of life on Earth. Like Mayo's other collections, this one is multicultural. There is a Native American story that explains how fire gets in trees, a Polynesian story about the sun, a tale from Ghana about human skin color, a tale from Iceland about salt in the sea, and one from Egypt which tells how the moon came to the sky. The work comes with a foreword and source notes. According to Susan Hepler in a *School Library Journal* review, Mayo speaks to her audience and offers "connections for today's youngsters." Writing in *Publishers Weekly,* a reviewer described Mayo's retellings as "lively" and "suspenseful" and called her a "masterful" storyteller.

*Mythical Birds and Beasts from Many Lands* provides ten tales of fantastic creatures from dragons to unicorns. A Thunderbird from Native American folklore and an ancient Aztec Quetzalcoatl are featured along with mermaids, serpents, and familiar creatures from Greek mythology. Once again, Mayo's storytelling talents were praised by critics. "Mayo lends the oral cadence of a storyteller's voice to these tales of enchantment," wrote a *Kirkus Reviews* contributor. In a *Publishers Weekly* review, a critic stated, "Mayo's energetically paced versions possess a lively intensity that never fails to entertain."

## BIOGRAPHICAL/CRITICAL SOURCES:

### PERIODICALS

*Booklist,* November 15, 1977, p. 552; November 1, 1993, p. 517; September 1, 1996, pp. 122-23.

*Growing Point,* April, 1975, p. 2605; November, 1977, p. 3203.

*Horn Book,* January-February, 1994, pp. 77-78.

*Junior Bookshelf,* August, 1976, p. 207; December, 1978, p. 302; February, 1981, p. 23; June, 1995, p. 101.

*Kirkus Reviews,* September 1, 1993, p. 1148; May 1, 1997, p. 725.

*Magpies,* May, 1995, p. 29.

*Publishers Weekly,* September 6, 1993, p. 91; May 1, 1995, pp. 58-59; October 21, 1996, p. 85; April 14, 1997, p. 73.

*School Library Journal,* May, 1993, p. 57; September, 1993, p. 226; May, 1995, p. 101; December, 1996, p. 116.

*Times Educational Supplement,* September 30, 1983, p. 48.

## McGAHERN, John 1934-

*PERSONAL:* Born November 12, 1934, in Dublin, Ireland; son of John (a police officer) and Susan (McManus) McGahern, married Madeline Green, 1973. *Education:* Attended Presentation College, Carrick-on-Shannon, Ireland, and University College, Dublin.

*ADDRESSES: Office*—c/o Faber & Faber, 3 Queen Square, London, WC1N 3AU, England. *Agent*—c/o Viking Press, Inc., 40 West 23rd St., New York, NY 10010.

*CAREER:* Writer, 1963—. Teacher at St. John the Baptist Boys National School, 1956-63; O'Connor Professor of Literature, Colgate University, 1969, 1972, 1977, 1979, 1983; British Northern Arts Fellow at University of Newcastle and University of Durham, 1974-76. Visiting professor at numerous colleges in England and Ireland.

*MEMBER:* Aosdana Irish Academy of Letters.

*AWARDS, HONORS:* A. E. Memorial Award, 1962, and Macauley fellowship, 1964, both for *The Barracks*; Society of Authors award, 1967; British Arts Council awards, 1968, 1970, 1973; Research Fellowship, University of Reading, 1968-71; American Irish Foundation Literary Award, 1985; Galway Festival Tenth Anniversary Award, 1987; decorated Chevalier Ordre des Arts et des Lettres, 1989; Irish Times-Aer Lingus Literary Prize, 1990.

*WRITINGS:*

NOVELS

*The Barracks,* Faber (London), 1963, Macmillan (New York City), 1964.
*The Dark,* Faber, 1965, Knopf (New York City), 1966.
*The Leavetaking,* Faber, 1974, Little, Brown (Boston), 1975.
*The Pornographer,* Faber, 1979, Harper (New York City), 1980.
*Amongst Women,* Viking (New York City), 1990.
*The Power of Darkness,* Faber, 1991.

SHORT STORIES

*Nightlines,* Faber, 1970, Atlantic (New York City), 1971.

*Getting Through,* Faber, 1978, Harper, 1980.
*High Ground,* Faber, 1985, Viking, 1987.

OTHER

*The Collected Stories,* Knopf, 1993, reprinted, Vintage, 1994.

Also author of radio play, "Sinclair," 1971, and the television plays, "Swallows," 1975, and "The Rockingham Shoot," 1987.

*SIDELIGHTS:* John McGahern is a contemporary Irish fiction writer whose works explore the vagaries of life in his native land. *Saturday Review* contributor Robert Emmet Long includes McGahern among Ireland's finest living writers, calling him "surefooted, elegiac, graceful when he moves in the confines of the land of his birth, his people speaking in accents of truth as they do." Long also describes McGahern as "an original voice, a writer who works without tricks within carefully controlled limits. . . . In . . . all of his best work, he examines the epiphanies in ordinary Irish lives." McGahern has been praised for his style, which some have compared to that of James Joyce, as well as for his controversial themes. Regardless of his topic, writes Patricia Craig in the *Times Literary Supplement,* McGahern "always writes well about the state of being Irish, its special deprivations and depravities." *Washington Post* correspondent John Breslin likewise concludes that McGahern "poignantly details the abrasions we inflict as well as the brief glimpses of delight we afford one another." According to Julian Moynahan in the *New York Times Book Review,* McGahern is quite simply "the most accomplished novelist of his generation."

The Ireland of McGahern's fiction is often dark and dour, a prison for the soul. His stories reveal the lives of the suffering poor, "human nature at its bitterest," to quote Long. *New York Times Book Review* contributor Joel Conarroe finds McGahern's characters "paralyzed by convention and habit, . . . unable to escape their parochial fates; their powerlessness suggests a central motif in James Joyce." Tom Pavlin elaborates in *Encounter:* "Running through McGahern's work is a fusion of sex, death and hopelessness. They are the presiding trinity of his imagination and are revealed in a series of epiphanies." Indeed, McGahern's work deals forthrightly with several taboo aspects of Irish social life—the Catholic church and its repressive tactics, sexuality, and family turmoil, Shaun O'Connell explains in the *Massachusetts Review.* "To stay within the circle of acceptability is, spiritually and sexually, to starve, but to range outside the province of the predictable in Ireland, particularly for sexual purposes, is to bring about retribution," writes O'Connell. "Repression is the means by which community is sustained." An important theme in McGahern is how his characters overcome this community repression, or conversely, how they are destroyed by it.

In *The Irish Short Story,* Terence Brown notes that McGahern, "while confident and skilled in portraying the provincial world he knows, recognises a need for modern Irish fiction to meet more stringent demands. It must be attentive to the recent major social changes in the country, in an art that more appropriately reflects the complex psychological currents that stir in its turbulent waters. So McGahern is consciously experimental in his work, welcoming the resonance of image and symbol to the enclosed worlds of rural and small-town Ireland, taking his protagonists away from their childhood farms and fields to the confused cultural settings of modern Dublin and London." Much of McGahern's work rests on the strength of his style, a feeling for "things like the everyday ecstasies" to quote Craig. *Newsweek* columnist Peter S. Prescott observes that McGahern "means us to read slowly, to hear the sounds, feel the weight of his words." *Encounter* essayist Jonathan Raban compares McGahern to that other experimental and widely-travelled Irish writer, James Joyce. "McGahern's and Joyce's prose styles bleed imperceptibly into one another like the voices of kissing-cousins," writes Raban. ". . . At his best, McGahern writes so beautifully that he leaves one in no doubt of his equality with Joyce: the similarities between the two writers spring from a sense of tradition which is thoroughly and profoundly shared. And that is something which one is so unused to encountering in 20th-century literature that it is tempting to mistake what is really a glory for a shabby vice."

McGahern was a teacher at the St. John the Baptist Boys National school in Clontarf when his first novel, *The Barracks,* was published in 1963. The novel set the tone for the author's early fiction; it details the last months in the life of Elizabeth Reegan, a rural Irish housewife afflicted with terminal cancer. *Studies* essayist John Cronin writes of Elizabeth: "Life has set her on a collision course and McGahern enters her experience at a point where his philosophy gives him complete and convincing command of her destiny and her doom." Moynahan finds the book memorable "for its dark portrayal of vindictiveness in the hateful feuding of a policeman with his superior, for the unusual

sensitivity and fullness with which a stepmother's domestic unhappiness and grave illness were rendered, and for its hell of tedium and of self-and mutual thwarting." In the *Dictionary of Literary Biography,* Patricia Boyle Haberstroh contends that the juxtaposition of life and death, "the need to find a way of getting through the mysterious cycle from birth to death, and the acceptance of life as a series of small deaths leading to the final mystery recur. The death that overshadows every life pervades McGahern's fiction." *The Barracks* won two of Ireland's most prestigious literary awards, the A. E. Memorial Award and the Macauley fellowship. McGahern was thereby enabled to take a leave of absence from his teaching post in order to write full time.

Public acclaim for McGahern's next novel, *The Dark,* came almost entirely from outside Ireland. The controversial book was banned by the Irish Censorship Board, and it ultimately cost McGahern his teaching job as well. A portrait of a confused Catholic adolescent and his abusive father, *The Dark* takes "a sombre, suffering malicious view of contemporary Ireland, [dwelling] with fond revulsion on the strange, brutal paradoxes that feed on and are fed by the 'Irish imagination,'" according to a reviewer for the *Times Literary Supplement.* The novel focuses on the young boy's dawning sexuality and his conflicting desire to become a priest. "We think at times we are reading a story of studious success or failure about which the author is excited," writes the *Times Literary Supplement* reviewer. "We discover we are reading grim and terrible farce. The writer who is capable of such a double take deserves esteem." McGahern's well-publicized battles with the Censorship Board and with the Catholic school hierarchy over *The Dark* made him anxious to leave Ireland. For several years he travelled through England and Europe, teaching at universities, lecturing, and writing.

Censorship and marriage outside the church, both experienced by McGahern, form the foundation of his novel *The Leavetaking,* published in London in 1974. In that work, the protagonist comes to know himself through his loss of his teaching job at a Catholic school and his marriage to an American woman. O'Connell suggests that in the novel, and his other recent works, McGahern "leads some of his characters through a door into the light, into a problematic freedom, out to an open field in which they first run free, but from which they eventually seek release, so some return to the familiar confines." McGahern's hero in *The Leavetaking* escapes; his central character in the 1979 book *The Pornographer* chooses to stay after examining his tawdry life and casual sexual encounters. In either case, notes Craig, "the gloom which permeated John McGahern's earlier novels is beginning to lift. It has been transformed into a reasonable despondency and flatness, tempered with irony—no longer a terrible Irish seediness and vacancy of spirit."

The protagonist of McGahern's novel *Amongst Women* is an abusive father named Michael Moran— "a prickly and embittered old man living 'amongst women'—his young second wife and three daughters," notes a reviewer for the *Los Angeles Times.* Critics emphasized McGahern's delineation of the intricate patterns of behavior that govern family relationships, as well as his portrayal of an Irish society in which the past—in the form of personal grudges and cultural rituals—continues to resist the forces of modern change. Richard Bausch in *Washington Post Book World* asserts that "*Amonst Women* is a disturbing novel, a story told simply, without flourishes or fanfares, of a single household which is at the same time a refuge and a tyranny; yet in the complexity of that fact, John McGahern finds, somehow, a source of light."

McGahern has also published several volumes of short stories. These, like his novels, "deal in love, frustrated or misplaced, and in intimations of mortality," to quote Michael Irwin in the *Times Literary Supplement.* Most of the fiction is set in Ireland, but *New York Times Book Review* contributor David Pryce-Jones finds it "free from the emerald sentiments that have been invested in [McGahern's] native land. He is his own master, and his stories owe nothing to anybody." Irwin feels that each tale "has resonance: some slight incident is made to disclose a mode of living and an attitude to experience." In the *London Review of Books,* Pat Rogers maintains that the author's short works "are unmistakably conservative: their freshness proceeds from close observation, a deep inwardness with the milieu, and a willingness to let events and description do their work unmolested by the urge to be wise about human affairs." Haberstroh concludes that an Irish sensibility informs McGahern's stories, "and the public and fictional history he creates from his personal life testifies to the degree to which art and life intertwine."

In his short-story collection *High Ground,* McGahern explores themes of human relationships, family, and the emotional conflicts associated with loyalty and tradition in the south of Ireland. Critics have empha-sized the work's vivid Irish setting, accurate style, and deft articulation of character. Joel Conarroe of the *New York Times Book Review* stresses the collection's concern with "passionate conflicts—between men and women, union members and those who 'cross the line,' Roman Catholic and Protestant, the older and younger generations, and even between poets and more prosaic folk." Patricia Craig notes that McGahern "writes, as always, with authority and gravity, and with an instinct for the most appropriate detail."

McGahern's *Collected Stories* publishes new short fiction with selections from three previous volumes. Tobin Harshaw in the *New York Times Book Review* comments on the volume's affinity with the theme of hardship that has characterized many of McGahern's previous works: "For more than three decades, [McGahern] has looked for that illuminating image by depicting the everyday life of the rural poor in his native western Ireland." Praising McGahern's use of language to portray problematic relationships and his evocative depiction of place, Elizabeth Shannon of *Commonweal* notes that "the language is sparse and justifies each word."

McGahern told the *New York Times Book Review:* "In my upbringing, there were very few books, and one would never have met a writer. But there was the pleasure of playing with words, and then you found that, almost without knowing it, you wanted to do this more than anything else." McGahern is widely praised for his prose fiction, and for refusing "the poet laureateship offered by the *status quo,*" according to Anthony C. West in *The Nation.* O'Connell claims that McGahern's "revised version of the Irish pastoral is edged in irony, weighted by expectation and sustained by compelling fictional energies." Raban feels that the author "has a genius—and that word does not overstate what he does—for mediating between the deep currents of feeling which belong to myth and history and the exact texture of the moment, seen so freshly that it comes off the page in a vivid cluster of sensations." Irwin observes that McGahern "writes with unobtrusive concision. So much of his skill lies in selection, or rather in omission, that his terse narrative seems free and full. He has the Irish gift of being able to move fluently and unselfconsciously between a simple and a heightened style. . . . Pace and proportion seem effortlessly adjusted: there is no sense of expository strain." Among the most compelling praise for McGahern's work comes from fellow writer John Updike. In *Hugging the Shore: Essays and Criticism,* Updike concludes that the artist "writes well, and for the usual reasons: he observes well, hears faithfully, and feels keenly."

## BIOGRAPHICAL/CRITICAL SOURCES:

### BOOKS

*Contemporary Literary Criticism,* Gale, Volume 5, 1976, Volume 9, 1978, Volume 48, 1988.

*Dictionary of Literary Biography,* Volume 14: *British Novelists since World War II,* Gale, 1982.

Dunn, Douglas, editor, *Two Decades of Irish Writing,* Carcanet Press, 1975.

Rafroidi, Patrick and Terence Brown, editors, *The Irish Short Story,* Colin Smythe, 1979.

Sampson, Denis, *Outstaring Nature's Eye: The Fiction of John McGahern,* Catholic University of America Press, 1993.

Updike, John, *Hugging the Shore: Essays and Criticism,* Knopf, 1983.

### PERIODICALS

*America,* July 31, 1993, p. 20.

*Catholic World,* January, 1968.

*Censorship,* spring, 1966.

*Chicago Tribune,* April 27, 1987; September 29, 1991.

*Commonweal,* January 14, 1994, p. 38.

*Critique: Studies in Modern Fiction,* Volume 19, number 1, 1977; Volume 21, number 1, 1979.

*Detroit News,* August 3, 1980.

*Encounter,* June, 1975; June, 1978.

*Globe and Mail* (Toronto), August 18, 1984.

*London Review of Books,* October 3, 1985.

*Los Angeles Times,* February 18, 1987; September 9, 1990, p. 6.

*Massachusetts Review,* summer, 1984.

*Nation,* November 7, 1966.

*New Leader,* March 31, 1975.

*New Republic,* December 15, 1979.

*New Statesman & Society,* May 11, 1990, p. 39.

*Newsweek,* February 17, 1975; November 5, 1979.

*New York,* January 25, 1993, p. 60.

*New Yorker,* December 24, 1979; March 8, 1993, p. 111.

*New York Review of Books,* May 1, 1980; December 6, 1990, p. 22; April 8, 1993, p. 22.

*New York Times,* July 12, 1980.

*New York Times Book Review,* March 6, 1966; February 7, 1971; February 2, 1975; December 2, 1979; July 13, 1980; February 8, 1987; September 9, 1990; February 28, 1993, pp. 1, 27.

*Saturday Review,* May 1, 1971.

*Spectator,* January 11, 1975; June 17, 1978.

*Studies,* winter, 1969.

*Studies in Short Fiction,* winter, 1994, pp. 118-20.

*Times Literary Supplement,* May 13, 1965; November 27, 1970; January 10, 1975; June 16, 1978; January 11, 1980; September 13, 1985.

*Washington Post,* March 23, 1987.

*Washington Post Book World,* December 23, 1979; September 30, 1990, p. 7.*

\* \* \*

## McINERNEY, Jay 1955-

*PERSONAL:* Surname is pronounced "*Mac*-in-er-ney"; born January 13, 1955, in Hartford, CT; son of John Barrett (a corporate executive) and Marilyn Jean (Murphy) McInerney; married Merry Reymond (a student), June 2, 1984 (marriage ended); married Helen Bransford (a jewelry designer), December 27, 1991. *Education:* Williams College, B.A., 1976; postgraduate study at Syracuse University. *Avocational interests:* Travel, skiing, tennis, fly-fishing, karate, wine.

*ADDRESSES: Home*—Franklin, TN and New York, NY. *Agent*—Amanda Urban, International Creative Management, 40 West 57th St., New York, NY 10019; and Deborah Rogers, Rogers Coleridge and White Ltd., 20 Powis Mews, London W11 1JN, England.

*CAREER: Hunterdon County Democrat,* Flemington, NJ, reporter, 1977; Time-Life, Inc., Osaka, Japan, textbook editor, 1978-79; *New Yorker,* New York City, fact checker, 1980; Random House (publishers), New York City, reader, 1980-81; Syracuse University, Syracuse, NY, instructor in English, 1983; writer, 1983—.

*MEMBER:* Authors Guild, Authors League of America, PEN, Writers Guild.

*AWARDS, HONORS:* Princeton in Asia fellowship, 1977.

## WRITINGS:

### NOVELS

*Bright Lights, Big City,* Random House (New York City), 1984.

*Ransom,* Random House, 1985.

*Story of My Life,* Atlantic Monthly Press (New York City), 1988.

*Brightness Falls,* Knopf (New York City), 1992.

*The Last of the Savages: A Novel,* Knopf, 1996.

OTHER

(Author of introduction) *New Japanese Voices: The Best Contemporary Fiction from Japan,* edited by Helen Mitsios, Grove/Atlantic (New York City), 1992.

(Editor) *Cowboys, Indians and Commuters: The Penguin Book of New American Voices,* Viking (New York City), 1994.

Also contributor to *Look Who's Talking,* edited by Bruce Weber, Washington Square Press, 1986.

*ADAPTATIONS: Bright Lights, Big City* was adapted for film by McInerney, starred Michael J. Fox, and was released by Metro-Goldwyn-Mayer/United Artists, 1988.

*SIDELIGHTS:* Jay McInerney gained critical success and a reputation rarely won by a first-time novelist for his work *Bright Lights, Big City.* The story concerns an unnamed young man who works as a fact-checker during the day at a stodgy, respectable magazine (some reviewers noticed that it resembled the *New Yorker,* where McInerney had been employed as a fact-checker in 1980) but stays out all night abusing alcohol and cocaine at New York City's popular nightclubs. Disillusioned and trying to cope with the death of his mother and his divorce from a shallow model, the narrator carouses with his friend and devil's advocate, Tad Allagash, who "envies him for his ability to find drugs and girls, to get into hip mischief and yet hold down a job, to do what he pleases without fatigue or remorse," according to Darryl Pinckney in the *New York Review of Books.* The narrator speaks in the second person, present tense, distancing himself from his feelings and describing people and events in, as John Lownsbrough commented in the *Globe and Mail,* an "insinuating" voice. Some critics quoted the novel's first passage, finding it indicative of the tone of the rest of the book: "You are not the kind of guy who would be at a place like this at this time of the morning. But here you are, and you cannot say that the terrain is entirely unfamiliar, although the details are fuzzy. You are at a nightclub talking to a girl with a shaved head. The club is either Heartbreak or the Lizard Lounge. All might come clear if you could just slip into the bath-room and do a little more Bolivian Marching Powder. Then again it might not. . . ."

"Bolivian Marching Powder" is a euphemism for cocaine; the frenetic social life of the narrator is analogous to the specious euphoria created by the drug, McInerney explained. As he told Joyce Wadler for the *Washington Post,* "[Cocaine] is the exact metaphorical equivalent of the idea that tonight, if you go to just one more party, one more place, that's gonna be the one . . . that somehow will fulfill you, and every time you do one more line, you think just one more. . . ."

Although a reviewer in *Kirkus Reviews* commented that the use of "you" throughout *Bright Lights, Big City* became "increasingly irritating," Terence Moran in the *New Republic* applauded the novel's style, writing, "McInerney employs an unusual and challenging narrative device; he tells the tale through the second person in the historical present tense and fashions a coherent and engaging voice with it, one that is totally believable at almost every moment in the novel." Moran also praised the work as "an accomplished and funny novel, full of clever verbal contraptions and hip social pastiches." A *Publishers Weekly* reviewer also remarked, "The best part of this promising debut is McInerney's humor—it is cynical, deadpan and right on target, delivered with impeccable comic timing." However, while the *New York Times*'s Michiko Kakutani extolled McInerney's "eye for the incongruous detail, his ear for language, his hyperbolic sense of humor, and his ability to conjure up lively characters with a few lines of dialogue and a tart description or two," a *Kirkus Reviews* writer criticized the "blatant padding throughout—tidbits of N.Y.C. observation, running gags lifted from Woody Allen, cutesy references to TV commercials."

After the release of *Bright Lights, Big City,* McInerney gained attention not only as an author but as a personality, embracing a celebrity lifestyle and socializing with some of his contemporaries at New York night spots. Authors Bret Easton Ellis (*Less than Zero*), Tama Janowitz (*Slaves of New York*), McInerney, and sometimes David Leavitt (*Family Dancing*) were called the "Literary Brat Pack" in the popular press because of their young ages at the time of their first success, the similar content of their novels, and their self-promotion and demand for high pay. The *Los Angeles Times*'s Nikki Finke said, "They're a new wave of writers soaring to stardom in the '80s at startlingly young ages with innovative writing styles and hip subject matter." Charles

Maclean in the *Spectator* reported that the group was "scorned for embracing celebrity, posing for fashion spreads, endorsing products and keeping the gossip columnists busy—all sensible ways of consolidating the appeal these writers have to their mainly young urban professional audience." Remarking on the content of the writing by McInerney, Ellis, and Janowitz, however, Jonathan Yardley opined in the *Washington Post,* "These writers want to have it both ways: to exploit and even glorify indulgence in sex, drugs and luxury on the one hand, and to draw cautionary morals from it on the other."

McInerney's second effort, *Ransom,* centers on Princeton graduate Christopher Ransom, an American expatriate who lives in Kyoto, Japan, teaching English to Japanese businessmen and studying karate. Events involving friends and family have left him numb: his mother has died; his father, in Ransom's opinion, has sacrificed his integrity by abandoning play writing to write for television; and he has lost his two traveling companions, Annette and Ian, in a drug-related incident at the Khyber Pass (Ian goes over the border of Pakistan and Afghanistan for drugs but doesn't return, and Annette dies, possibly of a heroin overdose). Ron Loewinsohn wrote in the *New York Times Book Review* that Ransom "feels guilty about the flabby privilege of his upper-middle-class background, and guilty by association with his father." In addition, blaming himself for the fate of his friends, he tortures himself with regrets and memories. In Japan, he hopes to find "a place of austere discipline which would cleanse him and change him," Loewinsohn explained; his immersion in the martial arts becomes "a form of penance and purification."

Many critics noted that the strength of McInerney's first two novels lies in his humorous delivery and unexpected irreverences. Kakutani attributed "a mastery of [the] idiosyncratic, comic voice" to McInerney and found most of his jokes "amusing and dexterously handled." Together, McInerney's sense of humor and his active interest in human pathos combine to create fiction which, Moran said, "not only jests at our slightly tawdry life, but also celebrates its abiding possibilities."

In *The Story of My Life,* McInerney returns to the New York club scene, but, as Kakutani reported in the *New York Times,* "Where the young magazine fact checker in *Bright Lights, Big City* merely visited this world, Alison, her roommate Jeannie and their friends are full-time residents here. . . . Cocaine and casual sex are their two obsessions; money to finance their

pleasures is a constant preoccupation." Kakutani criticized the author's characterizations, claiming, "Alison and her pals—who dither on endlessly, like adolescent ninnies, about clothes, makeup and their boyfriends' sexual endowments—all seem less like believable women than like a man's paranoid, cartoonlike idea of what such females might be." However, Sarah Sheard, writing for the *Globe and Mail,* applauded McInerney's "fabulous ear for dialogue," adding that he "captures a tortured and articulate spirit trying her hardest to hide inside the IQ of a lawn ornament. [The author] accomplishes this with wit and pacing, impeccable accuracy and, ultimately, compassion."

*Brightness Falls* is also set in New York in the 1980s—just around the time of the 1987 stock market crash—and comments on drug use, club-going and greed, but revolves around an older group, "thirtysomethings" in the publishing business. The main characters are Russell Calloway, an editor for a publishing firm; his wife, Corinne, a stockbroker; and their friend Jeff Pierce, a famous author with a drug habit and groupies. John Skow reviewing the book for *Time* called it "a funny, self-mocking, sometimes brilliant portrait of Manhattan's young literary and Wall Street crowd, our latest Lost Generation."

Some critics, and even the author himself, have compared *Brightness Falls* to Tom Wolfe's *Bonfire of the Vanities.* David Rieff writing for the *Washington Post Book World* related that McInerney declared in a *Vanity Fair* interview, "'What was going through my mind when I sat down to write this novel was: What if *Bonfire of the Vanities* had real people in it?'" Indeed, in the *Boston Globe,* Matthew Gilbert commented, "While *Brightness Falls* is a sociological critique like *Bonfire,* it's more human than Wolfe's knife-twister." Sven Birkerts, however, reviewing the work for the Chicago *Tribune Books,* noted that the author's gift of farce was still evident, claiming that McInerney was "quite adept at rendering the feel of the publishing milieu. We get bright, satirically edged shots of everything from the lunch-hour confabs over advances and reputations to the rituals of male bonhomie at the urinals." Also, Al J. Sperone in the *Village Voice Literary Supplement* stated that "McInerney has a gift for comic set pieces, and he's generous with snappy repartee, doling out wisecracks for everybody." Birkerts also lauded *Brightness Falls* as a "solid and durably plotted book," and added, "Fueled by its images of excess and rendered biographically interesting by its undercurrents of felt remorse, it makes for a quick and compelling reading experience."

McInerney's fifth novel, *The Last of the Savages*, features two characters: the narrator, a New York lawyer named Patrick Keane; and his old college friend Will Savage, now a famous record producer. Patrick, from the vantage point of middle age, recounts his lower-middle-class background and his neverending longing to be wealthy and aristocratic. While attending college at Yale, he meets Will, whose wealthy southern background is in stark contrast to his own. While Will goes on to achieve fame and even greater fortune as a record producer, Patrick abandons his dreams of a literary career for safe and solid work as a lawyer. Eventually, Patrick must come to grips with his homoerotic feelings toward Will.

Many critics were unmoved by McInerney's attempt to encompass a wider historical realm than he did with his earlier novels. Noting that the "central concerns" of the novel are "familiar adolescent ones"— youthful rebellion, social climbing, freedom—*New York Times* reviewer Michiko Kakutani remarked that "in order to broaden these coming-of-age quandaries and make 'Savages' seem like a larger novel, Mr. McInerney has tried to turn the story of Will and Patrick into an emblematic saga." However, Kakutani averred, "None of these efforts . . . really work." Other reviewers criticized the author for producing a contrived plot and using sloppy prose. *New York Times Book Review* commentator Geoff Dyer, for instance, noted McInerney's tendency "to coast linguistically," while Thomas R. Edwards in the *New York Review of Books* declared that "bad writing here becomes unexpectedly endemic." Edwards added: "Some of the ineptitudes of the novel's prose are just irritating or unintentionally funny. . . . Others flirt with disaster."

McInerney once told *CA:* "Since college, writing fiction is mainly what I've wanted to do, though I entered college writing poetry; I was convinced that was my metier. I changed, actually, in my senior year when I discovered a number of fiction writers all at once who hit me very hard and in such a way as to make me feel that fiction and narrative prose could be as exciting as lyrical poetry, which was what I was writing—and, ultimately, I came to feel, more exciting. Or I felt rather that my particular ambitions and proclivities were such that I would rather write fiction than poetry." Regarding who and what has influenced the humorous side of his work, McInerney revealed

that "[an author] that I read off and on quite a bit and like very much is Evelyn Waugh. I like P. G. Wodehouse, too, and Mark Twain. *Don Quixote* and *Tom Jones* are two novels that I would like to think have something to do with my comic sense. In more contemporary terms, the writer Thomas McGuane, although he's a very serious writer, is also very marvelous with comedy and has influenced me quite a bit, I'd say. J. P. Donleavy's *The Ginger Man* also. . . . And Joyce. The James Joyce of *Ulysses* is one of the funniest writers around, though most people are so daunted by some of his erudition that they forget to laugh."

## BIOGRAPHICAL/CRITICAL SOURCES:

*BOOKS*

*Contemporary Literary Criticism,* Volume 34, Gale, 1985.

*PERIODICALS*

*Atlantic Monthly,* December, 1984, p. 145.
*Boston Globe,* June 10, 1992, p. 43.
*Chicago Tribune,* September 27, 1984; April 1, 1988; April 24, 1988; August 29, 1988.
*Chicago Tribune Book World,* October 7, 1984; September 15, 1985.
*Christian Science Monitor,* October 29, 1985.
*Commentary,* September, 1992.
*Esquire,* May, 1985.
*Globe and Mail* (Toronto), November 16, 1985; September 10, 1988.
*Harper's* December, 1988.
*Interview,* June, 1985.
*Los Angeles Times,* September 21, 1984; September 13, 1987.
*Los Angeles Times Book Review,* October 6, 1985; August 28, 1988, p. 3; June 7, 1992, p. 3.
*Ms.,* August, 1985.
*Nation,* June 10, 1996, p. 30.
*National Review,* June 22, 1992, pp. 54-55.
*New Republic,* December 3, 1984, pp. 41-42; October 10, 1988, pp. 38-41.
*Newsweek,* October 21, 1985; September 26, 1988, pp. 72-73; June 8, 1992, p. 58.
*New Yorker,* July 27, 1992.
*New York Review of Books,* November 8, 1984, p. 12-14; May 23, 1996, p. 28.
*New York Times,* October 30, 1984; August 24, 1985; August 20, 1988; June 1, 1992, p. 13; April 30, 1996, p. C17.

*New York Times Book Review,* November 25, 1984,
p. 9; September 29, 1985; September 25, 1988,
p. 12; May 31, 1992, p. 7; March 3, 1996, p. 8;
May 26, 1996, p. 11.

*Publishers Weekly,* August 10, 1984, p. 76; July 19,
1985.

*Saturday Review,* November, 1984, p. 88.

*Spectator,* December 10, 1988, p. 36; May 30, 1992,
p. 32.

*Time,* October 14, 1985; October 19, 1987; September 19, 1988, p. 95; Jun 1, 1992, pp. 82, 86;
May, 20, 1996, p. 76.

*Times* (London), August 26, 1989.

*Times Literary Supplement,* May 24, 1985, p. 572;
April 18, 1986; August 26, 1988, p. 927; May
15, 1992, p. 20; May 27, 1994, p. 20.

*Tribune Books* (Chicago), June 7, 1992, p. 3.

*Vanity Fair,* May, 1992.

*Village Voice,* October 16, 1984, p. 52.

*Vogue,* June, 1992.

*Voice Literary Supplement,* October, 1988, p. 42;
June, 1992, p. 9.

*Wall Street Journal,* May 9, 1996, p. A16.

*Washington Post,* November 6, 1984; December 12,
1984; September 7, 1988.

*Washington Post Book World,* August 25, 1985; May
24, 1992, pp. 1, 14.*

\*    \*    \*

**McKAY, Simon**
**See NICOLE, Christopher (Robin)**

\*    \*    \*

**MCLANDRESS, Herschel**
**See GALBRAITH, John Kenneth**

\*    \*    \*

**MICHENER, James A(lbert) 1907(?)-1997**

*PERSONAL:* Born c. February 3, 1907, probably in
New York City; died of renal failure after choosing to
be removed from a kidney dialysis machine, October
16, 1997, in Austin, TX; foster son of Mabel (Had-
dock) Michener; married Patti Koon, July 27, 1935
(divorced, 1948); married Vange Nord, September 2,
1948 (divorced, 1955); married Mari Yoriko Sabu-
sawa (deceased, 1994), October 23, 1955. *Education:*
Swarthmore College, A.B. (summa cum laude), 1929;
Colorado State College of Education (now University
of Northern Colorado), A.M., 1936; research study at
the University of Pennsylvania, University of Virginia, Ohio State University, Harvard University,
St. Andrews University, University of Siena. *Politics:* Democrat.    *Religion:* Society of Friends
(Quakers).

*CAREER:* Worked variously as an actor in a traveling
show and as a sports columnist at the age of fifteen;
Hill School, PA, teacher, 1932; George School, PA,
teacher, 1933-36; Colorado State College of Education (now University of Northern Colorado), Greeley,
associate professor, 1936-41; Macmillan Co., New
York City, associate editor, 1941-42, 1946-49; freelance writer, 1949-97. Creator of "Adventures in
Paradise" television series, 1959. Visiting professor,
Harvard University, 1940-41, and University of
Texas at Austin, 1983. Chair, President Kennedy's
Food for Peace Program, 1961; congressional candidate from Pennsylvania's Eighth District, 1962; secretary of Pennsylvania Constitutional Convention,
1967-68. Member of U.S. State Department advisory
committee on the arts, 1957; U.S. Information
Agency advisory committee, 1970-76; committee to
reorganize U.S. I S, 1976; U.S. Postal Service advisory committee, 1978-87; National Aeronautics and
Space Administration advisory council, 1979-83; U.S
International Broadcasting Board, 1983-89. *Military
service:* U.S. Naval Reserve, 1942-45; became lieutenant commander; naval historian in the South Pacific.

*MEMBER:* Phi Beta Kappa.

*AWARDS, HONORS:* Pulitzer Prize for fiction, 1948,
for *Tales of the South Pacific*; D.H.L., Rider Col-
lege, 1950, and Swarthmore College, 1954; National
Association of Independent Schools Award, 1954,
1958; L.L.D., Temple University, 1957; Litt.D.,
American International College, 1957, Washington
University, St. Louis, 1967; Einstein Award, 1967;
Bestsellers Paperback of the Year Award, 1968, for
*The Source*; George Washington Award, Hungarian
Studies Foundation, 1970; U.S. Medal of Freedom,
1977; Franklin Award for distinguished service,
Printing Industries of Metropolitan New York, 1980;
cited by the President's Committee on the Arts and

the Humanities, 1983, for long-standing support of the Iowa Workshop writer's project at the University of Iowa; Lippincott Travelling fellowship, British Museum; U.S. Medal of Freedon; Distinguished Service Medal, NASA; Golden Badge of Order of Merit, 1988.

*WRITINGS:*

NOVELS

*The Fires of Spring,* Random House, 1949.
*The Bridges at Toko-Ri* (first published in *Life,* July 6, 1953), Random House, 1953.
*Sayonara,* Random House, 1954.
*Hawaii* (first section originally published in *Life*), Random House, 1959.
*Caravans,* Random House, 1963.
*The Source,* illustrated by Richard Sparks, Random House, 1965.
*The Drifters,* Random House, 1971.
*Centennial,* Random House, 1974.
*Chesapeake,* illustrated by Alan Philips, Random House, 1978, illustrated selections published as *The Watermen,* Random House, 1979.
*The Quality of Life, Including Presidential Lottery,* Transworld, 1980.
*The Covenant,* Random House, 1980.
*Space,* Random House, 1982.
*Poland,* Random House, 1983.
*Texas,* Random House, 1985, published in two volumes, University of Texas Press, 1986; chapter published as *The Eagle and the Raven,* illustrations by Charles Shaw, State House Press, 1990.
*Legacy,* Random House, 1987.
*Alaska,* Random House, 1988.
*Journey,* Random House, 1989.
*Caribbean,* Random House, 1989.
*The Novel,* Random House, 1991.
*Mexico,* Random House, 1992.
*South Pacific* (retelling of the musical *South Pacific*), illustrated by Michael Hague, Harcourt, 1992.
*Creatures of the Kingdom,* Random House, 1993, large print edition, Wheeler, 1994.
*Recessional,* Random House, 1994.

SHORT STORIES AND SKETCHES

*Tales of the South Pacific,* Macmillan, 1947.
*Return to Paradise,* Random House, 1951.
*Selected Writings,* Modern Library, 1957.
*A Michener Miscellany: 1950-1970,* Random House, 1973.

(Editor) *Firstfruits: A Harvest of 25 Years of Israeli Writing* (fiction), Jewish Publication Society of America, 1973.

NONFICTION

(With Harold Long) *The Unit in the Social Studies,* Harvard University Press, 1940.
*Voice of Asia,* Random House, 1951.
*The Floating World,* Random House, 1954.
(With A. Grove Day) *Rascals in Paradise* (biographical studies), Random House, 1957.
*The Bridge at Andau,* Random House, 1957.
*Japanese Prints: From the Early Masters to the Modern,* Tuttle, 1959.
*Report of the County Chairman,* Random House, 1961.
*The Modern Japanese Print: An Appreciation,* Tuttle, 1968.
*Iberia: Spanish Travels and Reflections,* Random House, 1968.
*America vs. America: The Revolution in Middle-Class Values,* New American Library, 1969.
*Presidential Lottery: The Reckless Gamble in Our Electoral System* (also see below), Random House, 1969.
*The Quality of Life* (essays; also see below), Random House, 1969.
*Facing East: A Study of the Art of Jack Levine,* Random House, 1970.
*Kent State: What Happened and Why,* Random House, 1971.
*About "Centennial": Some Notes on the Novel,* Random House, 1974.
*Sports in America,* Random House, 1976, revised edition published as *Michener on Sport,* Transworld, 1977, reprinted under original title, Fawcett, 1983.
*The Watermen,* Random House, 1979.
(With John Kings) *Six Days in Havana,* University of Texas Press, 1989.
*Pilgrimage: A Memoir of Poland and Rome,* Rodale, 1990.
*James A. Michener's Writer's Handbook: Explorations in Writing and Publishing,* Random House, 1992.
*My Lost Mexico,* illustrated with photographs by Michener, State House Press, 1992.
*The World is My Home: A Memoir,* Random House, 1992.
*Literary Reflections,* State House Press, 1993.
*Miracle in Seville,* Random House, 1995.
*This Noble Land: My Vision for America,* Random House, 1996.
*A Century of Sonnets,* State House Press, 1997.

*OTHER*

(Editor) *The Future of the Social Studies,* National Council for the Social Studies, 1939.

(Editor) *Hokusai Sketchbooks,* Tuttle, 1958.

(Contributor and author of foreword) Peter Chaitin, editor, *James Michener's U.S.A.,* Crown, 1981.

(Author of preface) John W. Grafton, *America: A History of the First 500 Years,* Crescent Books, 1992.

Many of Michener's works have been translated into foreign languages. Collections of his books and manuscripts are kept at the Swarthmore College and University of Hawaii libraries; the Library of Congress also has a large collection of his papers.

*ADAPTATIONS: Tales of the South Pacific* was adapted for the stage by Richard Rodgers and Oscar Hammerstein II as the musical *South Pacific*; the play was filmed in 1958. *Return to Paradise, The Bridges of Toko-Ri,* and *Sayonara* were all adapted into motion pictures, as were *Until They Sail* and *Mr. Morgan,* both from *Return to Paradise*; *Forgotten Heroes of Korea* was adapted into the film *Men of the Fighting Lady,* 1954; *Hawaii* was adapted into the films *Hawaii,* United Artists (UA), 1966, and *The Hawaiians,* UA, 1970; *Centennial* was adapted for television, 1978-79; *Space* was adapted into a television mini-series, 1985.

*SIDELIGHTS:* "As a literary craftsman [James] Michener has labored to entertain," said A. Grove Day of the popular novelist in the *Dictionary of Literary Biography*. Arthur Cooper characterized Michener as "the literary world's Cecil B. DeMille" in *Newsweek,* while *Time* reviewer Lance Morrow remarked that "practically entire forests have been felled to produce such trunk-sized novels as *Hawaii* and *The Source*." Cooper went on to praise Michener as "a popular novelist with an awesome audience for his epic narratives, an unpretentious, solid craftsman."

Citing *Centennial,* a novel that fictionalizes the history of Colorado from the beginning of time up to 1974, Morrow described a characteristic Michener drama: He "begins with the first faint primordial stirrings on the face of the deep and slogs onward through the ages until he hits the day before yesterday," said Morrow. "He is the Will Durant of novelists, less an artist than a kind of historical compactor." Day added, however, that the author's lengthy novels "also appeal to the thoughtful reader and are laden with details that reveal Michener's academic training and bestow information as well as enlightenment." As Day indicated, "he is a master reporter of his generation, and his wide and frequent travels have given him material for colorful evocation of the lives of many characters in international settings in periods going back to earlier millennia."

Reviewing the breadth of Michener's work, Webster Schott wrote in the *New York Times Book Review* that Michener "has found a formula. It delivers everywhere—Hawaii, Africa, Afghanistan, America, Israel, even outer space. The formula calls for experts, vast research, travel to faraway places and fraternizing with locals. And it calls for good guys and bad guys (both real and imagined) to hold the whole works together. It's a formula millions love. Mr. Michener gratifies their curiosity and is a pleasure to read."

Raised near Doylestown, Pennsylvania, by a foster parent, Michener never knew anything about his actual family background. The Micheners were far from wealthy, and the author told Bill Hutchinson in the *Miami Herald* that he had "a hell of a youth until I was 14 or 15 and discovered athletics, fell into the All-America pattern."

Michener became curious about the world outside of Doylestown at a young age, and he was keenly aware that he would have to make his own way. At the age of fourteen he hitchhiked for several months through forty-five American states. After he returned home, he delivered newspapers, excelled in sports, and wrote a sports column for the local paper. Michener won a sports scholarship to Swarthmore College, and during one summer vacation he traveled with a Chautauqua tent show. (Michener incorporated some of these experiences in his second novel, the semiautobiographical *The Fires of Spring*.) After graduation, he began teaching at a local school and won a Lippincott traveling scholarship to Europe, where he enrolled at St. Andrews University in Scotland, collected folk stories in the Hebrides Islands, studied art history in London and Siena, Italy, toured northern Spain with a troupe of bullfighters, and even worked on a Mediterranean cargo vessel.

After his return to the United States during the Great Depression, Michener taught, earned his master's degree, and served as associate professor at the Colorado State College of Education from 1936 through 1939. He published several scholarly articles on the teaching of social studies, became a visiting professor at Harvard University, and in 1941 was asked to accept an editorship with the Macmillan Company in New York. According to Day in his book *James A. Michener,* the author once told a college group that "no aspirant can avoid an apprenticeship to his literary craft. 'I *did* serve an apprenticeship,' he affirms, 'and a very intense one, and learned what a great many people never learn. I learned how to write a sentence and how to write a paragraph. . . . The English language is so complex, so magnificent in its structure that I have very little patience with people who won't put themselves through an apprenticeship.'"

Michener didn't publish his first work of fiction until around the age of forty, however, a fact he attributes to his disinclination to take risks, particularly during the Depression. And it was not until he volunteered for service in the U.S. Navy in 1942 that he began to collect experiences he could visualize as marketable fiction.

His first assignment as a lieutenant was at a post in the South Pacific, and from 1944 to 1946 he served as a naval historian in that region. During this tour of duty, Michener had the occasion to visit some fifty islands, and "as the war wound down," explains Day, "he retreated to a jungle shack and began writing the stories that were to appear as . . . *Tales of the South Pacific,*" which won the Pulitzer Prize in 1948.

Although *Tales of the South Pacific* is considered a collection of short stories, Michener considered it a novel due to the book's overall theme of America's fight in the South Pacific theatre during World War II. *New York Herald Tribune Weekly Book Review* writer P. J. Searles agreed, stating, "Romantic, nostalgic, tragic—call it what you will—this book seems to me the finest piece of fiction to come out of the South Pacific war." Michener "is a born story teller," *New York Times* writer David Dempsey added, "but, paradoxically, this ability results in the book's only real weakness—the interminable length of some of the tales. Mr. Michener saw so much, and his material is so rich, that he simply could not leave anything out." When the book was published in 1947, Orville Prescott in the *Yale Review* described Michener as "certainly one of the ablest and one of the most original writers to appear on the American literary scene in a long time."

After his discharge, Michener returned to Macmillan as a textbook editor. In 1949, Richard Rodgers and Oscar Hammerstein II adapted *Tales of the South*

*Pacific* into the successful musical *South Pacific*; a share of the royalties from the play—later to become a film—enabled Michener to become a full-time writer. In his book *James A. Michener,* Day reported that the author once told him that "I have only one bit of advice to the beginning writer: be sure your novel is read by Rodgers and Hammerstein." As for the Pulitzer, Michener once commented to Roy Newquist in *Conversations*: "There were editorials that declared it was the least-deserving book in recent years to win the Pulitzer; it was by no means the popular choice. In fact, it was an insulting choice to many. At least two other books had been definitely favored to win. . . . I had no occasion to develop a swelled head."

Throughout the 1950s and early 1960s, Michener continued to set much of his work in the South Pacific and Far East. He was assigned by *Holiday* magazine to write some feature articles about various places in the Pacific, so at the same time he wrote *Return to Paradise,* a collection of short stories and travel sketches. He then wrote some works of nonfiction about the area: *The Voice of Asia* and *The Floating World*. Several novels, including *The Bridges at Toko-Ri, Sayonara, Hawaii,* and *Caravans,* also date from this period in Michener's career.

It was with the novel *Hawaii* that Michener established the format that would see him through several subsequent novels and make him a best-selling author. Although *Tales of the South Pacific* won the Pulitzer Prize, it was not a best-seller, and as *New York Times Magazine* writer Caryn James explained, it was "only when he moved from small stories of people to monolithic tales of places—beginning with the fictionalized history of *Hawaii* in 1959 through Israel in *The Source,* South Africa in *The Covenant,* Poland, *Chesapeake* and *Space*—did he become the kind of brand-name author whose books hit the best-seller lists before they reach the bookstores."

James noted that "the Michener formula might seem an unlikely one for the media age: big, old-fashioned narratives weaving generations of fictional families through densely documented factual events, celebrating the All-American virtues of common sense, frugality, patriotism. Yet these straitlaced, educational stories are so episodic that they are perfectly suited to the movie and television adaptations that have propelled Michener's success."

In *James A. Michener,* Day described *Hawaii* as "the best novel ever written about Hawaii." It was published a few months after Hawaii was granted statehood in August, 1959. According to Day, the book "is founded on truth but not on fact." Michener drew from his own experiences in the Pacific region to develop *Hawaii* and also consulted a variety of other sources, including missionary accounts. As the author stated in his book *Report of the County Chairman,* his goal was to portray "the enviable manner in which Hawaii had been able to assimilate men and women from many different races."

Writing in the *New York Times Book Review,* Maxwell Geismar praised the book as "a brilliant panoramic novel about Hawaii from its volcanic origins to its recent statehood. It is a complex and fascinating subject, and it is rendered here with a wealth of scholarship, of literary imagination and of narrative skill, so that the large and diverse story is continually interesting." Day reported, "This is not a historical novel in the usual sense, for not one actual name or event is given; rather, it is a pageant of the coming of settlers from many regions; and the main theme might well be: Paradise is not a goal to attain, but a stage to which people of many colors and creeds may bring their traditional cultures to mingle with those of the others and create what may truly be an Eden at the crossroads of a hitherto empty ocean."

Nevertheless, some of the praise was qualified. A *Times Literary Supplement* writer indicated that "Mr. Michener's zestful, knowledgeable progress through the millennia is absorbing. He cannot, of course, with such enormous slabs of raw material to handle and shape, go anywhere deeply below the surface, but there are some splendid sustained passages in his book." William Hogan wrote in the *San Francisco Chronicle* that "as he has adjusted details in Hawaii's history to suit his fiction, the author is forced to adapt characters to fit into the big historical picture. And that is the book's main weakness." Although *Saturday Review* critic Horace Sutton was of a similar opinion, he maintained that *Hawaii* "is still a masterful job of research, an absorbing performance of storytelling, and a monumental account of the islands from geologic birth to sociological emergence as the newest, and perhaps the most interesting of the United States."

After publishing *Hawaii,* Michener became involved in national politics. He actively campaigned for John F. Kennedy and wrote a work of political nonfiction, *Report of the County Chairman,* in which he chronicled that involvement. A later Michener study, *Presidential Lottery,* presented an argument for reform in the method Americans use to select their president. He was also an unsuccessful candidate for the House of Representatives from Pennsylvania's Eighth District.

In 1963, however, Michener returned to fiction with *The Source,* a book researched while he was living in Israel, and described by Day as another best-selling "mammoth volume." In this novel, Michener described the archaeological excavation of Makor Tell, a mound that contains the remnants of various settlements built over the course of many centuries. As Day explained, "artifacts found in the various layers introduce chapters dealing with events in the Holy Land during the period in which the articles were made. . . . Prominent families of several nationalities are followed through the ages; the setting is limited to the invented tell of Makor, the surrounding countryside, and the shores of the Sea of Galilee." Day claimed that *The Source* is "one of the longest of Michener's books, and the best in the opinion of many readers. Although it may lack a clear general theme, its leading topic is certainly the various facets of religion."

Michener's nonfictional account of the Spanish peninsula, *Iberia: Spanish Travels and Reflections* was followed by *The Drifters,* published the same year as his report on the Kent State University shootings. *The Drifters* is a novelistic account that follows the adventures of six young members of the counterculture as they wander through Spain, Portugal, and parts of Africa. The story is narrated by a sixty-one-year-old man and reflects the author's own interest in modern times and contemporary issues. *Saturday Review* writer David W. McCullough pointed out that *The Drifters* is also "something of a guidebook loosely dressed up as fiction: a guide to quaint and colorful places especially on the Iberian peninsula, and to the life-styles of the rebellious young." According to Peter Sourian in the *New York Times Book Review,* *The Drifters* "is an interesting trip and Michener is an entertaining as well as a knowledgeable guide. The novel has a more serious purpose, however, which is exhaustively to examine the 'youth revolution.' Michener brings to this task narrative skill and a nicely adequate socio-psychological sophistication." And Thomas Lask of the *New York Times* claimed that "those interested in knowing how a sympathetic member of the older generation views some of the shenanigans of the younger will find *The Drifters* a tolerable interlude, especially as it is spiced with travelogue evocations of foreign climes. Dozens of readers will be making notes of the places they too will want to visit."

Michener returned to his historical panoramas with *Centennial*. The book is narrated by Dr. Lewis Vernor, who is writing a report on the village of Centennial, Colorado. The first part of the book covers the area's early geology, archaeology, and ecology before humans even appear. And then, according to Day, *Centennial* introduces some "seventy named characters . . . not including Indians, fur traders, trappers, cattle drivers, miners, ranchers, dry farmers, real estate salesmen, and assorted townspeople. Again national and ethnic interminglings in a limited region are recorded through many years, and little is omitted from the panorama of the developing American West."

The novel has few all-encompassing themes. As James R. Frakes wrote in the *New York Times Book Review,* "denying himself the luxury of 'flossy conclusions' and dogmatic theorizing, the author allows himself only a very few unqualified extrapolations from the text: the determining endurance of the land, for instance; the interdependence of man, animal, earth, and water; the possibility that white survival in some areas may require a return to the permanent values of the Indian."

In Michener's book, *Chesapeake,* according to Christopher Lehmann-Haupt in the *New York Times,* Michener "does for Maryland's Eastern Shore what he did for Colorado in *Centennial.* By telling the story of dozens of fictional characters who live in a partly imaginary locale, he tries to capture the real history of the area—in the case of the Chesapeake Bay, from the time in the 6th century when Indians and crabs were its chief inhabitants, down to a present when developers and pollutants have taken over."

Michener applied this same pattern to explore the history of South Africa in *The Covenant.* In this book, said William McWhirter in *Time,* the author "manages to cover 15,000 years of African history, from the ritual-haunted tribes of Bushmen to present-day Afrikaners obstinately jeering at appeals for 'human rights.'" Michener's method of combining fiction with nonfiction drew some criticism from reviewers. As Andre Brink noted in the *Washington Post Book World,* "in his portrayal of history the author adapts a curious method also characteristic of his earlier novel, *The Source:* even though well-known historical figures appear in it—the Trek leader Piet Retief, the Boer general De Wet, Prime Minister Daniel Malan and a host of others—many of their major exploits are attributed to fictitious characters appearing alongside of them. Imagine a novel prominently featuring

Abraham Lincoln but attributing the Gettysburg Address to a fictitious minor character." However, according to John F. Bums in the *New York Times Book Review,* "the book's accomplishment may be to offer a public inured to stereotypes a sense of the flesh and blood of the Afrikaners, the settlers who grew from harsh beginnings to a white tribe now nearing three million, commanding the most powerful economy and armed forces in Africa."

Writing in the *New York Times,* Stephen Farber described Michener's *Space* as a "fictional rendering of the development of the space program from World War II to the present." Michael L. Smith reported in the *Nation* that "real participants make occasional appearances, but Michener relies primarily on fictional approximations." In fact, said Smith, *Space* "is less a historical novel than a tract. In part, it is a celebration of space exploration as a glorious blend of science, American frontiersmanship and human curiosity. But more than that, it's an impassioned denunciation of what Michener considers one of the gravest dangers facing post-Vietnam America: the proliferation of an 'anti-science movement.'" Ben Bova in the *Washington Post Book World* added that the book "contrasts several varieties of faith, from the simplistic faith of the German rocket engineer who believes that technology can solve any problem, to the faith of the astronauts who believe that flying farther and faster is the greatest good in the world."

Michener began *Poland* in 1977 with the belief that the country would become a focal point within the decade. To write the book, explains Ursula Hegi in the *Los Angeles Times Book Review,* Michener "visited Poland eight times and traveled throughout the country. He talked to people of different backgrounds and enjoyed the assistance of 15 Polish scholars." The result was a novelization of the last 700 years of the country's history, including several invasions and partitionings, the Nazi occupation during World War II, and a modern struggle of farmers attempting to form a labor union. As Bill Kurtis reported in the *Chicago Tribune Book World,* "by now, Michener's form is familiar. History is seen through the lives of three fictional families: the nobility of the wealthy Counts Lubonski; the gentry or petty nobility of the Bukowskis; and the peasant heart of Poland, the family Buk. Around them, Michener wraps a detailed historical panorama; he combines fact and fiction to breathe life into nearly 1,000 years of battles, with far more Polish defeats than victories. If recited as dates and incidents, these would otherwise be dry as dust."

*Poland* received mixed reviews. Hegi claimed that "though Michener captures Poland's struggle and development, he presents the reader with too many names and personal histories, making it difficult to keep track of more than a few characters." Other critics cited omissions, historical inaccuracies, and oversimplifications in Michener's research. And Patricia Blake reported in *Time* that the work glosses over Polish anti-Semitism. However, *Washington Post* reviewer Peter Osnos described *Poland* as "Michener at his best, prodigiously researched, topically relevant and shamelessly intended for readers with neither will nor patience for more scholarly treatments." And, added Hegi, his "descriptions of the country—blooms covering the hillsides, the swift flow of the rivers, splendid groves of beech trees—are as detailed as his depictions of weapons, castles and costumes."

*Texas* was written when former state governor William Clements invited Michener to create a book that would be timed to appear for the 1986 Texas Sesquicentennial. According to Hughes Rudd in the *New York Times Book Review, Texas,* "at almost 1,000 pages, contains enough paper to cover several New England counties. The novel is so heavy you could probably leave it on a Lubbock, TX, coffee table in a tornado and find it there when everything else was still in the air over Kansas City, KS." The frame for *Texas* concerns a committee appointed by a Texas Governor to investigate the state's history and recommend what students should be taught about their state. The story begins early in the sixteenth century when the state was still an unexplored part of Mexico.

*Texas* received many of the criticisms that are frequently accorded Michener's work. According to Nicholas Lemann in the *Washington Post Book World,* none of the characters "stays in mind as embodying the complexity of real life. The reason is not exactly a lack of art on Michener's part; it's more that the form dictates that everything novelistic must be in the service of delivering history. Nothing ever happens that doesn't embody an important trend." For example, Lemann wrote, "when it's time to recount the story of the battle of the Alamo, [Michener] invents a handful of characters on both sides and has them engaging in dialogue with Jim Bowie, Davy Crockett, and General Santa Anna."

At 149 pages, *Legacy* qualifies as Michener's shortest novel. Prompted by Michener's disgust over events surrounding the Iran Contra scandal during the Reagan administration, the novel centers on the fictional Army major, Norman Starr, who has been called to testify at the Senate hearings involving the alleged cover-up of the president's National Security Council. As Starr and his lawyer, Zack McMaster, prepare his defense, Starr thinks about the roles of his ancestors in American history in chapters that discuss the nature of the country's Constitution. As Starr heads for the courthouse he realizes that his moral code and sense of propriety will not allow him to plead the Fifth Amendment as Colonel Oliver North and Admiral John Poindexter have in the novel. Published in 1987, as the U.S. celebrated the bicentennial of its Constitution, *Legacy*'s final pages consist of a complete reprinting of the Constitution. Acknowledging the appeal of the subject matter, critics nevertheless agreed that, in the words of John Ehrlichman, who reviewed it for the *Los Angeles Times Book Review,* "the brevity, research lapses and forced timeliness of [the novel] tarnish Starr's dramatic nobility and in some measure defeat the author's original, worthy objectives."

With *Alaska,* Michener returned to the genre of historical novel. *Alaska* traces the development of the land and its inhabitants from the time of the mastodons to the building of the state's highways. Finding Michener's research thorough and accurate, Chip Brown, in a review for *Book World,* noted further that Michener "is rightfully sympathetic to the native inhabitants of Alaska . . . exploring at length their customs, their shamans, their rituals and trials." In an effort to keep the novel under 1,000 pages, editors convinced Michener to delete a large portion of the *Alaska* manuscript. That portion, a story of a group traveling to the Klondike during the gold rush of 1897, was published the following year as *Journey.*

Discussing Michener's historical epic *Caribbean,* published in 1989, Karen Stabiner wrote in the *Los Angeles Times Book Review,* that Michener "has perfect best-seller pitch: enough intrigue to make life exciting; enough chronological and geographical distance to make the thrills thrilling, not threatening. While finding the characterizations in *Caribbean* "stiff and wooden" and the dialogue unrealistic, reviewer John Hearne, in the *New York Times Book Review,* nevertheless acknowledged that "what cannot be faulted, and what shines from the pages, is a great sympathy on Michener's part for the people who made the events happen."

In the 1990s Michener produced several works unique in his canon. *The Novel* is a work of fiction comprised of four segments, each narrated from a different point of view. It is a portrayal of the publishing world, with sections focusing on a writer named Lukas Yoder, his editor, Yvonne Marmelle, a literary critic, and a friend of Yoder who represents the reading public. Critics generally regarded *The Novel* as a failed experiment focusing on the interior lives of his characters—an area in which Michener's critics have generally found his abilities lacking—unlike the historical narratives at which he excelled. More favorable reviews emerged regarding the autobiographical *The World is My Home,* which documents Michener's extensive travels and literary endeavors. In the *New York Times Book Review,* Doris Grumbach noted that Michener considers himself a popular storyteller rather than a novelist; she asserted that while Michener's literary talents may be regarded by some as limited, his memoirs indicate that "there is every chance that he will be remembered . . . for being not an ordinary but a highly unusual fellow, almost a Renaissance man, adventurous, inquisitive, energetic, unpretentious and unassuming, with an encyclopedic mind and a generous heart."

Significantly shorter than many of his previous novels, Michener's 1995 work *Miracle in Seville* was classified by some critics as a novella or fable. Set in Spain, the story portrays the quest of Don Cayetano Mota, who faces his last opportunity to prove that his family's ranch can produce great bull-fighting bulls. Allen Joseph of the *New York Times Book Review* praised Michener's vivid evocation of Spanish culture and the suspenseful plot of the narrative: "What emerges most strongly is the real admiration and awe that lovers of bullfighting feel for the *toro bravo.*"

Michener's 1994 novel *Recessional,* concerned with the theme of old age and focusing on the pressures that face the elderly, also represented a departure from his usual fictional output. Reeve Lindbergh of the *Washington Post Book World* emphasized the volume's contrast with Michener's usual technique of depicting broad geographical areas and expansive family sagas in books that are "like going on a field trip with God." *Recessional,* in contrast, depicts the landscape of a human life by portraying Andy Zorn, a doctor who regains his ability to heal through his work at a retirement home. Offering praise for the novel, Mark Jackson of *Books* commented: "Meticulous, incomparable research and vividly drawn characters blend seamlessly within this richly told novel that is concerned with the choices, obstacles and rewards faced by older-but-wiser adults at the Palms retirement center in Florida."

"A Michener novel is a tribute to the industriousness of both author and reader," said James, "and, in addition to the easy-to-swallow data, it contains a morality tale about the heroism of hard work and guts. His thick, fact-filled books seem thoroughly impersonal, but several days in Michener's company show the novels to be perfect expressions of their author's anomalies—moral without being stern, methodical yet digressive, insistently modest yet bursting with ambition, full of social conscience yet grasping at facts as a way to avoid emotion."

Michiko Kakutani commented similarly in the *New York Times* that Michener's books contain many "bits of knowledge," which "served up in the author's utilitarian prose, are part of Mr. Michener's wide popular appeal: readers feel they're learning something, even while they're being entertained, and they're also able to absorb all these facts within a pleasant moral context: a liberal and a humanitarian, Mr. Michener argues for religious and racial tolerance, celebrates the old pioneer ethic of hard work and self- reliance, and offers such incontestable, if obvious, observations as 'war forces men to make moral choices.'"

James quoted literary critic Leslie Fiedler as commenting that Michener "puts a book together in a perfectly lucid, undisturbing way, so that even potentially troublesome issues don't seem so. *Hawaii* is about the problem of imperialism, yet one never senses that. *The Source* is about the Middle East, one of the most troublesome political issues in the world, but he's forgotten all the ambiguities. His approach is that if you knew all the facts, everything would straighten out, so it's soothing and reassuring to read him."

Such an approach has its flaws. *New York Times* critic Thomas Lask explained that Michener "likes to have his characters perform against the background or in accordance with the events of history. The quirks of personality, the oddities of character, the unpredictable Brownian motions of human psychology appear to interest him little. He prefers to represent a history in action." A *Time* reviewer summed up that Michener's "virtue is a powerful sense of place and the ability to convey great sweeps of time. His weakness is an insistence on covering murals with so much background and foreground that he has learned only a few ways of doing faces."

Jonathan Yardley reported in the *New York Times Book Review* that Michener "deserves more respect than he usually gets. Granted that he is not a stylist and that he smothers his stories under layers of historical and ecological trivia, nonetheless he has earned his enormous popularity honorably. Unlike many other authors whose books automatically rise to the upper reaches of the best-seller lists, he does not get there by exploiting the lives of the famous or the notorious; he does not treat sex cynically or pruriently; he does not write trash. His purposes are entirely serious: he wants to instruct, to take his readers through history in an entertaining fashion, to introduce them to lands and peoples they do not know." In Day's words, "as a scholarly novelist, Michener has won wide popularity without stooping to cheap melodrama."

Schott concluded that "while the arbiters of letters try to figure out what James A. Michener's fat books are . . . Mr. Michener goes on writing them as if his life depended on it." As Michener once told James, "I don't think the way I write books is the best or even the second-best. The really great writers are people like Emily Bronte who sit in a room and write out of their limited experience and unlimited imagination. But people in my position also do some very good work. I'm not a stylist like Updike or Bellow, and don't aspire to be. I'm not interested in plot or pyrotechnics, but I sure work to get a steady flow. If I try to describe a chair, I can describe it so that a person will read it to the end. The way the words flow, trying to maintain a point of view and a certain persuasiveness—that I can do." And he still has plenty of ideas for future development, he told *Insight* reporter Harvey Hagman in 1986. "I am able to work, and I love it. I have entered a profession which allows you to keep working at top energy. It's a wonderful job I have."

## BIOGRAPHICAL/CRITICAL SOURCES:

### BOOKS

*Authors in the News,* Volume 1, Gale, 1976.
Becker, G. J., *James A. Michener,* Ungar, 1983.
*Contemporary Literary Criticism,* Gale, Volume 1, 1973; Volume 5, 1976; Volume 11, 1979; Volume 29, 1984.
*Conversations with Writers,* Gale, 1978.
Day, A. Grove, *James A. Michener,* Twayne, 1964.
*Dictionary of Literary Biography,* Volume 6: *American Novelists since World War II,* Second Series, Gale, 1980.
Dybwad, G. L., and Joy V. Bliss, *James A. Michener: The Beginning Teacher and His Textbooks,* The Books Stops Here, 1995.

Groseclose, David A., *James A. Michener: A Bibliography,* State House Press, 1995.
Hayes, J. P., *James A. Michener,* Bobbs-Merrill, 1984.
Kings, J., *In Search of Centennial,* Random House, 1978.
Michener, James A., *Report of the County Chairman,* Random House, 1961.
Michener, *Iberia: Spanish Travels and Reflections,* Random House, 1968.
Michener, *About "Centennial": Some Notes on the Novel,* Random House, 1974.
Murrow, Edward Roscoe, *This I Believe,* Volume 2, Simon & Schuster, 1954.
Newquist, Roy, *Conversations,* Rand McNally, 1967.
Prescott, Orville, *In My Opinion: An Inquiry into the Contemporary Novel,* Bobbs-Merrill, 1952.
Severson, Marilyn S., *James A. Michener: A Critical Companion,* Greenwood Press, 1996.
Stuckey, W. J., *The Pulitzer Prize Novels,* University of Oklahoma Press, 1966.
Warfel, Harry Redcay, *American Novelists of Today,* American Book, 1951.

### PERIODICALS

*America,* August 31, 1963; September 23, 1978; January 24, 1981.
*Antioch Review,* fall-winter, 1970-71.
*Art America,* November, 1969.
*Atlantic,* March, 1949; July, 1951; September, 1953; April, 1957; October, 1958; September, 1963; May, 1968; June, 1971; November, 1974.
*Best Sellers,* September 1, 1963; June 15, 1965; July 1, 1968; December 15, 1970; June 15, 1971; November, 1976; September, 1978.
*Booklist,* December 1, 1993, p. 671.
*Bookmark,* June, 1951.
*Books,* October, 1971; January, 1995, p. 12.
*Books and Bookmen,* December, 1971.
*Book Week,* May 30, 1965.
*Book World,* May 5, 1968; June 1, 1969; November 9, 1969; July 4, 1971; July 18, 1971.
*Catholic World,* June, 1960.
*Chicago Sun,* February 9, 1949.
*Chicago Sunday Tribune,* May 6, 1951; November 25, 1951; July 12, 1953; January 31, 1954; December 26, 1954; March 3, 1957; November 22, 1959; May 7, 1961.
*Chicago Tribune,* January 17, 1982; September 29, 1983; June 27, 1985; October 17, 1985; July 2, 1989.
*Chicago Tribune Book World,* October 3, 1982; September 4, 1983; October 13, 1985.

*Children's Book World,* November 5, 1967.

*Christian Science Monitor,* February 5, 1949; May 1, 1951; July 9, 1953; December 23, 1954; February 28, 1957; September 11, 1958; June 3, 1965; May 9, 1968; June 17, 1970; September 18, 1978; November 10, 1980; October 6, 1982.

*College English,* October, 1952.

*Commentary,* April, 1981.

*Commonweal,* April 27, 1951; February 12, 1953; July 31, 1953; April 12, 1957.

*Congress Bi-Weekly,* June 14, 1965.

*Detroit News,* October 3, 1982; September 18, 1983; October 27, 1985.

*Esquire,* December, 1970; June, 1971.

*Good Housekeeping,* February, 1960.

*Guardian,* November 10, 1961.

*Harper's,* January, 1961.

*Insight,* September 1, 1986.

*Kirkus Reviews,* August 1, 1995, p. 1051.

*Library Journal,* October 7, 1970; November 15, 1993, p. 79.

*Life,* November 7, 1955; June 4, 1971.

*Los Angeles Times,* November 21, 1985.

*Los Angeles Times Book Review,* December 7, 1980; October 3, 1982; July 31, 1983; September 4, 1983; September 13, 1987; April 7, 1991.

*Nation,* February 12, 1949; May 12, 1951; April 20, 1957; January 31, 1959; December 12, 1959; July 19, 1971; March 5, 1983.

*National Observer,* May 27, 1968; June 7, 1971.

*National Review,* June 29, 1971; June 29, 1974; November 22, 1974; August 7 and 14, 1976; September 15, 1978; May 27, 1983; November 11, 1983.

*New Republic,* May 14, 1951; August 17, 1953; May 29, 1961; September 21, 1974; August 7-14, 1976.

*New Statesman,* June 25, 1960; November 29, 1974.

*Newsweek,* January 25, 1954; May 14, 1962; August 12, 1963; May 24, 1965; May 6, 1968; September 16, 1974; July 24, 1978; November 24, 1980; January 16, 1984; September 23, 1985.

*New Yorker,* February 19, 1949; May 3, 1951; January 23, 1954; March 16, 1957; August 14, 1978.

*New York Herald Tribune,* May 28, 1961.

*New York Herald Tribune Book Review,* February 2, 1947; February 13, 1949; April 22, 1951; May 20, 1951; October 7, 1951; July 12, 1953; July 19, 1953; January 24, 1954; December 12, 1954; March 3, 1957; August 10, 1958; November 22, 1959; December 20, 1959; August 11, 1963.

*New York Magazine,* September 2, 1974.

*New York Review of Books,* December 19, 1968; August 17, 1978.

*New York Times,* February 2, 1947; February 3, 1947; February 6, 1949; February 7, 1949; April 22, 1951; April 23, 1951; October 30, 1951; July 12, 1953; January 24, 1954; December 12, 1954; March 3, 1957; August 3, 1958; May 1, 1968; June 10, 1971; September 27, 1974; July 1, 1976; August 1, 1978; November 14, 1980; September 29, 1982; September 3, 1983; February 20, 1984; September 25, 1984; October 9, 1985; October 31, 1985.

*New York Times Book Review,* May 16, 1948; May 22, 1949; July 12, 1953; March 3, 1957; November 8, 1959; November 22, 1959; June 18, 1961; August 11, 1963; May 23, 1965; July 24, 1966; May 12, 1968; May 25, 1969; June 6, 1971; June 27, 1971; September 30, 1973; February 10, 1974; September 8, 1974; June 27, 1976; July 23, 1978; November 26, 1978; July 15, 1979; November 23, 1980; September 19, 1982; June 12, 1983; September 4, 1983; November 20, 1983; October 13, 1985; September 6, 1987; June 26, 1988; July 9, 1989; November 5, 1989; November 12, 1989; September 30, 1990; March 31, 1991; January 19, 1992; November 28, 1993, p. 26; October 16, 1994, p. 20; January 7, 1996, p. 20.

*New York Times Magazine,* September 8, 1985.

*Palm Springs Life,* October, 1974.

*Paradise of the Pacific,* September-October, 1963.

*Philadelphia Bulletin,* September 13, 1974.

*Publishers Weekly,* October 18, 1993, p. 54; August 21, 1995, p. 46.

*Reader's Digest,* April, 1954.

*San Francisco Chronicle,* February 4, 1949; May 6, 1951; July 12, 1953; January 29, 1954; December 19, 1954; February 28, 1957; August 17, 1958; November 24, 1959; November 25, 1959; May 3, 1961.

*Saturday Evening Post,* January, 1976.

*Saturday Review,* July 1, 1953; February 6, 1954; January 1, 1955; March 2, 1957; November 21, 1959; June 10, 1961; September 7, 1963; May 29, 1965; May 4, 1968; April 12, 1969; May 1, 1971; September 18, 1971; June 26, 1976; June, 1980; November, 1980.

*Saturday Review of Literature,* February 12, 1949; April 28, 1951.

*School Library Journal,* May, 1994, p. 143.

*Spectator,* June 25, 1954; September 15, 1955; November 10, 1961.

*Sports Illustrated,* May 12, 1980.

*This Week,* December 4, 1966.

*Time,* February 4, 1949; April 23, 1951; July 13, 1953; January 25, 1954; March 4, 1957; November 23, 1959; August 9, 1963; May 28, 1965; May 17, 1968; May 3, 1971; September 23, 1974; June 28, 1976; July 10, 1978; February 9, 1981; October 3, 1983; October 28, 1985.

*Times Literary Supplement,* October 26, 1951; July 9, 1954; May 17, 1957; February 19, 1960; June 17, 1960; November 17, 1961; October 14, 1965; November 7, 1968; July 23, 1971; November 22, 1974; July 22, 1977.

*U.S. News,* February 4, 1980.

*U.S. Quarterly Book Review,* June, 1947; September, 1951; September, 1955.

*Variety,* June 22, 1970; November 8, 1972; November 7, 1994.

*Vital Speeches,* July 15, 1979.

*Vogue,* November 1, 1966.

*Washington Post,* September 2, 1983.

*Washington Post Book World,* June 4, 1972; September 1, 1974; July 9, 1978; September 30, 1979; November 2, 1980; December 6, 1981; September 12, 1982; September 29, 1985; July 3, 1988; March 2, 1991; December 8, 1991; October 16, 1994, p. 1.

*Writer's Digest,* April, 1972; May, 1972.

*Yale Review,* spring, 1947; spring, 1949.


*OBITUARIES:*


*PERIODICALS*


*Chicago Tribune,* October 17, 1997.
*Detroit News,* October 17, 1997.
*Los Angeles Times,* October 17, 1997.
*New York Times,* October 17, 1997.
*USA Today,* October 17, 1997.
*Washington Post,* October 17, 1997.*


\*    \*    \*


**MILLER, Benj.**
  **See LOOMIS, Noel M(iller)**


\*    \*    \*


**MILLER, Frank**
  **See LOOMIS, Noel M(iller)**


**MOMADAY, N(avarre) Scott 1934-**

*PERSONAL:* Surname is pronounced *Ma*-ma-day; born February 27, 1934, in Lawton, OK; son of Alfred Morris (a painter and teacher of art) and Mayme Natachee (a teacher and writer; maiden name, Scott) Momaday; married Gaye Mangold, September 5, 1959 (marriage ended); married Regina Heitzer, July 21, 1978; children: (first marriage) Cael, Jill, Brit (all daughters); (second marriage) Lore (daughter). *Education:* Attended Augusta Military Academy; University of New Mexico, A.B., 1958; Stanford University, M.A., 1960, Ph.D., 1963.

*CAREER:* University of California, Santa Barbara, assistant professor, 1963-65, associate professor of English, 1968-69; University of California, Berkeley, associate professor of English and comparative literature, 1969-73; Stanford University, Stanford, CA, professor of English, 1973-82; University of Arizona, Tucson, professor of English and comparative literature, 1982-85, regents professor of English; former teacher at New Mexico State University. Artist; has exhibited his drawings and paintings in galleries. Trustee, Museum of American Indian, Heye Foundation, New York City, 1978—. Consultant, National Endowment for the Humanities, National Endowment for the Arts, 1970—.

*MEMBER:* PEN, Modern Language Association of America, American Studies Association, Gourd Dance Society of the Kiowa Tribe.

*AWARDS, HONORS:* Academy of American Poets prize, 1962, for poem "The Bear"; Guggenheim fellowship, 1966-67; Pulitzer Prize for fiction, 1969, for *House Made of Dawn*; National Institute of Arts and Letters grant, 1970; shared Western Heritage Award with David Muench, 1974, for nonfiction book *Colorado: Summer/Fall/Winter/Spring*; Premio Letterario Internazionale Mondelo, Italy, 1979.

*WRITINGS:*

(Editor) *The Complete Poems of Frederick Goddard Tuckerman,* Oxford University Press, 1965.

*The Journey of Tai-me* (retold Kiowa Indian folktales), with original etchings by Bruce S. McCurdy, limited edition, University of California, Santa Barbara, 1967, enlarged edition published as *The Way to Rainy Mountain,* illustrated by father, Alfred Momaday, University of New Mexico Press, 1969.

*House Made of Dawn* (novel), Harper, 1968, re-printed, 1989.

*Colorado: Summer/Fall/Winter/Spring,* illustrated with photographs by David Muench, Rand Mc-Nally, 1973.

*Angle of Geese and Other Poems,* David Godine, 1974.

*The Gourd Dancer* (poems), illustrated by the author, Harper, 1976.

*The Names: A Memoir,* Harper, 1976, reprinted, University of Arizona Press, 1996.

(Author of foreword) An Painter, *A Coyote in the Garden,* Confluence, 1988.

*The Ancient Child* (novel), Doubleday, 1989.

(Contributor) Charles L. Woodward, *Ancestral Voice: Conversations with N. Scott Momaday,* University of Nebraska Press, 1989.

(Author of introduction) Marcia Keegan, *Enduring Culture: A Century of Photography of the South-west Indians,* Clear Light, 1991.

*In the Presence of the Sun: A Gathering of Shields,* Rydal, 1992.

*In the Presence of the Sun: Stories and Poems, 1961-1991* (poems, stories, art), St. Martin's, 1992.

(Author of introduction) Gerald Hausman, *Turtle Island Alphabet: A Lexicon of Native American Symbols and Culture,* St. Martin's, 1992.

*Circle of Wonder: A Native American Christmas Story,* Clear Light, 1994.

Also author of film script of Frank Water's novel, *The Man Who Killed the Deer.* Contributor of articles and poems to periodicals; a frequent reviewer on In-dian subjects for the *New York Times Book Review.*

*WORK IN PROGRESS:* A study of American poetry in the middle period, *The Furrow and the Glow: Sci-ence and Literature in America, 1836-1866* (tentative title), for Oxford University Press; a book on storytelling, for Oxford University Press.

*SIDELIGHTS:* N. Scott Momaday's poetry and prose reflect his Kiowa Indian heritage in structure and theme, as well as in subject matter. "When I was growing up on the reservations of the Southwest," he told Joseph Bruchac in *American Poetry Review,* "I saw people who were deeply involved in their tradi-tional life, in the memories of their blood. They had, as far as I could see, a certain strength and beauty that I find missing in the modern world at large. I like to celebrate that involvement in my writing." Roger Dickinson-Brown indicates in the *Southern Review* that Momaday has long "maintained a quiet reputation in American Indian affairs and among distinguished

*literati*" for his brilliance and range, "his fusion of alien cultures, and his extraordinary experiments in different literary forms." Momaday believes that his poetry, in particular, grows from and sustains the Indian oral tradition, he commented to Bruchac. And his Pulitzer Prize-winning novel *House Made of Dawn* is described by Baine Kerr in *Southwest Review* as an attempt to "transliterate Indian culture, myth, and sensibility into an alien art form without loss." *The Way to Rainy Mountain* melds myth, history, and personal recollection into a narrative about the Kiowa tribe, while Momaday's *The Names: A Memoir* ex-plores the author's heritage in autobiographical form.

*The Names* is composed of tribal tales, boyhood memories, and genealogy, reports *New York Times Book Review* critic Wallace Stegner. Momaday's quest for his roots, writes Edward Abbey in *Harper's,* "takes him back to the hills of Kentucky and north to the high plains of Wyoming, and from there, in memory and imagination, back to the Bering Straits." Stegner describes it as "an Indian book, but not a book about wrongs done to Indians. It is a search and a celebration, a book of identities and sources. Momaday is the son of parents who successfully bridged the gulf between Indian and white ways, but remain Indian," he explains. "In boyhood Momaday made the same choice, and in making it gave himself the task of discovering and in some degree inventing the tradition and history in which he finds his most profound sense of himself." *New York Review of Books* critic Diane Johnson agrees that "Momaday does not appear to feel, or does not discuss, any conflict of the Kiowa and white traditions; he is their product, an artist, heir of the experiences of his an-cestors and conscious of the benignity of their influ-ence."

Momaday is only half Kiowa. His mother, Mayme Natachee Scott, is descended from early American pioneers, although her middle name is taken from a Cherokee great-grandmother. Momaday's memoir also includes anecdotes of such Anglo-American an-cestors as his grandfather, Theodore Scott, a Ken-tucky sheriff. His mother, however, preferred to identify in her imagination with her Indian heritage, adopting the name Little Moon when she was younger and dressing Indian style. She attended Haskell Insti-tute, an Indian school in Kansas, where she met sev-eral members of the Kiowa tribe; eventually she married Momaday's father, also a Kiowa. The author grew up in New Mexico, where his mother, a teacher and writer, and his father, an artist and art teacher, found work among the Jemez Indians in the state's high canyon and mountain country, but he was originally raised among the Kiowas on a family farm in Oklahoma. Although Momaday covers his Anglo-American heritage in the memoir, he prefers, like his mother, "to imagine himself *all* Indian, and to 'imagine himself' back into the life, the emotions, the spirit of his Kiowa forebears," comments Abbey. He uses English, his mother's language, according to Abbey, to tell "his story in the manner of his father's people; moving freely back and forth in time and space, interweaving legend, myth, and history."

Momaday doesn't actually speak Kiowa, but, in his work, he reveals the language as not only a reflection of the physical environment, but also a means of shaping it. The title of *The Names,* reports Richard Nicholls in *Best Sellers,* refers to all "the names given by Scott Momaday's people, the Kiowa Indians, to the objects, forms, and features of their land, the southwestern plains, and to its animals and birds." When he was less than a year old, Momaday was given the name Tsoaitalee or "Rock-Tree-Boy" by a paternal relative, after the 200-foot volcanic butte in Wyoming, which is sacred to the Kiowas and is known to Anglo-Americans as Devil's Tower. "For the Kiowas it was a place of high significance," points out Abbey. "To be named after that mysterious and mythic rock was, for the boy, a high honor and a compelling one. For among the Indians a name was never merely an identifying tag but something much more important, a kind of emblem and ideal, the determining source of a man or woman's character and course of life."

The Indian perception of the human relationship to nature is a central concern in Momaday's writing; he told Bruchac: "I believe that the Indian has an understanding of the physical world and of the earth as a spiritual entity that is his, very much his own. The non-Indian can benefit a good deal by having that perception revealed to him." And, he explained, his own particular "growing up" within the Indian culture was a "fortunate" upbringing. "On the basis of my experience, trusting my own perceptions, I don't see any validity in the separation of man and landscape. Oh, I know that the notion of alienation is very widespread, in a sense very popular. But I think it's an unfortunate point of view and a false one, where the relationship between man and the earth is concerned. Certainly it is one of the great afflictions of our time, this conviction of alienation, separation, isolation. And it is certainly an affliction in the Indian world. But there it has the least chance of taking hold, I believe, for there it is opposed by very strong forces.

The whole world view of the Indian is predicated upon the principle of harmony in the universe. You can't tinker much with that; it has the look of an absolute."

This view does not preclude conflict, however. Momaday's theme in his poem "Rainy Mountain Cemetery," Dickinson-Brown points out, "is as old as our civilization: the tension, the gorgeous hostility between the human and the wild—a tension always finally relaxed in death." And, ultimately, even the violent, discontinuous sequence of events in *House Made of Dawn* conveys what Vernon E. Lattin calls in an *American Literature* review "a new romanticism, with a reverence for the land, a transcendent optimism, and a sense of mythic wholeness." Momaday's "reverence for the land," according to Lattin, is comparable "to the pastoral vision found in most mainstream American literature," but with "essential differences." Dickinson-Brown argues that Momaday's use of landscape in *House Made of Dawn* "is peculiar to him and to his Indian culture. It is a landscape and a way of living nowhere else available." In Kerr's words, here, Momaday "may in fact be seeking to make the modern Anglo novel a vehicle for a sacred text."

Momaday's first novel, *House Made of Dawn,* tells "the old story of the problem of mixing Indians and Anglos," reports *New York Times Book Review* critic Marshall Sprague. "But there is a quality of revelation here as the author presents the heart-breaking effort of his hero to live in two worlds." In the novel's fractured narrative, the main character, Abel, returns to the prehistoric landscape and culture surrounding his reservation pueblo after his tour of duty in the Army during World War II. Back home, he kills an albino. He serves a prison term and is paroled, unrepentant, to a Los Angeles relocation center. Once in the city, he attempts to adjust to his factory job, like his even-tempered roommate, Ben, a modern Indian, who narrates parts of the novel. During his free time, Abel drinks and attends adulterated religious and peyote-eating ceremonies. He can't cope with his job; and, "because of his contempt," Sprague indicates that he's brutally beaten by a Los Angeles policeman, but returns again to the reservation "in time to carry on tradition for his dying grandfather," Francisco. The novel culminates in Abel's running in the ancient ritual dawn race against evil and death.

According to Kerr, the book is "a creation myth—rife with fabulous imagery, ending with Abel's rebirth in the old ways at the old man's death—but an ironic one, suffused with violence and telling a story of culture loss." The grandfather, he maintains, "heroic, crippled, resonant with the old ways, impotent in the new—acts as a lodestone to the novel's conflicting energies. His incantatory dying delirium in Spanish flexes Momaday's symbolic compass . . . , and around his dying the book shapes its proportions." Francisco is "the alembic that transmutes the novel's confusions," he comments. "His retrospection marks off the book's boundaries, points of reference, and focal themes: the great organic calendar of the black mesa—the house of the sun (which locates the title)—as a central Rosetta stone integrating the ceremonies rendered in Part One, and the source place by which Abel and [his brother] could 'reckon where they were, where all things were, in time.'"

Momaday meets with difficulties in his attempt to convey Indian sensibility in novelistic form, Kerr relates. The fractured narrative is open to criticism, in Kerr's opinion, and the "plot of *House Made of Dawn* actually seems propelled by withheld information, that besetting literary error," he writes. Of the novel's structure, Dickinson-Brown writes that the sequence of events "is without fixed order. The parts can he rearranged, no doubt with change of effect, but not always with recognizable difference. The fragments thus presented are the subject. The result is a successful depiction but not an understanding of what is depicted: a reflection, not a novel in the comprehensive sense of the word." Kerr also objects to the author's overuse of "quiet, weak constructions" in the opening paragraph and indicates that "repetition, polysyndeton, and *there* as subject continue to deaden the narrative's force well into the book." *Commonweal* reviewer William James Smith agrees that "Mr. Momaday observes and renders accurately, but the material seems to have sunken slightly beneath the surface of the beautiful prose." Lattin maintains, however, that the novel should also be regarded as "a return to the sacred art of storytelling and myth-making that is part of Indian oral tradition," as well as an attempt "to push the secular mode of modern fiction into the sacred mode, a faith and recognition in the power of the word." And a *Times Literary Supplement* critic points out Momaday's "considerable descriptive power," citing "a section in which Tosamah [a Los Angeles medicine man/priest] rehearses the ancient trampled history of the Kiowas in trance—like visionary prose that has moments of splendour."

John "Big Bluff" Tosamah, Kerr argues, "in his two magnificent 'sermons,' is really an incarnation of the author, Momaday's mouthpiece, giving us what we've been denied: interpretation of Indian consciousness, expatiation on themes." According to Lattin, he is "a more complex religious figure" than his thoroughly Christian counterpart, Father Olguin, the Mexican priest who works on the reservation. "In the first sermon, 'The Gospel According to St. John,' Tosamah perceives the Book of John as an overwrought creation myth, applies the lightning bolt concept of the Word to the Kiowa myth of Tai-me, and apotheosizes the Indian gift of the human need for a felt awe of creation," Kerr relates. Tosamah, he indicates, "is an intriguing, well-crafted interlocutor, but also a slightly caricatured self-portrait—like Momaday a Kiowa, a man of words, an interpreter of Indian sensibility."

Tosamah's sermon on Kiowa tribal history appears in a slightly altered form in Momaday's *The Way to Rainy Mountain,* and in a review of that book, *Southern Review* critic Kenneth Fields points out that Momaday's writing exemplifies a "paradox about language which is often expressed in American Indian literature." Momaday himself has written that "by means of words can a man deal with the world on equal terms. And the word is sacred," comments Fields. "On the other hand . . . the Indians took for their subject matter those elusive perceptions that resist formulation, never entirely apprehensible, but just beyond the ends of the nerves." In a similar vein, Dickinson-Brown maintains that Momaday's poem "Angle of Geese" "presents, better than any other work I know . . . perhaps the most important subject of our age: the tragic conflict between what we have felt in wilderness and what our language means." That Momaday must articulate in *The Way to Rainy Mountain,* Fields argues, is "racial memory," or "the ghostly heritage of [his] Kiowa ancestors," and "what it means to feel himself a Kiowa in the modern American culture that displaced his ancestors."

Described by Fields as "far and away [Momaday's] best book," *The Way to Rainy Mountain* relates the story of the Kiowas journey 300 years ago from Yellowstone down onto the plains, where they acquired horses, and, in the words of John R. Milton in *Saturday Review,* "they became a lordly society of sun priests, fighters, hunters, and thieves, maintaining this position for 100 years, to the mid-nineteenth century," when they were all but destroyed by the U.S. Cavalry in Oklahoma. And when the sacred buffalo began to disappear, Fields indicates, "the Kiowas lost the sustaining illumination of the sun god," since, as Momaday explains, the buffalo was viewed as "the animal representation of the sun, the essential and sacrificial victim of the Sun Dance." "Momaday's own grandmother, who had actually been present at the last and abortive Kiowa Sun Dance in 1887, is for him the last of the Kiowas," relates Fields.

Here, Momaday uses form to help him convey a reality that has largely been lost. His text is made up of twenty-four numbered sections grouped into three parts, The Setting Out, The Going On, and The Closing In. These parts are in turn divided into three different passages, each of which is set in a different style type face. The first passage in each part is composed of Kiowa myths and legends, the second is made up of historical accounts of the tribe, and the third passage is a personal autobiographical rendering of Momaday's rediscovery of his Kiowa homeland and roots. "In form," points out Fields, "it resembles those ancient texts with subsequent commentaries which, taken altogether, present strange complexes of intelligence; not only the author's, but with it that of the man in whose mind the author was able to live again."

By the end of the last part, however, writes Nicholas, the three passages begin to blend with one another, and "the mythic passages are no longer mythic in the traditional sense, that is Momaday is creating myth out of his memories of his ancestors rather than passing on already established and socially sanctioned tales. Nor are the historical passages strictly historical, presumably objective, accounts of the Kiowas and their culture. Instead they are carefully selected and imaginatively rendered memories of his family. And, finally, the personal passages have become prose poems containing symbols which link them thematically to the other two, suggesting that all three journeys are products of the imagination, that all have become interfused in a single memory and reflect a single idea." Dickinson-Brown considers the book's shape a well-controlled "associational structure," distinctively adapted to the author's purpose. The form, according to Fields, forces Momaday "to relate the subjective to the more objective historical sensibility. The writing of the book itself, one feels, enables him to gain both freedom and possession. It is therefore a work of discovery as well as renunciation, of finding but also of letting go."

Concentrating his efforts mostly on the writing of nonfiction and poetry, Momaday did not write another novel for twenty years after *House Made of Dawn.* "I don't think of myself as a novelist. I'm a poet," he told *Los Angeles Times* interviewer Edward Iwata. In

1989, however, the poet completed his second novel, *The Ancient Child.* Building this book around the legend behind his Indian name, Tsoaitalee, Momaday uses the myth to develop the story of a modern Indian artist searching for his identity. A number of reviewers have lauded the new novel. Craig Lesley, for one, says in the *Washington Post* that *The Ancient Child* "is an intriguing combination of myth, fiction and storytelling that demonstrates the continuing power and range of Momaday's creative vision." A "largely autobiographical novel," according to Iwata, *The Ancient Child* expresses the author's belief that "dreams and visions are pathways to one's blood ancestry and racial memory."

In addition to his poetry and fiction, Momaday is also an accomplished painter. His diverse skill is evident in *In the Presence of the Sun: Stories and Poems, 1961-1991.* The collection includes numerous poems from Momaday's early poetic career; twenty new poems; a sequence of poems about the legendary outlaw Billy the Kid; stories about the Kiowas' tribal shields; and sixty drawings by the author. "A slim volume, [*In the Presence of the Sun*] contains the essence of the ancestral voices that speak through him. It is a refined brew of origins, journeys, dreams and the landscape of the deep continental interior," remarks Barbara Bode in the *New York Times Book Review.*

Momaday turned his attention to children with *Circle of Wonder: A Native American Christmas Story,* published in 1994. The story revolves around Tolo, a young mute boy grieving for the loss of his beloved grandfather. On Christmas Eve, his grandfather's spirit unexpectedly leads Tolo to a mountain bonfire, where he meets an elk, a wolf, and an eagle and discovers new meaning to the Christmas tradition.

Momaday views his heritage objectively and in a positive light. He explains much of his perspective as a writer and as a Native American in *Ancestral Voice: Conversations with N. Scott Momaday,* the result of a series of interviews with Charles L. Woodward. *World Literature Today* contributor Robert L. Berner calls the volume "an essential tool of scholarship" in analyzing and understanding Momaday and his work. Discussing his heritage with Bruchac, Momaday commented: "The Indian has the advantage of a very rich spiritual experience. As much can be said, certainly, of some non-Indian writers. But the non-Indian writers of today are culturally deprived, I think, in the sense that they don't have the same sense of heritage that the Indian has. I'm told this time and time again by my students, who say, 'Oh, I wish I knew more about my grandparents; I wish I knew more about my ancestors and where they came from and what they did.' I've come to believe them. It seems to me that the Indian writer ought to make use of that advantage. One of his subjects ought certainly to be his cultural investment in the world. It is a unique and complete experience, and it is a great subject in itself."

*BIOGRAPHICAL/CRITICAL SOURCES:*

*BOOKS*

Allen, Paula Gunn, *Recovering the Word: Essays on Native American Literature,* edited by Brian Swann and Arnold Krupat, University of California Press, 1987, pp. 563-79.

*Authors and Artists for Young Adults,* Volume 11, Gale, 1993.

Blaeser, Kimberly, *Narrative Chance: Postmodern Discourse on Native American Indian Literatures,* edited by Gerald Vizenor, University of New Mexico Press, 1989, pp. 39-54.

Brumble, H. David, III, *American Indian Autobiography,* University of California Press, 1988, pp. 165-80.

*Contemporary Literary Criticism,* Gale, Volume 2, 1974, Volume 19, 1981, Volume 85, 1995, Volume 95, 1997.

*Dictionary of Literary Biography,* Volume 143: *American Novelists since World War II, Third Series,* Gale, 1994, Volume 175: *Native American Writers of the United States,* Gale, 1997.

Gridley, Marion E., editor, *Indians of Today,* I.C.F.P., 1971.

Gridley, *Contemporary American Indian Leaders,* Dodd, 1972.

Hogan, Linda, *Studies in American Indian Literature: Critical Essays and Course Designs,* edited by Paula Gunn Allen, The Modern Language Association of America, 1983, pp. 169-77.

Lincoln, Kenneth, *Native American Renaissance,* University of California Press, 1983, pp. 82-121.

Momaday, N. Scott, *The Way to Rainy Mountain,* University of New Mexico Press, 1969.

Momaday, *The Names: A Memoir,* Harper, 1976.

*Native North American Literature,* Gale, 1994.

Roemer, Kenneth, ed., *Approaches to Teaching Momaday's "The Way to Rainy Mountain,"* The Modern Language Association of America, 1988, 171 p.

Trimble, Martha Scott, *Fifty Western Writers: A Bio-Bibliographical Sourcebook,* edited by Fred

Erisman and Richard W. Etulain, Greenwood Press, 1982, pp. 313-24.

Velie, Alan R, *Four American Indian Literary Masters: N. Scott Momaday, James Welch, Leslie Marmon Silko, and Gerald Vizenor,* University of Oklahoma Press, 1982, 157 p.

*PERIODICALS*

*American Indian Quarterly,* May, 1978; winter, 1986, pp. 101-17; summer, 1988, pp. 213-20..

*American Literature,* January, 1979; October, 1989, p. 520.

*American Poetry Review,* July/August, 1984.

*American West,* February, 1988, pp. 12-13.

*Atlantic,* January, 1977.

*Best Sellers,* June 15, 1968; April, 1977.

*Bloomsbury Review,* July/August, 1989, p. 13; July/August, 1993, p. 14; November/December, 1994, p. 25.

*Canadian Literature,* spring, 1990, p. 299.

*Commonweal,* September 20, 1968.

*Denver Quarterly,* winter, 1978, pp. 19-31.

*Harper's,* February, 1977.

*Listener,* May 15, 1969.

*Los Angeles Times,* November 20, 1989.

*Los Angeles Times Book Review,* December 27, 1992, p. 6.

*Nation,* August 5, 1968.

*New Yorker,* May 17, 1969.

*New York Review of Books,* February 3, 1977, pp. 19-20, 29.

*New York Times,* May 16, 1969; June 3, 1970.

*New York Times Book Review,* June 9, 1968; June 16, 1974; March 6, 1977; December 31, 1989; March 14, 1993, p. 15.

*Observer,* May 25, 1969.

*Publishers Weekly,* September 19, 1994, p. 28.

*Saturday Review,* June 21, 1969.

*Sewanee Review,* summer, 1977.

*South Dakota Review,* winter, 1975-76, pp. 149-58.

*Southern Review,* winter, 1970; January, 1978; April, 1978.

*Southwest Review,* summer, 1969; spring, 1978.

*Spectator,* May 23, 1969.

*Times Literary Supplement,* May 22, 1969.

*Tribune Books* (Chicago), October 1, 1989; December 4, 1994, p. 9.

*Washington Post,* November 21, 1969; November 28, 1989.

*Western American Literature,* May, 1977, pp. 86-7.

*World Literature Today,* summer, 1977; winter, 1990, p. 175; summer, 1993, p. 650.*

## MORGAN, Robin (Evonne) 1941-

*PERSONAL:* Born January 29, 1941, in Lake Worth, FL; daughter of Faith Berkeley Morgan; married Kenneth Pitchford (a poet, novelist and playwright), September 19, 1962; children: Blake Ariel Morgan-Pitchford. *Education:* Attended Columbia University. *Politics:* "Radical Feminist." *Religion:* "Wiccean Atheist."

*CAREER:* Curtis Brown, Ltd., New York City, associate literary agent, 1960-62; freelance editor, 1964-70; writer, 1970—; *Ms.* magazine, contributing editor, 1977—, editor in chief, 1989-93, international editor, 1993—. International lecturer on feminism, 1970-76; guest professor at New College, Sarasota, FL, 1972; has given poetry readings all over the United States. Member of board of directors, Women's Law Center, Feminist Self-Help Clinics, Battered Women's Refuge, Women's Institute Freedom Press, and National Alliance of Rape Crisis Centers.

*MEMBER:* Women's International Terrorist Conspiracy from Hell (founding member), Authors Guild, Authors League of America, Women's Anti-Defamation League, Susan B. Anthony National Memorial Association, Poetry Society of America, National Women's Political Caucus, Women Against Pornography (founding member), Feminist Writers Guild (founding member), New York Radical Women (founding member), Global Fund for Women (advisory board), Media Women, National American Feminist Coalition.

*AWARDS, HONORS:* National Endowment for the Arts grant, 1979-80; Ford Foundation, 1982, 1983, 1984; Wonder Woman award for international peace and understanding, 1982; Feminist of the Year, Fund for Feminist Majority, 1990; D.H.L., University of Connecticut, 1992.

*WRITINGS:*

(Editor with Charlotte Bunch-Weeks and Joanne Cooke) *The New Women: A Motive Anthology on Women's Liberation,* Bobbs-Merrill, 1970.

(Editor) *Sisterhood Is Powerful: An Anthology of Writings from the Women's Liberation Movement,* Random House, 1970.

*Monster: Poems,* Random House, 1972.

*Lady of the Beasts: Poems,* Random House, 1976.

*Going Too Far: The Personal Chronicle of a Feminist,* Random House, 1977.

*Depth Perception: New Poems and a Masque,* Anchor/Doubleday, 1982.

*The Anatomy of Freedom: Feminism, Physics, and Global Politics,* Anchor/Doubleday, 1982.

(Contributor) Karen Payne, editor, *Between Ourselves: Letters between Mothers and Daughters,* Houghton, 1984.

(Contributing editor) *Sisterhood Is Global: The International Women's Movement Anthology,* Anchor, 1985, reprinted, 1990.

*Dry Your Smile* (novel), Doubleday, 1987.

*The Demon Lover: On the Sexuality of Terrorism,* Norton, 1989.

*Upstairs in the Garden: Poems Selected and New, 1968-1988,* Norton, 1990.

*The Mer-Child: A Legend for Children and Other Adults,* Feminist Press, 1991.

*The Word of a Woman: Feminist Dispatches, 1968-1992,* Norton, 1992.

*The Anatomy of Freedom: Feminism, Physics, and Global Politics,* Norton, 1994.

*OTHER*

"Our Creations Are in the First Place Ourselves" (in two cassettes), Iowa State University of Science and Technology, 1974.

Also author of "Their Own Country," a play, 1961. Works represented in many anthologies, including *No More Masks!,* edited by Howe and Bass, for Doubleday; *The Young American Writers,* edited by Kostelanetz, for Funk; and *Campfires of the Resistance,* edited by Gitlin, for Bobbs-Merrill. Contributor of articles and poems to about 100 literary and political journals, including *Atlantic, New York Times, Hudson Review,* and *Feminist Art Journal.*

*WORK IN PROGRESS: Tales of the Witches,* historical fiction; a book of poems; a cycle of verse plays.

*SIDELIGHTS:* "One discovery of this decade has been a hitherto unplumbed, forbidden, inexpressible depth of female rage. Robin Morgan—one of the most honestly angry women since Antigone—has rightly become a feminist heroine for her expression of it," notes Alicia Ostriker in the *Partisan Review.* Indeed, for more than twenty years, Morgan has been known as both an active leader in the international feminist movement and an accomplished poet. "I am an artist and a political being as well," Morgan once told *CA.* "My aim has been to forge these two concerns into an integrity which affirms language, art, craft, form, beauty, tragedy, and audacity with the needs and visions of women, as part of an emerging new culture which could enrich us all."

Morgan is best known for having edited "one of the first of the good anthologies of the women's movement, [*Sisterhood Is Powerful: An Anthology of Writings from the Women's Liberation Movement*]," notes Kathleen Wiegner in the *American Poetry Review*. Published soon after Kate Millett's *Sexual Politics*, Morgan's feminist reader has "profoundly affected the way that many of us think about women and the relations between the sexes," Paul Robinson says in a *Psychology Today* article. Reviewers concur with Jean Gardner of the *New York Times Book Review* that the collection maintains a distinctly anti-male tone; in fact, a *New Leader* contributor expressed a fear that its strident cast might eclipse "some basic truths: that women have indeed been discriminated against, their talents wasted or misused, by many institutions and many men for a very long time, and that an end to this inequality is still not in sight." Particularly hazardous are the book's dogmatic features, such as "The Drop Dead List of Books to Watch Out For," Gardner suggests. *Commonweal* contributor Kathy Mulherin sees these hazards as well, but recommends *Sisterhood Is Powerful* nonetheless because it relates "to the real conditions of women and is worth looking into."

She argues, "The worst aspects of the book can't really be helped; they are also the worst aspects of the women's liberation movement," which at that time was just beginning to address the concerns of women outside white middle-class status. Writing in the *Nation*, Muriel Haynes also defends the essays: "This is good personal journalism, some of it flecked with wit, though it is rarely amusing."

Morgan's next anthology, *Sisterhood Is Global: The International Women's Movement Anthology*, "clearly demonstrates that there is a vital international women's movement," observes *Choice* contributor S. E. Jacobs, who deems it, therefore, "one of the most important books to appear in the past decade." Reviewers such as Andrew Hacker question the validity and accuracy of certain statistics in the book; at the same time, Hacker, writing in the *New York Times Book Review*, admires the book's range: "By temperament, the editor and almost all the contributors veer toward the left. Yet, as Simone de Beauvoir points out in her article on France, if that side of the spectrum has been 'the chosen friend' of militant women, it has also been their 'worst enemy.'. . . Virtually every left-leaning regime has put women's issues on

the back burner or ignored them altogether." The collection's other successes include "the reports from feminists perhaps many of us did not know existed—Senegalese, Tahitian, Nepalese—who describe working, sexual, marital, political and economic life in their respective countries," remarks Vivienne Walt in the *Nation*.

Contributors to the anthology met with Morgan in New York City in 1984 to define a strategy for the Sisterhood Is Global Institute. Members of the institute plan to "address the problems of women everywhere, including illiteracy; the care of the elderly; refugee populations and war victims; the crisis of world population; [and] the welfare, health, rights, and education of children," one participant told Marilyn Hoffman for a *Los Angeles Times* article. It also aims to translate books by women's right activists; to investigate and impede the practice of sex tourism; and to expose religious groups they have identified "as being particularly adverse to women," Hoffman reports. Morgan, together with leaders from Greece, Portugal, New Zealand and Palestine, is one of the institute's founders.

"Morgan is a feminist, to be sure; she is also an accomplished and original poet," Jay Parini observes in a *Poetry* review. Because Morgan's political concerns are foremost, she sometimes deliberately relaxes her attention to poetic technique. As a result, says May Swenson in the *New York Times Book Review*, Morgan's first book of poems, *Monster*, offers some poems that are "strongly wrought" among others that are "polemical" and "formless." David Lehman, writing in *Poetry*, echoes this assessment, praising the poems that "attain an anger purer than prejudice, stereotype, or slogan." Particularly effective is the title poem, which records Morgan's reflections on the demands of political activism and in which she accepts the darker aspects of that role. "At her best," says Annette Niemtzow in the *Los Angeles Times*, Morgan possesses "a voice of passion, a gift of rhetoric and commitment, a verbal gesture which moves toward prophecy." Adrienne Rich, writing in the *Washington Post Book World*, values Morgan's "acute, devouring sense of her own potential, of the energy she and all women in patriarchal society expend in simply countering opposition—and of what that energy might achieve if it could be released from combat (and self-punishment) into creation."

Reviewing Morgan's second volume of poems, Wiegner comments, "*Monster*. . . dealt with female consciousness as an emerging political issue. Now, in

*Lady of the Beasts*. . . she melds this consciousness with the Jungian theory of archetypes to present women in their mythic roles as mother, consort, sister, and finally, divine. . . . Her work appears to give power to women by showing the reader how, in some historic or mythic past, women held power through roles which have, in recent times, fallen into disrepute." *Lady of the Beasts* surpasses *Monster* while it contains more "engage poetry, the most difficult of. . . modes," Parini notes. In all of the poems, he goes on, "Morgan commands a wealth of technical resources," but her skill, he feels, is most evident in the poems "Voices from Six Tapestries" and "The Network of the Imaginary Mother."

Both poems are ambitious, reviewers explain. "'Voices. . .' interprets the fifteenth-century *Lady with the Unicorn* tapestries, which hang in the Musee de Cluny in Paris, as the expression of a woman-centered pre-Christian religious system. It is also a moving, sustained love poem," Ostriker states. "The Network of the Imaginary Mother," notes Parini, is an "intricate long poem" that looks at Morgan's relationships with her mother, husband, woman lover, son, and self. Ostriker observes that this "descent into self has brought her to the sea floor where autobiography meets mythology." For example, its five sections "are laced together with horrifying lists of murdered prototypes of the women's liberation movement"—female veterinarians, herbalists, mystics, and others accused of witchcraft, Parini reports. These lists, he says, draw "taut the stitches between the concrete particulars of one life and their mythic potential." Though reviewers disagree about how well these poems serve the poet's intent, even those who see room for improvement find the poems successful on the emotional level. Ostriker, for example, comments, "I do not quarrel with Morgan's seriousness, her sense of the issues, or her conviction that poetry can make things happen. I have been touched and changed by her work, and presume that other contemporary women, and men, will be so also."

Morgan's later books place her continuing commitment to women's rights into context against a wider field of vision. *Depth Perception: New Poems and a Masque,* her third book of poems, takes her farther from "the unassimilated feminism of her first collection, *Monster,* and has gradually absorbed its ideas and concerns into an eloquent and forceful lyricism," says Parini in the *New York Times Book Review.* Essays in *Anatomy of Freedom: Feminism, Physics and Global Politics* claim a basis for human freedom

in quantum physics, where particles in motion sometimes behave erratically. *Dry Your Smile,* a first novel, treats some of the same concerns in a fictional account of one woman writer's feelings as she writes her first novel. *Going Too Far: The Personal Chronicle of a Feminist* contains autobiographical nonfiction giving insight into the range of her opinions from 1962 to 1977. Critics comment on the unevenness in this selection, even though Morgan had explained in a *Ms.* "Forum" article that she meant to honestly represent her development by including some weaker pieces: "Ten years ago my poems quietly began muttering something about my personal pain as a woman—unconnected, of course, to anyone else, since I saw this merely as my own inadequacy, my own battle. I think a lot these days about the intervening decade and the startling changes it brought about, especially since the current book I'm working on [*Going Too Far*] is an assemblage of my own essays on feminism, dating back to the early-1960s: a graph of slow growth, defensiveness, struggle, painful new consciousness, and gradual affirmation. My decision to leave each piece 'as it was'—warts and all—has necessitated an editorial process redolent with a nostalgia punctuated by fits of embarrassed nausea."

In *The Demon Lover: On the Sexuality of Terrorism* Morgan explores wide-ranging manifestations of male antagonism directed against women throughout history and the world. As Joanna K. Weinberg writes in the *New York Times Book Review,* Morgan repeatedly describes "a man's footsteps, a woman pursued. . . . She may be on her way home, a mother in a Beirut refugee camp or an inner-city teen-ager dodging drug gangs. He is a terrorist: not just the hijacker or fundamentalist extremist of our nightmares, but a neighbor, a friend, a lover. . . . Her fear is the book's motif." Drawing upon feminist theory and her own personal vision, Morgan denounces the oppression of patriarchal society and its perpetuation of both subtle and gross exploitation of women. "In her analysis," Barbara Ehrenreich comments in the *Washington Post Book World,* "terrorism is the manifestation—in fact, the 'logical incarnation'—of patriarchy." Noting the extent of Morgan's indictment, Ehrenreich adds, "What's worse, almost every imaginable form of human malfeasance, from rape to acid rain, turns out to be a form of terrorism, and hence of patriarchy." For such reasons Weinberg similarly finds Morgan's doctrinaire feminist discourse somewhat forced and artificial, particularly in her failure to recognize exceptional men and women who defy such characterization. However, praising Morgan's "compelling" poetic voice, Weinberg adds that Morgan's personal observations are "intense and at times magnificent; this is what makes the book important."

In the early-1990s Morgan produced several retrospective collections of her poetry and feminist writings. *Upstairs in the Garden: Poems Selected and New, 1968-1988,* brings together Morgan's classic early poems, including "Monster" and "The Network of Imaginary Mothers," along with many new pieces. Meryl Altman observes in the *Women's Review of Books,* "Morgan's recent poems continue to ask the old politics/aesthetics question, too. What is the proper place of the individual writer in the woman's struggle for a strong collective voice?" Altman praises Morgan's selections in the volume and concludes that her recent "post-feminist" poems, "which accept fragmentation even as they mourn the loss of wholeness, continue to testify to the integrity and urgency of the struggle." Barbara Bolz similarly concludes in *Belles Lettres,* "Morgan is a writer unquestioningly dedicated to women's lives and passions, deeply feminist in the most personal sense and passionately private in the most political sense."

*The Word of a Woman: Feminist Dispatches, 1968-1992* consists of eighteen previously published essays produced by Morgan over a quarter century. Renee Hausmann Shea writes in *Belles Lettres* that the essays, each accompanied by new prefaces and footnotes, "are shot through with optimism and pain. They are written with passion and humility and wit." According to Leora Tannenbaum in the *Women's Review of Books,* the volume "provides a comprehensive overview of feminist issues and slogans since 1968, and should be read by today's third-wave feminists." By asserting the commonality of female subjugation throughout the world, Morgan appeals to "universal sisterhood," a concept in which, as Tannenbaum writes, "[Morgan] imagines the possibility of a shared culture that could exist outside the realm of men and male domination—where battered and harassed women could seek refuge." The volume includes Morgan's well-known essays "Goodbye to All That" and "Theory and Practice: Pornography and Rape." As Tannenbaum notes, "Morgan represents the feminist struggle as trans-historical and trans-cultural."

Like other women writers who share her political concerns, Morgan has received "slings and arrows from all sides," she said in an interview for the *Women's Review of Books.* She concluded, "Somehow there has to be more support for these women. In a country where the written word is not particularly esteemed, and where the message of feminism is complex and vast and not monolithic—and threatening—part of the problems that we're all of us having, well, they just come with the territory. And we have to keep fighting. There are no simple solutions. We chose this."

*BIOGRAPHICAL/CRITICAL SOURCES:*

BOOKS

*Contemporary Literary Criticism,* Volume 2, Gale, 1974.
Morgan, Robin, *Going Too Far: The Personal Chronicle of a Feminist,* Random House, 1977.
Payne, Karen, editor, *Between Ourselves: Letters between Mothers and Daughters, 1750-1982,* Houghton, 1984.

PERIODICALS

*America,* February 17, 1973.
*American Book Review,* March, 1983.
*American Poetry Review,* January, 1977.
*Belles Lettres,* spring, 1991, p. 38; spring, 1993, p. 40.
*Black World,* August, 1971.
*Choice,* May, 1985.
*Christian Century,* March 31, 1971.
*Christian Science Monitor,* May 29, 1971; January 15, 1973.
*Commonweal,* April 2, 1971; January 15, 1973.
*Kirkus Reviews,* September 15, 1992, p. 1171.
*Library Journal,* December 1, 1970; July, 1990, p. 99.
*Los Angeles Times,* December 21, 1982; November 23, 1984.
*Motive,* March 4, 1969.
*Ms.,* September, 1975; March, 1977.
*Nation,* December 14, 1970; March 2, 1985.
*New Leader,* December 14, 1970.
*New Pages,* spring, 1987.
*New Statesman & Society,* June 23, 1989, p. 40.
*New York Times,* October 29, 1970.
*New York Times Book Review,* November 22, 1970; February 21, 1971; November 19, 1972; January 27, 1985; September 27, 1987; April 30, 1989, p. 17; July 15, 1990, p. 32.
*Partisan Review,* January 10, 1980.
*Poetry,* December, 1973; August, 1975; August, 1977.
*Progressive,* January, 1977; August, 1977.
*Psychology Today,* January, 1983.

*Publishers Weekly,* June 1, 1990, p. 53; May 3, 1991, p. 70.

*San Francisco Review of Books,* January, 1983.

*School Library Journal,* August, 1992, p. 156.

*Times Educational Supplement,* January 10, 1987.

*Times Literary Supplement,* November 12, 1982.

*Virginia Quarterly Review,* spring, 1971.

*Washington Post Book World,* November 19, 1972; December 31, 1972; June 12, 1977; June 25, 1989, p. 11.

*Women's Review of Books,* July 8, 1987; October, 1990, p. 16; May, 1993, p. 17.*

\* \* \*

## MOWAT, Farley (McGill) 1921-

*PERSONAL:* Born May 12, 1921, in Belleville, Ontario, Canada; son of Angus McGill (a librarian) and Helen Elizabeth (Thomson) Mowat; married Frances Thornhill, December 21, 1947 (marriage ended, 1959); married Claire Angel Wheeler (a writer), March, 1964; children: (first marriage) Robert Alexander, David Peter. *Education:* University of Toronto, B.A., 1949.

*ADDRESSES: Home*—Port Hope, Ontario, and Cape Breton, Nova Scotia.

*CAREER:* Author. *Military service:* Canadian Army Infantry, 1939-45; became captain.

*AWARDS, HONORS:* President's Medal for best short story, University of Western Ontario, 1952, for "Eskimo Spring"; Anisfield-Wolfe Award for contribution to interracial relations, 1954, for *People of the Deer;* Governor General's Medal, 1957, and Book of the Year Award, Canadian Association of Children's Librarians, both for *Lost in the Barrens;* Canadian Women's Clubs Award, 1958, for *The Dog Who Wouldn't Be;* Hans Christian Andersen International Award, 1958; Boys' Clubs of America Junior Book Award, 1962, for *Owls in the Family;* National Association of Independent Schools Award, 1963, for juvenile books; Hans Christian Andersen Honours List, 1965, for juvenile books; Canadian Centennial Medal, 1967; Stephen Leacock Medal for humor, 1970, and L'Etoile de la Mer Honours List, 1972, both for *The Boat Who Wouldn't Float;* D.Lit., Laurentian University, 1970; Vicky Metcalf Award, 1970; Mark Twain Award, 1971; Doctor of Law from Lethbridge University, 1973, University of Toronto, 1973, and Uni-

versity of Prince Edward Island, 1979; Curran Award, 1977, for "contributions to understanding wolves"; Queen Elizabeth II Jubilee Medal, 1978; Knight of Mark Twain, 1980; Officer, Order of Canada, 1981; Doctor of Literature, University of Victoria, 1982, and Lakehead University, 1986; Author's Award, Foundation for the Advancement of Canadian Letters, 1985, for *Sea of Slaughter;* Book of the Year designation, Foundation for the Advancement of Canadian Letters, and named Author of the Year, Canadian Booksellers Association, both 1988, both for *Virunga;* Gemini Award for best documentary script, 1989, for *The New North;* Take Back the Nation Award, Council of Canadians, 1991; L.H.D., McMaster University, 1994; L.L.D., Queen's University, 1995.

*WRITINGS:*

*NONFICTION*

*People of the Deer,* Little, Brown, 1952, revised edition, McClelland & Stewart, 1975.

*The Regiment,* McClelland & Stewart, 1955, revised edition, 1973.

*The Dog Who Wouldn't Be,* Little, Brown, 1957.

(Editor) Samuel Hearne, *Coppermine Journey: An Account of a Great Adventure,* Little, Brown, 1958.

*The Grey Seas Under,* Little, Brown, 1958.

*The Desperate People,* Little, Brown, 1959, revised, McClelland & Stewart, 1976.

(Editor) *Ordeal by Ice* (first part of "The Top of the World" series), McClelland & Stewart, 1960, Little, Brown, 1961.

*The Serpent's Coil,* McClelland & Stewart, 1961, Little, Brown, 1962.

*Never Cry Wolf,* Little, Brown, 1963, revised edition, McClelland & Stewart, 1973.

*Westviking: The Ancient Norse in Greenland and North America,* Little, Brown, 1965.

(Editor) *The Polar Passion: The Quest for the North Pole, with Selections from Arctic Journals* (second part of "The Top of the World" series), McClelland & Stewart, 1967, Little, Brown, 1968, revised edition, 1973.

*Canada North,* Little, Brown, 1967.

*This Rock within the Sea: A Heritage Lost,* photographs by John de Visser, Little, Brown, 1969, new edition, McClelland & Stewart, 1976.

*The Boat Who Wouldn't Float,* McClelland & Stewart, 1969, Little, Brown, 1970.

*Sibir: My Discovery of Siberia,* McClelland & Stewart, 1970, revised edition, 1973, published as *The Siberians,* Little, Brown, 1971.

*A Whale for the Killing,* Little, Brown, 1972.

*Wake of the Great Sealers,* illustrated by David Blackwood, Little, Brown, 1973.

(Editor) *Tundra: Selections from the Great Accounts of Arctic Land Voyages* (third part of "The Top of the World" series), McClelland & Stewart, 1973, Peregrine Smith, 1990.

(Editor) *Top of the World Trilogy* (includes *Ordeal by Ice, The Polar Passion,* and *Tundra*), McClelland & Stewart, 1976.

*The Great Betrayal: Arctic Canada Now,* Little, Brown, 1976, published as *Canada North Now: The Great Betrayal,* McClelland & Stewart, 1976.

*And No Birds Sang* (memoir), McClelland & Stewart, 1979, Little, Brown, 1980.

*The World of Farley Mowat: A Selection from His Works,* edited by Peter Davison, Little, Brown, 1980.

*Sea of Slaughter,* Atlantic Monthly Press, 1984.

*My Discovery of America,* Little, Brown, 1985.

*Woman in the Mists: The Story of Dian Fossey and the Mountain Gorillas of Africa,* Warner Books, 1987, published as *Virunga: The Passion of Dian Fossey,* McClelland & Stewart, 1987.

*The New Founde Land: A Personal Voyage of Discovery,* McClelland & Stewart, 1989.

*Rescue the Earth,* McClelland & Stewart, 1990.

*My Father's Son: Memories of War and Peace,* Houghton, 1993.

*Born Naked: The Early Adventures of the Author of "Never Cry Wolf,"* Key Porter, 1993, Houghton, 1994.

*Aftermath: Travels in a Post-War World,* Key Porter, 1995.

*FOR YOUNG ADULTS*

*Lost in the Barrens* (novel), illustrated by Charles Geer, Little, Brown, 1956, published as *Two against the North,* illustrated by Alan Daniel, Scholastic-TAB, 1977.

*Owls in the Family,* illustrated by Robert Frankenberg, Little, Brown, 1961.

*The Black Joke* (novel), illustrated by D. Johnson, McClelland & Stewart, 1962, illustrated by Victory Mays, Little, Brown, 1963.

*The Curse of the Viking Grave* (novel), illustrated by Geer, Little, Brown, 1966.

*OTHER*

*The Snow Walker* (short stories), McClelland & Stewart, 1975, Little, Brown, 1976.

Also author of television screenplays *Sea Fare* and *Diary of a Boy on Vacation,* both 1964. Contributor to *Cricket's Choice,* Open Court, 1974; contributor to periodicals, including *Argosy, MacLean's,* and *Saturday Evening Post.*

Mowat's books have been translated into more than thirty languages and anthologized in more than 200 works.

A collection of Mowat's manuscripts is housed at McMaster University, Hamilton, Ontario.

*ADAPTATIONS: A Whale for the Killing* (television movie), American Broadcasting Companies, Inc. (ABC-TV), 1980; *Never Cry Wolf* (feature film), Buena Vista, 1983; *The New North* (documentary), Norwolf/Noralpha/CTV, 1989; *Sea of Slaughter* (award-winning documentary; part of "The Nature of Things" series), Canadian Broadcasting Corporation (CBC-TV), 1990; *Lost in the Barrens* (television movie), Atlantis Films, 1990; *Curse of the Viking Grave* (television movie), Atlantis Films, 1992. Several of Mowat's books have been recorded onto cassette, including *Grey Seas Under, Lost in the Barrens, People of the Deer, The Snow Walker,* and *And No Birds Sang.*

*WORK IN PROGRESS:* Two feature films; an autobiography.

*SIDELIGHTS:* Farley Mowat is one of Canada's most internationally acclaimed writers. His many books for both young-adult and adult readers offer a reflective glimpse at the ill-fated future of wild species at the hand of humankind, and he presents a clear warning as to the consequences of our continued drain on the Earth's limited natural resources. Although often categorized as a nature writer, Mowat considers himself a storyteller or "saga man" whose works derive from his concern about the preservation of all forms of life. An outspoken advocate for the Canadian North with an irreverent attitude toward bureaucracy, Mowat has repeatedly aroused the ire of Canadian officials through his harsh indictments of government policies concerning the treatment of endangered races of people as well as endangered animal species. With characteristic bluntness, Mowat once remarked in *Newsweek:* "Modern man is such an arrogant cement head to believe that he can take without paying."

Mowat first became aware of humanity's outrages against nature in the late-1940s when he accepted a position as a government biologist in the barren lands of northern Canada. He took the assignment in part because it offered him a respite from civilization—Mowat had recently returned from the battlefields of World War II where he served in the Canadian Army and witnessed brutal combat during the invasion of Italy. "I came back from the war rejecting my species," he told Cheryl McCall in *People* magazine. "I hated what had been done to me and what I had done and what man did to man."

Mowat's assignment in the Barrens was to study the area's wolf population and their behavior. The federal government suspected that the wolves were responsible for the dwindling caribou population and enlisted Mowat to get evidence to corroborate their suspicions. However, after months of observing a male wolf and his mate—whom he named George and Angeline—Mowat discovered wolves to be intelligent creatures who ate only what they needed for survival. Subsisting primarily on a diet of field mice, the wolves would only eat an occasional sickly caribou—by killing the weakest of the species, the wolves actually helped strengthen the caribou herd.

Although the results of his study were quickly dismissed by the government, as were any expectations he may have had of further employment, Mowat eventually fashioned his findings into a fictional work, *Never Cry Wolf,* which was published in 1963. A *Chicago Tribune Book World* critic calls Mowat's experience "a perfect example of the bureaucrats getting more than they bargained for." Much to Mowat's dismay, according to a reviewer for *Atlantic,* "the Canadian government . . . has never paid any discernible attention to the information it hired Mr. Mowat to assemble." Fortunately, through his book Mowat's message was heeded by both the reading public and the governments of other countries. Shortly after a translation of *Never Cry Wolf* appeared in Russia, officials in that country banned the slaughter of wolves, whom they had previously thought to be arbitrary killers. Noting the long-range repercussions of the book, David Graber comments in the *Los Angeles Time Book Review* that "by writing *Never Cry Wolf* [Mowat] almost single-handedly reversed the public's image of the wolf, from feared vermin to romantic symbol of the wilderness."

Although not popular with officials of the federal government, *Never Cry Wolf* was welcomed by both readers and critics. Harry C. Kenney notes that the book "delightfully and instructively lifts one into a captivating animal kingdom" in his review for the *Christian Science Monitor.* "This is a fascinating and captivating book, and a tragic one, too," writes Gavin Maxwell in *Book Week,* "for it carries a bleak, deadpan obituary of the wolf family that Mr. Mowat had learned to love and respect. It is an epilogue that will not endear the Canadian Wildlife Service to readers. . . . Once more it is man who displays the qualities with which he has tried to damn the wolf."

During the months spent studying wolves in the Barrens, Mowat also befriended an Inuit tribe called the Ihalmiut, or "People of the Deer," because they depend almost solely on caribou for food, clothing, and shelter. After learning a simplified form of their native language, Mowat was able to learn that the Ihalmiut people had been dwindling in numbers for several years due to the decreasing availability of caribou. Mowat, enraged at the government's apathy toward preserving the tribe, immediately began to compose scathing letters that he distributed to government officials. When such letters only resulted in the loss of his job, he turned his pen to a more productive enterprise. In the book *People of the Deer,* published in 1952, Mowat put the plight of the Ihalmiut squarely before the Canadian people. As *Saturday Review* contributor Ivan T. Sanderson observes: "What [Mowat] learned by living with the pathetic remnants of this wonderful little race of Nature's most perfected gentlemen, learning their language and their history, and fighting the terrifying northern elements at their side, so enraged him that when he came to set down the record, he contrived the most damning indictment of his own government and country, the so-called white race and its Anglo-Saxon branch in particular, the Christian religion, and civilization as a whole, that had ever been written."

Other reviewers have expressed admiration for *People of the Deer.* A *Times Literary Supplement* reviewer writes: "The author traces with a beautiful clarity the material and spiritual bonds between land, deer and people, and the precarious ecological balance which had been struck between the forefathers of this handful of men and the antlered multitude." Albert Hubbell agrees: "It is not often that a writer finds himself the sole chronicler of a whole human society, even of a microcosmic one like the Ihalmiut, and Mowat has done marvelously well at the job, despite a stylistic looseness and a tendency to formlessness," he observes in the *New Yorker.* "Also, his justifiable anger at the government's neglect of the Ihalmiut, who are its wards, intrudes in places where it doesn't belong, but then, as I said, Mowat is something of a fanatic on this subject. His book, just the same, is a fine one." T. Morris Longstreth concludes in *Chris-*

*tian Science Monitor:* "Mr. Mowat says of his book, 'This is a labor of love, and a small repayment to a race that gave me renewed faith in myself and in all men.' It will widen the horizons of many who are at the same time thankful that this explorer did the widening for them."

Mowat has written several other books about the human mistreatment of wildlife. *A Whale for the Killing,* published in 1972, recounts the slow torture of a marooned whale in a pond in Newfoundland. But his most bitter account of humankind's abuse of nonhuman life has been *Sea of Slaughter,* published in 1984. "Built of the accumulated fury of a lifetime," according to Graber, *Sea of Slaughter* has been counted by critics as among the author's most important works. Tracy Kidder notes in the *Washington Post Book World* that compared to *Never Cry Wolf,* this book "is an out and out tirade." The book's title refers to the extinction and near-extinction of sea and land animals along the North Atlantic seaboard in the area extending from Cape Cod north to Labrador. Mowat traces the area's history back to the sixteenth century when the waters teemed with fish, whales, walruses, and seals, and the shores abounded with bison, white bears (now known as polar bears because of their gradual trek northward), and other fur-bearing mammals. Currently, many of these species have been either greatly diminished or extinguished because of "pollution, gross overhunting . . . , loss of habitat, destruction of food supplies, poachings and officially sanctioned 'cullings,'" writes Kidder.

Mowat depicts the stark contrast between past and present in a manner that is tremendously affecting, reviewers note. Although admitting that the book contains some inaccuracies and a lack of footnotes, *Detroit News* contributor Lewis Regenstein claims that these "shortcomings pale in comparison to the importance of its message: We are not only destroying our wildlife but also the Earth's ability to support a variety of life forms, including humans. As Mowat bluntly puts it, 'The living world is dying in our time.'" Graber believes that "the grandest anguish comes from Mowat's unrelenting historical accounts of the sheer *numbers* of whales, bears, salmon, lynx, wolves, bison, sea birds; numbers that sear because they proclaim what we have lost, what we have thrown away." And Ian Darragh writes in *Quill & Quire:* "Mowat's description of the slaughter of millions of shorebirds for sport, for example, is appalling for what it implies about the aggression and violence apparently programmed into man's genetic code. There is little room for humour or Mowat's personal

anecdotes in this epitaph for Atlantic Canada's once bountiful fish and wildlife." Concludes *Commonweal* critic Tom O'Brien: "*Sea of Slaughter* provides some heavier reading [than Mowat's other books]; the weight in the progression of chapters starts to build through the book like a dirge. Nevertheless, it may help to focus the burgeoning animal rights movement in this country and abroad. The cause has no more eloquent spokesperson."

*Sea of Slaughter* received some unintended but nevertheless welcome publicity in 1984 when Mowat was refused entrance into the United States, where he was planning to publicize the book. While boarding a plane at a Toronto airport, Mowat was detained by officials from the United States Immigration and Naturalization Service (INS) who acted on the information that Mowat's name appeared in the *Lookout Book,* a government document that lists the names of those individuals who represent a danger to the security of the United States. Mowat later speculated in the *Chicago Tribune* about some possible reasons for his exclusion: "At first, . . . the assumption was that I was excluded because of the two trips I made to the Soviet Union [in the late-1960s]. . . . Then some guy at the INS supposedly said I was being kept out because I'd threatened the U.S. Armed Forces by threatening to shoot down American aircraft with a .22 caliber rifle. The fact is the *Ottawa Citizen* [where the story supposedly appeared in 1968] can't find any record of it, but that doesn't matter. I admit it, happily." Mowat added that the suggestion was later put forth that the "gun lobby and anti-environmentalists" might have wanted to prevent efforts to promote *Sea of Slaughter.*

Mowat's works for children contain a gentler, more lighthearted echo of his message to adult readers—his nature books for young people have given him a reputation as one of the best known Canadian writers for children outside his homeland. *Lost in the Barrens* is a novel about a pair of teenaged boys who become lost and must face the winter alone in the tundra. *The Dog Who Wouldn't Be* and *Owls in the Family* are memoirs of eccentric family pets. "[Mowat] knows children and what they like and can open doors to adventures both credible and entertaining to his young readers," notes Joseph E. Carver in his essay in the *British Columbia Library Quarterly.* "His stories are credible because Mowat wanted to write them to give permanence to the places, loyalties and experiences of his youth, entertaining because the author enjoys the telling of them." Mowat continues to take his role as a children's author seriously, viewing it as "of vital importance if basic changes for the good are ever to be initiated in any human culture," he noted in *Canadian Library Journal.*

Mowat departs from his usual focus—the Canadian wilderness—in *And No Birds Sang,* a memoir describing his experiences in the Canadian Army Infantry during World War II. Written in 1979, thirty years after his return from the war, Mowat wrote the memoir in response to the growing popularity of the notion that there is honor in dying in the service of one's country. The book chronicles Mowat's initial enthusiasm and determination to fight, the gradual surrender to despair, and its culmination in a horrifying fear of warfare that Mowat calls "The Worm That Never Dies." Reviewers have expressed reservations about the familiar nature of Mowat's theme, but add that Mowat nevertheless manages to bring a fresh perspective to the adage, "War is hell." David Weinberger remarks in *MacLean's:* "Everybody knows that war is hell; it is the author's task to transform that knowledge into understanding." While noting that the book occasionally "bogs down in adjectives and ellipsis," Weinberger praises the work: "It takes a writer of stature—both as an author and as a moral, sensitive person—to make the attempt as valiantly as Mowat has." A similar opinion is expressed by Jean Strouse in *Newsweek:* "That war is hell is not news, but a story told this well serves, particularly in these precarious, saber-rattling days, as a vivid reminder." *And No Birds Sang* has been called by some reviewers a valuable addition to the literature of World War II. *Washington Post Book World* contributor Robert W. Smith calls the book "a powerful chunk of autobiography and a valuable contribution to war literature." *Time* critic R. Z. Sheppard writes: "*And No Birds Sang* needs no rhetoric. It can fall in with the best memoirs of World War II, a classic example of how unexploded emotions can be artfully defused."

In 1985, shortly after the death of noted primatologist Dian Fossey, Mowat was approached by Warner Books to write her biography. Although he initially refused—because he had never written a commissioned book—after reading one of Fossey's *National Geographic* articles, he reconsidered. Mowat told Beverly Slopen of *Publishers Weekly* that while reading Fossey's letters and journals he "began to realize that the importance of the book was her message, not my message. . . . I really became her collaborator. It was the journals that did it. They weren't long, discursive accounts. They were short, raw cries from the heart."

Mowat's biography *Woman in the Mists: The Story of Dian Fossey and the Mountain Gorillas of Africa* was published in 1987. The work relies heavily on Fossey's journal entries and letters to tell the story of her life: Her invitation by anthropologist Louis Leakey to study primates in the African Congo in 1967, an invitation that culminated in an escape to Uganda in the wake of political uprisings, and ultimately in her establishment of a research center on the Rwandan side of the Virunga Mountains where Fossey remained until her death. Fossey's murder has not been solved, but the book "goes a long way toward revealing what it was about her that made a violent death seem inevitable," notes Eugene Linden in the *New York Times Book Review.* Fossey was known to stalk gorilla poachers and she lived by the biblical motto, "An eye for an eye." She also angered government officials by opposing "gorilla tourism" and the development of park land for agrarian purposes. But Mowat's biography also reveals a side of Fossey that was generous, kind, witty, and romantic. She had a succession of affairs throughout her lifetime, including one with Leakey, and longed for a stable, monogamous relationship. Mary Battiata, a *Washington Post Book World* contributor believes that Mowat "puts to rest—forever one hopes—the shopworn notion of Fossey as a misanthrope who preferred animals to her own species." But, she goes on to add, "Though Mowat offers an intriguing and credible solution to the mystery of Fossey's unsolved murder, there is little else that is genuinely new here." *Chicago Tribune* contributor Anita Susan Grossman similarly observes that Mowat "limits himself to presenting excerpts from Fossey's own writings, strung together with the barest of factual narration. As a result, the central drama of Fossey's life remains as murky as the circumstances of her death." Although Linden concurs that *Woman in the Mists* does have several problems, including a lack of footnotes, Mowat's "pedestrian" prose, and "interlocutory words [that] add little to our understanding of Fossey or her world," he adds: "Despite these problems, this is a rare, gripping look at the tragically mingled destinies of a heroic, flawed woman and her beloved mountain gorillas amid the high mists of the Parc des Volcans."

Critical appraisal aside, Mowat states that the writing of Fossey's biography had a profound, sobering effect on him and that he will not undertake another biography. "It was a disturbing experience," he told Slopen. "It's almost as though I were possessed. I wasn't the master. I fought for mastery and I didn't win. It really was a transcendental experience and I'm uncomfortable with it."

Mowat returned to the war memoir genre with *My Father's Son*. Writing in *Books in Canada*, George Kaufman favorably compares the memoir to the earlier work documenting Mowat's experience in World War II, *And No Birds Sang*. While *My Father's Son* covers similar subject matter, notes Kaufman, this later work is distinguished by its more personal focus on Mowat's relationship with his father in the context of his traumatic wartime experience.

Also concerned primarily with the memory of the Second World War, Mowat's *Aftermath* chronicles his car trip through England, France, and Italy in 1952 after he had been commissioned to write the history of his wartime unit. Regarded as a mixture of memoir and travel documentary, the book was appraised by critics as an uneven but nevertheless original and interesting effort. "At its weakest," argues John Allemang in *Quill and Quire*, "*Aftermath* read like a wide-eyed chronicle of an uneventful motoring holiday, where every pub houses a character and every character has a tale to tell." John Bemrose in *MacLean's* similarly faults the memoir's "conventional" qualities and points to the different demands of travel writing as opposed to other forms of nonfiction. "Nevertheless," he concludes, "the sheer originality of the material occasionally asserts itself."

With another memoir, *Born Naked*, Mowat describes the roots of his passion for the natural world in his Canadian childhood, presenting himself, notes John Bemrose in *MacLean's*, "as a child of nature who generally felt much closer to animals than to people." While praising Mowat's evocative and frequently humorous depictions of his youthful encounters with wildlife, critics generally observed that the memoir backs away from deep exploration of personal experience. "It may be humility, or a laudable aversion to pseudo-psychology, that prevents Mowat from delving further into his peculiar understanding of the animal world," suggests Frances Stead Sellers in *Washington Post Book World*. "Or perhaps it simply can't be explained."

Although Mowat has spent nearly a lifetime trying to convince humanity that we cannot continue to abuse nature without serious and sometimes irreversible repercussions, he believes that "in the end, my crusades have accomplished nothing." Mowat continues in *People* magazine: "I haven't saved the wolf, the whales, the seals, primitive man or the outpost people. All I've done is to document the suicidal tendencies of modern man. I'm sure I haven't altered the course of human events one iota. Things will change

inevitably, but it's strictly a matter of the lottery of fate. It has nothing to do with man's intentions."

*BIOGRAPHICAL/CRITICAL SOURCES:*

*BOOKS*

*Authors and Artists for Young Adults,* Volume 1, Gale, 1988, pp. 175-88.
*Children's Literature Review,* Volume 20, Gale, 1990.
*Contemporary Literary Criticism,* Volume 26, Gale, 1983.
*Dictionary of Literary Biography,* Volume 68: *Canadian Writers, 1920-1959, First Series,* Gale, 1988, pp. 253-58.
Egoff, Sheila, *The Republic of Childhood: A Critical Guide to Canadian Children's Literature in English,* Oxford University Press, 1975.
Lucas, Alex, *Farley Mowat,* McClelland & Stewart, 1976.
Mowat, Farley, *And No Birds Sang,* McClelland & Stewart, 1979, Little, Brown, 1980.
*Twentieth-Century Children's Writers,* St. James Press, 1989, pp. 702-03.

*PERIODICALS*

*Atlantic Monthly,* November, 1963; February, 1993, p. 76.
*Audubon,* January, 1973.
*Best Sellers,* February, 1986.
*Books in Canada,* March, 1985; November, 1985; December, 1992, p. 52; December, 1993, p. 33; March, 1996, p. 15.
*Books of the Times,* April, 1980.
*Book Week,* November 24, 1963.
*Book World,* December 31, 1972.
*Canadian Children's Literature,* number 5, 1976; number 6, 1976.
*Canadian Forum,* July, 1974; March, 1976.
*Canadian Geographical Journal,* June, 1974.
*Canadian Literature,* spring, 1978.
*Chicago Tribune,* October 29, 1980; December 23, 1983; May 6, 1985; October 22, 1987.
*Chicago Tribune Book World,* November 13, 1983.
*Christian Science Monitor,* May 1, 1952; October 3, 1963; May 15, 1969; May 10, 1970; April 15, 1971; March 6, 1974.
*Commonweal,* September 6, 1985.
*Contemporary Review,* February, 1978.
*Detroit News,* April 21, 1985.
*Economist,* January 15, 1972.
*Globe and Mail* (Toronto), November 25, 1989.

*Illustrated London News,* September 20, 1952.

*Los Angeles Times,* December 13, 1985.

*Los Angeles Times Book Review,* March 16, 1980; April 28, 1985.

*MacLean's,* October 8, 1979; October 11, 1993, p. 76; December 11, 1995, p. 68; May 20, 1996, p. 16.

*Nation,* June 10, 1968.

*New Republic,* March 8, 1980.

*Newsweek,* February 18, 1980; September 30, 1985.

*New Yorker,* April 26, 1952; May 11, 1968; March 17, 1980.

*New York Times,* December 13, 1965; February 19, 1980.

*New York Times Book Review,* February 11, 1968; June 14, 1970; February 22, 1976; November 6, 1977; February 24, 1980; December 22, 1985; October 25, 1987; March 14, 1993; August 28, 1994, p. 16.

*Observer* (London), March 4, 1973.

*People,* March 31, 1980.

*Publishers Weekly,* October 2, 1987; February 16, 1990, p. 72; February 7, 1994, p. 78.

*Quill and Quire,* December, 1984; September, 1995.

*Saturday Evening Post,* July 29, 1950; April 13, 1957.

*Saturday Night,* October 18, 1952; October 25, 1952; November, 1975; May, 1996, p. 46.

*Saturday Review,* June 28, 1952; April 26, 1969; October 21, 1972.

*School Library Journal,* October, 1994, p. 162; December, 1994, p. 32.

*Scientific American,* March, 1964.

*Sierra,* September, 1978.

*Spectator,* November 21, 1952.

*Time,* February 18, 1980; May 6, 1985; October 26, 1987.

*Times Literary Supplement,* September 12, 1952; March 19, 1971; February 16, 1973.

*Washington Post,* October 9, 1983; April 25, 1985; October 25, 1985.

*Washington Post Book World,* February 24, 1980; May 12, 1985; October 25, 1987, January 10, 1993, p. 3; April 3, 1994, p.8.*

\*   \*   \*

**MURDOCH, (Jean) Iris 1919-**

*PERSONAL:* Born July 15, 1919, in Dublin, Ireland; daughter of Wills John Hughes (a British civil servant) and Irene Alice (Richardson) Murdoch; married John Oliver Bayley (a professor, novelist, critic), 1956. *Education:* Somerville College, Oxford, B.A. (first-class honours), 1942; Newnham College, Cambridge, Sarah Smithson studentship in philosophy, 1947-48. *Religion:* Christian.   *Avocational interests:* Learning languages.

*ADDRESSES: Home*—30 Charlbury Rd., Oxford OX2 6UU, England.

*CAREER:* Writer. British Treasury, London, England, assistant principal, 1942-44; United National Relief and Rehabilitation Administration (UNRRA), administrative officer in London, Belgium, and Austria, 1944-46; Oxford University, St. Anne's College, Oxford, England, fellow and university lecturer in philosophy, 1948-63, honorary fellow, 1963—; Royal College of Art, London, lecturer, 1963-67. Member of Formentor Prize Committee.

*MEMBER:* American Academy of Arts and Sciences, Irish Academy.

*AWARDS, HONORS:* Book of the Year award, *Yorkshire Post,* 1969, for *Bruno's Dream;* Whitehead Literary Award for fiction, 1974, for *The Sacred and Profane Love Machine;* James Tait Black Memorial Prize, 1974, for *The Black Prince;* named Commander, Order of the British Empire, 1976, Dame Commander, 1986; Booker Prize, 1978, for *The Sea, the Sea;* honorary doctorate, Oxford, 1987; medal of honor for literature, National Arts Club, 1990; honorary doctorate, Cambridge, 1993.

*WRITINGS:*

*NOVELS*

*Under the Net,* Viking, 1954, published with introduction and notes by Dorothy Jones, Longmans, Green, 1966, Penguin, 1977.

*The Flight from the Enchanter,* Viking, 1956.

*The Sandcastle,* Viking, 1957.

*The Bell,* Viking, 1958.

*A Severed Head,* Viking, 1961.

*An Unofficial Rose,* Viking, 1962.

*The Unicorn,* Viking, 1963.

*The Italian Girl,* Viking, 1964.

*The Red and the Green,* Viking, 1965.

*The Time of the Angels,* Viking, 1966.

*The Nice and the Good,* Viking, 1968.

*A Fairly Honorable Defeat,* Viking, 1970.

*An Accidental Man,* Viking, 1971.

*Bruno's Dream,* Viking, 1973.

*The Black Prince,* Viking, 1973.

*The Sacred and Profane Love Machine,* Viking, 1974.

*A Word Child,* Viking, 1975.

*Henry and Cato,* Viking, 1977.

*The Sea, the Sea,* Viking, 1978.

*Nuns and Soldiers,* Viking, 1980.

*The Philosopher's Pupil,* Viking, 1983.

*The Good Apprentice,* Chatto & Windus, 1985.

*The Book and the Brotherhood,* Chatto & Windus, 1987.

*The Message to the Planet,* Chatto & Windus, 1989.

*The Green Knight,* Viking, 1994.

*Jackson's Dilemma,* Viking, 1995.

*NONFICTION*

*Sartre: Romantic Rationalist,* Yale University Press, 1953, second edition, Barnes & Noble, 1980 (published in England as *Sartre: Romantic Realist,* Harvester Press, 1980).

(Contributor) *The Nature of Metaphysics,* Macmillan, 1957.

(Author of foreword) Wendy Campbell-Purdie and Fenner Brockaway, *Woman against the Desert,* Gollancz, 1964.

*The Sovereignty of Good over Other Concepts* (Leslie Stephen lecture, 1967), Cambridge University Press, 1967, published with other essays as *The Sovereignty of Good,* Routledge & Kegan Paul, 1970, Schocken, 1971.

*The Fire and the Sun: Why Plato Banished the Artists* (based on the Romanes lecture, 1976), Claredon Press, 1977.

*Reynolds Stone,* Warren, 1981.

*Acastos: Two Platonic Dialogues,* Chatto & Windus, 1986, Penguin, 1987.

*Metaphysics as a Guide to Morals: Philosophical Reflections,* Penguin, 1992.

*PLAYS*

(With J. B. Priestley) *A Severed Head* (three-act; based on the author's novel of the same title; first produced in London at Royale Theatre, October 28, 1964; produced in New York, 1964), Chatto & Windus, 1964, acting edition, Samuel French, 1964.

(With James Saunders) *The Italian Girl* (based on the author's novel of the same title; first produced at Bristol Old Vic, December, 1967), Samuel French, 1968.

*The Servants and the Snow* (first produced in London at Greenwich Theatre, September 29, 1970), Chatto & Windus, 1973, Viking, 1974.

*The Three Arrows* (first produced in Cambridge at Arts Theatre, October 17, 1972), Chatto & Windus, 1973, Viking, 1974.

*Art and Eros,* produced in London, 1980.

*The Servants* (opera libretto; adapted from the author's play *The Servants and the Snow*), produced in Cardiff, Wales, 1980.

*The Black Prince* (based on the author's novel of the same title), produced in London at Aldwych Theatre, 1989.

*OTHER*

*A Year of Birds* (poems), Compton Press, 1978.

Contributor to periodicals, including the *Listener, Yale Review, Chicago Review, Encounter, New Statesman, Nation,* and *Partisan Review.*

*ADAPTATIONS: A Severed Head* (based on her novel and play) was filmed by Columbia Pictures, 1971; the film rights to *A Fairly Honourable Defeat* were sold in 1972.

*SIDELIGHTS:* Described by *Commonweal*'s Linda Kuehl as "a philosopher by trade and temperament," Iris Murdoch is known for her novels full of characters embroiled in philosophical turmoil. Though originally aligned with the existentialist movement, Murdoch's philosophy quickly broadened, and critics now regard her works as "novels of ideas." In addition, her plays and non-fiction works encompass similar philosophical debates and add to her reputation as one of her generation's most prolific and important writers. Murdoch's body of work has proved influential in twentieth-century literature and thought; "she draws eclectically on the English tradition" of Charles Dickens, Jane Austen, and William Thackeray "and at the same time extends it in important ways," writes John Fletcher in *Concise Dictionary of British Literary Biography.*

Though born an only child of Anglo-Irish parents in Ireland, Murdoch grew up in the suburbs of London and earned a scholarship to a private school when she was thirteen. At Somerville College at Oxford, Murdoch was involved in drama and arts when not immersed in her literature and philosophy studies. Her left-wing politics led her to join the Communist party for a brief time in the early-1940s, an affiliation that caused the United States to deny her a visa to study in the country after winning a scholarship several years later. Following her distinguished scholastic career, Murdoch worked at the British Treasury during World War II and later for the United Nations Relief and Rehabilitation Administration. While working for the United Nations, she traveled to Belgium where she met Jean-Paul Sartre as well as the French writer Raymond Quenteau, whose writings greatly influenced her first novel, *Under the Net.* During the 1950s, Murdoch taught philosophy at St. Anne's College at Oxford, and said of the experience to Gill Davie and Leigh Crutchley in a *Publishers Weekly* interview: "I love teaching, and if I were not able to teach philosophy I would happily teach something else."

The existentialist movement, a philosophy that became popular in the 1950s in light of the wide-spread despair caused by World War II, was the impetus for Murdoch's first book. Popularized by such writers as Albert Camus and Jean-Paul Sartre, existentialism proposed that because human existence is meaningless, people must act according to their own free will and may never know the difference between right and wrong. *Sartre: Romantic Rationalist* chronicled the thoughts and influences of one of existentialism's most popular writers. Many critics began to view Murdoch as an emerging theorist of the philosophy, but as she professed to John Russell in the *New York Times:* "I was never a Sartrean, or an existentialist." Focusing on Sartre's influential *Being and Nothingness,* Murdoch examines Sartre's philosophy, and the events in his personal life that led him to his conclusions. Critics commended Murdoch's views; Wallace Fowlie in *Commonweal* calls it "one of the most objective and useful" interpretations of Sartre's works, and Stuart Hampshire in *New Statesman* hails Murdoch as "one who understands the catastrophes of intellectual politics, and who can still take them seriously."

Several critics noted similarities between Sartre and Murdoch. William Van O'Connor writes in *The New University Wits, and the End of Modernism,* that like Sartre, Murdoch views man as a "lonely creature in an absurd world . . . impelled to make moral decisions, the consequences of which are uncertain." Like Sartre, says Warner Berthoff in *Fictions and Events,* Murdoch believes that writing is "above all else a collaboration of author and reader in an act of freedom." Bertoff continues: "Following Sartre she has

spoken pointedly of the making of works of art as not only a 'struggle for freedom' but as a 'task which does not come to an end.'"

Though there are similarities, critics note some important differences between the two philosophers. Gail Kmetz writes in *Ms.* that Murdoch "rejected Sartre's emphasis on the isolation and anguish of the individual in a meaningless world . . . because she felt it resulted in a sterile and futile solipsism [a belief that the self is the only existent thing]. She considers the individual always as a part of society, responsible to others as well as to herself or himself; and insists that freedom means respecting the independent being of others, and that subordinating others' freedom to one's own is a denial of freedom itself. Unlike Sartre, Murdoch sees the claims of freedom and love as identical." Murdoch states in *Chicago Review* that "love is the perception of individuals . . . the extremely difficult realisation that something other than oneself is real," and that only when one is capable of love is one free. Murdoch recently told *CA* that she was critical of Sartre's concept of "a leap into pure freedom" and "his distinction between liberated free persons (intellectuals, artists, wild and courageous, etc.) and the dull, machine-like petty bourgeois [not quite unlike Derrida's later distinction]." But, she adds, "I do not 'follow' Sartre or Derrida."

One of Murdoch's major themes in her fiction is how best to respect the "reality" of others—how best to live "morally." Together with questions of "love" and "freedom," it comprises her major concern. "Miss Murdoch's pervasive theme has been the quest for a passion beyond any center of self," explains *New York Times Book Review* critic David Bromwich. "What her characters seek may go by the name of Love or God or the Good: mere physical love is the perilous and always tempting idol that can become destroyer." "The basic idea," says Joyce Carol Oates in the *New Republic,* "seems to be that centuries of humanism have nourished an unrealistic conception of the powers of the will: we have gradually lost the vision of a reality separate from ourselves. . . . Twentieth-century obsessions with the authority of the individual, the 'existential' significance of subjectivity, are surely misguided, for the individual cannot be (as he thinks of himself, proudly) a detached observer, free to invent or reimagine his life." The consequences of trying to do so are repeatedly explored in Murdoch's fiction, beginning with her first published novel, *Under the Net.*

Based on Austrian philosopher Ludwig Wittgenstein's idea that we each build our own "net" or system for structuring our lives—"the net," Murdoch tells *CA,* "of language under which we may seek for what is real"—*Under the Net* describes the wanderings of Jake Donaghue as he attempts to structure his. However, "planned ways of life are . . . traps," observes James Gindin in *Postwar British Fiction,* "no matter how carefully or rationally the net is woven, and Jake discovers that none of these narrow paths really works." Only after a series of comic misadventures (which change his attitude rather than his circumstances) is Jake able to accept the contingencies of life and the reality of other people. He throws off the net, an act which takes great courage according to Kmetz, "for nothing is more terrifying than freedom." *Under the Net* attracted much critical praise; Davie and Crutchley note that with just one novel to her credit, Murdoch became one of her generation's outstanding English writers.

Though situations vary from book to book, the protagonists in Murdoch's novels generally fashion a "net" of some kind. It may consist of a set of community mores, or a societal role. For Hilary Burde, protagonist of *A Word Child,* the net is a fixed routine. An unloved, illegitimate child, Hilary becomes a violent juvenile delinquent. When he is befriended by a teacher, he learns that he possesses a remarkable skill with words. In the rigid structure of grammar he seeks shelter from life's randomness. He is awarded a scholarship to Oxford and begins what should be a successful career, However, as *New York Times* critic Bromwich explains, "The structure of things can bear only so much ordering: his university job ends disastrously with an adulterous love affair that is indirectly responsible for two deaths." The story opens twenty years later, when Gunnar—the husband of Hilary's former lover—appears in the government office where Hilary holds a menial job. "The novel's subject," explains Lynne Sharon Schwartz in *Nation,* "is what Hilary will do about his humiliation, his tormenting guilt and his need for forgiveness."

What he does, according to Schwartz, is the worst possible thing. "He attempts to order his friends and his days into the kind of strict system he loves in grammar," she says. "This rigid life is not only penance but protection as well, against chaos, empty time, and the unpredictable impulses of the self. The novel shows the breakdown of the system: people turn up on unexpected days, they refuse—sometimes comically—to act the roles assigned them, and Hilary's

dangerous impulses do come forth and insist on playing themselves out." The tragedy of Hilary's early days is repeated. He falls in love with Gunnar's second wife; they meet in secret and are discovered. Once more by accident Hilary commits his original crime.

"At the novel's conclusion," writes *Saturday Review*'s Bruce Allen, "we must consider which is the illusion: the optimist's belief that we can atone for our crimes and outlive them or the nihilist's certainty (Hilary expresses it) that people are doomed, despite their good intentions, to whirl eternally in a muddle of 'penitence, remorse, resentment, violence, and hate.'" David Bromwich interprets the moral issue somewhat differently. "Hilary, the artist-figure without an art," he says, "wants to make the world (word) conform to his every design, and is being guided to the awareness that its resistance to him is a lucky thing. . . . Hilary must consent at last to the arbitrariness of an order imposed on him." Learning to accept the chaos of life without the aid of patterns or categories is a constant struggle for Murdoch's characters.

"I believe we live in a fantasy world, a world of illusion. And the great task in life is to find reality," Murdoch told Rachel Billington in a London *Times* interview. However, the creation of art, she told *Publishers Weekly,* should be the novelist's goal. "I don't think a novel should be a committed statement of political and social criticism," she says. "They should aim at being beautiful. . . . Art holds a mirror to nature, and I think it's a very difficult thing to do," Murdoch continues. The way Murdoch mirrors nature is by creating what she calls "real characters." According to Berthoff in *Fictions and Events,* these are "personages who will be 'more than puppets' and at the same time other than oneself." When asked why these characters are usually male, Murdoch told *CA:* "I find no difficulty in imagining men. . . . I am very much concerned about the (still distant) liberation of women. . . . [but] I do not want to write about 'women's problems' in any narrow, specialized sense. I have female narrators, too. I just identify more with the men."

However, Linda Kuehl explains in *Modern Fiction Studies,* Murdoch fails in her attempt to create these "real characters." Her propensity for nineteenth century characters produces many "types" that populate her novels, and "in each successive novel there emerges a pattern of predictable and predetermined types. These include the enchanter or enchantress—occult, godly, foreign, ancient—who is torn between exhibitionism and introspection, egoism and generosity, cruelty and pity; the observer, trapped between love and fear of the enchanter, who thinks in terms of ghosts, spells, demons and destiny, and imparts an obfuscated view of life; and the accomplice, a peculiar mixture of diabolical intention and bemused charm, who has dealings with the enchanters and power over the observers," analyzes Kuehl. "Though she produces many people," Kuehl continues, "each is tightly controlled in a super-imposed design, each is rigidly cast in a classical Murdochian role."

Lawrence Graver in the *New York Times Book Review* expresses a similar view: "In practice, the more she [talks] about freedom and opaqueness the more over-determined and transparent her novels [seem] to become. . . . Despite the inventiveness of the situations and the brilliance of the design, Miss Murdoch's philosophy has recently seemed to do little more than make her people *theoretically* interesting." Oates mentions this as well in *New Republic*, Murdoch's novels are "structures in which ideas, not things, and certainly not human beings flourish." In *The Novel Now*, Anthony Burgess compares Murdoch to a puppeteer who exerts complete control: "[Murdoch's] characters dress, talk, act like ourselves, but they are caught up in a purely intellectual pattern, a sort of contrived sexual dance in which partners are always changing. They seem to be incapable of free choice."

*The Message to the Planet*, Murdoch's twenty-fourth novel, published in 1989, encompasses many of Murdoch's familiar themes and conflicts. Marcus Vallar is a somewhat sinister mathematics genius-turned-philosopher; one of "'pure thought' who pushes his ideas to the point where they might actually kill him through their sheer intensity," says Anatole Broyard in the *New York Times Book Review*. A dying man believes Vallar has cursed him. The man sends his friend, Alfred Ludens, in search of Vallar, hoping that Vallar will be able to cure him. Miraculously, Vallar cures the man, and Ludens is so impressed by the event that he becomes Vallar's disciple. The book's other plot involves Luden's friend, Franca. In her quest for perfect love, Franca tolerates her husband's infidelities while she nurses the dying man. After he recovers, she must deal with her husband's affairs, and eventually she consents to letting one of his lovers move in with them.

Though these creatures of an educated middle-class live in a society that Toronto *Globe and Mail* reviewer Phyllis Gotlieb calls "hermetic," they "struggle vividly and convincingly to escape the chaos beneath their frail lives," Gottlieb continues. "The nature of discipleship is a subject Murdoch has made her own," claims Henry Louis Gates, Jr. in a *Village Voice* review of *The Message to the Planet*, "perhaps because it is the most compelling version of one of her great subjects—the character who desperately pursues his fantasy of someone else." Christopher Lehmann-Haupt of the *New York Times* adds to a common perception of Murdoch's writing by stating that "Murdoch's characters are paper thin and as contrived as origami decorations." Despite this, Lehmann-Haupt continues, "they burn with such moral passion that we watch them with the utmost fascination." He also notes that Murdoch's message is "predictably" that "humans are accidental beings with only love to make life bearable in a random universe."

With *Metaphysics as a Guide to Morals* Murdoch turned to a nonfiction presentation of her philosophical views. Diogenes Allen in *Commonweal* characterizes Murdoch's philosophical position in the book as consistent with her previous writings, "summarized as an update of Plato's allegory of the cave" and asserting the immanence of "the Good." Focusing predominantly on morality, Murdoch recommends that the Christian conception of God be replaced with a neo-Platonic conception of the Good. "Now she applies to her position the expressions 'neo-Christianity' and 'modern Christianity,'" comments Allen. *Metaphysics as a Guide to Morals* generated mixed responses from philosophers such as Simon Blackburn, who faults Murdoch's advocation of "salvation through Platonized religion" in his review in the *Times Literary Supplement*. Alasdair MacIntyre in the *New York Times Book Review*, however, notes potential critical disagreements with Murdoch's position but asserts that "it is important not to allow such disagreements to distract attention from what is to be learned from this book, both from its central theses and from an impressive range of topics . . . among them the relationship of artistic to moral experience, the relevance of deconstructive arguments and the nature of political morality."

In 1993's *The Green Knight*, Murdoch tries her hand at retelling the powerful tale of Sir Gawain and his unkillable foe, the Green Knight. In the original story, the Green Knight challenges any of King Arthur's knights to chop off his head; Sir Gawain obliges, but the beheaded Green Knight does not die. In Murdoch's tale, the role of Sir Gawain is played by Lucas Graffe, a historian who plots the murder of his brother, Clement. Before he can bludgeon his brother, though, a stranger—possibly a mugger—steps in and takes the blow. Months later the stranger, Peter Mir, returns, seeking justice from Lucas. "What an outline of the plot . . . fails to convey is the warmth and humour of this book, and the sheer narrative verve," writes A. N. Wilson in *Spectator.* "It is hard to put down."

"Reading [Murdoch's] work is like watching an expert needlewoman embroider, with fine silk thread and a dazzling array of stitches, a large, intricate, multicolored piece of fancywork," comments *New York Times Book Review* contributor Linda Simon. "But as the design becomes more complicated and the patterns more repetitious, one senses that the embroiderer may realize more pleasure than the viewer." Tom Shippey, writing in the *Times Literary Supplement,* also found problems with *The Green Knight*—in particular, a lack of plausibility. "It is not a poor grip on reality which strikes on first on reading this novel," he writes, "rather, its poor grip on *practicality.*" Still, the *New Statesman & Society*'s Kathryn Hughes proclaims the novel "a thoroughly good suspense" story.

Reviewing Murdoch's 1995 novel *Jackson's Dilemma* in *The Spectator,* Caroline Moore argues that Murdoch's detractors are members of what Murdoch has termed the "journalistic" (or realistic) school of modern fiction, which rejects elements of the romance tradition from which much of Murdoch's fiction is derived. "[Murdoch's] novels often adapt romantic genres—the love-comedy, the gothic tale," comments Moore. "And they are also romantic in subject and spirit." The premise of the novel is the disaster, mystery, and comedy surrounding the sudden disappearance of Edward Lannion's bride-to-be on the eve of their wedding day. While Lorna Sage of *The Times Literary Supplement* praises the work as "hilarious and horrible—a mystic farce," Michiko Kakutani of the *New York Times* expresses disappointment with the novel's "highly convoluted plot filled with improbable coincidences and disasters, and a glossy veneer of mythic allusions and philosophical asides."

Murdoch lived for many years in the English countryside (she now lives in the city of Oxford) with her husband, John Bayley, a respected literary critic, and enjoys gardening when she is not writing. She pays little attention to critical reviews of her work, even those that are favorable. Murdoch told *CA* that this is because "articles I have glanced at seem on the whole unperceptive, including the friendly ones." Her writing is deliberate and well thought out; she told *CA*

about the process: "I have always made a very careful plan of the whole novel before writing the first sentence. I want to keep the purely inventive stage (plot, characters) open as long as possible." In addition, all of her writing is done longhand. "I don't see how anyone can think with a typewriter," she told Davie and Crutchley. Her most recent novels average more than 500 pages each; a length that Murdoch insists is necessary because it enables them to encompass "more substance, more thoughts," she told a London *Times* interviewer. The London *Times* also reports that "her enemies are word processors . . . tight, crystalline, first person novels, existentialism, and analytical philosophy."

Despite Murdoch's implication that there is room for improvement in her work, (she confessed to the London *Times* in a 1988 interview that she would "like to understand philosophy, [and] I'm just beginning to now"), many reviewers praise the writing she has done. "She wears her formidable intelligence with a careless swagger," writes *Encounter*'s Jonathan Raban, "and her astonishingly fecund, playful imagination looks as fresh and effortless as ever. . . . Part of the joy of reading Iris Murdoch is the implicit assurance that there will be more to come, that the book in hand is an installment in a continuing work which grows more and more important as each new novel is added to it." Adds Broyard: "We have to keep revising our expectations of what her books are about—usually we find that we must travel farther and over more difficult terrain than we're accustomed to."

In 1995 Murdoch announced that she was suffering from severe writer's block, an admission that was later altered in 1996 when her husband John Bayley informed *The Daily Telegraph* of London that she in fact was a victim of Alzheimer's Disease. Realizing that her writer's block was attributable to biological forces beyond her control, Murdoch commented: "I'm afraid I am waiting in vain [to write]. Perhaps I had better find some other kind of job."

*BIOGRAPHICAL/CRITICAL SOURCES:*

*BOOKS*

Antonaccio, Maria, and William Schweiker, editors, *Iris Murdoch and the Search for Human Goodness,* University of Chicago Press, 1996.

Baldanza, Frank, *Iris Murdoch,* Twayne, 1974.

Berthoff, Warner, *Fictions and Events: Essays in Criticism and Literary History,* Dutton, 1971.

Bradbury, Malcolm, and David Palmer, *The Contemporary English Novel,* Edward Arnold, 1979, pp. 68-74.

Bradbury, Malcolm, *Possibilities: Essays on the State of the Novel,* Oxford University Press, 1973, pp. 231-46.

Burgess, Anthony, *The Novel Now: A Guide to Contemporary Fiction,* Norton, 1967.

Byatt, Antonia S., *Degrees of Freedom: The Novels of Iris Murdoch,* Barnes & Noble, 1965.

Conradi, P. J., *Iris Murdoch: Work for the Spirit,* Macmillan, 1985.

*Concise Dictionary of British Literary Biography,* Volume 8, Gale, 1992.

*Contemporary Literary Criticism,* Gale, Volume 1, 1973, Volume 2, 1974, Volume 3, 1975, Volume 4, 1975, Volume 6, 1976, Volume 8, 1978, Volume 11, 1979, Volume 15, 1980, Volume 22, 1982, Volume 31, 1985, Volume 51, 1989.

*Dictionary of Literary Biography,* Volume 14: *British Novelists Since 1960,* Gale, 1982.

Dipple, Elizabeth, *Iris Murdoch: Work for the Spirit,* University of Chicago Press, 1981.

Fletcher, John, *Iris Murdoch: A Descriptive Primary and Annotated Secondary Bibliography,* Garland, 1983.

Gindin, James, *Postwar British Fiction,* University of California Press, 1962.

Gerstenberger, Donna, *Iris Murdoch,* Bucknell University Presses, 1975.

Gordon, David J., *Iris Murdoch's Fables of Unselfing,* University of Missouri Press, 1995.

Heusel, Barbara Stevens, *Patterened Aimlessness: Iris Murdoch's Novels of the 1970s and 1980s,* University of Georgia Press, 1995.

Kellman, Steven G., *The Self-Begetting Novel,* Macmillan, 1980, pp. 87-93.

Kermode, Frank, *Modern Essays,* Fontana, 1971, pp. 261-66.

O'Connor, Patricia J., *To Love the Good: The Moral Philosophy of Iris Murdoch,* P. Lang, 1996.

O'Connor, William Van, *The New University Wits, and the End of Modernism,* Southern Illinois University Press, 1963, pp. 54-74.

Rabinowitz, Rubin, *Iris Murdoch,* Columbia University Press, 1968.

Spear, Hilda D., *Iris Murdoch,* St. Marin's Press, 1995.

Stade, George, editor, *Six Contemporary British Novelists,* Columbia University Press, 1976, pp. 271-332.

*Thinkers of the Twentieth Century,* St. James, 1987.

Todd, Richard, *Iris Murdoch: The Shakespearean Interest,* Barnes & Noble, 1979.

Todd, *Iris Murdoch,* Methuen, 1984.

Wolff, Peter, *The Disciplined Heart: Iris Murdoch and Her Novels,* University of Missouri Press, 1966.

*PERIODICALS*

*American Scholar,* summer, 1993, p. 466.

*Atlantic,* March, 1988, p. 100; March, 1990, p. 116; March, 1994, p. 130.

*Chicago Review,* autumn, 1959.

*Commonweal,* November 5, 1953; May 18, 1990, p. 326; June 14, 1991, p. 399; April 23, 1993, p. 24; April 8, 1994, p. 21.

*Economist,* October 24, 1987, p. 107; October 14, 1989, p. 104; September 25, 1993, p. 99.

*Encounter,* July, 1974.

*Globe and Mail* (Toronto), October 28, 1989.

*Interview,* November, 1992, p. 80.

*Listener,* April 27, 1978, pp. 533-35.

*Modern Fiction Studies,* (Iris Murdoch issue) autumn, 1959.

*Ms.,* July, 1976.

*Nation,* March 29, 1975; October 11, 1975; January 8, 1996, p. 32.

*National Review,* April 1, 1988, p. 52.

*New Leader,* April 16, 1990, p. 19.

*New Republic,* November 18, 1978; June 6, 1988, p. 40; March 5, 1990, p. 40.

*New Statesman,* January 2, 1954; January 8, 1988, p. 33.

*New Statesman & Society,* October 6, 1989, p. 38; September 17, 1993, pp. 39-40.

*New Yorker,* May 18, 1987, p. 113.

*New York Review of Books,* March 31, 1988, p. 36; March 4, 1993, p. 3.

*New York Times,* January 6, 1981; February 22, 1990; January 9, 1996, p. 24.

*New York Times Book Review,* September 13, 1964; February 8, 1970; August 24, 1975; November 20, 1977; December 17, 1978; August 10, 1980; January 4, 1981; March 7, 1982; January 4, 1987, p. 107; January 31, 1988, p. 1 and 26; February 4, 1990, p. 3; January 3, 1993, p. 9; January 9, 1994, p. 7; January 7, 1996, p. 6.

*Observer,* October 25, 1992.

*Publishers Weekly,* December 13, 1976; November 1, 1993, p. 64; October 23, 1995, p. 57.

*Saturday Review,* October 5, 1974.

*Spectator,* September 18, 1993, p. 42; October 7, 1995.

*Times* (London), April 25, 1983; January 23, 1988.

*Times Literary Supplement,* October 23, 1992; September 10, 1993, p. 20; September 29, 1995.

*Village Voice,* July 17, 1990, p. 73.
*Yale Review,* April, 1992, p. 207.*

\* \* \*

**NEY, Patrick**
See BOLITHO, (Henry) Hector

\* \* \*

**NICHOLSON, C. R.**
See NICOLE, Christopher (Robin)

\* \* \*

**NICHOLSON, Christina**
See NICOLE, Christopher (Robin)

\* \* \*

**NICHOLSON, Robin**
See NICOLE, Christopher (Robin)

\* \* \*

**NICOLE, Christopher (Robin) 1930-**
(Daniel Adams, Leslie Arlen, Robin Cade, Peter Grange, Nicholas Grant, Caroline Gray, Mark Logan, Simon McKay, C. R. Nicholson, Christina Nicholson, Robin Nicholson, Alan Savage, Alison York, Andrew York; Max Marlow, a joint pseudonym)

*PERSONAL:* Born December 7, 1930, in Georgetown, British Guiana (now Guyana); son of Jack (a police officer) and Jean Dorothy (Logan) Nicole; married Regina Ameila Barnett, March 31, 1951, (divorced); married Diana Mary Bachmann; children: (first marriage) Bruce, Jack, Julie, Ursula. *Education:* Attended Harrison College, Barbados, and Queen's College, British Guiana. *Avocational interests:* Sailing.

*ADDRESSES: Home*—Marlow House, St. Jacques, St. Peter Port, Guernsey GY1 1SW, Channel Islands, England. *Agent*—Maggie Noach Literary Agency, London W14 0AB, England.

*CAREER:* Writer. Clerk, Royal Bank of Canada in West Indian branches, 1947-56.

*WRITINGS:*

*West Indian Cricket* (nonfiction), Phoenix House (London), 1957.
*Off White,* Jarrolds (London), 1959.
*Shadows in the Jungle,* Jarrolds, 1961.
*Ratoon* (historical novel), St. Martin's (New York City), 1962.
*Dark Noon* (historical novel), Jarrolds, 1963.
*Amyot's Cay* (historical novel), Jarrolds, 1964.
*Blood Amyot* (historical novel), Jarrolds, 1964.
*The Amyot Crime* (historical novel), Jarrolds, 1965, Bantam (New York City), 1974.
*The West Indies: Their People and History* (nonfiction), Hutchinson, 1965.
*White Boy,* Hutchinson (London), 1966.
*The Self-Lovers,* Hutchinson, 1968.
*The Thunder and the Shouting,* Doubleday (New York City), 1969.
*The Longest Pleasure,* Hutchinson, 1970.
*The Face of Evil,* Hutchinson, 1971.
*Lord of the Golden Fan,* Cassell (London), 1973.
*Heroes,* Corgi (London), 1973.
*Introduction to Chess* (nonfiction), Corgi, 1973.
*Caribee,* St. Martin's, 1974.
*The Devil's Own,* St. Martin's, 1975.
*Mistress of Darkness,* St. Martin's, 1976.
*Black Dawn,* St. Martin's, 1977.
*Sunset,* St. Martin's, 1978.
*The Secret Memoirs of Lord Byron* (fictional autobiography), Lippincott (Philadelphia), 1978, published as *Lord of Sin,* Corgi, 1980.
*Haggard,* New American Library (New York City), 1980.
*Haggard's Inheritance,* M. Joseph (London), 1981, published as *The Inheritors,* New American Library, 1981.
*Brothers and Enemies,* Jove (New York City), 1982.
*Lovers and Outlaws,* Jove, 1982.
*The Crimson Pagoda,* New American Library, 1983.
*The Scarlet Princess,* New American Library, 1984.
*The Sun Rises,* Hamlyn (London), 1984.
*The Seeds of Rebellion,* Severn House (London), 1984.
*Red Dawn,* M. Joseph, 1985.
*The Sun and the Dragon,* Hamlyn, 1985.

*The Sun on Fire,* Arrow (London), 1985.
*Wild Harvest,* Severn House, 1985.
*Old Glory,* Severn House, 1986.
*The Sea and the Sand,* Severn House, 1986.
*The Ship with No Name,* Severn House, 1987.
*Iron Ships, Iron Men,* Severn House, 1987.
*The Wind of Destiny,* Severn House, 1987.
*The Power and the Glory,* Severn House, 1988.
*The High Country,* Century (London), 1988.
*The Regiment,* Century, 1988, St. Martin's, 1989.
*Raging Seas, Searing Skies,* Severn House, 1988.
*Pearl of the Orient,* Century, 1988.
*The Happy Valley,* Century, 1989.
*The Command,* Century, 1989.
*Dragon's Blood,* Century, 1989.
*The Triumph,* Century, 1989.
*Dark Sun,* Century, 1990.
*Sword of Fortune,* Century, 1990.
*Sword of Empire,* Century, 1991.
*Days of Wine and Roses,* Severn House, 1991.
*The Titans,* Severn House, 1992.
*Resumption,* Severn House, 1992.
*The Last Battle,* Severn House, 1993.
*Bloody Sunrise,* Severn House, 1993.
*Bloody Sunset,* Severn House, 1994.
*The Seeds of Power,* Severn House, 1995.
*The Masters,* Severn House, 1995.
*The Red Tide,* Severn House, 1996.
*The Red Gods,* Severn House, 1996.

UNDER PSEUDONYM LESLIE ARLEN

*Love and Honor,* Jove, 1980.
*War and Passion,* Jove, 1981.
*Fate and Dreams,* Jove, 1981.
*Destiny and Desire,* Jove, 1982.
*Rage and Desire,* Jove, 1982.
*Hope and Glory,* Jove, 1984.

UNDER PSEUDONYM ROBIN CADE

*The Fear Dealers* (thriller), Simon & Schuster (New York City), 1974.

UNDER PSEUDONYM PETER GRANGE

*King Creole* (historical novel), Jarrolds, 1966.
*The Devil's Emissary* (historical novel), Jarrolds, 1968.
*The Tumult at the Gate* (historical novel), Jarrolds, 1970.
*The Golden Goddess* (historical novel), Jarrolds, 1973.

UNDER PSEUDONYM NICHOLAS GRANT

*Khan,* Little, Brown, 1993.
*Siblings,* Little, Brown, 1994.

UNDER PSEUDONYM CAROLINE GRAY

*Treasures,* Fawcett (New York City), 1984, published in England as *First Class,* M. Joseph, 1984.
*So Grand,* Fawcett, 1985, published as *Hotel De Luxe,* M. Joseph, 1985.
*White Rani,* Fawcett, 1986.
*Victoria's Walk,* M. Joseph, 1986, Fawcett, 1988.
*Shadow of Death,* Severn House, 1987.
*The Third Life,* St. Martin's, 1988.
*Blue Water, Black Depths,* Severn House, 1991.
*The Daughter,* Severn House, 1992.
*Golden Girl,* Severn House, 1992.
*Spares,* Severn House, 1993.
*Spawn of the Devil,* Severn House, 1993.
*Sword of the Devil,* Severn House, 1994.
*Death of the Devil,* Severn House, 1994.
*A Women of Her Time,* Severn House, 1995.
*Child of Fortune,* Severn House, 1995.
*Crossbow,* Severn House, 1996.

UNDER PSEUDONYM MARK LOGAN

*Guillotine,* Macmillan (New York City), 1976, published as *French Kiss,* New American Library, 1978.
*Tricolour: A Novel of the French Revolution,* Macmillan, 1976, published as *The Captain's Woman,* New American Library, 1979.
*Brumaire,* St. Martin's, 1978, published as *December Passion,* New American Library, 1979.

WITH WIFE, DIANA BACHMANN; UNDER PSEUDONYM MAX MARLOW

*Her Name Will Be Faith,* New English Library, 1988.
*The Red Death,* New English Library, 1989.
*Meltdown,* New English Library, 1991.
*Growth,* Severn House, 1993.
*Arctic Peril,* Severn House, 1993.
*Where the River Rises,* Severn House, 1994.
*Shadow at Evening,* Severn House, 1994.
*The Burning Rocks,* Severn House, 1995.
*Hell's Children,* Severn House, 1996.

UNDER PSEUDONYM SIMON McKAY

*The Seas of Fortune,* Severn House, 1984.
*The Rivals,* Severn House, 1985.

*UNDER PSEUDONYM CHRISTINA NICHOLSON*

*The Power and the Passion* (historical novel), Fawcett, 1977.
*The Savage Sands* (historical novel), Coward (New York City), 1978.
*The Queen of Paris* (historical novel), Corgi, 1979.

*UNDER PSEUDONYM ROBIN NICHOLSON*

*A Passion for Treason* (thriller), Jove, 1980, published in England under the name C. R. Nicholson as *The Friday Spy*, Corgi, 1980.

*UNDER PSEUDONYM ALAN SAVAGE*

*Ottoman*, Macdonald Futura (London), 1990.
*Mughol*, Macdonald Futura, 1991.
*The Eight Banners*, Macdonald Futura, 1992.
*The Last Bannerman*, Macdonald Futura, 1993.
*Queen of Night*, Little, Brown, 1993.
*Queen of Lions*, Little, Brown, 1993.
*Eleanor of Aquitaine*, Severn House, 1995.
*Queen of Love*, Severn House, 1995.
*The Sword and the Scalpel*, Severn House, 1996.
*The Sword and the Jungle*, Severn House, 1996.

*UNDER PSEUDONYM ALISON YORK*

*The Fire and the Rope* (historical novel), Jove, 1979.
*The Scented Sword*, Berkley (New York City), 1980.

*UNDER PSEUDONYM ANDREW YORK*

*The Eliminator*, Hutchinson, 1966, Lippincott, 1967.
*The Coordinator*, Lippincott, 1967.
*The Predator*, Lippincott, 1968.
*The Dominator*, Lippincott, 1969.
*The Deviator*, Lippincott, 1969.
*Operation Destruct*, Holt (New York City), 1969, published as *The Doom Fishermen*, Hutchinson, 1969.
*Operation Manhunt*, Holt, 1970, published as *Manhunt for a General*, Hutchinson, 1970.
*Where the Cavern Ends*, Holt, 1971.
*The Infiltrator*, Doubleday, 1971.
*Operation Neptune*, Holt, 1972, published as *Appointment in Kiltone*, Hutchinson, 1972.
*The Expurgator*, Hutchinson, 1972, Doubleday, 1973.
*The Captivator*, Hutchinson, 1973, Doubleday, 1974.
*The Fascinator*, Doubleday, 1975.
*Dark Passage*, Doubleday, 1975.
*Tallant for Trouble*, Doubleday, 1977.
*Tallant for Disaster*, Doubleday, 1978.

*The Combination*, Doubleday, 1983.
*Tallant for Terror*, Severn House, 1995.

*ADAPTATIONS: The Eliminator* was filmed by United Artists under the title *Danger Route*, 1968.

*SIDELIGHTS:* Christopher Nicole, best known under his pseudonym Andrew York, is the creator of the secret agent character Jonas Wilde, the Eliminator. The Wilde novels, according to Frank D. McSherry, Jr. in the *St. James Guide to Crime and Mystery Writers*, "are to Ian Fleming's James Bond tales what a century ago the Martin Hewitt stories were to those about Sherlock Holmes: solid, if less spectacular stories modeled on a more famous hero whose popularity gave new life to an old form—in this case, the spy-adventure tale. Lacking the bizarre villains, tricky gadgets, and exotic color of far-off lands, the Wilde series has all the other characteristics of the Fleming formula: the secret agent authorized to kill, immensely attractive to women, and a connoisseur of wine and food, appearing in melodramatic fast-action adventures filled with violence and sex. Nevertheless, Wilde is no mere carbon copy; for example, he does not use a gun, killing with a karate blow behind the ear."

McSherry notes that in the Wilde books, "though the telling is deadly serious, the plot line is often parody, a wild black humor blowing through it, as if the author were unconsciously laughing at the Fleming form." In one adventure, for example, Wilde discovers that the people he has been assigned to kill as traitors have in fact been loyal British subjects; it is Wilde's own superior who is the traitor, using him to eliminate enemies of the Soviet Union. McSherry concludes that the Wilde novels are "well-written, suspenseful adventures" and Wilde himself "remains, perhaps, the best of all the men modeled on Ian Fleming's James Bond."

*BIOGRAPHICAL/CRITICAL SOURCES:*

*BOOKS*

*St. James Guide to Crime and Mystery Writers*, 4th edition, St. James Press (Detroit), 1996.

*    *    *

**NORTH, Andrew**
**See NORTON, Andre**

**NORTON, Alice Mary**
  See NORTON, Andre

\*    \*    \*

**NORTON, Andre 1912-**
  **(Andrew North; Allen Weston, a joint pseudonym)**

*PERSONAL:* Given name Alice Mary Norton; name legally changed, 1934; born February 17, 1912, in Cleveland, OH; daughter of Adalbert Freely and Bertha (Stemm) Norton. *Education:* Attended Western Reserve University (now Case Western Reserve University), 1930-32. *Politics:* Republican. *Religion:* Presbyterian. *Avocational interests:* Collecting fantasy and cat figurines and paper dolls, needlework.

*ADDRESSES: Home and office*—1600 Spruce Ave., Winter Park, FL 32789. *Agent*—Russell Galen, Scott Meredith Literary Agency, 845 Third Ave., New York, NY 10022.

*CAREER:* Cleveland Public Library, Cleveland, OH, children's librarian, 1930-41, 1942-51; Mystery House (book store and lending library), Mount Ranier, MD, owner and manager, 1941; freelance writer, 1950—. Worked as a special librarian for a citizenship project in Washington, DC, and at the Library of Congress, 1941. Editor, Gnome Press, 1950-58.

*MEMBER:* American Penwomen, Science Fiction Writers of America, American League of Writers, Swordsmen and Sorcerers Association.

*AWARDS, HONORS:* Award from Dutch government, 1946, for *The Sword Is Drawn*; Ohioana Juvenile Award honor book, 1950, for *Sword in Sheath*; Boys' Clubs of America Medal, 1951, for *Bullard of the Space Patrol*; Hugo Award nominations, World Science Fiction Convention, 1962, for *Star Hunter*, 1964, for *Witch World*, and 1968, for "Wizard's World"; Headliner Award, Theta Sigma Phi, 1963; Invisible Little Man Award, Westercon XVI, 1963, for sustained excellence in science fiction; Boys' Clubs of America Certificate of Merit, 1965, for *Night of Masks*; Phoenix Award, 1976, for overall achievement in science fiction; Gandalf Master of Fantasy Award, World Science Fiction Convention, 1977, for lifetime achievement; Andre Norton Award, Women Writers of Science Fiction, 1978; Balrog

Fantasy Award, 1979; Ohioana Award, 1980, for body of work; named to Ohio Women's Hall of Fame, 1981; Fritz Leiber Award, 1983, for work in the field of fantasy; E. E. Smith Award, 1983; Nebula Grand Master Award, Science Fiction Writers of America, 1984, for lifetime achievement; Jules Verne Award, 1984, for work in the field of science fiction; Second Stage Lensman Award, 1987, for lifetime achievement.

*WRITINGS:*

SCIENCE FICTION; "CENTRAL CONTROL" SERIES

*Star Rangers,* Harcourt, 1953, reprinted, Del Rey, 1985, published as *The Last Planet,* Ace Books, 1955.
*Star Guard* ("Central Control" series), Harcourt, 1955, reprinted, 1984.

SCIENCE FICTION; "ASTRA" SERIES

*The Stars Are Ours!* World Publishing, 1954, reprinted, Ace Books, 1983.
*Star Born,* World Publishing, 1957.

SCIENCE FICTION; "SOLAR QUEEN" SERIES

(Under pseudonym Andrew North) *Sargasso of Space,* Gnome Press, 1955, published under name Andre Norton, Gollancz, 1970.
(Under pseudonym Andrew North) *Plague Ship,* Gnome Press, 1956, published under name Andre Norton, Gollancz, 1971.
(Under pseudonym Andrew North) *Voodoo Planet,* Ace Books, 1959.
*Postmarked the Stars,* Harcourt, 1969, reprinted, Fawcett, 1985.

SCIENCE FICTION; "TIME TRAVEL" SERIES

*The Crossroads of Time,* Ace Books, 1956, reprint edited by Jim Baen, 1985.
*Quest Crosstime,* Viking, 1965, reprinted, Ace Books, 1981 (published in England as *Crosstime Agent,* Gollancz, 1975).

SCIENCE FICTION; "TIME WAR" SERIES

*The Time Traders,* World Publishing, 1958, reprinted, Ace Books, 1987.
*Galactic Derelict,* World Publishing, 1959, reprinted, Ace Books, 1987.

*The Defiant Agents,* World Publishing, 1962, reprinted, Ace Books, 1987.

*Key out of Time,* World Publishing, 1963, reprinted, Ace Books, 1987.

SCIENCE FICTION; "BEAST MASTER" SERIES

*The Beast Master,* Harcourt, 1959.
*Lord of Thunder,* Harcourt, 1962.

SCIENCE FICTION; "PLANET WARLOCK" SERIES

*Storm over Warlock,* World Publishing, 1960, reprinted, Gregg Press, 1980.

*Ordeal in Otherwhere,* Harcourt, 1964, reprinted, Gregg Press, 1980.

SCIENCE FICTION; "JANUS" SERIES

*Judgment on Janus,* Harcourt, 1963, reprinted, Del Rey, 1987.

*Victory on Janus,* Harcourt, 1966, reprinted, Del Rey, 1984.

SCIENCE FICTION; "MOON MAGIC" SERIES

*Moon of Three Rings* (Junior Literary Guild selection), Viking, 1966, reprinted, Ace Books, 1987.

*Exiles of the Stars,* Viking, 1971.
*Flight in Yiktor,* Tor, 1986.
*Dare to Go A-Hunting,* Doherty, 1990.

SCIENCE FICTION; "ZERO STONE" SERIES

*The Zero Stone,* Viking, 1968, reprinted, Ace Books, 1985.

*Uncharted Stars,* Viking, 1969.

SCIENCE FICTION; "FORERUNNER" SERIES

*Forerunner,* Tor Books, 1981.
*Forerunner: The Second Venture,* Tor, 1985.

SCIENCE FICTION; "STAR KA'AT" SERIES; WITH DOROTHY MADLEE

*Star Ka'at,* Walker & Co., 1976.
*Star Ka'at World,* Walker & Co., 1978.
*Star Ka'ats and the Plant People,* Walker & Co., 1979.

*Star Ka'ats and the Winged Warriors,* Walker & Co., 1981.

SCIENCE FICTION; OTHER

*Bullard of the Space Patrol,* edited by Malcolm Jameson, World Publishing, 1951.

*Star Man's Son, 2250 A.D.,* Harcourt, 1952, reprinted, Del Rey, 1985, published as *Daybreak, 2250 A.D.* (bound with *Beyond Earth's Gates,* by C. M. Kuttner), Ace Books, 1954.

*Sea Siege,* Harcourt, 1957, reprinted, Del Rey, 1987.

*Star Gate,* Harcourt, 1958.

*Secret of the Lost Race,* Ace Books, 1959, (published in England as *Wolfshead,* Hale, 1977).

*The Sioux Spaceman,* Ace Books, 1960, reprinted, 1987.

*Star Hunter* (also see below), Ace Books, 1961.

*Catseye,* Harcourt, 1961, reprinted, Del Rey, 1984.

*Eye of the Monster,* Ace Books, 1962, reprinted, 1987.

*Night of Masks,* Harcourt, 1964, reprinted, Del Rey, 1985.

*The X Factor,* Harcourt, 1965, reprinted, Del Rey, 1984.

*Operation Time Search,* Harcourt, 1967, reprinted, Del Rey, 1985.

*Dark Piper,* Harcourt, 1968.
*Ice Crown,* Viking, 1970.
*Android at Arms,* Harcourt, 1971, reprinted, Del Rey, 1987.

*Breed to Come,* Viking, 1972.
*Here Abide Monsters,* Atheneum, 1973.
*Forerunner Foray* (Science Fiction Book Club selection), Viking, 1973.

*Iron Cage,* Viking, 1974.
*Outside,* Walker & Co., 1975.
(With Michael Gilbert) *The Day of the Ness,* Walker & Co., 1975.

*Knave of Dreams,* Viking, 1975.
*No Night without Stars,* Atheneum, 1975.
*Voor Loper,* Ace Books, 1980.
*Voodoo Planet* [and] *Star Hunter,* (*Voodoo Planet*) also under "Solar Queen" series) Ace Books, 1983.

(With Susan Shwartz) *Empire of the Eagle,* Tor, 1993.

(With Pauline Griffin) *Redline the Stars,* Tor, 1993.

(With Griffin) *Firehand,* Tor, 1994.

FANTASY; "WITCH WORLD" SERIES

*Witch World,* Ace Books, 1963, reprinted, 1978.
*Web of the Witch World,* Ace Books, 1964, reprinted, 1983.

*Three against the Witch World,* Ace Books, 1965.

*Year of the Unicorn,* Ace Books, 1965, reprinted, 1989.

*Warlock of the Witch World,* Ace Books, 1967.

*Sorceress of the Witch World,* Ace Books, 1968, reprinted, 1986.

*The Crystal Gryphon* (first volume in "Gryphon" trilogy), Atheneum, 1972.

*Spell of the Witch World* (short stories), DAW Books, 1972, reprinted, 1987.

*The Jargoon Pard,* Atheneum, 1974.

*Trey of Swords* (short stories), Ace Books, 1977.

*Zarsthor's Bane,* Ace Books, 1978.

*Lore of the Witch World* (short stories), DAW Books, 1980.

*Gryphon in Glory* (second volume in "Gryphon" trilogy), Atheneum, 1981.

*Horn Crown,* DAW Books, 1981.

*Ware Hawk,* Atheneum, 1983.

(With A. C. Crispin) *Gryphon's Eyrie* (third volume in "Gryphon" trilogy), Tor Books, 1984.

*The Gate of the Cat,* Ace Books, 1987.

*Tales of the Witch World,* edited by Norton, Tor, 1987.

*Four from the Witch World,* Tor, 1989.

(With Pauline Griffin) *Storms of Victory,* Doherty, 1991

(With A. C. Crispin) *Songsmith: A Witch World Novel,* Tor, 1992.

(With Pauline Griffin and Mary Schaub) *Flight of Vengeance,* Tor, 1992.

(With Patricia Mathews and Sasha Miller) *On Wings of Magic,* Doherty, 1994.

(With Lyn McConchie) *The Key of the Keplian,* Warner, 1995.

*The Warding of Witch World,* Warner, 1996.

### FANTASY; "HALFBLOOD CHRONICLES" SERIES

*The Elvenbane: An Epic High Fantasy of the Halfblood Chronicles,* Doherty, 1991.

(With Mercedes Lackey) *Elvenblood: An Epic High Fantasy,* Tor, 1995.

### FANTASY; OTHER

*Rogue Reynard* (juvenile), Houghton, 1947.

*Huon of the Horn* (juvenile), Harcourt, 1951, reprinted, Del Rey, 1987.

*Steel Magic,* World Publishing, 1965, published as *Gray Magic,* Scholastic Book Service, 1967.

*Octagon Magic,* World Publishing, 1967.

*Fur Magic,* World Publishing, 1968.

*Dread Companion,* Harcourt, 1970.

*Dragon Magic,* Crowell, 1972.

*Lavender-Green Magic,* Crowell, 1974.

*Merlin's Mirror,* DAW Books, 1975.

*Wraiths of Time,* Atheneum, 1976.

*Red Hart Magic,* Crowell, 1976.

*Yurth Burden,* DAW Books, 1978.

*Quag Keep,* Atheneum, 1978.

(With Phyllis Miller) *Seven Spells to Sunday,* McElderry, 1979.

*Iron Butterflies,* Fawcett, 1980.

*Moon Called,* Simon & Schuster, 1982.

*Wheel of Stars,* Simon & Schuster, 1983.

*Were-Wrath,* Cheap Street, 1984.

*The Magic Books,* Signet, 1988.

*Moon Mirror,* Tor, 1989.

(With Shwartz) *Imperial Lady: A Fantasy of Han China,* Tor, 1990.

*The Mark of the Cat,* Ace Books, 1992.

*Golden Trillium,* Bantam, 1993.

*Brother to Shadows,* Morrow, 1993.

*The Hands of Lyr,* Morrow, 1994.

*Mirror of Destiny,* Morros, 1995.

### HISTORICAL NOVELS

*The Prince Commands,* Appleton, 1934.

*Ralestone Luck,* Appleton, 1938, reprinted, Tor, 1988.

*Follow the Drum,* Penn, 1942, reprinted, Fawcett, 1981.

*The Sword Is Drawn* (first volume of "Swords" trilogy; Junior Literary Guild selection), Houghton, 1944, reprinted, Unicorn-Star Press, 1985.

*Scarface,* Harcourt, 1948.

*Sword in Sheath* (second volume of "Swords" trilogy), Harcourt, 1949, reprinted, Unicorn-Star Press, 1985 (published in England as *Island of the Lost,* Staples Press, 1954).

*At Sword's Points* (third volume of "Swords" trilogy), Harcourt, 1954, reprinted, Unicorn-Star Press, 1985.

*Yankee Privateer,* World Publishing, 1955.

*Stand to Horse,* Harcourt, 1956.

*Shadow Hawk,* Harcourt, 1960, reprinted, Del Rey, 1987.

*Ride Proud, Rebel!,* World Publishing, 1961, reprinted, Juniper, 1981.

*Rebel Spurs,* World Publishing, 1962.

### SHORT STORIES

*High Sorcery,* Ace Books, 1970.

*Garan the Eternal,* Fantasy Publishing, 1973.

*The Many Worlds of Andre Norton,* edited by Roger Elwood, Chilton, 1974, published as *The Book of Andre Norton,* DAW Books, 1975.
*Perilous Dreams,* DAW Books, 1976.

EDITOR

*Space Service,* World Publishing, 1953.
*Space Pioneers,* World Publishing, 1954.
*Space Police,* World Publishing, 1956.
(With Ernestine Donaldy) *Gates to Tomorrow: An Introduction to Science Fiction,* Atheneum, 1973.
*Small Shadows Creep: Ghost Children,* Dutton, 1974.
*Baleful Beasts and Eerie Creatures,* Rand McNally, 1976.
(With Robert Adams) *Magic in Ithkar,* Tor, 1985.
(With Robert Adams) *Magic in Ithkar, Number 2,* Tor, 1985.
(With Robert Adams) *Magic in Ithkar, Number 3,* Tor, 1986.
(With Robert Adams) *Magic in Ithkar, Number 4,* Tor, 1987.
(With Martin H. Greenberg) *Catfantastic,* DAW Books, 1989.
*Grand Master's Choice,* Tor, 1991.
(With Martin H. Greenberg) *Catfantastic II,* DAW Books, 1991.
(With Martin H. Greenberg) *Catfantastic III,* DAW Books, 1994.

OTHER

(With Grace Hogarth, under joint pseudonym Allen Weston) *Murder for Sale* (mystery), Hammond, 1954.
(With mother, Bertha Stemm Norton) *Bertie and May* (biography), World Publishing, 1969.
*The White Jade Fox* (gothic), Dutton, 1975.
*Velvet Shadows* (gothic), Fawcett, 1977.
*The Opal-Eyed Fan* (gothic), Dutton, 1977.
*Snow Shadow* (mystery), Fawcett, 1979.
*Ten Mile Treasure* (juvenile mystery), Pocket Books, 1981.
(With Enid Cushing) *Caroline,* Pinnacle, 1982.
(With Miller) *House of Shadows* (mystery), Atheneum, 1984.
*Stand and Deliver,* Tor, 1984.
(With Miller) *Ride the Green Dragon* (mystery), Atheneum, 1985.
(With Marion Zimmer Bradley and Julian May) *Black Trillium,* Doubleday, 1990.
(With Robert Bloch) *The Jekyll Legacy,* Doherty, 1990.
(With Grace Hogarth) *Sneeze on Sunday,* Tor, 1992.

(With Bradley and Mercedes Lackey) *Tiger Burning Bright,* Morrow, 1995.
*The Monster's Legacy,* Atheneum, 1996.

Contributor to numerous periodicals and anthologies.

*SIDELIGHTS:* Although she has penned numerous books of historical fiction and mystery, among other kinds, Andre Norton is best known and admired for her science fiction and fantasy. Women writers were rare in the genre when she published *Star Man's Son, 2250 A.D.* in 1952, yet Norton quickly became a popular favorite, with some of her books selling over 1 million copies each. Despite frequent critical dismissal of her work as lacking complexity, both Norton's fans and peers have recognized her contributions to science fiction: she is one of the few writers to be awarded both the Science Fiction Writers of America's Grand Master Award and science fiction fandom's equivalent, the Gandalf Award.

"Those who know Miss Norton's work well appreciate her highly," notes a *Times Literary Supplement* writer. "She belongs to the group of writers whose books appear on the list for the young as a result of shrinkage in the adult novel, although her readers might be of any age over twelve." The critic adds that "the background of her stories is a literary one and includes myth and legend and the high tone and seriousness of epic, the dark and brooding matters of tragedy." Indeed, many critics have observed that solid research is the foundation of a Norton novel, a product of her early career as a librarian. As Francis J. Molson remarks in a *Dictionary of Literary Biography* essay: "The excitement and zest of great deeds or intrepid voyaging across galactic distances readers sense in Norton's science fiction and fantasy originate within her creative and prolific imagination, especially as it draws inspiration from and refashions material she has discovered in her extensive reading and research in history and related fields."

While critics may debate Norton's literary significance, many agree that her work has been overlooked for a variety of reasons. For instance, her first books were marketed toward juvenile readers, much as the early work of Robert Heinlein had been; thus, although they were read by all ages, Norton's novels were dismissed as relatively unimportant. Charlotte Spivack, however, proposes another explanation for Norton's lack of critical attention: "Her wide reading public has simply taken Andre Norton for granted, not as the author of a single masterpiece but rather as a steadily dependent writer who is always there with a couple of entertaining new paperbacks every year," as she writes in *Merlin's Daughters: Contemporary Women Writers of Fantasy.* "The would-be critic, on the other hand, is likely to be intimidated by the vast output and remarkable variety of this prolific writer."

Donald Wollheim similarly remarks in his introduction to *The Many Worlds of Andre Norton* that while science fiction and fantasy readers "may spend a lot of time discussing the sociology and speculations of the other writers, Andre Norton they read for pleasure. This is not to say that her works lack the depth of the others, because they do not," explains the critic. "But it is that these depths form part of the natural unobtrusive background of her novels." "It is possible that the pace and suspense of Norton's storytelling may so ensnare readers that they may overlook the themes or concerns her narratives embody," states Molson. But, the critic claims, "Norton's science fiction is actually serious on the whole—sometimes even explicitly earnest and didactic—as it dramatizes several themes and concerns. In fact, one theme, above all others, is pervasive in Norton's [work]: the centrality of passage or initiation in the lives of many of her protagonists."

Elisa Kay Sparks believes this theme figures prominently in Norton's work. In a *Dictionary of Literary Biography* essay, Sparks characterizes Norton's writings as "almost always. . . center[ing] on the process by which a somehow displaced, exiled, or alienated hero or heroine finds a new home or sense of community. From the first to the last her books insist on the necessity of cooperation between equals." "Frequently," relates Roger Schlobin in the introduction to his *Andre Norton: A Primary and Secondary Bibliography,* "the protagonists must undergo a rite of passage to find self-realization." The story of *Star Man's Son, 2250 A.D.* exemplifies this theme: a young mutant, scorned by a postwar society because of his differences, quests on his own to fulfill his father's legacy; in doing so, he discovers his own self-worth. As Molson describes it, the book "speaks directly and forcefully. . . through its convincing story of a boy's passage from a questioning, unsure adolescence to confident, assured young manhood."

The novels of the "Halfblood Chronicles" fantasy series similarly describe the heroic efforts of an alienated young girl who struggles to reconcile her individuality and to end the subjugation of humans in a world where they are enslaved by a merciless race of elves. In *The Elvenbane,* the first volume of the se-

ries, a human slave gives birth to Shana, a half-elven baby who is the feared "Elvenbane" of prophecy. Raised by a dragon in the desert, Shana masters her unique powers and leads the Elvenbane wizards in their struggle against the elven lords in the sequel, *Elvenblood.* With her ability to determine the interconnected fate of the humans, elves, and dragons by her actions, Shana realizes her capacity to chart her own destiny and to fight injustice in the world around her. Reviewers cite this series as an example of how Norton creates believable, compelling, character-driven fiction.

It is the focus on the internal struggles of her characters that makes Norton's work interesting, suggests Schlobin in *The Feminine Eye: Science Fiction and the Women Who Write It.* "Norton's reverence for the self, especially as it seeks to realize its potentials. . . is one of the major reasons why her plots are always so exciting. Her protagonists have to deal not only with dangerous external forces but also with their own maturation and personal challenges," states the critic. One such protagonist appears in *Forerunner: The Second Venture,* a 1985 work. While *Fantasy Review* contributor Carl B. Yoke finds other aspects of the story disappointing, the main character Simsa "is one of those stubbornly-independent, highly resourceful, intuitive, and intelligent characters that many of us fans have come to expect and admire in Norton's work."

In resolving this theme of self-fulfillment, Norton's work frequently expresses another idea of importance to her work: that to understand oneself, a person must come to understand and accept others. "In Norton's novels the heroic quest for self-realization ends typically in union with another," maintains Spivack. "The resolution of inner conflict is androgynous. For Norton the integration of Self and Other is of supreme importance, whether the Other is gender or species." The critic elaborates, observing that in the "Magic" series of books for younger readers, "in each case the self-knowledge of the protagonist results not only from the admission of one's own weaknesses but also from the discovery of the Other as worthy of respect." Schlobin similarly comments in his bibliography that Norton's "resolutions are androgynous: within themselves or in union with another, [Norton's characters] find the ideal combination of male and female characteristics. Most of all," continues the critic, "they discover a sanctity of ideas and ethics, and they recognize their own places within the patterns and rhythms of elemental law and carry that recognition forward into a hopeful future."

For instance, in what is her most popular series, the novels of the "Witch World," the resolution of many of the books lies in the cooperation of male and female aspects. The Witch World includes a society of female witches who remain virginal as a means of sustaining their power; this dictate is later shown to be unnecessary and even detrimental to the witches. As Spivack interprets this, "in Norton's view neither sex is complete without the other; self-fulfillment involves union with the opposite sex. Furthermore," she adds, "the relationship between the sexes should be based on equality, not domination. . . . Wholeness through balanced union of male and female, especially on the plane of values, tends to eliminate the need for aggression. Norton is thus the first of the women fantasists to combine the themes of the renunciation of power, the depolarization of values, and the vindication of mortality." Characters who reject such compromises make up a great number of Norton's antagonists, states Sparks: "Norton consistently associates evil with the denial of such bonds, or with a lack of appreciation for individuality and liberty; opportunism, willful destructiveness, and the urge to dominate through the imposition of mechanized forms of control are characteristic attributes of her villains."

Norton's monumental "Witch World" saga consists of more than twenty volumes, a number of which are collaborative efforts with several other authors. *Storms of Victory, Songsmith, Flight of Vengeance, On Wings of Magic,* and *The Key of the Keplian,* all produced in the 1990s, were created in part or entirely by others under Norton's editorial aegis. Critical reception of these volumes is generally favorable, though some reviewers lament Norton's limited role as the series creator and editor. Beginning with *Storms of Victory,* the novels are set in the aftermath of "The Turning," an apocalyptic battle that leaves the Witch World devastated. As in previous volumes, Norton and her collaborators examine the process of maturation and various conflicts between good and evil.

Critics observe that it is the mechanical, non-individualistic aspects of science that frequently provide the conflict in Norton's work; "though many of her novels are set in the future," remarks Schlobin, "she has no special affection for the technological and, in fact, science is most often the antagonist in her fiction." Rick Brooks similarly notes in *The Many Worlds of Andre Norton* that "in the battle between technology and nature, Miss Norton took a stand long before the great majority of us had any doubts. . . . Technology is a necessary evil [in her work] to get there for the adventure and to get some of the story

to work. And the adventure is as much to mold her universe to her views as to entertain," adds the critic. Norton revealed the reasons behind her distrust of technology to Charles Platt in *Dream Makers Volume II: The Uncommon Men and Women Who Write Science Fiction:* "I think the human race made a bad mistake at the beginning of the Industrial Revolution. We leaped for the mechanics, and threw aside things that were just as important. We made the transition too fast. I do not like mechanical things very much," the author explained. "And I don't like a lot of the modern ways of living. I prefer to do things with my hands; and I think everybody misses that. People need the use of their hands to feel creative." Brooks further notes: "Norton consistently views the future as one where the complexity of science and technology have reduced the value of the individual. . . . So Miss Norton is actually wrestling with the prime problem, that of human worth and purpose."

While some critics, such as Brooks, observe a higher purpose in Norton's writing, they consistently remark upon the author's ability to craft an entertaining tale. "Norton is above all committed to telling a story, and she tells it in clear, effective prose," asserts Spivack. "Not given to metaphors or lyricism, her style is focused on narrative movement, dialogue, and descriptive foreground. . . . Her scenes are moving and vivid, and both the outward action and inward growth are drawn convincingly and absorbingly." Molson concurs, calling Norton "a skilled teller of stories. . . . Characteristically, her stories, either science fiction or fantasy, are replete with incident; take place in the near or far future; feature alien or bizarre life forms, futuristic technology or exotic settings." In addition, the author not only provides her readers with new and exciting concepts but also with an opportunity to visualize these notions for themselves. As *Riverside Quarterly* contributor Barry McGhan summarizes, "[one critic] claims that a prime attraction of this author's writing is that she introduces many intriguing ideas that are never completely wrapped up at the end of the book, thus leaving something to be filled in by the reader's own imagination."

Yet for all Norton's skill in creating and presenting universes to her readers, she always includes ideas of substance in her fiction. "The sheer size of [Norton's] world, which is infinitely extended in time and space, and in which nothing is outside the bounds of possibility, is matched by the size of the themes she tackles," claims John Rowe Townsend in *A Sense of Story: Essays on Contemporary Writers for Children.* In a Norton novel, he adds, "there is always something beyond the immediate action to be reached for and thought about." Because of the breadth and scope of her work, maintains Brooks, "the chief value of Andre Norton's writing may not lie in entertainment or social commentary, but in her 're-enchanting' us with her creations that renew our linkages to all life." For example, in *Dare to Go A-Hunting,* the fourth installment in the "Moon Magic" series, Norton describes the interplanetary adventures of Free Trader Krip Vorlund, sorceress Maelen, and a young boy who sprouts wings, learns to fly, and sets out to find a legendary population of similar winged beings. "Not only does she succeed in holding her reader," observes Spivack, "but her cosmos lingers in the mind, with its unforgettable images of alien species, jewels and talismans resonant with psychic powers, and magical transcendence of time and space. At the center of this original universe, with its startling variety of life forms, is the individual, alone, heroic, supremely important."

Another quality that makes Norton's science fiction memorable, as Wollheim states, is her ability to evoke the "sense of wonder" that characterizes much of the genre. "Andre Norton is at home telling us wonder stories. She is telling us that people are marvelously complex and marvelously fascinating. She is telling us that all life is good and that the universe is vast and meant to enhance our life to infinity. She is weaving an endless tapestry of a cosmos no man will ever fully understand, but among whose threads we are meant to wander forever to our personal fulfillment." The critic continues: "Basically this is what science fiction has always been about. And because she has always understood this, her audience will continue to be as ever-renewing and as nearly infinite as her subjects." Schlobin similarly concludes in *The Feminine Eye:* "Andre Norton, then, like all special writers, is more than just an author. She is a guide who leads us, the real human beings, to worlds and situations that we might very well expect to live in were we given extraordinary longevity. . . . The Norton future is an exciting realm alive with personal quests to be fulfilled and vital challenges to be overcome," Schlobin continues. "Is it any wonder that millions upon millions of readers, spanning three generations, have chosen to go with her in her travels?"

## BIOGRAPHICAL/CRITICAL SOURCES:

### BOOKS

*Contemporary Literary Criticism,* Volume 12, Gale, 1980.

Crouch, Marcus, *The Nesbit Tradition: The Children's Novel in England, 1945-70,* Benn, 1972.

*Dictionary of Literary Biography,* Gale, Volume 8: *Twentieth-Century American Science Fiction Writers,* 1981, Volume 52: *American Writers for Children since 1960: Fiction,* 1986.

Elwood, Roger, editor, *The Many Worlds of Andre Norton,* introduction by Donald Wollheim, Chilton, 1974, published as *The Book of Andre Norton,* DAW Books, 1975.

Magill, Frank N., editor, *Survey of Science Fiction Literature,* Volumes 1-5, Salem Press, 1979.

Platt, Charles, *Dream Makers Volume II: The Uncommon Men and Women Who Write Science Fiction,* Berkley Publishing, 1983.

Schlobin, Roger C., *Andre Norton,* Gregg, 1979.

Schlobin, *Andre Norton: A Primary and Secondary Bibliography,* G. K. Hall, 1980.

Shwartz, Susan, editor, *Moonsinger's Friends: An Anthology in Honor of Andre Norton,* Bluejay Books, 1985.

Spivack, Charlotte, *Merlin's Daughters: Contemporary Women Writers of Fantasy,* Greenwood Press, 1987.

Staicar, Tom, editor, *The Feminine Eye: Science Fiction and the Women Who Write It,* Ungar, 1982.

Townsend, John Rowe, *A Sense of Story: Essays on Contemporary Writers for Children,* Lippincott, 1971.

### PERIODICALS

*Booklist,* February 15, 1991, p. 1180; May 1, 1992, p. 1587; December, 1992, p. 718; January 1, 1994, p. 811; July, 1995, p. 1866.

*Extrapolation,* fall, 1985.

*Fantasy Review,* September, 1985.

*Kirkus Reviews,* February 15, 1991, p. 219; November 1, 1992, p. 1340; April 1, 1994, p. 442.

*Library Journal,* August, 1990, pp. 138, 147; May 15, 1992, p. 123; June 15, 1993, p. 104; October 11, 1993, p. 73; October 18, 1993, p. 67; November 15, 1993, pp. 103, 1425; June 15, 1994, p. 99; June 15, 1995, p. 98.

*LOCUS,* January, 1990, p. 23; September, 1992, p. 29.

*Los Angeles Times,* December 27, 1984.

*New York Times Book Review,* September 20, 1970; February 24, 1974; January 25, 1976.

*Publishers Weekly,* June 22, 1990, p. 48; July 6, 1990, p. 61; February 8, 1991, p. 52; November 9, 1992, p. 77; May 17, 1993, p. 70; November 29, 1993, p. 58; May 23, 1994, p. 82; July 4,

1994, p. 56; February 20, 1995, p. 200; May 22, 1995, p. 52.

*Riverside Quarterly,* January, 1970.

*Science Fiction Chronicle,* January, 1990, p. 34.

*School Librarian,* July, 1967.

*School Library Journal,* December, 1992, p. 148; February, 1993, p. 126; September, 1993, p. 261; June, 1996, p. 154.

*Times Literary Supplement,* June 6, 1968; June 26, 1969; October 16, 1969, July 2, 1971; April 18, 1972; April 6, 1973; September 28, 1973; July 16, 1976.

*Voice of Youth Advocates,* August, 1991, p. 182; April, 1992, p. 45; June, 1993, p. 103; August, 1994, p. 158; February, 1996, p. 386.*

\* \* \*

**OLDFELD, Peter**
**See BARTLETT, Vernon**

\* \* \*

**PAULING, Linus (Carl) 1901-1994**

*PERSONAL:* Born February 28, 1901, in Portland, OR; died August 19, 1994, in Big Sur, CA; son of Herman William (a pharmacist) and Lucy Isabelle (Darling) Pauling; married Ava Helen Miller, June 17, 1923 (died December 7, 1981); children: Linus Carl, Jr., Peter Jeffress, Linda Helen, Edward Crellin. *Education:* Oregon State Agricultural College (now Oregon State University), B.S., 1922; California Institute of Technology, Ph.D., 1925; post-doctoral study at the universities of Munich, Copenhagen, and Zurich, 1926-27.

*CAREER:* Oregon State Agricultural College (now Oregon State University), Corvallis, assistant in quantitative analysis, 1919-20, assistant in chemistry and in mechanics and materials, 1920-22; California Institute of Technology, Pasadena, research associate, 1925-26, research fellow, 1926-27, assistant professor, 1927-29, associate professor, 1929-31, professor of chemistry, 1931-64; chair of the division of chemistry and chemical engineering, 1936-58, director of Gates and Crellin Laboratories of Chemistry, 1936-58, member of board of trustees executive committee, 1945-48; Center for the Study of Democratic Institutions, Santa Barbara, CA, research professor of the

physical and biological sciences, 1963-67; University of California, San Diego, professor of chemistry, 1967-69; Stanford University, Stanford, CA, professor of chemistry, 1969-74, professor emeritus, 1974-94; Linus Pauling Institute of Science and Medicine, Palo Alto, CA, president, 1973-75, fellow, 1973-94. Visiting lecturer in chemistry and physics, University of California, 1929-33, Massachusetts Institute of Technology, 1932; Foster Lecturer, University of Buffalo, 1936, 1953; George Fisher Baker Lecturer in Chemistry, Cornell University, 1937-38, 1988; Silliman Lecturer, Yale University, 1947; George Eastman Professor at Balliol College, Oxford, and Charles Lyall Lecturer at Exeter College, Oxford, 1948; Treat B. Johnson Lecturer, Yale University, 1953; Prather Lecturer, Harvard University, 1955; George A. Miller Lecturer, University of Illinois, 1956; Meade-Swing Lecturer, Oberlin College, 1956; Avogadro Commemoration Lecturer, Accademie dei Quaranta, Rome, 1956; National Institutes of Health lecturer, 1957; Beth Walton Moor Lecturer, Florida State University, 1958; Vanuxem Lecturer, Princeton University, 1959; Messenger Lecturer, Cornell University, 1959. Consultant to government agencies and research groups. *Wartime service:* Member of explosives division of U.S. National Defense Research Commission and official investigator for medical research committee of U.S. Office of Scientific Research and Development, 1942-45, member of U.S. Research Board for National Security, 1945-46; received U.S. Presidential Medal for Merit, 1948, "for exceptionally meritorious conduct in the performance of outstanding services to the United States from October, 1940, to June, 1946."

*MEMBER:* International Society of Hematology, International Society for Research on Nutrition and Vital Substances (honorary), International Society for the Study and Development of Human Relations (honorary), World Association of Parliamentarians for World Government, European Society of Haematology (honorary), American Chemical Society (president, 1949), American Philosophical Society (vice-president, 1951-54), American Association for the Advancement of Science (president, Pacific division, 1941-46), American Physical Society (fellow), American Association of Clinical Chemists (honorary), American Academy of Arts and Sciences, American Academy of Political Science, American Society of Naturalists, American Academy of Neurology, American Crystallographic Association, Mineralogical Society of America (fellow), National Academy of Sciences (chairman, chemistry section, 1940-45), Royal Institution of Great Britain (honorary),

Chemical Society of London (honorary fellow), The Royal Society of London (foreign member), Oxford Natural Science Club (honorary), Royal Society of Arts (Benjamin Franklin Fellow), Society for Social Responsibility in Science, Weizmann Institute of Science (honorary fellow), The Harvey Society (honorary), Longshoremen, Shipsclerks, and Walking Bosses Division of the International Longshoremen's and Warehousemen's Union (honorary), Alpha Omega Alpha Honor Medical Society (honorary). Institute of France, Academy of Sciences (correspondent, section of geology), Academie Nationale de Medecine de France (correspondent), Societe de Chimie Physique (France; honorary), Academie des Sciences, Inscriptions, et Belles Lettres de Toulouse (France; foreign member), Royal Society of Liege (Belgium; honorary fellow), Italian Chemical Society (honorary fellow), Academy of Sciences of Bologna (Italy; corresponding foreign member), Accademia Gioenia di Scienze Naturali di Catania, Sicily (Italy; honorary), The Academy of the Lynxes, Rome (Italy; foreign member), Bavarian Academy of Sciences, Mathematics-Natural Science Class (Germany; corresponding member), Deutsche Akademie der Naturforscher Leopoldina (Germany), Austrian Academy of Sciences (corresponding member), Swiss Chemical Society (honorary), Norwegian Academy of Science, Royal Norwegian Academy of Science, Royal Norwegian Scientific Society, Lisbon Academy of Science (Portugal; corresponding member), Soviet Academy of Sciences (foreign member), Indian Academy of Sciences (honorary), National Institute of Sciences of India (honorary), Chemical Society of Japan (honorary), Chemical Society of Chile (honorary).

*AWARDS, HONORS:* National Research Fellow in chemistry, 1925-26; John S. Guggenheim Foundation fellow, 1926-27; Irving Langmuir Prize in pure chemistry from American Chemical Society (ACS), 1931; elected to National Academy of Sciences, 1933; William H. Nichols Medal from New York section of ACS, 1941; Willard Gibbs Medal from Chicago section of ACS, 1946; Theodore William Richards Medal from Northeast section of ACS, 1947; Davy Medal from The Royal Society of London, 1947; Louis Pasteur Medal from Biochemical Society of France, 1952; Page One Award for work on proteins from Newspaper Guild of New York, 1953; Nobel Prize for Chemistry from Nobel Foundation for "research into the nature of the chemical bond and its application to the elucidation of the structure of complex substances," 1954; Thomas Addis Medal from National Nephrosis Foundation, 1955; Amedeo Avogadro Medal from Italian Academy of Sciences, 1956; John Phillips Memorial Medal for contributions to internal medicine from American College of Physicians, 1956; Pierre Fermat Medal, 1957; Paul Sabatier Medal, 1957; gold medal from French Academy of Medicine, 1957; medal with laurel wreath for contributions to international law from International Grotius Foundation, 1957. Named Rationalist of the Year by American Rationalist Federation, 1960; Cheers of the Year award form The Minority of One, 1960; grande medaille de vermeil from the City of Paris, 1961; Humanist of the Year award from American Humanist Association, 1961; Nobel Peace Prize, 1962; (with wife, Ava Helen Pauling) Janice Holland Peace Prize, 1962; Roebling Medal of the Mineralogical Society of America, 1967; Phi Beta Kappa Award in Science, 1971, for *Vitamin C and the Common Cold*; International Lenin Peace Prize from the Presidium of the Supreme Soviet of the U.S.S.R., 1972; U.S. National Medal of Science, 1974; 1977 Lomonosov Gold Medal from the Presidium of the Academy of the U.S.S.R. for work in chemistry and biochemistry, 1978; Award of Merit from the Decalogue Society of Lawyers, 1978; Chemical Sciences Award from the U.S. National Academy of Sciences, 1979; gold medal from the National Institute of Social Sciences, 1979; Annual Award from Women Strike for Peace, 1982; award for chemistry from Arthur M. Sackler Foundation, 1984; Priestley Medal for contributions to chemistry from ACS, 1984; Vannevar Bush Award, National Science Board, 1989; Tolman Medal, 1991; Rachel Carson Memorial Award from Lake Michigan Federation; gold medal from Rudolph Virchow Medical Society of New York; Modern Medicine Award for Distinguished Achievement from Modern Medicine Publications; Linus Pauling Medal from Puget Sound and Oregon sections of ACS; Gandhi Peace Prize; Eliasberg and Goedel Medallions in Anesthesiology; Vollum Award; Dr. Martin Luther King, Jr., Medical Achievement Award for pioneering work in determining the cause of sickle-cell anemia; Grand Officer of the Order of Merit of the Italian Republic; Ordre du Merite Social de Belgique; Medal of the Senate of the Republic of Chile. Numerous honorary degrees, including: Sc.D. from Oregon State College, 1933, University of Chicago, 1941, Princeton University, 1946, Cambridge University, 1947, University of London, 1947, Yale University, 1947, Oxford University, 1948, Brooklyn Polytechnic Institute, 1955, Humboldt University, 1959, University of Melbourne, 1964, University of Delhi, 1967, Adelphi University, 1967, Marquette University School of Medicine, 1969; Dr.h.c. from University of Paris, Sorbonne,

1948, University of Toulouse, 1949, University of Liege, 1955, University of Montpellier, 1958, Jagiellonian University, 1964, University of Warsaw, 1969, University of Lyon, 1970; M.A. from Oxford University, 1948; L.H.D. from University of Tampa, 1950; U.J.D. from University of New Brunswick, 1950; D.F.A. from Chouinard Art Institute, 1958; LL.D. from Reed College, 1959.

*WRITINGS:*

(With Samuel Goudsmit) *The Structure of Line Spectra,* McGraw (New York City), 1930.

(With E. Bright Wilson, Jr.) *Introduction to Quantum Mechanics, With Applications to Chemistry,* McGraw, 1935.

*The Nature of the Chemical Bond and the Structure of Molecules and Crystals: An Introduction to Modern Structural Chemistry,* Cornell University Press (Ithaca, NY), 1939, 3rd edition, 1960, shortened 3rd edition published as *The Chemical Bond: A Brief Introduction to Modern Structural Chemistry,* 1967.

*General Chemistry,* W. H. Freeman, 1947, 3rd edition, 1970.

*College Chemistry: An Introductory Textbook of General Chemistry,* illustrations by Roger Hayward, W. H. Freeman, 1950, 3rd edition, 1964.

*Molecular Structure and Biological Specificity,* American Institute of Biological Sciences, 1957.

*No More War!,* Illustrations by Hayward, Dodd (New York City), 1958, enlarged edition, 1962.

(With Hayward) *The Architecture of Molecules,* W. H. Freeman, 1964.

*Science and World Peace,* Indian Council for Cultural Relations (New Delhi), 1967.

*Structural Chemistry and Molecular Biology,* edited by Alexander Rich and Norman Davidson, W. H. Freeman, 1968.

(Editor) *Centennial Lectures: 1968 to 1969,* Oregon State University Press, 1969.

*Vitamin C and the Common Cold,* W. H. Freeman, 1970.

(Editor with David Hawkins) *Orthomolecular Psychiatry: Treatment of Schizophrenia,* W. H. Freeman, 1973.

(With son, Peter Pauling) *Chemistry,* W. H. Freeman, 1975.

*Vitamin C, the Common Cold, and the Flu,* W. H. Freeman, 1976, Berkley, 1981.

(With Ewan Cameron) *Cancer and Vitamin C: A Discussion of the Nature, Causes, Prevention, and Treatment of Cancer with Special Reference to the*

*Value of Vitamin C,* Linus Pauling Institute of Science and Medicine, 1979, revised and expanded edition, Camino, 1993.

*How to Live Longer and Feel Better,* Freeman, 1986.

(Editor) *World Encyclopedia of Peace,* Pergamon, 1986.

(With Daisaku Keda) *A Lifelong Quest for Peace: A Dialogue,* translated and edited by Richard L. Gage, Jones and Bartlett, 1992.

*Linus Pauling in His Own Words: Selections from His Writings, Speeches, and Interviews,* edited by Barbara Marinacci, Simon & Schuster (New York City), 1995.

*OTHER*

Featured on sound recordings, including *The Committed Scientist,* American Chemical Society, 1968; *Society and the Future, Science and the Future,* American Chemical Society, 1976; and *Vitamin C and Cancer,* Big Sur Recordings, 1976. Contributor of more than eight hundred scientific papers and of more than two hundred articles on social and political issues, especially peace, to periodicals. Associate editor of *Journal of the American Chemical Society,* 1930-40, of *Journal of Chemical Physics,* 1932-37, and of *Chemical Reviews.* Member of editorial board, American Chemical Society "Monograph Series."

*SIDELIGHTS:* "Linus Pauling is one of that select group of individuals whose lives have made a discernible impact on the contemporary world," proclaimed the *Antioch Review* in 1980. Two years later, writing of Pauling in *Discover,* John Langone deemed Pauling "one of the world's most distinguished scientists, the only American chemist whose name is a household word." Pauling "calls himself a physical chemist," explained Horace Freeland Judson in a 1978 *New Yorker* essay. "In over half a century in science," Judson continued, "in over five hundred scientific publications, Pauling has stretched that designation to cover everything from crystal structure and quantum mechanics, where he began, to molecular biology, molecular medicine, molecular psychiatry, and the structure of atomic nuclei." "The two-time Nobel laureate with the pioneering spirit has made headlines with countless achievements and an array of controversial causes," asserted Lidia Wasowicz in a 1985 *Chicago Tribune* report. "Pauling's contributions in such diverse fields as chemistry, molecular biology, immunology, genetic diseases, metallurgy and peace," Wasowicz assessed, "are part of textbook history."

A native of Portland, Oregon, Pauling was, according to Ted G. Goertzel, Mildred George Goertzel, and Victor Goertzel, in their *Antioch Review* article, "very much a product of American culture and society," what Wasowicz termed "one of the last of a breed . . . the American maverick." Pauling left Portland High School without a diploma following a dispute with the school's principal over American history course requirements; at age sixteen he enrolled at Oregon State Agricultural College and began to study what was already his abiding interest: chemistry. "I was simply entranced by chemical phenomena, by the reactions in which substances disappear and other substances, often with strikingly different properties, appear," Pauling wrote in *Daedalus*. He informed Judson: "I developed a strong desire to understand the physical and chemical properties of substances in relation to the atoms and molecules of which they are made up. This interest has largely determined the course of my research for fifty years."

After receiving his doctorate from the California Institute of Technology in 1925, Pauling traveled to Europe as a Guggenheim fellow to study with physicists pioneering quantum mechanics, a new concept in the investigation of the nature of matter. Working with Arnold Sommerfild in Munich, Germany, Erwin Schroedinger in Zurich, Switzerland, and Niels Bohr in Copenhagen, Denmark, Pauling began to use the principles of quantum mechanics to solve the problem of how atoms and molecules chemically combine. He returned to the United States in 1927 and accepted a position as assistant professor at the California Institute of Technology. A productive period in Pauling's life followed, for in the decade from 1926 to 1936, as Judson related, "Pauling and others working in the domain where physics shades into chemistry . . . were learning just how atoms are allowed in nature to behave in one another's intimate company."

"More than anyone else, Pauling has made the structure of molecules the central and most productive question of modern chemistry," Judson declared. In the 1920s and 1930s Pauling and his colleagues worked to understand the properties of chemical substances in relation to their structure. Applying the physics of quantum mechanics to the structure of molecules, Pauling arrived at his breakthrough theory of resonance in chemical bonding. "The principle of resonance states, for example," Judson explained, "that if a molecule can be described as having the bonds among its atoms arranged in either of two ways, then the molecule is to be considered as existing in both arrangements simultaneously." The theory of resonance, and other theories of chemical bonding, was described by Pauling in seven landmark articles published from 1931 to 1933. "By 1935," Pauling told Judson, "I felt that I had an essentially complete understanding of the nature of the chemical bond." Pauling's "investigation of the powers that bind substances," Wasowicz reported, constituted what Pauling considers "his greatest scientific contribution [and] revolutionized modern chemistry." In fact, Judson related, in the years following the publication of Pauling's ideas, "structures of the molecules of 225 substances were determined in Pauling's laboratory . . . and a great many others in other laboratories." The basis for modern theories of chemical bonding, Pauling's ideas explained the properties of many complicated substances and led to the development of drugs, plastics, and synthetics. His concepts were brought together and published in the 1939 book *The Nature of the Chemical Bond,* deemed one of the most influential chemical texts of the twentieth century. "His definitive book," Langone asserted, "ensured the dominance of his theories for years to come."

Molecular biology and biochemistry began to interest Pauling in the mid-1930s, when he investigated the molecular structure of hemoglobin, a component of blood responsible for oxygen transfer. Pauling told Judson that in 1935 he "asked what the structure of the hemoglobin molecule should be in order to account for the way it takes up oxygen." Then, Pauling continued, he "began to speculate more generally about the properties of the large molecules found in living organisms and about the problem of the structure of proteins," the essential constituents of all living cells. By 1937 Pauling was determined to arrive at a detailed structural understanding of proteins, which are composed of amino acids—molecules that combine to form larger molecules called peptides, which, in turn, combine to form chains of polypeptides, the complex components of proteins.

Pauling's subsequent work in this area was redirected by the onset of World War II, when the chemist became a member of the consultative committee of medical research for the U.S. Office of Scientific Research and Development. In this wartime capacity Pauling, using his protein research findings, helped to produce, in 1942, the first synthetic antibodies from blood globulins. In synthesizing these antibodies, and in uncovering the molecular structure of antitoxins, he helped to advance the frontier of immunology. While working for government agencies Pauling also supervised a project that in 1945 developed a gelatin-derived substitute for plasma, an essential blood component. Similar lines of inquiry attracted the chemist at the close of World War II. In April, 1947, he received a grant to study organic proteins and the debilitating polio virus. By 1949 Pauling had discovered a structural fault in blood hemoglobin responsible for the blood disease known as sickle-cell anemia. This discovery, which, according to Langone, represented "the first direct linking of a disease to a molecular defect," established a chemical basis for genetic diseases and carried wide-ranging impact in the fields of medicine, biochemistry, genetics, and anthropology.

Pauling's research activities in the early 1950s revolved chiefly around the problem he had first identified in 1937, namely, trying to determine the structure of protein molecules. By 1948, Judson recounted, "Pauling had come to realize that there was a general argument . . . for supposing that the structure he wanted would be a helix," or spiral staircase form. In 1951 Pauling, in a culmination of fourteen years of work with amino acids and peptides, presented a model for protein molecules called the "alpha helix." Together with his colleague, Robert B. Corey, Pauling accurately delineated the atomic structure of several types of protein molecules, outlining the first configurations to show protein's correct three-dimensional atomic arrangement. Termed by Judson "a rare triumph," the discovery of the alpha helix protein structure led to important developments in disease control, plastics, and synthetic fibers.

To his life of research and academic pursuits Pauling added a new set of concerns when World War II's conclusion was precipitated by American use of newly developed atomic bombs. In 1946 Pauling became a member of the board of trustees of the Emergency Committee of Atomic Scientists, which favored international controls on the use and development of atomic energy. Fulfilling a pledge he wrote in 1947, Pauling included in every lecture a comment about the importance of world peace. The chemist publicly declared that radioactive fallout produced in nuclear weapons testing threatens humanity. He explained that the radiation from nuclear fallout elements like strontium 90 and carbon 14 enters the food chain and leads to adverse biological effects, both direct and hereditary, such as leukemia, cancer, physical defects, and mental retardation.

Because of his advocacy of world peace and his outspoken opposition to atmospheric testing of nuclear weapons, Pauling was denounced in the early 1950s as a Communist subversive by U.S. Senator Joseph

McCarthy and was twice, in 1952 and 1954, refused a passport. "Even when accused of being un-American or a 'Communist sympathizer,'" the Goertzels wrote, "[Pauling] responded with an ironic smile and clever wit that consistently 'one-upped' his opponents." Pauling answered McCarthy's charges by denying that he was Communist and adding, "I am not even a theoretical Marxist." In an interview with Barbara Reynolds published in *USA Today* Pauling added a further twist, noting that he was also discredited in Communist-ruled Soviet Union: "Soviet chemists were forbidden to use my ideas in science, . . . which they said were incompatible with dialectical materialism." Pauling's wife played a major role in his crusade for world peace and nuclear disarmament, and when asked why he didn't abandon his efforts in the face of powerful attacks, the chemist told Wasowicz, "I continued because . . . I had to keep the respect of my wife." As Judson commented: "Pauling's political stand in the last years of the Truman Presidency seems mild now—a rather flamboyantly idealistic campaign against the Cold War, atomic weapons, and the development of the hydrogen bomb. In those days . . . Pauling's course required courage and principle."

"His politics had unpleasant consequences at the time," Judson continued. "At the end of April, 1952, Pauling was supposed to go to London to attend a meeting of the Royal Society [of London] on the structures of proteins, but at the last minute was refused a passport." By this time, Pauling had come to suspect that the helical form might also be the key to the structures of biochemical molecules other than proteins, especially nucleic acids, substances found in cell nuclei responsible for replicating and interpreting genetic messages. Scientists worldwide worked in the 1950s to determine the structure of one nucleic acid in particular, deoxyribonucleic acid (DNA), and new, clearer X-ray photographs of the molecule were available in the spring of 1952 to those who were able to attend the Royal Society meeting. Pauling's absence, termed a "scandal" by fellow scientists, deprived him of the opportunity to see the new DNA photographs. "Whether Pauling . . . could have learned enough [in London] to be the first to solve the structure of DNA is a question that must hang forever in the balance," Judson commented, for in 1953 James D. Watson and Francis Crick, scientists working in England with access to accurate photographs of DNA, solved the double-helix structure of the molecule, confirming Pauling's hunch. "There is no doubt whatever," Judson proclaimed, "that Pauling's lifetime of work on the structures of molecules provided information, insights, rules, techniques, and intellectual approaches that Watson and . . . Crick required" to formulate their history-making model of DNA. "The discovery of the structure of DNA by Watson and Crick," Judson continued, "was itself a tribute . . . to Pauling." When Pauling was asked why he didn't devote more of his research time to solving DNA's structure, Langone reported, the chemist replied, "Well, the fact is I didn't work harder at it partially because I had to put in so much time combating McCarthyism."

But Pauling's political views eventually gained acceptability, and Pauling himself gained widespread fame in 1954 when he was awarded the Nobel Prize in Chemistry for "research into the nature of the chemical bond and its application to the elucidation of the structure of complex substances." By 1955 other scientists were joining Pauling in uncovering and warning of the dangerous genetic and pathological effects of radioactive fallout from atomic explosions. That year Pauling participated in the first international Pugwash Conference, a gathering composed of scientists supporting nuclear disarmament. When internationally respected theologian and physician Albert Schweitzer, himself a Nobel laureate, broadcast a mandate for a ban on nuclear weapons testing, the appeal lent support to a petition Pauling circulated in 1957 urging international cessation of nuclear testing. Ultimately signed by more than eleven thousand scientists, the petition was presented to the United Nations in 1958; two years later Pauling successfully defied a U.S. Senate internal security subcommittee demanding the names of those who had aided the chemist in circulating the petition.

*No More War!,* Pauling's popular book on disarmament, was first published in 1958. That year Pauling engaged in a televised debate with hydrogen-bomb architect Edward Teller and brought an unsuccessful suit against the U.S. Defense Department and the U.S. Atomic Energy Commission in an effort to halt atomic weapons tests. In the early 1960s Pauling continued his campaign, cabling his concerns to Soviet Premier Nikita Khrushchev in September, 1961, and joining an April, 1962, protest in Washington, D.C., to decry atomic weapons testing. An enlarged edition of *No More War!* was published in 1962, and in November of that year the book's author received nearly 2,500 write-in votes in California's gubernatorial election. On October 10, 1963, the effective date for the provisions of a U.S.-Soviet nuclear weapons test ban treaty, Pauling was awarded the 1962 Nobel Peace Prize for his efforts on behalf of halting the

testing of nuclear weapons, thus becoming the first recipient of two unshared Nobel prizes. Accepting the Peace Prize in December, 1963, Pauling called for an end to the research, development, and use of biological and chemical weapons. Explaining why, of his two Nobel prizes, he valued his Peace Prize more highly, Pauling told Wasowicz: "The Peace Prize came for work I was doing as a sacrifice—lecturing and writing, hundreds and hundreds of lectures about radioactive fallout and about nuclear weapons and the need to world peace. I was taking time away from things I really liked to do because of a sense of duty."

In 1963 Pauling left the California Institute of Technology, with which he had been affiliated for four decades, to work as a research professor at the Center for the Study of Democratic Institutions, where he pursued peace and disarmament causes. In 1965 the scientist circulated a letter signed by eight Nobel laureates urging American withdrawal from the escalating Vietnam conflict. Two years later Pauling joined political philosopher Herbert Marcuse, educator and linguist Noam Chomsky, pediatrician Benjamin Spock, and others, in a "call to resist illegitimate authority" that branded as unconstitutional U.S. involvement in Vietnam and urged resistance to the conscriptive military draft. Pauling encountered opposition to his scientific endeavors because of these political positions. According to Langone, "he was barred from receiving federal research grants for many years, and President [Richard] Nixon, counseled by the White House scientific advisers, twice denied him the National Medal of Science (it was finally awarded to him by President [Gerald] Ford in 1975)." Commenting on his political and social involvement, Pauling told Langone, "I believe in democracy, the people making decisions as a whole. I don't say, for instance, that the *scientist* should refuse to work on nuclear weapons. The *people* should refuse to allow these weapons of mass destruction to be developed—and because the scientist has a better understanding of such matters, he has the obligation to help, to the best of his ability, his fellow citizens to understand what the problems are."

Scientific research pursued by Pauling beginning in the 1960s included an investigation of the molecular mechanism of general anesthesia that led to a new theory of the way in which anesthetics interfere with consciousness. In linking the abnormal molecular structure of genes to hereditary diseases and mental retardation, Pauling helped to create the field of molecular biology, proposing the concept of "molecular disease." Pauling's inquiry into what he terms "orthomolecular" medicine—therapeutic alteration of body chemistry—coincided with his establishment, in the mid-1970s, of the Linus Pauling Institute of Science and Medicine, a nonprofit research institute at which Pauling oversees empirical confirmation of his orthomolecular theories. According to *Newsweek,* neither of Pauling's Nobel prizes "has brought him the celebrity his 'orthomolecular medicine' has." Pauling's claim for his theories, as articulated by the Goertzels, states that "perhaps all of modern, drug-oriented medicine could be replaced by 'orthomolecular' medicine, which treats the body entirely with natural substances."

As put forth in his popular books *Vitamin C and the Common Cold, Orthomolecular Psychiatry: Treatment of Schizophrenia, Cancer and Vitamin C,* and *Vitamin C, the Common Cold, and the Flu,* Pauling's proposals for mental and physical health describe a program of chemical balance within the body that includes the introduction into body chemistry of large amounts of various vitamins, including vitamin C, or ascorbic acid. Identified by the Goertzels as "part of a broad countercultural movement against established medicine and in favor of natural foods and remedies," Pauling's position on vitamin C maintains that, in the words of *Listener* critic Henry Miller, "while minute doses of ascorbic acid may prevent scurvy, enormously larger doses are required to sustain good health." Pauling also proposes vitamin therapy to prevent or cure the common cold, cancers, influenza, and certain mental diseases. In his *Saturday Review* discussion of Pauling's books on orthomolecular medicine, author and editor Norman Cousins explained that Pauling's theory "is built on the well-known fact that the human body neither manufactures nor stores Vitamin C, yet cannot live without it. Therefore, he says, large amounts ought to be made available in case of need." Cousins noted Pauling's further claim that "massive doses of vitamins, with the emphasis on the Vitamin B family, plus ascorbic acid, enhance the body's ability to repair its 'orthomolecular' deficiencies and to provide for restored chemical balance in the brain." Cousins went on to characterize the reaction of the mental health establishment to Pauling's theories as "rigid to the point of being absurdly illogical in their opposition to megavitamin treatment."

Assessing *Vitamin C and the Common Cold,* Miller remarked that "the most disturbing thing about this highly unscientific book is the tenacious and emotive enthusiasm that Dr. Pauling brings to his profession of faith in ascorbic acid." Similarly, a critic quoted by Langone commented: "Twenty, thirty years ago, he was unerringly rational. Now his feelings about vitamin C are naive. He insists on taking a position that no self-respecting scientist would. There is absolutely no evidence, and Pauling's conclusions have not stood up." A *Newsweek* reviewer, however, noted that while "the scientific establishment sees [Pauling] as something of a crank . . . he continues to push his unorthodox views, and no one has absolutely refuted them." Concluding his review, Cousins advocated serious consideration of Pauling's theories, arguing, "Whether the issue concerns the common cold or mental disease or any of the areas that have claimed Dr. Pauling's interest, he should be confronted only on the highest ground. Professional prerogatives or even tradition should not be allowed to outweigh the possibility that his work could lead to a genuine improvement in the human condition." Reviewing *Vitamin C, the Common Cold, and the Flu* in the *West Coast Review of Books,* critic Henry Zorich acknowledged, "When Pauling speaks, you've got to listen." In a review of *How to Live Longer and Feel Better,* published in 1986, Jonathan Kirsch wrote in the *Los Angeles Times Book Review,* "When a man wins the Nobel Prize not once but twice, and manages to reach his 80s with both body and mind in sound condition, he deserves to be taken seriously." And Pauling mentioned to Wasowicz the attitude of some colleagues, noting, "They have said that I've been right so often in the past that I'm probably right this time, too."

Although his belief in megadose vitamin therapy is controversial, "Dr. Pauling, who now takes 18 grams of vitamin C a day, appears to be a living testament to his ideas," Craig McInnes remarked in a 1987 *Globe and Mail* article. "Twenty years ago, my health improved when I started taking three grams a day. I was livelier and felt better and didn't catch colds any more and that was about all that was bothering me," Pauling told McInnes. "People say I don't seem to have aged much in these 20 years."

Whether proposing new avenues of scientific inquiry or espousing social and political causes, Pauling commanded respect in his dual roles as scientist and humanitarian. "There is little danger when he is wrong and sometimes a great deal to be gained when he is right," the Goertzels wrote. "His unrelenting refusal to admit defeat," Wasowicz noted, "and his persistent crusades have, over the years, stirred up lingering hostilities of passionate proportions in some scientific and political circles—and a kind of folk-hero reverence elsewhere." Summarizing Pauling's career for Wasowicz, Stanford University chemist Hamden

McConnell remarked: "His contributions are hard to total up because they are so many, so diverse and so profound. Time has passed, and nobody remembers how it all got started. But so many things a modern chemist uses in his day-to-day work can be traced back to Linus Pauling." Still active in his eighties as a lecturer, humanitarian crusader, researcher, and author of scientific papers, Pauling informed Wasowicz: "I'm always being asked if I won't write my autobiography. But I have so many other things to do. Hashing over old stuff doesn't interest me as much as making discoveries."

Pauling died of prostate cancer in 1994 at the age of ninety-three. After his death, Barbara Marinacci of the Linus Pauling Institute of Science and Medicine gathered and edited a selection of Pauling's writings, speeches, and interviews and published it as *Linus Pauling in His Own Words.* Writing in the *New York Times Book Review,* John Allen Paulos remarked that "Pauling's prose is direct, devoid of panache or intimate revelation, yet his optimistic, ebullient public personality comes through strongly."

BIOGRAPHICAL/CRITICAL SOURCES:

BOOKS

Farber, Eduard, *Nobel Prize Winners in Chemistry, 1901-1961,* Abelard-Schuman, 1963.
Goertzel, Ted George, and Ben, *Linus Pauling: A Life in Science and Politics,* Basic Books, 1995.
Hager, Thomas, *Force of Nature: The Life of Linus Pauling,* Simon & Schuster, 1995.
Lipsky, Mortimer, *Quest for Peace: The Story of the Nobel Award,* A. S. Barnes, 1966.
Newton, David E., *Linus Pauling: Scientist and Advocate,* Facts on File, 1994.
Watson, James Dewey, *The Double Helix: A Personal Account of the Discovery of the Structure of DNA,* Atheneum, 1968.
Wintterle, John, and R. S. Cramer, *Portraits of Nobel Laureates in Peace,* Abelard-Schuman, 1971.

PERIODICALS

*Antioch Review,* summer, 1980.
*Chicago Tribune,* April 18, 1985.
*Daedalus,* fall, 1970.
*Discover,* November, 1982.
*Globe and Mail* (Toronto), May 16, 1987.
*Harper's Bazaar,* May, 1983.
*Listener,* April 22, 1971.

*Los Angeles Times Book Review,* February 9, 1986, p. 9.
*Los Angeles Times Magazine,* October 13, 1985.
*New Republic,* June 5, 1961.
*Newsweek,* November 15, 1954; July 4, 1960; October 21, 1963; September 29, 1975; October 27, 1980.
*New Yorker,* December 4, 1978.
*New York Times Book Review,* November 5, 1995, p. 28.
*Saturday Review,* May 15, 1971.
*Science,* February 2, 1996, p. 603.
*Tribune Books* (Chicago), January 21, 1996, p. 14.
*USA Today,* September 14, 1983.
*Washington Post Book World,* January 30, 1972.
*West Coast Review of Books,* March, 1977.

OBITUARIES AND OTHER SOURCES:

PERIODICALS

*Chicago Tribune,* August 21, 1994, sec. 2, p. 8; August 28, 1994, sec. 2, p. 6.
*Los Angeles Times,* August 20, 1994, pp. A1, A24; August 21, 1994, p. A3.
*National Review,* September 12, 1994, p. 18.
*New York Times,* August 21, 1994, pp. A1, B51.
*Time,* August 29, 1994, p. 25.
*Times* (London), August 22, 1994, p. 17.*

\*    \*    \*

**PHILLIPS, Bob 1940-**

*PERSONAL:* Born December 25, 1940, in Denver, CO; son of Richard Ross (in sales) and Evelyn (a homemaker; maiden name, East; present surname, Fordham) Phillips; married Pamela Joy MacDonald (a gift shop manager), November 28, 1964; children: Lisa Joy Phillips Ortman, Christine Lynne Phillips Anderson. *Education:* Biola College (now University), B.A., 1964; California State University, Fresno, M.A., 1977; Trinity Seminary, Newburg, IN, Ph.D. *Politics:* Republican. *Religion:* Baptist. *Avocational interests:* Karate, motorcycle riding, exploring caves.

*ADDRESSES: Home*—3224 West Tenaya, Fresno, CA 93711. *Office*—Hume Lake Christian Camps, 64144 Hume Lake Rd., Hume Lake, CA 93628.

*CAREER:* Hume Lake Christian Camps, Hume Lake, CA, assistant director, 1964-74; associate pastor of counseling ministries at a church in Fresno, CA, 1974-78; Fresno Counseling Center, Fresno, staff member, 1978-80; Hume Lake Christian Camps, executive director, 1980—. Licensed marriage, family, and child counselor.

*WRITINGS:*

PUBLISHED BY HARVEST HOUSE (EUGENE, OR), EXCEPT AS INDICATED

*The Great Future Escape,* Vision House (Ventura, CA), 1973.

*The World's Greatest Collection of Clean Jokes,* Vision House, 1974.

*More Good Clean Jokes,* 1974.

*The Last of the Good Clean Jokes,* 1975.

*Redi-Reference,* 1975.

(With Ken Poure) *Praise Is a Three-Letter Word,* Regal Books (Glendale, CA), 1975.

*The All-American Joke Book,* 1976.

*Lots o' Laughs,* Fleming Revell (Old Tappan, NJ), 1976.

(Editor with Tim LaHaye) *The Act of Marriage,* Zondervan (Grand Rapids, MI), 1976.

(Editor with Judy Messer) *To Know Him Is to Love Him,* Beta Books, 1976.

*A Time to Laugh,* 1977.

*The Pre-Marital Workbook,* 1977.

*How Can I Be Sure? A Pre-Marriage Inventory,* 1978.

*A Humorous Look at Love and Marriage,* 1981.

(With LaHaye) *Anger Is a Choice,* Zondervan, 1982.

*The World's Greatest Collection of Heavenly Humor,* 1982.

(With Charlie Tremendous Jones) *Wit and Wisdom,* 1985.

*The Return of the Good Clean Jokes,* 1986.

(With Jones) *Humor Is Tremendous,* Tyndale (Wheaton, IL), 1988.

*The Best of the Good Clean Jokes,* 1989.

*The Delicate Art of Dancing with Porcupines: Learning to Appreciate the Finer Points of Others,* Regal Books, 1989.

*The World's Greatest Collection of Daffy Definitions* [and] *The World's Greatest Collection of Riddles,* 1989.

*The All-New Clean Joke Book,* 1990.

*Good Clean Jokes for Kids,* 1991.

*Powerful Thinking for Powerful Living,* 1991.

*Awesome Good Clean Jokes for Kids,* 1992.

*Bob Phillips' Encyclopedia of Good Clean Jokes,* 1992.

*In Pursuit of Bible Trivia,* two volumes, 1992, published as *The Ultimate Bible Trivia Challenge,* 1992.

*Redi-Reference Daily Bible Reading Plan,* 1992.

*Bible Brainteasers: Heavenly Fun,* 1993.

*Friendship, Love, and Laughter: Inspirational Quotes to Live By,* 1993.

*Loony Good Clean Jokes for Kids,* illustrated by Norm Daniels, 1993.

*Phillips' Book of Great Thoughts and Funny Sayings,* Tyndale, 1993.

*The Best of the Good Clean Jokes Perpetual Calendar,* 1993.

*Ultimate Good Clean Jokes for Kids,* 1993.

*Wacky Good Clean Jokes for Kids,* illustrated by Daniels, 1993.

*Crazy Good Clean Jokes for Kids,* 1994.

*Goofy Good Clean Jokes for Kids!,* 1994.

*The Awesome Book of Bible Trivia,* 1994.

*The Great Bible Challenge,* 1994.

*The Unofficial Liberal Joke Book: For the Politically Incorrect,* illustrated by Nate Owens, 1994.

*More Awesome Good Clean Jokes for Kids,* 1995.

*Nutty Good Clean Jokes for Kids,* 1995.

(With Michael Reagan) *The All-American Quote Book,* 1995.

*The Bible Olympics,* 1995.

*The World's Greatest Collection of Knock Knock Jokes,* Barbour and Co. (Uhrichsville, OH), 1995.

*What to Do until the Psychiatrist Comes: How to Counsel Yourself and Others,* 1995.

(With Steve Russo) *Wild and Woolly Clean Jokes for Kids,* 1995.

*Jest Another Good Clean Joke Book,* 1996.

*The World's All-Time Best Collection of Good Clean Jokes,* Galahad Books (New York City), 1996.

*Tricks, Stunts, and Good Clean Fun,* 1996.

*Sillier Stunts and Terrific Tricks for Kids,* 1997.

*Silly Stunts & Terrific Tricks for Kids,* 1997.

(With Russo) *Squeaky Clean Jokes for Kids,* 1997.

*The Star Spangled Quote Book,* 1997.

*Totally Cool Clean Jokes for Kids,* 1997.

(With Howard Hendricks) *Values, Virtues, and Great Thoughts,* Questar Publishers (Sisters, OR), 1997.

*The Best Ever Book of Good Clean Jokes,* Galahad Books (New York City), 1998

Contributor to books, including *The Big Book of Questions and Answers: The Bible as Told in the Old Testament,* edited by David M. Howard, Jr., Publications International (Lincolnwood, IL), 1992.

*SIDELIGHTS:* Author of over sixty books, Bob Phillips once commented: "I am what is called a 'born again Christian.' I feel that as a Christian I have a responsibility to be an influence in my society with regard to the teachings of Jesus Christ. My writing is varied, from clean joke books to religious and family topics, and in all of these I have endeavored to carry forth my moral convictions. Martin Luther said, 'If you want to influence the world—pick up your pen.' I hope that in some small way my writings will influence my world for good."

*BIOGRAPHICAL/CRITICAL SOURCES:*

*PERIODICALS*

*Voice of Youth Advocates,* April, 1993, p. 57.


\*    \*    \*


**PULLEIN-THOMPSON, Denis**
  **See CANNAN, Denis**

# R

RAINEY, W. B.
See BLASSINGAME, Wyatt Rainey

* * *

RATUSHINSKAYA, Irina 1954-

PERSONAL: Some sources transliterate surname as Ratushinskaia or Ratouchinskaya; born March 4, 1954, in Odessa, Ukraine, U.S.S.R.; daughter of Boris Leonidovich (an engineer) and Irina Valentinovna (a teacher; maiden name, Bulgak) Ratushinsky; married Igor Geraschenko (an engineer), November 16, 1979. Ethnicity: "Russian." Education: Odessa University, M.A., 1976. Politics: None. Religion: Russian Orthodox.

ADDRESSES: Home—15 Crothall Close, Palmers Green, London N13 4BN, England. Agent—Andrew Nurnberg, 45-47 Clerkenwell Green, London EC1R 0HT, England.

CAREER: Teacher at primary school in Odessa, Ukraine, U.S.S.R., 1975-78; Northwestern University, Evanston, IL, poet in residence, 1987-89; writer. Spent four years in a labor camp in Mordovia, U.S.S.R., 1982-86.

MEMBER: International PEN.

AWARDS, HONORS: Poetry International Rotterdam Award, 1986; Religious Freedom Award from Institute on Religion and Democracy, 1987; award from Ross McWhirter Foundation, 1987; Christopher Award, 1988; El Comune di Milano Citizen Award,

city of Milan, Italy, 1989; Individual Templeton Award, United Kingdom, 1993.

WRITINGS:

Stikhi (poems; in Russian with translations into English and French), Hermitage (Ann Arbor, MI), 1984.

Skazka o trekh golovakh: Rasskazy-pritchi [and] A Tale of Three Heads: Short Stories (Russian text and English translation), foreword and afterword by Diane Nemec Ignashev, Hermitage, 1986.

Vne Limita: Izbrannoe (poems), Possev, 1986, selections in English and Russian, translation by Frances Padorr Brent and Carol J. Avis, published as Beyond the Limit, Northwestern University Press (Evanston, IL), 1987.

Ia dozhivu: Stikhi (poems; title means "I Will Survive: Poems"), Tsentr Kul'tury emigrantov iz Sovetskaya Soiuza (New York City), 1986.

No, I'm Not Afraid (poems), translated by David McDuff, introduction by Joseph Brodsky, Bloodaxe Books, 1986.

Grey Is the Color of Hope (memoir), translated by Alyona Kojevnikov, Hodder & Stoughton, 1987, Knopf (New York City), 1988.

Pencil Letter (poems), Bloodaxe Books, 1988.

In the Beginning (autobiography), Hodder & Stoughton, 1990, Knopf, 1991.

Dance with a Shadow (poems), Bloodaxe Books, 1992.

The Odessans (historical novel), Hodder & Stoughton, 1996.

Shadow of a Portrait (novel), J. Murray, 1998.

Wind in the City (poems), Bloodaxe Books, 1998.

Author of poetry collections published in Germany, Norway, the Netherlands, Poland, France, and the

Ukraine. Work represented in anthologies, including *Poetry with an Edge,* Bloodaxe Books, 1988; *Spirits of the Age,* Quarry Press, 1989; *Sing Freedom,* Faber, 1991; *Thin Ice,* Oxford University Press (Oxford, England), 1991; *Poetry Please,* BBC Books, 1991; *Seven Ages,* M. Joseph, 1992; *The Relaxation Letters,* Aquarian Press, 1993; *The Calling of Kindred,* Cambridge University Press (Cambridge, England), 1993; and *From the Republic of Conscience,* White Pine (Buffalo, NY), 1993.

*WORK IN PROGRESS: Dancers in a Minefield,* a historical novel, for Hodder & Stoughton, completion expected in 1998; *Female Virus,* a novel, 1999.

*SIDELIGHTS:* Irina Ratushinskaya told *CA:* "I like writing. When I write poetry, I just try to catch it, like a forgotten tune. It comes more easily if I walk alone. With prose, I do some research and then do my best to forget it (that's the longest part of the work). What remains in my memory then is exactly what I need for my writing. When I am ready, I have a honeymoon with my computer, enjoying myself. Then the whole project has a month's rest, and so do I. After a break I add the finishing touches and give the manuscript to my agent.

"I write about the things I find interesting. I have no idea why I get interested, and my instincts prevent me from searching the matter more deeply."

Charged with anti-Soviet agitation, poet Irina Ratushinskaya spent four years as a political prisoner in a labor camp in the Soviet Union. *New York Times Book Review* contributor Maria Carlson explained that Ratushinskaya was arrested for distributing her poetry and for her involvement in the Soviet human rights movement. She was released on October 9, 1986, the evening before the summit meeting between President Ronald Reagan and Soviet leader Mikhail Gorbachev in Reykjavik, Iceland. *Spectator* contributor Andrei Nazvrozov suggested that the coincidental timing of Ratushinskaya's release, almost four years before the end of her sentence, was a diplomatic political gesture to the West. Members of international human rights organizations such as International PEN were monitoring her situation and may have influenced her release. Gorbachev, regarded by many as a progressive reformer, has in recent years ushered in a welcome period of *glasnost* or openness between the United States and the Soviet Union, but the degree of progress in human rights in the Soviet Union has been disputed. Navrozov quoted Ratushinskaya in the *Spectator:* "It's non-

sense to talk about limited human rights. . . . It's like limited breath." In regard to Gorbachev's reforms, Ratushinskaya commented in a *New York Times Book Review* article, "It is too early to be so enthusiastic. . . . Gorbachev is like a dentist who fills a tooth for someone suffering from cancer." She added, "It is not cosmetic, but yet so much remains the same."

While imprisoned, Ratushinskaya composed some 250 poems, scratching them into soap and washing them away after committing them to memory. Her intimate, personal poems, now published in *Beyond the Limit,* show an intense appreciation for life, freedom, and the beauty of nature, which she was able to see through her prison window—colorful autumn leaves and the "prism ice" that formed on it. Carlson, who declared that Ratushinskaya "has already achieved a reputation as a poet of note and found an audience both in her homeland and abroad," asserted that the English translation of *Beyond the Limit* "does not convey the extraordinary range of this gifted poet, . . . [but] even in translation, reading her poetry is a profound emotional experience." According to Carlson, Ratushinskaya "transcends the prison experience, taking her reader with her into the world of unvanquished spirit, 'beyond the gates, beyond the boundary,' 'beyond the border / that cannot be crossed,' 'beyond the limit.'"

Ratushinskaya's life at the camp is further detailed in her memoir, *Grey Is the Color of Hope. Los Angeles Times Book Review* contributor Jacobo Timerman, who himself had been a political prisoner in an Argentine jail, remarked that Ratushinskaya "introduces us to a new manner of struggling against oppression: to take cognizance of the beauty of the world." Timerman added that it is "not the beauty of man [that fills her book], but the beauty of a world in which man is a very small particle and not the most commendable. It is a book in which the gray of a prisoner's uniform can be the color of hope." For Timerman, Ratushinskaya's narrative was a "true, moving revelation. There is something new, original and unexpected in Ratushinskaya's account of her life as a dissident and as a prisoner: humor, happiness, poetry."

Similarly, what *New York Times Book Review* critic Francine du Plessix Gray considered "some of the most startling passages" of *Grey Is the Color of Hope* were Ratushinskaya's depictions of "female ceremonies of domesticity and civility that helped her companions to maintain their loving ties." These ceremonies, which included elaborate birthday celebrations (given the circumstances), demonstrated different strategies of coping with prison than those associated with male prisoners. According to Gray, men usually played chess, discussed politics and dreamed of escape. Ratushinskaya relates how she and the other women dissidents supported each other, refusing to eat when one of them was mistreated. The women also united in devising and abiding by their own code of conduct, accepting certain prison rules and rejecting others as a way of preserving their sense of honor. For example, Gray reported that the women conscientiously performed their assigned task of making protective workmen's gloves "because such labor is honest and useful to any community." On the other hand, they balked at wearing identification tags, which they viewed as "a symbolic surrender of their autonomy," Gray explained. Ratushinskaya risked punishment in solitary confinement and missing a rare chance to see her husband when she refused to wear the tag.

Ratushinskaya maintains she is apolitical; that is not to say she is ambivalent toward world affairs. Her prison experience confirmed her dedication to human rights. According to Timerman, when Ratushinskaya, then free in England, was asked, "To what do you feel allegiance?," she replied, "To human rights."

Ratushinskaya told *CA:* "I was born a poet. For being an independent poet I was arrested in the U.S.S.R. I spent more than four years in prisons and labor camps, where I met people who struggled for freedom and human rights. I believe the most vital subjects are courage and the sense of personal responsibility for everything that is happening. I also think that for a poet, it is more important to keep in touch with God than with politicians."

## BIOGRAPHICAL/CRITICAL SOURCES:

### BOOKS

Ratushinskaya, Irina, *Beyond the Limit,* Northwestern University Press, 1987.

### PERIODICALS

*Los Angeles Times Book Review,* October 23, 1988.
*New York Times Book Review,* June 28, 1987; October 30, 1988.
*Spectator,* June 18, 1988.
*Times Literary Supplement,* October 31, 1986; August 26, 1988.

## REED, Rex (Taylor) 1938-

*PERSONAL:* Born October 2, 1938, in Fort Worth, TX; son of J. M. (an oil company supervisor) and Jewell (Smith) Reed. *Education:* Louisiana State University, B.A., 1960.

*ADDRESSES: Home*—Roxbury, CT. *Office*—c/o Macmillan Inc., 866 Third Ave., New York, NY 10022.

*CAREER:* Worked variously as a jazz singer, television performer, pancake cook, record salesman, and actor, 1960-65; film critic for *Women's Wear Daily,* 1965-69, *Cosmopolitan, Status,* and *Holiday,* beginning 1965; music critic for *Stereo Review,* 1968-75; film critic for *Vogue, New York Daily News, Gentleman's Quarterly,* and the *New York Post;* currently co-host of syndicated television series *At the Movies.* Syndicated columnist for Chicago Tribune syndicate. Member of jury at Berlin, Venice, Atlanta, and U.S.A. Film Festivals; lecturer. Actor in 1970 film *Myra Breckinridge;* cameo appearance in *Superman,* 1978.

*WRITINGS:*

*Do You Sleep in the Nude?,* New American Library (New York City), 1968.
*Conversations in the Raw,* World Publishing (New York City), 1970.
*Big Screen, Little Screen,* Macmillan (New York City), 1971.
*People Are Crazy Here,* Delacorte (New York City), 1974.
*Valentines and Vitriol,* Delacorte, 1977.
*Travolta to Keaton,* Morrow (New York City), 1979.
*Personal Effects* (novel), Arbor House (New York City), 1986.
*Rex Reed's Guide to Movies on TV and Video,* Warner (New York City), 1992.

Contributor to numerous magazines, including *Ladies' Home Journal, Esquire, Harper's Bazaar, New York Times, Playboy,* and *Vogue.*

*SIDELIGHTS:* As much a celebrity as many of the entertainers he writes about, critic and journalist Rex Reed is best known for interviews that strip the glamour from Hollywood stars. His incisive writing has earned him a reputation as the "hatchet man" of show business journalism, but Reed asserts that he never goes to interviews with preconceived ideas. "I give people the benefit of the doubt, and if they hang themselves that's their problem," he told a reporter from *Newsweek*. Nonetheless, according to John Simon writing in *National Review,* "clever bitchiness" is a hallmark of Reed's style. Although many literary critics have dismissed Reed as a lightweight, mean-minded commentator on popular culture, A. J. Kaul points out in the *Dictionary of Literary Biography* that Reed's early work in the 1960s earned him a spot in the "coterie of New Journalists who redefined nonfiction writing and resurrected its literary status."

The only child of an oil company supervisor whose work required extensive travel, Reed grew up in a succession of small Southern towns. By the time he graduated from Natchitoches High School in Louisiana, he had attended no less than thirteen public schools. He was, as he told the *Newsweek* reporter, "always the new kid," an experience that he found traumatic: "It was a terrible thing. I withdrew from it all and went to the movies every afternoon. Now when I go to interview movie people they say, 'But when did you see that?'" In college he became a columnist, critic and editorial writer for the campus newspaper and it was there he first established the reputation for controversy that would characterize his career. After attacking segregation in an editorial entitled "The Prince of Prejudice," he was burned in effigy by the Ku Klux Klan.

From the Baton Rouge, Louisiana, campus where he graduated with a degree in journalism, Reed moved to New York City. There he perfected his skills as a freelance writer while working at a number of odd jobs. His first big break came in 1965 when two celebrity interviews he conducted were published in the *New York Times* and *New York* magazine. Since that time, both his film criticism and his interviews have been in national demand.

In 1968, some of Reed's early *New York Times, Esquire* and *Cosmopolitan* articles were compiled in a provocatively entitled bestseller, *Do You Sleep in the Nude?* The publication was so successful that Reed has compiled his better celebrity interviews into book form ever since. Among those whom Reed has singled out for attention are Paul Newman, Jack Nicholson, Lucille Ball, Barbra Streisand, and such normally reticent stars as Walter Matthau and Geraldine Page. In fact, he is so renowned that "the Rex Reed treatment" has become "one of the hallmarks of success for an actor or director," according to Henry Flowers writing in the *New York Times Book Review.*

Despite the popularity of his books, many critics disparage Reed's style. "There is panic and fearful insecurity behind this frantic compulsion to mix with the famous and sniff the hem of power. But Rex sees neither the humor nor the mediocrity in a system that elevates his brand of witless ballyhoo to stardom," writes John Lahr in the *New York Times Book Review.* Of Reed's 1977 book, Lahr concludes, "*Valentines and Vitriol* is superficial even in its shallowness. Rex calls himself a 'critic,' as much a misnomer as 'sanitary engineer.'" While Flowers agrees that "Reed's is a severely limited talent," he tempers his assessment by acknowledging that "within his limitations he is excellent."

Yet Tom Wolfe, a journalist who has won widespread respect and praise for his writing, found Reed's work worthy of inclusion in his 1973 anthology *The New Journalism.* The piece he selected was a profile of film star Ava Gardner. According to Kaul, who described the Gardner piece as "poignant," Wolfe declared that Reed "raised the celebrity interview to a new level through his frankness and his eye for social detail. He has also been a master at capturing a story line in the interview situation itself." Wolfe added that "Reed is excellent at recording and using dialogue." Kaul went on to note that Reed's unique style of interviewing is "a mix of first-person commentary, observation, and extensive quotation candidly used to reveal the idiosyncrasies and foibles of the personalities he profiled."

Reed's first novel, *Personal Effects,* stays true to the author's showbiz leanings. The story of how a Hollywood journalist, Billy Buck, involves himself in the investigation of a famous actress's murder didn't win Reed many fans among reviewers. Karen Stabiner, for one, writing in the *Los Angeles Times Book Review,* sees *Personal Effects* as "a big candy box of a Hollywood novel—good for a quick sugary rush when ingested in small doses, but guaranteed to give you a bad case of mental bloat by the time you're through." Stabiner adds the dubious praise that *Personal Effects* "is a hoot, in the grand tradition of trashy Hollywood fiction, the kind of novel that keeps the word 'sprawling' in the top-10 of book-reviewing adjectives."

Summarizing Reed's career, Kaul allows that "few critics have bestowed upon his work the respect and dignity he hopes to earn. His notoriety and celebrity status may have prompted professional jealousies that found their way into the snide and caustic assessments of his writing." Kaul also quoted Reed as saying in a *Writer's Digest* interview: "All I would like for them to do is respect my work. I would like my body of work to be looked back on as honest and flavorful, but with respect and dignity."

*BIOGRAPHICAL/CRITICAL SOURCES:*

*BOOKS*

*Authors in the News,* Volume 1, Gale (Detroit), 1976.
*Dictionary of Literary Biography,* Volume 185: *American Literary Journalists, 1945-1995, First Series,* Gale, 1997.

*PERIODICALS*

*Florida Times-Union,* March 15, 1985.
*Globe and Mail* (Toronto), May 10, 1986.
*Los Angeles Times Book Review,* February 26, 1986.
*Minneapolis Star & Tribune,* March 11, 1986.
*National Review,* July 5, 1974.
*Newsweek,* January 8, 1968, p. 47.
*New York Times Book Review,* July 21, 1968; November 9, 1969; May 22, 1977.
*Philadelphia Inquirer,* March 9, 1986.
*Time,* August 23, 1968, pp. 54-55.
*Writers Digest,* September, 1973, pp. 10-21.*

\*     \*     \*

**REPLANSKY, Naomi 1918-**

*PERSONAL:* Born May 23, 1918, in New York, NY; daughter of Sol and Fannie (Ginsberg) Replansky; companion of Eva Kollisch. *Education:* Attended Hunter College, Bronx, NY, 1935-38; University of California, Los Angeles, B.A., 1956.

*ADDRESSES: Home*—711 Amsterdam Ave., #8E, New York, NY 10025.

*CAREER:* Poet. Worked at a variety of jobs, including office worker, factory worker, teacher, and computer programmer. Pitzer College, Claremont, CA, poet-in-residence, 1981; Henry Street Settlement and Educational Alliance, New York City, teacher of writing workshops, 1982-94.

*MEMBER:* PEN American Center, Poetry Society of America, Poets House, Phi Beta Kappa.

*AWARDS, HONORS:* National Book Award nomination, 1952, for *Ring Song.*

*WRITINGS:*

*Ring Song* (poems), Scribner (New York City), 1952.
(Translator) Bertolt Brecht, *St. Joan of the Stockyards,* produced in New York City, 1978.
*Twenty-one Poems, Old and New* (chapbook), Gingko (New York City), 1988.
*The Dangerous World: New and Selected Poems, 1934-1994,* Another Chicago Press (Chicago), 1994.

Contributor of poems and translations of the works of Hofmannsthal, Claudius, and Brecht to American and European magazines and anthologies, including *No More Masks! An Anthology of Twentieth-Century American Woman Poets,* edited by Florence Howe, 1993.

Collection of author's manuscripts is housed in the Berg Collection, New York Public Library.

*SIDELIGHTS:* Poet Naomi Replansky arose to prominence in the early-1950s when her first full-length collection of poems, *Ring Song,* was nominated for the National Book Award. However, such kudos were accompanied by blistering reviews by several critics. Replansky published only occasionally for four decades, finally emerging with *The Dangerous World: New and Selected Poems, 1934-1994.*

Written primarily during the poet's 20s and 30s, *Ring Song* reflects the creativity of a "self-taught, working-class woman who learned the craft of poetry while working in factories and stores," according to *Contemporary Women Poets* essayist Denise Wiloch. While several critics had praise for the collection—among them M. L. Rosenthal of the *New Republic,* who deemed Replansky's verses "alive and bright with color and feeling"—there were also criticisms, issuing mainly from the "patriarchal poetry establishment" of the mid-1950s, according to a reviewer in the *Bloomsbury Review.* Lawrence Ferlinghetti, reviewing *Ring Song* in the *San Francisco Chronicle,* maintained that the volume contained choppy writing and surmised that Replansky neglects the use of "her mind . . . when writing, as if merely to observe were enough." Unfortunately, Ferlinghetti, continued, such skills of observation were not yet mature.

After publication, Replansky kept a literary silence for some years. Though some have interpreted that silence as a reaction to hostile reviews, Replansky explained to *CA* that it was more likely "the smothering effect of the McCarthy era, as well as the long gestation period for each of [my] poems" that were to blame. However, she continued to write, and the best of her work over the first sixty years of her writing career were collected and published in the mid-1990s as *The Dangerous World*. A collection that a *Publishers Weekly* reviewer characterized as "offer[ing] stark and sturdy urban wisdom," *The Dangerous World* contains twenty-five poems from *Ring Song,* many of which are revised, and an additional forty-two more recently penned verses that take as their subject such themes as poverty, work, love destroyed, love fulfilled, aging, and the fragile essence of life itself. While Replansky's verses reflect the circumstances of her own life as a single, working-class woman with such a life's attendant difficulties, the tone of *The Dangerous World* is not pessimistic. As Florence Howe characterized Replansky's book in her *Women's Review of Books* article, "the single volume, read for plot, offers an outline, names the themes. . . . [She] writes brief, often exquisite lyrics that glance across the pain to insist on survival." Beyond simply maintaining emotional survivor status, the poet's voice is "secure and happy," in the opinion of Wiloch, who credits a late-in-life lover with Replansky's positive outlook. *The Dangerous World* showcases its author's "gift for writing delicate lyrics," continued Wiloch, "that celebrate in simple, sculpted language the joys and beauties of her life."

*BIOGRAPHICAL/CRITICAL SOURCES:*

*BOOKS*

Blair, Virginia, and others, editors, *Feminist Companion to Literature in English,* Yale University Press (New Haven, CT), 1990.
*Contemporary Women Poets,* St. James Press (Detroit), 1997.

*PERIODICALS*

*Bloomsbury Review,* January/February, 1995, p. 20.
*Booklist,* September 1, 1952, p. 49; October 15, 1994, p. 395.
*Lamp in the Spine* (St. Paul, MN), 1973-74.
*Nation,* September 12, 1952.
*New Republic,* January 5, 1953, p. 128.
*New York Times,* August 31, 1952, p. 11.

*Publishers Weekly,* September 26, 1994, p. 60.
*San Francisco Chronicle,* September 7, 1952, p. 21.
*Women's Review of Books,* December, 1995, pp. 11-12.

\*   \*   \*

**RICKMAN, H(ans) P(eter) 1918-**

*PERSONAL:* Born November 11, 1918, in Prague, Czechoslovakia; son of Ernst (a lawyer) and Grete (Wollin) Weisskopf; adopted by stepfather, 1929; married Muriel Edith Taylor, May 5, 1947 (died May 28, 1981). *Ethnicity:* "Caucasian." *Education:* Educated in Czechoslovakia, 1924-38 (with one year at a university); University of London, B.A. (with honors), 1941, M.A., 1948; New College, Oxford, D.Phil., 1943.

*ADDRESSES: Home*—12 Fitzroy Ct., 57 Shepherds Hill, London N6, England. *Office*—Department of Social Sciences and Humanities, City University, London, England.

*CAREER:* University of Hull, Hull, England, staff tutor in philosophy and psychology, 1949-61; City University, London, England, senior lecturer, 1961-67, reader, 1967-82, visiting professor of philosophy, 1982—. Imperial Cancer Research Fund, life governor. *Military service:* British Army, served in intelligence and education posts, 1944-47.

*MEMBER:* International PEN, Aristotelian Society, Royal Institute of Philosophy, Association of University Teachers, Society of Authors, Oxford Union.

*WRITINGS:*

*Meaning in History: Dilthey's Thought on History and Society,* Allen & Unwin, 1961, published as *Pattern and Meaning in History,* Harper (New York City), 1962.
*Preface to Philosophy,* Schenkman (Cambridge, MA), 1964, published as *The Use of Philosophy,* Routledge & Kegan Paul, 1973.
*Living with Technology,* Zenith (New York City), 1966.
*Understanding and the Human Studies,* Heinemann, 1967.
(Editor) Wilhelm Dilthey, *Selected Writings,* Cambridge University Press, 1976.

*Wilhelm Dilthey: Pioneer of the Human Studies,* University of California, 1979.

*The Adventure of Reason: The Uses of Philosophy in Sociology,* Greenwood Press (Westport, CT), 1983.

*Change,* Nan-Un-Do, 1985.

*British Universities,* Nan-Un-Do, 1987.

*Dilthey Today,* Greenwood Press, 1988.

*Haunted by History* (suspense novel), Book Guild, 1995.

*Paper Chase* (suspense novel), Book Guild, 1995.

*Philosophy Today,* Associated University Presses, 1996.

Author of the book *Philosophy in Literature.* Contributor to *Encyclopedia of Philosophy,* 1967, *Symposium Volume on VICO,* 1969, 1981, and *The Hero in Transition,* 1983. Also contributor of about sixty articles to *Fortnightly, Hibbert Journal, German Life and Letters, International Studies in Philosophy,* and other periodicals.

*SIDELIGHTS:* H. P. Rickman told *CA:* "One of the major concerns of my research and writing is how philosophy can help the social sciences to become more relevant and rigorous without aping the physical sciences."

He added: "Writing has been a compulsion throughout my life. Philosophically I have been most influenced by Kant and also Dilthey, the subject of several of my books. For writing, I need regular, undisturbed hours, starting in the early morning.

"In my recent book *Philosophy in Literature,* my persistent interest in philosophy is turned on my lifelong love of poetry and fiction. My two thrillers are a response to decades of reading crime fiction."

\*    \*    \*

### ROSS, Lillian 1927-

*PERSONAL:* Born June 8, 1927, in Syracuse, NY; daughter of Louis and Edna (Rosenson) Ross; children: Erik Jeremy.

*ADDRESSES: Office*—c/o *New Yorker* Magazine, 25 West 43rd St., New York, NY 10036.

*CAREER: New Yorker,* New York City, 1948—, staff writer, 1949—, including fiction for "Profiles" and "Reporter at Large" sections and stories in "The Talk of the Town" section.

*AWARDS, HONORS:* Books-across-the-Sea Ambassador of Honor Book, English-Speaking Union, 1985, for *Takes: Stories from "The Talk of the Town."*

*WRITINGS:*

*Portrait of Hemingway* (originally published as a "Profile" in the *New Yorker,* May 13, 1950; also see below), Simon & Schuster (New York City), 1961.

*Picture* (account of the making of the film *The Red Badge of Courage,* originally published in the *New Yorker;* also see below), Rinehart (New York City), 1952, with foreword by Anjelica Huston, Anchor (New York City), 1993.

(With sister, Helen Ross) *The Player: A Profile of an Art* (interviews), Simon & Schuster, 1962, Limelight Editions, 1984.

*Vertical and Horizontal* (short stories), Simon & Schuster, 1963.

*Reporting* (articles originally published in the *New Yorker,* including "The Yellow Bus," "Symbol of All We Possess," "The Big Stone," "Terrific," "El Unico Matador," "Portrait of Hemingway," and "Picture"), Simon & Schuster, 1964, with new introduction by the author, Dodd (New York City), 1981.

*Adlai Stevenson,* Lippincott (Philadelphia), 1966.

*Talk Stories* (sixty stories first published in "The Talk of the Town" section of the *New Yorker,* 1958-65), Simon & Schuster, 1966.

*Reporting Two,* Simon & Schuster, 1969.

*Moments with Chaplin,* Dodd, 1980.

*Takes: Stories from "The Talk of the Town,"* Congdon & Weed (New York City), 1983.

*Here but Not Here: A Love Story* (memoir), Random House, 1998.

*SIDELIGHTS:* In *Book Week,* Robert Manning describes interviewer and reporter Lillian Ross, who is not related to *New Yorker* founder Harold W. Ross, as "a contemporary journalistic equivalent of Goya the court painter. . . . With an Ampex ear, a scalpel for her palette knife and a cool, clear head for structure and style, [she] stands back from the situations she has chosen to chronicle or the subjects (one is strongly tempted to call them victims) who have somehow been beguiled into sitting for her." According to Irving Wallace in the *New York Times Book Review,* "She is the mistress of selective listening and viewing, of capturing the one moment that entirely illumines the scene, of fastening on the one quote that Tells All. She is a brilliant interpreter of what she hears and observes. And she is the possessor of a unique writing style—spare, direct, objective, fast—a style that disarms, seemingly only full of wonder, but one that can suddenly, almost sneakily, nail a personality naked to a page."

Ross has always been extremely careful to guard the details of her own life. One of the few personal facts known about her is that she was born in Syracuse, New York, and she has publicly lamented letting that piece of information become common knowledge. "Ross's reluctance to reveal much about herself may be based, at least in part, on principles about writing and reporting that she holds dear," notes Thomas B. Connery in *Dictionary of Literary Biography.* The critic goes on to explain that Ross believes strongly that the reporter should not become a noticeable part of his article. "Ross views celebrity journalists as distractions to genuine reporting and counterproductive to depicting the truth of the persons, places, or events being covered," advises Connery. "Thus, the less the reader knows about Ross, the more the reader is able to focus on her subjects."

Yet Connery further notes that "if there is a contradiction in Ross's views of reporting/writing, it would be in her contention that as long as she stands back from a scene and exhaustively records details for her readers, she remains a neutral observer and the facts tend to speak for themselves. Her primary reporting technique is to be as unobtrusive as possible, to listen and watch carefully, to use a fly-on-the-wall approach . . . and take lots of notes. She never uses a tape recorder. . . . Her presence in an article is barely and rarely felt, except as the narrator who serves as the reader's eyes and ears."

Some reviewers have referred to the text on the dust jacket of Ross's *Reporting* for its description of her work. It reads, in part: "Over the years, the reporters of the *New Yorker* have, among them, produced a new literary tradition: reporting as an art. None of them has done more to develop that art than Miss Ross. . . . She creates the illusion that the reporter has vanished altogether and that life is transferring itself, with startling immediacy, to paper. In her 'Profile' of Ernest Hemingway, she employs very much the same method to form an entire portrait in terms of narrative—a minute-by-minute account of what Hemingway did, and how he looked and talked (with friends and family), in a few hours of his life."

About her 1950 *New Yorker* profile of Hemingway, Ross once told *CA* that despite some published reports to the contrary, the piece did not draw a large volume of unfavorable mail: "The overwhelming reaction when it was first published was one of great enthusiasm and appreciation. Some people did not like it and said so; hence the 'controversy.'" (It remained controversial into the 1960s, with attacks by such critics as Irving Howe, although Hemingway himself read the article prior to publication, made a few corrections, and supported Ross when criticism of it appeared.)

J. F. Fixx of *Saturday Review* labels *Reporting* "a vivid and valuable example of the journalist's art [that] deserves to be recommended to any reporter interested in a postgraduate course in his craft." Referring to *Talk Stories,* Marya Mannes of *Book Week* considers Ross an excellent reporter who "knows how to record the revealing phrase, the defining gesture. [In *Talk Stories*] she allows these to make their own comment, withholding hers. Because of this, and because of their vitality and humor, the stories have stood as miniature documentaries of cosmopolitan life peculiar to the *New Yorker*'s best tradition."

In *Takes: Stories from "The Talk of the Town,"* Ross presents a collection of articles from the section of the same title in the *New Yorker*. Art Seidenbaum observes in the *Los Angeles Times* that "these pieces are models of reporting, of proving how the discrete detail can tell a more credible story than the big generalization, of showing how the participating writer may attend everything without distorting anything, of finding profound emotion in the most mundane enterprises."

*Portrait of Hemingway* was translated into Russian.

*BIOGRAPHICAL/CRITICAL SOURCES:*

*BOOKS*

Connery, Thomas B., editor, *A Sourcebook of American Literary Journalism: Representative Writers in an Emerging Genre,* Greenwood Press (New York City), 1992, pp. 231-37.

Dennis, Everette E., and William L. Rivers, *The New Journalism in America: Other Voices,* Canfield Press (San Francisco), 1974.

*Dictionary of Literary Biography,* Volume 185: *American Literary Journalists, 1945-1995, First Series,* Gale (Detroit), 1997.

*PERIODICALS*

*Book Week,* March 15, 1964; May 1, 1966.
*Chicago Tribune Book World,* July 27, 1980, p. 3.
*Los Angeles Times,* March 30, 1983.
*Los Angeles Times Book Review,* March 27, 1983.
*New Republic,* August 7, 1961.
*Newsweek,* December 18, 1961, p. 102.
*New York Times,* May 7, 1998.
*New York Times Book Review,* June 2, 1963; May 15, 1966; December 16, 1984.
*Saturday Review,* May 25, 1963; March 14, 1964.
*Time,* May 9, 1964, pp. 67-68.
*Variety,* May 24, 1993, p. 63.
*Washington Post Book World,* January 13, 1985.\*


\*    \*    \*


**RYDER, Jonathan**
   **See LUDLUM, Robert**

# S-V

## SACK, John 1930-

*PERSONAL:* Born March 24, 1930, in New York, NY; son of John Jacob (a clerk) and Tracy Rose (Levy) Sack. *Education:* Harvard University, A.B., 1951; Columbia University, graduate study, 1963-64.

*CAREER:* Writer and journalist. United Press, correspondent in Peru, 1950, Japan and Korea, 1953-54, and Albany, NY, 1954-55; Columbia Broadcasting System, CBS News, documentary writer and producer in New York City and Paris, 1961-66; *Esquire,* New York City, correspondent in Vietnam, 1966-67, contributing editor, 1967-78, correspondent in the Persian Gulf, 1991; *Playboy,* Chicago, IL, contributing editor in Los Angeles, 1978—; KCBS-TV, Los Angeles, newswriter and producer, 1982-84. *Military service:* U.S. Army, 1951-53; served in Korea; war correspondent, *Pacific Stars and Stripes,* 1952-55.

*MEMBER:* Writers Guild of America, Screen Actors Guild, American Federation of Television and Radio Artists.

*WRITINGS:*

*The Butcher: The Ascent of Yerupaja,* Rinehart (New York City), 1952 (published in England as *The Ascent of Yerupaja,* Jenkins [Lancaster, England], 1954).
*From Here to Shimbashi,* Harper (New York City), 1955.
*Report from Practically Nowhere,* Harper, 1959.
*M,* New American Library (New York City), 1967.

*Lieutenant Calley: His Own Story,* Viking (New York City), 1971 (published in England as *Body Count: Lieutenant Calley's Story,* Hutchinson [London], 1971).
*The Man-Eating Machine,* Farrar, Straus (New York City), 1973.
*Fingerprint,* Random House (New York City), 1983.
*An Eye for an Eye,* Basic Books (New York City), 1993.
*Company C: The Real War in Iraq,* Morrow (New York City), 1995.

Author of television documentaries. Contributor to magazines, including *Harper's, Atlantic Monthly, Holiday, Town and Country, Playboy, Eros,* and *New Yorker.*

*WORK IN PROGRESS:* "Searching in the People's Republic of the Congo for the last living dinosaurs," and writing about them for the Associated Press, CBS News, *Playboy,* and Random House.

*SIDELIGHTS:* "John Sack's devotion to accuracy and fairness places his writings among the best examples of the ability of literary journalism to capture truth," declares James Stewart in the *Dictionary of Literary Biography.* "Working within a school of reporting often criticized for its use of literary license, Sack, one of New Journalism's pioneers, has built a career on accuracy. His stories are as vivid and compelling as those of others using that style, and yet, despite the assumptions of some critics, he has made it his practice not to fictionalize."

Sack's reporting career began when he was just fifteen years old and took a job as a stringer for the *Mamaroneck Daily Times,* a Long Island newspaper.

By the time he was in college, he was a stringer for the United Press and for the *Boston Globe.* Working as a correspondent in Peru for United Press, he accompanied an expedition up Yerupaja, which was then the highest unclimbed mountain in the Americas. Out of this experience came his first book, *The Butcher: The Ascent of Yerupaja.* His next, *From Here to Shimbashi,* records his years in the Army, including his service in the Korean War.

Sack once told *CA* that his "best or best-known book" is "*M,* which was excerpted in 1966 as the cover story in *Esquire,* the longest article in *Esquire*'s history." *M* is the story of "M" Company of the 1st Advanced Infantry Training Brigade. "John Sack followed the company from the inanity of a training inspection at Fort Dix to the senseless killing of a seven-year-old girl in Viet Nam," writes Stewart Kampel in the *New York Times.* "He has produced a gripping, honest account, compassionate and rich, colorful and blackly comic, but with that concerned objectivity that makes for great reportage." Writing in *Book Week,* Dan Wakefield praises *M* as "one of the finest, most perceptive books of reportage in recent years. One must go back to Orwell for appropriate comparisons of journalistic excellence." And Robert Kirsch's *Los Angeles Times* review names *M* as "the whole story, one of the most compelling ever told about men in war. This is the way it is." Sack's *Lieutenant Calley* is the story of the My Lai massacre in Viet Nam. In a letter to *CA,* the author notes that it is his "most infamous book . . . in the course of writing which the federal government arrested and indicted me but never prosecuted me." *Lieutenant Calley* has been translated into German, Spanish, French, Portuguese, Italian, and Finnish.

The 1983 book *Fingerprint* has been compared by reviewers to Laurence Sterne's *Tristam Shandy.* Like that classic, writes Michiko Kakutani in the *New York Times, Fingerprint* "begins with the events leading up to the author's conception and birth, and it similarly boasts a narrative positively crammed with digressions and asides." Kakutani continues: "Gifted with an eye for physical detail and a canny ear for dialogue, Mr. Sack is at his best when he sticks closely to the facts of his own life. . . . It is when he attempts to pontificate on the large evils of society that he becomes trite and moralistic." Reviewing *Fingerprint* in the *Washington Post Book World,* Joseph McLellan criticizes Sack's "polemic, which is . . . a diatribe against what he calls 'efficiency'. . . . In a sense, his complaints resemble what one of his beard follicles might have to say about his efficient habit of

shaving. Still, he does write well and there is a germ of truth in what he has to say. . . . In an age when we are teaching computers to become more and more "user-friendly," we may hope to see better days ahead—speeded, perhaps, by amorphous howls such as *Fingerprint.*"

"Sack has hung about since the '50's, participating in the kinks and enthusiasms of the succeeding times while writing about them critically but on the whole amiably," notes Richard Eder in the *Los Angeles Times Book Review.* "He is a sunny man, or a sunny writer, at least: *Fingerprint,* though a concentrated denunciation of what he sees as the central fallacy of our civilization, draws its originality not so much from the fierceness or cogency of the denunciation as from its exuberance."

In 1993 Sack became the center of controversy again with the publication of *An Eye for an Eye,* a story of abuse in the internment camps set up by the postwar Communist Polish government to hold ethnic Germans and Poles suspected of collaborating with the Nazis. Some of the commandants of these camps were Polish Communist Jews—including people who had themselves been held in concentration camps during World War II—who took out their resentments on their German prisoners. In a series of interviews with some of these commandants, Sack presented a drastic picture of anti-German brutality that, according to some reviewers, distorted historical truth. In addition, historians complained that Sack's free, journalistic style and the unorthodoxy of his documentation made it difficult or impossible to check his sources.

Basic Books, Sack's publisher, attracted criticism for its sensational marketing of the book and its hurried publication. Sack's book was very nearly never published; according to the author, reports Jon Wiener in the *Nation,* "no one else [but Basic Books] would publish the book: It was rejected by something like a dozen publishers, until Steve Fraser of Basic Books signed it up." One of the reasons that Basic Books accepted *An Eye for an Eye* so quickly was because *60 Minutes* was doing a piece on one of Sack's interviewees. The book was rushed through publication within two months, about one-fourth of the time normally taken. "The publication date of the book did coincide with the *60 Minutes* broadcast," Wiener explains, "but the result was that the book that Basic published, as Fraser says, was virtually identical to the text that Sack submitted. A manuscript that desperately needed editing got virtually none."

A number of critics agree that the events Sack describes in *An Eye for an Eye* did happen—that some Communist Polish Jews who had been held by the Nazis in concentration camps during World War II were appointed by the Communist government of Poland in 1945 to command camps interning ethnic Germans and suspected German collaborators, and that some of these Polish Jews took their frustrations out on their prisoners. However, they question his conclusions and implications as well as his methods. Daniel Jonah Goldhagen, an assistant professor at Harvard University's school of government and one of Sack's earliest and harshest critics, declares in his review for the *New Republic* that *Eye for an Eye* "strings together facts and pseudo-facts about individual Jews in the aftermath of the Holocaust with the effect of creating a sometimes subtle and sometimes not so subtle indictment of Jews in general." "The book fails disgracefully in much of what it does present—misshapen stories and wild innuendo—and in all of what it does not present, namely a serious consideration of the context and the meaning of the events that it describes," Goldhagen concludes, "and the analytical and moral concepts that it employs." "There's one more problem with Sack's claim that the Jews in his book 'became like Nazis'—they didn't," asserts Wiener. "The Holocaust was not just sadistic SS men whipping and killing Jews; it was bureaucratic, scientific and comprehensive in its mobilization of the resources of Europe's leading industrial society for the purposes of extermination."

Some reviewers attacked Sack's critics, claiming that the Jewish community objected to the presentation of Jews as persecutors of Germans at the end of World War II. According to John Lombardi in *New York* magazine, "Alarms went off that Sack had produced a tract that would prove useful to . . . traditional anti-Semites and right-wing crazies interested in denying the Holocaust and showing that Jews were as 'bad as Nazis': and excitement grew at Basic Books, which signed Sack up, and *60 Minutes,* which dispatched its own researchers to verify Sack's reporting." Carolyn Toll Oppenheim writes in *Progressive* that, although she "questioned the book's failure to blast the Polish Communists" who may have placed the abusive camp commanders in their positions, and objected to the fact that "Sack never refers to the ultimate fate of many of those Polish Jewish Communists," she nonetheless felt that "rather than take on the task of supplying such context, some of Sack's critics chose simply to discredit his entire story." In particular, Oppenheim refers to a *60 Minutes* interview with "Elan Steinberg, director of the World Jewish Congress, [who] told Sack . . . 'You'd better be damn sure you have your evidence there. Because if you don't you're . . . insulting the memory of six million martyrs.'"

Oppenheim herself took a less harsh view of Sack's conclusions. "Inside," she concludes, "the book is far more balanced and empathetic toward the Jewish avengers than the jacket advertises. Sack, a literary journalist, records his interviews and archival research in a novel-like, 'in-your-face' style with recreated dialogue that packs the brutal punch of a war story. . . . What comes out is not nice, and it wasn't meant to be nice. It's meant to try to get to the truth about war, violence, and other ugly things most of us want to ignore."

In 1991, Sack returned to his role as war correspondent when he accepted an assignment from *Esquire* magazine to cover the Persian Gulf war. He tried to use the same methods that had worked for him in *M,* attaching himself to a company in the First Infantry Division and intending to follow them from training grounds to battlefield. Severe restrictions on the military press held him back at headquarters when the air war began, however. Yet Sack disguised himself in army garb and managed to rejoin his unit. "Of the fifteen hundred accredited journalists covering the conflict, Sack was the only one to stay with a frontline unit throughout the war," asserted Stewart. His experiences eventually became *Company C: The Real War in Iraq.*

"The 241-page book presents a view of the war unseen by most Americans, who formed their impressions of the conflict from television coverage," declared Stewart. "Far from the video-game image created by broadcast coverage, the combat, as Sack described it, was as brutal, confusing, and frightening as in any other war."

The John Sack Collection at Boston University includes manuscript drafts, notes, audiotapes, videotapes, and correspondence related to Sack's career.

*BIOGRAPHICAL/CRITICAL SOURCES:*

*BOOKS*

*Dictionary of Literary Biography,* Volume 185: *American Literary Journalists, 1945-1995, First Series,* Gale (Detroit), 1997.

Polsgrove, Carol, *It Wasn't Pretty Folks, But Didn't We Have Fun?* Esquire *in the Sixties,* Norton (New York City), 1995.

Schroeder, Eric James, *Vietnam, We've All Been There: Interviews with American Writers,* Praeger (Westport, CT), 1992, pp. 12-31.

*PERIODICALS*

*Book Week,* March 12, 1967.

*Christian Science Monitor,* April 6, 1967.

*Fort Scott Tribune* (Kansas), May 20, 1995, p. 1.

*Los Angeles Times,* March 8, 1967.

*Los Angeles Times Book Review,* January 2, 1983.

*Nation,* October 23, 1967; June 20, 1994, pp. 878-82.

*New Republic,* December 27, 1993, pp. 28-34.

*New York,* May 9, 1994, pp. 18-21.

*New York Times,* March 7, 1967; January 31, 1983; November 1, 1994, p. 3.

*New York Times Book Review,* May 14, 1967.

*Progressive,* September, 1994, pp. 39-44.

*Washington Post Book World,* March 5, 1983.

*OTHER*

"The Commandant" (transcript), *CBS News-60 Minutes,* Burrelle's Information Services, November 21, 1993.*

\* \* \*

**SANDFORD, Cedric Thomas 1924-**

*PERSONAL:* Born November 21, 1924, in Basingstoke, Hampshire, England; son of Thomas (a Methodist minister) and Louisa (Hodge) Sandford; married Evelyn Belch (a teacher), December 1, 1945 (died March 19, 1982); married Christina Katarin Privett (a registered nurse), July 21, 1984; children: (first marriage) John, Gillian. *Ethnicity:* "Anglo-Saxon." *Education:* Victoria University of Manchester, B.A. (economics), 1948, M.A., 1949; University of London, B.A. (history), 1955. *Religion:* Methodist.

*ADDRESSES: Home and office*—Old Coach House, Fersfield, Perrymead, Bath BA2 5AR, England.

*CAREER:* Burnley Municipal College, Burnley, Lancashire, England, assistant lecturer, 1949-51, lecturer in economics and history, 1951-59; Bristol College of Science and Technology, Bristol,

Gloucestershire, England, senior lecturer in general and social studies, 1959-60, head of department, 1960-65; University of Bath, Bath, Avon, England, professor of political economy, 1965-87, professor emeritus, 1987—, head of School of Humanities and Social Sciences, 1965-68, 1971-74, and 1977-79, director of Centre for Fiscal Studies, 1974-86. University of Delaware, visiting professor, 1969; Australian National University, visiting fellow, 1981 and 1985; Victoria University, Wellington, New Zealand, visiting fellow, 1987 and 1990; University of Melbourne, visiting fellow, 1990; University of Newcastle, Newcastle, Australia, visiting fellow, 1994. Meade Committee on Reform of the Direct Tax System, member, 1975-78; South West Electricity Consultative Council, member, 1981-90; Bath District Health Authority, member, 1984-92; Office of Water Services, Wessex, member of customer services committee. Consultant to International Monetary Fund, World Bank, Organization for Economic Co-operation and Development, National Federation of the Self-Employed and Small Businesses, Irish Tax Commission, Australian Treasury, Canadian Finance Ministry, British National Audit Office, and British Inland Revenue. *Military service:* Royal Air Force, pilot, 1943-45; became flight sergeant.

*MEMBER:* Liberal International, Economic Association (past president), Sonnenberg Association.

*WRITINGS:*

*Taxing Inheritance and Capital Gains,* Institute of Economic Affairs, 1965, 2nd edition, 1967.

*Economics of Public Finance,* Pergamon, 1969, 3rd edition, 1984.

(Editor with M. S. Bradbury, and contributor) *Case Studies in Economics,* three volumes, Macmillan, 1970-71.

*Realistic Tax Reform,* Chatto & Windus, 1971.

*Taxing Personal Wealth,* Allen & Unwin, 1971.

*National Economic Planning,* Heinemann Educational, 1972, 2nd edition, 1976.

*Hidden Costs of Taxation,* Institute for Fiscal Studies, 1973.

(With J. R. M. Willis and D. J. Ironside) *An Accessions Tax,* Institute for Fiscal Studies, 1973.

(With Willis and Ironside) *An Annual Wealth Tax,* Heinemann Educational, 1975.

*Social Economics,* Heinemann Educational, 1977.

(With Willis) *The Taxation of Net Wealth, Capital Transfers, and Capital Gains of Individuals,* Organization for Economic Co-operation and Development, 1979, new edition, 1988.

(With Alan Lewis and Norman Thomson) *Grants or Loans?,* Institute for Economic Affairs, 1980.

(Editor with Chris Pond and Robert Walker, and contributor) *Taxation and Social Policy,* Heinemann Educational, 1981.

(With M. R. Godwin, P. J. W. Hardwick, and M. I. Butterworth) *Costs and Benefits of VAT,* Heinemann Educational, 1981.

*The Case for the Abolition of Non-Domestic Rates,* National Federation of the Self-Employed and Small Businesses, 1981.

*Wealth Tax: The European Experience; Lessons for Australia,* Centre for Research in Federal Financial Relations, Australian National University (Canberra, Australia), 1981.

*Value-Added Tax: The UK Experience; Lessons for Australia,* Centre for Research in Federal Financial Relations, Australian National University, 1981.

*The Economic Structure,* Longman, 1982.

(With Ann Robinson) *Tax Policy-Making in the United Kingdom,* Heinemann Educational, 1983.

(With Oliver Morrissey) *The Irish Wealth Tax: A Study in Economics and Politics,* Economic and Social Research Institute, 1985.

*Taxing Wealth in New Zealand,* Institute of Policy Studies, Victoria University (Wellington, New Zealand), 1987.

(With Godwin and Hardwick) *Administrative and Compliance Costs of Taxation,* Fiscal Publications, 1989.

(With Hasseldine) *The Compliance Costs of Business Taxes in New Zealand,* Institute of Policy Studies, Victoria University, 1992.

*Successful Tax Reform: Lessons from an Analysis of Tax Reform in Six Countries,* Fiscal Publications, 1993.

(Editor and contributor) *Key Issues in Tax Reform,* three volumes, Fiscal Publications, 1993-97.

(Editor and contributor) *Tax Compliance Costs: Measurement and Policy,* Fiscal Publications, 1995.

Contributor to accounting and tax journals.

*SIDELIGHTS:* Cedric Thomas Sandford told *CA:* "I had nothing published before the age of forty. It was then that a threat to my job and my self-respect led me to be bold and try my hand at writing. May others have the courage without the provocation."

*BIOGRAPHICAL/CRITICAL SOURCES:*

PERIODICALS

*Spectator,* September 18, 1971.

---

**SAUNDERS, Susan 1945-**
　　**(Sara Hughes)**

*PERSONAL:* Born April 14, 1945, in San Antonio, TX; daughter of George S. (a rancher) and Brooksie (Hughes) Saunders; married John J. Cirigliano, September 7, 1969 (divorced, 1976). *Education:* Barnard College, B.A., 1966. *Avocational interests:* Gardening, animals.

*ADDRESSES: Home*—P.O. Box 736, Westhampton, NY 11977. *Agent*—Amy Berkower, Writer's House, Inc., 21 West 26th St., New York, NY 10010.

*CAREER:* John Wiley, New York City, copyeditor, 1966-67; CBS/Columbia House, New York City, 1967-70, began as proofreader and assistant to production manager, became copyeditor, then staff writer; Greystone Press, New York City, copyeditor, 1970-72; *Lighting Design and Application* (trade magazine), New York City, associate editor, 1972-76; Visual Information Systems (radio and video production company), New York City, editor, 1976-77; Random House, New York City, editor, 1977-80; freelance writer, scriptwriter, editor, copy editor, proofreader, and researcher, 1980—. Professional ceramicist.

*MEMBER:* Authors Guild.

*AWARDS, HONORS:* Notable Children's Trade Book in the Field of Social Studies, National Council for the Social Studies/Children's Book Council, 1982, for *Fish Fry.*

*WRITINGS:*

*Wales' Tale,* illustrated by Marilyn Hirsh, Viking (New York City), 1980.

*A Sniff in Time,* illustrated by Michael Mariano, Atheneum (New York City), 1982.

*Fish Fry,* illustrated by S. D. Schindler, Viking, 1982.

*Rat's Picnic,* illustrated by Robert Byrd, Dutton (New York City), 1984.

*Dorothy and the Magic Belt,* illustrated by David Rose, Random House, 1985.

*The Get Along Gang and the Treasure Map,* illustrated by Carol Hudson, Scholastic (New York City), 1985.

*Dolly Parton: Country Goin' to Town* (nonfiction), Viking, 1985.

*Mystery Cat,* Bantam (New York City), 1986.

*Sir Silver Swine and the Missing Rain*, Scholastic, 1986.

*The Daring Rescue of Marlon the Swimming Pig*, illustrated by Gail Owens, Random House (New York City), 1986.

*Mystery Cat and the Chocolate Trap*, Bantam, 1986.

*The Right House for Rabbit*, Western Publishing (New York City), 1986.

*Mr. Nighttime and the Dream Machine*, Scholastic, 1986.

*The Golden Goose*, illustrated by Isadore Seltzer, Scholastic, 1987.

*Margaret Mead: The World Was Her Family* (nonfiction), Viking, 1987.

(Adaptor) Johanna Spyri, *Heidi*, Troll (Mahwah, NJ), 1988.

*The Mystery of the Hard Luck Rodeo*, Random House, 1989.

*Tent Show*, illustrated by Diane Allison, Dutton, 1990.

*Jackrabbit and the Prairie Fire: The Story of a Black-Tailed Jackrabbit*, Soundprints, 1991.

*Seasons of a Red Fox*, Soundprints, 1991.

*Tyrone Goes to School*, illustrated by Steve Bjoerkman, Dutton, 1992.

*"CHOOSE YOUR OWN ADVENTURE" SERIES; PUBLISHED BY BANTAM*

*The Green Slime*, 1982.

*The Creature from Miller's Pond*, 1983.

*The Tower of London*, 1984.

*Runaway Spaceship*, 1985.

*Ice Cave*, 1985.

*Attack of the Monster Plants*, 1986.

*The Miss Liberty Caper*, 1986.

*Blizzard at Black Swan Inn*, 1986.

*The Haunted Halloween Party*, 1986.

*Light on Burro Mountain*, 1986.

*You Are Invisible*, 1989.

*"MORGAN SWIFT" SERIES; AS SARA HUGHES; PUBLISHED BY RANDOM HOUSE*

*Morgan Swift and the Treasure of Crocodile Key*, 1985.

*Morgan Swift and the Kidnapped Goddess*, 1985.

*Morgan Swift and the Lake of Diamonds*, 1986.

*"BAD NEWS BUNNY" SERIES; ILLUSTRATED BY LARRY ROSS; PUBLISHED BY SIMON & SCHUSTER (NEW YORK CITY)*

*Third-Prize Surprise*, 1987.

*Back to Nature*, 1987.

*Stop the Presses!*, 1987.

*"SLEEPOVER FRIENDS" SERIES; PUBLISHED BY SCHOLASTIC*

*Patti's Luck*, 1987.

*Starring Stephanie*, 1987.

*Kate's Surprise*, 1987.

*Patti's New Look*, 1988.

*Kate's Camp-out*, 1988.

*Lauren's Big Mix-up*, 1988.

*Stephanie Strikes Back*, 1988.

*Lauren's Treasure*, 1988.

*Patti's Last Sleepover?*, 1988.

*Stephanie's Family Secret*, 1989.

*Stephanie's Big Story*, 1989.

*Patti's Secret Wish*, 1989.

*Patti*, 1989.

*Stephanie*, 1989.

*Patti Gets Even*, 1989.

*Lauren's Sleepover Exchange*, 1989.

*Kate's Crush*, 1989.

*A Book of U.S. Presidents*, 1989.

*Lauren Takes Charge*, 1989.

*Kate's Sleepover Disaster*, 1989.

*Lauren I*, 1990.

*Starstruck Stephanie*, 1990.

*Trouble with Patti*, 1990.

*Lauren's New Friend*, 1990.

*Stephanie and the Wedding*, 1990.

*The New Kate*, 1990.

*Kate's Surprise Visitor*, 1990.

*Lauren's New Address*, 1990.

*Kate the Boss*, 1990.

*Lauren's Afterschool Job*, 1990.

*A Valentine for Patti*, 1991.

*Lauren's Double Disaster*, 1991.

*The New Stephanie*, 1991.

*"FIFTH GRADE S.T.A.R.S." SERIES; PUBLISHED BY KNOPF (NEW YORK CITY)*

*Twin Trouble*, 1989.

*Rent-a-Star*, 1989.

*"PONY CAMP" SERIES; PUBLISHED BY HARPERCOLLINS (NEW YORK CITY)*

*Pam's Trail*, 1994.

*Maxine's Blue Ribbon*, 1994.

*"DOUBLE R DETECTIVES" SERIES; PUBLISHED BY HARPERCOLLINS*

*The UFO Mystery*, 1995.

*Double R Detectives No. 3*, 1997.

*Double R Detectives No. 4*, 1997.

*"TREASURED HORSES COLLECTION" SERIES; ILLUSTRATED BY SANDY RABINOWITZ, PUBLISHED BY ERTL (DYERSVILLE, IA)*

*Riding School Rivals: The Story of a Majestic Lipizzan Horse and the Girls Who Fight for the Right to Ride Him,* 1996.
*Kate's Secret Plan: The Story of a Young Quarter Horse and the Persistent Girls who Will Not Let Obstacles Stand in Their Way,* 1996.

*ACK CAT CLUB" SERIES; PUBLISHED BY HARPERCOLLINS; ILLUSTRATED BY JANE MANNING*

*The Ghost Who Ate Chocolate,* 1996.
*The Haunted Skateboard,* 1996.
*Curse of the Cat Mummy,* 1997.
*The Ghost of Spirit Lake,* 1997.
*The Revenge of the Pirate Ghost,* 1997.
*The Phantom Pen-Pal,* 1997.
*The Case of the Eyeball Surprise,* 1998.
*The Creature Double Feature,* 1998.
*The Creepy Camp-out,* 1998.
*The Chilling Tale of Crescent Pond,* 1998.

*ADAPTATIONS: The Daring Rescue of Marlon the Missing Pig* was adapted for videocassette recording, 1990.

*SIDELIGHTS:* Texas-born writer Susan Saunders has branded her many books for preteen readers with her love of animals, her sense of humor, and her sensitivity to the interests of young people. "I was an only child for a long time and books were my favorite entertainment, especially fairy tales from other lands, preferably with wizards, elves, dark forests, and rushing rivers," Saunders once told *CA*. Magic finds its way into Saunders' first children's book, *Wales' Tale,* and her picture book *A Sniff in Time*. In *Wales' Tale*, a young girl on her way to the local market encounters a talking donkey who requests her help in ending the spell that changed him from a handsome prince. In *Sniff in Time*, James, bored by his uneventful life as a farmer, longs for a way to leave his landlocked home. A visiting wizard offers James the power to see into the future if he gives him a bowl of hot soup. With only turnips to give his aged guest, James is granted an abridged wish—the power to smell into the future. His new gift proves difficult to harness, but at last he becomes adept enough at foretelling the future that he earns a reward from the king—a boat, which James puts on a trailer and rolls to his farm, finally content with his lot. "A very

good tale for the telling," Helen Gregory commented in her review for *School Library Journal*.

Animal characters figure prominently in both Saunders' nonfiction works, such as 1991's *Seasons of a Red Fox,* picture books like *Wales' Tale* and *The Daring Rescue of Marlon the Swimming Pig,* and numerous installments in her series of novels for preteen readers, particularly the "Pony Camp" series inaugurated in 1994. In *The Daring Rescue of Marlon the Swimming Pig,* a three-hundred-pound pig goes on the lam after he discovers that he is scheduled for a visit to the livestock auction. "Briskly paced action throughout this chapter book will delight young readers," according to *Booklist* contributor Philip Wilson. In *Tyrone Goes to School,* its time for obedience training for tail-wagging Tyrone, who gets straight A's in doggy school but promptly forgets his lessons once he is out the door. Fortunately, Tyrone's young owner, the equally distractible Robert, understands the problem—a short attention span—and a helpful teacher directs both puppy and master into a schedule that allows them to settle in to their studies. While noting that the story is "a little unlikely," a *Kirkus Reviews* commentator praised *Tyrone Goes to School* as "briskly told and mildly funny," and Stephanie Zvirin deemed it a "sprightly, easy-to-read tale" in her *Booklist* review.

Among Saunders' most popular books for young readers has been her *Tent Show,* which profiles the life of nine-year-old Ellie. Ellie is disappointed after her older sister drops out of college to get married, giving up opportunities for education and a career. When she vents her feelings about her sister's choices to an elderly actress named Sara during the wedding reception, the woman tells Ellie about her own childhood, and helps the young girl to accept the fact that she cannot change or judge others' choices, but must concentrate her energies on making decisions regarding her own life. Praising the book's short chapters as a help to more reluctant readers, *School Library Journal* contributor Nancy P. Reeder added that the elderly actress, Sara, "is particularly well developed . . . and it will be easy for readers to see the child in the adult." And in *Booklist,* Kay Weisman called *Tent Show* "a bright and funny story with memorable characters." In addition to this popular work, Saunders has written several multi-volume series for middle-graders, including "Fifth Grade S.T.A.R.S.," "Sleepover Friends," and her "Black Cat Club" books, which *School Library Journal* contributor Christina Dorr praised as "sure to satisfy early chapter-book readers."

Saunders has always loved children's books. She once explained to *CA,* "There is a magic to them, especially picture books, that I think doesn't exist anywhere else in literature." Of her writing style, Saunders admitted: "I write in spurts: I can have an idea for a long time, but will only commit it to paper when it's almost all written in my head, or when the suspense is killing me."

*BIOGRAPHICAL/CRITICAL SOURCES:*

BOOKS

Saunders, Susan, *Wales' Tale,* Viking (New York City), 1980.

PERIODICALS

*Booklist,* October 15, 1987, p. 400; September 15, 1990, pp. 163-64; March 1, 1993, p. 1240.
*Bulletin of the Center for Children's Books,* April, 1987, p. 156.
*Kirkus Reviews,* May 1, 1980, p. 578; April 15, 1982, p. 487; February 1, 1986, p. 213; May 1, 1987, p. 725; December 15, 1987, p. 1736; December 1, 1992, p. 1508.
*Publishers Weekly,* June 27, 1986, p. 91; December 11, 1987, p. 63.
*School Library Journal,* October, 1980, p. 139; August, 1982, p. 105; September, 1986, p. 139; March, 1987, p. 165; February, 1990, pp. 92-93; October, 1990, pp. 118-19; April, 1993, p. 102; November, 1996, p. 92.*

\*   \*   \*

**SAVAGE, Alan**
  See NICOLE, Christopher (Robin)

\*   \*   \*

**SCHWARTZ, Stephen (Alfred) 1948-**
  (S. Solsona)

*PERSONAL:* Born September 9, 1948, in Columbus, OH; son of Horace Osman (a bookseller) and Mayme Eileene (a social service employee; maiden name, McKinney) Schwartz; married Mary Uhran, March, 1969 (divorced, 1974); married Rebecca Rae Long (a filmmaker), March 22, 1984; children: Matthew.

*Education:* Attended City College of San Francisco, 1970-72; University of California, Berkeley, 1972-73, 1976, and 1989; and University of London, 1985—. *Politics:* "Conservative anti-fascist." *Religion:* "Jewish by affection, Catholic by association, Muslim by sympathy, Buddhist by nature." *Avocational interests:* Linguistics, non-European art.

*ADDRESSES: Office*—San Francisco Chronicle, 901 Mission St., San Francisco, CA 94103. *Agent*—Felicia Eth, 555 Bryant St., Ste. 350, Palo Alto, CA 94301.

*CAREER: City of San Francisco* (magazine), San Francisco, CA, staff writer, 1975; Re/Search Publications, San Francisco, staff writer, 1977-81; *The Alarm,* San Francisco, editor, 1980-83; *Pacific Shipper Weekly,* San Francisco, senior editor, 1981-84; Sailors Union of the Pacific, San Francisco, historian, 1983-86; Institute for Contemporary Studies, San Francisco, senior editor and fellow, 1984-89; *San Francisco Chronicle,* staff writer and op-ed editor, 1989—. U.S. Department of State, consultant, 1987-88; U.S. Institute of Peace, research associate, 1988. Also active in Brotherhood of Railway and Airline Clerks and member of board of Albanian Catholic Institute, University of San Francisco; frequent lecturer and commentator at conferences and on television and radio.

*MEMBER:* The Newspaper Guild, Dictionary Society of North America, Historians of American Communism, Korea America Friendship Society.

*AWARDS, HONORS:* Earhart Foundation fellowship, 1986 and 1989, Olin Foundation fellowship, 1988.

*WRITINGS:*

(Translator) *Antinarcissus,* self-published (San Francisco, CA), 1969.
*Hidden Locks,* Radical America (Cambridge, MA), 1972.
*A Sleepwalkers Guide to San Francisco,* La Santa Espina (San Francisco, CA), 1983.
*Brotherhood of the Sea,* Transaction Books (New Brunswick, NJ), 1986.
(Editor) *The Transition,* ICS Press (San Francisco, CA), 1986.
(With Victor Alba) *Spanish Marxism vs. Soviet Communism,* Transaction Books (New Brunswick, NJ), 1988.

*Heavens Descent,* Transition (San Francisco, CA), 1990.

*A Strange Silence,* ICS Press (San Francisco, CA), 1992.

*Incidentes de la Vida de Benjamin Peret con Anotaciones Sobre el Comunismo de G. Munis,* Editorial Balance (Barcelona, Spain), 1994.

*From West to East: California and the Making of the American Mind,* Free Press, 1997.

Author under the pseudonym S. Solsona of *Incidents from the Life of Benjamin Peret,* published in *The Alarm,* 1981.

Contributor to books, including *What Is Surrealism?: Selected Writings of Andre Breton,* Pluto Press, 1978; (with Gjon Sinishta) *Mediterranean Europe Phrasebook,* Lonely Planet, 1992; *Yearbook on International Communist Affairs,* edited by Amb. Richard F. Staar, Hoover Institution Press, 1989, 1990, and 1991; and *Fighting the War of Ideas in Latin America,* edited by John C. Goodman and Ramona Marotz-Baden, National Center for Policy Analysis, 1990. Contributor to numerous periodicals, including *American Spectator, Commentary, World Affairs* and the *New York Times Book Review.*

*SIDELIGHTS:* A writer on political subjects for the *San Francisco Chronicle,* Stephen Schwartz has also authored several books on such political subjects as Marxism in Latin America and the history of radical movements in California.

Schwartz's *From West to East: California and the Making of the American Mind* traces the history of revolutionary and bohemian movements in California and the effects these movements have had on the rest of America. Citing California's frontier history, Schwartz argues that the state has always been the home of those exploring the edges of acceptable behavior. While detailing the activities of California writers and artists who broke with convention, Schwartz contrasts these ground-breaking artists with the state's radical totalitarian movements such as the Communist Party. A major goal of Schwartz's history, Harold Meyerson recounts in the *New York Times Book Review,* is "to demonstrate the moral and esthetic toll Stalinism took on the California left, and to resurrect the reputations of artists, intellectuals, and unionists who were too democratic, bohemian or just plain ornery to toe the party line." Calling Schwartz's study an "ambitious, unorthodox history," the critic for *Publishers Weekly* cites the author for producing "a 'hidden' or 'secret' history of

Californians' forging of a nonconformist cultural identity." According to Harold Johnson in *National Review, From West to East* contains "a wealth of information ignored or underreported in conventional histories. . . . If there is a rambling quality to much of Schwartz's book, it is reflective of the creative energies he describes, which at their best and most positive are the antithesis of the totalitarian cultural strains that he labors to expose."

Schwartz told *CA:* "I was born in Columbus, Ohio, in 1948, but shortly thereafter moved with my family to San Francisco, where I have lived ever since. My parents were very active in the left-literary scene in the city during the 1950s. My father ran a 'little magazine' called *Goad,* which published the poetry of such notable figures as Kenneth Rexroth, Lawrence Ferlinghetti, and Robert Creeley.

"My literary work began in my teens, in the mid-1960s, simultaneously with the beginning of my twenty-year involvement in revolutionary Marxism. At fifteen, I attended a Communist Party 'night school' in San Francisco, the S.F. School of Social Science, where I was trained in dialectical materialism, political economy, and contemporary politics. My writings first consisted of poetry, and of translations from Latin American poets. The latter association proved extremely durable, since I ended up seriously studying the Spanish language and becoming a fully bilingual writer.

"I began in the youth branch of the Communist Party of the United States, then shifted to Trotskyism, and then to an 'ultra-leftist' position, in affiliation with a European grouping, Fomento Obrero Revolucionario. In 1983, I broke with the left, and in 1984 I joined a 'free-market' think-tank, the San Francisco-based Institute for Contemporary Studies.

"As a late teenager I frequented the 'Beat' circle, meeting and cultivating friendships with Ferlinghetti, Allen Ginsberg, and Gary Snyder, the last of whom introduced me to Buddhism. In 1968, I met Philip Lamantia, the leading American surrealist poet, who became a mentor.

"Until 1973, my dual commitment to poetry and radical politics was supplemented by academic study in linguistics. I then dropped out of Berkeley to become a full-time transportation worker, first in the merchant marine and then in the railroad industry. I was active in union reform movements as well as in revolutionary agitation and propaganda, while publishing poetic texts here and there.

"In 1975, I was invited to join the staff of a new weekly magazine, *City of San Francisco,* published by film magnate Francis Ford Coppola. The magazine did not endure, but I began a trek back from my emphasis on Marxist politics to full-time literary activity.

"In 1977, I joined a group of friends in starting *Search & Destroy,* a punk rock/new wave magazine that was one of the main such periodicals in the country, and which was to expand into the Re/Search label, today known for its authoritative books on body art and related post-modernist phenomena. I also managed a well-known punk band, The Dils, whose music had a Marxist edge.

"By 1984 I had regained a certain youthful poetic energy and began writing and publishing poetry more extensively than ever before. My turn to ICS Press and a 'free-market' position also led me to begin contributing to neoconservative journals such as *Commentary.* I also wrote extensively on politics in the Hispanic world, the fall of the Soviet regime and its aftermath, and on the war in former Yugoslavia.

"I travel widely and remain interested in new areas of study and acquisition of other languages. I am one of the leading U.S. experts on newly-independent and stateless nations in Europe, including Croatia, Bosnia and Herzegovina, Macedonia, Ukraine, Catalunya, and Euzkadi.

"My advice to young writers is to cultivate mentors, resist ideology, ignore negative criticism, work through blocks, and don't ever stop. The only writers who succeed are those who write because they cannot stop themselves, because they have no other choice than to write."

*BIOGRAPHICAL/CRITICAL SOURCES:*

*PERIODICALS*

*National Review,* April 20, 1998, p. 50.
*New York Times,* April 7, 1998.
*New York Times Book Review,* March 15, 1998.
*Publishers Weekly,* February 2, 1998, p. 75.

## SCOTT, Ann Herbert 1926-

*PERSONAL:* Born November 19, 1926, in Germantown, Philadelphia, PA; daughter of Henry Laux (a newspaperman) and Gladys (a homemaker, singer and painter; maiden name, Howe) Herbert; married William Taussig Scott (a professor of physics) September 29, 1961; children: Peter Herbert, Katherine Howe; (stepchildren) Jennifer, Christopher (deceased), Stephanie, Melanie. *Education:* University of Pennsylvania, B.A., 1948, graduate student, 1948-49; Yale University, M.A., 1958. *Politics:* Democrat. *Religion:* Society of Friends.

*CAREER:* Editor, writer, and lecturer. Rider College, Trenton, NJ, teacher of English, 1949-59; New Haven State Teachers College (now Southern Connecticut State College), New Haven, part-time teacher of English, 1956-58; Wider City Parish, New Haven, coordinator of volunteer work, 1958-61; American Friends Service Committee, Northern California Office, member of Reno area committee, 1966-84; co-founder and member, Children's Literature Interest Group, 1980—; director, All the Colors of the Race, Nevada Humanities Committee Conference on Ethnic Children's Literature, 1983; founder and chairperson, SIERRA Interfaith Action for Peace, 1986.

*MEMBER:* Society of Children's Book Writers and Illustrators, National Association for the Advancement of Colored People, Phi Beta Kappa, Mortar Board, Sphinx and Key.

*AWARDS, HONORS:* American Institute of Graphics Arts Children's Books, 1967-68, and Notable Book, American Library Association (ALA), 1967, for *Sam;* Children's Books of the Year, Child Study Association of America (CSAA), 1968, for *Not Just One,* 1972, for *On Mother's Lap,* 1993, for *A Brand Is Forever* and *Cowboy Country,* and 1996, for *Brave as a Mountain Lion;* Nevada State Council on the Arts Grant, 1987; Best Books, *School Library Journal,* 1993, for *Cowboy Country;* Notable Books, ALA, 1995, for *Hi.*

*WRITINGS:*

*FOR YOUNG PEOPLE*

*Big Cowboy Western,* illustrated by Richard W. Lewis, Lothrop (New York City), 1965.
*Let's Catch a Monster,* illustrated by H. Tom Hall, Lothrop, 1967.

*Sam,* illustrated by Symeon Shimin, McGraw (New York City), 1967.

*Not Just One,* illustrated by Yaroslava, Lothrop, 1968.

*Census, U.S.A.: Fact Finding for the American People, 1790-1970* (young adult), Seabury (New York City), 1968.

*On Mother's Lap,* illustrated by Glo Coalson, McGraw, 1972.

*Someday Rider,* illustrated by Ronald Himler, Clarion (Boston), 1989.

*One Good Horse: A Cowpuncher's Counting Book,* illustrated by Lynn Sweat, Greenwillow (New York City), 1990.

*Grandmother's Chair,* illustrated by Meg Kelleher Aubrey, Clarion, 1990.

*A Brand is Forever,* illustrated by Himler, Clarion, 1993.

*Cowboy Country,* illustrated by Ted Lewin, Clarion, 1993.

*Hi,* illustrated by Coalson, Philomel (New York City), 1994.

*Brave as a Mountain Lion,* illustrated by Coalson, Clarion, 1996.

*OTHER*

Contributor to periodicals, including *Reno Gazette-Journal* and *Nevada Highways.*

*ADAPTATIONS:* "Books about Real Things" (based on *Sam,* along with discussion of author's work; filmstrip and cassette), Pied Piper, 1982; "On Mother's Lap" (based on book of same name; sound recording), 1994.

*SIDELIGHTS:* Over the last three decades, Ann Herbert Scott has published many stories for younger readers that share a simple narrative format and realistic dialogue and description. Through these stories, she evokes such universal themes as, in her own words, "the security of a mother's love, the yearning to be big and important, the courage to deal with fear or jealousy." "I believe the pull toward children's writing comes from something childlike within me," Scott has written. "The sense of delight and wonder little children bring to the here and now seems to awaken something deep in me. In contrast to writing for adults, which is often dreary and difficult for me, writing for children is often fun; it springs up unexpectedly in familiar places with some of the same spontaneous independence as forgotten daffodils in a leaf-covered bed.

"In general I work over material for some time, usually simplifying and resimplifying, often cutting out favorite phrases because they are not necessary to the thrust of the story. When there is something I am unsure about, six-year-old children's ideas about monsters, for example, I do a lot of talking with children. Otherwise I work from memory and imagination. I always *see* picture books as I write them; the sense of the graphics helps the development of the manuscript."

"As a writer who specializes in picture books for young children, my work has peculiar aesthetic concerns. Although I am not an artist, I continually work with images in mind, leaving much of the telling to the skill of the illustrator. My work is often described as 'simple,' and so it is. However, it is the simplicity of discovering the organic shape of an idea, eliminating all that is unessential, depicting the large in the small. My manuscripts often go through twenty to thirty revisions."

Remembering the inspiration for her first publication, *Big Cowboy Western,* the author once told *CA:* "When I worked in New Haven in the 1950s, I was appalled by the lack of children's books picturing either urban neighborhoods or dark-skinned families. . . . I dreamed that someday I would write true-to-life stories that would be set in the housing project where I [once] worked, stories in which my New Haven friends could find themselves. However, it was not until I had moved to Nevada that *Big Cowboy Western* evolved." The book is about an inner-city boy who gets a cowboy outfit for his fifth birthday but feels unimportant because he has nobody to play with—until an understanding fruit peddler gives him a job watching his horse. The book was praised by Zena Sutherland of the *Bulletin of the Center for Children's Books* for its "excellent" depiction of relationships and the value of its "particular urban setting."

The author's conversations with children about monsters led to 1967's *Let's Catch a Monster,* in which a small boy on Halloween tracks down a monster that turns out to be a cat. The story was described as an "appealing anecdote" by a *Publishers Weekly* reviewer. That same year, Scott's *Sam* appeared. *Sam* is the story of a small African-American child whose parents and older siblings are all too busy to pay attention to him. The story was widely praised. What one reviewer writing in *Booklist* called a "touching family story" was described by a later *Booklist* critic as "perceptively interpreted in expressive drawings," referring to the work of artist Symeon Shimin.

*On Mother's Lap* and *Grandmother's Chair* both illustrate Scott's 'make-it-simple' ideal. In the first story an Eskimo boy happily snuggles with his mother, gradually adding his favorite toys until he is sure there is no room for his baby sister, and yet there is. "The simplicity and familiarity of the situation are universal," said Zena Sutherland in the *Bulletin of the Center for Children's Books*. In *Grandmother's Chair,* children learn concepts of relationships and family trees from the story of a family heirloom that has been handed down through three generations. "Scott's text is plain and clear," wrote *Booklist* reviewer Leone McDermott. "Its understated warmth comes from the sense of continuity as the chair passes from one little girl to the next."

Scott once commented to *CA* that "an opportunity to interview a number of old buckaroos was provided by a Nevada State Council on the Arts grant in 1986-87, inspiring a number of partly finished stories and a book entitled *Someday Rider*." In *Someday Rider,* Kenny wants to join his dad and the cowboys on their western ranch, but his parents have put off teaching him to ride. After Kenny practices riding a goose, a sheep, and a calf, his mother finally shows him the basics, and the two then both join the roundup. "Would-be cowpokes should hanker to read this coming-of-age story," concluded reviewer Charlene Strickland. A *Kirkus Reviews* critic praised Scott for the "warmth" of the story. Mining the same western lode, Scott next wrote *One Good Horse: A Cowpuncher's Counting Book. Horn Book* reviewer Elizabeth S. Watson noted that the book's theme would surely gain "warm reception" from the "spurs-and-six-gun set."

In four more recent books, *A Brand is Forever, Cowboy Country, Hi,* and *Brave as a Mountain Lion,* Scott has continued to explore mostly western subject matter and universal themes, using the same pared-down approach. *A Brand is Forever* is basically "a warm family story" and "a good yarn" about a girl on a ranch and her pet calf, according to *Horn Book* reviewer Elizabeth S. Watson. Critic Roger Sutton praised "Scott's quiet but plain-speaking tone." But isn't branding a cruel practice, and isn't Annie's mistress-pet relationship behind the times? the reader may ask. Reviewer Ilene Cooper tackled these questions in an extended essay-review in *Booklist* and reached several conclusions. On one hand, "it's a bit disconcerting to see the pleasures of ownership cel-

ebrated quite so blatantly, especially when the item being owned is a living animal," contended Cooper. At the same time, Cooper added, "Scott makes a good case for the practical reasons behind branding, and readers with some knowledge of branding are likely to agree . . . that the procedure is necessary." For Cooper, the bottom line is that "the book should be judged on [its] merits, not on how well it fits the attitudinal climate of the times."

Drawing on her research and interviews with old Nevada buckaroos, Scott's next book, *Cowboy Country,* shows an old-timer guiding a young greenhorn in both the work and the lore of the cowboy, contrasting present practices with earlier methods. "Youngsters swept up by space-opera technomyths may rediscover the wonders of the West with this book," maintained *Bulletin of the Center for Children's Books* reviewer Deborah Stevenson. Elizabeth S. Watson of *Horn Book* found that "the strength of the book is the atmosphere created."

In *Hi,* Scott returns to the theme of persistence that she first treated in *Sam*. Margarita and her mother are waiting in line at the post office. The toddler calls out "Hi" to each person in the line, but when she gets no response her greeting becomes progressively weaker. Finally the "post-office lady" to whom she gives her package responds warmly, and Margarita's confidence is restored. "A delightful moment in time perfectly captured," commented reviewer Anna Biagioni Hart in *School Library Journal*. "It's a simple scenario but Scott captures a child's emotions nicely," noted a critic for *Publishers Weekly*.

In 1996, to wide acclaim, *Brave as a Mountain Lion* was published. Spider, who lives on a contemporary Shoshone reservation, is afraid of participating in a school spelling bee. But, encouraged by other family members, and finally through his own efforts, to think of himself as "brave as a mountain lion, clever as a coyote, silent as a spider," he wins second place. "Scott knows how to take a universal childhood anxiety and particularize it to the needs of a story," commented Roger Sutton in the *Bulletin of the Center for Children's Books*.

*BIOGRAPHICAL/CRITICAL SOURCES:*

*BOOKS*

De Montreville, Doris, and Elizabeth D. Crawford, editors, *Fourth Book of Junior Authors & Illustrators,* H. W. Wilson (Bronx, NY), 1978.

PERIODICALS

*Booklist,* February 15, 1968, p. 702; May 1, 1973, p. 836; November 15, 1990, p. 667; April 1, 1993, p. 1434; May 15, 1994, p. 1684.
*Bulletin of the Center for Children's Books,*.
*Bulletin of the Center for Children's Books,* December, 1965, p. 68; December, 1972, p. 64; November, 1990, p. 70; April, 1993, p. 263; November, 1993, pp. 98-99; February, 1996, pp. 202-03.
*Horn Book,* July-August, 1990, p. 447; November-December, 1992, pp. 741-742; May-June, 1993, p. 330; November-December, 1993, p. 760; July-August, 1994, p. 445.
*Kirkus Reviews,* August 15, 1989, p. 1251; May 15, 1994, p. 706.
*Publishers Weekly,* October 9, 1967, p. 60; July 18, 1990, p. 53; March 23, 1992, p. 71; May 30, 1994, p. 56.
*School Library Journal,* December, 1989, p. 88; April, 1990, p. 96; July, 1994, p. 89.*

\*     \*     \*

**SEDARIS, David 1957(?)-**

**PERSONAL:** Surname pronounced "seh-*dar*-iss;" born c. 1957 in Raleigh, NC; partner of Hugh Hamrick (a painter). *Education:* School of the Art Institute of Chicago, attained degree in 1987.

**ADDRESSES:** *Home*—New York City. *Agent*—Don Congdon Associates, 156 5th Ave., Suite 625, New York, NY 10010-7002.

**CAREER:** Diarist, radio commentator, essayist, and short story writer. Has taught writing at the School of the Art Institute of Chicago; has held a number of other part-time jobs, including employment as a moving company worker, an office worker, an elf in SantaLand at Macy's Department Store, and an apartment cleaner.

**WRITINGS:**

*Origins of the Underclass, and Other Stories,* Amethyst Press (Washington, DC), 1992.

*Barrel Fever: Stories and Essays,* Little, Brown (Boston), 1994.
*The SantaLand Diaries* (play), produced Off-Broadway at the Atlantic Theater, November, 1996.
*Naked,* Little, Brown, 1997.
(With sister, Amy Sedaris) *Little Freida Mysteries* (play), produced at the Club at la Mama, New York City, February, 1997.
*Holidays on Ice,* Little, Brown, 1997.

Also author of commentaries for National Public Radio, 1992—, and of satirical plays, written with his sister Amy, a member of Chicago's Second City comedy troupe.

**WORK IN PROGRESS:** A novel for Little, Brown.

**ADAPTATIONS:** "Diary of a Smoker," an essay from *Barrel Fever,* was adapted by Matthew Modine into a thirteen-minute film shown at the Sundance Film Festival and on Public Broadcasting System (PBS), 1994. Audio-cassette versions of *Naked* and *Holidays on Ice* were released by Time Warner Audio Books in 1997.

**SIDELIGHTS:** Humorist David Sedaris grew up in North Carolina and moved to Chicago while in his twenties, where he attended school and performed readings from his diaries for audiences. After his move to New York in 1991, Sedaris began reading excerpts from his diaries on National Public Radio (NPR), where his "nicely nerdy, quavering voice," in the words of *Newsweek* commentator Jeff Giles, delivered monologues praised for their acerbic wit and dead-pan delivery. John Marchese commented in the *New York Times:* "In the five radio pieces that he has done, Mr. Sedaris has shown remarkable skill as a mimic and the ability to mix the sweet and the bitter: to be naive and vulnerable and at the same time, jaded and wickedly funny." *Entertainment Weekly* contributor Margot Mifflin remarked: "Sedaris is a crackpot in the best sense of the word."

Sedaris's comic, and often satirical, monologues draw primarily on his experiences in the odd day-jobs that he held before his work with NPR heated up his artistic career. Of his long-standing position as an apartment cleaner, Sedaris told Marchese in the *New York Times:* "I can only write when it's dark, so basically, my whole day is spent waiting for it to get dark. Cleaning apartments gives me something to do when I get up. Otherwise, I'd feel like a bum."

Sedaris has received numerous job offers, both for cleaning and for writing, as a result of his appearances on NPR. The immediate result was a two-book contract with Little, Brown, who in 1994 published *Barrel Fever,* a collection of Sedaris's essays and short stories.

*Barrel Fever* includes several pieces that brought Sedaris to national attention when he read them on the radio, including "Diary of a Smoker," in which the author declares that the efforts of nonsmokers to extend his life by not allowing him to smoke in front of them only gives him more time to hate nonsmokers, and "SantaLand Diaries," in which the author chronicles his amorous and aggravating experiences playing one of Santa's elves in Macy's Department Store one Christmas. Critics remarked on the humorously exaggerated self-delusion of Sedaris's narrators in the short stories, including a man who brags on talk-shows about his affairs with such stars as rock singer Bruce Springsteen and boxer Mike Tyson, and a homosexual man with a persecution complex who "bemoans his suffering at the hands of society in a style so over-the-top as to be laughable," according to a critic in *Kirkus Reviews.*

Critical response to *Barrel Fever* was generally positive, with reviewers appreciating Sedaris's humorous, yet accurate, portrayal of such American foibles as the commercialism of Christmas and the self-righteousness of health fanatics. "Without slapping the reader in the face with a political diatribe," wrote a critic for *Kirkus Reviews,* "the author skewers our ridiculous fascination with other people's tedious everyday lives." A contributor to *Publishers Weekly* commented: "Sedaris ekes humor from the blackest of scenarios, peppering his narrative with memorable turns of phrase and repeatedly surprising with his double-edged wit." And although *Newsweek* critic Giles found some of Sedaris's commentary relatively shallow, he nonetheless concluded: "This is a writer who's cleaned our toilets and will never look at us the same way."

Sedaris's second collection of essays, *Naked,* appeared in 1997. As these essays reveal, according to a reviewer for *Publishers Weekly,* "NPR commentator Sedaris can hardly be called a humorist in the ordinary sense. . . . Sedaris is instead an essayist who happens to be very funny." In his characteristic deadpan style, Sedaris tells stories "about nutty or bizarre experiences, like volunteering at a hospital for the insane," Craig Seligman observed in the *New York Times Book Review.* Others include Sedaris on hitchhiking, working in Oregon, his personal battle with his childhood nervous disorders, and the title piece, about Sedaris at a nudist colony. In still others, the essayist turns his eye on his family, especially his mother. And for Seligman, "the funniest [essays], and ultimately the saddest, have to do with the writer's family." In these autobiographical tales, wrote Margot Mifflin in *Entertainment Weekly,* "Sedaris covers a impressive emotional range . . . from the comically corrosive title piece . . . to 'Ashes,' his account of his mother's death from cancer—a direct, unsentimental hit to the heart." This inclusion of essays that go beyond his sarcastic take on the bleaker side of life, that touch the heart, suggested to Seligman an evolution in the essayist. "He's in the process of figuring out how to go beyond the short humor piece," noted Seligman, "and the essays in 'Naked' feel transitional." As Ira Glass, the producer for Sedaris's NPR commentaries told Peter Ames Carlin in a *People* profile, "People come to his work because he's funny. . . . But there's a complicated moral vision there."

## BIOGRAPHICAL/CRITICAL SOURCES:

### PERIODICALS

*Advocate,* December 10, 1996, p. 54.

*Booklist,* June 1, 1994, p. 1762.

*Chicago Tribune,* February 2, 1996, sec. 7, p. 2.

*Entertainment Weekly,* July 29, 1994, p. 55; December 13, 1996, p. S10; March 21, 1997, p. 68.

*Kirkus Reviews,* April 1, 1994, p. 430.

*Library Journal,* May 1, 1994, p. 104.

*Los Angeles Times Book Review,* October 16, 1994, p. 6; July 2, 1995, p. 11.

*Newsweek,* August 15, 1994, pp. 66-67.

*New York Times,* February 19, 1997, p. C14.

*New York Times Book Review,* July 4, 1993, p. 5; March 16, 1997, p. 10.

*People,* October 20, 1997, p. 129.

*Publishers Weekly,* April 25, 1994, p. 58; January 27, 1997, p. 88; April 7, 1997, p. 22.

*Variety,* November 11, 1996, p. 66.

*Washington Post,* March 22, 1997, p. B1.

*Whole Earth Review,* winter, 1995, p. 63.

\*    \*    \*

**SEIFERT, Elizabeth**
  **See GASPAROTTI, Elizabeth Seifert**

**SEYMOUR, (William Herschel Kean) Gerald 1941-**

*PERSONAL:* Born November 25, 1941, in Surrey, England; son of William Kean (a poet) and Rosalind (a novelist; maiden name, Wade) Seymour; married Gillian Mary Roberts, May 3, 1964; children: Nicholas, James. *Education:* University College, London, B.A. (with honors), 1963.

*ADDRESSES: Agent*—Michael Sissons, Peters Fraser & Dunlop, 5th Floor, The Chambers, Chelsea Harbour, Lots Rd., London SW10 0XF, England.

*CAREER:* Writer. Independent Television News, London, England, staff reporter, 1963-78.

*AWARDS, HONORS:* Pye Award, 1983, for television play.

*WRITINGS:*

NOVELS

*Harry's Game,* Random House (New York City), 1975.
*The Glory Boys,* Random House, 1976.
*Kingfisher,* Collins (London), 1977, Summit Books (New York City), 1978.
*Red Fox,* Collins, 1979, published as *The Harrison Affair,* Summit Books, 1980.
*The Contract,* Collins, 1980, Holt (New York City), 1981.
*Archangel,* Dutton (New York City), 1982.
*In Honour Bound,* Norton (New York City), 1984.
*Field of Blood,* Norton, 1985.
*A Song in the Morning,* Collins, 1986, Norton, 1987.
*An Eye for an Eye,* Morrow (New York City), 1987, published in England as *At Close Quarters,* Collins, 1987.
*Home Run,* Collins, 1989, published as *The Running Target,* Morrow, 1990.
*Condition Black,* Morrow, 1991.
*The Journeyman Tailor,* HarperCollins (London), 1992, HarperCollins (New York City), 1993.
*The Fighting Man,* HarperCollins, 1993.
*The Heart of Danger,* HarperCollins, 1995.

OTHER

Also author of television scripts, including *Harry's Game,* 1982, *The Glory Boys,* 1984, and *The Contract,* 1988, all based on his own novels.

*ADAPTATIONS: Red Fox* was adapted for film in 1991.

*SIDELIGHTS:* Gerald Seymour, once a staff reporter for London's Independent Television News, has become a successful suspense novelist with book sales of over 4 million copies. Often grouped with such writers as Graham Greene, Charles McCarry, and John le Carre, Seymour uses his understanding of covert government to create believable characters and cinematically energized action. Herbert Mitgang in the *New York Times* calls Seymour "one of Britain's most authoritative thriller writers."

Seymour sets his thrillers in trouble spots throughout the world, including the grim confines of war-torn Belfast, in the midst of political instability in the Middle East, and in the Afghan hills during the rebel struggle against Soviet occupation. Robert Cohen explains in his review of *Field of Blood* in the *New York Times Book Review* that Seymour utilizes his first-hand experience as a world reporter to make Belfast more than a mere backdrop to the action: "What distinguishes this novel is neither the driving, unilinear plot nor the prose. . . . Instead, the power accrues through short takes of the gray, brooding city itself, and from the harsh, slangy music of its voices."

Seymour's sharply rendered settings are echoed in his realistic depiction of characters, who often face internal as well as external struggles. Frederick Busch explains in a *Tribune Books* review of *The Running Target,* "Seymour's focus has always been on the moral imperative—on men and women gripped by their conceptions of duty and honor. . . . This novel is a moral as well as a physical adventure." Mitgang offers similar praise, proclaiming that "Seymour proves that a writer with opinions and ideas can handle a difficult subject and rise above the thriller genre." One illustration of Seymour's "opinions and ideas" becomes evident through his unique portrayal of women. In his review of *Field of Blood,* Mitgang writes that "the female characters are not just adjuncts to the main action but very much a part of it. Few male writers take the time, or have the ability, to give women in suspense novels lives of their own."

Some critics have compared Seymour's fictional vision to that of author Graham Greene. Karl G. Fredriksson in the *St. James Guide to Crime and Mystery Writers* notes: "Seymour's special historical and philosophical vision—or perhaps even outlook on life—contributes to the sense of reality in the novels. These individuals are all fighting heroic combats for their countries, their political beliefs, their fellow human beings. But Seymour shows us that all their heroics are futile in the end. The 'heroes' are only puppets, manipulated by the puppet-masters, puppets in a cynically written play where they never know the whole script or the whole cast." Similarly, a *Publishers Weekly* critic describes *The Heart of Danger,* set in war-torn Bosnia, as "a harshly detailed novel about a dirty little war, peopled with a wide variety of deeply etched characters and suffused with a nearly palpable sense of despair and weariness."

By unconventionally offering more than fast-paced action, Seymour invites his reader to think about his/her own conceptions of society, country, and government. Speaking of *The Harrison Affair* in the *Washington Post Book World,* Stanley Ellin trusts that "Most readers will emerge from it as I did, with a headful of troubled thoughts and the sense of having undergone a journey of discovery through strange and alarming territory."

*BIOGRAPHICAL/CRITICAL SOURCES:*

*BOOKS*

*St. James Guide to Crime and Mystery Writers,* 4th edition, St. James Press (Detroit), 1996.

*PERIODICALS*

*Booklist,* June 15, 1981, p. 1334; November 1, 1982, p. 355; May 15, 1984, p. 1296; July, 1985, p. 1475; December 1, 1989, p. 705; July, 1991, p. 2034.
*Critic,* winter, 1975; winter, 1976.
*Guardian,* March 6, 1995, p. 26.
*Library Journal,* May 15, 1997, p. 118.
*New Yorker,* September 16, 1985, p. 124; March 1, 1993, p. 115.
*New York Times,* October 16, 1976; February 9, 1978; August 2, 1985, p. 17; February 28, 1990, p. C19; July 16, 1991, p. C16; March 3, 1993; June 29, 1994.
*New York Times Book Review,* October 5, 1975; October 17, 1976; March 5, 1978; May 27, 1984, p. 16; October 6, 1985, p. 28; September 4, 1988, p. 16; March 11, 1990, p. 33; April 25, 1993, p. 22.
*Observer,* January 2, 1983, p. 46; January 29, 1984, p. 53; March 24, 1985, p. 26.
*Publishers Weekly,* October 16, 1995, p. 44.

*Times* (London), March 16, 1995, p. 14.
*Times Literary Supplement,* December 9, 1977; December 26, 1980, p. 1458; June 5, 1992, p. 21.
*Tribune Books* (Chicago), February 18, 1990, p. 7.
*Washington Post Book World,* February 17, 1980; September 22, 1985, p. 6; August 4, 1991, p. 6.*

\* \* \*

## SHAPPIRO, Herbert (Arthur) 1899-1975 (Burt Arthur, Herbert Arthur, Arthur Herbert)

*PERSONAL:* Born 1899, in New York, NY; died March 15, 1975, in New York, NY; wife's name, Hortene; children: Budd (a writer under name Budd Arthur).

*CAREER:* Novelist. Also worked as a newspaperman, advertising agency executive, editor, screen writer, and playwright.

*WRITINGS:*

*The Black Rider,* Arcadia (New York City), 1941 (published under pseudonym Burt Arthur, J. Curley [South Yarmouth, MA], 1985).
*The Valley of Death,* Arcadia, 1941.
*Chenango Pass,* Arcadia, 1942.
*Mustang Marshall,* Phoenix (New York City), 1943.
*Trouble at Moon Pass,* Phoenix, 1943 (published under pseudonym Burt Arthur, J. Curley, 1987).
*Silver City Rangers,* Phoenix, 1944.
*Gunsmoke Over Utah,* Phoenix, 1945 (published under pseudonym Burt Arthur, Macfadden [New York City], 1969, reprinted under pseudonym Burt Arthur, J. Curley, 1992).
*Woman in the White House,* Tech Books (New York City), 1945.
*High Pockets,* McBride (New York City), 1946 (published under pseudonym Burt Arthur, Macfadden, 1968, reprinted under pseudonym Burt Arthur, J. Curley, 1992).
*The Texan,* McBride, 1946 (published under pseudonym Burt Arthur, J. Curley, 1985).
*The Buckaroo,* Arcadia, 1947 (published under pseudonym Burt Arthur, J. Curley, 1993).

*Boss of the Far West,* Phoenix, 1948 (published under pseudonym Burt Arthur, Macfadden, 1969).

*Sheriff of Lonesome,* Phoenix, 1948 (published under pseudonym Burt Arthur, J. Curley, 1990).

*The Long West Trail,* Phoenix, 1948.

*UNDER NAME BURT ARTHUR*

*Lead-Hungry Lobos,* Phoenix, 1945, J. Curley, 1989.

*Nevada,* Doubleday (Garden City, NY), 1949, published as *Trigger Man,* New American Library (New York City), 1957, reprinted as *Nevada,* J. Curley, 1993.

*Stirrups in the Dust,* Doubleday, 1950.

*Trouble Town,* Doubleday, 1950.

*Thunder Valley,* Doubleday, 1951, reprinted, J. Curley, 1986.

*The Killer,* Doubleday, 1952, reprinted, J. Curley, 1988.

*Gunplay at the X-Bar-X* (also see below), Avon (New York City), 1952.

*Killer's Crossing,* Lion (New York City), 1953, reprinted J. Curley, 1987.

*Two-Gun Texas,* Lion, 1954.

*Killer's Moon,* World's Work (Kingswood, Surrey, England), 1953.

*The Drifter,* Ace (New York City), 1955, Chivers (Bath, England), 1986.

*Texas Sheriff,* Avalon (New York City), 1956.

*Return of the Texan,* New American Library, 1956, reprinted J. Curley (South Yarmouth, MA), 1985.

*Gunsmoke in Nevada,* New American Library, 1957, reprinted, J. Curley, 1990.

*Ride Out for Revenge,* Avon, 1957.

*Outlaw Fury,* Avon, 1957.

(With son, Budd Arthur) *The Stranger,* Doubleday, 1959, reprinted, J. Curley, 1990.

*Duel on the Range,* Berkley (New York City), 1959, reprinted, J. Curley, 1991.

*Swiftly to Evil,* Consul (London), 1961.

*Quemado,* Wright & Brown (London), 1961.

(With Budd Arthur) *Three Guns North,* R. Hale, 1962, Macfadden (New York City), 1964.

(With Budd Arthur) *Big Red,* New American Library, 1962.

*Shadow Valley,* Wright & Brown, 1962, reprinted as *Thunder Valley,* J. Curley, 1986.

*Flaming Guns,* Paperback Library, 1964, Chivers, 1988.

(With Budd Arthur) *Ride a Crooked Trail,* Avon, 1964.

(With Budd Arthur) *Requiem for a Gun,* Avon, 1964, reprinted, J. Curley, 1991.

*Sing a Song of Six-Guns,* Macfadden, 1964, reprinted, J. Curley, 1990.

*Empty Saddles,* Macfadden, 1964, reprinted, J. Curley, 1986.

*Two-Gun Outlaw,* Paperback Library (New York City), 1964, reprinted, J. Curley, 1987.

*Gun-Law on the Range,* Paperback Library, 1964.

(With Budd Arthur) *Walk Tall, Ride Tall,* New American Library, 1965, reprinted, J. Curley, 1992.

*Gunsmoke in Paradise,* Macfadden, 1965, reprinted, J. Curley, 1992.

(With Budd Arthur) *Ride a Crooked Mile,* Avon, 1966, reprinted as *Ride a Crooked Trail,* J. Curley, 1991.

(With Budd Arthur) *Action at Truxton,* Avon, 1966.

*The Free Lands,* New American Library, 1966, reprinted, J. Curley, 1989.

*Action at Ambush Flat* (also see below), Paperback Library, 1967.

*Deadman's Gulch,* Belmont, 1967.

(With Budd Arthur) *The Saga of Denny McCune,* Belmont (New York City), 1979, reprinted, J. Curley, 1990.

(With Budd Arthur) *Westward the Wagons,* Belmont, 1979, reprinted, J. Curley, 1990.

(With Budd Arthur) *Canavan's Trail,* Nordon (New York City), 1980, reprinted, J. Curley, 1991.

(With Budd Arthur) *Brothers of the Range,* Hale (London), 1982, reprinted, J. Curley, 1993.

*The Black Rider,* J. Curley, 1985.

*Boss of the Far West,* J. Curley, 1989.

*Action at Spanish Flat [and] Gunplay at the X-Bar-X,* J. Curley, 1992.

*UNDER NAME HERBERT ARTHUR*

*No Other Love,* Pleiades Books, 1952.

*Action at Spanish Flat,* Allen (London), 1953.

*UNDER NAME ARTHUR HERBERT*

*Bugles in the Night,* Rinehart (New York City), 1950 (published under pseudonym Burt Arthur, J. Curley, 1988).

*The Gunslinger,* Rinehart, 1951.

*Freedom Run,* Rinehart, 1951.

*OTHER*

Also author of more than fifty additional westerns, and of numerous plays and screenplays, some in collaboration with his son, Budd Arthur.

*SIDELIGHTS:* Best known under the name Burt Arthur, Herbert Shappiro was the author of numerous pulp Western novels, some of which he co-wrote with his son, Budd. Although he has been dead for a quarter century, Shappiro still has a readership, thanks to reprints of even his oldest novels. His books have been issued in many countries and in many languages, and during his lifetime he estimated that about 32 million copies had been sold.

Shappiro was born in New York City, but he spent much of his youth in Texas. It was there that his interest in the West was cultivated, and the desert Southwest proved to be a recurring setting for his works. He began publishing novels in mid-life and continued to produce sometimes as many as two or three books per year through the late 1960s. His son, who published as Budd Arthur, began collaborating with him in 1957 and continued to do so until Shappiro's death in 1975.

The father-son collaboration—indeed the entire Shappiro opus—is rather confusing. Sometimes Burt and Budd Arthur wrote books together from scratch. Sometimes Budd Arthur re-wrote his father's older novels or their earlier collaborations. A number of these joint efforts appeared under the "Burt Arthur" name; others were published under both names. Shappiro admitted that he was himself unsure of which books were his own work and which were collaborations. To further confuse things, some of Shappiro's earlier Westerns were reprinted under the name Burt Arthur.

Whatever their provenance, the novels of Herbert Shappiro have been characterized in *Twentieth-Century Western Writers* as "rather typical pulp Westerns, less violent than the popularly held stereotype of the form but with memorable acting scenes when violence does occur." Certain plot devices and characters reappear from book to book, but Shappiro's stories are notable for their sharply-drawn minor characters, including all sorts of horses. Shappiro also enjoyed writing phonetic dialogue based on the accents he remembered from his youth. To quote R. Jeff Banks in *Twentieth-Century Western Writers,* a Shappiro book, especially from early in the author's career, contains "forests of apostrophes." Banks con-

cluded that Shappiro's work "can best be appreciated in small, infrequent doses, but he should certainly not be neglected altogether."

*BIOGRAPHICAL/CRITICAL SOURCES:*

BOOKS

*Twentieth-Century Western Writers,* 2nd edition, St. James Press (Detroit, MI), 1991.*

\* \* \*

**SHEPHERD, Michael**
  **See LUDLUM, Robert**

\* \* \*

**SIMPSON, Doris 1913-**
  **(Anthea Cohen)**

*PERSONAL:* Born August 26, 1913, in Guildford, England; married Mark Simpson, 1947. *Education:* Educated at convent school in England. *Politics:* Liberal. *Religion:* Society of Friends (Quakers).

*ADDRESSES: Home and office*—3 Camden Court, Dover St., Ryde, Isle of Wight PO33 2AQ, England. *Agent*—Vanessa Holt Associates, Claranc Rd., Leigh-on-Sea, Essex, England.

*CAREER:* Writer. Former registered nurse at hospitals in Leicester, Chelsea and Ryde, Isle of Wight. Teacher of creative writing.

*WRITINGS:*

UNDER PSEUDONYM ANTHEA COHEN; MYSTERY NOVELS

*Angel without Mercy,* Quartet (London), 1982, Doubleday (New York City), 1984.
*Angel of Vengeance,* Quartet, 1983, Doubleday, 1984.
*Angel of Death,* Quartet, 1983, Doubleday, 1985.
*Fallen Angel,* Quartet, 1984.
*Guardian Angel,* Doubleday, 1985.
*Hell's Angel,* Quartet, 1986.
*Ministering Angel,* Quartet, 1987.
*Destroying Angel,* Quartet, 1988.
*Angel Dust,* Quartet, 1989.

*Recording Angel,* Constable (London), 1991.
*Angel in Action,* Constable, 1992.
*Angel in Love,* Constable, 1993.
*Angel in Autumn,* Constable, 1995.
*Poison Pen,* Constable, 1996.

OTHER

*Be Patient: Your Life in Their Hands,* Butterworth (London), 1967.
*Popular Hospital Misconceptions,* International Publishing Corp. (London), 1969.
*Dangerous Love* (young adult novel), Pan Books (London), 1984.
*Substance and Shadows,* Pan Books, 1986.

Author of several short stories; also author of columns in *Nursing Mirror,* 1970-73, and "Green Girl" in *Scholastic,* 1978. Columnist for *World Medicine.* Contributor to trade journals and women's magazines. Many of Cohen's works have been translated into German.

SIDELIGHTS: Anthea Cohen's "Angel" mystery novels feature the unusual character Agnes Carmichael. L. M. Quinn in the *St. James Guide to Crime and Mystery Writers* describes Carmichael as a nurse who "in the course of her life, from her childhood in an orphanage and throughout her career as a nurse, . . . solves all her problems by simply disposing of anyone unfortunate enough to stand in her way. The unwitting victims may have directly thwarted her ambitions, for example Nurse Pearson who is strangled because she is having an affair with the object of Agnes's affections, or they may merely have annoyed her in some small way on an already bad day. The outcome is always the same—another unsolved crime for the police and a reestablished sense of power for the homely and introverted nurse."

Because of Carmichael's murderous nature, which she justifies to herself in various ways as it suits her, the "Angel" series is not so much a series of mystery or crime novels as a continuing examination of one psychopathic personality. "Cohen's chief preoccupation," Quinn writes, "[is] the inner workings of the mind of a psychopath. Her books are more accurately thrillers, in the sense that they deal with the murderer's motivation and method rather than the detective's logic and deduction. It is a perspective which sets Cohen apart as an original and refreshing writer in the genre."

BIOGRAPHICAL/CRITICAL SOURCES:

BOOKS

*St. James Guide to Crime and Mystery Writers,* 4th edition, St. James Press (Detroit), 1996.

PERIODICALS

*Listener,* April 21, 1988, p. 30; September 21, 1989, p. 32.

\*　　\*　　\*

**SIMPSON, Mona (Elizabeth) 1957-**

PERSONAL: Born June 14, 1957, in Green Bay, WI; sister of Steven Jobs (cofounder of Apple Computer and technology entrepreneur); married Richard Appel (a public prosecutor), 1995; one child. *Education:* University of California, Berkeley, B.A., 1979; Columbia University, M.F.A., 1983.

ADDRESSES: *Agent*—Amanda Urban, International Creative Management, 40 West 57th St., New York, NY 10019.

CAREER: Writer. Creative writing instructor at Bard College, Annandale-on-Hudson, NY.

AWARDS, HONORS: Whiting Writers' Award and National Endowment for the Arts grant, both 1986; John Simon Guggenheim Memorial Foundation fellowship and Hodder fellowship, Princeton, both 1988.

WRITINGS:

*Anywhere but Here* (novel), Knopf (New York City), 1986.
*The Lost Father* (novel), Knopf, 1991.
*A Regular Guy* (novel), Knopf, 1996.

Work represented in anthologies, including *Twenty under Thirty,* Scribners, 1985; *Louder than Words,* 1990; *The Pushcart Prize: Best of the Small Presses XI;* and *Best American Short Stories of 1986.* Contributor to periodicals, including *Harper's, Iowa Review, North American Review, Paris Review,* and *Ploughshares.*

*SIDELIGHTS:* Mona Simpson is a highly regarded novelist from the generation of writers that emerged in the 1980s. Her novels explore the complex ties in families torn apart by divorce or abandonment, usually focusing on daughters, their wayward mothers, and absent fathers. *Anywhere but Here,* Simpson's critically acclaimed first novel, set the framework for her fiction. In this book, Adele August, the mother, is a twice-married woman who longs for her daughter Ann's success as a child star in Hollywood. When Ann is twelve, Adele drives her from Wisconsin to luxurious Beverly Hills, California, hoping to make important connections with the film world's upper echelon there. Once in Beverly Hills, however, mother and daughter find life less than promising. Adele deludes herself with imagined love affairs while working mundane jobs, and Ann enjoys only limited success as a television performer. By novel's end, the emotionally trying—and occasionally violent—mother-daughter relationship is altered by Ann's growing need for independence.

Upon publication in 1986, *Anywhere but Here* was recognized as an important new work. Richard Eder, writing in the *Los Angeles Times Book Review,* describes Simpson's debut as a "remarkably gifted novel," and Laurie Stone, in her *Village Voice* appraisal, calls *Anywhere but Here* a "brilliant, true first novel." Further accolades came from the *New York Times*'s Michiko Kakutani, who praises Simpson's book as "stunning," and from *Newsweek* reviewer Laura Shapiro, who describes *Anywhere but Here* as a "big, complex and masterfully written . . . achievement" that readily establishes Simpson as one of America's "best younger novelists."

As the accolades continued for *Anywhere but Here,* Simpson revealed in various interviews that producing her first novel was a demanding task. The book underwent several drafts—with some episodes revised as many as ten times—and was the subject of often severe criticism from friends and peers. Even after the novel was finally published and the acclaim came, Simpson expressed some dissatisfaction. "You really want to be proud of your work," she told *Washington Post* writer Paula Span. "You want the work to be as good as the vision you started with. For me, it never has been, so far."

Simpson continued to pursue her vision in *The Lost Father,* the sequel to *Anywhere but Here.* Ann, now grown, has left the West Coast—and the Hollywood dream to be a star—for the East Coast and medical school in New York City. She is a gifted student with high expectations, but under the pressures of medical school, her long suppressed questions about her absent father bubble to the surface and then consume her life. She knows that her lost father, John Atassi, was an Egyptian immigrant who came to study in the United States and then started a career as an academic. Along the way, he started and then abandoned a family. As her search takes on a life of its own, Ann Stevenson becomes Mayan Atassi, the name given to her by her father. She searches the United States and even takes a trip to Egypt to query her undiscovered family there. In the end, she finds him, a restauranteur in California with a new wife. When she at last finishes her quest, Ann/Mayan finds no answers, no satisfaction.

Ann/Mayan's quest for her father is long and all-consuming, characteristics which, according to a number of reviewers, create significant challenges for readers of Simpson's book. "There are problems in dramatizing such single-mindedness," notes Jim Shepard in the *New York Times Book Review,* "and the novel doesn't escape all of them." For, as Richard Eder points out in the *Los Angeles Times Book Review,* "Mayan is alive, believable, and real; and as with any live, real and engaging person who talks endlessly about herself and doesn't look up or out, you wish she would."

Yet, even with such qualifications, Shepard finds *The Lost Father* "a superb book." "The author's language can be breathtaking in the simple beauty of its imagery," he comments. "And," he writes, "the portrait of Mayan that emerges is marvelous in its acuity and richness." Eder commends Simpson for treating the familiar theme of parental abandonment in a way that makes it come alive by keeping it personal. "What Simpson does," he observes, "is to work out in enormous, sensitive and highly imaginative detail the pattern this abandonment describes in one individual." *London Review of Books* contributor Jonathan Coe admits that Mayan's deeply personal quest seems to plod along at times, but he finds that "eventually the narrative is allowed to get up a good head of steam, and the excitement of the final stages of the search—involving the inevitable trip to Egypt—is topped only by the exhilarating rightness of the novel's anti-climax, when Mayan does find her father and realises that she is no closer to solving the mystery which has been dogging her all her life."

*A Regular Guy,* Simpson's third novel, is another story of a daughter, her unconventional mother, and her absent father. In this case, Jane and her mother,

Mary, are long forgotten by Tom Owens, Mary's high school sweetheart and Jane's father. Owens never finished college, but he did not need to. A biotechnology wizkid, he has built his own company (named Genesis) from a home project into an extremely lucrative concern. (Reviewers have noted a parallel with real-life wizkids such as Bill Gates and Simpson's brother Steve Jobs.) The novel begins as Jane, not yet a teenager, learns to drive from her wayward mother and then sets out in a rickety truck in a journey from the California mountains to the California valleys to force her father to accept her. The resulting tale is "a luminous family saga," according to Sybil S. Steinberg in *Publishers Weekly*. Steinberg adds, "Echoes of the Book of Genesis resonate throughout the novel, lending it an enchanting, allegorical air without overwhelming the uneasy, acutely observed family chemistry that is its focal point."

Because of the similarity of its theme with Simpson's earlier novels, reviewers have been quick to compare *A Regular Guy* with *Anywhere but Here* and *The Lost Father*. In the opinion of *New York Times* reviewer Michiko Kakutani, *A Regular Guy* is "a novel that lacks the emotional immediacy of her earlier books, a stilted and strangely detached novel that feels as if it had been forcibly willed into creation." This detachment affects Simpson's characterization, according to Roxana Robinson in the *Washington Post Book World*. She writes, "The characters—who are hard to like—never take on the psychological mass necessary to command our attention and sympathy. Never clearly defined, they cannot develop relationships or change through experience." *Library Journal* contributor Adam Mazmanian concedes differences between this and earlier novels, but he comes to a more positive evaluation. "Though this beautifully written novel lacks some of the humor of Simpson's earlier work," he observes, "the fully realized characters and the well-cast mood of ambivalence make this her best novel yet."

Martha Duffy also faults Simpson for continuing to mine the same theme in the same ways, this time with less energy. She writes in *Time*, "*A Regular Guy* has the same theme as much of her earlier work—a child searching for a lost father—and it lacks the energy and rude gusto of *Anywhere but Here*." Laura Shapiro recognizes similar origins for these novels, but draws a different conclusion about the final products. "Simpson shows no sign of being tempted to write the same novel over and over," she maintains in a *Newsweek* review. "Her books may be inspired by similar emotional preoccupations, but her imagination works strictly from scratch. For "A Regular Guy," she has created a voice, a perspective and a style that are entirely fresh and that give her prodigious talents a challenging new playing field." She believes that "Simpson has never written a novel so teeming, nor one so technically daring." Steinberg concludes, "It is Simpson's delicate grasp of family planning and misplanning, of legitimate versus illegitimate parenting and the machinations of creativity and selling-out that make this rich and winding story so mesmerizing."

Taken together, Simpson's novels offer her unique vision of American family life and its particular effect on young women. As Devoney Looser comments in *Contemporary Novelists*, "Simpson's novels are remarkable for their unsentimental versions of contemporary womanhood. Her female narrators are strong characters but not invincible heroines; they are victimized but not merely victims." The books appeal directly to readers, suggests Looser, because they "read much more like memoir, providing readers with intricate and painful windows into her characters' psyches."

## BIOGRAPHICAL/CRITICAL SOURCES:

### BOOKS

*Contemporary Literary Criticism,* Volume 44, Gale (Detroit), 1987.
*Contemporary Novelists,* 6th edition, St. James Press (Detroit), 1996.

### PERIODICALS

*Cosmopolitan,* February, 1992, p. 18; November, 1993, p. 234.
*Entertainment Weekly,* February 14, 1992, p. 50.
*Library Journal,* August, 1996, p. 114.
*London Review of Books,* July 23, 1992, p. 22.
*Los Angeles Magazine,* October, 1996, p. 26.
*Los Angeles Times Book Review,* January 4, 1987, p. 3; February 9, 1992, p. 3; October 6, 1996, p. 2.
*Los Angeles Times Magazine,* November 17, 1996, p. 18.
*Maclean's,* March 16, 1992, p. 54.
*Nation,* April 13, 1992, p. 494.
*Newsweek,* February 2, 1987, p. 69; February 3, 1992, p. 62; October 7, 1996, p. 78.
*New York,* October 7, 1996, p. 48.

*New York Times,* December 24, 1986; January 24, 1987; January 21, 1992, p. C17; October 15, 1996, p. C15.

*New York Times Book Review,* January 11, 1987, p. 7; February 9, 1992, p. 10; October 27, 1996, p. 16.

*New York Times Magazine,* January 12, 1997, p. 14.

*Observer,* June 28, 1992, p. 66.

*People,* March 9, 1992, p. 29; December 2, 1996, p. 36.

*Publishers Weekly,* August 19, 1996, p. 52; November 4, 1996, p. 50.

*Time,* November 4, 1996, p. 95.

*Times Literary Supplement,* May 22, 1992, p. 28.

*Tribune Books* (Chicago), January 19, 1992, p. 1; October 20, 1996, p. 1.

*USA Today,* February 14, 1992, p. D4; January 7, 1997, p. D6.

*Village Voice,* February 3, 1987, p. 47; October 15, 1996, p. 45.

*Voice Literary Supplement,* March, 1992, p. 6.

*Wall Street Journal,* February 7, 1992, p. A11.

*Washington Post,* January 27, 1987; February 4, 1992, p. D2.

*Washington Post Book World,* February 1, 1987, p. 7; October 6, 1996, p. 4.


\*     \*     \*


**SINFIELD, Alan 1941-**


*PERSONAL:* Born December 17, 1941, in London, England; son of Ernest and Lucy (Seabright) Sinfield. *Education:* University of London, B.A. (with first-class honors), 1964, M.A., 1967. *Politics:* Socialist. *Religion:* Atheist.


*ADDRESSES: Home*—4 Clifton Pl., Brighton BN1 3FN, England. *Office*—School of English and American Studies, Arts Building, University of Sussex, Brighton BN1 9QN, England.


*CAREER:* University of Sussex, Brighton, England, lecturer, 1965-82, reader, 1982-90, professor of English, 1990—. University of California, Berkeley, Beckman Professor, 1989; Northwestern University, Avalon visiting professor, 1997.


*AWARDS, HONORS:* D.Litt., University of London, 1987.

*WRITINGS:*

*The Language of Tennyson's "In Memoriam,"* Basil Blackwell, 1971.

*Dramatic Monologue,* Methuen, 1977.

*Literature in Protestant England 1560-1660,* Croom Helm, 1983.

(Editor) *Society and Literature 1945-1970,* Methuen, 1983.

(Editor with Jonathan Dollimore) *Selected Plays of John Webster,* Cambridge University Press (Cambridge, England), 1983.

(Editor with Dollimore) *Political Shakespeare: New Essays in Cultural Materialism,* Manchester University Press (Manchester, England), 1985, 2nd edition, 1996.

*Alfred Tennyson,* Basil Blackwell, 1986.

*Literature, Politics and Culture in Postwar Britain,* Basil Blackwell, 1989, published as *Literature, Politics, Culture: Consensus to Conflict in Postwar Britain,* University of California Press (Berkeley, CA), 1989, 2nd edition, Athlone Press, 1997.

*Faultlines: Cultural Materialism and the Politics of Dissident Reading,* University of California Press, 1992.

(Editor) *"Macbeth:" William Shakespeare,* Macmillan, 1992.

*The Wilde Century: Effeminacy, Oscar Wilde, and the Queer Moment,* Columbia University Press (New York City), 1994.

*Cultural Politics—Queer Reading,* University of Pennsylvania Press (Philadelphia, PA), 1994.

*Gay and After,* Serpent's Tail, 1998.


Editor, *Textual Practice,* 1995—.


*WORK IN PROGRESS:* A study of theatre and homosexuality since Oscar Wilde.


*SIDELIGHTS:* Alan Sinfield told *CA:* "My literary criticism began with a formalist study of Tennyson's poetry in which I experimented with the methods of structural linguistics. Then I moved increasingly towards the belief that literature can be properly understood only in its historical context. I explored this approach in relation to the writing of Shakespeare's time and the current disturbing and provocative religious orthodoxy. As this work was progressing, developments in critical theory, especially those deriving from Marxism, helped me to see that the literary text is always interpreted in the specific historical and political conditions in which it is read, and this led me to write again about Tennyson and

Shakespeare, and to pursue a study of the conditions and determinants of intellectual life in our own time."

He adds, "In the more repressive atmosphere in Britain since the 1980s, it seems necessary to address the resources of gay history, culture, and politics, as a way of helping to consolidate and defend a beleaguered minority. Most of my work is about sexualities."

*BIOGRAPHICAL/CRITICAL SOURCES:*

*PERIODICALS*

*Times Literary Supplement,* June 22, 1984, November 14, 1986.

\*     \*     \*

**SINGER, Mark 1950-**

*PERSONAL:* Born October 19, 1950, in Tulsa, OK; son of Alexander Simon (a geologist) and Marjorie (Teller) Singer; married Rhonda Klein (an attorney), May 27, 1973 (divorced, 1996); children: Jeb Lincoln, Reid Teller, Timothy Goodman. *Education:* Yale University, B.A. (with honors), 1972. *Religion:* Jewish.

*ADDRESSES: Office—New Yorker,* 25 West 43rd St., New York, NY 10036. *Agent—*Joy Harris, c/o The Lantz Office, 888 7th Ave., New York, NY 10106.

*CAREER: New Yorker* magazine, New York City, staff writer, 1974— ; writer.

*AWARDS, HONORS:* Distinguished Service Award from the Society of Professional Journalists, 1985.

*WRITINGS:*

*Funny Money,* Knopf (New York City), 1985.
*Mr. Personality,* Knopf, 1989.
*Citizen K: The Deeply Weird American Journey of Brett Kimberlin,* Knopf, 1996.

Author of introductions *In Cold Blood,* (commemorative edition), by Truman Capote, Random House (New York City), 1986; *Miss Thistlebottom's Hobgoblins,* by Theodore M. Bernstein, Noonday Press (New York City), 1991; *I Am Thinking of My Dar-ling,* by Vincent McHugh, Yarrow Press (New York City), 1991. Also author, with Garrison Keillor, of foreword to *The Honest Rainmaker,* reprinted edition, by A. J. Liebling, North Point Press (San Francisco), 1989.

*SIDELIGHTS:* Mark Singer, a native Oklahoman renowned for his witty, offbeat writing in the *New Yorker* magazine's "Talk of the Town" column, has also received critical acclaim for his nonfiction books. *Funny Money* is Singer's 1985 account of the rise and collapse of the Penn Square Bank in Oklahoma City. Penn Square was an unassuming institution located in a small shopping mall that nevertheless grew to colossal proportions during the energy boom of the late-1970s and early-1980s. In the extravagance of the times, the bank's chief officers discovered that there was great profit in making liberal and virtually unconsidered oil and gas loans which could then be sold to large national banks such as the Continental Illinois and Chase Manhattan.

In *Funny Money* Singer chronicles the Oklahoma oil-boom years with, according to *New York Times* critic Christopher Lehmann-Haupt, "a gift for mimicry and an amusing sense of hyperbole. He speaks the American vernacular. He makes comic poetry of the art of turning liabilities into assets." S. C. Gwynne commented in the *Los Angeles Times Book Review* that the book's charm lies in the characters it portrays. Penn Square's energy loan officer, Bill "Monkeybrains" Patterson, for example, delights in wearing Mickey Mouse ears or a duck cap to work and getting into food fights in restaurants. Susan Lee wrote in the *New York Times Book Review* that "Mr. Singer does a great job describing the yahooism, generally called Okiesmo, that captured Oklahoma City during the boom years." Lee, while applauding the wit and charm of *Funny Money,* regretted the author's lack of political analysis, summarizing that "although Mr. Singer has an eye for vulgar excess and an ear for self-serving bluster, he doesn't fit the gossip into a broader context."

Singer's 1989 publication, *Mr. Personality,* is a collection of reprints of thirty-one profiles written by the author for the *New Yorker.* The subjects of Singer's pieces are as varied as the people on a Manhattan street. Included are a zipper repairman, the inventors of the automatic "Doggie Washer," five brothers who superintend luxury apartment buildings, a dealer of rare prints, an auto wreck renter, a knife sharpener, two retired television news producers, a court buff, a radio humorist, and the title character, a clarinetist who calls himself "Mr. Personality" and plays on the subway. A *Publishers Weekly* reviewer, calling the Oklahoma-born Singer "a genuine New Yorker," praised the "delightfully whimsical interviews with fellow townspeople" that Singer conducted for the work. Clarence Petersen, in his *Tribune Books* review, labelled the pieces "witty and urbane and usually offbeat."

In 1996, Singer published a book that grew out of a *New Yorker* piece called "The Prisoner and the Politician." It concerned Brett Kimberlin, a convicted drug smuggler serving time at a federal penitentiary in Oklahoma. During the 1988 presidential campaign, Kimberlin had alleged that Republican vice-presidential nominee Dan Quayle had purchased marijuana from him in the early 1970s. When Kimberlin attempted to hold a press conference, he was placed in detention and the story suppressed. Singer was interested in the story not only because he found Kimberlin credible, but because he wondered why Quayle should be held above suspicion.

In his article and book, Singer portrayed Kimberlin as an intelligent, disciplined individual. The writer focused on the reaction of prison officials and journalists to Kimberlin's allegations about Quayle. "Based on his own extensive study, Singer concludes . . . that Kimberlin 'has become a political prisoner,'" informed Susan Weill in the *Dictionary of Literary Biography.*

Singer's article was a finalist for the prestigious National Magazine Award, and it was expanded and published in 1996 as *Citizen K: The Deeply Weird American Journey of Brett Kimberlin.* During the course of his continued research, however, Singer became convinced that Kimberlin, whose credibility he had strongly defended, was in fact lying to him. "Repudiating the conclusions he had drawn in his *New Yorker* article, Singer turns *Citizen K* . . . in part, into a mea culpa in which he frankly admits to having been duped," advised Weill. Yet the book drew mostly favorable reviews. Ben Yagoda, a writer for the *New York Times Book Review,* "found it remarkable that Singer, whom he praises as a first-rate reporter and a diligent researcher, candidly placed himself in an unfavorable light as he spun his cautionary tale about the dangers inherent in the journalist's relationship to his source," said Weill. Perhaps being right is not as important to Singer as simply being an observer. Weill quoted him as say-

ing: "What has always driven me as a writer is that I'm curious about people. I just want to know."

## BIOGRAPHICAL/CRITICAL SOURCES:

### BOOKS

Connery, Thomas B., *A Sourcebook of American Literary Journalism: Representative Writers in an Emerging Genre,* Greenwood Press (Westport, CT), 1992.

*Dictionary of Literary Biography,* Volume 185: *American Literary Journalists, 1945-1995, First Series,* Gale (Detroit), 1997.

Hollowell, John, *Fact and Fiction: The New Journalism and the Nonfiction Novel,* University of North Carolina Press (Chapel Hill), 1977.

Sims, Norman, editor, *Literary Journalism in the Twentieth Century,* Oxford University Press (New York City), 1990, pp. 82-109.

Sims, editor, *Literary Journalism: A New Collection of the Best American Nonfiction,* Ballantine (New York City), 1995.

Sims, editor, *The Literary Journalists,* Ballantine, 1984.

Wolfe, Tom, and E. W. Johnson, editors, *The New Journalism,* Harper (New York City), 1973.

Zinsser, William, *Speaking of Journalism,* HarperCollins (New York City), 1994.

### PERIODICALS

*Chicago Tribune Book World,* April 27, 1986, p. 44.

*Journal of Popular Culture,* spring, 1982, pp. 142-49.

*Los Angeles Times Book Review,* July 7, 1985, p. 2; May 27, 1990, p. 10.

*New York Times,* May 30, 1985.

*New York Times Book Review,* June 23, 1985; November 10, 1996.

*Publishers Weekly,* November 18, 1988, pp. 60, 62.

*Tribune Books* (Chicago), June 3, 1990.

*Washington Post Book World,* May 25, 1986, p. 13.*

\* \* \*

**SMITH, Adam**
  See GOODMAN, George J(erome) W(aldo)

## SNEVE, Virginia Driving Hawk 1933-
(Virginia Driving Hawk)

*PERSONAL:* Surname rhymes with "navy"; born February 21, 1933, in Rosebud, SD; daughter of James H. (an Episcopal priest) and Rose (Ross) Driving Hawk; married Vance M. Sneve (a teacher of industrial arts), July 14, 1955; children: Shirley Kay, Paul Marshall, Alan Edward. *Education:* South Dakota State University, B.S., 1954, M.Ed., 1969. *Politics:* Republican. *Religion:* Episcopal.

*ADDRESSES: Home*—10501 Woodstock Court, Rapid City, SD 57702.

*CAREER:* Teacher of English in public schools, White, SD, 1954-55, and Pierre, SD, 1955; Flandreau Indian School, Flandreau, SD, teacher of English and speech, 1965-70, 1975-80, guidance counselor, 1980-85; Rapid City Public Schools, Rapid City, SD, bicultural resource teacher, 1986-90, high school counselor, 1988-95. Ogalala Lakota College, associate instructor, 1987-95. Brevet Press, Sioux Falls, SD, editor, beginning in 1972; Episcopal Church of South Dakota, historiographer, beginning in 1976. Member of Rosebud Sioux Tribe; United Sioux Tribes Cultural Arts, member of board of directors, 1972-73. Corporation for Public Broadcasting, member of board of directors, Native American Consortium, 1975-80. Member of South Dakota State University Foundation Board and Devereaux Library Friends Board, South Dakota School of Mines; member of Native American advisory board, Rapid City Museum Alliance and *Rapid City Journal.*

*MEMBER:* South Dakota for the Arts, Word Craft Circle of Native American Writers.

*AWARDS, HONORS:* Manuscript award, American Indian category, Interracial Council for Minority Books for Children, 1971, for *Jimmy Yellow Hawk;* Woman of Achievement Award, South Dakota Press Women, 1974; award for "special contribution to education," South Dakota Indian Education Association, 1975; named National Woman of Achievement, National Federation of Press Women, 1975; Doctorate of Letters, Dakota Wesleyan University, 1979; award for "distinguished contribution to South Dakota history," Dakota History Conference, 1982; named Writer of the Year, Western Heritage Hall of Fame, 1984; Native American Prose Award, University of Nebraska Press, 1992; Spur Award, fiction category, Western Writers of America, 1994, for

*Betrayed;* Human Services Award, South Dakota Education Association, 1994; Books for the Teen Age, New York Public Library, 1996, for *Completing the Circle;* Human Rights Award, South Dakota State Counselors Association, 1996; Author-Illustrator Human and Civil Rights Award, National Education Association, 1996; Spirit of Crazy Horse Award, 1996.

*WRITINGS:*

*FOR YOUNG PEOPLE*

*Jimmy Yellow Hawk,* illustrated by Oren Lyons, Holiday House (New York City), 1972.

*High Elk's Treasure,* Holiday House, 1972, reprinted with illustrations by Lyons, 1995.

*When Thunders Spoke,* Holiday House, 1974, reprinted with illustrations by Lyons, University of Nebraska Press (Lincoln), 1994.

*Betrayed,* Holiday House, 1974.

*The Chichi HooHoo Bogeyman,* illustrated by Nadema Agard, Holiday House, 1975.

*The Twelve Moons,* Houghton (Boston, MA), 1977.

(Editor and contributor) *Dancing Teepees: Poems of American Indian Youth* (nineteen poems from Native American oral tradition and more contemporary sources), illustrated by Stephen Gammell, Holiday House, 1989.

*The Trickster and the Troll,* University of Nebraska Press, 1997.

*"FIRST AMERICANS" SERIES; ILLUSTRATED BY RONALD HIMLER; PUBLISHED BY HOILDAY HOUSE*

*The Sioux,* 1993.

*The Navajos,* 1993.

*The Seminoles,* 1994.

*The Nez Perce,* 1994.

*The Hopis,* 1995.

*The Iroquois,* 1995.

*The Cherokees,* 1996.

*The Cheyennes,* 1996.

*The Apaches,* 1997.

*OTHER*

(Editor) *South Dakota Geographic Names,* Brevet Press (Sioux Falls, SD), 1973.

*The Dakota's Heritage,* Brevet Press, 1973.

*They Led a Nation,* illustrated by Loren Zephier, Brevet Press, 1975.

*That They May Have Life: The Episcopal Church in South Dakota, 1859-1976,* Seabury (New York City), 1977.

*Completing the Circle* (nonfiction), University of Nebraska Press, 1995.

Contributor to books, including *Ethnic American Woman,* Kendall/Hunt (Dubuque, IA), 1978; *A Common Land, a Diverse People,* Nordland Heritage Foundation (Sioux Falls, SD), 1987; and *Growing Up in Siouxland,* Nordland Heritage Foundation, 1987. Contributor of articles and poems to periodicals, including *Country Living, Plainswoman, Dakota West, Wanbli Ho Journal,* and *Indian Historian.* Contributor to educational units on American Indians. Contributor to periodicals, including *Boy's Life.* Some writings appear under the name Virginia Driving Hawk.

*SIDELIGHTS:* Born on the Rosebud Sioux Reservation in South Dakota, Virginia Driving Hawk Sneve has called upon her Native American roots to create many respected works of fiction and nonfiction for young people and adults. She has been determined to create stories for young people that would portray Native Americans and their history more accurately, informatively, and accessibly than had much of the existing literature. Of her purpose as a writer, Sneve commented in the *Seventh Book of Junior Authors & Illustrators:* "All of my adult life I have been involved in education, from kindergarten through college. My writing is an extension of being a teacher and counselor because I strive to be honest and accurate about the Native American experience portrayed in my work. In so doing, I hope to dispel stereotypes and show my reading audience that Native Americans have a proud past, a viable present, and a hopeful future."

*Jimmy Yellow Hawk,* Sneve's first story for children, was published in 1972. This coming-of-age tale set on a Sioux reservation in South Dakota features Little Jim Yellow Hawk, a youth who desires to earn a grown-up name for himself by contributing something to the community and to his tribe. Inspired by his grandfather's story of another boy who succeeded in saving his village from starvation by trapping rabbits, Little Jim sets his own traps and captures a precious mink. After witnessing this feat his friends no longer use the epithet "Little" to describe him, much to Jim's delight. Like most reviewers, Beryl Robinson of *Horn Book Magazine* commented, "the chief value of the story . . . is the realistic picture it gives of modern Indian life on a reservation," such as the rodeo and annual Dakota Reservation Pow Wow that form the background to this story." *High Elk's Treasure* is another of Sneve's books that celebrate Sioux heritage. Forced to seek shelter in a cave by a violent thunderstorm, Joe High Elk discovers an old treasure bundle. In the confusion of the storm, however, Joe loses a valuable horse, the last animal in his family's ancestral herd. Later, he learns that the bundle belonged to his great-grandfather, a mighty Sioux warrior in the Battle of the Little Big Horn, and locates the missing horse. Despite its relatively simple plot, *High Elk's Treasure,* like *Jimmy Yellow Hawk,* has been favorably received by critics. A reviewer for the *Bulletin of the Center for Children's Books* noted that the strong point of the book is that "it makes clear without a sociological commentary the attitudes of contemporary Indians of different generations."

Sneve assesses the contemporary status of Native American culture from a slightly different perspective in *When Thunders Spoke.* Fifteen-year-old Norman Two Bull is a Sioux who rejects the traditional beliefs of his culture. Yet, when Norman uncovers an ancient and magical coup stick that seems to bring his family good luck, his skeptical notions soon begin to disappear. A *Publishers Weekly* reviewer called *When Thunders Spoke* "a wonderfully powerful story, written with skill."

*Betrayed* recounts the events of the 1862 Santee Sioux uprising in western Minnesota. Sneve explores the desperation of several Native Americans provoked to violence by the broken promises and overt greed for land of the U.S. government during this era. Some commentators observed that Sneve's handling of this still delicate subject at times sinks to equivocation, but many, like Cathleen Burns Elmer in the *New York Times Book Review,* noted the author's successes in the work, including her compelling presentation of native language "in gravely simple, spring-clear prose of unmistakable authenticity."

In the 1990s Sneve's writing has been refocused somewhat to a number of nonfiction volumes that form the "First Americans" Series, devoted to the clear and authentic presentation of Native American history and culture. Appearing regularly since 1993, each installment begins with a retelling of the respective tribe's creation stories and launches into a discussion of its history, beliefs, traditional ways of life, important leaders, and contemporary concerns. Each text is also enlivened with colorful maps and quotes from Native American literature and legend. In a review of *The Navajos* and *The Sioux,* the first two books of the series, *Booklist* contributor Karen Hutt hailed the "First Americans" books as "excellent introductions, with a tribal focus that clarifies the unique characteristics and beliefs of each group." Reviewing *The Cherokees,* Elizabeth S. Watson of *Horn Book* commented on Sneve's simple account of the tragic past of the Cherokees: "The delivery of information is straightforward, with no editorial comment, but the facts alone speak volumes."

*BIOGRAPHICAL/CRITICAL SOURCES:*

BOOKS

*Children's Literature Review,* Volume 2, Gale (Detroit, MI), 1976.
Holtze, Sally Holmes, editor, *Seventh Book of Junior Authors & Illustrators,* H. W. Wilson (Bronx, NY), 1996, pp. 301-03.

PERIODICALS

*Booklist,* December 15, 1993, p. 759; October 1, 1994, p. 331; May 1, 1995, p. 1549.
*Bulletin of the Center for Children's Books,* February, 1973, pp. 97-98.
*Horn Book,* August, 1972, pp. 383-84; May-June, 1996, p. 353.
*Library Journal,* May 15, 1995, p. 77.
*New York Times Book Review,* January 19, 1975, p. 8.
*Publishers Weekly,* May 27, 1974, p. 65; November 8, 1993, p. 80; April 10, 1995, p. 49.
*School Library Journal,* April, 1994, p. 146; July, 1995, p. 91; October, 1995, p. 151; April, 1996, p. 130.

\* \* \*

**SOLSONA, S.**
  **See SCHWARTZ, Stephen (Alfred)**

\* \* \*

**SOREL, Julia**
  **See DREXLER, Rosalyn**

**STUART, Dabney 1937-**

*PERSONAL:* Born November 4, 1937, in Richmond, VA; son of Walker Dabney, Jr., and Martha (von Schilling) Stuart; married Suzanne Bailey, 1960 (divorced, 1962); married Betty Kantor, 1963 (divorced, 1964); married Martha Varney, 1965 (divorced, 1977); married Sandra Westcott, 1983; children: Martha, Nathan von Schilling, Darren Wayne. *Education:* Davidson College, A.B., 1960; Harvard University, A.M., 1962.

*ADDRESSES: Office*—Department of English, Washington and Lee University, Lexington, VA 24450.

*CAREER:* College of William and Mary, Williamsburg, VA, instructor in English, 1961-65; Washington and Lee University, Lexington, VA, instructor, 1965-66, assistant professor, 1966-69, associate professor, 1969-74, professor of English, 1974-91, S. Blount Masson professor of English, 1991—. Visiting assistant professor of English, Middlebury College, 1968-69; McGuffey Professor of Creative Writing, Ohio University, spring, 1975; lecturer in creative writing, University of Virginia, fall, 1981. Resident poet, Trinity College, Hartford, CT, spring, 1978. Visiting poet, University of Virginia, Charlottesville, 1981, 1982-83. Has given poetry readings at numerous colleges and universities throughout the United States.

*MEMBER:* Authors League of America, Authors Guild, American Association of University Professors.

*AWARDS, HONORS:* Dylan Thomas Award, Poetry Society of America, for "The Two Lindens," 1965; Howard Willett Research Prize, for poetry manuscript; Borestone Mountain Poetry Awards, 1969, 1974, and 1977; National Endowment for the Humanities summer stipend, 1969; National Endowment for the Arts fellow, 1974 and 1982; first Governor's Award for the Arts (Virginia), 1979; Guggenheim fellowship, 1987-88; Pulitzer Prize nominee, 1987, for *Don't Look Back,* and 1990, for *Narcissus Dreaming.*

*WRITINGS:*

POEMS

*The Diving Bell,* Knopf (New York City), 1966.
*A Particular Place,* Knopf, 1969.

(With others) *Corgi Modern Poets in Focus 3,* Corgi (London), 1971.

*The Other Hand,* Louisiana State University Press (Baton Rouge), 1974.

*Friends of Yours, Friends of Mine* (poems for children), Rainmaker Press (Richmond, VA), 1974.

*Round and Round: A Triptych,* Louisiana State University Press, 1977.

*Rockbridge Poems,* Iron Mountain Press (Emory, VA), 1981.

*Common Ground,* Louisiana State University Press, 1982.

*Don't Look Back,* Louisiana State University Press, 1987.

*Narcissus Dreaming,* Louisiana State University Press, 1990.

*Light Years: New and Selected Poems,* Louisiana State University Press, 1994.

(With Carroll Cloar) *Second Sight: Poems for Paintings by Carroll Cloar,* University of Missouri Press (Columbia), 1996.

*Long Gone,* Louisiana State University Press, 1996.

OTHER

*Nabokov: The Dimensions of Parody* (nonfiction), Louisiana State University Press, 1978.

*Sweet Lucy Wine: Stories* (fiction), Louisiana State University Press, 1992.

*The Way to Cobbs Creek* (fiction), University of Missouri Press, 1997.

Work is represented in about sixty anthologies. Contributor of essays, reviews, and poetry to *Poetry, New Yorker, Tar River Poetry, Triquarterly* and other periodicals. *Shenandoah,* poetry editor, 1966-76, editor-in-chief, 1988-95; poetry editor, *New Virginia Review,* 1983. A collection of Stuart's manuscripts is housed at Virginia Commonwealth University.

*SIDELIGHTS:* Of the Southern poets in the second half of the twentieth century, Dabney Stuart has established himself as one of the best and most consistent poets of his generation. Though his work has grown stylistically from formal verse to associative non-metrical free verse, what has remained relatively consistent are his themes and subject matter. Stuart explains to Fleur Adcock and Tod Marshall in *Contemporary Poets* that his themes include "family relationships, particularly those involving parents and children, levels of consciousness mirrored in language, the unforeseen and ubiquitous past, shifting perspective, cultural icons, isolation, dreams, the hidden self," as well as those of "son/father and father/son, the aloof self-regard of women, the illusion of solidarity and perspective, death and punning" which he identified in *Poets in the South*. R. S. Gwynn, writing in the *Dictionary of Literary Biography,* notes that Stuart works these themes beyond the literal by using post-Freudian psychology to elevate "parents, lovers, and children to the level of archetypes," and thus it is that Stuart has "chosen autobiography, rather than any external system of values, for the mythos that underlies his work."

*The Diving Bell* established Stuart's reputation as a skillful and intelligent traditionalist, while in *A Particular Place* the poet moved into more open forms and a more contemplative tone to craft poems about the Shenandoah Valley or the Charles River, places where "the music and the river/ Lapping the stones/ Become one sound." *The Other Hand* presented, with an honest tone and from an occasionally surreal position, the social tensions of American culture in the early 1970s, when Stuart "could hear history groping/ Like a blind man in a strange room." *Round and Round* offered readers a series of *persona*—Poet, Slut, Fool—and character sketches of sideshow performers, including a hermaphrodite and a snake charmer, often employing song-related stanza patterns which Gwynn believes "constitutes a major tour de force." *Common Ground,* "a turning point" in Stuart's career, according to Adcock and Marshall, presents variations on father and son relationships, and redefines the poet's relationship with his past.

*Don't Look Back,* which earned Stuart a Pulitzer Prize nomination, found the poet exploring his own middle age as well as his relationships with his ex-wives and his children. In the acrostic poem, "Discovering My Daughter," Stuart describes re-establishing a relationship with his long-estranged daughter after many years, noting how "We've come the longer way / Under such pressure, from one person to / Another. Our trip proves again the world is / Round, a singular island where people may come / Together." A second Pulitzer nomination came for *Narcissus Dreaming* as, according to Gwynn, Stuart "for the most part moved[d] away from autobiography toward encounter with others," as in the title poem where a fisherman catches "his reflection off the water / as if it were a laid-out suit / of clothes lifted / by its center" and puts it on, finding it "a perfectly imperfect fit."

*Light Years: New and Selected Poems* was praised by a *Publishers Weekly* reviewer for its "closely textured, resonant voice" and "seemingly effortless beauty." *Long Gone* offered poems of love, memory, and the search for lost innocence; also included are poems reflecting Stuart's travels to New Zealand as well as poems showing the poet's "concern with the power of language to create both reality and fantasy," according to a *Publishers Weekly* reviewer.

The short story collections, *Sweet Lucy Wine* and *The Way to Cobbs Creek,* indicate Stuart's interest in crafting fiction. The former collection centers eight of its ten pieces around a young boy, Mark Random, who lives in a small Southern town, so that the collection can nearly be read as a novel. The latter volume includes stories which show Mark Random as a father himself, exploring his relationship with both his own children and his own father. The *Publishers Weekly* critic praises Stuart's foray into fiction, calling him a "gifted writer." As such, Dabney Stuart stands as an example of both a contemporary Southern short story writer and poet of merit.

*BIOGRAPHICAL/CRITICAL SOURCES:*

BOOKS

Abse, Dannie, editor, *Corgi Modern Poets in Focus 3,* Corgi (London), 1971.
*Contemporary Poets,* 6th edition, St. James Press (Detroit), 1996.
*Dictionary of Literary Biography,* Volume 105: *American Poets Since World War II,* Second Series, Gale (Detroit), 1991.
Flora, Joseph M. and Robert Bain, editors, *Contemporary Southern Writers,* Greenwood (Westport, CT), 1991.
Rubin, Louis D. and others, editors, *The History of Southern Literature,* Louisiana State University Press, 1985, pp. 540-543.
Williams, Miller, editor, *Contemporary Poetry in America,* Random House (New York City), 1973.

PERIODICALS

*Bloomsbury Review,* April, 1992, p. 8.
*Booklist,* October 1, 1990, p. 249; February 1, 1992, p. 1011; October 15, 1994, p. 396.
*Chatahoochee Review,* winter, 1991.
*Chronicles,* March, 1989, pp. 28-30.
*Davidson Review,* fall, 1993.
*Georgia Review,* winter, 1990; summer, 1991, p. 383; winter, 1992-93, p. 786.
*Greensboro News and Record,* June 7, 1987.
*Hollins Critic,* June, 1993.

*Kentucky Poetry Review,* Volume 27, number 1, spring, 1991.
*Kirkus Reviews,* December 15, 1991, p. 1556.
*Poetry,* July, 1967; July, 1975; August, 1978.
*Poets in the South,* fall, 1984, pp. 35-42.
*Prairie Schooner,* spring, 1993, p. 157.
*Publishers Weekly,* October 19, 1990, p. 53; January 1, 1992, p. 48; October 15, 1994, p. 56.
*Roanoke Times,* March 27, 1983; August 30, 1987.
*Sewanee Review,* October, 1991, p. 101.
*Shenendoah,* autumn, 1966; autumn, 1969, pp. 70-76.
*Southern Review,* autumn, 1976.
*Studies in Short Fiction,* spring, 1992, p. 225.
*Virginia Quarterly Review,* August, 1987.
*Washington Post Book World,* November 7, 1982.

—*Sketch by Robert Miltner*

\* \* \*

## THORPE, D. R. 1943-

*PERSONAL:* Born March 12, 1943, in Huddersfield, England; son of Cyril and Mary (Avison) Thorpe. *Ethnicity:* "British." *Education:* Selwyn College, Cambridge, B.A. (with honors), 1965, M.A. (with honors), 1968.

*ADDRESSES: Home*—94 Grange Rd., Banbury, Oxfordshire OX16 9AY, England.

*CAREER:* Charterhouse, Godalming, England, schoolmaster, 1965-97; Oxford University, Oxford, England, fellow of St. Antony's College, 1997—.

*WRITINGS:*

*The Uncrowned Prime Ministers: A Study of Sir Austen Chamberlain, Lord Curzon, and Lord Butler,* Darkhouse Publishing, 1980.
*Selwyn Lloyd,* J. Cape, 1989.
*Alex Douglas-Home,* Sinclair-Stevenson, 1996.

Contributor to periodicals.

*WORK IN PROGRESS:* An authorized biography of Sir Anthony Eden, for Sinclair-Stevenson, completion expected in 2002; biographical research on twentieth-century British politics.

*SIDELIGHTS:* D. R. Thorpe told *CA:* "As a teacher of British political history, it struck me how much attention was paid to prime ministerial and presidential figures, whereas, with failure sometimes being more interesting than success, those who had just failed to attain the top of what nineteenth-century prime minister Benjamin Disraeli called 'the greasy pole' sometimes had as great an influence. For this reason I embarked on my study of three of the most celebrated 'near misses' of British politics: Austin Chamberlain was an important figure of the Chamberlain dynasty, and Lord George Curzon a crucial figure in Britain's imperial history, but of the three it perhaps could be claimed that Lord Butler left the most important legacy with his 1944 Education Act and his work in reforming Conservative philosophy and policy in the late 1940s. Selwyn Lloyd, the subject of my second book, though never a serious candidate for the highest office, was a crucial figure in the post-war Conservative Party, making important contributions in broadcasting policy and occupying two key roles—the foreign secretaryship and the chancellorship of the exchequer—at times of great controversy. His career was one that needed assessment and fortunately his full papers at Cambridge University made that a possible and rewarding task."

*BIOGRAPHICAL/CRITICAL SOURCES:*

PERIODICALS

*Country Life,* February 23, 1989.
*New Statesman and Society,* February 17, 1989.
*Observer,* February 19, 1989.
*Scotsman,* February 18, 1989.
*Times Educational Supplement,* February 17, 1989.
*Times Literary Supplement,* March 17, 1989.

\*     \*     \*

**UHER, Lorna**
    **See CROZIER, Lorna**

\*     \*     \*

**URQUHART, Jane 1949-**

*PERSONAL:* Born June 21, 1949, in Geraldton, Ontario, Canada; daughter of W. A. (a mining engineer) and Marianne (a nurse; maiden name, Quinn) Carter; married Paul Brian Keele (an artist), January 1, 1969 (deceased); married Tony Urquhart (a pro-

fessor and visual artist), May 5, 1976; children: (second marriage) Emily Jane. *Ethnicity:* "Irish/English." *Education:* University of Guelph, B.A. (English), 1971, B.A. (art history), 1975.

*ADDRESSES: Home*—24 Water St., Wellesley, Ontario, Canada N0B 2T0.

*CAREER:* Canada Manpower Center, Trenton, Ontario, student placement officer, 1971-72; Royal Canadian Navy, Halifax, Nova Scotia, civilian information officer, 1972-73; University of Waterloo, Waterloo, Ontario, tutor and coordinator of art history correspondence program, 1973—. University of Ottawa, writer in residence, 1990; Memorial University of Newfoundland, writer in residence, 1992; University of Toronto, writer in residence, 1993.

*MEMBER:* International PEN, League of Canadian Poets, Writers' Union of Canada.

*AWARDS, HONORS:* Grants from Ontario Arts Council, 1980-86, and Canada Council, 1983, 1985, 1990; France's Prix du Meilleur Livre Etranger, 1992; Trillium Award, 1993; Marian Engle Prize, 1994; D.Lett., University of Waterloo, 1997.

*WRITINGS:*

*False Shuffles* (poems), Press Porcepic, 1982.
*I Am Walking in the Garden of His Imaginary Palace* (poems), Aya Press, 1982.
*The Little Flowers of Madame de Montespan* (poems), Porcupine's Quill, 1983.
*The Whirlpool* (novel), David Godine (Boston, MA), 1986.
*Storm Glass* (short stories), Porcupine's Quill, 1987.
*Changing Heaven* (novel), McClelland and Stewart, 1990, David Godine, 1992.
*Away* (novel), Viking (New York City), 1994.
*The Underpainter* (novel), Viking, 1997.

Work represented in anthologies, including *Four Square Garden: A Poetry Anthology,* edited by Burnett, MacKinnon, and Thomas, Pas de Loup Press, 1982; *Illusions,* Aya Press, 1983; *Meta Fictions,* Quadrant Editions, 1983; *Views from the North,* Porcupine's Quill, 1983; *Best Canadian Stories,* Oberon Press, 1986; *Magic Realism and Canadian Literature,* University of Waterloo Press (Waterloo, Ontario), 1986; and *The Oxford Book of Stories by Canadian Women,* Volume 2, 1988. Also contributor to magazines, including *Canadian Fic-*

*tion, Descant, Poetry Canada Review,* and *Antigonish Review.*

*SIDELIGHTS:* Jane Urquhart is known for her fascination with the Victorian era and her talented use of language. She has become one of the most popular of Canada's current generation of novelists, with a reputation that transcends her native country.

Urquhart was born on June 21, 1949, in Geraldton, Ontario, Canada, to W. A. and Marrianne Carter. Her family lived in a small mining settlement called Little Long Lac until she was five or six years old and then moved to Toronto. As a child she loved to read, and her favorite book was Emily Bronte's *Wuthering Heights.* Despite her interest in literature, she dreamed of becoming a child actress, but she never made it to Broadway as she had hoped. In 1967 she left for Vancouver to attend junior college and then returned to Ontario to attend the University of Guelph, where she received her B.A. in English in 1971. While at the university she met and married visual artist Paul Keele, who later died in a car accident. Urquhart returned to the University of Guelph, this time studying art history, and she recieved another B.A. in 1975. She met another visual artist, Tony Urquhart, who she married on May 5, 1976. Together they had a daughter Emily. While caring for Tony's four other children in addition to Emily, Urquhart began to write. She first wrote poetry, publishing several volumes, and then turned her attention to narratives, publishing a collection of short stories and several novels.

Many of Urquhart's stories come from her own family history. The undertaker's widow in *The Whirlpool* is based on her husband Tony's grandmother, and her novel *Away* is based on her family's history as Irish Canadians. Her love of *Wuthering Heights* also enters her fiction, especially in *Changing Heaven,* in which the ghost of Emily Bronte appears and discusses her work with the ghost of another character, Arianna Ether. An important element in much of Urquhart's work is its setting in the nineteenth century. *Whirlpool, Changing Heaven,* and *Away,* are all set in the nineteenth century, a favorite era of Urquhart's which allows her to expound upon history and her fascination with the elements. Urquhart's fiction is also filled with mysticism and the supernatural; ghosts are common characters. In *Away* Urquhart explored Celtic myths and the Irish concept of "away," which means being taken by a spirit and returned forever changed. Landscape is an important element as well—Urquhart evokes a strong sense of place through details about the setting of a novel.

Urquhart's novels have received mixed reviews from critics. Most critics praise the language and conception of her fiction, though some complain that she does not follow through with a strong structure. Her short stories, especially, have been criticized for lacking plot. Although many critics praise her poetic language and mystical storylines, some think she pushes the limits too far. Reviewers specifically point out her introduction of the nineteenth-century English poet Robert Browning as a character in *The Whirlpool.* One critic opposed her dramatization of Browning's death as a maudlin romantic addition designed to give the novel the weight of literature. Other critics point to the scene between the ghosts of Emily Bronte and Arianna Ether as problematic and say that Urquhart's attempt to demystify Bronte was a failure.

*BIOGRAPHICAL/CRITICAL SOURCES:*

*PERIODICALS*

*American Book Review,* May/June, 1988, pp. 10, 21.
*Belles Lettres,* fall, 1993, pp. 23, 43.
*Bloomsbury Review,* May/June, 1990, p. 21.
*Booklist,* March 15, 1993, p. 1296.
*Books in Canada,* January/February, 1987, p. 26; June/July, 1987, p. 14; October, 1993, p. 44.
*Canadian Forum,* August/September, 1987, pp. 41-3.
*Canadian Literature,* spring, 1992, pp. 209-10.
*Chicago Tribune,* March 21, 1990.
*Detroit Free Press,* August 17, 1994, p. 3D.
*Globe and Mail* (Toronto), December 6, 1986; March 17, 1990.
*Maclean's,* September 21, 1987, p. 54.
*New York Times Book Review,* March 18, 1990; June 26, 1994, p. 28.
*Poetry,* August, 1984, p. 305.
*Quill and Quire,* October, 1982, p. 33; March, 1983, p. 66; May, 1984, p. 35; November, 1986, p. 25.
*Saturday Night,* March, 1990, p. 55.
*Village Voice,* October 18, 1988, pp. 52-53, 101.
*Village Voice Literary Supplement,* June, 1993.
*World Literature Today,* summer, 1991, p. 487; winter, 1995, pp. 143-44.

## URSINI, James 1947-

*PERSONAL:* Born May 10, 1947, in Pittsburgh, PA; son of Vincent (a tailor) and Marie (Riccardelli) Ursini. *Ethnicity:* "Italian-American." *Education:* University of California at Los Angeles, A.B., 1969, M.A., 1972, Ph.D. (cinema), 1975. *Politics:* Socialist. *Religion:* Roman Catholic. *Avocational interests:* Music, books, theater, travel.

*ADDRESSES: Home*—Santa Monica, CA. *Office*—Department of Communications, El Camino College, 16007 South Crenshaw Blvd., Los Angeles County, CA 90506. *E-mail*—usher50@aol.com.

*CAREER:* El Camino College, Los Angeles, CA, instructor in communications, 1972—.

*MEMBER:* American Federation of Teachers, American Film Institute.

*WRITINGS:*

*The Fabulous Life and Times of Preston Sturges: An American Dreamer,* Avon Books (New York City), 1975.
(With Alain Silver) *Supernatural Horror in Literature and Film,* Leslie Frewin, 1975.
(With Silver) *The Vampire Film,* A. S. Barnes (San Diego, CA), 1976, *The Vampire Film: From Nosferatu to Bram Stoker's Dracula,* second edition, Limelight (New York City), 1993, *The Vampire Film: From Nosferatu to Interview with the Vampire,* third revised edition, Limelight, 1997.
(With Silver) *David Lean and His Films,* Frewin, Ltd., 1977, second edition, Silman-James, 1993.
(Editor with others) *More Things Than Are Dreamt Of: Masterpieces of Supernatural Horror from Mary Shelley to Stephen King in Literature and Film,* Limelight, 1994.
(With Silver) *Film Noir Reader,* Limelight, 1995.
*Whatever Happened to Robert Aldrich? His Life and His Films,* Limelight, 1996.

*Noir Style,* Viking-Overlook (New York City), 1998.
*Roger Corman, Metaphysics on a Shoestring,* Silman-James, 1998.

Also contributor of articles to periodicals, including, *Cine Fantastique, Cinema* (U.S.), *DGA Magazine, Femme Fatales, Midnight Marquee,* and *Photon.*

*  *  *

## VINCENT, K(enneth) Steven 1947-

*PERSONAL:* Born November 13, 1947, in Hot Springs, AR; son of Kenneth C. and Elizabeth (Moulton) Vincent; children: Daniel Kenneth. *Education:* University of California, Berkeley, B.A., 1970, M.A., 1972, Ph.D., 1981.

*ADDRESSES: Office*—Department of History, North Carolina State University, Box 8108, Raleigh, NC 27695.

*CAREER:* North Carolina State University, Raleigh, assistant professor, 1981-86, associate professor, 1986-91, professor of history, 1991—.

*WRITINGS:*

*Pierre-Joseph Proudhon and the Rise of French Republican Socialism,* Oxford University Press, 1984.
*Between Marxism and Anarchism: Benoit Malon and French Reformist Socialism,* University of California Press (Berkeley), 1992.

*BIOGRAPHICAL/CRITICAL SOURCES:*

*PERIODICALS*

*Times Literary Supplement,* July 26, 1985.

# W-Y

## WABER, Bernard 1924-

*PERSONAL:* Born September 27, 1924, in Philadelphia, PA; son of Henry and Pauline (Fleishman) Waber; married Ethel Bernstein, 1952; children: Paulis, Kim, Jan Gary. *Education:* Attended University of Pennsylvania, Philadelphia College of Art, 1946-50, and Pennsylvania Academy of Fine Arts, 1950-51.

*ADDRESSES: Home*—3653 Bertha Dr., Baldwin Harbor, NY 11510.

*CAREER:* Commercial artist for Conde Nast Publications, New York City, and *Seventeen,* New York City, 1952-54; *Life,* New York City, graphic designer, 1955-72; author and illustrator of children's books, 1961—; *People,* New York City, graphic designer, 1974—88. *Military service:* U.S. Army, 1942-45; became staff sergeant.

*AWARDS, HONORS:* Children's Spring Book Festival picture book honor, *New York Herald Tribune,* 1962, for *The House on East 88th Street; An Anteater Named Arthur* was selected one of the American Institute of Graphic Arts Children's Books, 1967-68; Notable Books, American Library Association, 1970, and *Boston Globe-Horn Book* honor book for illustration, 1971, for *A Firefly Named Torchy; Ira Sleeps Over* was included in the Children's Book Showcase of the Children's Book Council, 1973; *But Names Will Never Hurt Me* was selected one of Child Study Association's Children's Books of the Year, 1976; Lewis Carroll Shelf Award, 1979, for *Lyle, Lyle, Crocodile; The Snake: A Very Long Story* was selected one of International Reading Association's Children's Choices, 1979.

*WRITINGS:*

SELF-ILLUSTRATED; FOR CHILDREN; PUBLISHED BY HOUGHTON (BOSTON), EXCEPT AS NOTED

*Lorenzo,* 1961.
*The House on East 88th Street,* 1962, published in England as *Welcome, Lyle,* Chatto, Boyd & Oliver, 1969.
*How to Go about Laying an Egg,* 1963.
*Rich Cat, Poor Cat,* 1963.
*Just Like Abraham Lincoln,* 1964.
*Lyle, Lyle, Crocodile,* 1965.
*"You Look Ridiculous," Said the Rhinoceros to the Hippopotamus,* 1966.
*Lyle and the Birthday Party,* 1966.
*Cheese,* 1967.
*An Anteater Named Arthur,* 1967.
*A Rose for Mr. Bloom,* 1968.
*Lovable Lyle,* 1969.
*A Firefly Named Torchy,* 1970.
*Nobody Is Perfick* (collection of short stories), 1971.
*Ira Sleeps Over,* 1972.
*Lyle Finds His Mother,* 1974.
*I Was All Thumbs,* 1975.
*But Names Will Never Hurt Me,* 1976.
*Good-bye, Funny Dumpy-Lumpy,* 1977.
*Mice on My Mind,* 1977.
*The Snake: A Very Long Story,* 1978.
*Dear Hildegarde,* 1980.
*You're a Little Kid with a Big Heart,* 1980.
*Bernard,* 1982.
*Funny, Funny Lyle,* 1987.
*Ira Says Goodbye,* 1988.
*Lyle at the Office,* 1994.
*Do You See a Mouse?,* 1995.
*Gina,* 1995.

*A Lion Named Shirley Williamson,* 1996.
*Bearsie Bear and the Surprise Sleepover Party,* 1997.
*Lyle at Christmas,* 1998.

Waber's manuscripts are included in the Kerlan Collection, University of Minnesota.

*ADAPTATIONS: The House on East 88th Street* (filmstrip with record or cassette), Miller-Brody; *Lovable Lyle* (filmstrip with record or cassette), Miller-Brody; *Lyle, Lyle, Crocodile* (filmstrip with record or cassette), Miller-Brody; *Lyle and the Birthday Party* (filmstrip with record or cassette), Miller-Brody; *Lyle* (play; based on "Lyle" books), first produced at the McAlpin Rooftop Theatre, 1970; *Ira Sleeps Over* (film), Phoenix/BFA Films; *Ira Sleeps Over* (cassette; filmstrip with cassette), Live Oak Media (Somers, NY), 1984; *Lyle, the Musical* (animation), Home Box Office, 1987; *Ira Says Goodbye* (filmstrip with cassette), Live Oak Media, 1989; *Lyle* (musical stage production), first produced in Chicago, 1989; *Lyle* (play), Minneapolis Children's Theater, 1990-91; *Lyle, Lyle, Crocodile* (adapted from *The House on East 88th Street* [videotape]), Hi-Tops Video.

*SIDELIGHTS:* Popular picture book author and illustrator Bernard Waber is perhaps best known for his books about a crocodile named Lyle. Featuring the author's penchant for rhymes and wordplay and his characteristically droll, understated wit, many of Waber's other stories for primary graders have been similarly well-received. "Armed with a clear understanding of the anxieties, taunts, and humor that go hand in hand with childhood," *Children's Books and Their Creators* contributor Lynn Sygiel noted, "Waber provides the readers of his more than twenty-four books with a mirror of their childhood experiences." Fick similarly asserted that in the "Lyle" books, "text and illustrations merge dynamically to balance fantasy with the exploration of feelings and relationships" that are central to the lives of children.

Lyle, the humorous and endearing cartoon reptile appears for the first time in *The House on East 88th Street,* where he is discovered in the Primm family's bathtub. "With aplomb and dazzling showmanship, Lyle entertains and enchants" the Primms, according to *Twentieth-Century Children's Writers* contributor Martha J. Fick, and along with the Primms a host of children who have responded with enthusiasm for each of Lyle's five subsequent picture-book adven-

tures. "It's hard to go wrong with Lyle," asserted *Booklist*'s Ilene Cooper in a review of *Lyle at the Office,* a sentiment underscored by a *Kirkus Reviews* commentator, who maintained in a discussion of the same book that "most would follow the lovable Lyle anywhere."

*Ira Sleeps Over* tells the story of a young boy who, chided by his older siblings, struggles to determine whether he really should leave his teddy bear behind for an overnight visit to his friend Reggie's house. Ira makes a second appearance more than a decade later in *Ira Says Goodbye,* which explores a somewhat similar dilemma: best friend Reggie is moving away, and his initial excitement over the move hurts Ira's feelings. "The author's portrayals of the confusing array of emotions are wryly accurate," maintained a *Publishers Weekly* reviewer, who concluded the book "warm, wise, and ultimately reassuring." Elizabeth S. Watson of *Horn Book* noted that Waber "uses an understated style that is perfect for suggesting the grief of parting with a best friend, without putting a burden on the story."

*Gina,* "another winner from the redoubtable Waber," according to *School Library Journal* contributor Virginia Opocensky, is also deals with friendships and is directed toward very young children. Gina has just moved into a new apartment building in Queens, and to her dismay there are no other girls in the building but only "boys, boys, boys galore . . . on every floor." After tiring of playing alone, the spunky young protagonist gains new friends by demonstrating her skills in such important particulars as baseball, tree climbing, and biking. A *Publishers Weekly* reviewer praised "the domesticated daffiness of [Waber's] action-packed watercolors."

In the spirit of his highly regarded "Lyle" books, Waber has written other comical fantasies for children revolving around the adventures of endearing anthropomorphic animals. A showcase for his whimsical, cartoon-style art, such works as *Do You See a Mouse?* and *A Lion Named Shirley Williamson* have been praised for their ability to capture the imagination of beginning readers. In *Do You See a Mouse?* a complaint has been registered at the elegant Park Snoot Hotel: someone has seen a mouse. "Do you see a mouse? I do not see a mouse" is the common refrain throughout, as employees and other guests find it difficult to imagine a rodent at Park Snoot. "Delighted youngsters, however, will squeal 'Yes!' as they spy the mouse on the subsequent pages of this predictable yet engaging tale," noted a *Publishers*

*Weekly* reviewer. Hanna B. Zeiger of *Horn Book* asserted: "Waber's characterizations are full of sly humor, and readers of all ages will have to smile at the antics of the little rascally rodent who successfully bamboozles one and all in this comic adventure."

*A Lion Named Shirley Williamson* begins with the odd naming of a new lion at the public zoo due to a miscommunication between the zoo director and a representative of the Wildlife Trading Company. Shirley joins the zoo's other lions—Goobah, Poobah, and Aroobah—and is an instant hit with the public and with the zookeeper, who gives her special treatment. However, the jealousy of the other lions and the firing of the zookeeper, along with the humiliation of the zoo director's renaming her "Bongo," causes Shirley to run away. "Waber is back in full form with a story that is both hysterical and poignant," enthused Ilene Cooper of *Booklist.* Cooper added that the book "succeeds at every level," citing a lively plot, "characters that show the inevitable tangle of emotions life elicits," and artwork that appeals to both children and adults.

*BIOGRAPHICAL/CRITICAL SOURCES:*

*BOOKS*

Kingman, Lee, and others, compilers, *Illustrators of Children's Books: 1967-1976,* Horn Book (Boston), 1978.
Silvey, Anita, editor, *Children's Books and Their Creators,* Houghton (Boston), 1995, pp. 666-68.
*Twentieth-Century Children's Writers,* 4th edition, St. James Press (Detroit), 1994, pp. 987-88.

*PERIODICALS*

*Booklist,* August, 1987, p. 1753; June 1, 1994, p. 1846; September 1, 1996, p. 128.
*Horn Book,* September-October, 1987, p. 604; November-December, 1988, p. 779; July-August, 1995, pp. 454-55.
*Kirkus Reviews,* August 15, 1987, p. 1246; July 15, 1994, p. 997.
*New York Times Book Review,* March 5, 1989, p. 31.
*Publishers Weekly,* July 8, 1988, p. 54; January 23, 1995, p. 70; August 14, 1995, p. 83; September 15, 1997, p. 75.
*School Library Journal,* September, 1995, p. 188; October, 1995, p. 123; December, 1996, pp. 108-09.

**WATER, Silas**
**See LOOMIS, Noel M(iller)**

\*     \*     \*

**WEINHOUSE, Beth (R.)  1957-**

*PERSONAL:* Born May 19, 1957, in Boston, MA; daughter of Melvin (a physician) and Eleanor (a teacher; maiden name, Taub) Weinhouse; married David Galef; children: Daniel. *Education:* Brown University, A.B., 1979; Columbia University, M.S., 1980.

*ADDRESSES: Home and office*—Oxford, MS. *Agent*—Suzanne Gluck, International Creative Management, 40 West 57th St., New York, NY 10019.

*CAREER: Ladies' Home Journal,* New York City, assistant articles editor, 1981-82, associate articles editor, 1982-85, acting executive editor, 1985, senior editor, 1985-88; *Self,* New York City, contributing editor, 1988-91; free-lance writer, 1991—.

*WRITINGS:*

*The Healthy Traveler,* Simon & Schuster (New York City), 1987.
(With Leslie Laurence) *Outrageous Practices: The Alarming Truth about How Medicine Mistreats Women,* Fawcett (New York City), 1994.

Author of "Your Health," a monthly column in *Redbook,* 1991-92, and "Capsules," a column in *Rx Remedy,* 1992-95. Contributor of articles, columns, and reviews to periodicals, including *American Health, Elle, Family Circle, Glamour, Good Housekeeping, New Woman, Parenting, Travel and Leisure, Women's Sports and Fitness,* and *Working Mother.* Contributing editor, *Rx Remedy,* 1992-95.

*WORK IN PROGRESS:* Another investigative medical book.

*BIOGRAPHICAL/CRITICAL SOURCES:*

*PERIODICALS*

*Clarion-Ledger* (Jackson, MS), October 19, 1994.
*Connecticut Post,* October 16, 1994.
*San Francisco Examiner and Chronicle,* January 15, 1995.

*USA Today,* October 7, 1994.
*Washington Post,* December 1, 1987; January 31, 1995.

\*    \*    \*

## WESTALL, Robert (Atkinson) 1929-1993

*PERSONAL:* Born October 7, 1929, in Tynemouth, England; died of respiratory failure caused by pneumonia, April 15, 1993, in Cheshire, England; son of Robert (a foreman and fitter at a gas works) and Maggie Alexandra (Leggett) Westall; married Jean Underhill (an administrator), July 26, 1958 (divorced, 1990); children: Christopher (deceased). *Education:* University of Durham, B.A. (first class honors), 1953; University of London, D.F.A., 1957. *Politics:* "Left-wing Conservative." *Religion:* Church of England. *Avocational interests:* Designing, building, and sailing model yachts; Gothic architecture; local history; film; sculpting; religion and the supernatural; "cats (you have to *earn* their friendship), old clocks, Buddhist statues, bird-watching and people-watching, other people's gardens, ruins and the sea."

*CAREER:* Erdington Hall Secondary Modern School, Birmingham, England, art master, 1957-58; Keighley Boys' Grammar School, Yorkshire, art master, 1958-60; Sir John Deane's College, Northwich, art teacher and head of department, 1960-85, head of careers guidance, 1970-85; antiques dealer, 1985-86; writer, 1986-93. Director of Telephone Samaritans of Mid-Cheshire, 1965-75; writer, Whitehorn Press, Manchester, 1968-71. *Military service:* British Army, Royal Signals, 1953-55.

*AWARDS, HONORS:* Carnegie Medal from Library Association of Great Britain, 1976, for *The Machine-Gunners,* and 1982, for *The Scarecrows;* Guardian Award commendation, 1976, for *The Machine-Gunners; Horn Book/Boston Globe* Honor Books citations, 1978, for *The Machine-Gunners,* 1982, for *The Scarecrows,* and 1983, for *Break of Dark;* "Best Books for Young Adults" citation, American Library Association, 1979, for *The Devil on the Road;* Leseratten Prize (Germany), 1988, for *The Machine-Gunners,* 1990, for *Futuretrack Five,* and 1991, for *The Promise;* Senior Smarties Prize and Children's Book Award commendation, both 1989, both for *Blitzcat;* Carnegie Award commendation and Sheffield Children's Book prize, both 1991, both for

*The Promise; Guardian* Award, 1992, for *The Kingdom by the Sea.*

*WRITINGS:*

NOVELS FOR YOUNG ADULTS

*The Machine-Gunners* (also see below), Macmillan (London), 1975, Greenwillow (New York City), 1976.
*Fathom Five,* Macmillan, 1979, Greenwillow, 1980.
*Futuretrack Five,* Kestrel (London), 1983, Greenwillow, 1984.
*The Witness,* Macmillan, 1985, Dutton (New York City), 1994.
*Urn Burial,* Viking Kestrel (London), 1987, Greenwillow, 1988.
*Cat!,* Methuen (London), 1989.
*Stormsearch,* Blackie (London), 1990, Farrar, Straus (New York City), 1992.
*The Kingdom by the Sea,* Methuen, 1990, Farrar, Straus, 1991.
*Size Twelve,* Heinemann (London), 1992.
*Falling into Glory,* Heinemann, 1993, Farrar, Straus, 1995.
*A Place for Me,* Macmillan, 1993.
*Time of Fire,* Macmillan, 1994, Scholastic (New York City), 1997.

FANTASY NOVELS FOR YOUNG ADULTS

*The Wind Eye,* Macmillan, 1976, Greenwillow, 1977.
*The Watch House,* Macmillan, 1977, Greenwillow, 1978.
*The Devil on the Road,* Macmillan, 1978, Greenwillow, 1979.
*The Scarecrows,* Greenwillow, 1981.
*The Cats of Seroster,* Greenwillow, 1984.
*Rosalie,* Macmillan, 1987.
*The Creature in the Dark,* illustrated by Liz Roberts, Blackie, 1988.
*Ghost Abbey,* Macmillan, 1988, Scholastic, 1989.
*Blitzcat,* Macmillan, 1989, Scholastic, 1990.
*Old Man on a Horse,* Blackie, 1989.
*If Cats Could Fly . . . ?,* Methuen, 1990.
*The Promise,* Macmillan, 1990, Scholastic, 1991.
*Yaxley's Cat,* Macmillan, 1991, Scholastic, 1992.
*Gulf,* Scholastic, 1992.
*The Wheatstone Pond,* Penguin (London), 1993.

SHORT STORY COLLECTIONS FOR YOUNG ADULTS

*Break of Dark,* Chatto & Windus (London), 1981.
*The Haunting of Chas McGill,* Greenwillow, 1983.

*The Other: A Christmas Story,* Macmillan, 1985.

*Rachel and the Angel and Other Stories,* Macmillan, 1986, Greenwillow, 1987.

*Ghosts and Journeys,* Macmillan, 1988.

(Editor) *Ghost Stories,* Kingfisher (London), 1988.

*The Call and Other Stories,* Viking Kestrel (London), 1989.

*Echoes of War,* Viking Kestrel, 1989, Farrar, Straus, 1991.

*A Walk on the Wild Side: Cat Stories,* Methuen, 1989.

*The Christmas Cat* (also see below), Methuen, 1991.

*The Stones of Muncaster Cathedral: Two Stories of the Supernatural,* Farrar, Straus, 1991.

*The Christmas Ghost* (also see below), Methuen, 1992.

*The Fearful Lovers,* Macmillan, 1992, published as *In Camera and Other Stories,* Scholastic, 1993.

*A Trick of Light: Five Unnerving Stories,* Scholastic, 1993.

*Demons and Shadows,* Farrar, Straus, 1993.

*Blitz,* HarperCollins (London), 1994.

*Christmas Spirit* (omnibus; includes *The Christmas Cat* and *The Christmas Ghost*), Farrar, Straus, 1994.

*Shades of Darkness: More of the Ghostly Best Stories of Robert Westall,* Farrar, Straus, 1994.

*OTHER*

(Editor) *The Children of the Blitz: Memories of Wartime Childhood,* Viking (London), 1985.

*The Machine-Gunners* (play; adapted from his own novel), Macmillan, 1986.

*Antique Dust: Ghost Stories* (short stories; for adults), Viking, 1989.

Staff writer for *Cheshire Life,* 1968-71. Art and architecture critic for *Chester Chronicle,* beginning 1962; art critic for *Guardian,* 1970.

*ADAPTATIONS: The Machine-Gunners* was used as the basis for a British television series.

*SIDELIGHTS:* "The only way to read Robert Westall is to give yourself up to the spell of his storytelling," wrote Margaret Meek in the *School Librarian.* Westall's award-winning fiction for young adults aroused heated controversy for its realistic detailing of violence, sexuality, family tensions, the rampaging emotions of the teen years, and the horrors of war, but it is widely accepted that his novels and short stories exude "a remarkable authenticity of atmosphere," in the words of Margery Fisher in *Grow-*

*ing Point.* While many of Westall's books deal with the supernatural, time travel, and fantasy, he was careful to create characters who a *Junior Bookshelf* writer claimed "are clearly drawn in all their idiosyncratic oddity." Westall himself believed that writers for the teen-aged group "must look for the hotline to the reader. . . . It lies, I think, in children's love of inevitable catastrophe."

Westall won Britain's prestigious Carnegie Medal for his first novel, *The Machine-Gunners,* a story of five young teens in England during World War II, who find and hide a machine gun after the crash of a German plane. They plan to use the gun to bring down other enemy aircraft. The group's leader, Chas McGill, keeps his comrades silent and loyal with a violent ferocity that eventually proves his undoing. As a tale of unsupervised youth, *The Machine-Gunners* has often been compared to William Golding's *Lord of the Flies* and has generated similar controversy.

Aidan Chambers, reviewing for the *Times Literary Supplement,* felt that *The Machine-Gunners* is the "best book so far written for children about the Second World War." However, the book's grim details of life during the blitz and its realistic portrayal of the tough teens, which includes strong language, led Chambers to suggest: "There will inevitably be those who will wonder about offering ten or eleven year olds a book so uncompromising in language and incident as this." Ann Thwaite described these adult qualms in the *Times Literary Supplement:* "A Welsh librarian recently recalled that he had asked a group of teachers to read *The Machine-Gunners* for a seminar. Had they all enjoyed it? Yes. Did they think their pupils would enjoy it? Yes. Would they be using it in school? No, unanimously no."

In an article in *Signal* magazine, Westall described how the adverse criticism of *The Machine-Gunners* influenced his subsequent works: "To my shame, I tried [to please the critics]. Crawlingly and contemptibly, though unconsciously, I tried. The amount of swearing in my books dropped; the intellectual content, the scholarship and research grew. I began writing books for the children of publishers, librarians, and the literary gent of *The Times.* . . . Now that I am at last conscious of what I was doing, I look round and see so many 'good' children's books written for the same bloody audience. Books that gain splendid reviews, win prizes, make reputations and are unreadable by the majority of children."

Westall's books after *The Machine-Gunners* dealt with a variety of topics, from witch-hunting in the seventeenth century, to ghosts that haunt other ghosts, to a race of intelligent cats. *The Scarecrows,* which won Westall his second Carnegie award, is typical of his best work. It relates the tale of Simon Brown, a teenage boy whose father recently died. His mother's remarriage fills Simon with an almost uncontrollable rage, particularly toward his stepfather. This deep anger rouses the spirits of the past at an old mill near Simon's home; these ghosts manifest themselves as three scarecrows in the nearby fields. "Simon identifies them as participants in a pre-war tragedy of passion that ended in murder and closed the mill forever," observed Sara Hayes in the *Times Literary Supplement.* "The events of the past are going to be re-enacted unless Simon can break the power of the mill." Hayes noted that despite the spooky storyline, the way in which "people talk and relate to each other, to their families and to themselves is what Westall's work is really about. And despite its earnest intent, his story is exciting, agonizing, tender and terrifying by turns, and never fails to grip."

Although Westall toned down his writing after the negative reaction to *The Machine-Gunners,* he still aroused controversy from time to time. Critics seemed to become more willing to accept his evaluation of his audience's tastes, however. In a *Times Literary Supplement* review of *Fathom Five,* Thwaite made the admission: "It would be a pity . . . if timid teachers and librarians steered clear of this book. Certainly children won't be shocked by it." "Westall has never patronized his readers," wrote Sarah Hayes in a *Times Literary Supplement* review of *The Cats of Seroster.* And Lance Salway, reviewing *The Wind Eye* for the *Times Literary Supplement,* noted: "Whether the book is viewed as exciting time fantasy or as a perceptive study of family behavior, the reader is kept in thrall until the final page. And, above all, it reinforces Robert Westall's reputation as an exciting and stimulating new writer for the young."

Westall died suddenly after contracting pneumonia, leaving behind several completed manuscripts "to witness to his genius," in the words of *St. James Guide to Fantasy Writers* contributor Jessica Yates. In her opinion, Westall "made a unique contribution to the development of the teenage or young-adult novel in the 1980s and 1980s. Typically a young-adult novel on the American model deals with a young person's awakening sexuality and/or antago-nism towards parents and society. . . . Westall added supernatural elements, confidently moving between or combining the genres of science fiction, fantasy, ghost story and horror, as well as writing realistic, non-magical fictions. He wrote with passionate commitment: faced with an anthology of anonymous short stories, one would always be able to pick out the Westall story."

Westall once told *CA:* "Like many writers, I have been aware of the future splitting away from the past. Since I write for young people, I have always used the experiences of my own childhood a lot—a childhood now over thirty years away and growing more distant all the time. A childhood where everybody over the age of fourteen expected to have a job. A childhood where our fathers understood nearly all the factors in their lives that could affect them, and could largely control them. My father needed to understand four things to feel secure: the machinery of the works where he was foreman, the plants in his large garden, the world of buying and selling, and the temperament of my mother. All these he managed pretty well.

"But the young people I write for are moving into a world made dark and mysterious by the new technology. They look to me for answers I have not got. Will I get a job I like? Will I get a job at all? Where will I live? How much power will the government have over me?

"I do believe that all the best stories become myths which have a real power to guide, which become focal points in the minds of those who read them. *Dr. Jekyll and Mr. Hyde,* 'Pandora's Box,' 'Bluebeard,' *Beauty and the Beast,* Sidney Carton in *A Tale of Two Cities,* all have survival value for any human mind seeking to bring order out of the sea of chaos. But who will make the myths for the new times?

"It is no comfort to say that human nature is unchanging. Human nature is infinitely variable. There are countries in the modern world where the activities of the Spanish Inquisition would not be tolerated for a moment; there are others where something similar to the Inquisition is tolerated as a daily event. A handbook on human relationships issued to General Motors executives would be spiritually as well as imaginatively incomprehensible to a Greek fisherman or a Buddhist monk.

"People everywhere are bedevilled by a flood of media information they do not want and cannot use; at the same time, they are often deliberately or uncaringly denied the information they really need to live happily and effectively.

"I thought perhaps all these thoughts were caused by middle-age creeping up on me. But recently, an old pupil came to see me. He was aged thirty-eight, with a wife of thirty-three, a successful teacher himself. Yet he said, 'I find myself turning more and more to the past. I choose to live in a solid old home, with antique furniture. Our interests are in the past: history, growing things in our garden as our fathers did. Nothing that is coming from the future seems worth having. . . .'

"I suppose you could call these challenging times for a writer. Yet all I can think of to say is that the main thing to avoid is belonging to any big organization, whether it's the Roman Catholic Church or the Communist Party—it's paying someone to do your thinking for you. Any man is worth listening to, when he's telling you something he's worked out for himself, something he's noticed himself; big beliefs, big organizations, are like junk-car yards—worth looking at, to see if you can find something useful to pull off, buy and use. I *like* weird customized beliefs, like I like weird customized cars."

*BIOGRAPHICAL/CRITICAL SOURCES:*

BOOKS

*Authors and Artists for Young Adults,* Volume 12, Gale (Detroit), 1994.
*Children's Literature Review,* Volume 13, Gale, 1987.
*Contemporary Literary Criticism,* Volume 17, Gale, 1981.
*Something about the Author Autobiography Series,* Volume 2, Gale, 1986.
*St. James Guide to Fantasy Writers,* St. James Press (Detroit), 1996.

PERIODICALS

*Growing Point,* October, 1975.
*Horn Book,* August, 1976.
*Junior Bookshelf,* April, 1979.
*New York Times Book Review,* May 16, 1982.
*School Librarian,* June, 1979.
*School Library Journal,* April, 1993, p. 144; June, 1993, p. 134.

*Signal,* January, 1979.
*Times Literary Supplement,* September 19, 1975, p. 1056; December 10, 1975; December 14, 1979; March 27, 1981, p. 339; July 23, 1982; November 30, 1984; October 11, 1985.
*Voice of Youth Advocates,* June, 1993, p. 96; December, 1993, pp. 315-16; August, 1994, pp. 161; October, 1995, p. 226; April, 1996, pp. 31-32.
*Washington Post Book World,* November 7, 1976; November 11, 1979.

OTHER

*Junior DISCovering Authors* (CD-ROM), U*X*L (Detroit), 1994.

*OBITUARIES:*

PERIODICALS

*New York Times,* April 20, 1993, p. B8.
*School Library Journal,* June, 1993, p. 22.*

\*          \*          \*

**WESTON, Allen**
 **See NORTON, Andre**

\*          \*          \*

**WILLARD, Nancy 1936-**

*PERSONAL:* Born June 26, 1936, in Ann Arbor, MI; daughter of Hobart Hurd (a chemistry professor) and Margaret (Sheppard) Willard; married Eric Lindbloom (a photographer), August 15, 1964; children: James Anatole. *Education:* University of Michigan, B.A., 1958, Ph.D., 1963; Stanford University, M.A., 1960; additional study in Paris and Oslo.

*ADDRESSES: Home*—33 College Ave., Poughkeepsie, NY 12603. *Office*—Department of English, Vassar College, Raymond Ave., Poughkeepsie, NY 12601. *Agent*—Jean V. Naggar Literary Agency, 336 East 73rd St., Suite C, NY 10021.

*CAREER:* Poet, author of children's literature, literary critic, and short-story writer. Vassar College,

Poughkeepsie, NY, lecturer in English, 1965—. Instructor at Bread Loaf Writers' Conference, 1975.

*MEMBER:* Children's Literature Association, Lewis Carroll Society, George MacDonald Society.

*AWARDS, HONORS:* Avery Hopwood Award, 1958; Woodrow Wilson fellowship, 1960; Devins Memorial Award, 1967, for *Skin of Grace*; O. Henry Award for best short story, 1970; Lewis Carroll Shelf Award, 1974, for *Sailing to Cythera and Other Anatole Stories,* and 1979, for *The Island of the Grass King: The Further Adventures of Anatole*; National Endowment for the Arts grant, 1976, fellowship, 1987-88; Special Honor Book Plaque, Society of Children's Book Writers, 1981, John Newbery Medal, Caldecott Honor Book award, American Library Association, and American Book Award nomination, all 1982, all for *A Visit to William Blake's Inn: Poems for Innocent and Experienced Travelers*; Creative Artist Service Award; National Book Critics Circle award nomination (poetry), 1990, for *Water Walker*; Michigan Author award, Michigan Library Association, 1994.

*WRITINGS:*

*POETRY*

*In His Country: Poems,* Generation (Ann Arbor, MI), 1966.
*Skin of Grace,* University of Missouri Press (Columbia), 1967.
*A New Herball: Poems,* Ferdinand-Roter Gallerias (Baltimore), 1968.
*Nineteen Masks for the Naked Poet: Poems,* Kayak (Santa Cruz), 1971.
*The Carpenter of the Sun: Poems,* Liveright (New York City), 1974.
*Household Tales of Moon and Water,* Harcourt (San Diego), 1983.
*Water Walker,* Knopf (New York City), 1990.
*Poem Made of Water,* Brighton Press (San Diego), 1992.
(With Jane Yolen) *Among Angels* (for children), Harcourt, 1995.
*Swimming Lessons: New and Selected Poems,* Knopf, 1996.

*CHILDREN'S BOOKS*

*Sailing to Cythera and Other Anatole Stories,* Harcourt, 1974.

*The Merry History of a Christmas Pie: With a Delicious Description of a Christmas Soup,* Putnam (New York City), 1975.
*All on a May Morning,* Putnam, 1975.
*The Snow Rabbit,* Putnam, 1975.
*Shoes without Leather,* Putnam, 1976.
*The Well-Mannered Balloon,* Harcourt, 1976.
*Simple Pictures Are Best,* Harcourt, 1977.
*Strangers' Bread,* Harcourt, 1977.
*The Highest Hit,* Harcourt, 1978.
*The Island of the Grass King: The Further Adventures of Anatole,* Harcourt, 1979.
*Papa's Panda,* Harcourt, 1979.
*A Visit to William Blake's Inn: Poems for Innocent and Experienced Travelers,* Harcourt, 1981.
*The Marzipan Moon,* Harcourt, 1981.
*Uncle Terrible: More Adventures of Anatole,* Harcourt, 1982.
*Household Tales of Moon and Water,* Harcourt, 1982.
*The Nightgown of the Sullen Moon,* Harcourt, 1983.
*Night Story,* Harcourt, 1986.
*The Voyage of the Ludgate Hill: A Journey with Robert Louis Stevenson,* Harcourt, 1987.
*The Mountains of Quilt,* Harcourt, 1987.
*Firebrat,* Random House (New York City), 1988.
*The Ballad of Biddy Early,* Knopf, 1989.
*The High Rise Glorious Skittle Skat Roarious Sky Pie Angel Food Cake,* illustrated by Richard J. Watson, Harcourt, 1990.
*Pish, Posh, Said Hieronymous Bosch,* illustrated by Leo Dillon, Harcourt, 1991.
*Beauty and the Beast,* illustrated by Barry Moser, Harcourt, 1992.
*The Sorcerer's Apprentice,* illustrated by Leo and Diane Dillon, Scholastic, Inc. (New York City), 1993.
*A Starlit Somersault Downhill,* illustrated by Jerry Pinkney, Little, Brown (Boston), 1993.
*An Alphabet of Angels,* Scholastic, Inc., 1994.
*Gutenberg's Gift* (pop-up book), illustrated by Bryan Leister, Harcourt, 1995.
*The Good-Night Blessing Book,* Scholastic, 1996.
*Cracked Cattle Corn and Snow Ice Cream: A Family Almanac,* illustrated by Jane Dyer, Harcourt, 1996.
*The Tortilla Cat,* Harcourt, 1997.
*The Magic Cornfield,* Harcourt, 1997.

*ILLUSTRATOR*

John Kater, *The Letter of John to James,* Seabury, 1981.

Kater, *Another Letter of John to James,* Seabury, 1982.

OTHER

*The Lively Anatomy of God* (short stories), Eakins (New York City), 1968.
*Testimony of the Invisible Man: William Carlos Williams, Francis Ponge, Rainer Maria Rilke, Pablo Neruda* (criticism), University of Missouri Press, 1970.
*Childhood of the Magician* (short stories), Liveright, 1973.
*Angel in the Parlor: Five Stories and Eight Essays,* Harcourt, 1983.
*Things Invisible to See* (novel), Knopf, 1984.
*East of the Sun and West of the Moon: A Play,* Harcourt, 1989.
*Telling Time: Angels, Ancestors, and Stories,* Harcourt, 1993.
*Sister Water* (novel), Knopf, 1993.
*A Nancy Willard Reader: Selected Poetry and Prose,* University Press of New England (Hanover, NH), 1993.

Work represented in anthologies, including *Rising Tides.* Contributor to periodicals, including *Esquire, Field, Massachusetts Review, Redbook, New Yorker,* and *New Directions.*

ADAPTATIONS: A filmstrip based on *A Visit to William Blake's Inn: Poems for Innocent and Experienced Travelers* was produced by Random House/Miller Brody.

SIDELIGHTS: Loved by her readers, well-respected by critics, and admired by her students, Nancy Willard is an accomplished author of poetry, children's literature, and adult fiction. Although her first published works were books of poetry followed by two collections of short stories and a volume of literary criticism, most of Willard's recent writings have been aimed at young readers.

Several reviewers have speculated on the reasons for her success. For example, Hilda Gregory points out in *Prairie Schooner* that "Willard is a teacher, a storyteller. . . . She speaks to the child in us, the student, the wonderer." Donald Hall states in the *New York Times Book Review:* "Willard's imagination—in verse or prose, for children or adults—builds castles stranger than any mad King of Bavaria ever built. She imagines with a wonderful concreteness. But also, she

takes real language and by literal-mindedness turns it into the structure of dream."

Willard produced a succession of well-received children's books in the 1990s, including re-interpretations of two classic tales. Her version of *Beauty and the Beast,* set in the late-nineteenth century with Beauty's father recast as a wealthy New York merchant, was praised in *Kirkus Reviews* as a "felicitous retelling." Linda Boyles writes in *School Library Journal* that Willard's version "startles and surprises." A critic in *Publishers Weekly* similarly commends Willard's "lavish language," concluding that the book has "the assured look of permanence." In *The Sorcerer's Apprentice,* Willard updates the traditional tale with a contemporary heroine who rides a bicycle and replaces Disney's magical brooms with an uncontrollable sewing machine. Gary Wolfe praises Willard's "ingenious verse revision" in *Locus,* while Michael Dirda describes the book as "masterly" in a *Washington Post Book World* review. Commending Willard's retelling, *Booklist* reviewer Hazel Rochman notes that "Willard tells her story in lively rhyme that jumps with the unexpected."

Willard also displays her imaginative, lyrical verse in *A Starlit Somersault Downhill,* a children's story about a hospitable bear who invites a rabbit into his winter den, though the rabbit soon thinks better of the arrangement and leaves. As Shirley Wilton observes in *School Library Journal,* Willard effectively communicates inherent dangers in nature as well as contrasting the safe life with that of risk and adventure. In *An Alphabet of Angels* and *The Good-Night Blessing Book* Willard incorporates her own photographs of angel figurines and statuary in a rhyming alphabet and litany of everyday items around the theme of angels. *Publishers Weekly* praised *An Alphabet of Angels* for the "sheer loveliness of her cryptic poetry" and *The Good-Night Blessing Book* for Willard's "arresting and sometimes humorous" photographic images.

In *Gutenberg's Gift,* Willard reinterprets events precipitating the invention of the printing press. Though historically inaccurate, as noted in the afterword by the curator of the Morgan Library, Willard's engaging tale describes Gutenberg's determination to produce a printed Bible for his wife in time for Christmas. The traditions of not only Christmas but other seasons of the year are showcased in *Cracked Corn and Snow Ice Cream: A Family Almanac,* a nostalgic view of family life in the rural Midwest that a *Publishers Weekly* critic calls an "exquisitely designed and compulsively readable. . . . American quilt of fact and folk wisdom."

As with her children's verse, critics have responded enthusiastically to the pleasant and heartwarming nature of Willard's poetry, which some reviewers have characterized as surrealist despite its seemingly mundane subject matter. Willard "seems very much at home with herself and her world," comments Stanley Poss in *Western Humanities Review.* "Her poems don't draw blood or blow your head off. . . . Her subjects are cooking, food, sports headlines, marriages that're doing OK, pregnancy, kids, animals, unwashed feet, plants, flea circuses, but her domestic is not merely cozy, and she's not merely domestic. . . . What I think I'm saying is that I like her because her poems are poised, assured, calm, they bid us not to be too hard on ourselves." In agreement, Francine Dranis writes in *Modern Poetry Studies,* "Willard's poetry, bright, graceful, and often playfully radiates womanly fullness, contentment, and reverence."

*Hudson Review* contributor John N. Morris calls Willard's 1974 poetry collection *Carpenter of the Sun* "a book full of poems about flowers and vegetables and animals and her son . . . and with not a single hard word to say about her husband and the difficulty of being a poet and a wife." Morris continues: "Since the skill is considerable, since it makes poems, it would be a piece of impertinence to tell her that it is her duty to go out and suffer more so that she might entertain us with the tally of her sorrows. Surely we are right to believe that nowadays no subject is foreign to poetry—not even good luck and decent contentment." In a review of *Carpenter of the Sun, Open Places* contributor Jonathan Holden remarks that, like many of Willard's other works, these poems "are filled with a shy wonderment, a tenderness toward Creation that is rare in contemporary poetry. They celebrate; but they're not effusive, they're not wrung from the spirit by any mechanical operation; they are inspired. Their quiet is the stillness of rapt attention. They are exquisite miniatures, each filled with the luminosity and reverence for detail of a Vermeer painting."

Willard's 1982 poetry collection, *Household Tales of Moon and Water,* find the poet adopting a more playful approach than in her earlier works. "Here begins a lasting immersion in Zen-like composure," in the opinion of *Contemporary Women Poets* essayist Maril Nowak. "Simultaneously," Nowak adds, "the adult voice wrenches truths from simple observa-

tions" and the poet "shows an increasing need to let go." In the career-spanning *Swimming Lessons: New and Selected Poems,* thirty new verses are joined with selections from Willard's poetic oeuvre to produce an overview that shows Willard's "imagery [to be] both elemental and ethereal, her characteristic forms the litany, elegy and ballad," according to *New York Times Book Review* contributor Gardner McFall. Her poems focus on the ordinary—bathtubs, a pulled tooth, the hardware store—and then transform it. "What consistently happens in [Willard's] poetry is that which should happen naturally in all verse," Nowak maintains: "detail, movement, and instantaneous transformation. The reader is lifted, even propelled, into new remembrances of simple objects and circumstances in our common experience. . . . Willard reminds us most powerfully that, more than acting as servants or descriptive devices in the world, words create worlds." *Swimming Lessons* "crowns Nancy Willard as the magician of the simile and the stunning metaphor," concludes *Poetry* contributor John Taylor.

Reviewers have found the use of imagery and the quality of contentment and good humor that characterizes Willard's verse to be also apparent in her fiction. Reviewing the 1973 short-story collection *Childhood of the Magician,* Joseph M. Flora writes in *Michigan Quarterly Review:* "There is an abundance of good humor in these stories. At the same time, Nancy Willard excellently evokes the pathos of life. . . . Life is sad and wonderful and ultimately incomprehensible. There is no self-pity in these stories, no fatigue over the weariness or absurdity of life. Nancy Willard gives us something closer to blessing and benediction."

While reviewers such as Poss and Flora point out that Willard's writing is optimistic in nature and is concerned with many of life's simpler and more basic pleasures, critics do not find her writing to be simple-minded or shallow. "If the writer's voice is not angry nor desperately troubled, neither is it complacent nor trite," states Judith S. Baughman in the *Dictionary of Literary Biography.* Other reviewers acknowledge Willard's commitment to nature and to the basic order that unites us all. Willard is aware and appreciative of her surroundings and in tune with nature; she is also dedicated to the precise representation of her feelings and thoughts. Dabney Stuart explains in *Library Journal* that Willard "is a creature among creatures and sees her nature everywhere: as she turns she marvels, variously, at the flea . . . or praises unwashed feet. . . . Willard knows where she is and has invented a way to speak of it so we know, too. . . . She writes, as proud and humble before creation."

Also characteristic of Willard's work is the caring, compassionate manner in which she tells her story and portrays her characters. "Willard has . . . a sensitive, almost delicate feeling for tender childhood relationships, and real skill in shaping and bringing off a story," Doris Grumbach remarks in *New Republic.* And contributor Bill Katz points out in *Library Journal* that Willard "shows a strong feeling for individuals—grandmothers, old soldiers, hunters—and the things of nature." Offering *Childhood of the Magician* as an excellent example of her sensitivity, a critic writing in *Publishers Weekly* praises Willard for "the special texture of her [characters]" coupled with her "vivid remembrance of what it was like to believe literally in the homilies of adults."

Willard's first adult novel, 1984's *Things Invisible to See,* is set in the late-1930s and early-1940s and tells the story of a pair of twin brothers, Ben and Willie—one gregarious, intuitive, sentimental, the other shy, reserved, methodical. The story is also about a girl named Clare, who becomes accidentally paralyzed when Ben hits her on the head with a baseball. Clare later falls in love with Ben. "The point of this luminous first novel," writes Ann Tyler in the *Detroit News,* "is that the miraculous and the everyday often co-exist, or overlap, or even that they're one and the same." While the novel is filled with out-of-the-ordinary events, "what makes this book so moving," according to Tyler, "is not the presence of the magical in the ordinary, but the presence of the ordinary in the magical." Michiko Kakutani comments in the *New York Times* that Willard "writes of small-town life during World War II with a genuine nostalgia—neither sentimental nor contrived—for the innocence Americans once possessed; and she makes a teen-age love story . . . reverberate, gently, with larger, darker questions about the human condition." The reviewer praises Willard's "pictures of daily life so precisely observed that they leave after-images in the reader's mind," and notes that "in the end, the novel probably most resembles an old-fashioned crazy quilt—eclectic and a little over-embroidered, but all in all a charming work of improvisation, held together by the radiance of its creator's sensibility."

In 1993's *Sister Water,* her second novel, Willard explores the challenge to a family's love and cohesion that are posed by death. As seventy-something

Jesse, now suffering from progressive memory loss and troubling encounters with the angel of death, awaits her calling into the next world, her daughter copes with the loss of her husband in a tragic automobile accident and the haunting dreams that follow. While praising Willard's characterizations, Gregory Blake Smith notes in his review for the *New York Times Book Review* that "the reader is teased with the idea that the quirky allure of image and character [in *Sister Water*] will ultimately coalesce into a vision" uniting the literal and metaphoric lands Willard had created. "We wait for revelation, but . . . the novel keeps its secrets to itself." However, Gale Harris finds the novel more satisfying, writing in *Belles Lettres* that "Willard describes a benevolent but retributive cosmology that lies behind the visible everyday world." Though members of the family experience acute fear and despair, Harris adds, "Willard's triumph is that she makes even this darkness alive with meaning and promise."

Willard's outlook on writing, especially poetry, is similar to that of the authors she examines in her critical study *Testimony of the Invisible Man: William Carlos Williams, Francis Ponge, Rainer Maria Rilke, Pablo Neruda.* She observes that although these authors were born in different countries and wrote in four different languages, they are united by their philosophy of poetic creation or, as Willard herself suggests, "the rhetoric of things." Willard explains in *Testimony of the Invisible Man:* "Art is not a [mere] selection from the world but a transformation of it into something that praises existence."

Baughman comments in the *Dictionary of Literary Biography:* "These four writers . . . are united, [Willard] says, by their scrupulous examinations of concrete things. For these poets, Willard contends, the truth of the world resides in particular objects themselves, not in the conventional ideas that men impose upon these things." And Priscilla Whitmore writes in *Library Journal:* "Each [poet] rooted his poetic ideas in observation of things—of the outside world—as opposed to the exclusive self-scrutiny found in confessional poets." It is this association with the art of living and the observation of things of nature that students of Willard's work believe she shares with these great authors.

Another poet Willard has admired since her childhood is William Blake. According to Barbara Karlin, writing in the *Los Angeles Times,* "Blake not only inspired author/poet Nancy Willard to write *A Visit to William Blake's Inn: Poems for Innocent and Experienced Travelers,* he is an integral part of many of the poems." "The title should not suggest that this picture book is merely a chronicle of the mystical English poet-painter," Michael Patrick Hearn explains in the *Washington Post Book World.* "Instead, it is a collection of lyrical nonsense poems inspired by a reading of [Blake's] *Songs of Innocence* when Willard was a little girl." And Donald Hall comments in the *New York Times Book Review* that "in this book, William Blake, poet and engraver, is transformed into an innkeeper. . . . These new poems, made with adult skill, successfully embody a 7-year-old's imagining of the poet who keeps an inn for the imagination. Color and verve are everything; import is nothing."

In *Telling Time: Angels, Ancestors, and Stories,* a collection of thirteen essays, Willard offers personal reflection on the process of creative writing. Through the use of poetry, parable, and fiction, she conveys the maxim, "Show don't tell; and write from what you know." In one story, "How Poetry Came Into the World and Why God Doesn't Write It," Willard portrays Adam and Eve lamenting their losses, including poetry, to an insurance claim agent. Donna Seaman writes in *Booklist,* "Willard is intrigued by the often perverse inspirations of fear and fancy; she delves into the legacy of ghost stories and confesses to an obsession with angels." Praising Willard's skill and insight, Marie Lally writes in *Library Journal* that the collection will "enrich and entertain all aspiring writers."

## BIOGRAPHICAL/CRITICAL SOURCES:

### BOOKS

*Children's Literature Review,* Volume 5, Gale (Detroit), 1983.
*Contemporary Literary Criticism,* Volume 12, Gale, 1977.
*Contemporary Women Poets,* St. James Press (Detroit), 1997.
*Dictionary of Literary Biography,* Gale, Volume 5: *American Poets since World War II,* 1980, Volume 52: *American Writers for Children since 1960: Fiction,* 1986.
Rubin, Stan Sanvel, *The Post-Confessionals: Conversations with American Poets of the Eighties,* Farleigh Dickinson Press (Rutherford, NJ), 1989.

Willard, Nancy, *Testimony of the Invisible Man: William Carlos Williams, Francis Ponge, Rainer Maria Rilke, Pablo Neruda,* University of Missouri Press, 1970.

### PERIODICALS

*Belles Lettres,* spring, 1994, pp. 40-1.
*Booklist,* November 1, 1992, p. 504; October 1, 1993, p. 245; November 1, 1993, p. 529; September 15, 1994, p. 141.
*Choice,* October, 1968; January, 1971.
*Detroit News,* January 20, 1985.
*English Journal,* April, 1990.
*Horn Book,* August, 1982.
*Hudson Review,* autumn, 1975.
*Kirkus Reviews,* October 15, 1992, p. 1318; August 1, 1993, p. 1009; July 1, 1996, p. 977.
*Library Journal,* May 1, 1968; December 15, 1970; February 15, 1975; September 15, 1975; September 15, 1993, p. 76; October 1, 1995, p. 88.
*Locus,* February, 1994, p. 62.
*Los Angeles Times,* November 29, 1981.
*Los Angeles Times Book Review,* January 20, 1985; January 2, 1994.
*Michigan Quarterly Review,* winter, 1975; spring, 1984; winter, 1986.
*Modern Poetry Studies,* spring, 1978.
*New Republic,* May 25, 1974; January 4, 1975; January 11, 1975.
*New York,* October 4, 1982.
*New Yorker,* December 7, 1981.
*New York Times,* January 12, 1985.
*New York Times Book Review,* September 25, 1977; May 21, 1978; May 27, 1979; July 12, 1981; November 15, 1981; October 23, 1983; February 3, 1985; July 12, 1987; November 8, 1987; September 25, 1988; July 7, 1989; July 18, 1993; January 16, 1994; December 18, 1994; January 26, 1997.
*Open Places,* fall/winter, 1975-76.
*Poetry,* January, 1998, p. 232.
*Prairie Schooner,* summer, 1976.
*Publishers Weekly,* October 1, 1973; June 18, 1979; December 14, 1984; October 12, 1992, p. 76; July 5, 1993, p. 71; August 1, 1994, p. 77; October 10, 1994, p. 28; November 27, 1995, p. 68; August 5, 1996, p. 440; September 30, 1996, p. 81; July 28, 1997, p. 73.
*School Library Journal,* October, 1992, p. 123; September, 1993, p. 221.
*Times Literary Supplement,* March 26, 1982.
*Washington Post,* January 9, 1984.

*Washington Post Book World,* November 8, 1981; November 14, 1993; December 10, 1995.
*Western Humanities Review,* autumn, 1975.*

\*　　\*　　\*

## WINEGARDNER, Mark 1961-

*PERSONAL:* Born November 24, 1961, in Bryan, OH; son of Gary and Beverly Winegardner; married Laura Ryll, August 11, 1984. *Education:* Miami University, Oxford, Ohio, B.A., 1983; George Mason University, M.F.A., 1987.

*ADDRESSES: Home*—9447 Arlington Blvd., No. 304, Fairfax, VA 22031.

*CAREER:* Writer. Instructor at Writers' Center, Bethesda, MD, 1987—; George Washington University, Washington, DC, lecturer, 1988—.

*MEMBER:* Phi Beta Kappa.

*AWARDS, HONORS: Playboy* College Fiction finalist, 1986, for "Summer in Blue"; Irene Leache Fiction Award, 1987, for "More Than a Casual Fan."

*WRITINGS:*

*Elvis Presley Boulevard: From Sea to Shining Sea, Almost* (nonfiction), Atlantic Monthly Press (New York City), 1988.
*Prophet of the Sandlots: Journeys with a Major League Scout* (nonfiction), Atlantic Monthly Press, 1990.
(With Steve Fireovid) *The 26th Man: One Minor Leaguer's Pursuit of a Dream,* Macmillan (New York City), 1991.
*The Veracruz Blues* (novel), Viking (New York City), 1996.

Contributor to magazines, including *Playgirl, Family Circle, Gargoyle,* and *Phoebe: The George Mason Review.*

*SIDELIGHTS:* Mark Winegardner writes about baseball, both as myth and as reality, in the form of fiction as well as nonfiction. His *Prophet of the Sandlots* follows one of baseball's most successful scouts, Tony Lucadello, as he makes the rounds one last season, searching for another future star. In Winegardner's novel, *The Veracruz Blues,* the author

mixes fact and fiction to recreate the baseball season of 1946, known as the Season of Gold, when a wealthy Mexican businessman was able to lure a number of American major league baseball players to the Mexican league by offering them more money and, for several black players, a chance to play professionally in an officially color-blind league. Winegardner's familiarity with his subject, and the extensive research he conducted for his novel in particular, were singled out for praise by critics.

Over the course of fifty years scouting talent for the Chicago Cubs and the Philadelphia Phillies, Tony Lucadello discovered, and signed to contracts, forty-nine future major league baseball players, including such figures as Mike Schmidt, Ferguson Jenkins, Jim Brosnan, and Mike Marshall. Winegardner's *Prophet of the Sandlots* follows Lucadello on what turned out to be his last season scouting. "As they drove from game to game, Lucadello's chatter revealed a gentle but wily character," Diane Cole observes in the *New York Times Book Review.* Cole adds: "Winegardner's engaging portrait of a scout's life is at its best when he simply allows Lucadello to talk," noting that the author's own narrative voice necessarily pales in comparison. Similarly, the critic for *Kirkus Reviews* complains that Winegardner fails to attempt to uncover the roots of some of Lucadello's more eccentric behavior, but concludes that *Prophet of the Sandlots* makes for "good reading nonetheless."

Winegardner's first novel, *The Veracruz Blues,* also takes its cue from baseball history, and the accuracy of the historical details that crowd his complex narrative structure was an issue for several of the book's critics. The author expands on a fairly spectacular set of facts when he sets his novel in 1946, the year Jorge Pasquel decided to make the Mexican baseball league competitive with the American big leagues by luring a number of American players and potential big leaguers barred from the majors by their race to play in Mexico. To this true-life scenario Winegardner adds a fictional sports writer who interviews the major characters decades after the period in question, as well as cameo appearances by such historical figures as Ernest Hemingway and the artists Diego Rivera and Frida Kahlo. "As a milieu, baseball begs writers to indulge in the pleasures of tall tales and broad characterization," notes the reviewer for *Publishers Weekly,* "and Winegardner . . . excels at it."

As in reviews of *Prophet of the Sandlots,* Winegardner's facility with prose was the object of some negative criticism in reviews of his novel. "If *The Veracruz Blues* has a problem, it is its structure," claims Tom Miller in *Washington Post Book World,* adding that the device of including interviews about events long past as well as contemporary editorial asides "makes for occasionally clunky writing and dialogue." In addition, Larry Eldridge, a reviewer for *Christian Science Monitor,* notes factual errors in some of Winegardner's baseball history and complains of feeling "confused and unsatisfied" by the author's "hybrid method" of mixing fact and fiction. For others, such issues were not a problem. "[*The Veracruz Blues*] is a wonderfully entertaining and enlightening look at Mexican baseball's *temporada de oro,* the golden season that changed the face of professional baseball forever," avers Kevin Baxter in the *Los Angeles Times.* Roberto Gonzalez Echevarria, a contributor to the *New York Times Book Review,* went further: "*The Veracruz Blues* is not just a baseball novel; it is the best baseball novel that I have read."

Aside from his books about baseball, Winegardner is also the author of *Elvis Presley Boulevard: From Sea to Shining Sea, Almost,* a nonfiction account of a two-month road trip the author took with a college friend in the weeks before Winegardner's wedding in 1984. *Booklist* reviewer Ray Olsen compares it to John Steinbeck's *Travels with Charley* and Jack Kerouac's *On the Road,* but dubs *Elvis Presley Boulevard* "a whole lot sweeter, thanks to Winegardner's ingenuous narrative voice."

*BIOGRAPHICAL/CRITICAL SOURCES:*

PERIODICALS

*Atlanta Journal-Constitution,* May 6, 1990, p. F2.
*Booklist,* January 15, 1988, p. 825; February 1, 1990, p. 1063.
*Boston Globe,* April 1, 1990, p. B44; February 25, 1996, p. B42.
*Christian Science Monitor,* March 15, 1996, p. 11.
*Denver Post,* March 3, 1996, sec. F, p. 8.
*Esquire,* December, 1995, p. 60.
*Houston Chronicle,* March 31, 1996, sec. Z, p. 23.
*Hungry Mind Review,* May, 1990, p. 31.
*Kirkus Reviews,* December 1, 1987, p. 1668; December 15, 1989, p. 1818.
*Library Journal,* January, 1990, p. 116; December, 1995, p. 161.
*Los Angeles Times,* February 15, 1988.
*Los Angeles Times Book Review,* March 31, 1996, p. 6.

*New York,* March 19, 1990, p. 109.
*New York Times Book Review,* April 1, 1990, p. 18; April 7, 1991, p. 32; March 31, 1996, p. 6; April 7, 1996, p. 14; December 8, 1996, p. 84.
*People,* May 14, 1990, p. 31.
*Publishers Weekly,* December 4, 1987, p. 68; December 8, 1989, p. 48; November 6, 1995, p. 81; February 24, 1997, p. 88.
*St. Louis Post-Dispatch,* April 26, 1990, p. E6.
*Sporting News,* August 12, 1991, p. 47.
*Tribune Books* (Chicago), April 1, 1990, p. 1; March 31, 1996, p. 11.
*Voice of Youth Advocates,* June, 1990, p. 132.
*Wall Street Journal,* April 20, 1990, p. A12.
*Washington Post Book World,* February 18, 1996, p. 6.
*West Coast Review of Books,* April, 1990, p. 65.

\* \* \*

## WOOD, Edward John 1931-
### (Jack Barnao, Ted Wood)

*PERSONAL:* Born April 22, 1931, in England; immigrated to Canada; naturalized Canadian citizen, 1960; son of Alexander (police officer) and Jessie (a homemaker; maiden name, Hooper) Wood; married Mary Gwendoline Pearsall, June 23, 1951 (deceased); married Mary Patricia Lawson Barnao (a columnist), December 21, 1975; children: Anne Elizabeth, Heather Mary, Edward John; three stepchildren. *Politics:* Conservative (Progressive Conservative Party). *Religion:* Catholic. *Avocational interests:* Fishing, canoeing.

*ADDRESSES: Home and office*—239 Wellington St., Whitby, Ontario, Canada L1N 5L7. *Agent*—Richard Curtis, Richard Curtis Associates, 164 E. 64th St., New York, NY 10021.

*CAREER:* Writer. London & Manchester Assurance, sales representative, 1953-54; Toronto City Police, Toronto, Ontario, Canada, constable, 1954-57; MacLaren Advertising, copywriter, 1957-66; Foster Advertising, creative director, 1966-69; worked for Cockfield Brown Advertising, 1969-74. *Military service:* Royal Air Force, served in coastal command as air gunner and flight engineer, 1949-53; became sergeant.

*MEMBER:* Crime Writers of Canada (chair), Writers Union of Canada, Literary Guild, Aircrew Association.

*AWARDS, HONORS:* Ontario Arts Council grant, 1974; Scribner Crime Novel Award for first mystery, Charles Scribner's Sons Book Awards, 1983, for *Dead in the Water.*

*WRITINGS:*

"REID BENNETT" SERIES; UNDER NAME TED WOOD

*Dead in the Water,* Scribner (New York City), 1983.
*Murder on Ice,* Scribner, 1984, published as *The Killing Cold,* Collins (London), 1984.
*Live Bait,* Scribner, 1985, published as *Dead Centre,* Collins, 1985.
*Fool's Gold,* Scribner, 1986.
*Corkscrew,* Scribner, 1987.
*When the Killing Starts,* Scribner, 1989.
*On the Inside,* Scribner, 1990.
*Flashback,* Scribner, 1992.
*Snowjob,* Scribner, 1993.
*A Clean Kill,* HarperCollins (New York City), 1995.

"JOHN LOCKE" SERIES; UNDER PSEUDONYM JACK BARNAO

*Hammerlocke,* Scribner, 1987.
*Lockestep,* Scribner, 1988.
*Timelocke,* Macmillan, 1991.

OTHER

*Somebody Else's Summer,* Clarke, Irwin, 1973.
(With others) *Mister Scrooge* (play), produced in Toronto, Ontario, 1983.
(Photographer) Jeremy Schmidt, *In the Village of the Elephants,* Walker, 1994.
(With Schmidt) *Two Lands, One Heart: An American Boy's Journey to His Mother's Vietnam,* Walker, 1995.
(Photographer) Guy Garcia, *Spirit of the Maya: A Boy Explores His People's Mysterious Past,* Walker, 1995.
*Iditarod Dream: Dusty and His Sled Dogs Compete in Alaska's Jr. Iditarod,* Walker, 1996.

Author of television scripts, including *It's Not Like Stealing,* (episode of *Sidestreet* series), 1974; *Susan* (adapted from his story "Somebody Else's Summer"), 1974; *The People You Never See,* 1976. Work represented in anthologies, including *Cold Blood,* Mosaic Press, 1988, 1989.

*SIDELIGHTS:* Edward John Wood is the author of two mystery series, one featuring Reid Bennett as the detective protagonist and the other with John Locke. Wood won the Scribner Crime Novel Award for his first Bennett book, *Dead in the Water.* Reviewing Wood's work in the *St. James Guide to Crime and Mystery Writers,* Carol Barry writes that the Bennett books are "action-packed police procedurals" with "clear-cut good against evil plots."

Bennett, the chief of police in the fictional town of Murphy's Harbour, and Sam, his German shepherd, were introduced in *Dead in the Water.* Discussing the Bennett series in the *St. James Guide to Crime and Mystery Writers,* Wood says that he placed Bennett in a small-town police force because his own experience in the police was "gained in a pre-electronic time, under circumstances which are now found only in a small town."

*Dead in the Water* was praised as "an attractive first novel" written in "civilized prose" by Newgate Callender in the *New York Times Book Review.* The book is written as a first-person narrative by Bennett, who is investigating a murder in Murphy's Harbour. Wood starts *Dead in the Water* with a prologue, which introduces Bennett, and then quickly goes on to the narrative, which reveals the murder Bennett will investigate. Jean M. White stated in a *Washington Post Book World* review that Wood writes "tough, spare prose," and setting the book in the Canadian countryside is a welcome "scene shift from the mean big-city streets of most police procedurals." Callendar notes the "fine narrative line, natural speech and a lovely feel for the outdoors."

Wood's use of this setting was distinctive to several reviewers, including Margret Cannon reviewing *Fool's Gold* in the Toronto *Globe and Mail.* The book, another Bennett adventure, is set in a tiny logging town in Canada. Cannon feels that "Wood's use of his northern Ontario setting is excellent." Toronto *Globe and Mail* contributor Derrick Murdoch praises Wood's books for their action-packed narrative, but, like Cannon and White, Murdoch most admires the Canadian countryside setting in Wood's work. Wood's writing style reflects the simple, country setting he describes. Callendar, reviewing the book *Corkscrew,* cites Wood's "functional prose without any padding. It is unpretentious writing, but more subtle than would appear." Speaking of the Bennett books as a whole, Barry claims that with "their strong series character, action and adventure in a rugged setting, and satisfying plots, Wood's mysteries are an exciting addition to the genre."

Wood's other detective character is John Locke, who is termed a "one-man army who hires himself out as a bodyguard," according to a reviewer writing in the *New York Times Book Review*. Wood introduced the character in *Hammerlocke,* in which Locke is working as the companion of a rich woman touring Florence with her grandson. The narrative follows Locke through the investigation of the grandson's kidnapping.

Wood has also written or illustrated several nonfiction books for young people. In *Two Lands, One Heart: An American Boy's Journey to His Mother's Vietnam,* Wood and co-author Jeremy Schmidt chronicle the true-life story of a boy named TJ visiting Vietnam for the first time. "The bulk of the book follows TJ's often funny adventures on the family farm," writes the critic for *Publishers Weekly,* who notes that "the writing is unexceptional, but the content is strong enough to compel the reader's attention." In *Iditarod Dream: Dusty and His Sled Dogs Compete in Alaska's Jr. Iditarod,* Wood focuses on the famous dogsled race and young Dusty Whittemore's efforts to win first prize. "Dusty's stamina, courage and sportsmanship," writes the reviewer for *Publishers Weekly,* "will shine through to young readers."

Wood told *CA:* "I have written since childhood, and I believe it's more important to write than to study writing and other writers. My police and air force experience gave me a solid grounding for my books. I have also traveled a fair amount, which has been useful.

"My first novel, *Dead in the Water,* was submitted to a host of Canadian publishers, all of whom turned it down. They claimed the Canadian locale was trite. Finally I answered an advertisement placed by Richard Curtis, telling him I wasn't interested in a reading fee arrangement but had sold many stories and one book. He took the novel and sold it to Scribner's within a week. It's since been picked up in England, France, Holland, and Japan. Moral of the story: never give up hope."

*BIOGRAPHICAL/CRITICAL SOURCES:*

BOOKS

*St. James Guide to Crime and Mystery Writers,* 4th edition, St. James Press (Detroit), 1996.

PERIODICALS

*Globe and Mail* (Toronto), October 27, 1984; May 18, 1985; May 24, 1986.
*New York Times Book Review,* December 18, 1983, p. 29; January 17, 1988, p. 35.
*Publishers Weekly,* June 7, 1993, p. 54; February 28, 1994, p. 89; February 20, 1995, p. 206; November 20, 1995, p. 78; March 4, 1996, p. 66. .
*Washington Post,* May 4, 1985.
*Washington Post Book World,* October 16, 1983, p. 10.

\* \* \*

**WOOD, Ted**
**See WOOD, Edward John**

\* \* \*

**WRIGHT, A. D. 1947-**

*PERSONAL:* Born June 9, 1947, in Oxford, England; son of David H. and Mary D. (Groom) Wright. *Education:* Merton College, Oxford, B.A., 1968; attended British School at Rome, 1969-71; Brasenose College, Oxford, M.A., 1973, D.Phil., 1973.

*ADDRESSES: Office*—School of History, University of Leeds, Leeds LS2 9JT, England.

*CAREER:* University of Leeds, Leeds, England, lecturer, 1974-92, senior lecturer in history, 1992—. University of Edinburgh, visiting fellow at Institute for Advanced Studies in the Humanities, 1983.

*MEMBER:* Royal Historical Society (fellow), Ecclesiastical History Society, Accademia di San Carlo.

*WRITINGS:*

*The Counter-Reformation: Catholic Europe and the Non-Christian World,* St. Martin's (New York City), 1982.
(With Romeo De Maio, L. Gulia, and A. Mazzacane) *Baronio Storico e la Controriforma* (title means "Baronius as Historian and the Counter- Reformation"), Centro di Studi Sorani (Sora, Italy), 1982.

*Catholicism and Spanish Society under the Reign of Philip II, 1555-1598, and Philip III, 1598-1621,* Edwin Mellen (Lewiston, NY), 1991.

*WORK IN PROGRESS:* Editing the five-volume *History of the Papacy* for Longman.

*BIOGRAPHICAL/CRITICAL SOURCES:*

*PERIODICALS*

*Times* (London), April 8, 1982.
*Times Literary Supplement,* October 15, 1982.

**YORK, Alison**
**See NICOLE, Christopher (Robin)**

\*    \*    \*

**YORK, Andrew**
**See NICOLE, Christopher (Robin)**

\*    \*    \*

**YORK, Georgia**
**See HOFFMAN, Lee**